EYE CONTACT

The Mysterious Death in 2000 of Kassidy Bortner, and

the Wrongful Convictions of Chad Evans and Amanda Bortner

by
Morrison Bonpasse
with
Chad Evans

BonPasse Exoneration Services (a Maine non-profit corporation)
P.O. Box 390
Newcastle, ME 04553
207-586-6078
Morrison Bonpasse, Executive Director
morrison@bonpasseexonerationservices.com
www.bonpasseexonerationservices.com

EYE CONTACT - The Mysterious Death in 2000 of Kassidy Bortner and the Wrongful Convictions of Chad Evans and Amanda Bortner

ISBN-10 0983798524
ISBN-13 9780983798521

TABLE OF CONTENTS

Page

i Letter from Chad Evans

1 Preface

8 Introduction

CHAPTERS

11 1. Tragedy - 9 November 2000 through 12:38 p.m.

18 2. Kassidy Caitlyn Bortner - 4 February 1999 to 8 June 2000

31 3. Kassidy Bortner - 9 June 2000 to 8 November 2000

82 4. Investigating Chad Evans- 9 November 2000, after 12:38 p.m.

194 5. Investigating Chad Evans- 10 November 2000 to 20 August 2001

298 6. Trial of Chad Evans - Preparation - 21 August to 3 December 2001

332 7. Trial of Chad Evans - The Evidence for the Jury - 4 December to 17 December 2001

441 8. Trial of Chad Evans - Closing Arguments, Charge/Instructions to Jury, and Verdict: 18 to 21 December 2001

478 9. Sentencing, Prison, and Appeals for Chad; Preparation for Amanda's trial - 23 December 2001 to 17 November 2002

505 10. Trial and sentencing of Amanda Bortner: 18 November 2002 to 3 March 2003

541 11. Appeals, Prison, and New Hampshire "Kassidy Bortner Law": 2003 to the present

576 12. Conclusion: The Wrongful Convictions of Chad Evans and Amanda Bortner

597 13. Campaign for Chad

603 Appendix Photographs of Kassidy Bortner. June-November 2000.

To the reader of this book:

Thank you so much for being open-minded by investing the time to read this book. It is never a comfortable feeling to go against the grain or question what society has accepted as truth. The reality is that our criminal justice system is not infallible. Many are aware that the Innocence Project has now freed over 275 people who were convicted of guilt "beyond a reasonable doubt." In each of those cases, irrefutable evidence was offered to prove innocence, ultimately resulting in freedom for the wrongly convicted. Knowing these facts, it is still uncommon for people to question a conviction. I suspect this is due to the human desire for security. I appreciate your courage to investigate alternate possibilities.

Unfortunately, this case doesn't have the type of "black and white" proof to secure my freedom as those mentioned above. (At least not yet) If it did, I would be home with my son because I simply DID NOT kill Kassidy. The truth is, no one knows what really caused Kassidy's death. The investigation was pursued strictly as a homicide, and from there the investigation was structured and facts were sought merely to support that theory.

Morrison has worked tirelessly to break down the facts and investigate the possibilities of what caused Kassidy's death. First he needed to be sure of my innocence. What lies ahead of you in your reading is the truth as I know it, corroborated by facts that Morrison has uncovered. He has laid all of this out in a manner that allows you to come to your own conclusions.

It has been 11 years since Kassidy's tragic death. My memory is not perfect. Comments, questions, and feedback are always welcome. Our journey is one of seeking absolute truth.

While I cannot say for certain what the cause was of Kassidy's untimely death, I can assure you it was not from abuse that I perpetrated. I have done everything asked of me and will continue to do so with regards to proving that I have been wrongly convicted. In 2010 I submitted to a VSA lie detection test which I passed with "No Deception Indicated." Those results were individually verified by five different professionals in the field. We are contemplating other methods that can also verify my honesty and add to our position.
No matter what happens as a result of this book, and our search for the truth, there are no "winners." Kassidy's death has caused ripples that will last forever in at least two extended families. I have wrestled for many months with the terms "Wrongly convicted" vs. "Innocent." There are only two innocent people in this case: Kassidy and her would be step-brother, Kyle. Every adult involved in Kassidy's life failed Kassidy in some manner. This failure and regret are what I was referring to when I spoke at my sentencing: the decisions I could have made, the actions I could have taken, the awareness I should have shown .... How can I ever feel anything other than failure where Kassidy is concerned? None of us has the ability to turn back time. If that was an option, I know the exact day I would rewind to. Unfortunately, life can only be lived in the present and for the future.

Everyone in this tragedy deserves to know the absolute truth. Thanks again for showing your interest in Kassidy's justice.

Chad Evans

PREFACE

I was introduced in January, 2003, to the world of wrongful convictions when a friend urged me to read the book, Human Sacrifice, by James Moore. It's about the wrongful conviction of Dennis Dechaine in Maine in 1989 for the murder of 12 year-old Sarah Cherry. Feeling that such injustice should not be tolerated in Maine, or any state, I began working as a volunteer member of the group, "Trial and Error," supporting Dennis. We built a website for him, www.trialanderrordennis.org, found him a new lawyer, and mobilized public support for his claims of innocence. By 2005, a Maine public opinion poll which we sponsored found that a majority of Mainers favored a retrial for Dennis, which was remarkable considering the public fear and outrage after Sarah Cherry's murder. I know of no other public opinion polls which have been conducted in the U.S. regarding the question of whether a convicted murderer should be granted a new trial. Recently, I searched the internet for "public opinion poll" and "new trial" and found a 2000 New York Times article which reported that Peruvians were polled in 1999 on whether the American, Lori Berenson, should be retried in a civil court, years after her military court conviction. Twenty-four percent approved of the decision, after the fact, to give her a civilian trial.

Since 1993, Dennis has been a client of the Innocence Project, and he would have been exoneree #15, approximately, after the Innocence Project began working on the case, and exculpatory DNA was found underneath Sarah's thumbnail. However, the Maine Attorney General, like his ill-advised successors, opposed efforts to re-open the case. As of October, 2011, and 18 years later, over 275 people have been exonerated in the U.S. by the Innocence Project, mostly with DNA testing. Yet Dennis continues to languish in the Maine State Prison while continuing to press for a retrial. The Maine Legislature supported that claim by modifying the DNA statute in 2006 and Dennis filed for a retrial in 2008. More DNA testing has been done, but the Motion for a Retrial has not yet had a hearing. The reluctance of the Attorney General of the State of Maine and the courts to re-examine Dennis's case has been shameful.

In 2006, Alfred Trenkler's brother called me to assist Alfred in his efforts to overturn his wrongful conviction in Boston Federal Court in 1993 for building the "Roslindale Bomb" which killed Boston Police Bomb Squad officer, Jeremiah Hurley, Jr., and maimed his partner, Francis Foley. Replicating the strategy of Dennis Dechaine's campaign for justice, we built a website for Alfred, www.alfredtrenklerinnocent.org, and I wrote a 727 page manuscript about his case, Perfectly Innocent. Of the five jurors whom I was able to find, and who would communicate with me, four read the manuscript. All four wrote letters to the Federal Judge in the case, Rya Zobel, to disavow their votes for a Guilty verdict, and they asked for justice and a new trial. The fifth wrote the judge too, saying to me that he was the "holdout juror" during the jury's deliberations, and didn't need to read my book.

Alfred's supporters have asked for a re-investigation of the case, but the U.S. Attorneys in Boston, Michael Sullivan and his successor, Carmen Ortiz, have decided to stay the course and resist any re-examination of the facts. As the five jurors concluded, those facts do not support the Government's case.

In 2009, U.S. Attorney General Holder said to a group of newly-sworn Assistant U.S. Attorneys, *"Your job is not to win cases. Your job is to do justice. Your job is in every case, every decision that you make, to do the right thing. Anybody who asks you to do something other than that is to be ignored. Any policy that is at tension with that is to be questioned and brought to my attention. And I mean that."* (Boston Globe, April 9, 2009, "US Attorneys told to expect scrutiny.") Efforts since then to bring this case to his personal attention, including letters from U.S. Senators, have failed. His subordinates at the Dept. of Justice in Washington have decided, so far, to stay the course, and support Alfred's wrongful conviction. I sent to the Dept. of Justice a list of "29 Questions," the answers to which would lead reasonable people to conclude that there were severe flaws in the Alfred Trenkler case, but the Dept. of Justice has declined, so far, to answer those questions. In April, 2011, I sent a followup letter to Attorney General Holder, and enclosed copies of 15 previous letters to him. There has been no response.

Alfred Trenkler remains in Federal prison as life passes him by. His mother and stepfather have died, in 2008, and 2009, respectively. The facts in Alfred's case make his conviction absurd, and even Officer Hurley's widow has said publicly that she wants the truth to be told, but the wall of prosecutorial opposition remains standing.

In December 2009, Chet Evans, the father of Chad Evans, called to ask me to help Chad, who had read of my work in a November 22 Boston Herald front page article about Alfred Trenkler. Chad was convicted in 2001 of assaulting and murdering Kassidy Bortner, the 21 month-old daughter of his girlfriend, Amanda Bortner. As with the other two cases, it did not take too many days of reading and investigating to see that it was likely that Chad Evans was also wrongly convicted. Now, more than a year and a half later, his innocence is increasingly clear. His website is www.chadevanswronglyconvicted.org, and public interest in the case is growing.

Like the books for Dennis Dechaine and Alfred Trenkler, this book is part of Chad's Campaign for Justice and the efforts to persuade the people and government of New Hampshire that an injustice was done to Chad and to Amanda Bortner. In addition to this book, Chad's letters to me during 2010-2011 have been collected as "Letters from New Hampshire Prison" and posted at the homepage of his website. At 657-plus pages, and growing, these letters give a remarkable view of Chad Evans, his understanding of the case, and his struggle for exoneration. In this book, these letters are often excerpted and quoted as it's crucial for people to see Chad's own words, as he describes his life, and his life with Amanda and Kassidy Bortner.

All three of these men, and Amanda Bortner, deserve justice and exoneration. If outright exoneration is not politically acceptable, then the prosecutors in each case should schedule a retrial if they think there is even a chance that a jury could again be persuaded of guilt beyond a reasonable doubt. One likely reason for prosecutorial reluctance for a retrial in each case is that the prosecutors in each case understand that their cases are now very weak.

At Boston University Law School in the early 1970's, I don't recall hearing the term "wrongful conviction." We students knew that injustice to Blacks in the South was prevalent, but I do not recall learning that there was much questioning of inherent fairness of the American criminal justice system and the sanctity of its standard of guilt "beyond a reasonable doubt." We learned the oft-used mantra that it was better that nine guilty people remain free rather than one innocent person be found guilty. The DNA revolution, led by the work of the Innocence Project in New York, has shattered that faith in our justice system. However, DNA is a factor in a very small percentage of crimes. There is no reason to believe that wrongful convictions occur more often in DNA-rich rape and murder cases than for other types of crimes.

It's been estimated that between 0.5-5% of the approximately 2 million people[1] in prison or jail in the U.S. were wrongly convicted and are innocent of the crimes for which they were convicted. (See a 2003 ABA study, a 2006 study by Prof. Michael Risinger and a 2007 article by Prof. Samuel Gross.) and a 2010 online Summary by the 'Skeptical Juror'.) That means between 10,000-100,000 people, which is a horrendously large number in a society that believes that it doesn't convict people of crimes, and thus deprive them of their liberty or lives, unless they are guilty beyond a reasonable doubt. For many, it appears that the standard was "guilty, even with some doubts."

Even in New Hampshire, with its relatively low crime rate, and even looking only at the State Prison population of almost 3,000, that means that between 15-150 innocent men

---

[1]. This footnote explains that this book will not be using footnotes in the traditional manner. Instead, to the extent practicable, it will link items to online references. Such items will appear in blue/underlined text. When reading this book online, the linked items can be brought to the screen. If you are reading this book in print form, you may want to have the online version opened on a nearby terminal screen for easy viewing of the linked document, or photo. Note: sometimes the "Discovery" page numbers in collections of documents are out of order, so it may be necessary to skim the collection to find the correct page.

and women are in New Hampshire prisons today. Again, that's between 15-150 Chad Evans's and it represents a staggering burden to ensure justice and overcome their wrongful convictions. A close examination of the documents and photographs in the Chad Evans case on his website and in the 657+ pages of his 2010-11 Letters to me, and in this book, show how much work is often necessary to overcome even the most glaring of wrongful convictions.

New Hampshire could begin its path to ensure justice for its citizens by candidly agreeing that its justice system is fallible, just like those of the other 49 states. It would be helpful for New Hampshire to acknowledge that wrongful convictions can happen here. While its immediate neighbor to the south, Massachusetts, is different in many ways from New Hampshire, its larger population of 6.5 million, compared to New Hampshire's 1.3 million, doesn't explain the difference in the number of exonerations of clearly innocent people in each state since 1976: 38 in Mass. to zero in New Hampshire. Former New Hampshire Attorney General Philip McLaughlin has written in an article, "The Risk of Injustice is Real" (p. 28) of prosecutions during his term in office of two innocent people who almost went to trial for murder where convictions would have been likely. However, in both cases, the real perpetrators were identified, prosecuted and convicted. There have been a few exonerations in New Hampshire since 1976, but none with the defendant so clearly innocent as to warrant counting them in the same tally as the Innocence Project's 275 since 1989, or Massachusetts' 38 since 1976.

For the rest of Northern New England, Maine has not seen an exoneration of a wrongfully convicted man since the early 1950's. Vermont's best connection to the widening world of wrongful convictions was the 1820 exoneration of Jesse and Stephen Boorn in Vermont, who had been convicted for the 1812 murder of Russell Colvin. This was the first U.S. exoneration of a serious crime in the U.S., and it came about because the alleged victim returned to his hometown alive. With a combined population of almost one-half of Massachusetts, Northern New England has not seen any exonerations from wrongful convictions in the period since 1976.

New Hampshire could follow the example of California and North Carolina and establish an Innocence Commission to ensure that those who claim wrongful conviction are heard. Another example to follow is that of Dallas County, Texas, which now has a Conviction Integrity Unit. New Hampshire does not need to wait until a court determines that one or more of its inmates who claim innocence is actually innocent.

It is a myth that most prisoners claim their innocence. That number is closer to 15% than 100%, and that 15% is close to the real percentage of wrongful conviction. Even a percentage as low as one tenth of one percent should not be tolerated in our democratic society. One tenth of a percent of 2.2 million is 2,200, and one tenth of a percent of New Hampshire's 2,615 prison inmates, (the count in 2007, according to a 2009 study), is 2.6, or two. Chad Evans is one of those two. If the percentage of wrongful conviction in New Hampshire is only 1%, which is still less than the U.S. number, the count of wrongfully convicted people in New Hampshire prisons would be 26, and Chad would be included in that number, too.

I only work for clients who I believe to be innocent, and I tell each client explicitly at the beginning of a relationship that if I learn information that indicates that s/he may have committed the crimes for which convicted, then my work for him or her will cease. For the three mentioned above, that point has not come, and never come close. I'm often asked, "*How do you know that your clients are innocent?*" Initially, the decision process is the same as that followed by the police and prosecutors. I evaluate the evidence and keep asking questions. A good ongoing indication of whether I am on the right track is to continually evaluate which way the newly discovered evidence is pointing, and there is always more to discover. In the cases above, and in the Kassidy Bortner cases, State vs. Chad Evans, and State vs. Amanda Bortner, the newly discovered information has either been neutral or has pointed in the direction of innocence. One challenge is to avoid the mistake that police and prosecutors make in cases, and make in spades in wrongful conviction cases, which is to request and see only the evidence that you want to see and discount the rest. We humans tend to see and believe what we want to see, and must guard vigilantly against that tendency. If you find evidence of biased fact searching or fact reporting in this book, please let me know.

In 2010, I formed the non-profit corporation, BonPasse Exoneration Services, to do this work. Its website is http://www.bonpasseexonerationservices.com.

There is one common element for The Alfred Trenkler and Chad Evans cases, which is that both involve stepfathers. Alfred's stepfather, Jack Wallace, worked tirelessly for the last 17 years of his life to find justice for Alfred. Chad Evans was a stepfather to the first son of his wife, Tristan Evans. If Kassidy had survived the fall of 2000, in both senses of the word, Chad would likely have become her stepfather. I, too, am a stepfather, after marrying the mother of two children in 1978. They are now in their 40's and have children and stepchildren of their own. In our stepfamily, we had rules about the biological Mom being the source of discipline. However, sometimes I would, as her agent, be the adult to insist on obedience to some rule of the house. Two very painful memories, and for which I've apologized, are when I spanked each of my stepchildren, both of them hard. Both times, I was very frustrated, angry and affronted, but I should not have done it. In neither case were there bruises. Thus, I did what Chad was accused many times of doing which was to hit Kassidy Bortner. He did not spank or hit Kassidy, and I **did** spank my stepchildren; and he is in prison.

To rid his home of mice, Chad used humane traps that captured mice, and Chad would release them elsewhere. My mousetraps kill mice with a snap that either breaks bones or cuts off breathing or both.

Working on this book has brought back another memory, of when I was a young boy in the 1950's. I remember my mother washing out my older sister's mouth with bath soap as a punishment for lying. This method of punishment would surely be frowned upon today and probably was frowned upon then. My mother was a college graduate, with a specialty of child psychology. If my sister had died of any suspicious causes soon thereafter, and if my mother was a suspect, her disciplining could have been included in the charges as abusive.

The tragedy of Kassidy Bortner also reminded me of the powerful effect of the loss of a child on a family. We had a quarter-acre pond at our property and a small 8-foot rowboat. Also, I had my own boat, a primitive kayak, which we called a "banana boat," because of its shape. The family next door had two sons, both younger than me, and the older boy had a birthday party during a warm summer day. The younger son, perhaps about three years old, wandered away from the party and apparently pulled my "banana boat" to the water. He paddled toward deeper water, and when he tipped over, he drowned. My family was devastated, and I was ordered to destroy the boat, and the neighbors were irreparably scarred. It was thought then that bearing a tragedy quietly was more proper than talking about it. They moved to another part of town and had a third child, but the mother was permanently saddened and scarred and their marriage failed.

The title of this book comes from the parenting practices of Chad's grandfather, Emery Evans, which were passed to Chad's father, Chester (Chet), and to Chad. Emery, who died after Chad's conviction, believed that effective communication is enhanced with eye contact between the individuals. Sometimes, the Evans parent would hold the chin of the child to ensure that eye contact, but most of the time such holding was not necessary. Chad Evans effectively used that family advice to establish eye contact when communicating with his employees, his son, Kyle, and his stepson, Brent. When communicating positive and disciplinary messages to Kassidy Bortner, Chad sometimes held her chin with the palm of one hand to ensure that she had eye contact with him. A few times, when holding her chin, Chad caused bruises, and those bruises contributed to a colossal by-product of miscommunication: Chad's wrongful conviction.

I fully understand that this book is being written and published 11 years after the death of Kassidy Bortner, which has its advantages and disadvantages. The advantage is that we have the perspective of time, and some advances in science and medical knowledge. The disadvantage is that memories fade and become distorted with time, and many records have not been saved.

It is argued here that many people in this case made mistakes, including Chad Evans, and that hindsight is often better than contemporary judgment. I have great respect for the police and prosecutors, judges, defense lawyers, media people, and others who worked on or touched this case. They did the best they could given the circumstances, the information that was available at the time, the decisions of others, and the requirements of our adversarial criminal justice system. I began working on this case with the assumption that they thought that what they were doing was right, and I have not found proof otherwise.

The media covered this case extensively, sometimes sensationally. A Portsmouth Herald article called the case, "*one of the most high-profile murder cases in recent memory*." A book could be written about the media coverage and its possible effect on the trial, but the goal here is to present the facts about the Kassidy Bortner cases. To learn more about the actual articles, readers can follow the links provided here, with the associated headlines, and go to Chad's website to read other articles.

A few notes on the writing of the book.

Chad Evans and Amanda Bortner and their friends and relatives are often referenced by their first names after their introduction in this book. Officials, lawyers and judges are referenced always by their full names or by their title and last names, or by last name, only.

Where there are quoted statements, which are always in italics, I've sometimes added information in brackets [ ] which might fill in a missing word or a correct word or a word or two of clarification, but they are not words said by the speaker.

Instead of cumbersome footnotes and citations, this book uses two methods of referring readers to the source materials. Where it seems to fit with the flow of a sentence, the hyperlink will be imbedded in the text, and if the referenced document has more than a few pages, the page number will be referenced in parentheses. At other times, the entire cited source is placed in parentheses at the end of the sentence, such as with the links to the document with Chad's "Letters from New Hampshire Prison." Where the cited document was part of the Discovery materials which were provided by the State to the defense in Chad's trial, the Discovery page numbers are used. Otherwise, the page number within a particular document is used.

To the extent possible, the legal technicalities of the trial are avoided, with little discussion of the rules of evidence including "hearsay," a prohibited form of testimony which is when one person states what another person said in order to present some truth in the statement. There are many exceptions to that prohibition which is why several witnesses were able to present the statements of others at Chad's and Amanda's trials. For the book, the statements are simply presented, without the legal analysis of their admissibility.

Most of the book is organized chronologically, but sometimes issues or testimony are combined to present them coherently. Emphasis is placed here on dates, because there was so little emphasis on time during the investigation and during Chad's trial. As noted in the text, there were many times where everyone involved could have been more specific about the dates of events or statements. When the dates were not certain, I've used the expressions, "around this time," or "approximately." The book seeks to present a comprehensive view of the death of Kassidy Bortner and the Chad Evans and Amanda Bortner cases. It also seeks to explain how the jury could have reached its verdict, by showing what it knew and didn't know. However, what is lost is a clear view of what the jury heard and saw, and when. To obtain that view, one must read the transcripts.

Readers will sometimes find repetition here, but hopefully not too often. A major reason for such repetition is that there are several times in the story where details and summaries can be added. For example, the events of November 9, could be presented as they occurred (See Chapter 1), and as viewed by participants in their police interviews, and at Chad's and Amanda's trials and in the views of others such as appellate courts, and in newspaper accounts.

It's emphasized in the book that the absence of a clear sense of time and timing contributed to Chad's and Amanda's wrongful convictions. The website has an extensive

"Chronology" section, and even that section doesn't include all the dates of police interviews and trial dates which are in the "Investigation" and "Transcripts" sections of the website. Thus, it's a challenge to present time-related information clearly. From time to time, this book uses a one-line time-line consisting of 153 dots, with one for each of the 153 days that Kassidy and Chad knew each other, from June 9 through November 9, 2000. The generic form looks like this:

....

9 Jul**1** Aug**1** Sep**1** Oct**1** Nov**1** **9**

At other times, monthly calendars are used. Since before 2000, the New Hampshire courts have kept audio recordings of trials. A copy of the Chad Evans trial, which the defense attorneys may have purchased, could not be found. I do not know if the prosecution ever obtained a copy. The courts have destroyed their copies.

This book was first published as an ebook on July 17, 2011. Copies were sent to all of the police originally involved in the case for whom email addresses could be found, and to the prosecutors of Chad and Amanda. Copies were sent to Chad's lawyers, and his family and supporters. Each forwarding email requested that readers send me feedback about errors and omissions, with the goal of making the book as accurate as possible. After a few changes, the "second draft edition" was published as a printed book with "comb" binding on August 10, 2011. The temporary binding was used to convey the message that the book was still a work in progress. After the first 20 copies were sold or given to libraries or others, another 20 were printed on September 25, 2011. It was named "draft Edition 2b," as there were more changes. Especially helpful have been the edits and recommendations from Sandy Gelinas, a co-chair of the Rochester Chapter of the Chad Evans Wrongly Convicted Committee.

The official publication date of the first paperback edition was November 9, 2011, eleven years after Kassidy's death. This edition is also posted on the Chad Evans website, www.chadevanswronglyconvicted.org, where comments, criticisms and suggestions are welcomed. Please email such feedback to me at the address of my first name @ Chad's website.

Chad Evans has read all of this book, and has made many suggestions about its content and editing. To the extent that he had any personal knowledge of the contents of this book, he agrees with what is stated here even as we may differ about emphasis or about what's not in the book. Nonetheless, as the author, I am responsible for the contents, and welcome the opportunity to change or clarify anything in the book in the interest of truth and justice.

INTRODUCTION

The death of 21-month old Kassidy Caitlin Bortner, on November 9, 2000, shook the states of Maine and New Hampshire. When the police and EMT's arrived at the Kittery, Maine home of her babysitter, Jefferey Marshall, shortly after noon, Kassidy showed no signs of life. Not knowing the hour and minute of her last breath, the First Responders tried valiantly to revive her on the apartment porch and on the way to the York Hospital, in York, Maine.

Kassidy's 18-year old mother, Amanda Jean Bortner, had brought her to the apartment of her sister, Jennifer Bortner Conley, and her boyfriend, Jeff Marshall, around 8:30 that morning. Jennifer and Amanda had both used their stepfather's name, Conley, at Sanford High School, Maine, and Jennifer still used it. As if Jeff and Jen needed confirmation, Amanda told them that Kassidy's "*face looks like shit*," or that "*her eye looks like shit*" [Transcript, 5 Dec 2001., p 142] due to the presence of several bruises.

Since late June/early July of 2000, Amanda and Kassidy had lived with Amanda's boyfriend, 28-year old Chad Emery Evans, of Rochester, New Hampshire. Chad was the father of a three year old son, Kyle Evans, and the stepfather to his wife's older son, Brent Lincoln. Chad was not Kassidy's father.

Investigators from the town of Kittery, Maine, the city of Rochester, New Hampshire, and the State Police of Maine and New Hampshire proceeded with the assumption that Kassidy's death was a homicide, and that someone was responsible for intentionally harming and killing her. They quickly assembled a short list of four suspects: Amanda, Chad, Jeff and Jennifer. The two women were rapidly excluded, and the police asked Jeff for a voluntary statement from Jeff, which was assembled in two parts in seven pages. The investigation train was on its way to Conviction Station. A key question in the case was what it would take to persuade the police and prosecutors that the train was going in the wrong direction and/or was going too fast. Chad began his interrogation at 7:10 p.m. on November 9, the day Kassidy died. Feeling extremely badly about the shocking death of Kassidy, but knowing that he did not intentionally injure her, Chad talked openly of the causes of several of Kassidy's bruises, including those on her lower cheeks by his own hand. He described how he would hold her chin in his hand, or her face within the palms of both hands, in order to make eye contact to ensure she understood what he was saying. However, in further explanation of those bruises, he also told them the "trampoline story," much of which was a lie. This was the third and last time he told anyone the "trampoline story." By approximately 9:30 p.m., Maine State Trooper Lance McCleish told Chad that he was the primary suspect.

When police in a criminal case decide who is responsible for a crime, they naturally look for evidence which supports that view and they tend to ignore evidence which doesn't. This is a natural tendency of anyone seeking to validate a hypothesis. In the case of the death of Kassidy Bortner, the focus on one person had the dramatic effect of moving the responsibility for the investigation and prosecution from Maine to New Hampshire. With Chad Evans as the primary suspect, the location of the crime was stated to be his car in New Hampshire or his home in Rochester, New Hampshire, and the focus shifted away from the Kitttery, Maine home where Kassidy spent the last four and a half hours of her life, and died.

The case attracted considerable media attention, but Chad's attorneys advised him to say nothing to reporters. Feeling that his employer, a franchise operator of McDonald's restaurants, could be hurt by the bad publicity for the case, Chad quickly asked for a leave of absence from his $80,000 a year job as an Area Supervisor of 10 restaurants. During the next year while free on bail, he prepared for his trial and found other work. He struggled with his feelings of responsibility for not taking Kassidy to the hospital, or insisting that Amanda do so when Kassidy's health was declining. Chad continued to see, and sometimes live with, Amanda despite a condition of his bail that he not communicate with her. The condition was imposed because the prosecutors were concerned that Chad might harm Amanda, as he did have some history of fighting with his ex-wife, Tristan Evans, and police had been told of domestic violence against Amanda. Also, prosecutors were concerned that their case could be contaminated with communications between their defendant and the mother of the victim.

In August 2001, Chad's bail was revoked after the police found evidence of Chad's contacts with Amanda, and Chad was jailed at the Strafford County Jail until his trial, which began in late November 2001.

At that trial, several witnesses told the jury about bruises on Kassidy's face and body which began to appear in the fall of 2000. Jeff described his babysitting for Kassidy and his actions on November 9, and denied the defense accusations that he was responsible for Kassidy's death. The penultimate prosecution witness was the Chief Medical Examiner for Maine, Dr. Margaret Greenwald, who described approximately 100 bruises, injuries and fractures suffered by Kassidy and visible on Kassidy's body after her death. Dr. Greenwald said that Kassidy's death was caused by the release of fat emboli into her blood stream which caused her heart to stop. This release of fat emboli was said to be caused by blows to Kassidy's head and/or abdomen delivered within 24 hours of her death.

Chad's attorneys called only one defense witness, despite the availability of many of Chad's friends and relatives who knew him as a moral person and excellent father. They knew that Chad could not have intentionally caused Kassidy's death. The defense's only witness was nationally renowned forensic pathologist, Dr. Michael Baden. He testified that the blows that killed Kassidy likely were delivered within the last few hours of her life, i.e. when she was in Jeff's care. The defense lawyers thought Dr. Baden's testimony was sufficient to establish the reasonable doubt needed for a not-guilty verdict. Chad took his attorneys' advice not to testify. They feared a negative jury reaction to Chad's testimony, and the possibility that he might become angry at the prosecution and their tactics. I don't know why the other potential witnesses were not called to testify.

Their assessment of the case, that enough seeds for reasonable doubt had been planted, was wrong. Instead, the jury found Chad guilty of most of the charges: second-degree murder, five counts of second-degree assault, endangering the welfare of a child and simple assault against Amanda. When Chad was sentenced in April, 2002, he again took his attorneys' advice not to proclaim his innocence, in order to avoid angering Judge Tina Nadeau. Chad expressed sincere regret for his actions, by which he meant his failure to do more to help Kassidy. Nonetheless, although Judge Nadeau acknowledged Chad's good deeds in his life, she chastised him for showing insufficient remorse, and sentenced him to 28 years to life in the State Prison in Concord. That conviction was upheld by the New Hampshire Supreme Court in December 2003.

The State of New Hampshire appealed the sentence to the state's Superior Court Sentence Review Board which had recently been authorized by statute hear petitions from prosecutors to change a defendant's sentence. Previously, only defendants could appeal a sentence. After challenges to the prosecutors' request were set aside by the New Hampshire Supreme Court, the Sentence Review Board imposed a consecutive sentence of five to ten years in prison on one of the counts of second-degree assault and an additional consecutive 10-30 year sentence on another count of second-degree assault, with each sentence consecutive to previous sentences. The net effect was to increase Chad's sentence by a minimum of 15 years, transforming his 28 year to life sentence into a 43 year-to-life sentence.

In November, 2002, Amanda was tried and found guilty of child endangerment and sentenced to two years in the Strafford County Jail. Before and after her sentence, she continued to communicate with Chad and to write and telephone him in her belief that Chad was not responsible for the death of her daughter. After her sentence was completed, and after overcoming objections, she visited him, lived in Keene with Chad's parents, and planned to marry Chad.

Jeff Marshall filed a civil lawsuit in 2003 against Chad for slander for accusing him of being responsible for Kassidy's death. That accusation allegedly caused Chad's former employer to cancel Jeff's landscaping contracts. In 2004, each man was deposed by the other's attorney. In the second session of his deposition at the State Prison, Chad continued to heed legal advice from his lawyers and inmate advisors, to remain silent under oath when asked about his role in Kassidy's death, and he "took the Fifth." Jeff dropped his civil suit after his attorney declined to continue working on the case.

In September 2006, the New Hampshire Supreme Court denied Chad's appeal of the 15 year increase in his sentence, and he sought relief in the Federal courts.

In June, 2010, Chad's Motion for Habeas Corpus before the U.S. District Court for New Hampshire was denied. In that Motion, Chad challenged the legality under the U.S. Constitution of the 15 year increase in his sentence. The judge's denial was appealed to the U.S. Court of Appeals for the First Circuit in Boston, and that court affirmed the denial in June, 2011. There is no current challenge in the courts to his wrongful conviction, for which he has spent more than ten years in prison, but other motions for judicial relief are anticipated.

To introduce readers to the characters of this story, the 46 people most affected or involved in this case are listed below. The more complete list of "Who's Who?" at Chad's website has 157 people.

Aube, Bruce. A best friend of Chad, in Rochester, NH. Lived with Jessica Edmands.
Baden, Dr. Michael. Forensic Pathologist. Chad's only defense witness at his trial.
Blodgett, Angela. Detective, Maine State Police.
Bortner, Amanda Jean (Mandy). Mother of Kassidy Caitlyn Bortner, and Chad's girlfriend.
Bortner, Kassidy Caitlyn. Daughter Amanda Bortner & Robert Sheehan, born 4 Feb. 99.
Brown, Simon R. New Hampshire Asst. Attorney General and prosecutor at Chad's trial
Chick, Melissa. Best friend of Amanda from high school, since seventh grade.
Conley, Emily. Springvale,ME. Amanda's friend from school; not related to her stepfather.
Conley, Jacqueline. Mother: Charles, Jennifer, Amanda &Joshua Bortner & Scott Conley.
Conley, Jennifer (also Bortner). Girlfriend of Jeff Marshall, and sister of Amanda Bortner.
Conley, Joshua Bortner. Younger brother of Amanda Bortner.
Creamer, Robert. Patrolman, Kittery Police Dept.
Cronheim, Alan J., Attorney for Chad Evans, together with Mark Sisti.
Delker, N. William, ("Will"). NH Asst. Attorney General, prosecutor at Chad's trial.
Evans, Chester (Chet). Father of Chad and Jason Evans and Nicole Evans Harvey, Married to Pam Evans.
Evans, Chad Emery. Son of Chet and Pam Evans. Father of Kyle, boyfriend of Amanda.
Evans, Kyle Chester. Son of Chad and Tristan Wentworth Evans.
Evans, Pamela Martin. Mother of Chad and Jason Evans, Nicole Evans Harvey. Married to Chet Evans.
Evans, Tristan Wentworth. Former wife of Chad Evans and mother of Brent Lincoln and Kyle Evans.
Foley, Tracey. Of Springvale, Maine. Friend of Amanda Bortner.
Gagne, Shannon. Friend of Amanda Bortner from high school.
Greenwald, Dr. Margaret. Chief Medical Examiner, State of Maine.
Hamel, Steven. Detective with the Kittery, Maine, Police Dept.
Harakles, Scott. Maine State Police Detective. Interviewed Jeff Marshall and Travis Hunt.
Harvey, Brandon. Husband of Nicole Evans Harvey, brother-in-law of Chad Evans.
Harvey, Nicole Evans. Younger sister of Chad Evans. Now Nicole Evans-Mahoney.
Hinton, Jeremy. A best friend of Chad Evans. Manager of McDonald's in Portsmouth.
Hocter, Patricia. Case worker: NH DHHS, Division of Children Youth & Families (DCYF).
LeClair, Richard. Maine State Police. Interviewed Amanda Bortner & then Chad Evans.
Linscott, Jeff. Maine State Trooper. Participated in several interviews.
Magee, William F., III. Sergeant of NH State Police. Conducted Nov. 10 search of Chad's home.
Mansson, Vanessa. Friend of Chad and Amanda in Keene, New Hampshire.
Marshall, Jefferey(Jeff). Boyfriend of Jennifer Bortner and babysitter for Kassidy.
Martin, Crystal. Friend of Amanda Bortner, after high school. Crystal had a son, Devin.
McCleish, Lance. Detective, Maine State Police. Interviewed Chad Evans, November 9, 2000

McDougall, Robert. Supervisor of Chad Evans, at the McDonald's licensee, Colley/McCoy. Nadeau, Tina L., Judge, at Chad's. Now Chief Justice of New Hampshire Superior Court.

Nuernberg, Cathy. Friend of Amanda Bortner from high school. Lived in San Antonio, Texas.

Peirce, William C. Next door neighbor to, and landlord of, Jeff Marshall in Kittery, Maine.

Rockey, Jill. Trooper, NH State Police. Interviewed Travis Hunt and Jeremy Hinton.

Rothstein, David M. NH Deputy Chief Appellate Defender. Chad's appellate attorney.

Ruoff, David. Asst. Attorney General. Prosecutor in the case NH vs. Amanda Bortner.

Sisti, Mark L. Attorney, together with Alan Cronheim, for Chad Evans.

Timoney, James. Orthopedic surgeon who examined Kassidy in Sept., 2000.

Varney, Glen. A friend of Chad, who lived on Baxter Lake, where Chad kept his boat in 2000.

White, James. Detective-Sergeant, New Hampshire State Police. Chief NH investigator in case.

Wiberg, Patricia S., Attorney for Amanda Bortner. 2001-02.

CHAPTER 1: TRAGEDY - 9 NOVEMBER 2000, to 12:38 P.M.

"Come on Kassidy. Come on Kassidy. Come on ..." - Jeff Marshall

For the melded Evans/Bortner family at 191 Milton Road, the day almost began at 4:30 a.m. or 5:30 a.m. when Kassidy began crying. Amanda asked Chad, "*Chad, yell to her and tell her to go to sleep,*" and Chad called out, "*Kassidy, go to sleep, baby.*" Kassidy went back to sleep, and saved Chad, Amanda, and Kyle another 45 minutes or more of sleep. So far, the morning seemed normal.

At 6:15 a.m., or later, Kassidy began crying again, and wakened Chad and Amanda, which was fortunate, as they had overslept their 6:00 a.m. goal. Chad wrote in his Nov. 2000 letter to his attorneys,

...she did fall back to sleep. It didn't seem odd because she had done that a lot the last couple of weeks. I usually went in and got her and brought her in to sleep with us. But this morning I was too dead tired to move. I remember thinking, "Oh shit!" when I read 6:39 on the alarm clock. I woke Amanda up and told her she was going to be late if she didn't get a move on, as she had to work at 8 am. I got up with her initially. She walked into Kassidy's room and I started towards Kyle's. When she entered Kassidy's room, Kassidy woke up and said, "Mamma." Kassidy got up and walked to the edge of the bed and put her arms out for Amanda.

Amanda changed Kassidy's diaper and dressed her for the day and was able to see Kassidy's entire body before getting her dressed. Even with her 20/800 vision, Amanda could see, without her contact lenses, the bruises on Kassidy's forehead. Amanda said in her first interview,

I saw a bruise on her, right here and here. On her eyes. I didn't notice anything on her body, but when I got her dressed this morning, I didn't have contacts in and my vision's 20/800 so ... I didn't notice that it was hurting or anything." (p. 863)

Among the few bruises on her body was the bruise from hitting her head, near her right eye, on a table on Sunday evening, November 5. Amanda and Travis Hunt, a McDonald's employee friend of Chad, and basement tenant, were with Kassidy at the time. Kassidy slid off the couch and into the table. The other bruise on her head came from being hit in the eye the previous evening with a "*hard rubber ball*" or "*starter baseball*" or Tee-Ball. It was hit by 3-year-old Kyle, after being tossed a pitch by Chad. Kassidy had scratches over her left eye from her newly acquired kitten. Perhaps there was another bruise on her head from falling in Chad's driveway the previous afternoon, but neither Chad nor Amanda noticed such a bruise. Also, the previous evening, Chad had noticed a sore spot on Kassidy's lower lip, but it wasn't noticed by Amanda that morning and Chad doesn't remember commenting on it to Amanda.

Chad carried Kassidy on his hip downstairs around 7:00 - 7:10 a.m and sat her on the kitchen counter with her legs over the edge. He asked Kassidy which cereal she wanted. Then he reached for the cereal boxes on top of the refrigerator and pointed to a box he thought she preferred. She shook her head sideways, to indicate "*No*," and pointed to the cereal which she wanted: Reese's Puffs. Chad packed enough cereal for breakfast and a snack in a Ziploc bag, or "baggie," for Kassidy for the trip to Jeff's and Jennifer's home. He filled her sippy cup with juice, and placed a few snacks into the diaper bag. Amanda said in her police interview that she *"noticed that she wasn't really hungry and didn't eat very much."* (p. 863)

In 2011, Chad remembered,

We were behind schedule....I do have a distinct memory of picking Kassidy off the counter after I packed her chosen cereal in a baggie and set her standing up on the kitchen floor. She stood there looking at me with her juice cup in hand. I then asked Kassidy if she wanted to watch cartoons for a minute. She said "Yes," and then to get her there quicker, I picked her up and carried her to the couch. (Letter, July 29, 2011)

At some point that morning, Kyle saw the bruise on Kassidy's left eye and asked, "*Daddy, did I do that?*" At some point, Kassidy said, "*Drink,*" to Amanda. After rushing breakfast and packing lunch for Kyle, Amanda went out the door with Kassidy. Amanda was expected at work at 8:00 a.m., and she already knew that she would be late. Still, she had agreed to take Kyle to day care because it was on her way. It added only an additional 15 minutes, to the trip to Jeff's and Jennifer's apartment to drop Kassidy off, and get to work. Chad wrote in 2010, with some overlap with the description above,

Kyle was eating cereal at the dining room table and Kassidy was sitting on the couch watching cartoons. I yelled up to Amanda and asked her if she wanted me to feed Kassidy or pack her food for Jeff's. She yelled down to pack it up because Kassidy would take too long to eat and she was already late. While Kyle ate his breakfast, I carried Kassidy into the kitchen and set her on the counter by the sink. We kept the cereal on top of the refrigerator, on the other side of the kitchen. I asked Kassidy, "What kind of cereal do you want?" I recall we had 3 different boxes which I held out to her, and she pointed to the Reese's Peanut Butter Puffs. (This was a semi-new cereal at the time and came in little chocolate looking puff balls similar to Cocoa Puffs or Kix.) I put the cereal in a baggie. I can't recall what else, but I packed some other things for Kassidy to eat throughout the day. We had a lot of kids' snacks- cheese and crackers, chips, fruit, juice, I can't recall if I made her a sandwich that particular day. If there is a description from that day of what was found for food in Kassidy's bag at Jeff's house, we will know what I packed. Once Amanda finished her shower and got dressed, we got the kids' coats on and carried them to the car. I believe that I had both of the kids in my arms and Amanda had their bags. I put Kassidy into her car seat directly behind Amanda's seat and Amanda buckled her in while I went around the other side and buckled Kyle in. Amanda was going to drop him off at school in Dover on the way to Kittery. I kissed Kyle as Amanda got into the car. I ran around and reached through the driver's door to kiss Amanda. She barely gave me a peck. She was rushing and I believe she was still mad at what she perceived as my laziness/unwillingness to help her when we woke up. I backed away from the car toward our steps as she got ready to back out and I realized that I hadn't kissed Kassidy goodbye so I came back toward the car screaming, "Wait!" As Amanda rolled down her window I said, "I didn't kiss Kassidy yet." I quickly opened the backseat door and kissed Kassidy on the forehead. "I love you, have a good day baby." That is when I noticed she had somehow gotten hold of her Ziplock cereal baggie, had opened it and was eating some of her cereal. I was amazed that she could open it. I believe I said out loud. "You little shit. I didn't know you could open these." I said to Amanda, something like, "Baby, she opened her cereal bag. Did you know she could open them?" Amanda sounded a little irritated and replied something like, "She's been able to do that for a while. I am late. I've got to go!" The reason that this is such an important sequence is because Kassidy sat on the counter, and she chose her cereal, and she opened her own baggie, etc. These are all things that they told Amanda would have been impossible for Kassidy to do in the condition that Dr. Greenwald said she would have been in that morning. God as my witness, this is all true. She left our house that morning awake, though apparently tired. (Letter, Apr. 29, 2010)

Off they went, for the 15 mile/24 minute trip to Kyle's day care. This was the last time Chad saw Kassidy Bortner. At that time, as far as he knew, it was the hectic beginning of another workday. In addition, he knew that Kassidy...

-was not at her best, but he was ever hopeful that she would improve, after the lethargic behavior of the previous day.
-had a bruise from the injury by a Tee-ball the previous night.
-had a bruise under her right eye from a scratch from their new kitty.
-had a bruise under her right eye from falling into the coffee table in his living room, when Amanda and Travis were with her.
-had a bruise under her chin, perhaps caused by the fall in his driveway yesterday.
-had a lump on the back of her head from the fall from Jeff's truck on Saturday, October 28.
-had a sore, of unknown origin, inside her lower lip, which led him to skip her toothbrushing the previous night.
-had a bruise on the side of her head.
-had some dry skin protrusions on the bottoms of her feet, which he understood were

caused by exposed tacks on Jeff's flooring.
-possibly had some miscellaneous typical childrens' bruises on arms and legs, but nothing extraordinary that caught Chad's attention.

That was all he knew about bruises and injuries. He wasn't sure if there were any bruises from his holding Kassidy's face in order to obtain eye contact, but he knew that he hadn't held her face strongly during November because of her apparent fatigue and illness, and because he and Amanda had realized that such holding could cause bruising. Normally, Chad drove Kyle to Cross Road Kindergarten and Child Care in Dover, but he and Amanda agreed that it was easier for her to take Kyle on this fateful day. Chad had to finish a report that was due for work. Amanda's variable work schedule at the Kittery, Maine, Old Navy store gave her a start time on this day which made the trip to Kyle's day care convenient, with only a 15 minute detour.

At about 7:40 a.m., Amanda left Kyle at Cross Road, by driving up to the door, with its protective portico at the entrance. She let Kyle out of the car and walked him in, while keeping an eye on Kassidy in the car. Then, Amanda and Kassidy left for Jeff's and Jennifer's home at 51 Rogers Road in Kittery, Maine, which was 16.5 miles away, or about 28 minutes.

Chad began his workday at home with his report, and then by calling the Rochester McDonald's at 8:10 a.m. for 13 minutes. This restaurant was the site of Chad's first managerial position for his employer franchisee, Colley-McCoy. As it was located exactly three miles from his home, he watched its operations closely.

Life seemed to be good that morning for Chad. He was in love with Amanda, and looking forward to a life with her and Kassidy. He expected that word would be coming soon from the Probate Court about the finalization of his divorce from Tristan. He would have felt better if he had known that it had already been completed on October 4, and that there had been a delay in mailing the paperwork to him. Amanda was in the first full week of her new job at Old Navy, not including the previous week's training. Both she and Chad looked forward to her finding a better day care situation than the temporary babysitting at Jeff and Jennifer's home. One reason was that there were no other children at Jeff's, and Amanda knew that it would be good for Kassidy to play and learn with other children. More importantly, there were difficulties the previous day with Kassidy, which showed, once again, that Jeff's babysitting was not good for her. There were too many accidents, and watching TV was Kassidy's primary learning activity.

Amanda and Kassidy arrived at Jeff and Jennifer's home shortly after 8:00 a.m. Amanda carried Kassidy into the apartment, rather than having her walk because she was rushing. Another reason for carrying her was that Kassidy was still limping, whether from an accident a few days previous where Jeff had stepped on her foot, or from Chad playing with Kassidy at home, or from her toed-in problem, or from another cause. Amanda sat Kassidy on Jeff and Jennifer's bed, with her bag of Reese's Puffs, juice in a sippy cup, and diaper bag. Kassidy was wearing her new "Basic Editions" red pajama pants and a red and white dress-like pajama top with a white dog on the chest. During the investigation, it was called a "dress." Under the dress, she was perhaps also wearing a red fleece sweatshirt. Kassidy was wearing her new "Elmo" slippers. It was November, and she was wearing her new pink hooded jacket. The diaper bag had spare diapers and a container of A&D Ointment for treatment of diaper rash, and food snacks packed by Chad. Amanda commented to Jeff and Jennifer about the bruises, "*She looks like shit, doesn't she*?" Also, Kassidy was obviously tired, and Amanda and Chad thought perhaps she had caught a bit of the flu that Kyle had suffered earlier in the week and month. Amanda had no clue that Kassidy was seriously sick, and was even more unaware that Kassidy was no more than four hours away from her death. Jeff and Jennifer were equally unaware. Jeff testified at Chad's trial (p. 168) that he tried to pick Kassidy up and stand her on the floor, but that "*she didn't want to be picked up*," so he left her on the bed. He turned on the television to a channel with cartoons, and went into the living room to watch the continued coverage of the election returns, especially the Bush-Gore presidential race.

Jennifer said in her first police interview that she asked Kassidy "*Do you want to go sit in the bathroom while I put my makeup on*?" as that was their usual practice. Kassidy liked it when Jennifer would also put some makeup on her. On this morning, said Jennifer, "*...she did not want to get up. She started like crying, took the bed stuff off her, she started crying. So, I was, 'Okay. okay.' So I covered her back up and gave her, you know, her Cocoa Puffs,* (p. 925-26) " *or Cocoa Krispies whatever she was eating and she started eating those."* (p. 918) Similarly, she asked, *"You want to get up and walk around and stuff like that?" And she started crying when I took the covers off of her."* so Jennifer restored the covers. (p. 918)

Jennifer said did not get a good look at Kassidy because she was fully clothed, but she did notice that *"she had a little scratch here* [pointing to her right eye] *from my cat scratching her."* (p. 926) A small misunderstanding between Amanda and Jennifer was whether Jennifer's cat, Toby, or Kassidy's new unnamed, kitten, caused the scratch. Amanda was planning to pick Kassidy up at Jeff's after her work shift ended around 5:30 p.m.. Perhaps she was planning to bring Kassidy to go candlepin bowling with Chad and his best friend, Bruce Aube, and Travis, or meet them at their habitual Thursday evening spot, "Bananas Bar and Grill," in Portsmouth. Kyle would be picked up at Cross Road Kindergarten and Child Care by his mother, Tristan Evans, and taken to her home for a few days, pursuant to the joint custody arrangement between her and Chad. Alternatively, Amanda may have been scheduled to work late that evening, for a full 12-hour shift and may have planned to ask Chad to pick up Kassidy, as he had done the previous day. (First Amanda interview, p. 863.)

Amanda left Jeff's home around 8:20 a.m. for work at Old Navy, which is only 2.3 miles away. The Kittery Police Station is between the two locations.

Jeff talked by telephone at 8:49 a.m. with William Peirce, who lived next door, and told him that Kassidy was not walking and was sitting in front of the television eating cereal. Peirce was Jeff's friend, occasional employee and, most recently, landlord, as Peirce had purchased in October the 51/53 Rogers Road duplex property.

Jennifer told the police during her first interview that Kassidy was eating her "Cocoa Puffs," but they were actually "Reese's Puffs." They looked almost like "Cocoa Puffs," but they had a chocolate and peanut butter flavor. (See photo of box at Chad's house.) Also, Jennifer reported that Kassidy said, "*Kitty, Kitty, Kitty*," to Jeff and Jennifer's cat, Toby. Those words may have been her last words, but she may not have said them on that day, either, as Jennifer testified (p. 113) at Chad's trial that she didn't actually see Kassidy eating her cereal.

Close to 9:00 a.m. Jennifer kissed Kassidy "*Good-bye*," and Kassidy made a "kiss" sound. as Jennifer left for work at Perfumania, a shop at the Kittery Mall, a few storefronts away from Amanda at Old Navy. She was scheduled to work until 2:30 or 4:30 p.m., so she would have returned home before Amanda, and would have likely spent some time with Kassidy.

Shortly after 9 a.m., Patricia Hocter of the New Hampshire Division of Children, Youth and Families (DCYF) called the Chad Evans home phone and left a message to call. (Chart of Calls This "Chart of Calls" was prepared by the Office of the Attorney General or the New Hampshire or Maine State Police and faxed to Chad Evans's defense counsel on 30 November 2001, just before Chad's trial.) As Ms. Hocter did not know who would retrieve the message and how confidential information might be treated, she said nothing about the reason for the call, which was to followup on an anonymous call to DCYF on 31 October reporting bruises on Kassidy. The message referred to "*the children*" and not to any particular child. (Magee report, p. 3091) Chad was in the shower at the time, and did not hear the phone. After getting dressed, he made two calls from his home phone, heard Patricia Hocter's message and then called her at 9:32 a.m. He was not familiar with the initials DCYF, and had no idea what the call was about. He waited for 120 seconds, but there was no human response. At 9:35 a.m., he called DCYF again, and left a message for Patricia Hocter in the DCYF "general mailbox." (Chart of Calls) According to Ms. Hocter's testimony (p. 54) at Chad's trial, he stated that he was going out of town and wouldn't be back until Tuesday, and asked that she call him back between 3:00-4:00 on that day.

The planned trip was to Maine for a McDonald's business meeting and celebration which he was planning to attend with Amanda. At her hiring at Old Navy, Amanda had specifically requested that time off. Chad's employer, Colley-McCoy, was a large McDonald's franchisee, and it was doing well. Chad was planning to leave with Amanda on Friday afternoon and not return until late Monday, and expected that Tuesday morning would be busy; hence the suggestion that Ms. Hocter could reach him in the afternoon.

A few minutes later, Chad Evans called his childhood friend, Vanessa Mansson, at her workplace in Peterborough, New Hampshire, to learn more about the state agency, DCYF. After being referred to a different number, he called again, at 9:40 a.m., and talked with Vanessa for more than five minutes. (Chart of Calls) Chad wrote in his Nov. 2000 letter to his attorneys,

Vanessa told me that it wasn't [related to child support issues]*, she said it has to do with abused or neglected kids. We both had a little laugh and she said, "Yeah right, as if Kyle is so abused."(She really didn't know Kassidy, but knew I spoiled Kyle and Brent rotten.) So I went about my business until it dawned on me, "Wait a minute, maybe they are calling because of Kassidy. The poor girl has a limp, bump on her head, bruise on her forehead, etc."*

At 9:47 a.m., Chad called Jeff's cell phone, but did not connect, so he called again with the two goals of reminding Jeff to fix the problems with a tree at the Greenland, New Hampshire, McDonald's restaurant, and to ask about Kassidy, given her difficulties the previous day. (Chart of Calls) Chad wrote about that 13 minute call,

So I then called Jeff and told him I got a call from DCYF. He asked me what they were and I told him. I said, "I wonder what they are calling about and who called them." He said, "Oh it was probably Amanda's friend Emily (Another entire story) and that it was nothing to worry about she was a bitch anyway." I said to him, "Well Jeff, 1 don't know what they are calling about but if it is anything to do with the baby, she and Amanda are going to come stay with you until it blows over. You are the one that stepped on her, dropped her out of the truck onto her head, and bruised her head. I am going through a divorce right now and until it is final I don't need to be involved with any shit or give Tristan anything to screw me with." He said, "Oh no, don't worry about it. They can if that is it." I then asked, "How is the little princess?" He said, "She is fine. She is sitting right here with me." I could hear her cooing in the background. Then he said, (laughing as he said it) "Man, her eye looks like shit. I told you to call me if you were going to beat her up so I could watch." I said, "Man you're fucked up. I didn't hit her. I told you last night she got hit by Kyle's ball!" He could tell I was pissed. He said, "I know, 1 know, I was just kidding." (The thing I don't understand is if her face was so fucked up like he told the cops that Amanda brought her that way. Why did he just say her eye looked like shit and not her entire face?) He made a similar comment the night before and I think it was during our last conversation when I said she was acting weird like she wasn't even in there. He said before we got off the phone, "Ok, well, don't beat her too hard without me." I got off the phone with him and arrived at my first restaurant. (Nov. 2000 Chad letter to his attorneys.)

According to Jeff's testimony (p. 171) at Chad's trial, Chad began the call with, "*How's Kassidy*?" and Jeff replied that she was "*fine*."

At Chad's trial, Jeff testified that before Chad's call, he went into his bedroom to check on the mischief that his cat, Toby, might have caused, as it had jumped from a desk in the living room, apparently taking something, and ran into the bedroom and under the bed. In his initial statement to the police, Jeff said that he had observed Kassidy sleeping, and at Chad's trial, he said the same thing. (Transcript, Dec. 6, p. 169)
Jeff has stated that shortly after noon, he went to his mailbox on his porch for mail and returned and checked on Kassidy, who seemed lifeless. He brought her into the kitchen and splashed water on her face to try to arouse her.

At 12:24 p.m. he started calling.

1st Call: From his home phone, he made his first call about Kassidy's condition - to Chad's cell phone, but Chad was in a meeting and didn't answer.

2nd Call: At 12:25 p.m. Jeff called Chad again with the same result,

3rd Call: Jeff tried a third time immediately thereafter. (Chart of Calls)

4th Call: At 12:26 p.m. in his fourth call after finding Kassidy in distress, Jeff called Jennifer for advice on what to do, and she recommended during the 46 second call that he call the hospital, and she went back to work. (interview, Nov. 9, p. 942) In her trial testimony (p. 136) she stated that she recommended that Jeff call the hospital. (Chart of Calls) He didn't call the hospital or 911. According to Detective Steve Hamel's report, Jennifer's recommendation during this first call was for Jeff to call Amanda, which is what he tried to do, after calling more calls to Chad. In Jeff's Nov. 9 interview, he said that Jennifer's advice during this first call was to "get a hold of Mandy." (interview, p. 1297)

5th Call: At 12:28 p.m., Jeff called Chad's cell phone a fourth time, but did not reach him.

6th Call: Seconds later, he tried calling Chad a fifth time.

7th Call: He called Chad a sixth time. In one of these calls, Jeff left the message, "*Chad, This is Jeff. Call me as soon as you get this, bye!*" (Letter, Feb. 22, 2010) Chad was in a business meeting, so he did not see the message until he checked his cell phone messages at 2:24 p.m. (Chart of Calls)

8th Call: At 12:32 p.m., in his eighth call after finding Kassidy in distress, Jeff Marshall called "411" for "Information" for the phone number for the Old Navy store in Kittery, where Amanda Bortner worked. In my own recollection of babysitting as a teenager, I remember the familiar instruction from a parent, "Here's the phone number where we will be, if you need us." Jeff didn't have Amanda's work number, on this fourth, or more, day of babysitting while Amanda was working at Old Navy.

9th Call: After getting the Old Navy phone number, Jeff's ninth call was to Amanda at 12:34 p.m., but did not get past the phone messaging system. (Chart of Calls)

10th Call: From his home phone at 12:37 p.m., Jeff's tenth call was to Jennifer again, and he said, according to Jennifer's testimony, (p 137) that *"the baby was - was coming through, and the ambulance was on its way, and not to worry."* Jennifer referred in her police interview, and testimony at Chad's and Amanda's trials, to Kassidy most often in the third person, as "*the baby*," or "*the kid*." (Chart of Calls) Jennifer then called Amanda at work to tell her that Kassidy was in distress and that Jeff was taking her to "*the hospital*." Jennifer apparently felt that the problem was minor or under control, and she returned to her customers.

11th Call: At 12:38 p.m., Jeff's eleventh call was to 911. The call went to the Kittery Police Dept. which reported the call at 12:39 p.m. Fortunately, the Police Dept. was down the street at 200 Rogers Road, Extension, and less than a mile away from Jeff's home at 51 Rogers Road. (Chart of Calls) According to the 911 transcript, the call began as follows with "DIS" being the 911/Kittery Dispatcher and "JM" being Jeff.

DIS ... What town are you calling from?
JM Kittery.
DIS What's your problem?
JM I've got a little girl that I'm baby-sitting and she just went into like shock.
DIS Ok, what's the address?
JM 51 Rogers Road.
DIS 51 Rogers Road?
JM Yep.
DIS Ok. Let me get the ambulance started. Hold on please. Kittery, Kittery 9, can you go to 51 Rogers Road for a juvenile female that's just went into shock and is unconscious.
AMR American Medical Response, is this an emergency?
DIS Hi. Karen calling from Kittery.
AMR Hi.
DIS We have a female juvenile who just went into shock unknown cause. And this is at 51 Rogers Road.
AMR Fifty-one Rogers?
DIS Yep.
AMR And how old again was she ma'am?

DIS Unknown.
AMR Unknown.
DIS Yep.
AMR Thank you.
DIS You're welcome.
AMR Bye-bye.
DIS Kittery ... Kittery 14. Hi, is she breathing?
JM Barely.
DIS Ok. And do you know has she swallowed anything ... or?
JM Nope. Nope. She fell on the ground I guess yesterday at home. Like I said, I'm babysitting. I'm her uncle. And, ah, she was laying in bed and I was in the, ah, other room.
JM (Inaudible) I'm like trying to press on her stomach.
DIS Ok. Don't press on her stomach, ok, just in case there's an injury there. Ok, is she ... if she's breathing ...
JM She's barely ...
DIS Okay. She is breathing though?
JM A little bit.
DIS Ok. Can you just try talking to her and she if can ...
JM It's like her eyes are like out.
DIS Ok. Keep saying her name.
JM **Come on Kassidy. Come on Kassidy. Come on ...**
DIS Say Kassidy talk to me and stuff like that.
JM Kassidy come on talk to me. Talk to me come on. Come on ...
DIS Kittery, Kittery 9, if you can expedite she's barely conscious.
JM Come on Kassidy. Come on Kassidy.
Kit9 10-4, is there an ambulance coming?
DIS Affirmative.
JM I'm out on the porch. They can just pull up right out front.

Simultaneous with this series of calls was Patricia Hocter retrieval of her phone messages, at 12:30 p.m. including the 9:35 a.m. call from Chad.

At 12:41 p.m. Kittery Patrolman Robert Creamer arrived at Jeff's home as the first "First responder." Officer Creamer's report said he was called "*about 12:30 p.m.*," but the report gave the time of the "*incident*" as 12:41 p.m.

By this time, it was too late, as Kassidy was dead according to the testimony of Dr. Margaret Greenwald, the Maine Medical Examiner, at Chad's trial. She said, at page 231 "*Well, she died around 12:30.*" Similarly, the Emergency Room doctor at York Hospital, Dr. Anthony Bock, estimated during his testimony (p. 29) that Kassidy was dead by the time of the arrival of the Emergency Medical Technicians (EMT's) at 12:46 p.m. Officer Creamer reported that all of Kassidy's body was cold to the touch, except her armpits. The EMT's tried valiantly to resuscitate Kassidy, including the insertion of IV's, (intravenous fluids), but to no avail. At 1:06 p.m., they carried her body to the ambulance and drove to York Hospital, about 8 miles north.

Now, the challenge was to discover why and how Kassidy Caitlyn Bortner died, and if someone was responsible, to prosecute and punish that person or persons.

CHAPTER 2: KASSIDY CAITLYN BORTNER - 4 FEBRUARY 1999 TO 8 JUNE 2000

"The thing that attracted me to him the most was how great of a father he was." - Amanda Bortner

Friday, 22 May 1998

Kassidy Caitlyn Bortner's life began inauspiciously as the result of at least one crime, serving alcohol to a minor. This crime was soon supplemented with a lie. Someone served enough alcohol to Amanda Bortner on May 22, 1998 to reduce her defenses to having unprotected sex with Robert Sheehan, who she had been dating for about a month, and whose 20 year birthday party she was attending. Amanda was 16 and a half years old and almost finished her sophomore year at Sanford High School. She leaned toward having an abortion, but her mother persuaded her to continue with the pregnancy and birth. (Stephen Carlisle Presentence Report, (PSI) page 8) Amanda did not return to school in the fall.

Thursday, 4 February 1999

Kassidy was born at the Southern Maine Medical Center in Biddeford, Maine. Her maternal grandmother, Jacqueline Conley, formerly Jacqueline Bortner, was there, and cut the umbilical cord. At birth, Kassidy weighed 8 1/2 pounds and was 21 1/2 inches tall. Her birth was slightly premature at 36.7 weeks, with normal gestation for children being 37-42 weeks. The early birth was apparently not significant enough to affect her future development. Amanda and Kassidy returned to Amanda's home in the village of Springvale, within the town of Sanford. She lived there with Jacqueline and her stepfather, Paul Conley, and older sister, Jennifer Bortner Conley and two younger brothers, Joshua Bortner Conley, and Scott Conley. Amanda convinced her long time boyfriend, Gabe Snyder, 18, and perhaps herself, that he was Kassidy's father. Gabe and Amanda, now 17, and Kassidy moved to an apartment together in early Spring. Also living with them was Amanda's close friend, Emily Conley, and her boyfriend Cory. Amanda hoped to raise Kassidy with a father, and hoped for a life for herself with a man and away from her parents. These were difficult decisions for a 17 year-old, high school dropout. The young family seemed to be making a start, despite the handicaps, and Gabe became attached to Kassidy.

However, enough people were at Robert Sheehan's birthday party to cause the rumor to circulate that Gabe possibly was not Kassidy's father. Gabe's and Amanda's relationship deteriorated and he moved out early in the summer. He also asked for a paternity test, and the results, later in the year, showed that he was not Kassidy's father. Immediately thereafter, Amanda and Kassidy moved to live with her friend, Cathy Nuernberg, and Cathy's sister, in a downstairs apartment of a home owned by Cathy's mother. Kassidy was initially with them, but her grandmother, Jacqueline Conley, increasingly provided most of the care for Kassidy. Amanda moved back home for a while, where she and her mother shared caring for Kassidy.

Amanda was not ready for motherhood, as so few teenaged, unmarried girls are. She was born in Anchorage, Alaska to Charles and Jacqueline Bortner and her family moved several times. They returned to their home state of Pennsylvania, and then moved to New Hampshire and in 1993, they moved to Sanford, Maine. Sanford is the largest town in Maine, with a town hall that is as large as most City Halls in the state, and is located just east of the New Hampshire border city of Rochester. It's connected to Rochester by U.S. Route 202/State Route 11.

In Pennsylvania, Amanda's father and mother divorced, and times were tough for the Bortner family. Jacqueline then married Paul Conley, and they had a son together, Scott Conley. Amanda had an older brother, Charles Bortner, who had developed epilepsy. Her sister, Jennifer, was one year older, and stayed at Sanford High School for most of her senior year with the class of 1999, before leaving. Later, she received her G.E.D. from Sanford. Amanda's brother, Joshua Bortner, was three years younger than Amanda, and Scott Conley was more than ten years younger.

Both the girls were attractive blondes and had many friends in high school. Jennifer later competed in several Miss Maine contests. Amanda's teenage friends included Melissa Chick, Emily Conley, Shannon Gagne, Crystal Martin, Cathy Nuernberg, and Vikki Normand. Amanda's middle school/high school boyfriend was Gabe.

Amanda's stepfather, Paul, was a mechanic and later a long-distance truck driver. Amanda and Jennifer worked during high school delivering newspapers. In the summer of 1998, Amanda was working at Shain's Ice Cream on Main Street in Sanford, and Jennifer was working in the kitchen at Goodall Hospital in Sanford.

While working at Shain's, Amanda met Tracey Foley who had a stepson and toddler daughter, Chandler, and Amanda began babysitting for her. After Kassidy was born in February 1999, Amanda would bring Kassidy with her to Tracey's for babysitting, and Gabe Snyder would join in the babysitting as well. After Tracey and her husband separated, Amanda wasn't needed for babysitting, and Tracey and Amanda lost contact.

In the late Spring of 1999, Jennifer Bortner was working at a video store in Sanford, Video Gallery. In the early summer she opened up a new Video Gallery store in Kittery, Maine, on the coast about 30 miles southeast of Sanford, bordering New Hampshire to the south. When working there, a customer, F. Jefferey Marshall (Jeff), introduced himself and asked Jennifer out for a date. Their relationship blossomed quickly and she moved to his apartment at 51 Rogers Road, in Kittery, a few weeks later. He had lived there since 1996.

Jeff Marshall was born in 1975, and thus was 24 when he met Jennifer, age 19. He was the older of two sons born to Frank D. Marshall and Janis Adams Marshall of Newburyport, Mass. Jeff's younger brother, Frank Joshua, was born in 1981. Jeff's parents divorced and Janis and her sons moved to York, Maine in 1986. His mother continues to live in York, which borders Kittery to the south. Also in 1986, tragedy struck the family, when Joshua was diagnosed with neuroblastoma, a form of childhood cancer. The disease is hard to detect as the symptoms can include fatigue, loss of appetite, fever and joint pain. During his struggle with the disease, he excelled in school, and was a member of the Cub Scouts and played, soccer, basketball and baseball. He wrote of his experiences in a book, Hospital is a Nightmare, which was privately published and presented at the Dover, New Hampshire Jimmy Fund Telethon. Before his tragic death on October 3, 1992 at the age of 11, he had achieved two Make-a-Wish goals of meeting Roger Clemens in 1987 and 1992 and going to Disney World in July, 1992. His death had a significant and uncertain effect on his older brother. Jeff said in his November 9, 2000 police interview, "*I don't have any kids, no,... like I said I like kids, you know. I have a little brother that died of cancer when he was 11, you know.... This is why this bothers me quite a bit....* (p. 1273) In terms of age, Joshua was between Jennifer and Amanda.

Jeff attended York High School, in the class of 1994, and in 1992 was the president of the school's chapter of VICA (Vocational Industries Clubs of America). In his senior year, the mornings were spent at the Regional Technical School in Sanford, now called the Sanford Regional Technical Center. Two weeks before graduation, he dropped out of school. He did not subsequently obtain a GED (General Equivalency Diploma). At his deposition in a civil suit in 2004, Jeff said of that period,

I was having a hard time dealing with my brother's death....Hated the world, you know. Thought everything was, you know, the world's fault because my brother passed away. (p. 9)

During high school, he played soccer, basketball and flag football, and was a member of the track team and earned his "letter," in that sport. Outside of school he was a member of York Police Explorer Post #393 which was affiliated with the York Police Dept. Although the Law Enforcement Explorer Program is organized through an affiliate of the Boy Scouts of America, girls are active participants, Of the 16 Explorers listed in the Post's 1994-95 fundraising cookbook, six were girls, and Jeff was not listed. In 2004, he described this activity as being a "*junior police officer*" and his goal was to become a State Trooper. (deposition, p. 12) Jeff explained that his participation in the post declined after the death of York Police Officer Charles Brown, a leader of the Post. (p. 14) However, Brown died in June, 1996, two years after Jeff's senior high school year.

He was a member of "Rainbows," a social service volunteer organization that assisted families who had suffered losses, just as Jeff had lost his brother. Jeff recalled,
...we'd go and kind of counsel them as far as saying, "You know. We've been there. We've done that." And, you know, kind of help... (deposition, p. 11)

Jeff started his business, Marshall Brothers Landscaping in 1994, which was a year-round business, including snowplowing in the winter. The "Brothers" part of the name was in honor of his brother, Joshua. At some point, Jeff adopted for his company the slogan, "Dirty Deeds, Done Dirt Cheap," from the 1976 song and album by the same name by the Australian rock group, "AC/DC." Most customers probably thought it simply a clever slogan for a landscaping company. The lyrics of the song, however, are far from landscaping, as excerpted below:

If you're havin' trouble with your high school head/He's givin' you the blues/
You wanna graduate but not in 'is bed/Here's what you gotta do
Pick up the phone, I'm always home/Call me anytime/
Just ring: three-six-two-four-three-six, hey, I lead a life of crime
Dirty deeds done dirt cheap/ Dirty deeds done dirt cheap/Dirty deeds done dirt cheap
Dirty deeds and they're done dirt cheap/ Dirty deeds and they're done dirt cheap
You got problems in your life of love/You got a broken heart/
He's double-dealin' with your best friend/
That's when the teardrops start FELLA, well/Pick up the phone, I'm here alone/
Or make a social call/Come right in, forget about him/We'll have ourselves a ball,
Dirty deeds done dirt cheap/ Dirty deeds done dirt cheap/Dirty deeds done dirt cheap
Dirty deeds and they're done dirt cheap/ Dirty deeds and they're done dirt cheap
You got a lady and you want her gone/But you ain't got the guts/
She keeps naggin' at you night 'n' day/Enough to drive you nuts/
Pick up the phone, leave her alone/ It's time you made a stand/
For a fee, I'm happy to be/Your back door man.
Dirty deeds done dirt cheap/ Dirty deeds done dirt cheap/Dirty deeds done dirt cheap
Dirty deeds and they're done dirt cheap/ Dirty deeds and they're done dirt cheap
Concrete shoes Cyanide T.N.T Done dirt cheap
Ooo, neckties Contracts High voltage Done dirt cheap, yeah
Dirty deeds, do anything you want me to, done dirt cheap
Dirty deeds, dirty deeds, dirty deeds, done dirt cheap

Jeff had several encounters the the law, apart from his Explorer Post membership. On December 11, 1993, in his senior year at high school, he was arrested for "simple assault" in Newington. Jeff pled Guilty on April 28, 1994, and his sentencing was postponed at later hearings. The last entry in the docket is for a "show cause hearing" on April 13, 1995.

On May 19, 1994 a complaint was issued in York County District Court for "Harassment" against Jeff. It was later filed for one year without a finding. He paid a fine of $100.00.

On January 24, 1995 Jeff pled guilty to the offense of "Violation of Protection from Abuse" order in York County District Court. He was a fine of $220 and paid compensation to the victim.

On March 29, 1995 A complaint of "Criminal Threatening" in York County District Court against Jeff was dismissed "without prejudice" after he had been ordered to pay reimbursement of $800.00 to the victim. The source incident for that complaint occurred on August 22, 1994 when Jeff was arrested.

On January 2, 1996 Jeff was arrested in Exeter, New Hampshire for "Criminal Mischief" and "Driving after Revocaton or Suspension." In March, 1996, the case was "continued for one year, good behavior."

On March 2, 1998 An "Order for Protection from Abuse" was issued against Jeff in York County District Court by Judge Thomas Humphrey, who later became the Chief Judge of the Maine Superior Court. The order was on behalf of Jeff's former girlfriend,

Nicole Mitchell. A temporary order had previously been issued on February 12, 1998. On July 20, 1998, two criminal complaints were issued in York County District court against Jeff for violation of the Protection from Abuse Order, and for "Criminal Threatening" for placing Jeffrey Foye "in fear of imminent bodily injury by threatening, '*I'm going to kill you.'* " Both cases were transferred to York County Superior Court on September 1, 1998. On February 10, 1999 Jeff pled guilty in York County Superior Court to "Criminal Threatening" against Jeffrey Foye, and was fined $250.00. The charge of "*Violation of Protection* [order] *from Abuse*" was "*dismissed in view of plea to Criminal Threatening.*" It's not known how much of this background Jennifer knew when she met Jeff, but he was liked within the Bortner/Conley family. During the entire case, no mention was made in any document of the connection Jeff may have made between his late brother, Joshua, and Jennifer's brother, Joshua, by virtue of their common name. In another name coincidence, one of Jeff's previous girlfriends was named Jennifer.

Approximately in November, 1999 Kassidy was babysat by her aunt Jennifer and Jeff, at least once, at Jeff's home in Kittery, Maine. During visits to Auburn that year, Jeff had become familiar with Kassidy, and the other members of the family.

In November or December 1999, Amanda took Kassidy to a photo studio for a portrait photo. It was a favorite among Amanda's family members.

In December, Amanda applied for public assistance with the Maine Department of Health and Human Services (DHHS). In her autobiographical essay, "My Life Story," Amanda wrote,

...then in December I filed for assistance. I heard about the Aspire program. It was a program for underage teenagers who were going nowhere because there was no way to work for minimum wage, not get child support, have to pay for daycare and the cost of living. It is almost impossible to not go to college these days and pay the bills. The program paid for college, daycare, and gas money, also car repairs. I even applied for housing. They also sent me a check every month. Well that's when I found out my mother had been trying to get child support. The whole time I was living there raising Kassidy myself, she was trying to get money from me. I still owe $800.00. I refused to pay it. When I confronted her she said she called them right when I moved in but they must've forgotten. Yeah right!

In January 2000, Amanda turned 18, and changed her status with the Maine TANF program (Temporary Assistance for Needy Families) which was administered by DHHS.

Friday, 4 February 2000

For Kassidy's one year birthday, there was a family party at the Bortner/Conley's. It was her first and last birthday.

Kassidy had one medical emergency, with a high fever in 1999 or early 2000, and grandmother Jacqueline took her to the Goodall Hospital Emergency Room in Sanford.

In early spring, Jennifer's work with Movie Gallery ended and she began work for Zales Jewelers. On Saturday, April 22, there was an altercation at the Muddy River Smoke House in Portsmouth, between Scott Cormier, a co-worker of Jennifer's at Zales Jewelry and Jeff, from whom Jennifer had recently separated. This resulted in Jeff's arrest on May 8, and he was "*charged May 8 for simple assault and criminal threatening.*" (See Portsmouth Herald Police Log Report.

In her "My Life Story," Amanda wrote about this period,

Okay. I don't even no where to start about... Jeff Marshall. Let me see.. . . Okay I did kind of like him when I first met him, only cause I probably saw them once or twice. I didn't really know him. At that point me and my sister were still kind of enemies. Until they broke up. We were living in Auburn by then. Jen moved back home. She took every single thing back home. (When Jen cheated on him). That's when Jeff went nutty. He called the house constantly. Begged for her back. Threatened her. She was even scared to be alone with him. That's when Jen finally told us about the real Jeff. How he never let her do anything, how he's a real jerk, how she thought he was cheating on her, how they have nothing in common, how he's so boring, and etc.. . . The list went on. My mom was really worried for my sister. I remember her even saying , "We better be careful what we say to him too,....!"

Next thing you know he's manipulating my mother and Paul on the phone, and I think then they convinced my sister to actually see him. And that's when they got back together. I barely ever saw them until, I met Chad. Chad and I never even really talked to them until the last 2 months. Well I might have talked on the phone with my sister, but not really. Well basically, I wanted to go on that Aspire Program. But I needed to use a Maine address, so I used theirs. At that point I was practically living at Chad's house.

Around March-April 2000, Amanda and Kassidy lived for several weeks with her friend, Crystal Martin and her son Devin, at the home in Sanford of Crystal's mother, Gayle. Crystal's former relationship with Kassidy's father, Robert Sheehan, was an obstacle that was overcome.

Around this time, Amanda and Kassidy moved with their family from Sanford to Auburn.

In May of 2000, Amanda and Kassidy were living with the Conleys, full-time in Auburn. Amanda was working as a waitress at the Martindale Country Club in Auburn, which was a few minutes away by car.

Tuesday, 9 May 2000

Amanda took Kassidy to a pediatrician, at Pediatric Associates, in Lewiston, Maine, the sister city to Auburn, and across the Androscoggin River. Kassidy weighed almost 24 pounds and was 32 1/2 inches tall, and both measurements were at 75% for her age group. She received the scheduled immunizations. Dr. George Glass reported that Kassidy passed all of the milestones listed for this 15 month checkup: "*Vocabulary (3-6+ words); Listens to story; Points to one or more body parts; Gestures what they want; Understands simple commands; Walks, stoops, climbs stairs; Stacks blocks; Feeds self with fingers* [with a note that she uses a spoon]*; Drinks from a cup;* [and] *Social Play*." He noted, by hand, "*0 meds. Eats & sleeps good. 0 problems*." There was no mention of bruising or "easy brusing." The next exam was to be scheduled in three months. Amanda was able to obtain medical care for Kassidy through the Maine Dept. of Health and Human Services (DHHS). Amanda had been receiving Medicaid assistance for herself from the Dept. since 1995.

I don't know what pediatricians treated Kassidy from the time of her birth until the May 9, 2000 appointment with Dr. Glass. The Maine Chief Medical Examiner has 70 pages of Kassidy's medical records which may have that information, but confidentiality rules, in the absence of a court order, make that information inaccessible.

Friday, 9 May 2000

Amanda earned her GED degree from the Edward Little High School in Auburn. She earned that high school equivalent diploma several weeks before her former classmates at Sanford High School received their diplomas at their formal graduation.

Friday, 2 June 2000

Amanda, 18, met Chad, 28, through a blind date arranged by her sister, Jennifer, age 20, and her boyfriend, Jeff, age 25. At the time Amanda thought Chad was about 25-26 and Chad was led to believe that Amanda was 19, and thus they had a mutual misunderstanding of their 10 year age difference as a 6-7 year difference. The four gathered for dinner at the Applebee's restaurant on Woodbury Avenue in Portsmouth. Afterwards, Chad and Amanda went to the Hampton Beach Casino to see a concert performance by the rock group "Staind," one of Chad's favorite rock groups. Chad had purchased four tickets, but Jeff said at dinner that he didn't want to go, so Chad sold the two extra tickets later at the Casino. Amanda drove back to her parents' home in Auburn, and to Kassidy, that evening. He had a pre-arranged date later that evening, about which he was honest enough to tell Amanda, but that was his last date with another woman. The initiative for the blind date came from Jeff, as Chad described in his November 2000 letter to his attorneys,

Before I met Amanda Bortner, my girlfriend, Jeff Marshall did work for us at my McDonald's locations snowplowing, landscaping and cleaning play places. My opinion of

him was that he was a nice guy. When I was going through my separation with Tristan he would at times come into my office in Portsmouth and just shoot the shit. He said things like. "I know what you are going through. I myself had a similar situation with my girlfriend, Nicki." I told him all about my breakup and what had happened. He seemed genuine.

Not two weeks after I had been talking to Jeff about my breakup with Tristan, I ran into him and Jen doing a job for me at the McDonald's at the Rochester Wal-Mart. He said, "I got a great idea. Why don't you take Jen's little sister Mandy out." He and Jen went on to describe her as a cute girl that had recently had a kid and was starting to get her shit together. They then told me she was only 19 and I was like, "Are you nuts, I am 28." I then jokingly said to them. "Well, find out if she is still single and wants to go on a date with an older man." Jeff piped right up and said, "Oh yeah she will," and swished his fingers around as if to indicate dollar signs. I laughed and finished up my conversation and then left. I ran into Jeff a few days later (This must have been around mid-May.) He mentioned something about Mandy again. I told him that I was actually seeing a few different people and he made some comment like, "Well just take her out ...I don't give a shit. She has a kid so ...." He laughed and said, "No, seriously, she is a nice girl. Just go out to dinner and see if you like each other." I think he would make comments like this to me trying to be funny. I agreed to a double-date thinking, "What the Hell."

Amanda wrote about that first date in her spring 2001 essay, "My Life Story,"
It was June second. I remember when I got out of the car and saw him I thought he was gorgeous. At the time he had a great body, nice tan, and a cute smile. We went to dinner at Applebee's. The date went great. Almost too great! We had good conversations, a couple laughs, and found out we had a lot in common. We both shared a lot of the same goals in life. ***The thing that attracted me to him the most was how great of a father he was.*** *That was exactly what I was looking for. I wanted a good father for Kassidy. And he seemed perfect. He also said be wanted a girl who spent quality time with their kids, not one who's going to sit them in front of the television everyday.*
From then on we couldn't get enough of each other. We would go to the park all the time, have dinners together, go to the zoo, play wiffle ball, and just do family things. Stuff I never got to do. I really wanted this kind of life for Kassidy. I thought things were finally going my way. Although it hadn't been long, it was the first time I actually considered myself happy.

Backing up, Chad Emery Evans was born on October 15, 1971 to Pam Martin Evans and Chester (Chet) Evans of Keene, New Hampshire. He was Pam's first child, and Chet's third as he had two children in a prior marriage. Chad was followed by Jason in 1973 and Nicole in 1976. Thus, in June, 2000, Jason was 27 and Nicole, 24. Chet and Pam were from Vermont families, with Chet growing up on a dairy farm in Guilford, which is near Brattleboro. Pam was one of the seven, locally-famous, Martin sisters. Chet had moved to Keene where he started "Chet's Rubbish Removal Service." Chad remembers Saturdays as special days when he would ride the truck and help his Dad at work.

Keene had a population of approximately 20,000 and is the home of Keene State College whose students make up about one-quarter of the city's population.
In 1983, Chad and his older half-brother, Ronnie Evans, were injured when they were in a motorcycle accident on Ron's cycle. This was the beginning of Chad's problems with his back, and elbow. In 1988, he went to Children's Hospital in Boston for surgery to repair that elbow.

In November, 1986, at the age of 15 and in his freshman year at Keene High School, Chad began working at the McDonald's restaurant in Keene. Before his 16th birthday the following October, he had been promoted to crew trainer, crew chief and shift manager. At the time of the promotion to shift manager, he was the youngest shift manager in Colley-McCoy, the McDonald's franchisee. As a sophomore in high school, he was in charge of 20 people, and the money was attractive. At school, he played on the football team, but stopped after a bout with spinal meningitis.

Like York, Maine, Keene had a Police Explorer program, but that was not one of Chad's activities. Nicole was an Explorer for about a year, where she learned CPR.

On Chad's 17th birthday, on 15 October 1988, his mother gave him a letter, in which she wrote, "*The world is just opening up and waiting for you. So many good things are waiting for you. I hope you never change. You have a lot of love in you , so you'll get whatever you go after in life.*"

On August 3, 1989, Jim Rice played his last game for the Boston Red Sox. Shortly thereafter, Chad, now a 17-year old eleventh grader, wrote a Letter to the Editor of the Keene Sentinel as he didn't feel that Rice was being treated well in his last days as a Red Sox player. He wrote, "*I think the fans in New England can be both your best friend and worst enemy at the same time.... The fans of New England treat their stars like gods until they make a few mistakes. Then the fans would like to throw them to the dogs like they never did anything good for them.*" Chad would find eleven years later that the transition, in the eyes of others, from hero to monster could be quick, indeed.

In March, 1990 Chad was recognized for HIGH HONORS grades for the second term of his senior year. He achieved high honors in the fall, as well.

In June, Chad graduated, and chose to pursue his career with McDonald's and not go to college. His work at McDonald's was his major activity during his high school years, and he was very successful. On June 18, Chad wrote a Letter to the Editor of the Keene Sentinel to thank those who worked on "Project Graduation," a chemical-free party for Keene High School seniors. He concluded, "*It was a night I will always remember and a night I will be sure to take part in for years to come.*"

On December 7, 1990, Chad completed a McDonald's four-day training course and was designated the outstanding student out of 15, according to his Evaluation. On January 4, 1991, he won the "Oustanding Student Award" in Colley-McCoy, according to a letter from senior manager, Peter Napoli.

In November, 1991, at the age of 20 and one year out of high school, Chad ran for a seat on the Keene Board of Education, and became the youngest person ever elected to that position. Because of a ballot mistake which put his father's name on the ballot, rather than his own, he was not confirmed by a court as the winner in that uncontested race until March, 1992. This would probably remain his best experience with the judicial system. The Keene Sentinel ran the glowing articles, "Chad Evans looks toward fast lane" and second page, "Keene's youngest school board members: a quick study"

On April 18, 1992, Chad graduated from "McDonald's University" in Oak Brook, Illinois, with a "bachelor of hamburgerology" degree. The Keene Sentinel reported that Chad was named to the dean's list and that he "*completed the school's advanced operation course, required for all McDonald's restaurant managers, franchisees, mid-management and company executives.*" In September, he was promoted to be Store Manager at McDonald's in Rochester, New Hampshire. Because of this transfer, he had to resign from the Keene Board of Education. He moved to an apartment in Rochester where he was living when introduced to Mary Paquette at a Colley-McCoy Christmas party in 1992. Mary moved to Chad's apartment in the summer of 1993, and in May, 1994, they moved together to the single family, two-story, home which Chad purchased at 191 Milton Road/Route 125 in Rochester. His monthly mortgage payment was $710.00.

Shortly after moving in, Chad acquired his dog, Kato, from a friend, Sarah Walsh. He wrote in a letter on February 21, 2010, "*My dog's name was Kato. He was a beautiful white German Shepard. I got him as an 8 week old puppy shortly after I bought my house in Rochester and Mary and I moved in. He was our 'child'. I swear he was almost human. I was a big Bruce Lee fan and though I had never seen an episode of The Green Hornet, I loved the name Kato.*" (See photo of Chad with his new puppy.) That fall, Kato was hit by a car which veered off Route 125 in front of Chad's home. His left front leg was shattered and required extensive surgery, including metal plates. (See photo of Chad with Kato, whose leg is in a cast.)

On June 28, the Colley-McCoy owners Richard McCoy and Peter Napoli submitted Chad's name in a letter to Corporate McDonald's in Chicago for consideration as "*outstanding restaurant manager.*" They made the same nomination a year later, too.

In January, Chad and Mary went on a group trip to New York City with his friend, Matt Skidds and his girlfriend, Maureen, and Bruce Aube and his girlfriend, Jessica Edmands.

They saw the show, "Cats," at the Wintergarden Theater on Broadway, and took the ferry to the Statue of Liberty, among other tourist attractions. New York City was always a special place for the boy and young man from New Hampshire.

In December 1995, Chad met a McDonald's employee, Tristan Wentworth, and their relationship grew, as the relationship with Mary was fading. In the Spring of 1996, Tristan and her son, Brent, moved to Chad's home in Rochester.

In April 1996, Chad was promoted to General Mgr. in Colley-McCoy, by a letter from Peter Napoli, who was then the Senior Vice President. The stores for which he was responsible were: Rochester and the store in the Rochester Walmart and the seasonal store at Hampton Beach.

Around this time Colley-McCoy acquired a number of restaurants in Massachusetts and offered Chad the opportunity to move there to manage those restaurants. Chad turned down the offer as he wanted to raise his family in Rochester, and an addition was not long in coming. In the fall of 1996, Chad was at a meeting with Colley-McCoy managers to discuss the acquisition of the seasonal McDonald's franchise in Kittery, Maine. It was during this meeting that Tristan paged Chad twice, with their own *"911"* code, and told him that she was pregnant when Chad called her back. Chad returned to the meeting, all smiles, and shared the news in a whisper with his friend and manager, Larry Lane. Later, the Kittery McDonald's became Chad's fourth store. The next "911" in Chad's life would be a disaster.

On the evening of November 1, 1996, there was a car crash on Route 125 near Chad's home, and he and a neighbor, Marie Altobelli, rescued three men from a car which was burning. Chad's wife, Tristan, also assisted by dousing the flames on one survivor. Foster's Daily Democrat covered the story with the article, "Two rescue people from burning car." The next spring, the Governor of New Hampshire, Jeanne Shaheen, and the publisher of the Union Leader, Nackey Loeb, recognized Chad and Ms. Altobelli as "heroes" for that rescue. (See the Union Leader story, "Lifesavers Get Heroes' Welcomes," and photo of Chad and Governor Shaheen.)

For Chad, one of the nicest parts of that recognition, was the congratulatory letter to him from one of his fifth grade teachers at Fuller Elementary School. Jean Corriveau wrote, "*...So often, in this day and age, heroic efforts like yours are lost in all the negative news....I am very proud of you and not surprised in the least, that you were willing to get involved.... I'll bet your face got red! Love, Miss Corriveau.*"

On Nov. 24, 1996, Chad and Tristan were married. Chad's brother, Jason, was his best man, and ushers were Larry Lane, Bruce Aube and Matthew Skids. The maid of honor was Tristan's sister, Tiffany, and the bridesmaids were Dot Plaisted (now Urrutia), and Chad's sister, Nicole.

Chad was on the way to career and family success. A short time after his marriage Chad visited his friend, Stephanie Chick, who worked part-time at a jewelry store in the Fox Run Mall in Newington, New Hampshire. Stephanie, whom he had met when she was running the print shop next door to the Rochester McDonald's, was trying to encourage Chad to buy something for Tristan. She went to the back office to check his credit rating and get pre-approval for a purchase, and returned to him, with an exclamation within earshot of others, "*Holy cow, Chad, you have the highest credit rating I have ever seen." Seconds later, she said, "Now you HAVE to buy something*," but he didn't. (Letter, Aug. 11, 2010) He was trying to be extra careful about avoiding unnecessary expenditures and, on the other hand, actively saving money for the future.

That became easier as he earned more money in salary and bonuses. In December, 1996, Peter Napoli awarded Chad a $1,000 bonus for outstanding performance. (See the Napoli letter.)

Around this time Chad and Tristan decided together that it would be better for their future family if they both didn't work crazy hours for the same company in the restaurant business. Tristan left Colley-McCoy and went to New Hampshire Technical Institute to learn to be an X-Ray technician. Chad's salary was enough for her tuition and raising the children, and for saving for the future.

In July 1997, Kyle Chester Evans was born. "*The most amazing day of my life*," wrote Chad in a March 5, 2010 letter. In September, 2010, Chad wrote a poem, "THE GIFT" as part of a 4-week poetry prison education class "*with the hopes of inspiring Kyle to do things outside his 'comfort zone.'*" The last stanza of the poem reads:

But I've never been more blown away:
Than when I witnessed my beautiful baby boy thrust with urgency
onto his mother's belly, waiting for me to cut the cord.

A few days latter, Colley-McCoy co-owner Richard McCoy and V.P. Peter Napoli submitted Chad's name, once again to Corporate McDonald's for consideration as "*outstanding restaurant manager*." (See their letter.)

On August 31, Chad Evans and Bruce Aube, and their fathers, Chet Evans and Bruce Aube, went to Foxboro, Mass., to see the first football game of the New England Patriots season. The "home team" defeated the San Diego Chargers 41-7. Chad remembered the day well because that evening he heard the news of the death of Princess Diana in Paris. As is often the case, his memory was correct, as she died on August 31. He wrote in a July 7, 2010 letter, "*One of my fondest memories was of Bruce and I taking our dads down to see the first Patriots game of the regular 1997 season. We stayed overnight in a hotel, smoked cigars, and played cards the night before. It was a chance for Bruce and I to see our dads get away from the 'old ball and chain' and let loose a little.*"

Chad's career success continued. In September, 1997, Colley-McCoy owner Richard P. McCoy announced in a memo to all of his restaurants the promotion to Area Supervisor of "*two outstanding individuals,*" Chad Evans and Sal Napoli, son of co-owner Peter Napoli. Chad's restaurants now included: Rochester, Rochester Walmart, Hampton Beach, Portsmouth and Greenland. Sal's were in Massachusetts: Ayer, Leominster I and II, and Searstown Mall.

It was around this time that Chad first met Jeff Marshall, who was doing landscaping work for the Dover McDonald's which was in the area supervised by Chad's former boss, Larry Lane.

On October 27, Chad and his brother, Jason, and friends, Bruce Aube and either Matt Skidds or Jeremy Hinton, went to the Patriots/Green Bay Packers game. The occasion was to celebrate Chad's 26th birthday, which was on the 15th. Chad recalled in 2010 that it was cold and was in the old Foxboro stadium, and that the Patriots had lost to the Packers the previous year in the Super Bowl. They lost this October 27 game as well. A check with the Patriots' websites for the 1996 Patriots Schedule and 1997 Patriots Schedule showed that he was correct. The Patriots lost in the 1996 Super Bowl 35-21, and lost this game 28-10. Chad's memory is very good.

On December 7, 1997 Chad won a gift certificate for $1,700 or cash for that amount, for placing "*first overall in the RAYSWAY contest,*" named after the founder of McDonald's, Ray Kroc. Chad's manager at Colley-McCoy, Peter Napoli, wrote in his letter, "*Congratulations on your outstanding performance in the areas of Quality, Service, Cleanliness and profit in 1997.*"

In a July 23, 2010 letter, Chad remembers a comment from an employee that meant as much to him as the awards and the money. Chad wrote,

Larry Giarard was a former area supervisor, like myself... I thought it was going to be a little awkward when he came to work for me, running the Greenland McDonald's, but he was great. He was an area supervisor when I started as a 15 year old, so he had been around ***forever****. We got along great, and he made my day once several months after working for me in Greenland when he said, "I have enjoyed working for you Chad more than anyone else in my career. You pitch in, you listen, you care and your enthusiasm is refreshing."*

In July 1998, Kyle celebrated his first birthday with a party. In 2010, Chad wrote captions for Kyle for two photos taken at that party. For the first photo, "*I know I am not one yet but I still get a piece of cake right?*" and for the second photo, "*Finally, I got to try the cake, not bad. Waiter, can you get me something to clean up, I'm a bit sticky.*" Even wrongfully convicted inmates can have a sense of humor.

Around this time, the landscaper contracted by Chad for the Rochester McDonalds, Glenn Couture, told Chad that he would be discontinuing his work for McDonald's. Knowing that Jeff was recommended by Larry Lane as being a low cost landscaper, Chad asked Jeff to contract for the landscaping work at Rochester. That work went reasonably well, and Jeff began work at other McDonald's restaurants which Chad managed. Chad and Jeff were friendly, but it was a business relationship. In 1998, Chad had several parties at his home and welcomed many friends and people he knew from work, including Jeff. At some point, Chad asked Jeff when he would get the opportunity to meet his brother, i.e. of "Marshall Brothers Landscaping." It was then that he learned about the death of Jeff's brother, Joshua, before Jeff started his company.

Chad's career success continued with a December 1998 award from Colley-McCoy executive Peter Napoli of a $600 bonus for his "*outstanding performance in the areas of Quality, Service, Cleanliness and profit in 1998*." One source of his success was that he hired good people to work in his restaurants, and that included several family members. His brother, Jason, ran the Rochester McDonald's and moved to Rochester. In January, on behalf of McDonald's, Chad and Jason received a "Business Appreciation Award" from the Rochester, Jaycees at their 40th annual Distinguished Service Awards ceremony. A Foster's Daily Democrat article carried the story, "Rochester Jaycees Honor Community Members." The Colley-McCoy Hamburger Press, published Chad's article, about the award, "Outstanding in Rochester's Eyes."

In addition to hiring good people, Chad believed in education and training. In February, 1999, Chad's friend, Jeremy, wrote the article for the Hamburger Press, "Swingin' with Larry & Chad," with a photo of the two men. Wrote Hinton, "*Larry Lane and Chad Evans hosted their third annual swing manager's convention at Rochester High School. The event was a huge success attended by over 75 swing managers from ten different restaurants*." As part of the program, Chad donned a cape and Superman gown and was called "*Super Chad McMuscle*" in the Hamburger Press. (See photo.)

All did not continue well at home, however. On the evening of March 27, Tristan went out for the evening and Chad had a few drinks at home. When Tristan came home in the early morning, which was several hours later than expected, Chad was very upset. According to Tristan's account, Chad accused her of having an affair and she slapped him. In the ensuing fight, a cap on one of Tristan's teeth was broken off. She called the police and Chad was arrested. (See the Rochester Police report.) After that, Tristan and Chad tried to recover their marriage. They stayed together, but in April, Tristan went to Chad's office and told him she wanted a separation.

As a result of the arrest, the Rochester District Court ordered that Chad enroll in a 26 session Domestic Violence program at the Strafford (County) Guidance Center which Chad began in April. He and Tristan tried again to live and love together.
In May of 1999, Tristan graduated from New Hampshire Technical Institute and began working as an X-Ray technician.

Colley-McCoy believed that community service was good for the community and good for business, and one of the activities it supported was the Special Olympics. On Saturday, June 5, Chad was part of a Colley-McCoy team that provided McDonald's food at the 30th Annual New Hampshire Special Olympics Summer Games. Tristan and Kyle were there, too. (See the Colley-McCoy Hamburger Press article by Larry Lane, and the group color photo with Chad on the right, holding Kyle.)

In mid-June, Chad, Tristan, Brent, Kyle and Chad's parents went to "Castle in the Clouds," in Moultonborough. It was the hilltop estate of Thomas Plante, a 19th Century industrialist. Despite difficulties, Chad and Tristan were trying to make their relationship work.

The next week, Chad and Tristan attended the kindergarten graduation at Cross Road Kindergarten in Dover for Chad's stepson, Brent. Also attending was the stepson's father, with whom Chad had a strained but formally amicable relationship.

In July, 1999, Chad and Kyle went to Canobie Lake Park, an amusement park in Salem, New Hampshire, with Chad's mother, Pam, who was visiting for a few days. Also joining them were Chad's friend and fellow Colley-McCoy employee, Jim Kennedy, and his wife and son, who was about six months older than Kyle. Wrote Chad, "*Our sons had a blast together that day*." (Letters, Sept. 7, 2010) (See photo.)

Chad believed that employees should work hard, but also should have fun together. In September, 1999, he took most of his McDonald's restaurant managers to the Six Flags of New England Amusement Park, in Springfield, Massachusetts. (See photo.) .

On September 28, Chad finished the court-ordered 26 session domestic violence counseling program, and received a "Letter of Completion." However, he felt that it wasn't sufficiently helpful for him to manage his temper and occasional anger, primarily relating to the loss of his marriage and feared loss of his unitary family.

In October, Chad began treatment with a Rochester chiropractor, Dr. Michael Clark, for back pain which arose periodically from his motorcycle accident when he was about 11-12 with his older brother, Ronald. Previously, Chad's back treatments were with Dr. Craig Anderson in Brattleboro, Vermont, which was closer to Keene than Rochester.

In December 1999, Chad and Tristan had a severe argument after a Christmas party in a hotel and they separated again. Chad suggested that she, Kyle and Brent stay in their house, but she chose to return with Kyle and Brent to her parents' home in the neighboring town of Milton. Chad and Tristan developed a joint custody arrangement for Kyle, who was with Chad about half of each week.

Soon afterwards, Chad voluntarily sought out additional counseling at Strafford Guidance Center and began work with Gray Fitzgerald, a counselor who was also a minister. Chad met with Gray for 12 meetings, until the voluntary termination of services approximately in April, 2000. One outcome from these sessions was a "Checklist" with steps to take to prevent or reduce anger, which Chad kept in his wallet and stuck to a wall upstairs in his home. Fitzgerald has since written a book, "The Bible Confronts The Bible." In 2010, Chad contacted him, seeking his friendship and support, but Fitzgerald declined, without explanation. He may have chosen to believe the newspapers' and the court's caricature of Chad rather than the person he had come to know in counseling sessions. Chad has lost touch with many former friends who seem to have made the same choice.

On December 31, 1999, Chad's younger sister, Nicole, married Brandon Harvey in Belmont, New Hampshire. A believer in financial security and planning, Chad gave Nicole $500 for an IRA (Individual Retirement Account). See photo of family and photo of Chad.

Over the weekend of Feb 12-13, 2000, Chad went to Keene to spend time with, and pick up, Kyle, who had been with his grandparents for the week. (See the photo of Chad sitting with his niece, Malana, and son, Kyle on the 13th. Chad wrote humorously of that weekend and that photo in a 2010 letter, "*Ok, I don't know what my excuse is here for needing a nap. :) I'm sure I was out with Kyle and Malana all day pulling them up the hill at Robinhood Park in a sled, making "Frosty" the Snowman, etc. Not to mention, while in Keene my mother never stops feeding me these tasty, heavy meals. Hey, any excuse to play with Kyle will do. Two hour drive home I have to get rested up for....*" (Letter, Sept. 5, 2010)

Over the weekend of Feb. 19, 2000, Chad's parents and sister came to Chad's home in Rochester for the weekend, to help celebrate Jason's 27th birthday. Jason was still managing the Rochester McDonald's. Soon afterwards, he left that job to move back to Keene to be closer with his daughter, Malana, who was born in August, 1998.

During the week of March 13, Chad and Bruce Aube took a week's vacation for a self-directed "Hall of Fame Tour" during which they went to the Baseball, Basketball and Football Halls of Fame in New York, Mass. and Ohio. While in Ohio, they went to President McKinley's home and tomb. In Ohio, they also visited an Amish community, where Chad purchased a hand-made wooden hand-operated "steam shovel" set, which he gave to Kyle at his upcoming birthday. (See the date-stamped photo of Kyle and shovel at his July, 2000 birthday party.)

Represented by Attorney Stephen E. Gaige, Chad pled guilty on March 24, 2000 to two counts of simple assault arising from the fight with Tristan the previous year. In 2011, Chad said, "*I was guilty, so I pled guilty. This was far different from the circumstances of*

Kassidy's death." Also, he said, "*I wasn't going to have my lawyer try to tear my son's mother apart.*" He was assessed a fine of $750 and was placed on probation for one year. There was a no-contact requirement prohibiting most contact with Tristan, except for what was necessary to provide for the shared custody of Kyle. His lawyer specifically requested that the judge include in the Order that Chad had the statutory right to seek an annulment of the verdict in three years.

In March 2000, Colley-McCoy, purchased the franchises for the McDonald's restaurants on Route 1 in Hampton and in Seabrook. The Hampton restaurant was demolished and a new restaurant was built about a mile down the road. This new restaurant was added to Chad's area, to bring the total to nine, and it opened for business on May 18, with a larger staff which Chad hired and trained. This project took a lot of his time in May and some in June. (See the Hamburger Press article, "Hampton Beach Reopening" and staff photo, including Chad, second from left. See also, a management photo on the occasion, with Chad's identifications: from left to right, "*a gentleman. but not McDonald's employee, Tim McCoy-Ops manager of company, Steve Slipp, Manager of Exeter, John Collins, our controller, Frank Morse in background, Peter Napoli, Bob McDougall, my direct boss.*")

In May, Chad took Kyle and a woman he was dating to Boston for a day Included was a visit with a clown near Faneuil Hall Marketplace. (See the photo with a clown holding Kyle's face toward Chad for "camera contact.") That was one of the last dates for Chad with another woman before meeting Amanda.

For an excellent summary of Chad's life, see Probation Officer Stephen Carlisle's 2002 Pre-Sentencing Report.

Saturday, 3 June 2000

The morning after Chad and Amanda's first date, Chad and Larry Lane went to the University of New Hampshire Field House and set up the McDonald's (Colley-McCoy) booth for the annual New Hampshire Special Olympics. From that booth were served McDonald's lunches (fajitas, apples and cookies) to the competitors. At mid-afternoon, Chad and Larry drove to the Dover McDonald's, and then Chad drove to Milton to pick up his son, Kyle, at Tristan's mother's and had him for the rest of the weekend. He wasn't sure about what would come next with Amanda.

Sunday, 4 June 2000

By this date of Kassidy's 16th month, she had been walking for about six months and was saying more words. To everyone who knew her, she was a happy, normal, beautiful baby. At the Conley home, she loved to play with the family cat, "Reggie" and dog, "Sampson," and to dance to the 1976 song, "Dancing Queen" by the Swedish group, Abba. She was said to have liked bananas, cookies, pizza and spaghetti, and bubble baths.

Amanda and her friend, Cathy Nuernberg, were roller blading in Sanford, Maine and Amanda called Chad, who invited them to come over, and they spent the night. Chad was in love. He wrote in an August, 2010 letter, "*I was as good as done, 'Stick a fork in me.' After that Sunday evening, Amanda was a constant and we were pretty much inseparable.*" Impressed with Amanda's strength and athletic ability, Chad recalled that Cathy and Amanda rollerbladed most of the way from Sanford, but Amanda remembers that they drove in Cathy's car. This was an example of how memory can be altered, by assumptions and wishful thinking. Because they didn't arrive for about two hours, Chad had the impression that the women rollerbladed the 18 mile distance. His high regard of Amanda's athletic abilities supported that assumption. It was a mistake, but one the least harmful mistakes in this story.

Monday, 5 June 2000

After work, Chad picked up Kyle at day care at Chad and Linda Dallesandri's and then took him to Chad's friend, Glen Varney's, home in Farmington, New Hampshire on Baxter Lake. (See date-stamped photo of Kyle on Glen's float with his pontoon boat.)

Chad hadn't yet purchased his own boat. There were several friends there that evening, including Jeff Jacobs, who did electrical work for some of Chad's restaurants.

Tuesday, 6 June 2000

Amanda came to Rochester on Tuesday and took the date-stamped photo of Chad in the hallway of his home, just after returning from work. This is the photo on the cover of this book. In an April 5, 2010 letter, Chad wrote,

"*There was no occasion. It was Amanda that took the photograph. I told you, after that first weekend we were pretty much inseparable. She pretty much was always there. I look happy because I was extremely happy. After a rough six months and the dissolution of my marriage, I found someone that made me happy to my core. We thoroughly enjoyed each other's company. For the first time in my life, I couldn't wait to get back home from work. A lot of mornings I dreaded leaving Amanda, Kassidy, and Kyle.*"

CHAPTER 3: KASSIDY BORTNER - 9 JUNE 2000 TO 8 NOVEMBER 2000

"Hey there. Do you want to go see mama and get a snack?" - Chad Evans

Friday, 9 June 2000

Kassidy Bortner was 16 months old when she met Chad at Chad's home in Rochester when Amanda brought her for the night. Chad wrote of that night,

I asked her to bring Kassidy so that I could meet her. It was one of my nights to have Kyle so I thought it would be cool to see them play together. I believe Amanda had met Kyle a night or two prior. I'll never forget, I was sitting on the living room floor playing with Kyle when Amanda walked in with Kassidy in her arms. She sat her down on one of the couches and said, "This is Kassidy." She was sooooo cute. She had this short blonde hair up in a ponytail on top of her head, a cute little button nose and these adorable little blonde eyebrows, and beautiful blue eyes.... Kassidy just sat there taking the entire room in.

Amanda and Kassidy joined Kyle and I on the floor and all played with the toy we were playing with for a while. Kassidy was very quiet and understandably clung tight to Amanda. Amanda and I had plans that evening to make a Greek type salad for dinner, so we had Kassidy and Kyle help us. Back in those days Kyle loved to help with whatever I was doing. When dinner was ready we sat to eat. I couldn't believe that Kassidy had such a good appetite. She ate everything! Romaine lettuce, feta cheese, black olives, and even tried the red onion with a little wrinkle of her nose. It took me by surprise that a 16 month old would try so many foods. Kassidy always had the best appetite, and ate so much for her size. I used to joke with Amanda that whoever she marries is going to have to get second job to afford the groceries. The only thing dainty about her was going to be her size. Kassidy literally ate more than Kyle who was twice her size. As time went on Kassidy continued to try everything we fed her. I loved that she was so willing to try new foods because Kyle was pretty picky. On the rare occasion that Kassidy bit into something she didn't like, she would just spit it out to the side of her tray on the high chair.

After dinner we had some ice cream. Kyle was sitting in Amanda's lap eating his and I was feeding Kassidy hers. I guess it was a chance for us to meet and spend time with each other's child. Amanda spent that night with Kassidy and then went back home with her to Auburn, where her parents were living. (Letter, Jan. 20, 2010)

Amanda returned to Auburn with Kassidy as she had a day shift at the Martindale Country Club on Saturday the 10th.

Chad was falling for Amanda, and Kassidy was a beautiful and welcome addition to his family, which had gone through several recent changes. His parents' family, in Keene, New Hampshire, was a melded family, and he had been a stepfather for four years. Chad knew a lot about the necessary flexibility and adjustments in a melded family.. The biggest adjustment would be for Kassidy, who was initially very jealous of her closeness to Amanda. It had been a long time since she had lived with a man who loved her mother. She would get upset and throw tantrums when Chad was affectionate toward Amanda. Amanda wrote of Kassidy's early days with Chad in her essay, "My Life Story,"

When Kassidy first met Chad she was just really quiet and hung all over me. She wouldn't let Kyle or Chad go near me. If Chad would kiss me or even go near me she would kick and scream. She'd bang her head into anything. She didn't care where she was. She'd even do it in the bathtub if I didn't let her have the shampoo bottle. That's just an example.

Saturday, 10 June 2000

Amanda and Kassidy returned to Auburn, where Amanda was working for the day. Chad's parents came to Rochester for a weekend visit, and watched a Little League game, in which Chad's stepson, Brent, was playing. Pam Evans remembers that day well, as it was when she took her favorite photo, of Chad holding Kyle. On Sunday, Chad and Chet played baseball with Kyle and Brent at Chad's home in Rochester. (See photo of Chet and Kyle, with the two-year old, almost three-year old, Kyle holding his large red Fisher-Price plastic bat.) That day, Brent was using a yellow bat, as he had graduated through the thick-to-thin series of red to brown to yellow bats. The red bat was the fattest Fisher-Price bat, which enabled children to have more hitting success. It was early in Chad's relationship with Amanda, so the "Meet the Parents" event didn't occur that weekend, but it wouldn't be long. Amanda was spending more days and nights with Chad, and sometimes with Kassidy. The longer the visits, the less frequent were the hour and three-quarters trips in an old car to Auburn.

Friday, 16 June 2000

Amanda and Chad went to a "3 Doors Down" concert at the Hampton Beach Casino Ballroom, and she spent the night at Chad's. (See the dimly-lit date-stamped photo of the band. The date stamp incorrectly said 6 17 00, but the concert was on the 16th, so this was another occasion where the date on the camera was set incorrectly by a day.) Kassidy was in Auburn with Amanda's mother, Jacqueline, and family, who loved having her stay with them.

Saturday, 17 June 2000

Amanda drove to her mother's home in Auburn, Maine, and brought Kassidy to Chad's home for another visit. Chad had Kyle for the weekend, and he picked him up at Tristan's mother's home in Milton. It was a Saturday morning, instead of the usual Friday night pickup, due to Chad's concert attendance the previous night. Chad took Kyle to work with him, but went home early and waited for Amanda and Kassidy.

Sunday, 18 June 2000

In Chad's words,

"*we took the kids to one of the elementary school playgrounds. We stopped by the Stop-and-Go Deli and picked up subs, chips, and soda and had a picnic with the kids at the playground. We played ball, swung on the swings, slides, played tag, etc: It was a blast. At that time, Kyle was not quite 3 years old. He could already hit a wiffle ball with his brown wiffle ball bat, but he also had a large, fat, red bat that we would take to the park. He could really kill the ball with that bat and there was plenty of room for him to do it at the park. Like many boys I suspect, Kyle got more enthused when he hit the ball hard and far. Of course, as his dad, I was willing to do anything to keep him interested and on the path to being the next Ted Williams.*" (Letter, April 5, 2010)

Tuesday, 20 June 2000 (approximately)

Chad went to Auburn to "Meet the Parents." Chad wrote,

Amanda wanted me to come up and meet her mom. They were planning a cookout. So I stopped and bought a huge Boston Creme Pie for dessert. I offered to bring a dish but they had it all planned. It was very casual. I was there, Amanda, Kassidy, her two younger brothers, the parents and Jen + Jeff for a while. It was clear from their interactions Jeff had a well established relationship with them. I visited with the family for a while and Scotty was dying to have someone play ball with him. Amanda described how I played with Kyle all the time and would play with him. I went to the back yard and played with Scotty for well over an hour. I had to show him how to hold the bat, how to swing, etc. It was really fun. I think I made a good impression with her mom. I know I did with Scotty, he was all over me. That is how it usually is for me and kids. Jen + Jeff left after the cookout. I stayed visiting a while longer. Around 9:30 or so, I told Amanda it was a long ride and I needed to get heading home. She said, "No, you are staying over with me." This made me pretty uncomfortable. We just started dating, I just met her parents and I had no intentions of staying over. Amanda persisted. "Stay, it's late. My mom doesn't care. Mom, tell him." Then her mom said, "Yeah, it's fine. You can stay." This made me even more uncomfortable. I went with the flow and figured I would be sleeping on the couch. But when bed time came both Amanda and her mom said, "The couch isn't comfortable. Sleep in Mandy's room." I am pretty brash and have really open minded parents but wouldn't think of doing something like that in their house 2-3 weeks into a relationship. Needless to

say, Amanda won and she and I stayed in her single bed together with Kassidy in the crib beside us. I left real early in the morning. (Letter, March 20, 2010)
As people in families of divorced or separated parents know, life, love and logistics can be complicated.

Wednesday, 21 June 2000

Chad and Tristan held a seventh birthday party for Chad's stepson, Brent, at the Chuck E. Cheese restaurant in Newington, New Hampshire. Also there were Tom and Dot Urrutia and family and Tristan's sister, Tiffany, all of whom were in Chad's and Tristan's wedding.

Thursday, 22 June 2000

Chad took a day off from work and he and Amanda took Kyle and Kassidy to York's Wild Animal Kingdom, in York Maine. (See photo, one of many taken that hot and humid day. See also the five photos in the Appendix.) Chad wrote about that memorable day,
Kassidy and Amanda were basically living with Kyle and I at this point. Amanda and I had decided a few nights prior that we wanted to do something fun with the kids so we settled on York's. It was fairly early in the season so we figured it wouldn't be too packed.
I took the day off from work and we left fairly early in the morning. It was a great day other than it was extremely hot and humid. By the time the photograph was taken at the prairie dog enclosure the kids were hot and tired. It was a great photo of all of them. I just wish I had taken it earlier because they were all smiles then.

We walked through all the animal exhibits and fed the deer. There was this gumball type machine where you could put a quarter in and get grain. Kassidy was a little timid to let the deer eat out of her hand at first but there was a tiny deer that I lured to the front and she held her hand out and let it eat the grain. It was so cute because Kyle was holding his hand out and showing her, "Do it like this, Kassidy." With Amanda's encouragement she did it. When the deer licked Kassidy's fingers she giggled.

The park had animal trainers giving rides on an elephant and a camel. I tried to get Kassidy to go for a ride on the elephant with Kyle but she wanted no part of that. Kyle was especially enamored with a white tiger at the park. We had to stay at that exhibit for at least 20 minutes. He wanted to hear it roar. Finally, he gave up and we moved onto the smaller animal displays. I believe we ate lunch at a spot near water that had ducks and other water animals. The kids enjoyed throwing bread scraps to them. We ate junk food, got the kids balloons and overall had an awesome day.

As we were leaving the park I got a page from my McDonald's field consultant, Dick Bisbee. He was at my Greenland Restaurant and there were problems. They were extremely busy and understaffed. He said if he was grading the visit it would be an F. In a departure from my normal routine, I informed Dick that I was taking a day off with my family and wasn't available. I told him I would call one of my other restaurants in the area and have them send some crew people over to help out.

Normally, I would drop what I was doing, even if I was on vacation, and run to the rescue. For the first time, in my life, I was truly putting my family first. McDonald's had basically run my life for so long. It was a big cause to the end of my marriage. After Tristan left I had a mindset change. I wasn't about to lose Amanda and Kassidy the same way. This is the reason I started working less, doing more fun things, buying toys like a boat, 3 wheelers, etc.

I'm pretty sure that we drove to York Beach and walked around the beach and some of the shops with the kids that day after we left the Wild Animal Park. (Letter, May 20, 2010)
By this time Amanda and Chad were seeing each other nearly every day. There was no formal "move-in" date as she brought her belongings gradually with each trip. At some point, perhaps as a symbol of Amanda's and Kassidy's moving in, Kassidy's December, 1999 portrait photo was placed on the mantle in the living room at Chad's home. At Chad's trial, the prosecution seemed to accept this move-in date, as Will Delker asked Amanda, "*Now, you've been in Chad's house from July onward, right?*" (Amanda testimony, Dec. 7, 2001, p. 73)

Below is the first of several calendars in this book which will show days or periods of no bruises observed on Kassidy. Each such day is marked, **NB** for No Bruise. As the life cycle of a bruise for Kassidy appears to have been about five days, from the date of the appearance of the bruise to the date of its disappearance, the observations of No Bruises (**NB**) are preceded by **NI** for No Injury to mark that five day period of no injuries or bruises being newly caused. In this three-month calendar, June 22 is marked as a No Bruise day because we have photographs of her, apparently bruise-free.

June 2000						
Su	**Mo**	**Tu**	**We**	**Th**	**Fr**	**Sa**
					9	10
11	12	13	14	15	16	**NI**
NI	**NI**	**NI**	**NI**	**NB**	23	24
25	26	27	28	29	30	

July 2000						
Su	**Mo**	**Tu**	**We**	**Th**	**Fr**	**Sa**
						1
2	3	4	5	6	7	8
9	10	11	12	13	14	15
16	17	18	19	20	21	22
23	24	25	26	27	28	29
30	31					

August 2000						
Su	**Mo**	**Tu**	**We**	**Th**	**Fr**	**Sa**
		1	2	3	4	5
6	7	8	9	10	11	12
13	14	15	16	17	18	19
20	21	22	23	24	25	26
27	28	29	30	31		

Sunday, 25 June 2000

At Chad's home was held one of the joint Brent and Kyle birthday parties. Other parties for Kyle were at Tristan's, and at his paternal grandparents' in Keene a few days later. It was at this party in Rochester that Chad gave Kyle and Brent the trampoline, that would play a central role in the case later. Chad wrote about the trampoline purchase in his September 21, 2010 letter,

You asked about the trampoline that I bought for Brent and Kyle. When did I get it, and where, etc. Did I ever mention that BJ's Wholesale Club was my favorite store? he he!! I was wandering through BJ's one night in either May or June and there was this huge trampoline hanging from the ceiling. It was the biggest one I had ever seen. Immediately I said, "Yup, the boys need this." I'm sure I purchased it with my credit card. I always used my credit card at stores like BJ's. Like I said, it was much easier to track your expenses. I borrowed someone's truck, possibly John Seppy's, and bought the trampoline within a day or two. I stored it in the garage until the boys' birthdays got closer. Larry Lane helped me set it up for them. What a blast. That was the best gift I could have ever purchased. We all had a blast on that thing. Kyle still uses it today.

When initially purchased from BJ's, the trampoline did not have a safety fence around it. (See a 2002 photo of the trampoline, with the safety fence.)

At age seven, Brent and his biological father, Joseph Lincoln, were now moving closer together, so Chad saw him less often. Brent spent the night at Chad's only a few nights over the rest of the summer, so Kassidy was moved into his room, when he wasn't there.

In his police interview, Jeremy said that Chad's probation officer made a surprise visit to Chad's home during the party, and found no alcohol, which was prohibited by the terms of his probation. (p. 1766) Chad recalls that Jeff and Jennifer and Amanda and Kassidy were there. In her third police interview, on November 10, 2000, Jennifer said that she recalled that her half-brother, Scott Conley, was also there and that Kassidy had fun jumping on the trampoline.

Another birthday party was held later at Chad's parents' home in Keene and another at Tristan's.

End of June 2000 (approximately)

With their own successful experience of double-date introductions, Amanda and Chad arranged a double-date for Amanda's friend, Emily Conley, to meet Chad's friend, Jeff Jacobs. They went to Whale's Tale on Ocean Boulevard in Hampton, a short distance from the Hampton Beach McDonald's, one of the restaurants for which Chad was responsible. Despite the same surname, Emily Conley was not known to be related to Amanda's stepfather's family.

It was around this time that Amanda quit her job as a waitress at the Martindale Country Club in Auburn, and that long distance commute was terminated. Without the need for her mother's day care for Kassidy, Amanda brought her to Rochester, again without a formal "move-in" date. In part, Chad and Amanda were reluctant to call this big change a formal "move-in" as it had only been three weeks since Amanda and Chad had met. Chad and Tristan had filed for an amicable divorce, and Chad was pleased with the custody arrangements for Kyle, but he did not want to upset those arrangements in any way. Thus, a dynamic developed where Chad was trying to understate his love and commitment to Amanda, until his divorce became final.

Although Tristan didn't seem jealous of Chad's earlier, post-separation, girlfriends, Tristan could surely sense that this relationship with Amanda was different. Chad was concerned that it might be used against him in the divorce process. One visible result, or invisible, was that Chad asked Amanda to park her car across the street, so Tristan would not see it as she drove by every day to and from work. Of course, when Tristan would leave or pick up Kyle, she would see Amanda at her former home, but it was not the same as every day. When there were family events at Chad's where Tristan was expected to come, Amanda and Kassidy would go elsewhere, often to friends in Sanford.

Saturday, 1 July 2000

In the evening, Chad and Amanda went boating on Baxter Lake with Chad's friend, Glen Varney, who lived on the lake, and his girlfriend, Deb. As Deb's daughter was elsewhere, and not available as a playmate for Kassidy, Amanda arranged for Kassidy to spend the night with Jeff and Jennifer. This was the first babysitting for Kassidy that Chad can recall at Jeff and Jennifer's, since he met Kassidy on June 9. It was certainly her first overnight there since June 9.

First week of July 2000

Perhaps from Monday through Friday, July 7, Pam Evans stayed at Chad's home with Chad and Amanda and, as often as possible, with Kyle. Pam's friend, Liz Cox, was with her, and on Tuesday, July 4, both of them filled in to work a few hours at the Hampton Beach McDonald's, which was a very busy restaurant over the 4th of July week. (See date-stamped photo of Liz, on left, and Pam.) Around this time, Chad and Amanda took her sister, Jennifer, and Jeff, to dinner at Newick's on Dover Point in Newington as a "thank-you" for introducing them to each other. Later, the four walked in Prescott Park in Portsmouth, but Chad recalls that Jeff didn't want to do more, so the evening social foursome broke up. Kassidy was being babysat by Jacqueline, or by a friend of Amanda's, or by Chad's mother, whose visit may have coincided with that date.

Second week of July 2000

During this week, Pam Evans and her friend, Liz Cox, were again visiting Chad. They watched the Hampton Beach fireworks, conducted weekly during the summer, from the McDonald's roof. Toward the end of that period, perhaps, Friday, July 14, Amanda drove to her mother's home in Auburn and brought Kassidy back to Chad's home. During this visit, Pam noticed that Kassidy's feet were perhaps "pigeon-toed," which could have contributed to her apparent lack of balance and frequent falling. Pam told Chad about her observation and Chad recommended to Amanda that Kassidy be examined by a doctor. Pam specifically recalls spending time with Kassidy on the back steps, while the others played ball and jumped on the trampoline. To Pam, Kassidy seemed quiet and withdrawn. Amanda and Chad drove Pam home to Keene on that same Friday, and Kassidy rode in the back seat with Pam. Chad, Amanda and Kassidy spent Friday and Saturday at Chad's parents for their first of two overnight visits to Keene.

The calendar below represents these two periods of No Bruising (NB), whether observed by Jacqueline or Pam, and No Injury (NI)

June 2000						
Su	Mo	Tu	We	Th	Fr	Sa
					9	10
11	12	13	14	15	16	**NI**
NI	**NI**	**NI**	**NI**	**NB**	23	24
25	26	27	28	29	30	

July 2000						
Su	Mo	Tu	We	Th	Fr	Sa
						1
2	3	4	5	6	**NI**	**NI**
NI	**NI**	**NI**	**NB**	**NB**	**NB**	**NB**
NB	17	18	19	20	21	22
23	24	25	26	27	28	29
30	31					

August 2000						
Su	Mo	Tu	We	Th	Fr	Sa
		1	2	3	4	5
6	7	8	9	10	11	12
13	14	15	16	17	18	19
20	21	22	23	24	25	26
27	28	29	30	31		

Thursday, 20 July 2000 (approximately)

Chad, Amanda and Kassidy visited Amanda's parents in Auburn, and they took Jeff and Jennifer to dinner at "Margaritas," a Mexican restaurant in Auburn. Chad recalls that Amanda and Jen wanted to go dancing afterwards, but Jeff wanted to get home to Kittery. Chad wrote of that visit,

The next time I stayed was about a month later. Amanda was up there for a few days and wanted me to come up. Jen + Jeff were there again when I arrived. I played ball with Scotty again. This was where I saw that Jeff had no relationship with either of the boys. I don't recall how it ended up this way but Me, Amanda, Jen + Jeff went to dinner at Margarita's Mexican restaurant. I paid for dinner. I offered to take the entire family but Jackie didn't want to go for some reason. After dinner Jen + Jeff left. Amanda and I took Kassidy and the boys to some local school playground. It was dark out by this time. I pushed Kassidy and Scotty on swings as Amanda swung beside them. I let Josh drive my car around the empty school parking lot. Pretty dumb in hindsight because he was under age but it sure made him pretty happy. We drove back to the house and they had a TeePee or Tent pitched out in the yard. We decided to camp out. Kassidy stayed inside with Gramma and me, Amanda, and Scotty camped out. It was a blast. In the morning when I left, Jackie said I will have to bring Kyle up next time so they can meet him. I said I would. Unfortunately, it just never happened. I think because of the allegations of sexual abuse, Amanda had a very strange dynamic with her family. Amanda's mom didn't drive and sometimes in Rochester when she hadn't seen her mom in a while, Amanda would complain about missing her. I would tell her to just go up and get Jackie and bring her down for a few days if you want or go spend it with her. She would never do it. She would just say, "I will" or "I'm ok, I'll just call her." (Letter, March 20, 2010)

As Amanda was with Kassidy in Auburn during the week following the return from Keene on Sunday, July 16, next week is marked NB (No Bruise) as Kassidy was in the shared care of her grandmother, Jacqueline.

June 2000						
Su	Mo	Tu	We	Th	Fr	Sa
					9	10
11	12	13	14	15	16	**NI**
NI	**NI**	**NI**	**NI**	**NB**	23	24
25	26	27	28	29	30	

July 2000						
Su	Mo	Tu	We	Th	Fr	Sa
						1
2	3	4	5	6	**NI**	**NI**
NI	**NI**	**NI**	**NB**	**NB**	**NB**	**NB**
NB	**NB**	**NB**	**NB**	**NB**	21	22
23	24	25	26	27	28	29
30	31					

August 2000						
Su	Mo	Tu	We	Th	Fr	Sa
		1	2	3	4	5
6	7	8	9	10	11	12
13	14	15	16	17	18	19
20	21	22	23	24	25	26
27	28	29	30	31		

Over the weekend of July 22-23, Chad and Amanda went with Bruce Aube and others to his parents' camp in Pittsburg, New Hampshire. Kassidy was with Amanda's mother. (See date-stamped photo of Jason Evans, Tommy Urrutia, Jeremy Hinton, Travis Hunt and Amanda in the red shirt.)

Thursday, 27 July 2000

After work, Chad, Amanda and Kassidy went to Laconia, New Hampshire, on Lake Winnipesaukee to look at a 1986-ish 16 foot outboard "Glastron" boat for the family. It had an 85 horsepower "Johnson" engine and was very fast. Chad's brother-in-law, Brandon Harvey, worked at a boat yard and found the boat for Chad. They all went for a test ride and Chad made the purchase right there, for $1,600, cash. They had dinner afterwards with Nicole and Brandon. Chad used the boat several times a week throughout the summer, and most of the time he was with Amanda, Kassidy, and Kyle. Having a friend, Glen Varney, with a waterfront home helped a lot. Chad wrote about his boat in 2010,

When I first bought it I kept it on a trailer at my house and I would go launch it in Baxter Lake by Glen's house. After a week or so, Glen offered to let me keep it docked in the water at his house. That worked out perfect because I bought it late in the season, July August area and it was the first boat I had owned since I was 17 so I wanted to get used to it on a small lake. Glen's was great because the kids were small and very close to my house so some weeks we went 2-3 times right after work. Glen only lived 10-15 minutes away from me. He was an experienced boater. The lake was small so I didn't really have to worry about the kids if something happened in the middle of it. Most nights, we had the oversized pond to ourselves. The first night that I test drove it on Winnipesaukee it was me, Amanda, Kassidy, Brandon and the owner. After that I believe that Brandon came down once and went out with me on Baxter lake. I believe that Bruce and Jeremy went out with me one time. I went out with Jeff and Glenn several times. This was shortly after I purchased it. I believe Deb and her sister went out with us and her daughter one time. I know that Travis went out with me once in the very beginning of September with two Irish girls, one girl that Travis was dating throughout the summer, and her friend. We stopped in the middle of the lake and swam for a while. I would do that on occasion for Kyle too. We'd stop and he'd jump in. Kid was fearless. I think I brought my Dad and brother out once in 2000 also but am not sure. Typically on most nights it was Amanda, me, Kyle and Kassidy. There was a seat right next to the driver's seat where Amanda would often sit holding Kassidy and I'd have Kyle in my lap helping me steer. We switched it up sometimes but Kassidy had very little interest in driving. There was a long bench seat in the back of the boat and Amanda would sometimes sit in the back right in the middle with Kassidy and Kyle on either side of her. I had some great photos of this. All three looking at me smiling. They liked sitting there on hot days as I could sway side to side, change speeds and get the water splashing them. As you can see the boat rides low in the water so you could reach over and touch it. Other times they would ride in the bow of the boat. Sometimes Amanda would drive and I would hold the kids. It was a blast. Sorry I can't get more specific with dates and things. (Letter, Aug. 31, 2010)

Chad estimated in 2010 that Glen saw Kassidy with Chad and Amanda on the boat, or at shared picnics no fewer than ten times.

In 2011, the boat still rests on a trailer at Chad's grandmother's home in Vermont, waiting for Chad to return.

Friday, 28 July 2000

This was the effective date of Chad's voluntarily termination of his counseling sessions with Gray Fitzgerald at the Strafford Guidance Center, now named Behavioral Health Services. However, the actual end of the counseling with Fitzgerald was in April. Sometime thereafter, Amanda persuaded Chad to remove the small notepaper "Checklist" about managing anger from a wall in his home. She said he no longer needed it.

Saturday-Monday, 29-31 July 2000

Over the three day weekend, Chad, Amanda, Chet, Jason, Brandon and Nicole took a long-anticipated canoe trip down the Saco River, which is popular among overnight canoeists for its sandbars and slow water flow. The 26 mile trip began at SacoBound in Center Conway, New Hampshire, and ended at the Brownfield Bridge in Brownfield, Maine. (See date-stamped photo of Chad paddling, taken by Amanda. In the second date-stamped photo are, from the left, Jason Evans, Nicole Evans Harvey, Chet Evans and Chad. Taking the photo was either Brandon Harvey or Amanda.) Kassidy was with her grandmother, Jacqueline, and Kyle was with his mother, Tristan. Even though Amanda and Chad were both parents, they shared the parenting with others who were also devoted to their children. The result was that Amanda and Chad had many dates, and some weekends without either Kassidy or Kyle.

Below is the updated calendar showing the periods of observation of No Bruises (NB) and No Injury (NI) which could have caused bruises. Again, Kassidy's time with her grandmother is assumed to be a time of no bruises, given her strong reaction to bruises which she heard about in October, and which she related at Chad's trial.

June 2000						
Su	**Mo**	**Tu**	**We**	**Th**	**Fr**	**Sa**
					9	10
11	12	13	14	15	16	**NI**
NI	**NI**	**NI**	**NI**	**NB**	23	24
25	26	27	28	29	30	

July 2000						
Su	**Mo**	**Tu**	**We**	**Th**	**Fr**	**Sa**
						1
2	3	4	5	6	**NI**	**NI**
NI	**NI**	**NI**	**NB**	**NB**	**NB**	**NB**
NB	**NB**	**NB**	**NB**	**NB**	21	22
23	**NI**	**NI**	**NI**	**NI**	**NI**	**NB**
NB	**NB**					

August 2000						
Su	**Mo**	**Tu**	**We**	**Th**	**Fr**	**Sa**
		1	2	3	4	5
6	7	8	9	10	11	12
13	14	15	16	17	18	19
20	21	22	23	24	25	26
27	28	29	30	31		

August 2000

According to her new supervisor, Heather Hamilton, Jennifer began work at Perfumania, in Kittery, in August. However, Jennifer recalled in her November 9 police interview (page 10) that she began that job in early October. This was one of the many discrepancies about dates which was left unresolved throughout the investigation and trial processes. By itself, Jennifer's start date was not critical for understanding the changes in Kassidy's behavior and health, but such a date was often used as a reference date for other events. Ascertaining one would help determine the other.

In "My Life Story," Amanda wrote about Kassidy and motherhood,

I had spoiled her for a long time. I didn't know I was doing it. Just every time she'd cry for something I'd give in to her and that'd be it. She didn't know how to share, I never taught her "please" and "thank you." I'd always say it, thinking maybe she'd copy, but her favorite word was "gimme" at the time. She basically ruled me. Whatever she said went. Well that was until I saw her with kids her own age. She didn't know how to play with them. At first she'd just stare at them. And then when she felt comfortable she'd try playing with them. If she wanted a toy or something she would just take it out of the other kids' hands.

And then they would fight. Sometimes even bite or pinch each other. So I really had to start disciplining her. Her fits were getting worse and worse. Even when we went to the grocery store if I didn't get her candy in the check-out, she would scream and throw her fits. So Chad and I decided to put her in her bedroom every time she'd throw her fits. In the beginning she'd just run out of the room and scream some more, so I would put a sock in the door so she wouldn't get out, and she could kick and scream all she wanted to. A couple months went by and she was doing much better. We barely had to put her in her room. And she didn't scream when Chad or Kyle came near me. The bedroom thing had worked. Our daily routine was she'd come in usually and wake Chad and I up. Or a lot of the time she'd wake up in the middle of the night and Chad would bring her in and she'd sleep in between us. That became a lot more frequent before she died. In the morning, Chad would put her on his shoulders or back and bring her downstairs for cereal. She loved cereal. She could not go a day without it. She'd then go upstairs, throw toys down the stairs and play in front of the television, while I did laundry and cleaned. Then she'd eat lunch. Sometimes I'd bring her and a bunch of toys in the basement with me while I went tanning. Then she'd take a good long nap. Usually around two and half hours. Sometimes even longer! That's when I took a shower and had a little bit of time to myself. When she'd wake up, we usually did flash cards, read books, go on the swing set, and jump on the trampoline almost every day. Kassidy and Kyle absolutely loved painting, and doing art stuff. We did that stuff a lot too. Unless, I went to the grocery store, or ran errands. Also after dinner we'd sometimes go to the park, all of us, or we'd go outside and jump on the trampoline again. Then Chad and I would give them baths. Most of the time Chad would read her a book and I would read to Kyle. Just so we could kind of get a little one on one time. She was becoming really smart for her age. Her and Kyle were also starting to play nicely. Well most of the time.

I thought we were doing great! I was very proud of myself, and was really enjoying being a mother. She was learning and so was I at the same time.

Tuesday, 1 August 2000

This was the date that started the period of the subsequent indictment charge against Chad for Endangering the Welfare of a Child, and for which Chad was later convicted. Specifically, from August 1 to November 9, it was charged that:
While Evans lived with Kassidy and Amanda and provided care and supervision for Kassidy, Evans inflicted bodily injury to Kassidy. Evans bruised Kassidy's body and fractured her bones by repeatedly grabbing Kassidy by the face, throat, arms, and legs and by propelling Kassidy into the walls of the home, causing Kassidy to strike the walls. Evans also withheld Kassidy from proper medical treatment for those injuries.
The indictment said that Kassidy was 20 months old during this period, but it began when she was 17 months old and ended when she was 21 months old.

Thursday, 10 August 2000

Amanda brought Kassidy again to Dr. George Glass at Pediatric Associates of Lewiston. (See Vaccine Record and "18 Month Well Child Exam report" and "Physcal Growth Charts.") Kassidy weighed 23 1/2 pounds which put her at less than "normal" range and her height was 34 1/2 inches or 100% of normal. Amanda asked Dr. Glass or the nurse, Adrienne Platt, about the "pigeon-toe" characteristic which Pam Evans had noticed, and he wrote on his report for "Gait" that there was "toeing-in." Dr. Glass thought it was enough of a concern to refer Kassidy to an orthopedic specialist for closer examination of her legs and feet. In view of what happened later in the cases against Chad and Amanda, it is noteworthy that it was not Amanda's family, or her sister or her friends who observed the "toeing-in" characteristic of Kassidy's feet. It was Chad's mother; and Chad urged Amanda to take Kassidy to a doctor.

In her first police interview, Amanda estimated that Kassidy had been walking since about nine months old, or since around November, 1999. (Interview, page 854)

Dr. Glass also made a note about the "*Wart on R index finger*" and recommended, "*Return for Histofreeze*," or removal. That followup appointment was never made. Chad had urged Amanda to have a doctor remove the wart, and he recalls giving Amanda cash for that minor operation.

Kassidy's medical "Problem List" was empty. There was no mention of bruises, or of "easy bruising" on Kassidy in these medical records. The orthopedic surgeon appointment was scheduled for 3:00 p.m. on September 11, 2000. (See "Referral Forms") The next pediatric appt. was scheduled for "six months," i.e. the 24-month checkup at approximately mid-February 2001.

Below is the updated NB (No Bruise) NI (No Injury) calendar:

June 2000							**July 2000**							**August 2000**						
Su	**Mo**	**Tu**	**We**	**Th**	**Fr**	**Sa**	**Su**	**Mo**	**Tu**	**We**	**Th**	**Fr**	**Sa**	**Su**	**Mo**	**Tu**	**We**	**Th**	**Fr**	**Sa**
													1			1	2	3	4	**NI**
					9	10	2	3	4	5	6	**NI**	**NI**	**NI**	**NI**	**NI**	**NI**	**NB**	11	12
11	12	13	14	15	16	**NI**	**NI**	**NI**	**NI**	**NB**	**NB**	**NB**	**NB**	13	14	15	16	17	18	19
NI	**NI**	**NI**	**NI**	**NB**	23	24	**NB**	**NB**	**NB**	**NB**	**NB**	21	22	20	21	22	23	24	25	26
25	26	27	28	29	30		23	**NI**	**NI**	**NI**	**NI**	**NI**	**NB**	27	28	29	30	31		
							NB	**NB**												

Saturday, 12 August 2000

Chad and Amanda went with their friends, Michelle and Bruce Truell, to a party in Newport, New Hampshire, organized by the Freelancers Motorcycle Club. Later, this party was remembered by attendees as the "Harley Party." Kassidy stayed overnight with Jeff and Jennifer. This was the second overnight for Kassidy at Jen and Jeff's since Amanda met Chad on June 2.

Sunday-Tuesday 13-15 August 2000

Together with Jaime Hinton, brother of Jeremy, Chad attended the annual McDonald's store manager conference, for selected managers, in Boston for three days and two nights. As neither the prosecutors nor Chad's attorneys requested Chad's personnel file at Colley-McCoy, the exact dates are unavailable. In his August 14, 2010 letter, Chad estimated that the conference was in August.

Week of Monday, 14 August 2000

Scott Conley and Joshua Bortner visited Amanda, Kassidy and Chad for a few days. On Wednesday, the 16th, Amanda took her brothers and Kassidy to "Water Country" Water Park in Portsmouth. (See photo1 and photo2 of Kassidy at Water Country. See also, a photo of Amanda, probably taken by her brother Joshua, of Amanda coming down the water slide. The photos of Kassidy can also be seen in the Appendix to this book) Chad commented in 2010,

Awesome photographs of Kassidy. These were taken by Amanda in August of 2000 when she took Kassidy and her brother(s) to Water Country in Portsmouth. I was busy in Hampton so I couldn't make the trip, but I picked up tickets for Amanda to take the kids. I don't have the chronology handy but I know that you do. Amanda and I did a lot during August. Jackie watched Kassidy a lot. One of the times when Amanda went to pick Kassidy up, she brought her brothers back to spend a few days with us. Amanda may have gone with one of her friends as well. Obviously from the develop date it was prior to Aug 16, 2000. The important thing is look how HAPPY Kassidy is? Photos are close enough to see no bruises. She is wearing a 2-piece bathing suit which show NO BRUISES on her abdomen.... Wish I had thought of using these photos during the trial. As a matter of fact, I don't recall my attorneys asking for ANY photos. Amanda and the kids had a great day. We grilled out that night and I believe walked up to Lone Oaks and got ice cream later. (Letter, Apr. 11, 2010)

Chad wrote about Joshua's and Scott's visit in another letter,

I recall Josh staying longer than Scottie. I know we walked to Lone Oaks to get ice cream all together. I know I purchased tickets so that Amanda could take them all to Water Country. I couldn't attend as I was busy at work. We have some photographs of that trip. I also know that we grilled on the BBQ and ate dinner together in the dining room. This was the time that Kassidy heard Amanda's brothers call her, "Mandy" so she repeated it. Amanda said, "No, to you I'm 'Mama' " Amanda went to the kitchen to get one of the boys some more juice and Kassidy whispered quietly, "Mandy" and we all burst out laughing. We played ball in the front yard I also recall giving Amanda some money and she took her brothers shopping. I think she bought them clothes or sneakers. She was pretty happy to be able to do something nice for them. I'm not sure what she did with the boys during the day most days. (Letter, Oct. 5, 2010) (See photo of new sneakers at Jeff and Jennifer's on November 9.)

Below is the updated NB (No Bruise) NI (No Injury) calendar which included NB for the Water Country photographs,which show no bruising.

June 2000

Su	Mo	Tu	We	Th	Fr	Sa
					9	10
11	12	13	14	15	16	**NI**
NI	**NI**	**NI**	**NI**	**NB**	23	24
25	26	27	28	29	30	

July 2000

Su	Mo	Tu	We	Th	Fr	Sa
						1
2	3	4	5	6	**NI**	**NI**
NI	**NI**	**NI**	**NB**	**NB**	**NB**	**NB**
NB	**NB**	**NB**	**NB**	**NB**	21	22
23	**NI**	**NI**	**NI**	**NI**	**NI**	**NB**
NB	**NB**					

August 2000

Su	Mo	Tu	We	Th	Fr	Sa
		1	2	3	4	**NI**
NI	**NI**	**NI**	**NI**	**NB**	**NI**	**NI**
NI	**NI**	**NI**	**NB**	17	18	19
20	21	22	23	24	25	26
27	28	29	30	31		

Friday, 18 August 2000

Amanda, Chad and Bruce and Michelle Truell, went to see comedian/singer "Dr. Dirty," John Valby, at the Hampton Beach Casino Ballroom. Kassidy spent her third overnight with Jeff and Jennifer.

Sunday-Monday, 20-21 August 2000

Chad, Amanda, Elaine and Jay Shunk, Jeremy Hinton and April Blaise went to New York City to watch a Yankees baseball game. The game was either on Sunday or Monday. On Sunday, the Yankees lost to the Anaheim Angels, 5-4. On Monday, the Yankees beat the Texas Rangers, 12-3. The group spent the night in New York and returned on Monday. They stayed at a hotel in Manhattan where weekend rates were lower. Amanda's mother remembers that it was a Marriott hotel, because Amanda brought back a souvenir towel when she picked up Kassidy the following Saturday. (See photo of Chad in a New York pub. The photo is dated August 21, but Chad remembers that the camera was incorrectly set a day ahead, so the actual date of the photo was Sunday, 20 August.)

Tuesday, 22 August 2000

Chad and Amanda went to a "Creed" concert at Great Woods, in Mansfield, Mass. Their other favorite group, "3 Doors Down" was the opening act. They went with their close friends, Michelle and Bruce Truell, Glen Varney and his girlfriend, Deb.

Wednesday, 23 August 2000

Chad, Amanda, Jason and his friend, Jeff Porter, went to another "Creed" concert at the Civic Center in Portland. Amanda and Jeff Porter were ticketed for possession of alcohol as a minor, in Portland. All four returned to Amanda's and Chad's home in Rochester.

Thursday, 24 August 2000

Chad went to work, and Jason, Jeff and Amanda went to "Water Country" in Portsmouth.

Friday, 25 August 2000

On Friday of that week, Chad and Amanda attended a McDonald's, Colley-McCoy, dinner at the Exeter Inn, Exeter, New Hampshire. On the way home, they argued about a woman there whom Chad had previously dated. Amanda slapped Chad and he reached out with his right arm and pushed Amanda into the seat, and told her to stop the argument. He wrote about the incident, "*...it was a disagreement that lasted for 30 seconds*." (Letter, Apr. 20, 2010)

It was a busy week for Chad and Amanda, and an enjoyable week for grandmother Jacqueline, who had Kassidy for the whole week.

Saturday, 26 August 2000

Amanda went to her mother's home to pick up Kassidy. Below is the updated NB (No Bruise) NI (No Injury) calendar:

June 2000						
Su	Mo	Tu	We	Th	Fr	Sa
					9	10
11	12	13	14	15	16	**NI**
NI	**NI**	**NI**	**NI**	**NB**	23	24
25	26	27	28	29	30	

July 2000						
Su	Mo	Tu	We	Th	Fr	Sa
						1
2	3	4	5	6	**NI**	**NI**
NI	**NI**	**NI**	**NB**	**NB**	**NB**	**NB**
NB	**NB**	**NB**	**NB**	**NB**	21	22
23	**NI**	**NI**	**NI**	**NI**	**NI**	**NB**
NB	**NB**					

August 2000						
Su	Mo	Tu	We	Th	Fr	Sa
		1	2	3	4	**NI**
NI	**NI**	**NI**	**NI**	**NB**	**NI**	**NI**
NI	**NI**	**NI**	**NB**	**NI**	**NI**	**NI**
NB	**NB**	**NB**	**NB**	**NB**	**NB**	**NB**
27	28	29	30	31		

Sunday, 27 August 2000

Jacqueline remembered this date, August 27, as the day of her operation for removal of a tumor. However, she had two weeks notice before the operation, so it wasn't an emergency, but the 27th was still a Sunday. Regardless of the exact day of the week, this operation made babysitting for Kassidy at Jacqueline's home less feasible in the short term after that date. This date, or the time of Jacqueline's operation, was later used as a reference point for ascertaining the dates of other events or incidents.

So far, it was a busy August. Wrote Chad,

"*....most years in August I didn't do much, but on this particular August it seemed like we were out doing stuff every night. Not much time for sleep with all that we had going on. If we weren't at these concerts and things, we were doing things with Kyle and Kassidy. I felt bad that we had so much going on that month without the kids.*

It was going to be great when they were a couple of years older as we could then take them with us to enjoy many of these activities." (Letter, Sept. 3, 2010)

Sunday-Monday, 27-28 August 2000

For the last weekend of the month, family returned to center stage. On Sunday and Monday, Chad, Amanda, Kassidy and Kyle went to Keene for their second weekend together at Chad's parents' home. The first such trip began on Sunday, July 16, when they brought Pam back to Keene from her visit in Rochester. The occasion in August was Chad's niece Malana's birthday party, which was Sunday. (See date-stamped photo of Chad encouraging Kyle to jump into his arms.) Chad wrote about the photo and this trip to Keene,

This photo is of Kyle and I in the pool at my parents' around the time of Malana's birthday party. This is an important photo for several reasons. I think it is a great photo of the relationship Kyle and I shared. I was teaching him how to leg kick when swimming that day. I was intently focused on getting him to jump into my arms again and trust the process after he swallowed some water. I also believe this may have been our second trip to Keene with Kassidy and Amanda. I'm not sure if it was Amanda or my mother that took this photo. I believe they were both sitting on the pool deck with Kassidy. The photo is date stamped Mon. the 28th of August. This is likely the date we were there. Because the pool is empty of other people. I believe Malana's party was on Sunday the 27th and I took that Monday off. I wrote my own schedule so this is likely. I would have called the restaurants in the morning and had Melissa Allard collect all of the weekly figures. (Letter, Apr. 5, 2010)

During this visit, Pam saw Kassidy fall onto the concrete at the pool without putting her hands out in front to block her fall, and she hit her head. Pam had no recollection in 2011 of a resulting bruise. Inside the house, recalled Chet in 2011, Kassidy walked into the brick chimney in the living room and fell backwards.

Below is the updated NB (No Bruise) NI (No Injury) calendar:

June 2000						
Su	**Mo**	**Tu**	**We**	**Th**	**Fr**	**Sa**
					9	10
11	12	13	14	15	16	**NI**
NI	**NI**	**NI**	**NI**	**NB**	23	24
25	26	27	28	29	30	

July 2000						
Su	**Mo**	**Tu**	**We**	**Th**	**Fr**	**Sa**
						1
2	3	4	5	6	**NI**	**NI**
NI	**NI**	**NI**	**NB**	**NB**	**NB**	**NB**
NB	**NB**	**NB**	**NB**	**NB**	21	22
23	**NI**	**NI**	**NI**	**NI**	**NI**	**NB**
NB	**NB**					

August 2000						
Su	**Mo**	**Tu**	**We**	**Th**	**Fr**	**Sa**
		1	2	3	4	**NI**
NI	**NI**	**NI**	**NI**	**NB**	**NI**	**NI**
NI	**NI**	**NI**	**NB**	**NI**	**NI**	**NI**
NB	**NB**	**NB**	**NB**	**NB**	**NB**	**NB**
NB	**NB**	29	30	31		

September 2000

In September, Amanda enrolled in the Maine Dept. of Health and Human Services ASPIRE Program. The acronym stands for "Additional Support for People in Retraining and Employment" and was part of the TANF (Temporary Assistance for Needy Families) program through which she had received some benefits. Through the ASPIRE Program, Amanda pursued options for further education and for working, and was eligible for day care assistance. It was to fulfill the requirements of this program that Amanda found a regular job in November at Old Navy in Kittery. At Chad's trial, she described the program as one "*... that helped young mothers. They would pay for college if you had a job, and they pay for - - they give you a check every month to help you take care of your child. And they pay for car problems and daycares, actually, too.*" (Amanda testimony, Dec. 5, 2001, p. 72-3) She said in her first police interview that she had received payments of "*$395 a month... a couple of times.*" (Amanda, interview, Nov. 9, 2000, p. 52)

Regarding "car problems," Chad wanted to help Amanda get a safer car, but respected her wishes. He wrote in his June 29, 2010 letter,

Amanda drove a light blue Chevy Corsica. It was this little "junker" car that she bought for like $500 just prior to meeting me. To be honest, it was one of the things that attracted me to her. Early on I mentioned buying her something a little more reliable and she said, "I love my little car. It drives great." I was worried about the drive from Auburn to Rochester with her and Kassidy. It was a pretty independent statement and I loved it. In the beginning, she either really wanted to do things on her own or could read me like a book, and knew this would make me even more attracted to her and give me the desire to do even more for her. As time went on and the car started having some mechanical issues that come with buying a $500 car we talked about it again. I wanted to buy her one of the McDonald's supervisor fleet cars. We sold them back to the dealer when they were 1 ½ to 2 years old and had 60,000 miles on them. I could pick one up for around $6,000 and I knew which supervisors took care of their cars. Not bad for a car that we bought new for $18,000 - $20,000 two years earlier.

In September, Jeff and Jennifer were doing landscaping work, including semi-annual hedge trimming, at the Rochester McDonald's, and Chad was there, coincidentally. Taking advantage of the coincidence, he called Amanda to invite her and Kassidy to come to the restaurant to have lunch with him, and Jen and Jeff. Chad remembered that lunch in 2010,

After we ate, I brought Kassidy into the play area for a few minutes and let her play in the ball pit while Amanda visited with them. On the way back to the table I stopped by one of the party rooms to get Kassidy a treat (the rooms were all glass and the cabinets in them were filled with trinkets.) Once in the room, you can see into the restaurant's main lobby and Kassidy could see Amanda, Jen, and Jeff. I said to her, "Uh, Oh Kassidy, how do we find mama?" She ran over to the glass wall and started banging on it and crying. I said to her, "Oohh, I'm just kidding honey, the door is right there." I grabbed her some stickers and we headed back to the table. I felt bad, because I was trying to get her excited, and not to scare into thinking she couldn't have mama or something. (Letter, Apr. 18, 2010)

Also in September, and as he did the previous year, Chad took his McDonald's managers and spouses/significant others on a day trip to the amusement park, "Six Flags" in Springfield, Mass. Amanda came, and Kassidy stayed with either Jeff and Jennifer or with a friend of Amanda's.

Friday, 1 September 2000

On this day began the period of the first of six charges in the indictment of Second Degree Assault by Chad against Kassidy. This period ended on September 30, during which time, allegedly *"Evans knowingly caused bodily injury to Kassidy Bortner, age 20 months. Evans caused bruising to Kassidy by grabbing and squeezing her face."* During this period Kassidy turned from 18 to 19 months old.

Saturday, 2 September 2000

Kassidy was at her grandparents' in Auburn, and on this day her uncle Scotty celebrated his birthday. Her grandmother, Jacqueline recalls that she took a photo of Kassidy, but Chad believes that the photo may have been taken later in the fall at his home. [See the Appendix for photo.] There were no bruises reported to be observed on Kassidy during this visit, and there were no reports of injuries. Kassidy was wearing the same sweater as she was wearing in the photo taken of her and Amanda in Belmont on October 20.

Below is the updated NB (No Bruise) NI (No Injury) calendar:

June 2000

Su	Mo	Tu	We	Th	Fr	Sa
					9	10
11	12	13	14	15	16	**NI**
NI	**NI**	**NI**	**NI**	**NB**	23	24
25	26	27	28	29	30	

July 2000

Su	Mo	Tu	We	Th	Fr	Sa
						1
2	3	4	5	6	**NI**	**NI**
NI	**NI**	**NI**	**NB**	**NB**	**NB**	**NB**
NB	**NB**	**NB**	**NB**	**NB**	21	22
23	**NI**	**NI**	**NI**	**NI**	**NI**	**NB**
NB	**NB**					

August 2000

Su	Mo	Tu	We	Th	Fr	Sa
		1	2	3	4	**NI**
NI	**NI**	**NI**	**NI**	**NB**	**NI**	**NI**
NI	**NI**	**NI**	**NB**	**NI**	**NI**	**NI**
NB	**NB**	**NB**	**NB**	**NB**	**NB**	**NB**
NB	**NB**	**NI**	**NI**	**NI**		

September 2000

Su	Mo	Tu	We	Th	Fr	Sa
					NI	**NB**
3	4	5	6	7	8	9
10	11	12	13	14	15	16
17	18	19	20	21	22	23
24	25	26	27	28	29	30

October 2000

Su	Mo	Tu	We	Th	Fr	Sa
1	2	3	4	5	6	7
8	9	10	11	12	13	14
15	16	17	18	19	20	21
22	23	24	25	26	27	28
29	30	31				

November 2000

Su	Mo	Tu	We	Th	Fr	Sa
			1	2	3	4
5	6	7	8	9		

Monday, 4 September 2000

Chad worked at the Hampton Beach McDonald's on this Labor Day. Amanda brought Kassidy and Kyle to the beach, so they could spend some holiday time with Chad. Kassidy was 19 months old on this date.

Tuesday, 5 September 2000

Kyle began attending Cross Road Kindergarten and School in Dover, and his half-brother, Brent, began first grade at the affiliated school, Tri-City Christian Academy in Somersworth. Brent had previously attended the Cross Road Kindergarten and had graduated in 1999.

Saturday-Sunday, 9-10 September 2000

The weekend saw the annual Seafood Festival at Hampton Beach. Amanda, Crystal Martin and Kassidy came to the beach. Chad remembers taking some time off and carrying Kassidy on his shoulders, as the three adults worked through the extremely packed crowds.

At Chad's trial in December 2001, where dates were often confused or omitted, and not referenced with a calendar, Amanda's friend, Melissa Chick, specifically testified that she began work at Sanford YMCA's day care facility on September 10. (Transcript, Dec. 10, 2001) However, that was a Sunday, and therefore it was an unlikely start date for work at a day care center. Also at Chad's trial in December 2001, she stated that she babysat for Kassidy before this reference date.

Monday, 11 September 2000

At 3:00 p.m., Amanda brought Kassidy to an appointment with Dr. James Timoney of Auburn, Maine, for an examination of her "toeing in," per the referral from Dr. Glass at Pediatric Associates. The doctor determined that no medical action was required, and Amanda understood that Kassidy would grow out of it. He made no mention of bruises. Below is the updated NB (No Bruise) NI (No Injury) calendar:

June 2000

Su	Mo	Tu	We	Th	Fr	Sa
					9	10
11	12	13	14	15	16	**NI**
NI	**NI**	**NI**	**NI**	**NB**	23	24
25	26	27	28	29	30	

July 2000

Su	Mo	Tu	We	Th	Fr	Sa
						1
2	3	4	5	6	**NI**	**NI**
NI	**NI**	**NI**	**NB**	**NB**	**NB**	**NB**
NB	**NB**	**NB**	**NB**	**NB**	21	22
23	**NI**	**NI**	**NI**	**NI**	**NI**	**NB**
NB	**NB**					

August 2000

Su	Mo	Tu	We	Th	Fr	Sa
		1	2	3	4	**NI**
NI	**NI**	**NI**	**NI**	**NB**	**NI**	**NI**
NI	**NI**	**NI**	**NB**	**NI**	**NI**	**NI**
NB	**NB**	**NB**	**NB**	**NB**	**NB**	**NB**
NB	**NB**	**NI**	**NI**	**NI**		

September 2000

Su	Mo	Tu	We	Th	Fr	Sa
					NI	**NB**
3	4	5	**NI**	**NI**	**NI**	**NI**
NI	**NB**	12	13	14	15	16
17	18	19	20	21	22	23
24	25	26	27	28	29	30

October 2000

Su	Mo	Tu	We	Th	Fr	Sa
1	2	3	4	5	6	7
8	9	10	11	12	13	14
15	16	17	18	19	20	21
22	23	24	25	26	27	28
29	30	31				

November 2000

Su	Mo	Tu	We	Th	Fr	Sa
			1	2	3	4
5	6	7	8	9		

Friday, 15 September 2000

The seasonal McDonald's at Hampton Beach closed, and Chad's friend and McDonald's employee, Travis Hunt, began living in the basement unit of Chad's home. He transferred to the Portsmouth McDonald's, managed by Jeremy Hinton.

Saturday or Sunday, 16-17 September 2000

Over this weekend, Chad and Amanda went to the 125th annual Rochester Fair with a couple. Chad had recently met Christine Wentworth (no relation to Tristan), at Dunkin Donuts, and they had socialized at the wedding of his friend, Stephanie Chick. Kyle was with Tristan, and Kassidy was likely being babysat by Jeff and Jennifer. Amanda and Chad planned to bring Kyle and Kassidy to the fair later, during its 10 day run from 15-24 September, but it didn't happen. (Letter, Oct. 22, 2010)

Fall-2000

Sunday,-Wednesday, 24-27 September 2000

Beginning on Sunday, September 24, through Wednesday, Amanda and Chad went to Martha's Vineyard, and stayed in a rented home. Chad's friend and manager, Larry Lane, had purchased a week's stay at the home at a Special Olympics benefit auction the previous winter, and he and Kim Grace stayed at the home for the remainder of the same week. Kassidy was with her grandmother, Jacqueline, during Amanda's and Chad's trip. Upon their return, Chad called an attorney in the office of Mike Bolduc, the husband of his friend, Stephanie Chick, about Chad's upcoming divorce and child support matters. As his relationship with Amanda was growing, he was getting more eager to get his divorce from Tristan finalized.
Below is the updated NB (No Bruise) NI (No Injury) calendar:

June 2000

Su	Mo	Tu	We	Th	Fr	Sa
					9	10
11	12	13	14	15	16	NI
NI	NI	NI	NI	NB	23	24
25	26	27	28	29	30	

July 2000

Su	Mo	Tu	We	Th	Fr	Sa
						1
2	3	4	5	6	NI	NI
NI	NI	NI	NB	NB	NB	NB
NB	NB	NB	NB	NB	21	22
23	NI	NI	NI	NI	NI	NB
NB	NB					

August 2000

Su	Mo	Tu	We	Th	Fr	Sa
		1	2	3	4	NI
NI	NI	NI	NI	NB	NI	NI
NI	NI	NI	NB	NI	NI	NI
NB	NB	NB	NB	NB	NB	NB
NB	NB	NI	NI	NI		

September 2000

Su	Mo	Tu	We	Th	Fr	Sa
					NI	NB
3	4	5	NI	NI	NI	NI
NI	NB	12	13	14	15	16
17	18	NI	NI	NI	NI	NI
NB	NB	NB	NB	28	29	30

October 2000

Su	Mo	Tu	We	Th	Fr	Sa
1	2	3	4	5	6	7
8	9	10	11	12	13	14
15	16	17	18	19	20	21
22	23	24	25	26	27	28
29	30	31				

November 2000

Su	Mo	Tu	We	Th	Fr	Sa
			1	2	3	4
5	6	7	8	9		

Thursday, 28 September 2000

In the morning, Chad called his financial advisor, Darren Janakis, and initiated a discussion about the creation of an education IRA for Kassidy, just as he had already established for Kyle and his stepson, Brent.
That afternoon, he called Jeff at his home phone for four minutes, probably about the landscaping at one of his restaurants.

Friday or Saturday, 29-30 September 2000

On either evening, Chad, Amanda, Kassidy and Kyle went to the Deerfield Fair with Bruce and Michelle Truell and their daughter, Ashley. Chad took Kassidy on several rides, including the "Kiddie Roller Coaster." Chad recalls that when that ride started, the cart lurched forward, and Kassidy bumped her head on the side of the cart. "*She cried for a few seconds but seemed fine.*" (Letter, March 7, 2010) Chad didn't recall any bruising on Kassidy's forehead from that accident.

October 2000

Around the beginning of October, Amanda began her work of inputting data from surveys into a formatted report, for Chad's best friend, Bruce Aube. She did this work on Chad's home computer. To ensure uninterrupted work time, she began taking Kassidy more often to Jeff's and Jennifer's for babysitting. As Jennifer was working at Perfumania, the actual babysitting was performed mostly by Jeff. About this time, as Chad recalled in

2010, Kassidy resumed having her jealousy tantrums, similar to those she showed back in June and July, and which had subsided during August and September.

Around this time, Thomas McNeil, a friend of Jeff Marshall, held Kassidy Bortner in his arms, approximately 4-6 weeks before her death, and saw no bruises. The summary of his interview, a year after Kassidy's death, reported,

He said she seemed to be tentative and slow, and he thought maybe she was slightly retarded...was slow to react with a smile when one talked to her and when one talked to her, she seemed slow to react in general... McNeil said he did not see any bruises on her at that time... he had never seen Kassidy walk, explaining that the times he saw her, she was being carried...he has [sic] *never seen* [sic] *Kassidy talk, either.* (Interview, Nov 13, 2001)

Note that there is no "No Bruise" entry here for a calendar entry because McNeil's observation could not be dated more precisely.

Sunday, 1 October 2000

Amanda and her friend, Cathy Nuernberg, brought Kassidy to her grandmother's home in Auburn, from which she and the family were moving to Buckfield on that weekend. All the family members saw Kassidy on that day, and family photographs were taken, and no bruises were noticed, and thus, there appeared to be no bruise from the Deerfield Fair cart forehead bump. One of those photos was of Kassidy sitting in a chair holding her bunny rabbit. At Chad's trial, Jacqueline remembered the setting of that photo, which became State Exhibit 19, because that chair was about the last piece of furniture left in the house. [See also the Appendix for this photograph.] By this time, Kassidy and Amanda had been living with Chad for approximately 90 days. Kassidy died 40 days later.

On this day began the period of the second of six charges of Second Degree Assault by Chad against Kassidy. This period ended on October 7, during which time *"Evans knowingly caused bodily injury to Kassidy Bortner, age 20 months. Evans caused bruising to Kassidy by grabbing and squeezing her face."* This was the only one of the six Second Degree Assault charges with a Not Guilty verdict. The logical reason for that verdict was the presence of the October 1 photograph.

Below is the updated NB (No Bruise) NI (No Injury) calendar:

June 2000

Su	Mo	Tu	We	Th	Fr	Sa
					9	10
11	12	13	14	15	16	NI
NI	NI	NI	NI	NB	23	24
25	26	27	28	29	30	

July 2000

Su	Mo	Tu	We	Th	Fr	Sa
						1
2	3	4	5	6	NI	NI
NI	NI	NI	NB	NB	NB	NB
NB	NB	NB	NB	NB	21	22
23	NI	NI	NI	NI	NI	NB
NB	NB					

August 2000

Su	Mo	Tu	We	Th	Fr	Sa
		1	2	3	4	NI
NI	NI	NI	NI	NB	NI	NI
NI	NI	NI	NB	NI	NI	NI
NB	NB	NB	NB	NB	NB	NB
NB	NB	NI	NI	NI		

September 2000

Su	Mo	Tu	We	Th	Fr	Sa
					NI	NB
3	4	5	NI	NI	NI	NI
NI	NB	12	13	14	15	16
17	18	NI	NI	NI	NI	NI
NB	NB	NB	NB	NI	NI	NI

October 2000

Su	Mo	Tu	We	Th	Fr	Sa
NB	2	3	4	5	6	7
8	9	10	11	12	13	14
15	16	17	18	19	20	21
22	23	24	25	26	27	28
29	30	31				

November 2000

Su	Mo	Tu	We	Th	Fr	Sa
			1	2	3	4
5	6	7	8	9		

Monday, 2 October 2000

Amanda went to the Portland, Maine District Court to respond to the charge of possession of alcohol as a minor at the "Creed" concert on August 23. She was found guilty and fined $100. As her driver's license likely said she lived in Auburn, the court reported her residence as "of Auburn." She and Jason Evans and Jeff Porter rented a car in New Hampshire to be sure that they would make it to court, without mishap, in Portland. Amanda brought Kassidy with her, where a lot of people saw her, including her "temper tantrum," while at the courthouse.

Wednesday, 4 October 2000

This was a notable day, but it may not have been noted in the Evans/Bortner household. Kassidy Bortner was 20 months old on this date, though there was no comment or celebration.

Also, Chad's and Tristan's divorce became effective on this date. However, Chad did not receive the written notice until after Kassidy's death. Thus, he and Amanda were still thinking in October and November that he was legally married to Tristan, and still trying to avoid alienating Tristan and avoid any slipup with the agreed-upon custody arrangements. This was a major cause of tension between Chad and Amanda during that period, and a reason that Amanda considered finding her own apartment.

Friday-Sunday, 6-8 October 2000

Chad wrote, in his November, 2000 letter to his attorneys,

The first sign of trouble came somewhere during the week of Oct. 6-8. Jeff brought Kassidy home one of those nights with three little bruises on her cheek. The odd thing was he had tried to cover them with makeup. He told Amanda, when he brought Kassidy home, that she was standing on the bed and he said to her, "Mamma's here." She repeated, "mamma, mamma" and walked off the edge of the bed. I know it was that weekend because I went to Bruce's (one of my best friends) for football on Sunday and was bitching to Jeremy (my other best friend) about the whole makeup thing.

Chad recalls that Jeff told him that it was a joke or a trick to tell Kassidy that Amanda had arrived, when, in fact, she had not. At Chad's trial, Jeff denied saying "*Mamma's here*," if Amanda was not, in fact, there. He said that he used that expression only when Amanda actually arrived, but Amanda never told Chad or anyone that Kassidy had fallen while trying to run to greet her at Jeff's.

Saturday, 7 October 2000

Around 9:00 a.m., from his Sprint cell phone, Chad called Jeff at his cell phone for four minutes. (Sprint phone bill, Oct. 2000) During the day, Amanda, Kassidy, Chad, and Bruce bowled at Bowlaway Lanes, in Rochester.. Chad had recently taken up candlepin bowling, and he, Bruce and Jeremy were bowling 2-3 times a week. Amanda often joined them, with Kassidy. Chad described in 2010 how he and Bruce began bowling:

We were sitting around at his house, enjoying a beer or a good cigar and one of us said, "We should go bowling." Next thing you know, we were at the bowling alley making it happen. This is how he and I did things. (Letter, May 3, 2010)

Sunday, 8 October 2000

On this day began the period of the third of six charges of Second Degree Assault by Chad against Kassidy. This period ended on October 14, during which time, according to the indictment, *"Evans knowingly caused bodily injury to Kassidy Bortner, age 20 months. Evans caused bruising to Kassidy by grabbing and squeezing her face."*

Early October 2000

Amanda's friend, Crystal Martin, babysat Kassidy for an evening and Kassidy spent the night, "*3 weeks to a month before her death.*" according to the summary of her interview. Crystal bathed her son, Devin, and Kassidy at the same time, and she saw no bruises on Kassidy. On this evening Kassidy's arm touched a hot hair curling iron, but Crystal could see no bruise or mark. Crystal said she took Kassidy to Emily Conley's, but Amanda called Emily to say she could not pick up Kassidy until the next day.

Around this time, while Chad was carrying Kassidy downstairs on his shoulders from a nap, Kassidy hit her head on the low overhang. Chad wrote of the accident in 2010,

*I am pretty sure it was in October. I am going to guess that it was sometime during the weekend of Oct. 8th because I believe Amanda was working on Bruce's survey project then. I believe it was a Sunday because as I recall, I was bringing Kassidy down the stairs from a nap. I wasn't often there for afternoon naps. She usually woke up pretty happy. I likely said something like, "**Hey there. Do you want to go see mama and get a snack?**"*

Those two things, seeing mama, and food always brought a smile to her face and she'd reply "Yesssss." Whenever Kassidy said, 'Yes,' she dragged the "sss" at the end. Just thinking back to it now, it was so cute, sometimes I would lift her onto my shoulders or back, other times, I would sit down on the bed and she'd wrap her arms around my neck for a piggyback or if I sat on the floor she would wrap her little legs around my shoulders. It was really one of those stupid, freak accidents. I had a really low overhang going down the stairs. Most of the time I carried the kids on my hip or piggy back going down the stairs. I had carried her down on my shoulders before and ducked just fine. On this particular occasion, I didn't duck enough and she bonked her head on the ceiling/overhang. It must have hurt like hell because she started crying. Amanda came running in from the computer room. She hit her forehead, towards one side of her face, (I can't remember which side.). I don't recall it swelling or anything which is something that often happens with forehead injuries. We put a few ice cubes in a washcloth (I believe). Kassidy didn't like that at all. It made a bruise in the area that she hit. (Letter, May 3, 2010)

Around this time, for the first time Chad and Amanda noticed that his holding Kassidy by the jaw to get "eye contact" might have caused some bruising on her lower face. When they saw such bruising a second time, their hunch seemed more correct, though still hard to believe. He resolved not to press so hard again. He had used his hand before to hold Kassidy's face, but it never caused bruises. He wrote in 2010 about "eye contact" with his boys and Kassidy, in an April 8, 2010 Letter,

There were occasions throughout the summer where I would speak to Kassidy and ask her to look me in the eyes, no differently than I did with both Kyle and Brent. The boys would automatically look me right in the eyes, listen to what I had to say and then move on. With Kassidy, it was different. She wouldn't look me in the eyes unless we were playing or something. I wasn't smart enough then to realize like in the Dr. Sandy video that maybe she was nervous or whatever and some children learn differently. Eye contact is how I learned, and how I taught the boys, etc. I would bend down to her level, put my fingers on her chin or palm her checks to get her to listen to me. I remember once specifically she was going near Kato's dog dish while he was eating. I had trained Kato to back away from his dish whenever the kids went near his food but you never know. He was a German Shepherd and besides, she may be around other dogs which would attack if they thought you were going to take their food. I gently explained to Kassidy not to go near "doggies" when they are eating because they don't like to share.

He wrote again about **eye contact** in a May 3, 2010 Letter,

I think the most important thing to note was whenever we did anything, whenever I demanded eye contact, we ALWAYS explained things. I can't remember a time where I ever reprimanded her where I didn't make a point of explaining why I was doing something. After the fit and everything was over, there was always an explanation, always a hug, a kiss, and "I love you." From the first time I ever got after Kassidy for something, I got down with her at eye level and explained the problem and why I was upset. Back then, Amanda would kind of laugh at me and say, "She doesn't understand a word of what you are saying." I would reply, "I know, but someday she will and I want her to get used to the fact that we will always talk and explain things." This is something that my father did while raising me, this is what I ALWAYS did with Kyle and Brent, and something I would do with any child I am involved with. They were/are the most important thing in the world to me and I remember when my dad took the time to explain things to me, I always felt like I was the most important thing to him. Anyone that has ever seen me around the kids should be able to speak to this. I believe this is an example of what Amanda was talking about when she said, "That I helped to make her a better person, a better parent." Amanda quickly saw the power of this and adopted it if she ever had to speak to Kyle or Kassidy about anything.

Monday, 9 October 2000

On this day began the period of the two charges of First Degree Assault by Chad against Kassidy. This period ended on November 9, during which time, "*Evans recklessly caused serious bodily injury to Kassidy Bortner, age 20 months. Evans caused a fracture to Kassidy' s leg by grabbing and pulling on her legs.*" The second of the two alleged that "*Evans recklessly caused serious bodily injury to Kassidy Bortner, age 20 months. Evans caused a fracture to Kassidy's arm by grabbing and pulling on her arms.*" Chad was found not guilty of the first fracture charge, i.e. the leg, and the second charge was dismissed by Judge Nadeau before the case went to the jury.

Wednesay, 11 October 2000

Chad renewed the registration on his Mazda RX-7. Also, his calendar had a note to sign up Tom Urrutia and Chad's sister, Nicole, for the upcoming financial management class. Tom's wife, Dorothy also attended the class as Tom's guest, and Amanda attended the class as Nicole's guest. Chad believed strongly that people needed to plan for their financial futures.

Thursday, 12 October 2000

In the morning, from his cell phone, Chad called Jeff at his cell phone for a short two minute call. As a measure of the closeness of their relationship, or lack of it, Jeff did not tell Chad about his court date later that morning, arising from the charges of "simple assault" and "criminal threatening" from the previous April 22 in Portsmouth and his arrest on May 8. These charges were never mentioned in any police interview or trial testimony relating to Kassidy's death. The Portsmouth District Court, Jury Division, continued the Simple Assault case "*without a finding for one year, good behavior.*" Previously, Jeff had requested a jury trial. The Criminal Threatening case was "*nol-prossed*" by the Assistant County Attorney Patricia Conway Capsalis. (See "Misdemeanor Sentencing Order and Case Summaries.")

On Chad's shopping list for Thursday were: "*Milk, OJ, Fruit, Veggies, Turkey, Bread, Grape Juice, Raisins, Shake N Bake, Ice Cream Sandwiches, Ovaltine.*" He wrote in a 2010 letter, "*As you can see, we ate pretty healthy. We ate mainly 'Whole Foods' rather than overly processed. Much better for you.*" (Letter, April 15, 2010) This was an interesting observation for a McDonald's manager. Also in Chad's book collection was a book about cooking with yogurt by Gary Hirshberg, CEO of New Hampshire's Stonyfield Yogurt.

mid-October 2000

Around this time, Amanda gave her friend, Emily Conley, who was pregnant, a ride to the obstetrician's office for a pre-natal checkup. Kassidy was with them, and Emily noticed bruises on her and Amanda told her the "trampoline story" which she and Chad had developed very recently, in anticipation of this doctor's appointment for Emily. It was likely the first time that Amanda had told anyone that story. Chad wrote in 2010 about the origin of that story,

The trampoline story was false but based on a true incident. We had a giant trampoline, and as you can imagine the kids all loved it. Kassidy was too light to really get herself bouncing so we (Amanda and I) would bounce her lightly. There is a safety enclosure to keep you from bouncing off the edge, but we never installed it that first summer. I don't know if you've ever been on a trampoline, but it's very uneven and you don't control exactly where you land. A little bit of extra pressure can send you flying. Anyway, on this particular day I was bouncing Kassidy and she was too close to the edge. She fell backward. Luckily, I was close enough to grab her hand. Obviously, this second of free fall scared both Kassidy and I, and we stopped jumping that day. When Amanda got home, I relayed this to her. At some point later, I believe it was around my birthday in October, Kassidy was having one of her fits when I went close to Amanda. I grabbed her cheeks in a palming fashion to get eye contact (eye contact was my big thing.) Sometime after that she had bruising and Amanda told that to one of her girlfriends and "melded" the stories of the trampoline fall to the appearance of bruising, for some reason. I remember asking why she did that and she said, "I didn't want her to think you were beating Kassidy or something." This certainly made my grabbing her less embarrassing. I wish I could say this woke me up to how stupid that behavior was. Of course, I had no idea how the "trampoline story" would acquire a life of its own. Unfortunately, it just gave me a cover. I never set out to hurt Kassidy, but I did leave bruises. I believe there was a time when Kassidy did actually fall off the trampoline when she was with Amanda. In fact, Jen might have even been at the house that day. Anyway, I remember she landed on one of her legs and limped for a few days but seemed ok. (Letter, January 28, 2010)

Around this time, Chad and Tristan, and the father of Chad's stepson, Brent, attended an evening variety show at the Cross Road Kindergarten and School. Brent was in the show. As the "significant other" in Chad's life, but not yet official because Chad believed he was still married to Tristan, Amanda did not attend. Her relationship to Brent was not as close as to Kyle, but the exclusion was surely a cause of tension at Chad's home.
Also around this time, Amanda and Chad acquired a kitten for Kassidy, from a friend of Jennifer's. The kitten wasn't in the home long enough to decide upon a name, so Kassidy's name for it remained, "Kitty."

Around this time, Amanda called her friend, Crystal Martin, and discussed the idea of getting an apartment together as she and Chad considered the idea that Amanda should get her own apartment, at least for a while. About three weeks before Kassidy's death, according to Crystal Martin's police interview, Amanda also described to Melissa Chick the temporary difficulties with Chad. Shortly thereafter, Amanda and Chad resolved whatever issues led to the discussions with Crystal and Melissa, and the idea of Amanda's sharing an apartment with Crystal was dropped. What the police never learned, in part because they never asked, was that Chad and Amanda also talked about getting married and about having a child and family together.

Around this time, a burn mark appeared on the top of one of Kassidy's feet. Crystal Martin stated that it was likely caused by a curling iron at her house when she was babysitting Kassidy.

Around this time Jeff was babysitting Kassidy more. Chad wrote, in his November 2000 letter to his attorneys,

Other times Jeff watched her in October.
-When Amanda went shopping 4 or 5 times with Jen,
-while Amanda looked for a job 2 or 3 days,
-while Amanda landscaped for him twice,
-while Amanda went to a money management class I sent her to, and

-while we went to a concert.
-A couple of times when I took Amanda out,
-once or twice when she went over to her friend Tracey's house.

Around this time, as Chad wrote, in his November 2000 letter to his attorneys, Jeff and Chad talked,

So I never got further into the conversation about how I would discipline her other than to say sometimes Kassidy's crying got on my nerves and I would occasionally put her into time outs. He said to me, "The other night she was being a little bitch so I let her have it. I smacked her ass." I assumed when he said this that he spanked her pretty age-appropriately. He said to me, "Now when Jake (his dog), sees her coming he and the cat are psyched, they say to themselves, 'Oh good here she comes again. She can take the beating we would have gotten.' "The way he described it, I just started chuckling because he was so determined. I never thought he was serious. He then proceeded to pretty much convince me Kassidy was slow. "I mean it, Chad, she is like Children of the Corn. It freaks me out. She just will sit there and stare at walls like a retard."

The reference to "Children of the Corn" is to a 1977 short story by Stephen King, from which a movie by the same name was produced. The children of a midwest horror town kill everyone else and commit other atrocities.

Finally, around this time, Kassidy's relationship to Chad seemed to be strengthening. In his January 2008 interview of Amanda, Ron Rice began the following exchange:

RR: *How was Chad and Kassidy's relationship before Jeff started watching Kassidy in October?*

AB: *... it was good and it was getting a lot better .... she was just so ... um.. she was a mommie's girl. If anyone came near me she would freak out. . ... and it was like a guy thing, girls she was fine with .. but I think it was a guy thing. . ..... I thought she loved him .... they played together ....*

Friday, 13 October 2000

From his Sprint cell phone on Friday morning, Chad called Jeff at his cell phone, for two minutes, probably for the purpose of confirming their trip the next day to Concord to the state's surplus property auction. (Sprint phone bill, Oct. 2000)

Also on Friday, Amanda brought Kassidy to her mother's home in Buckfield to pick up a $100 check so she could buy Chad a birthday present. Amanda's brother, Joshua, was at home and saw them both. Amanda's uncle, Robert Conley, also saw Kassidy briefly when he was coming home from work, and Amanda and Kassidy were leaving. Chad wrote in a February 21, 2011 letter,

I really have no idea who Amanda went to Buckfield with, because I didn't know she was going. Amanda had a free schedule to come and go as she pleased. I knew Amanda had no money for a birthday present for me and when she mentioned going to her mom's to get some of her money that her mom had, I told her that was silly, and that I didn't need a birthday present. I think I told her that a nice back massage would have been the best birthday present she could ever give me. Material things weren't that big a deal to me. If I wanted something, I bought it. Apparently it was important to her, so she went.

Amanda's mother, Jacqueline, was away on a trucking trip with her husband, Paul. Upon her return the next day, Joshua mentioned to his mother that he had seen bruises on Kassidy.

Later on Friday afternoon, Amanda visited her friend, Melissa Chick, at the YMCA in Springvale, Maine, where Melissa Chick worked as a child care worker. Coincidentally, Amanda saw her friend, Tracey Foley, whose child was in day care at the YMCA. Later, Amanda and her two friends went to Tracey's home, including Kassidy. Amanda and Kassidy spent the night at Melissa's, according to Melissa Chick. Both Melissa and Tracey saw bruises on Kassidy, and Amanda told them the "trampoline story."

Chad wrote, in his November 2000 letter to his attorneys, that originally,

Amanda had arranged to stay Saturday night at Jeff and Jen's house and I talked to him on Friday and he said, "Oh man doesn't she have some other place to go? We don't really want them here." He stated to me, "We don't mind Mandy staying over but Jen and I

don't really want to have the kid here too." I was silent in disbelief and he then said, "Well it is Jen. When she gets out of work after working all day you want to come home to some peace and quite. The last thing you want is to listen to a screaming brat." I said to him, "Wow, Jen is her aunt. Maybe she ought to tell Amanda how she feels." I told Amanda about this when she got home that Friday night and she went and stayed at her friend Tracey's house. It worked out well because Tracey needed a babysitter anyways.

Also, around this time, Jeff's dog, Jake, knocked Kassidy down, causing a bruise on her face. Jeff and Jennifer put makeup on Kassidy, in order to hide the bruise when they went shopping.

Saturday, 14 October 2000

Chad and Jeff drove to Concord to the semi-annual New Hampshire state surplus property sale, which began at 9:00 a.m. They drove in Jeff's truck in case they made a purchase. Chad was hoping to find a three-wheeler, but neither man purchased anything. Chad wrote, in his November 2000 letter to his attorneys,
During the ride up to the auction Jeff bitched the whole time about Kassidy, the boys, Josh and Scottie (Amanda and Jen's brothers), Amanda's parents. etc.

At 12:24 p.m. Chad called his friend, Glen Varney, at his home where Chad docked his boat.

At 3:23 p.m., Chad called Jeff at his cell phone for six minutes, and again at 3:31 p.m. for two minutes. These calls were about landscaping for McDonald's and not about babysitting. Amanda made all the babysitting arrangements with Jeff and Jennifer, her friends and mother.

Upon her return from a trucking trip with her husband, Paul Conley, Jacqueline learned from her son, Joshua, and perhaps from her brother-in-law, Robert Conley, of bruising on Kassidy's face. She was concerned and called the home of Amanda and Chad. Chad answered the phone and explained the bruises with the "trampoline story." It was the first time he had told that story, since it had been created a few days earlier, either by Amanda or by Chad and Amanda, together.

Chad wrote about that call in his November 2000 letter to his attorneys,
She then wished me a happy birthday and we got off the phone. She then called Jen and Jeff's house and they told her the same thing. Jeff then called me and was laughing telling me that Amanda's mom called questioning Jen if; "Chad would do anything to Kassidy." Jen said, "No he never would" and then Jeff proceeded to tell me, "I was yelling behind Jen that that little bitch needed discipline. She was acting up over here last week and I smacked her ass and liked it." I just kind of laughed because I was glad to see they knew better and that was the last thing that I wanted was for Amanda's mom to think I was beating Kassidy. I was going through a somewhat easy divorce with Tristan, but I was scared to death that she could turn at anytime so the last thing I would want is to give her any reason to turn.

Amanda returned to Tracey's home, visiting, and stayed overnight, including Kassidy. During this visit, Tracey observed more closely the bruises on Kassidy's face, and discussed them with Amanda.

Sunday, 15 October 2000

On this day began the period of the fourth of six charges of Second Degree Assault by Chad against Kassidy. This period ended on October 21, during which time, according to the indictment, *"Evans knowingly caused bodily injury to Kassidy Bortner, age 20 months. Evans caused bruising to Kassidy by grabbing and squeezing her face."*

Chad's 29th birthday was on Sunday. His parents came to Rochester with Jason and Nicole, but Amanda was in Maine, and did not bring Kassidy to the party at Chad's house. Later the Evans family returned to Keene, and the party continued at Bruce's house. Later that afternoon, Amanda drove to Bruce's, with Kassidy in the backseat, and gave her two presents for Chad to Bruce. Then, Amanda and Kassidy returned to their Milton Road home and Chad soon joined them.

Tuesday, 17 October 2000

Tristan was at the home of Chad Evans and made the first of two observations of Kassidy, which led to her calling DCYF two weeks later, on Tuesday, the 31st.

That evening, at 8:34 p.m., from his Sprint cell phone, Chad Evans called Jeff Marshall at his cell phone, for three minutes. (Sprint phone bill, Oct. 2000) The call was likely to see if Jeff could help with Chad's planned purchase and pickup of a 3-wheeler in Saugus the next day. Jeff wasn't available, so the next day, Bruce and Chad drove to Saugus, Mass. in Bruce's father's truck to pick up a Honda 200X 3-wheeler.

That afternoon, at 3:56 p.m., from his Sprint cell phone, Chad called Darren Janakis, his financial advisor, to continue their discussion about an education fund for Kassidy. Two weeks later, they talked again about this plan. (Sprint phone bill, Oct. 2000)

Below is the updated calendar of bruises with NB (No Bruise) NI (No Injury) and B for (Bruise). This shows the observations of bruises over the period from October 13 through October 17.

June 2000						
Su	Mo	Tu	We	Th	Fr	Sa
					9	10
11	12	13	14	15	16	NI
NI	NI	NI	NI	NB	23	24
25	26	27	28	29	30	

July 2000						
Su	Mo	Tu	We	Th	Fr	Sa
						1
2	3	4	5	6	NI	NI
NI	NI	NI	NB	NB	NB	NB
NB	NB	NB	NB	NB	21	22
23	NI	NI	NI	NI	NI	NB
NB	NB					

August 2000						
Su	Mo	Tu	We	Th	Fr	Sa
		1	2	3	4	NI
NI	NI	NI	NI	NB	NI	NI
NI	NI	NI	NB	NI	NI	NI
NB	NB	NB	NB	NB	NB	NB
NB	NB	NI	NI	NI		

September 2000						
Su	Mo	Tu	We	Th	Fr	Sa
					NI	NB
3	4	5	NI	NI	NI	NI
NI	NB	12	13	14	15	16
17	18	NI	NI	NI	NI	NI
NB	NB	NB	NB	NI	NI	NI

October 2000						
Su	Mo	Tu	We	Th	Fr	Sa
NB	2	3	4	5	6	7
8	9	10	11	12	B	B
B	B	B	18	19	20	21
22	23	24	25	26	27	28
29	30	31				

November 2000						
Su	Mo	Tu	We	Th	Fr	Sa
			1	2	3	4
5	6	7	8	9		

Thursday, 19 October 2000

From 7-9:30 p.m., Nicole and Amanda went to their first of three weekly, Thursday evening, sessions of a money management seminar. It was held at the complex at the former Pease Air Force Base in Portsmouth, as was recommended, and paid-for, by Chad. Chad babysat Kassidy, after meeting Jeff in the Sears Parking lot in the Fox Run Mall in Newington to pick up Kassidy. She had been with Jeff for at least part of the day. Chad wrote in 2010,

I recall the incident well. It was one of the nights that Amanda and Nicole were going to their money mgt. class. So this was mid to late October. I'm not sure why we were meeting there other than that the Spaulding Turnpike was how I returned from any of my restaurants so we met there. I'm not sure where he was prior to the Sears parking lot, but I suspect I was returning from one of my restaurants in the lower seacoast or Methuen. Otherwise, I likely would have had Amanda drop her right off to me because as I recall, Jeff was only watching her for a short while that day. I think that is one of the things that surprised me about Jeff yelling at Kassidy that day. She had only been with him for a short while. What could she have possibly done to upset him. Jeff was in his pickup and didn't see me pull up two spaces from his passenger door. I walked up to the truck and heard her crying hysterically and him screaming something to the effect of "Stop being a fucking brat today." I cranked open the passenger door and he looked like he had seen a ghost or something. Kassidy immediately stopped crying and put her arms out and ran to me (she wasn't in a car seat). To be honest, it felt really good to have her run to me like this, and this is what makes the entire exchange memorable. As I buckled her car seat, I asked Jeff what his problem was and why he was screaming at her. I don't recall his answer or if he even really gave one. It's hard to explain. (Letter, March 7, 2010)

Friday, 20 October 2000

At 7:33 a.m., from his cell phone, Chad called Jeff, at his home phone, for one minute, probably to confirm the plans for their trip together to Maine on Sunday where Chad was purchasing another 3-wheeler. He needed Jeff's help with his truck to bring it to Rochester.

In the afternoon, Chad, Amanda and Kassidy visited Chad's sister, Nicole, and her husband, Brandon Harvey, in Belmont, New Hampshire. Brandon and Chad talked about Chad's 3-wheeler acquisitions - past and upcoming. During this trip, Nicole took a photo of Amanda holding Kassidy. [See this photo in the Appendix.] Everyone ate dinner that evening at the "Nothin' Fancy" Mexican restaurant in Weirs Beach. There were no questions and no discussions during this family gathering about bruises on Kassidy, so the bruises of the previous weekend had diminished enough to make them not observable or worth a comment.

Below is the updated calendar of bruises with NB (No Bruise) NI (No Injury) and B for (Bruise).

June 2000

Su	Mo	Tu	We	Th	Fr	Sa
					9	10
11	12	13	14	15	16	**NI**
NI	**NI**	**NI**	**NI**	**NB**	23	24
25	26	27	28	29	30	

July 2000

Su	Mo	Tu	We	Th	Fr	Sa
						1
2	3	4	5	6	**NI**	**NI**
NI	**NI**	**NI**	**NB**	**NB**	**NB**	**NB**
NB	**NB**	**NB**	**NB**	**NB**	21	22
23	**NI**	**NI**	**NI**	**NI**	**NI**	**NB**
NB	**NB**					

August 2000

Su	Mo	Tu	We	Th	Fr	Sa
		1	2	3	4	**NI**
NI	**NI**	**NI**	**NI**	**NB**	**NI**	**NI**
NI	**NI**	**NI**	**NB**	**NI**	**NI**	**NI**
NB	**NB**	**NB**	**NB**	**NB**	**NB**	**NB**
NB	**NB**	**NI**	**NI**	**NI**		

September 2000

Su	Mo	Tu	We	Th	Fr	Sa
					NI	**NB**
3	4	5	**NI**	**NI**	**NI**	**NI**
NI	**NB**	12	13	14	15	16
17	18	**NI**	**NI**	**NI**	**NI**	**NI**
NB	**NB**	**NB**	**NB**	**NI**	**NI**	**NI**

October 2000

Su	Mo	Tu	We	Th	Fr	Sa
NB	2	3	4	5	6	7
8	9	10	11	12	**B**	**B**
B	**B**	**NI**	**NI**	**NI**	**NB**	21
22	23	24	25	26	27	28
29	30	31				

November 2000

Su	Mo	Tu	We	Th	Fr	Sa
			1	2	3	4
5	6	7	8	9		

Saturday, 21 October 2000

Chad and Amanda spent the day and evening with their friends, Bruce and Michelle Truell, in Newport, New Hampshire, and Kassidy had an overnight babysit with Jennifer and Jeff. This was her fourth overnight with Jeff and Jennifer since June 9.

Since the June 2 fix-up by Jeff and Jennifer, Amanda's and Jennifer's relationship was strained by their competition with each other. In her "My Life Story," Amanda wrote of how her older sister was favored, even though, she, Amanda was the better student and more athletic.

Jen was very jealous of Chad and my relationship. Just the little things, for example: When we went shopping, Chad would give me a couple hundred dollars without batting an eyelash and I didn't even work. Jeff gave Jen an allowance of like $50 every two weeks and she worked her ass off. Chad was always bringing me little gifts like one time he even went into her perfume store to get me perfume, and she was all mad because Jeff was never thoughtful. Chad would take me places, we went out, went on little vacations (Jeff would never take Jen out say nothing about going on a vacation.) We basically loved the same things and Jen would always tell me how lucky I am.

Sunday, 22 October 2000

On this day began the period of the fifth of six charges of Second Degree Assault by Chad against Kassidy. This period ended on October 31, during which time, according to the indictment, *"Evans knowingly caused bodily injury to Kassidy Bortner, age 20 months. Evans caused bruising to Kassidy by grabbing and squeezing her face."*

Chad and Amanda returned from Bruce and Michelle's and Jeff later brought Kassidy back to Chad and Amanda's home. Leaving Amanda, Travis and Kassidy in the kitchen, Chad and Jeff made a trip north to Maine to pick up a three-wheeler. The 3-wheeler was a Honda 250SX, with an automatic clutch, reverse gear and electric starter. It was for Amanda.

Chad wrote about that trip, in his November 2000 letter to his attorneys,
He showed up at my house around 2PM on Sunday afternoon, dropped Kassidy off and we left. When we were getting ready to leave I ran out to get some stuff out of my car and Jeff was left in the kitchen alone with Travis (my roommate), Amanda, and Kassidy. I didn't find out at the time but two days later I found out Jeff said to Amanda, "Her ass might be a little sore because I spankcd it." Immediately after Jeff and I got underway he started talking about how fucked up their family was. He talked about Scottie and Kassidy being retarded. He said Josh is the next "unabomber." He then stated that the girl's parents were "useless, lazy trash, that had kids so they could take their paychecks." He proceeded to tell me how Jen worked and her mom would always take her checks, they had borrowed money from him several times, they always cried poor, that I had better watch Mandy's money or they would spend it too. (Come to find out her mom did cash two of her checks.) He said, "The mom is totally fucked. She had Josh call me and ask to come down and work. I told him, "Hello, it is the middle of October. You should be in school." He talked about how they were raising Kassidy up there he said she was a cute kid, but he thought maybe Josh was the father, because she is "fuckin' retarded." He said, "She lacks discipline. They baby the shit out of the little bitch." They all let her have her own way. It is not Mandy's fault because she seems like she wants to do the right thing, but they all will go pick her up or whatever." (At the time I thought he really had a lot of respect for Mandy. I have since realized....)

He described an incident at his house where he was teaching Kassidy a lesson about listening. When watching her the previous week, she started crying and he threw her in on the bed; and she started crying louder. So he then threw a pillow over her head and said, "Cry into that you little bitch. I have neighbors you know." He let Kassidy get up once she was quiet and she sat still in the chair until it was time to go home after that. At this point I just sat in amazement listening.

At Chad Evans' trial, Jeff Marshall recalled the trip to purchase the 3-wheeler, but did not recall .. making a statement to Amanda about spanking Kassidy. (Transcript, December 7, 2001, pp. 10-13)

In his police interview, Travis Hunt recalled that Jeff said to Chad, " *'You know,' he said, 'she's being a real bitch this weekend'... And he said he had to slap her ass or whatever.*" (Interview, Nov. 22, 2000, page 359)

While Chad and Jeff were in Maine, Amanda saw the dark and extensive bruises on Kassidy's buttocks when she changed Kassidy's diaper. Jennifer came to visit, and Amanda showed her the bruises on Kassidy. Jennifer asked Amanda not to tell Chad right away, to give Jennifer time to discuss it with Jeff.

In a 2008 interview with Ron Rice (RR), Amanda recalled Jennifer's and Jeff's reactions to the black and blues:

RR: *What was Jennifer's reaction when you showed her the bruises on Kassidy's butt after Kassidy ..... ?*

AB: *.. Jen started crying with me and um, saying 'I can't believe that Jeff would do that, my gosh' - and then she screamed at Jeff when he walked through the door.*

RR: *And what did Jeff say?*

AB: *"I didn't know I did it that hard," ... he looked like he really felt bad.*

Thus, for that moment, Jeff was in the same position as Chad was when he and Amanda first realized that his palming Kassidy's face was causing bruises. For some reason, perhaps beginning in October, Kassidy was bruising more easily than before. Also during that visit, Amanda and Jennifer and Kassidy were playing on the trampoline and Amanda asked Jennifer about the bruises on her own leg. Amanda then told her sister that she could stay with her, Chad and Kassidy if she wanted.

In "My Life Story," Amanda described that evening,

One night Jen came over after she was done work, only cause Jeff was with Chad picking up a three wheeler for me, four hours a way up ME. We were jumping and doing flips on the trampoline and she said this is so fun, but it is killing my leg. She then showed me big bruises all up and down her one leg. She said, "Promise you won't tell mom?' I said "Yeah". Then she said, "Jeff and her had gotten in a fight and he punched me." I told her she could move in with us if they were fighting. She said I at least have to wait until I get my new car because she had been giving him her paycheck every week, plus she sold her old car and he kept that money. She said as soon as she was done paying off his truck, then she'd get whatever car she wanted. Oh yeah I think I'm not too positive, but I think that's when I told her that Chad grabbed my throat before and left a mark on me, only so she would feel better about it. It was all talk. Just something to keep the conversation rolling.

This acknowledgment by Amanda that she had said something bad about Chad in order to make her sister feel better was important, and was likely a reason why Jennifer's opinion of Chad declined and why it apparently because easier for her to think ill of him by the time of her police interviews and Chad's trial.

Chad wrote about that evening in his November 2000 letter to his attorneys,

When we got home that night, Jen was over. Amanda was not in a great mood. We were all sitting at the table shooting the shit and the subject of Kassidy came up. Jeff chimed in that she needed discipline in her life. I agreed that she was a bit spoiled at times. I told them that she was freaking out one time so bad that I had to splash cold water on her face to get her to calm down. I could see Amanda getting a little upset. Jeff was in the middle of a story and Amanda got up from the table and said, "I don't think you should hit anybody else's kid Jeff." Kassidy was acting up about going to bed and I took her up and loudly told her to lay down and go to sleep. When I came back down the stairs and was rounding the corner Jeff said to me while I was coming out of the bathroom, "Let me know if you are going to beat her. I want to watch." I gave him a real fucked up look and then he kind of laughed off what he said. They left soon after and Amanda was a little mad at me for saying Kassidy did need discipline every now and then. (I had no idea why she was so upset at this point.)

Chad went to Bruce's to watch a Sunday Night football game.

Below is the updated calendar of bruises with NB (No Bruise) NI (No Injury) and B for (Bruise)

June 2000						
Su	**Mo**	**Tu**	**We**	**Th**	**Fr**	**Sa**
					9	10
11	12	13	14	15	16	**NI**
NI	**NI**	**NI**	**NI**	**NB**	23	24
25	26	27	28	29	30	

July 2000						
Su	**Mo**	**Tu**	**We**	**Th**	**Fr**	**Sa**
						1
2	3	4	5	6	**NI**	**NI**
NI	**NI**	**NI**	**NB**	**NB**	**NB**	**NB**
NB	**NB**	**NB**	**NB**	**NB**	21	22
23	**NI**	**NI**	**NI**	**NI**	**NI**	**NB**
NB	**NB**					

August 2000						
Su	**Mo**	**Tu**	**We**	**Th**	**Fr**	**Sa**
		1	2	3	4	**NI**
NI	**NI**	**NI**	**NI**	**NB**	**NI**	**NI**
NI	**NI**	**NI**	**NB**	**NI**	**NI**	**NI**
NB	**NB**	**NB**	**NB**	**NB**	**NB**	**NB**
NB	**NB**	**NI**	**NI**	**NI**		

September 2000						
Su	Mo	Tu	We	Th	Fr	Sa
					NI	NB
3	4	5	NI	NI	NI	NI
NI	NB	12	13	14	15	16
17	18	NI	NI	NI	NI	NI
NB	NB	NB	NB	NI	NI	NI

October 2000						
Su	Mo	Tu	We	Th	Fr	Sa
NB	2	3	4	5	6	7
8	9	10	11	12	B	B
B	B	17	18	19	20	B
B	23	24	25	26	27	28
29	30	31				

November 2000						
Su	Mo	Tu	We	Th	Fr	Sa
			1	2	3	4
5	6	7	8	9		

Monday, 23 October 2000

At 2:07 p.m. from his cell phone, Chad called Jeff at his home phone for four minutes. Chad recalled in 2010 that this call was likely about landscaping at a McDonald's restaurant.

That evening at 6:57 p.m., again from his Sprint cell phone, and after returning home, Chad called Jeff at Jeff's home phone for nine minutes. (Sprint phone bill, Oct. 2000) Chad recalled in 2010 that this call was when he informed Jeff that his landscaping contracts with Chad's McDonald's restaurants would not be renewed for 2001. Normally, the Colley-McCoy contractors are told about non-renewals of contracts in the Spring. However, as a favor to a friend, and boyfriend of Amanda's sister, and possible future brother-in-law, Chad gave Jeff an early "heads-up." Chad recalls that Jeff did not protest or otherwise respond openly.

Meanwhile, Amanda was ready to tell Chad about Kassidy's condition the day before, when Jeff brought her home. Chad wrote, in his November 2000 letter to his attorneys,

The next night[Sunday] *I came home right before lifting, and Amanda was changing Kassidy's diaper. She was visibly upset and I asked her what was wrong. She said with tears in her eyes, "Look at her butt." I had never seen anything like it. Her ass was completely black. Amanda did not tell me how hard Jeff had beaten her ass because Jen asked her not to, the night before. Jen said, "She will talk to Jeff." If she had shown me while he was there the night before I would have beaten him senseless. Up to this point I had given Amanda no real direction. I let her come and go and do as she pleased because I did not want to control her and lose her like I did Tristan. I knew this was wrong though. I stated to her, "I don't think Jeff should watch her anymore." Amanda told me that she talked to Jeff and he apologized. I went off to lift and watch "Monday Night Football" at Bruce's house. That night Jeremy came and stayed at the house as we were leaving at 7 AM the next morning for a company golf outing.*

Chad shared with Amanda that he and Jeff had discussed the spanking during their Sunday trip to Maine, but not its severity. The Monday night NFL football game was between the Miami Dolphins and New York Jets. Jeremy and Chad returned home to Chad's early in the morning.

Tuesday, 24 October 2000

Jeremy recalled at Chad's trial that on the morning of October 24, he awoke after not much sleep for himself and Chad. Then he went into Chad's and Amanda's bedroom to awaken Chad. Kassidy was in bed between Chad and Amanda and enjoying herself. That morning, Amanda showed Chad the bruises on Kassidy's buttocks, which had occurred during Kassidy's last babysitting with Jeff the previous Saturday. Chad wasn't sure what to do, so he gave it a day to mull over.

Chad wrote, in his November 2000 letter to his attorneys, that on the way to their McDonald's golfing tournament at the Overlook Golf Club in Hollis, New Hampshire, "*Jeremy made a comment to me... 'Does the baby always sleep with you guys?' I said, 'No, she just crawls in with us.'*" As Jeremy noted in his interview, this surprised him because of Chad and Amanda's active sexual life. However, he underestimated Chad's joy in being with Kassidy.

That day, Jeff, Jennifer and Amanda, with Kassidy, did landscaping fall cleanup work at customer sites. It must have been a day off for Jennifer from Perfumania, as she often worked weekends. Jeff took Kassidy with him back to his home for most of the day as he was doing business paperwork. Amanda worked for minimal or no wages, but, unbeknownst to Chad, she had a barter-like arrangement with Jeff. She gave him and Jennifer some or all of her Maine food stamps for his and their babysitting. Amanda calculated correctly that Chad would not want to have her buying food with government food stamps while living with him, as he would interpret it as a statement that he was not providing enough for her and Kassidy. It's simply wrong for people who don't need government assistance to use it.

Chad wrote about that evening in his November 2000 letter to his attorneys,
We got home that night and Kassidy had a few fresh bruises on her face. Jeremy looked at her and said, "Chad, what the fuck happened to her face, it wasn't like that this morning?" I said, "I don't know" (it didn't really alarm me because like any 20 mo. old baby, she was sometimes very clumsy.) "But look at this." I said to him and proceeded to pull her diaper down. He said, "Holy shit, who the hell did that?" I told him Jeff did, and asked him what he thought I should do if anything? He replied, "You have to beat his ass or at least talk to him. If anyone ever hit my kid like that they would be dead." I said you are right and then Amanda heard us talking from the computer room. Jeremy went into the room and she confirmed the story. Amanda also told him that Travis was standing right there when Jeff said it.

Late-October 2000

Around this time, Chad had been notified by a state labor inspector that his Hampton Rte. 1 and Greenland stores were going to get a state labor audit.
Around this time, Amanda talked with Tracey Foley about Amanda coming to her home for an overnight with Kassidy, but Amanda didn't come. Amanda said she was very busy, including the survey work for Bruce Aube. Later, with hindsight, such non-acceptance of invitations was interpreted by some as part of an effort to hide Kassidy.
Around this time said Amanda, Kassidy hit her head on the driver's seat of Amanda's car when Amanda hit the brakes hard to avoid a collision. Kassidy's car seat-belt was not securely fastened. (Angela Blodgett report, November 21, 2000.)

Around this time, according to what was related to Chad, Jeff "*was changing her diaper, and leaving her standing on the bed while he went to get wipes with her pants around both ankles and she fell face first.*" (Chad, November 2000 letter to his attorneys)

Wednesday, 25 October 2000

Chad wrote, in his November 2000 letter to his attorneys, about his response to the bruises on Kassidy.

The very next day I called Jeff to confront him on the situation I said, "Jeff, I guess the hell you smacked Kassidy's ass." I had expected him to apologize to me as he did Amanda the day before and let me know that he just let his anger get the best of him. Instead, he replied, "Yah! My friggin hand was killing me too." As if he was proud of what he did and that I would be too. I went off. I said, "You dumb shit. You beat her ass that hard through her diaper. You ever do that again and I will beat your ass. Do you understand me'?" He then piped down and told me how sorry he was and he didn't mean to do it that hard. I told him that I didn't want to hear it. I made my threat and no one had ever not listened so I figured he would listen as well.

Chad recalled in 2010 that he had the above conversation with Jeff on Tuesday, and that Jeff said to him, "*Yeah, I spanked her so hard, my hand stung.*" (Letter, March 23, 2010)

Thursday, 26 October 2000

Nicole and Amanda went to their second of three weekly evening sessions of their money management seminar, in Portsmouth. Amanda's car was in the VIP-Rochester shop for brakes and exhaust, so Jeff picked up Kassidy at Chad's and Amanda's in Rochester for overnight babysitting at Jeff's and Jennifer's in Kittery, for her fifth and last stay with them overnight. See "List of Overnight Babysitting." Amanda described what became a three-day, two-night babysitting period in her three-page notes ("Flashbacks"), which she wrote shortly after Kassidy's death. They begin, "*These are some flashbacks that are coming into mind.*"

Friday, 27 October 2000

Jeff was expected to bring Kassidy back to Amanda, and Amanda called him to arrange the time. Amanda wrote in "Flashbacks ," "*So I call early morning. I remember really missing her. And he said he 'was gonna be over in a couple of hours.' He never showed. Finally....*" Jeff said, " *'I'll drop her off soon,'* " but he didn't. Amanda wrote, "*So I waited & still he didn't show. He kept call*[ing] *a couple* [of] *times & said he'd be there soon.*" Later, Jeff called Amanda and said he would bring her back on Saturday, and Amanda said, "*Okay*."

Amanda had an optometrist appointment with Dr. Daniel Roy in Sanford, for an examination to get new contact lenses. She must have been given a ride there by a friend, or borrowed a car.

When Chad arrived home that Friday evening, Amanda was very upset about Jeff's failure to bring Kassidy home. Chad offered to drive to Kittery to get Kassidy, but Amanda declined the offer and decided to wait until the next day for Kassidy's return. She was reluctant to ask for Chad's help in resolving this dilemma.

Saturday, 28 October 2000

Amanda picked up her car at "VIP Auto" and paid for it with Chad's Gold Card, but she didn't drive to Kittery to get Kassidy because Jeff said that he would return her "*today*." She wrote in "Flashbacks," "*Finally he drops her off around 4 or 5:00. She was so sick and hungry.*" Jeff told Amanda that during Kassidy's time with Jeff and Jennifer, Kassidy opened a bottle of Windex and drank some. According to Jennifer, Kassidy " *'got sick, really sick and we were feeding her and she kept throwing up...really, really, really sick.'* " (Jennifer Interview, Nov 9, 2000. p 925.) Jennifer said that Jeff called "*Poison Control and they told him what to do and stuff like that and she was fine.*" (Jennifer Interview, Nov 9, 2000. p 923.). In addition to the dehydration and hunger, Kassidy had two large bumps on the back of her head. Amanda told the police at her first interview, *Well, um, about 2 weeks ago, she, Jeff was babysitting her and he brought her back and he told me that she fell out of the truck.... and she had a bump on her head. And, um, she came home that day and she was really sick. She was like dehydrated and she wanted drinks and stuff, so I gave her Pedialyte and I gave her Tylenol and I kept giving her water to get some fluid in her and the next day she was fine. (*p. 828)

Chad or Amanda went to Brooks Pharmacy to purchase the Pedialyte which was to ameliorate Kassidy's dehydration. Amanda wrote in "Flashbacks,"

And I held her and cuddled with her. Jeff suspiciously stayed there for a while, watching me care for her. He just said she was sick and acting weird. And dazed. The flu was going around. ..[That] *was my first thought. Then he told me about her falling out of the truck on to the ground. And I started getting mad. (But I never thought he would do anything intentionally.) He also forgot her bag & diapers. So I asked him to watch the kids* [Kyle and Kassidy] *while I went to Market Basket to get diapers. I came back right away, cause he said he had a place to clean. So I got back & held her all night. And watched TV with her. Kept giving her fluids. Then she was sitting on my lap and she... falling asleep. Then she rolled her eyes back (But I thought she was sleeping & just tired*) *& then she fell asleep. I laid with her and then put her to bed. Chad and I slept beside her that night. He was really concerned and wanted to help. The next day she seemed fine. She was doing her ABC's 123's. And seemed happy.* ("Flashbacks")

Chad recalled the incident in his November, 2000 letter to his attorneys,
Amanda stated to me that the baby was starving, she said to Amanda "Hungry, Hungry." She gave Kassidy a bowl of cereal. Kassidy had learned table manners and usually she ate very well with a spoon and fork, but at this time she stuck her face in the bowl and

drank every bit of the milk out. Amanda then filled the milk back up and she did it again. Amanda also told me that she witnessed Kassidy's eyes roll into her head for a second approximately an hour before I had gotten home. I asked her at that point, "Do you think we should take her to the hospital?" She said, "No, I think she will be ok." Amanda then asked me to get some Pedialite. We both stayed up with Kassidy that night, taking turns holding her and walking with her as she cried. Amanda described the way Kassidy ate as if she hadn't been fed the entire time she was at Jeff's house.

Interestingly, and as yet another example of non-communication, Chad wrote in the same letter that he didn't learn about the Windex swallowing incident until after Kassidy's death.

Monday, 30 October 2000

Tristan was at Chad and Amanda's home and made the second of two observations of bruises on Kassidy, which she reported to DCYF the following day.
Below is the updated calendar of bruises with NB (No Bruise) NI (No Injury) and B for (Bruise) including the goose egg bumps on Kassidy's head, as observed on the 28th.

June 2000

Su	Mo	Tu	We	Th	Fr	Sa
					9	10
11	12	13	14	15	16	NI
NI	NI	NI	NI	NB	23	24
25	26	27	28	29	30	

July 2000

Su	Mo	Tu	We	Th	Fr	Sa
						1
2	3	4	5	6	NI	NI
NI	NI	NI	NB	NB	NB	NB
NB	NB	NB	NB	NB	21	22
23	NI	NI	NI	NI	NI	NB
NB	NB					

August 2000

Su	Mo	Tu	We	Th	Fr	Sa
		1	2	3	4	NI
NI	NI	NI	NI	NB	NI	NI
NI	NI	NI	NB	NI	NI	NI
NB	NB	NB	NB	NB	NB	NB
NB	NB	NI	NI	NI		

September 2000

Su	Mo	Tu	We	Th	Fr	Sa
					NI	NB
3	4	5	NI	NI	NI	NI
NI	NB	12	13	14	15	16
17	18	NI	NI	NI	NI	NI
NB	NB	NB	NB	NI	NI	NI

October 2000

Su	Mo	Tu	We	Th	Fr	Sa
NB	2	3	4	5	6	7
8	9	10	11	12	B	B
B	B	17	18	19	20	B
B	23	24	25	26	27	B
B	B	31				

November 2000

Su	Mo	Tu	We	Th	Fr	Sa
			1	2	3	4
5	6	7	8	9		

Tuesday, 31 October 2000

At 12:49 p.m. Tristan called DCYF, anonymously, to report the bruises on Kassidy. An internal DCYF "Assessment Referral Information" report summarized the call, *Reporter was at the home two weeks ago and child had large bruises on left side of face and across her neck. Reporter asked mom who said, "She fell down the stairs." Two days later, Reporter asked mom's boyfriend, Chad Evans, who said, "Child fell off from trampoline.' Reporter is divorced from Chad Evans due to DV. Reporter was in the home last evening and child has new bruise on right cheek. Report did not ask how this occurred. Reporter goes into the home due to her own children residing in the residence.* (p. 410)

The form had a box for "substance abuse" which was checked and contained the comment, "*Chad Evans is an alcoholic,*" (p. 410) but it's not known why, as Chad is not an alcoholic. As the "reporter" indicated that she was divorced from Chad Evans, it wasn't totally anonymous, which didn't matter to Chad, when he learned later about her call. Chad said to Tristan on the evening that Kassidy died, when Tristan told him of her call to DCYF, that he was pleased she had called, and that he was sorry either that she didn't call sooner or that DCYF hadn't responded sooner.

On the evening of Tristan's call, she and Chad took Kyle and Brent trick-or-treating for Halloween in the neighborhood around Tristan's parents' home in Milton. Amanda stayed home with Kassidy, who appeared to be ill.

Around this time, Amanda noticed that Kassidy was losing clumps of hair. Chad recalled in his February 26, 2010 letter, that

I believe it was a few days after Kassidy came home from Jeff's and this fall from his truck episode. I came home from work and saw one of the saddest things in my life. Amanda was sitting on the dining room floor holding Kassidy and crying hysterically. Big clumps of Kassidy's hair was coming out of her head (close to where the eggs were).

Amanda was rubbing Kassidy's hair and looked up at me to say, "What's happening to my baby?" It was like a baby holding her baby.

Early-November 2000

Around this time, Amanda learned that she had been hired at Old Navy, a retail clothing store in the Kittery Mall. She had been applying for jobs pursuant to the requirements of the ASPIRE program. The Old Navy acceptance came sooner than expected, so she accelerated her efforts to find day care for Kassidy, and concentrated her search on the Kittery area. She said in her first police interview (p. 863) that if Jeff hadn't offered to babysit for Kassidy, she would not have accepted the Old Navy job.

Chad wrote, in his November 2000 letter to his attorneys, about that week and the job. *She told me that she had found one at Old Navy and they wanted her to start right off. She said her hours would be 8 to 8. I asked her how she planned on working that out and she said that she was going to get a daycare for Kassidy and that Jeff had volunteered to pick her up and watch her after day care closes at 5 or so until when she got out of work. I wasn't really fond of the idea. 1. He hadn't proven to be good with her. 2. I liked having Amanda at home. But I also understood she was going stir crazy. She was hopefully starting school in January and I did not want to control her. Well, getting a daycare was not as easy as she thought. She had called like seven places and was on the waiting list for two. So Jeff ended up watching her that 1st entire week of work.*

Around this time, Amanda brought Kassidy to Olympia Sports in Sanford "*Two, a couple of days before she died.*" to exchange a pair of shoes. Kassidy was "*running around, she and Dawnya* [sic]*...I was chasing her around the store.*" (Interview with Amanda, by Ronald Rice, Jan. 25, 2008, p 17) However, Shannon seemed to remember, also in 2008, that the occasion was in October. (Interview with Shannon, by Ronald Rice, Feb. 12, 2008) At Amanda's trial in 2002, Melissa Chick recalled going to Olympia Sports with Amanda and Kassidy, shortly before Halloween in 2000. (Testimony, p. 104) Because finding day care was difficult, Chad spoke with Susan Edgar, the director of the Cross Road Kindergarten and School in Dover about enrolling Kassidy for day care and he briefly explained his reasons for dissatisfaction with the existing arrangements for Kassidy. Susan advised Chad that she could make an exception for Kassidy as she was under the age limit, but she could not make an exception to the school's policy that children were not admitted for day care until after they had been toilet trained. Chad said that Kassidy had not yet reached that milestone. Amanda stated in a 2008 interview, that Chad had told her, at the time, about his conversation with Mrs. Edgar.

BJ's Wholesale Club was Chad's favorite store, as he wrote in his March 14, 2010 letter, "*Always buying kids stuff at BJ's. Kid's videos, cereal, snacks. Kyle loved beef jerky, Kassidy loved Swedish Fish, muffins, toys, etc. I just loved the store.*" Around this time, Chad was window shopping at BJ's, and almost purchased a play house. He wrote in his April 6, 2010 letter,

Getting back to Kassidy for a minute, I DESPISE this notion that I wanted to get rid of Kassidy. It is just so RIDICULOUS. Anyone who knows me will tell you how much I loved BJ's and I am a "chick" when it comes to Christmas shopping. I love it. I believe it was the Fox Run Mall that I was wandering around one night trying to kill some time when I saw this huge wood doll house cut in half in front of a store. I immediately wanted to buy it for Kassidy for Christmas. I thought she would love it. I asked the sales lady about it and she told me it was a kit that I could buy. I was like, "Oh no, I wanted to buy

the display or one put together. I have no skills for that stuff!" She laughed. I told Amanda about it later. I wish I had done my usual impulsive thing and purchased it on the spot...
He wrote again about the doll house in a July 22, 2010 letter,

If I was done for the day, it is VERY likely that the large doll house box would have been loaded into my car. I was addicted to BJ'S Wholesale Club and couldn't stop there unless it was the end of my day because I'd leave with a car load full. When I made my comments in letter 83, I was thinking about how much fun it would have been to see Kassidy play with this doll house that was bigger than her. I guess it wouldn't have mattered if I had purchased it that day. Kassidy died in November and would never have had the chance to play with it. Who knows, maybe if one of the officers searching my house came upon it, he would have scratched his head and said, "This doesn't make a lot of sense that this guy who we believe wanted to get 'rid' of Kassidy went out and spent all this money on a doll house for her." Probably not though, they ignored everything else that didn't make sense.

Wednesday, 1 November 2000

On this day began the period of the sixth of six charges of Second Degree Assault by Chad against Kassidy. This period ended on November 9, during which time *"Evans knowingly caused bodily injury to Kassidy Bortner, age 20 months. Evans caused bruising to Kassidy by grabbing and squeezing her face."*

Patricia Hocter, a DCYF caseworker, received the "referral file" which was created after the anonymous call to DCYF on the previous day about bruises on Kassidy Bortner. (Hocter testimony, Dec. 7, 2001, page 49).

Thursday, 2 November 2000

Amanda may have gone to Old Navy to be trained for her work, and, if so, she would have left Kassidy with Jeff for babysitting. The only record of such training was the November 21, 2000 interview with Amanda's co-worker, Kristin Parsons,which was summarized by New Hampshire State Trooper, Jill Rockey.
Nicole and Amanda went to their third and last weekly, evening session of the money management seminar, in Portsmouth. Jeff Marshall babysat for Kassidy for much of the day, as Amanda had likely gone to Old Navy for training in the morning and was doing survey data entry work at home. Chad recalls the rendezvous at the Newington McDonald's near the entrance to the former Pease Air Force Base where the seminar was being held,

[Jeff] *had to be somewhere and I couldn't get to Newington fast enough so Nicole and Amanda met him at the McDonald's and picked up Kassidy. I recall Nicole later telling me how upset Kassidy was, crying and screaming when she was with Jeff and she immediately calmed down when she saw Amanda. They waited a few minutes for me and when I arrived, Kassidy remained calm. I scooped her up in my arms and said, "You want to go get some French fries baby?" She said, "Yesssss ," I buckled Kassidy into the car seat and proceeded to take her through the drive-thru to get some French Fries as Nicole and Amanda left for their class.* (Letter, May 17, 2010)

Friday, 3 November 2000

At 8:09 a.m., Chad called Jeff's home phone from his home phone, for 32 minutes. (See Chad Evans home phone AT&T Nov00 bill.) Chad had purchased a third 3-wheeler from a man in Maine, who was going to be driving to Massachusetts on this day. They planned to execute the sale at the Greenland, New Hampshire McDonald's, one of Chad's stores. Chad called Jeff Marshall for assistance in transporting the 3-wheeler to Chad's Rochester home. Later, Jeff did go to the Greenland McDonald's and took the 3-wheeler, and Chad gave him a $50 bill. However, as Jeff had other work to do with his truck, he brought the 3-wheeler to his apartment, with the plan to bring it to Chad's later. The 3-wheeler never made it to Chad's. Later, after Kassidy's death, Chad asked Amanda to ask Jeff, via Jennifer or their mother, to bring the 3-wheeler to the Conley's in Buckfield as a present to Joshua. Chad doesn't know if Joshua ever received it.

From 12:49 p.m. to 2:46 p.m., from Chad's home phone, Amanda made six calls to day care facilities to find an opening for Kassidy. She wanted good day care, similar to what Kyle was receiving. She and Chad both knew that Jeff was not a good babysitter for Kassidy, and his care was only a temporary expedient. (See Amanda's one page List of names and numbers of day centers called on this day and on the following Wednesday, November 8. This list was Defendant's Exhibit A at Chad Evans's trial. See also Chad Evans home phone AT&T Nov00 bill.. See also Amanda's testimony at Chad's trial on Dec. 5, 2001, p 105-06, regarding her day care center calls.)

That evening, Amanda and Kassidy came to Portsmouth and had dinner with Chad either at Shorty's Mexican Restaurant or Applebee's and then they went to BJ's after dinner. Kassidy's preferred fare was chicken fingers. Chad wrote in a letter on July 30, 2010,

I'm not sure if we purchased anything or not, but I can almost guarantee that we stopped and walked around BJ's for a little while together. Especially if we were at Applebee's, which was just down the road. For some reason, I was addicted to BJ's. It was always full of cool and different stuff.

Saturday, 4 November 2000

On this day, Kassidy was 21 months old. At 10:14 a.m. from Chad's home phone, Amanda called Jeff's and Jennifer's home for eight minutes. (AT&T Nov00 bill.) At 1:37 p.m. from Chad's home phone, Amanda called a number for one minute in North Sanford, Maine, where several of her friends lived. Two minutes later, she called Melissa Chick for 31 minutes. (AT&T Nov00 bill.)

In the afternoon and evening Chad, Amanda and Kassidy were at home, and went to Spinale's restaurant with Bruce and Travis. Amanda called Jeff's and Jennifer's home four times that evening: 8:13 p.m. (3 min), 9:32 p.m. (3 mins), 10:09 p.m. (1 min), and 11:04 p.m. (1 min). These calls, and a 2 minute call at 9:07 a.m. on Sunday morning were probably devoted to making plans for the next day, as Jacqueline was staying with Jeff and Jennifer and the two sisters and their mother were going to go shopping the next day. (AT&T Nov00 bill).

Sunday, 5 November 2000

At 9:30 a.m., from the home phone, Amanda called her new employer store, Old Navy, for two minutes, probably to finalize details of her starting regular, post-training, work the next day. (AT&T Nov00 bill.). Then, Amanda went to Kittery and Buckfield to spend the day shopping with her mother and sister. Amanda focused on buying clothes for Kassidy with the $300 which Chad had given to her for that purpose. Among the new items were the pink hooded insulated winter jacket. It's likely that her "Basic Editions" red pajamas, composed of red pants with a red and white striped dress-like top, were also purchased that day as Amanda described them as "*brand new*" in first her police interview. (p. 827) Perhaps a red fleece sweatshirt was a third piece to the pajamas, but that was never recovered.

Around 10:00 a.m., after an hour and ten minute drive, Chad brought Kassidy to his sister Nicole's in Belmont, New Hampshire, for the day, until approximately 6 p.m. On the way, Chad and Kassidy went through the drive-thru at the Dunkin Donuts in Alton where the sales person

saw Kassidy sitting in the car seat behind me and said something like, "Oh my God. She is adorable." She then proceeded to ask me how she was, etc. I had already purchased some Munchkin mini-donuts, but she asked anyway if she [could] *give one to Kassidy. I said, "Sure," and pulled the car ahead a foot or so, rolled down the window and the lady handed Kassidy a Munchkin through the window. Kassidy smiled. The lady commented on Kassidy being beautiful and we left. The exchange wasn't that long, but more so than the typical "grab your food and go" experience. Kassidy and her adorableness gets the credit for that.* (Letter, July 29, 2011)

Kyle was scheduled to be with Chad that weekend, but Tristan requested a swap of weekends, so Kyle was with Tristan for the weekend. Chad went to Belmont to help Nicole and her husband, Brandon, work on the rebuilding of their home, and all three adults watched Kassidy. Also there were Brandon's parents. His mother, a long-time school nurse observed no problems with Kassidy. Prior to Chad's 2002 sentencing, she wrote on February 1, 2002, to Judge Nadeau about that occasion,

I'm a child health nurse, an RN, who has worked with at-risk children and families for over 30 years. I have seen how children behave around adults who have hurt them either physically or emotionally; the guarding and the reluctance to be close to them or be touched by them. Several days before Kassidy Bortner died, I saw Chad with her. She climbed onto his lap and lay her head against him. This was within an informal family context, as Chad is the brother of my daughter-in-law. I have also seen Chad with his own son on more than one occasion and saw nothing except a loving and comfortable relationship." (Harvey letter, Feb. 1, 2002)

Brandon Harvey also wrote a pre-sentencing letter to Judge Nadeau and he also wrote about the family gathering on this day. He wrote,

On a Sunday a few days before Kassidy died I did have an opportunity to see Chad with Kassidy. We were working on our house (that is all I did weekends and evenings for about a year, fixer upper) Chad had told us he wanted to help us and come up and see us. When he got here he had Kassidy with him, he said Amanda had gotten a job cleaning a house so he was watching her for the day. She spent most of the day in the other part of the house with Nicole (we had a temporary wall up dividing off the half we were working on at the time) but at least once an hour if not more Chad would go out to check on her. She seemed very attached to him she would go over and sit on his lap while he fed her a banana or gave her a drink. He would talk to her and she was doing her best to talk back. I was somewhat surprised that they already had such a bond knowing that Kassidy had lived with her Grandmother the majority of the time Chad and Amanda were together. My Grandfather who was also there that Sunday thought that Kassidy was Chad's kid because of the way that they were interacting. Chad had been working with her on counting and both of them were excited to demonstrate her progress especially to Nicole who at the time was teaching a preschool class." (Brandon Harvey Letter, undated, 2002.

See also, Brandon's police interview on November 9, pages 985-86, and the summary of Nicole Evans Harvey's interview, and the full transcript of that interview, pages 1809-14) Chad's sister, Nicole, remembered that Sunday gathering in a January 21, 2011 email to me,

A few things I can recollect are Brandon's grandfather, Tom, asking me if that was Chad's little girl because he was so good with her. I also remember being proud of Chad for packing her a lunch with so many choices, peanut butter and jelly sandwich, banana, oreos, crackers and juice boxes. She did sit on his lap and ate pizza with him at lunch time. I can't remember if it was delivered or if that was when Gerri stopped by. It was from a local pizza place down the road from us on rte 106. I remember her taking a nap on my lap singing her to sleep brushing her hair from her eyes like I do with my own daughter Aliza.

"Skinnamainki dinky dink skinamirinki doo, I love you" and "freckled frogs". It got noisy in there so I remember taking her out to my car for awhile to sleep in the front seat of my car on my lap for at least an hour and a half. I remember Chad being like a proud

peacock with her singing ABCs and counting for me knowing how proud I would be of him because he had been teaching her. And I was. I also remember him asking me (because I'm also a hairdresser) if it was normal for children to lose their hair. He showed me a spot on the top of her head where a small patch was gone. I assured him It was very normal. Children don't get their actual head of hair until 4 or 5 years old. Their baby hair eventually falls out like their teeth. I remember teasing him about changing her diaper because he always compared my mom and I to oil changers because we were so fast at it.

In his January 14, 2011 letter, Chad described his day with Kassidy at Belmont and return home,

In the morning, I woke up early, I would say, 7 a.m. or so. I was excited to be going up to lend Nicole and Brandon a hand with their house. I am not much of a builder, so this was a great opportunity for me to learn things as Brandon's father, Steve, was excellent. Amanda got up with me, as she was excited to be going shopping with Jennifer and her mom for the day. She dressed Kassidy while I got her some cereal ready and packed a bag with diapers and snacks. I remember. Kassidy had very little in the way of fall and winter clothes that fit her so I gave Amanda, I believe $300 or $400, to go shopping. I wasn't really thinking that Jackie would probably really like to see Kassidy. I was thinking of Amanda. She had been working her butt off on the survey project and I thought she would enjoy a "girl's day out" shopping.

At approximately 8 a.m., Kassidy and I were on the road headed to Belmont. Amanda was still home. I know I stopped at the Dunkin' Donuts in Alton, I believe. I loved their poppy seed bagels with veggie cream cheese. It was one of the only times I was interested in drinking coffee back then. I know I bought Kassidy some Chocolate Munchkin Donut Holes. Kassidy loved them and ate them even though she had just eaten cereal. I remember she had a chocolate crumbs all over her by the time we reached Nicole and Brandon's house.

We got to Belmont around 9 a.m. Nicole and Brandon were there as was Brandon's dad, Steve, and Brandon's grandfather, I believe. I introduced Steve and Brandon's grandfather to Kassidy. They thought she was adorable. Nicole loved kids: she was excited to be spending some time with Kassidy. I had some toys and things packed in Kassidy's back and Nicole had brought some stuff as well. The work we were doing that day involved hanging some sheetrock, insulation. wiring, etc. Nicole was very involved in the house building but on this particular day, my skill set was more in need, i.e. lots of lifting.

As I recall, we left Nicole and Kassidy sitting in what was the former kitchen and we headed to the bathroom and guest bedroom area. Every so often, I would poke my head in to see how Nicole and Kassidy were doing. One time, Nicole was singing, and at another time, she was holding Kassidy in her lap, rocking her as she slept. Another time, she was doing ABC's and other word games. I'm pretty sure Nicole took her outside to walk around for a while. Around lunchtime, we stopped for a break. I believe this is when Mrs. Harvey, Brandon's mom, came. I know we had pizza for lunch. I am not sure exactly how the pizza got there. Perhaps Mrs. Harvey brought it. Kassidy was still in the kitchen area with Nicole when the pizza arrived. I had packed Kassidy a lunch because I did not know what our plan for lunch was going to be but I fed her pizza instead, knowing that she loved it. I recall piking Kassidy up off Nicole's lap, giving her a kiss on the forehead and in a soft voice saying, "Do you want some pizza baby?" She was groggy looking, as if she had just woken up again.

Kassidy slept A LOT that day. We assumed at the time that she was just getting over the flu because Kyle had it just prior. I recall laughing with Brandon and Steve saying something to the effect that nothing seems to affect her appetite. I sat Kassidy down and cut up a piece of pizza to feed her. She walked over and crawled into my lap and I fed Kassidy each bite. She was old enough and usually fed herself, but we didn't have running water at the house yet; and it was fun to baby her. I can't recall who, but someone commented on how well she ate. I commented, I only wish I could gel Kyle to tend to business the way she does.

After our lunch break, we went back to work for a while. Approximately an hour or TWO later we took a drink/bathroom break. I came into the kitchen and Kassidy crawled

into my lap and rested her head on me. I am not sure if this is when Mrs. Harvey observed this. I know that this is how Kassidy typically sat with me. It felt good when she would do this even if I was only second fiddle to "mama." We went back to work and an hour or so later, as I recall, Kassidy had the horrible poopy diaper that I wrote about a few months back. I could hear Nicole laughing and hollering my name from the other end of the house. We went into hysterics laughing about who was going to change her. Try as I may, Nicole wouldn't budge. I almost gagged but got through it. I believe we quit working around 5 or 6 PM and Kassidy and I left for Rochester shortly after. I don't believe Amanda was home yet. I think I grilled some chicken breast for all of us for dinner and Amanda arrived shortly after. She had bags of clothes and was happy to show me all the outfits she bought for Kassidy. her new winter coat. etc. Amanda was proud of the great deals she had gotten and I believe even had a few new shirts for Kyle. We ate dinner together and then played on the floor with Kassidy for a while before bed.

In Chad's Nov. 2000 letter to his attorneys, he quantified his above comment that Kassidy slept "A LOT," by estimating that she slept five hours in Belmont.

At 7:00 p.m., a 21-minute call from Chad's home phone was made to Jeff and Jennifer's home. (AT&T Nov00 bill.) Presumably, it was from Amanda, and some of the call included arrangements for Monday's babysitting of Kassidy at Kittery. Later that evening, Kassidy fell off the couch in Chad's living room, in the presence of Amanda and Travis Hunt, and hit her right eye on the glass coffee table in the living room. Amanda said to the police,

"*Yeah. She hit the corner of the table. She's really, she's really like disoriented. She falls, well, she fell, a lot. But she's always been like that, klutz, kind of, too.... I was there for like the glass table in the living room.... Probably like three (3) or four (4) days ago.*" (Amanda, interview, Nov. 9, 2000, page 831)

Around the same time, Kassidy was playing with her new kitten and received a scratch under the same eye.

Below is the updated calendar of bruises with NB (No Bruise) NI (No Injury) and B for (Bruise) including the goose egg bumps on Kassidy's head, as observed on the 28th, and the bruise on Kassidy's right cheek which Tristan saw on Monday, October 30 and with continued to be visible when Nicole and Brandon Harvey noticed it on Sunday, November 5.

June 2000

Su	Mo	Tu	We	Th	Fr	Sa
					9	10
11	12	13	14	15	16	**NI**
NI	**NI**	**NI**	**NI**	**NB**	23	24
25	26	27	28	29	30	

July 2000

Su	Mo	Tu	We	Th	Fr	Sa
						1
2	3	4	5	6	**NI**	**NI**
NI	**NI**	**NI**	**NB**	**NB**	**NB**	**NB**
NB	**NB**	**NB**	**NB**	**NB**	21	22
23	**NI**	**NI**	**NI**	**NI**	**NI**	**NB**
NB	**NB**					

August 2000

Su	Mo	Tu	We	Th	Fr	Sa
		1	2	3	4	**NI**
NI	**NI**	**NI**	**NI**	**NB**	**NI**	**NI**
NI	**NI**	**NI**	**NB**	**NI**	**NI**	**NI**
NB	**NB**	**NB**	**NB**	**NB**	**NB**	**NB**
NB	**NB**	**NI**	**NI**	**NI**		

September 2000

Su	Mo	Tu	We	Th	Fr	Sa
					NI	**NB**
3	4	5	**NI**	**NI**	**NI**	**NI**
NI	**NB**	12	13	14	15	16
17	18	**NI**	**NI**	**NI**	**NI**	**NI**
NB	**NB**	**NB**	**NB**	**NI**	**NI**	**NI**

October 2000

Su	Mo	Tu	We	Th	Fr	Sa
NB	2	3	4	5	6	7
8	9	10	11	12	**B**	**B**
B	**B**	17	18	19	20	**B**
B	23	24	25	26	27	**B**
B	**B**	**B**				

November 2000

Su	Mo	Tu	We	Th	Fr	Sa
			B	**B**	**B**	**B**
B	6	7	8	9		

Monday, 6 November 2000

Amanda started her first regular, non-training, day of work at Old Navy at 9:00 a.m. and Kassidy went to Jeff's and Jennifer's for babysitting. As Jennifer worked 9 a.m. to 5 p.m. at Perfumania on that day, the babysitting was primarily by Jeff.

Chad Evans had an appointment with his chiropractor, Dr. Michael T. Clark, of Rochester, because he had lifted something heavy at work with the wrong technique. He knew that his back could go "out" if not treated preventively. He was looking forward to the upcoming weekend with Amanda in Maine, without physical problems.

At 1:46 p.m., a four minute call was made from Chad Evans' home phone to Jeff's cell phone. (AT&T Nov00 bill.)

On this day, according to her testimony at Chad's trial Patricia Hocter, of the Rochester office of DCYF, said that she called Chad's home and left a message to call on this date, but Chad, Amanda and Travis have stated that the message was not received. (Transcript, Dec. 7, 2001, p. 49) Chad has stated that the message system on his home phone was very reliable, and that there was no such message. He states that if there had been such a message on that phone, he would have returned the call. As the call was a local call, there was no phone company record.

After work, Amanda picked up Kassidy at Jeff's and Jennifer's and drove her home. During an evening around this time Chad and Amanda discovered minute marks, scabs or abrasions on the bottoms of Kassidy's feet. Chad wrote in 2010,

I first noticed the pinpricks on the bottoms of Kassidy's feet when I was carrying Kassidy up to bed. I often gave her airplane rides up the stairs and on this night I felt something rough on her feet. I was on the stairs and screamed for Amanda. It really freaked me out. Amanda came in and noticed all the pricks and started crying. I knew she couldn't have gotten them at my house. There was nothing she could have stepped on like that. Amanda told me that she was going to talk to Jeff. The next day I asked her about it and she said that he said he had some carpet strip exposed, and she must have stepped on it. It is the only thing that sounded plausible but I was dumbfounded that he could be that stupid. I told Amanda to yell at him to fix it and not let her go barefoot. In hindsight, I feel like a retard. (Letter, Jan. 26, 2010)

Tuesday, 7 November 2000

Tuesday was Election Day and Chad voted at the McClelland Elementary School on Brock Street in Rochester. Also on this day, Chad purchased six tickets at the University of New Hampshire Whittemore Center for an upcoming December concert by the rock band, "Disturbed." He was planning to go with Amanda, Bruce and Michelle Truell, Travis and Chad's brother, Jason.

On Tuesday, Amanda worked a full twelve-hour day at Old Navy, 8:24 a.m. to 8:02 p.m., and Kassidy was at Jeff's. Jennifer worked 1 p.m. to 9 p.m. at Perfumania, so she was with Kassidy in the morning.

Around this time, a "*day or two before Kassidy's death,*" William Peirce, a neighbor and landlord of Jeff, saw Jeff catch Kassidy as she began to fall from her car seat in his truck. Acc. to the summary of Peirce's interview, Marshall said, "*See, she just falls out of the truck.*" (Summary of Interview, Dec. 6, 2000) Peirce earned a living by purchasing properties and rehabilitating them for resale or rent. Coincidentally, for this case, his aunt, Gareth Peirce, is a well-known defense lawyer in the United Kingdom who was active in several wrongful conviction cases there. One case was of the "Guildford Four" who were wrongly convicted of carrying out a deadly IRA bombing of a pub in Guildford, England. One of the four was Gerry Conlon, whose role Daniel Day Lewis played in the movie, "In the Name of the Father."

At lunchtime Chad sought to surprise Amanda with a visit for lunch, and he planned to pick up Kassidy first at Jeff's home, and then take Kassidy to see Amanda and take them both out to lunch. However, when he arrived at Jeff's, Amanda was already there, on some kind of a longer-than-usual break. Jen was also there, before starting work for the day. Jen and Amanda went to Perfumania to take Jen back to work in Amanda's car and Chad brought Kassidy to meet Amanda there. Chad then took Amanda and Kassidy to the "drive-thru" at McDonald's in Kittery to pick up lunch. After lunch, Chad drove Amanda back to her work at Old Navy and took Kassidy back to Jeff's. Chad wrote in 2010 about this and similar rendezvous,

For some reason we didn't end up going anywhere. I went through the McDonald's drive-thru in Kittery with Amanda and Kassidy for a couple of salads and a Happy Meal. We parked on the far side of Perfumania where Jen worked, ate and talked. I believe this was the day that I was playing with Kassidy in the back seat while Amanda was talking. Amanda said, "You're not even looking at me." and I teasingly replied, "No, I'm looking at Kassidy because she's cuter." It was a good lunch. Jen and/or Amanda may have been at Jeff's and heading to work on this particular day. I'm not sure but I know I asked Jeff for directions so that I could pick up Kassidy. I thought it was a cool way to spend a quick half hour together and planned to surprise Amanda in the future, showing up with Kassidy from time to time for lunch or a quick visit.

I know that I ALWAYS enjoyed it when she or Tristan would show up with the kids sometimes at a restaurant I was working at. It breaks up the day and that little smile, hug, and kiss from Kyle, Kassidy, or Brent can make the entire day better. Not to mention, kids are like our little trophies. It sounds horrible but it's awesome to see how everyone fawn all over them and get all giddy around them. Believe it or not, at McDonald's it made the entire mood lighter when someone's child showed up for a few minute surprise visit. I loved taking the kids back behind the counter to let them make their own ice cream sundae. (Letter, April 18, 2010)

This surprise, and memorable get-together may have occurred the previous Thursday, while Amanda was in training at Old Navy.

After work, Chad picked up Kyle at Cross Road for his weekly Tuesday through Thursday stay.

Around this time, Jeff Marshall tripped over Kassidy causing her to "*walk funny*." Said Amanda in her first interview,

"... *he* [Jeff Marshall] *tripped over her the other day, like 2 days ago, and she hurt her leg and she was walking funny and... he told me that when I picked her up that she's walking funny because he had tripped over her. She was standing right behind him and I was like okay, and I like, was feeling her legs and I was asking her if it hurt because usually she says, 'Ow' and she didn't say 'Ow' or anything.*" (Amanda, interview, Nov. 9, 2000, p. 829)

At 7:37 p.m., there was a one minute call from Chad's home phone to Jeff and Jennifer's home. (AT&T Nov00 bill.) The purpose of the call, presumably from Chad, is not known, and it was not the subject of questions during police interviews or of questions at Chad's trial. Perhaps it was to see if Amanda had been there yet to pick up Kassidy. After her work ended at 8:02 p.m., Amanda picked up Kassidy at Jeff and Jennifer's and drove her home.

Wednesday, 8 November 2000

Chad's workday began at 7:03 a.m. with a work call from Chad's friend and service provider, Jeff Jacobs, at Jacobs Electric. The call to Chad's cell phone was a short 24 seconds. (Chart of Calls) In 2010, Chad recalled that morning,

I do recall starting my day in Rochester. I can't recall anything specific about that morning but I am fairly certain that if Kyle was there, I saw both the kids that morning before I left for work. Unless I was leaving very early, between 6 and 7 am, I usually spent a few minutes with them eating breakfast, playing, or holding one or both. If I did see Kyle and/or Kassidy on Wednesday morning it would have been very brief. I had a lot going on with my end of month meeting to prepare for on the 9th and labor audits in two restaurants the following week. In addition to my regular duties. (Letter, July 8, 2010)

Amanda did not have to be at work until 5:00 p.m., and she chose to take Kyle later in the day to Cross Road.

At 8:35 a.m. from Chad's home phone, Amanda called her mother's home in Buckfield for six minutes. This was an important call, because in 2011, Amanda stated that the purpose of this call was to seek and confirm babysitting for Kassidy for the upcoming weekend, while Chad and Amanda were in Kennebunkport for the Colley-McCoy meeting. (AT&T Nov00 bill.) This call was not a subject of later inquiry, either, and it was 28 hours before Kassidy died.

From 9:30 a.m. to 9:55 a.m., Amanda called two daycare providers in Sanford. Chart of Calls) In between those calls, she called Old Navy for two minutes. (AT&T Nov00 bill.)

Approximately at 10:00 a.m., Travis awoke, and prepared for work. In his interview on November 9, he said he noticed that no one was at home and he left for work for the day. He was due at 11:00 a.m. for 11-7 shift. (Interview, Nov. 22, 2000, page 20) Perhaps Amanda and Kassidy went to the local store for the few minutes between 9:55 a.m. and her next call at 10:24 a.m., and he missed them, or perhaps he misunderstood what day the police were asking about. He may have been thinking about Thursday morning. During his interrogation, Chad had once mistaken those two days as well.

At about 10-10:30 a.m., Chad arrived at the Portsmouth McDonald's store, managed by his friend, Jeremy, and where Travis worked. Chad worked there for about an hour.

At 10:24 a.m. from Chad's home phone, Amanda called Jeff and Jennifer's home phone and conversed for six minutes with Jeff or Jennifer as Jennifer was scheduled to work from 1:00 to 9:00 p.m. (Selected Discovery Phone Pages, pages 2494, 2771)

At 11:14 a.m., Chad called Amanda for two minutes from the Hampton McDonald's on Route 1, Hampton. (Chart of Calls)

At 11:57 a.m..Tristan's mother, Sharon, called Chad on his cell phone for 24 seconds. (Chart of Calls) Perhaps it was to coordinate Kyle's transportation that evening from school, back to Chad's.

Around 12:30-12:45 p.m., Amanda brought Kyle Evans to day care at the Cross Road Kindergarten and School in Dover. According to Erin Entrekin, a teacher at the center, Amanda had said that Kyle had been fed and that she had taken him to a doctor's appt. Amanda had taken Kyle to Cross Road about five times before. However, perhaps Ms. Entrekin was thinking of another parent, with respect to the doctor's appointment. In 2010, neither Chad nor Tristan recalled that Amanda had taken Kyle to a doctor's appointment.

In his only police interrogation, Chad stated that Amanda picked up some brake parts for him on Wednesday. (Interrogation, Nov. 9, 2000, page 1541) In 2010, he explained, *...I said that Amanda picked up some brake parts for me around noon on the 8th. You asked a bunch of questions about this.... It is likely I gave her cash to pick up the brake parts. I cannot recall this incident exactly. I am guessing that it was either for the RX-7 I had or for Amanda's car. I usually brought my company car to a garage for service. I had a couple of "Ma and Pa" type garages in the Rochester area that I had to do my personal work if I wasn't doing it myself. I may have been planning to do this myself. I don't remember. Sometimes I would do brake jobs and small repairs with my dad. It was a nice way for him and I to spend some time together. When I was a child my dad worked non-stop. Some of my best memories of spending quality time with him were when we were working on his old work trucks. I would spend hours laying on the ground with him, handing up tools.* (Letter, June 30, 2010)

At 1:05 p.m., from the Hampton/Route 1 McDonald's phone, Chad called Amanda at home for three minutes, 34 seconds. She had likely just walked in the door, after taking Kyle to day care. (Chart of Calls)

Shortly thereafter, and until 1:21 p.m. from Chad's home phone, Amanda called five more day care providers. The last call of this series was to "Care Link" in Sanford for 6 minutes 18 seconds. (Chart of Calls) This brought the total for the day to 8 calls to potential day care providers, and brought the total number of providers called over the past week to 14, with two additional calls to unidentified numbers in Sanford, which may also have been to potential day care providers.

At 2:35 p.m., Amanda made a short call to Jeff from Chad's home phone, probably to say that she would soon be on her way to Jeff's with Kassidy. (Chart of Calls) Shortly after 3:00 p.m., Amanda left Kassidy at Jeff's and Jennifer's apartment. Earlier in the week, Amanda had discussed with Chad her schedule to work late on this night and her plan to have Kassidy stay overnight. Chad was uncomfortable about having Kassidy spend the night, given both Amanda's and Chad's concerns about the quality of babysitting at Jeff's, so Chad said he would pick her up after his work.

When leaving Kassidy with Jeff around 3:00 p.m., Amanda forgot to leave the car seat, as the new plan was for Chad to pick up Kassidy later in the afternoon. Jennifer had already left for work, as her schedule at Perfumania was from 1 p.m. to 9:00 p.m. Heather Hamilton, Jennifer's supervisor at Perfumania, said that Amanda came to visit her sister around 3:00 p.m., and earlier she said that she hadn't seen Kassidy since October, so Kassidy was not with Amanda on that Wednesday, November 8 visit by Amanda to see Jennifer. Jeff stated in his "Statement" to the Kittery Police that it was 4:20 p.m. when Amanda brought Kassidy to his home. (handwritten Statement, and rekeyed Word Copy). This apparent conflict in time between Amanda's estimate of the drop-off time of 3:00 p.m. and Jeff's estimate of 4:20 p.m. was never resolved. However, Amanda's estimate makes more sense and is consistent with her other activities and the observations of others. From 3:15-5:00 p.m., Amanda searched for a dress for dinner on Saturday, November 11 for the McDonald's (Colley-McCoy) weekend gathering in Maine, likely Kennebunkport. Prior to beginning work at Old Navy on Monday the 6th, Amanda had asked that she have the weekend of the 11-12th off. After that, she would have been scheduled for one or both weekend days. The plan for Kassidy for the weekend was for her to stay with her grandmother, Jackie, in Buckfield, Maine. Amanda was not hiding Kassidy from her mother.

At 4:42 p.m., Chad Evans called his boss, Bob McDougall, at the McDonald's licensee, Colley-McCoy Management offices for 33 seconds. (Chart of Calls) He called again at 4:44 p.m. and they talked for 11 minutes. They discussed the upcoming State Labor Dept. inspection, and Chad assured Bob that everything was in order. (Chart of Calls)

Chad wrote in 2010,

This is significant because I was working with my assistant, Melissa Allard, in the Hampton Rte. 1 store on Nov. 8 doing a final run through in preparation for the audits that were scheduled for the following week. I was quite happy on the afternoon of the 8th because after reviewing all of the paperwork it was clear we had no violations. (Letter, April 15, 2010)

At 4:55 p.m., Chad finished his work for the day on a labor report, with his secretary, Melissa Allard, and went to the Hampton Shop 'n' Save, and purchased a "Met Rx" energy bar and said "*Hello*" to Melissa's daughter, and Chad's friend, Mandy Allard. He felt good. Everything was in order.

From his cell phone at 4:56:34 p.m., Chad called Jeff's cell phone. The call lasted 15 seconds. (Chart of Calls. This call is not on the one-page report of Chad's Sprint Calls 11/8-11/9 at Discovery page 809.)

At 4:56:58 p.m., from his cell phone, Chad called Jeff Marshall's home phone for 70 seconds. Chad called Jeff to get directions to Jeff's home, as Chad had been there only once before, which was for his surprise lunch with Amanda and Kassidy earlier that week. Also, to save him some time, Chad asked Jeff if they could meet elsewhere to transfer Kassidy, but it was agreed that Chad would come to Jeff's home. (Chart of Calls.)

At 4:58 p.m., Bob McDougall, Chad's boss at the Colley-McCoy Management, called Chad for 72 seconds. (Chart of Calls)

During Jeff's babysitting for Kassidy, according to Jennifer at her first police interview, "*Jeff called me yesterday while I was at work and she's* [he's] *like* 'she's *been sleeping for like the past 4 hours. It's like she's been sleeping all day long.'* " (Jennifer interview, Nov. 9, 2000, p. 917). This would have been a local Kittery call, so it doesn't appear in telephone records. Kassidy was at Jeff's for approximately two hours, 30 minutes on this day, from 3:00 p.m. to 5:30 p.m. Jeff did not mention this call in his police statement or interview and he was not asked about it at Chad's or Amanda's trials. Jennifer may have been confused about the day, or the number of hours, as Kassidy was not with Jeff for four hours on the 8th. Nonetheless, regardless of the day, the content of that call should have been explored for more information about Kassidy's condition during her last few days.

At 5:00 p.m., Amanda began her third day of work at Old Navy. She stated in her November 12, 2000 interview that she went to work around 5:00 p.m.
At 5:15 p.m., Chad stopped at Moonlite Reader, an adult store, on Route 1 in Portsmouth, between the Portsmouth Circle and the River, to correct an overcharge for a previous purchase. This transaction took about 15 minutes. After Chad's arrest on November 16, and release on bail, he returned to Moonlite Reader and the same clerk waited on him as with the transaction on November 8, and the clerk recognized Chad from his photograph in the newspapers. The clerk said, "*Man, you seemed fine when you were in here, it doesn't make sense. We were joking around when you were in here. That sucks man, I hope everything works out for you.*" (Letter, June 30, 2010)

At 5:22 p.m., Jeff checked his messages on his cell phone, a short process which took 25 seconds. (Chart of Calls)

At 5:32 p.m., Chad picked up Kassidy at Jeff's and Jennifer's, and drove to pick up Kyle at day care in Dover. Chad described the pickup in his November 2000 letter to his attorneys,

While I was bent over in the car buckling her up, he was standing behind me and talking to me. Jeff said in a very determined tone. "Amanda has to find something else to do with this kid. I don't mind helping out but I am tired of watching her. I want a kid that will do something. All this little retard does is sit around and either bawl or stare off into space. She fuckin' freaks me out. It is like she is one of the kids in Children of the Corn." (This is not the 1st time he has said that to me.) I was kind of surprised because this conversation seemed to be coming from out of the blue. I said, "Jeff, I am really late getting Kyle so I don't really have time to get into it but as far as I knew you were only watching her for a little bit until she found a day care. She has called some, but is put on waiting lists or something. But if you really feel this way you should probably talk to her." I then shut the car door and he was still talking a little bit. I told him, "Listen I have to go to get Kyle. I will call you in my car or at home." I didn't really have much to say to him but I hate being rude to people. I started pulling out of the driveway and he started inside. He turned around and signaled to me from the steps and then came running back to the car. He said (In a totally different mood than he was just in. Dr. Jekyll - Mr. Hyde anyone?) All smiles, "So what did you get at Peter's Palace? Anything good?" I said, "No, as I said to you on the phone, I just had to run in real quick because they screwed up my credit card receipt last month. It was a movie or something." He said, "Oh." I then said, "I got to go, I will call you soon."

Chad recalled in 2011 that he took his own jacket off and folded it and placed it between Kassidy's seatbelt and her lap, to try to make up for the lack of a child's car seat. He recalled that she was wearing her "Elmo" slippers.

On the way to Cross Road Kindergarten, according to Chad, Kassidy seemed lethargic and "*spacey*," and her head drooped forward. Her eyes were "*glassy*" and she was drooling.

At 5:44 p.m., from his cell phone Chad called Jeff's home phone to ask what had happened to Kassidy at Jeff's during the afternoon. They talked for nearly 11 minutes. (Chart of Calls)

In his November 2000 letter to his attorneys, Chad described the trip to Dover,
I left and was headed to Dover and noticed about 5 minutes later that Kassidy was being even more quiet than usual. I started talking to her once I got on the Spaulding Turnpike, and she wasn't talking back. I reached back to grab her leg and say, "Hey, are you being shy?" She still didn't answer. I then looked back it was dark by now so I saw her not real clearly, but I could see her little head was hanging over the seat belt and she looked like she was drooling or something. I called her name and she didn't respond . I immediately called Jeff and asked him, "What the hell did you do to her?" He replied, startled, "Nothing, why? What is she doing?" I explained what she was doing and he said, "I told you she was fucking retarded." We talked for several more minutes. I asked if she was normal when she was dropped off? What time she came, etc.
At 6:05 p.m., Chad and Kassidy picked up Kyle, the last child to be picked up, at Cross Road Kindergarten and School in Dover.

At 6:35 p.m., Chad arrived home with Kassidy and Kyle. Chad released Kassidy from her seatbelt and stood her on the paved driveway, and then went around to the other side of the car to release Kyle. Then, returning to Kassidy, Chad saw that she had fallen in the driveway, face first, and lay there with her hands to her side before being picked up by Chad. He brought Kassidy and Kyle inside, and Kyle saw a mousetrap and said, "*Daddy, you got another mouse*." Kassidy pointed to the mousetrap, too. Chad put Kassidy in her high chair to give her some food. Later, Chad saw a little black and blue mark on Kassidy's face which he assumed was caused by the fall in the driveway. (Chad interview, page 58)

At 6:39 p.m., from his home phone Chad called Jeff at his home phone. "No connection." (Chart of Calls)

Around 6:40 p.m., Chad began feeding Kyle and Kassidy. Kassidy ate only half a banana. Chad cooked a grilled cheese sandwich, and Kassidy may have taken one bite, but her appetite was clearly diminished. Chad brought both Kyle and Kassidy into the living room for a few minutes, and later brought them upstairs, for play and a bath for Kassidy.

At 6:40 p.m., from his home phone, Chad called Jeff again, because of Kassidy's fall in driveway and how she was acting. Chad described the call in his November 2000 letter to his attorneys

I called Jeff again immediately. This time I was less than nice. I explained what had happened in detail. I said, "You had to have done something. This baby is all fucked up." We went through everything again and by the time I got off the phone, he convinced me she was just tired or something and that nothing happened at his house. While on the phone with him I was fixing her and Kyle something to eat for dinner. Once I was off the phone with him I was holding her in the living room talking to Kyle about school and I noticed her eyes fluttering up in the back of her head. It really freaked me out I grabbed her head in one hand and patted her face similar to what you would see in a boxing match when the guy gets his bell rung. Her eyes stopped doing it and I got up.

The relationship between the two men had already turned cold because of Chad's decision not to renew Jeff's landscaping contracts. It probably would not have helped much if Chad's question had been put in a more neutral way, such as, "Did anything happen to Kassidy today?"

It was a 19 minute, 19 second call, including time he was on hold, and the time when Chad took a call from his friend, Bruce, and told him he would call back. (Chart of Calls)

In his November 2000 letter to his attorneys, Chad wrote,

I decided I was going to give her a bath. She hardly touched her supper and I figured I would just put her to bed early. I set her down again standing up in the hallway to start her bath water. I heard this thud. Apparently, she took a step and fell back hitting her head on the wall. I ran out to see what happened and her eyes did it again. I picked her up by her shoulders and brought her right up to my face and said, "You are freaking me out kid," and she kind of smiled at me. I was really worried though and decided to postpone the bath a little while. I tried calling my mom twice to tell her what was going on and to see if she felt I should bring her to get checked. There was no answer at her house so I said, "Ok, well, I am taking you with me wherever I go now." I had a nightly ritual to play ball with Kyle and I took her in with me.

Chad's mother was not home, and there was no answering machine at the Evans home in Keene.

At 6:43 p.m., Tristan called Chad's cell, but the call only registered 17 seconds, so it's likely that Chad didn't answer that call. (Chad's Sprint Calls 118-11/9. This call is not listed in (Chart of Calls) At 6:44 p.m., from her unlisted home or cell phone, Tristan called Chad's home phone, and they talked for one minute, 51 seconds. (Chart of Calls) Around 6:50 p.m., Chad called his close friend, Bruce, and talked about football and betting for about 15 minutes. It was a local call, so it didn't appear on phone records. In his police interrogation the next evening, Chad stated that he ended the call with Bruce because he had water running for Kassidy's bath. (p. 1520)
At 7:05 p.m. and 7:06 p.m., from his home phone, Chad called his cell phone to check messages. 24 and 35 seconds. (Chart of Calls)

Around 7:15 p.m., in Kyle's bedroom, he and Chad practiced hitting balls of all types. Kyle often practiced hitting balls with his thick brown Fisher Price fat plastic bat. He was not yet skilled enough to graduate to the yellow, long thin wiffle ball bat, but he had graduated from the even thicker red bat which he used the previous summer. (See photo of Sgt William Magee holding a brown bat at Chad's trial.) There was usually a toy wheelbarrow in the room, with about 20 balls, most of which were wiffle balls. While sitting on Kyle's bed, with Kassidy on his right lap, and after pitching with his left hand a series of wiffle balls to Kyle, Chad picked up a Tee-ball. For a split second, he felt its weight and hardness and considered whether to toss it to Kyle or set it aside and get up from the bed and pick up the rest of the wiffle balls and start again.

Unfortunately, he chose to toss that ball to Kyle and Kyle hit it into Kassidy's face, just below her left eye, and she fell backward into Chad's chest as she sat on his lap. Although the ball which hit Kassidy is commonly known as a "Tee-ball," it was identified by Chad during his 9 November police interrogation as a "*hard rubber ball*" and "*starter baseball.*" (p. 1536) Softer than a leather-covered "hardball," a Tee-ball has the appearance of the stitching and colors of a "hardball." It weighs about the same as a "hardball," one-third of a pound.

Chad described the aftermath in his November 2000 letter to his attorneys,

She whimpered for a minute and then was fine. I was like, "Wow, she is pretty tough." I sat her on the floor and ran down to get an ice pack to put on her. She hated that and it didn't stay on too long. By now she was playing away and acting like none of the previous events happened. This put my mind at ease a lot. About then the phone rang and it was my ex-wife Tristan. I told her briefly what had happened: the fall, the eyes rolling, the ball and now she was acting completely normal. I asked Tristan what she thought to get a mom's perspective and she said, "If she is talking and acting normal now I wouldn't worry about it." So I felt even more relieved.

Around this time, Chad started bath water for Kassidy, holding her on his hip. Also, during Tristan's call, Kyle talked with her, and said he was sorry that he hit "*Akassidy*" (as he called her) with a ball. As Tristan lived in Dover at the time, her calls to Rochester were "local" calls, and thus do not appear in phone bills. It would be another day, and a tragic day, before Chad would learn that Tristan had called DCYF on the 31st. Even on this night of November 8, with Chad talking with the "anonymous reporter" to DCYF, neither she nor Chad saw enough symptoms which might be alarming in Kassidy's condition to warrant a trip to the Emergency Room, or to a doctor the next morning. They seemed to feel that the ills they saw, or heard about, were not sufficiently serious. Chad started giving Kassidy her bath, after the conversation with Tristan.

Around 7:20 p.m., Travis came home.

At 7:23 p.m., Travis made two calls to his workplace from which he had just left, the Portsmouth McDonald's. The first, at 7:23 p.m., had no connection. The second, also beginning at 7:23, lasted for 14 seconds. (Chart of Calls)

Around 7:45 p.m., Travis went upstairs where Chad was bathing Kassidy. According to Travis, Kassidy was not happy with hair shampoo. During the bath, Chad observed (as related in his October 6, 2010 Letter) a "*soreness on her lower lip*" on Kassidy, which led him to skip having Kassidy brush her teeth that night. He also observed a faint bruise under her chin. Travis held Kassidy for a few minutes while Chad went into Kassidy's room to get a diaper and pajamas. Also, Kassidy had a bruise on her cheek, as Chad told the police in his interrogation the next day. (p. 1532) In November 2010, Chad learned that the medical examination or autopsy of Kassidy revealed blood underneath all ten of her fingernails. He wrote,

I gave Kassidy a bath that evening. I changed her, and put lotion all over her body. I certainly would have noticed if her fingernails appeared "dirty" with red/brown stains. If I had noticed something like that, I would have spent more time washing them. Kassidy was a very clean baby. Amanda always had her dressed nice and clean. I certainly wouldn't have left myself open to Amanda being able to criticize my lack of bathing skills. The point I'm getting at is I didn't see anything under her fingernails. I know Kassidy was in the bath tub for at least 15 minutes that evening and had her hands submerged playing for much of that. (Letter, No. 7, 2010)

Kyle came into the bathroom to say, "*Hello,*" to Travis. Without prompting, Kyle told Travis that he hit "*Akassidy*" by accident. Both Travis and Chad looked at the red mark starting to form under Kassidy's left eye. Chad described the scene in his November 2000 letter to his attorneys,

Kassidy was being her normal self, talking away and saying words. He was standing there as I took her out to dry her off. I turned real quick to let the tub water out and she started to fall back. (This was the last time I forgot about her leg.) I asked Travis, "Can you just hold her for a second while I go and get her jammies. And a diaper?" He said, "Sure" and picked her up and held her.

Travis and Kyle went into Kyle's bedroom where Travis pitched a few more balls to him for about 10 minutes. Travis then went downstairs to change clothes.

After Kassidy's bath, Chad put Johnson & Johnson baby lotion all over her body, and dressed her in pajamas and a new diaper. He combed her hair and noticed that a bump from a previous injury was still on her head, perhaps from falling from Jeff's truck as was thought to be the cause, 12 days earlier. At 7:44 p.m., Amanda clocked out for a break at work.

At 7:47 p.m., from his home phone, Chad called Jeff for almost eight minutes on his home phone about the Tee-ball accident. (Chart of Calls) Jeff then called Jennifer at Perfumania and Jennifer then told Amanda.

At 7:54 p.m., after hearing about the baseball accident, Amanda called Chad's home phone from Jennifer's workplace, Perfumania, to hear directly from Chad what happened to Kassidy during the day, including the Tee-ball accident. The discussion continued into the next call, which Chad placed back to Perfumania at 7:58 p.m. for another seven minutes. (Chart of Calls) Chad recommended to Amanda that they should make arrangements, other than Jeff, for watching Kassidy, and he asked again about the search for day care. There was some bitter irony in this for Amanda, because the most dramatic and visible injury from that day was the ball hitting Kassidy's head which was Chad's responsibility and not Jeff's. Invisible were the symptoms that Chad had described as occurring that afternoon in his car, after picking up Kassidy at Jeff's, such as drooling, and head bobbing.

Chad mentioned to Amanda seeing a bruise under Kassidy's right eye and he thought that may have happened at Jeff's. Chad wrote that Amanda replied, "*Oh no, she fell forward yesterday and hit the coffee table. I saw her do it.*" (Chad, November 2000 letter to his attorneys)

At 8:04 p.m., from her unlisted home or cell phone, Tristan called Chad's home phone. 1 minute 26 seconds. (Chart of Calls)

8:04 p.m. Jeff called an unknown, probably local, number from his home phone. 2 min. 13 seconds. (Chart of Calls) This was probably Jeff's call to his friend, landlord and neighbor William Peirce, about Chad's call to Jeff about the Tee-Ball incident. (Peirce, Summary of Interview, 6 Dec 2000, Discovery page 401)

At 8:07 p.m., from his home phone, Chad called Jeff again, on his home phone, for this 11 minutes, 3 seconds call. (Chart of Calls) Chad wrote about this call, and the evening in his November 2000 letter to his attorneys

I then called Jeff back and finished my conversation with him. I went through Kassidy's behavior for the night and asked him if he thought it was strange? Trying a little different angle and he just replied, "I told you she is retarded." I explained how for a while tonight she acted like she wasn't even in there. I told him, "I was like 'Kassidy, Kassidy'," he started laughing and said, "Oh yeah, it's like children of the fucking corn. She is either crying or looking at you like she is dumb." It was just the way he said it that made me laugh. Somehow, we then got onto the presidential election. I asked him something about the Electoral College. He then started going off about the Democrats about how they liked giving money to the poor and the people that cry poor. He said, "You know people like Mandy's parents. Or single mom's like Mandy that you and I pay for." I guess at this point I did as I usually did, just rationalized away everything with Kassidy thinking he would somehow give something up if he was really doing something. I always felt paranoid after because I didn't want to think badly of people, and I felt a little stupid at the time for questioning him. I guess when I think back to that night there were three main reasons I didn't take her to the hospital and God do I wish I had:

1. She was fine after a while and I got confirmation from Tristan who works with doctors all the time that she was sure Kassidy was fine.

2. I knew Kassidy's eyes rolled into her head before, based on what Amanda had told me. She told me that the night Jeff dropped Kassidy out of his truck window it had happened, so I didn't think it was a life and death situation.

3. I was going through a divorce with Tristan. Things were almost final and I didn't want anything to screw it up. Kassidy had a mark under her eye from the coffee table and two faint bruises on her forehead that I have no idea where they came from. She also had a huge bump on the back of her head where she fell out of the truck and thinning hair in the back (caused from the bump on the head.) Not to mention she still walked with a limp. I didn't really want to take her to the doctor's and have them start pointing the finger at me. I knew I was not responsible for her condition, but I didn't want to be questioned either and have things screwed up for visitation with my son. I had a sweet deal arranged, and Tristan or the state could have screwed it up if they thought I had done something to Kassidy. Had I known or even suspected that whatever happened to Kassidy was life threatening, I would have taken her to get checked in a second. Looking back I was being very selfish. I hate myself for this, it should have been so clear, the condition she was in.

At 8:14 p.m., Amanda clocked back in from her break at work.

Around 8:20 p.m., Chad took Kyle and Kassidy downstairs for a snack. Kyle had a mint "ice cream sandwich," and Chad fed Kassidy a Popsicle on his lap. (See photo of "Ice Cream Sandwich" box in kitchen trash.) Although Kassidy was generally an adventurous eater, she didn't like mint ice cream. Travis came up from his basement room and saw Chad in his office with Kassidy in his lap and Kyle was on the couch in the living room. Later, Kyle and Kassidy sat on the couch together, watching a few minutes of TV. Chad asked Kyle to take a one-minute time-out because he was having a hard time "sharing" the couch with Kassidy. After his one-minute, he returned from the corner, saying, "*Daddy, I'm ready to share, now.*"

At 8:23 p.m., Chad called an unknown, possibly local, number and the call lasted two min. 13 seconds. Perhaps it was Bruce. (Chart of Calls)

Around 8:30 p.m., Chad put Kassidy to bed and kissed her good night, with "*about 50 kisses. She went to bed and seemed to be fine.*" (Nov. 2000 letter to his attorneys) Chad was reading a bed-time story to Kassidy from the book Snappy Numbers, and doing "ABC's" with her when Travis went to, and returned from, the Mobil convenience store across the street. Shortly afterwards, around 8:45 p.m., Chad put Kyle to bed.

After putting the kids to bed Chad did some survey-inputting work on his computer, to help Amanda with that project. With her quick hiring at Old Navy, terminating her survey work was another task that wasn't completed in time for her start date the previous Monday. The other was finding day care.

At 9:05 p.m., Travis left for Irene Ricci's house in Gonic, about 15 minutes away. Shortly afterwards, at 9:10 p.m., Irene called Chad's, and Travis's home to ask where Travis was, as she was expecting him. Chad was in his home office and told her that Travis would be there shortly, as he had just left. Chad had a specific visual memory of seeing her phone number appear on his Caller ID system.

In Kittery around this time, Jennifer came home from work, after the end of her shift at 9:00 p.m. She and Jeff then went to Wendy's to purchase dinner and bring it home to eat. (Jeff testimony, page 141) This was the source of the Wendy's "wrapper" that was mentioned during the Chad Evans trial.

Around 9:30 p.m., Chad checked on Kassidy and Kyle. Chad recalls that Kassidy saw him and said, "*Kiss*," and Chad kissed her.

At 11:02 p.m., Amanda's six hour workday ended, but she had to wait for others to lock or unlock doors before she could leave. Around 11:30 p.m., Amanda arrived home and argued with Chad about the stress of working, and, between them, who was working harder. Chad either grabbed or pushed Amanda, which was the basis of the subsequent Simple Assault charge against Chad. Such physical contact has to be evaluated within the overall context of their relationship, about which Chad wrote in 2010,

I had a very physical relationship with both Amanda and Tristan. I love a girl who can dress up, look beautiful and command the attention of a room when they walk in. But I also like a girl that is a bit of a tomboy. Who likes to wrestle, who enjoys throwing a pair of sweats on and playing some one on one basketball with me. I love a girl who likes to take chances, be adventurous and try new things. Both Amanda and Tristan were awesome. I couldn't have asked for better partners to share my life with. They were both tough and could hold their own which I loved. Amanda and I were VERY playful. She did a lot of things that would result in me chasing her around the house, catching her and start a wrestling match. For example, Amanda may be washing dishes, and I would go to get a glass of water, and she flicks water at my face with her fingers, I say, "You do that again and you are going to get it." She giggles and of course does it again and then breaks off in a run. Kato starts barking, I start chasing Amanda, she scampers around the house and up the stairs where she has no place to go. I jump on her on the bed. She laughs. I pin her hands down. She attempts to buck me off her with her hips. Sometimes she does, other times, not so successfully. Either way we struggle back and forth, start kissing and typically this leads to making love. Amanda would often initiate these matches doing other things. Typically, she would throw something at me, I'd playfully threaten her, she would do it again, I would chase her, etc. We had an incredible relationship in so many ways. I never felt such passion for someone. When I wasn't with her I wanted to be. I couldn't wait to get home at night to be near her. I couldn't wait to go to bed at night to hold her. I often would drop in during the workday to give her and Kassidy a little surprise snack, Muffins, donuts, a Happy Meal or McDonald's Salad. Those five minutes with them, a couple of kisses from each was like a "fix" for me and helped me make it through the day until I got back home. I honestly had never been happier overall. (Letter, May 27, 2010)

In his June 29, 2010 Letter, Chad further described his physical relationship with Amanda, and "*How we wrestled hard, I would throw her on bed, chase each other through the house, Amanda's come from behind, jump on my back, headlocks, etc.*"

Before being charged for assault from that argument, Chad had written in his Nov. 2000 letter to his attorneys, simply, "*Amanda returned home around midnight we argued and then we cuddled on the couch for a few minutes, and then went up to bed.*"

At around 11:45 p.m., Chad and Amanda went upstairs, checked on the children, kissed them "*Good Night,*" and went to bed. Amanda and Chad noticed that Kassidy needed another diaper change, but Amanda said that she wouldn't wake her at that time, and would change it when they all woke in the morning. Amanda testified that Kassidy was awake with open eyes and that she and Chad went to bed about 1-1:30 a.m. Thursday morning. (Transcript, Dec. 5, page 136) However, Chad believes she was actually recalling the bedtime of the previous evening, when he did some of Amanda's remaining survey work for Bruce.

At some point that evening Chad said to Amanda, "*We have to do something different Amanda, I'm serious. I realize she is your daughter, but Jeff is not good with her.*"

Below is the updated calendar of bruises with NB (No Bruise) NI (No Injury) and B for (Bruise) including the goose egg bumps on Kassidy's head, as observed on the 28th, and the bruise on Kassidy's right cheek which Tristan saw on Monday, October 30 and which continued to be visible when Nicole and Brandon Harvey noticed it on Sunday, November 5. Continuing through November 8, the calendar reflects the scratch from the kitten and Kassidy's hitting her head into the glass table in the living room at Chad's.

June 2000

Su	Mo	Tu	We	Th	Fr	Sa
					9	10
11	12	13	14	15	16	**NI**
NI	**NI**	**NI**	**NI**	**NB**	23	24
25	26	27	28	29	30	

July 2000

Su	Mo	Tu	We	Th	Fr	Sa
						1
2	3	4	5	6	**NI**	**NI**
NI	**NI**	**NI**	**NB**	**NB**	**NB**	**NB**
NB	**NB**	**NB**	**NB**	**NB**	21	22
23	**NI**	**NI**	**NI**	**NI**	**NI**	**NB**
NB	**NB**					

August 2000

Su	Mo	Tu	We	Th	Fr	Sa
		1	2	3	4	**NI**
NI	**NI**	**NI**	**NI**	**NB**	**NI**	**NI**
NI	**NI**	**NI**	**NB**	**NI**	**NI**	**NI**
NB	**NB**	**NB**	**NB**	**NB**	**NB**	**NB**
NB	**NB**	**NI**	**NI**	**NI**		

September 2000

Su	Mo	Tu	We	Th	Fr	Sa
					NI	**NB**
3	4	5	**NI**	**NI**	**NI**	**NI**
NI	**NB**	12	13	14	15	16
17	18	**NI**	**NI**	**NI**	**NI**	**NI**
NB	**NB**	**NB**	**NB**	**NI**	**NI**	**NI**

October 2000

Su	Mo	Tu	We	Th	Fr	Sa
NB	2	3	4	5	6	7
8	9	10	11	12	**B**	**B**
B	**B**	17	18	19	20	**B**
B	23	24	25	26	27	**B**
B	**B**	**B**				

November 2000

Su	Mo	Tu	We	Th	Fr	Sa
			B	**B**	**B**	**B**
B	**B**	**B**	**B**	**B**		

CHAPTER 4: INVESTIGATING CHAD EVANS - 9 NOVEMBER 2000, AFTER 12:38 P.M.

"...our investigation clearly indicates that you are the cause of these injuries." - Lance McCleish

"I think everybody lies." - Angela Blodgett

"I don't live with them, so I don't really know exactly what goes on there, but..." - Jennifer

"...***but he's like the best father. You can ask anybody."*** - Amanda

"The big thing with me is eye contact " - Chad

"Kassidy did not die of natural causes." - Jeff Smith

12:38 p.m.

The investigation of Kassidy's death can be said to have begun when Kittery Police Patrolman Robert Creamer was notified of Jeff's 911 call at 12:38 p.m. Creamer arrived at 51 Rogers Road at 12:41 p.m. Seven hours later, at approximately 9:40 p.m., Maine State Police Detective, Lance McCleish said to Chad, "***our investigation clearly indicates that you are the cause of these injuries***." Chad responded, "*Ah, no way*." (Chad interrogation, Nov. 9, 2000, p.1370) We will never know what facts might have swayed the police from their quickly formed, and quickly announced, conclusion.

Officer Robert Creamer's first efforts were to try to save Kassidy's life, but that work was assumed by the EMT's who arrived quickly, and Officer Creamer began absorbing and recording information about a possible crime. This is the full text of Officer Creamer's report, in CAPS, as it was in the original:

I WAS ON PATROL IN A MARKED POLICE VEHICLE. I RECEIVED A CALL FROM DISPATCHER SULLIVAN AT ABOUT 12:30 P.M. OR SO TO GO TO 51 ROGERS RD. DISPATCHER SULLIVAN TOLD ME THAT A YOUNG CHILD THAT WAS IN SHOCK WITH SHALLOW BREATHING.

I ARRIVED AT 51 ROGERS RD. COMING IN FROM THE SOUTH, I CAME UP TO #51 AND SAW A WHITE MALE ON A PORCH KNEELING OVER A SMALL CHILD. THE MALE LOOKED AS IF HE WAS TRYING TO GIVE THE SMALL CHILD CPR. HE WAS PRESSING DOWN ON THE CHILD CHEST AREA, AND FANNING THE MOUTH AREA OF THE CHILD. I CALLED DISPATCHER SULLIVAN AND TOLD HER TO EXPEDITE THE AMBULANCE. I THEN RAN TO THE PORCH WHERE THE MALE AND SMALL CHILD WAS. THE CHILD WAS A SMALL WHITE FEMALE ABOUT 1 1/2 YEARS OLD. SHE WAS LAYING ON A SHEET OF SHEET ROCK. SHE HAD ONLY A DIAPER ON. HER EYES WERE OPEN AND FIXED. I ALSO SAW BLACK AND BLUES MARKS ALL OVER THE FACE, CHIN AND NECK AREA. THERE WERE BLACK AND BLUE MARKS ON THE STOMACH AREA. ALSO. I ASKED THE MALE WHAT HAD HAPPENED TO THE...[cutoff, end of page]

I ASKED THE MALE HOW THE CHILD HAD GOT ALL THE BLACK AND BLUE MARKS. HE TOLD ME HE DIDN'T KNOW FOR SURE. HE TOLD ME HIS GIRLFRIEND'S SISTER HAD DROPPED THE CHILD OFF THAT MORNING FOR HIM TO WATCH BECAUSE THE CHILD HAD BLACK AND BLUES ALL OVER, AND SHE DIDN'T WANT THE DAY CARE TO SEE THE BLACK AND BLUES MARKS. I WAS NOW DOING CPR ON THE CHILD. AS I WAS DOING THIS I COULD SEE THAT THE HANDS AND FEET WERE VERY BLUE LOOKING. I TOUCHED THE CHILD'S ARMS AND HANDS AND THEY WERE COLD. HER LEGS AND FEET WERE ALSO COLD AND VERY BLUE. THE ONLY WARM AREA I FOUND WAS UNDER THE CHILD'S ARM PITS. AS I WAS GIVING MOUTH TO MOUTH I COULD TELL THAT THE CHILD'S FACE AND LIPS WERE ALSO VERY COLD. THERE WAS A SMALL AMOUNT

OF BLOOD COMING FROM THE NOSE OF THE CHILD. THIS WAS ALSO COLD, AS I WIPED IT FROM THE MOUTH AREA TO DO MORE CPR.

I TOLD DISPATCHER SULLIVAN TO TELL THE AMBULANCE TO HURRY IT UP AND FOR HER TO CALL THE CHIEF AND DET.'S TO THE SCENE ASAP.

I ASKED THE MALE HOW THIS YOUNG GIRL GOT ALL THE BLACK AND BLUES ON HER FACE AND HE TOLD ME HE WASN'T SURE BUT SAID HIS GIRLFRIEND SAID SHE WAS HIT BY A BASEBALL. I SAID HOW MANY TIMES WAS SHE HIT, BY THE BASE BALL, BECAUSE SHE HAD SO MANY BRUISES.

I KEPT CHECKING THE CHILD FOR SIGNS OF LIFE BUT DIDN'T FIND ANY. THE MALE KEPT ASKING IF SHE WAS ALIVE OR NOT, I TOLD HIM I DIDN'T KNOW. I ASKED HIM WHY SHE WAS OUTSIDE ON THE PORCH AND HE TOLD ME THAT HE HAD CHECKED ON HER IN THE HOUSE AND FOUND HER WITH HER EYES OPEN, AND SHE WASN'T RESPONSIVE TO HIM. HE THEN CALL 911, PICKED HER UP AND TOOK HER OUT SIDE ON THE PORCH TO WAIT FOR THE POLICE AND AMBULANCE TO ARRIVE.

THE MALE SEEM[ED] *TO BE UPSET ABOUT WHAT WAS GOING ON BUT ALSO DIDN'T SEEM TO KNOW MUCH ABOUT THE CHILD OR WHAT WAS WRONG WITH HER. THE AMBULANCE ARRIVED AND THEY TOOK OVER THE CPR FROM ME. THE KITTERY DET.'S SGT. RON AVERY AND DET. STEVE HAMEL ARRIVED ABOUT THE SAME TIME THAT THE CHIEF OF KITTERY ARRIVED. I TOLD THEM WHAT I KNEW AT THIS POINT AND POINTED OUT THE MALE THAT WAS TRYING TO DO CPR ON THE CHILD. THERE WAS ANOTHER MALE THERE NOW BUT I DON'T KNOW WHERE HE CAME FROM. HE SEEM*[ED] *TO BE A FRIEND OF THE MALE DOING THE CPR ON THE CHILD WHEN I ARRIVED.*

THE AMBULANCE PEOPLE ASKED ME IF I COULD HELP DO CPR AGAIN, AND I DID. THE AMBULANCE PEOPLE GOT THE CHILD ON IV, AND MOVED HER TO THE AMBULANCE, WHERE SHE WAS TAKEN TO YORK HOSPITAL.

I WAS TOLD TO STAY AT THE SCENE AND NOT LET ANYONE IN THE APT. UNTIL THE STATE POLICE TOOK IT OVER. I WAS RELIEVED BY A MAINE STATE TROOPER AT ABOUT 20:45 P.M.

Officer Creamer's report of blood coming from Kassidy's nose was never again addressed. He did not testify at Chad Evans's trial, but his report contained the foundation of the prosecution's case. He understood Jeff to say that he was caring for Kassidy only because her mother didn't want to send her to her regular day care provider, because of bruises. However, Officer Creamer, in the rush of the moment in these first few minutes of the investigation, didn't know that despite Amanda's efforts, she had not yet been able to find a regular day care provider for Kassidy, and that inability had arisen from the shortage of suitable day care spaces and not from any reluctance, for any reason, to place Kassidy into an available position. However, Jeff's statement that the motivation for his babysitting was because a regular day care person would see the bruises was soon set in stone.

The identity of the "*another male*" was not clear. Will Peirce was at the scene almost immediately and he later made a statement and was interviewed. Tom McNeil, the neighbor at 53 Rogers Street was also at the scene, but that was not confirmed until he was interviewed a year later, on November 13, 2001.

In quick succession, Officer Creamer and the EMT's were joined by Kittery Police Chief Edward Strong, Detective Steve Hamel, Sergeant Ronald Avery and Detective William Hackett. Reports were filed by Avery, Creamer, Hamel and Hackett, but none is available from Chief Strong. Only Hamel testified at Chad Evans's trial. Hackett reported that he took three rolls of photographs at Jeff Marshall's home and at the York Hospital. Detective Hamel reported,

... As I approached the front porch, I noticed that the infant was noticeably bruised about the head and face area. At this time my attention was drawn to a male who was on the porch at the side of the infant. This male was visibly shaken and was trying to assist the medical personnel with the care of the infant. This male was subsequently identified as

FRANK JEFFREY MARSHALL

AKA: JEFF or JEFFREY MARSHALL

Marshall was the caretaker of the child on this day. Also present at the residence at this time was one: WILLIAM C. PEIRCE

This officer, thereafter, initiated an interview of Marshall while Det. Sgt. Ronald Avery conducted an interview of Peirce. At this time the following information was obtained from Jeffrey Marshall:

Marshall indicated that baby Cassidy had been dropped off at his residence by her mother, one: AMANDA J. BORTNER

AKA: MANDY BORTNER

at around 8:30 A.M. that morning. Marshall recalled that the mother, he and his girlfriend, Jennifer Connelly (the baby's aunt), saw a great deal of bruising around the baby's face and head. According to Marshall, the baby's mother, Amanda Bortner, made the statement, "Look at her face." Marshall also indicated that he noticed the baby had a hard time walking. Because of this, the baby was placed in bed to watch T.V. According to Marshall, the baby was wearing red pajamas when dropped off and was eating Coco-Puffs out of a clear baggie....

Marshall stated that he was in the living room watching T.V. when his girlfriend, one:

JENNIFER M. CONNELLY

AKA: JENNIFER M. BORTNER

left for work that morning. Marshall watched T.V. all morning, but remembered checking on the baby who was still sleeping in the bed in the master bedroom sometime between 9:30 A.M. and 10:00 A.M. According to Marshall, he went out to get his mail around noontime and. upon his return to the house he again went to check on the baby. At this time, Marshall found the baby having difficulty breathing and noticed the baby's eyes were rolled back. Marshall, at this point, took the baby from the bed and checked for a pulse. Finding a slight pulse, he brought the baby into the kitchen sink in an attempt to wake the baby by splashing cold water on her face. Marshall indicates that he was unable to revive the baby, so he began to do CPR. Marshall indicates that he called Jennifer at work to get advice from her on what to do. According to Marshall, Jennifer was busy at work and unable to talk long on the phone, but she did tell him to contact Amanda, the baby's mother, at her workplace (Old Navy at the Tidewater Mall in Kittery). Marshall attempted to contact Amanda at Old Navy but was unable to make contact with her. Again, Marshall called Jennifer at work. It was at this time that Jennifer told him that if the baby was that bad that he should call the ambulance. Marshall then called 911. According to Marshall, he kept performing chest compressions on the baby until the police and ambulance arrived.

Through further questioning of Marshall, I learned that Marshall had been watching the baby on and off over the past few weeks while the mother was working. Marshall further indicated that he had watched the baby the day before for approximately one hour (from 4:30 P.M. to about 5:30 P.M.). At this time the mother's live-in boyfriend, one

CHAD E. EVANS

came to pick up the baby at Marshall's Rogers Road address. Marshall indicated that the baby seemed normal and did not have the bruising on her face at that time. Shortly after the baby had been picked-up by Evans, Marshall received a cell phone call from Evans who stated he was calling from the area of the Dover Toll Booth on the Spaulding Turnpike. Evans, at this time, said that the baby was acting weird, kind of out-of-it. Marshall thought this was strange because the baby had just left his residence and, according to him, was acting fine. Marshall received a second call from Evans approximately a half hour to forty-five minutes after the first call. During this second call Evans indicated that when he arrived home he (Evans) had placed the baby on her feet outside the car and when he returned to get her she had fallen face first onto the driveway. This, again, struck Marshall as odd, as he questioned why Evans called him and not the baby's mother to report or explain this. Marshall received a third call from Evans between 9:00 P.M. and 9:15 P.M. During this third call, Evans told Marshall that the baby had been hit in the face with a baseball, but was alright now. Again, Marshall felt that this phone call was strange....

By his statements to Officer Creamer and Sgt Hamel, Jeff had laid the groundwork for suspecting Chad:

1. He told Creamer that he was babysitting in order to avoid a day care provider who might see bruises on Kassidy.

2. He told Hamel that Kassidy "*seemed normal and did not have the bruising on her face*" and "*was acting fine*" the previous day.

3. He told Hamel that, given Kassidy's normal behavior the previous day, he thought that Chad's calls to him the previous afternoon and evening were "*strange*."

4. He did not tell Hamel that among his 10 calls on this day, for help, and before calling 911, six of his first seven calls were to Chad.

In addition to trying to resuscitate Kassidy's cold body, the EMT's also gathered information about the case. EMT Robert Frechette reported

PT [patient] *has had bruises recently, throughout her body.* __ *Also* [Marshall] *states PT was acting abnormally today. -- Lethargic and bumping into things. He* [Marshall] *states PT fell and/or was struck in the head* [by] *baseball ~~ two days ago or possibly yesterday.*

Sergeant Avery reported that when he arrived, Officer Creamer was "*attending to an infant with ambulance personnel on the front porch... In approaching the infant, I noticed that bruises were clearly visible, particularly around the head and facial area.*" (p. 13) Avery interviewed Will Peirce who told him that he saw Amanda leave at approximately 8:20 a.m. and Jennifer left at approximately 9:00 a.m., and that he did not see anyone else enter or exit, until the ambulance arrived at approximately 12:40 p.m. Avery wrote that *approximately two (2) weeks ago, reportedly Jeff Marshall spoke with Mr. Peirce, telling him that he had observed bruises near Cassidy Bortner's eyes; and secondly, approximately seven to ten days ago Jeff was said to have informed Peirce that bruises were visible on the child's chin (as if she had been grabbed and held.) ... Jeff Marshall had also told him that he suspected Chad Evans as the person responsible for inflicting bruises on infant Cassidy Bortner.* (p. 14)

12:53 p.m.

From her workplace at Old Navy, Amanda Bortner called Jeff Marshall's cell phone at 12:53 p.m., but there was no answer. (Chart of Calls) She then clocked out of work at 12:59 p.m. and drove to Portsmouth Regional Hospital. She thought her sister, Jennifer, had told her by phone that Kassidy was at that hospital. Even though her workplace was two miles north of Jeff's and Jennifer's apartment, it was still a shorter distance to the Portsmouth Regional Hospital, even though in another state, than to the York Hospital. Thus, embarking for Portsmouth seemed reasonable. If she had driven straight to Jeff's and Jennifer's she might have arrived in time to see Kassidy on the porch with the EMT's, but she had been told by Jennifer that Jeff had taken Kassidy to the hospital himself, as that was Jennifer's understanding at the time, before she returned to her customers.

1:06 p.m.

The ambulance left Jeff's home with Kassidy's body to go to the York Hospital in York, Maine, which was 8.13 miles north. The Portsmouth Regional Hospital was only 4.85 miles south, but the EMT's and the police were from Maine. Perhaps they had calculated that there was no need to save a few minutes in travel time to the hospital because Kassidy was already dead.

When Amanda arrived at the Portsmouth Regional Hospital, no one there knew of a patient or recent arrival by the name of Kassidy Bortner. Surely panicked, Amanda then called Jennifer back to say that Kassidy was not there, and Jennifer recommended calling the York Hospital. Jennifer still was apparently not alarmed by the situation, and remained at work.

Amanda called the York Hospital, and the person with whom she talked did not yet have a record of Kassidy, whose body had just arrived at the hospital. (Amanda interview, p. 841-42) Amanda then frantically called Jeff's cell phone at 1:25 p.m. from the

Portsmouth Hospital's main phone. (Chart of Calls) Jeff advised her to come to the Kittery Police Station, without saying more about Kassidy's condition.

Amanda arrived at the Kittery Police Station and was told of Kassidy's death. Kittery Detective Steve Hamel's report states that he

was present during the death notification... which took place in the Chief's Conference Room at the Kittery Police Station. At the time of the notification, it was apparent to me, having delivered numerous death notifications in the scope of my duties as a Law Enforcement Officer, the spontaneous reaction by Amanda Bortner was not of genuine grief. In observing Amanda Bortner during this time, I noted that she seemed able to control her emotions, turning them on and off when she needed to. At the time of the death notification, Amanda Bortner made statements that I recorded in my notes. The statements made by Bortner are as follows:
1) "Did the baby fall or something?"
2) "I feel like such a bad Mom."
3) "How could this happen to me?"
4) "I don't feel like living anymore."

Despite Detective Hamel's experience as a policeman, he had never been a teenage mother and likely never lost an infant child. Going forward, this case saw several people who were forthright in their opinions about how other people should behave in certain situations. In this instance, an 18-year old single mother was informed in a police station about the death of her child with very few details about the cause of death. It was not as if Amanda had been told that Kassidy had run after a ball into a street and been hit by a car or that she had some other specific accident. Thus, Kassidy's death had an even greater sense of unreality than it otherwise would. Also, Chad had told Amanda about Kassidy's falling in the driveway and her behavior on the way home the previous day, and that Kassidy was hit by a ball the previous night, and she knew that Kassidy seemed tired and lethargic that morning. She must have had some terrible wrenching feeling that she and Chad had missed the signs of a serious problem. What an awful feeling for a parent: to hear that your child has died and to realize that you might have been able to prevent that death. The swirling emotions in Amanda must have been very intense and complex and hard to decipher, even by a policeman who has seen notifications of death before.

Virginia Grover was the secretary to Kittery Police Dept. Chief, Edward Strong and was present when Amanda arrived. Grover was interviewed the next day by Maine State Police Detective Angela Blodgett who wrote,

Amanda was crying and very upset so Virginia got her some water and sat with her in the conference room and kitchen areas of the police station. Virginia also sat outside with Amanda for about 45 minutes after Amanda stated she was feeling sick and needed some fresh air. She tried to comfort Amanda and make sure Amanda didn't feel alone, while she waited for her family to arrive...

...Amanda made several spontaneous statements including the following: 'What am I going to do now? I had a baby when I was young, and now I've lost a baby when I'm young. I should have taken the baby to the doctor. She was sick and I gave her Tylenol. It's all my fault.' Amanda's sister arrived... and Virginia sat in the conference room... with the two women."

There was no indication from Virginia Grover or from Angela Blodgett that Amanda's reactions to the death of her daughter were not genuine.

2:10 p.m. - William Peirce statement

Jeff Marshall's neighbor, friend, and landlord, William Peirce, began writing his two-page statement for the Kittery Police. He wrote....

Jeff has occasionally been babysitting Cassidy for a number of months.
Jeff Marshall has been babysitting Cassidy for about two weeks, regularly. He showed me that Cassidy had bruises on her face when he first started babysitting regularly. He speculated that she was being hit by her caretakers. He also said that she fell easily and that could be the cause of her bruises.

He told me that she fell out of his bed when he asked her to get up one time. He also said that she fell in the living room. She had bruises on her cheeks.

About a week ago he showed me that Cassidy had two bruises on her lower jaw bones. He pointed out that it resembled a pattern of a grip, as if someone had grabbed her face. She also had marks on her cheekbones. I remarked that Cassidy did not show protective flinching behavior (defensive reactions to mistreatment) in my experience. He said that he did not see any either. We pulled down her diaper halfway and did not see any marks there.

Previous to these conversations, Jeff and I discussed discipline methods in childrearing. He said that Chad was physically disciplining Cassidy....

I probably asked him to bring the child outside to play on the grass while we worked. He definitely told me that she had been hit in the head by a baseball the night before while playing indoors with the name of a child that I did not recognize. He told me that she was not walking and therefore could not come outside. He told me that he put her in front of the TV with a bowl of Coco-Puffs.... (See, also, Rekeyed WORD copy of Peirce statement.)

Shortly after 2:00 p.m. York Hospital Nurse Janet Jones marked a body chart form with the locations of bruises and "*petechia*" on Kassidy's body. A "*petechia*" is defined by Merriam- Webster as "*a minute reddish or purplish spot containing blood that appears in skin or mucous membrane as a result of a localized hemorrhage.*" She showed the scabs on Kassidy's feet and bruises on her abdomen and "old bruising" on her back at shoulder level, and "hair loss" on the back of her head. Those were the only notations apart from her face, on which she marked three locations with "petichia" and eight bruises, plus a note about bruising on the inside of her lower lip. Two of the bruises were at the front of her chin, and one was on each side of the bottom of her nose, and one was underneath her left eye. Two were on her forehead above her nose and one above her left eye. Thus, Amanda was correct when she told Jeff and Jennifer earlier in the morning that Kassidy, or Kassidy's face, "*looks like shit.*"

At 2:12 p.m. the Kittery Police Dept. called Chad's cell phone and left a message to call. Chad was in a business meeting in Hudson, New Hampshire, with his boss, Bob McDougall, and at 2:22 p.m. he received a "page" from a Kittery phone number which he didn't recognize, but he knew that Amanda worked in Kittery and Kassidy was being babysat in Kittery, so the call was not likely to be a good call. Chad checked his cell phone for messages at 2:24 p.m., and told Bob that he needed to go to Kittery, but he still did not know the reason for the police request to go to Kittery. The police station was about 60 miles, and an hour and a quarter away. Included in the messages were Jeff's urgent calls when he was trying to revive Kassidy around 12:35 p.m. At 2:25 p.m., from his cell phone, Chad called Jeff's cell phone to ask, "*What the hell is going on?*" He didn't reach Jeff, but left the message in the 38 second call. (Chart of Calls)

2:25 p.m. - Jeff Marshall statement

At that same time, 2:25 p.m., Jeff began writing, by hand, a statement on a "Witness Statement Form." He signed the first two pages, and an additional five pages, unsigned, apparently were written later on a different form, "Kittery Police Follow-up Report." He wrote:

I, Jefferey Marshall of 51 Rogers Rd Kittery ME. My girlfriend, Jennifer Bortner, who lives at the same address as me. Me and her would take Cassidy to baby sit her overnight so her and Chad could go out. This was at first, but then we took her because she had bruises on her. They said it was because she had fallen many more times. She came over with more bruises on her and we took her because Mandy did not want to bring her to day care.

I and my girlfriend said to each other that it was weird that she had bruises on her face that look like she have been grabbed by the face. We don't know but we thought Chad had done it on Cassidy. Cassidy came over and stayed more times because Mandy was going out to school and Chad's sister was coming over so they did not want Cassidy to be seen by Chad's sister or parents. About every time she came over she looked like she had bruises on her body. Kind of like hand prints on her face like she was grabbed. I will say this. Casidy was clumbsy and not a very active child. She was very quit[sic] *and did not walk around like you would suspect a little one to do. (One time though she...* [crossed out].*) I would tell you that I told Mandy that the baby seemed weird and she did not seem to now what she was doing all the time. One time at are house, she did get in to windeck's and I assumed she had swallowed some. So I tried to get her to spit it out but other than that she was very quiet and kind of studd there up against the wall in less you put her in bed and even then sometimes she would get out of bed and stand up against the wall. I was told by Chad that she would go and get put in the corner if she was bad. So we thot that she was so us to this and this would happen all the time I would say there was many time's that* [crossed out] *we should have thought twice about the bruises on her face. Because my next store neighbor saw her face and that that it was bad and Stanley Staley who worked for me said that it look like she was not taken care of.*

SIGNED Jefferey Marshall /s/

I believe that one night, it could be during a day in the last week or so Mandy called me and Jen and told us Casidy was walking funny because she said Chad did something to Cassidy leg by pulling her or picking her up by it. We still watched Casidy for them because Mandy had to work at Old Navy Store. She told us she was going to get a babysitter again. Mandy told us that Chad had hit her because she was bad. Me and Jen should have probibly done something but you would have never thought it was this bad. Casidy came over a few days ago and could hardly walk that day. The only problem I say was she could not walk around that day. She was in bed most of the day. The one thing that was wierd was she must have gut out sometime because the phone rang and I got up and rain to get the phone. I was in the living room and Casidy was in the bed room, but when I went around the corner I tripped over her because she was just standing there by herself. She did not say anything. She just looked tired and domfounded look on her face. She had no brusses on her face from me tripping over her. Just the one's that look like some one had grabbed her face. Me and Jen watch her again and this time the brusses look like they got worse but not that thay were new but that she had got grabbed by the face in the same place. Yesterday the 11/8/00 she came over and she looked fine, not to many busses but she was still acting strang. She was over at 4:20, I think, and was pick up at about 5:30 or so. He called me at home and said he was going to pick her up at home and asked me if I could meet him at the Peter Palace in Portsmouth NH on Rte 1. I told him, no, and he said he would come over and get her. So got her coat on and brought her out to the car. She did not have any brusses on her at this time. I then went in to the house and watched TV. Chad called me and said Casidy was acting wierd in his car. I told him I did not know what he should do.

He called me latter that is, Chad, to tell me he was at home and Casidy fell down again on the driveway. When he got in he said he put her standing up on the driveway and went to get his sun out of the car. At that time he went around the car and Casidy was on the ground face down. He said he took her in the house and he said she had dirt in her hair. He called me again latter and said that he was playing baseball in the house with his sun and he hit a ball at her face by accident. It was earlier then or latter I think he called me later and he did say very worried because he said she was not looking very good. Her eyes were in the back of her head and she was not responding to him at this time and was not lookin good on the bed. He then said more worried she rail does not look good and ask if this ever happened over at my and Jen's house. I then said, no, and he said she was coming out of it and we got off the phone.

Jen came home and me and her talked about it. She said that Mandy talked to Chad [sic] *her work and Mandy left mad. So me and Jen thought that this was because Chad had told her about what had happened with Casidy. Then this morning Mandy brote Casidy over the house and in to are bed room and said look at her face. It did not appear a baseball could have done that kind of brusses on her face because it was all over her face. She tried to walk around and Casidy fell on the floor. Jen was there. We then tried to let her walk again but she would not move out of the bed. We put the blankets over her and put on cartoon's on TV so she could lay there and watch them. She was very quit and not very coherrent but was still watching TV. I went out and watch TV in the other room the living room. I went in the room I believe onecs before because the cat was jumping up on the desk in the living room and ran into the bed room and I went in there to see what he might have got to hide under the bed. She was from what I remember sleeping. I then went back and watched the voteing on TV. About an hour or an hour and a half later I went to check the mail and outside on the deck I broght the mail in the house and walked in to the bed room with it. I looked at Casidy and could tell there was something wrong with her, so I took the blanket's off of her and tried to wake her up, but I got no reaction from her. I did not know what to do. I felt her pulse and could feel it I thoght that she was doing the same thing that Chad said she did last night but it was worst. She was not breathing so I tried punging her stomich with my hand's to get her to breathe, but she wasn't coming to. I called Jen. I called Chad and called Mandy. I could not get a hold of Chad. Jen did not know what to do and I could not get a hold of Mandy. So I called 911 and tried to wake her up by splashing water on her face. She would not come to. I ran outside for the ambulance and the cops came and at that time we both tried to get her to come to.* (See Rekeyed WORD copy of Jeff's statement, using original spelling.)

This was the second of the only two statement requests of anyone in this case: from Will Peirce and Jeff Marshall. In the law, there is a dichotomy between substance and procedure, and sometimes procedure says a lot. In this case, what did it mean that only two people were asked for statements? Why Will and Jeff, and not Jennifer nor Amanda nor Chad? Requesting such statements would have provided police with information unfiltered by police questions and body language and subtle hints or intimidation. While much was written that pointed toward Chad Evans, these two statements contained several indications or problems or injuries or bruises which did not point in that direction..

1. Peirce: *" He also said that she fell easily and that could be the cause of her bruises."*
2. Peirce: "*...she fell out of his bed when he asked her to get up one time."*
3. Peirce: *"He also said that she fell in the living room."*
4. Jeff: "*Casidy was clumbsy and not a very active child."*
5. Jeff: *"One time at are house, she did get in to windeck's and I assumed she had swallowed some..."*
6. Jeff: *"she was very quiet and kind of studd there up against the wall in less you put her in bed and even then sometimes she would get out of bed and stand up against the wall."*
7. Jeff: "*when I went around the corner I tripped over her..."*
8. Jeff: *"She tried to walk around and Casidy fell on the floor. Jen was there."*

At 2:26 p.m., from his cell phone, Chad called his home number, looking for Amanda, thinking , or hoping, that she was home, safely. Then, Chad called telephone information (411) to get phone numbers for Amanda at Old Navy and Jennifer at Perfumania. At 2:27 p.m., he called Jennifer at Perfumania, and was put on hold while other employees looked for her. He was told that Jennifer was going to a hospital. (Chart of Calls) However, she didn't go to a hospital and was still at work when her mother called her later.

At 2:27 p.m., The Kittery Police called Chad's cell phone, and left a message in a 24 second call. Apparently, the caller acknowledged receiving Chad's earlier call. (Chart of Calls)

Meanwhile, the grim task of notifying family members of Kassidy's death continued. After Amanda, the police next called Jacqueline, who was called by a Kittery Police officer at 2:28 p.m. She left immediately with her brother-in-law, Robert Conley, for the Kittery Police Station, a distance of about 97 miles and a two hour drive. Before leaving, she call Jennifer to tell her that Kassidy died. For Jennifer, it had been almost two hours since her two calls with Jeff, and her one call with Amanda, and since she had resumed her normal workday. She apparently assumed that Jeff had taken Kassidy to the hospital and was okay. She apparently assumed that after talking with Amanda, who had gone to the wrong hospital, Amanda had eventually found Kassidy and was probably okay. After receiving the call from her mother, Jennifer called Chad's cell phone from Perfumania's main line at 2:36 p.m., but did not reach him. (Chart of Calls) Then she went to the Kittery police station, as her mother had said that's where she was going.

Jeff Marshall's mother lived in York, Maine, about three miles north of the Kittery Police Station, and worked a few miles further north, but she was not able to come to the police station on this day. She was never interviewed by investigators, and neither was Jeff's father who lived in Newburyport, Mass. Neither were Chad's parents, both of whom had known Kassidy.

Also at 2:36 p.m., the Kittery Police Dept. called Chad again and left a message. Shortly afterwards, Chad called Jeff's cell phone, but there was no answer, and Chad did not leave a message. Chad called again, a few seconds later at 2:38 p.m. while stopped at a gas station and pumping gas, and a policeman answered. (Chart of Calls)

I called them and they told me that there was a problem with Kassidy and they wanted to see if I could help them. I said, "Holy shit, what is wrong?" The officer said, "we can't discuss it over the phone." I said, "Ok I will be there in an hour and a half or so."(I was in Hudson NH and they wanted me to drive to Kittery.) When I got to my car I noticed that my cell phone had some messages so I checked them. The 1st one was around 2 p.m. with the Kittery police asking me to call them. The second one was from Jeff around 12:30 or so that was frantic. He said, "Chad, This is Jeff. Call me as soon as you get this, bye!" He sounded scared shitless. So I then called him and left a message and then called him right back. Some guy answered and I asked for Jeff. He said, "Hold on," and handed Jeff the phone. Jeff was very rude on the phone. I asked him what was going on and he said very loudly, "I am at the police station, What the hell did you say you did to Kassidy last night? Hit her in the face with a ball?" I was like, "What?" He said, "Just get your ass down here now." I said to him, "You know damn well what happened to her last night, and don't talk to me like that or I will kick your ass." He then calmly replied, "Just come here." And I said, "I am already on my way." When I hung up I immediately thought to myself that bastard got caught doing something to her and said all of that shit loud enough to get the cops thinking I did it. (Chad, Nov. 2000 letter to his attorneys)

A policeman came to the phone again, and Chad reassured the policeman that he was on his way to the police station. Even after this three and half minute call, Chad still did not know what had happened to Kassidy. (Chart of Calls)

At 2:42 p.m. one of Chad's two best friends, Jeremy, called Chad at his cell phone from the Portsmouth McDonald's where Jeremy worked, but the 2-second call was interrupted by a call from Chad's secretary, Melissa Allard, about the State of New Hampshire labor audit being performed at a McDonald's restaurant. Chad told Jeremy he would call back, as the call with Melissa would take a while, and it took 14 minutes. (Chart of Calls)

In Maine, all homicides are prosecuted by the Office of the Attorney General of the state, and most are investigated by the Maine State Police. At 2:50 p.m., the first Maine State Police detective, Jeffrey Smith, arrived at the Kittery Police Station to join the investigation.

Also at 2:50 p.m. Jeremy called Chad again from the Portsmouth McDonald's and Chad told him that something had happened to Kassidy and that he, Chad, was on the way to the Kittery Police Station. He said that he would be stopping, briefly at the Portsmouth McDonald's to leave soup cookers and other items. (Chart of Calls) The Portsmouth McDonald's is about a mile southeast of the Portsmouth Rotary, adjacent to Interstate 95, and the Rotary is on the way to the Kittery Police Station. Chad asked Jeremy if Travis was at the Portsmouth McDonald's and then Chad talked with him about Kassidy, and about Travis's observations the previous night. Chad was seeking some reassurance, as Jeff had just asked Chad about the ball hitting Kassidy during his brief conversation earlier in the afternoon, and in the presence of a Kittery policeman.

Chad wrote in his Nov. 2000 letter to his attorneys,

After Jeff's phone call, I went to Portsmouth real quick. I had to start soup the next day, so I dropped their kettles off. (Keep in mind this entire time I had no idea Kassidy was dead.) I wanted to just get the kettles there so that if she was really hurt or something I could be with her and Amanda uninterrupted. When I got there I went through the grill with the kettles. One of the grills was not cooking properly so I went to fix it. I knew it would only take a minute or so to fix. I saw Travis there on my way out and I said to him, "Something is wrong with Kassidy. I don't know what but I got a phone call from the police department. I am going up there to answer a few questions for them and then heading to the hospital. I don't know which hospital she is at, but I will call you when I find out anything. Or you can call around and find her." And then I said to him, "If anyone asks, you have seen me with her." He said, "Oh yeah, you are great." (I was thinking of Jeff and my little phone conversation and his, what seemed to me, attempt to push anything that happened onto me. I then left the store. About 5 minutes down the road, I remembered that I left my office door unlocked, so I called Portsmouth to have Jeremy lock it up. While driving to Kittery, I got to thinking and freaked myself out. I called my best friend Bruce. My calling Bruce and talking to Travis were solely because of my paranoia with regards to the cops. It is a long story but they intimidate the shit out of me. I called Bruce, and briefly explained what had happened and he said to just go there and answer their questions. I was freaking and said, "You know how the cops are they are going to twist everything, they have done it to me once already." He said, "Well just don't say anything to them, then. You know you tend to get worked up Chad. I'm sure you are worrying about nothing."

At 2:56 p.m.Chad called the Kittery Police Department for directions, and assured an officer that he was on his way.

At 3:00 p.m. Tristan called Chad, and they discussed arrangements for picking up Kyle at Cross Road Kindergarten and the unknowns about Kassidy. While on the way to the Kittery Police Dept. via the Portsmouth McDonalds', Chad called the Rochester McDonald's at 3:13 p.m. to ask Tommy Urrutia to leave a message for Chad's secretary, Melissa Allard, regarding the upcoming labor audit. (Chart of Calls)

At 3:51 p.m., while on his way to Kittery, and from the parking lot at the Portsmouth McDonald's, Chad called his other best friend, Bruce. Chad left a phone message, with his concerns about how his police station visit might affect his probation status, from his 1999 guilty plea for domestic assault of Tristan. (Chart of Calls)

At 3:55 p.m., Chad called the Portsmouth McDonald's to ask Jeremy to lock his office door, which he just left a few minutes previous. (Chart of Calls) Then Chad talked with Tristan regarding meeting him at the Portsmouth traffic rotary, as he was still uncertain about how to get to the Kittery Police Dept. Tristan met Chad at the rotary and then led him to the station.

Back in Rochester, Rochester Police Detectives William Carlberg, Lisa Gero, and Paul Callahan accompanied one or more employees of DCYF to the home of Chad Evans. It was known to all that a child from that home had died in Kittery that day. No one was home.

At approximately 4:10 p.m., Chad and Tristan arrived at the Kittery Police Station, but Tristan initially did not want to enter with Chad because of her no-contact restraining order against him, and she didn't want the police to see her with Chad. Later, Chad called her to tell her that Kassidy had died, and Tristan came into the police station and waited for her turn to assist in the investigation.

4:12 p.m. - Jeff Marshall Interview

Jeff (JM) began his two hour interview with Maine State Police Detectives Jeffrey Linscott(JL) and Scott Harakles(SH). At some point during the investigation, Linscott was designated as the lead investigator for the Maine State Police in this case. After reading Jeff his Miranda rights, even though he wasn't under arrest, Linscott assured Jeff "*...and we certainly haven't accused you of anything...*" (p. 1270)

Linscott described one objective of the interview, "*... we're trying to figure out what happened with... Kassidy and putting a timeline together...*" (p. 1270) Except for a very short timeline assembled a few days later by New Hampshire State Police Sergeant Jim White in an Investigative Plan, there was no other timeline in this case produced by the investigators. At least none was made known or available to Chad's lawyers or to the media or the public. Later, Linscott repeated the police goal, "*...we just want to get the* *truth on all this stuff.*" (p. 1277) Sincere though he was, this interview and the others were focused on gathering information about Chad, as well as gathering the facts about Kassidy,

Jeff stated his desire to help in several ways, e.g. "*I'll tell you everything I know,*" (p. 1271) but about 15 minutes into the interview, another goal appeared in this exchange:
JM The problem was, I want to kick some ass, you know ...
SH I hear you ...
JM I mean he called me up, you know, right out here.
SH It's a very natural response that you're having, so,... why don't we try to take it from the beginning.
JM You know, he'll probably end up getting away with it.
SH Well, we'll see what we can do. (p. 1272)

Jeff said that he and Jennifer first babysat for Kassidy about a year ago, "*basically she'd go for rides in the truck if I had to go the store and get something, you know, I mean we took her shopping, I mean when we had her with us we treated her like she was our own really, I mean ...I don't have any kids, no,... like I said I like kids...*(p. 1273) He said that he became the primary babysitter during the day
about a couple weeks ago.., the main focus of that was, and me and her sister had taken Kassidy a few other times because there were bruises on Kassidy and they felt that it wasn't the right time to, you know what I mean, they didn't want his parents to see her, you know, and being stupid, you know we kind of, I'll admit, you know, kind of say, well, what happened? They said she fell and we kind of like, you know I understand if you don't, we won't jump to conclusions, they kind of, they, you know what I mean? (p. 1273-74) Harakles asked a timeline question, *"When did you first start noticing bruises on this kid in the kid's lifetime?"* and Jeff responded, *"I guess when she was around Chad. I, I don't, let me first of all say this, okay, because Chad is, I consider him a friend of mine....We do landscaping for the guy, I got those two together, you know, I knew he had kind of a history, as far as abuse goes..."* (p. 1274). Later, he added information about the "*abuse*," saying, "*...he was going through a divorce for beating up his ex-wife,...*" (p. 1283)

When Jeff mentioned this part of Chad's history, he didn't mention the court restraining orders against himself, which had been brought by women. He didn't mention the "criminal threatening" and "simple assault" complaints which were resolved in Portsmouth District court 27 days before this interview. Of course, being in a police interview is not the best time to present one's own criminal history, but the better reason for Jeff's not offering that information is that the interview was not about him. It was about Chad's alleged role in Kassidy's death.

Harakles asked again about when Jeff first started seeing bruises on Kassidy, and Jeff responded, "*...when she was around Chad,*" and that began "*About three, four months ago, something like that when I got them two together,...*" (p. 1274) Thus, Jeff was telling the police that the bruises began in early June. More accurately, it had been five months, or 160 days since Jeff and Jennifer introduced Amanda to Chad, and 153 days since Chad had met Kassidy and had her first overnight at Chad's.

Jeff described a call from Amanda, *" '...can we bring Kassidy over to you guys to watch her because we're going up to see mom and dad and I don't want mom and dad to think that Kassidy got hit by Chad?' "* (p. 1274) Harakles and Linscott didn't know that Amanda and Chad visited her parents in Auburn twice since June, and on both visits Kassidy was with them, and so were Jeff and Jennifer. Jeff said nothing about those visits. On both those occasions, Chad stayed overnight. Not once in those 153 days that Chad knew Kassidy did Jeff and Jennifer babysit for Kassidy when Amanda and Chad visited her parents.

Harakles returned again to the issue of time and asked about the bruising "*over the course of the past six months...was it always on the arms or on the face or....?*" and Jeff said there was no bleeding or cuts, and that the bruising was "*Mainly on the face..., maybe on her legs and stuff like that, but you never, You know, I mean kids fall down...Like wounds, just chap lips...just a couple scratches under her eye, but they just got a kitten....* (p. 1275)

Jeff described the changes in Kassidy's behavior since he first knew her,
...she was kind of active baby but then we started noticing like when she got start walking she just, even if she came over to the house she just stand there, you know, and she just stand there and sometimes I'd be in the living room watching TV, Kassidy [would] *be there and she'd just stand and I don't mean for a little while, I mean for hours, you know, like this kid was lost, you know, that this kid was out there and you'd be like "Are you alright?" and she just like look at you and whether she's like, you know, confused because she's brought to a different home here, you know what I mean, I don't know, but when it happens over and over and you try to play, you know, you get a doll for her and you're like "Here you go" you know, and she still does the same thing or you go to bed at night - this is a fine example - went to bed at night, heard something out in the living room,* [I] *said, "Jen, something is weird," because we left her out on the couch, got up walked in the living room, she's standing there in the pitch dark. Now, no little kid does that, just stand there facing the wall, so we asked Mandy, what, you know, there's something, you know, I kind of told you, I guess, she's a little lost or something and, uh, just basically asked Mandy and she says, "Well, when Chad tells her to get in the corner, you know, makes her sit in the corner, stand in the corner, she does something bad," so I think it kind of, you know what I mean, whether she, I don't know why she would think: she was doing something bad, but that's the way she just kind of, she wouldn't walk around, she wouldn't. ..* (p. 1276)

As seen in this book, several people had observed behavioral changes in Kassidy, especially during the last month of her life, but Jeff was the only person to make a causal connection between Kassidy's "time-out's" and such changes.

Linscott asked whether Kassidy had *"ever required any,...medical treatment for anything you've seen, ever any trips to the hospital, to the ER or anything like that?"* Jeff answered, *"She got sick, uh, over at our house and I kind of thought she should have went to the hospital then, but,... they kind of wanted to wait because obviously she had bruises, you know, on her face and they were more concerned with ..."* and he said that Amanda said that to him directly. (p. 1276) The only other references in police reports or trial testimony to Kassidy being sick when at Jeff and Jennifer's were to the three-day/two-night babysitting from Thursday, October 26 to Saturday, from which Kassidy came home hungry and dehydrated.

Jeff continued with the theme of Amanda and Chad hiding Kassidy, saying "*And... that was, and that's basically the reasons for her being at my house. It wasn't because Uncle Jeff was, quote unquote, going to baby sit her because they couldn't go somewhere else, because they had options to go other places. It was because she was at my house because she had bruises and they didn't want those other places to see her and then think something,..."* Asked whether Amanda actually told him that, Jeff said, *"Yeah."* (p. 1276-77) By saying that hiding Kassidy was "*basically the reason*" for Jeff and Jennifer babysitting, Jeff missed other good reasons, such as:

1. Jennifer was Kassidy's aunt, and thus the only available relative within short driving distance,
2. Jeff and Jennifer lived in Kittery which was convenient, especially after Amanda began working at Old Navy, and
3. Babysitting with Jeff and Jennifer was inexpensive, with payment partly through barter and, according to Amanda, with Amanda's food stamps.

Harakles asked Jeff what Amanda had said about Chad's role in causing bruises, and Jeff responded,

Like I went to go give Kassidy a bath over at the house, she was sick one day and she had throw up all down her, and, I changed her clothes, put a new pair on she threw up again so I said, well I'm just going to keep her in her diaper, you know. I told Jen, I said I'm just going to give her a bath this kid freaked out, I mean freaked out on me, couldn't even get her, like I opened up the curtain to bring, put her in the bathtub, didn't want nothing to do with it, now I know kids don't like water, you know, might be a little afraid of water, but this was like terror, so I was like, okay, so I washed her up, you know, got sick again so I brought her back and she just terrified of the shower, so I said to Mandy, you know, I called Mandy up, I think I called Mandy or she called me because I had talked to her on the phone or she might of called to see how Kassidy was, I said, you know, put her in the sh[ower?], *you don't want to do that, she got, I guess Chad put her head under the sink in the kitchen, I think it was, I don't want to assume nothing, but, said put her head under the sink and had water sprayed on her face, now ...* (1277-78)

Jeff was not asked for the place in the timeline, as all he said was "*one day*." If this was an occasion other than the dehydration/bumps-on-head babysitting stint, its date is not known, and there is no other mention of it. If Harakles and Linscott had asked the "When" question, they might then have followed up with questions about what had happened with bathing Kassidy at Amanda's and Chad's, and even at Jeff's, since then. As most parents bathe their toddler children regularly, this would have been an easy issue to investigate. Later, Linscott asked if this water incident was an instance of Chad punishing Kassidy, and Jeff responded, "*I believe so...Discipline kind of action, from the way I took it...*" Then Jeff added a perspective which could have been applied to the whole interview, "*...obviously there's going to be two sides, you know, to what I have to say...*" (p. 1279)

Harakles asked if Amanda ever said *"that Chad acted inappropriately, like, well Chad lost his temperature* [sic, but probably "temper"] *one night and did she ever say that to you, I mean I don't want you to guess. I want you to tell me."* Jeff responded, *"Yeah, yeah, I know that Chad hit her* [Amanda], *you know."* (p. 1278) Rather than explore the details of that firmly stated allegation, Harakles asked, "*How about the baby?* and Jeff answered, *"I believe that's what she said to me too that she, Chad has hit her and stuff, and, you know, she stuck up for the baby in front of Chad, but, it's like, I guess looking back now you kind of see that, and, by all, all accounts, you know, we could be talking about a kid that just fell off of something, you know, it could be the truth."*
Jeff may have been referring to Kassidy's alleged fall from his own truck during his babysitting of October 26-28, but, as he stated, what people say about accidents, "*could be the truth.*" (p. 1278) That is, paraphrasing Freud, sometimes an accident is just an accident.

Linscott said simply, *"We're going to look at everything,"* and Jeff volunteered what seemed to be the "trampoline story," but with an acknowledgment of a real trampoline accident that neither Amanda nor Jennifer mentioned in their interviews.
I don't know, but when she tells me, you know, well, you know, bruise here, bruise there from him, you know, pulling her in the corner, something like that, or, you know, and then he starts telling me, well, she was jumping on the trampoline with my little son and she fell off, you know and I knew of one time she did fall off when Jen and Mandy were out there because Jen brought it up to me... (p 1278)

Without a new question, Jeff described Kassidy's proclivity for falls and failing to protect herself with her hands,
... you'd be like "Mumma's here," [and] *she'd get right up, her arms, like stayed down and she would run like you were supposed to catch her or something off the bed and land right on the floor... I mean, it was amazing as far as, you know where kids, I think a person's first instinct is protect their head, you know, protect themselves, that was not her instinct whatsoever, you know....* (p. 1278-79)

Linscott asked about bruising in general, and Jeff said,
..what happens is, the bruises would tend to fade, you know, because after a while I guess they start going away ... and then, like the next day, come back, bruises are there again, so it's like, being grabbed again, you know, the same place, you know, except be a little darker, you know this time around still have the yellow from, uh, other side and I pointed out to my next door neighbor again, I came out, I'm like and we checked her body over, you know, lift up her shirt and stuff and, he was like, you know, we should do something, you know, say something. I said "I know," you know, but, you know, their excuse when you talk to them, "Oh, she fell off the bed or she fell off of this," in my eyes, I can believe some of that because I've seen just how she is as far as running off of stuff, I think because the same as far as her just being clumsy like that, but I think when it starts happening over and over, you know what I mean, because right here you know ... [1279]
Jeff told the police,

I know Chad wasn't fond of having a little kid around, you know what I mean, as far as that stuff goes, but we always took it, we would never say no, in taking Kassidy, I don't, and actually I would say yes more than Jen would, you know, Jen would be mad,... (p. 1282)

Jeff explained to Harakles and Linscott his business relationship to Chad, but he didn't mention that Chad had told him late in October that his contracts would not be renewed after the current contract period. Said Jeff,

He's actually, and this is what makes it real hard for me, alright, because I don't want to see anybody in trouble. I'm pissed because, of, what's been going on in the past day or so, past of couple days, and now this, but me and Chad, had like a business kind of relationship, my company does work for McDonald's, and he's the area rep..., so he oversees some of the stores that we take care of, you know, he was going through a divorce,... (p. 1283)

Several times during the interview, Jeff made general statements about Chad's character that fit into the police profile of a manipulative child and wife abuser. Jeff said, "*...he's like that, he's controlling..,*" and then moved on to something else. (p. 1283) About Amanda's relationship to Chad, he said, "*Mandy is very much into Chad, you know what I mean, she'd do anything for him, I really believe that,... it was like, bend over backwards, you know, make him happy, I mean, and, you know, she's young, so, she's 19 or whatever....*" (p. 1283) His point would have been stronger if he had told the police Amanda's correct age of 18, but they would soon learn that from Amanda's interview and their search of police and government records. The one person in the case who didn't know Amanda's true age, yet, was Chad. Incredibly, it would take him another nine months before he fully realized that Amanda was 18 when he met her.

Jeff had views about when to talk about others and when not to do so. He said that Amanda told him that Tristan had said to her, "*Get out of there, you know, he's going to hurt you...*" Later he described that advice as "*kind of weird.... to have an ex come over to your house...I would never go over to somebody else*['s] *house... whether you're there to pick up the kid or not, keep your mouth shut...*" (p. 1284-85) As with much of this case, this is an example of where there are many other possible interpretations of events or statements. For example, Tristan may have been wanting to discourage Amanda's relationship with Chad as ex-spouses sometimes want to hold on, in some way, or don't want their ex-spouses to get into new relationships, generally.

Jeff said, "*...I've gone to a couple parties at his house, you know, he gets kind of mad, he's got a temper on him ... Oh yeah, oh yeah, he got into a fight one night I was over at his house having a party,.....*" (p. 1284-85) There was no request by the police for more details about the alleged "*fight.*"

Jeff volunteered observations about Amanda and Jennifer's mother and stepfather, "*I don't want to say 'the in-laws.'* " He said that he and Chad "*both had conflicts with her parents, as far as how they, try to use their kids for money and stuff like that, so me and Chad would always talk about that, you know, it kind of ticked off the girls a little bit... we'd always talk about them, you know, these guys are, you know, are low lifes, you know what I mean....*" (p. 1285) Chad doesn't recall any conflicts with Amanda's parents, and he didn't know anything about Amanda's financial issues with her parents until after Kassidy's death. He didn't know, either, that Amanda was giving Jeff and Jennifer her State of Maine-provided food stamps in partial payment for babysitting. Chad did not even know that Amanda was receiving food stamps.

Asked about Chad's drug use, Jeff said, "*I don't want anyone mad at me...but... like he was not into marijuana, which I assumed he was, but he had done coke, and I thought that kind of odd, but that's what Mandy said...*" (p. 1285)

About Kassidy's condition on Wednesday, Jeff said, "*like yesterday, we were at our house, she had no bruises, she was awfully quiet though, this real like, kind of, you know, and she kind of laid in bed, and she was only there for an hour or so, maybe a little over an hour... her legs were bothering her.*" (p. 1287) He wasn't asked anything more about his care for Kassidy that afternoon, such as what she ate, or did he change a diaper, or how often did he check on her. The entire babysitting stint was more like two and half hours, according to Amanda's and Jennifer's descriptions of their afternoons, but Kassidy clearly had on Wednesday the bruise on her right eye from hitting the glass table in Chad's living room, and the kitten scratch under the same eye. A few minutes later, Jeff added an observation, "*...the scratches that were on her face, I can't remember what side they were on, but they were there yesterday, you know, but as far as the black and blues go, she might a had a little black and blue down here, right here...*" (p. 1289) Those were the scratches from Kassidy's new kitten. She may also have had a recent set of bruises from Chad holding her chin when obtaining eye contact, but Chad does not recall any such incident in the few days before Kassidy's death.

Then Jeff described the Wednesday pickup of Kassidy at his home and the two subsequent phone calls from Chad,

I got a phone call, he was on the, supposedly over by the Dover, uh, toll booth and he was in traffic and he said, you know, he's like, "Something is weird with her," and I said, "What, what's weird with her?" And he says that, "Kind of, looking kind of dazed," and I said, "Well, she's kind of like, dazed today too," and he says, "Yeah that's really weird," you know, and then all of a sudden he gets to the house, I get a phone call,... "You won't believe what happened to her," and I said, "What?" and he says "I put her outside of the car, I went over to get" his son out of the, out of that side of the car, got the son, he came around the corner and "she was flat on her face on the cement." So I said to him then, I said, "What'd you do?" He says, "Well, I picked her up, she had dirt on her hair, I guess," and I said, "Well, not good," but then we kind of, I said well, she kind of, she's not all there most of the... I felt a little bit suspicious but not, and then, after that I got another phone call, that supposedly they were playing baseball in the room, and, his son hit a baseball hit her in the face... he's like, "You won't believe this, she's like dazing out, like her eyes are going in the back of her head," (p. 1287-88)

Linscott asked about Chad's motivation for calling Jeff that third time, "*Is he calling you for advice or something, or?*" and Jeff responded, "*Yeah, I, I really believe that... he kind of felt like, he probably done something, and didn't know... instead of calling 911 like Mr. Marshall did...*" (p. 1288.) At the time, the police officers likely didn't know that Jeff's call to 911 was his 11th call, and was made14 minutes after finding Kassidy in the bed. Ironically, Jeff's first three calls on the 9th were to Chad.

Jeff indicated his skepticism about Chad's relaying of the ballplaying incident, saying that on Thursday morning, after seeing Kassidy, "*... I said to Jen, 'Does that look like a baseball to you?' you know, because, and,... but it was hard to tell what it was that actually could do it, you know, because I don't play baseball, and I don't want to say what a bruise looks like from a baseball, but, it just looked like a bunch a little bruises,...* (p. 1289)

Relaying what happened that morning, Thursday, Jeff said,

... so she brought her in, she laid her in bed with us, you know, she was eating Cocoa Puffs, ... chocolate cereal or whatever, she has a baggy, she got into bed and when she was coming over to get into the bed, she's kind of walking funny, now that wasn't no surprise to me because earlier we had heard of a situation where Mandy called us in the middle of the night, or not in the middle of the night, but I believe at night or it was during the day it was some, but she did call us on the phone and said, "You won't believe this, Kassie's walking weird now." I guess Chad did something to her leg, and I assumed, pulled her leg or something because, and she came over and all this week she's been kind of limping, you know, favoring her leg, and, today she comes in, she's a little, favoring her legs, you know, uh, so I said, Jen, I said, "You got to see this, man." She wasn't with it, you know, she was just kind of laying there, you know, when you went to go pick her up, when she was laying in bed, she didn't want to move, you know, it was just like she was like ...Chad did something to her leg, you know... (p. 1289)

Regarding the cereal, Jeff later said, "*...that was the only thing I saw her eat this morning,...I don't think I actually saw her eat one. She kind of... had them next to her...*" and then he said that he didn't give her anything else to eat, and nothing to drink either, "*I didn't see a bottle, or, something...*" (p. 1300). When talking about Kassidy's legs, Jeff didn't mention that a few days earlier, he had tripped over Kassidy's foot, which was a possible cause of her limping. He did mention that accident in his statement, along with others, but the police did not ask Jeff about anything in his statement.

Linscott asked if Jeff had seen any bruises on Kassidy's legs and Jeff said, "*Nope, from changing her diapers and stuff, no bruises on her leg or whatever...*" (p. 1290) One useful detail to ask would have been the dates and times of Kassidy's recent diaper changes at Jeff's. At Chad's trial, Detective Herbert Leighton testified that when he searched Jeff's and Jenn's home on the night Kassidy died, there were no used diapers anywhere in the home. (Transcript, p. 202) The date of Jeff's last diaper change for Kassidy is not known.

Linscott asked if Jeff had seen anything unusual on her body, in addition to bruises on her face, and he answered, "*I mean, she had bruises on her butt, ... supposedly they're from falling down or something...*" (p. 1290) Jeff gave no indication of the timing of this observation and his interviewers did not ask, as the subject changed again.

Jeff described the Windex incident,

....like she got into Windex one day, you know, and started drinking from the Windex bottle,... but once again, it was very rare that you actually saw her active, as far as doing that, but she was kind of sneaky too, you know, it's like, you leave a room, just, I suppose every kid has, you know, (inaudible) Windex I was like, okay, and you're trying to wash her up, you're trying to (inaudible) you've got to spit this up, you can't be, I don't know if she actually took a lot, but she definitely was playing with it, you know, because I heard the bottle fall on the floor, I came out and there she was, .." (p. 1290)

Jennifer stated in her first interview that the Windex bottle was in the open, on the kitchen table when Kassidy found it. (p. 940) Harakles asked for the date of the Windex incident and Jeff answered, "*a couple... weeks ago, I think. Jen would know better than I do as far as time goes. She's better at that... I called Jen because I'm like, 'What do I do?' you know... I love kids, but it's like what do you do....I didn't know if I should call the... hospital...*" (p. 1290) The Windex incident actually occurred during the three-day/two-night babysitting beginning Thursday, October 26, so his estimate of two weeks was exactly correct. However, Jennifer said in her interview that she was there when Jeff spanked Kassidy for getting into the Windex, whereas Jeff said during this interview that he "*called*" Jennifer. Jeff also testified (p. 112, 235) that Jennifer was at home at the time, so maybe his use of the word "*called*" meant "call to the next room" rather than "call on the phone." At the end of describing the Windex incident, Jeff said, "*... but she seemed fine after that.*" (p. 1290) which was a recurrent theme in this tragic story. Kassidy would have a problem or an accident and she would recover, and the hopeful adults around her would think that "*she seemed fine*."

Jeff repeated the reason for Amanda using him as a babysitter, "*...but one of the main reasons is, due to the fact of the bruises, you know.*" (p. 1291) Jeff and Jennifer were concerned about bringing Kassidy out in public,

But that was the other thing, you feel, it's like Jen's like yesterday, you know, she said, "You want to bring her to the store with you and stuff and you feel kind of weird," because here's a kid that's obviously, you know, I don't care how many bruises the kid has, you know, it's not my kid first of all and I feel kind of weird going out in public, you know, and have somebody saying, "Oh my god, you know, she's got bruises here and here," you know what I mean,... (p. 1292)

Ironically, Jeff's and Jennifer's concern of being wrongly accused of abusing Kassidy was the same concern that Chad had expressed, twice, to Amanda. The first time was after she had taken Kassidy with her to a medical appointment in October with her friend, Emily Conley. The only other time when Chad implicitly expressed that concern was on the evening of November 8, when he suggested that Amanda take Kassidy to see a doctor, after her bruises disappeared.

Jeff did not mention to the police the time that he and Jennifer put makeup on Kassidy's face to hide a bruise or bruises when they took her shopping.

Jeff returned to the subject of Kassidy's general behavior,

... like I said the time she has, she's either cried or when she's sleeping, this is another thing, you should verify with her mother, she'll be sleeping and then all of a sudden you

hear (JM demonstrating child sobbing sounds) like, you know, just like, when you're a little kid and you're out there and you're like, you're crying so much and you're like (JM demonstrating child sobbing sounds) you know, you get that (JM demonstrating child sobbing sounds) she'd sleep, you know, she's sound asleep and all of a sudden (JM demonstrating child sobbing sounds) you know, she'd do that all the time, and it kind of made me wonder, what the hell is she dreaming about, you know, she's, you know, she's dreaming of crying or what, you know.... she'd cry in the middle of the night and she'd get up, which is normal for a little kid, you know, to cry. So you'd bring her in the bed with you, you know and have her sleep in bed, you know, and while she's sleeping, she'd start crying again, you know, and its like, and Jen witnessed that, you know, many a nights she'd just sit there and start crying, okay, and auntie would say, "Put her out there, let her, you know, she'll cry herself to bed." You put her out there and cry herself to bed, then again, we heard things that she gets up in the middle of the night, we'd go in there in the dark and there she is just standing there, and I don't mean standing there with something in her hand or something, I mean, looking at a dead wall, just, you know, her arms down, you know, and you're like, "What can possibly be going through this kid's head, as far as what she thinking, what she doing," you know, and, "Kassidy, it's time to go to bed," now the minute you go pick her up she start crying, you know, it's like she's in her own world as far as whether she's being abused, and, you know what I mean, she's kind of going through that dreaming or something of it, but, I don't know. (p. 1293-94)

Linscott asked how many times Kassidy had stayed overnight with Jeff and Jennifer, and Jeff responded, *"I don't, I don't know.... More than once, I couldn't say an exact time."* Linscott asked further, *"I mean, more than, more than 10 times,..."* Jeff seemed to respond affirmatively, *"Probably, I would, I would say, I guess, um,..,"* and he resumed talking about Kassidy crying in the night. (p. 1293-94) The question deserved to be clearly put, and it deserved a clear answer. The answer was that Kassidy was babysat overnight at Jeff and Jennifer's for six nights, over five babysitting stints since June 9. (List of Overnights.) The last overnight was the three day/two night babysitting of October 26-28.

Jeff described Chad's call the previous evening after the Tee-ball accident,

...he says, "I don't know what to do," you know, it was a frantic, it wasn't like, it was like a frantic, "I don't know what to do, you know, her eyes are back of her head now, she's kind of sitting there and, you know, what do I do," you know, she's not coherent, you know, and, and then all of a sudden it's like, "she's snapping out of it," you know, and that's when we got off the phone... (p. 1294)

Chad's call to Jeff, as retold by Jeff, was eerily similar to Jeff's frantic calls the next day to Chad, Jennifer, and 911.

Jeff then described Chad's call to him that morning of Kassidy's death, at 9:47 a.m. during which Chad said he had received a call,

...from the town of Rochester,... I thought he said DHS, or, you know, the Department of Human Services or something like that,... saying, you know, talk to him or left a message or something, he was very concerned about that, you know, he's like "1 don't want to be putting up with this shit, you know, they're asking me about child abuse over her, it's like, 1 ought to have her and her mother out." You know, and 1 was just like, "You know, we don't know what it is, it could be for court fee, you know," but this was, it could have been for court, you know, for his ex-wife, he has custody over the kids, you know, it could be making sure he's getting ... (p. 1294-95)

He said that Chad did ask him how Kassidy was doing and Jeff responded, "*...I'm, ' she's just laying there,' you know ...*" (p. 1295)

Jeff returned to the subject of the previous day's pickup of Kassidy by Chad,

... let me say this much. 1 know when she left my house last night, and this is the part that pisses me off the most and this gets me quite mad about him, is that when she left my house last night, she wasn't, 1 don't want to say overly spunk or anything, she just kind of sat there and stuff, but that was her way... But she had no real facial bruises, nothing that would, you know, besides her walking problem, and besides, these are, these are starting to clear up, you know, the ones right here. I brought her outside in that car, you know, she was going off with him to go home, and that was it, you know, he didn't have a safety belt,

whether that's against the law or not, you know, that's, 1 don't know if that's considered child abuse or not, but, to me, it's like, you know, let's just get car seat down the street and, I'm sure parents do it all the time,... (p. 1295)

Harakles then asked about Kassidy's appearance that morning, the 9th, and Jeff said, *It looked like something had happened... She had bruises all over her face. I mean, how can you not see something different?... these were fresh, these weren't something that just, you know, and they certainly didn't happen over at my house yesterday, you know, without a doubt, they didn't happen yesterday over at my house,...*

...but today she was just like laying there, you know, and I was like (inaudible) put the blankets over her. She had blankets on her, she's just sitting there watching TV, and that's basically, you know, how I left her and then, I got up, went outside, grabbed the news, uh, the, post office box stuff, came in, went in to check on her and she's sitting in there, and the look on her face, I mean, it scared me, because I'm like, what the hell, you know what 1 mean, just like her eyes were like in the back of her head just laying there, and I mean, 1 hadn't paid any attention to her for like, a, probably an hour, hour and a half or so, you know, because I was too busy laying down watching TV, you know, and, uh, it's just like she was in shock, I took down the blankets, I'm like, "Kassidy, Kassidy, are you there?" and I started like, you know, I didn't shake her violently but I just kind of, I'm like, "Kassidy, Kassidy," you know, and then I started, she was like gargling or something, like,... breathing kind of (JM demonstrating child labored breathing sounds) like that, you know, something like that, and I was like, alright, so I started pumping on her stomach, you know, and.... I didn't know what to do, and then I called up my,...girlfriend at work, I said, "Something's wrong with Kassidy," and she's like, "Well, I'm too busy," you know, like, "You got to get a hold of Mandy." What do I do, you know. Tried calling 411 to get a hold of Mandy. Couldn't get a hold of her. Called back Jen. Jen said, "Get, call 911," [I] *called 911, you know.... Brought her out to the kitchen. Put water on her face, you know, trying to revive her or whatever, you know, I could do, um, carried her out, got her out of the house. Brang her down that way the ambulance could just pull right up...I couldn't do anything.... but, uh, I lost a little brother with cancer, (inaudible), I was in the same room with him when he passed away, you know, he just laid there and he kind of died and I was like, you know, I did not think, they said that she passed away. I did not think that she was, at that point, I thought, you know, she's just going through the same thing she went through with Chad, you know, kind of dazed. And I just kept pumping on her stomach, kept trying to get some breath into her and I felt up here, I believe it was right here, I felt on her, you know, she had blood pressure going, or whatever you call it, you know, and I was like, everything's going to be good, and then the cop came, and, said, "Well, no, you don't want to push on her stomach, you want to pump, pump right here." I said, "Okay," so we started pumping right there, he started giving her mouth to mouth ...* (p. 1296-98)

Jeff described his second conversation with Chad on this day, the 9th. Although Jeff didn't state the exact time, it was at 2:38 p.m. and Jeff told his interviewers, "*... I'm like, 'We're at the police department, you know, you need to come down here.'... like, he didn't even know, that anything was wrong...*" (p. 1302) Jeff 's observation was correct, as Chad didn't know that Kassidy had died until he arrived at the police station.

Scott Harakles asked Jeff, *"Do you remember what were times, like did you check on her at 9:30, or 10, when Barney's on, or do you, do you remember anything like that?"* and Jeff responded, *"No, I just came in because my shoes were in the bedroom, you know, I got my shoes, and put my shoes on and, you know, at that time, you know, she was kind of, not sleeping or whatever, you know, and kind of...* (p. 1303) At Chad's trial, Jeff said that his only mid-morning observation of Kassidy was when he followed his cat, Toby, into the bedroom, thinking that that Toby had taken something. (Transcript, Dec. 6, 2001, p. 169) Jeff described his discovery, after getting the mail, of Kassidy in distress, *"...and I'm like, I see her and I'm like, 'Kassidy,' and she's like .."* (p. 1303)

Harakles returned to the subject of Chad's call the previous evening and asked about the ball that Chad said had hit Kassidy, "*Did he say baseball, like an actual...*" and Jeff responded,

Yeah, I don't know... Probably a wiffle ball... You know, I can't be sure though.

...But this is the other thing I want to make very clear to you, okay?..., I think Mandy was kind of getting sick of the bruises,... Mandy's going to college, took some college classes, and, ... Chad's sister would come over, and,... pick Mandy up, and Chad didn't want Kassidy around the house because she had bruises, and, I, you know, ...I think I can remember like Mandy saying, "It's because, you know, we don't want them to think that something's happening with ... ," you know, it was always kind of like, "Can you watch her?" You know, we were kind of the ones that watched her, she had a bruise, or, you know what I mean, that way I kind of, no one else would kind of see it. (p. 1304-06)

When he said, "*going to college*," Jeff was referring to the money management seminar that Amanda and Nicole attended on three Thursday evenings, October 19, October 26, and November 2. Chad babysat for Kassidy for the first session, and Jeff babysat for the second, which became the three-day/two-night babysitting stint. On November 2, Jeff babysat for Kassidy during the day, and brought Kassidy to a rendezvous spot in Portsmouth, where he gave her to Amanda and Nicole, and where they, in turn, gave her to Chad, who arrived a few minutes later and took her home.
Most of the babysitting by Jeff in October was to enable Amanda to work at home, uninterrupted, on the survey work for Bruce. On those occasions, there was no issue of anyone seeing Kassidy because she and Amanda were home alone during the day. Thus, sending Kassidy to Jeff's to prevent people from seeing her at Chad's home was not a likely motive.

Scott Harakles conversed with Jeff about people being accountable for their actions, and Jeff said, "*I would say, after getting phone calls like I did last night....and the phone calls today, I kind of swing towards the fact that, you know, something happened last night, and...**I should have probably told him** last night when she was going in a daze, but 'You need to bring this kid to the hospital,' you know, or something...*" (p. 1308, emphasis added) Something did happen on Wednesday night, which was that Kassidy was hit in the head with a Tee-ball, but Jeff and Scott Harakles appeared to be talking about something more criminal that they believed "*happened.*" At Chad's trial, Jeff testified that he said to Chad that evening, " '*You know, you need to bring her to the hospital.*' " (Transcript, Dec. 6, 2001, p. 138) That's different from what he told Harakles and Linscott which is that "***I should have probably told him***..." (emphasis added)

Scott Harakles then said to Jeff, "*...from what you're saying, uh, I think you're a pretty special guy in that, you cared quite a bit for this little girl that, wasn't even a blood relative, um, and I don't know too many young people your age ..,*" and Jeff responded, *"I should have done something, that's what I should have fucking done."* (p. 1306) A few minutes later, Harakles made his, and the police's, view of the case more clear,

Well, you got to also remember,... you're a bit of a victim here as well, because what you had in this guy is trust, right? He was your friend, so you had some trust, and he betrayed your trust, let's say that that's what he did, betrayed your trust, don't take it so hard. I mean, is it your fault if someone puts one over on you? I mean, I don't know if you should beat yourself up about that. Yeah, you and I both know, because you're a big boy. You and I both know that it would have been nicer had you been able to maybe report it, or call someone, but you didn't do it. You had trust in your friend. That's not a crime, you believed in him, you didn't believe he was a nasty person....when they take advantage of you like this,.... sounds like you have a trusting nature about you and somebody pulled the wool over your eyes on some things. (p. 1308)

Thus, Chad Evans was already labeled a "*nasty person.*" This appraisal was made approximately, an hour and a quarter into Jeff's interview, making the time approximately 5:30 p.m. Jennifer and Amanda were still in their interviews, and Chad had not yet been interviewed. It had been five hours since Kassidy's death.

Harakles and Linscott said to Jeff several times during the interview, variations of the message, "*I don't want to put words in your mouth...*" and then they did just that. Linscott asked about Amanda's arrival at Jeff's that morning, "*Did she say Chad did anything to Kassidy?... Do you think she was inferring, when she said, 'Look at her face,' do you think she was inferring, you know, 'Look what Chad did to her face?'*" Jeff responded, "*Yeah, oh yeah.*" (p. 1309)

Asked about the relationship between Amanda and Jennifer and their discussions, Jeff said, "*...I know that Mandy has talked to her about Chad, you know, grabbing her by the throat, grabbing Mandy by the throat or hitting her or something like that, or, you know, being kind of, a little abusive with her, and I know Mandy's friends, had said the same thing,...*" (p. 1310)

Linscott asked about Chad's abuse of his wife, and Jeff said,

... I know he went to court over the assault and stuff ...his name's in the newspaper, you know, he, they quote, unquote, called it "the worst beating in New Hampshire, in a domestic abuse beating in New Hampshire," that's what, you know, everyone at the stores had said, uh, but 1 never really, 1 guess this is where the stupid part from me comes out, because 1 never said, "I got these two together," ... She [Amanda] *always thought it was probably because his wife cheated on him, you know, and well, what made his wife cheat on her, make her leave, you know, urn, but recently 1 had said that, I told that to Jen, you know, I said, "You know, he is kind of abusive." And Mandy talked about going to a party or something for McDonald's. They went there and they got into a fight, you know, he grabbed her by the throat....* (p. 1311)

Regarding Jeff's understanding of the fight between Chad and Tristan on March 28, 1999, it's a tragic truth that the "*worst beatings*" suffered in domestic violence cases result in death. The basic source of Jeff's statement was apparently Amanda and she apparently based her statement upon what Tristan told her during a heart-to-heart conversation. However, Jeff embellished the story, as no newspaper had ever called the incident a "*worst beating in New Hampshire.*" There were no separate articles in any newspaper about the incident, and Foster's Daily Democrat did not include the incident in its regular section, "Police Log" for Rochester. The "Police Log" in the April 6, 1999 Rochester Times did contain five entries for March 28, including this entry,

2:48 a.m. - Chad Evans, 27, of 191 Milton Road is charged with second degree assault, a weapon offense and criminal restraint.

There was no followup about that McDonald's party, and thus there was no question about the date, which was Friday, August 25.

Jeff mentioned bruises on Amanda, "*...she did come over with bruises too, ... I'm trying to think where they were.... I don't know where they were exactly. I want to say around the throat... on her arm but I can't be quite sure, you know.*" Jeff said that when he and Jennifer argued, "*...it's usually just us yelling at each other... and that's it. You don't get into a physical altercation....*" Scott Harakles then left the interview, saying, "*Well, you guys touch on that...and... probably wrap it up shortly...*" (p. 1312)

Jeff correctly observed that Chad was more of a physical contact person than he was, saying, "*I'm not the kind of a guy that comes up to you and goes you know, hits you on the shoulder.... He is, as far as he'll come up... He uses himself in that sense...*" (p. 1312) Chad was a person who is very comfortable with touching others, and being touched as well. With Amanda, he was comfortable with touching, hugging and chasing in a loving and playful way. Not everyone is. For such people whose relationships with others is more physical, the line between permitted physical contact and non-permitted contact is sometimes hard to discern.

Linscott asked what Amanda had said about her own bruises, and Jeff said,

Oh yeah, "These are from Chad," you know, and, you know, "did this."... like I said, I think it was around here, you know, it was a pretty good one, you know and she's the kind of girl, though, that will go right back at him but even so, even if she did go back at him, he had fucking no right to be hitting her....there were other arguments, you know,...as far as the bruises go, you know, ones that I could see, that was probably one of the few times that I saw the actual... black and blues, yeah. (p. 1313-14)

Linscott then tried to nail down the dates and times of Jeff and Jennifer's recent babysitting for Kassidy. Trying to sort out his and Jennifer's schedules, Jeff said, "*... Jen doesn't like doing it* [babysitting for Kassidy] *if it's her day off, you know, because she's worked all week, you know... but she's good about that as far as taking care of her.*" (p. 1315) Jeff thought, correctly, that he had babysat Kassidy on Monday and Tuesday, but not during the previous weekend.

Jeff Linscott asked Jeff if Kassidy, "*ever pick*[ed] *up any of those bruises on her from your place, do you think?*" and Jeff responded,

Oh yeah, I mean, I'm sure she did. I'm sure she picked up a few here or there, um, put her in the truck one day and had her standing up there to go somewhere else, and she fell out of the [truck], *she didn't hit her face or nothing, she seemed like she didn't have any bruise on her, but that's just, you know what I mean, she's just standing there and you try to get the safety belt thing locked at her ...You know, you're like, "Oh," you know, and you pick her up, wipe her off and she doesn't cry, you know, she didn't cry so...* (p. 1317)

Linscott did not ask about the date of that fall. It wasn't clear if Jeff was talking about a fall from his truck two weeks previous, during the three-day/two-night babysitting beginning on Thursday, October 26, or an incident one or two days before the interview which Will Peirce witnessed. However, in the latter incident, Jeff and Will later stated that Jeff caught Kassidy before she touched the ground, so there would have been no need to "*pick her up*" or "*wipe her off,*" so it's likely that Jeff was referring to the previous fall, or to another.

Linscott asked about other accidents or discipline at Jeff's, and Jeff responded,
The only, the only time she got disciplined over at our house is when I slapped her on the ass one time and that was it, we never, you know, for getting into stuff, anyway, and I believe Jen was there, but I'm not quite sure, but, you know, and that, I mean I'm not one that, we're talking about a little kid that's, obviously, from a little bit of weight could, do some damage so, she's just a little kid.

Harakles returned to the interview from his conversations with other investigators, and he asked, *"You smacked with your hand?"* Jeff implicitly agreed, saying that it was *"on the butt,"* and that she had a diaper on. Asked if she cried, Jeff said, "*No, not, not really, not really.*" (p. 1318)

Linscott asked Jeff about what Chad may have told him about disciplining kids in his home. Jeff said,

Oh, he's strict, he's strict.... I'm trying to think, ... he said he turned the corner, you know, he slapped her little ass, you know, if she misbehaved,... he'd get mad, like, if he tries to teach her how to talk, you know, like give her a grape, and, if she said, you know, he tried to make her say "please." you know, he'd lose control about that, you know, he'd grab her arm or something, I mean, you know, but Mandy really said that, you know, it got a little abusive, I mean, she was the one that kind of told us as far as, you know, Chad smacked her if she came downstairs,.... She was in bed but she got out and now she's downstairs and he smacked her on, you know, that kind of stuff... not... right by any means. Officially that's not your kid, and it wasn't his kid. (p.1319-20)

Jeff's understanding of the relationship between Chad and Kassidy was dramatically different from Chad's. First, Chad never said to Jeff that he spanked her or "*slapped her little ass,*" because he didn't spank Kassidy during the entire 153 days that he knew Kassidy.

The interview with Jeff then moved to identifying other people in Chad's life. Jeff estimated that five-year old Brent was five years old and he said that he believed Chad had adopted Brent. In fact, Chad and Tristan had considered that option, and talked with a Rochester lawyer about it, Stephen Brown, but the idea was dropped. Even when the police later confirmed that Chad didn't adopt Brent, they still might have asked themselves why a man who was thought willing to adopt his wife's son by another man would later abuse his girlfriend's daughter by another man.

Scott Harakles asked if Chad's alleged cocaine use was "*a joke about an incident he did a long time ago or that he might still be dabbling in even now?*" and Jeff responded, "*Still be doing...But like I said, I never seen the stuff on them, I never seen it over at his house, I never seen, you know, anything.* (p. 1326) As was the case about so much of what Jeff said about Chad, his knowledge was not by his own observation, but was second or third hand. Asked about his own use of drugs or alcohol, Jeff said that Chad, "*knows I'm straight and narrow... that's part of the reason why I don't get invited over at many parties anymore...*" (p. 1327)

Then Jeff requested that the tape recorder be turned off and what was said during that "time-out" was not revealed. When the recorder was turned back on, he said,
Whether that [the subject of the discussion while the tape recorder was off] *matters or not, but,... she* [Amanda] *said to me, you know, "It's really weird how he spends all this money and stuff," you know, and he does because, I been over there and he's been gambling on football games and stuff, and I said, how much money can one person, you know, I knew he probably makes about a grand a week from McDonald's, or maybe a little bit over, but I said that's an awful lotto money when you're down 900 bucks on a pool for one week. That's a lot a money to me, you know, I'm like, damn, and uh, she said, "Yeah, it's really weird," you know, I'm like, "Well, where else does all the money go?" I said, "What does he do, marijuana?" "No, no. He used to but he doesn't anymore," she says, "Don't say anything, but he does coke every now ... ," you know what I mean?* (p. 1328)

Jeff said that conversation occurred a week-and-a-half to two weeks ago.
The interview was closing down and both officers asked if there was anything else Jeff wanted to add, and there was this exchange

JM *This is a god damned little girl, okay, something happened, I'm pissed off, but I'm, I'm sad but I'm pissed off, I'm pissed off that, this asshole, you know, just like out there I said I don't want to be in here when he comes in.*

SH And Lord only knows what he's going to say, I mean, you're not a dumb kid. Lord only knows what this guy's going to say.

JM I'll confront him about anything he has to say.

SH Don't worry, that's what we're here for, and you got to trust us to do a good investigation.

JM As long as you've got enough guards, you can put me in the same room with him, I mean, I'm so cross I'll confront him on anything he has to say.

SH Just trust us to do a decent investigation here and get to the truth, but,... you know him better than we do, you know... how he handles things with his ex-wife, ...

JM I just, I believe in God so much, you know, I got a little brother, I believe the angel in my life, and I just don't want to, get up there someday and have her be mad at me that we didn't do nothing all along, you know, and now here I am, oh, we're finally doing something, finally telling people about this stuff, you know, and I, a little too fucking late, you know.

SH Well, like I told you,... if everything that you're telling me is, is how it really is ...

JM I'll confront him 100 and ...

SH Just listen to me, if you got duped, I don't know how much you should beat yourself up about it, you know what I mean, you trusted someone, you trusted a friend, so I don't know how much you should, like I know this is going to hurt you and I know you're going to hurt for awhile, but just remember that I said this to you, it's not all your fault, it might feel like your fault, you might feel like you should have done something, but, you trusted a friend, which is something we do all the time, you trusted this kid, not to be hurting your, maybe future sister- in-law .. (p. 1330)

Jeff then agreed to searches of his home and truck which the officers asked for, but not because a baby died at his home that day. Instead, the stated reason for the search seemed to be bureaucratic box checking. Linscott asked for permission almost apologetically, "*...if at some point,... if someone else out there may say, you know, 'Look at.. Jeff. He was doing something shaky.'... Would it be a problem if... say I... wanted to look through your apartment for any reason?*" Jeff responded, "*Go ahead...and you can talk to my neighbors, you can talk to my friends, you can talk to anybody.*" (p. 1331)

Harakles asked Jeff if he would be willing to take a polygraph, lie detector test, and Jeff responded, "*I'd probably be willing to do it, like I, you know, I have, like I said, I have nothing to worry about.*" Harakles said that if "*he* [Chad] *points the finger at you, the person I interviewed, ... we take offense to that because we sat here and talked to you....*" Jeff also asked if he could be present during their interview with Chad, but the offer was implicitly declined. For the officers, Jeff's openness to a polygraph was important. Said Harakles, "*...just your willingness, if I could tell my boss that, yeah, he would be willing to take a polygraph test, you may never have to take one.*" (p. 1332) Later, Jeff's polygraph test was scheduled for the following Tuesday, November 14. Jeff's interview ended at 6:15 p.m. and he remained at the police station for several more hours, as Jennifer was still being interviewed, and other members of the Bortner/Conley extended family and friends were to be interviewed. To the extent possible, the key people were kept in separate rooms.

4:15 p.m. - Jennifer Bortner Interview

At almost the same time as Jeff's interview, Jennifer(JB) began her one-and-a half hour interview, excluding a 50 minute break, by Maine State Police Detective Jeffrey Smith(JS) and Kittery Police Detective Steve Hamel(SH). The interview was in Hamel's office. Going over Jennifer's family history and relationships, she said Jeff was, "*My fiance. See my ring,*" (p. 909) and that their relationship began when he "*harassed me for a date.*" (p. 910) It was a tense time for everyone that afternoon and evening, and little lapses occurred in most interviews. Jennifer's first such lapse came when she was asked for Chad's last name, "*Chad, what the hell is his name? I can't believe that I'd forget his last name.*" (p. 910) It came to her about five minutes later.

Jennifer's grasp of dates and time was relatively accurate. She estimated that she had introduced Chad and Amanda 6-7 months earlier, where as the actual number was five. Later in the interview, she correctly gave Amanda's age as 18. (p. 939) She estimated that Amanda had moved in with Chad "*about three or four months ago,*" (p. 912) and that was a good estimate, as it was closer to the other side of four. Jen said she had worked at Perfumania, *"About, almost a month. It's more like 3 weeks. I work with Jeff in the summer."* (p. 913) Later she said that she started work on October 1. (p. 976) Given the relative accuracy of her other estimates of time, and given that her start of work at Perfumania was more recent than those earlier events, and given her use of a specific date, October 1, her estimate that she had worked at Perfumania three to four weeks was probably close to accurate.

Jennifer said that "*...Mandy just got a job at Old Navy and.... that's why were watching the kid for the last week and a half almost two weeks we've been watching the kid.*" (p. 914) This was another indication that Amanda spent some number of hours the previous week at Old Navy in training. She said that the arrangement was "*Just until, cause Mandy was supposed to find a babysitter.*" Later, she repeated this statement of purpose, "*I said I'd watch Kassidy until she found a regular babysitter, and she's been applying to a bunch of...day cares, because they're a full time babysitter.*" (p. 935) She said that after Amanda's visit to Perfumania the previous evening, when she talked with Chad about how Kassidy, "*got hit in the face with a baseball...Mandy got all mad and she like stormed out of the store... and went home.*" (p. 915) Jennifer later repeated that misunderstanding, "*So she went home...*" (p. 944) In fact, Amanda went back to work at Old Navy and worked until 11:00 p.m.

Jeffrey Smith asked about other injuries Jennifer had seen other than "*getting hit with the baseball?*" and Jennifer said, "*I know she had bruises on her butt. Like a couple little ones...I've seen her do it, too, on the stairs. Drag her little butt on the stairs. You know what I mean so she wouldn't fall down the stairs.* (p. 917) Jennifer later noted that the only stairs in their apartment were the few steps from their porch to the ground level. However, Chad recalled in 2010 that Kassidy would slide down the stairs from the second to the first floor at his house the same way and that some bruises would show. He wrote, in a March 19, 2010 letter,

Kassidy would lay down at the top of the stairs almost as stiff as a board and literally FLY down the stairs. It was like fun to her. This habit started out with her sitting on the stairs and going down them one at a time on her butt. Eventually she found that it was faster and more fun to slide down them. I don't know how she did it but once while I was sitting on the living room sofa I observed this little blonde streak coming down the stairs on her back. She somehow got going too fast, got caught up in one of the railing rungs, or the carpet and got herself turned completely turned around and crashed down the last 3-4 stairs face first and landed at the bottom, (which wasn't carpeted) on her head. She got up and ran over to me crying. Within several minutes she was fine. At least I thought so at the time.

My point is the very next day she was sliding down the stairs again. Unfortunately, we weren't smart enough to put the child gates back up. It just seemed like her having fun.

Returning to Jennifer's interview and regarding Kassidy's health, *Jennifer said, "Kassidy hasn't*[?] *been sleeping like a whole lot lately.... Jeff called me yesterday while I was at work and she's like she's been sleeping for like, the past 4 hours. It's like she's been sleeping all day long."* (p. 917) Jennifer was likely referring to Tuesday's, or even Monday's babysitting because Kassidy was with Jeff for 12 hours and 8 hours, respectively on those days. Later, Jennifer repeated the assessment, "*But she's been sleeping a lot lately, he* [Jeff] *said. Like he'll come in the bedroom and she'll be sleeping. She was sleeping a lot."* and Jennifer said that *"Mandy said it was because she was sick, you know what I mean? She's just getting better."* (p. 941) Even later, she put it more strongly, "*She's been sleeping like nonstop ever, you know, almost every day she's been with us.*" (p. 964)

She continued,

Chad and Jeff said there was something wrong with her like in the head like she was dumb or something. And 1 didn't feel, like, "don't think so."... Jeff used to be like, "That kid's a retard." Because the kid wouldn't sit there and play with toys like a regular kid would do. The kid would, she'd stand there and look at the wall sometimes. You know what I mean? For like a half hour and you'd go, "Kassidy, Kassidy, you okay?" And then like she'd turn around, walk over and sit down in your lap. She didn't play like a normal kid. You know what I mean? (p. 919)

Later, Jennifer said that Chad's and Jeff's statements were "*just an opinion because she just stands there. Whenever she's standing there looking at the wall,*" which Jennifer said had "*only been for the past couple of weeks, too.*" (p. 937)

About the babysitting work, Jennifer said, "*It's been okay. It's like, we were getting sick of it, you know what I mean cause we don't, you know we were just doing it as a favor....No, we don't get paid or anything like that."* (p. 918) In 2010, Amanda said that she was giving Jeff and Jennifer her Maine-issued food stamps as compensation, along with her labor for Jeff's landscaping company.

Harakles asked, "*...do you guys feed her breakfast when she gets there?*" Jennifer responded, *"Nope. She comes with breakfast... she's usually already fed. Yup. I do feed her Spaghetti-O's for lunch."* (p. 920) When Det. Leighton searched Jeff and Jennifer's home, there was an empty can of Spaghetti-O's in the sink, which could have been there from Wednesday, Tuesday, or even Monday. Detective Leighton spoke with Jeff after his search of the apartment later that evening, and Leighton reported that Jeff said that the Spaghetti-O's were "*fed to the baby the day before.*" (p. 1195) However, Amanda brought Kassidy to Jeff's at about 3:00 p.m., or as Jeff recalled, around 4:15 p.m. As Chad picked her up at 5:30 p.m., it seems unlikely that Jeff gave her the Spaghetti-O's on Wednesday afternoon, because of the shortness of her stay that day.

Jennifer said the Windex incident,*" was a long time ago... like a week, you know, two weeks ago." (p. 921)* It occurred during the three-day/two-night babysitting, which began Thursday, October 26, which was two weeks earlier, so she was very close.

Jennifer implicitly confirmed that Jeff had, on occasion, changed Kassidy's diapers because she said that Jeff would call her to complain occasionally that there were not enough diapers, so she purchased some during her lunch breaks and brought them home. She said that, "*... he doesn't like changing diapers... There's diapers all over the house. He doesn't put them in the garbage.*" (p. 938) As noted earlier, Detective Leighton had not found any used diapers in the house on the night of Kassidy's death on the day of this interview, so it must have been several days since Kassidy's last diaper change at Jeff's and Jennifer's. Also, Jeff must have picked up and disposed of all the diapers of which Jennifer spoke. Of her own diaper changing, she said, *" I haven't changed her diapers for a long time."* (p. 931) Later, she said, "*Once or twice in the past 2 weeks, 2 or 3 weeks.*" (p. 938)

She said that in the beginning, Kassidy was not used to being around men, so it took a little while for her to adjust to Jeff. She said "*I've never really seen her around Chad...I've rarely ever seen Chad with Mandy, with the kid alone....*" (p. 122-123) Later, she said, "*I don't see them together, him and the baby together unless they're all together....*" (p. 980) Jennifer referred to "Kassidy" by name about 29 times during her interview, and as "*the kid*" about 33 times, and as "*the baby*" 10 times. The three times that it's known that she saw Chad in the presence of Kassidy were during the two visits by Jeff and Jennifer and Amanda, Chad and Kassidy to Auburn on June 20 and July 20, and then in October. That third occasion was when Jeff and Jennifer were doing landscaping work at the Rochester McDonald's and Chad called Amanda to bring Kassidy with her for lunch.

About the arrival of Kassidy earlier that day, Jennifer said, *"The baby was fine this morning. She sat there eating her, you know, her food.... Cocoa Puffs."* (p. 924) At Chad's trial a year later, Jennifer would acknowledge that she didn't see Kassidy eating, and she explained the change in her recollection. Jennifer said that Kassidy "*was sleeping when I left. Falling asleep, watching TV.*" (p. 942)

Jennifer said that, "*a week ago she got sick, really sick and we were feeding her and she kept throwing up, ...Really,really, really sick and ...*" (p. 925) Steve Hamel asked, *"Could it be from the Windex do you think?* and Jennifer responded, *"That could have been."* However, Jennifer said that *we called Mandy up and Mandy came over, you know, came over to pick her up, you know, early...She took her home and she said the kid was really sick that night. Throwing up all night. They fed him,..., that Pedialyte and then she started to get better, you know....She stopped throwing up and stuff like that....But, it was the, it was the Windex, the new Windex, the country fragrance. (p. 925)*

Chad recalls that the dehydration/hunger incident was the same weekend as the three-day/two-night babysitting, beginning on October 26, which was two weeks previous. According to Amanda's "flashbacks" notes, Jeff brought Amanda to Rochester that Saturday morning the 28th, and thus, if true, Amanda did not drive to Kittery to pick up Kassidy after the Windex incident. On the 29th, two purchases with Chad's Gold Card were posted at Brooks Pharmacy for $27.96 and $4.49, and the latter purchase was likely the Pedialyte on the previous day.

Continuing with her recollection of Kassidy the morning of the interview and Kassidy's death, Jennifer said that Kassidy,

didn't want... to get picked up which is kind of, kind of odd. We thought she fell out of the bed and, you know, I was like, "Do you want to go sit in the bathroom while I put my makeup on?" Because I usually put lipstick on her lips in the morning,...and she did not want to get up. She started like crying, [I] *took her bed stuff off her. She started crying. So, I was, "Okay, okay." So I covered her back up and gave her, you know, her Cocoa Puffs.* (p. 925-26)

Later Jennifer said that when she pulled the covers back, she could see that "*She had slippers on and she had her pajamas on...*" (p. 931) They were Kassidy's favorite "Elmo" slippers. Later, describing Kassidy's clothes, Jennifer said, "*It was a pair of sweatpants and a sweatshirt.*" (p. 941) When Kassidy arrived that morning, "*She had a big pink jacket with a hood.*" (p. 942) The pink jacket would later be significant because it was very recently purchased on the previous Sunday, four days before Kassidy died. No sweatshirt for Kassidy was found at Jeff's and Jennifers, so perhaps Jennifer mistook the dress-like pajama tops for a sweatshirt, or perhaps Kassidy usually wore a sweatshirt for the top garment. Perhaps she really did wear a red fleece sweatshirt top and it was not recovered from the Rogers Road apartment.

Asked about what she saw unusual this morning and she said "*Just the bruise....and she had a little scratch here from my cat.* [pointing to an area under her own eye].. *It was black and blue."* (p. 926) Later, she seem to modify the "*my cat*" statement, "*She had scratches on her face from the cat. That's what Mandy told me. It was from a cat.*" (p. 955)

Asked about discipline used at Jeff's and Jennifer's for Kassidy, she said,

She got sent to the corner... She got spanked on her butt once and I, you know, I was like, "Oh, no, no, no spanking." Out of there. Jeff picked up and goes "pchew." And then I was like you know, okay. So he's been sending her into the corner every other time because

that's what Mandy told him to do 'cause it works. She goes in the corner, you know? Jeff said he was outside on the porch once and he opened the window 'cause she was, she had to go to the corner. She's standing in the corner and, all of a sudden she looks around, walks around the kitchen, starts digging into things. But, that's what she got, she got sent to the corner.

Asked what would lead to such discipline, Jennifer answered, *"Getting in the Windex and stuff like that."* (p. 926-27) That mild spanking was a week after Jeff's alleged spanking Kassidy on Saturday, October 21 for unknown reasons. Jeff did not mention this incident in his interview, but Amanda and Chad both discussed it. (See below.) Later, in his interview, Travis also said that Jeff had acknowledged spanking Kassidy after that overnight.

Jeff Smith asked Jennifer if she had *"heard anything about Kassidy falling out of a vehicle?"* Jennifer responded,

She was sitting in the chair, the passenger seat, and Jeff was doing something, talking to the neighbor [Will Peirce] *or something like that, and she fell out off the passenger seat like trying to get out of the car...It was the truck so it was like that high up...And she fell out onto the ground.... Dodge. 3/4 ton pickup truck.... Like two weeks ago, three .... like the first time we started babysitting....She had a bruise. Jeffrey said she just cried. He picked her up and she was just fine...* (p. 928-29)

Later, Jennifer reaffirmed that Kassidy seldom cried when hurt, but one occasion was, "*like when she fell out of the truck.*" (p. 972) The time given, "*two weeks ago*," would have been during the three-day/two-night babysitting stint beginning Thursday, October 26. It was after Jeff's returning of Kassidy on the following Saturday to Rochester that Amanda, Chad, and Travis saw the two large bumps on the top rear of Kassidy's head. Emily Conley stated in her interview that she saw them, too, but she did not testify at Chad's trial.

Hamel asked, "*...have you ever seen the baby's eyes kind of roll or whatever?* Jennifer responded, *"In the back of her head? No.....Mandy told me she saw it once....but yesterday when she came in. She's like, 'Something must be going on with her.' Cause the kid's been sick lately. Like sick. coughing and stuff like that. ....And she said, ' something's going on with her. She rolled her eyes in the back of her head last night.' "* (p. 929-30)

At 4:40 p.m. Steve Hamel stepped out of the interview for ten minutes and likely talked with other investigators and compared a few notes before returning at 4:50 p.m. to resume the interview with Jeffrey Smith. Jennifer said that her older brother, [Charles], had epilepsy and seizures. Jennifer continued that when Jeff called [shortly after noon on this day],

...he saw something was wrong with her and he's like, "Something's wrong with her. She's rolling her eyes down in the back of her head." And I'm like, "Oh, my God. You know. She must be having a seizure." Cause I like looked back to when Chuckie's [her older brother] *always had seizures, you know.....And I'm like, "Call the hospital." You know. "Call the ambulance. And he's like "Okay." And so .... He said he wanted to check on her because she was quiet, you know what I mean?... Not because she was watching TV and he was in the living room and she was rolling her eyes in the back of her head and moaning and that's what Chuckie used to do after he had a seizure...* (p. 932-33)
Later in the interview, she said, "*...that's what happened to Chuckie. He got hit in the head and that's how he started his epilepsy*." (p. 948)

Jennifer continued,
Mandy said she'd seen her do it [eyes in the back of her head] *before. Um, hum... She said ever since she fell out of the truck. She fell out of the truck, like she's been sick. Sick, you know, like she couldn't hold food down. She got better. She's been better for the past week. You know what I mean?*

Steve Hamel asked, *"And where was she when she fell out of the truck?"* and Jennifer responded, *"She was in our parking, our driveway.* (p. 933) This was the fall from Jeff's truck during the three-day/two-night babysitting, beginning on Thursday, October 26th.

Jeff Smith asked Jennifer, *"Do you know who Amanda sees for a pediatrician?"* She said, "*I have no clue. I don't,*" but she did know that Amanda was on the ASPIRE program. (p. 934) Unfortunately, no detective asked Amanda and her mother, Jacqueline, to what doctors and pediatricians they had taken Kassidy since her birth. There is nothing in the 3000-plus pages of Discovery materials that the police or prosecutors obtained information about and from those doctors and pediatricians. The only reference was in an Investigative Plan by New Hampshire Sgt. James White who wrote as "*To Do*" item, "*Cassidy's last medical exam.*"

Steve Hamel asked, *"...in your opinion, does Jeff do a good job with the baby?"* and Jennifer responded, *"He's not the best baby*[sitter]. *He doesn't play with the kid. you know what I mean? The kid will watch TV all day and Jeff will watch TV. He's not the best babysitter, but he's not like, you know what I mean, he doesn't treat the kid bad or anything like that. I've never seen him treat the kid bad. "* She agreed that there was one spanking, *"Yeah, and I was there, you know, it was like a little swat and it wasn't even hard,..."* (p. 935) Later, Jennifer described some of Jeff's activity with Kassidy, *"And usually, whenever Jeff has her, he's out with her during the day, you know? Going places. Running errands like to Walmart and stuff with her.... Because he'll give me a call and stop in with Kassidy while I'm at work, drop me off food, you know what I mean?"* (p. 941) There was no mention here of Jeff's concern about bringing Kassidy out in public.

Steve Hamel asked, *"Have you noticed anything else strange over the past two weeks?"* Jennifer said, *"Just her looking at the wall. I've seen her doing that...but she talks normal....she actually walks normal. but Mandy said that she wasn't walking right for some reason, but she's walking fine now. She was walking fine."* Hamel asked for the time period that Kassidy "*wasn't walking right*" and Jennifer's vague response of "*like a while ago,... before we babysat her, like...maybe she stubbed her toe on something...*" was left to stand, without further effort to date that problem more precisely. Jennifer also acknowledged, "*I haven't really seen her walk,*" so her knowledge of any limping problem was secondhand. (p. 937)

The interview returned to Jeff's two calls to Jennifer on this day, the 9th.
Jeff called me and said, "Something's wrong with the kid. She's like rolling her eyes in the back of her head." And I'm like, "Well, call the hospital." You know what I mean?...And I had customers in the store so I had to let him go....So, I gotta go, you know? You know, "Call the ambulance and then give me a call back whenever you hear anything," you know what I mean? ...And he gave me a call back and he's like, "We're going to the hospital. Something's wrong with her." And he's all worried, all crying and stuff. He's crying. He's wicked upset. And I was like, "Oh, my God." You know. "Something's wrong with her." So, I went on with my day, you know. (p. 942)

Later in the interview, Jennifer said that Jeff said during that first call that Kassidy was moaning while her eyes were "*rolling in the back of her head.... I told him to call the ambulance, because he asked me if she has a doctor he could call and I was like, 'Don't you think you should call the ambulance?' He was wicked nervous. His brother died.*" (p. 946)

Later, Jennifer elaborated, that after Jeff said that he was taking Kassidy to the hospital, "*He said, 'She's doing fine, now. She's walking around,' and he's like, 'I'm going to take her to the hospital.'... She was like eating food again and stuff like that, but I told him to take her to the hospital just in case."* (p. 947)

Later, she said about the first call, "*She was alert, watching TV with... Jeff hung up and then he called and said he'd take to the hospital.*" (p. 949) She said, "*And he was all upset, you know, and he just took her, right after I spoke to him, he took her to the hospital....*[he] *Told me, like normal, just sitting there watching TV, like speaking to him and stuff like that, you know what I mean. Like saying, 'Kitty.' and stuff like that,..."* (p. 947-48)

At Chad's trial she would recall that her statement about Kassidy eating, and being normal, was incorrect, and likely reflected assumptions on her part, as Jeff "*didn't seem as upset the second time he called.*" (p. 948) Also, it's noteworthy that at this time of the interview, around 5:00 p.m., Jennifer still thought that Jeff had taken Kassidy to the hospital. She said later that she hadn't talked with Jeff since that second call. (p. 949) At the end of the interview, the officers told her that Jeff had called 911, and had not taken

Kassidy to a hospital. (p. 981) Also, she did not know yet that the doctors would later estimate that Kassidy was dead at the time Jeff began making his calls for help. She said the two calls were a "*minute and a half*" apart. (p. 947) According to the "Chart of Calls" the calls were 11 minutes apart, as they were made at 12:26 p.m. and 12:37 p.m. Jennifer said that she then called Amanda after the second call, as Jeff did not have Amanda's phone number. (p. 947) However, at the end of the 11 minute gap in the calls to Jennifer, he called 411-Information for the Old Navy number, and had tried to call Amanda, but she was unavailable.

Jennifer described her last call at work that day. *"Then I got a phone call from my mother. She's balling her eyes out, and she's like, 'Kassidy's dead.' You know what I mean?"* (p. 942) That call was nearly two hours after the two calls with Jeff, and Jennifer's conversation with Amanda about Kassidy going to the hospital.

Smith asked, "*What do you think happened?*" and Jennifer said, "*I don't know... I know she got hit by the face with a friggin baseball, yesterday....*" (p. 942) Jennifer may have been the first person to recognize the possible role of the Tee-ball accident in contributing to Kassidy's death.

Hamel asked, *"Did she* [Amanda] *say anything to you this morning about it?"* and Jennifer responded,

No, I said, "Look at the bruise on her face." She's like. "I know. He hit her. The baseball hit her hard." You know what I mean? It's like a little bruise right here. It's not like a big, huge bruise, but you could tell she got hit right like right around here....She's got a, she had a bruise like right here this morning.... And, you know, everything else I've ever seen on her body has been like so minute, you know, like little bruises like that, you know, from like falling down and stuff like that. (p. 944)

Jennifer said that Kassidy had thin hair and that it was usually in a pony tail. She said that Amanda carried her into the home this morning, as she did every morning, and "*just put her in the bed.*" (p. 945) Jennifer estimated that she was at the home with Kassidy and Jeff for about an hour before she left for work.

Smith and Hamel asked Jennifer if they could take a break, at 5:10 p.m., as they likely wanted to further compare notes with other investigators, but that was the end of the first part of Jennifer's interview. (p. 951) They resumed the interview at 6:00 p.m.

4:20 p.m. - Amanda Bortner Interview

At 4:20 p.m., Amanda(AB) began her first of four interviews, beginning with Maine State Police Detectives Angela Blodgett(ACB) and Richard LeClair(RCL). This first interview was for one hour, 44 minutes, and the second interview was for an additional 25 minutes, for a total on that first, fateful, tragic day of two hours and 10 minutes.

Early in the interview Amanda told the police two lies. First, she said that her address was "*53 Rogers Road. I just moved from my mom's because, well, they just moved to Buckfield and I live*[d] *in Auburn.*" 53 Rogers Road was the duplex unit next door to Jeff's and Jennifer's unit. She had used that address for her ASPIRE application and was probably trying in the interview to avoid being caught living in New Hampshire, but receiving welfare benefits from Maine. She might have had a grace period of six months after moving to New Hampshire, but it was not something she had examined beforehand, so she just used the same address when responding to the officers.

Second, she said, "*....I kind of live with my boyfriend, but not really.*" (p. 822) It was not a good start, and surely aroused suspicion, as she was minimizing her relationship to Chad. The police probably thought she was minimizing the relationship because she was hiding Chad's responsibility for Kassidy's death, but she was really minimizing because of the Maine residency/ASPIRE problem. Another problem with her responses was that they led the police to misunderstand the critical timeline of her relationship with Chad.

She said that she took two diet pills a day, metabolite. (p. 823) After hearing her Miranda rights, she agreed to remain for the interview though she stated a preference to postpone it, *"I'd rather talk when I've moved, like in a couple days when I've moved out of state, but if you have to talk with me now, I will.*" (p. 826) It's not known what she had in mind when she mentioned a move to another state.

Amanda said that she awoke to Kassidy's crying at 6:15 a.m. "*I had to be at work at 8:00. I got there at 8:20 though, but I got her ready first to leave. I gave her actually cereal in a bag to take because we were in a hurry.*" (p. 826)

Angela Blodgett asked, "*How was everybody this morning?*" and Amanda said, "*She was really tired and like I don't know why I didn't think of her being sick, but she was really tired.*" She was dressed in "*...actually, a brand new outfit. A fleece sweatshirt, fleece pants, I put on her Elmo slippers because I couldn't find her sneakers and her winter jacket and a hat.* (p. 827)

This was the clearest statement of what Kassidy was wearing that morning. The sneakers were at Jeff and Jennifer's. (See Nov. 9 photo1 and photo2 of Kassidy's new sneakers at bedside.) The "*fleece sweatshirt*" and "*fleece pants*" were later described as pajamas. There was no clear description of her red-top dress-like pajama tops with a white image of a dog's face, which is what she was wearing when the EMTs arrived. The lower portion of the dress-like pajama tops had horizontal red and white narrow stripes. No sweatshirt or "*fleece sweatshirt*" was found at Jeff's and Jennifer's.

Amanda began to describe the previous evening's activity, "*...last night on the phone, see I worked till 11, but didn't get home till 12, because it's like a half-hour drive. My boyfriend, well I called him on my break to see how she was doing and, just as I was calling,...they play wiffle ball a lot, and he was playing in the bedroom with both of the kids and the little boy was throwing the bat around. They fight a lot. He's at that age, you know?... And he hit her in the eye with the ball, with the bat. They fight all the time.*" (p. 827)

When she arrived home, Amanda said she saw a bruise "*on the side of her eye,*" and said that Chad

told me that she was acting funny... I didn't bring her to the doctor's because she's been so good. She was being so smart lately like she was surprising me. Like Kyle said, '1, 2, 3, 4, 5' the other day and she said,'6, 7, 8, 9' and I couldn't believe it, you know? And then she says, she's been saying the ABCs and she's been painting things out, you know? But I didn't think she was sick, I thought she was all better. (p. 828)

Rick LeClair asked if she was sick earlier, and Amanda said,

Well,... about 2 weeks ago, she, Jeff was babysitting her and he brought her back and he told me that she fell out of the truck...he said that she was sitting on the front of the car seat and, like Will, the neighbor, said something like to pass a break or something, I don't know, something like that and he moved and then Kassidy fell out of the truck and she had a bump on her head. And,... she came home that day and she was really sick, she was like dehydrated and she wanted drinks and stuff, so I gave her Pedialyte and I gave her Tylenol and I kept giving her water to get some fluid in her and the next day she was fine. I was going to bring her to the doctor's, but I thought she was better, you know, and actually that night, actually she was really tired, it was like 10 o'clock and her eyes went back a little bit and,... I thought it was just because she was tired, but now,... (p. 828-29)

She said it occurred "*like 2 weeks ago. Maybe 3 weeks ago.*" She was close, as it occurred during the three-day/two-night babysitting by Jeff which began on Thursday evening, October 26, which was exactly three weeks earlier. (p. 829)

Blodgett asked if Amanda talked with Kassidy about that fall, and Amanda said that Kassidy, "*doesn't talk that well...Like I'll ask her, if I ever asked her if she feels good she, and .,. he* [Jeff] *tripped over her the other day, like 2 days ago, and she hurt her leg and she was walking funny and ...*" (p. 829) She said that Jeff "*told me that when I picked her up that she's walking funny because he had tripped over her. She was standing right behind him and I was like okay, and I like, was feeling her legs and I was asking her if it hurt because usually she says, 'Ow' and she didn't say' ow' or anything.*" She described Kassidy's walking after the incident, "*It was just like a little limp, not even like a limp, but....*" (p. 829) and said that the incident occurred "*two days ago.*" (p. 830) As noted above, and at about the same time on November 9, 2000, Jeff attributed this same limp, in his interview, to Chad. (Jeff interview, p. 1289)

Blodgett asked about the "*injury to the bottom of her foot.... Did she burn her foot or something?*" Amanda responded, "*No, actually, I saw that and,... she came home from*

Jeff's house and he said that Jeff and Jen thought that, because there's like nails sticking up from the bottom of their floor, so that's why I brought over, brought her, put her in slippers also.... He said that they have like, kind of, not like nails, but like, you know, sharp things." (p. 830)

Blodgett said that Kassidy *"has a lot of bruises on her,"* which surprised Amanda, *"She has bruises on her body?... She had bruises on her body? They said that?"* (p. 831) She acknowledged only bruises on her head, "*Just what was on her eye, right here and right here... Yeah, she hit the corner of the table. She's really, she's really like disoriented. She falls, well, she fell, a lot,"* which she said was a recent phenomenon, "*probably like three or four days ago,*" but *"...she's always been like that klutz kind of, too."* (p. 831) She said she was with Kassidy when she hit the glass table. She didn't mention him, but Travis Hunt was with her, too.

Blodgett asked if anyone smoked around Kassidy, because the hospital *"doctor thought that marks on her foot looked like a cigarette."* (p. 831) Amanda said that Kassidy was not around people who smoked, but she didn't remember to mention the curling iron burn which was thought to have occurred at Emily Conley's home during an October babysitting. Initially, that was thought to have resembled a cigarette burn.

Asked to describe Kassidy's behavior on November 9, Amanda said*, "..she said, 'Drink.' I gave her a drink... at the house and I gave her cereal in a baggie.... She hasn't been eating very well, like last night, actually, Chad was telling me on the phone she didn't eat much and she was acting funny.... , like kind of sick. She didn't feel well, tired."* (p. 832)

Chad recalls that while Amanda usually was the one who packed cereal for Kassidy, it was Chad who packed the Reese's PB Puffs for her that morning.
Beginning with this exchange, Amanda made the first of several statements, which showed her disbelief about what was happening, saying, "*Oh, my God, I can't believe this."* (p. 832)

Rick LeClair asked about the timeline, *"How long has Chad been in the picture?"* and Amanda said, *"Probably for like, helping me take care of her for like four months probably. But I've been with him for almost 6 months."* It was actually five months and a week, or 160 days, and when asked by Angela Blodgett, *"How long have you been living over there full time pretty much?"* Amanda said, *"probably like 3 or 4 months....maybe not even that long,"* but four months was the better estimate, i.e. since early July. (p. 832) In any case, with these responses, she was not minimizing her relationship to Chad.

Blodgett followed up to ask about the expression, *"helping me take care of her"* and Amanda said*, "...like picking her up and stuff... He doesn't like, he's babysit her like twice by himself... actually, he just first, recently changed a diaper... The other day. He watched her all day when I went to my mom's with my sister. I hadn't seen her in a while."* (p. 833) Chad recalls only three occasions when he was babysitting for Kassidy, and for most of that time he was with others. The first was the night of Thursday, October 19, which was during Amanda's first money management class. The second was, *"the other day,"* as Amanda referenced it, which was the Sunday, November 5, day with his sister, Nicole and her in-laws and friends. The third was the previous night, Nov. 8, most of which was also with Kyle, and some of which was with Travis.

Regarding diaper changes, Chad recalled in 2010, *"I know anytime I gave her a bath I obviously put on a fresh diaper. I changed a bunch of Kassidy urine diapers. Kassidy was a pleasure to change. She didn't flail around the way Kyle would.*" (Letter, Apr. 27, 2010) The most recent diaper change was the previous night, November 8. Amanda's statement, *"he just first, recently changed a diaper,"* probably refers to Chad's memorable diaper change on Sunday, November 5 at his sister's. He wrote in 2010 about that *"funny story,"* which he shared with Amanda when she returned from shopping with Jennifer and their mother,

Changing girls diapers always made me a little uncomfortable. I know it is a natural process but they have "girl parts." That last Sunday, November 5th, when I took Kassidy up to Nicole and Brandon's in Belmont before her death, Kassidy pooped about mid-day. It was funny because Nicole was holding her in what was the old kitchen and I was in another room and I began to smell it. I went to Nicole and she informed me that Kassidy needed a change. I could tell that it was going to be a bad one and just then it dawned on me that I had "escaped" ever changing a poopy diaper for her. I immediately went into my male, "whiney" voice asking Nicole if she would change it. Nicole wasn't as easily persuaded by my whiney voice as mom, Tristan, and Amanda had been. Nicole was holding her nose and giggling and saying, "No way, this is horrible." I replied, "I'm busy nailing." She replied, "I'll go nail for you." It was apparent that Nicole wasn't going to let me off the hook so I retrieved the diaper bag. I laid Kassidy down and proceeded to remove her diaper. It was the worst mess I had ever seen. Nicole and I were in hysterics laughing. Her feces was the consistency of a mud puddle just after all the water was absorbed into the ground. It had covered the inside of her diaper, down her legs, it had worked its way up her back, and of course into her genitals. I recall getting this shiver when I looked and pleaded one more time, "C'mon Nicole, help me out." Nicole was taking great pleasure in standing over my shoulder, laughing and saying, "No way, you're on your own." (Apparently, Nicole was getting me back for some torture that I no doubt put her through during her childhood). Nicole wasn't going to help me but she sure relished the chance to "supervise." I was laughing so hard my eyes began to water. Brandon came into the room to see what was so funny and immediately had to cover his nose from the smell. When I got to Kassidy's genitals I gave them a cursory wipe and Nicole quickly reprimanded me. "Chad you have to get in the cracks a little because she has poop there and make sure you wipe down or she'll get an infection." I was like, "Jesus, you have to do this, I don't want to dig around in her girl parts." As you may have guessed by now, I ended up doing it with only verbal assistance by Nicole. But I was pretty uncomfortable about wiping out her genitals. I am glad I did, though, because she had feces packed in there. The entire time this whole thing was going on, Kassidy just laid there patient, with those blue eyes staring up at me. I got the diaper on, bent over and kissed her forehead. I recall pulling her face close to mine and saying in a semi baby talk voice, "How can something so big and stinky come out of something so small and pretty?" I remember Nicole agreed with my assessment.

Returning to Amanda's interview, Angela Blodgett asked about the frequency of Jeff's babysitting. Amanda described part of it, *"...well, this week a lot. I started landscaping for him, and I did it like twice, and he watched her both days while me and my sister landscaped."* Then she paused in stunned reflection on what had really happend on this day, *"Oh my gosh."* Amanda said that Jeff had watched Kassidy before the current week, *"But not every day."* (p. 833)

Blodgett asked, "*Have you ever accidentally or just without thinking hit Kassidy or...?*" and Amanda responded, "*No, never.*" (p. 833) In a subsequent interview, Amanda did remember one incident where she had driven with Kassidy and opened the car's back door to get her out of the car and after doing that, she pushed the door into Kassidy's head, without realizing she was still there.

The questions were getting closer to her, and Amanda stated, more defensively, *"... Like if you had talked to anybody about that* [possible accidents], *they'll tell you how much she loved me.... She was always like, "Momma." And she just, just doesn't like anybody but me. Like she'll cry and she doesn't like guys." (p. 834)*

Blodgett asked *"Did she have any marks on her hands? Or her fingers?...No cuts on her hands?"* and Amanda responded with a gasp, "*Oh my God,*" and she said Kassidy had a wart. Unfortunately, she didn't explain to the detectives that Chad had recommended that the wart be removed and that Kassidy's pediatrician had recommended that a wart removal appointment be scheduled. After Detective Blodgett assured Amanda that the cuts she was asking about were not deep cuts, Amanda said, *"Oh, we have a cat. We just got a kitten. Could be scratches."* (p. 834)

Detective Blodgett then asked, *"Have you ever, have either Chad or Jeff or even Jennifer really, have ever done anything that made you feel like they got frustrated with Kassidy easily or have they ever done anything that you had to say, 'hey' ?"* Amanda responded, *"No, just yell at her... They don't touch her. Like I would never let anybody touch her."* Blodgett then asked the followup question, *"...what do you think happened then?"* Amanda said,

I have no idea like I didn't know about any of this. I knew about her feet and I knew about her eye, and that's what he told me right when it happened. And like you telling me about these bruises and I have no idea about any of this, and then he told me she had bruises on her chin and then asked me if I saw it this morning and I didn't see anything. Oh, my God. (p. 834)

LeClair asked, *"Is Chad a good guy?"* and Amanda answered, *"Yeah, he's a really good guy...."* LeClair followed up with, *"I mean, has he ever been in trouble with the law?"* Amanda replied, *"Yeah, he's been... once, **but he's like the best father. You can ask anybody**."* (p. 834) No police interviewer on that day asked whether Amanda, or Jeff or Jennifer had been in trouble with the law. What was important was not the truth of the answer, as the police had their own databases with the answer. Rather, it was important to know who was aware of what, and who was telling the truth, and how often.

After explaining that Kyle lives with Chad and Amanda, *"four or five days a week, more with us than his mom,"* Amanda was asked, by Angela Blodgett, *"...does he ever lose his temper? Do you have any reservations about..."* Amanda responded, *"No,"* before the question was completed. (p. 835) Blodgett continued, *"I mean 1 1/2 can be a pretty frustrating age..."* and Amanda responded about Kassidy, in the present tense, *" She's more whiny than, like, he's used to boys and she's a girl so he'd yell at her, but he'd never hurt her."* (p. 835)

Rick LeClair asked, *"Do they play rough?"* and Amanda answered, *" Actually, I'll tell you that like I'd yell at him because he'd play a little too rough with her. He'd swing her around and stuff,"* and Amanda added, *"I play with her like that, but she laughs and stuff... He wouldn't do it like she would cry or anything, but I would just be like, 'Be careful,' you know?.. Just like pick her up and go around the house and stuff and play airplane and stuff."* (p. 835)

Had Chad been in the room, he might have noted that he had received similar caution from Janet Lane, the wife of his friend, Larry Lane, who asked Chad to be careful when he was playing with her daughter, Chelsea. Thirty years ago, I dropped my nephew onto his head while playing with him. We all should have been more careful.

Returning to the interview, Amanda volunteered, almost spontaneously, to describe Kassidy's stair descents, as Jennifer had described earlier,

And when she goes down the stairs she goes on her back, so she might have, she always had like a little spot back there. She would just like rolled down the stairs. That's how she would do it. If that's what they are talking about. That's what I can think of, you know?...She always goes on her butt, her back. She goes like that." (p. 835)

Amanda explained that Travis Hunt was a housemate, and lived in the basement, but she said that he never babysat for Kassidy. Later in the interview, Amanda was asked whether Travis "*had ever been alone with* [the] *kids for any time*," and Amanda said, "*I don't know, but Kassidy really likes him*." (p. 858) In 2010, Chad wrote that

On page 38 of my interview I stated that Travis babysat for the kids twice. I know on one of these occasions, it was for like a half hour. Amanda was out somewhere and I had Kyle and Kassidy at home. Travis was also there. I got an urgent phone call from my Rochester restaurant, because the fryolaters had gone into shutdown mode. I had to go there and get them up and running. Hard to run a McDonald's when you can't sell your world- famous French Fries. Travis stayed with the kids until I got back about a half hour later. As I recall, I played with them for a little bit and then put them to bed. The second time I recall Travis watching Kyle and Kassidy I forget exactly what we were doing but I believe Amanda and I went somewhere, perhaps the movies. I think it was for only a couple of hours.

Rick LeClair asked if Chad always uses the car seat when transporting Kassidy, and Amanda said, "*Always*," but Chad hadn't yet told her that he didn't use a car seat the previous day when picking up Kassidy at Jeff's. LeClair continued, "*What would you say if he didn't?*" and Amanda said, "*Oh, I would yell at him, like scream at him*." LeClair dropped the matter without telling Amanda what he knew from what Jeff had said.

Amanda didn't yet realize that she hadn't left the car seat at Jeff's when she dropped Kassidy off that morning of the 8th.

Detective Blodgett then opened a line of questioning relating to the police theory that Chad was frustrated and angry on November 8th. She asked, "*Was he upset? I had been told that he was, was he annoyed when he had to pick her up yesterday because you had to work? When you talked to him, did he seem mad?"* Amanda correctly stated, *"He offered to do it."* (p. 837) The only possible source for Blodgett's *"I had been told"* comment was Jeff. Perhaps she had been told that Jeff had correctly observed that Chad was annoyed with the clerk at Moonlite Reader and he was annoyed that Amanda forgot to leave Kassidy's car seat at Jeff's. However, she, or another policeperson, must have combined those particular frustrations with the police theory that Chad harmed Kassidy out of frustration and that a likely source of frustration was having to pick up Kassidy. With Amanda stating that Chad offered to pick up Kassidy, that source of possible frustration was eliminated. The police explored every other possible source they could develop to support their theories.

The questioning then returned to basic biography, and Chad's job at the McDonald's franchisee. Amanda answered, "*Holly - McCleod,*" meaning Colley-McCoy, and then she volunteered, "*He would never do anything like this*." (p. 838)

Blodgett asked again about *"cuts on her feet?* And said that the doctors *"thought they were burns."* Amanda said, *"No, they were like little, little tiny ones... I saw them this morning and I didn't think they were bad...they're not even like cuts. They really look like a little flesh burn, you know." (p. 838)* She said she saw those marks on Kassidy's feet after her last bath which was *"two or three days ago."* (p. 838) Then LeClair asked Amanda to describe what other bruises she had seen at the time of that bath, and "*we'll work from the feet up*." (p. 838)

Nonetheless, she started with the "*cut on her eye*" from hitting the coffee table. "*She fell off the couch...She falls off the couch a lot*." Then repeating an observation she made earlier in the interview, Amanda said, "*She's just really disoriented....She was really like... klutzy, and she falls...she's always been klutzy. I've noticed it a lot worse lately."* Fortunately, Rick LeClair asked if Amanda had talked with a doctor about this, and Amanda said, *"Yeah, I did. I took her to the doctor's this summer because I thought it was her feet, because she walks with a limp and like I was thinking she would get leg inserts."* (p. 839) When asked, Amanda gave them the name of Pediatric Associates of Auburn, which was correct for the August 10 appointment with Dr. Glass. The followup question was not asked about exactly when during the summer was the appointment.

Showing how confused Amanda could become, regarding dates, Rick LeClair asked, "*She's never been to anything down... this way for a doctor*." and Amanda responded, "... *not since I've been down here*." She may have thought that she was being asked if she had been to a New Hampshire doctor, or otherwise misunderstood the question. The visit to Dr. Glass of Pediatric Associates, referenced above, was on August 10, which was clearly since Amanda had been "*down here*." Even more clearly, was the appointment with the orthopedic surgeon, Dr. James Timoney, on September 11, which Amanda referenced without further comment or notice by the interviewers, "*the last time she went to the doctor's she got checked for her legs...*" In any case, the police apparently did obtain the records of these visits, but they were never provided to Chad's lawyers, and not later to Amanda's lawyer.

Asked about other hospital or medical appointments, Amanda said,

My mom took her once.... I think she just had a fever. I know it was a long time ago, but also like I was going to bring her to the doctor's as soon as, urn, she bruises really easily and, I don't know, you poke her and next ... I thought she had anemia because my mom has anemia....My mom said that she might have anemia....I don't eat much red meat, so she [Kassidy] *doesn't eat much red meat, either...."* (p. 840)

Stating that her mother made that diagnosis indicated that Amanda had talked with her mother about Kassidy's bruises. In 2010, Amanda said that she bruises easily, too.

Rick LeClair tried to bring the interview back to question of what bruises did Amanda see on Kassidy's bruises during the last bath which Amanda gave Kassidy, which was on

Monday or Tuesday, November 6 or 7. He asked, "*Did she have any marks on her back?* and Amanda responded, "*I don't think so...I think I would have noticed. I might not have my glasses on, but my prescription is 20 over 800 so it's really bad. Like, right now I have one contact in.*" (p. 840)

Asked about Kassidy's behavior in the bath, Amanda said, confusingly, "*Oh, she hates water. She doesn't like water, but she loves all of that.*" Blodgett asked about Kassidy's possible flinching, as when touching an injury on her arm, "*and they pull away or something like that*?" Amanda replied, "*Oh, no. No, no*." (p. 840)

Amanda agreed with Blodgett's restatement that Kassidy had not been eating well, and that "*She went to the bathroom a lot. I though thought it was normal.*" Blodgett asked, "*Pee or poop or both?*" and Amanda said, "*Both,*" and she had "*a little bit of a diaper rash.*"(p. 841)

Amanda related the call from Jennifer that morning, "*...she said that, ... Kassidy, her eyes rolled back or something like and that's what really scared me because I thought that, like the last time, you know, and she says nothing really bad, but just go to the hospital...*" (p. 841)

Trying to find a motive for abusing Kassidy, Rick LeClair asked "*...your relationship with Chad, and your home life, are there any problems?*" and Amanda said, "*None at all.*" He tried another, "*You have any money problems?*" and Amanda responded, "*Oh, no. Not having any money problems.*" (p. 842) Then he asked, then "*why did you go to work?*" which was a curious question, as a lot of people work who don't have money problems, including the spouses of police detectives. Amanda responded, "*Because I'm on the Aspire program... I have to work right now until I was going to go to school and, hopefully, in January... I couldn't go to school until I had taken some tests and stuff..*" (p. 842)

Blodgett didn't ask for more information about the ASPIRE program, which would have been a good source of information about Amanda and Kassidy. In particular, there were records, now destroyed, of Amanda's appointments at the Sanford ASPIRE office of the Maine Dept. of Health and Human Services. A detective could have talked with Amanda's counselor and others who saw Amanda and Kassidy during appointments in the fall of 2000. In 2000, the records still existed of the distribution of food stamps to Amanda and other assistance payments to her and her mother.

Amanda said, *"I feel like I'm going to puke,"* and when offered a drink or a chance to go to the ladies room, she said, *"No. I just want to get this over with."* (p. 843) Then Amanda asked some questions, "*Do you think somebody hurt her?... Do you think she was sick at all?"* Detective Blodgett responded, *"I think someone's been hurting her. I think that she's sick because she's been getting hit....I think that may be where you're talking about her eyes rolling back and stuff. I'm not a doctor, but I do a lot of infant deaths. I think that she's been getting hit in the head or has been suffering head injuries. "* (p. 843-44) Amanda then defended both Jeff and Chad, "*But they wouldn't like hurt her. I don't think they'd like hit her on the head or hit her, you know? Like I said, she fell out of the truck and she had like a bruise right here and a big bruise right here and that's when she did that night and that's what worried me. "* (p. 844)

Amanda continued, *"And she is really klutzy."* LeClair asked, *"She had two bruises on her head from one fall?"* and Amanda replied, *"Like, he said like, yeah, it was like one right here and one right here."* Knowing that some people would be listening to, rather than watching, this recorded interview, LeClair said, *"Okay, and you're, you pointed to the back side, top back side of your head?... But, there were two bruises?"* and Amanda said, *"They were pretty big. I put ice on them and took her inside.... Yup, two." (p. 844)* LeClair and Blodgett asked good followup questions, *"Now you know, I mean, if you think about it, the reason we ask is because that's really weird, that's either ... One fall you get one bruise..., You fell hard enough to bounce and hit twice.. You've gotta have impact twice to get two bumps..."* and Amanda replied, *"Yup. He* [Jeff] *said .. "I think she like when she fell she like hit the bottom of the truck and then she hit her head on the ground.* (p. 844-45)

LeClair asked how often Kassidy had been alone with Chad or with Jeff and Amanda said, *"... I haven't left her alone much with Chad, but with Jeff, he's had her like all day while I was at work and like if I needed to go to a doctor's appointment, he'd take her. Lately, he's had her a lot."* Perhaps not wanting to hear that message, LeClair asked again, *"Now, Chad is, Chad's had her a lot?"* and Amanda corrected him, *"No, Jeff's had her a lot.* (p. 845)

Since the September 11 appointment for Kassidy with Dr. Timoney, Amanda did have an appointment with her optometrist, Dr. Daniel Roy, on Friday, October 27. That was during the three-day/two-night babysittting by Jeff and Jennifer, so Amanda was right, that at least on that occasion, Jeff and Jennifer did babysit for Kassidy when Amanda had a doctor's appointment. The police didn't followup with questions about the dates of those medical appointments.

Detective LeClair's question about who was with Kassidy alone was a good question. Below is a primitive chart showing the number of hours that Amanda, Chad or Jeff was alone with Kassidy during different time periods, beginning backwards, from 12:38 p.m. on Thursday, November 9. For the purpose of this chart, if Kyle was present with Chad and Kassidy, then Chad and Kassidy were not alone.

	Last 12 Hours W/T Midnt	Last 24 Hours Wed. Noon	Last 36 Hours T/W Midnt	Last 48 Hours Tues Noon	Last 72 Hours Mon Noon	Last 96 Hours Sun. Noon
Amanda	0	2.5	8.5	9.5	10.5	11.5
Chad	0	.5	.5	.5	.5	1.5
Jeff	4.5	7.0	7.0	15.0	20.0	23.0

In response to a question, Amanda described her call the previous night with Chad, *"On the phone whenever she got hit with the wiffle ball... Let me think,... they were playing. He was like... Kyle hit her with a wiffle ball... and Kyle whacked her right in the eye... And I was like, 'Oh, great'...there was a big mark around her eye.... It was red."* (p. 846) Not only did Amanda misunderstand the type of ball that hit Kassidy, she also didn't seem to understand the circumstances. She said, "*Yeah, they fight a lot really. Pinch each other, bite each other. He was really like he kicks her and stuff. Like that could be a lot of bruises, you know.... Yeah, they act like brother and sister."* (p. 846-47) Kyle's hitting Kassidy with the Tee-ball was part of hitting practice, and had nothing to do with his occasional fighting with Kassidy. Kassidy was on Chad's lap on the bed at the time.

After some softer time spent with questions about family biographical information, LeClair asked, "*Has Chad ever hit you?*" and Amanda responded with, "*No. Never."* (p. 848) When asked, Amanda said that Chad had not been in any trouble with the police since she had known him and that his previous trouble was "*just like drinking and stuff...nothing bad.... I really don't know.*" (p. 848) LeClair asked about "*Jen's husband, Jeffrey? Has he been in any trouble?*" and Amanda responded, "*No, not that I know of.*" (p. 848-49) She didn't correct LeClair about the relationship between Jeff and Jennifer. Was Amanda consciously hiding what she knew about Chad's domestic violence with Tristan? Or perhaps she didn't regard that as "*trouble with the police?*" Did she know about Jeff's court orders and arrests? Did her sister, Jennifer, know? (p. 848-49) Neither Jeff nor Jennifer were asked that question.

Then, for the first time in the interview, the detectives asked Amanda about what they had heard from others, i.e. Jeff, although unnamed. Angela Blodgett said, "*On the...Kassidy not liking to take baths, I've been told that Chad had put her head under a faucet and that since then she doesn't like to take baths. Do you remember that happening?*" As an example of the power of suggestion, Rick LeClair then asked Amanda, "*Can I get you some more water?*" Responding to Blodgett, Amanda said, "*Yeah...he got mad at her once and he did that....That was like 3 months ago maybe. Well, she was just screaming and screaming and she wouldn't stop and that's what he did. I yelled at him and screamed at him."* (p. 849) There was no followup question about exactly what happened, when Chad sprinkled some water in Kassidy's face to break the tantrum, and it worked. There was no follow question about the timing. That is, if the incident was three months previous, what have baths been like since then? The answer would have been that Kassidy was fine with baths, and there was zero problem. As recently as the previous night, on November 8, Kassidy had a bath and Chad, Travis and Kyle were there, and Travis would later report that she was splashing water and having a good time, although she didn't like the shampoo. Amanda, however, was not there that night, but she had given Kassidy a lot of baths since "three months ago," including the bath she had just mentioned on Monday or Tuesday. Instead of more followup on the timeline between Chad's water splashing incident with Kassidy and her subsequent baths, Blodgett moved on to another allegation from Jeff. "*...I've also been told that he pulled her leg once and laughed because it made her walk funny. Do you remember him pulling her leg so she walked funny?* and Amanda responded, *" No. I don't remember that."* (p. 849)

Regarding her conversation with Tristan and the need to be careful, Amanda said, *" I thought she was just lying and stuff....She told me... that he hurt her when they were married....*" Amanda asked, in response to the Blodgett's refrain*, "I've been told."* Amanda asked, *"Who did you talk to?"* and Blodgett said, *"We're talking to everybody...Chad, your sister, Jeff, all the neighbors."* Amanda then asked specifically, *"You talked with Chad already?"* and, after previously claiming that the police had been talking with Chad, Blodgett and LeClair avoided the question. About 20 minutes later in the interview, Amanda asked again, *"When did you guys speak to Chad?"* and LeClair again avoided the question*, "Oh, all they're speaking, we've probably got 15 guys working now on this."* An honest answer would have been, *"No, that was a mistake to say, earlier, that we have talked with Chad. We haven't yet talked with Chad."* (p. 862) The only other interviews so far had been with Jeff and Jennifer.

Angela Blodgett asked, "*... when was the last time your mother saw the baby?"* and Amanda said, *"probably like a month and a half.*" (p. 849) She said later that she talked by phone "*almost every day*" (p. 855) with her mother. Most recently, according to Amanda's recollection in 2011, she had talked with her mother the previous morning, Wednesday, about her babysitting for Kassidy during the upcoming weekend when Amanda and Chad were going to Kennebunkport.

Blodgett continued, *"People are telling me that they know that Kassidy had bruises and have talked to you about this and that's one of the reasons why you weren't taking her to daycare and taking her to Jeff's and not taking her up to see your mother was because she had all these bruises from Chad."* Amanda responded, *"Really?... No, that's not why. I just been on a waiting list since last fall, but I'm on Care Link and they're sending me a package and everything."*

Detective Blodgett then pressed harder, *"... you're not doing Chad any service here. I mean, your baby's dead. I think your priorities should be to at least be honest... for her about what's been going on."* (p. 850) Amanda replied, "*Yeah, but I've never seen him actually like hurt her...he would just get mad at her. Like he would put her in the corner and... be rough with her and he'd play rough with her saying to, like tough her up, play like a boy, you know?*" (p. 850)
Amanda said she meant by "*rough*," swinging Kassidy by her arms, as would later be called, "Airplane" and "Superman."

Detective Blodgett asked, "*... did she have all of these bruises and all of these falls and all of these strange explanations before you were with Chad?*" and Amanda said "*Never.*" (p. 850) It probably seemed like a compelling question to Amanda, but what Blodgett described didn't start happening consistently until early October, which was two and half months after Kassidy moved to Chad's home. There were one or two observations of bruises on Kassidy's face in September, but they were not seen by Dr. Timoney on September 11 and not seen by Jacqueline during a four day babysitting stint in late September, from the 24th to the 27th and not seen on Sunday, October 1, during which day the photo was taken of Kassidy with her bunny rabbit at the Conley's Auburn home.

Blodgett, said, "*I think that deep down, you've had concerns that she had a head injury. I think that you're pretty smart and that you recognized this lethargic behavior and the eyes rolling back in the head as something mildly serious to some degree.*" Amanda replied, with the implicit reference to the fall from Jeff's truck that was previously discussed, "*... When it happened, I just thought she was like tired. I mean, she never had like really bad bruises, you know what I mean? ... I don't know.*" (p. 851) As Amanda had mentioned earlier in the interview, about Kassidy coming home on October 28 from that three-day/two night babysitting with Jeff and Jennifer, there were two other symptoms, dehydration and hunger, and they could have masked the symptoms of the head injuries.

Changing to a different subject, Amanda answered, "*No,*" to Blodgett's question of whether she had "*ever seen him do anything to his son.*" Blodgett continued, "*Does he treat his son the same way that he treats your daughter?*" and Amanda said, "*Yeah,*" and then explained that there were obvious differences, "*He doesn't throw fits like she would. She would throw her head back if she didn't get anything she wanted. She would throw her head back and bang her feet on the ground and she would have temper tantrums like that.*" Blodgett acknowledged, "*That's pretty normal.*" Amanda continued, "*And he would get mad over that because he wasn't used to it.*" (p. 851) This was one of the better examples in the case where the use of a single word would carry incorrectly placed weight. If Amanda had said that Chad was "frustrated" by Kassidy's temper tantrums, that would have implied a more patient and accepting approach than the more assertive and egotistical word, "*mad.*"

Blodgett asked, "*...how would he discipline her?*" and Amanda said,

...I was very lenient. And that's what he didn't like. Like I would just hold her and, you know, be the mom and that's when he... thinks that she should be disciplined.... at first, we would just send her to her room when she does that, but then he would get really mad because she would just go to bed... And it wasn't discipline. So he'd stick her in the corner." (p. 851)

That difference in the approach by a parent and father figure, to temper tantrums, perhaps should have seemed as "*normal*" to Detective Blodgett as temper tantrums themselves.

Blodgett asked about "*other forms of discipline? I mean, since you preferred like a time-out thing?*" Actually, as Amanda presented it, both she and Chad agreed about time-outs, with the difference being that Chad preferred a time-out in the corner of a room and Amanda preferred a time-out in Kassidy's upstairs bedroom. Chad recalled in 2010 that the bedroom time-out was his idea, in a section of his October 11, 2010 Letter, about parenting and discipline,

Regarding putting Kassidy into her bedroom for a time out or nap... Ultimately, I have to take responsibility because I believe it was me that put Kassidy into her bedroom the first time. I recall that Kassidy wanted a cookie and Amanda replied, "after dinner," which was almost ready. Kassidy become very agitated and even my attempts to distract her with a toy were not successful. Kassidy started pulling at her hair and screaming. I had honestly never seen anything like it before. All that kept going through my head was Jeff's claims about how spoiled, "that kid" is. Jeff would often say things like, "Jackie spoiled the shit out of her and she needs discipline." This tantrum certainly appeared like one from a spoiled child. (Shamefully, I must admit, I was taking parenting observations from Jeff who had no children.) This was fairly early on, and I thought he knew Kassidy much better than I did. Jeff certainly had been with Jen much longer than I with Amanda and he had established relationships with each member of the family where I never had the chance. This became very clear when the police started doing their interviews and sharing with the interviewees who they felt was responsible. None of these folks really knew me. Anyway, at this point, I have no idea what I was thinking. It's not a very good excuse but as with the times Jeff would tell me stories about Paul and Jackie, filling my head with all kinds of garbage, he could be very persuasive. He allegedly had seen with his own eyes how "spoiled" Kassidy was.

Anyway, I picked Kassidy up and brought her to the corner for a 30 second time out. She freaked even more and threw herself onto the floor. This was in the kitchen where we

had very hard ceramic tiles. I didn't want her to hurt herself so I scooped her up and carried her upstairs and put her on her bed. After a minute or so she calmed down and I went in to pick her up. Anytime there was any form of discipline such as a time out for her or Kyle, it ended with them sitting on my lap where I could calmly explain why I gave the time out or whatever. I'd follow this with a kiss, hug, and an "I love you." Amanda laughed at me saying that Kassidy couldn't understand what I was saying. I said, "I know, but she will in time and it's important to me to be consistent and always explain things." I wanted Kassidy to know that it was always about the action and not her personally. I loved Kassidy. (It was impossible to meet her and not love her. She was adorable.) I wanted her to understand that love was always unconditional even when certain behaviors weren't ok. I always wanted what was best for Kassidy. Was bringing her to the room right or wrong? I don't know...

I had been sent to my room before as a child and also sent Brent and Kyle in the past when I felt it necessary. I guess at the time I thought I did the right thing. In hindsight, I'm not so sure. Perhaps Kassidy was too young and I shouldn't have used my childhood or Brent and Kyle as the benchmark. Maybe I should have tried harder to distract her thus, focusing her attention somewhere other than, "no cookie." It's easy to sit here and second guess but at the time I did what I knew.

Looking back, I ask myself, "Who cares if she was a little spoiled, would that be the end of the world? It's not like we couldn't have worked on it over time. What would it have hurt if we just let her have the damn cookie before dinner? I mean, she was an awesome eater anyway. The magazines and stuff telling you how to raise your kids aren't always right either." Hindsight is a tough thing. I know I sit here wishing that I had more of the tools that time and reflection seemed to have given me. All I know for sure is that I loved Kassidy and tried to do the best I could for her.

After this first incident I know that Amanda on occasion would put Kassidy in her bedroom for a time out. As you may recall, I wrote earlier that I believed that Amanda was doing the vast majority of the parenting of Kassidy since birth. Where Amanda was just learning, it appears that I taught her this.

Oh, and this whole sock-in-the-door thing that I have heard about has been blown way out of proportion. The door needed to be shaved down to close properly. The door wouldn't close so we always had a sock in the door so that all the other household noises wouldn't wake Kassidy up if she was taking a nap. The door wouldn't stay shut without the sock. There was a crack in the door so we could always hear her when she woke up.

I will say that I think people have overstated how often Amanda put Kassidy in the bedroom for a time out. It happened occasionally but usually only when Kassidy was having the worst of tantrums or was over tired. Actually, I'm sure I brought her up on a couple of occasions. For the most part though, this was a last resort thing and lasted for minutes. I can't speak for when Josh or Scott were at the house because I was really only there with them for a few hours at night but the majority of the time Kassidy was only brought to her room for naps and bed time. Occasionally Kassidy would fuss and cry. What child doesn't? That is part of growing up. Most evenings, one of us would lie there with Kassidy and/or Kyle until they fell asleep. In fact, on Nov. 8th I did just that with Kassidy. This reminds me of something I never told you. I remember when I put her to bed she didn't go to sleep right away. We laid there for a few minutes went around the room pointing things out and she named them. She was so good at that. It appears she had favorite dolls at both houses. At ours, it was the Tella Tubby, Tinky Winky. She had Tinky tucked under her arm. A few minutes later I kissed her on the forehead and said, "Goodnight."

In 2010, Chad wrote about the previously noted time-out for Kyle on the evening of Nov. 8.

O*n page 47 of my interview I presented a "couch scene" with Kyle and Kassidy watching TV on the night of the 8th. You provided my exact statement and asked me about the incident. Despite the view widely held by the police, I disciplined Kyle when he was misbehaving as well. It was after Kassidy's bath and prior to me taking her into the office for the Popsicle if I recall correctly. I sat them on the couch and Kyle was trying to hog* *the entire couch and saying that he didn't want Kassidy on it with him. Just like every brother and sister, they had their moments of jealousy of each other as well as times of getting along. Because of my concern for Kassidy's odd behavior that night, I was paying more attention to her, and I think Kyle was feeling a bit jealous. I told Kyle that the couch was huge and he didn't need the entire thing. I then took the throw pillows and set them up, splitting the couch down the middle informing Kyle that he and Kassidy now each had their own side. Kyle was still not happy with this and kicked the pillows on the floor and tried to hog Kassidy's side too, saying "No, Daddy, I want the whole thing." Kyle was just being bratty so I picked him up off the couch and told him that he needed to go stand in the corner. I can't remember if he just went or if I had to carry him which sometimes was the case. This corner happened to be next to the downstairs bathroom. We didn't have set "corners," so whichever was closest to the event worked. Kyle faced the corner for one minute. This was the general practice because I thought it best that he stare at a "blank canvas" (the wall) and think about the event that led to the time-out. After a minute or so, Kyle came back over and said, "Ok, Daddy, I can share now." As ALWAYS was my practice, I pulled him up on my lap and explained it to him. I'm not sure of the exact words I used but I'm sure it was something very close to, "Kyle, we are a family and as a family we share everything and show each other love. This couch is just as much Kassidy's as it is yours. I hate sending you to time-out probably more than you hate going there, but sometimes your actions leave me no choice. Now give me a hug and can you give Kassidy one too, please?" It is one of my biggest core values that you always share and look out for your family members. I believe the best way to get kids to think this way is to show them the value in it, model it yourself, and talk about its importance.* (Letter, June 30, 2010)

Back to Amanda's interview. Instead of responding to the question about discipline, Amanda switched to the question about Chad's playing with Kassidy, *"... Actually, when he plays rough with I really, you know, I just, I'm forgetting things, but he like picked her up by her head once and I screamed at him, and said, 'You don't do that', you know? And he's like it doesn't hurt her and..."* (p. 851) How many mothers of daughters and sons have had this exchange with the father of the children? I can remember holding a nephew upside down once and my sister was very upset. She was right about being careful, because I remember vividly that I dropped him. Later, Angela Blodgett returned to this incident, "*...when Chad picked Kassidy up by her head, what was going on then? I mean was he angry with her? Was he playing? What?*" and Amanda said, "*He was just playing. She wouldn't cry, either, so I don't think it was like hurting her.*" (p. 853) Despite Amanda's explanation, this image of Chad picking Kassidy up by her head became one of the core phrases of the subsequent newspaper coverage, e.g. "*...and picking her up by the head when he was angry.*" (Foster's Daily Democrat, Dec. 6, 2001.)

Returning to discipline, Angela Blodgett asked a neutral question, and then a leading question, *"... what other things would he use to discipline besides sitting in the corner? I mean would he throw her in the corner?"* Amanda responded, *"Not like throw her, but... just like roughly put her there, you know."* And more leading questions, *"And would he pull her by her arms?... To get her over there? Did he drag her over and put her down, plop her down?"* and Amanda said, *"Yeah."* (p. 851) Later, the press and the prosecutors would talk of Chad throwing Kassidy into a corner, but those began as Angela Blodgett's words, and not Amanda's. She agreed to Blodgett's characterization, as it was easier than disputing her.

Blodgett asked again, *"What other things for discipline if she acted out?"* and Amanda responded, *"My mind's just running right now."* The 18-year old mother had just lost her daughter about five hours earlier and her mind was spinning. *"That's all right,"* said Detective Blodgett, and then she continued with her leading questions without a pause, *"Did you ever see him throw her hard against the wall or anything like that?"* (p. 852) Amanda responded, "*I don't think so,...*" Blodgett pounced on Amanda's wavering, saying, "*You don't think so? That makes me think that ...*" and Amanda continued, *"I don't remember seeing him throw her against the wall."* (p. 852) In the years after this interview, Amanda would tell others, "*If they had told me that the Pope killed my daughter, I would have believed them.*" In the case of Marty Tankleff on Long Island, born two months before Chad Evans, Tankleff was sure that he had slept well before awakening on the first day of his senior year in high school in 1988. Then he found his parents dead or near dead in his bloody home. By the end of the day, the police had convinced him that he had murdered his parents in his sleep, and they had a confession. He was there, after all, and someone had to be held responsible. Police often underestimate their power of their persuasion, which was a particularly interesting issue in Chad's case, because it was alleged that Chad was the "persuasive" one, i.e. that he persuaded Amanda to stay with him despite his alleged abuse to Kassidy.

Blodgett asked, *"And do you have suspicions that he threw her against the wall?"* Amanda answered, *" Well, whenever she used to stand in the corner downstairs, I'd make sure she's okay, you know?... Sometimes he does lose his temper, and I don't know...* (p. 852)

Rick LeClair asked, *"Whose truck did the baby fall out of?"* Amanda said it was Jeff's truck, in his driveway at his home, "*getting her in to bring her home for me.*" (p. 852) She said that on "*that day he did* [bring Kassidy home] *Because I went to a money management course and I got home really late. So he just took her overnight.*" (p. 853) Amanda was either confused or she had forgotten that the plan for that Thursday night, October 26, was for Jeff to keep Kassidy overnight, and to return her the following morning, Friday. However, he didn't bring Kassidy home on Friday and kept her with him and Jennifer until Saturday afternoon. Thus, it was on Saturday afternoon, October 28, when Kassidy fell from Jeff's truck. This was 13 days before she died.

Angela Blodgett turned to the subject of Kassidy's hair, which was brought to the attention of the police by the doctors at York Hospital, and asked, *"What happened with her hair?"* In another room, Steve Hamel had shown Jennifer a photo of Kassidy's head and said that her hair wasn't normal. Amanda said*, "Like, I brush her hair and put it in hair things everyday and I thought maybe it was just I was thinking it could be because she has bald spots from sleeping on it because baby's get bald spots. But I just noticed hair falling out. Not like big clumps, but little pieces and it concerned me."* Blodgett asked, *"...is it falling out in clumps or do you think it was pulled out or ... ?"* and Amanda answered, *"No, I just think like thin her side. She sleeps on her side."* Angela Blodgett, whose experience with young children was not explained to Amanda, said*, "That doesn't really make* [sense]*, I sleep on my side and my hair's never fallen out."* Amanda said, *"Well, I thought baby's hair was ..."* Blodgett argued again, *"Not that I've ever heard of. She's not an infant. She's a toddler."* (p. 854)

In 2011, Chad's sister, who was an elementary school educational assistant and a hairdresser, wrote in an email of her observation of Kassidy on Sunday, November 5, "*I remember her taking a nap on my lap singing her to sleep brushing her hair from her eyes like I do with my own daughter Aliza.... I also remember him* [Chad] *asking me(because I'm also a hairdresser) If It was normal for children to lose their hair. He showed me a spot on the top of her head were a small patch was gone. I assured him It was very normal, children don't get their actual head of hair until 4 or 5 years old. Their baby hair eventually falls out like their teeth.*"

After Amanda said that she talked with her mother "*almost every day*," Rick LeClair asked, "*What do you tell mom?*" and Amanda said, "*Nothing*." LeClair asked if Amanda had discussed "*any of the* [bruises] *with her mother*," and she said, "*I might have... I don't even remember right now*," and described her early motherhood, "*Like when she first was born, my mom took care of her and I didn't because for some reason couldn't handle it and, I don't know if it was postpartum depression or something like that.... And I remember that I moved in again and I lived with her forever and, then I like, like whenever I moved down here that's the first time I ever had her away from my mom."* (p. 855) There was at least one sighting of bruises that Jacqueline must have discussed with Amanda, which was the observation made by Amanda's brother, Joshua and uncle, Robert Conley, on Friday, October 13. It caused enough concern for Jacqueline to call Amanda on the day that she returned from the truck-driving trip with her husband. On that call, she reached Chad, but it surely must have come up in the daily phone calls between Amanda and Jacqueline the following week.

Rick LeClair asked about Kassidy's schedule, and Amanda said, "*...she used to wake up really, really late, like 10 or 11, and I thought she would sleep a lot..... But then she started waking up really early just recently... She goes to bed at 8:30....when I lived in Auburn...She would sleep from like 8 till like 9 or 10.*" (p. 856) Amanda said that Kassidy would take *"a three hour nap,"* starting around *"one o'clock or something like that....She'd cry and say, 'I don't want to go nap,' but I'd ...give her a nap anyway. Then, she'd fall asleep...."* (p. 856) Before her nap, Amanda said she would watch "Blue's Clues" and they would do flash cards together, "*She's really smart.*" (p. 856) Much of the conversation about Kassidy was in the present tense. It was not easy to say, "She **was**..." After Kassidy's nap, continued Amanda, "*..I'd give her a snack. She'd usually want something to drink...and then we'd go on the trampoline outside... And if I had to do an errand or something, we'd do that. Then I'd make dinner...usually* [for] *just her and me....usually I give her a bath around 7:30 and... put her to bed by 8:30...I always did her hair in the morning.*" (p. 857) This was Amanda's description of life before beginning work at Old Navy, which dramatically altered the routine. She said that her mother cut Kassidy's hair "*probably, two months ago,*" (p. 857) which was likely during the babysitting from Sunday, September 24 through Saturday, September 30.

Angela Blodgett asked, *"Did she like CHAD or not?"* and Amanda responded, *"Yeah, she did,...he's the one that taught her a lot of ABCs and the numbers. He'd teach her a lot....Like colors and stuff."* (p. 858) She said that Chad's schedule was usually from around 7:00 a.m. to 5:30 p.m.

Rick LeClair asked, *"Okay, does Chad like to drink?"* and Amanda said, "*He doesn't really drink much. Probably, he hasn't drank in like probably a month. Not usually.*" (p. 859) And he didn't often go to "*clubs*," with the last one being, "*three months ago, 2-3...*" (p. 859) At this point, at 5:20 p.m., an hour into the interview, the officers changed the tape on the audio recorder, and asked about the relationship between Chad and Amanda. Amanda said it began "*six months ago.*" (p. 859) Asked about Chad's separation and divorce from Tristan, Amanda said it was amicable and LeClair asked about child support, apparently looking for stress in the relationship, "*Does he have to give them a lot of money weekly or....?* (p. 860) Amanda knew little, "*... I think he gives them money, but I'm not too sure about it...I don't know how much or anything....*" (p. 860) For some reason, she added, "*Probably not too much.*" It was perhaps some kind of reflex negative answer which filled a space in time, but it made no sense. She knew that Kyle was going to a private school/day care, because Amanda drove him there many times, but she may not have known that Chad also paid for Brent's education. She apparently did not know about the several education funds Chad had established for Brent and Kyle. She knew that Chad had given her money for Kassidy, most recently the $300 for clothes, the previous Sunday. She knew that he had purchased a boat that summer and she knew that he had purchased three 3-wheelers that fall, and they had taken trips together. Amanda told the officers that Chad earned "*around $70,000 a year*," (p. 861) which was correct. LeClair was interested, judging from his question, "*He was able to keep the house?*" that Chad was able to keep living in his home, when Tristan and her sons moved out. That would have been a good question to ask Chad or Tristan, but it wasn't asked.

Rick LeClair asked, "*...what did you do this summer with the baby for... fun*?" and Amanda's first response was, "*Went swimming at his mom's...we went twice... They're in Keene... Oh my God.*" (p. 861) Perhaps LeClair or Blodgett might have thought to themselves, "*We've been told by Jeff that you kept Kassidy away from his parents....*" They might have made a note to plan interviews with Chad's parents, but no such interview, not even a telephone interview, was ever conducted. They would have told the police a lot about Chad and about those two visits. Chet would also have told them of his vivid memory of Kassidy walking into the brick chimney in his living room and falling backward to the floor.

Rick LeClair returned to Kassidy's death, "*...we need to get the... truth out of everybody... the Emergency Room doctors said it appeared to be... a major assault....*" and

Amanda replied, "*Something must have happened today, then. While I was at work.... I don't know.* (p. 862) LeClair pressed, "*Now are you telling us that... when you dropped Kassidy off there was absolutely nothing wrong with her?*" Amanda corrected him, "*I told you she was like really tired, and .... I saw a bruise on her right here and here. On her eyes. I didn't notice anything on her body, but when I got her dressed this morning, I didn't have contacts in and my vision's 20/800 so ... I didn't notice that it was hurting or anything. I noticed that she wasn't really hungry and didn't eat very much. I don't know why I didn't think to bring her to the doctor."*
(p. 863) This was one the few occasions when Amanda or anyone caught the police with an exaggerated question or recollection.

LeClair asked about the babysitting arrangements with Jeff, and Amanda said that he charged her *"Nothing...until I found a daycare. Well I had landscaped for him for free."* In 2010, Amanda added that he gave him her food stamps given to her by the State of Maine.

Asked about the logistics of care for Kassidy on the 8th, Amanda said that "*Well, I was supposed to get out of work at 8:00. I was going to call Chad and see if he'd pick her up...I was going to call him to pick her up at like 5:30.*" (p. 863) This would have meant a 12 hour day for Amanda, and a late pickup for Kassidy, so Amanda anticipated or hoped that Chad could pick up Kassidy at about the same time as on the 8th.
In a June 2, 2010 letter, exactly ten years after he met Amanda, Chad recalled the modification of the November 8 babysitting arrangements,

I think Amanda had arranged for Kassidy to stay at Jen and Jeff's overnight because she was working until 11 P.M. or so Wednesday and then had to be to work early the next day so Amanda would have just been bringing Kassidy back to Jeff's early the next morning. At some point, possibly the day before, I offered to Amanda that I would pick Kassidy up because I knew I was feeling uneasy about Jeff watching Kassidy. My thinking was, if Jeff watched Kassidy for a few hours, that was one thing, but she shouldn't be there for any more overnights and certainly, she should be with Amanda or I as often as possible until we could get Kassidy into some proper day care. I didn't outright know what the problem was, but I had a very uneasy feeling about him watching Kassidy. That is why I approached Mrs. Edgar about her taking Kassidy early at the Cross Road day care program. Things were sitting in the back of my mind, ex. Kassidy fell out his truck window, he spanked her ass so hard it black-and-blued, and he claimed his hand stung. He admitted putting a pillow over her face, and he stepped on her foot, and there were unexplained bruises on her cheeks. Then there were the pinpricks that I found on Kassidy's feet after she came back from spending the day with him, etc. My intuition wasn't working, and connecting the dots, the way it should have been; but it wasn't completely asleep. All of these things were seeming to happen too often. I was outright telling Amanda that we needed to get her into regular day care, but I was trying to be careful at the same time. This was her daughter and the last thing I wanted was for Amanda to think I was trying to control her in any fashion. Also, this was about her sister and her sister's boyfriend (also a friend and business associate of mine), and not just any babysitter." (Letter, June. 2, 2010)

Rick LeClair asked, perhaps with some sexist assumptions, *"I mean, how did Jeff get stuck with this?"* and Amanda replied, *"He offered to babysit her. I wasn't even going to take the job because I couldn't work the hours because of her, but he was like, oh, 'I'll take her because I don't have to work right now.' "* (p. 863) She explained that his landscaping work was between the busy seasons of summer and winter.

Angela Blodgett asked about the ballplaying accident the night before, and said, "*It just seems like you're downplaying it to us now, but that you were really concerned that Chad had been hurting the baby again last night.*" That explained Blodgett's theory of the case which was that Chad was abusing Kassidy, but Amanda responded, "*I thought it was Kyle, his son....He* [Chad] *doesn't lie, though. He's really honest. At least to me.*" Blodgett replied, "*... **I think everybody lies.** I think you know enough to know that. Did you ask, did you talk to Kyle about it?* (p. 864) Amanda said that she didn't talk with Kyle, and she probably didn't yet know that Kyle had talked with his mother, Tristan, about the accident, and she didn't know that Travis had talked with both Chad and Kyle about the accident, too. When Amanda came home the previous evening, she knew a little about Kassidy's ride home with Chad, and only a little about the ballplaying accident. She didn't press for a full accounting, as she didn't know yet how crucially important Kassidy's last 24 hours were.

Blodgett pressed Amanda,

Did you really, I mean, I just, I'm not buying either you're really naive and you just are oblivious to the concerns of your child or you don't or you didn't want to have to leave Chad so you were just ignoring all this stuff that was going on and you really did have concerns that he was hurting the baby. I think that that's it. I think that you wanted this to work... And that, you knew that he had anger control issues and wasn't really coping...What, I mean, would he tell you what he would do or would he make up these silly little stories? (p. 865)

Now seeing that the police were beginning to blame her, Amanda's answers and statements seemed to change to what the police wanted to hear. Was this change because she was being more truthful, or because she was trying to please the police, or perhaps because she was starting to believe their theory of Chad being the perpetrator? Maybe she didn't like being called "*naive*," and "*oblivious to the concerns of your child*."

Amanda responded, *"No, I would see,... like I saw him hurt her like he would get mad and grab her by the back of the neck and like toss her into the ... Corner. Like bang her head on the closet door so it would keep her there... Like every, like three times a week.... Maybe more."* (p. 865) This last statement was confusing on its own terms. It may relate to an incident that Chad has described in a letter about Kassidy hitting her head on a closet door, in the context of other time-outs.

You asked about me roughly placing Kassidy in the corner where she hit her head against the closet door in our bedroom. I can't remember exactly when it was but I believe it was sometime in October after Jeff started watching Kassidy. That is when those extreme tantrums started again. I am fairly confident Amanda and Kassidy were laying on our bed and I came into the room and jumped on the bed with them. I leaned over to give Amanda a kiss and Kassidy started flipping out. Crying and pushing me away. Obviously, she didn't want me near mama. I picked her up and set her on the floor standing up. This is normally how I would start this type of discipline. "If you don't want to share mama then you don't need to lay with her." If she got off the bed and stopped fussing within a minute I would bring her right back up on the bed. If she had a bigger fit, which in this instance she did, I would send her to the corner for a timeout. I would say, "You need a time-out, go to the corner." Here she said, "No," so I picked her up and said, " 'No' doesn't work for me." I quickly put her into the corner. When I sat her down she fell forward into the closet door. The closet was one of those hollow, Lauan doors. I didn't push her head into the door or anything like that. I recall on a few occasions putting Kassidy into the corner in our bedroom and having to physically carry her there. One time, she was being so defiant about facing the corner that I physically had to hold her head facing that direction. No real force necessary. On a few occasions she would actually be going so fast running herself to the corner she would "throw herself into it." I swear this was for dramatic effect. Another time she tripped over a blanket or dirty clothes laying on our bedroom floor and actually banged her head pretty hard. This was, I believe, soon after the closet door incident and the only time I recall something resulting in a bruise to her forehead. Kassidy got up crying real tears and running back toward us. The time-out was quickly dismissed as Amanda and I cuddled her because of what we perceived a real injury. After this I think we pretty much stopped sending her to the corner for time-outs. (unless we carried her there). (Letter, April 30, 2010)

Instead of asking for more details about the "*closet*," Blodgett asked, "*...what, what other things have been going on? I mean has it been getting worse?"* and Amanda responded, *"No, it was getting fine for a while and, then, um, like I don't know what happened last night because I wasn't there... Because I wasn't there.... That ... the wiffle ball bat, what I told you."* (p. 865)

Blodgett challenged Amanda, *"And did you confront him about that? About whether or not that was true?....Because a little plastic wiffle ball bat isn't going to leave a, I mean, it looks like someone got slapped in the face."* Why should Amanda "*confront*" Chad about the ballplaying accident? She never thought that Chad was a liar. She was annoyed with him for being so stupid and careless, but the only lie that she knew about was the lie that she and Chad created, the "trampoline story," and she hadn't yet discussed that story with the police. She didn't even discuss the ballhitting incident enough with Chad to clarify exactly how it happened, i.e. with a bat or a wiffle ball or other type of ball. It was a stupid accident and the truth was not the issue. Amanda saw the bruise, and that bruise was not there in the afternoon. The issue was whether the accident had any lasting effect. Blodgett and LeClair continued to press on the wiffle ball issue, saying, *"You're not going to get black and blue over that, like that...That's why they're plastic. That's why they let kids play with them.... Not with a plastic bat. Because they know. Fisher Price knows that they're going to bop each other over the head with it."* (p. 866) The detectives were correct that the bruise on Kassidy's eye was not likely made by a wiffle ball, or even by a plastic bat, but the problem was that they answered their doubts with the conclusion that Chad was lying, instead of asking themselves whether their understanding, and Amanda's understanding, of the accident was correct. Now, because Amanda thought that Chad had told her that Kassidy was hit with a wiffle ball, she surely began to think that Chad did lie to her. As their telling of the "trampoline story" to others showed, once you burst the dam of trust, you unleash a torrent of suspicion, which the police were eager to exploit - because it supported their quickly-formed theory of the case.

Blodgett asked, *"Now, other marks on her face? Were those there last night? Are those new? What were those from?"* Initially, Amanda asked, *"What marks?... I didn't see them?"* Did she not remember other bruises? Or did she intentionally act like she didn't know? Or was she simply too defensive as a mother? Or too confused and shocked by the day's events? Any of these feelings could have triggered an initial defensive reaction to deny knowledge. LeClair said, "*...they're very visible. People have seen them and it's, you know, you would have seen them, I don't care if you didn't have your glasses on."* Recovering and remembering, Amanda said, "*Yeah, that was from when he would get mad at her and he'd grab her like·this."* (p. 866) One problem is that it appears that she was taking LeClair's word that there were other bruises on Kassidy's lower chin, rather than recalling them on her own, and then she was guessing as to the cause. The other problem here was that Amanda described Chad's actions, but not the motivation. Holding Kassidy's face to ensure her attention, and accidentally holding it too hard, so as to cause bruises, is not the same as holding Kassidy's face intentionally hard enough to punish with pain.

Rick LeClair asked Amanda, "*...this has got to be hard for you. I mean, do you live in Buckfield, Maine, or do you live down here in Rochester with a guy who's making $70,000 a year? Where money isn't a problem.... I mean, you're 18 years old."* Now Amanda was beginning to be persuaded by the police, saying, *"Yeah. It looks like my fault....I know, but it is because I didn't leave. I should have seen it."* (p. 867) For Amanda, the dream was collapsing, and another man had let her down, because the police must be right, as she and Jennifer would say, "*Do you know what I mean?*" First, her father, and then her stepfather, and then Kassidy's father, and her boyfriends, and now Chad. She had survived the earlier losses, and she was struggling to survive this.

Blodgett continued, *"I mean why, why didn't you, did you confront him at all about what he was doing and what did he say?"* and Amanda replied, *"Yes. I don't know why I didn't think it was that bad. Now, I do, but I didn't think it was like hurting her or traumatizing her and I just thought like he would make, because he was like disciplining her and I thought it was good, you know? I don't know why I thought that, but I did."* (p. 867)

Angela Blodgett opened another area of inquiry, *"... the doctor at the hospital and I have seem some photographs. Her genitals really looks irritated. Had you noticed that"* Amanda responses to this and followup questions were, *"No, not at all.... Never.... No, not at all.... No. and Oh my God... he was not like that at all. Because I was sexually abused when I was a kid and he knows that."* (p. 868) Blodgett continued, "*...I mean, I'm not sure, but if the doctor's final conclusion is that someone's been penetrating her with, you* *know, an object or her finger, with their finger or something like that, I mean, what is your take on that?"* Amanda's shock continued, *"Oh, my God. I've never even, I've never seen anything like that down there. And I'm really paranoid about that because I'd always, every time I changed a diaper, I'd always look and I've never seen anything like that."* (p. 868) Later in the interview, the subject of sexual abuse was presented again, and Amanda's responses were firmly the same. (p. 881)

Amanda said that she changed Kassidy's diaper on this morning, the 9th, because, *"she pooped really bad."* (p. 868) Actually, she and Chad noticed the smell just before they went to bed the previous night, but they postponed the diaper change. Thus, Kassidy pooped between Chad's diaper change and Amanda's arrival home. Blodgett asked again about "*the area around her vagina being raw and irritated and...*" and Amanda responded, "*... I mean when Jeff would babysit her, he would leave her in her diaper, like a wet shitty diaper and, then by the end of the day, he wouldn't change it... and I would change it* [after bringing her home.] *Maybe that's why she was irritated.*" (p. 868)

Rick LeClair asked a very important question, *"Who besides Jeff, Jen, you and Chad has been with the baby in the last week?... Have you gone out to eat? Have you gone to the store?"* (p. 868) Amanda responded only to the *"out to eat"* portion of the question, and said, *"went out to eat."* and described a meal at a restaurant in Rochester the previous Friday with Chad, Kassidy, Bruce Aube and the roommate, who was Travis Hunt. Chad wrote in his February 12, 2010 letter about that evening,

You asked about the dinner that Amanda testified to us going to dinner with Bruce, Travis and Kassidy the Friday before she died. I am not sure if it was The "103 Main Street" or Spinale's Italian Restaurant about 4 miles up the road from our house in Milton. We loved both places. On this particular night, I am pretty sure (about 90%) that it was Spinale's, and I have an idea that Amanda had her days mixed up and she is describing Saturday evening. First, because she describes Travis being with us. As the Asst. Manager, Travis would likely have been the closing mgr. in Portsmouth. Second, I am pretty firm on what we already have for that Friday in the chronology. Saturday is a much slower night in the fast food industry than Friday typically, and it is more likely Travis would have been with us then. Also, for some reason, I recall splitting a steamed mussels-in-sauce appetizer with Bruce at Spinale's. We did that from time to time. Lastly, we have Amanda making phone calls on Saturday evening from our home phone, setting up plans for the next day with her sister. I had a big day planned for Sunday so it makes sense that we were close to home.

The two things that stick out in my mind about this is:

1. We were out in very public places on both Friday and Saturday with Kassidy, just days before her death and she wasn't all BEAT up.

2. We were with friends, who were also around Kassidy that evening. It is not likely they would remember this one night from 10 years ago without sharing some recollections, but this is where Travis and Bruce's help would be great.

There was no further police followup with Bruce or Travis or Amanda about that restaurant outing, only five or six days before Kassidy died, except for Rick LeClair's subsequent questions, below, to Amanda during this interview.

Returning to the interview, Amanda then switched to the immediate concern of where she was going to sleep on the night of the interview, but it was unresolved.

Unfortunately, although the police did return to the question of who saw Kassidy the previous week, it wasn't fully explored. They asked if Amanda had seen any of her friends the previous week, and she said "*No.*" (p. 871) In addition to those just mentioned by Amanda as being at the restaurant the previous weekend, that list would have included many more people.

Among those to be interviewed by the police were:

Kyle Evans - most days and nights during last week.

Tristan Evans - during a pickup or drop off of Kyle at Chad's home.

Brandon Harvey - husband of Nicole Evans, Sunday, Nov. 5.

Nicole Evans Harvey - sister of Chad and wife of Brandon Harvey, Sunday, Nov. 5.

Travis Hunt - several of last seven days.

Tom McNeil - at the time of the Nov. 9 emergency, and perhaps earlier.
Will Peirce, - around Nov. 7, during partial fall from Jeff's truck, and Nov. 9.

Among those never interviewed by the police were:

Lisa DeVoe - friend of Brandon and Nicole Evans Harvey, Sunday, Nov. 5.
Jessica Edmands - girlfriend of Bruce Aube, who was probably at the Fri./Sat. restaurant dinner.
Gerri Harvey - mother of Brandon Harvey, Sunday, Nov. 5.
Steve Harvey - father of Brandon Harvey, Sunday, Nov. 5.
Tom Harvey - grandfather of Brandon Harvey, Sunday, Nov. 5.

Places Kassidy was taken to:

Olympia sports - Saturday, Nov. 4(?) or in October?
McDonald's drive-through, Kittery , Tuesday, Nov 7, or Thursday, Nov 2.
BJ's Wholesale Club, Friday evening, November 3.
Spinales (or 103 Main St.) , Rochester, on Saturday, Nov 4.
Dunkin' Donuts drive-through, in Alton, Sunday, November 5.

By this time, police were forming a picture of Chad, and it wasn't good. Blodgett mentioned Chad's "*temper, ... lack of coping skills, low level of frustration,*" but the police never seriously asked his employer about those alleged traits, which were certainly not characteristic of successful managers. There were only two contacts with Colley-McCoy by the police which were both with Chad's manager, Bob McDougall. New Hampshire State Police Sergeant James White called him on January 2, 2001 to confirm the time, date and place of the Exeter Inn celebration on Friday, August 25. Later, on January 11, White interviewed McDougall at his office. There were no requests for Chad's employment records or his work schedules

Rick LeClair returned to the Amanda's interview to ask about Kassidy's behavior at the restaurant dinner the previous Friday, and Amanda responded, "*She was good. She just sat there. She was real good. She drank chocolate milk and I gave her,...I fed her.* [sitting in a] *High Chair.*" (p. 872) Rick LeClair asked about the person Amanda described as a good friend in Rochester, and Amanda gave him her phone number, from memory, but no policeperson ever contacted Jessica Edmands. She was at the Kittery police station on the evening of the 9th, according to Bruce in his Nov. 15 interview. (p. 1349)

Amanda said that Kassidy did not form complete sentences, but she called her grandmother, Jacqueline, "*Nana*," and Aunt Jennifer, "*Auntie*," and that "s*he would surprise me when she said, "seven, six, seven, eight, nine." I'd be like, "Wow."* (p. 873) She said that her favorite toys were "*a Teletubbie that she loved and a bunny*." (p. 873) She described Kassidy's bedroom, which was actually Chad's stepson, Brent's, but "*...we'd get to see him, probably like once a month he comes by. So it's not really, it's like her room, but you know, she plays with all his toys and I have all her clothes there, everything. Like her, we live there. We just didn't want to say that we actually live there,...*" (p. 873) This was an honest statement of her living status with Chad. Because of the fear that living together would interfere with the terms of Chad's upcoming, or thought to be upcoming, divorce or because of the ASPIRE residency requirements or because of Amanda's mother's anticipated disapproval, Amanda and Chad were reluctant to openly state the truth, that they were, in fact, living together. Many of us have been in that situation, but only a few have been asked about it inside a police interview room after the death of a child.

Rick LeClair asked, *"Does, did Chad buy clothes for the baby?"* Amanda's response was an apparently reflexive, *"No,"* as if she was trying to deny her dependence upon him, but then she said, *"I was going to pay him back, but I never did yet."* LeClair asked further, *"Did he give you an allowance?"* and Amanda responded, *"Yeah... he gave me like $300 for shopping."* (p. 873-74) As with so many other questions and answers in this and other police interviews, there was more to be said, and what was said was misleading. Chad didn't give Amanda an allowance as the term is commonly understood to mean a regular payment of a specific amount of money. Instead, he gave her money for her own needs and for purchasing items for the shared home, such as groceries and toilet items. When they discussed what she needed, he would give it to her, with some to spare. The

$300 that she mentioned was a specific gift of money to purchase clothes for Kassidy on Sunday, November 5. It was not a loan, and Chad didn't expect any of it back. That night, when Amanda showed Kassidy and Chad what she had purchased, they all shared the pleasure. If the police had explored the use of that $300, they would have asked for more information about that critical day of Sunday, November 5, when so many people saw Kassidy, and saw so little wrong with her.

Responding to leading questions, Amanda partially described Chad's treatment of Kassidy. Rick LeClair asked, "*... how would Chad be when he gets home from a hard day's work at McDonald's and then you sit down for supper and all of a sudden the kids start, start being kids, acting up?*" Amanda responded, "*It's not really like, more like that night when she wouldn't go to bed. That's when he would get frustrated with her and when she would, it's when she cries... Like if he would kiss me and she's there or when he would come into the room when I was in the room.... And he'd grab her by the face and tell her to be quiet.*" (p. 874) Chad has written in 2011 that he never grabbed Kassidy's face and told her to be quiet. Instead, he would explain to her that she and he could share Amanda's love, sometimes, to ensure eye contact, he would hold her face. If she didn't stop crying, he'd tell her that she needed a time-out. Also, as he explained in a letter, he developed a better strategy of kissing Kassidy first when he walked into a room with both of them. This paragraph describes the initial adjustments,

Things moved quickly. Of course, for the kids there was a small adjustment period. They were both young so it helped. In Kyle's case he went from his mom and dad living together to daddy alone to daddy with Amanda. For Kassidy, she hadn't had a daddy figure in her life. There were some testy moments from time to time in the beginning. Kassidy would occasionally have a fit if Amanda came up to me or if I approached Amanda. They weren't like fits I'd ever seen before. When Kassidy was having one she would scream at the top of her lungs. If Amanda happened to be holding her and put her down to stand during one of these outbursts, Kassidy would throw herself backwards landing on the floor and pound the back of her head off the floor hoping that Amanda would pick her back up. Of course, she usually did. We didn't want her to hurt herself, but it was clear that Kassidy had learned very early how to manipulate her mother. I didn't think it was big deal. I just knew it was something we would have to work on. If limits or boundaries aren't set, then children rule the roost. I think that Kassidy was just used to having mama to herself and was letting me know in those moments that Amanda was hers. Every child is an individual anyway and I was used to boys, so I had to adjust too. I soon learned that if I came home and went up and played with, hugged, and kissed Kassidy before approaching Amanda, she was fine. I would say that by early July everything was fine. Everyone had adjusted. Kassidy wasn't throwing those temper tantrums and we were clicking along. (Letter, Jan. 20, 2010)

Then Blodgett asked about Chad's treatment of Kyle, and Amanda said that Tristan told her that Chad would never hurt his son. Amanda said that Kyle "*...threw up once and he* [Chad] *slapped him on the butt, but it wasn't nothing like nothing.*" There was no followup question to that odd statement. What kind of a parent would spank their child because the child was sick? Unless, of course, you are the Chad Evans that the police have envisioned. It should have been obvious to the police that there was more to that story. Chad comments on this part of Amanda's interview in his March 22, 2011 Letter,

I have no idea what Amanda was talking about here. I don't believe that I would EVER spank a child for getting sick. If you think back to other parts of Amanda's interview, she would describe me being the most patient with Kassidy when she was sick. Didn't you have a quote from Amanda that said something close to this: "He was really good with her, (Kassidy) holding her and helping me walk her all night."? I would like to see the surrounding parts of the interview so I can get a context. I can only speculate from the small amount that you have provided, that Amanda was extremely nervous and wasn't liking the direction the interview was going. Amanda was likely feeling the intense pressure the police were applying that I was an unfair disciplinarian to Kassidy and Amanda was trying to give a sample of how I disciplined Kyle as well. In this instance, I suspect that Amanda made it up.

As I read more and more books on wrongful convictions, law review articles and case studies, I have found that it is not that uncommon for a person during interrogations to "adlib" especially during uncomfortable silences or instances were it is obvious to the person being questioned that the police are off base. Unfortunately, the police are the professionals and filling these "pauses" or trying to convince them of something is often detrimental. Amanda's ending "but it was nothing like nothing" tells me that after she said it, she immediately regretted it or knew that it was nothing/not true. Put it this way. I am so confident that it didn't happen that if you asked Amanda today, "Do you ever recall seeing Chad spank Kyle after he threw up?" she would not have a memory of saying it to the police.

Blodgett asked more about Chad parenting, "*Do you think that he treated Kassidy harder? Was he harder on her? ... Demanding things that maybe weren't very realistic from a one and a half year old?"* and Amanda responded, *"Yeah, I think he was a little bit. A little bit more mean to her.... I'd always say, 'She's not three,' You know,' she's going to throw a fit.' "* Blodgett asked, *"...do you have concerns about anyone else mistreating Kassidy other that Chad?"* It was an interesting question, because Amanda had told the officers about Jeff's babysitting of Kassidy, and of injuries received at his home, but Angela Blodgett had already decided to focus on Chad, despite what Amanda said to her and LeClair. Amanda responded, "*She's not around anybody else. I mean, her and Kyle would fight and stuff and they'd hit each other and bite each other, but there's nothing, I didn't think that was bad."* (p. 875)

Blodgett asked, *"Did you ever notice bruises and things like that after Chad would discipline her by, you know, grabbing her by the face and stuff?* Amanda responded, *"Yeah, like after he'd grab her face, she'd have a little bruise here and there."* Rick LeClair pointed out that, *"...it takes quite a lot to make a bruise on a baby because I've done the same thing to my kids and I never, ever have even left a red mark grabbing them on the face. There's got to be a lot of anger displayed. What were you thinking when that was going on? I mean that's not just going like that, that's a crush that makes those bruises."* (p. 875) Even though the interview had previously considered the idea that Kassidy bruised easily, the question focused only on Chad, rather than on the bruising. LeClair was right that it would be very difficult to cause a facial bruise on a normal child by holding his or her face. No one in the room thought to clarify the frequency of such bruising. Chad estimates that he held Kassidy's face perhaps about 12 times, with bruising resulting about 3-4 times, during the months of October and early November. There was no followup question about possible medical reasons for easy bruising, such as anemia.

LeClair said, and it wasn't a question, "*You must have been petrified yourself.*" And Amanda replied, *"I don't know what was wrong with me, like I seriously don't. I don't know why I didn't do anything about it. I'd yell at him.* [and Chad would say] *'She's a brat, she's bad....She needs to get disciplined or she's going to keep being like this.' "* (p. 875)

Blodgett asked, *"Did he say something about her being stupid?"* Amanda responded with another topic, *"Like when she's been sick. Like she was sick for a while. She was kind of like, you know, I always thought she was tired. That's when she was dehydrated when she came back from falling out of the truck."* Then she connected the truck fall with Blodget's question, *"He was like 'well, she's not very smart for her age,' and he would say things like that."* (p. 876) It was again apparent that the police were willing to believe anything bad about Chad, and this was another bizarre example. What parent or father figure would say that a child who comes home with two large bumps on head and is hungry and dehydrated is "*not every smart for her age*." The police had already heard Amanda tell them that Chad helped Kassidy with her ABC's and 123's. In this incident, Chad and Amanda were up most of the night, on Saturday, October 28, sharing the holding of Kassidy as she was clearly sick.

Blodgett asked, *"What about the walking funny thing?... He made fun of her walking funny or was that?* and Amanda said, *"It made me mad. I don't know about ... Oh, yeah, he would make fun of her because she walked inward."* (p. 876) There's a difference between laughing at a child who trips or stumbles and laughing at a child with a handicap who does the same thing. When you are a police person trying to find the truth about a child's death, humor is not always appreciated. It's been noted earlier in this chapter that Chad and his mother urged Amanda to have a doctor look at Kassidy's feet and her walking. Amanda again told the officers that she took Kassidy to the doctor's for that problem, and "*They said it would get better*," without the need for surgery. (p. 876) It was not such a severe problem that everyone noticed it, because Chad's mother was the first to suggest that it was a condition that should be examined by a doctor.

Chad wrote another time about the incident when both he and Amanda laughed when Kassidy tripped when rushing on her own into the "corner" for a time-out .

You asked about the time we sent Kassidy to the corner in our bedroom and she tripped over a pile of clothing or blanket on the floor, and went head first into the corner causing a bruise on her forehead. (As you can see from the photos of our bedroom, there always seemed to be some clothes on the floor). Yes, I believe this was the incident where Kassidy started crying. Amanda and I rushed over to her, and then joked with each other that we would have to put padding on the closet door/corner area. Kassidy had also, for lack of a better word, "thrown" herself into the corner on a couple of occasions also. You have to remember that Kassidy had been walking for less than a year so her balance was an issue, as with all babies. I am reminded of that as I watch my now 16-month old niece, Aliza, navigate the toys and obstacles in the visiting room. If we had informed Kassidy she needed to go to the corner for time-out, this became a very dramatic experience from time to time. Depending on how tired she was, what she had done, if voices were raised, etc. In these instances, Kassidy would tilt her head back, squint her eyes up, start crying loudly and running toward the corner. More than once, I have witnessed this run where Kassidy was going faster than her little legs could gracefully carry or stop her against momentum prior to hitting the wall. In those few instances what stopped her was the corner itself. Kassidy wasn't actually walking up to a wall and "throwing" herself into it as the police/prosecutors characterized it from my interview. Under the conditions of an interview, I was describing as quickly as I could what seemed to fit and "throwing herself into walls" were the short words for something much more elaborate. To me it was obvious that Kassidy wasn't purposefully "launching" herself into walls. Had I known at the time that the police weren't going to use more common sense or ask me to describe something more thoroughly that they didn't understand, I would have attempted to be much clearer in describing what I had witnessed. It seems that this case is full of instances where something was said but meant far differently than how the police and others interpreted it. This has become very evident over our last several letters. Sadly, once something is said and misinterpreted, you rarely get a chance to explain how it was meant or even if you do, the sincerity is questioned. I believe I just hit on the head why I had preferred, until now to say nothing and have such a phobia of talking to the media and others. (Letter, March 8, 2011)

The interview then turned to logistics. Amanda said, "*... I want to see someone that I know. I've been alone for, since it happened....like I need somebody here with me,*" and she asked again, "*Did you guys talk to Chad? Did you find him?*" Blodgett answered, while noting that it was 5:51 p.m., "*Oh, yeah. Yup, he's here.*" (p. 877)

Shaken by what the police had told her about Kassidy and their theories about Chad, Amanda was ambivalent, "*He's going to be mad at me, now.*" and "*I just want to like see him again.*" (p. 877)

Returning to the substance of the interview, LeClair asked, "*... have you ever caused any injuries?* and she responded, "*Never. Well, like I would hit her like a little bit. Once I did it just so he wouldn't hit her hard. You know? Like I hit her on the butt, so he wouldn't touch her and I was like, 'Don't touch her. I will. I'll do discipline.' ... I did that once because I was mad about it.*" (p. 878) Again, Amanda began her answer with a defensive and reflexive negative to a challenging question, as she said, "*Never.*" Then, with time to think, she responded substantively. LeClair said, "*And your explanation is that she was...a jealous person...*" and then he speculated, despite what Amanda had said earlier about Kassidy liking Chad, "*Maybe she knew more than us. She didn't, she didn't like him.*" Now believing the police theory, Amanda said, "*Yeah. People would, my friends would tell me maybe it's a sign. I feel like so stupid, now. Like I didn't do enough.*" (p. 878)

Rick LeClair asked a very good question, *"When's the last time you saw him hurt her?"* Amanda answered obliquely, *"Well. I don't know what he did last night because I wasn't there, but ..."* (p. 879) Unfortunately, LeClair didn't press for an answer to his question. If one assumes that if LeClair was referring to occasions when Chad held Kassidy's face hard enough to cause bruising, no matter how easily, then the answer might have been about several or more days before Kassidy's death. The next time previous could have been about a week to two weeks before that, and so on for a total of 3-4. That was it. He never spanked or hit Kassidy.

Instead of getting an answer to his question, LeClair asked a different followwp question, *"What did he tell you last night? Can you be truthful with us?* By now, Amanda was agreeing with the police theory, and she responded, "*Yeah. ... I'm being totally truthful now. Before I was,... I don't know what my problem was, but I don't even want to see him again now, so I'll tell you everything.... I don't know, I don't remember totally."* (p. 879)

This statement showed how shaky Amanda was. A few minutes earlier, she asked for Chad, "*I just want to like see him again*," even though she had just said, "*He's going to be mad at me, now.*" (p. 877) When a police interviewer is doubting the responses of an interviewee and the interviewee then announces, "*so I'll tell you everything*," that's like a winning a slot machine jackpot, which reinforces the previous belief. Intermittent reinforcement is powerful.

Amanda volunteered, *"I don't think he would care if she like hurt herself."* LeClair was correctly astounded, *"Excuse me? He wouldn't care if she got hurt?* and Amanda confirmed, *"I don't think so."* (p. 879) No followup questions were asked, after this bizarre statement, which conflicted with what Amanda had said earlier, and with the truth.

LeClair asked, *"Okay, you said you were going to be truthful. Last night, what happened last night?"* The only change from what she had previously said was that *"He swings the bat and the ball hit her."* Previously, the police had introduced some idea that perhaps it was a bat that hit Kassidy. Amanda clarified that she came home after work around midnight and saw Kassidy, who was asleep, "*I remember touching her head.... I looked at her face. It wasn't that bad. It was kind of like a little red around.*" Blodgett asked, "*And then this morning she was just kind of out of it?"* and Amanda agreed, *"Yeah. She was out of it."* (p. 879)

Blodgett asked, "*When she was crying and you woke up, is that normal? Does she usually cry when she wakes up?"* and Amanda replied, *" No, well, yeah. Like in the middle of the night. Like Kyle will, then she will. If dog barks and stuff like that."* Again, the initial response to a question which may have implied any kind of fault or imperfection in Kassidy, was, *"No,"* and then was followed by a thoughtful response. When LeClair asked, *"And when she woke up this morning, was there anything that concerned you?"* Amanda answered, *"No, she was just tired and she didn't want to eat. So I gave her cereal in a bag because we were running late. We were late.... I think she took a couple bites of that. I'm not sure, though....I didn't actually see her put it in her mouth."* LeClair asked, *"Was she, yeah, was she able to eat cereal in a bowl? In a spoon?"* and Amanda answered, *"Usually she, you can ask anybody. Like she used to eat so much like more than, she ate more than me some days....Yeah, she would eat a lot, but lately she hasn't been eating much."* (p. 880-81)

LeClair asked, *"What's the worst you've seen him do?"* Amanda answered, *"I, basically, well, when he put her head under the water. He didn't really, he just put her face under the water.... Cold water."* LeClair asked, *"What, what was he saying? When he was doing this?"* and Amanda replied that Chad said, *" 'She won't stop crying,' and I was screaming at him because of it....he just held her up to the sink. He didn't, like he just splashed water on her face, he said."* LeClair asked if Amanda had seen this incident, and she responded, *"No. I heard him and he said he splashed water on her face. But then I, now she's, since she's scared of water. So that's why I was mad over it. She was never before...Like I turn the sink on and she would cry."* (p. 882) The fear that Amanda described was likely not of water, generally, as she had regular baths, but a more specific fear, such as a reaction to a sink faucet being turned on.

Chad recalled the incident in letters in 2010, writing that it was "*was a completely innocent attempt to get Kassidy out of hysterics so that she could breathe.*" and it worked. (Letter, Feb. 3, 2010.

During the exchange about the water splashing incident, Rick LeClair, asked, "*Do you believe anything the guy says?*" (p. 882) Chad was in the police station at the time, waiting to be interviewed, in another hour or so, and no one had yet talked with him. In their interview with Amanda, the police had found no lies by Chad, despite their hopes and predictions. The closest thing to a "*silly little story*" to use Angela Blodgett's phrase, was the "trampoline story," which was not Chad's story, alone, and Blodget and LeClair hadn't yet asked Amanda about that.

Asked LeClair, "*What else did he do?*" Amanda answered, *"... grab her face and, then, throw her on the bed.... Yeah, and grab her arm, too, at the same time. Like pick her up by her arm and hold her by her face."* LeClair tried to picture it, *"How would he do it?"* and Amanda said, *"It's always different. I don't know."* Blodgett asked, *"Was he enraged?"* and Amanda's answer was not responsive, *"Whip her around. That's the thing."* (p. 882-83) Amanda was likely describing play, rather than was LeClair was seeking which was evidence of abuse. There were no further questions about this incident or these incidents, but LeClair was combining descriptions of "eye-contact" holding and playful activity all into one malevolent combination. There was no effort to put such behavior on a timeline.

LeClair moved on to another set of questions, *"Did he ever hit her in the head with anything? Djd he ever throw her in the corner where she hit something solid with her head?*

Amanda responded, *" Yes....Like the closet door....the closet door isn't like a hard door..." Asked "When?"* Amanda responded, *"I don't know. Not too long ago,"* but agreed with Blodgett that it was less than a week previous. (p. 883) By responding *"Um. Um"* Amanda said that she didn't see any bruises on Kassidy afterwards, and Kassidy did not lose consciousness at the time, and not *"ever."* (p. 883) This closet door incident was described in Chad's April 30, 2010 Letter, and earlier in this Amanda-interview section of this chapter

Angela Blodgett asked, *"Okay. You've never seen him pick her up by her hair or anything like that?* and Amanda replied, *"No. Never."* Looking for an answer to what she had probably heard about patches of Kassidy's head without hair, Blodgett asked, *"... would she pull out her hair when she was stressed?"* and Amanda said, *"Yeah, actually like she'd pull on her pigtails and stuff when she would throw a fit. She'd never throw fits with me, though. Only, when he came around.... She was really good with me. Like I was on the computer for a while. I was doing this computer survey thing and she had to watch TV a lot during the day. I'd just have her watch TV or something and she was so good. She'd come out, 'Can I have a drink?' and I'd get her a drink."* (p. 884) What Amanda didn't have time to say, or because the questions were not open-ended, was that Kassidy would get jealous when Amanda showed affection to Kyle, too. Thus, it wasn't an anti-Chad jealousy, but a possessive-Mama jealousy.

Trying to understand the mixed messages, LeClair asked, *"What is it about Chad that you like?"* and Amanda responded, *"Like his personality. Except when he lost it sometimes. I don't think I was, it wasn't really the money thing. It was just like a security thing, I guess.... I never really even had anybody that I could count on, you know."* (p. 884) Now the police had temporarily persuaded her that she could not count on him, either. In the subsequent hours, that changed, and she never wavered again in her belief in Chad. However, what she said to the police during this interview, and the next would help the police make their case and convict Chad, no matter how much she tried to retract what she said.

Angela Blodgett returned to the subject of the morning routine, *"Will she come into the bedroom to wake you up?... How is he with that? Is that allowed? Does she ever sleep with you guys?"* Amanda responded, *"Yeah. He's really good about that stuff like he cuddles her and stuff. Like some days she would let him and some days she wouldn't."* (p. 884)

In a 2010 letter, Chad described such cuddling, and more about their morning routine, *You asked about Kassidy sleeping with Amanda and me and indicated how this counteracts the view that I wanted to get rid of Kassidy. Boy, this is probably another good question to ask Amanda. I know we probably shouldn't have let her sleep with us in society's eyes because of the SIDS thing, but man, it was the best. Do you know how awesome it is to have this cute little blonde snuggle up to you or to wake up with one arm wrapped around "Tinky Winky" and the other wrapped around your neck? Most nights she started out in her bed, but halfway through the night she would wind up with us. Amanda and I usually slept with the door open and Kassidy would sometimes wander in and stand at the bottom of the bed. I would sometimes feel her at our feet early on. She was too small to crawl in, so I would lift her onto the bed. Other times she would have a bad dream or something and start crying. One of us would go to her room and pick her up, and bring her in, usually me. I have always been a very light sleeper.*

I would guess that it was once or twice a week on average that she slept part of the night with us. Amanda and I loved it. I think we both thought of it as a guilty pleasure. If you were looking down from the ceiling, Amanda would be on the left closest to the bathroom and I slept on the right, closest to the front of the house. I loved to sleep on the right so that I could wrap my left arm around Amanda's back if she wasn't sleeping in the crook of my right arm with her head on my chest. Man do I miss this. When Kassidy came in she usually would slip right in between us, in the middle of the bed. Occasionally she would sleep on Amanda's or my side wrapped in our arms (more often Amanda's than me). It was great to cuddle with her this way but we would transfer her to the middle of the bed after she fell asleep. Our bed was pretty high, and we were worried about her rolling out of it. Once she was with us, she usually stayed until the morning, similar to the way Jeremy described seeing her in our bed the morning of the golf outing.

Some of the best nights Amanda and I had, and I am confident Amanda would agree, were when both Kyle and Kassidy ended up in our bed. They were so cuddly then. It's hard to describe but to me it was what life was all about. I'd get to make love to this beautiful woman, and several hours later we had these two tired little babies sleeping between us; looking for protection for whatever was chasing them in their dreams. It's too bad we weren't so good at protecting one of them in real life. Thinking back, I really loved watching Amanda and Kassidy sleep together. Amanda had long hair and Kassidy was always somehow wrapped up in it. Some of my best memories of Kassidy are mornings where it was just she and I awake, she'd open her little blue eyes as happy as could be, and breathe her pungent breathe in my face. I'd say, "You want to go get some breakfast?" and she would have this huge smile on her face and in her eyes and say "yaaa" in a whisper.

I would take her down, strap her into her high chair and feed her some cereal, donuts, toast, or something else. I LOVVVEEEDD watching her eat. She was the best little eater. I always said that I wished Kyle would tend to business the way she did. It was so funny too because she would eat almost anything. I can't remember what it was, but we fed her some vegetable and she didn't like it. She carefully leaned forward in her high chair and spit it out on a spot with no food on it. She was determined not to put it in the same spot as the food she was eating. It was adorable. It may have been tomatoes. I bet Amanda would remember. I feel like an idiot. How can I forget these things? (Letter, Apr. 6, 2010)

Rick LeClair asked another general question, "*What would piss him off the most?*" and Amanda responded,

When she would cry when we would just come into the room, when she was there and all the sudden and not even if he was kissing me. like he would just ... First he would be like, 'Be quiet' and then she wouldn't stop and then he'd grab her by the face. And usually the face.... if she screamed louder. If she screamed louder, it was worse.... Yeah. He'd call her a bitch. (p. 885-86)

Rick LeClair concluded his questions or statements, "*...we're on your side. We want to get to the bottom of this.*" Amanda asked, "*Can I see my family, my sister?*" This first interview ended at 6:04 p.m.

Unfortunately, neither Blodgett nor LeClair asked Amanda about Kassidy's behavior during the first few days of the current week, especially, Wednesday. There were no questions about how she was before being left at Jeff's around 3:00 p.m. There was no discussion of her food and diaper changes, if any. These questions might have been asked if the inquiry was aimed at gathering information about Kassidy's death, instead of already making the case against Chad. In her answers to questions, Amanda did not describe the black and blues which she saw on Kassidy's buttocks after Jeff brought her home on Sunday, October 22. According to Chad in his interview, Jeff had told him that he had spanked Kassidy hard during the Saturday and overnight babysitting stint.

Outside that interview room, Chad had arrived at about 4:10 p.m., which was about the same time that the first three major interviews began, with Jeff, Jennifer and Amanda.

At 4:23 p.m.,Tristan called Chad's cell phone from the parking lot of the Kittery Police Station for an update. Inside the police station, Chad asked Tristan to call Bruce with whom Chad previously had made plans for bowling that evening, in order to cancel those plans. After work, Amanda would have picked up Kassidy at Jeff's and brought her to bowling as well. Also, Chad asked Tristan to call Travis, perhaps about bowling, but mostly so he could go to Chad's home and let Kato outside. ("Chart of Calls") Chad's plan for the evening was to go to a favorite pub/restaurant, "Banana's" in Portsmouth, with Jeremy and then bowling with Bruce and Travis.

At 4:30 p.m. Kristine Keeler, a DCYF supervisor who had been assigned after Kassidy's death to assist Patricia Hocter, called the Kittery Police Dept. and talked with Chad. Earlier she had been working with Rochester Detective Paul Callaghan, and went to Chad's house, but found no one there. Callaghan had given her the Kittery Police Dept. number. Chad told Keeler about his son and stepson and the living arrangements. Keeler wrote in her report,

When I asked him if Amanda lived at his residence, he said yes, with her daughter, Cassidy, but he was not the father and she is involved in a work program in Kittery, making it sound like she does not always reside there. He said he has Kayle [sic] *from Tuesday through Thursday. Tristen was supposed to have Kayle for the night. He also said that he tried to make contact with the Division earlier that day and left a message. At that time I told him I would call him back.* (p. 162)

This was Chad's first substantive conversation with anyone from New Hampshire's DCYF, or even from the police. Among other motivations, he was trying to protect Amanda, not from charges of abuse and homicide, which he didn't understand yet, but from possible charges of welfare fraud. He knew that she was receiving assistance from Maine, even though she had been living in New Hampshire for five months.

Shortly afterwards, at approximately 4:30 p.m., Sergeant Matthew Stewart of the Maine State Police informed Chad that Kassidy had died. Because of the separation and intentional isolation of potential interviewees, he had been unaware until this point of her death.

In 2010, Chad wrote about those terrible minutes,

I sat there in the lobby for a while and finally Sgt. Matthew Stewart from Maine State Police came out to see me. He informed me that something had "happened" to Kassidy. I said, "Oh my God, is she ok?" He told me that she was not. "Unfortunately, she is dead." I was in shock and unable to comprehend what he was saying. I asked how that could be, I had just seen her that morning. "I was just holding her in my arms last night. There has to be some mistake. This isn't possible." I remember I was crying and had this urge to puke. There is a bathroom in the lobby. I went in and dry heaved. I came out and Stewart was still sitting there, calmly. I asked, "How could this happen? How did she die?" (I was dumbfounded). Stewart said, "Well, that's what I was hoping you could tell me. Do you know how she died Chad?" This question pissed me off, it was almost accusatory. I angrily replied, "How the hell should I know? She left my house fine around 7 this morning." Stewart seemed to back off. "Ok, we have to ask these type of questions of everyone to get to the bottom of it. Are you willing to sit by for a few until I can get an officer to talk with you?" I asked how Amanda was, if I could see her? I told him, "Of course I would be here to do anything I could to help." I didn't like how he questioned me if I knew anything, but of course I was concerned and wanted to help. At this point, I still had no idea what had happened to Kassidy. She could have been hit by a car for all I knew.

I sat there for a while longer. It seemed like forever. Then Tristan arrived. We hugged and cried as I told her Kassidy had died. A while later, Amanda's mom, Jackie arrived. She immediately came over and hugged me, crying, asking, "What did he do to my baby, Chad?" I was bawling and said, "I don't know." We embraced for a few. Jackie obviously knew that Kassidy was alone with Jeff. After a while longer the police pulled me back into the heart of the station. Tristan and Jackie were still in the lobby at this point and Tristan overheard some of Jackie's conversation with her brother-in-law. (Letter, Jan. 28, 2010)

It was a very busy afternoon, with a lot of conversations. Unfortunately, Sgt. Stewart did not write a report of this interaction with Chad. If he did, it was not provided to Chad's attorneys. That short conversation between Chad and Jacqueline was the last time they talked as the police soon separated them. Without such charges against Chad, Jacqueline and he could have learned a lot from each other about Kassidy during a normal grieving process.

Shortly afterward, Kristine Keeler called Chad again, and "*asked if we could request that Brent and Kayle stay with their mother until Monday. Until Patricia Hoctor had an opportunity to speak with him.... Mr. Evans stated that he was supposed to have Kayle this weekend and that he has him every other weekend, but he still agreed for the children to stay with Tristen for the weekend.*" (p. 163) Perhaps because of its tardy response to Tristan's anonymous call, the DCYF sought to ensure that Chad's son and stepson were protected from him and did not want anything else to go wrong or reflect badly on DCYF. Already, the implications of the early suspicion of Chad, and the characterization of him as a murderer, were being felt. This conversation shows how rattled Chad already was by Kassidy's death. He knew he was going away for the weekend and that he would not have Kyle for the weekend, but perhaps he hadn't yet made those arrangements with Tristan, as she did have Kyle the previous weekend. Chad would never have Kyle for a weekend again.

Ms. Keeler continued, "*I asked him* [if] *he was going to be ok and at this time it was evident that he was upset about the death of Cassidy. He said, 'This is all very hard.' I asked him if he was going to be ok and if he had someone that was going to be with him and he said he was going to be with his best friend, he was supposed to meet him to go bowling.*" (p. 163) At least, Ms. Keeler was not yet treating Chad like a child abuser and murderer.

According to Detective Baker's "Continuation Report" he and New Hampshire State Trooper Jill Rockey went from the Kittery Police Station to York Hospital, "*to view Cassidy and take photographs.*" (p. 147)

At 4:53 p.m., Tristan Wentworth called Chad Evans' cell phone. Chad was in the police lobby, waiting, and informed Tristan of Kassidy's death, and she then came into the police station. ("Chart of Calls")

At 5:00 p.m., New Hampshire State Police (NHSP) Sergeant James White arrived at the Kittery Police Dept. to join the investigation as the lead investigator for the NHSP. This was another indication that the Kittery and Maine State Police now believed that crimes relating to Kassidy, who died in Maine, had occurred in New Hampshire.
Around 5:15 p.m., Chad was brought to Kittery Police Dept. Detective Ronald Avery's office where he spent more than an hour with Avery. Chad captured part of this time in the excerpt, above, from his Jan. 28, 2010 Letter. While Det. Avery was still with Chad, Chad used Det. Avery's phone, with his permission, to call his mother to tell her that Kassidy had died. Chad was crying and told his mother how he had tried to call her the night before, because of the way Kassidy was acting. Detective Avery did not file a report about this hour-plus period of time with Chad. If he did write a report, it was not provided to Chad's attorneys. In his January 28, 2010, Letter, Chad wrote,

While out back, I sat there forever in a Kittery cop's office. I think he was the Chief or something. His name was Avery. He was really nice. He let me call my mom and I told her

Kassidy was dead. I was bawling my head off. I remember telling Officer Avery how "None of this makes sense. I just had her last night, she was tired, and a little sick but she seemed fine this morning. She even picked out her own cereal, Reese's peanut butter puffs. How can it happen one minute I'm holding her doing the picture game and the next minute she's gone." I think I was thinking out loud, trying to make sense of things. Officer Avery listened well, seemed friendly, almost empathetic. He said, "I know it's horrible." What I couldn't see was it was all just a set up. The state cops would come in every now and then and just say, we'll be with you soon. (All nice as can be.) Meanwhile, in separate interview rooms they were compiling their case against me. When you line it all up, it was like they weren't even interested in theories other than my guilt.

Chad wrote in his Nov. 2000 letter to his attorneys about the same period in Sgt. Avery's office,

I then went back into one of the Kittery captains' offices. He sat with me and just shot the shit for a while. I completely lost it back there. I think it finally hit me that she was dead. I bawled for an hour straight. He let me call my mom and let me break the news to her. He was really nice and understanding. He put his hand on my shoulder and said you will get through it. I just kept saying, "I can't believe it, I just gave her a kiss this morning. I just read her a story last night and did the alphabet with her. I am never going to be able to do those things again. She was just a baby. What could have happened to her?" This officer was very understanding. Finally, after hours and when I had no more tears, they pulled me into a room for questioning. [at 7:10 p.m. See below.]

At 5:25 p.m., MSP Detective Erik Baker interviewed Dr. Anthony Bock at the York Hospital, and Baker summarized that 10-minute interview. Dr. Bock said that Kassidy "*had multiple bruising on her head and face... her feet had small scabs on the bottom,* [which] *appeared to be small needle-like pricks*." The X-rays showed "*no signs of broken bones.*" (p. 1686) Dr. Bock issued his own "Emergency Room Report" as well, and wrote that there were "*no obvious fractures*." (p. 40-42)

After the interview of Dr. Bock, Baker wrote, "*I photographed Cassidy in the Emergency Room, with the assistance of New Hampshire Trooper Jill Rockey.*" (p. 148) Thus, there were now four sets of police photographs of Kassidy's body:

1. ~12:50 p.m. On Jeff Marshall's porch, by Kittery PD. Chief Edward Strong
2. ~ 1:00 p.m. On Jeff Marshall's porch, by Kittery PD. Detective William Hackett.
3. ~ 1:30 p.m. At York Hospital, by Kittery PD. Detective William Hackett. (for total of three rolls by Det. Hackett)
4. ~ 5:40 p.m. At York Hospital by Det. Erik Baker.

At approximately 5:40 p.m. Kristine Keeler of DCYF called the Kittery Police Dept. again and talked with Chad about arrangements for caring for his stepson and son. She wrote in her report , "*It was evident that he was upset about the death of Kassidy.*"

Keeler reported that she then called Tristan's cell phone,

...to confirm that it would be ok for the children to stay with her for the weekend. She said it would. She was very upset and said she just spoke with Chad. I inquired about Brent and Kayle getting physicals and she said Chad would never hurt them, and he wouldn't have done anything to Cassidy. She stated that she never had concerns that he was hurting Cassidy, [but] *that someone else may have. When I asked if she was the reporter to DCYF assessment received this month she said, "Yes," but it was not that she thought Chad was doing anything to Cassidy....*

About this time, Chad's friend Jeremy, age 25, arrived at the Kittery Police Station. He was interviewed later in the evening when he describe his short conversation with Jeff upon his arrival, "*I asked Jeff when I got here, well, 'Jeff did you touch that kid?' And he goes, 'Ah, I spank her, but I don't spank her that hard to kill her.'* " (p. 1770)

At 6:00 p.m., Det. Jill Rockey signed a York Hospital form "Authorization to Release Medical Records," for the Emergency Room records, as the "*patient, parent (or other agent for patient)*." (p. 29) However, Rockey was not such a person. As Amanda had been at the Kittery Police Station since about 1:45 p.m., and was only about seven miles away, and thus readily available, it's not known why York Hospital didn't require Amanda's approval for the release of the Emergency Room records. If she declined, the police could have easily obtained a court order for the information, most of which was already known to the police as Detectives Baker, Hackett, and Rockey had been to the hospital. Detective Baker completed another "Authorization to Release Medical Records," on this date.

At the Kittery Police Dept., Jennifer's second interview began at 6:00 p.m., and would continue until 6:40 p.m. when she was able to meet with Amanda and her mother. Jeff's interview ended at 6:15 p.m., and it was his last interview of the day. Amanda's first interview ended at 6:04 p.m.

At 6:20 p.m., Kassidy's body was transported by hearse from the York Hospital to the office of the Chief Maine Medical Examiner in Augusta, Maine.

6:00 p.m. - Jennifer Bortner Second Interview (pages 950-983)

When they resumed at 6:00 p.m., Jeff Smith again advised Jennifer of her Miranda rights, and said, "*We've talked to many, many people,... Jeff, Chad,... Amanda and, ... the information we're getting from people is not consistent with what we're hearing* [from you, Jennifer] *It isn't fitting together....I also have a problem with some of the stuff you are telling me that is not true.*" (p. 953) He was wrong about talking with Chad, as his interview didn't begin until 7:10 p.m., so the only two people interviewed so far, and still in their interviews, were Jeff and Amanda. At least one of those interviews was in a room with a device or one-way mirror so it could be viewed and heard by others, as was explicitly the case for Chad's interview, though not known to him. From the other interview, as happened with Jennifer's interview, one of the two interviewers might step out for a few minutes and exchange observations with other investigators. However, the major change for Jeff Smith's and Steve Hamel's new approach to Jennifer was that they had seen the police photographs of Kassidy's body on Jeff's porch and at the York Hospital. There may have been some use of Polaroid film, or some regular film was taken to a quick-develop location nearby.

"*Oh my God,*" was Jennifer's response when seeing a few photographs, and they seemed to show more bruises on Kassidy's face than Jennifer had mentioned. Smith said, "*These injuries didn't happen today.. You suppose these weren't there yesterday? Were they there yesterday?*" (p. 956) They put the question this way, even though Jennifer had already told Smith and Hamel that she didn't see Kassidy the previous day, Wednesday. The last time Jennifer had seen Kassidy, before the 9th, was Tuesday morning. Jennifer responded without reflecting about the characterization of "*yesterday,*" and said, "*Yes. There were some on her face yesterday, but they weren't that bad.*" (p. 956)

Jeff Smith told Jennifer, "*We do this for a living. We go to many, many death scenes...*" (p 953) Later, he said, "*Let me show you another photograph. This is called lividity, this colorization here.... This happens after someone has been dead for a period of time....A lengthy period of time...She was dead 4 to 6 hours before this photograph was taken...This, this lividity takes a while to happen. Lividity is caused by blood settling.... It makes it dead when she arrived at your place.*"
Jennifer responded starkly, *"She wasn't dead when she arrived at our place this morning.... she was alive when I left this morning."* (p. 958) Hamel asked, "*Have you seen anybody else hit this child*" and she responded, *"No. I've seen MANDY hit the child on the butt when she's throwing a fit."* (p. 958) As with some of Amanda's responses to difficult questions, Jennifer's first reflexive response was, "*No,*" and then, essentially, a "*Yes.*"

Smith asked her about apparent cuts on Kassidy's fingers, and Jennifer said, "*That's from the cat. That has to be from a cat....Because she's got a little kitten... I just gave my sister a little kitten at the house.*" (p. 958) Jennifer didn't know the cause of a bruise on Kassidy's abdomen or on her chin.

Hamel then told Jennifer that photographs were taken at 1:30-1:45 p.m. and he insisted that blood in a dead person "*Does not settle in an hour and a half... Doesn't happen. It's medically incapable of happening.*" (p. 959) Thus, the photos were among those taken by Detective Hackett at York Hospital. Jennifer insisted, *"The kid was alive when I left for work this morning,"* and Smith responded, *"She couldn't have been,"* and again, *"She couldn't have been."* Jennifer stood firm, *"She was in the bed eating Cocoa*

Puffs." About her not seeing the bruise under Kassidy's chin, Jennifer said that in the morning, Kassidy *"had a sweatshirt like up to her chin...."* (p. 959)

This dramatic exchange reminded me of one of my favorite scenes in the TV program of the 1960's, "Dragnet," where Sgt. Friday grills a burglary subject and tells him that the victim homeowner saw him in her large house's library, and the alleged burglar responded, "*She couldn't have, the lights were out.*" There was no such made-for-TV resolution at this interview with Jennifer, and the time of Kassidy's death would still be a controversy a year later at Chad's trial, but it seemed that she died around 12:30 p.m., around the time of Jeff's calls for help.

Smith pressed Jennifer, "*...we need to get at the truth. This is a serious matter. I need to hear from you.... I know you want to protect somebody in this."* and Jennifer responded, *"Yeah, Chad."* (p. 960)

This must have seemed to the police to be a breakthrough, as they had, by dramatic confrontation, persuaded Jennifer to say what she hadn't said before, and it seemed to confirm what Jeff had told Scott Harakles and Jeff Linscott about Chad's alleged abuse.

Smith asked, *"What's Chad been doing?"* and Jennifer responded, *"When she, when she's bad, he like, he just grabs her face like that, but, basically, that's it."* (p. 960) Smith told her that probably the ballplaying story "*probably wasn't just an accident. It probably happened intentionally.*" (p. 961) As tempting as it must have been, the police during the first few hours of an investigation should not have been telling interviewees what they thought of any part of their investigation. As soon as interviewees learned the police theory, and given the nearly universal desire to help the police solve the mystery of Kassidy's death, the recollections and statements of interviewees tended to contain what the police wanted to hear, to confirm their own theories.

Jennifer said, "*She's always had, red, red, like red marks all over,..?"* (p. 962) but this observation was never checked with anyone else, such as Amanda, Chad, or Jacqueline. If even partially true, and despite Hamel's and Smith's insistence that it was lividity, it might have been a clue for understanding what was happening to Kassidy. Perhaps such marks were simply not worth mentioning by Kassidy's pediatricians or others, but now, given Kassidy's tragic death, they might have some significance.

Hamel and Smith pressed Jennifer with the possibilities: Either it was Amanda or Jeff, both of which Jennifer dismissed. Smith insisted, "*Who did? I need to get the truth. You're only dancing with me. You only tell me parts of what you either know or believe happened.*" (p. 962)

Jennifer then said, *"I believe that Chad hurt her. Because Chad had squeezed her face... Mandy's told me stories."* (p. 963) One of those stories was "*Like one time she was crying and she wouldn't stop crying so he picked her up and put her face under the faucet*" (p. 963) However, it was Chad who told Jeff and Jennifer about that water splashing incident, when the four of them were sitting at Chad's dining room table on Sunday, October 22. This was after Jeff and Chad had brought the 3-wheeler that Chad purchased for Amanda back from Maine.

Smith and Hamel asked about sexual abuse of Kasssidy, and Jennifer again dismissed Amanda and Jeff as possibilities, but "*What about Chad*?" asked Hamel. Jennifer said, "*I don't know. I don't know. .... I've heard stuff about, from Mandy, about what Chad's, you know, done...but I don't think he....*" (p. 963) For the police, the doubts about Chad were weaker than they were for Amanda or Jeff, and that was enough to help push them toward Chad being the abuser.

Smith then assessed the case, "*This child was tortured over a period of time. This just didn't happen one day.*" (p. 964) This was the first characterization of Kassidy as being tortured.

Jennifer insisted that Kassidy's real complexion that morning "*wasn't as dark,*" as the photographs. She said about the bruises, "*...she's always had bruises on her. On her face... But they weren't... they weren't nearly that bad. And I've always said something to Mandy, ... I went like...she's got a black streak on her face? Because he did squeeze her face like that a lot. And you can see, see where the squeeze marks were because it's like ???*" (p. 966)

Steve Hamel showed Jennifer a photo of Kassidy's head and hair, saying, "*Little kids at 18 months do not lose their hair like that.*" Responded Jennifer, "*She has real thin hair....*" (p. 966) and then defended herself, "*I've never, you know, I don't. I'm not with her all the time. I can show you my work proof... My schedules and stuff. Like this week, I saw her about twice and that was like this morning.*" (p. 966) Later, Jennifer said that she didn't see Kassidy on Wednesday, but did see her Tuesday "*for a couple hours..*[and] *she had a little bit of bruises, but they weren't that bad.. They weren't that dark.*" (p. 967)

Pointing to Chad, Jennifer said, "*But that's... that's Mandy's boyfriend... she told me what's going on...She told me it was going to stop... The only reason I didn't call anybody is because I didn't want the baby taken away from Mandy.*" (p. 967-68) Hamel followed up, "*So you've been concerned a while about the bruises?*" and Jennifer said, "*Yeah. So has my mother. ...my mom's known about them and Mom's known it's from Chad...*" (p. 968)

Continued Jennifer, *"Chad's wife left him because he beat her."* (p. 968) With Mandy, "*..he used to choke Mandy... she said it didn't hurt, but it hurt after...*" (p. 969)

Trying to present the timing, Jennifer said, *"They've been together for 6 or 7 months, but, and the bruises didn't start until she started moving in with Chad." (p. 969)* It was more precisely five months and a week, or 160 days since Jeff and Jennifer introduced Amanda and Chad to each other. Hamel tried, again, to date the time that Amanda moved in with Chad, which was the time that Jeff and Jennifer said that Kassidy's bruises began, and he guessed, "*Which was about 3 weeks ago*?" Jennifer, reconfirmed, "*Yeah. Whenever she moved in with him, yeah."* (p. 969) Earlier in the interview, she had correctly stated that Amanda had moved in with Chad "*three or four months ago,*" (p. 912) If the four month mark is used, and the actual move-in was before July 9, that's a lot earlier than the "*three weeks ago*" mark. In fact, the "*three weeks ago*" date marks the beginning of the three-day/two-night, Oct. 26-28, babysitting of Kassidy by Jeff, from which she came home dehydrated with bumps on her head. By that time, Amanda and Kassidy had been living with Chad for about three months. Jennifer's agreeing with Hamel's leading question, "*about 3 weeks ago,*" was a good example of how interviewees agreed with their police questioners, without thinking about it. Maybe Hamel's substitution of "*weeks*" for "*months*" was a Freudian slip.

The interviewers would sometimes ask leading questions, instead of "Tell us more about..." or "What happened with....?" Steve Hamel asked, "*What about water in the face? ... hold the baby under water?"* and Jeff Smith joined, "*Did he dunk her head under the water?"* (p. 969-70) Jennifer responded less dramatically, "*No, just, he put some, sprinkled water and put her head underneath it, but, yeah.*" (p. 970) Later, she characterized the incident as, "*..Chad put her face under water.*" (p. 974) However, she was 29 miles away when it happened, and only knew about the incident because Chad told her and Jeff about it. The earlier use of the term, "*sprinkled*" was more accurate.

Smith asked about the "*injuries on the bottoms of her feet. Do you know anything about those?"* and Jennifer explained, *"Yeah, me and, me and Mandy talked about* [that]. *We, we came to the conclusion that because I got linoleum on my floor and she's walking around with bare feet there's little tips to nails that are sticking up that she walks over that, .."* (p. 970)

Responding to questions about smoking, Jennifer said, *"I know she came home from another babysitter once with burn marks on the bottom of her feet...Mom, my mom was all upset about it.... Mandy was like, 'I don't know, she came home from the babysitter like that.'.. I think it was Emily Conley???...I don't know where in Sanford. I just know her name.* Steve Hamel asked, *"Your mom noticed it? Your mom confronted Amanda about it?"* and Jennifer said, *"Um, hum. It happened months ago, months ago."* and that the burns were *"On the bottom of her feet....Maybe like two.... One foot. I think. I don't know. I didn't see. I never saw Kassidy before like this past like week and a half, you know, whenever we started babysitting her. It wasn't like a usual thing. We didn't babysit her that often."* (p. 971-72) During her interview, and subsequent trial testimony, Jacqueline Conley was not asked about the alleged burn marks, and she never offered information about them. The only bruises which she acknowledged knowing about were those which her son, Joshua, and brother-in-law, Robert Conley, saw on October 13, and which were the subject of her call to Chad on Saturday, the 14th. In her own interview, below, she said that she talked with Amanda on Sunday the 15th about those bruises. (p. 891, 896)

Jeff Smith returned once again to Kassidy's condition on the morning of her death, and asked, "*...how do you know she was alive?"* and Jennifer again reported Kassidy's activity, *"Cause she was talking to me and she was, you know, gave me a kiss good bye, you know what I mean? I mean I like kiss her and she goes (kissing sound). You know and I left for work. She was alive when I left for work.... She was eating. Cocoa Puffs.... She was,* [saying] *"kitty, kitty, kitty." Cause Toby was on top of the bed. Toby is my cat."* (p. 972)

Jennifer said that Chad and Amanda had talked about the bruises, but it wasn't clear whether she was talking about all the bruises and alleged abuse or only on Kassidy's face. She said that during such a discussion, as related to her by Amanda, *"Chad cried and said he'd change and not touch her again..."* (p. 969) She said, "*... Mandy told Jeff that it was gonna stop...that the bruises would stop because Chad said he wouldn't do it any more... like squeeze her face like that.*" (p. 974)

Jeff Smith asked if Jeff was protecting Chad and Jennifer said that Jeff knew that "*Chad was doing that to Kassidy's face and stuff like that.*" Smith stepped out of his interviewer role, and said, "*I mean, I have friends, but if any of my friends did this to a child. That's crazed. That's insane.*" (p. 974) As happened so often in this case, comments were made about something, but it wasn't clear what that something was. Jennifer was referring to the bruises which Chad had caused on Kassidy's lower cheeks, but Smith was likely referring to what he saw in the photographs. What was "*crazed*" and "*insane*" was Smith's theory about what had happened, and not Chad's behavior.

Smith returned to the issue of the fall out of the truck, and Jennifer said that Kassidy had no bruises from that fall, and Smith said, *"Everybody's telling us that. That she didn't have bruises like that when she fell out of the truck."* (p. 975) Smith, once again, overstated the "*Everybody*," as only three interviews had begun by that point: with Amanda, Jeff and Jennifer. Although Jeff and Jennifer may have stated there were no bruises after the fall from the truck, Amanda certainly did. Jennifer did reconfirm, however, the effects of the fall, "*She was acting weird after she fell out of the truck though. That's why they're, probably everybody brought it up cause that's when she started looking at the wall and stuff like that. You know, just standing there. She wasn't acting like her normal self, but ..."* Smith was incredulous, "*...doesn't a bell go off? Doesn't an alarm? Lights go on?... The child's dead. No one can bring that child back. Someone is responsible.*" (p. 974) However, hindsight can be 20/20. No one at the time seemed to understand the potential seriousness of Kassidy's fall, or whatever caused the two large bumps on the top of her head that week.

When asked whether anyone "*confronted*" Chad about the bruises, Jennifer related that Amanda had told her the "trampoline story." The police were convinced that Kassidy's death was a homicide and that the railroad must proceed to "Conviction Station." Soon, the train would accelerate on one track.

Sometimes the officers had the timeline almost correct. Said Smith*, "... She is showing up with repeated injuries over a period of time, over a 3 week period,"* and Hamel*, "And the baby's been showing up like this for 2 weeks."* Jennifer, however, combined the coincidence with causation, *"She's had bruises on her. She's always had bruises on her ever since her and Chad got together. You know, little bruises her and there, but not on her face. I've never seen a bruise on her face until her and Chad got together."* (p. 975) The primary difficulty with that connection was that there was no coincidence of time between Amanda and Kassidy's move to Chad's in June and July and the appearance of the bruises. A few minutes later she said that the face holding bruises began "*About 3 week*[s], *4 weeks ago. When I started working. I started October 1st.*" (p. 976)

Jeff Smith asked, "*What were Mandy and Chad's plans?"* and Jennifer answered*, "I don't know. I think they were gonna get married and stuff like that. Mandy wants to, wanted to marry him. You know what I mean? But not anymore. Mandy and Chad talked* *about it. Supposedly, and CHAD was like ??? stop, you know. Mandy didn't want him disciplining her* [Kassidy] *at all or anything like that anymore."* (p. 978) As a child in a melded family, with a stepfather, Jennifer surely understood that this issue is an issue in all such families.

Jennifer said that she and Amanda were both minors so they didn't drink alcohol, but, *"I know Chad has drank, gotten really drunk a lot, you know. He drinks a lot. They do go to bars a lot."* (p. 978) On such occasions, for babysitting, she said that *"Me and Jeff usually have Kassidy, ...Take Kassidy all night and drop her off in the morning..."* However, she added, "*we haven't done that in a long time... We haven't had the kid overnight for a long time.*" That most recent overnight for Kassidy with Jeff and Jennifer was the three-day/two night babysitting beginning Thursday, October 26, or exactly three weeks before the interview. Prior to that, Jeff and Jen had Kassidy overnight on only four occasions since June 2, when Chad met Amanda. They were July 1, August 12, August 18 and October 21. None of those five babysitting occasions, with six overnights, was when Amanda and Chad went to a bar. Are six nights over a period of five months enough to describe the routine as "*usually*"?

Jennifer said that Chad "*treats his child a lot better than Kassidy... he used to tell Mandy that Kassidy was stupid and like, you know, brain dead. And shit like that. And Mandy, you know, and I was like, 'The only reason she keeps getting stupid is cause you keep hurting her.' "* (p. 978-79) Steve Hamel asked, *"Anything else that you noticed, even when the four of you were together, whatever, that how he treated this little child?"* Jennifer responded, *"He didn't treat her like it was his... He treated his kid like all kinds of terms better than Kassidy. Like if Kassidy cried, he'd walk away...."* (p. 979) Jennifer did not mention that the only time she had ever seen Chad with Kassidy was during the two trips to her parents' in Auburn around June 20 and July 20 and Kyle was not with Chad on those occasions. It's hard to see why anyone would expect Chad to treat Kassidy as his child on those occasions at Amanda's and Jennifer's parents' home. There was no indication that Kassidy cried during those visits. Jennifer had never seen Kassidy and Kyle together with Chad.

Steve Hamel then introduced what became a major police theory of the case, *"Do you think he's jealous of this kid? Kassidy?"* Jennifer didn't know, *"I think he.... He might be...."* Then with prophetic understatement, she said, ***"I don't live with them, so I don't really know exactly what goes on there, but..."*** (p. 979)

To support the jealousy theory, Jennifer said, "*...Mandy had pictures of ...the guy that she thought Kassidy was from, cause they broke up, and she hooked up with another guy, and then... and he* [Chad] *got all mad. And he didn't want those pictures in the house. Like he's jealous, I think.*" (p. 979) This issue was addressed with Amanda, and Jennifer's understanding of it was false. Chad expressed an interest in Kassidy knowing her father, and did not oppose having his photograph in his house, but it was never there, and it wasn't an issue. See Amanda's interview, below. The "photograph of father" story originated with Chad's seeing a photograph at Amanda's parents' home in Auburn, as is described later.

At the end Harakles said that Hamel had seen Kassidy at Jennifer's home "*before rescue arrived.*" This was when Jennifer learned that Jeff didn't take Kassidy to the hospital himself as she had previously understood and incorrectly communicated to Amanda. (p. 981)

The interview ended at 6:40 p.m. Jeff had finished his interview at 6:15 p.m. Amanda was on a break from 6:04 p.m. until 6:55 p.m. when her second interview began in the kitchen of the Kittery Police Dept.

At 6:15 p.m. at the York Hospital, Det. Baker "*took possession of the clothing that Cassidy had on, when she was brought in by the ambulance. The funeral home of Wilson & Cooper, from Kittery, were at the hospital. The driver, Mark Sousa, had the clothing, which he turned over to me.*"

At 6:20 p.m. Baker "*escorted Cassidy Bortner's body to the hearse with the driver, Mark Sousa. Sousa was directed by the Medical Examiner's Office to take Cassidy directly to Augusta.*" (Baker report, p. 148)

Chad was still waiting in Sgt. Avery's office to talk with the police, when Maine State Police Detectives Angela Blodgett and Richard LeClair began their second, and shorter, interview of Amanda. It went for 25 minutes.

6:55 p.m. - Amanda Bortner Second Interview

During the break, Detectives Blodgett and LeClair were able to compare notes with other detectives and with documents and photographs which were arriving. Angela Blodgett began, "*...one of the things that we've been told, you had said that Chad had never hit you...Did you have bruises on your neck at a work picnic that came from Chad?... for like McDonalds or something. And you had bruises on your neck. Do you know what that would be about?"* Amanda said she didn't remember what the event was about, but Blodgett was referring to the Exeter Inn celebration on August 25 of the new McDonald's in Exeter, and Amanda responded, *"He got mad at me before and he's done this before and I had a bruise right here and a bruise right here."*

LeClair commented, *"We're trying to get to the bottom of this... and Mommy's lying."* Amanda protested, *"But he's not... He's not like, I don't know. Well, I yelled at him and he never did it again."* In response to Angela's followup question, Amanda said that the event was *"a month ago."* (p. 53) However, it was Friday, August 25, or more than two and half months or 76 days, earlier. Thus, it was during the first half of Amanda's and Chad's relationship.

LeClair pressed harder, *"Huh? Now Amanda, ... we're going to have to go over some things again because other people are being truthful, okay, other people who are in the know, and you're not. And you know that, right?"* and Amanda responded, *" Yeah. ... well, he just grabbed my throat and stuff."* (p. 53-54) The "*other people*," he was referencing were Jeff and Jennifer, and only Jeff and Jennifer. At Chad's trial, Jennifer acknowledged that she wasn't telling the truth when she told the police during these interviews about Kassidy's condition that morning of November 9. Jeff's statements to his interviewers about Kassidy's first fall from his truck were substantially different from what Amanda told Blodgett and LeClair that Jeff told her about the same incident on the day that it happened. However, the police chose whom they wished to believe.

LeClair continued to challenge Amanda's veracity, without apparent consideration of the veracity of his sources, "*This isn't the only incident we're talking about..... about truthfulness.... everyone else is telling us a lot more and they say that they know this because you told them.... Amanda, why are you, can I ask you why you're trying to minimize what happened here?"* She responded, *"I don't know why."* (p. 54) LeClair continued, "*If I were to ask you yesterday what was the most important thing in your life, what would your answer be?"* and Amanda answered, predictably, *"My daughter."* LeClair pushed the Kassidy button,

Well, guess what? She's not here anymore. And you know, you have a good reason or a good idea as to what happened. You've been sleeping with Chad for how long? You know what happened, and you have to tell us. There are other people who are telling us things but then we can't even get the truth out of her mother. Yesterday she was the most important thing to you. This is the last thing you can do for her.

Amanda responded, "*Um. hum.*" (p. 54)

Then, at approximately 7:05 p.m., and five minutes before any policeman talked with Chad about the case on tape, Angela Blodgett told Amanda the police theory of the case, *"I think that you know that he killed your daughter. He beat her to death. And that's not, I know that it's difficult, but I need you to tell me what's been going on. And she deserves that."* (p. 55)

LeClair told Amanda, *"You know, auntie and uncle love your daughter."* At least LeClair was honest about his "everybody" sources. And Amanda answered, *"So what do you want me to tell you?"* (p. 55) Blodgett challenged Amanda, *"He didn't tell you about calling Jeff?"* Still without seeing what lies her interviewers were accusing her of, Amanda said, *"He told me he had a conversation with Jeff, and they were just saying that... after the bruises go away, I should take her to the doctor's because she's acting weird."* (p. 55)

Blodgett sought to show that Chad was lying to Amanda, *"And did he talk to you...about falling, calling Jeff saying she fell out of the truck? And that she was laying on the ground and her eyes were falling in the back in her head."* Thinking that Blodget was referring to the Saturday, October 28 fall from Jeff's truck, Amanda said, *"No that happened with Jeff, when she was with him."* Blodgett insisted, *"No. This was last night."* and LeClair backed her up, *"No. This happened last night, too."* When two uniformed police interviewers are seeking to persuade a grieving 18-year-old mother that her boyfriend is lying to her, it would appear essential that the police understand the facts, but they didn't. There was no fall from Jeff's truck on Wednesday afternoon or night. They were misunderstanding, and their only sources were Jeff and Jennifer, and what Chad had told Jeff about Kassidy's falling in Chad's driveway after Chad had brought her out of his car and left her standing in that driveway. Again, no policeman had asked Chad yet about any aspect of this case. Amanda responded, *"What happened last night? She fell out of the truck, truck again? All I heard about last night was wiffle ball."* She did hear about more than the wiffle ball, but it wasn't a fall from Jeff's truck, and it wasn't at "*night*." Amanda appeared to interpret "*night*" as being different from late afternoon or early evening, and later in the interview she told them that Chad did tell her about Kassidy falling in their driveway, when he and Kyle and Kassidy arrived home. (p. 60) Also, she continued, unknowingly, her misunderstanding of the ballplaying accident (p. 55) However, not understanding a police question, and not understanding what Chad had told her about the ballplaying accident, and not agreeing with a police statement are not the same as lying.

Blodgett changed direction, and asked, *"What did he say, he told you over the phone that she was acting funny?* and Amanda agreed, *"Yeah,... Like spacey...He told me, um, I was like, well, I'll bring her to the doctor's and he's like, well, 'you should wait until the bruises go away'."*

LeClair asked, *"Why's that?"* and Amanda said, *"Because he was paranoid about this, about him getting in trouble with her* [Tristan]*."* LeClair asked for Amanda's opinion, *"Do you think he should be?"* and she said, *"Yes."* (p. 56) She was right, but we don't know exactly what she meant, but it was not necessarily for the reason that LeClair had intended. She could have meant that it was wise for Chad to feel paranoid because people would unfairly accuse him of abuse, because that was precisely what was happening in this case, before anyone had talked with him. On the other hand, Blodgett and LeClair may have thought that her "*Yes,*" meant that she agreed that Chad should have been in trouble with Tristan and that the bruises he periodically had caused on Kassidy's face should affect his child custody and visitation rights.

Coincidentally, Chad's interview began at about the time of this exchange in Amanda's interview.

LeClair and Blodgett thought they had caught Amanda in a previous lie when they asked again in this second interview what time she left work, and she said, *"Like around 11 :00,-11:30."* She said, *"No,"* she did not go home early. Blodgett said, *"Your sister swears that you stormed out of the store and went home early."* Amanda responded with the only exclamation recorded in the transcript of the interview, *"No! I went back to work. Call my work."* The Convict-Chad train was moving forward, and the detectives' faith in *"other people who are being truthful"* was apparently unshaken even though Jennifer was simply wrong on this point.

The detectives challenged Amanda about the ballplaying accident. First, Blodgett said, "*Did you believe him? I mean, did you think it was just garbage and that he had done something?*" Then, Rick LeClair began one of his statements where he addressed her by name, "*You know, Amanda...*" and Amanda interrupted him, and agreed with them, "*No, I think about it and I don't believe it.*" (p. 57) As noted earlier, it was reasonable for Amanda not to believe that a wiffle ball caused the bruise at Kassidy's eye, because it didn't happen that way. However, it wasn't because Chad was feeding her "*just garbage.*" It was because the police AND Amanda misunderstood the incident. In a few minutes in his own interview, Chad would tell his interrogators that the ball that hit Kassidy was a "*starter baseball,*" or a "*hard rubber ball.*"

From time to time in these interviews, Rick LeClair reminded Amanda that he was a father and he knew about parenting. He said, "*Obviously, something happened, because if I got a call right now and someone told me my son just got hit with a hockey puck, which is a lot harder than a wiffle ball, it wouldn't bother me a single bit.*" (p. 57) He was right that, "*Obviously, something happened,*" but what happened was an accident with a "*hard rubber ball*" or "*starter baseball*" or what is commonly called a Tee-Ball. Setting aside his misunderstanding about the ball, could he have sincerely meant that it wouldn't bother him if his son was hit in the head by a hockey puck? Isn't that why hockey players of all ages, especially goalies, wear protective helmets? One month after the interview, Foster's Daily Democrat published a story about a 12-year old boy in Springfield, Massachusetts, "Boy dies after being hit with puck."

LeClair then appealed, "*Did your motherly instincts kick in and you, you think something, something more's happening there?*" Again, something more was happening, but that point has been made above. Amanda responded,

I was thinking,... more when he was talking on the phone because he said something like he didn't want anything to do with her anymore, on the phone... Yeah. He was like I don't want to get in trouble. He was worried about it.... he was like "Amanda..., I'm worried about her. Every time I'm with her it seems like she always hurts herself or falls down or something.".... and that whole story about Kyle doing it. And then he's like, "I don't, I don't think I should have anything to do with her anymore." Maybe he was feeling bad about it and, but, I even thought bad and I was like really mad at him and I left and went to work, back to work." (p. 57-58)

Yes, Chad was feeling stupid and bad about the accident. Period.

Amanda volunteered that, *"I've been trying to get an apartment... but then I was like, I don't know. I thought that it, you know, would get better and, I don't know."*

Rick LeClair said, *"I mean, you've got auntie and uncle there spilling their guts telling us everything they know, and we have to come to you two times to get the truth on something."* (p. 58) This was the second time that LeClair called Jeff an uncle to Kassidy, and he wasn't. It was another effort to make Jeff's position appear to be more legitimate. It's unclear what "*two times*" he was referring to, unless it was to the fact that this was the second interview. It is clear, however, that his source, Jennifer, was wrong about Amanda leaving work early, and LeClair and Blodgett were wrong about the Tee-ball and were confused about the truck fall incident. Jeff was wrong about Chad's alleged gambling debts and wrong about his drug use. The detectives hadn't yet shown a single instance where Amanda was wrong. LeClair may have stepped out of the interview shortly after this observation, because the transcript does not reflect his continued presence. Perhaps he and Blodgett agreed that she was making more progress with her, so she became the lead questioner. He clearly was gone from the interview when it ended at 7:20 p.m., because he participated in the upcoming interview with Chad, which began at 7:10 p.m. The videotape will have the answer, but I haven't yet found or seen it.

After a brief discussion about Kassidy's hair, and Amanda's statement that "*she's always had, like a weird hairline,*" and denying, once again, that Chad ever pulled her by her hair, Blodgett and LeClair attacked Amanda's credibility on another issue, the length of her relationship with Chad. Blodgett asked, "*...how long have you been living with him, with Chad?*" and Amanda answered, "*Probably like, there everyday, probably like three months.*" and the same for Kassidy. Once again referring to "*other people,*" Blodgett said, "*...other people are telling us, like two weeks.*" (p. 59) Amanda asked, "*Who told you that*?" and Blodgett responded directly, "*Like your sister and... Jeff.*"

Once again, the Convict-Chad train was traveling over a shaky trestle bridge of mis-information. Amanda was probably conservative on her moving date to Rochester which was late June or early July, and Kassidy's move date could be said to have been mid-July, both of which dates are far earlier than the detectives' representations of two weeks, which would have meant a move-in date of Thursday, October 26. All they needed to do was obtain the phone records from Chad's home for the months of June through October, but they were never gathered and are now unavailable. Most records for October and November were saved, fortunately.

In this second interview, where the detectives were trying show that Amanda and/or Chad were lying, this was the third instance where the detectives were simply wrong. Amanda said, "*My mom would know the exact* [date?] *because that's when I left her, my mom's...*" but Amanda correctly predicted that "... *Chad would say less than that* [three months] *just because he,...*" (p. 60) Were Blodgett and LeClair going to question their sources more closely? Were they going to slow down the Convict-Chad train and look more carefully at available evidence before getting locked into their theory? Were they going to explore with Jeff the inconsistencies between what he and Amanda said about the fall from his truck on Saturday, October 28? Most of the remainder of the interview was conducted by Angela Blodget, as LeClair apparently left the room, after his last recorded statement at page 59.

Blodgett asked about Kassidy's recent behavior, *"Has she gotten slower? I mean, her, her ability to function... People are describing that she would just stand and stare for hours?"* (p. 60) Even though it was obvious who the *"people"* were, Blodgett seemed unwilling to be truthful about her source or sources. Perhaps she thought that referring to a source in the vague plural form made the source more reliable. This was not an issue of protecting the identity of a source to protect his or her confidentiality, or from retribution. In any case, it was increasingly apparent to Amanda that the police had believed all of what Jeff and Jennifer had told them, and that they were not believing her and Chad.

Amanda knew the source, saying,

Yeah. She never did that to, to me and I, whenever Jeff told me that she did that I just thought that maybe she didn't know where she was because she was always with me. She just woke up and she was like, didn't know where she was. He told me she did it once in the middle of the night. But she never did that with me.... I noticed that she was like tired and she was spacey and that one time,... when she fell out of the truck that day, that night, and her eyes, I thought she was just tired, and I thought that was kind of weird. Then, the next day, she was fine. And that's why I didn't really think it was that bad. (p. 60-61)

After noting that "...*my mind's like, can't think straight. I remember when she had her bruises on her face from this,*" Amanda said that, *"Chad was all paranoid about it*[the bruises], *and he was like 'you shouldn't bring her to your mom's' because I was always planning on going up there....Because of the bruises and stuff. And my mom like said something one day about it. So he was, he was all worried about that, and,..., he made up an excuse about saying that he was on the trampoline and she like fell and he grabbed her by the feet to hold her up."* (p. 61) Here, it would have been helpful to discuss the timeline. The officers did not yet know that Amanda had taken Kassidy to see her mother on Sunday, October 1 They didn't know that, yes, her mother did talk with Chad on Saturday, October 14, about bruises that her son Joshua had seen on Kassidy on Friday, the 13th. They didn't know that Chad had taken Kassidy to visit with his sister and family as recently as Sunday, November 5, so he wasn't hiding Kassidy from his family. They didn't know that according to Amanda's recollection in 2011, Amanda had talked with her mother two days before about babysitting for Kassidy during the upcoming weekend, November 11-12. Chad wrote in 2010, "*I always encouraged Amanda to go visit* [her mother]. *Gave her money when she wanted to, etc. Like my mom, Jackie didn't drive. From time to time Amanda would say that she missed her mom. I told her on several occasions to go pick her up and bring her down to stay for a few days. I thought that would be cool. Amanda did bring her brothers down from time to time.*" (Letter, Jan. 20, 2010) Mother-daughter relationships can be complicated, and seen from different perspectives simultaneously.

Amanda addressed the "trampoline story" and told Blodgett that Chad, "*made up an excuse about saying that he was on the trampoline and she like fell and he grabbed her by the feet to hold her up.*" (p. 61) Surely, she meant to say "*face*" instead of "*feet.*" Even if she didn't acknowledge her own role in developing the "trampoline story," Amanda was telling the police that it wasn't true, and it wasn't.

In response to Blodgett's question, Amanda denied that she had "*asked anyone not to call Social Services and report these injuries.*" Blodgett told Amanda, "...*everyone we're talking to knows that he's been hurting the baby and hasn't been calling* [Social Services] *because they felt bad for you and didn't want you to lose your child because you weren't being a protective mother. You were letting someone kill the baby slowly.*" (p. 61-62) It was a strong allegation, and surely gave Amanda pause. Maybe the police were right, and she missed the signs?

Blodgett then returned to the question of sexual abuse of Kassidy, "*... what... as far as Chad's sexual history, does he have any strange, or is there anything that looking back now, knowing what I've told you about the doctor's concerns about the irritation in your daughter's vaginal area...*" She asked if Chad had ever asked Amanda to have sex in front of the children, and whether they walked naked in front of the children. Amanda said she didn't believe that Chad was the source of the irritation, and that he never suggested sex in front of the children and that they wore towels when the children were around. She correctly said, "*... Chad wouldn't even change the diapers in the beginning....*" (p. 62) As the incident was only four days earlier, Amanda may not have discussed with Chad his diaper changing of poop-laden Kassidy on Sunday, November 5, and his reluctance to clean Kassidy's genital area.

Amanda volunteered, "*... he just loses his temper....he just has a really bad temper.. Can't control it. Anger.*" (p. 62) Blodgett didn't followup with this issue, and thus didn't know about Chad's voluntary counseling with Gray Fitzgerald, and Amanda's telling him that he didn't need to keep the "anger management" checklist on the bedroom wall because he didn't need it anymore.

Blodgett asked "*What about him pulling her leg and that's when she started walking funny*?" and Amanda responded, "*...when that happened, I thought it, he was pulling her around her legs playing with her, and he had told me that she was walking funny, and I, I was like 'it's probably from you throwing her around and that stuff.'...He picked her up by her legs before.... No. In fun. Not when he was mad....*" (p. 63) Again, Amanda had reminded the officers of Chad's playing with Kassidy, but they didn't seem to hear it. They were thinking child abuse.

Then Amanda opened a new issue, "*When he's mad, he'd like, goes like this and does like this and chokes. When she was bad....And she was just like, he would do this and that's what he would do to me.*" Amanda then demonstrated for the officers, using her hands, "*This is what he would do to me. Not that,*" but the video is not yet available. She said, "*And then, he wouldn't even do it and she'd automatically make herself gag.*" Blodgett tried to describe what she was seeing Amanda demonstrate, "*He'd push on your throat and knock the air out?...Push down on her like, trachea? That hole?*" (p. 63) About the touching of Kassidy's throat, Chad wrote in 2010,

You asked about the touching of the throat thing on Kassidy. I laid my finger over Kassidy's throat, horizontally, around the middle of her neck, near where her Adam's Apple would be. There really wasn't much pressure, just enough to make her voice sound deeper. I wasn't angry in any way. It was just stupid on my part. I was sitting in front of her watching her have this incredible tantrum. Sometimes these tantrums frustrated me. This one just amazed me. I think at one point Kassidy realized that Amanda and I were laughing at her and she got even more angry. She started making this fake gagging sound and at first I think Amanda thought I was doing something to her but then her eyes were directly on Kassidy and saw her making the sound and I wasn't even touching her. Amanda was smiling and said, "Oh my God Kassidy, stop it." (Letter, March 20, 2010)

In 2011, Chad added that he and Amanda had tried several techniques, and he thought that if Kassidy heard her own voice sounding differently, it might defuse the situation. Like the water sprinking idea, this worked, too.

Amanda volunteered another issue, "*...he headbutted me once.*" It wasn't explored further in Amanda's interview, but Chad addressed the question in a letter,

It was in the summer, I left work early to take Amanda and the kids out on the boat for the afternoon. I don't know if it was a miscommunication or Amanda just deciding to change plans but her friend, Cathy, showed up at the house and Amanda was going to go somewhere with her instead. (This is another reason I think the boat was purchased earlier than we believe. Cathy and Amanda really hung out the most toward the beginning half of our relationship). I was upset about this. I went down to the basement to get Kyle's swim trunks out of the dryer I believe, and Amanda followed me. Amanda and I argued a little. I probably said something that upset her. Let me tell you, Amanda wasn't a "meek lamb" when it came to arguing. She wasn't afraid of me, didn't take my shit and I liked this about her. She got right in my face. I'm talking noses an inch apart. Mine a little higher because I am a couple of inches taller. We were talking animatedly, and I either leaned forward some or bent to pick up something and our heads bumped together. I didn't headbutt her. It was an accident. There was no bruise, no bump, no anything. Amanda may have thought I did it on purpose but she quickly realized it was an accident. (Letter, March 25, 2010)

Angela Blodgett asked, *"Did you have any concerns that she was suffering brain damage?"* Amanda started to answer, *"When she fell out of the truck, that was ..."* but Blodgett then finished her question, *"From lack of oxygen? Or from banging her head so much? I mean she. .. seemed to be slowing down and getting spacey and ...."* Amanda said, *"I didn't even think about that...Like, one day, I did. And then the next day she was like, talk, like, like doing smart things so I didn't think that, I didn't think to do anything."* (p. 63-64) Blodgett's question about brain damage was a good one. Unfortunately, the investigation never pursued that idea. No doctor was consulted about the changes which were observed Kassidy's behavior after October 28.

Returning to another important issue, the timeline, Blodgett asked, "*How long has this stuff been going on?"* without defining *"this stuff."* Amanda fumbled with an estimate of *"two months,"* and repeated her estimate of the context, *"I've probably been living there for like three months.*

Blodgett again presumed, with the advantage of 20/20 hindsight, *"... And obviously, you both knew ... You and Chad both knew that this was bad and that's why ..."* Amanda said, *"I don't, I don't think he thought it was bad....like last night, he said 'you should take her to the doctor after she gets rid of the bruises.' "* (p. 64) To achieve an effect rather than to gather information, Blodgett said, "*Well, I mean, that's apparently wasn't quick enough because she's dead.*" Amanda acknowledged, "*I, I know that.*" (p. 64)

Blodgett said, *"So he must have known he had done something wrong...why would he care if the baby had bruises."* Chad was concerned that something might BE wrong, but not that HE had done anything wrong. He cared about the bruises, because he was afraid that someone would think that he was intentionally abusing Kassidy, instead of unintentionally pressing too hard when obtaining eye contact with her, and that the result of such a misunderstanding might ricochet back to affect his custody arrangements with Kyle. Even as late as November 9, he still did not know that his divorce, and custody arrangements, had been finalized on October 4. As his prosecution and conviction showed, his concerns about the misunderstanding of the bruises and the consequences to him were tragically correct.

Amanda said that she was spanked as a child, but never hit.

Blodgett asked, "*What about Chad's current use of cocaine? Do you think that it's a problem?*" After the expression of her initial astonishment, "*Current use of cocaine?*" Amanda said, "*Oh no. That was a long, long time ago. We had done it once...He doesn't do coke. ... He's on probation, so he can't really ..anyway...*" (p. 65)

Moving to another allegation about Chad from Jeff, Detective Blodgett asked, *"Alright, because people are telling me that, that's a problem and that he also has some gambling problems. He's like a $1,000 behind?"* Responded Amanda, *"Oh, he gambles,"* but the allegation that Chad owed money was left on the table. In fact, Chad was ahead for the year, and that very week was to receive a payment. He wrote in 2010,

I had just started betting that very year. I had never been really interested in gambling prior to that. Jeremy introduced me and I loved it. Bruce and I would study all of the lines for the week and discussed the games we liked. We would sometime "tease" a couple of games which may give us more points to play with but you had to win both games. It didn't matter what we did; we routinely cracked the bookies. We settled up weekly so that $900 that Jeremy had for me was from the previous week and Bruce and I usually split 50/50 unless one of us made a bet that the other didn't agree with. We often bet Patriots, [and] *watched nearly every Patriots game, and parts of others. I would bring* *a bunch of the kids' toys and play with them on the floor or on Bruce's coffee table. During halftime we would go throw balls around with the kids or take them to a field to play.* (Letter, July 22, 2010)

Following up on on Amanda's mentioning Chad's probation, Angela asked about it, and Amanda said, *"When I talked to Tristan, she told me that he hurt her and,... she told me to go to the police station and look at pictures but I never did."* It was an unusual suggestion by a separated wife, who also knew about Chad's counseling and who also knew that Chad never hurt his son and stepson. It was this discussion that was likely the basis for Amanda's alleged statement to Chad and to Jeff and Jennifer that Chad's domestic violence against Tristan was "*the worst beating in New Hampshire*," as Jeff stated in his interview, above. Blodgett then said, "*I guess, I just don't know why you were ignoring all this. Why you just stood there and let this happen.*" Amanda responded, *"I just, I don't really know."* Like Marty Tankleff not remembering that he had killed his parents in his sleep, Amanda seemed to think that she must have been missing something. However, although the police made them feel otherwise, neither she nor Marty Tankleff missed anything in their respective situations.

Apparently referring to Chad's visit the previous day to Moonlite Reader to correct a duplicate charge for previously purchased sex-related items that were for both he and Amanda, Blodgett asked, *"What about going to a strip club the other day?... or looking for someone to go to one?"* There's nothing in the transcripts for Jeff and Jennifer's interviews about strip clubs, but Blodgett may have received information shared off line, that is, not as part of a recorded interview. In any case, Chad wrote in 2010 about one visit to a strip club, and Amanda probably shared it afterwards with Jennifer. He wrote,

On August 18, 2000, which was a Friday, Amanda and I went to see Dr. Dirty, John Valby at the Ballroom. I am 90% sure Bruce + Michelle and possibly Glen + Deb went with us. I think Me, Amanda, Bruce + Michelle, went to Tens, a local strip club after the show. We didn't stay long. Amanda had never been and it was kind of a dare to the girls. I believe Jen + Jeff likely watched Kassidy. Busy week. Creed concert + Exeter Inn too,... (Letter, March 21, 2010)

Blodgett brought up Chad's decision the previous day to use an adult seatbelt for Kassidy, which Chad hadn't yet shared with Amanda. Chad and Amanda had talked by phone while she was at Jennifer's workplace, and they had talked and argued when she had come home around midnight, and they scrambled to get going in the morning. There was a lot going on, and not everything was covered, which is typical of any close relationship. Detective Blodgett said, "*Jeff said he* [Chad] *just threw her in the car and put the seat belt on her yesterday. No child seat or anything.*" Amanda was surprised, *"Jeff said Chad did that?... Oh, because I had her car seat in my car so he probably went to work and got it.... Well, I know he had one car seat. I know he wouldn't do that. Like, he, I don't think ..."* It was regrettably true that Chad, in the rush to get to Cross Road by 6:00 p.m., and he was the last parent to arrive, made the quick decision to use only the adult seatbelt for Kassidy. He didn't have time to even add the ten minutes it would take to go to Amanda's car at Old Navy, even if he had thought of the idea. In any case, he made a decision that loving and careful parents sometimes make and usually without consequence, like a decision to run into a store leaving a child in the back seat, when a car thief then steals the car. In Chad's case, his child passenger died the next day, so the microscope was then turned on. Fortunately, the absence of a car seat had nothing to do with Kassidy's death. Later in the evening, if Kyle's swinging his bat had sent the Tee-ball into a wall or even through a window, Chad's split decision to toss that ball to Kyle would have disappeared into family history. Tragically, it was that ball that was batted into Kassidy's head.

Blodgett urged Amanda to make the transition from her not thinking that Chad would make such a decision, about driving Kassidy without a car seat, to, *"Did you think he would kill the baby?"* She responded, *"No, but, he would just like,* [have a] *bad temper. If I would ever do that he would scream at me. Maybe he did."* (p. 67) If the next 24 hours had not gone tragically wrong and Amanda and Chad had talked about the Wednesday, November 8 car seat mixup, they might have come to some reasonable understanding of their mutual mistakes.

Blodgett then asked, *"... if the only reason that Kassidy died is because she had head injuries from being beaten, who would be responsible for that? Only Chad or anybody else?"* and Amanda answered, *"Chad."* Blodgett continued, *"Chad? Do you feel that he is responsible her death?"* and Amanda agreed, *"Yeah. I know he is."* (p. 67-68) Blodgett asked, "*What if the testing shows that she had been sexually abused?*" and Amanda said, "*Well, I... I don't think it would. I don't know. Because Jeff's been with her a lot. I'm not gonna, ...*" (p. 68)

Blodgett then moved to another topic, *"Now Chad was pretty possessive,... how it's getting explained to us is not so much that your daughter was jealous but that Chad didn't like the attention you gave the baby?"* Amanda responded, *"Yeah. He thought I spoiled her,"* but that's a different question. Then Blodgett gave specifics of what Jennifer had told police, *"And then he made you throw out some pictures of her father? Did you have pictures of the baby's father?"* Amanda replied simply, *"I never had pictures of him* [i.e. Robert Sheehan]*."* Blodgett then revealed her obvious source, *"I thought that your sister had said that he ...,"* and Amanda corrected her, *"Me and my boyfriend. My ex-boyfriend* [i.e. Gabe Snyder]*."* Blodgett returned to the initial allegation, *"Did he* [Chad] *make you throw out pictures of your old boyfriend?"* Amanda said, *"I don't think I, I think he did like made fun of it when he* [Chad] *came over one day. But I never threw it away. It's all at my mom's house, so, but he was, he was not really controlling. He just,... wanted to know where I was and what time I'd was going to be home and all that."* (p. 68)

Chad addressed this allegation about jealousy and a photo of either Sheehan or Snyder allegedly at his house,

You asked about a part in Jen's interview where she claimed to have knowledge of me being upset about Amanda having some photos of Kassidy's father and that I "didn't want them in my house." This is absolutely false. I had addressed this in a letter several months ago that Amanda and I NEVER had a discussion about her having photos or past memorabilia. You may recall I indicated that my house was very large and she could have very easily hid something there if she was concerned that it would upset me. I believe it was Jen or Jeff that indicated that Amanda was keeping some photo albums at their house and Amanda claimed that I didn't want them in my house. This is false. I was 28 years old and very aware that people had a past. Jealousy was part of the downfall of my marriage to Tristan and I wasn't going there again. When I was married to Tristan, I had a strong dislike for Brent's father but never had a problem with Brent having photos of his dad in his room or whatever. ***What kind of a monster do people think I am?*** *We now know that Amanda was a teenage girl then and thus, used to dealing with teenage problems and insecurities. I have a feeling that this resulted in Amanda telling Jen + Jeff that I didn't want the photos in my house to make it easier on herself, avoiding what she felt would lead to an argument. Amanda was feeling a little bad about what she was doing, keeping pictures of old lovers, and it was easier to be sneaky and blame it on me. Let me state for the record. I have NEVER seen a photo of Robert Sheehan and have no idea what he looks like. In fact, I had never seen a photo of Gabe, Amanda's former boyfriend, until you grabbed them from that website Jackie Conley had them on last year. I kept some of my old photos, so why couldn't Amanda keep hers? ESPECIALLY, for Kassidy if they were of her dad!* (Letter, Feb 1, 2011) (emphasis added)

In his June 24, 2011 letter, Chad remembered that he had seen a photo of Gabe Snyder before, and it was at Amanda's parents' home and not his own. He wrote,

You have asked this question a few times before but I never knew what the hell you were talking about until I saw it in the context of the full exchange between Blodgett and Amanda. I was confused because I knew I had never seen photos at my house, and as far as I knew, Amanda had never had Gabe or Bobby Sheehan at my house, at least that she ever told me about. ...[It] *was during my 2nd trip to Amanda's mom's in Auburn Maine. I was visiting in July when I noticed a framed photo of Gabe in Amanda's room. (I knew by this point Gabe wasn't Kassidy's dad). I made a comment to Amanda, something like, "Awww isn't he cute." It was priceless for me to see this photo and make FUN OF IT because it allowed me to innocently rib Amanda. Amanda was always giving me crap about Tristan's photos being up with the kids around our house. I tried explaining when*

Amanda would mention the photos that Tristan is the boys' mom and I was just trying to keep things somewhat normal for them when they were at the house because they had obviously gone through a big change with Tristan and I splitting up. (Eventually the plan was to take them all down and move them to the boys' bedrooms). Obviously Amanda and I both had a past, but it didn't seem like she ever wanted to hear it, so finding this photo was great. I wasn't upset at all. In fact, Amanda didn't elaborate to Blodgett on how I made fun of the photo. After I said, "Aww isn't he cute." I said with a big smile, "Hey, why don't we hang his photo up at our house right next to Tristan SO you can stop giving me so much grief about her photos". I laughed and Amanda laughed and she likely backhanded me in the gut, saying, "That's different you jerk." Of course, Amanda knew that it WASN'T different and that she just wanted her "Cake and to eat it too."

When I would sometimes describe Amanda as a "little nutty," it's this type of double standard with which I was referring. I can totally see how Cathy N. described Amanda as controlling all past relationships. Amanda was very used to getting her way, including with me. Ultimately though, the answer to the photo question is I was not jealous of Gabe Snyder or Robert Sheehan in any way nor did I make Amanda get rid of photo's. I knew Amanda was interested in going forward not back. I also would have never done that to Kassidy, knowing photos of her dad may be important to her someday, I would never gotten in the way of Kassidy having a relationship with Robert if he was interested, because I feel all kids deserve to have as many people love them as possible.

Then, Blodgett asked about Travis, *"... what do you think, ... your roommate is going to have to say about what's been going on?* and Amanda said, *"He knows... Like, I told him....I don't know if he'll say anything because he works with Chad. I've cried to him. I cried to him like last week with, well whatever that head thing because I stressed out over it and I was like, you know, and then the next day she was fine so I didn't do anything about it."* (p. 69) After Amanda said, "*He knows*," the question was not asked, "What does Travis know?" Amanda would have likely answered that Travis simply had a good sense of the lives of Amanda, Chad and Kassidy, but the police likely thought that Amanda was saying that Travis knew about abuse. Over and over, ambiguous statements were made and the ambiguity unexplored, and the police assumptions seemed to be supported.

Amanda said that the *"head thing"* she referenced was the fall out of Jeff's truck and Blodgett asked, *"Did she really fall out of the truck..."* Amanda replied cryptically, *"Ask Jeff."*

Blodgett then responded, *"... because Jeff didn't tell us anything about that? Whether he just forgot about it or, it was Jeff that told you that himself?... because he's completely at a loss."* Amanda said, *"Yeah. Jeff told me, ... she fell out of the truck and she was really sick when she came over.... When she came, when he dropped her off."* (p. 69)

Mistakenly referring to Travis as "*Treavor*," Amanda said she didn't know how helpful he would be, "*Just because it's his boss*," [i.e. Chad] Blodgett then upped the ante further, "*Well, it's also a murder though. So I would hope he would have some... respect*." (p. 70) Ironically, Travis would be the only non-expert defense witness to testify at Chad's or Amanda's trials. In 2010, he said he would take a lie detector test in support of what he said ten years ago.

According to the transcript, Amanda's second interview ended at 7:20 p.m., just ten minutes after Chad's began, with her saying, "*I'm trying to think, like, if I didn't remember anything, you can just come back and ask me because I, I can't remember anything right now.*" (p. 71)

7:10 p.m. 9 November 2000 - Chad Evans Interrogation [See copy of annotated interrogation with Chad's 2010 annotations, referenced here as A. for "annotated," i.e. p. A-0000]

At 7:10 p.m. Maine State Police Detectives Rick LeClair(RL) and Lance McCleish(LM) and, later, Sgt. Matthew Stewart(MS), began their interrogation of Chad Evans(CE). The term "interrogation" is used here, and not for the other interviews, because a police "interview" is conducted when police are searching for information. In an interrogation, police seek incriminating information, and even a confession, from the primary suspect. By this time, almost seven hours after Kassidy's death and four hours after Maine State Police detectives arrived at the Kittery Police station, Chad Evans was already the primary suspect, and the New Hampshire State Police were getting involved and would soon take control of the case. They wanted a confession and/or incriminating statements.

Chad was anxious as he had been waiting for three hours and been mulling over Kassidy's death and the events of the last several days. Also, he felt that he had been roughly treated by the Rochester police when they came to arrest him in March, 1999, so he was wary of the police.

Sergeant Stewart introduced LeClair and McCleish to Chad and left the interrogation, but probably continued to participate by watching through a mirror or electronic video device. After small talk about sports and a review of Chad's biographical and career information, Rick LeClair advised Chad of his Miranda rights, including his right to decline to answer questions and to have a lawyer present. LeClair had participated in the first two interviews with Amanda, so he was familiar with her understanding of the situation. This was McCleish's first interview of the day. There were a lot of interviews that day in several rooms at the Kittery Police Station, and it was impossible to position the optimal interviewers in each interview. Ideally, the second interviewer with Chad would have been Linscott or Harakles, who had already completed their interview of Jeff. Regarding LeClair's statement about Chad's right to an attorney, Chad asked, "*Do you think I need one?*" and LeClair answered, "*That's, that's totally up to you... like I said you don't have to answer questions.*" (p. 1489) A more honest answer would have been to tell Chad that he was already the primary suspect, as the police had already told Amanda, Jeff and Jennifer, and that he should consider carefully his right to get an attorney or to not answer questions. However, the interrogator's job was to use whatever legal means possible to obtain information and even a confession, and honesty was not legally required for the interrogators. It was expected of the suspect.

LeClair asked the first substantive question, "*...we're investigating the death of Kassidy. Tell us what went on the last day or so with... Kassidy.*" (p. 1490) After agreeing to begin with a narrative of Wednesday's activities, Chad began with Thursday morning, but then he switched back to Wednesday afternoon. He was nervous. As Amanda's schedule on Wednesday at Old Navy was 5 to 11, Chad said to LeClair and McCleisch "*...I told her it wouldn't be a big deal. I'd pick her* [Kassidy] *up... because I had to pickup Kyle, my son...went to pick Kyle up.. I talked with Kyle's teacher for a minute. Then we went home..*" (p. 1491) Then he volunteered,

I'm sorry,... what keeps going through my mind right now is...having the other detective... just tell me that she was dead, and it just like, hey, rewind, rewind, rewind.... I mean last night I fed them, her and Kyle and we were playing. I gave her a bath, gave Kyle a bath and put her to bed. I put Kyle to bed. I did her alphabet with her before she went to bed, and now I get a phone call today ... telling me she's dead....I've been sitting and thinking about things that, kind of feeling guilty like maybe I could of prevented things if I had just taken her to the hospital." (p. 1491-92)

LeClair asked, "*What happened?*" and Chad said, "*She just was acting funny. You know I don't even know if I want to continue. I do but I don't. I don't want to like, I don't know anything, so I don't want to get anyone in trouble.*" (p. 1492) He explained the decision to bring Kassidy home without a car seat, "*...Amanda didn't give me her car seat. She didn't leave it at, at Jeff's house so I had to strap her in the back seat... But I just strap her in because I had to get Kyle, the school closes at six. I didn't have time to go buy one or anything so I strapped in.*" Chad was worried about the car seat, "*I'm probably gonna get a ticket for telling you guys this because it's against the law.*" and LeClair reassured him, "*No, we're not gonna give you a ticket for that.*" (p. 1492) Chad did not yet know how serious this interrogation was for him, and that the car seat issue was very small potatoes, compared to the death of a beautiful, blonde toddler, for which someone must be held responsible.

Chad said that when driving from Jeff's, Kassidy,

wasn't talking, but she's kind of a quiet kid. Like my sister spent the weekend with her and she spent six hours straight with her and Kassidy sat in the chair the whole time, didn't move, didn't, you know which is kind of weird for a little baby to do you know. (p. 1492)

By "*weekend,*" Chad meant Sunday, November 5.

On the way to Kyle's day care, said Chad,

...she's just sitting there like leaning forward like this,... on the seat belt. I'm like, "what the hell is wrong with her?" And like she was, kind of drooling, which she doesn't usually drool unless she's cutting a tooth or something. I'm like what the hell. So actually I - then I called Jeff up on the phone. I said, you know I was kind of joking when I said this I said "What the hell did you do, beat this kid or something?" And he, he started laughing or whatever and he said, "No why?" And I'm like, "I don't know. She's acting strange like laying against the seat and whatever." (p. 1492)

Chad continued his summary description, saying that after arriving home, he made her a *grill cheese she wouldn't eat whatever. I was like "What the hell." So I gave her a banana and she mowed it, half of it and then didn't want the rest which was kind of ... because she's got a really good appetite for a baby that young. So I thought it was a little strange. But any way so she ate her banana or whatever and then. You know I fed her, fed Kyle, then we went upstairs, and you know I played with - It's hard because you know Kyle is a boy he's three and she's you know 20 months a girl... I played with him for a few minutes and then I go play with her and then you know him and then her.*" (p. 1493)

Five days before, on February 4, Kassidy had passed the 21-month mark. Chad described Kassidy's recent walking problem, saying that Jeff,

stepped on her the other day, like on her foot. So she's having a hard time walking. And so like what I eventually I would just carry her around,.. She doesn't like to walk anyway. She likes to be held. But usually I don't want to baby her, you know I make her walk, do her thing, but she was hurting. So I carried her from her room. (p. 1493)

Chad described how he had made some calls about opening his schedule for this evening and to notify people of Kassidy's death. He said about Tristan, "*But yeah we still, we still talk and everything and we just - a lot of times don't get along about stupid things but. So anyway I told her. I started crying and she started crying, Oh my God.*" (p. 1495)

Asked about Jeff's role, Chad replied, "*...he's been watching her because she hasn't been able, like just checked with a couple day care she* [Amanda] *said she can't get in them yet. I get her into one and then she checked into one down here that had openings, but it was too close to the road so she didn't want it.*" (p. 1496) What Chad meant by "*I get her into one*" was that he had talked with Susan Edgar, the director of Cross Road Kindergarten and School, about enrolling Kassidy there. However, Kassidy wasn't yet toilet trained, so she was ineligible. This was one of several examples in Chad's interview where the stress overwhelmed his speech coherence. At another time, he called his male dog, Kato, a "*she.*" As Chad wrote when preparing the annotated version of the transcript of this interrogation, "*It is so much easier to think and respond when you didn't find out about your child's death just hours earlier* "

LeClair asked if Kassidy was on any waiting lists. Chad didn't know but explained some other aspects of his relationship to Amanda and Kassidy,

...you know she just, she - we haven't been together all that long. I really, there's a lot of things that I mean are going through my head right now that I'm, that you know that I just don't know.... I don't really tell her how to run her kid and I don't really, we did get into a ton of conversations you know I tell her how she should ... with my wife... I followed up everyday. Like, "Did you get this day care thing?" "Have you done this," and you know. With her I felt like I kind of raised one, one (inaudible) not raised but you know what I mean kind of, I don't want to do that again. (p. 1496)

Chad loved Kassidy, but he didn't want to raise her in a family where he over-managed her mother, and risk losing another family. Amanda and Chad talked about getting married and having a child together.

Rick LeClair asked Chad how he met Amanda and how he knew Jeff, even though he already knew that information through his two interviews with Amanda. Chad explained, and then noted that Jeff "*is a landscaper for my restaurants.*" (p. 1497) Although there was no surprise, LeClair responded, "*Oh really*!" In a case characterized by mis-remembered facts and dates, Chad said that he and Amanda went to a "Sting" concert on their first date, "*I think it was in July.*" (p. 1497) The group was "Staind," and it was Friday, June 2. Whether consciously or unconsciously, Chad was minimizing his relationship to Amanda, but that had the effect of bringing the start of the relationship a little closer to the start of the bruising, which was not the desired effect of such minimizing. To the extent that it was conscious, it was to protect Amanda's Maine residency status for her eligibility in the ASPIRE program.

Further commenting on his relationship to Jeff, Chad said, "*I've been talking to him about kind of what happened in my life with my wife and you know he'd been talking. You know he had a similar situation with an ex-girlfriend and ...*" (p. 1497) If Chad was talking about their common experience with court restraining orders, he wasn't specific and the interrogators didn't ask. With their access to judicial and police databases, they surely already know a lot about both men and their criminal records.

Chad told LeClair and McLeish that he was separated from Tristan and that his divorce was almost final. McCleish asked, "*So you, you and Amanda living together?*" and Chad made the first serious mistake of the interrogation when he responded, "*No. Well, not really. See it's kind of odd...she's a nice girl, and she's totally in love with me and I really like her a lot. But I'm so burnt from the last thing that...*" (p. 1499) In fact, they had been living together since early July and in love. When Chad said, "*No, not really*," LeClair and McCleish knew that Chad was mis-characterizing the relationship. However, what he said afterwards was true. It's common for people to misrepresent the status of their love relationship to others, especially when they still believe they are legally married to someone else; but this was a police interrogation about a death of a child and not a casual inquiry. Also, Chad was trying to protect Amanda's Maine residency for her ASPIRE program. Three hours earlier, Amanda had told Angela Blodget in her interview that her residence was at "53 Rogers Road," i.e. Jeff's and Jennifer's, but that was a lie because she had never lived there. Of her relationship to Chad, she said, "*I kind of live with my boyfriend, but not really.*" (p. 822) She, too, was minimizing the relationship.

A few weeks after Kassidy's death, Chad wrote about his interrogation in his Nov. 2000 letter to his attorneys,

One thing I know for sure about my questioning is I really tried to down play my relationship with Amanda. She recently got involved with some program with the state of Maine where they were going to pay for her college. She was talking about getting her own place in Kittery soon anyways, so I didn't think it was a big deal that she wasn't living in Maine at the time. But when I started getting questioned I really didn't want her to get into trouble. I will explain my entire relationship with Amanda later, but the major mental block I had going through my head was that I was very badly hurt in my relationship with Tristan and I didn't want to fall for anyone again or admit to myself I had. She basically lived with me from July but when she ever talked about moving her dresser in, I had a fit. I would say, "I am not ready for a live-in girlfriend," and she would get pissed and say "What the fuck, I do live here Chad. I haven't been home in months." My feeling on the education front was, I was paying for everything for Amanda and Kassidy and had no problems doing so, but I wasn't about to put another woman through school and have her leave me also. If she moved to Maine and I couldn't have lived without her, I would have brought her back, moved her in, and paid for her education but I wanted to see how things would be first.

LeClair asked about Kassidy's health, and Chad responded, "*Healthy wise she got sick a lot like colds and things like that.*" Chad then volunteered other information about his relationship with Tristan and how she seemed to be coming over to his house more often now that Amanda was "*a girlfriend.*" (p. 1501) Chad added that Tristan said to him about Kassidy,

She goes, "I'm not trying to be mean or anything but is she like retarded?' And I'm like, "I don't know, Tristan." I mean she doesn't really talk a lot, doesn't really you know she just doesn't seem ...developed a lot for a kid... sometimes she goes into things where

she'll go forever just blabbing away talking, not really saying but talking and whatever. But then other times she'll just sit there and like zone out, like weird." (p. 1502) Chad estimated that he had known Kassidy for four months, which was close to the actual five months, or 153 days.

LeClair asked, "*Has she been to the doctor or anything in the four months you've known her?"* Chad responded, *"She went once I think to - Yeah you know what, she's got, she's got a problem with her feet. And I didn't really notice it. My mother noticed it.*" (p. 1502) Unfortunately, Chad didn't remember the dates of Kassidy's two medical appointments, on August 10 and September 11. He may not even have known about one or both of them. He didn't think to mention that he had recommended to Amanda that she take Kassidy to a doctor to remove the wart on her index finger of her right hand, or that he had passed on his mother's recommendation that a doctor examine Kassidy for her toed-in problem. On the other hand, the detectives didn't seem to feel the date was important, either. Otherwise, they could have asked Chad, and before him, Amanda, to find those dates and let the police know.

Continuing with Kassidy's feet problems, Chad said that she fell a lot, at his parents' home around the pool and in Rochester. Also, "*I have a kitchen table that's, it's all glass and she's walked in that a few times*." (p. 1503) In 2010, Chad added,

We had a glass kitchen table that was about head height for Kassidy. She ran into that several times playing "Fetch" with our dog, Kato. In the living room, we had a glass table sitting right in front of the sofa. Several times Kassidy landed and did a face plant right into the table. She actually did it once while home with Travis and Amanda, several days before her death. Amanda and I finally smartened up and pulled the table out more, away from the sofa." (p. A-1503)

LeClair asked Chad, *"When was the last time you, you saw Kassidy alive?*" and Chad described the morning sendoff, "*...it must of been about 7:15, gave her a kiss, put her in the car whatever and she waved 'bye-bye.'* " (p. 1504) Asked by LeClair, "*What was - when she got up, how would she get up? Is she the type of child who would wake up crying every morning*?" Chad said,

I've noticed that for the last month now that you bring that up. Every morning it seems like probably 4 or 5 o'clock she starts bawling and then comes in and crawls in bed with Amanda and I. Not, not maybe two or three weeks you know.... But most of the time she'd wake up pretty happy you know. I mean wake up and she'd be like, I'm like you, you want to eat. "Yeah." You know and ...Loves to eat, that kid. (p. 1506)

Later, Chad again described Kassidy's sleeping and waking habits,

...like I said in the last couple weeks I noticed that she would wake up. Like it was weird because sometimes like, usually I consider myself to be a pretty light sleeper but sometimes like she wakes up like that and I look over and there's Amanda on the other side and she's right in the middle. I'm like, "How in the hell did you get there?" (p. 1510)

LeClair asked, *"Would you change diapers*?" and Chad responded,

Yeah I've done it a few times. Unfortunately I've changed my first shitty diaper from her this weekend. Let me tell you she's got a little shitter on, a little shitter. I never really was around her you know like when she shit. Sorry... Usually when she'd do that she, Amanda was there to change her. But usually right before, like a lot of times you know I'd given her a bath on the nights that, so I'd put a new diaper on her but. But I found out you know like after this weekend, actually my sister was there and it stunk so bad I couldn't talk her into changing it. And I found out why I'm glad I didn't have a girl: you know." (p. 1506)

Unfortunately, no more details about the family gathering on Sunday, November 5 were requested or offered.

Lance McCleish asked, "*If, if say Kassidy or, or one of your boys is over the house and someone does something you know that's bad or whatever, who's usually the person to, to kind of discipline them or you know tell them that...?*" Chad answered,

...we both do. I mean she [Amanda] *struggles with that a little bit because Kyle's got a mind of his own and, but I've made it very important that she's the one telling him a lot. Like what to do or whatever.... I mean we, you know for the most part you know both of us we, I mean she's a lot of times, I mean a lot of times like with Kassidy she'll say, "no,*

mama" or whatever and You'll know, so then I'd be like "No, Kassidy, you got to do what mom says," or whatever. I'll pick her up. ***The big thing with me is eye contact****.... I would say to my son, Kyle "look me in the eyes" because he's big enough to know.* (p. 1508)

McCleish asked how Kassidy was responding to Chad and that technique, "*Oh yeah, she's never, she's never really said, 'No' to me. She just said, 'No' to me once and I'm like, 'Well, you're gonna be going time-out you know.'* " (p. 1508)

Asked if Kassidy cried a lot, Chad said,

Yeah, Just, not really cry, whine....I mean, she she was a tough kid some things, you know that you think a kid would freaken bawl about... But then if you know like she would had fits a lot you know. Like if I was sitting next to Amanda. I guess she never really had a guy you know. If I sit near Amanda or something like that, you know especially at the beginning she'd stomp her feet and throw herself on the floor. I mean, you know I'm like what is that? And I'd immediately pick her up, "You need to go stand in the corner," you know. And then she'd throw herself in the corner or throw herself into the wall like, I mean like I'd never seen her [do before]. *I'm like, "*[This] *is a girl thing.*" (p. 1510)

Lance McCleish then suggested, "*Think she was maybe a little jealous.*" and Chad agreed,

Yeah very, very jealous you know but. I mean but you know one of the things I try to do and actually Amanda made that point the other day you know. She was having a fit because, it's like, "Stop look at me," you know. I met her for lunch. We were at Old Navy and you know Kassidy is in the back seat and I'm doing eyes, ears, whatever and she'd point to all the things. She[Amanda] *says, "You pay more attention to her than me" and I'm like, "Well, it's because she's cuter than you," just kind of make ...* (p. 1510-11)

This was Thursday, November 2, or Tuesday, November 7, which was important, as it was so close to November 9.

In 2010, Chad wrote about that impromptu get-together:

Amanda had just started her job, and I was in the area so I was going to Kittery to pick up Kassidy and surprise Amanda by taking her to lunch, or if she couldn't go to lunch, I knew she would love a quick visit from Kassidy. Something strange happened though, I made the arrangements with Jeff to pick Kassidy up but when I got there, Amanda was there with Jen. She had messed up her schedule or something and wasn't due into work for like another 30 minutes. So I ended up taking Kassidy anyway and we met at the Perfumania parking lot. Amanda got into my car and we took Kassidy through the Kittery McDonald' s drive-thru to get a happy meal. (Letter, Aug. 14, 2010)

LeClair picked up on that point, "*So you try to pay attention to her.*" Chad agreed and gave an example of his parenting tactics, "*Yeah, well... what I found worked was if I went home and, and talked to her first you know. I hate that thing like you kissing up to kid but yeah whatever. You know if I talk to her first I didn't hear a lot of crying you know.*" (p. 1511)

Chad expanded on this in his 2010 annotations of the transcript to the interrogation:

Kassidy had serious tantrums when Amanda and I first got together and I went near Amanda or showed Amanda attention. This quickly stopped and I think what helped it was when I got home I would go to Kassidy and show her love and attention first. Then we'd both go to Amanda. Around October 1st or so, the tantrums started again. Throwing herself on the floor, raging, banging her hands and head on the floor. Even on occasion she would pull her hair. The only major change in her life around October 1st was that Amanda started working, first on a survey project and later at Old Navy. Kassidy began spending significant amounts of time with Jeff. Maybe the separation from Amanda so suddenly caused it. (p. A-1511)

Chad noted that Kyle was colicky as a baby, and "*I learned a new sense of patience, you know.*" (p. 1511) Then Chad noted, "*I didn't even realize you guys were, were taping this. That's all right.... Like I said, I have nothing to hide.*" (p. 1511) That previous lack of awareness of the taping may account for some aspect of his responses to questions, but it's difficult to discern any difference in his post-tape-discovery responses.

Lance McCleish asked about the stress level at Chad's work, and Chad said,

It can be great....I went through a lot of shit before I was married, I mean before I met Amanda you know and we you know being from like the, the things that I did. I would a lot of times with Tristan I'd come home and, and have like a bad attitude you know. Not like really say anything to her but just be quiet and whatever. And I had a guy that, that works for me in Rochester. He's an old, old fellow. He's a good guy. We talk all the time and he... said "Chad you work your ass off." He goes, "You got to stop and smell the roses along the way." you know. And you know when you go home you leave work at work and as much as you can. Because I was [a] *typical company man you know, do whatever.* (p. 1512)

In 2010, Chad added,

What I meant to say is, I sometimes brought the stress of work home with me when I was married to Tristan. It was part of our downfall. I lived in a constant state of worry. When Amanda came into my life, I was determined to do things differently. I left work problems at work. I focused on her and the kids when home. I went and purchased some family toys to enjoy with them - a trampoline, a boat, some 3-wheelers, etc. (p. A-1512)

LeClair asked, "*...have you ever been physical with your wife or Amanda over.. a domestic situation*," and Chad responded quickly, "*Yeah, Tristan. ...I'm sure you guys, you're not dumb guys. You're cops. You know that I was arrested for. ..*"

LeClair then said, "*No I didn't, I don't know,*" but he had just interviewed Amanda and she told him about Chad's probation, and Tristan's warnings to Amanda, and to go to the Rochester police station to see her photographs. He knew, but as Angela Blodgett had observed in that same interview with Amanda, "*I think everybody lies.*" The challenge in this case was that some lies were more important, and more justifiable, than others. Also, the police believed that it was okay for them to lie, as it was justified by the higher purpose of solving crimes and punishing criminals. They did not believe it was okay for other citizens to lie.

Chad continued to respond to LeClair's question,

Never been in trouble my life, model citizen, got elected to the school board at 18, one of those guys just never ... Very, very political. My goal was to be the mayor. You know what I mean? Big into ... Jaycees ... and I always had life by the balls, you know what I mean it's really, I'm the man you know.... I would come home sometimes and have an attitude with her but we never really fought or anything like that you know. But Tristan and I once we had a couple of altercations with domestic things. Basically, she was out having an affair and ... (p. 1513)

Actually, Chad was 20 when elected to the Keene Board of Education, but was still the youngest person ever elected to that position. He was asked again about "*problems with the police*," and he related the story of a fight with three men which 20 witnesses were ready to say was started by the other three. The three men didn't appear in court, so the matter was dismissed.

LeClair asked Chad, "*Do you know if Jeff has any criminal history?*" and Chad knew about one incident, "*I guess she* [a former girlfriend] *screwed around on him once and he went and beat the guy up or something.*" (p. 1513) So far, as of about 8:15 p.m. on November 9, nobody had asked Jeff that question, about his criminal history, and it was never asked in future interviews.

Chad was asked who were his best friends, and he named Bruce and Jeremy, and then described friendship, generally,

...they're friends in that you know, they know everything about you... It was the hardest thing in the world to talk to, it was like telling my parents that, "I'm ashamed, guys, I got in a fight with Tristan and this is what happened," you know. And to listen to them say, "I mean, Chad, what the hell is the matter with you? You're a big guy, you know I mean no matter if she started it whatever you got to just walk away." You know what I mean? They're true friends, you know what I mean. They didn't judge me for it but they certainly let me have it. (p. 1516)

Chad described Travis and his babysitting, "*A couple of times he would watch them for us. Usually it was like right before they were going to bed though, you know. He's, he is great with kids as well.*" (p. 1517)

LeClair asked, "*...over the last two or three weeks, who's been, been watching Kassidy? Who she been around*?" and Chad responded, "*Amanda and Jeff mostly. Because I've been you know working quite a bit.*" He then noted that Amanda had just begun work at Old Navy, but she was working hard before that on the survey inputting work for Bruce.

Chad said,

She does like five or six thousand surveys and you input them in the computer, like six questions of each. She made a cool 1800 bucks and ... to be home and ... able to spend time with your kid you know.... I'd say it took her a good solid two weeks to do it in between. Like you know, you really can't stare at the computer screen for eight hours so she'd do it for two hours....Go do something else, go do the laundry you know. (p. 1518)

LeClair asked an important question, "*How often? How many times have you watched her?*" Chad began,

Jesus. I just put Amanda in money management class to teach her how to... Off early and she appreciated it you know right learn about IRA's and stuff.... I signed her up about a month ago. It's a three session class for two and a half hours in Portsmouth. I sent her with my sister to the class. And along with a couple of my employee[s].... I watched her probably from 7 to 8:30 on two of the nights. And one of the nights she just stayed with Jeff the whole time and I think I've watched her twice since she's worked. And I really can't think of many times other than that been alone. As a matter of fact, last night was the only time I think that I had her alone for any period, we were alone for about half an hour or so before Trav came in. Most of the time I have her and the kids, I just go, I mean her and the kids. Her and Kyle and I would go to my friend Bruce's house.... he has a live-in girlfriend that loves yeah, and a couple of dogs and they just sit there and play with them all night. And I'd go out and work out with Bruce or something and you know have dinner together and by that time Amanda is coming back from work."(p. 1519)

As noted in Chapter 3, the first of the three money management classes was Thursday, October 19, and Chad took over the babysitting from Jeff who had been with Kassidy during the day. The next Thursday was the beginning of Jeff's three-day/two-night babysitting. The last was on November 2, and the babysitting split was the same as on October 19. Before Saturday, November 4, except for the money management seminar, Kassidy was always either with Amanda or Jeff. Chad forgot to mention his approximately nine hours with Kassidy the previous Sunday, November 5 at Nicole's and Brandon's. Bruce's "*live-in girlfriend,*" was Jessica Edmands, who was never interviewed by the police. Chad, Amanda, and Kassidy and Kyle may have been with Bruce and Jessica on Monday evening, November 6, for Monday-night-football, and possibly Tuesday. On Wednesday, the only time Chad was alone with Kassidy was during the 30 minute drive from Kittery to Dover to pickup Kyle at Cross Road Kindergarten. For the rest of the evening, Kyle was home, as was Travis for a brief period.

LeClair asked about the specific events and times for the previous evening, and Chad described his call to Bruce "*...for a good 15 - 20 minutes because I do a little football betting*." McCleish acted surprised, "*Oh really!*" but Jeff had already told the police about Chad's football gambling, and LeClair and Blodgett had asked Amanda about it. There was discussion about football and the New England Patriots. Then, Chad said that he told Bruce the previous night, "'*...all right I got to go because I have bath water running and I'm trying to do it all you know, be Mr. Mom.' And he's like, 'All right man, call you in a little while,' because I usually get the kids in bed by 8 - 8:30 so I know it's a good time to call.*" (p. 1520) In the interrogation, there was more "guy-talk" about weightlifting and supplements and Chad's motorcycle accident and bad back, as the police tried to put Chad at ease. They were his friends, at least for a while longer.

Then, Rick LeClair, called "*Ricky*" by McCleish, asked Chad, "*Did you give her a bath the night before*?" (p. 1525) Chad described how Kyle preferred to have a bath separate from Kassidy. Provoking a bit of humor, LeClair asked, "*Did Kyle and Amanda fight? Like brother and sister?...*" and Chad corrected him, "*Kyle and Kassidy, you mean? I'm like Kyle and Amanda? Oh I hope that she'd win that.*" (p. 1526)

LeClair asked whether Kassidy and Kyle considered themselves as "*brother and sister... were there any jealousies?*" Chad said, "*There were jealousies.... There was a lot of jealousies*," and Chad described the "shared couch" episode of November 8th, as was noted earlier in this chapter with the discussion of "time-outs" in the section with Amanda's interview. In his 2010 annotations, Chad added, "*As with any children, but they also acted like brother and sister and had that type of relationship. Kyle is very protective and was with Kassidy. If Amanda or I were disciplining Kassidy for some reason, Kyle would come into the room and say, 'Stop yelling at AKassidy.' He called her, 'AKassidy.'* " (p. A-1526)

Rick LeClair asked, "*Now last night at the, the bath, did you notice anything funny about the way Amanda was, was behaving?*" After correcting him with, "*Kassidy?*" Chad responded,

Yeah. I noticed a lot of things last night.... She was in a daze last night. She was really weird. Like I don't know why I didn't, like not talking and I... she was, you know I'm just picturing it in the car like you know, she's sitting there in the car you know hanging over that car seat with like, kind of like drooling a little bit you know and... She was looking forward so I'm like, I thought maybe she was just getting ready to go to sleep because sometimes she does that you know.... She's got you know daze look. But she didn't really fall asleep. When Kyle got in the car she didn't say "Hi Kiko" like she always did, you know what I mean? She just kind of sitting there looking at the house, freaken weird. And I don't know. (p. 1528)

Chad said that Jeff carried Kassidy from his apartment to Chad's car, and at that time, Kassidy, "*was the same way, just fucken like lethargic, just kind of there you know.*" McCleish asked what Jeff said about Kassidy's behavior, and Chad responded,

He, he didn't really say, that's kind of why I called him, because I'm like, "What the hell?" You know, I mean how long have you had her? He said, "Oh well, I haven't had her that long." ...because Amanda didn't go to work until like 4 or something like that and this is like almost 6. You know it's about, probably an hour and half whatever. And I said," well, did she, was she fine[? and he said] *"Oh, she seemed fine over here." But I mean it was dark you know....And I wasn't really paying attention to her until like I'm like when she wasn't talking. I'm like, "What the hell is going on?* " (p. 1529)

Chad agreed with LeClair who asked, "*Did you maybe think she was tired or something at first?"* and then LeClair asked *"how was she when, when she got home? I mean did she act like she had the flu or was she running around? What did she do?*" Chad answered,

She was weird. Like last night she, as a matter of fact I mean I, I called Jeff then too afterwards but she, I, I spoke to Amanda about it. That the weirdest things happened. Like one of the things that she does sometimes is like, she'll just you know be running along and fall, but unlike a typical kid she doesn't like to put her hands to stop herself. I don't, you know what I mean? ... That's what makes me wonder if she might be a little slow like you know.... Because I mean even Kyle when he always fell at that age you can always put your hands out to stop. But you know she was sitting in the car and I went and got her out of the car and that kind of like bothered me a little bit but... I set her down ... She was out, in the car, I opened the car door, I set her down in front of the door standing up. I'm like, "Wait a minute," because Kyle is on the other end of the car screaming "Daddy get me out, get me out," whatever. So I opened his car door and let him out. I go back to the other side of the car and she's not standing anymore. She's laying face down on the ground ... With her hands to her side, not crying or anything. I'm like, "What the hell is going on with you"...actually Kyle came around the corner and saw her. He goes, "Daddy why is she laying on the ground?" ... so I picked her up and carried her inside....When we went inside, I sat her down on the counter and I opened up the mouse trap, I caught a mouse. She actually acknowledged it, [and] *pointed* [to] *it. And Kyle is "Daddy you got another mouse." You know whatever. And then I set her in her seat and I, I think that's when I started... talking to Bruce. I started the bath water. Trying to be multitasked. Feed 'em, clean 'em....When I fed her she ate pretty good.... Well I tried to give her a grilled cheese.... I gave her a banana.... I fed her and she went, brought them in the living room for a few minutes. And I brought them upstairs and, and here's another, here's another thing that happened that was, that was kind of odd. I called Jeff and I, I was talking to him*

about it. And I just thought it was really strange but he was acting kind of weird on the phone like I thought you know just like wasn't, like we always make little jokes you know, like I mean. But he, he wasn't like I'm just -" what the hell, what did you do to her when she was at your house?" He goes "nothing" you know but... (p. 1529-30)
Chad continued, "*I told him that she fell, you know and didn't even like flinch. But she, but that's not really uncommon to be honest with you. She's done that a million times. Travis, you know, has seen it. You know Amanda has seen it. Like if Amanda 'What the hell is wrong with her? Why does she do that?' She'll just be walking along, fall and like ... Like 'Why don't you put your hands up and catch yourself?'* "

LeClair asked Chad if he "*suspected Jeff of being assaultive?*" A few minutes earlier in the interview, Chad had said clearly "*... the last thing I want to do is like accuse somebody of doing something that, you know unless you actually physically seen somebody you know what I mean, or whatever.*" (p. 1528) And he didn't start by directly answering LeClair's question. Instead, he said,

Because last night she was you know, didn't seem right whatever. You know and she was acting kind of funny. I'm thinking maybe I should just take the kid to the doctor's. Because she had some you know, black and blues on her whatever; And I'm like, you know, like I went through my thing with Tristan and I know how people have kids. I don't want anybody thinking I'm bringing this kid to the hospital. (p. 1531)

He didn't want anyone to think that he was abusing Kassidy. Yes, he had caused the bruises at the bottom of her cheeks, and the final round of such bruises was fading or gone, but they may have been still there, and they were accidental. He didn't mean to hurt Kassidy and initially didn't realize that he was holding her firmly enough to cause the bruises. It wasn't until the second or third observation of bruises on Kassidy's lower cheeks that Chad and Amanda realized that Chad's "eye contact" face holding was causing them.

Lance McCleish asked, "*She had marks you're saying?*" and Chad said, "*Yeah like, she had like a black and blue on her cheek or something,*" and McCleish, asked the followup question, "*...where did that come from those same things?*" Chad then made one of the most important mistakes of his life. He lied about the bruises he caused. Not about all the bruises, but about the bruises on Kassidy's lower cheeks from his holding for "eye contact." He said, "*To be honest with you I don't know.*" (p. 1532) He did know. At least, he knew about the cheek bruises.

Chad said, "*I mean, I mean you know like I said she does walk into things,*" and then he explained his motivation for not wanting to be accused. He told the officers that Tristan had said, in the context of their divorce, "*She said, 'No matter what he did to me or what we got in a fight in he's been the best father in the world and I would never try to take the kids from being able to see him,' or whatever. And like the last thing I'm gonna do is like have anybody tell me that I can't see my kid.*" However, by avoiding the truth about his "eye contact" bruising, he allowed the police to continue with their theory that he did a lot more to Kassidy than hold her face to make "eye contact." He was afraid that if he told them about his role, the police would accuse him of enough other bruising to affect his custody arrangements for Kyle. He knew, and it's never even been suggested otherwise by anyone since then, that the bruises on Kassidy's cheeks that he caused had absolutely nothing to do with Kasidy's death. Thus, by not telling the police the truth about them, he reasoned, he wasn't impeding their investigation, and he wasn't risking, he thought, his custody arrangements for Kyle. Instead, by lying, he allowed them to enhance their theories about his credibility and his abuse and murder of Kassidy.

Then without a specific question, and beginning with, "*I mean I didn't think it was that huge a thing,*" Chad said, "*...as I was saying, like a month ago Jeff was watching her and Amanda, him and I went out the next day and got some three wheelers. And he's telling me how he spanked her so hard his hand stung. And I kind of laughed because I thought he was kidding you know, thinking you know that's kind of you know there's no way you can hit a kid that hard you know.*" (p. 1533) Chad was scrambling the words, but on Sunday, October 22, Jeff brought Kassidy home from babysitting on Saturday and an overnight, and then he and Jeff went north to Maine to pick up a 3-wheeler in Jeff's truck.

Amanda did not go with them. Chad told LeClair and McCleish of his understanding that Jeff's spanking was through a diaper.

Chad said that Amanda showed him the black and blue that evening, but it was likely the following Tuesday morning because, according to Amanda, "*Jennifer said, "'Don't show that to Chad.' because she knew I'd be kind of bullshit about it.*" Chad told LeClair and McCleish, *"I've never seen a big black and blue like that before. I'm like, 'holy shit'.... I mean like last night on the phone I suggested to Amanda, I said and I mean, swear on a stack of bibles and this is what's kind of weird. Like I was talking to her I said, 'Amanda I don't know if I want to watch Kassidy,' I'm like, 'The weirdest shit happens.'"* (p. 1534)

McCleish asked if Chad had asked Jeff about the bruises, and Chad said,

...I said, "Jesus you really hit her hard." And he's like "Yeah" and he was kind of like you know laughing about it, whatever. And I'm like, "Amanda is pretty pissed off about that," you know what I mean. That's really the only conversation we had. I meant it, you know, I know it's wrong. But[it's] *like that whole back to not butting my nose into everything. If it was Kyle I would of.* [said or done more.] (p. 1535)

Chad continued,

...last night on the phone I said, "Amanda I just don't," I said, "I think you really should you know we talked about him just watching her a little bit. I really think that you should find another place." He's 24 years old; he doesn't have any kids of his own, he doesn't understand how to handle them... I don't think that he's a good person to be watching her." (p. 1534)

By "*another place*," he meant another place for day care for Kassidy.

Then, Chad described the Kassidy fall-from-Jeff's-truck incident as it was told to him,

...she's got a big ole' egg on her head that been there for a week and a half when he left her alone in the truck and she fell out of it... Big ass freaken bruise and like right here on the back of her head. And I wasn't home. I hadn't been, I think I was away for a day or something because I came home and I'm like, "What the hell happened to her, Amanda?" And she said "Oh Jeff said she was sitting in her seat and fell out of it." Out of the truck or something. (p. 1535)

Rick LeClair had already heard Amanda describe this incident, which came at the end of the three-day/two-night babysitting from Thursday, October 26 through Saturday, the 28th.

Chad related another incident that he recalled in 2010 which Jeff had told him during the October 22 trip to Maine for the 3-wheeler,

And another time he was baby-sitting her he left her in the, I guess he left her in the room, he changed her diaper. She shit....He changed her diaper but he le[f]*t her. She was standing on the bed and he left her pants around her ankles and what do you think is gonna happen? ...And what did she do?...Smack, you know.* (p. 1535)

Rick LeClair asked, "*What did she have last night for bruises when you were bathing her?*" and Chad responded,

Well she got one from, she got a bruise from Kyle....Well I'm a little embarrassed to say it. My mother always told me never play with balls in the house. I have this thing with him where you know if you can't go out whatever.... I'll just throw balls to him in his room. He can hit like the dickens. I throw wiffle balls to him you know....She can't really walk or whatever. So I have her sitting beside me you know. I'm sitting on the bed just tossing in the air and he's wailing on them. But he's, you know, throwing all over and he's catching the things or whatever. She was sitting on the right hand side and you know I threw the ball and he hit it and, but it was like, it was a hard rubber ball and he whacked her right on the side of the face, like right here.... With the ball....Well it's like, you know one of those starter baseballs... it's hard, but it's got a rubber coating on it. (p. 1536)

Chad described the effects,

...she just dropped back on the bed and just whimpered like "hahh". I was like what the hell? But then I started like looking at her. I'm like Jesus, are you all right you know. And Kyle is like "Sorry daddy, sorry Kassidy" and I'm like Kyle it's okay you didn't do it on purpose. She didn't really cry, I mean she just had that like whimper you know...I don't know I mean, she did. You know you think that's why I was saying a little earlier about her

being like tough, you'd think that something like that is gonna hurt. Immediately got, she got like a little puffy you know.... Oh yeah, it [is] *definitely hard. I mean he hit me with it once, you know when he was throwing it so I felt it you know. So anyway, you know, so I'm like, "It's all right Kyle. You didn't do it on purpose," or whatever. But I'm like looking at her and like she had a little black and blue that I'm assuming is when she hit the driveway*." (p. 1537)

Chad said that he didn't notice the driveway-fall bruise when he was bathing and shampooing Kassidy, "*but the whole time I was there I give her a bath I was talking to Travis so I wasn't really looking at her because he was standing right beside and we were shooting the shit.*" (p. 1538)

Asked more about Kassidy's bath, Chad said that she was completely naked. He said that he didn't suspect Jeff or anyone of sexually abusing Kassidy, but he wasn't told what Amanda was told about the physical signs of such abuse on Kassidy's body. The question reminded him of his diaper change, on Sunday, November 5, as was described earlier in this chapter, "*I felt really weird wiping her diaper, her dirty diaper because she had it* [feces] *all the way up herself.*" (p. 1539) However, Chad said nothing about that occasion and the date. About possible sexual abuse of Kasssidy, Chad said, "*And like that whole, so you know that whole thing kind of makes me sick. I never really thought about anybody doing that kind of shit you know.*" (p. 1539)

Chad said that the fall from Jeff's truck, "*was like a week ago... And she's still got a bump the size* [of] *her shoe today.*" (p. 1539) The fall occurred on Saturday, October 28, or 13 days before Kassidy's death. Chad told LeClair and McCleish what Amanda had said that Jeff had told her about the incident. He didn't recall at the time that Jeff had told him that the accident occurred, according to Chad in 2010 when Kassidy, "*was leaning out the truck window when parked in his driveway and fell out, and landed on her head." (p. A-1540)* Unknown to Chad, Amanda had already told LeClair what she knew. A blow to Chad's and Amanda's credibility came at Chad's trial when Chief Maine Medical Examiner Margaret Greenwald said that she did not see evidence of such a bruise or swelling on Kassidy's head when she began the autopsy on Friday, November 10. The police doubted the story entirely, just as they doubted the November 8 ballhitting story, and the "trampoline story." During the stress of the interrogation, Chad didn't have the opportunity to think clearly about the two goose eggs on the top of Kassidy's head, and that Amanda, Jeremy and Travis also saw them when Kassidy returned home. Emily Conley said in her Nov.21 interview that she saw them, too.

Lance McCleish asked, "*Is she coming back from like Jeff's house you know, did you ever feel like you know why does she seem to come from there with bruises and injuries and stuff a lot?*" and Chad answered,

That's kind of what I was leading to I think with Amanda last night was I said to Jeff, I'm like, "what the hell did you do her?" "Nothing" But then I talked to Amanda on the phone. I said, "She's got like a little mark on her left eye Amanda, what happened?" You know because I hadn't seen her all day and Amanda had her all day. She's like "Oh I don't know that was there a couple days ago." I'm like, "How in the hell did I not notice something like that?" you know. It wasn't huge but she's got like, it looked like a cat scratch, you know. (p. 1541)

Thus, Chad had told the detectives that on Wednesday night, he knew about a bruise from the fall in his driveway, and about the "*hard rubber ball*" hit, and about the cat scratch bruise.

LeClair asked Chad about the previous day's activities for Amanda and Kassidy and he noted that Amanda took Kyle to his kindergarten, and said, "*I know she picked up some brake parts for me at noon and she still had Kassidy then because I called her and I heard Kassidy in the background and I'm like you know,* [heard her] *just say something like 'Big Bird is on TV,' or something.*" That three minute call was at 1:05 p.m. (Chart of Calls) Chad continued, "*I'm like what* [is] *she doing?* [and Amanda said] *'She's like being a little bitch'. I'm like, 'what is she doing now, she's watching TV.*" Asked if "*being a little bitch*" was a "*common expression*," for Amanda, Chad said,

Lately she's been very frustrated with her because she's been very fussy. And she's been less fussy with me than she has with Amanda which is kind of odd....Because at first you know she had a big jealous streak for me. You know now it's like she didn't have a problem ...She's warmed up to me to the point where like you know, I'll put my arms up and she'll come right to me you know what I mean. (p. 1541)

This description of Kassidy at 1:05 p.m. on Wednesday, is one of the only descriptions of Kassidy's behavior during the entire day of Wednesday, until Chad picked her up at 5:30 p.m. Still, "*being a little bitch*" is more descriptive than no description, and it provides a baseline to measure her behavior at 5:30 p.m.

Continuing to comment on Amanda's phrase, "*being a little bitch,*" Chad noted that during the summer, when he and Amanda took several trips, there were breaks from caring for Kassidy, but since mid-October, "*she had two solid weeks of, three solid weeks of complete Kassidy time you know.*" (p. 1542)

Lance McCleish asked, "*How was Kassidy acting? Normal?*" and Chad responded, *Yeah she seemed, she seemed - before she went to bed because I checked on her a few times just because I was you know, just weird and she was fine. Like as a matter of fact I think the last time I checked on her was like 9:30, I went in, I sneaked in I looked at her ... She was fine. She actually rolled over gave me, said "kiss" ... And gave me a kiss and then she then you know... she seemed a lot better you know.... and usually before I go to bed I make a trip into both kids*[rooms]*, give them a kiss goodnight. Ah pretty typical. And I kissed her. And I think it was probably about midnight that I went upstairs because I had to use the bathroom and I could smell she had a shitty diaper. And I told Amanda about it. She goes "I'm not waking her up to change it" so....* (p. 1542-43)

LeClair asked, "*Did, did you notice anything with her this morning on the bruises when you saw her?*" and Chad initially responded, "*No, I didn't. This morning I was late...*" but then he confused the morning of that day, Thursday, with the previous day. He continued with the right recollection for Thursday, saying that Amanda, "*came downstairs, Kassidy was still in bed, she got Kassidy up, brought her down. I said Amanda what, actually she went and got Kyle's lunch together. I'm like what do you want me to do? Do you want me to feed Kassidy right now? Do you want me to put cereal in a bag? She said put cereal in a bag and I you know, so I asked her* [Kassidy] *what kind she wanted and whatever.*" (p. 1542) In 2010, Chad said that Kassidy pointed to the Reese's Puffs box, and that's what he put into her baggie for the day. In the police photographs of Chad's home, that box was on the counter by the sink, and not with the other cereals on top of the refrigerator, which corroborates Chad's recollection. Also, in further corroboration, the Ziplock baggie was seized at Jeff's, and it had the same cereal in it.

McCleish asked, "*So then this morning she, she seemed all right?*" and Chad replied, "*Yeah. This morning she picked out her cereal, she was mowing it out of a baggie.*" (p. 1544) In 2010, Chad noted that "*mowing*" was "*a slight exaggeration. I was trying to make the point that she definitely was dipping her little hand into the baggy and eating cereal, because it felt like they were in disbelief that she was actually eating. I recall during the autopsy the contents of Kassidy's stomach was a brown liquified goop, consistent with the cereal I described her eating." (p. A-1544)* [See Chapter 1 for a full description of November 9, until Kassidy's death at approximately 12:30 p.m.]

Asked about Kassidy's bruises on that morning, Chad said he saw a previously unnoticed "*lump on one side of the head that was a little black and blue,*" (p. 1544) Chad said, about the bruise from the previous night,

...Kyle made a comment about it this morning. He said "Daddy, did I do that?" you know. And I'm like, "yeah that's - Kyle, it's okay," you know, because, you know sometimes he'll do malicious things to her you know...like he'll just take her ball, I mean take her - She'll come over and take something he's eating or whatever and you know he'll take it back and push it down on the floor or something and he's much bigger than her. She's a little peanut. (p. 1544)

Chad explained that he knew of no bruises on Kassidy on the 9th that had been caused by the kids' fighting.

Rick LeClair asked an important question, "*...let me ask you Chad. Have you ever, have you ever caused any bruises on Kassidy?*" and, again, Chad did not explain the "eye contact" bruising, and the reason for it. He said,

No. Well. I remember one time when I you know, she did something... and then she said "No, No, No" to me and whatever, and I'm like..."What did you say?" She's like, "No." So I went over and just - that's, that's one thing about her it's like I didn't really ever want to touch, she's like one of those kids it seemed like you touch her,... I always told Amanda that you know but. I think she had a bruise like right here and I'm like, "Oh." But then I saw Kyle touch her there. (p. 1545)

Chad seemed to be saying that he never hit Kassidy, and he didn't, but that he held her face; and also that she bruised easily.

Lance McCleish seemed to understand, "*So you kind of just like grabbed her face kind of thing?*" and Chad said that he would say to Kassidy, "*just like you know, 'You listen to me,' just like this with two fingers ...'No, you listen to me' ...*" And McCleish again indicated that he understood, saying, "*like my parents.*" and Chad finished his sentence, and responded to McCleish, "*Looking me in the eyes. Exactly.*" (p. 1545) This would have been a good time for Chad and McCleish to explore the communication technique of **eye contact**, and how Chad used that technique with Kassidy in disciplinary and non-disciplinary communication; but it was a police interrogation, and not a parenting seminar. Chad continued, "*You know, 'Look me in the eyes' and then she'd look* [at] *me. I think the only reason I did that because she wouldn't even look me in the eyes before that. So I'm like, 'No. You look me in the eyes.'* " (p. 1546) McCleish asked Chad when that happened, and Chad wasn't sure, but less than a week, and he agreed that such holding "*left a little bruise,*" but later said, "*I don't know that I actually left a bruise or not...*" (p. 1546) In 2010, Chad believed that on November 9, Kassidy's face may still have shown the faded remnants of a bruise from the most recent of about three overly firm "eye-contact" face-holding incidents.

Chad wondered if Kyle's occasional scrapes with Kassidy, or the throwing of toys, might have caused bruises, and said, "*I know he did right around her eye area,...*" and then when asked about bruises at Kassidy's chin, Chad said, "*...he's three years old. I don't think he could, I don't know. How the Hell do I know?*" (p. 1547) In 2010, Chad wrote, "*I still don't understand how I caused the bruises on her jaw. I don't believe I applied that much pressure. I only held her jaw to get Kassidy's attention, or correct a behavior or stop a tantrum. Every discipline with both children was followed by an explanation as well as kisses and hugs." (p. A-1547)*

McCleish asked if there were any "*...other times when you know there might of been a bruise or something like that that you know accidentally or trying to you know put her over here or you know like say, 'Go stand in the corner,' type thing when you think like maybe a bruise might of come from when you might of touched her?*" and Chad replied, " *most of the time my contact was like right there you know .... just like... it be like, 'No, you didn't listen to me, you know you need to look me in the eyes.'* " (p. 1547-48)

McCleish asked again, "*Did that ever cause any other bruising in the past? You know maybe, you know once or twice something like that?*" and Chad said, "*Yeah I'm sure. But I mean not, Jesus I don't want you guys to ...think I .... You know, but I'm sure, Because one other time, there was one when I was actually jumping with her on the trampoline.*" and he told the detectives the "trampoline story," which was a big mistake. (p. 1548) Amanda had already told LeClair that it wasn't true. It was true that he had been on the trampoline with Kassidy, and she had started to fall off, but not how he reached out to her. In 2010, Chad added,

I actually grabbed her hand as she was falling backwards. This near accident was the basis for the "trampoline story" which Amanda would later tell some of her friends to cover for the finger tip marks I left on Kassidy's jawline while trying to get her to make eye contact with me. I believe this trampoline incident occurred just prior to my birthday, October 15. I was nervous and sure this story would be told to the police by others, so I felt I needed to continue the fib rather than taking responsibility for causing the fingertip size bruises when holding Kassidy to make eye contact. The complete truth would have been more believable, and might have reduced the officer's suspicions. (p. A-1548)

Yes, indeed. He had told LeClair and McCleish about his belief in "eye contact" when communicating with people, especially children. This interrogation was the best time to tell them that the "trampoline story" was developed because the "eye contact" truth was either too embarrassing or took too long to explain or other reason. If not now, the best course of action would be to talk with Amanda and see what she told Blodgett and LeClair and then develop a plan so they both would tell the police and others the truth about the "trampoline story." However, given the tragedy at hand, Amanda and Chad did not discuss the "trampoline story" the first day after Kassidy's death, nor the second, nor at any time thereafter. Thus, the story continued its life, and was part of the prosecution's presentation to the jury. Chad did not foresee the impact of the withholding of the truth about this "white lie" from the police.

Chad told LeClair and McLeish about flicking Kassidy's lips after she said a swear word. In 2010, he wrote,

Kassidy was obviously just repeating something she heard one of us adults say. I flicked her lips with the back of my fingers no harder than you would shoo a fly away from your corn on the cob. It was very gentle, and didn't leave a bruise or mark of any kind. It didn't hurt Kassidy and she didn't cry. I was just telling the officers about this in the interest of full disclosure, as I was trying to think of anything, or any way I might have disciplined Kassidy." (p. A-1549)

Chad said,

Amanda made a comment she's like if you - she's like, "Don't hit her face. I don't want any bruises." Because she's always falling, always you know what I mean?... But I guess the reason I was bringing that up was because she made a comment, she's like if you're going to reprimand her, hit her in the legs. That's what I do and I've only seen one time that I really noticed that I thought she did something. There was like four or five black and blues on her leg." (p. 1549)

In 2010, Chad explained,

I'm not sure why I launched into this long explanation. Amanda would on occasion lightly swat Kassidy's diaper if she was misbehaving. Kassidy at one point laughed it off and Amanda got angry and lightly swatted Kassidy's legs. I honestly don't believe the bruises I saw were from this. I believe the bruises that I saw on the back of Kassidy's legs were part of the spanking episode from Jeff.... Any other bruises I ever witnessed on Kassidy's legs I believe were normal everyday kids' stuff: running into things, falling off of something, etc. They never concerned me because I had seen similar bruises on Brent and Kyle. Despite the fact that Kassidy was a peanut, she was tough and played hard. (p. A-1549-50)

Chad said to the officers, *"I'm just trying to be completely honest with you,"* and McCleish replied, *"Yeah. That's all I want, just your honesty."*

Chad told them that he asked Amanda about a bruise, "*...you know 'what the hell is that from" and whatever and she's like 'you know' because I think Jeff was kind of starting to watch her at that time she's like, 'I did that" ...But see that's - Amanda would sometimes hit her but she'd literally would be like that hard. Sometimes she'd bruise from that....*" and McCleish filled in the rest of the sentence, "*Bruised easily*?" Chad agreed, and added, "*...So I said to her 'Jesus Amanda maybe your kid is anemic, you should start feeding her some red meat or something.*" (p. 1550) Unfortunately, they didn't seek a doctor's opinion. He wrote in 2010, "*I wish we had seriously looked into this problem. It may seem to be a convenient excuse, but Kassidy really did bruise easier than anyone I had ever met. I guess because of her very fair skin tone, I assumed it was natural.*" (p. A-1550)

McCleish asked whether Chad had done anything like McCleish's own father who would *"grab me by the arm, 'You're going there, buddy.' "* Chad agreed, saying, *"A common thing for her actually speaking about the corner, sometimes she wouldn't go and I'd actually go right there just like hold her there,*" and he demonstrated that to the officers. (p. 1550) Chad described one incident that didn't require such holding.

I was sitting on the bed, you know I don't remember what she did but I was like you know "you got a time-out go in the corner." So she ran and started crying, run over the corner and slam right into the thing and she just gets like freaken bruise. I'm like, "Jesus Christ." Amanda is like, "Oh God" and she started laughing, she was sitting right there and she's like, "we got to have padded corners for her don't send her to the corner without... putting your hand in from of the thing because she does that every time like we send her to the corner," fucken slam. (p. 1551)

In 2010, Chad wrote,

In our bedroom, we often had a pile of clothes on the floor. On one particular occasion, Kassidy tripped on the pile and did a "face plant" right into the corner (near our closet). You have to remember that Kassidy had the baby clumsiness of a 21-month old. In addition, she was pigeon-toed and the majority of the time, when she started running, it would result in a fall. Amanda wasn't laughing maliciously. It was just funny in the moment because we could see it in like slow motion. Kassidy was very smart. I'm not so sure that she didn't figure out that flying into a time-out enough to make a thud got her out of trouble. We literally would sometimes follow her over to the corner and hold her hands up so she couldn't whack her head into the wall. (p. A-1551)

There was a break in the interrogation so the officers could get Chad a glass of water. Chad asked, "*How's Amanda doing?... I really want to see her.*" (p. 1552)

Rick LeClair resumed the questioning of Chad, and asked about the previous night, and Chad's observations of Kassidy. Chad repeated his description of the bruises he remembered, and said, "*...when I was combing her hair, I felt it, 'Holy shit.' The thing still hasn't gone away.*" (p. 1553) Chad wrote in 2010,

As I recall the two bumps were kind of side by side on the top, back half of her head. You asked about the cause. They were there after the fall from Jeff's truck....I know that several times as I child I get hit in the head and almost immediately a HUGE egg formed where it happened. I recall one time specifically in a little league baseball game, I was in a pickle between 1st and 2nd base and the 2nd baseman hit me right in the forehead with the ball. It hurt like hell, within a minute or two, I looked like a unicorn and could see this huge bump on my forehead. In hindsight, that fluid bump on my forehead went away within a couple of days. Kassidy's eggs lasted much longer. I think that may have been why I was more worried and surprised when I felt these slight raises in her head on the 8th when I combed her hair. (p. A-1553)

Chad mentioned the bruise on Kassidy's foot, explaining, "*Jeff said he stepped back on her but I don't know.*" (p. 1554) He continued, "*She has a scar... On the top of her foot. Amanda was over one of her friend's house or something and the - I think she leaned up against the curling iron or something.*" (p. 1554) LeClair and Chad's response was inaudible, but from the statements of others, it appears to have been caused in early October at either Emily Conley's or Crystal Martin's homes.

Lance McCleish shifted back to questions about Wednesday afternoon, and then he asked about Chad's relationship with Amanda, "*Has anything ever gotten physical between you two, as far as you know maybe a fight or an argument or something like that getting, not totally out of control but maybe a little bit?*" Chad responded,

Yeah I believe we got into an argument. She's got a - I've, I've got a little bit of a temper but not one of the things that, I mean after the whole thing with Tristan I went and found out that you sometimes I can be a control freak you know. And I went and saw a counselor, kind of like help me deal with a lot of stuff you know. Like I never got worked up after that you know... With a lot of stuff you know. But we got into it a few times over the stupidest things ... you know like she'd get freaked out about, you know like an ex-girlfriend calling or something like you know, she always like throw shit.... You know so she'd throw shit at me. It's probably I can only think it was like twice you know but.... (p. 1558)

McCleish continued, "*Did you guys ever hit each other?*" and Chad replied,

No never hit. Just mostly you know, she would, yeah actually she did slap me a few times...But that - usually it start with her throwing something and I'd chase her you know and it's kind of actually more fun than any but she, she'd be like "Why are you such an

asshole? I can't believe you still talk to her and her whatever" and then slap me whatever. So then I'd grab her and just throw her on the couch or something. Say "don't fucken slap me" because I don't need to get into this physical shit, you know what I mean....I want to make it very clear, not physical. I mean not if I like beat her up, if I hit her, have I done anything like that? Absolutely not. (p. 1558-59)

Then McCleish for the first time, told Chad that he was asking him about something that Amanda had told the police. He asked, "*What would you say if I told you that, that she told us that things might of gotten out of control at a McDonald's party one night.*" (p. 1559) Already nervous, Chad was thrown off by the word, "*party.*" He didn't think of the August 25 Colley-McCoy dinner celebration of the opening of a McDonald's in Exeter as a party, and he couldn't remember what McCleish could be referencing. He asked for more details, "*...can you get more specific like when, where, or anything?*" and the officers wouldn't oblige. Instead, LeClair asked, "*Well, how about did you ever choke her?*" and Chad said, "*No.*" (p. 1559) LeClair tried again, "*Did you ever assault her?*" and after confirming that LeClair meant "*Like hit her, anything like that?*" Chad said, "*No.*" (p. 1560) In 2010, Amanda agreed that Chad never hit her, but grabbed her a few times, as Chad had described in his interview. She was physical with him, too, and sometimes slapped him.

McCleish pressed Chad for "*just the truth*" about the physical aspects of some of his arguments with Amanda, and Chad said, "*... I think I've been very good about giving you the truth.*" McCleish said, "*You have up until this point,*" but he really didn't believe that. It would have been more honest for him to say that he and LeClair did not believe the "trampoline story," for example. (p. 1560) Chad kept trying to remember a "*McDonald's party,*" as the officers' pressed him for other recollections of arguments. He said, "*..If she'd, ...hit me with something or throw something at me or whatever... you know I mean that's happened like I said a couple of times. And then one time I mean I did like physically sat on her, like, 'Stop. You got to calm down.' And then she's like, 'Oh leave me alone. You just calm down.'*" (p. 1561) Chad said that was at their home.

McCleish asked the question again, "*You don't remember having an argument with her at some party where she was choked by you, is that what you're telling me?*" and Chad responded, "*Yeah that's exactly what I'm saying. I can't remember a thing where like I went anywhere with her like and where we got - I remember going to a dinner function.*" Finally, he remembered the event that the officers were referencing. McCleish said, "*Ok,*" and Chad started to explain, and McCleish cut him off, "*Why don't, why don't we move on from that, Ok.*" It's not known why they didn't now want to discuss the event that they had been pressing Chad about for several minutes. If they had continued to ask about that event at the Exeter Inn, Chad would have explained that there was another woman at the event that Chad had dated, and Amanda became jealous, as was described in Chapter 3.

McCleish said, "*I want to talk about Kassidy now okay?*" and said that "*we talked to a lot of people,... And everybody that we've talked to has been very up front with us...* " but, in fact, the police had talked only with Jeff, Jennifer and Amanda. Chad repeated what he had said earlier about "*very rarely am I ever alone with her. There's three times that I've watched the girl.*" (p. 1562)

McCleish pressed further, "*I'm gonna tell you. As far as your friend, Jeff goes, those bruises and those marks didn't come from Jeff.... I think where they came from is probably you might of had something to do with it.*" (p. 1563) Chad was incredulous, and McCleish offered, "*Well I'll tell you why I think that.... Because there's some incidences here that you haven't told me about.*" Chad, asked, "*Like what?*" and McCleish responded, "*There's some things, there's some things that we've you know talked to everybody else about and, and some stuff that, that I want to, you know, ask you about.*" (p. 1563)

Instead of proceeding directly to the specifics of what McCleish was charging, Chad defended himself and his love for children, including his son and stepson, and that, "*I've been the best parent in the world for my kid.*" (p. 1564) Now feeling accused, Chad said, "*... And now maybe we're to the point where it's like I feel like you're accusing me, maybe I should stop asking questions or something, answer questions.*" (p. 1564)

Instead of asking Chad about the specific allegations that he had said "*everybody*" had told the police, McCleish asked generally what Chad thought "*should happen to the person who would do this?... Cause injury like that to her, that that would cause her death okay*?" (p. 1564)

Chad responded, "*Probably should string him up by the nuts or whatever. Certainly I mean kids no matter what you know, you know like I told you before one of the things that I've learned since being a parent is patience...*" (p. 1564)

McCleish tried to reassure Chad that sometimes good people do bad things when under stress, "*So what, what I'm trying to tell you is you know if something happened, if it did, if it was a spur of the moment type thing or maybe she got some marks from you more than what you're telling me about, you know it be helpful for us to know that.*" However, Chad had already denied being under financial or work stress. (p. 1566) In 2010, he told me that the summer and fall of 2000, with Amanda and Kassidy and Kyle, were the happiest months of his life.

Feeling more accused, Chad said, "*I'm kind of sick to my stomach now....I wasn't around her for two minutes today...*" (p. 1567-68) Even for those two minutes in his kitchen and in his driveway, he wasn't alone with Kassidy.

Instead of returning to the specific incidents that "*everybody*" had told the police about, LeClair returned the general subject of child abuse, by asking, "*...what kind of person could do this to a child?*" (p. 1568) Chad answered by acknowledging his responsibility for the domestic violence with Tristan, but insisted,

I've never ever hit that girl, [Amanda] *never. Because I'm like there's no way I'm going there again, there's no way. So to answer your question you know on, on how I feel about it or whatever it's like, you know I believe wholeheartedly that that the thing with, with the kids. I mean what kind of person could do that? I don't know. Maybe somebody under stress fine, but that's, that's not me.* (p. 1568)

McCleish returned to request for explanations from Chad , "*...like I said, we've talked to some, a lot of other people and ...*" and Chad responded before the sentence was finished, "*So I mean throw it on too. Tell me what they're telling you, I'll tell you if it's true or not. I mean, you, you try to understand.*" (p. 1570)

McCleish then told Chad that Kassidy didn't die from injuries inflicted today, on November 9, and,

...you were with her last night okay. She died from major trauma. She didn't die from, from a baseball to the face or falling down out of the car or whatever. She died of a major trauma.... And you were with her last night okay.... She died of a major trauma.... And what I'm telling you is, after talking to everybody here ***our investigation clearly indicates that you are the cause of these injuries***." (p. 1569-70)

Stunned, at approximately 9:40 p.m., and nine hours after Kassidy's death, Chad replied, "*Ahh, no way...No way.*" (p. 1570) McCleish said, "*I don't want to hear that, I don't want to hear 'no way'. What - clearly it indicates that this is what happened okay.*" I remember learning in law school that if a lawyer argues to a judge or jury that something is "clear," it probably isn't.

By telling the other interviewees, and now by telling Chad that he was their target, they cut off Chad as a source of further information. If he hadn't been accused, he could have been called back the next day for more questions, after the police had compared their observations for the first day's interviews. Despite their beliefs about the case, there should have been no doubt that Chad was motivated to help them, and there were a lot more questions to ask. However, the police were driven, apparently, and perhaps by the expected media interest, to assess responsibility as soon as possible.

Similarly, the quick designation of a primary suspect reduced the likelihood of getting unbiased information from others, as people now knew what information the police wanted to hear, and there were many people who wanted to please the police, and many people who wanted to help them solve this mysterious death of a beautiful blonde toddler girl.

Chad reminded LeClair and McCleish that Kassidy was with Jeff the previous day, too, and McCleish said, "*...why don't we leave Jeff out of the picture here?*" (p. 1570)

Chad was angry, "*See what is this, is like this big witch hunt that you bring me in last...and like listen to everybody else's bullshit all day ...?*" McCleish said, "*No, it's not a witch hunt. You arrived here last.*" That wasn't fair, as he, of the four adults closest to Kassidy, was the last be asked to come to the Kittery Police Station and the last to be notified of her death. He arrived at the police station at approximately the same time that the interviews of Amanda, Jeff and Jennifer began. However, Chad was correct that McCleish's "*clearly indicates*" came from information gathered in the other interviews and that conclusion was formed before Chad's interrogation began at 7:10 p.m. The police didn't wait for the end of Chad's interrogation, and they didn't wait for the autopsy report. For some reason, they chose to lock in on their theory as soon as possible. The Convict-Chad train was now on one track and accelerating.

However, the interrogation continued for a few more minutes, as McCleish insisted that "*these injuries didn't come from accidents. These injuries came from somebody inflicting them on her, that's what happened to her.*" Chad was devastated, "*Oh my God!...This is impossible, I can't believe this.... I told you every single thing that happened last night.*" (p. 1572) He wasn't asked about the argument when Amanda arrived home late the previous night, but he told the officers a lot about the previous night; and there has never been any evidence to contradict what he told the officers about that night. They just didn't believe part of what he said, because it conflicted with their theory of the case.

McCleish finally responded with a specific example of what "*everybody*" was telling the police about Chad and Kassidy. He said, "*Okay, you didn't tell me about holding her face under the water of the faucet. You didn't tell me about that and I know that you've done that to her, okay. Why didn't you tell me? Okay. Right. So what's up with that? You didn't tell me about that so you expect me to believe now...*" (p. 1572) Chad responded, *No that's not exactly what I did. I didn't hold her face under the faucet.... She was having one of her screaming fits ...with Amanda or whatever, she wouldn't listen to me and she wouldn't to her and I brought her to the bathroom sink ... And I just splashed water on her.... And I just splashed water on her face and she just like stopped screaming....No I did not hold her head under water. No I did not. That's ridiculous, I can't even believe that shit.... Is that what you were told, I - I held her head under the water?* (p. 1573-74)

In 2010, Chad wrote, "*I did it to shock her system. Kassidy was having such a tantrum that she was gasping for breath. I got scared when it seemed she could not breathe. Cold water was the only thing I could think of - and it worked." (p. A-1573)* McCleish didn't say what he would do about the conflicting reports of the same incident. In the non-law enforcement world, when people are presented with conflicting information, they try to resolve the differences in recollection or understanding. In the second and third interviews to come there was no effort by the police to ask "*everybody*," about Chad's version. In this instance, this only meant Amanda, as she was the only one of the other three adults at their home with Kassidy at the time of the water splashing incident, and she was in another room. She had told the police that she thought the incident involved splashing water. The more violent version came from Jeff and Jennifer. Then, McCleish asked about something else, "*Okay some of the bruising on her face and stuff was, was pretty fresh okay....Did you, did you maybe grab her face last night that.. .?*" Chad responded, "*No,...Absolutely not,*" but then he wavered, "*Let me think.*" (p. 1574) McCleish asked again, "*Okay, there's extremes here so did you grab her face and that might of caused that last night?*" and Chad responded, "*No I - Just like I said I picked her up went inside, no I wasn't mad at her at all last night. I was worried about her last night.*" (p. 1575)

McCleish returned to the primary question, "*How do you explain these injuries then that she's, she's died from?*" Chad responded, first with a hypothetical and then, "*I can't even believe I'm... Holy shit...I can't believe this.*" (p. 1576)

The two officers began an important line of inquiry, i.e. the timeline. Said LeClair, "*...shortly after you came into the picture the baby started showing bruising. And this came from from Jeff and Jen. Prior to that everything, everything is all set.*" McCleish confirmed the idea, "*Right.*" Then LeClair added, "*The day he comes in the picture she shows bruises.*" (p. 1596) If LeClair and McCleish had stopped there to ask Chad about the timeline, there might have occurred an important discussion. When, for example, did he first start seeing bruises on Kassidy? If they had asked Chad or Amanda, or even Jeff and Jennifer about any photographs that might have been taken of Kassidy, such a discussion would have been enhanced. Instead, they seem to have taken Jeff's word that the bruises on Kassidy began, "*I guess when she was around Chad.*" (Jeff interview p. 1274) At Chad's trial a year later, Jeff said the same thing, "*Like I said, she started getting bruises when she started moving in with Chad. I can't say an exact date.*" (Trancript, 6 December 2001, p. 201)

However, the exploration of the timeline would have to wait, until 2010. Instead of asking Chad to respond to the charge that the bruises began "*the day he* [Chad] *comes in the picture*," LeClair immediately shifted to that morning, November 9, but there was no clear question for Chad. McCleish, then said, "*people have seen things okay you know, there's no reason to hold back here because you know I'm asking you questions and a lot of these questions I know the answer to okay....Have you ever picked her up by part of her body other than her arms or her legs*?" (p. 1577) Chad then started to describe his playful activity with Kassidy, "*Like one of the things that I was you know getting at before was Amanda said to me before 'Jesus she's not Kyle you know, she's not a boy.' Because like I'll pick her up like you know and swing her around and go on the bed and wrestle with her and whatever.*" (p. 1577)

Chad wrote in 2010,

I was trying not to be defensive here, but it was getting more frustrating. The police were listening to a bunch of crap and were not willing to listen to the facts. Yes, I wrestled with the boys (and with Amanda, too) and we would include Kassidy. She loved to have horsey rides on my back, with me on all fours, and she loved our spinning 'helicopter rides,' with me turning around and around while holding her by both her arms. She loved to be tossed onto the bed. She enjoyed flying like a superhero, as long as we didn't zoom around the room too fast. She loved to swing by her arms and also tip upside down and walk around on the ceiling. I never picked up Kassidy by her head. I had this thing that I always did with the boys that they loved and also I did with Kassidy. I would put my hands on either side of their head. They would then wrap their hands on my forearms and I would lift them. It gave them the illusion that I was lifting them by their head, when really it was my forearms and their hands which were bearing the weight. They would giggle and kick their feet as if they were running on air. For Kassidy, it was even easier, and she loved it. Amanda was not used to such play and sometimes felt that Kassidy wasn't ready for such physical games, but Kassidy enjoyed them, and she was never hurt by them. (p. A-1577)

McCleish asked Chad, "*I want you to show me how you picked her up.*" (p. 1577) Chad showed him and then said, "*Not, no* [never] *have I picked her up like maliciously by the neck .... The thought of that is, you know....*" He might have been planning to say, "repulsive," but McCleish interjected, "*Well, these are things that people are telling us, okay... they've seen you do this stuff.*" Chad responded, "*No, that's totally - Do you know what?...If I'm, if I'm a freaken abuser don't you think I'd be a little smarter than to hit her in the face? ...*" (p. 1578)

Lance McCleish then left the room, presumably to talk with his supervisor, Sergeant Stewart. Rick LeClair returned the questioning to this morning, November 9, and asked Chad what clothes Kassidy was wearing, and Chad said, "*I have no idea,*" and then was asked again about Wednesday night. Chad said, "*I can't believe this shit.*" (p. 1579) and LeClair went to other subjects, including Jeremy's name and contact information. McCleish returned to the interrogation and, Chad, perhaps thinking that Jeremy saw the bruises on Kassidy's buttocks on

Tuesday, October 24, brought the interrogation back to that incident. Chad told LeClair and McCleish,

Jeremy was at the house and [asked], *"What the hell happened to her face?" I said, "I don't know man, I said but look at this too." And I pulled her diaper down and showed him her ass. And he said "holy shit" - and he goes "Who did that?" And we were kind of talking quietly because you know I, I don't know it was just Kyle sitting on the couch any way (inaudible). And I told him Jeff did it. He's like, "Holy shit man, if anyone ever did that to my kid,"... and then he went in and he talked to Amanda about it, I believe.* (p. 1581)

The timeline continued to be a challenge for everyone, but since the police believed that the abuse to Kassidy began simultaneously with Chad's relationship to Amanda, it was critical to understand it. McCleish said to Chad, *"What's been going the last, like say two months. You know you get hooked up with Amanda they, they kind of you know, you guys get involved and ..."* and Chad corrected him, "*Well, that's like four months,*" and even that date was conservative by a month. As he had already spent about two hours explaining a strong and loving relationship with Amanda and Kassidy, it no longer made sense to minimize it. It was what it was. Then McCleish reframed slightly the question to ask about whether during the last couple of months, "*...has anything been bothering you, you know, as far as any pressures or?* The only pressure that came to Chad was from Amanda, *"...she wants me to just come out and say 'I love you' all the time. And, and I've just couldn't, I stuck to my guns and saying, 'Look Amanda, don't you want it to be real. Don't you want to be like when I'm feeling it. Don't you want it to be,' I mean - but like pressures at work. I mean work is easy.*" (p. 1581) That was not the kind of pressure that McCleish was thinking about, and certainly not the kind of pressure that leads someone to abuse and kill the daughter of the woman you love.

In response to McCleish's questions, Chad explained again that his financial condition were "*fantastic*." Chad's mortgage and credit debt totaled less than his annual income. McCleish then realized, "*You make more than I do*." (p. 1581)

With an ironic metaphor, McCleish then asked, "*... I want to put all the cards on the table here. And we talked about, remember how we talked about football?... What's going on with that*?" Then there was a rapid exchange:

LM: Do you have some debt in that?
CE: Do I have any debt, no.
LM: You don't have any gambling debts?
CE: No, none.
LM: You have no gambling debts? Because we're ...
CE: Zero.
LM: ... we were told you have some gambling debts.
CE: Not at all. Notta.[Nada]
LM: See you told me you were ahead. You told me you were ahead.
CE: Absolutely. As a matter of fact I mean I made, see you know I'm trying to do shit that's illegal, well I mean obviously it's a small scale but let me let her rip. I made 450 bucks, actually yeah about 450 bucks last week, you know. I mean we, we're not talking big money. I don't bet like thousands of dollars. I'm talking we do, me and my buddy Bruce bet 25 bucks a game you know what I mean. I mean 25 bucks each on a game or whatever.
LM: Okay.
CE: ... I mean and we, we're just very good at betting football you know.

If McCleish was starting to wonder about the accuracy of what "*we were told*," he didn't show it. Jeff had told Harakles and Linscott that Chad was in debt and that Chad was down $900 for one week. Chad told McCleish and LeClair that his only losing week for the year was for $500, and his share of that loss was $250. In a nearby room, Detective Erik Baker and New Hampshire Trooper Jill Rockey were interviewing Jeremy and he independently described his and Chad's and Bruce's success with football gambling, and that he had their winnings from the previous week, $900 in cash, in his car.

McCleish seemed to want to backtrack on his earlier indication that Chad "*clearly*" was the person who killed Kassidy, saying, "*I just want to get your side of everything that's going on in your life. Everything that's going on in Chad's life.*" (p. 1585) Unfortunately, due to the pressures of the moment, and the nature of criminal investigations, neither officer ever asked Chad about the good things in Chad's relationship with Amanda and Kassidy, about their good times. The subject of "airplane" and "Superman" fun only came up during questioning about bruises. In any case, Chad responded to McCleish's comment, "*I've been completely honest and up front about everything. I mean from the ...*" McCleish, retorted candidly, *"Okay. I don't think you have been. I think that you've been less than truthful on certain issues*." (p. 1586)

Unfortunately, as the tone of the interrogation was again more civil and Chad had seemed to slow the Convict-Chad train a little, McCleish didn't followup with a single example of where he thought Chad was less than truthful. If Chad had had another chance to admit that the important part of the "trampoline story" was false, he might have taken it, especially if LeClair had told Chad that Amanda had already said that it was false. If he had had another chance to review the timeline of his relationship with Amanda, that would have helped to further erase his earlier minimizing of the length and intensity of the relationship.

Chad was critical of himself, *"If I had probably any wits about me... And the first time that her ass... came back like that I would of said... you know you need to leave Amanda or you need not to have a kid. " (p. 1586-1587)* Fortunately McCleish did not misunderstand what Chad had just said. In fact, he said, *"I do understand that. And I don't want to hear about anymore about Jeff okay. So let's just put Jeff away."* However, LeClair and McCleish had earlier asked Chad what he thought had happened to Kassidy. Unbeknownst to Chad, and maybe even to his interrogators, no policeperson ever said to Jeff, or Jennifer, "I don't want to hear any more about Chad, okay. Let's just put Chad away."

McCleish then told Chad more about his theory of the case and what "*I know*." He said, "*I know that the reason why you don't take that child to a day care is because she's got all those marks and bruises on her okay. And I know that's the real reason. It's not because ...* " (p. 1587) It was not a question, and Chad was not invited to respond.

McCleish continued, "*I also know that you know there there have been some other instances where you picked her up, you grabbed her, thrown her around a little bit. I know that's the facts because they've told me that.*" Chad then asked again, "*Who's they?*" and McCleish responded, "*Amanda...has told me that*." (p. 1587) That wasn't true. She said something like that to Rick LeClair and Angela Blodgett, but not to McCleish. LeClair might have interjected, "*Actually, she said that to me*," but he didn't, or McCleish could have clarified that other officers told him that Amanda had said that, but he didn't either.

McCleish tried again, "*Okay. She went in and she said, 'Look at, look at her face,' again this morning when she took, brought the kid over to Jeff's house."* (p. 1587) Chad, of course, was not there to hear Amanda's comment, which a mother might have made to a babysitter if there was only one bruise on her daughter, let alone the three or four which Chad had already acknowledged that he saw and knew about. Chad simply said, "*Yeah*," as he was seeing that the effort to stop the Convict-Chad train was not succeeding. He had only learned about it an hour earlier, but McCleish still seemed convinced of what he thought he knew.

McCleish continued, "*I know you've done certain things to her and I just want you to be you know up front with me on it. If, if all I'm saying is a lot of these things might not happen intentionally type of thing okay*." (p. 1588) Chad simply exclaimed, "*Oh my God!*" Said McCleish, "*If you know you grab her or something like that and you even said yourself, you know I've grabbed her face sometimes and it left a mark.... And what I'm saying to you is lots of times ...*" Chad answered, "*Done that twice that I can think of.*" (p. 1588)

McCleish noted that Chad was a "*big dude*," and "*lots of times I know for me anyway that sometimes I can do things and not even know I'm that strong*." Chad picked up on this, saying, that he "*Didn't really believe any of that crap....Until I start wrestling with Amanda and she's like 'Jesus Chad you don't even know your own strength'... Okay, put that wherever, we're fucken around you know and having fun*." (p. 1589) Although he may not have been thinking about it at the time, there was one occasion during his relationship with Amanda that their sexual play involved his touching of Amanda's neck. The next day, Chad noticed a bruise, and said something like, "*Jesus, Amanda, we better not try that again.*" He thus had learned that Amanda bruised easily, too. However, as was so often the case in this tragedy, children are different. As Chad wrote in 2010, "*I never hurt Kassidy in any way when wrestling with her, alone or with Kyle or Brent. Even though I was a strong adult, I was perfectly capable of knowing my strength when playing with children."* (p. A-1589)

McCleish continued to find a way to persuade Chad that he might have hurt Kassidy, even if unintentionally, saying, "*It could of been completely accidental, just tell me about that. Okay.*" (p. 1590) However, the police had already disbelieved one of the accidents, which was the Tee-ball hitting Kassidy the previous evening. By this time in the interrogation, Chad didn't feel motivated to think about other accidents, such as bringing Kassidy downstairs on his shoulders and having her head hit the ceiling, or carrying Kassidy on his hip and swinging around and having her head hit a door.

McCleish seemed to be trying to persuade Chad that he delivered traumatic injuries to Kassidy without being aware of what he had done, just as police on Long Island persuaded Marty Tankleff that he had killed his parents, without knowing it, in his sleep. Said McCleish,

I don't think that you're a person who goes and hurt ...hurting kids all the time. Okay, well or does things like that on purpose. I don't think that that's the kind of person you are okay. I don't doubt that you're a good parent. I don't doubt that you love your kid and that you love Kassidy. There's no doubt in my mind that you love that little girl okay. There's no doubt in my mind about that. Or even if you didn't love her that you at least cared about her... Because she was your girlfriend's kid. ... What I'm saying is I know things can happen on the spur of the moment. I know sometimes you know things can happen and you go Jesus that was, that was you know I wish that hadn't happened okay. And I know that guys like you and me sometimes we don't even know our own strength and that's no fault of our own okay. (p. 1591)

McCleish continued to insist that Kassidy's fatal injuries occurred before she was left at Jeff's that morning, and Chad responded,

I babied the shit out of her last night, more than usual because she was sick ... she was just laying there whatever.... No she's been sick, like she's had a cold or something for like a week but, what I mean sick is like she was just like - So I'm like what the hell. So I just fed her I whatever. (p. 1592)

Detective McCleish then said that the doctors had said that Kassidy had died of a "*closed head injury, which means something happened in there, in her head.... That isn't like falling down and you know hitting your head on the floor ...*" (p. 1592-93) McCleish was wrong on that point, because a fall can cause just as much damage to a head as an intentional blow. It's only a matter of how long is the fall, and how strong is the blow. Dr. John Plunkett has written, "*A fall from less than 3 meters in an infant or child may cause fatal head injury and may not cause immediate symptoms.*"

McCleish then offered to show the photographs he had of Kassidy's body, saying, "*I'd be more than happy to show them to you?*" Did he mean to say, "*more than happy?*" He continued, "*If you want to see them I'll show them to you. I'll show you what I'm talking about with these injuries.*" (p. 1593) However, the photographs do not show the severity of any injuries, as they only show multiple smaller injuries. In any case, Chad declined the offer, saying, "*I don't know that I want to see a dead baby.... I'd be in the medical field ...if that's what I wanted to do.*" (p. 1593)

The conversation then returned to the bottom line, "*...But what I'm telling you is, is everything that we've done, everybody that we've talked to, our investigation indicates that you are responsible for these injuries.*" and Chad responded again, "*No way.*" (p. 1595) McCleish said, "*Chad you have hurt her before okay, whether it was intentional or not. She's got bruising, we got mom saying and we got sister and ...*" However, Kassidy had a lot of bruises, and Chad already acknowledged causing only a few bruises to Kassidy face from holding her, but McCleish was painting here with too broad a brush. Almost all of the 100 bruises or injuries that the autopsy would reveal had absolutely nothing to do with Kassidy's death, such as the cat scratch.

LeClair rejoined the exchanges, "*There's a reason you didn't go to the day care. You told us that yourself that you didn't bring her to the doctor's because you didn't want the doctor to see the black and blues.*" (p. 1596) Chad wrote in 2010.

At the time that I made that comment about not wanting a doctor to assume that I was the source of bruises on Kassidy, I was thinking not only of the faint bruises that I had caused on Kassidy's lower cheeks while seeking eye contact with her, but also of the other bruises

which I didn't cause at all. Among them was the black and blue that Jeff caused with the diaper incident at his apartment. I should have asked the police to ask Amanda how many times I told her to take Kassidy to the hospital to have a wart removed from her finger because it obviously bothered Kassidy." (p. A-1596)

He also could have reminded of the calls Amanda made to day care providers, and his own conversation with Mrs. Edgar at Cross Road, but he had already made these points, and the police ignored them.

The three men continued to argue about the facts of Chad's care for Kassidy, including the water faucet sprinkling incident. He even agreed that splashing the water, " *...was the wrong thing to do. I admit it.*" (p. 1597) However in 2010, he wrote,

I was eager to please these officers where I could, so I agreed with them that splashing water on Kassidy was wrong, but at the time it was a reasonable response to the situation, and it worked. I shouldn't have agreed with them. The police never explained to me what they would have done in such a situation, and what they would have done if their efforts failed. (p. A-1597)

Chad kept trying, with this result:

CE: *Let me explain something to you.*
LM: *No I don't want you to explain.*
CE: *So what I'm trying to tell you though is why ...*
LM: *I don't want you to explain.*

And another exchange

LM: *And I'm telling you that it clearly indicates that you are responsible for these.*
CE: *Clearly bullshit. I did not do these injuries...*
LM: *Okay everyone is telling us what they've seen you do to that girl before.*
CE: *Yeah.*

Finally, Chad said, "*I feel like I'm the defense here, I'm defending my fucken. I don't even want to talk anymore just, you're gonna think I murdered some baby whatever. Just I'll..*" (p. 1598-99) Trying to save the conversation McCleish asked, "*Do you want to take a break?*" and Chad replied, "*No. Fuck it I just want a lawyer, I don't want to talk anymore because you, you're gonna accuse me....*" Instead of stopping the interrogation, as Chad's lawyer later argued at his trial should have happened, the detectives tried to save it, saying, "*Chad, sit tight. Be right back.*"

Said Chad, "*This is bullshit. Unbelievable.*" (p. 1599)

Chad took a bathroom break, and he heard what he thought was Jeff talking.

He was being questioned in the room beside me, they were out in the hallway talking and I heard him say, "I want to help in any way I can. I really cared about that little girl." I wanted to puke because he never did anything but bitch about her and call her a retard. I then went out in the hall to use the bathroom while he was in a room. He was writing something out on a piece of paper and I said, "Jeff." He looked up saw me and put his eyes right down to the ground as if to say "Oh shit." He couldn't look me in the eye. (Chad, Nov. 2000 letter to his attorneys)

Afterward, Chad returned to his own interrogation and the conversation continued a little longer. Chad told them about his conversation with Tristan the previous evening, and he repeated other facts already stated to the detectives. McCleish left the room, presumably for some consultation with Sergeant Stewart, and then returned. He tried to keep the conversation going, but acknowledged Chad's request to consult with an attorney.

Chad made several concluding comments, including,

And [I] *told you exactly how I feel and what and what I've done and everything and that and I don't, and then it's like you, you're twisting things and... I feel like I'm just talking in circles. You guys are just gonna try to pin this thing on me any ways, so no I'm done talking.... You know, whatever. Arrest me.* (p. 1603)

McCleish then said, before leaving the room, "*Okay. No, no. Okay Chad. Let me find out what's gonna happen okay. I'm gonna leave you here, just sit tight.*" (p. 1603) Sergeant Stewart came into the room and Chad confirmed that he wanted a lawyer. He wanted to help the investigation, "*but I need somebody to tell me what you should answer and what you shouldn't answer ...*" (p. 1604)

Stewart finally agreed that the discussion was over, and said, "*And once again we appreciate you coming in. Ah what's gonna happen from this point on okay is that we are securing a search warrant, New Hamsphire State Police is securing a search warrant for your residence in Rochester.*" (p. 1606) Unlike for Jeff, the police didn't ask Chad if he would consent to a voluntary search. If he had been asked, he would have consented. He said later, that he was pleased with the plan to search his car and home because he knew that the police would find no evidence of abuse, because there was none.

As a sign of how frazzled Chad was, he expressed concern that Kato be fed and not be harmed and referred to him as a "*her*". Chad said, "*I mean I had that dog for six years. I don't want to hurt her or anything like that.*" He assured the police again that he wanted to help, and that his request to consult with an attorney was not a sign of guilt, *"And I know beyond a shadow of a doubt I did nothing ..to that baby.*" (p. 1608)

Sgt. Stewart said the door was always open for Chad to return to talk with the investigators. In a closing request , and similar to Jeff Marshall's request, Chad said, "*I hope you guys investigate and talk to everybody that I know about what kind of a person I am.*" (p. 1608). The interrogation ended at 10:43 p.m. and Chad met Jeremy in the lobby and left the building for the parking lot.

In hindsight, it can be asked whether Chad hurt himself by agreeing to a police interview. He did hurt his claim of innocence, but the police would certainly have concluded that refusing to assist in their investigation was an indication of guilt. In a criminal trial when a defendant doesn't testify, a jury is told that a defendant has a constitutional right not to testify, and that the jury should not draw any inferences from such a refusal. However at the investigation level, the police can draw any inferences they wish then a person declines to assist with an investigation.

The best result would have been for Chad to initially decline to meet with the police, but to quickly retain a lawyer and then offer to meet with the police and his lawyer, as often as they wanted. Another alternative would be to ask for the police to submit their questions in writing.

7:50 p.m. - While Chad was being interrogated, Maine State Police Detective Scott Harakles secured voluntary agreements from Jeff, Jennifer and Amanda to search Jeff's apartment and all the possessions therein, including those belonging to Amanda.

8:00 p.m. - Tristan Evans Interview

New Hampshire State Police Detective John Marasco and MSP Detective Jeff Linscott, began their interview of Tristan. This was the first interview in the case in which the New Hampshire State Police shared in the interview. Linscott had already particpated in the interview of Jeff.

Tristan said she was Chad's ex-wife even though she, like Chad, had not yet received the final divorce decree with an effective date of October 4. She told Linscott and Marasco that she came to the Kittery Police Station to talk with Chad, and "*a week ago I called DCYF on him about Kassidy because I had seen bruises on her...*" (p. 1074) Linscott asked what prompted the call to DCYF and Tristan said,

...maybe two weeks before, I had gone over to Chad's house...and at first I thought she had dirt all over her face or something and then I got closer and it wasn't dirt. It was bruises all over her face and across her neck. And I just bent down and I was like, "Oh my, Kassidy, honey, what happened to you?" And she never says anything, which I think is odd. And... Amanda just looked at me and I said, "What happened to her?"... and she goes, "Oh, she fell on the stairs....." they were like little and then I said to Chad the following day..."What happened to Kassidy's face?"... he said she was on the trampoline... and she went to fall off the edge and he caught her....And I said, "....Well, Amanda said she fell down the stairs." He goes, "I don't know." And I'm like, "Okay." And then just what actually made me call DCYF last week was she had another bruise on her right cheek and it was almost like a black bruise. I was like a deep bruise and I was like, "Okay,

so maybe I'm overly reacting. Maybe I'm not," but I said [to myself] *"I'm going to give them [DCYF] a call and it's just because it's not normal. She doesn't even act normal." And then I saw her two days ago and she had another bruise on her cheek....I started mentioning to Chad after I saw the bruises... And I said, "she's not acting normal...but is there something mentally wrong with her?" I said, "because she doesn't do things that a one and a half year old do*[es]*." .. I said, "She doesn't talk. She doesn't play. She just sits there. You sit her in a chair and she would just sit there for hours. And not move." I'm like, 'you need to start asking some questions here." Two days ago I said to him, cause... she was just like crying when ...I've gone over to the house before and she'll be upstairs shut in the bedroom, just like bawling. And I'm like, I hate that because she's only one and a half... I mean I'd never do that to a kid.... and I just thought it was weird I just had a feeling that something else was going on. And I was like, "I'm just going to give DCYF a call" ...and I made it anonymous because if I was wrong, I didn't want anybody pissed off at me.* (p. 1075)

Linscott asked what Tristan told DCYF in the anonymous call and she said that she didn't know Amanda's or Kassidy's last name, but that

they were residing in Chad's house. He was my ex-husband and that I wanted to remain anonymous. I said that he does have an abusive past with me. Never with my children. Not even a concern of mine by any means or else they wouldn't be there.. I said, but she just had bruises [which] *aren't normal like kid bruises.... I said maybe I'm wrong,... but I would feel more comfortable letting somebody else know and maybe it can be looked into...* (p. 1076)

Tristan said that she had talked with Amanda a few times, and *"she didn't really have Kassidy until recently.... And she did not have Kassidy like hardly even until probably two months ago. And she was with Amanda's mother. Up until that point. And just recently, she's had her all the time."* (p. 1076) Tristan said that the custody schedule for Kyle is that "*Chad has our son Tuesday's and Wednesday's, Friday's and every other weekend.... the past Tuesday, I picked Kyle up because he* [Chad] *was at a meeting. And then he came over to my apartment and picked him up...it's very flexible*." (p. 1076)

Tristan said she did not mention her concerns about Kassidy's mental development to Amanda, but she did mention them to Chad, "*Is there something mentally wrong? She doesn't seem like she's there*." (p. 1078) Tristan also said to Chad that she didn't want Amanda to be involved with raising Kyle if she was "*not going to be a permanent fixture... because I don't want people in and out of his life*." (p. 1079) She said that Chad had responded that as long as she and Chad were not reconnecting that Amanda would be there. Thus, by this measure, Chad's plan was for a long relationship with Amanda and Kassidy.

Tristan told Lincsott and Marasco that "*When I saw the bruises on Kassidy's face and neck, I did body checks every time he* [Kyle] came back from that house and I outright told him [Chad], *'... if he ever comes home with any bruises, I'll kill you. I'll kill whoever is doing it.' " It's never been a problem."* She said laughingly, "*Actually, he refused to discipline Kyle*." (p. 1080)

Tristan said that "*Kyle actually adores the ground that Amanda walks on. She does projects with him. She paints with him. She makes signs with him. Everything.... She picks him up from daycare half the time if Chad's working*." (p. 1081)

Linscott asked Tristan about Chad's domestic abuse. Initially, she said, it involved "*a lot of slapping, pulling hair, with the bruises beneath her clothing, and thus not visible. Um this last time* [which was in December, 1999] *was the worst time. There was punching. He was kicking. He was pulling hair.....*" (p. 1081)

Marasco asked if there was any particular issue that would trigger Chad's violence. She said that "*...he was usually like irritated or something else to begin with. Like... his work... is very stressful. ..* [If] *he had like a really, really bad day at work, then he'd bring it home. But I ... wouldn't say anything like really in particular*." (p. 1082)
Tristan said that Chad would resume their marriage "*now if I let him*." (p. 1082) She said that their divorce was no longer causing him stress, as it was in the beginning, and, regarding stress in general, "*he doesn't care half as much about work. He cares more*

about the boys..... when we were married, he used to spend 90 hours a week at work. Now, he's usually home by 6:00. And he was never home before like 11 or midnight....He's home. He's ten thousand times better than he used to be." (p. 1082-83)
John Marasco commented that "*And I know that it's* [Kassidy's bruising] *is not a trampoline or falling down the stairs.*" (p. 1083)

Tristan said that Kyle had said nothing to her about the treatment of Kassidy at Chad's and Amanda's home, and Tristan had not asked. She said,
...he is the biggest eyes most ever. He's got the biggest ears, you've ever seen, and the biggest loud mouth himself. And he's never ever said anything. He likes and he talks about Kassidy all the time, and that's going to be one of the hardest things, because she's not going to be there. Because, you know, he sees her every single time he's there. And he talks about her all the time. He talks about Amanda. He talks about Chad and he's never said anything, never [about abusive treatment.]" (p. 1084)

Tristan said that Chad was not a drug user, and he never used cocaine to her knowledge while they were married. She said that he rarely drank in recent years, and even more rarely, now that he was on probation for the 1999 assault.

Marasco asked, "*... what would you say, from talking with Chad, what his feelings were about Kassidy? Did you ever catch him saying anything about the little girl... negative and it's obvious that .. like you said maybe that she didn't act correct all the time or normal?*" and Tristan answered, "*...he said that Kyle and her got along great. 'She was a cute little shit.' .... I don't know if it's a guy thing or not. But he doesn't really pay attention to what she does or how really he was just like, ah, she's just a little girl.*" (p. 1087) Marasco asked again, "*He never said, 'ah, she's kind of a pain in the ass.' or 'she cries too much?' Ever make any comments like that?*" Tristan said, *"No.*" (p. 1087) Marasco asked how Chad was as a father to Kyle. She said, "*Kyle will push your buttons. Kyle is the biggest three year old you'll ever meet in your life.*" (1088) Marasco asked, "*Was there ever a time when you were married with... Chad, ever any thoughts or statements from him, you know, 'I've got to get out of the house or I'm going to do something to that kid. He's crying too much. He's driving me banana's?*" Tristan repled, "*Nope. Absolutely not. ... I used to get irritated at him because he wouldn't give him* [Kyle] *a time-out. I'm like, do I need to be the big* [disciplinarian?] *on him all the time?' Cause he* [Chad] *was just like... a little baby. He's just a little kid.*"

Tristan said that no one from DCYF contacted her after her initial call, until today, the day of Kassidy's death. During that call, she was told that Chad cannot "*be around the kids at least until after Monday.*" (p. 1088)

Jeff Linscott asked, "*But if it came down to,... you know Tristan, your, your ex-husband is the person, you know, last with the kid who could have inflicted this stuff, would, would that surprise you or shock you?*" Tristan answered,
I don't think he would ever do it. Never. And the thing that is weird cause you said not to by hearsay, when Jeff was just out there, he said something about Kassidy coming to his house blank this morning. Chad called me last night after he picked Kassidy up from Jeff's saying that she didn't seem like she was all there. He said... "you know, you told me to watch, and you know, cause...she just seems blank, like she's not there, like she's not anywhere in the room." He said he went home and he got her out of the car, and he stood her beside the car and he went on the other side and got Kyle out and theen back around. Kassidy was lying face down on the ground. And she scratched somewhere on her face like her nose or her chin or something. He said.. "Well, you know Kassidy," and then he picked her up and they went inside and they were like playing like nurf ball baseball or some kind of baseball with like Kyle. Upstairs and he said Kyle hit the ball and it hit her. He said, and she didn't do anything. He goes, "it's just like she wasn't there. She was sitting there like dumbfounded." He, and for him to call me and ask me that like is everything ok, I said, "Chad, it's not normal." I said, "who does she stay with? Who babysits her?" Because, I said, "It's not normal." I said..." whoever she's spending time with, I said, is not treating her like they should, because that's not normal...." (p. 1090)

Tristan said that she didn't believe the "trampoline story," and thus, she was among the several doubters of that one story. Otherwise, she was a reliable witness to Chad's character and parenting skills. Her interview ended before 9:00 p.m.

8:00 p.m. - Jacqueline Conley interview

Detectives Scott Harakles and Jeffrey Smith interviewed Jacqueline Conley. Harakles had previously interviewed Jeff Marshall and Travis Hunt, and Smith had interviewed Jacqueline's daughter, Jennifer. Smith reported that the first ten minutes of the interview was not recorded due to a mechanical malfunction. (p. 887) Thus, the first line of the transcript is Jacqueline's answer to an unknown question. As Kassidy's virtual second mother, she was "*... all upset, I'll tell you.*" about Kassidy's death. (p. 888)

Jacqueline summarized the early months of Kassidy's life where she and Amanda lived in her home, and when they left to live elsewhere, and then returned. Harakles asked, "*...when Kassidy and Amanda have now basically made their residence down south here, we'll say Sanford or Kittery or wherever,... how often did you see Kassidy?*" Was he intentionally minimizing Rochester? Jacqueline specifically recalled August 27th as the day of her hysterectomy, and as a day that she saw Kassidy, and that she had seen her during September and "*part of October, well, early part of October.*" (p. 889)

Jacqueline estimated that Amanda met Chad in July, though she acknowledged, "*I don't remember.*" (p. 890) She said that she first met him when he "*came a couple times in August to visit us.*" (p. 890) She was correct that Chad visited twice, but they were around June 20 and July 20. Was Jacqueline already minimizing the relationship between Chad and Amanda?

Harakles asked about Jacqueline's concerns about Amanda and Chad, and she mentioned the large age difference, and then mentioned her trucking trip with her husband, "*a couple of weeks ago,*" which was actually the week of Thursday, October 12, or 28 days earlier. She said that her "*sixteen year old son,*" who was Joshua, "*said he saw some bruises on Kassidy's face.*" (p. 891) Later in the interview, she again referred to "*My 16 year old son.*" (p. 895) As Joshua was born in January 1985, he was fifteen, as Amanda correctly stated in her interview. Was Jacqueline saying "*sixteen*" to enhance Joshua's credibility? Later, however, Jeff Smith asked, "*Scott"s 15?*" and Jacqueline responded, "*No, no, Joshua's 15. Scott's 7*" (p. 898)

Jacqueline said, about her call on October 14, "*Now I called them. I said, 'What's going on? Why is she hurt? Why is there bruises on her face*?" She said she talked with Chad on that day and he told her the "trampoline story," and Amanda later confirmed it during a call Jacqueline made to her the next day. (p. 891, 896) Jacqueline said that Jennifer never said anything about other bruises to Kassidy, but Jennifer also told her the "trampoline story," when Jacqueline asked her about the bruises which Joshua had seen on October 13. (p. 897)

Jacqueline said that she had expected to see Kassidy when she and Jennifer and Amanda went shopping "*this past Sunday,*" i.e. November 5, but Amanda had told her that Chad had taken Kassidy to the zoo with his two sons, and that Chad was "*Trying to bond with Kassidy. You know, that's what I thought.*" (p. 892) Going to York's Wild Animal Kingdom was the original plan. I don't know why Jacqueline didn't know of the change in plans, because York's was closed. It doesn't appear likely that Amanda told her mother of the change.

Jacqueline said that she talked with Amanda almost every day and that she did know about her starting work at Old Navy and "*then she was trying to go to college.*" (p. 893)

Harakles asked if Amanda had said anything to Jacqueline about Kassidy being sick, and Jacqueline responded, "*...not this week, but the week before, Jeff and Jen told me that Kassidy had a little cold and they, Jeff, was babysitting her... they said she was coughing and stuff and that she was crying. You know, she was crying a lot and I said, 'Well, ... is she okay?' and then I called Mandy and they said she just had a little cold. That was two weeks ago.*" (p. 894)

In response to a question, Jacqueline said that Amanda never expressed any concern to her about the care for Kassidy at Jeff's and Jen's. However, as she has just noted that

Jennifer didn't say anything to her mother about Kassidy's bruises, it's safe to assume that each sister was careful not to say negative things to their mother about the other sister. Later Jacqueline observed, "*Yeah. Seems to me they're keeping some secrets.*" (p. 899)

Returning to the subject of the October 13 visit of Amanda and Kassidy to Buckfield, Jacqueline said "*No. Mandy didn't know I was going on the trip. It was a spur of the moment thing....*" (p. 896) That was a critical observation because Kassidy did have bruises at that time and Amanda was bringing her to Jacqueline's home. Thus, Amanda was not hiding Kassidy from her. When she went to Buckfield with Kassidy, she expected to see her mother, and expected her mother to see Kassidy.

In response to a question about Chad's treatment of Amanda, Jacqueline said that Amanda, "*said one time he grabbed her throat, and I said, 'If he's going to be that way, don't let him treat you like that'....And she said, he's never done it again.*" (p. 897) Jacqueline said that her first husband, i.e. the father of Chuck, Jennifer, Amanda and Joshua was abusive, but the children "*didn't see it.. They knew about it.. My first husband was not a nice person.*" (p. 897)

Showing the strong love she had for Kassidy, Jacqueline said, "*I never saw the bruises. If I had known that, I would have went down there. I would have found a way, when my husband got home, we would have been down there..... Oh, God.*" (p. 899)

Jacqueline said that she hadn't been around Chad long enough to "*judge the person,*" but that "*I've been around Jeff a lot. I really liked Jeff,*" but that "*I've heard that he's mistreated other girls...I think he hits girls....I think he did his ex-girlfriend, but I'm not sure about that....*" She said that she had never seen, herself, any sign of such violence. (p. 900) Thus, even if the police had not completed their own arrest and court record checks, this was the second interviewee who told them about Jeff's record with domestic violence. The first was Chad who mentioned a "*similar situation*" to his own. When asked, Amanda had said that she didn't know of such issues with Jeff. Jacqueline's interview ended at 8:25 p.m.

8:45 p.m. - Bruce Aube Interview

New Hampshire State Police Detective John Marasco and Maine State Police Detective Jeff Linscott interviewed Bruce Aube, age 28, one of Chad's two best friends. He, too, had come to the Kittery Police Station to see what he could do to help Chad. No friends of Jeff Marshall came to the police station that evening, and neither did his mother, who lived in York, Maine, the next town to the north, but she explained at Amanda's trial that she was unavailable that day. The two detectives had just completed their interview with Tristan, and Linscott had previously interviewed Jeff, together with Scott Harakles.

Jeff Linscott began with the mis-information that Kassidy was 18 months old, but then fairly explained his role, "*...we're investigators. It's our job to figure out what happened....the medical examiner's office - they're the people who look at the child and they've got to figure out whether it was a natural death* [or] *... an unnatural death,* [i.e.] *a homicide....We're extensions of the medical examiner's office. We're fact finders for them.*" (p. 1461)

After the background questions, and telling Bruce that he was not a suspect, Linscott asked about Kassidy. Bruce said that she was "*different*" and that he saw her at his house about once a week, for a "*couple of months.*" (p. 1469). He noted that he didn't have children, but that he had been around Chad's son and that his brother and sister had children. He first met Chad when he was in college and Chad was the manager of the Rochester McDonalds. Of Kassidy, he said, "*She's... very quiet.... doesn't talk a lot... more easily* [now] *than she did.*" (p. 1467) About her speech, he recalled she said "*See doggy,*" as Bruce had two dogs.

Linscott asked specifically about Chad's temper, and Bruce agreed that "*he has a temper,*" and one example was when an employee stole three thousand dollars from one of his McDonald's restaurants. Bruce said that Chad would never hurt his kids. (p. 1469) Bruce said that he had never seen Chad physically harm anyone, including his former wife, Tristan.

Linscott asked , "*...there was an incident at a party at his house where...everyone's hanging around drinking out of kegs. And some person went by and made some comments and.. he got bent out of shape about that and went over and dealt with that person.*" (p. 1471) Bruce said he was not aware of such an incident, and, as a close friend, "*I think I would of, you know what I mean.*" (p. 1471)

Chad believes that Linscott was referring to an incident involving a friend, Scott Lloyd, and Chad wrote about it in a January 21, 2011 letter.

Regarding Scott Lloyd. Perhaps it would be best to find and ask him. I believe Sandy knows him so I will ask her to do so. What I recall is that Scott was an employee of mine in the early to mid 90's at the Rochester McDonald's. I liked Scott and we always got along well. I was having a party at my house one evening. Probably 30 or so of my friends were over and Nicole came up with her boyfriend of the time. I believe Scott did think Nicole was attractive and, as sometimes happens when you add alcohol, people say and do crazy things. Scott and my sister's boyfriend were having words about something, and Nicole stepped between them and then Scott was in my sister's face. I am very protective of my family and immediately walked over to Scott and shoved him toward the kitchen door. As I recall the door was open, Scott was still talking and I escorted him out of the kitchen to get some air. I believe everything was fine after that. Scott apologized the next day and all was good.

In days of old, it used to be an obligation of men in a family to defend the honor of their mothers, wives, sisters and daughters.

Bruce said he knew of no violence between Chad and Amanda, and that he would be completely comfortable leaving children in their care, "*Yeah, absolutely.*" (p. 1473)

John Marasco asked if Bruce had "*ever noticed Kassidy with any marks on her,*" and Bruce said that he had, "*last week, I guess. Give or take a couple days.... like on both cheeks... like on her cheek bones...the size of your pen cap.*" (p. 1474) Marasco then rephrased the description as "*about the size of a half the size of a penny?*" (p. 1474) and Bruce agreed. He also said that about a "*week or two ago,*" he had seen other bruises on Kassidy's face, in a different area, but still on her cheeks. He said that there were "*two or three*" other occasions when he saw bruises on Kassidy, and one of those might have been on her forehead. (p. 1475)

John Marasco asked, "*...how long of a time span are we talking about from the first time that you noticed them until this one last week?*" (p. 1477) Bruce's response was inaudible, according to the transcription. Marasco asked what was Bruce's reaction, which was, "*What the hell happened?*" but Bruce said that it might have been his girlfriend who actually asked Amanda or Chad. The response that he heard was that Kassidy "*had fallen or I, I don't know specifically.*" (p. 1477)

Bruce was asked if he asked Chad directly, and he didn't remember, "*I probably did once, but I don't remember exactly what I said, and I'm sure he said something that, 'she fell, she's clumsy,' or....*" (p. 1477) When that answer was challenged, Bruce said, "*I'm not a dumb person...there's no way I would sit here and lie to you about anything about the little girl that died. I promise you that.... I'm not getting offended by you...I wouldn't lie to you. I don't remember.*" (p. 1477) Bruce thought that the question, "*What the hell happened?*" was put to Chad or Amanda at the time that he (Bruce) and/or his girlfriend first saw bruises on Kassidy. Bruce was not asked his girlfriend's name, but it was Jessica Edmands. He said the he hadn't asked since that first time, but it wasn't because he was afraid to ask. He said, "*... no, I'm never afraid to talk to him and if he was sitting here right now... If I thought he fucked something up, I'd tell him... I'd be very straight with him. So that's, No, no I wasn't afraid to ask him...*" (p. 1479) The interview ended abruptly when the tape ended for that side of the cassette.

Usually, during this investigation, an interview was either transcribed from a tape recording or it was summarized, sometimes with the benefit of a tape, but usually from notes. Occasionally, an officer would write a summary in addition to the transcript, and John Marasco's summary of Bruce's first and second interviews is one example. Marasco wrote about Bruce, "*At times... he appeared to be reluctant to offer all the information he possessed about the baby and Evans*. (p. 1069) What Marasco perceived as reluctance could also have been the result of Bruce's being intimidated by the police.

8:50 p.m. - Jeremy Hinton Interview

MSP Detective Erik Baker and NHSP Trooper Jill Rockey interviewed Chad's close friend, Jeremy Hinton. Neither officer had participated in any of the other interviews in the case. Jeremy had come to the Kittery Police Station after work, because he hadn't heard from Chad since seeing him at work in the mid-afternoon. One of Chad's best friends, Jeremy's estimate of the move-in date for Amanda, came from Amanda, and "*she said she's been there straight probably for four or five weeks now, but she's been staying there off and on pretty much since halfway through the summer*." (p. 1767) Jeremy didn't say when Amanda had given him that estimate. For an unknown reason, Amanda was minimizing her relationship with Chad at the time.

Of Kassidy, Jeremy said, "*I've honestly never seen her talk. She just sits there on the couch*." (p. 1768) He spent the night on Monday, October 23, before going to play golf with Chad at a company outing the next day. The next morning, "*... I saw Kassidy in Amanda's, Chad's bedroom and I'm like, 'Is she sleeping with you guys or something?' That's kinda odd, 'cause, you know, they're kind of sexually active.... He said that, no, she fell out of the bed that night. And I'm like, 'Well, that's not good.'* [Chad said,] *'Ah, well, she always falls out of the bed.'* " (p. 1768)

"*That night... it was the first time like I ever said anything to Chad about the bruises...*" (p. 1768) "*Chad goes, 'Oh, come here,' and then called Kassidy over and Kassidy came over, and showed me her butt. I said, 'Chad, that's..what's that?' ... that's not right, you know. I don't care how close my friend is. I'm like, 'Chad, did you do that?' Because I knew his sister and Tristan wouldn't. He said, 'Jeremy, I wouldn't touch kids.' I'm like, 'Okay, who did it?' ...He said it was Jeff. And I said, 'Yeah, are you going to fucking kill him or something?' I mean. That's wrong*." (p. 1769) At that same time, Jeremy saw "*just a couple of bruises on her neck.... an odd place to have a bruise, I thoughtt....*" He asked Chad about them, but he did not get an explanation. (p. 1770) Chad and Jeremy observed those new jaw bruises together, and they were not there in the morning before they left for their golf tournament on Tuesday, October 22. Kassidy was with Jeff for a good part of that day, while Amanda and Jennifer did landscaping work for Jeff.

Jeremy said that Chad "*said, he just talks to him* [Jeff]. *He just spanks her really hard*." (p. 1770). Then Jeremy added what was noted above, "*I asked Jeff, when I got here, 'well, Jeff, did you touch that kid?' And he goes, ...'I spank her, but I don't spank her that hard to kill her.'* " (p. 1770) This confirmed what Jeff and Jennifer had told their interviewers about Jeff spanking Kassidy, but there was no consensus on the severity.

Jeremy said,

I do remember the only other time. It was probably a month ago. I was talking to Amanda and I said, 'you know, you going home this weekend?' or something and, ah, that was back when she was still like making trips home. And she said that, 'no' her mom would flip out if she saw the bruises on Kassidy's face, and I looked at Kassidy and I go, 'I don't see any bruises.' I didn't really ask her anything. She just said she [Kassidy] *was really klutzy. She'd fall, and I said, "Oh.' So that was probably a good month ago. It was before that period where she stayed consistently at Chad's house. She was probably going there for two nights and coming back for two nights. She wasn't working. It was... in September. She hadn't started school, but she was going to start school; and then she didn't start school.* (p. 1771)

As Jeremy was one of Chad's two best friends, Jeremy reciprocated by naming Chad as his best friend. As did Chad, Jeremy believed that a measure of friendship was frank feedback. He said,

I've been around Chad's kids and I, I was probably the first person to tell him that what he did to his wife was wrong. You know, I mean he did the typical guy thing, "Ah I really didn't hit her that much." And, .. I was quite honest with him.... because I talked to Tristan and I said I don't believe it, you know, "I want to talk to you about it." You know,

... he went through a phase when I wouldn't talk as much at first, but... I've never seen him lay a hand on one of his two kids. I mean I would never....I've never seen him so much as spank either one of them. (p. 1771-72)

Erik Baker asked, *"Did he ever compare his two kids to Kassidy?"* and Jeremy said, "*No, he never... I mean the two kids that he's kinda responsible for, the oldest one isn't even his. And he's always treated him, if anything, better than Kyle.*" (p. 1771)

Jeremy described Chad's stop at the Portsmouth McDonald's that afternoon around 3:30 p.m..

He just said, "Jeremy, I don't know what's going on. The Kittery Police paged me," and I go, "What did they say?" and he told me they said, "We'll talk about it when you get here." I said, "Did they say anything else?" He said, "No." He goes, "I'm just nervous, Jeremy, because I'm on probation," He goes, "I haven't..." [I asked him] *"Did you hit Amanda or anything?" He goes, "Ah, no. I've never laid a finger on her." He says, "I'm not dumb, you know." and I says, "What about Kassidy? Does it have something to do with Kassidy?"... He said that ... Kassidy was in Kittery at Jeff's place for the day.... I said, "Wasn't she supposed to be starting day care today, cause last night Amanda told me she was starting daycare today".... He thought she was going to a day care place in Kittery. ... And it must have been Jeff. Because when I called Chad's house last night, Amanda was on the phone and she was looking for daycare. I says, "Oh." Cause she started working again.* (p. 1772-73)

Jeremy later said that his conversation with Amanda was the previous afternoon, Wednesday, and she told him that she was looking for "*a more reliable daycare other than Jeff.*" (p. 1774) Jeremy said that his call with Amanda was "*before I worked out at 5:00.*" (p. 1773) However, it must have been before Amanda left to take Kassidy to Jeff. Her last call from her and Chad's home was to Jeff at 2:35 p.m. Jeremy later said that he called Chad's home as he was trying reach him.

Jeremy said,

I was like, "Chad, did she start that new day care?" I'm like, "Did the day care see the bruises?" I did ask him that at work, today....I said, ..."maybe she went to the daycare and they saw the bruises and called the police." He said, "I don't know," Jeremy. ... he was visibly upset. He didn't know if Amanda was all right and he didn't know if Kassidy was all right. He just knew that he didn't have a good experience with the whole police thing. (p. 1774)

Baker asked if he had seen Chad ever hit anyone, and Jeremy said, "*Never, the only time I've ever seen him hit another person... was one night at a party when Tristan, his ex-wife, hit him and he just kinda grabbed her. He didn't really slap her. He just kinda grabbed her and held her up against the wall, and said, 'Don't hit me.'*" (p. 1775)

Erik Baker asked, "*What type of a temper does he have?" and Jeremy responded, "He has a temper, but... it's not one of those tempers ... where... he's always angry... I takes a lot to piss him off.... I've worked for him for four years... he's never yelled at me at work or anything like that.... I know he's yelled at a couple of the other managers before.... But he's not the type of person that just snaps...*" (p. 1775)

The police seemed to have believed Jeff's statements about Chad having gambling debts. Baker asked Jeremy, "*Does he seem like he's hurting for money right now?*" and Jeremy said, "*Oh no, not at all.*" That seemed to catch Baker by surprise, "*Not at all?*" Baker pressed, "*...does he owe anybody money for gambling....*" And Jeremy gave him the same response, *"No. He doesn't owe anybody any money.*" Baker was still surprised, "*Are you sure*?" and then "*...I'd hate to see you lie to me about something that is so simple.*" (p. 1776-77) It was very hard to persuade the police that their image of Chad Evans, formed primarily from the interview with Jeff, was substantially incorrect. Jeremy added, "*I just picked up a good chunk of money for him tonight* [from gambling winnings]." (p. 1777) Later in the interview, Baker returned the gambling issue as if he hadn't heard Jeremy's earlier answers, asking, "*But he's... probably pretty heavily in debt with the gambling?*" Jeremy said that they settle up every Thursday evening with their bookie and Chad was on the winning side. Still disbelieving, Baker asked, "*Just recently on the winning side of it*?" and Jeremy responded, "*No, all year.*" (p. 1783) The good news was that Baker kept on asking. The bad news was that he didn't believe Jeremy. It seemed to be a classic illustration of someone not wanting the facts to get in the way of theory.

Jeremy said he was nervous telling the police about Chad's illegal gambling, and Jill Rockey urged him, "*Jeremy take a deep breath...you're not going to get in trouble here, but as you know, these things can affect how people act, okay?*" Then she added, "*And we do have some information... and that's why you're being questioned about that... As far as you know is this the only source where he gambles?*" (p. 1778) Jeremy said, "*No, it's the only place we gamble...he met the person through me...*" (p. 1778) Still later in the interview, Rockey returned to the gambling issue, "*Let me ask you, because we're getting different information,... especially about the gambling...we were led to believe that Chad was in financial trouble,*" though she didn't say from whom the information came. It came from Jeff. No other interviewee had mentioned the football gambling to the police. Rockey said again, "*...we've talked to a lot of people tonight...*" (p. 1786) Jeremy told Baker and Rockey that he had $900 cash for one week's winnings in his car. After being assured that no harm would come to the bookie, Jeremy gave them contact information for him. There is no indication in the case discovery materials that the police ever contacted that bookie. They did, however, discuss the football gambling later that evening with Chad and his responses confirmed those from Jeremy. As the issue was important enough to the police to spend much interview time about it, after the allegations were first made by Jeff, it's unfortunate that the police never asked Jeff again about his allegations, or questioned his motives for making them. It would have been a good test of credibility for Jeff's other allegations. Either Chad was losing money on football betting or he wasn't. The bookie knew. Chad knew, and Jeremy knew. Jeff's information came second hand from Chad or third hand from Amanda, via Jennifer.

Baker added, "*But we need to find out a full background. And we're all ready asking you a few questions we know answers to.*" (p. 1778) However, the answers Baker thought he knew were correct were actually wrong. He wasn't the only officer that evening to say that s/he was asking questions to which the answers were already known. Then Baker summarized the problem with lying to the police, "*...and when you give us the untruthful answer... We begin to question what type of person we're really talking to...*" (p. 1779) It was a message that could have been communicated to all the interviewees in this case. They questioned Amanda's credibility and Chad's and Jeremy's, but apparently not Jeff's.

Even after Jeremy told Baker and Rockey about Chad's illegal gambling, thinking that it was better to tell them about that illegal activity than for them to believe an untruth about him, i.e. that he owed money, Baker still accused Jeremy of protecting Chad, saying "*...how far do you want to go for a friend that you've only known for four years? How much protection do you feel you need to give him?*" There was a curious assumption there about the duration of bonding friendships. Baker's implication was that four years was not enough. Many Medal of Honor winners, and many policemen, have died trying to protect fellow soldiers and policepeople they've known for only a few months or a few days.

Jeremy responded,

...if I thought for ...a minute that Chad did that to my [child] *I wouldn't ever try to protect him... I didn't tell you that because I wanted to protect him at all. I told you that because I saw a kid with bruises that I've never seen before in my life....I really admire him for what he's done for Brent... even after the divorce. Obviously, he's not legally obligated to... pay for a dime for Brent, ... and he's put money away for them for an education IRA still.. He... treats him like he's his own....and he's canceled plans before, to spend time with his.. kids.*" (p. 1779-80)

Instead of asking more questions, Trooper Rockey seemed to argue with Jeremy, "*But those are his kids Jeremy!*" (p. 1780) Rockey ignored, for the moment, the fact that Brent was Chad's stepson, and not his biological son. Therefore, the only differences between Brent and Kassidy were their gender and their mothers' marital status. Chad was married to Tristan, but was not married to Amanda. After Jeremy again noted that Chad had told him that he talked with Jeff about the black and blue on Kassidy's buttocks, Rockey made the point that Chad really did treat Kassidy differently from Brent and Kyle because if he

had seen such bruises on either of the boys, he would have beaten "*the crap out of somebody.*" (p. 1780) She seemed to ignore three key aspects of Jeff's babysitting:
1. Jeff was the boyfriend of Amanda's sister, and
2. Chad was trying very hard to defer to Amanda regarding Kassidy's upbringing, and
3. Jeff had no children of his own.

Then Jill Rockey told Jeremy, "*... you knew those bruises were not caused by a spanking. You knew that. You don't have any children, but you grew up and you looked at that child's body and you knew that that was not caused by a spanking.*" (p. 1780) Jeremy asked Rockey, "*...how else would it get there if it wasn't caused by a spanking?*" and she responded, "*...not by a normal... not when you discipline a child. There's a spanking and there's abuse.*" (p. 1781) Rockey did not appear to believe that the black and blue that Jeremy saw on Kassidy's buttocks after returning from Jeff on Sunday, October 22 came from Jeff's spanking, or even that they were caused by Jeff at all.

Baker asked Jeremy what Chad said about the bruising that Jeremy saw on Kassidy's neck, and Jeremy answered, "*He didn't give me one. He just said, 'Check this out,' and showed me and that was it... I said, 'Chad, that looks like someone's been hitting,' and that's what he showed me.*" (p. 1782) Jeremy said that the neck bruise was on the left side of Kassidy's neck, as he recalled how she and he were sitting together on the couch in Chad's living room.

Baker asked if Chad was right or left handed, and Jeremy replied "*left-handed,*" and Baker moved on to another question. He might have pursued that inquiry, but the results are not conclusive. If a left-handed person slaps or hits a person who is facing him or her, the blow will come to the right side of the victim. Of course, there are no statistics on how many such victims are hit when facing toward their assailants or facing away. Still, it was Erik Baker who asked the question, so he must have thought it worth asking. As with other answers from Jeremy and others, it may have been that the answer didn't fit his theory, i.e. that Chad was right-handed, so he ignored it. That was one of the problems in this investigation, that when facts conflicted with theory, the policed either ignored or rejected the facts, or offerings of fact, and stuck with the theory. The Convict-Chad train continued.

Baker said that "*...we've got a dead child that's laying on a piece of metal slab...*" and said that he and Rockey "*went and looked at the child tonight...*" (p. 1784) Baker had gone to the York Hospital and interviewed Dr. Bock, above. Rockey said that the bruises were "*not disciplinary*" and Baker said, "*She has been, she, she suffered and suffered... you would not want to face what we saw tonight.*" (p. 1784-85)

Baker asked if Jeremy ever saw Amanda discipline Kassidy, and Jeremy recalled, "*I've seen Amanda like just leave her upstairs in her room and the kid's crying and she won't do anything about it.*" Baker then commented, without a question, "*Well, did... Chad goes up stairs and takes care of it,*" without saying what he had in mind. Jeremy said, "*...and Chad would bring her downstairs,*" and Baker seemed surprised again, "*What would he do? He'd go upstairs and do what?*" (p. 1785) Baker seemed to assume that Jeremy was describing an occasion where Chad would beat Kassidy. Said Jeremy, "*He would just bring her downstairs, and Amanda's like, 'She's never gonna learn....if you go get her when she cries every time you pick her up.*" Baker kept looking for a problem with Chad, "*Would Chad get frustrated with it?*" and Jeremy said, "*No, he never would.... I* [have] *only seen her cry a few times... I'm not kidding you. She just sits there on the couch. And obviously, for obvious reasons now, but she just sat there.*" (p. 1785) Unfortunately, it was not obvious to anyone who knew Kassidy, why she stared into space so often, or didn't put her hands out in front of her when she fell. No one knew why, and some of these problems began before the fall from Jeff's truck on Saturday, October 28.

Jill Rockey again sought to find stress in Chad's life, saying, "*Oh. I'm sorry. Financial problems can create a great deal of stress in people's lives.*" Jeremy then summarized Chad's financial information, "*...he just bought a couple three-wheelers recently...he is very sound investment wise ...he probably has at least $40 thousand put away for their* [Brent and Kyle] *education... And he has plenty of money. He doesn't have a car bill.... You know that guy Travis that lives with him, Chad gave him a car...*" (p. 1787-88) He might have added that Chad recently paid for Amanda and Nicole to attend the money management classes, being conducted by his own financial advisor, Darren Janakis.

Baker continued the search for Chad's problems. "*Ok, what about drug use*?" and Jeremy responded, "*I've never seen him touch the stuff,* " but then described Chad's experience with alcohol, "...*He doesn't drink much anymore, but I'd say ...his whole marriage thing with Tristan, that was one of the reasons that led to his problems. He'd drink a lot. Not really a lot, but when he drank, he drank a lot.*" Rockey asked, "*How was he when he drank too much*?" and Jeremy candidly said that he, Jeremy, "*usually passed out before I saw...I've never seen him violent or anything when he was drunk.*" Baker then followed up, "*Well, why would you call him a problem drinker then, if you've never seen him?*" Jeremy returned with one of the more memorable statements in the case, "*He drank a fifth of vodka and a case of beer in a night... you'd call that a problem.*" (p. 1788-89) The officers asked again about Chad's drug use, but Jeremy insisted that Chad was not a current drug user.

Baker and Rockey both restated how upset they were about the "*murder*" of Kassidy, and Jeremy described again the bruises he saw, which observations were made on Tuesday evening, October 24. He said, "...*when I saw the butt and the legs, I mean it just wasn't the butt. ...it went all the way down to the back of her legs. That's how I knew it wasn't just... a spanking. I mean. It was very, it was sick.*" (p. 1791) Baker asked how Chad reacted to Kassidy's bruising, and Jeremy said, "*Chas was whispering it to me in the living room. She* [Amanda] *was in the office doing the survey thing she was doing at the time. And ... she said, 'what are you guys whispering about?' And then Chad's like, 'I just was showing him what Jeff did to ... Kassidy.' And then I was walking out before and I said, 'Bye, Amanda.'* " (p. 1792)

Baker asked about Chad or Amanda "*acting up*," and Jeremy said that he hadn't seen Amanda around Kassidy that much. Generally, about "*acting up*," he said, "*they didn't seem like they had that violent thing that... Tristan and Chad had. Tristan and Chad differently had a violent, you know, it was a mutual* [thing]." (p. 1792)

Baker then asked about the length of Tristan's relationship with Chad, and after Jeremy estimated "*about four years,*" Jill Rockey said "*So, maybe they haven't gotten to that point yet?*" (p. 1793) She was apparently suggesting that such violence was probably coming, but showing that she didn't hear or believe Jeremy's earlier assessments of Chad, and that the violence between Tristan and Chad was at least partly mutual, and of the differences between Chad's relationships with Tristan and Amanda. Also, there was no apparent police interest in talking with the woman who lived with Chad before he met and married Tristan, Mary Paquette, and with whom there was zero violence.

After Jeremy noted that Jeff introduced Chad to Amanda, Baker asked about Jeremy's relationship to Jeff, and he said, "...*we hang out.... he's not someone I hang out with on a regular basis, even though we see each other* [when] *he's wrapping up, mowing my lawn or doing plowing. We'll go out for a beer, hang out or something. I mean, we've hung out a few times socially, but we never... I wouldn't know his home phone number or anything like that.*" (p. 1793)

Jeremy said that his seeing Jeff this evening, November 9, was the first time he had seen him since seeing the bruises on Kassidy. Again, the officers did not seek to clarify that date, but it was Tuesday, October 24.

Baker asked Jeremy if he asked Jeff, this evening, about the bruises and he replied, "*Oh yeah, I asked him.... because he came out and he was pretty much talking like Chad did it. And I said, 'Jeff, you spanked her.' He said, 'I just spanked her. I didn't put those bruises on her.' And at that point, I just, I didn't talk to him. I just said, 'whatever,' And me and Bruce left.*" (p. 1793) Thus, Bruce heard that conversation, too, but he wasn't asked later in his interview whether he knew Jeff or had ever talked with him.

Baker asked what Jeremy knew about Jeff's background, and he said, "... *the only personal information I know about him is he just talks about girls he's dated and stuff. I know he had a problem with one, where she was married, and I'm not sure if that's why the restraining order was involved. I just know he had a restraining order on him for that.*" (p. 1793) Jeremy thought that incident was probably before 1999.

Baker asked, "*Who else hangs out at ... Chad's with you. Who else was some of his friends?*" and Jeremy replied, "*No one really hangs out at that house, except for his family. His sister, Nicole, his brother, Jason, and his mom and dad.*" (p. 1794) He gave the parents' names as Pam and Chetty (Chet) and said that they were last at Chad's house over his birthday weekend, Octobrer 14-15, after arriving on Friday afternoon and leaving before the Sunday football game at noon. Jeremy remembered one incident from the Saturday of that weekend, when he had observed a blonde toddler talking a lot and he had made the observation to Chad that Kassidy was talking a lot more. Chad told him that the girl was not Kassidy, but his brother's daughter, Malana, who was a few months older than Kassidy.

Jeremy continued about that birthday weekend, saying

Amanda didn't go over to Chad's that Saturday night... I wasn't sure why and then she came over that Sunday to ... drop presents off at Bruce's, and stuff, before she was bringing Kassidy to the babysitter's or something and... I said, "Why isn't Kassidy staying here," [and Amanda said,] *"she*['s] *got bruises on her." I said, "Amanda, she*['s] *got bruises all the time." ...that's when she said, "I know. I talked to Jeff," and I thought* [it] *was kinda funny, and I'm like it's really strange she didn't seem that upset about it. That's her own kid, but she didn't.... I don't want to say who is a good mother or a bad mother, but she's never been one to, she just doesn't strike me as a good mother. I just wouldn't ... bring my kid over to a house that someone I was just dating didn't stay there all the time... I wouldn't go off to New York and leave her with my mom for three days, but that's just me, you know.... Nobody's going to watch my kids except me and my wife.. She never... she just doesn't seem too concerned.* (p. 1795)

Jeremy added, later in the interview, about his conversation with Amanda on Sunday, October 15, "*I said, 'Are you bringing her to your mom's?' She's like, 'No, I can't bring her to my mom's. Mom would flip out if she saw the bruises on her.' ... I don't know why I didn't say anything then, but I mean she wasn't flipping out about it either.*" (p. 1798) Now married to his 2000 girlfriend, April, Jeremy has two children.

Jeremy said that when he saw Kassidy on "*the night of the Jets* [game, Monday, October 23], *she was walking fine and he "didn't see her limp or anything. I've seen* [her] *get up and like go upstairs.*" Jeremy said, "*I, I'm starting to feel like I could have done something,*" and Baker agreed, "*Maybe, it sounds like a few people could have done something. You are just one of many....But the only good feeling that may come out of this is if we figure out exactly how this happened. When someone tells us the complete truth about what happened... and you need to think about long and hard about what's going on.*" (p. 1796) Again, there was the implication that Jeremy was not being truthful. On the one issue where their information "*from everybody*" i.e. Jeff, conflicted with Jeremy's information, the gambling issue, the officers had a good opportunity on a specific collateral issue to determine the truth. They must have done some fact checking, because the issue was never mentioned at Chad's trial.

Jeremy asked, "*... is Chad like the one that's suspected?... or is it Jeff?*" and Baker answered, "*A couple suspects.... We're not ruling anybody out at this point.*" (p. 1797)

Returning to Chad and Kassidy, Baker asked Jeremy if he thought that "*Chad was capable to causing bruises on... to her?*" and Jeremy restated what he had said earlier, "*I don't think Chad's capable of... I've never seen him spank Kyle and I've never seen him spank Brent... No, I've never seen him hit Kassidy, either.*" (p. 1798-99) Baker asked, "*When he's picked up Kassidy, how did her pick her up?*" and Jeremy responded, "*Just put her in his arms like this*," and demonstrated. Again apparently surprised, Baker said, "*So, he didn't pick her up by the arms and drag her... or pick her up in any way that you thought was a little bit rougher...*" and Jeremy said, "*No.*" (p. 1799)

Jill Rockey asked, "*Was he affectionate with his own children?*" and Jeremy said "*Yeah, Chad was very affectionate toward them...Kyle... is always, you know, kissing him* [Chad] *and saying, 'I love you.' I mean, me and Chad joke about it, cause I've never kissed my dad on the lips. You don't kiss your son on the lips. That kind of thing. He says, 'I kiss my son on the lips. I love him, you know. Brent, the same way.'*" Rockey then asked, "*Did he ever show affection with ... Kassidy?*" Jeremy said, "*No, except for the times when he would go upstairs and get her cause she was crying... But not like affection. Just kind of held her to get her to stop crying.*" (p. 1799) Jeremy added, "*... he's had Kyle show affection, you know, 'This is Kassidy, you know, say Good Night and give her a kiss,' and that thing, so.*" (p. 1799)

The interview returned to Chad's hitting Tristan, and Jeremy explained that his frank conversation with Chad about those two domestic violence incidents with Tristan came when Chad asked for Jeremy for help in reconciling him with Tristan. Jeremy agreed that Chad minimized his actions at the time. Jeremy told the officers that during the first incident, one of Tristan's teeth was chipped. Chad had insisted that he never hit Tristan with a closed fist, but with an open hand. That doesn't make it right, of course, but it was another reason for the officers to believe Chad to be a violent liar. However, what they didn't know, and never did acknowledge during the entire case was that the affected tooth was previously capped, and it was the cap that broke off, which took less force. Even if they knew that important piece of information about this issue, the police would have probably minimized, themselves, the distinction, and still considered him to be violent. Everybody has a tendency to minimize what we don't want others to hear, paraphrasing Angela Blodgett's statement to Amanda, *"I think everybody lies."*

Near the end of the interview, Jeremy reflected, "*... I'm thinking, there's no way in heck that Chad did it* [killed Kassidy.]" (p. 1801) and Rockey asked, "*Why do you think he could beat his wife, but not a child?*" Jeremy said, "*I've never seen him beat Amanda. I've never seen him, I know he didn't hit the girlfriend before ... Tristan.*" (p. 1802) That girlfriend was Mary Paquette, and there was no indication that the police ever tried to contact her. However, the New Hampshire State Police did later talk with a high school girlfriend at her own initiative, Barbara Hamel, as will be seen in the next chapter. Rockey asked, "*How do you know that*?" and Jeremy acknowledged that he only knew what people told him, but he did make direct observations of Tristan, and he continued, "*... I asked Tristan about it, and Tristan said he never... they were both violent people... I've seen Tristan hit Chad ten times more than I've ever seen Chad yell at her.*" (p. 1802)

As the interview closed down, Jeremy asked Baker for a business card in case he thought of something more. Baker urged Jeremy to, "*really start thinking about calling some people...*" *and sharing the truth... and think about that little 18 month old girl that's laying on that slab right now..*" Added Jill Rockey, "*and how she was tortured.*" (p. 1804) Rockey, for one, had apparently excluded any possible role in Kassidy's death for genuine accidents, or a chronic condition. The interview ended at 9:55 p.m. It didn't make a significant difference that Kassidy was actually 21 months old, having passed that milestone on November 4th. There could have been a lot more precision in this case about time and dates.

Almost an hour earlier, at 9:07 p.m. MSP Detective Herbert Leighton began a "consent search" of Jeffrey Marshall's home at 51 Rogers Road. He conducted his search, alone, until about 11:45 p.m. He took photographs and seized items which might become evidence of crimes. As happened with some of the Chad Evans family photos, the date stamp was off by a day, "00 11 10," because the wrong date was input. He seized several items: pajama bottoms, baby slippers, pink baby coat, yellow napkin, bag with cereal, bed sheets, pillow covers and a comforter. Missing in the inventory of the seized items was the Sippy cup which Amanda brought with Kassidy, the pajama tops, i.e. "sweatshirt" (Jennifer) or "*fleece sweatshirt*" (Amanda), if worn on that day, and her diaper bag, with A-D Ointment, diapers and snacks. Until 2011, no one noticed that these items were missing. Detective Leighton appeared to have considered the question of what Kassidy was drinking because he wrote on his "Continuation Report" that *"No used diapers or baby formula were found in the apartment.*" (p. 1192) However, there was no recognition that items were missing.

Detective Leighton did not search the basement, as he apparently did not know that there was a basement. Thus, he did not check all the doors in the small one-bedroom apartment, and didn't do a walk-around on the outside, during which he would have seen the bulkhead.

9:33 p.m. - Travis Hunt Interview

Maine State Police Detective Scott Harakles interviewed Travis Hunt, age 26. Harakles had previously interviewed Jeff Marshall in the late afternoon. It's not known why the Travis interview was not recorded, even if it was intended to be a short interview because of the late hour. Perhaps there was simply a shortage of recording devices. There were other people waiting to be interviewed. However, by this time in the evening, the police knew that Travis was at least one of five adults to see Kassidy during her last 24 hours, and lived under the same relatively small roof as Amanda, Chad, Kassidy and Kyle. Thus, he was an important witness.

In his summary of Travis's interview, Harakles wrote that Travis said that he "*had been Chad Evans' roommate for a little over a month and that he had known Chad Evans for approximately six years.*" (p. 1213) As was the case with others throughout the trial, the accuracy of dates and lengths of periods was not emphasized by the interviewers. Still, "*a little over a month*" was reasonably close to the actual 55 days since his September 15 move-in. Also, he was a tenant, or a housemate, but not a roommate.

Harakles said that Travis believed that Amanda and Kassidy had lived with Chad for "*approximately three weeks to a month.*" (p. 1213) His most important reference point was the date that he moved to 191 Milton, and thus his estimate of Amanda's move-in date was after his own. He did not distinguish between Amanda's move-in and Kassidy's. As he lived in the basement, and as Amanda and Chad made their four day trip to Martha's Vineyard in late September, and as both Amanda and Chad were verbally downplaying the actual status of Amanda's and Kassidy's living with Chad, Travis didn't know that actual status.

According to Harakles' summary, Travis described Kassidy as

always having bruises on her face and that she would not use her arm to break her falls. Travis felt that she might be a little slow or mildly retarded, but he was not sure....he never witnessed anything suspicious, or what he considered inappropriate discipline practices toward Kassidy. He said that ... bedtime ... seemed to be the most stressful time in the house, as Kassidy cried a lot during that time.... (p. 1213)

Regarding last night, Wednesday, November 8, Travis said that when he arrived home, *Chad was giving Kassidy a bath, and Travis did notice fresh marks on Kassidy's face. Travis told me that Chad explained to him that Kyle, Chad's 3 year old son, had hit Kassidy with a wiffle ball. Travis told me that Kyle did repeat that story to him shortly after Chad told it. Travis described Kassidy as coherent and happy the last time that he saw her for those few moments. Travis then went out for the evening and did not come home until well after Kassidy's bedtime. Travis did add that Chad Evans contacted him today, approximately late afternoon, and told him that the police wanted to talk to him It was at that time that Chad reminded Travis about the wiffle ball story and that Travis had witnessed those injuries.* (p. 1213-14)

10:00 p.m. - Nicole Evans Harvey interview

Detective Angela Blodgett interviewed Chad's sister, Nicole Evans Harvey, age 24. Previously, Blodgett had participated in Amanda's two interviews, along with Rick LeClair. Nicole said she worked as a Special Education Assistant at a Belmont, New Hampshire elementary school. That was the same school system where her mother-in-law, Gerri Harvey, was the school nurse at the Middle School. Before the interview, Nicole waited in the reception area, along with several others, and she noticed that she could not make **eye contact** with Jeff.

At the beginning of the interview, Blodgett asked how well Nicole knew Kassidy, and she said, "*... Not that much... She came over to our house on Sunday... with Chad, and I watched her for the day...*" (p. 1808) It was not emphasized during the interview that "Sunday" was actually, Sunday, November 5th, i.e. four days before Kassidy died. Asked about bruises, Nicole said, "*Yeah, she did have a bruise on her cheek.... like a little touch mark...*" (p. 1809) In 2011, Nicole stated that the referenced cheek was Kassidy's right cheek, and thus it was likely one of the same bruises observed by Tristan. She said she saw no other bruises,

I didn't at all, she slept on me for a little [while]. *She fell asleep in my arms.... She seemed kinda disoriented. I don't know because she just always kinda seemed like that. Like she just sat there for a long time at the table and didn't say anything. Like I was singing songs with her. I was a preschool teacher before. I was playing games....Not responsive at all, and she didn't say hardly anything... She seemed mentally delayed... she definitely seemed delayed in some sense...She was really clumsy, and she wouldn't, like when I put her on the floor she, she would fall down, but she wouldn't put her arms down. She would just fall down...without bracing herself. And then, she'd just per her arms like this, and I would pick her up, but she didn't... cry. She didn't make any noises. She just wasn't really responsive. Actually, after she fell asleep on me for a little while....* (p. 1809-10)

Blodgett asked if Chad had discussed with Nicole any problems he and Amanda might have been having, and she replied, "*Not at all. She seemed like always extremely in love with him and always talking about him... no, I wouldn't have suspected any problems at all.*" (p. 1811)

Blodgett asked if Nicole asked "*your brother about the bruise on her face,*" and Nicole answered, "*Yeah, I did. I've always asked him, because I saw on* [her] *one before, too.... It was on her forehead, I think.... There was something on her foot because we were jumping on the trampoline one day when I was over. It was like a, some kind of ring.*" Nicole said that she asked, " '*What happened to her*?" (p. 1811) Although Blodgett asked about Chad's explanations, Nicole seemed to describe conversations with Amanda, saying, "*She's like, 'Oh, she fell down,' or 'She was at the babysitter's and... she turned her head for a second and Kassidy was on the floor, but she wasn't crying or anything,' so, I don't know what happened.*" (p. 1811)

Detective Blodgett asked, "*... when you asked your brother about the face, did he have a response... for that on Sunday*?" By that question, Blodgett seemed to understand that they were talking about the previous Sunday, November 5. Nicole responded, "*He really didn't have an idea. He said, 'I don't know. She's just always bruised. She bruises really easy and, ...always falling down and stuff.*" (p. 1812)

Chad recalled in 2010,

You asked about one bruise that Brandon mentioned in his interview on Kassidy's cheek. I looked at Nicole's interview and she mentions the same thing, seeing one bruise on her cheek. I do not believe this was an eye contact bruise. Nicole indicated she asked me about it. I might have not willingly told someone I did that but if my sister asked me directly, I doubt very much I would lie to her. I believe I was told Kassidy obtained that bruise by Jeff's dog knocking Kassidy over. As I recall it was in the middle of her cheek and not some place I held. When I palmed Kassidy' s cheeks trying to get her to look me in the eyes, I would hold her near the lower jaw areas On the occasions that I either held her too firmly or too long, it left 2-3 small bruises on one side and one small finger tip sized bruise on the other side of her face where my thumb was. So the short answer is no, I don't believe the bruise that Nicole and Brandon observed was one of the "eye contact" bruises. I could be wrong but the evidence suggests otherwise. (Letter, December 3, 2010)

Nicole understood the Evans "eye contact" tradition, so if there were any "eye contact" bruises on Kassidy on that day, this would have been the easiest time to explain the circumstances to her. However, Chad recalls no such bruises at that time.

Asked whether Chad or Amanda had "*temper problems or frustration problems in dealing with their kids*," Nicole said, "*Oh, definitely not with their kids*." She said that she hadn't seen Amanda with Kassidy much, but "*she came down to my parents' once and she came up to our apartment once...*" (p. 1812) About Chad and discipline, she said, "*No, No. Chad, Chad cries if he has to put Kyle in time-out*." (p. 1812)

Asked about Chad's background and possible unresolved problems, Nicole recalled his childhood and a story that showed that he was "*always like the kind of person that, at 10 years old...this guy was sitting at the table eating all by himself and he would bring his lunch over and eat with him..He was always like, really compassionate, like, and an awesome brother... Amanda I don't know very well. I know that she does have a brother I think who's epileptic... We kinda talked a little bit on the way to class.*" (p. 1812-13) She was referring to the money management class that Chad had enrolled them into, and that she attended with Amanda for the three sessions.

Nicole said that her father-in-law, Steve Harvey, "*thought that* [Kassidy] *was his* [Chad's] *daughter, ... because he seemed like such a good dad to her.*" (p. 1813) Nicole was again referring to the Harvey family gathering the previous Sunday, November 5.

About Chad, Nicole said that one reason for his enrolling Amanda in the money management course was "*so she could start an IRA and a college fund for Kassidy....he encouraged... doing things for her daughter like he did for his sons. And kind of teaching her in a way to be a good parent...she really didn't know.*" (p. 1816) This statement confirms Chad's 2010 recollections of conversations with his financial planner about setting up funds for Kassidy, by Chad and by Amanda.

About Amanda, Nicole said,

"*...she's talked about family issues and how she lives. She really likes my family because, you know, we're really close and my parents are married and we all do everything together and...I think she sometimes felt she doesn't really know about parenting...and I don't think she's really realized there were any signs that she need*[ed] *to be looking for, and thought about, like taking her* [Kassidy] *more regularly for checkups and things... I reminded her one day to put a jacket on her* [Kassidy]*....And... I don't even have children.*" (p. 1816) Nicole now has a toddler daughter, Aliza.

Nicole said about Kassidy,

...I've seen her fall and you get a bruise, and I know how little iron and people can bruise real easily...and I thought maybe developmentally she was delayed and... that's why she wasn't reaching out when she fell and...the concepts were a lot slower and things that she needed to learn because she didn't really speak very much either." (p. 1817)

At the end of the interview at 10:15 p.m., Angela Blodgett supported Nicole's contact with Amanda, "*I'll bring you... back out to your sister-in-law...*" even if the relationship was not yet that formal. (p. 1818)

In addition to the transcript of Nicole's interview, Angela Blodgett also wrote a two page summary, and in that summary, she correctly noted that "*Nicole last saw Kassidy on Sunday 11/05/00. On that date, Chad stopped by her home with Kassidy.*" That "*stopped by*" period was 8-9 hours, and warranted far more interest from the police and, later, Chad's lawyers. This interview was one of the few times during the investigation that a transcript and a summary were prepared for the same interview.

10:05 p.m. - Brandon Harvey interview

Maine State Police Detective Jeff Smith interviewed Nicole's husband, Brandon Harvey. Smith had shared in the afternoon interview of Jennifer, and at 8:00 p.m. of Jacqueline Conley. Smith asked Brandon when he last saw Chad and Kassidy, and Brandon replied, "*Sunday.*" As the interview was on Thursday, the 9th, the implication was that he meant the previous Sunday, November 5. He said that Chad and Kassidy arrived at his home "*...probably 10, 11 o'clock... somewhere in there,*" and stayed until "*about 7 o'clock, I think. 6,7 o'clock.*" (p. 985) Smith tried to explicitly clarify the date for the "Sunday," saying "So, this is last Sunday, the date would be....*like November 2, somewhere around there....Halloween was on Friday.*" Was Smith unconsciously trying to minimize the immediacy of Kassidy's public appearance only four days before her death? He tried again, "*The 30th. So it was like the 1st, the 31st,*" and Brandon replied, "*Yup. What's today's date? Oh, it's just this past Sunday. It was this past Sunday.*" (p. 986)

Smith asked how Kassidy acted on that day, and Brandon said, "*...she's pretty quiet.... she pretty much sat there and slept on the cold slab for 2 or 3 hours and...ate some donuts..*" (p. 987) Given what happened four days later, expression "*cold slab*" was coincidental and chilling. He described "*a bruise... on her cheek maybe... as sort of off color tannish.*" As was the case with Nicole, this was the only bruise that Brandon observed. Smith did not ask who else was at that family gathering at Brandon's home on that day.

Brandon said this was the third time he had seen Kassidy. The first time was when, *"they came up and bought a boat from a guy I work with. Amanda and Kassidy came up....*

during the summer. Late summer." Actually it was Thursday, July 27. He said that Chad and Kassidy's relationship seemed "*good.*"

The second time was on a week night, when he and Nicole were just passing through Rochester, and stopped at Chad's and Amanda's for about a half hour. He made no observation of Chad and Kassidy at that time, but said, "*I think he gets along with kids...I don't think he had anything to do with* [Kassidy's death] and Smith responded, "*so you'd be surprised if I said different?*" (p. 989) Then Smith added, "*The people we're talking to, everyone indicates that they've known about this and they've kept it a secret... Chad hurting, physically assaulting or touch*[ing] *or hitting Kassidy.*" (p. 990) Brandon picked up on the "*everyone*" claim, and asked, "*Everyone else seems to think that?... I don't know, I never...I have a pretty hard time believing that.*" (p. 990)

Asked about Chad's drinking, Brandon said he hadn't seen him drinking since before Brandon's wedding to Nicole which was December 31, 1999. Brandon mentioned some parties "*last summer*" and said, "*...we had a buddy with us that was pretty intoxicated and Chad was, 'No, you're not going anywhere. Give me your keys.*" (p. 992)
The interview ended at 10:15 p.m., when Jeff Smith said, "*Yeah, **Kassidy did not die of natural causes.***" (p. 993)

10:25 p.m. - Robert Conley interview

After completing the interview with Brandon, Jeff Smith interviewed Robert Conley who was Amanda's and Jennifer's uncle and Kassidy's great uncle. He described Kassidy, "*When she lived with us in Auburn, she was a very happy child, active, energetic. She was learning to talk, learning to feed herself.... there were no bruises on her. Very seldom did you see her fall down. She's very curious...*" (p. 995) He continued, "*So, there are no bruises on her, physically, from falling down or anything like that... a few weeks ago, Jackie was on a trip with my brother and Mandy brought Kassidy up, and I noticed some marks on her, on her ankle area and Mandy said that... I guess the babysitter had used a cigarette on her.*" (p. 995) Conley was the only person interviewed to suggest that a babysitter, or anyone "***had used a cigarette on***" Kassidy, which would have been a dramatic indication of intentional child abuse. (p. 996) (emphasis added) He may have developed that impression because the mark may have looked like a cigarette burn, but it was likely the burn caused by a curling iron at the home of Amanda's friend, Crystal Martin. Later Conley said that he understood that the babysitter lived in Rochester, New Hampshire, and he thought it happened in August. (p. 996)

It was a very serious allegation, and the first of any of the interviews of intentional, non-discipline-related, non-play related, abuse, but there were no followup questions about this allegation. Smith did not ask if anyone else had seen the alleged burn mark. He did not ask if he had discussed his observation with his sister-in-law, Jacqueline Conley, and what was her reaction.

Conley said that Amanda would leave Kassidy with him, his brother, and Jacqueline Conley when Amanda and Chad would go on vacation. "*Every time that she dropped her off, she was fine. Every time she picked her up she was fine. These incidents or incident, now, is recent. And the last time I saw her, which was just prior to her moving to Buckfield, she was still fine. She was still very active, energetic, and everything else.*" (p. 996) That was Sunday, October 1, which was the day that the Conley's moved to Buckfield. Later, Conley said that he last saw Kassidy "*about mid-September,... Jackie had gone into the hospital in September for a hysterectomy.*" (p. 996) Jacqueline stated that her operation was on August 27.

Conley continued, "*Since she's been down there, that's when the problem starts. And we do happen to know that they came up on a visit and Chad was telling her* [Kassidy] *to take a time-out. To go stand in a corner. And for somebody that small, it's awful to stay in a cor*[ner], *or put them in a corner. It's not very nice to them. Or put them in a room because they're crying.*" (p. 996) It's not clear whether Conley actually saw such a "time-out" order or whether someone told him about it. Chad and Amanda and Kassidy went to Auburn only twice, on June 20 and July 20. In 2011, Chad wrote that he has no recollection of putting Kassidy in a corner for a time-out on either trip. Even if his memory has failed him in this case, it seems highly unlikely that a boyfriend would, on his own, be undiplomatic enough to try to discipline his hosts' granddaughter in their own home. Even if he felt that Kassidy needed discipline at that home, he would have made a recommendation to Amanda, out of earshot of her mother and stepfather and stepuncle. These two visits were 19 days and 39 days after Chad met Kassidy. Once again, the investigation would have been helped if calendars and timelines had been used.

Jeff Smith asked how he knew the burn marks occurred in August, and Conley said it was before Jackie's operation. Also, he recalled seeing bruises on Kassidy's neck in August. And he said that Amanda had explained the bruises, saying that Kassidy "*had fallen down and another time it was* [that she] *fell off the trampoline.*" (p. 997) Later, in October, he noticed other bruises on Kassidy's lower neck, when Amanda came to get clothes from the house. Conley said he was just getting home from work, and Amanda was coming out of the house. That must have been the Friday, October 13 visit, when Joshua Conley also saw Kassidy, because Conley said that Jackie called Chad, who told her the "trampoline story." (p. 998)

Jeff Smith said that Jackie told him that Amanda called her almost "*every day, every couple days*" and Conley said that Jennifer calls more often than Amanda.

One difficulty with Robert Conley's recollection was the confusion in timing of his first observation of bruises on Kassidy's neck, sometime in August, because Jacqueline had never mentioned such an observation in her interview. According to Jacqueline, her first knowledge of any bruises on Kassidy came when she returned from a trucking trip with Paul Conley on Friday, October 13 or Saturday and Joshua told her what he had seen. Also, in her interview, she didn't mention the burn marks either. In her interview, Jennifer had said that Jacqueline did know about the burn mark and was upset about it. The burn from Crystal Martin's curling iron occurred around Sunday, October 8.

Conley had heard that Amanda might be soon getting her own apartment and also the conflicting information that she and Chad planned to marry after his divorce from Tristan was final.

Robert Conley seems to have seen Chad in the Kittery Police station before his interview, because he said, in a comment about Chad, "*And even tonight, I could see the way he was acting. And unfortunately, I know a little about people because that's what I used to do for a living. I think something kind of strange here.*" (p. 999) Previously, he had said that his current work was repairing airplanes. He continued, "*I don't know what, but it just seems strange because every time I saw him, he's always, ah, making eye contact was difficult... If he made eye contact at all...And he's always, kind of on edge.*" (p. 999) Whereas Chad has emphasized eye contact when actually communicating with people, Conley seemed to be, ironically, taking the establishment of eye contact one step further, by interpreting the absence of eye contact with a person, negatively, even if there was no explicit communication between them. Conley continued his recollection of his observation of Chad,

I saw him tonight and he still doesn't make eye contact... I saw him out with Jackie and it sounded like he was crying and all that... It was like he was playing a game... And..see I'm a former Marine NCO... so they teach you a lot of that stuff...as soon as he turned away from Jackie and he started walking back toward the door, he didn't make eye contact with me...He was acting like he was crying, but he wasn't crying. And I just, something's not right. (p. 1000)

Of course, something "*wasn't right.*" The 21-month old daughter of his girlfriend, whom he saw alive about 14 hours earlier, had died. As the older, more experienced, parent in the household, Chad felt very, very badly that he hadn't seen what might be coming, and hadn't done enough to avoid it by insisting that Amanda seek medical attention for Kassidy, or seeking it himself for Kassidy. It doesn't make sense that he was actively avoiding Robert Conley's eyes, after embracing, and crying with, Jacqueline Conley only seconds before. There was too much speculation in this tragedy about how people SHOULD act, communicate or feel at any one time.

As the interview was concluding, Conley said, "*..all these problems with Kassidy started when he came into the picture....*[all ok] *until she left a... month and a half ago.*" Thus, his estimate of Amanda's move to Rochester was about late September instead of late June. In addition to bruises on Kassidy, Conley said, "*we have seen Mandy and I've seen marks on her....face.*" (p. 1000) However, he didn't say when he had made those observations, and he said he didn't say anything at the time, because he figured that Jacqueline would say something.

By this time on Thursday evening, November 9, Conley had heard of the ball playing accident of the previous night. He said, "*...I've seen Chad throw a wiffle ball, he played with Scott at Auburn. It would really take some doing to hit a wiffle ball to leave a bruise.*" Jeff Smith echoed the thought, "*That's why they call it wiffle ball.*" (p. 1000) Each man seemed to be doing what happened so often in this case, which was to resolve uncertainty and ambiguity in a way that assumed Chad abused and killed Kassidy and that he was lying about the ballhitting incident of November 8. Earlier, Conley had interpreted the failure to have eye contact in a negative way. Each man seemed to assume that since a wiffle ball couldn't cause a bruise, Chad must have been lying, and, even worse, the bruise was caused by some criminal action. Neither man seems to have considered the idea that it wasn't a wiffle ball, but a Tee-ball, and such balls can easily cause bruises to children. Conley came close to the answer when he said, "*You should not be playing ball with a kid who, he was saying, was not doing too good. Something's wrong with the kid. They should have been, you know, throwing something else. That's common sense.*" (p. 1000) If Chad and Robert Conley had talked that evening, and even made eye contact, Chad would have agreed with him on that point. He lacked common sense when he tossed that Tee-ball to Kyle. The interview ended at 10:35 p.m. There was only one reference to Jeff during the entire interview, and Conley knew him for a longer period of time than he knew Chad. That single reference was when Conley stated, without a question from Jeff Smith about Jeff Marshall, that Jeff Marshall and Jennifer had been to the new Conley home in Buckfield, whereas Chad had not.

Ten minutes later, the police interrogation of Chad ended, and Chad left the police station, accompanied by Sgt. Matthew Stewart who told Chad about the need to impound and search his car. Sgt. Stewart restated his belief that Chad was responsible and Chad offered to take a lie detector test "*Hook me up, now,*" he said. Sgt. Stewart said that because Chad had asked for a lawyer, such a polygraph exam was no longer possible, which may have been a reasonable prediction, but was not an accurate portrayal of the law. Sgt. Stewart gave Chad his business card. As Sgt. Stewart didn't write a report of his interactions with Chad on this day, this recollection of the moments after leaving the police station is Chad's.

Chad then saw others in the parking lot, including Jeff Marshall. Each man viewed the other as responsible for Kassidy's death. Chad said to Jeff, "*Son of a bitch. I hope you rot in hell for what you did to Kassidy. And then you go and try to blame it on me.*" Chad recalls that Jeff said that he had said nothing to the police to blame Chad, but that wasn't true. Actually each man had talked about the other and his care for Kassidy, though Jeff had said a lot more about Chad than vice versa, and much of what Jeff said about Chad was false.

Around 11:00 p.m., Chad went to the home of his friend, Bruce, in Rochester, along with his sister, Nicole, and brother-in-law, Brandon.

After leaving the Kittery Police Station, Jeff and Jennifer and Amanda went to Dunkin' Donuts and then to Jeff's home at 51 Rogers Road. Initially, they went to William Peirce's home, next door at Johnston Court, as the police were still at Jeff's, and there they talked with Will and Amanda's mother, and uncle, Robert. Jeff said, "*Mandy got real mad cause Mandy's mother said, 'fuckin ...Chad killed her,' like that and Amanda freaked.*" [Jeff interview, Nov. 10, p. 1619] If Jacqueline had said these words, it would have been approximately seven hours after she said to Chad in the afternoon when they first met at the police station, "*What did he* [Jeff] *do to my baby?*"

At 11:42 p.m., Maine State Police Detective Herbert Leighton completed his search of Jeff's home. The search took one officer about two hours and 35 minutes. At 11:45 p.m.,

Detective Leighton talked briefly with Jeff at Jeff's home about items seized during voluntary search, and Jeff signed a receipt. Det. Leighton also asked Jeff about the "Wendy's napkin" with a stain and about the Spaghetti-O's in the sink. (p. 1195) The Spaghetti-O's were probably eaten by Kassidy the previous day, Wednesday or even Tuesday.

In her "My Life Story," Amanda described her view of late Thursday evening, *After I got out of the police station that night Jeff, Jen, and I went straight to their house. After we talked at Will's for like 15 minutes. Get this. There was no police there. Just tape around their house. Which means the cops probably stayed there for maybe a couple hours. I remember them at Chad's house for almost three days. They obviously didn't check Jeff's house very good.*

Another weird thing was when we got to Jeff's house he practically ran in the house, and was rummaging in the house freaking out because they took a couple things. Then I kept complaining, saying I wanted to leave. I did not want to be there cause she had died there that day. After he was done rummaging through his stuff, he said, "Why don't you and Jen go wait in the car. I'll be out in a minute." So we did. Now that I think about it now if he had something there he obviously got rid of the evidence. After finally about I don't know, an hour or so, we finally were headed to a hotel. But of course, Jeff had to stop at Dunkin Donuts. He parked in front and said I think we need to talk, and I was like, "No, I am not going in there I just lost my baby, I don't want to talk. I want to lie down and just die." So he went through the drive through. And let me tell you, he didn't get your everyday midnight snack. He bought and ate a ton of food. My baby practically died in his arms and he wanted to sit, talk, and eat. Also he showed no emotion whatsoever. He was even cracking jokes and just laughing, like nothing happened.

At 11:59 p.m., Chad went to his home and put his dog, Kato, into the kennel and took Kassidy's kitten with him. There was a police officer present and he allowed Chad only to open the door to let the animals out. Subsequently, until November 15, he and his parents and sister, Nicole, resided with Chad's friend, Bruce, in Rochester. During that time, the police had full control of Chad's home and spent many hours searching for evidence and taking photographs.

At midnight Jeff, Jennifer and Amanda went to the Anchorage Inn in Portsmouth for the night. Amanda had indicated strongly that she didn't want to spend the night in the apartment where her daughter died the same day, and she didn't want to go with her mother and stepuncle to Buckfield.

As of November 9, it had been five months to the day since Kassidy had been introduced to Chad by Amanda on Friday June 9. For some, that was enough of a coincidence to believe that Chad caused Kassidy's death.

CHAPTER 5: INVESTIGATING CHAD EVANS 10 NOVEMBER 2000 TO 20 AUGUST 2001

"Chad didn't do it. You twisted around everything I said." - Amanda Bortner

"... it was almost a family joke that no one other than Marshall and his girlfriend Jennifer Conley could babysit Cassidy,.. "
- attributed to Jeff Marshall by Sgt. Jim White.

"I have a hard time with people making accusations about someone they don't know." - Jeremy Hinton

Friday, 10 November 2000

By the beginning of the second day of the investigation into the death of Kassidy Bortner, the police had developed their theory of the case, which was that her death was a homicide and that a person was responsible and that person was Chad Evans. The Convict-Chad train was moving forward on one track and accelerating.

At the Anchorage Inn in one bedroom, Amanda was with her sister, Jennifer, but also with Jeff at whose home and in whose care Kassidy died. Seeking to make sense of her tragedy and seeking the company of the man she loved, Amanda called Chad at Bruce's house, despite the police efforts to persuade her not to have contact with him. The cell phone batteries in Jeff's phone ran low, so Amanda called from the motel room phone using Jeff's credit card, and one call was for 115 minutes.

As was agreed in their calls, Chad and his sister came to Amanda, Jeff and Jen's room around 6:00 a.m. and Amanda went downstairs to talk with them. Later, she returned with Nicole to the room, retrieved her belongings and then left with Nicole and Chad. She was struggling with the choice that the police had forced upon her: between her family and the police on one side and Chad and his family on the other.

Shortly after Amanda left with Chad and Nicole, Jeff called the police and advised them that Amanda had talked with Chad during the long night and the police agreed to meet him and Jennifer at their home at 51 Rogers Street..

At 9 a.m. on the 10th, the initial autopsy of Kassidy's body began, and continued until 2:45 p.m. Detective Erik Baker attended the autopsy. To evaluate Kassidy's height and weight in comparison with others, the Chief Medical Examiner's office used a "Ross Growth & Development Program" chart for "Girls: Birth to 36 Months - Physical Growth, NCHS Percentiles. Kassidy was 33 inches tall, which was right at the 50% mark, whereas at birth, she was 21.5 inches tall, which was at the higher end of the range for children her age.

At death, she weighed 22 pounds which was between the 10th and 25th percentile in frequency. She weighed 8 ½ pounds at birth. Thus, at death she was at average height and below average weight. The autopsy report did not indicate the source of the information about Kassidy's height and weight at birth, but it was from the Southern Maine Medical Center, where Kassidy was born. During her third interview, Amanda told Angela Blodgett that Kassidy weighed eight pounds and 13 ounces, so she wasn't the source of that birth information. (Interview, page 80)

At 9:00 a.m., Sergeant James White arrived at the Rochester Police Dept with a Search Warrant for Chad's home. At 10:50 a.m. a number of police from Rochester and the New Hampshire State Police, and with Det. Linscott from the Maine State Police assisting, began the search. Sgt. William Magee was responsible for taking photographs and Sgt. Susan Forey took videos and drew the diagrams of the home. The search lasted for 9 hours and 45 minutes, until 8:15 p.m. when the home was released to Travis. See assorted search documents, including careful diagrams and a narrative of the search. (p. 3077-3120) The items which were seized were listed as "*Assorted bats, balls, bed linens, diapers, blankets, comforters, clothing, miscellaneous drugs and drug paraphernalia.*" (p. 3085) Three presumably soiled diapers were seized. One was found on Chad's and Amanda's bed where Amanda changed Kassidy's diaper on the morning of November 9.

Its location on the bed was an indication of the family rush that morning. The other two were in the bedroom wastebasket. (See search report, pp 3099, 3106, 3115, 3118) The referenced drug was marijuana, of which only residue was found in the basement bedroom, where housemates had lived, and where Travis lived in the fall of 2000. (p. 3078) While the bats and balls were clearly associated with the ballhitting accident which Chad described to the police, none of the evidence seized was ever shown to have any connection to any of the injuries or blows which were thought to have caused Kassidy's death. DNA tests were done on the items and the results were negative for blood or other evidence of crime.

There were many photographs taken of every room of the house, including the basement. In the kitchen, photographs were taken of the trash barrel and its emptied contents where could be seen the half-eaten banana which Chad had told police Kassidy had eaten on the evening of the 8th. (Chad interrogation, p. 1493) However, no photographs appear to have been taken of the trash contents in Chad's study which is where he was sitting with Kassidy after her bath and where she was eating a popsicle. If photographs had been taken, the discarded wrapper and wooden stick would have been seen, and they would have added further confirmation to Chad's and Travis's recollection of the events of the evening of Nov 8.

To support his application for a search warrant, Sgt. White prepared an Affidavit based on the interviews and reports of the previous day. It included the circumstances of Kassidy's death.

From Dr. Bock came this information:

-multiple pin-prick marks all over [the bottoms of] *both feet;*
-bruising on Kassidy's arms, stomach, chest, face, and head.
-multiple bruises the size of a dime or quarter all over Kassidy's head.
-bilateral and diffused retinal hemorrhages... indicative of closed head injury.
-Cassidy's hair appeared unusually thin in the back.
-Cassidy's vagina was irritated and visibly swollen, [and] *suspicious.*
-irritation to Cassidy's anus.
-[Kassidy's lethargy] *would be consistent with a head injury.*

White's affidavit continued to spell Kassidy's first name with a "C." Perhaps the error was symbolic of the overall quality of the investigation where some basic information was omitted and not requested, such as photographs of Kassidy and a time-line for the entire period of Chad's relationship to Kassidy. The six page affidavit is remarkably detailed, given that the police interviews had not yet been transcribed.

The affidavit stated the information about Chad which had been received from identified sources. From Jeff came the information that on Wednesday, Kyle had "*hit Kassidy in the head with a baseball,*" which was a correct term for the type of ball, but not precise. Included were three statements that Chad's calls to Jeff about Kassidy on Wednesday and Thursday were "*very unusual because Evans had rarely, if ever, expressed concern for Cassidy's welfare in the past.*"

About his babysitting, Marshall stated "*that* ***it was almost a family joke that no one other than Marshall and his girlfriend Jennifer Conley could babysit Cassidy,*** *due to concern that anyone else would report the injuries.*" This allegation is not in any transcript of the first, or any, interview of Jeff, but it would be reported later in the newspapers.

About the incident of Kassidy's fall from his truck on Saturday, October 28th, "*Marshall stated that approximately two weeks ago he was babysitting Cassidy. When he took Cassidy out of his truck, he placed her in the bed of the truck. Marshall was fixing some straps in the front of his truck. When he turned around Cassidy fell over. He stated that Cassidy was not bruised as a result of this incident and was fine afterward. He stated that she might have had a scratch from falling.*" This description had more information about the fall than was in the transcript of Jeff's interview of November 9 where he said, *she fell out of the* [truck], *she didn't hit her face or nothing, she seemed like she didn't have any bruise on her,...* (Interview, p. 1317) The "*two weeks ago*" estimate of the date of the fall didn't come from Jeff's interview, but may have come from Jennifer's interview, at page 928-29, where she said, "*Like two weeks ago, three...,*" or from Amanda's interview.

The affidavit stated, "*Marshall stated that Evans is an abusive person and a heavy drinker. He also stated that Evans takes cocaine. Marshall indicated on one occasion he observed marks around Amanda Bortner's neck. Marshall stated that Bortner told him that Evans had caused this bruising on her neck.*"

From Angela Blodgett's interview with Amanda came the information that "*Evans had abused Cassidy for approximately 4-6 weeks. Bortner related several instances when Evans would abuse Cassidy. She stated that Evans would grab Cassidy's face and cause bruising. He would also grab Cassidy's arm and throw her against the wall....that Evans' son hit Cassidy in the head with a wiffle ball...*

From Scott Harakles' interview of Travis came the information that Kyle had "*hit Cassidy in the eye with a ball....*[and] *Evans' son confirmed that he hit Cassidy in the eye.*" From Chad's interview came the information that "*Cassidy was hit in the eye by a hard rubber ball,*" Information from Bruce's and Tristan's interviews was also included.

The affidavit concluded, "*Based on the foregoing there is probable cause to believe that evidence of the crime of homicide will be found in the house at 191 Milton Road in Rochester.*"

Asst. Atty General Delker filed a "Motion to Seal Application for Search Warrant, Affidavit in Support of Application, and any Resulting Search Warrant," (p. 218) and it stated, "*Premature disclosure of the information ... may compromise the integrity of an on-going criminal investigation by revealing the identities of witnesses and investigative information known to authorities... and any warrants that may issue may result in prejudicial pretrial publicity.*" The Attorney General's concern about publicity was warranted as the newspaper coverage was already extensive, and the motion was approved by Judge Jones of the Rochester District Court.

Back in Kittery, Sgt Jeff Smith reported that at 9:45 a.m., he and Detective Hamel met Jeff and Jennifer at their home. Jeff told the officers of Amanda's calls with Chad earlier that morning from the motel and how Amanda left with Chad and Nicole. Smith added, "*I received from Jeffrey Marshall a baby car seat that Jennifer Conley and he had used to transport Kassidy Bortner in his truck while baby sitting. Jeffrey Marshall removed the car seat from his truck last night at approximately 11:00 p.m. and he left it on the porch of his residence.*" (p. 177) One question that could have been asked was when was the car seat put into Jeff's truck. Amanda's routine was to take it out of her car and leave it on the porch when bringing Kassidy in to the apartment. If it was left on the porch on Thursday morning the 9th, when did Jeff put it into the truck?

Steve Hamel interviewed Will Peirce outside of Jeff and Jennifer's apartment for a few minutes, and returned to the Kittery Police Dept. At 10:45 a.m., reported Detective Smith, Hamel called Jeff and Jennifer and asked them to come to the police station for more recorded interviews. They arrived at 11:15 a.m. and at 11:30 a.m., Jennifer's interview began.

Jennifer Bortner, second interview.

MSP Detectives Jeffrey Smith and Lance McCleish conducted the second interview with Jennifer at the Kittery Police Dept. Smith participated in Jennifer's first interview the previous day, but McCleish was substituted for Jennifer's other first interview investigator, Steve Hamel. McCleish had interviewed Chad the previous evening. The transcript says that the interview began at 9:45 a.m. and ended at 10:30, but these times conflict with Detective Smith's timeline in his "Continuation Report" of his activities that morning, which said that he interviewed Jennifer at 11:30 a.m.

Jennifer said about Amanda's calls the previous night at the Anchorage Inn,
She [Amanda] *was telling Chad that she knows he killed Kassidy. She told Chad that... he threatened to kill her like he said that he wished she was dead and she wasn't even born...she's telling him how he strangled her* [Amanda]... *My sister told me that he did that once, too...She told me that a while ago. How he did it to her once when they got in a fight.*

[and to Kassidy, too] *...and it cut her* [Kassidy's] *air off... He hurt her really bad.* (p. 1143-44)

Later, Jennifer said that this was the first time she had heard anything about Chad saying such a thing to Amanda. She continued,

Oh God. That's my niece...I kinda had a suspicion something was going on because of all the bruises on Kassidy on her face all the time. Ever since she started dating Chad....And they came up with excuses and I believed them. (p. 1144)

After Jennifer explained her feeling of regret, "*...I should of said something,*" Jeff Smith said, "*... I really believe Chad is responsible for Kassidy's death. For whatever reason, your sister wants to protect Chad.*" Jennifer responded, "*And I hate Chad. I never want to see him.*" (p. 1146) Several times in the interview, Jennifer said that she didn't say anything to anyone because she didn't want Amanda to "*lose her kid.*" (p. 1152) Jennifer made a new allegation that Amanda had said that Chad had told Amanda that "*...he'd hold her* [Kassidy's] *nose shut whenever she was crying just to shut her up...*" (p. 1146)

Trying to make Jennifer feel better about her inaction, Lance McCleish referred to the tragedy of Kassidy's death as "*just like a train wreck. This is just craziness what's going on.. obviously you feel bad...people make mistakes all the time.*" (p. 1147) He told Jennifer his perspective on the case so far, "*...these injuries didn't come from a baseball, and didn't come from falling down, didn't come from walking into a wall or a coffee table, okay.... these injuries happened from being inflicted by another person.*" (p. 1149) It had been almost 24 hours since Kassidy's death.

Drawing a distinction between hitting and spanking, Jennifer said, "*I've never seen my sister hit that kid. I've never seen her hit her kid....*" A few seconds later, Jennifer said, "*I've seen her swat her on the butt when she's been with me... but that was just a, 'No,' ...it wasn't so bad that she's bruised...*" (p. 1152)

About Amanda's departure that morning with Nicole and Chad, Jennifer said, "*I begged her not to leave this morning. I begged her not to talk to him on the phone. I cried.. How can she...take his side... he fucking killed her kid.... he doesn't deserve to live.*" Amanda told Jennifer that morning, when leaving, that she needed to pick up some new contact lenses and do some errands. Then Jennifer described her own last moments with Kassidy, "*...I was leaving, she's all 'Kiss's.' I gave her a kiss.*" (p. 1153)

Amanda's ambivalence about what happened to Kassidy was reflected in Jennifer's recollections. She recalled from hearing Amanda's calls with Chad, that the two of them discussed Kassidy's problems, "*and they were saying* [it was] *because she fell out of Jeff's truck. They were saying...that's what happened.*" At another time Jennifer "*heard her screaming, 'I know you killed my kid. I know you killed my kid.' And she goes, 'and you remember* [t]*hat you didn't want the kid to be around, and you wished the kid wasn't alive...'* " (p. 1153) As Amanda always referred to Kassidy as "*Kassidy*," or "*Kass*," "Baby," or "*my baby*," it's unlikely that Jennifer's recollection of Amanda using the expression, "*my kid*" is correct.

Jennifer described how her family was torn about Kassidy's death and tensions were high. She said that her "*...mother said* [to Amanda], *'That man's bad. That man's bad.' ...You know, but Mandy called my mother a bitch and told her to shut up, and my mom started crying."* (p. 1156)

Thus, the family lineup was Amanda on one side and all the other members of the Bortner/Conley family, including Jeff, on the other.

Jennifer repeated several of the allegations of the first interview, such as that Chad called Kassidy stupid, or a bitch, and that Kassidy was afraid of Chad, and no one else.

Jennifer said that she and Jeff babysat for Kassidy over a weekend "*because he was going to his family's house and he didn't want them to see the kid 'cause the kid had a big hand print on her face... It looked like... he picked her up by her head... a big man's handprint...we babysitted her for those two nights cause she* [Amanda] *went to his family's house and he didn't want them to see the bruises.*" (p. 1158) The officers did not ask for a date estimate on that weekend babysitting stint. Chad and his parents maintain that Chad and Amanda visited them only twice together, in July and August, and both times Kassidy was with them. Amanda told Blodgett and LeClair that she and Kassidy had been to Chad's parents' home twice for "*fun*." (Amanda interview, p. 861) Chad told LeClair and MacLeish that Kasssidy often fell at his parents' pool. (Chad, interrogation, p. 1503) If Amanda's and Chad's and his parents' recollections are correct, then Jennifer's was false. The police never interviewed Chad's parents.

Jennifer said that she had bathed Kassidy once and changed her diapers an uncertain number of times. Asked about other bruises, she said, "*The only thing that I've ever noticed on her butt was, because she used to go down the stairs on her butt. And she did it at my house, too....She slides... instead of walking down the stairs...*" (p. 1159) Jennifer had described this practice by Kassidy in her interview the previous day. (p. 917) Amanda described it in her first interview on the 9th. (p. 835) Thus, there was no question that Kassidy used this method to come down the stairs. The question remained about the frequency, location and severity of the resulting bruises.

Later, Jennifer said that the one bath she gave Kassidy was during an overnight babysitting early in Chad's and Amanda's relationship. (p. 1168) This would have been in July or August. She seemed to imply that there were no bruises on Kassidy at that time. Of the five overnight babysitting stints for Kassidy at Jeff and Jennifer's, the first three were on July 1, and August 12 and 18. After a gap of two months, the last two were on October 21 and 26 and 27. McCleish accused Jennifer of previously withholding information, compared to what Jeff told them, "..*he had a lot* [to say]. *You gave us about one-quarter of what he gave us, okay?*" Jennifer assured them, "*No. I've told you everything*." (p. 1160)

Jennifer described the moving-in process for Amanda, after first meeting Chad, "*...she was with my mom like two days a week, and then she'd come down and stay with Chad the rest of the week...she hasn't been like officially moved in with him for like probably about three, three and a half weeks....*" (p. 1163) Jennifer said that the abuse by Chad began "*when she started dating him... when they were started to get serious...it's been getting a lot worse ever since she moved in with him.*" (p. 1163)

Regarding the dating of Amanda's and Kassidy's move to Chad's, Jennifer said "*...then she* [Amanda] *moved in with Chad because they moved up to Auburn* [actually, Kingfield] *and they didn't have enough room for her. And..she wasn't there anyway, you know. You know, she wasn't there at all, ever. So her and Kassidy were always with Chad...*" (p. 1164) To anchor those observations, the Conley's move to Buckfield was on October 1.

McCleish asked Jennifer about an incident on a Kassidy overnight, and Jennifer said, "*...we were sleeping one night in bed, me and Jeff, and... she slept on the couch...we came in and checked on her... in the middle of the night... and she's standing up on the middle of the room looking around...*" (p. 1164-65) Jennifer was not asked for a date for this staring-at-the-wall incident. Most likely it occurred during the October overnights, as this period included other reports of Kassidy's behavior changes.

McCleish asked "*have you seen...Chad say, 'Look at how stupid she is. She just* [is] *standing there. She won't even play.' Or did he tell you about this stuff?*" (p. 1165) Jennifer responded, "*I've seen him say that.*" During Chad's 153 days of knowing Kassidy, after meeting her on Friday, June 9, Chad, Kassidy and Jennifer were together in the same place only four times. They were during the two overnight visits to Auburn by Chad, Amanda and Kassidy on June 20 and July 20, and at an afternoon barbecue at Chad's on Sunday June 25 and at a quick lunch at the Rochester McDonald's in October.
Chad never said to anyone, anywhere, that Kassidy was stupid, and especially not in her grandmother's home. Later, seemingly contradicting her earlier comment Jennifer said, "*I didn't really see them together... we were all together once basically like an outdoor barbecue at Chad's house, and Kassidy was playing on the trampoline with all the other kids. .. and she was doing fine. Scotty, my little 5-year old brother, was over and she was playing with Scotty...*" (p. 1166) That barbecue was on Sunday, June 25. Given the fun that Jennifer described, that, too, seems like an unlikely time for Chad to call Kassidy stupid.

Jennifer described another "standing-staring" incident as related to her, "*Jeff told me one time he was sitting there watching TV and she was just standing there watching TV, standing up watching TV.... I mean falling asleep.... while she was standing up, and he went over and he picked her up and put her on the couch.*" (p. 1165) Before Kassidy's death, neither Amanda nor Chad ever heard of these observations of Kassidy standing and staring, from either Jeff or Jennifer.

Returning to the belief that Kassidy's bruises "*started to get really bad*" when Amanda and Kassidy moved in with Chad, Jennifer said "... *I've never changed her diapers.... I mean, we'd have her for like an hour and then he'd pick her up...*" (p. 1167) It was a curious statement, as she stated at other times during both interviews, so far, that she **had** done a diaper change. Also, she said during the previous day's interview that she had given Kassidy a bath. A few minutes earlier, during this second interview, she answered "*Yeah*" about whether she had ever changed Kassidy's diapers, at page 1158. During her interview the previous day, she said, "*...I've changed her diapers, and she's been fine.*" (p. 938) Also, she did say that she had applied some "boom-x" to Kassidy's butt for her diaper rash, which could have been done without changing a diaper, but that seems unlikely. In 2011, Chad recalled that this diaper rash cream was "Balmex."

Also, regarding the implication of a routine that "*....he'd pick her up,*" Chad picked up Kassidy at Jeff's and Jennifer's apartment only once during the 153 days he knew her, and that was on Wednesday, November 8. The other two times that Chad could be said to have "*pick*[ed] *her up*" were on two of the three Thursdays of Amanda's and Nicole's money management classes. On those two occasions, he met Jeff at Newington, New Hampshire, Sears parking lot, on October 19, and he met Nicole and Amanda at the Newington McDonald's parking lot on November 2.

Jennifer added to previous allegations of Chad holding Kassidy's "*mouth,*" by saying that Amanda "*freaked out on him and told him never to touch her* [Kassidy] *again. And he said he'd change and he was crying and everything like that. They had a confrontation about it...within the past month.*" (p. 1168) While pointing out that discipline was only a small part of his relationship with Kassidy, Chad estimates that the communications with Kassidy which he thought were important enough to ensure that he and she had eye contact, from July 9 through November 9, occurred approximately 2-3 times a week, or 50-75 times. The moments of eye contact were not all disciplinary. Sometimes, eye contact was sought to communicate important messages about safety, such as staying away from Kato when he was eating or drinking water from his dishes. Of those, he estimated that he held Kassidy's face to ensure such contact about 12 times, and of those, 3-4 caused bruising. Chad has long thought that one of those 3-4 times was close enough to the time of Kassidy's death that the bruises on her lower cheeks were a fading remnant. However, no such bruises were observed at the family gathering at Nicole's on Sunday, November 5, and Dr. Greenwald did not record an observation of such bruises. Chad recalls a discussion with Amanda when they both discovered that some bruises on Kassidy's lower cheeks likely came from his handholding, and that he should not squeeze so hard; but there was no "confrontation" about the issue, and Chad did not cry during any such discussion.

Jennifer said that Amanda told her that, "*Kassidy would... freak out whenever Chad was trying to kiss* [Amanda]*...Mandy told me ... that he would be like* [to Kassidy] *'Be quiet, be quiet... knock it off,' and she'd throw a fit.... and Chad's* [response] *would be... that's when Chad would hold her mouth shut. Picked her up and put her under burning* [later corrected by Jennifer to '*running*'] *water because every time Chad picked her up and she was crying, she'd start screaming, like screaming at the top of her lungs. Amanda's like, 'don't touch my kid.'*" Later in the interview, Jennifer's understanding of the incident was more accurate, "*...it was just running water and* [he] *sprinkled it on her face to make her shut up...*" (p. 1173) It must be remembered that after the end of August, Jennifer saw Kassidy and Chad together once, at the brief lunch at the Rochester McDonald's in October, and that get together was initiated by Chad.

Everything she just related to the police was what she recalled from her conversations with Amanda. As with the classic story of what happens when a story is told to the first of a number of people in a circle or line, the story that emerges at the end of the line is always different. In this instance, the flicking water in Kassidy's face, which effectively stopped her from hyperventilating, was not holding her under running water. As was described during Chad's interview, the sprinkling of water on Kassidy's face was not "*to make her shut up*," but to stop a temper tantrum that was causing Kassidy to have difficulty breathing.

Lance McCleish returned to another allegation by Jennifer, that Chad "*had choked Kassidy at one time?*" and Jennifer said, "*Yeah, Mandy said it wasn't that hard...she just told me it once...*" (p. 1170) McCleish asked, "*Is that the first time that you heard about him choking* [Kassidy]?" and Jennifer responded, "*I heard about him choking Mandy... all along... maybe, I've made an assumption... That he was doing it to Kassidy....And she* [Amanda] *said that to him on the phone* [last night], *'Remember when you put your hands around Kassidy's neck? You know, and Kassidy was choking, you cut her off. She couldn't breathe for a few minutes...*" (p. 1171) Aside from sexual play, Chad never choked Amanda, and never sought to cut off her breathing, and never came close to such behavior with Kassidy. As Jennifer said, "*Maybe, I've made an assumption.*"

Lance McCleish asked generally about "*every conversation you had last night with your sister about what kind of abuse he did to her?*" (p. 1172) Jennifer said that when they went to the hotel room, at the Anchorage Inn, Amanda,

started balling and she's like, "He killed her." You know, "He choked her"...he would hold her nose shut. He'd pinch her mouth, and she'd seen him do it. She said she'd freak out at him, when he did it, but she had seen him do it....and name calling.. Always talking about her being stupid. He, Jeff, would joke around ...Chad would be like, "That kid's fucking stupid," and Jeff's like, "There is something wrong with her," ... Jeff would just joke around about it with Mandy, too.... they were teasing Mandy about her kid being stupid. (p. 1172)

This was the only time that anyone alleged that Chad held Kassidy's nose shut or pinched her mouth, even if in a playful matter, and that didn't happen either. Jennifer said that once she responded to such conversation, "*I was like, 'The only reason she is being stupid is because she keeps getting bruises on her face and you guys are accidentally hurting her.'*" (p. 1173)

Then, Jennifer explained some of her resentment of Chad, who, "*... is talking about my family and how my parents didn't teach us how to... spend our money. He sent my sister to a money management course... We were really poor when we were growing up. We were just poor kids on our own. ... I gave my mother every paycheck I had...And he* [Chad]*... tried to tell Jeff that... my parents needled my money off of me and that's why I'm not good at managing money...*" (p. 1173) Chad had no idea about how Jennifer managed her money, and he never suggested that she might benefit from the money management course that Amanda and Nicole attended.

Jennifer told McCleish and Smith that Chad was "*pinching the* [Kassidy's] *nose*" but there was no further discussion of that allegation. The transcript of the interview ended with an audiotape malfunction.

11:40 a.m. Friday, 10 November. Jeff Marshall, second interview.

Kittery Police Detective Steve Hamel and MSP Detective Scott Harakles conducted a second interview with Jeff Marshall at the Kittery Police Dept. Harakles had interviewed Jeff the previous day, and Hamel replaced Jeff's other previous interviewer, Jeff Linscott. Jeff noted that when bringing and picking up Kassidy from his babysitting, "*they're always late... she was supposed to drop the child off at, I believe, at 8:00....never showed up till quarter past...*" (p. 1611) In this time-challenged case, every clarification of time is important. For the babysitting of Kassidy during the last week of her life, Monday-Thursday, the drop-off time for Kassidy was 8:00 a.m. on two of the four days, Tuesday and Thursday. On Monday, it was about 8:30 a.m. and Wednesday, about 3:00 p.m. Regarding the bruising on Kassidy's face Jeff said, in seeming contradiction, "*She always had bruises right here on her face... but they'd go away and then they would come back... it was like he was somewhat, was continuously, grabbing her face... and that was the only injury to her at that time. They were kinda fading away...*" (p. 1612) He distinguished between the "*pigeon-toed*" problem and an injury to Kassidy's leg in causing her "*trouble walking*" on Wednesday, November 9. Jeff said, "*Oh yeah, he* [Chad] *grabbed her leg.*

Mandy called our house and said, 'Chad did something to her leg...you know, I'm sure [it's] *in the autopsy. I'm sure they can tell there was something wrong because the girl could not walk...*" (p. 1612)

Jeff said that there was a bruise on Wednesday on Kassidy's chin. (p. 1613) Later, in apparent contradiction, he said, "*...she had no bruises when she left my house* [Wednesday] *and that's why yesterday morning* [Thursday] *when she came to my house and Mandy says, 'Look at her face,' ... I mean, something happened.*" (p. 1616) Jeff said that while he was waiting for Chad to arrive to pick up Kassidy on Wednesday, he put Kassidy in the truck, and moved it within the parking areas, "*I didn't have a car seat to put her in. She sat in the front seat of the truck...waiting for him to come... went back in, and then his lights pulled in the driveway and I brought her out with her little bag...*" (p. 1614)

Jeff said that when Chad called from the Dover Tolls area to tell Jeff, "*... she's acting really weird...she's kinda babbing* [bobbing] *back and forth,' and I'm like, obviously, I said, 'You should take her to the hospital....'* " (p. 1616) Chad has no recollection of Jeff making that recommendation, and Jeff didn't mention it in his first interview the previous day. He did say in that first interview that during a subsequent call on Wednesday evening, that "***I should have probably told him last night***" *to take Kassidy to the hospital.* (Jeff Interview, November 9, 2000, p. 1308, emphasis added here) This was an example of what I call "recollection enhancement," which occurred at various times during the investigation and trial, and it usually occurred to support the theory of the case held by the person, on both sides of the case, making the statements.

Jeff described Chad's second call to him that afternoon about Kassidy's fall in the driveway, and then the third call, "*...he's like, 'Oh, man,... she got hit by a baseball... I was tossin' the baseball to my son and he can hit some good ones.... She got nailed in the face by a baseball..'* ." Jeff said it was "*odd to get these phone calls... and the other part that bothers me...he called his ex-wife and told her the same god damn thing. That bothers me as far as why is he calling me...*" (p. 1617) What Jeff didn't know was that Chad and Kyle called Tristan almost every night before Kyle went to bed at Chad's house.

Even though Jeff said "*baseball*" four times in his answer to the previous question, Scott Harakles, responded, "*So he tells you the wiffle ball story?*" (p. 1617) The police didn't believe that there was a ball-hitting accident. As noted before, they didn't understand that the injuring ball was a Tee-ball, or "*starter baseball*" or "*hard rubber ball*" as Chad had told McCleish and LeClair the previous night. Instead, they stuck to their understanding that it was a bogus "*wiffle ball*" story, and another example of Chad lying. It was around this time that a policeman identified only as "HAM" joined the interview, and asked several questions. Instead of being initials, which was how the interview transcripts identified participants, "HAM" may have been a shorter version of "Hamel" for Kittery Detective Steve Hamel, who had previously interviewed Jennifer that morning.

Asked to describe Kassidy's condition or appearance on Thursday morning, Jeff said, "*... she had bruises all over her face.*" and the previous afternoon, "*she didn't even have... red face... a beginning of bruises or nothing...*" (p. 1618)

Jeff recalled his confrontation with Chad the previous evening at the police station, and Jeff's recollection was similar to Chad's, "*he's like, '...I can't believe you told 'em this.... how could you do that to me?..'* " except that Jeff recalled in addition, that Chad said, *"he's like, 'I loved that child...'* " (p. 1619) By this point each man had accepted a key part of the police's theory of the case, which was that Kassidy's death was a homicide. Each man believed that the other was her killer.

Scott Harakles asked Jeff about what he knew of Chad's sexual relationship with Amanda, hoping perhaps to find some type of deviance, which would relate to the preliminary indications of sexual abuse of Kassidy. He asked, "*... I gotta ask you... do you know if Chad is the kind a guy that uses a dildo in sex...is the kind a guy that does that stuff?*" Jeff said, "*I don't know... I question the fact because they have one of those strap on dildo things ya know and ... I said, 'what the hell does have this for'... and nothin' was ever said to me about why...*" (p. 1623) Jeff was not asked how he knew this information, or whether he had actually seen such a device. In fact, Chad and Amanda had an excellent, satisfying sexual relationship, and that did not include a dildo or any kind of "*strap on*" device. As Jeremy said in his interview, they were "*sexually active.*" Harakles didn't ask Jeff about his own sexual relationship to Jennifer, but Jeff offered, "*... we get a little kinky, we never use toys like that though...*" (p. 1623) Neither Chad nor Amanda was asked for details about their sexual life, but Jeff was asked about Chad and Amanda, as was Melissa Chick. Freudians would argue that sexually happy people are less likely to abuse people, but Harakles was interested in finding sexual deviance and not whether Chad and Amanda were happy.

Moving to the primary reason for the second interviews for Jeff and Jennifer that morning, i.e. Amanda's calls and activities since midnight, Jeff said that Amanda had gone out to Chad's car around 6:20 a.m., and had come back about an hour and a half later with Nicole to retrieve Amanda's belongings. Jeff said that Amanda and Chad talked, it seemed, *"all night long*" and "*we finally got her off the phone and... she's like, 'I can't believe, I don't believe he did this. I love him...*" (p. 1620) Jeff said that he and Jennifer strongly advised Amanda not to go with Chad, just as they had discouraged her from talking with him from their hotel room. However, Jeff did permit Amanda to use his credit card for most of the calls. They told Amanda that they would be calling the police, "*...'cause this is bullshit,'* " to tell them about Amanda's calls and her leaving with Chad. (p. 1621)

Jeff then said, "*I don't really wanna see this guy* [Chad] *but I'll do anything I can... whether it means having a tape recorder or something on me... and trying to catch him speak. If I can get anything out of em... or even her.... I do think she knows something....*" (p. 1624) The police didn't pursue Jeff's offer, but he followed up on the idea later, with a secret taping of Amanda.

Jeff told the police that he and Jennifer thought that maybe Amanda had a sexual relationship with Travis..."*we... thought...maybe she was screwing around with Travis...cause things... were a little bizarre.*" (p. 1624) The transcript of the interview ended abruptly with a tape change. It's not known why Jeff said that Travis's situation at Chad's home was a "*little bizarre.*"

The transcript resumed as Jeff was describing the trip he and Chad took to a state auction for 3-wheelers in Concord, which was Saturday, October 14. On the way back, they stopped at a Wendy's restaurant. Impressed with the sales woman's service, Chad talked with her, and gave her his card to try to recruit her for McDonald's. Jeff drew different conclusions, as he told the police he suspected Chad was being unfaithful to Amanda and trying to pick up the woman. He told them, "[I] *probably should 'a' said something, and* [Chad] *gave the girl behind the counter his number....just how old is this guy... and I tell Jen...it's probably she* [Amanda] *shouldn't get too close to him...I don't even know what to say...*" Hamel responded, "*Strange*," (p. 1625) but there is nothing strange about a good manager always looking for good employees. What was strange was Jeff's interpretation of the interaction between Chad and the saleswoman and his belief that it was sufficiently important and credible to share with the police.

During this short interview, there were no questions about Jeff's criminal record. After their interviews, Jeff and Jennifer returned home and were joined by Amanda, and the three went to Buckfield to be with the Bortner/Conley family.

At 2:20 p.m. Maine State Police Detective Erik Baker spoke with Dr. Greenwald at the end of the first session of the autopsy on Kassidy's body. He wrote that she said, *that Kassidy died of blunt head trauma with the possibility of Shaken Baby Syndrome. Kassidy's brain was slightly swollen, too....Dr. Greenwald stated that the optic nerve appeared to have hemorrhaged. The abdomen had hemorrhaging, which is a deep injury. This injury is definitely an impact injury...* (Summary. p. 1687)

At 3:50 p.m. Detective Erik Baker delivered to the Maine State Police Crime Lab the first collection of evidence, as documented by an "Examination Request/Evidence Receipt" (p. 1689) Included among the nine listed items were a rape kit, soiled diaper, a red and white dress with a white dog image and a "known bloodstain card [? sic] of Cassidy Bortner." That document, listed Chad Evans as the "*Suspect/Defendant*" in a "Homicide" and no one as the "*Complainant.*" An earlier, 3:00 p.m. handwritten version of that same form, with no "discovery" page number, listed Jefferey Marshall as the "*Complainant*," and one of the six listed items was a "*DNA blood sample*" from Kassidy's body.

At 4:00 p.m. Detective Angela Blodgett interviewed Virginia Grover, who was the secretary for the Kittery Police Chief, Edward Strong about her interaction with Amanda the previous day.

That afternoon at 4:10 p.m., according to Det. Rick LeClair's report, a search warrant was obtained for a search of Chad Evans's car. The pursuit of search warrants, instead of asking for Chad's consent, seemed to be another illustration of how the police were treating Chad and Jeff differently. For Jeff, the police simply asked him to consent to a search. For Chad, there was a court order. Perhaps asking for consent from a man they believed to be a child abuser and killer was something that seemed too friendly or polite, and politeness was not a side the police wanted to show to such a man as they perceived Chad Evans to be. Perhaps the difference just reflected the different criminal investigation practices of Maine and New Hamsphire.

Sgt. Stewart's and Detective LeClair's request for the search warrant for Chad's car initially included, among the items to be seized, "*sperm, seminal fluid*," and listed among the crimes to which evidence might be related, "*Gross Sexual Contact and/or Unlawful Sexual Contact*," but these references to sexual crimes were initialed out by Judge Andre Janelle on November 14. This was documentation that the police had decided that there were no sexual crimes committed against Kassidy.

Like Sgt. White, Sgt Stewart also prepared an affidavit in support of that request. The six-page affidavit was very similar, and in some sections the same, as Sgt. White's two affidavits.

These affidavits soon became available to the media, as "court documents," and their inaccuracies were never corrected, except for the spelling of Kassidy's name. The media continued to repeat them, and the police and prosecution seemed to continue to believe them.

Detective Herbert Leighton, who had searched Jeff's home on the 9th, searched Chad's company car, a red Ford Taurus, on the afternoon of November 15.

Thus, Friday was a relatively quiet, though methodical, day for the Kassidy investigation.

Only Jeff and Jennifer were asked for their second interviews, and that was because Jeff called the police with an update for what happened in their hotel room the previous night. By the end of the day, the first stage of the autopsy of Kassidy's body was completed and Chad's home had been searched. Several items were seized, but, using the language of the search warrant, there was no "*evidence of the crime of homicide*" found.

On Friday afternoon, with the publication of the afternoon newspaper, Foster's Daily Democrat, came the first media coverage of the case, with the front page story, "Toddler's death suspicious," by Jennifer Saunders. She reported that "*Just the day before* [Kassidy's death] *Peirce recalled, he had held her in his arms. She would say, 'Give us loves,' and give you little kisses here,' he said, touching his cheek.*" Peirce didn't mention in his two-page handwritten statement that he had seen or held Kassidy on Wednesday, November 8, or in his brief interview with Sgt. Avery at Rogers Road on November 9. Peirce was not interviewed by the police at the Kittery Police Station where he wrote that statement. His substantive interview in the case came on December 6, as is described later in this chapter. He said in 2011 that he was in the presence of Kassidy for a total time of only about five minutes during 2000, and he did not recall ever hearing her say anything.

The Foster's article cited a "*neighbor*" as the source of several bits of information about Kassidy, but that neighbor was never identified nor interviewed by the police. The article said, "*As one neighbor put it, signs of child abuse were always there, but they did not recognize them.*" As Peirce was identified when he was quoted, it was not he, and it wasn't Jeff's neighbor, Tom McNeil, who was also quoted and who had recently moved to 53 Rogers Road, the apartment next door to 51 in the two unit duplex. McNeil had seen, and been close enough to, Kassidy to say, " '*She was so precious...Your natural instinct is just to love and protect. That anyone could do something else is just inconceivably horrible.'* " McNeil knew that Kassidy had "*large blue eyes...* [and] *wore her long, dark blonde hair in a high pony-tail...She loved to be hugged..*" The article said, "*McNeil never saw bruises on little Cassidy, but recalled her as both a shy girl and a little girl who longed for affection.*" McNeil was not interviewed by the police until a year later, on November 13, 2001. (Summary of interview by Sgt. James White.) The article correctly reported that Amanda was 18 years old, but it spelled Kassidy's name as "*Cassidy*."

Saturday, 11 November 2000

By this time, the State's morning newspapers and other media had picked up the story. The Union Leader's short story was headlined, "21-month old death." and in the Portland Press Herald, "Police Probing Toddler's Death." In both articles, Kassidy was "*Cassidy*." In Buckfield, Amanda and Jennifer and Jeff were visiting Amanda and Jennifer's mother and stepfather. Everyone was trying to cope with and understand what had happened to Kassidy and the family. In her essay, "My Life Story," Amanda described briefly the atmosphere,

Oh yeah, and after she died the next day we were all at my mom's in Buckfield, and all I did was lay on my mom's bed trying to be sane. It wasn't working. But Jeff kept coming in the room trying to talk to me. He wouldn't leave me alone. He kept asking me to go for a walk. As if I could go for a walk!!! That night I freaked out on Jeff yelling at him saying, "I don't know what happened to her,..."

That evening, at 7:05 p.m. Jeff called Maine State Police Detective Jeffrey Linscott to advise that he had secretly taped a conversation that day among himself, Amanda and Jennifer, in Buckfield. Of the three, only Amanda did not know of the recording of their conversation. (See Transcript of the recording. Also, see the Word copy with Chad's comments.) Linscott advised Jeff to bring it to the police, which he did on the following Monday. In New Hampshire, now the center of the investigation, it's illegal to tape a conversation without the consent of all those being recorded, but Jeff was lucky, as the recording was made in Maine. The transcript shows that Amanda was torn between the police and her family telling her that Chad killed Kassidy and Chad and his family on the other side. She struggled to make sense of the tragedy. During the discussion, Jeff and Jennifer tried to convince Amanda that Chad mistreated her and killed Kassidy. Excepted here are some of Amanda's responses or comments,

I didn't think it was that bad. I didn't think, he like, really hurt her. Do you know what I mean?... Once, I mean, it was just, but it wasn't like abuse. Do you know what I mean. I don't know... you just had to be there... No Jen. I don't want to hear about this. You guys don't like understand, anyway. (Inaudible)... you've never had a kid and I just want some peace of mind and all I keep hearing is shit.... It never really hurt me.... I don't know. I don't know, obviously. And you don't know either 'cause it's never happened to you. It's a fucked-up situation.... but I loved him and that's why.... I never thought it was that bad, Jeff....

That morning, Chad called the Portsmouth office of the law firm of Sisti and Twomey, one of the law firms recommended by a friend at work. Chad remembers being surprised when attorney Alan Cronheim answered the phone, on a day off for most people, Veterans' Day, and a Saturday. They scheduled an appointment for Chad to come to his office later that day. Cronheim told Chad of the retainer fee he would need to pay, and then waited for the police investigation to run its course. It must be remembered that at the time, Chad knew almost nothing about what others had told the police. Cronheim knew less, and he knew very little about Chad. He didn't ask Chad if he had lied to the police or if he had lied to anyone else involved in the case. Even if he had, and even if he had learned the truth about the "trampoline story" and about the length and depth of Chad and Amanda's relationship, it's a rare defense lawyer that would then pick up the phone and ask to set up a second interview with the police. At the time, he knew very little. The legal game had begun and, to continue the sports metaphor, Cronheim's style was truly defense. His initial instructions to Chad were to not talk with the media and not to talk further with the police.

Shortly after noon, from his home phone, Chad called the senior manager of Colley-McCoy, Peter Napoli, at his home, to discuss Chad's situation. They agreed to meet early the next week to discuss how Chad's work might be affected.

Saturday afternoon's Foster's Daily Democrat continued its coverage with Jennifer Saunders' story, "*Toddler's Autopsy Complete - Officials withhold cause of death pending further study of body of Rochester girl, 1 1/2*." Saunders wrote that the autopsy "*results are being withheld pending further study*." She wrote that the Maine State Police "*remained at the Kittery Police Department throughout the day, Friday, conducting interviews related to the case.*" As noted above, the only interviews on Friday were of Jeff and Jennifer, Dr. Greenwald and Virginia Grover.

Karen Dandurant wrote the Portsmouth Herald's story, "*Cause of toddler's death is under scrutiny; police call it suspicious.*" Because they were afternoon papers, the Portsmouth Herald and Foster's Daily Democrat could cover the events earlier in the publication day. By the end of the day, Sergeant James White had prepared a supplemented seven-page affidavit which included the information of the previous day's six-page affidavit, and added new information about the case, including the correct spelling of Kassidy's name, but primarily the preliminary results of the autopsy, which was conducted on Friday morning. He wrote,

Greenwald's autopsy revealed that Kassidy died as a result of head trauma consistent with blunt injury to the head.... Dr. Greenwald also identified hemorrhaging in the muscle tissue of Kassidy's abdomen. In her opinion, that hemorrhaging was consistent with being caused by strong, blunt force such as a punch or kick. Dr. Greenwald's preliminary finding is that these injuries occurred within 2-24 hours before the time of death...Dr. Greenwald concluded that the abrasions were likely caused when a dull instrumentality, such as a hairbrush, dull pin, or tines of a fork, was used to strike Kassidy's feet. Dr. Greenwald further stated that, in her opinion, it was unlikely that these injuries were self-inflicted or otherwise the result of an accident, such as Kassidy jumping on a dull, pointed object. Dr. Greenwald's preliminary conclusion was that these abrasions were inflicted within, at most, a few days of Kassidy's death." (p. 317-18)

He also added details to the summary of what McLeish and Harakles had told him about Chad's interview. White wrote,

While Evans denied abusing Kassidy, he admitted that on one occasion he used both hands to pick the child up by her head. Evans claims he did this to prevent Kassidy from falling off a trampoline. Evans also admitted that several times he grabbed Kassidy's face to discipline her. Finally, Evans said that he played with Kassidy in a "rough" fashion to "toughen her up."" (p. 322)

White had to work from the officers' and memories. That last statement, about "*rough*" and "*toughen her up*," came not from Chad's interview but likely from Amanda's first interview with Blodgett and LeClair where she said, "*Like he would put her in the corner and... be rough with her and he'd play rough with her saying to, like tough her up, play like a boy, you know?*" (Amanda interview, p. 850)

This revised Affidavit was used to obtain a second search warrant for the search of Chad's home on the night of his upcoming arrest on November 16.

Sunday, 12 November 2000

The only newspaper coverage on this day was in the Union Leader, "Toddler's Death Probed," but there was nothing new reported.

At 1:00 p.m. Detective Jeff Linscott interviewed by telephone a Sanford friend of Amanda, Vikki Norman, age 19, and employed at VIP Discount Auto in Sanford. Linscott's summary of the interview said that Norman told him that, of Amanda's friends, Emily Conley babysat Kassidy the most. The summary stated that "*approximately two weeks ago, Amanda Bortner left Kassidy Bortner with Emily Conley to be babysat. While at Emily Conley's residence, Norman, Emily Conley and Shannon Gagne all saw bruises on Kassidy Bortner's neck.*" Linscott wrote that each of the three asked Amanda independently about the bruises and Norman was told the "trampoline story." Finally, "*Norman stated she never saw any bruises on Amanda Bortner.*"

The observations by Vikki, Emily and Shannon may have been around October 12, it was around this time when Amanda gave Emily a ride to an obstetrician appointment, and it was the day before Amanda brought Kassidy to Auburn to pick up money for Chad's birthday present. However, "*approximately two weeks ago*" would have placed it closer to Sunday, October 29. In her Wednesday, November 15 interview, Emily stated that she saw bruises on Kassidy "*three weeks ago*," which would have been around Wednesday, October 25. In any case, these observations were in mid-to-late October.

At 1:15, Linscott interviewed by phone Shannon Gagne, age 18 and not employed. His summary of the interview said that Shannon
last saw Amanda Bortner and Kassidy Bortner about three weeks ago when she went to Rochester, NH to see them and meet Chad Evans. Gagne stated she saw a bruise on Kassidy Bortner's forehead. Gagne said that Amanda Bortner told her that Chad Evans was holding Kassidy Bortner in his arms when he walked around a corner and hit her head on the wall. (p. 1263)

That would have been approximately the weekend of October 21-22.

In a February 28, 2010 letter, Chad mentioned one bruise to Kassidy's forehead,
While on this subject, I just remembered Kassidy got a bruise once in the middle of her forehead, from the glass top kitchen table. Kassidy was chasing a ball around with Kato, tossing it and he would bring it back to her, dropping it at her feet. The ball rolled over to the kitchen table once and Kassidy ran after it. She ran smack into the edge of the octagon table as it was all glass and you could not see it. She fell on her butt and started crying. It bruised quickly. Within an hour or so, I'd say. It had to be close to November or so when this happened because she would have been too short otherwise. Perhaps it was the metal frame under the table hard to tell for sure. I wonder if this was the bruise on the forehead that I think it was Heather Hamilton or Tristan said she had seen.

Chad also recalled in two letters, the incident that Amanda may have described to Shannon as causing the forehead injury she saw. From Chad's letter of March 20, 2010
I wrote to you about carrying Kassidy down the stairs on my shoulders. I didn't duck enough and Kassidy's forehead smacked the overhang. It may have bruised her forehead. I believe Amanda was sitting in the living room and witnessed/yelled at me for not being more careful.

Later, in a May 3, 2010, letter, Chad wrote,
It was really one of those stupid, freak accidents. I had a really low overhang going down the stairs. Most of the time I carried the kids on my hip or piggy back going down the stairs. I had carried her down on my shoulders before and ducked just fine. On this particular occasion, I didn't duck enough and she bonked her head on the ceiling/overhang. It must have hurt like hell because she started crying. Amanda came running in from the computer room [later thought by Chad to be the living room]. *She hit her forehead, towards one side of her face, (I can't remember which side.). I don't recall it swelling or anything which is something that often happens with forehead injuries. We put a few ice cubes in a washcloth (I believe). Kassidy didn't like that at all. It made a bruise in the area that she hit.*

Returning to Linscott's summary of the Shannon Gagne interview, he wrote,
Gagne said that in the past she has seen bruises on Kassidy Bortner's forehead and Amanda Bortner has explained these bruises by saying that Kassidy had fallen down. Gagne said she remembered a bruise on Kassidy Bortner's eye and Amanda Bortner told her the bruise was caused by a little girl Kassidy Bortner was playing with had hit her while playing.

Linscott wrote that Shannon said that Amanda had taken Kassidy to
Kittery to be babysat overnight because Chad Evans' parents were coming to Rochester, NH to stay at Chad Evans' house and she did not want the parents to see the bruises on Kassidy Bortner. (p. 1263)

While that may have been a plan that Amanda considered, she had her own reasons from not wanting to be at Chad's home on his birthday weekend of October 15. In particular, she was feeling impatient about Chad's pending divorce, and his wife, Tristan would be participating in the birthday celebrations. Instead, Amanda stayed with Kassidy at Melissa Chick's on Friday the 13th and at Tracey Foley's on Saturday, the 14th. She didn't take Kassidy to Kittery that weekend.

Finally, Shannon said that she had seen Amanda and Kassidy, "*about three times since Amanda Bortner started dating Chad Evans.*" It would have been helpful to specify what the other two occasions were, and details about them, such as where, and who else was there. Also, she could have been asked if she saw bruises on Kassidy on those two other occasions.

At 6:30 p.m., Amanda Bortner began her third police interview, which was with Maine State Police Detective Angela Blodgett. The location was the Maine State Police Troop B Barracks in Gray, Maine. Amanda was driven by her mother to the interview from her parents' home in Buckfield. The previous day, Saturday, she had called Chad and wanted to see him and pick her up after the interview. Chad and his sister, Nicole, and her husband, Brandon, and Chad's friend, Bruce Aube, drove to Gray in two cars to meet Amanda after her interview and bring her home.

The transcript of the interview began in the "polygraph" room, but Amanda recalled that she had several exchanges with Angela Blodgett in another room before the tape recording began. There is no transcript of that first part of the interview, approximately 15 minutes. Amanda referred in the interview to her friend, "*Jessica*," (p. 73) who was Jessica Edmands, and Bruce's girlfriend, but the police never followed up to interview her. For the first time, and perhaps because she had just spent two days at his home, Amanda told Blodgett that her stepfather had "*sexually molested me and no one believes me.*" (p. 73) This experience, and the family's response to it, deeply affected Amanda's sense of trust, and mistrust, in her family.

Amanda said that "*... my mom keeps saying...'I think you know something you're not saying.' But I don't.... I'm saying everything I know...And it's like, I don't know...*" (p. 73-74) Detective Jeff Linscott joined the interview, as was planned, but Blodgett asked him to leave her to interview Amanda alone. According to his report, he watched the interview from a "*separate observation/taping room.*" Asked about Kassidy's conception, Amanda said that it was the first time she had sex with the father, Robert Sheehan, and "*...it was the first time I ever got drunk. He took advantage of me.*" (p. 75) Although the police later interviewed Sheehan, there was never any prosecution of him for serving alcohol to a minor. It's not known if the State of Maine sought to collect child support from him, after Amanda applied for TANF assistance. Amanda said, "*I even tried to get child support and stuff, but it would just take me forever.*" (p. 80)

Amanda said of the early period of her relationship with Chad, "*he was really good with her* [Kassidy] *in the beginning...I thought he was a great father...and that's the one thing that attrracted me to him.*" (p. 85) She continued,

...at first he was making me to be a good, better mom. He would say things like, 'I don't like a girl that doesn't spend quality time with her kids and...so I would make sure that I did... I'd do flash cards with her...she had a really good attention span...she recently learned letters and numbers.. The flash cards were like 'cat'... We did paints and stuff...There's tons of that at his house, too... one day we took a Polaroid camera and took a picture of her and I just drew a hand print and...she knew red and blue. But that was it. And pink... Chad read to her, too.'" (p. 88-89)

Amanda said that in the beginning Kassidy was reluctant to sit and listen to Chad read to her, "*But after a while, I did it with Kyle and her, and then they started doing it together.*" (p. 89) Amanda had no concerns about Kassidy's development until "*that two week period*," (p. 89) which seemed to be the two weeks beginning on Thursday, October 26 three-day/two night babysitting with Jeff and Jenn, including ingestion of Windex and the fall from Jeff's truck on the 28th.

Blodgett asked specifically when Kassidy last saw a doctor and Amanda said, "*This summer...She had all her shots up to date.*" (p. 90) Unfortunately, Blodgett did not ask for a more precise date, and didn't ask for any copies of Kassidy's medical records, or ask for Amanda's help in obtaining such records.

Even after living with Chad for most of the time since June, Amanda had moments of doubt. Around the time of her mother's move to Buckfield on October 1, said Amanda,

...I was going to move with them because I didn't, Chad wasn't, I didn't think Chad was ready for a live-in or anything because he was ... going through the divorce, finally... like he was confused...then he was like, 'I miss you, I want you.' " (p. 86)
Thus by that date, her move-in at Rochester notched up to a higher commitment.

Amanda said that she had never seen, what Chad had seen, which was that Kassidy did not put her hands out in front of her to block or stop a fall. Later, in his interview, Travis reported the same observation. (Travis, Interview, Nov. 22, p. 364) Asked about Kassidy's appetite, Amanda said, "*She ate like a pig. She ate a lot....She ate, seriously, more than I ate,*" and she noted, "*...like Chad's mom was like, 'Wow, you give her that much?'* " (p. 93) Blodgett did not ask when Chad's mother, Pam, was with Amanda and Kassidy, but it was likely during one of her two July, 2000 visits to Rochester, or Kassidy's two visits to Keene, with Chad and Amanda in July and August. No one ever interviewed Pam Evans.

Blodgett asked, "*.....when was the first time... that something happened with Kassidy, either that you got frustrated or* [with?] *a babysitter or Chad, when was the first time something happened that concerned you?*" and Amanda said,
...if Chad.. would like totally lose his temper with her and he would like grab her face, like I told you. He was really, really rough with her, but I never thought, like I never seen him hit her head... I've seen him like throw her on the bed, but I never thought it was really bad, and I would always yell at him. But I never thought it, like, 'never do that to her again.' " (p. 93)

The first part of that response was about holding Kassidy's face to get her attention, and the second part was during playful activity in Chad's and Amanda's bedroom; but the distinction between discipline and play was not often clear. Focusing on her frustration theory, Blodgett asked, "*Was it always because she was crying?*" and Amanda said, "*...no.. if she would just cry or something, he wouldn't do it... It confused me because... she was sick once and he was like all there for her, helping her out.... Cuddling with her.*" (p. 93) Amanda appeared to be describing her and Chad's care for Kassidy when she returned from the three day/two night babysitting with Jeff on Saturday, October 26.

Amanda estimated that Chad held Kassidy's face "*Maybe like twice a week...I thought that, like him, disciplining her was good because she wasn't throwing like the fits...*" (p. 94) Amanda estimated that Kassidy's last temper tantrum was "*not too long ago. Like three weeks ago.*" (p. 96)

Later, Amanda said, "*...one time... he threw her on the bed and I picked her up and I'm like, 'don't ever touch her again. I'm going to do the discipline.*" (p. 96) Chad recalls that the tossing of Kassidy and Kyle onto their bed was part of playful activity and that Amanda was confusing play with discipline. He recalls that she made the strong statement, "*I'm going to do the discipline,*" to Jeff, Jennifer and to Chad, about her doing the disciplining when Kassidy came back from Jeff's with black and blue on her buttocks, on Sunday, October 22. In melded families, biological parents sometimes have to remind other adults that, "*I'll do the disciplining.*"

Several times during the interview, Blodgett would characterize what Amanda had said in an earlier interview or in that same interview in a more severe or harsh way than originally stated, and Amanda would apparently agree, even she didn't say the same thing explicitly. For example, Blodgett said, "*...the other day we talked about him picking her up and just kind of throwing her on the bed or throwing her into a corner,*" and Amanda replied, "*Um hum.*" (p. 96) Blodgett asked, "*...how hard would he yank her arm and toss her?.... did her jerk her arm when he would pick her up...*" and Amanda replied, "*Yeah.*" (p. 96) And again, "*...so he would grab her face and push her into a corner,*" and Amanda, "*Yeah.*" (p. 97) Later, Blodgett characterized Chad as someone who would "*...wing her* [Kassidy] *across the room.*" (p. 98) The words, "*throwing her into a corner,*" "*yank,*" "*toss,*" "*jerk,*" and "*wing*" were Blodgett's.

At other times, Blodgett seemed to ask neutral questions, "*...did you ever try to talk to him about... instead of punishing her because she cries when you kiss me, maybe, if you give her attention, too, at the same time, then she wouldn't feel so scared?*" Amanda agreed, "*We tried that.. he would, everyday, he would give her... kisses and hugs and she'd* *give him kisses and she'd sit on his lap and pinch his nose and say all this stuff.*" (p. 98) Continuing with the positive view of Chad, Amanda said, "*He talk* [taught] *her a lot of things...he taught her numbers and stuff, too... He did that like two days before it happened...He would like read her books...* " (p. 98) Summarizing her views, she said, "*It's just like all confusing to me...*" (p. 98)

Blodgett asked about Chad's pressing on Kassidy's throat, "*... we had talked about choking... and you had told me how he would put pressure on like her esophagus?....how.. long would he do that? Until she was quiet or until she passed out...?*" (p. 99) Amanda said that it happened once or twice, but the idea of pressing until Kassidy "*passed out,*" was Blodgett's. This incident, and Chad's 2010 explanation were discussed in the previous chapter, with Amanda's first interview.

Then Blodgett asked about Chad "*pushing the flat of his hand against your throat?*" (p. 99) and Amanda described the incident when driving home on Friday, August 25, from the McDonald's "*dinner thing*" at the Exeter Inn. She said, "*... and he was really, really, really drunk and he was driving and I didn't have a license at the time, so I didn't want to drive....he would grab me by the throat and he was really, really rough with me, and I would try hitting him back and stuff, but it never hurt him...he never really did anything that would seriously hurt me and when he did it, it didn't really hurt me really bad.*" (p. 99-100) As noted earlier, the event was a business celebration for fewer than 20 people with a professional bartender and sit-down dinner. In the presence of Chad's supervisors and fellow managers, it's extremely unlikely that Chad was "*really, really, really drunk.*" Incidentally, Chad had never in his life been arrested or otherwise cited for driving under the influence of alcohol.

Regarding Amanda's "*not having a license at the time,*" the Discovery records in the case do not reflect that any criminal records check was done on Amanda or Jennifer as was done for Chad and Jeff. Neither was there a license check as was done for Melissa Chick, Gabe Snyder and Tracey Foley. A check for Amanda would have shown two speeding tickets, on May 4 and May 11, 2000, which led to two suspensions of her license for the combined period from June 25 to October 8. None of the police questions to Amanda related to those suspensions.

Amanda described the argument she had with Chad when they were in Chad's basement and they both bent down to pick up a piece of clothing at the washing machine and their heads collided. Amanda said, "*he... got really mad and like head-butted me, and it didn't leave a mark or anything, but it hurt a little bit....*" (p. 100) Blodgett never was told that the collision was an accident. This incident and Chad's explanation are described in the previous chapter.

Amanda talked about Kassidy's behavior on Wednesday, November 8th, at home while Amanda was calling to find day care openings, "*And, she was fine. She was watching TV.... She was pointing at everything. Telling me what it was.... And I was pointing at everything, like we would do that all day long, because I wanted her to learn....*" (p. 101) Amanda said that she left Kassidy at Jeff's at "*three o'clock, I think... Three, three-thirty...*" (p. 102)

Amanda described what happened on her work break Wednesday evening, when she went to Perfumania to visit Jennifer,

...first my sister told me that Jeff said that he never wanted to babysit again.. they never told me, they told me she would, ... she acted funny. Jeff would. My sister wouldn't. But they would make fun of her [Kassidy], *so I...didn't know if they were serious or not. I didn't think they were. They would call her retarded, just joking around and stuff.... Jeff just said "she's really slow and like, she acts stupid"'...and then I called Chad, and he was on the other line with Jeff... and he told me about the ball and the bat, like the wiffle ball.* (p. 103-04)

Amanda said that when she came home late that night, "*I went upstairs and gave her a kiss on the cheek and touched her hair and looked at her face, and I just saw the red mark right here and the one where she fell off the couch...it was like little, little right way over here and that's all I saw....*" (p. 105)

Amanda described the argument she had with Chad that evening,

...we actually got into a little argument. I was like, "Wow, I'm really tired. I haven't worked in a long time."....I was going from not working at all to working 8 or 9 hours, 12 hours....Tired, but nothing that I couldn't handle. And I was just like, "I need a back massage."...we got in a fight... I was like, "I work hard... but you don't have a backbreaking job. I have to go up the ladder all day," you know....And he got mad over that... he didn't like grab me or anything, but we just got in a little argument over it. He got really mad about it. (p.106)

This was the foundation for the charge against Chad of Simple Assault on the evening of November 8, when Chad allegedly, "*placed his hands around Bortner's neck.*" In this initial telling, Amanda said that *"he didn't like grab me or anything."*

The next morning, Kassidy,

...had a really bad diaper. [I] *changed her diaper in the morning and I got her dressed... She was acting normal like. I gave her cereal. Well, actually Chad gave her cereal in a bag. I asked him to...And I got Kyle ready. I was getting really bad like because I'm like not used to like having to go to work and get everybody ready, you know?*" (p. 107) Amanda said that Kassidy was on the couch watching TV for some part of that rushed getting-out-the door period.

Amanda said that when she dropped Kassidy off at Jeff and Jennifer's, the bruise from the ballhitting "*looked like a circular thing...*" (p. 108)

Blodgett asked about what happened when most of the people left the police station on Thursday night, and Amanda said about Chad and her internal conflict,

He says,... "I didn't kill her, I didn't kill her." He's like, "You know I didn't kill her, Amanda." I'm like,"Yeah." I just talked to you [Blodgett] *and I was just like, "I don't know." I don't know what I was feeling....and for some reason I don't know why like I ever want to see him. Like I still do.* (p 110)

Amanda was torn, and in the middle. Later she said to Blodgett, "*... but then when I talk to you, I feel better about the whole, not wanting to talk to him...*" (p. 122) Chad, Nicole, Brandon and Bruce were waiting nearby to bring Amanda to Bruce's home according to the plan arranged the previous day.

Amanda described the phone calls with Chad on the morning of November 10th, "*I was trying to get him to admit what he did to her. He would like hurt her and stuff and he was like, 'Yeah, Amanda, but I could never really,...' He felt really bad. He was saying, 'I'm sorry, sorry.'*" (p. 110) This exchange highlighted a critical distinction which was that Chad felt badly that he hadn't done more to prevent Kassidy's death, but the police saw that regret as an indication of guilt for causing her death.

During those calls Chad described to Amanda Kassidy's behavior in the car coming home from Jeff's, "*...he told me that... her tongue was out of her mouth and like her eyes were glazed over and I was like, 'Why didn't you do anything about that? That's like a big thing, you know?...He was like, 'I don't know. I don't know why I didn't, and she was fine after.'*" (p. 111) In 2010, Chad explained that this was a critical point about Kassidy's behavior on that Wednesday which was that she would alternate between being OK and looking spacey. He kept on focusing on the OK periods, and hoping that she was, in fact, OK. He was guilty of wishful thinking.

Blodgett asked more about the calls on Thursday morning, and Amanda described another source of her torment which was, "*everybody's saying, 'Don't talk about everything.'.. and I'm trying to be smart about it. I'm trying not to say anything. Even today, talking about it, we shouldn't have...I have a friend, Michelle, her husband's named Bruce. I just talked to her today. But they were like, 'Don't talk about anything.'*" (p. 112) Perhaps Amanda's friends, including Michelle Truell, whom the police never interviewed, were replaying traditional Victorian advice which was not to think about unhappy thoughts or events. That advice echoed the police messages which were to discourage their potential witnesses from talking with one another, in order to avoid contaminating future testimony. It also echoed the advice from Chad's new lawyer, which was not to talk with the police or the media. That advice was not helpful to Amanda. In the face of such a tragedy, Amanda should have felt comfortable talking about it with her family and friends. Later she said that her stepfather said, "*like last night, he was like, 'You're not taking any more phone calls.'* " Amanda said it was "*kind of helping me out a little bit,*" that "*people are calling me who haven't called me in forever...*" (p. 123) Thus, Amanda's grieving was being short-circuited by well-meaning family members and others who felt that talking was not useful. In fact, it is one of the essential parts of grieving.

Amanda mentioned that Chad was seeking a lawyer and Blodgett asked, "*Did he say why he was looking for a lawyer?... Does that makes sense to you?...That he doesn't want to talk to us and wants a lawyer?... I believe that the other day he left and didn't want to talk to them anymore*" (p. 113) Blodgett was trying to convince Amanda that Chad's seeking a lawyer was an indication of his guilt and unwillingness to help the police. She didn't tell Amanda that the police did not ask Chad to interview with them again, until the 16th, when he was arrested. An arrest is not the most friendly way to persuade someone to sit down and discuss something. Chad had told the police on the 9th that he wanted to talk with him, but wanted to protect his rights and did not feel good about the accusation that he killed Kassidy.

Amanda said, "*My mom's like asking me questions......people keep asking all these weird things and I just want to be left alone.*" (p. 113) She didn't mention, until later, the many questions she was asked that morning by Jeff and Jennifer the previous day, Saturday. She didn't yet know that they secretly recorded the conversation. She said, "*He,* [Jeff] *keeps asking me questions.*" (p. 123) Interestingly, Amanda said about "*Chad's family, they make me feel better for some reason.*" (p. 113) One reason was that Chad's family was sharing in the grieving and not trying to force upon Amanda their own perspectives on how Kassidy died.

Blodgett then explained to Amanda what she understood about what killed Kassidy, "*Basically, it's a bruised brain. Like you* [have] *been hit on the head and your brain shakes back and forth. So, like shaken baby...you get hit on the head hard enough so that your brain bangs against one side of your skull and then against the other side of your skull and the pressure builds up and... eventually, will kill you. Ah cause your brain can't function.*" Amanda asked an excellent question, "*Do you think it was when she fell out of the truck?*" (p. 114) Blodgett she didn't think so because "*That's going to have been too long ago, I think,*" without know exactly when the October 28 fall actually occurred. She also said that she had been taught that such an injury as Kassidy's would not be caused "*unless you fall from higher than eight feet.*" (p. 114) It's not known where that number came from. As noted in the previous chapter, Dr. John Plunkett has written, "*A fall from less than 3 meters in an infant or child may cause fatal head injury and may not cause immediate symptoms.*" Three meters is 9 feet, 10 inches. Falls from a lesser height might not be fatal, but they could still cause serious damage, which can be more serious damage than shaking a baby.

Blodgett was not interested in pursuing possible causes of Kassidy's death, other than Chad's recent actions. She said about the earlier fall (or whatever was the cause of those two bumps on Kassidy's head on October 28th), "*... I mean she may have had a concussion... but I really think that she was hit on the head sometime the night before* [i.e. Wednesday night] *and I think that's why she was kind of sleepy looking, groggy....*" (p. 115) Amanda asked, "*Do you think that Chad might have done that to her?*" and Blodgett said, "*I do. I think that he did.*" (p. 115) Amanda did not ask Detective Blodgett for the reasons for her thinking that Chad hit Kassidy on Wednesday.

Amanda asked whether Kassidy's fall in Chad's driveway might have contributed to her death, and Blodgett said, "*No,*" and she cited Dr. Greenwald, "*she said, 'No, it wouldn't. I would have to be something with a lot of force...*" (p. 115) No one has done, or was aware of, an analysis of the kinetic force of a line-drive Tee-ball, weighing approximately one-third of a pound, from about six feet away. A Tee-ball weighs approximately six times as much as a wiffle ball.

Blodgett asked if Chad had "*ever shaken her when he was mad at her?*" and Amanda said, "*I've never seen him shake her.*" Blodgett tried again, "*I mean...holding the baby and launch her across the room into the wall...*" The phrase "*launch across the room into the wall,*" was Blodgett's own. Amanda again did not accept the characterization, "*I've never seen him do that either.*" (p. 115-116) and said "*He would really play with her and he would play really rough with her, grab her by the legs and swing her around by her arms and stuff.*" In another context, such a description of playing with a child would be welcomed, but Blodgett asked, "*But he wouldn't let go of her?*" and Amanda replied, "*No.*" (p. 116)

Amanda continued about Chad's relationship with Kassidy, *"Like whenever I wasn't around with him with her. He was actually really, really good... Like I... come back after he had her for a while she'd be with him, hugging him....*" (p. 116) Blodgett was struggling, "*I just don't see how you get a head injury like that without something, some sort of traumatic incident... somebody had to have done something to her. Or seen something like fall off the porch roof. I mean, something big happened to her.*" (p. 116-17) Blodgett discounted the ballhitting incident as a cause, saying, "*I talked to the doctor, Dr. Greenwald, about getting hit in the face with a baseball isn't going to do it..*" (p. 117) However, it's not known whether that conversation was about a wiffle ball hitting Kassidy or a real baseball, or Tee-ball. As many a baseball player will attest, a baseball or Tee-ball can do damage.

Blodgett challenged Amanda's assertions that Chad was good to Kassidy when she, Amanda, wasn't around, saying, "*Or do you think he just tells you she's so good.*" (p. 117) Amanda responded with yet another reference to the previous Sunday, November 5, just a week previous, which neither Blodgett nor the police cared to pursue, "*... like Nicole... she was over there that Sunday...when I was at my mom's house with my sister and he was... really, really good with her...*" (p. 117) Amanda said that Nicole told her about that day with Kassidy.

Amanda then changed the subject, and said, "*Well, she would .... say things like, 'Where's Chad? Where's Chad?' When Chad was at work...*" (p. 117)

In 2010, Chad had memories of the same refrain, "*Where's Chad?*" and a story. He wrote in his August 6, 2010 letter,

Amanda would tell me upon arriving home, "Kassidy has been asking for you all day. She keeps looking for you and saying, 'Where's Chad?' "

Whenever I heard this, it made my day. How could it not? I recall one time several weeks to a month before Kassidy died, Amanda called my cell phone and said, "Someone's been asking for you all day. Hold on a minute." Next thing I hear is Amanda whispering in the background say "Hi," and then I hear Kassidy's little voice saying "Hiiii." It was perfect timing because I am 99% sure I was in Greenland having a rough day and this made it all better. I bet if we can get hold of those cell phone bills and my October calendar, I could pin down the day. I don't mean to sound sarcastic, but I don't believe 20-month old Kassidy was looking for me because she was afraid of me coming home to abuse her. As I have told you since the beginning, I had some bonding issues with Kassidy those first few weeks. I was some happy when months later Amanda would tell me that Kassidy was saying "Where's Chad?" all day, looking for me. Those are happy memories, I will never forget. I know they made Amanda pretty proud too.

Chad's recollections show how smart Kassidy really was. Not every toddler can talk that well at the age of 20-21 months.

Blodgett continued to try to demonize Chad, saying "*he denied ever holding her face under water. Remember we talked about him putting her face under the faucet. He just said that he splashed water on her,*" but she didn't wait for Amanda to further clarify that it was, in fact, a "*splashing*" and not "*putting her face under water*". (p. 118) Instead, Blodgett, for the first time told Amanda that Chad was accusing her of abusing Kassidy, "*...then he started saying that you had, that he had thrown her in corners, I think, but that you did it, too.*" Amanda responded, "*No, I never threw her in a corner. Ever. I can't believe he would say that.*" (p. 118) Feeling defensive about the additional allegation that she grabbed Kassidy's face, too, Amanda said, "*Never. Never. I never lost my temper with her. I was like. I don't lose my temper, you know. I'm not that kind of person.*" (p. 118)

Chad never said in his interview that he had "thrown" Kassidy into corners, and he never said that Amanda had done that, either. Whether Blodget actually believed what she told Amanda is unknown. It may have been wishful thinking on her part, similar to the upcoming exchange in Jeremy Hinton's interview on November 14 where Detective Baker and Trooper Jill Rockey told Jeremy that Jeff had taken a polygraph test, but he didn't. The police may have become so invested in their theory about Chad and Amanda that they may have started to confuse the theory with the facts.

Later, they returned to the water incident, and Amanda said, "*Well, I didn't see it. She was totally screaming at the top of her lungs and I was in the other room... and he said, 'I put water on her face to get her to stop crying*." Blodgett responded, "*But she's been afraid of faucets ever since?.. So it makes you think that he did a little more than just splash some water in her face?*" (p. 118) Amanda countered by recalling that "*...she wasn't afraid of water at all. She loved bubble baths. She'd give me bubbles just to get me to give her a bubble bath.*" As faucets are used to fill bathtubs for baths, Kassidy's fear, if it could be generalized, was slightly different than a simple fear of a faucet, or faucet being turned on.

Blodgett said, "*I have serious concerns about Chad,*" and asked if Amanda supported giving a polygraph/lie detector test to him, and Amanda agreed, and she would "*feel better about it,*" if Jeff were also given such a test. Blodgett agreed, and said later, "*...but Jeff was really up front with us and told us about the spanking thing*." However, Blodgett was apparently referring to Jeff's acknowledgement that he spanked Kassidy when she drank some Windex, but Jeff didn't tell the police about the spanking he gave Kassidy a week before the Windex incident, on Saturday, October 21 when his alleged spanking caused considerable bruising on Kassidy's buttocks. Blodgett also said that Jeff had told them about Kassidy's fall from his truck, "*and he was very concerned about how that might have contributed to... her being sick or something like that. Someone, there's like a neighbor... saw her fall out of the truck... and, I mean, he's just completely up front...*" (p. 124) Later, in his December 6 interview by Sgt. White, Jeff's neighbor, Will Peirce, stated that he only saw Kassidy fall, partially, and into Jeff's arms. According to White's summary, this occurred "*just a day or two before Kassidy's death*." (p. 401)

In November 2001, another friend, Tom McNeil, was interviewed by Sgt. White because the police understood, perhaps from Jeff, that he witnessed the fall that hurt Kassidy's head; but he said he never witnessed such a fall. At Chad's trial, the two falls were confused for one another. Blodgett was pleased with what Jeff had told the police because it confirmed their theory, that Chad was responsible. She didn't tell Amanda what efforts the police had made to fact-check what Jeff had said about Chad's gambling, drug use, sexual deviance and giving Tristan "*the worst beating in New Hampshire*." She didn't tell Amanda that during his interview on Friday the 10th, Jeff had told the police about what he and Jennifer had guessed about Amanda, "*we... thought...maybe she was screwing around with Travis.*" (Jeff, interview, p. 1624)

After reminding Amanda that "*you told me, the other day, he would yell at her and call her stupid, call her a bitch, grab her face*," (much of which was not true or an exaggeration), and Amanda said, "*... I don't want to go see him or anything. I do, but, you know, I'm not going to....*" (p. 119) Nonetheless, she knew that at the end of the interview she was meeting and planning to stay with Chad.

Blodgett then tried to be Amanda's feminist therapist by advising that she was in an unequal relationship, where "*he's paying the light bill and that sort of stuff, but you're still doing everything else and you're not only taking* [care of] *yourself, but now you're taking care of him and his kid when his kid's there. You know, ironing his clothes, and that sort of stuff. I mean, that's not a partnership.*" Amanda agreed, and Blodgett added, "*... I don't think you went there intending to be instantly, you know, Alice and Carol rolled into one.*" and Amanda agreed with that, too. However, it wasn't clear to whom the reference was made. Was it to the characters played by Dyan Cannon (Alice) and Natalie Wood (Carol) in the movie, "Carol, Bob, Ted and Alice," which was released in 1969, 13 years before Amanda was born? Or was it to Alice the housekeeper and Carol the wife in "The Brady Bunch," the TV series from 1969 to 1974, or to the 1995 movie by that name. In any case, it wasn't Blodgett's job to tell citizens how they should relate to their partners and how to share the relationship's responsibilities.

Blodgett returned to the theme that Jeff was honest and upfront and helpful and Chad was not. Jeff, she said, was *"so upset about this and... telling us every little detail that he can think of, even if it's stuff that he felt he did was wrong....and then.. Chad was saying that I know are lies because I talked to you.... Jeff, I think called us Friday and wanted to know... was there anything else that we need, was there any other way I can help.*" (p. 124) Blodgett didn't tell Amanda that the previous day, Saturday, Jeff had called the police to advise that he had secretly taped Amanda in a conversation at her parents' home. Blodgett continued with her demonization of Chad, "*...he doesn't seem to want to help. I'm just trying to find out what happened to her. And if it was a head injury that's fine, but if someone kicked her in the head, threw her across the room...*" (p. 124) The phrase, "*kicked her in the head,*" was Blodgett's.

Blodgett then attacked Travis's credibility, saying that Travis was lying for Chad, "*Would Travis lie for Chad? He seems to be...He denied that he had ever, because you told me that you had confided some concerns to him about that you should take her to the doctor... you'd never talked to him at all about anything.*" Amanda said, "*Oh, my God, wow.*" (p. 125) Travis' interview by Detective Jeff Linscott was not recorded, so we only have Linscott's summary where he wrote, "*...Travis did not recall Amanda Bortner ever sharing her concerns for Kassidy with him.*" (p. 1213) For Blodgett, if a friend of Chad Evans could not recall something, s/he was a liar. For others, there was a kinder label.

Amanda then recalled that her conversation with Travis about Kassidy "*was Halloween night. I remember because he* [Chad] *had just left with Tristan and the boys.*" (p. 126) That was Tuesday, the 31st, which was three days after Jeff brought Kassidy home with two big bumps on her head on Saturday the 28th. She recalled that she was crying, "*when I told him about Kassidy. I said, ... there's bruises on her cheek and stuff.. I told him all about Kassidy... and he was like, 'Amanda, you don't have to put up with that.... I'm always there for you...*" (p. 126) Blodgett noted, "*Obviously not.... He's saying nothing. He knows nothing.*" Travis was the fifth most important adult during Kassidy's last 24 hours, as he observed her on Wednesday evening, November 8. His interview with Det. Linscott was not recorded and lasted only 30 minutes. On November 22, that relative neglect was corrected and he was interviewed and recorded for an hour an a half. In that interview Travis was not asked about that conversation that Amanda recalled so vividly. There were no leading questions to go in a direction the police did not want to go.

Blodgett suggested that Amanda not consider Travis a friend, and she replied, "*A friend? Oh, I don't anymore.*" (p. 126) Such was the collateral damage of this investigation. Suspicion among friends was sown, and bonds of trust and friendship were broken. All it took at that time to cause Amanda to disavow her friendship with Travis was for Blodgett to tell her that Travis was "*obviously not*" always there for her. That's how fragile Amanda was at that time.

Amanda then talked about her friends, and the obligation to do what's right. She referred to Chad's sister, Nicole, and Jessica Edmands as her friends. Jessica was never interviewed.

Also not interviewed was her friend, Michelle Truell, in whom Amanda said she confided, "*She knew that he* [Chad] *hurt me.*" (p. 127) Amanda said that Michelle offered her a place to stay. Blodgett concluded this line of discussion, "*Where are your friends... and where are your enemies*?" (p. 128)

Amanda reconfirmed that Chad brought the abrasions on Kassidy's feet to her attention and that she, Amanda, called Jeff and Jennifer right away and "*they said, 'Oh, it must be the nails... or something that stick out from the bottom of the floor.'*" (p. 129)

As the interview was closing down, Amanda gave Blodgett the phone number at Michelle Truell's house. Amanda had said during the interview about Michelle, "*... she told me to come to her house. She'd come and get me... So I told her I'd call her after this.*" (p. 127)

Blodgett advised her about contacts with Chad, without being asked for such advice, "*My suggestion would be, if you want to talk on the phone with him, ... I'm not going to tell you not to. I wouldn't see him like face-to-face, I think that, emotionally, that's just like too much right now.... I think that... there's some more questions* [that] *should be answered.*" (p. 131)

At the same time, Blodget wanted Amanda to talk with Chad, specifically about a polygraph test. Amanda said that she would talk with Chad and encourage him to take a polygraph test. She later did have that conversation, and he agreed to the idea. Amanda told Angela Blodgett about Chad's agreement to such a test in her next interview. Still, the police never asked Chad to take such a polygraph, and they never asked his attorneys. Returning to the current interview, Blodgett asked Amanda if she was willing to take a polygraph, and she said "*Definitely, I'll take one.*" (p. 135) Such an exam for Amanda was listed as "*pending*" on the "Investigative Plan." (p. 449) apparently prepared by Sgt. White. This plan was apparently prepared before Jeff's planned exam on November 14, but the polygraph examination for Amanda was never scheduled or conducted. Detective Blodgett then left the room for a few minutes to confer with Jeff Linscott, and then returned with some post-mortem photographs of Kassidy, which she showed to Amanda. She said "*These are pictures of Kassidy in the hospital. People were working on her.*" That latter phrase, "*working on her*" implied that Kassidy was still alive at the time. However, these photos must have been the series taken by Kittery Detective Hackett, and Kassidy had been dead for about an hour. Amanda responded, "*Oh my God. Oh, my God.*" (p. 132)

Blodgett asked about the bruises, "*all up on the side of her head, I mean is that something you remember?*" and Amanda said, "*No, nothing I remembered. Oh my God.*" (p. 132) Blodgett showed a photo of Kassidy's chin, "*See, like up under her chin, is that anything that you remember*?" and Amanda again said, "*No.*" However, later Amanda said, '*... she had a bruise on her chin.*" (p. 135) If Blodgett believed Amanda, her statements that the bruises on her shortly after noon on the 9th were not there when she dropped Kassidy off at Jeff's might have been food for thought. If she didn't believe her, then she might have asked her directly again about a lie detector test.

Amanda said she could not look at the photos any more, and it was stopped. Blodgett returned to ask about Chad's alleged drinking, "*No, barely ever...*", and cocaine, "*Oh, no.*" Still trying to find a motivation or a frustration which would lead Chad to abuse Kassidy as she , Blodgett, believed he had done, she asked, "*Where is his money going?*" (p. 132) Amanda surely disappointed Blodgett by responding, "*He's got college fund*[s] *for his kids...*" (p. 132) It's probably safe to say that not many people convicted of murdering children have college funds for the other children in the melded family. Nicole had told Blodgett during her interview on November 9, of Chad's encouragement to Amanda to set up an education fund for Kassidy. (p. 1816)

Blodgett asked another leading question, "*Okay. So ... when he would get angry and grab you or mistreat Kassidy, it didn't have to do with alcohol or drugs?*" and Amanda replied, "*Oh, no,*" without realizing that the question depended upon an unchallenged assumption by Blodgett that Chad was mistreating Kassidy. (p. 133) Blodgett asked another leading question, whether Chad "*was frustrated or he wasn't getting his own way?*" Amanda said, "*He had an anger control problem, I think.*" (p. 133) Amanda said that Chad had received counseling, and said that Chad had not been seeing a counselor during their relationship. She was almost right, as Chad voluntarily terminated his weekly sessions with Gray Fitzgerald in the spring, but effective on Friday, July 28. Amanda might have added that she told Chad that he didn't need to use the short list of techniques that Chad had stuck to a wall upstairs in his bedroom. He agreed and she threw the list away.

Blodgett asked Amanda about Jeff's and Jennifer's assertions that she said to Chad on the phone on Friday morning, the 10th, "*I know that you killed her. You know I love you anyway.*" and Amanda countered, "*Yeah, they keep saying that. I did not say that.... that's probably one of the reasons they* [Jeff and Jennifer] *make me mad... I think I said, 'I don't know if he killed her.'* " (p. 133-34)

Amanda said that she recalled saying to Chad that she didn't "*ever want to see a bruise on her, and he actually, I think he was all paranoid about it, too... and Jeff was, too... she had a bruise right here pretty bad from Jeff's .... I think it was like she fell or something, but he was all paranoid about it, too. Because when she fell out of the truck, he told me he was like, 'Oh, God, Amanda's going to kill me.' I remember him saying that.*" (p. 136)

Asked about the allegation of avoiding a doctor or day care because of bruises, she said that she didn't take Kassidy to the hospital when she was dehydrated, which was when she came home from Jeff's on Saturday, October 28, "*because she got better so fast.*" (p. 136) Thus, not going to the hospital was not because of the bruising. As happened so often, Kassidy recovered, and hopeful adults didn't think she needed additional medical treatment.

Regarding bruising and day care, Amanda said that *"about two or three weeks ago,"* she told Chad, " *'I'm going to day care tomorrow to see how it is and see if I like it and if they'll take Kassidy and he's like, 'you're not taking her now with bruises on her face.'* " (p. 137) However, Amanda said she was not very concerned, "*... I never thought it was like a big... I'd go to the grocery store* [with Kassidy] *and I'd never think twice about it... in my head, I thought she bruised easily and I just didn't think, like, it was that big of a deal. I didn't think it was that bad. I didn't think she was hurting from it, you know. To me, like, she was getting disciplined. He kept telling me she needed discipline...*" (p. 138) The implication was that the only bruises on Kassidy at that time, "*two or three weeks ago*" were bruises from Chad's palming Kassidy's face, but that wasn't necessarily correct. Without knowing the exact date of "*two or three days ago,*" it's safe to say that Kassidy had other bruises as well, during the month of October.

Blodgett then spent a few minutes asking Amanda about Chad's sexual interests, and Amanda dismissed them as a "*guy thing,*" and "*Well, he's definitely a pig. I'll give him that, but I think he knows his boundaries...*" (p. 139) There was no discussion of Jeff's allegation of a "*strap on dildo*" and no discussion of sexual deviance.

Detective Blodgett again asked Amanda what she saw for bruises on Kassidy on Thursday morning, November 9, and Amanda reminded Blodgett of her bad vision. At the time, she was wearing one contact lens. Coincidentally, she picked up new lenses the day after Kassidy died, as they were authorized by Amanda's ASPIRE program case manager on October 31.

Blodgett asked specifically about "*bruises on the top of her head, like around the front of the forehead on top of her head.... they were at different stages of healing. Some seemed old. Some seemed new.*" (p. 140) At first Amanda said "*I have no idea,*" later said, "*... I was holding her once and I hit her on the door by accident... but I didn't think it was hard enough to even bruise her.*" (p. 141) Amanda said that Kassidy didn't cry, and gave another example of when she didn't cry which was when Amanda pierced Kassidy's ears. That was before Sunday, September 24, which was when Chad and Amanda went to Martha's Vineyard. During that trip, when Kassidy was at Auburn, Amanda's mother took out Kassidy's earrings.

Amanda said that she never saw bruises on Kassidy's stomach.

Blodgett asked, "*How many times do you think Chad had thrown her into a corner or someplace where she hit her head?*" and Amanda responded, "*I can't count how many times. Probably...about twice a week.*" (p. 143) The problem was that Amanda never agreed that Chad "*threw*" Kassidy "*into a corner,*" so the quantity guess answer she gave may have been the number of times a week that Kassidy had a time-out in a corner.

Blodgett asked another leading quesiton, "*And that would be part of the whole. She's crying at an inappropriate time, and he would get frustrated and go grab her face and grab her arm and toss her into the nearest corner...*" and Amanda agreed, "*Yup. Yeah. Yeah.*" However, Amanda had previously said that Chad didn't discipline Kassidy because she cried too much. He held her face only to get eye contact and not to inflict pain or punishment, and he never "*tossed*" Kassidy for any disciplinary reason into a corner or anywhere. (p. 143)

Blodgett then left the room to talk with Jeff Linscott and then return with one question which was about the "*magic marker, like scribbling, drawing on the wall* [at Chad's house]." Surely, the police were hoping that Kassidy did it, so it would provide one example of where Chad might have become enraged and hit Kassidy. Amanda said that Kyle did the scribbling when she was babysitting him, and that Chad did get upset, and "*He just smacked him in the butt and made him go upstairs. I think he did that. His mom got even more mad about it.*" (p. 144) Chad wrote in 2011 that Amanda's recollection is incorrect, as he never spanked Kyle. Amanda said that she wasn't really mad, "*I just scrubbed it off.*" However, enough of the marking was still evident for Detective Linscott to notice during his participation in the search of Chad's home.

When closing, Blodgett again emphasized the lie detector tests, "*We could schedule polygraph tests for Chad and Jeff, as I pointed out that it's not really fair to expect them to do it without you to do it, too...*" and Amanda again agreed, "*Oh, okay. I'll do it.*" (p. 144)

Finally, they agreed that Blodgett would use Amanda's mother's phone as the primary phone contact number, and the backup would be Michelle Truell's. Amanda was not telling Blodgett that another number to call might be Bruce Aube's.

Amanda's two hour interview ended at 8:30 p.m. As was her original plan, Amanda called Bruce's cell phone and Bruce, Nicole, and Brandon came to the State Police barracks to pick up Amanda. Then they brought her to where Chad was waiting. Amanda and Chad drove back to Rochester together, alone, in one car.

The "Investigative Plan" referenced above was undated and the name of the author was not on any of its four pages. It's likely to have been written by Sgt. James White as he was the NHSP lead investigator. As it referred to Jeff's polygraph as a future event, and as it spelled Kassidy's name with a "C," it's thought that it was written by Sgt. James White before his November 11, 2000 revised Affidavit, in which he spelled "Kassidy" correctly. The "Plan" is noteworthy in several respects.

First, it contains a time-line, albeit a short one that begins at 3:30 p.m. on Wednesday, November 8 when Amanda was thought to have brought Kassidy to Jeff's, and ends with Jeff's 911 call on the 9th. (p. 447) Also, the "Plan" included a list of observations of Kassidy by Amanda, Chad, Jeff and Jennifer on Wednesday and Thursday. (p. 449)

Second, it lists incidents of "*Confirmed Prior Abuse*" as related to inverviewers by Amanda, Chad, Jeff and Jennifer, starting with Amanda, "*1. Cassidy thrown by Evans. Strikes wall, etc. Several times/week. 2. Evans grabs Cassidy by face. 3. Evans chokes Amanda and Cassidy a few times.....*" (p. 448) These allegations were definitely not yet "*confirmed,*" but that was the label that White assigned to them.

Third, the "Plan" listed 12 "To Do" items regarding the gathering of evidence. (p. 450) Item #6 was "*Cassidy's last medical exam,*" which could have been titled, "All of Cassidy's medical exams," as all of them would have been important for each side of the case to see. However, it's not known which of these records were obtained by the New Hampshire State Police, as none of these records was provided to Chad's attorneys in Discovery. The Maine Chief Medical Examiner had some of the records, but it's not known which, if any, of those records was sent to New Hampshire.

Item #9 was "*Maine DHS records,*" and these would have been very helpful, as Amanda had appointments in the fall of 2000 with her ASPIRE/DHHS counselor and she took Kassidy with her to those appointments. Amanda wrote in "My Life Story," *Actually that whole month before she died and week, I was in and out of the Department of Human Services quite frequent*[ly] *with her. If she was all banged* [up] *they would be the people to report something.*

It's not known if the New Hampshire State Police obtained those records, but they were not included in the Discovery documents provided to Chad's lawyers. Because 2000 was more than seven years ago, DHS has now destroyed all of those records, except for minimal entries for initiation of Medicaid authorization and other services.

Item #11 was "*Psyc. Eval with Chad through NH DCYF (NHSP)*" It's not known what this item encompassed, but in the interest of gathering truth, such an evaluation of Chad and of the other three adults in this tragedy would have been helpful.

Monday, 13 November 2000

Stephanie Bolduc, a friend of Chad, talked with him by phone at 10:30 a.m. and later called the Rochester Police Dept. and talked with NHSP Sgt. James White and Rochester Detective Paul Callaghan. From White's report, Stephanie reported that Chad was "*crying and upset*" and "*commented to her that 'It's awful. I can't believe she died. I can't believe this.'* " She said that she had never seen Chad with Kassidy but that

Amanda had commented to Bolduc about how good C. Evans was with her daughter. Chad had commented to Bolduc about how good a mother Amanda was. Very mature and responsible. Bolduc told us that C. Evans family seemed loving. She was not aware of any drug or alcohol abuse by C. Evans, and she did not know of any gambling problems he might have.

At 11:40 a.m., Detective Eric Baker interviewed Kris Keeler of DCYF who said that the anonymous call of October 31 had reported that "*Kassidy was observed with large bruises to the left side of* [her] *face and across her neck. This was seen approximately two weeks ago. The reporter was in Chad's home the night before the report and observed new bruising to the right side of her face.*" (p. 1688)

At 2:30 p.m. Sgt. James White talked by telephone with Chad's probation officer, Kevin Callaghan, who reported, "*that he had met with C. Evans that morning....C. Evans submitted to a drug screen. Callaghan said C. Evans was nervous and stressed out.... splitting his time between his house and Bruce Aube's house since Kassidy's death. Callaghan told me that C. Evans had never been a problem as far as probation was concerned.*" (p. 250)

Amanda's friends, Tracey Foley and Melissa Chick, had read about Kassidy's death in the newspapers, and had tried unsucessfully to reach her. To assist in the investigation, they drove to the Kittery Police Station and were interviewed by Maine State Police Detective Jeffrey Smith. At 3:15 p.m. Tracey began her 15-minute interview which was summarized by Smith. Foley had reported that she and Melissa had run into Amanda and Kassidy "*two months ago at the YMCA in Sanford,*" which was actually Friday, October 13, or 31 days previous. She reported that "*Amanda had a large bruise on the side of her face and Kassidy's whole face was covered with bruises,*" and that Amanda had told her the "trampoline story" to explain Kassidy's bruising. Tracey said that the bruise to Amanda was caused "*when Chad had hit her during an argument,*" and that Amanda declined Tracey's offer for her and Kassidy to move in to live with Tracey. (p. 182)

At 3:35 p.m., Smith interviewed Melissa, and stated in his summary that she said that the reconnection with Amanda had occurred "*four to five weeks ago,*" and that *Kassidy's face was covered with black and blue bruises all over except around the sides of her nose which was white. Chick stated, "We could barely see her face with all the bruises all over her face." Chick described in detail a mark coming from across Kassidy's face starting behind her left ear and coming down to her chin. The mark was very clear and in a straight line. Chick stated that Amanda had told her Chad's son had hit Kassidy with a bat. Chick also observed a bruise on Amanda's face and asked* [Amanda] *about it. Chick told me that later that night she bathed Kassidy and observed a bruise to Kassidy's stomach area, marks on her arms and legs...*[and] *a bruise line across the back of Kassidy's fingers... Amanda told Chick the injuries are a result of kids' play. Chick told me that Kassidy may* [have] *had a blood deficiency that may be causing the bruising..* (p. 180)

The bruises on Kassidy's face were the same bruises seen by Joshua Bortner the day before, on Friday the 13th, and by Tracey Foley.

After reporting Chick's recollection of what Amanda had told her about her sexual relationship with Chad, Smith reported that

Chick told me that she had talked to Amanda three weeks ago on the telephone and Amanda had told Chick that her relationship was shaky. Chad wanted her to move out and it was not working living together....Chick told me that a week ago was the last time she had spoken with Amanda. Amanda described everything as being much better and Chad and she were getting along fine, now. Chad had bought Amanda a three-wheel all-terrain vehicle and they were not fighting." (p. 181)

This was the 3-wheeler Chad and Jeff picked up on Sunday, October 22. Sometime in the afternoon, Jeff brought to Maine State Police Det. Jeff Linscott the tape recording of the conversation among Jeff, Amanda and Jennifer in Buckfield.

Around this time, Chad Evans met with Peter Napoli, a senior manager at Colley McCoy. As a loyal employee Chad did not want the names of McDonald's or Colley-

McCoy to be dragged into his case, so he asked for, and was given, a six month leave of absence, without pay.

The afternoon Foster's Daily Democrat story about the case was headlined on page 1, "Officials still investigating toddler's death - Autopsy results withheld pending further analysis." Beyond the information in the headline, there was no new information in the article. As did so many of the newspaper articles, it reviewed the prosecution's case against Chad for Kassidy's death.

At 6:30 p.m. Tracey Foley called Detective Smith to tell him, according to his report, that she had just spoken with Amanda and that Amanda was with Chad at his home. (p. 178) Her motivation for the call was not stated, but it seemed apparent that she understood that the police did not want Amanda and Chad to be together.

Tuesday, 14 November 2000

At 10:40 a.m., Sheila Thayer at the Office of the Chief Medical Examiner began searching for Kassidy's medical records, and called the office of Kassidy's most recent pediatrician, Pediatric Associates of Lewiston. Then she called the hospital of Kassidy's birth, Southern Maine Medical Center in Biddeford. Records from both places were soon sent to the Office of the Chief Medical Examiner. (See the four-page "Report of Death," completed by Thayer.)

At 11:32 a.m. Jeremy Hinton began his second interview, which was with NHSP Trooper Jill Rockey and MSP Detective Erik Baker. Jeremy said that Chad and Amanda and Chad's family had been staying at Bruce's home and that "*the main gist of the conversation*" had been, "*should Chad and Amanda be around each other*." He said that Chad's parents had asked him to "*be there*" for Chad, but "*try not to discuss as many specifics as you can. You know, cause obviously it just makes you more involved.*" (p. 253) Everyone was struggling about how to respond to the tragic circumstances of the loss of Kassidy, the ongoing investigation and suspicion of Chad, the upcoming funeral, and what could be discussed.

Jeremy said that friends and co-workers of Chad were calling him for information and to support Chad. In response to Erik Baker's request, Jeremy named Stephanie Chick, Larry Lane, Bob McDougall, Melissa Allard and Mandy Allard. Of those five, the only person later contacted by the police was Bob McDougall, who was called by Sgt. James White on January 2 2001. The sole purpose of that call was to establish the date of the McDonald's dinner function at the Exeter Inn on Friday, August 25, and that Amanda and Chad were present. Later, White interviewed McDougall in McDougall's office. As one aspect of the police's theory of the crime was that Chad was frustrated and angry on the afternoon of Wednesday, November 8, it would have been useful to interview Melissa Allard, his secretary, with whom he worked that afternoon, and Melissa's daughter, Amanda Allard, who had seen Chad briefly when he purchased an energy bar on his way to Jeff's.

Jeremy said that Chad had acknowledged to him that he had "*grabbed her that one time*" and held Kassidy by the chin. (p. 254) Rockey said, "*...we've done exhaustive interviews. Would it surprise you to learn that other people have witnessed Chad doing more than that to Kassidy*," and Jeremy said, "*Yeah, it would definitely surprise me.*" (p. 255) This was Jill Rockey's second interview of Jeremy, who was the only person she had interviewed. The only person who had said s/he had witnessed Chad's physical contact with Kassidy was Amanda. There were no "*other people*" who had "*witnessed Chad doing more than that to Kassidy.*"

Rockey continued, "*We've had people tell us that Chad has done more than grab her by the face... We've gotten similar stories from several people. So he is lying to you...*" (p. 255) Of all the people interviewed by the police, Jeremy was the person quickest to challenge the police view, and he asked, "*Who's, who's told you this*?" and Rockey said she couldn't say. As she was relying on only one eye witness, Amanda, who was a fragile, grief-stricken, teen-aged mother who wanted to believe what the police initially told her, Rockey was quick to label Chad as a liar.

Detective Baker responded to the challenge with his own direct challenge to Jeremy, "*I'm having a real problem here with you, okay.....you're protecting someone...you're not a clean person yourself... we do a little bit of backgrounds...you've had contact with the law before.*" Jeremy responded, "*I have*?" (p. 256) Baker said, "*Sure*," and Baker indicated that he would show Jeremy his records later on. At the end of the interview, Jeremy remembered these allegations that he had a police record, and Baker said he was talking about Jeremy's having an un-inspected vehicle, which is not the type of criminal record he was trying to allege here. The interview was off to a confrontational start. Interestingly, the police had done this kind of criminal records check on Jeremy, but they hadn't done a similar check for Amanda or Jennifer, and they hadn't asked Jeff about his record.

After Jeremy acknowledged that Chad was his supervisor, Baker expressed concern "*that maybe you're not telling us everything because ... I get that sense, and when I get that sense, usually I'm correct.*" (p. 257) The police in this case were confident of their instincts and their skills. Later, Jeremy said, "*I think I'm just as good at judging character as you are.*" (p. 264) Part of Baker's assessment of Chad was, "*He's a control freak as much as anybody else I've seen in my life.*" (p. 261) He said to Jeremy, "*I have a hard time with people protecting people,*" and Jeremy responded, "***I have a hard time with people making accusations about someone they don't know.** You know, Amanda said to me, 'Jeff hit that kid.'* " (p. 261) Baker didn't respond to the raising of Jeff's name. This interview was not about searching for the causes of Kassidy's death. It was about Chad.

Jeremy preferred to discuss his own direct experience, and about his own experience with Kassidy, he said, "*... the only time I ever saw Kassidy, I tried playing with her a couple times. She didn't play with me. She just, all she ever did was sit there on the couch.*" (p. 263)

Jill Rockey then told Jeremy her view of the case, "*I'm just telling you, you're putting your faith in the wrong person*," and then she described Kassidy's world, "*That girl went through a hell of a lot for the five weeks she lived in that home... broken bones... in pain. Physical pain and she had nobody comforting her. Nobody telling her they loved her...*" No witness had told the police that Kassidy wasn't loved. This was the first reference in an interview to broken bones and the only evidence of broken bones was from the Maine Medical Examiner, who contradicted what Dr. Bock said he saw in the X-rays on November 9th. No witness had said that s/he had seen Kassidy in pain.

Jeremy agreed with the police theory that someone was responsible for Kassidy's death and that three people, Amanda, Chad and Jeff were highest on the list. Rockey thought she had a gotcha moment and asked, "*Okay. Which one of those three people has been arrested for assault?*" and Jeremy answered, "*Jeff,*" and then there was discussion about Jeff. (p. 267)

Jeremy said about Jeff and his restraining orders, "*...I'm not friends with Jeff and he would brag about them, you know, to me. Ah, to me that doesn't sound like a guy that's playing with a full deck.*" (p. 268)

Baker and Rockey supported the credibility of their source, with Baker saying, "*Jeff's taken a poly. Jeff's taken a polygraph,*" and Rockey echoing, "*Jeff's taken a polygraph test.*" (p. 268)

Rockey asked, "*Who's got an attorney and won't talk to the police?*" Jeremy said that Chad told him that the police hadn't called him back for a second interview and that it was just "*common sense*" to seek an attorney if you are accused of a crime. (p. 268) Later, Rockey said to Jeremy, "*I'm gonna tell you right now in the real world... unless people have something to hide, they don't ask for an attorney...*" (p. 285) In the real world, in the world of the Innocence Project, thousands of innocent people have been convicted in this country of serious crimes, and 275 have been exonerated through DNA evidence as of November 9, 2011.

Baker asked Jeremy, "*So you think Chad's going to be willing to come in and take a polygraph and talk to us again?*" and Jeremy responded, "*I would say he would be, yeah.*" (p. 270) The police never asked Chad to take a polygraph. They later explained to Jeremy their understanding that once a suspect retains a lawyer, the police cannot ask to talk with him. (p. 282) However, on the evening of Chad's arrest, the police did seek to talk directly with Chad, and they knew Chad had an attorney, and they even knew that his attorney had called to advise Chad not to talk with the police. The only way that Chad knew about that advice was that he overheard the police end of the conversation at the Rochester Police Department. After he declined to talk with the police without his attorney, they told him that his attorney had called.

Rockey returned to the "three people" approach and said, "*Jeff is going up to take a polygraph today. And, and I'm gonna guarantee you that's gonna eliminate him as a suspect.*" Jeremy saw the change in what he was told about Jeff and the polygraph, "*You said he's taking it. You just said he's already taken it....*" (p. 271) Rockey tried to backtrack, "*It's today. It's today,*" and Baker said, "*...he is.I don't know what time it was. I'm not sure,*" but that wasn't enough for Jeremy who said, "*I have a question for you guys... are you guys telling me the truth about, you know, when you say to me... I mean, you just told me that he's taken a polygraph test already and passed.*" Jeremy was reasonable in thinking that the police said that Jeff passed a polygraph, because they wouldn't have been so willing to say that he had taken a test, but Baker and Rockey did not explicitly say that Jeff passed. Baker denied entirely his earlier statement, "*He's taking it, and I'm sure he's going to pass, but I didn't mention he has,*" and Jeremy insisted, "*But I'm just telling you if you rewound that* [tape]... *you told me he took it and he's passed.*" Baker again insisted, "*I didn't say he's passed. I said he's taking it and he's probably going to pass.*" (p. 271) Jeremy was correct about what Baker and Rockey had said earlier about Jeff's having <u>taken</u> a test, even if not about the <u>passing</u> part. There was never an acknowledgement or apology to him for the error.

Baker then took a backup position which was that "*Hey, the guy's coming up to take the test. That's a step in* [the] *right direction... You've got to give him that, okay.*" Jeremy was now the interviewer, and asked, "*What happens if he fails it, though?*" Baker said, "*If he fails it, we're going to deal with it in that manner. But I can tell you right now from everything that I see, if he fails I'd be very, very surprised. Like I said, I've done this long enough to know.*" Then Baker raised the ante, "*... you're a smart man... to get involved in this type of case and sit back and not help to try to help it and get it taken care of could be a black mark against you later in your career. I don't know how. I mean it could be, ... if you get charged for some reason because you..withheld information....*" This threat came from a person who, together with his co-interviewer, was just caught lying, or communicating a false statement, and who refused to admit it and did not apologize for it. (p. 271-72)

Rockey argued to Jeremy that Chad "*...did not seek medical attention for her, ever... They did not take that kid to a doctor from the time that girl moved in. She did not go to the doctor once with all her physical ailments...*" (p. 273) Amanda had already told Angela Blodgett that she had taken Kassidy to a doctor "this summer" which easily overlapped the period that Kassidy had moved in with Chad. Also, the search for Kassidy's medical records was on the <u>Investigative Plan</u>, apparently prepared by Sgt. James White. Those records, if actually obtained by the police, were never shown to Chad's attorneys. They showed, however, that Kassidy's most recent visit to a doctor was on September 11. Even if Jeremy's interviewers did not yet have actual knowledge of Kasssidy's doctor appointments, the police did know about Amanda's statement of "*this summer,*" and summer ends on September 21. Thus, the police accusations to Jeremy that Chad was at fault for not seeking medical attention for Kassidy were overbroad, even without considering the question of Chad's responsibilities as a boyfriend.

Rockey insisted that Chad was minimizing his abuse of Kassidy as he did of his abuse of Tristan, saying, "*... I guarantee you he's minimizing it.. I guarantee it. He's minimizing what he did to his wife. And I'm sure she did, too.*" (p. 275) Jeremy insisted that his friend, Chad, was not lying to him, "*You know, I don't think the guy would lie to me. .... if you sit down and you look him directly in the eye and you ask him a question, and he loves and respects your opinion....*" (p. 277) Jeremy, too, believed in **eye contact**.

Ostensibly relying upon police records, Rockey told Jeremy that Chad had "*run-ins with the police as an adult,*" and Jeremy said that after Chad's high school years, "*the only one I know of is the Tristan one.*" Rockey responded, "*Okay, so again there's another thing that he hasn't been forthcoming with you about, right?*" (p. 277) However, Jeremy was right, in that Chad had no run-ins with the police after high school, at least not according to the Discovery records provided to Chad's defense lawyers. Rockey did not tell Jeremy what "*run-ins*" she was referencing, but he had been alerted to the police technique since Baker had told Jeremy early in the interview that he, Jeremy, had problems with the law, and Jeremy knew that wasn't true.

Regarding the time-line of Chad's relationship with Amanda, Jeremy said that "*she never had her daughter all summer long when she came up... I saw Kassidy... a couple of occasions..*" and one was a cookout when Amanda's brother, Joshua, was there. He said, "*I really didn't start seeing Kassidy a lot until probably... around the beginning of October, when she pretty much started staying at Chad's from this point.*" (p. 279-80)

Rockey returned to Jeff and his plan to take a polygraph test, "... *whether he's taken it already, he's.. consented to a polygraph, and you know why? Cause he wants to be cleared of this... He doesn't want the stigma of being somebody who beat a child to death on him...*" (p. 282) She continued, "*And people care about.. proving themselves innocent,... Jeffrey knows he didn't do anything. He has admitted to spanking her. Chad, all the instances we've gotten from different people, Chad's not fessing up to anything. Anything.*" (p. 285) That wasn't true, as Chad did tell LeClair and McLeish that he held Kassidy's cheeks in order to obtain eye contact. He did not "*fess up*" to the accusations made by the police, who were relying upon Jeff and Jennifer, because they were not true. Later, Rockey reaffirmed her belief that a person who takes a lie detector test is more reliable than one who is not, saying about Jeff, "... *and been cooperative, and going to take a polygraph or has taken a polygraph. Um, Jeff's been a stand up guy.*" (p. 294) This was Jeremy's last interview with the police until late the following summer. By that time the issue of Jeff's polygraph had faded from view. If there had been an additional interview in November or December 2000, Jeremy would likely have asked the obvious followup question about Jeff's decision not to submit to a polygraph exam. Jeremy could also have asked why the police had not asked Chad or Amanda to take such a test by that time.

Jeremy and the officers exchanged views on the hypothetical question of what would have happened if Amanda and/or Chad had taken Kassidy to see a doctor with her bruises. Said Jeremy, "*...if Chad takes.. Kassidy to the doctor's, and let's say here, 'I believe the babysitter is hitting my kid.' What happens? He loses his kids....*" (p. 290) Baker and Rockey disagreed with Jeremy's conclusion from the hypothetical, but that was Chad's primary fear when he suggested, once, to Amanda, that taking Kassidy to see a doctor about her general health might lead to a problem because of potential misunderstandings about the causes of her bruises.

About the bruises, Jeremy said that "*the first time I asked Amanda about the bruises was that weekend of Chad's birthday,*" i.e. October 15th. (p. 280) Jeremy said that he had seen bruises "*two Tuesdays*" ago, but that was after the McDonald's golf tournament on Tuesday, October 24, and thus was three Tuesdays previous.

As he had done in his first interview, Jeremy described his conversation with Jeff at the Kittery Police Station on the 9th. He said,

I talked to Jeff outside the police station....I said, "Jeff, did you ... ever hit this kid?" and he said, "No." He's like, "I never saw bruises on her before in my life. Until," he said, "Thursday morning." Now, I saw those bruises two weeks ago on Tuesday. If he's watching for that kid and he's changing her diaper, I guarantee you, you guys, [he] *saw the same bruises I saw. They were that bad.... For him to sit there and tell me he's never seen bruises until Thursday, I know the guy's lying to me....they were from here down to the back of her legs. And they weren't bruises. They were black.* (p. 293)

What Jeremy didn't know until Chad's trial was that Jeff had told the police that he had seen bruises on Kassidy almost continuously since Chad came into her life.

Toward the end of the interview, Baker and Rockey tried being softer toward Jeremy as he wasn't buckling from their hardnose approach. Jeremy suggested that perhaps more than one person was responsible for Kassidy's death, and Rockey said, "*Now, come on, Jeremy. I mean we've a lot of people trying to point us in the wrong direction.*" (p. 296) She and Baker were quite confident that they were going in the right direction on the Convict-Chad train. Rockey acknowledged, "*Of course, people are gonna try and lay the blame elsewhere. All I'm telling you is right now, Jeffrey is the only one talking. Jeffrey is the only one willing to take a polygraph....*" (p. 296)

That last statement was not true as Chad had indicated to Sergeant Stewart on Thursday night the 9th, that he was willing to take a polygraph. Also, Amanda had indicated that she was willing to do so as well. The record is silent on whether Jennifer was asked or whether she was willing. Rockey said that she wasn't seeing such cooperation "*from your friend, Chad,*" and Jeremy said, "*...I'm sure it's gonna be a conversation I have with him very soon.*" (p. 296)

Chad's attorneys were old-school defense-oriented defense lawyers and they didn't often proactively contact the police and ask for meetings for their clients; and they barely knew Chad. In this case, it would have been far better for Chad and his attorneys to seek to affirmatively present Chad's knowledge of Kassidy and his relationship to Kassidy, to the police, and the sooner the better. For now, the Convict-Chad train was moving forward, and the police were not interested in statements or facts that contradicted their theory, unless perhaps they were affirmatively and coherently presented.

Rockey said, "*...I'm sorry... I'm sure you've felt ... a little hostile earlier... you know we both felt from the beginning that you've been nothing but a stand up guy...You know, you are a Christian....*" (p. 296) Baker echoed, "*We just don't want you to have your eyes tunnel-visioned on what's going on here.. You need to really open your eyes up...*" (p. 296) That advice, of course, could have cut both ways, as the Convict-Chad train had been in a tunnel for five days.

Jeremy explained that when the allegations emerged about Chad hitting Tristan, his friends split about 50/50 on whether he did or didn't assault her. However, regarding the allegations of abusing, assaulting and murdering a child, Jeremy said, "*Of the people I've talked to, not one person has even had a reservation as* [to] *Chad for a minute...And I've talked to people that don't particularly care for Chad as a manager.... even his ex-wife doesn't even think* [he hurt Kassidy]" (p. 298)

Jeremy noted that Chad had gone to counseling since the violence with Tristan and Baker asked the rhetorical question, "*But has it worked? We don't know.*" (p. 300) Unfortunately, the police never sought to answer that question. They never sought records or information from Chad's counselor, Gray Fitzgerald, nor obtained his appointment schedule with Chad, or any of his records of that counseling or even the records of his court-ordered counseling. Jeremy tried to answer Baker's question, "*I've seen signs in his everyday life that it's different....he was a bear sometimes at work, and now he isn't...*" (p. 300) Although he said that he was "*not going to say he's not a control freak,*" (p. 299) Jeremy again said, "*But, I, honest to God saw, ... emotional changes in Chad from the time he started to go to counseling.*" (p. 300) Baker had said earlier that Chad was a "control freak," but what did that mean to him, and what did it mean to Jeremy? Did Chad know where Amanda was on the weekend of his birthday? No. One person's "control freak" might be another person's character who pays attention to details.

Rockey told Jeremy one of her theories of Chad's actions was that he became frustrated with Kassidy and lost control and beat her on Thursday morning, November 9th, "*I don't think he is a malicious person ...I think something happened in that house that morning that he didn't want to happen but did. Because he lost control.*" (p. 302) The difficulty with Rockey's theory is that there was absolutely no evidence to support such a theory. It was purely an idea to support the existing police conclusion which was that Chad was the abuser and killer of Kassidy. There was no physical evidence and no circumstantial evidence. Now all the police needed to do was figure out when the violence happened, and how and why. Another theory was, "*let me assure you that, that little girl... was beaten over a period of time and it was severe.*" (p. 305) Where was the evidence for that theory? There were some reports of some bruising due to several different causes during Kassidy's last 40 days. There were also reports of accidents.

At the end of the interview, and it became more conversational, Jeremy asked, "*Why was Chad's car the only one taken? I mean, cause as far as I know, Chad didn't drop her off that morning?*"(p. 310) Baker and Rockey dodged the question by saying that their supervisors make the decisions. It was a good question, and most of the answer was that they were no longer looking at other suspects, or other causes for Kassidy's death. They were looking for evidence against Chad, and not for anything else.

Baker and Rockey told Jeremy that he interviewed well. Even Jill Rockey implicitly endorsed a belief in **eye contact** for effective communication, by noting, "*how you've responded to things and looking us in the eye when you're talking to us.*" (p. 311)

Because there was apparently no appropriate question, Jeremy did not tell Baker and Rockey about his observation of three new bruises on Tuesday, October 22, after Kassidy had been with Jeff for the day, and while Jeremy and Chad were golfing.

At 11:30 a.m. on this same day, Jeff arrived at the Alfred, Maine State Police barracks for the scheduled polygraph examination. This was the same time that Jeremy had arrived at the Kittery Police Station for his second interview, during which there was statements made about Jeff's taking a polygraph test. Shortly after his arrival at Alfred, Jeff declined to take the exam, according to a report by Det. Jeff Linscott. There is no transcript of any discussion on that day with the police about this decision. At his deposition in his civil lawsuit against Chad in 2004, Jeff explained why he decided against taking the polygraph exam, after talking with police and a friend, Ron Donnell. He concluded, "*To me, it wasn't a big deal. You know, I'll take the test.*" (pp. 46-51)

In subsequent interviews, Jeff was not asked again about the polygraph test. Despite the police reliance on Jeff's credibility, and on the scheduled polygraph as anchor for that credibility, the matter was closed. No report was ever provided to Chad's attorneys regarding the police preparation for Jeff's examination, which would have contained the questions that were going to be asked, and the name of the scheduled polygraph examiner. Before this day, he was a suspect who had made several claims about Chad, but whose credibility had not yet been tested by a polygraph. Now, he was a suspect who had refused to take such a test. No one else in the case had been offered such a test, and no one else had refused.

At 1:30 p.m., the second session of the autopsy for Kassidy Bortner's body was conducted, and completed at 2:30 p.m.

The afternoon Foster's Daily Democrat page 1 story by Jennifer Saunders, was *"Investigation into toddler death could take months"* and it simply said that the investigation was continuing. Similarly, the Portsmouth Herald story by Amy Wallace, "*Officials Await Child Autopsy Results*, reported that the investigation was continuing and that Kassidy's death was considered to be "*suspicious.*"

Wednesday, 15 November 2000

The morning, statewide, newspapers had no coverage of the Kassidy Bortner story as the police were saying only that the case was under investigation.

At 11:15 a.m., MSP Detective Jeffrey Linscott and NHSP Detective John Marasco conducted the second interview with Bruce Aube, which began with a discussion of the trip on Sunday, November 12, to the Gray State Bolice barracks to pick up Amanada. Then Bruce described the rules at his home where Chad and Amanda and his family had been staying, "*...rule number one is, 'I don't want to hear ... any of it. I'm just here to be supportive... I don't even want you talking to your parents or anything....*" (p. 1344)

As with others who knew Kassidy, Bruce felt badly that

... maybe... I could have have done something about this... I had seen bruises on her face... why didn't I say anything? ... I knew a particular instance where she had a lot of cold sores on her mouth... It's easy to talk in hindsight, I guess...maybe they aren't cold sores. I don't know what they are. But she had a lot of them....That's what I was told they were. (p. 1346-47)

Bruce said that his belief in Amanda's general credibility was shaken when his girlfriend, Jessica, had heard Amanda's mother at the police station on the 9th say that she was Kassidy's primary caregiver during her first six months. Bruce recalled that when Amanda and Chad returned from their trip to Martha's Vineyard, Amanda told Bruce and Jessica that the trip was her first time away from Kassidy since she was born. (p. 1349) However, maybe she meant this was the first time she was far away, i.e. out-of-state.

Nonetheless, Bruce's faith in Chad was strong, and he said, "*I don't think in a million years that he could of done that to that little girl. No possible way... there's just no, there's no way.... and nobody's gonna change my mind about that...* " (p. 1351)

Bruce was uncomfortable. Linscott reminded Bruce that he was going to return to the police station after his first interview and prepare a written statement, but he didn't come. Bruce explained, "*I hated this place. I didn't like the thought of coming back here again.... we talked about doing the park bench thing... we don't even have to be in this building.... I don't have anything to hide. I guess what I've been telling myself this whole time, so why the hell am I nervous. Some shitty stuff has happened....*" (p. 1360-61) Bruce asked about the written statement request, "*...I'm wondering, was I the only one that was asked, and why was I the only one that was asked?*" (p. 1361) Linscott told Bruce he was not the only one and that he had "*a couple... of written statements in my folder....*" (p. 1361) The only written statements prepared in the case were from Jeff and Will Peirce. Except for Bruce, no one else was asked, and no other requests were recorded in an interview transcript or summary of interview report.

John Marasco asked Bruce to describe his friendship with Chad, an Bruce said it began when he was 16 and working at McDonald's. Chad saw the transcript of this interview in 2010 and noted that Bruce was 20 when they met, but he understands how nervousness during a police interview can lead to such incorrect answers. Bruce continued,

"*He's ...always been someone I could... count on... he's the type of guy you know that you know bend over backwards to help someone else out...*" Asked for specifics, Bruce said, "*...let people that didn't have a place to live, live in his house.*" (p. 1367) Then he remembered, "*...that he had pulled some guys out of a car that had blew up... in front of his house. He saved them. He got some award from the Union Leader for that...*" (p. 1368) That information didn't seem to impress the police, but later in the interview, Marasco said about Chad, "*This guy has probably done a lot of good things in his life. He may have saved people from a burning car. Unfortunately, that's not what this is about. This is about the facts and circumstances involved in the death of a twenty-one-month old baby.*" (p. 1417) Marasco asked Bruce why "*... you can't off the top of your head... tell me anything definitively that makes him so great.*" (p. 1370) Despite telling them about the Union Leader award, Bruce felt badly that he could not tell them more clearly why his belief in Chad was so strong, "*Yes, see, and I, I'm feeling totally guilty about that.*" (p. 1371)

Bruce expressed his concern about the interview, "*I feel like you're trying to change my, what my opinion is..,*" and Marasco responded, "*No... absolutely not. Ah, we would never do that.*" (p. 1374) Marasco and Linscott were asking Bruce why he had asked people not to talk about the case with him, and he seemed to say that he didn't want to get involved in the case and didn't want people to be tripped up later by their statements. Also, he said, Chad's lawyers had asked them not to talk about the case. Despite Bruce's efforts not to be involved or hear anything, Marasco said, "*...now you're here. In the middle of this thing....that means now you do have to answer some questions. Now, you got to help us...and you have to explain that comment... Because that comment's gonna hurt you.*" (p. 1385-86)

Then Marasco asked Bruce about his home, for which there was no mortgage, and about his car, and said,

...you have a lot at stake...this thing is not gonna go away... you got a lot to lose now...This is a different interview today... so Bruce Aube now has a lot to lose...Blanket statements are made, and yet they can't be backed up. Bruce, you're in a world of hurt. In a world of hurt, man. Cause this could affect you now....friends come and go, but comments don't. And statements don't, and trials don't... I'd hate to see you lose a house, lose a car, lose a job, lose anything you got going for you...For somebody that you've only known for 8 years...you've played with fire a little bit. By letting these people, staying so close to these people... there's a death involved...this is not a book.... This could affect you the rest of your life. (p. 1389-90)

Bruce said, "*... you got all the suspicion in the world that I know something, and I don't.*" (p. 1391)

Marasco kept on the pressure, "*... the 21-month old kid, dead.... Wasn't natural causes. Need I say more... We're looking at civil suits.... We're looking at prison time. .... I mean ... this is the real deal.*" (p. 1391) Linscott joined, "*You're not the first one, Bruce. It's like this all the time... it's always the nice guy, the innocent guy that gets drawn in to something.... Someone gets sucked in...*" (p. 1392) And Marasco, "*...Nice guys finish last...*" (p. 1392)

Bruce wasn't intimidated yet, "*... I don't think I'm gonna finish last. I mean unless... this whole system's really shitty.... If you guys think I've done something wrong, I wish you'd tell me and I would try to fix it, you know?... the messages I'm getting sent to me is these people shouldn't be in there at your house.* " (p. 1392-93)

Marasco revealed the pressures on the police to solve the case, as he asked Bruce, "*...have you seen the stuff on the news? I hear it in the car all the time... Have you heard it on the news? Or seen it?... or read the paper?... the internet?*" (p. 1393)

Bruce said that his father didn't think that Chad killed Kassidy, and Marasco responded, "*...So, another blanket statement that can't be backed up?*" (p. 1395)
The pressure continued. Said Marasco,

Let me explain it to ya. It's very simple... if Chad had involvement with this, ok? ... Chad is gonna try to do the best thing for Chad, hands down. Amanda's gonna do the best thing for Amanda, hands down. They have nothing to lose. You do. ...And what the hell's gonna happen. But you know what's gonna happen to you?... Nobody's gonna give a shit about Bruce Aube. I hate to break it to ya." (p. 1396-97)

Finally, Bruce said, "*Can I ask you guys a couple things?...I'm worried.*" and Marasco said,

You should be....What you need to do is, you need to back peddle away from where you are....and not just physically. Physically back pedaling doesn't solve it for ya....you to start helping us to think of every little thing... that's gonna help us finally solve this case.... only then can we say, Bruce Aube, you helped us...Now you can go on with your life, Bruce. And you'll never hear from Maine and New Hampshire State Police again.... You got a father, you got a girlfriend, you got stuff you need to do." (p. 1397-98)

Bruce still felt the pressure was wrong, "*Yeah, don't, don't... you told me this stuff, and this is your job.. but I'm almost insulted that you keep continually bringing this up. Cause I heard you.*" (p. 1398)

Then the officers peppered Bruce with direct questions and finally Bruce acknowledged that Chad had told him, since the 9th, that he had, in Marasco's words, "*grabbed the baby by the face.*" (p. 1402) As he later acknowledged, he already knew about the face grabbing (p. 1409), but Bruce was feeling the pressure, "*I been fuckin' sick to my stomach... she* [Kassidy] *was in my house, too..... if I'm telling you everything that I know, I'm not gonna be in trouble. Am I right or wrong?*" (p. 1403) Marasco responded, "*I can't answer that. I don't know.*" (p. 1404)

After a pause to change tapes, Bruce told Marasco about hearing from Chad, about a month earlier, that Tristan had visited Amanda and told her that she suffered from Chad, "*the worst beating in New Hampshire history...* " (p. 1407) Bruce thus confirmed that the "*worst beating*" story came from Tristan via Amanda. As both Bruce and Jeff (see Chapter 4) used the phrase, "*worst beating*" it seems clear that Amanda used that phrase when passing the story on to Chad and also on to Jennifer and Jeff. What isn't known is what Tristan actually said to Amanda, or whether it was an exaggeration by Amanda. In any case, it wasn't true.

Marasco returned to his allegations that Bruce may have legal problems because of his help for Chad and Amanda, saying, "*... you're asking me.. can you be ever, in any trouble here? Be charged criminally? And I told you,... it's gonna take until the end of the investigation...The problem is... depending on how this thing turns out, you may be living with a felon.*" Now more concerned, Bruce asked, "*...should I be fixing this right this second?*" (p. 1407) Marasco responded, "*...what I'm saying to you is, yes. Fix it. And you* *know how to fix it. Separate yourself from him by telling us what you know about him.*" (p. 1408)

Bruce said that he talked with Chad before coming to the interview and Marasco guessed that Chad tried to influence what he said. Bruce said that Chad said, "*something along the lines of, 'I'm glad I have a logical, you know, guy on my side,' or something like that.*" (p 1411) Bruce also talked with Chad's father, and wondered what to say to the police.

Marasco tried again to return to Bruce's conversation with Chad when Chad acknowledged that he had grabbed Kassidy's face, and Bruce responded changed gears, saying,

...There's a note at my house right now that she, that Amanda wrote that includes that in the letter. I went, after I had read that, I was like, you know, what the fuck is going on here?.... I think when I originally had ... talked with you guys, I had said that she had been hit in the head with a ball? Right? That's what he had told me?... And I had said, 'it's a wiffle ball?'... and then found out it wasn't a wiffle ball... It was a harder ball... And then I read the, in the note about the face thing." (p. 1413)

Marasco asked, "*Can we follow you back to your house and get the note? When we're out of here? We need the note. Bruce, that's... an easy one...You got evidence at your house...we can get out of here and we'll go back to the house, and you can give us the note...*" (p. 1413-14) Marasco and Linscott asked for Bruce's help in obtaining that document which Amanda had written, but Bruce didn't want a police car anywhere near his home.

Bruce relayed a conversation he had with Amanda and Chad, which included a confused discussion of several events relating to Kassidy. Marasco continued to try to persuade Bruce that his friend was not as good as he thought. He recounted what Bruce said that Chad had told him about Tristan going to Amanda "*saying he gave me the worst beating in New Hampshire's domestic violence history. Is it really a long reach from that to us looking at him for causing some injuries to a child*?" (p. 1415)

After a confusing exchange about Chad and Tristan's conversations on the afternoon of the 9th, Marasco asked Bruce, "*Who do you think committed this crime?*" and Bruce responded, "*I hope, I hope to God that it wasn't a crime*," and then he mentioned that Amanda "*had done some work for me... She started data entry contracted to her.*" (p. 1430) With all the focus on Bruce's relationship with Chad, the police ignored Amanda's work for Bruce, and they didn't followup on his statement here, either. Bruce was never asked for any work records from Amanda's work for him. Such records perhaps would have helped everyone understand the time-line for her use of Jeff as a babysitter.
Bruce recounted conversations he had had with Chad early in his relationship with Amanda where they wondered together whether getting involved with a woman with a toddler, who was sometimes a nuisance, was a good idea. "*He said something along the lines of... she had the kid,... having... prevented him from doing other things occasionally.*" Linscott agreed that these conversations were "*just expressing normal woes that many parents have?*" (p. 1432)

Bruce discussed some of the comings and going of the previous week, as Chad and his family went back to Keene for a night, and then returned to Rochester, and checked on Chad's dog, Kato. Chad had decided to sell his 3-wheelers to his brother, Jason, to help raise money for his defense, and to sell his comic book collection, which was back in Keene.

Several times during the interview, the police reminded Bruce that he had told the police during his first interview that he had seen Kassidy four times with bruises on her, and another time with cold sores, but there were no additional questions during this interview about those four bruises, or cold sores. There were no questions about the dates of those observations.

Linscott and Marasco asked what Bruce would say to the others about this interview, and the first one, and they were especially interested in Chad's reaction - which Bruce couldn't remember. He said the he hadn't had **eye contact**, "*I don't think I've looked him in the eye since this whole thing's happened.*" (p. 1445) Marasco expected more of a reaction, "*Somebody must have acknowledged that... that you made that comment. Somebody must have acknowledged that you said that to us.*" (p. 1445) Marasco seemed to think that the recognition of any bruises or cold sores was somehow an acknolwedgement of criminal activity. Instead, it may have just been an acknowledgment of bruises and cold sores.

Marasco asked what Jeremy said during these discussions and Bruce said that Jeremy had "*Heard stuff about Travis had seen a big black and blue on her ass that was.....*" (p. 1445) There were no followup questions about that allegation.

Bruce said that he would ask Chad and Amanda to leave his home, but what about Chad's parents, "*should I tell them they should leave, too? And his sister and...*" Marasco's response was, "*But what I'm saying is this, you care about this baby?*" (p. 1451) The implication was that if Bruce cared about Kassidy, he would tell Chad's family to leave, too.

Marasco tried to persuade Bruce to call Chad, apparently to ask him if he killed Kassidy, perhaps on the theory that Chad's response might be different if his friend asked him, "*Better yet, better yet, would you be willing...rather than do it face to face, would you be willing to call on the phone? Would he tell you on the phone?*" (p. 1451) Bruce answered, "*When he tells me, when he tells me that he didn't do anything, what happens then?*" (p. 1452) And later, "*I don't think it would work. I just don't think so...*" Marasco then said,

That's common sense, yeah, ok. Yup. ...what about a body wire?...I'm just throwing these options out to ya as options to remove yourself from the situation that you're in now....maybe if you were willing to help us, then we'll make the charge go away...If you wore a body wire, they wouldn't be able to see it...then at the moment, you know, have a couple beers, and... sit down and... this thing is really getting to me. My head is spinning.... (p. 1453)

Bruce finally said,

It's not my, it's not my fucking way at all....I can't, you can't. My answer right now would be 'No.'..... I can't fucking believe this, man....I don't fucking know... I don't know what I'd fucking do if he told me that to my face, that he did that. I'll tell you that right now...He's [Chad] *my boring fucking life, you know? I have to talk to somebody about what we just did here. Do you realize that? I have to at least talk to my old man about this. Because I'm gonna go fucking nuts.* (p. 1454)

Marasco kept trying,

Cause you could, you could, you could expose the truth.... It would take courage.... But if he were to admit to you on tape, ok? 'I did this. I did this. I did that.... well, yeah, you know, you may inside like you betrayed a friend. What you've really done is... you've done justice.... (p. 1455)

Bruce seemed to say "*No,*" at least temporarily to such assistance to the police, "*I got to say 'No' now, but I don't want to say 'No' to you totally....*" (p. 1458)

At the end of the interview Bruce asked about Jeff, "*... you don't think the other guy did it?.. That Jeff guy?*" and Marasco responded,

I don't know. We think we know, obviously, that Chad's been involved with abuse of the child.... I mean, let's face it. Anybody that would pick up a little girl by her face, has some problems. I mean, that's, that's something you don't even see in the movies. That's just sick.... He's full of shit. That's man to man. He's full of shit. (p. 1460)

It was a powerful, but hard to visualize, image that Trooper Marasco presented, "*pick up a little girl by her face,*" but he seemed to be combining Chad's acknowledged holding of Kassidy's face to obtain **eye contact**, with Amanda's description of Chad's playing roughly with Kassidy. Still, even though he acknowledged that such an image was so sick that "*you don't even see in the movies,*" he stuck with that image, instead of questioning it.

John Marasco wrote a summary of both interviews with Bruce, and the aftermath of the second. He wrote that he offered to Bruce the

possibility of wearing a body wire while residing at the house with Amanda and Chad. Aube stated that he would have to think about it....Aube returned to meet me at the police department a short time after traveling to his house. When Aube returned, he was visibly upset. He stated that Chad had taken the note and given it to his attorney. Aube stated that he told Chad and Amanda to leave the residence. As I stood in the parking speaking with Aube, I saw a vehicle circle the police parking lot. Aube identified a male and female subject inside the vehicle to be Amanda and Chad. At one point, while standing in front of Aube, he began to cry. He also threw his vehicle keys forcibly to the ground. Aube identified [sic]*that he was upset because he had asked Amanda and Chad to move out.* (p. 1069-70)

Marasco wrote that he understood that Amanda's note "*makes reference to the fact that Chad picked up Cassidy by the face on a previous occasion.*" In fact, Amanda's note , below, states, "*To me, he was rough and when mad and grab her face, but I don't think he could or would be capable of what happened.*" Wednesday evening, Chad and Amanda were back at Chad's home, and Bruce's friendship with Chad was permanently harmed.

The three-page handwritten note by Amanda that Linscott and Marasco were seeking to obtain from Bruce was given by Chad to his attorneys, who then gave it to the prosecutors in May of 2001. The rekeyed WORD version of the note appears below:

These are some flashbacks that are coming into mind. Right now I can't even think straight. But I do remember this. I was going to a money management class, and I asked Jeff to watch her. He picked her up at my house in Rochester. (My car was in V.I.P. Chad was gonna pickup ......at the time... meet him ... halfway. So he took her. I said, well, might as well take her overnight 'cause it's late. I didn't have my car. So, the next day I call. He says, 'I'll drop her off soon.' Never did. He said he had a lot to do. (And I thought he was just being lazy.) and didn't feel like driving. (He's very lazy.) So I waited & still he didn't show. He kept call[ing*] a couple* [of] *times & said he'd be there soon. Then I call and said where is he? He's like, "Well, it's getting late, might as well take her XXXXXXXXXX"* [crossed out four or five words]. *So I said, "Okay." I don't know. Almost. So I call early morning.* [the next day?] *I remember really missing her. And he said he was gonna be over in a couple of hours. He never showed. Finally...*

I got my car in the morning, but since he said he was gonna drop her off, I didn't drive to Kittery to get her. (I also was on the computer a lot. (I was typing in surveys for money. I did almost 9,000 of them. But I had a deadline. So I had to get them done asap. So, for me at the time, it was more of a favor.

But I never used him too...

Finally, he drops her off around 4 or 5:00. She was so sick and hungry. I sat her down on her chair and gave her a bowl of cereal. (She usually eats great with a spoon, but she XXXX put her mouth in the bowl and tried to suck the milk out of the bowl. Then she puked it up 'cause I kept giving [her] *water. but she was drinking really fast. Then I gave her Tylenol and Pedialyte. Finally, she was done drinking. And I held her and cuddled with her. XXXXXX Jeff (suspiciously stayed there for a while, watching me care for her.) He just said she was sick and acting weird. And dazed. The flu was going around.* [That] *was my first thought. Then he told me about her falling out of the truck on to the ground. And I started getting mad. (But I never thought he would do anything intentionally. XXXXXX He also forgot her bag & diapers. So I asked him to watch the kids while I went to Market Basket to get diapers. I came back right away, cause he said he had a play place to clean. So I got back & held her all night. And watched TV with her. Kept giving her fluids. Then she was sitting on my lap and she XXXX XXXXXXX falling asleep. Then she rolled her eyes back (But I thought she was sleeping & just* [tired?] *& then she fell asleep. I laid with her and then put her to bed. Chad & I slept beside her that night. He was really concerned and wanted to help. The next day she seemed fine. She was doing her ABC's 123's. And seemed happy. Chad did lose his temper with her. But could NEVER XXXXXXXX intentionally abuse her. To me he loved her. And wanted the best for her. To me, he was rough and when mad and grab her face, but I don't think he could or would be capable of what happened.*

Dare to Conquer
Amanda Bortner
603-336-3151 or 3757 or 3751

At 2:50 p.m. Det. Jeff Linscott interviewed Emily Conley, age 19, for an hour at the Sanford, Maine Police Dept. Linscott did not record the interview, but wrote a two-page summary, instead. Excerpts of the report stated,

Conley said she last saw Amanda about three weeks ago and told Amanda that she didn't want anything to do with her anymore. Conley said this decision was based on the quality of Amanda's mothering....Conley said that Amanda said that Chad grabbed Amanda's [Kassidy's?] *face in anger 5-6 times. Conley said she saw bruises on Amanda's face on one occasion. Conley said she saw bruises on Kassidy once also. Conley said that 3 weeks ago she saw a burn on the top of Kassidy's foot. Conley said Amanda was very irresponsible and that she would send over Kassidy to be babysat very dirty. Conley said that a couple of weeks ago, Amanda said that Chad was a very controlling person and that she wanted to get her own apartment. Conley said the bruising she saw on Kassidy was 3 weeks ago and she saw Kassidy's face completely bruised. Conley said that Amanda said Chad did it to Kassidy, but said Kassidy was jumping on the trampoline and Chad grabbed Kassidy by the face to keep her from getting flung off. Conley said she later asked another mutual friend, Shannon Gagne, about bruises on Kassidy and Shannon said Amanda said that Kassidy was on Chad's hip and Chad walked around the corner and hit Kassidy's head on the wall or door jam.*

Conley stated that Amanda asked her if she would take part in a threesome with Chad, which Conley declined. Conley said that Amanda took nude photographs of _______ for Chad. Conley said that Amanda said Chad had his ex-wife's wedding cake still in his freezer and that Chad had a bag of bra's of women he had slept with....Conley stated she has met Chad and thinks he is stuck on himself. Conley said that Chad always talked a lot about weightlifting. Conley said that Chad was hard on Amanda about her looks, that she has been taking diet pills to look good for him. Conley said her advice to Amanda was to get out of the relationship and get her own apartment.

....Conley stated that Amanda wanted someone to baby-sit for the whole weekend on Chad's birthday because Chad's parents were coming to stay with them, and she did not want them to see the bruises on Kassidy. Conley said she told Amanda to tell the parents the trampoline story, but Amanda said the parents would think they abused Kassidy. Conley said that her boyfriend, John Perreault, saw the burn on top of Kassidy's foot along with her.

Once again, dates were important to establish. Emily was reported to have said that she saw Kassidy's face "*three weeks ago*" and it was "*completely bruised.*" She also said that Amanda had talked with her about the possibility of babysitting Kassidy during the weekend of Chad's birthday, which was Saturday/Sunday, October 14/15, and that weekend was exactly 25/26 days before Kassidy's death and 31/32 days before this interview. Thus, the easy question would have been whether she saw Kassidy's "*completely bruised*" face before or after the weekend of Chad's birthday. It was likely afterwards. Vikki Norman had said that Emily had babysat Kassidy "*two weeks ago*," i.e. two weeks prior to her November 15 interview, which would have made the babysitting date for Emily, about November 1.

Linscott didn't establish the date of the last time that Emily actually babysat Kassidy. In a subsequent interview, in January 2001, of Crystal Martin, she said that she babysat Kassidy *"3 weeks to a month before her death"* and she bathed Kassidy and her own son together and saw no bruising. That would have been between Thursdays, October 12 and 19. As October 13 was the day that Joshua Bortner saw bruises on Kassidy, and as there were no bruises for the October 1 photograph, then it's likely that Emily's babysitting was a week earlier, over the weekend of October 7/8.

Emily was unemployed and a few months away from becoming a single mother, like Amanda, and their mutual friend, Crystal. As she was known to be pregnant around the end of June when she was introduced by Chad and Amanda to Jeff Jacobs, she surely was obviously pregnant at the time of this interview on November 15. To assist in establishing dates, Emily's obstetrician appointments were an obvious source of clear dates. This was especially important because Amanda told Jim White in her December 19 interview that she was "*planning on driving*" Emily to a doctor's appointment. (p. 618) However, the date of that appointment has not been established.

Regarding the accident when Chad was holding Kassidy on his hip, Chad wrote in a March 20, 2010 letter, that he was "*holding Kassidy on my hip with my hand under her butt. I swung around real quick and she fell back with the momentum. She hit the corner of the door or the casing. It left a slight bruise on her face as I recall. I believe Amanda witnessed it.*"

About the bras, Chad wrote in a January 7, letter,

This seems like another one of those things that started out with a grain of truth and by the time it gets through 2-3 different people it has changed drastically. The only thing that I can imagine Amanda may have told her is one of two things.

1. On occasion after Tristan moved out, __ would come spend the night. I know at one point, she left a complete change of clothing, which I kept in my dresser. Can't recall if Amanda ever knew this or not.

2. I was married to Tristan and lived with her for nearly 4 years. When Tristan moved out she left many things behind and would take them on occasion. Our lives were intertwined. I do remember at one point I found a few of Tristan's bras in my closet. Knowing it would upset Amanda I shoved them in my top dresser drawer with the intentions of giving them to Tristan at some point. Amanda found them and got very upset, demanding that I throw them out. I was a bit stubborn myself, and didn't do well with demands. I informed Amanda that I was going to return them to Tristan along with some other items that were hers, in the bureau drawer. After that, I deliberately left the items in the bureau for a while until Amanda stopped mentioning it. Then I returned them to Tristan as I recall. It was so important that I "win" that it caused Amanda to feel like shit and share who knows what with one of her girlfriends. Then this girlfriend shares a story with the police that makes me look like a first class pervert. Anyway, I think that is it.

Emily didn't mention the double date that Amanda and Chad arranged, as Chad described in his August 2, 2010 letter:

You asked about the double date with Emily Conley. I could give you an exact date if we could get some help from these credit card companies. We went for dinner and drinks at the Whales Tale. I believe I paid for it on my credit card. I want to say it was late June or early July. Kyle would have been with Tristan. It's likely that Kassidy was at Jackie's. Amanda may have been still working in Auburn at this point. I was aware that Emily was pregnant when we went out on the double date. Amanda had informed me that her ex boyfriend was a real jerk and wanted to fix Emily up with someone nice. Jeff Jacobs, like me, had recently split from his wife. I met Emily and thought she was really nice. I knew Jeff Jacobs was a great guy. I informed him that Emily was pregnant. Jeff was a father to a young son, and this did not phase him. If things had worked out between Jeff and Emily, Jeff is the kind of guy that would have stepped up. I didn't put a ton of thought into it. Mostly, I just went on Amanda's word and wishes. I thought it could be potentially good for both of them. Emily, because no one should have to go through a pregnancy alone, which is the way Amanda described to me. It would be good for Jeff because he was taking his pending divorce hard.

On this day, Amanda Donnell, age 20, of Somersworth, New Hampshire, saw Amanda, whom she knew, and Chad in a cash register line at TJ Maxx and called them, to their faces, "*baby killers*." Later, she contacted the police to advise of her exchange with Amanda and Chad. The Kittery Police report by Detective Steve Hamel said that Donnell's observation was "*two days prior to Evans' arrest*," which occurred on the 16th, but Chad's Gold Card reflects purchases at TJ Maxx in Somersworth for $209.95 on the 15th. Amanda, Chad and Chad's mother were purchasing clothes for Kassidy's body for burial, and for something for Amanda to wear at the funeral. Chad paid for the purchases. Hamel's report stated

As a result of that interview the following information was obtained: Ms. Donnell indicated that she observed both Chad Evans and Amanda Bortner at the T.J. Maxx store in Somersworth, New Hampshire just two days prior to Evans' arrest. Ms. Donnell indicated that she was taken back and aggravated at seeing these two individuals together.

Ms. Donnell explained that she knew Amanda Bortner for just a few months and described their relationship as being acquaintances, noting that they were not close friends. Ms. Donnell knew Evans through an introduction from Bortner. Ms. Donnell indicated she was aggravated because she observed Bortner and Evans laughing and joking, which she felt was inappropriate after having just lost the baby. Donnell indicated that during the entire time she was able to observe Bortner and Evans together she observed no remorse of any kind or to any degree. To the contrary, they constantly laughed and joked. According to Donnell, Evans was purchasing a new winter jacket for Bortner at the time. While at the T.J. Maxx check-out, Ms. Donnell realized that Evans and Bortner were right behind her in the line. Again, Ms. Donnell described their behavior at this time as laughing and joking and not at all normal considering the recent death of an infant. Being aggravated by this, Donnell turned to Evans and Bortner and said, "Baby killer" as she stared at Evans. In response, Evans gave Donnell the middle finger and they both (Evans and Bortner) began to laugh as if nothing bothered them, which caused Donnell to repeat the words "Baby killer" to them.

In 2011, Chad has no recollection of ever meeting Amanda Donnell before seeing her in that TJ Maxx store on that day. Hamel's report did not indicate that Donnell realized that Chad's mother was with him and Amanda.

Like the Kittery Detective Steve Hamel, Ms. Donnell had opinions about how young mothers should grieve for their deceased children. She had her own difficulties with the law, with her arrest for a September 16 altercation with a woman in Rochester, during which a tooth was broken. Foster's Daily Democrat covered the story on December 5, with the article, "Somersworth woman granted bail in assault." Amanda Donnell's father, Ronald, was the man with whom Jeff had discussed his upcoming polygraph exam, before he declined.

On this day, November 15, the Maine Chief Medical Examiner, Dr. Margaret Greenwald, completed a four-page "Report of Inquiry and Examination by Medical Examiner" which stated that Kassidy died of "*multiple blunt force*" injuries. It gave some medical history for Kassidy, who was said to have been born "*full term... no significant complications. Birth weight 8 lbs. 12 oz. length 21 1/2 inches, head circumference: 13 1/2 inches, chest circumference: 12 1/2 inches.*

In September 1999, was seen by Dr. James Timoney for evaluation of 'in-toed' gait. On that date, no injuries are noted by the physician. There is no indication of X-rays, but an orthopedic examination is performed. The decedent is described as cranky, but this is attributed to her missing her nap. Mother says that the growth milestones have been normal and she began walking at about 8 months." (p. 1099)

By this report, it was clear that Dr. Greenwald had obtained medical records from at least two sources, Southern Maine Medical Center, where Kassidy was born, and Dr. James Timoney. Of perhaps critical importance was the error, by a year, in the date of Dr. Timoney's examination, which occurred on September 11, 2000 and not "*September of 1999*." On September 4, 1999, Kassidy was eight months old, and thus barely walking, and an "in-toed" gait would have been barely noticeable. In fact, it wasn't noticed by anyone until mid-summer 2000 by Chad's mother. When Chad's attorneys received this report as part of a batch of discovery materials in the spring of 2001, they missed the implausibility of the 1999 date, and thus missed the reminder to obtain all of Kassidy's medical records. If this report had said, "In September of 2000," Chad's attorneys would have seen the opportunity to challenge an important part of the case against Chad, which was that abuse began on August 1, and that the period of one of the assault counts began on September 1.

The afternoon Foster's Daily Democrat story was on page 3A, *"No new info in probe of toddler's death"*.

Thursday, 16 November 2000

Shortly after Noon, on the 16th, Amanda Bortner went to the Kittery Police Station with her friend, Melissa Chick, and Amanda had her fourth police interview, with Maine State Police Detective Angela Blodgett and New Hampshire State Police Detective James

White. The 30 minute interview ended at 12:55. Amanda signed the "Authorization" form releasing Kassidy's body to the Andrews funeral home in Buckfield, Maine. It was one of the few forms in the case to correctly list 191 Milton Road as her home address, but it spelled Kassidy's name with a "C" until Amanda corrected it by hand.

White introduced himself to Amanda, and she said, "*I do want to see a counselor because, like, I don't know... I just don't understand like why I still want to see Chad, and I can't... prevent myself from calling him, you know what I mean?*" (p. 1003) By this time, the police had convinced her that Chad was responsible for Kassidy's death, but another part of her knew that he was not. Blodgett said she "*can get in touch with a couple places*" (p. 1004) for counseling, but none was ever offered by the Maine or New Hampshire Police Departments. At some point in the investigation and prosecution of Chad, and then Amanda, a Victim/Witness Advocate, Allison Vachon, from the New Hampshire Attorney General's Office was assigned to assist Amanda. However, that assistance evaporated when Amanda later affirmed her belief that Chad didn't kill or assault Kassidy. Amanda was transformed from victim to defendant.

Amanda said that she had been staying with Chad at Bruce's but that her best friends, Melissa Chick and Cathy Nuernberg, were "*all saying that I shouldn't be with Chad.... And I know I know I shouldn't be, but I don't know why....*" (p. 1004) Amanda said that Chad had told her he was "*sorry for what he did. You know? He thinks he made a mistake. He just tells me he loves me and...*" Blodgett asked if Amanda understood his apology to be for the "*general abuse that we've gone over*" and Amanda said, "*Yes.*" (p. 1004) However, Amanda misunderstood Chad's regret, which wasn't for any alleged abuse of Kassidy, but for his failure to do more to prevent Kassidy's death, whatever was the cause.

Blodgett asked Amanda "*What about Chad saying... that he wished you had never had her* [Kassidy] *and he wish*[ed] *she was dead?*" (p. 1005) Amanda said, "*I thought he was joking around. He did that only once.*" (p. 1005) Blodgett asked for more details, and it became clear that the context was an argument and not a joke. Amanda said, "*... I was in the bedroom, and... he had grabbed her face and I yelled at him and I like pulled her away. And I was just like, 'Go downstairs... I was really mad and he made that comment as he was going downstairs.*' The incident began when "*she just started crying when he came in the room, but, because he came near me.... because that's when she would cry... She was just really jealous. And he had grabbed her face and was like threw her on the bed.*" (p. 1006) Significantly, Amanda clarified, "*... I don't think he used the word, 'dead.' I think he said, .. 'I wish she wasn't here' or something like that. You know it was like he was just really frustrated... So I never really thought about it.*" (p. 1006)

In 2011, Chad recalled that argument, and wrote in his April 1, 2011 Letter.

You asked about the allegation that I said to Amanda that I wish Kassidy was dead! Or never been born! Apparently, Jennifer said that she had first heard about such a statement when overhearing the conversation between Amanda and me in the early morning hours of Nov. 10, 2000. ***I NEVER SAID.*** *"I wish Kassidy was dead or hadn't been born!!" I don't recall Amanda saying this to me on the phone that evening, but I suppose it is possible that she could have said something, though not using those words. The bulk of Amanda's questioning to me on the phone that evening had to do with asking me why I didn't take Kassidy to the hospital the night before if she was acting messed up upon picking her up from Jeff's and then she fell in the driveway and got hit by a ball, making matters worse. The statement originally came from an argument Amanda and I were having as I recall, a few months before Kassidy died. Kassidy was in the middle of her jealousy phase. Kassidy was absolutely fine with me one minute, but in the next, if I walked in the room and went near Amanda, she would cry and freak out. Kassidy could be playing on the other side of the room and do this. Ten minutes later, everything was fine, and I'd be on the floor playing with both of them. 30 minutes later I'd leave the room and come back in. If I took a step towards Amanda, Kassidy flipped out again. Because nothing happened to cause Kassidy to act this way, I just thought she was being bratty. It was frustrating for me. I couldn't understand it.*

This exact scenario played out once in our bedroom. Usually, Amanda got upset when Kassidy acted like this too. We both mutually decided to give Kassidy a time-out for 30 seconds or so when she acted like this. Amanda was laying on the bed and Kassidy was on the other side of it, playing with something, I walked into the room and went to kiss Amanda and Kassidy started crying. I think it had already happened a couple of times that day so I went to pick Kassidy up to actually give her the time-out. Amanda said, "No, she just loves her mama" or something close and sat up with her arms out to take Kassidy from me." So I dropped Kassidy into her arms and said, "Fine, but this is the kind of bullshit, not following through, and being divided that will continue to let her know these fits are ok." According to Amanda I left the room muttering, "I wish she wasn't here." (RIGHT THEN not forever) Perhaps in that moment, I wished her biological father was involved in her life. I don't know. It was a stupid thing to say in that moment of frustration. It certainly isn't what I felt in my heart. Basically, I just needed a time-out myself for a minute and went outside to play with Kato. Fifteen minutes later, everything was fine. I may have had a rough day at work, who knows, I'm not even convinced I said this. I think I may have said, "I wish I wasn't here." And that is why I went out to play with Kato. In any event, I KNOW I NEVER WISHED KASSIDY NEVER BORN OR DEAD. I NEVER FELT THIS WAY ABOUT HER.

These are horrible things to say. In any event, I bet 50% of all parents feel they are going "nuts" at certain moments in time and say things that they don't mean. I know that I have. It's absurd to think that if someone says something out of frustration they will possibly act on it. I can't tell you how many times in my life I have said to someone, "you do that again, and I am going to kick your ass." It is a horrible choice of words but is something I have hardly ever acted on.

Returning to Amanda's interview, Blodgett asked Amanda about Chad and a polygraph and she said that Chad said, "*...yeah, I'll take one...*" but nobody had yet asked him to take the test. (p. 1006) Chad recalled well when Amanda asked him. He wrote in an April 12, 2011 Letter,

Yes, Amanda came to me at Bruce's after one of her police interviews. We were sitting in his living room. I believe Bruce or Jess and my mom may have been sitting there. Amanda said, "They want me to ask you if you would take a lie detector test." Without hesitation, I looked Amanda right in the eyes and said, "Absolutely I will." Amanda looked up at me, smiled and gave me a kiss and then rested her head on my chest. "I can't wait to tell them this because they told me that they didn't think you would." I believe it was during Amanda's next interview that she happily relayed this fact back to Blodgett who acted surprised and said something like, "Oh really," and then quickly changed the subject. From what I can remember, the only conversation Amanda and I had about her taking a polygraph was right then on Bruce's couch. She said, "I would too. I think everyone should."

Blodgett again offered to assist Amanda with getting counseling and a place to stay, away from Chad, but she insisted that Amanda make a commitment not to see Chad; and Amanda couldn't do that, saying, "*He's like the most important person...that's there. He's like the most comforting to me.*" (p. 1007) Without apparently considering the possibility that Chad was an innocent and grieving and loving partner, Blodgett asked "*...do you think it's because of guilt? Because he killed her?*" and Amanda said, *"I don't know. I don't know.*" (p. 1007)

For Blodgett, the case seemed simple, after Amanda denied killing Kassidy,
If you didn't kill her and Jeff didn't kill her, who else had contact with her? I mean, I really, I don't believe that a stranger broke into your house and hit up side the head and punched her and kicked her in the stomach ... and all that stuff during the night..There's one person left... You killed her or Chad killed her. Right now, I'm pretty convinced that Jeff didn't kill her....Nobody did anything for Kassidy when she was alive... you just stood there and you let her get beat on. Her life sucked.... she really had a shitty last six months...your daughter the most beaten child I have seen so far in seven years... I don't know how you can be sleeping with someone that killed your child.." (p. 1009-10)
Amanda buckled, "*I won't talk to him any more...I'm not going to be with him.*" (p. 1009-10)

After suggesting that Chad might not have intended to kill Kassidy, Blodgett demonized him further, "*I think he's glad she's gone. Had a little football party, right? Did you know that Sunday, was it Sunday? Yeah, Sunday afternoon, he had a big party with beer. They're dancing and jumping on the trampoline and...*" and Amanda said, "*No, I don't think so...At his house?*" (p. 1010-11) Blodgett didn't reveal her source for that information, but it was false. In fact, Chad and his family were at Bruce's and Jessica's in the late afternoon, until they drove to Gray to pick up Amanda after her Sunday evening interview with Angela Blodgett. This allegation of glee at Kassidy's loss must have seemed odd to Sgt. Jim White, as his only previous interview in the case was the telephone interview with Stephanie Chick who told him that Chad was crying and agonizing over Kassidy's loss.

Earlier on Sunday, Chad and his family were at his house. In his interview on Wednesday, the day before Amanda's fourth and current interview, Bruce had been confronted by Jeff Linscott with the same accusation, "*...Sunday when you, when you took the trip to... Maine and ... picked up Amanda... outside the barracks there,,, Were you over at Chad's house earlier that day? Early in the afternoon... who's all over there anyway?*" and Bruce said, "*Me, him* [Chad], *his dad, and ... his brother-in-law.*" Linscott asked Bruce, "*Bounced on the trampoline and stuff?*" and when Bruce said, "*No,*" Linscott asked again, "*Didn't play on the trampoline?*" Bruce said, "*No.. the primary need for going there... we went earlier...we found out the dog leash was broken... His mother and dad went and bought a new chain and... I walked the dog outside and stuff.*" Linscott pressed further, "*So it was not like a big, ah, big, big party that day? Big beer drinking, football watching party or anything going on?*" Bruce said, "*No....Chad... sad about this whole thing... we left.. around the early afternoon. The Patriots game wasn't even over yet.*" (Bruce interview, p. 1141)

A day after Bruce's interview, Blodgett was telling Amanda the same false story about a big party at Chad's house on Sunday. It seemed that the police had shared the information that confirmed their theories of the case, but didn't share the information that didn't support those theories. The source for this story about the alleged party was never identified. Jeff also knew about the alleged party and described his understanding in his interview on Thursday afternoon, November 16.

Amanda again believed the police. This time, the false story she believed was about the alleged party. After gasping, "*Oh my God,*" to the story about the alleged party at Chad's Amanda said, *"I'm not going there anymore*," and that she would stay with her friend, Melissa Chick. (p. 1011) However, she saw an immediate practical problem which was that she had, the previous day, given Chad a check for $1,000, made out to her, as Amanda Conley, from her work for Bruce. Chad was going to put it in his bank account, as she didn't yet have a bank account, even after her three weeks of money management classes. Blodgett said the Rochester Police would help her get her money. In 2011, Chad recalled when the police called his attorney, Alan Cronheim for his assistance with the money. Chad wrote,

I felt somewhat embarrassed that I was being asked this, as if I would keep Amanda's money from her. It was clear in my mind that none of these people know who Chad Evans is, to think such a thing. If Amanda had contacted me directly, I would have written the check in a second. When Alan told me about Amanda's situation, my heart ached for her. I offered to write her a check for more than the $1,000 I had deposited. Alan instructed me not to and that just the $1,000 was sufficient. (I'm sure he was thinking of my best interest and appearances) The thing is, I loved Amanda and Kassidy and loved providing for them just as I enjoyed providing for Kyle and Brent. I was happy with the family we had started so the request for the $1,000 was the least I could do. I guess part of me felt as though my integrity was called into question. If Amanda had asked for it, she had to have known she would have gotten it. Maybe my mind works too much, because then I started thinking bad things such as, "How can Amanda not know me, and know that I would give her the money?" (Letter, March 22, 2011)

The police were doing a lot more than insulting his integrity.

Blodgett gave Amanda her business card and said Amanda could call her 24 hours a day, and left the interview, apparently to talk with Amanda's friend, Melissa, about Amanda's staying with her. Sgt. White was now the lead New Hampshire investigator on the case, and conducted the remaining few minutes of the interview. He asked a few questions, but Amanda said she had already answered them with Blodgett. Regarding her residence arrangements, he said, "*..we just wanted to be sure you're safe...and that you've got somewhere to go. You said that you really feel like you need to get away from Chad...and you shouldn't be talking to him, you said....You've got to make that decision...for this to move forward, we're really counting on your cooperation and your help.*" (p. 1013) Blodgett and White seemed to be concerned that Chad might hurt Amanda, even though she had expressed no such concern. They also wanted Amanda's support in prosecuting Chad, so they made her feel that it was somehow wrong or inappropriate for her to be Chad. Her continued love for him, despite the momentary hesitations that were encouraged by the police, did not fit with their theory. How could a mother continue to love a man who killed her daughter, they reasoned. Instead of questioning their theory about Chad's guilt, they questioned Amanda's integrity and reasonableness, and eventually prosecuted her. They didn't ask themselves if they had ever heard of a similar situation in real life or in literature where the mother of young child remains in love with the killer of that child. I do not know of such an instance.

Amanda said about Chad, "*He keeps saying things like you guys are going to convince me that he did it...just because of the circumstances.*" White asked Amanda, "*What do you think?.. You have a mind of your own,*" and she responded, "*It's not like you guys are lying to me or anything. And I'm not stupid, you know? I don't know what my problem is.*" (p. 1015)

White asked about Amanda's view of Jeff, "*Do you think Jeff's responsible?*" And she responded, "*I think that he obviously hurt her. Like he spanked her and she had bruises all over her butt...*" White countered, "*Yeah, but there's a big difference between spanking and some bruising and the other things you've talked about, grabbing her by the face and by the head.*" White thought that Jeff's spanking was an isolated incident, and Amanda said, "*...and then... she came home once with like little* [?] *and he told about the one accident where she fell out of the truck, and he just called her like, 'little bitch.' and, I don't know. But he would joke around, like. I didn't think it was serious, you know? I don't know.*" (p. 1016)

Blodgett returned to the interview, after talking with Melissa and confirmed that Melissa and Amanda were next driving to Buckfield to Amanda's mother's, and that "*... she agrees with me that being away from Chad is a good thing.*" Blodgett didn't seem aware that Melissa and Amanda were going to Chad's home next, and then they were going to Buckfield.

She discussed alternative housing for Amanda, "*And it will be a place, where he...wouldn't know where you were ... I mean, if you change your mind, and you're going to go back to see him or talk to him or something, at least give me a call first and just let me know.... just so that I'll know where to find you.... I'm not going to lecture you...*" (p. 1017-18)

At 1:15 p.m., according to a report (p. 1338) by Det. Jeff Linscott, Jeff re-enacted for the police his administration of CPR to the stomach of Kassidy Bortner on November 9. The re-enactment was videotaped so that doctors, and the Maine State Medical Examiner could evaluate his efforts, and consider whether any of the bruising to Kassidy resulted. That afternoon, Melissa Chick and Amanda returned to Chad's home in Rochester and then they and Chad went shopping at the Fox Run Mall in Newington for burial shoes and a doll for Kassidy. Chad paid for the items at Filene's and perhaps another store, and Melissa and Amanda drove the items to the Andrews Funeral Home in Buckfield.

Amanda then returned to Chad's home that evening and they went for a drive. Amanda told Chad that the police didn't think it was good for her to continue to see Chad. At 2:00 p.m. Jeff had his third interview with MSP Detective Jeff Linscott and NHSP Detective John Marasco. They did not ask him, on tape at least, about his refusal two hours earlier to take the scheduled polygraph examination. There were no questions about his criminal record. It had three pages with 35 items, including minor traffic violations and the restraining orders mentioned earlier, were pulled in an undated computer search report by the Kittery Police Dept.. Thus, the information must have been available by the time of this third interview of Jeff. Also, at 3:15 p.m. that day, Detective Jeff Smith received residence and license records for Chad (p 183-198) and Jeff (p. 199-212) in response to his requests. In that same report, he stated that he gave those records to Detective Linscott on December 12. (p. 178)

Jeff described Kassidy when he found her in distress on November 9, *...she was laying up on the pillow, eyes in the back of her head. And, she sounded like she was breathing hard....I believe I ran to the other room, grabbed a Wendy's...kind of looked inside her mouth with it... I'm like, "Wake up, wake up," ran out, called Jen, called everybody on the phone....started pressing on her stomach... she was like, making taking deeper breaths... she sounded like she was...then I picked her up, flipped her over...didn't know if she had something lodged in her mouth...I had her, I believe in this arm.... and flipped her back over and back down on the bed. Now, this is when I called 911...I took her, and once again, started pressing on her stomach.... I ran out to the kitchen, on the phone 911, they're just like, "Is she still breathing?" From what I can remember... I turned on the faucet... took water, splashed it on her face, to wake up...this kid's like, basically just limp....I'm like, 'what do I do?'.... she says, "Is she still breathing?"... and I said, "Barely, you know, you guys have got to hurry up." And then I went outside ...I could feel her pulse....* (p. 1626-29)

When he went to the porch, Jeff said he carried Kassidy in one arm and the cordless phone in the other, and continued to talk with the 911 dispatcher.

Linscott asked, "*Did you ... feel like you were causing any injuries when you were giving the CPR compressions*?" and Jeff responded, "*I don't want any lawsuits... coming back to me*." (p. 1629) Jeff was critical of himself for not knowing CPR, saying, "*Always do the wrong way, though, always do the wrong way...I didn't know you blow into her mouth... I didn't know you press right here...you press on the chest...*" (p. 1634)
Jeff described Chad's call earlier that morning, which began, "*How's Kassidy*," and Jeff said that she was "*fine*." Then Chad described the phone message from DCYF and wondered what it was about. Jeff suggested that it might be related to Chad's divorce, and Chad said, according to Jeff, " *'Oh yeah, it could be, but it's probably one of her friends saying that I hit Kassidy... They're calling me. I bet this is about Kassidy...her friends are saying this crap...Supposedly me abusing her...'* " (p. 1637)

Jeff continued, "*...as this story unfolds, I hear that they* [Amanda and Chad] *accused her* [Emily Conley] *of like, cigarette burns.....Before this happened, he* [Chad] *didn't like Emily anyway... her boyfriend got mad at Chad... this guy called his house a couple of times in the middle of the night...*" (p. 1638) The boyfriend apparently thought Chad was improperly close to Emily, and Jeff said, "*I asked him and he denied that anything happened... I was always trying to get the scoop.... but he did say that there was another girlfriend* [who] *had spent the night over at their house...there was a threesome... and he said that him and his ex-wife used to do that, too....*" (p. 1639) This comment about Chad and Amanda's sexual relationship was unsolicited, and it's unclear why Jeff felt it was necessary or even useful to provide this information to the police.

About Chad, Jeff said, "*...I'm a little calmer than I was, ... I still want him dead...probably now, I should keep my mouth shut a little more...*" (p. 1640)

Jeff said that he had talked with the Newington McDonald's store manager, "*...cause we're good friends..*" and Jeff had brought up the subject of Chad's *"football party... I had heard that he had a football party*," which may have been the party that Amanda and Bruce were asked about in earlier interviews that week. His friends denied there was such a party, saying, " *'That's not what we heard. There's no way that could have happened. Police just released his house.' And I said, 'really,'....*" Also, Jeff was told that his friends "*got told to get different snow plowing guy, cause obviously they didn't know what was happening with me*." (p. 1640) Jeff expressed concern about the loss of the McDonald's contracts, but said nothing about his conversation with Chad in October about the end of those contracts.

Jeff said that the Kittery McDonald's manager, Dave Bowen, had talked with Jeff about Chad, "*... he's known Chad for like ten years... he can remember working with him...he would always get into fights... there's history... you guys know... you got my record, you got his record.... I'm very vocal and very opinionated, and, that's what gets me in trouble all the time.*" (p. 1640) This was the only mention during all of Jeff's interviews of his own police and court record. There was no discussion in the interviews about Jeff's arrests, restraining orders, and criminal cases.

The referenced manager, "*David Bowen,*" was actually Daid Heon, as identified by Chad in his April 15, 2011 letter. Chad wrote,

I certainly did not always get into fights. What a vague statement.... David was a long time assistant manager in the Dover McDonald's. I only worked directly with David for a few months when he got promoted to restaurant manager of Kittery. By then, I was a supervisor and had calmed considerably. Very simply, hotheads and/or violent or stupid people didn't get promoted to supervise people in Colley-McCoy, and usually not anywhere. David and I never really cared too much for each other. He is a very competitive individual that often trash talked when playing [basketball]. *He has almost gotten into it with a number of individuals including me at different times while playing a game.*

Switching back to the morning of the 9th, Jeff remembered that Amanda handed Kassidy to him and that he placed her onto the bed. (p. 1636) He said that when Toby ran into the bedroom, and when Jeff was chasing after it, the cat went under the bed, which is how Jeff's attention was drawn to Kassidy, who seemed to be sleeping with her head on the pillow, as if she was still watching television. Jeff said, "*But it wasn't uncommon for her to be.... you stand her some place, unless you kind of physically pick her up and kind of move her somewhere, she's just.... she'd stand there right at the wall. Very strange as far as...*" (p. 1649)

He said that the mail was delivered to his home at unpredictable times, sometimes as early as 9:00 a.m. He thus checked the mail on his porch four or five times a day. He again described what he saw when he return inside the home after retrieving the mail,

"*...her head was back, her eyes were up in her head... And she's [making labored breathing sounds]...it seemed that there was a pulse... I could feel it with my fingers...I felt thump, thump, thump... of a heart... I didn't know if she had swallowed something... she had gone through the same thing last, the night before, supposedly.*" (p. 1651-52)
After calling 911, Jeff said, "*... I assumed I was getting response from her when I was pressing on her stomach... and because, she, seemed like she was taking more breaths...*" and Jeff simulated Kassidy's breathings sounds for Linscott and Marasco. Jeff didn't recall that the 911 dispatcher had told him to stop pressing on Kassidy's stomach.

Jeff recalled that Amanda brought Kassidy to him on Wednesday afternoon "*...around 4, 4:30, somewhere along there.*" (p. 1653) Actually, it was about 3:00 p.m. He explained that Chad came to pick up Kassidy around 5:30, "*...because their main concern was, they didn't want to over use our generosity, as far as, watching her.*" (p. 1655) Amanda's original plan was for Kassidy to spend the night, as Amanda had a late-night shift, but Chad was concerned about Kassidy's care at Jeff's and offered to bring her home, on his way to pick up Kyle at day care at Cross Road. Ironically, Jeff said later, "*I wish she had stayed over to our house....*" (p. 1663) This could be characterized as one of the big "WHAT IF's" of this case.

Jeff continued,

...I got her ready, put her jacket on. She had a pink coat that her mother had just bought her.... put that on, fully zipped it up... and brought her outside, because I said I'd meet him outside.... I put her and her diaper bag in the truck and ... we kind of sat there for a couple minutes... we went back into the house and waited in the kitchen....then when he came over... we did to out to the truck. I'm pretty sure that she was out on the porch.... She had a hard time walking, but she did fly down the stairs. But I can't remember if she walked all the way to the truck...

Later he clarified that when Chad arrived, he "*carried her out, brought her out to him.*" (p. 1657)

Then Jeff described the call from Chad from the Dover toll booth, "*...said she was acting weird in the back seat...bobbing around...he always said she was retarded, so...then as more time went on, the more I saw her, the more you hear... like there might be something wrong with her... she might be a little retarded.*" (p. 1660) Jeff said that he and Chad also talked about the Presidential election and how the Electoral College worked. Quoting Chad from his interview, almost word for word, Linscott asked, "*Did he say anything to you like, 'Jeff, what the hell did you do to her? She's acting weird,'* " and Jeff said, "*I don't think so.*" (p. 1660)

Jeff said about Kassidy's appearance on Wednesday afternoon, "*...the only thing that was on her at that time was from where he had grabbed her before, or supposedly bumped into something, but, you know, it was fading away.*" (p. 1663)

Jeff described the two subsequent calls from Chad that afternoon and evening, about Kassidy's fall in the driveway and the ballhitting incident, about which Jeff said, "*...she got hit pretty good...he didn't say what kind of baseball...I've heard several things, that it was a baseball, and I heard that it was a wiffle ball...*" (p. 1664) Jeff recalled the ballhitting conversation,

...it was a frantic one...he kept yelling out her name, "Kassidy, Kassidy, Kassidy, Kassidy,"... and he says, "I can't get her to respond, Jeff," He's like, "She's just standing there, you know, and her eyes were in the back of her head, and she's just laying there." ...he said there was no response... I was like, "Get her help," and he's like, "Well, I think she's coming back... She's all right... She'll be all right..". (p. 1665)

A few seconds later Jeff painted a different picture,

...at the end of our con, it wasn't a long conversation, but he said, 'She just, she's not coming to,'.... her eyes are in her head, and she's like, out cold.'... I obviously... should have probably called the cops myself... but he said she was coming to. And I figured... you think that the person will do the right thing... You know, do what I did, as far as call the med, medics..." (p. 1666)

Jeff's comment that Chad should have done "*what I did.*" was ironic. On Thursday, the 9th, Jeff's first three, and first six out of seven, calls were to Chad and not to 911. During his police interview, Jeff said he thought it odd that Chad called him about Kassidy.

As with Chad's call from the highway, Jeff said that third call, the ballhitting call, turned to politics. Jeff said, "*He asked me* [about the election], *cause I think he had a bet going with somebody...cause he always bet...that was his nature...*" (p. 1666-67) This was an enhancement of the allegation made by Jeff about Chad, that he was a gambler.

Chad wrote in his April 15, 2011 letter,

I NEVER bet on politics. He was just trying to make me look bad. I had never bet on anything prior to Jeremy getting me involved in betting football that year. I am not much of a risk taker. If I was going to gamble, it was in the stock market. When I went to the casinos a few times with my friends, I might blow $25 or $50 and then spend my time eating at the buffet or watching people. I spoke to Jeff about politics because he was actually much more knowledgeable than I was. He watched the election and debates so much it bordered on obsession. I recall picking his brain about electoral votes, what each candidate's top issues were and why he hated Democrats so much.

Twice during the interview, Jeff said that Chad's former wife, Tristan, "*called social services on him.*" (p. 1663, 1671) However, the DCYF report of Tristan's call said that she was not concerned about Chad hurting Kassidy, but "*that someone else may have.*" Jeff appeared to feel resentful of Chad, and said that during his conversations with Chad, "*...he said these things, and it's like, 'What? Are you stupid, Marshall?'* " (p. 1671)

Then came the only reference to Jeff's secret tape recording of his conversation with Jennifer and Amanda the previous Saturday, when Jeff reminded the officers that Amanda had said on that tape that the "trampoline story" wasn't true. (p. 1672) He didn't know that Amanda had told Angela Blodgett and Rick LeClair it wasn't true in her second interview on November 9. (p. 61) Chad didn't learn that Amanda had acknowledged that the story was untrue until he read transcripts of her interviews in his lawyer's offices in the spring of

2001. Chad recalls in 2011 that he told his attorneys that the story was not true before reading those Discovery materials.

Of his confrontation with Chad on the evening of November 9, Jeff said,
...he came out [from his interview].... *all his friends, were sitting on that bench, and I just walked up to him, cause I was kind of by myself inside the building, I wanted to get some air. I walked up to him, ... I sat on the bench by myself, and that's when.... he walked over and, he's like, "How can you tell them that?... How can you say that stuff?... Why'd you tell on me? Why'd you do this?" and I basically said, "I didn't say anything"...if he didn't do it, then... I feel bad for saying those things, but that's what happened...* (p. 1673)

Jeff then talked generally,
.... *and this is the other thing that kind of bothers us* [him and Jennifer] *as more time goes on. Amanda called her mother up yesterday and says, "Can I make any food for the funeral?" I'm thinking to Jen. I'm saying, "This is the mother." All right, her last thing on her God damned mind is to be making food for a funeral for her child. This is, yeah, it makes me sick... if I could take those two and sit them in an electric chair right now, I'd grab them and, like I said, do me a favor, bring them down to the woods somewhere and... turn your back and Marshall* [martial?] *law.... that bothers me, and then, I didn't know this, but she* [Amanda] *kept some of Kassidy's stuff at our house, so she had Kassidy's baby books at our house. Why she didn't bring those to Chad's house is beyond me. And, obviously,... I made a special trip up to her mother's house, so that way her mother could have them.*" (p. 1674)

This was yet another instance where someone, such as Detective Hamel and Amanda Donnell was willing to pass judgement on how Amanda grieved for Kassidy.

Jeff said that he decided to purchase a tape recorder, to record Amanda's statements, after she denied saying on the phone to Chad that "*I know you killed my baby...*" (p. 1676) Jeff said that Amanda told him, "*I never said that. You must have been dreaming.*" (p. 1677)

In her "My Life Story," Amanda described her call to Chad from the Anchorage Inn,
I tried going to sleep. That didn't work, so I called Chad. I was dying to hear what he had to say. Now, he showed so much emotion. He was crying, saying how did this happen. He told me he loved her, how he wanted so much to be her daddy. He was a mess just like me. I could tell he really loved her. Later in the conversation I was telling him what they told me how they said, "You slowly killed my baby," and Jeff ran to the cops saying I said that to Chad. He heard the whole conversation,...

Returning to the interview, Jeff continued his criticism of Amanda,
..she knows something... We always thought she knew something...It doesn't seem like there's any remorse....she says 'I didn't think he would kill her,'....well, if you know this in you heart, why are you even talking to this asshole? I mean, sorry for swearing, but it doesn't make sense...." (p. 1677-78)

Jeff's views about the loss of a child were affected by an abortion undergone by an earlier girlfriend, "*behind my back...*" and by the loss of his brother, Joshua, in 1992. Jeff said, "*...I just can't imagine... losing a child, and I know what my mother went through with my brother....we knew my brother was going to pass away...we knew, we saw, every day.*" He again criticized Amanda, "*You would think it's a huge loss.... you don't ask if you can bring food to.... it just bothers me.... That bothers me.*" (p. 1679) It's not known why this upset Jeff so much, as it's customary to prepare food for receptions at memorial gatherings or funerals, in the U.S. and most other cultures.

The interview ended with the police cautioning Jeff about his behavior if Chad came to Kassidy's funeral.

The afternoon Foster's Daily Democrat carried the case again on the page 1, *"Custody case may have link to baby's death"* The story reported that Tristan had filed a motion in court to revoke Chad's rights to see Kyle. According to the article, this motion was encouraged by DCYF, which was perhaps now trying to be over-protective after it failed to abide its own guidelines for responding within 72 hours to Tristan's anonymous call on October 31. Kassidy might have survived if DCYF had responded quickly and appropriately. Regardless of who was responsible, the court denied Tristan's motion, but did rule that future visits for Chad with Kyle and Brent would have to be supervised. This was Chad's nightmare, and the result that had led him to once urge caution to Amanda about taking Kassidy to see a doctor, which was that a doctor and social service people might overreact and blame Chad, and restrict his ability to see Kyle. Now, that had happened, but worse was coming. Tristan was very supportive of Chad's innocence during this time, and she resisted DCYF pressure to treat Chad like a criminal.

That evening at 8:54 p.m., the police came to Chad's home to arrest him. There is no record of whether the police considered calling Chad's attorney and asking him to surrender Chad at the police station without all the drama of a number of police cars encircling a home along a state highway. It's also not known whether Chad's attorneys had made the offer, even though it was apparent that an arrest was coming.

Sgt. James White had obtained the Arrest Warrant (p. 313) from Judge Franklin Jones at the Rochester District Court at 8:12 p.m. From the Rochester "*Police Log*" in the Rochester Times was this short note, "*8:54 p.m. Chad Emery Evans, 29, is charged with the manslaughter of an infant.*" Answering the door was his father, Chet Evans. Said Chad to one of the arresting officers, New Hampshire State Trooper William Graham, "*This is bullshit.*" (Report, p. 230)

The other arresting officer was Rochester Patrolman Anthony Deluca III, who wrote in his report that he asked Chet, "*if Chad Evans was home. He advised that he was and inside the home and invited us inside. I....handcuffed him without any problems. At first, it appeared that he was pulling away. However, I believe that he was only going to say 'Good-bye' to his parents and another female who were walking behind him.*" (p. 339) This was a good example of how an initial perception was incorrect, and that it could be corrected. In the larger case, the initial perceptions became set in concrete.

Also at Chad's home at the time were his mother, Pam and sister, Nicole, and Amanda. Chad took a few seconds to write a short note to his family, saying, "*I love you guys. w/ all my heart. Be strong. We will make it, I hope.*"

Amanda Bortner was there at the time, and called her friend, Cathy Nuernberg, in San Antonio, Texas to tell her about Chad's arrest, and to confirm plans for Cathy's arrival for Kassidy's funeral on Saturday and Amanda's plan to return to Texas with Cathy afterwards.

Amanda then drove to her friend, Tracey Foley's, home in Sanford and spent the night.

Back at Chad's home, after 9:00 p.m., his family had left because the police announced they had another search warrant to look for "*objects capable of inflicting the pin-point abrasion injuries on Cassidy Bortner's feet, described in the attached affidavit.*" See assorted search documents. (p. 3121-33) The search warrant and supporting affidavit were also sealed by Judge Jones upon the Motion by the Office of the Attorney General. The police seized these items, "*two plastic handled grill brushes, one metallic meat tenderizer, two wire dog brushes, seven hair brushes, one wooden pasta* [?] *One plastic pin imprint toy, two metal headbands, two plastic toilet brushes, one wood, metal wire brush.*" (p. 3125) Also during the search according to a report by Sgt. Conte, Detective Carlberg found a box of live ammunition near the tanning bed in Chad's basement. Chad's probation officer, Kevin Callaghan, was notified and he advised the search team to leave the ammunition there, and he would pick it up at some future time. (p. 1072)

At the conclusion of the search, at about 1:00 a.m., Chad's family was permitted to re-enter Chad's home, according to a report by Rochester Detective William Carlberg. (p. 337) It was late at night, but this would have been a good time for the police to talk with Chad's parents and schedule interviews with them. They had seen Kassidy several times, at Rochester and at Keene, and Pam was the person who observed Kassidy closely enough to see that her feed were toed-in.

Tests found that none of these items could have caused the pattern (or lack of pattern) of abrasions on Kassidy's feet. One report of the analysis of a meat tenderizer brush, stated, "*Physical examination of exhibit JMC 2 failed to reveal deposits characteristic of blood, tissue or hair.*" (p. 392)

At 10:48 p.m., according to a courageous report by Rochester Sgt. Anne Brideau, Alan Cronheim, the attorney for Chad Evans, called Rochester Police Dept. and sought to speak with his client, and sought to preclude the police from interviewing Chad Evans. Sgt. Brideau wrote that she told Cronheim that she had no control over the NHSP, and that people were busy, but that she would give Cronheim's home phone number to Evans. She wrote that she discussed Cronheim's call with Asst. A.G. Delker "*who advised me to tell Attorney Cronheim that no one was available to speak with him at this moment and that his client was tied up.*" (p. 342) Surely, no pun was intended. Frustrated by the lack of response, Cronheim specifically asked Sgt. Brideau, according to her, "*to make a note to the report that at 2155* [sic, it was 2255] *hours he called the station after receiving a message from someone from the NHSP and that he was trying to invoke his client's right to not speak with the police.*" (p. 342)

Sgt. White reported that at 10:50 p.m. [2250] he and Detective Linscott asked Chad if he would be willing to talk with them, and that "*C. Evans said he was willing to speak with us and commented, 'I know you guys wouldn't have done this (made the arrest) if you didn't have a case.'*" While Sgt. Conte and Det. Linscott were setting up to audiotape an interview with Chad, White wrote that he spoke with Chad, "*generally about his work with McDonald's, where he grew up, and about his family. During the conversation about his family, C. Evans commented 'I'm just wondering what Kyle will do without a father around.'*" (p. 341) It's likely that Sgt. White believed that both of these quotes were somewhat incriminating, but at most, they were ambiguous. In the first quoted statement, Chad could very well have said, "*... if you didn't THINK you have a case.*" For the second, Chad could very well have been thinking about what Kyle would do over the next few days or weeks, or what Kyle would do if the Convict-Chad train was not derailed soon, and he ended up in prison. It's generally okay for people to wonder aloud, except when a policeman is listening and later reaches a computer and summarizes what s/he remembers. At 11:04 p.m. Sgt. Brideau gave to Chad Evans Alan Cronheim's phone number and allowed him to use phone to call his attorney. (p. 342) Chad recalls that he received Cronheim's phone number and talked with Cronheim **after** his abbreiated interview with the police.

At 11:05 p.m. NHSP Sgt. Russell Conte and MSP Detective Jeff Linscott began an interview with Chad Evans. Conte told Chad of his Miranda rights and Chad and he had several exchanges about what that meant. Chad then said,

"*...I want to answer every question you have. I want to be as helpful as I can, but...I got a million and one things going through my head...I think I'd like to have my attorney present while I answer a few questions.... He called like 20 minutes ago... and said that he'd come down.... I'm not trying to be a pecker head. I want to help you in any way I can. I want to answer any question.... But you know, when I went through that last questioning...I got too many things going through my head. I'd rather. There's two of you. There's one of me. I* [would] *just feel comfortable answering any question with him sitting here beside me...I'm not trying to be difficult.*"(p 345-47)
The seven minute interview concluded at 11:11 p.m.

Friday, 17 November 2000

The Union Leader was the only morning paper to cover the case, "Man charged in death of toddler," and with Kassidy's name spelled correctly.
By order of a New Hampshire Complaint against Chad for Manslaughter "*for causing Kassidy's death by inflicting blunt force injury to her head,*" on November 8th or 9th, he was arraigned at a hearing which began at 8:30 a.m. Afterwards, he remained in the Strafford County Jail, until the "probable cause" hearing which was scheduled for the next Wednesday, November 22.

At 12:30 p.m. Rochester Detectives Callaghan and Lisa Gero interviewed Erin Entrekin, a teacher at Cross Road School in Dover. Det. Giro prepared the report and wrote that Erin saw Amanda bring Kyle to school and that around 12:30-45 p.m. on November 8, she "*observed ... a small female child in the driver side rear seat. The child was wearing a pink coat and possibly a white hat or a hat with a white trim.*" Gero continued that Amanda *"stated to Erin that Kyle had just come from a Doctor's appointment and that he had eaten something already."* (p. 349)

It was true that Kyle had eaten lunch, but it was not true that the reason for coming to school late was because of a doctor's appointment. In 2010, neither Chad nor Tristan could recall that Amanda took Kyle to a doctor that day.

The report continued,

Later that same evening, at approximately 5:20 p.m., Chad Evans came to the Kindergarten to pick up Kyle.... Chad walked into the K3 room, where the children were watching a movie, VEGGIE TALES. They always watch a movie from 5-5:30 p.m. and Erin remembered Chad showing up near the end of the movie. He questioned Erin as to where he could get the movie for Kyle. Chad then got Kyle's lunch box from his cubby and left. Erin estimated that he was present for approximately 2-3 minutes. Erin did not observe any unusual behavior. She stated that Chad was wearing a suit and tie.

In the afternoon at the Rochester Police Dept., Rochester Detective William Carlberg and Det. Callaghan interviewed the first of the inmate informants who appeared in Chad's case, eager to help the police, and themselves. John LaCroix, age 39, was in the Strafford County Jail for violating a protective order, and was in the same cell with Chad the previous night and early on this morning. The interview was audiotaped, and Det. Carlberg also prepared a summary. He said that he and Callaghan told LaCroix that they were not going to discuss the charges against him. In other words, the report put on the record that there was no *quid-pro-quo* for LaCroix in return for him voluntarily coming forward with information about Chad.

The summary stated, "*LaCroix stated that he could not remember the conversation word for word, only bits and pieces.... but he did know that Nicole was his* [Chad's] *sister...* " The rest of the "*bits and pieces*" from LaCroix were quite accurate. (p. 352-53) He said that "*Chad then asked about prayer and if he thought that it helped and LaCroix said that it did.*"

The 11 page transcript largely corroborates Carlberg's summary. In addition, LaCroix did not know Chad's last name, but he said of Chad,

He said that he would pick up the baby and then take it home and remove the diaper and see bruises black and blue marks on the baby's bottom and he said to himself, "Man, that looks like, you know, somebody whacked the baby through the diaper"...he then went on to finding the lumps on the baby's side... of the head...he also...said the baby was always coming home to the mother and to him and she was always crying, "I'm hungry, I'm hungry," and then almost immediately grabbing a bowl of cereal.... he mentioned about this guy having the baby in a truck and somehow or other the baby fell out of the truck....OUT of the truck!...at one point he was going to take the baby home and the baby was in the back seat in a ... car and he looked back at the baby and the baby's eyes were rolling....and he said that the baby was sorta hunched over the baby seat and he, you know, pushed back a little.... a day and a half or so later... he said, "I got a call telling me that the baby was dead"....he was really scared that the police officers and the detectives were going to talk to his girlfriend and try to twist her mind around. And he loves her. And he didn't know if it was going to stay that way after the police got to talk with her....he asked me if I believed in God and if I believed in praying and if I thought he heard the prayers. And then he asked my religion....he asked me to call his sister.... tell them that I'm all right, that I'm ok and that I love them and that he needed commissary. (p. 2978-82)
Approaching the end of the interview, Det. Callaghan asked LaCroix if Chad "*was concerned about having other inmates ... wonder what he's in there for?*" LaCroix recalled that Chad had said he didn't want to be known as a "*skinner. A skinner is a child molester.*" The previous night, Chad and LaCroix had seen how an inmate known as a "skinner" had been showered with contempt by other inmates. (p. 2982) It was at that time that Chad learned the meaning of "skinner," which was the first of many prison slang words he would learn over the next ten years.

As quoted by LaCroix, Chad was right about the ability of the police to "*twist*" Amanda's mind, and twist it they did. Amanda didn't stop loving him, until years of separation by incarceration wore her love out.

The afternoon Portsmouth Herald, now spelling Kassidy with a "K," covered the arraignment and began Chad's trial in the media with several allegations after noting Alan Cronheim's assertion of Chad's innocence. Wrote reporter Amy Wallace, "*But the prosecution said witnesses have described Evans as having a violent temper and has been abusive to Amanda Bortner by 'butting her in the head and choking her.'* " There was no indication that the reporter asked Chad or his lawyer about those allegations, but the answer likely would have been something like, "No Comment," as Chad had been advised not to talk with the media and his attorneys were following their own advice, after the initial broad denial of the charges, and a statement in support of his request for bail, that he would not flee. The article reported that Asst. Attorney General Christopher Carter at the arraignment, "*said Evans has also violated his probation for an assault charge, related to a domestic violence incident in March.*" This was misleading as it was only his arrest the previous evening that violated the probation requirement that he not be arrested in a felony charge. Otherwise, he thought he was fully complying with the terms of his probation until the box of ammunition was found in his basement during the search of his home.

The afternoon Foster's Daily Democrat carried Jennifer Saunders' story on page 1, "Man charged in baby's death - Rochester suspect faces manslaughter, was boyfriend of little girl's mother" and quoted Assistant Attorney General Carter as saying that "*Evans is 'a very real danger.' and described his history of domestic abuse as well as his temper. Carter also said Evans could pose a threat to witnesses in this case.*" The article stated that ammunition was found in Chad's home, in violation of the terms of his probation. Chad had forgotten about that box in his basement and hadn't given it to his probation officer.

Tracey Foley traveled to London and Amanda and her friend Cathy Nuernberg stayed at Tracey's home Friday and through the weekend.

Saturday, 18 November 2000

Showing the dual-state interest in the case, the Portland Press Herald's story ran, "N.H. Man Held In Beating Death Of Girlfriend's Baby." Correcting its earlier error, the paper spelled Kassidy's first name correctly, but there were no witnesses cited for the "beating." The paper also published Kassidy's obituary which stated that she had been "*raised by her mother, grandmother and uncle, Joshua.*"

The Union Leader published the first article with positive news about Chad, "Former 'hero'charged in girl's beating death" Alan Kerr wrote about Chad's saving of three lives in 1996 and his subsequent "Hero Award" by the Union Leader. No law enforcement was quoted with a comment about the apparent inconsistency between police and prosecutor characterizations of Chad, and his life-saving history. He saved three lives **once**, and he was arrested for domestic violence **once**, and he would henceforth be known as a man with a history of domestic violence and not as a man with a history of lifesaving.
Most of the article was about the arraignment, and the police view of this "hero." The article quoted Assistant Attorney General Christopher Carter, "*Quite simply, he's charged with beating Kassidy to death.*" He described the victim as "*utterly helpless and defenseless.*"...

Carter argued that Evans represents a danger to others, especially Kassidy's mother and members of her family. Bortner, his 18-year-old live-in girlfriend, maintains that Evans has hit her and head-butted her in the past, according to Carter. Evans is known to have a "*violent, volatile temper,*" Carter said.

Defense attorney Alan Cronheim countered that his client has co-operated with police and has no intention of leaving town. "*He vehemently denies responsibility for this,*" Cronheim told the judge. "*Believe me, he wants to stay so he can deal with this.*"
At 11:00 a.m. a memorial service was held for Kassidy at the Andrews Funeral Home in Buckfield, Maine, a few miles east of Kassidy's cemetery plot in Buckfield. Amanda had told Chad that she wanted Kassidy to be buried in the Evans family plot in Guilford, Vermont, but it's not known if that wish was communicated to Jacqueline. Kassidy had essentially two mothers, and there was some struggle between them for control of Kassidy's burial.

Attending for the Evans family were Chad's father, Chet, his brother Jason, and his sister, Nicole and her husband, Brandon. Detective Blodgett was there and she recorded the names of some other attendees, including Cathy Nuernberg, Crystal Martin and her mother, Gayle Martin, and Melissa Chick. Also attending were Will Peirce and Janis Marshall-Colby, the mother of Jeff Marshall. (p. 45) Presumably, Jennifer Bortner and Jeff were also there. Earlier in the week, there was speculation about whether Chad would attend, but he was jailed on the 16th and was still in jail. Otherwise, he would have been there.

According to a Foster's Daily Democrat article, Jennifer thanked Amanda for making her Kassidy's godmother and said that she hoped, one day, to have a child as beautiful as Kassidy. Amanda spoke about how difficult it was to be a teenage mother. The service was conducted by Pastor Paul Swihart. Kassidy's body was buried at the Damon Cemetery in Buckfield, where it now rests, alone, with the spot marked with a heart-shaped gravestone. Also buried with her body were a doll from Jeff and Jennifer, her bunny rabbit doll which was given to her by Jacqueline, and with which she was photographed on October 1, and a Barbie doll from Amanda, which she had purchased with Chad the previous Wednesday. Amanda kept Kassidy's favorite doll, a purple Teletubby named "Tinky Winky," that Amanda and Chad had given to her.

After the services, Amanda and her friend, Cathy Nuernberg, called Detective Blodgett at 6:41 p.m. Blodgett later reported that they called to tell her that Amanda would be going to Texas with Cathy, and they gave Det. Blodgett Amanda's contact information for Cathy's home in San Antonio, Texas. (p. 45)

The Portsmouth Herald recapped the story of the arraignment, "Death of toddler is 'senseless'". Amy Wallace quoted Alan Cronheim about Tristan's role, "*His ex-wife is here today to show her support.*" Tristan continued to support Chad through the trial the next year.

Foster's Daily Democrat highlighted the story with a three stories united by a large banner headline across the top of the front page, **"Who is to blame?"** Despite all the coverage, the paper still spelled Kassidy's name with a "C." Teresa Robinson's lead article, "Authorities look for deeper answers," said "*authorities are looking at other people who might be responsible,*" and specifically that Amanda, 18, "*has not been charged.*" The article quoted a New Hampshire Attorney General press release which said that Chad was charged "*with recklessly causing Cassidy's death by inflicting blunt trauma.*"

Kimberly Houghton wrote the article, "State DCYF official won't deny agency knew about abuse." DCYF Associate Commissioner John Wallace did not share with the reporter the information that Tristan Evans had called DCYF 10 days before Kassidy's death, and that DCYF's slow response violated DCYF's guidelines. Perhaps to compensate for its failure, DCYF had urged Tristan the previous Wednesday to seek a court order to prohibit contact between Chad and his son, Kyle. The court denied the request, but did give Tristan sole custody of Kyle.

Jennifer Saunders wrote in "Family prepares for funeral as suspect faces charges," that "*...authorities are painting a picture of senseless abuse, which culminated in the death of an innocent, helpless child...*" On the front page was the first photo of Kassidy to appear in the newspapers. It had the credit, "*Courtesy photo.*" In this article, the photo was explained as, "*a photograph given to Foster's Daily Democrat by a relative, the toddler smiles out at the world, her blue eyes full of hope. In reality, however, authorities are painting a picture of senseless abuse, which culminated in the death of an innocent, helpless child.*" The phrase "*senseless abuse*" was often used in the Kassidy Bortner case, but surely the prosecutors did not mean to suggest that they viewed some child abuse as sensible.

No date for the photo was given, but it was taken in late 1999 in a studio where Amanda had taken Kassidy, six months before she met Chad. It's not known if the Foster's Daily Democrat reporters asked for the date and source of the photo, or if they asked if there was a recent photo. If the family had provided the October 1 photo of a bruise-less

Kassidy, and told the media of the date of that photo, the sensational press coverage might have been muted.

Similarly, the police and prosecutors, and also Chad's defense lawyers should have been asking everyone for photographs of Kassidy. The October 1 photo of Kassidy in a chair holding a toy rabbit was not made known to Chad's attorneys or the media until Sunday, January 21, 2001. Amanda and Chad had many photos of Kassidy as she appeared during the period of June 9 through November 9, but they were advised not to talk with the media.

Monday, 20 November 2000

In Rochester District Court, Judge Franklin Jones set bail for Chad at a total of $100,000 ($50,000 on the manslaughter charge, and $50,000 for violation of probation) with a condition that he have no contact with the victim's family, including Kassidy's mother, Amanda Bortner.

Nancy Harris, the Director of the Strafford Country Victim/Witness Program interviewed Kyle Evans in order to learn more about Chad and his treatment of Kassidy. The interview was witnessed by Sgt. White, Detective Jeff Linscott, Carol Ann Jensen of the Strafford County Victim/Witness Program, and Patricia Hocter and Kristine Keeler of DCYF.

Kyle said that he lives with "*Daddy*" and that "*Amanda*" and "*Kassidy*" lived there, too, "*and Kassidy's now with God.*" (p. 1735-36) Harris asked what Kyle and Kassidy did together, "*Play. But and Kassidy pooped all the time.*" (p. 1738) Kyle said Kassidy had a "*mark.... right where her belly's, right here.... Somebody pushed her, and she got a mark.*" Harris asked who pushed her and Kyle said, "*Probably Amanda did.*" (p. 1740) Then he said that "*daddy could*" have pushed her and "*Everybody pushed her.... I pushed everybody.*" He seemed to acknowledge that he had hurt Kassidy by accident, and "*It wasn't by purpose. It was a little bit by purpose... When I pushed her a little bit.*" (p. 1741-42)

Kyle said about Kassidy, in the context of her falling down, "*She was a bad girl...She screams by herself. Can I color on your wall?... I colored on my dad's wall... I got in trouble.*" Harris asked what happens to him when he gets in trouble, "*I don't know.*" (p. 1745) Harris asked about time outs and Kyle said that "*My dad*" gives him time outs, "*over in the corner.*" Harris asked, "*Did you ever see your dad push Kassidy?*" and Kyle responded "*Yes, I did,*" and then changed the subject to the paper he was drawing on. Asked about other bruises on Kassidy, Kyle referred again to her belly, but then, said, "*She didn't get bruise on her belly. She got it right over here.*" (p. 1748) At one point, he referred to a bruise on her leg. Three times in succession Harris asked, "*Who put bruises on Kassidy?*" and Kyle responded, (1) "*Um, probably you do when you're a little girl,*" (2) "*When you were a little girl like this,*" (3) *And I'm gonna take (inaudible) thing. Hey I got good idea.*" He was easily distracted. Perhaps more could be surmised about many of his answers to questions, but he was a three-year old. Near the end of the interview he responded directly to a few questions. Harris asked, "*Kyle, do you ever get more than a time out? Do you ever get a spanking? Or anything like that?*" and he said "*No, I just go in the corner.*" Harris asked, "*Did Kassidy get spankings?*" and he responded, "*Yes.*" He said that "*Daddy*" gave the spankings and "*Amanda doesn't.*" (p. 1751) Then a series of questions:

Harris: *Does your daddy think that Kassidy's a good girl or a bad girl?*
Kyle: *Bad girl*
Harris: *Ok. What did he do about Kassidy being bad? What would happen to her?*
Kyle: *He. she was being punished.*
Harris: *How did she get punished? What did dad do?*
Kyle: *I think she went up to the green one. She said, "Amanda, daddy, don't use that word." And when she went up to yellow one, she said, "Why you doing dad?" And then she went up to this, um, bad one, and she went up to what are you doing, dude? And then she went up to this yellow one after that, this one.*

Harris: *Are you going to talk about the yellow crayon? I think we are almost finished...* (p. 1752)

The last series of questions related to the ballhitting incident, with Harris asking, "*Did Kassidy ever get hurt by one of your toys?*" and Kyle answered, "*No.*" (p. 1760) Again, "*Did you ever hit Kassidy with one of your balls? By accident or on purpose?*" Kyle laughed, and gave no verbal response. Perhaps a more specific question about the night of November 8, which was the last time that Chad and Kyle played baseball at the Milton Road home, would have found a more substantive response. This exchange was one of the reasons that Chad later decided not to have Kyle testify at Chad's trial, a full year later.

Tuesday, 21 November 2000

At 9:30 a.m., from Texas, Amanda called MSP Detective Angela Blodgett with the recollection "*that on or about 10/31/00, Kassidy fell forward in her car and hit her head on the back of the driver seat in Amanda's vehicle. This occurred because the belt holding Kassidy's car seat was not 'clicked all the way in' and Amanda had to hit her brakes suddenly to avoid a collision. Kassidy did not cry or seem injured after the incident.*" (Report p. 45.)

According to Kimberly Houghton's article in Foster's Daily Democrat, "Bail set for accused man in baby's death," Asst. Attorney General Carter "*said it is imperative that Evans have no contact with the witnesses, maintaining that he could 'intimidate' them and possibly influence their testimony.*" As would become clear over time, Chad's mantra to his friends was always "*to tell the truth,*" and it was never alleged by anyone that he tried to influence their recollections or upcoming testimony. To Amanda, and others, the police in uniform were more intimidating than Chad, and the police had no restrictions placed on their ability to talk with witnesses.

Though not in the headline, the article included a surprise for the readers of Foster's Daily Democrat, which was the story of Chad's heroism in 1996 in saving the lives of three men from an auto crash. Wrote Houghton, "*Although Evans is now behind bars, just four years ago he was deemed a hero for saving three area residents from a burning vehicle. A different side of Evans was brought to light November 1, 1996 when he risked his own life....*" That was the last reference to Chad's 1996 heroism in the Foster's Daily Democrat. There was nothing in the media about his other good characteristics and his public service in the Keene Board of Education, for example, (except in the Keene Sentinel) because, in part, Chad and his family had been advised not to talk with the press. The other reason was that the police and the media were confident that Chad Evans was a child abuser and killer.

At 12:40 p.m. New Hampshire State Trooper Jill Rockey and Detective Linscott interviewed Kristin Parsons, a co-worker at Old Navy of Amanda. (p. 354) Trooper Rockey wrote the summary of the unrecorded interview:

Parsons said Amanda started work on November 2. Once Amanda finished training and started working, they began talking. One day they were talking about Amanda's boyfriend. Amanda said he had a lot of money. He was great, Amanda said. Nice, good looking. A half an hour later, the story changed. Amanda started telling Parsons she wanted to get away from him. She said he was an asshole. Parsons asked Amanda why he was an asshole. Amanda didn't answer, then walked away. Amanda told Parsons, Chad was 29. Amanda wanted to go out. Chad wanted to go to dinner parties. Amanda told Parsons, "I am getting sick of him. I want to break up with him."

Amanda told Parsons Chad had a 3 or 4 year old. Amanda had to get both kids ready. Pick out their clothes. He (Chad) didn't do anything in the morning.

Parsons said Amanda didn't talk about her daughter much. Amanda was young when she got pregnant. Amanda told her it was a one time thing....

On November 9th, Amanda got the call. She came back from the phone crying. She said, "My baby. My Baby." She (Amanda) said, "My little girl fell off a truck and now she's at the hospital. My sister's boyfriend was watching her." Amanda told Parsons this as she was running toward the door. Amanda said she fell off the truck 3 or 4 times. She has (was in) a coma.

Amanda said she had been running late that morning. At 8:00 she was still trying to get the kids ready."

There are several inaccuracies in this report, but it's uncertain whether they came from Parsons or from Trooper Rockey or from Amanda. The most clear error is the last sentence's statement that at 8:00 a.m. the kids were still getting ready. Amanda must have meant or said 7:00 a.m.

Parsons' estimate of Amanda's start date as November 2, a Thursday, might be correct. Other records had indicated that it was Monday, November 6, but there was little allowance for training. It may have been that Amanda was in training on Thursday and Friday, November 2-3. That would explain Chad's recollection that his surprise lunch was before the week of Kassidy's death. However, it's odd that the precise date of Amanda's starting work was not clearly specified in documents and recollections early in the investigation.

At 1:10 p.m. Detective Linscott interviewed Emily Conley a second time. In his seven line summary of the 15 minute telephone interview, he wrote,

Emily Conley stated that Amanda Bortner told her that Chad Evans would grab Kassidy Bortner by the face when Chad was kissing Amanda as that would upset Kassidy. Conley stated that Kassidy had bumps on the back of her head after she fell out of the back of Jeff Marshall's truck. Conley stated that Amanda told her that Chad told Amanda to tell people the trampoline story to explain the bruises on Kassidy. Conley stated that Amanda's friend in Texas, she may be staying with is Kathy Nuernberg.

It wasn't clear whether Emily actually saw the bumps on Kassidy's head, which Chad remembers as being on the top of her head, or whether she was telling Linscott what Amanda told her.

At 2:35 p.m., in the Kittery Police Dept. Conference Room, Jeff Linscott interviewed Heather Hamilton, age 21, who was Jennifer's manager at Perfumania. During the 11 day period between Kassidy's death and this interview, Hamilton and Jennifer had worked together approximately during 4-5 shifts. Below are excerpts of Linscott's summary of the 55 minute interview.

Heather Hamilton stated that Jennifer Conley has been employed by the store since August, 2000...Jennifer has been talked to about Amanda staying too long during her visits... Hamilton stated that she has gotten other complaints from employees about the length of Amanda's visits and of Amanda being behind the counter when store policy states that friends or relatives of employees are not allowed behind the counter.

Hamilton stated she did not speak much with Amanda because she thought Amanda was "snobby." Hamilton stated that Chad came into the store once and asked to speak with Jennifer....she heard Chad ask Jennifer if Jennifer would ask Hamilton out for Chad.

Hamilton stated that in approximately September, a couple of weeks after Chad had come into the store, Amanda came into the store with Kassidy and Hamilton saw bruises on Kassidy's face....Hamilton said she asked Amanda about the bruises on Kassidy's face and Amanda "laughed it off" and said Kassidy fell off the trampoline and Chad caught her by the face. Hamilton said the bruises looked like a big hand print on Kassidy's face and Amanda's story did not sound plausible.... Hamilton said that when Amanda left the store that day, Jennifer said, "Chad wasn't a nice guy."....

Hamilton said that on the day of Kassidy's death, Jennifer received a telephone call at work from Jeff about Kassidy.... Hamilton said that Jennifer said the baby arrived this morning and had been lying on the bed eating cocoa puffs. Hamilton stated that Jennifer held her fingers up as quotation marks and stated "supposedly Kassidy got hit in the head with a baseball." Hamilton said that Jennifer said she thought Chad caused all the injuries to Kassidy, including the baseball bruises. Hamilton stated that Jennifer told her that she witnessed Chad put Kassidy's head under a water faucet to quiet her down....

Hamilton stated that Jennifer told her after Kassidy's death about Chad hitting Amanda. Hamilton stated she never saw any bruises on Amanda. Hamilton stated another store employee had also seen the bruises on Kassidy - Crystal Grimes, who is out of work on maternity leave.

Hamilton's seemed to dislike Amanda, which may have colored her other recollections. It seems extremely unlikely that she overheard Chad asking Jennifer, sometime in August or September, for help in asking Heather out, when Chad and Amanda were in love and Amanda and Kassidy were living with Chad in Rochester. It was unlikely that Chad was interested in anyone else, but even more unlikely that he would ask his lover's sister for help in dating her sister's boss. Still more oddly, the only other person to allege that s/he had seen Chad trying to cheat on Amanda was Jeff who had told police in his second interview, on November 10, that he had seen Chad try to pick up a Wendy's employee on October 14, after Chad and Amanda had been living together for an even longer time.

Heather's understanding of the water faucet/Kassidy incident was also wrong, as Jennifer was not at Chad's home at the time. Even Amanda didn't actually see it. It was Chad who told Jeff and Jennifer about it, and Kassidy's head was not held under a water faucet.

No interview with Crystal Grimes was ever conducted.

Wednesday, 22 November 2000

Around this time, Chad's lawyer, Mark Sisti, had plea bargaining discussions with the prosecution and he communicated an offer to Chad for pleading guilty to manslaughter in return for a less-than-maximum prison sentence. Chad's response to Mark was, "*I'm not taking a plea bargain for something I didn't do.*" The idea was not addressed again by either side.

A probable cause hearing was scheduled for this day at 1:30 p.m., but it was postponed to December 4.

The $100,000 bail was paid by Denis Bail Bonds of Raymond, New Hampshire, and Chad Evans was released from the Strafford County Jail, in time for Thanksgiving. Articles (e.g. "Unknown person posted Evans' bail") about the release said that Chad's attorney, Alan Cronheim, did not know who provided the $10,000 fee and security for the bail, but it was Chad's parents, and their home in Keene was the security.

After his release, Chad continued to work on a long letter for his attorneys which contained many details of his relationship with Amanda, Kassidy and about Jeff. He concluded that letter with an acknowledgment that he had been evasive with the police about his eye contact efforts with Kassidy,

As I said earlier, I can't remember everything about my interview with the cops, but I know it wasn't pretty. I suspect you will know what I mean if they ever send us our discovery. I know I was evasive and told what I thought was a small lie to them. I had lost my temper with Kassidy. I had squeezed her cheeks [to get eye contact with her]*; I even had bruised them. I knew this had nothing to do with her death though and I didn't want their attention diverted from what really mattered, I never thought this would steer their entire approach.*

Unfortunately, together with Jeff's allegations, Chad's evasiveness on this point did help steer the police toward him. It would have been helpful if Chad had told his attorneys at that time that he also told the police the "trampoline story," and that story was also evasive. He didn't clarify with his attorneys the truth of that story until shortly before his trial.

At 12:30 p.m. Travis Hunt was interviewed by MSP Detective Scott Harakles and NHSP Trooper Jill Rockey at the Rochester Police Dept. Harakles told Travis that he was viewed as a "*cooperating witness*" and that he was free to leave, and that "*We're taping because we are in New Hampshire, and this is the law in New Hampshire. This is what you have to do.*" (p. 356) Trooper Rockey didn't object, but taping did not seem to be required of at least one other interview in New Hampshire, which was Amanda's by Jim White on December 19 in the Offices of the Attorney General.

The interview of Travis by Harakles at Kittery on the evening of November 9 was not taped and Harakles wrote a two page summary. The transcript of this interview on November 22 contains 54 pages, which made it far more useful than a two page summary.

Travis said that he moved to Chad's "*A little over a month ago,*" which would have been approximately October 15. Chad remembers the date as early September, after the closing of the Hampton Beach McDonald's. He said that he "*was moving in like slowly pretty much I moved stuff in there or whatever.*" (p. 357) This was similar to Amanda's "moving-in" which was incremental and not officially precise. Asked when he first saw bruises on Kassidy, Travis responded, "*Actually, I wouldn't say the first time, um, pretty much like right when, when I lived there....*" (p. 357) When asked for locations, he said, "*...she always had like.... right here, around her face. Sometimes she's have a.... and I seen one on her arm. ... she had one on her butt once... around the jaw areas.... Just bruises.*" (p. 358) Asked about causes, he responded,

I've seen her fall down a lot... I've seen her like on the couch. We have a coffee table. It's like right in front of it and I've seen her fall and hit that before.... and I've seen her .... she goes down the stairs, when she goes down the stairs, she'd go down like laying down....And sometimes, she'd.. fall off at the bottom...Well, the one on her buttocks was from she came home with it after being babysat.... Jeff Marshall had given her a spanking or whatever." (p. 358)

Harakles said, "*why don't we talk about that. I do know all about that story. It's, it's out in the open and talked about.... but from your point of view, how long ago was that?*" (p. 358) Travis said, "*three, three or four weeks ago.*" (p. 359) As the referenced spanking by Jeff occurred on Saturday, October 22, which was 31 days prior to Travis's interview, his estimate was very close. Travis said that when Jeff brought Kassidy home, which was on Sunday the 23rd from an overnight babysitting, Jeff said, " *'You know,' he said, 'she's being a real bitch this weekend,' to Chad. And he said he had to slap her ass or whatever.*" (p. 359) Harakles asked if the people present at that time, who were Chad, Travis, Amanda and Jennifer, took Kassidy's diaper off at that time "*and take a look or what?,*" and Travis responded, "*No....later, like I don't know. Later on in the day, or maybe even the next day or whatever, Amanda was changing her or whatever and she showed me.*" Already familiar with Travis's knowledge in the case, Harakles asked the leading question, "*She brought the baby to you and said look at this?*" and Travis concurred, "*Yeah, and said that... she and her sister gave Jeff 'Holy Hell,' or whatever.*" (p. 359)

Travis said the bruise was "*Black and blue... right, well, across the buttocks...*" (p. 360) Asked what he thought at the time, he said, "*I knew she bruised easy, so, but... I didn't really think too, too much about it... Because she did bruise easy, but... after the fact... and in regards to all this, all that's happened, or whatever. I thought maybe through a pamper, through pants, that was a little much black and blue.*" (p. 360) Jill Rockey asked, "*How do you know she bruised easily?*" and Travis answered, "*... she just always had bruises, or whatever...even if she barely fell, she'd bruise, ... pretty easy. And she was light complected, so I, I really didn't think anything about it.*" Asked for specific incidents, or falls, Travis said that he saw, "*I'd say, maybe three or four... like I said.. she hit her head on the... coffee table...going down the stairs, she'd fall a lot... and get, like probably,... on her arms....*" Harakles asked specifically, "*... did you ever see her do anything that caused the bruising right in here,.... to the cheek area*?" and Travis said, "*No.*" (p. 361)

Asked to describe the fall from the couch to the table, Travis said, "*...right head first on her chin...she was... trying to get off the couch and just kinda stumbled off and...like this, standing up on the couch, trying to get off. And fell off, boom.... and hit the coffee table.*" He said that the injury from the glass table was "*in the front or underneath*" her chin, and Kassidy cried. (p. 362) During this interview, Travis was not asked for the date and time of this particular fall, but it was likely on the evening of Sunday, November 5, after Amanda had returned from her shopping day with her sister and mother, and Chad had returned from his sister's in Belmont.

Harakles asked about the manner of Kassidy's falls, "*...on this same subject, you had described to me what she was like when she would fall.... it was a little bit different than what most kids do... you even described her as possibly being a little slow.*" (p. 362) Travis agreed, and said, "*The thing that made me think she was slow would be... she's 1 and 1/2. 1 1/2 year olds are usually... in to everything, pretty much... And... she'd just sit on the couch all day. Or,... in her high chair. When it was time to eat. She was... she'd just sit there, quiet.*" (p. 363) Travis affirmed that Kassidy's quietness had been consistent since he first knew her, "*...except for when... her mother would...she's pretty much working from the house doing surveys.... when she got up, she'd get up... when Amanda got up, Kassidy would get up.*" (p. 363)

Again relying on his earlier interview of Travis, Harakles asked, "*...what I was getting at was about these falls... I thought you had described to me that the way she would fall was kind of strange. And... that she wouldn't protect herself?*" And Travis responded, "*Yeah, she wouldn't...I've seen it before... when she fell, she wouldn't put her arms out, like to stop herself, like instinct.*"(p. 363) Specifically, with the coffee table incident, "*She didn't really put her arms out, no. She just kinda fell into it.*" (p. 364)

Jill Rockey asked about the bruise on Kassidy's buttocks, as she had understood that it could be seen with diaper on, and Travis said that it was not visible with Kassidy diapered.

Travis said that he never heard the "trampoline story."

Asked about Amanda's and Chad's roles in the disciplining of Kassidy, Travis said, "*...it was pretty much the both of them, I would say.... punishment usually consisted of time-out, going to the room,*" and he did witness Amanda and Chad giving Kassidy time-outs. Harakles asked if there was "*any touching involved in this time-out, like, ... take her by the arm...?*" and Travis responded, "*Most of the time you, you'd just tell her, 'Go upstairs,' and she'd go.... she'd put up a little bit of a fuss, but she'd go pretty much." (p. 365)*

Harakles asked, "*...did you ever witness any physical punishment, like a spanking or a slap on the hand?*" and Travis said, "*Never.*" Asked further, about Chad or Amanda "*kind of at the end of their rope, losing patience with her,*" and Travis said, "*...he yelled for her to be quiet when it was, bedtime, or whatever. She'd always throw a fit around bedtime.*"

Det. Harakles asked for Travis's opinion, whether he had ever seen any disciplining "*that you thought was a little bit inappropriate?*" (p. 366) and Travis responded, "*... locking her in her bedroom when it was bedtime.... I definitely wouldn't do that. ... I've only seen it maybe twice, but even then... Amanda would close the door and she'd put a sock in the top of it.... So she couldn't open it. Once she, Kassidy just opened the door and come right out."* (p. 366-67) Harakles asked a parenting question of whether Kassidy was sleeping in a bed or crib, and Travis said it was a bed. For a 20-month old child, it may have been too soon to move from a crib to a bed, but neither Chad nor Amanda was on trial for that decision. In his December 14, 2010 letter, Chad wrote about Kassidy's falls from her bed,

Kassidy usually slept toward the middle of the bed and Amanda or I typically put one of her pillows on the side of the bed or lined up a pillow or thick blanket on the floor in case Kassidy fell out of bed. Once, approximately a week or so prior to her death, Kassidy rolled out of bed headfirst in the middle of the night. She immediately started crying and I went and picked her up and brought her into bed with Amanda and me. She had a small egg right in the middle of her forehead for a day or so from that.

Harakles asked for more examples of "*something you wouldn't condone,*" and made the point that "*you are my best witness being that you lived in the house. Was there anything else, ... maybe grabbing by the arms or grabbing by the ears, just certain things parents do that if I saw would raise my eyes and say, 'the kid's too small to be doing that?*" and Travis recalled nothing else, despite Harakles' leading questions. (p. 367)

Jill Rockey asked, "*Did you ever notice the bruises... and say something to Chad or Amanda about them?*" and Travis said, "*... I never said anything, but Amanda said something to me...She was going to put her in day care. She had just started working or whatever, and she said she couldn't because of her bruises.... because obviously, a day care... teacher... the person that watched them would say something....she mentioned.. the way Chad handled her* [Kassidy] *was a little... not right and whatever.... I said, 'Well, I don't know.' I said, 'I've never seen anything like that happen, so I don't know,' I said... I don't remember what I said.* " (p. 368-70) Travis said that Amanda described and demonstrated to him how Chad grabbed Kassidy's face. Neither the officers nor Travis seemed to understand that Chad's palming Kassidy's face was not to hold firmly to cause pain as punishment by itself, but it was to hold her face to ensure that had **eye contact** so she would pay attention to what he was saying to her. There's a difference.

Harakles returned to the subject of seeking day care for Kassidy, "... *were you aware of the real reason she was going to Jeff's?*" and Travis said, "*She didn't want to put her in day care.*" Harakles asked if "*it was just Amanda who didn't want to do it, or was that Chad's advice... that the two of them didn't want to.*" Travis replied, "*I figured it was just her.*" (p. 373) Harakles told Travis, "*it's actually my understanding that Amanda didn't think anything of it. And was, and was gonna look into day cares. And that Chad stopped her. And he advised her against doing that because of the way Kassidy looked.*" (p. 373) Once again a police interviewer was telling the interviewee his or her view of the case. Travis said he wasn't aware of those dynamics, and Harakles wasn't aware of Chad's efforts to get Kassidy into day care at Cross Road Kindergarten. Travis agreed with Harakles' statement "*that the real reason she went to Jeff rather than a normal day care was because of the bruising.*" (p. 373) In reality, Travis didn't know the reasons for using Jeff and Jennifer as babysitters, and he probably didn't know about Amanda's calls to 17 day care providers during Friday, November 2 and Wednesday the 8th. The power of suggestion by the police was formidable, and Travis agreed to Harakles' leading question.

The questioning then shifted to Wednesday, November 8, and Travis said that he arrived home at "*probably 7:30, 7:45, around there,*" and hadn't see Chad before on that day. Travis went upstairs and Chad was bathing Kassidy in the bathtub and Travis saw a "ring" on Kassidy's face and asked Chad about it, who, "*said he was playing... baseball with Kyle or whatever, wiffleball and... that he had hit Kassidy in the eye, 'cause I noticed it. She had like a ring.*" (p. 377) Travis said that at the time, he was not told what kind of ball hit Kassidy, but, "*...after, he told me it was like a rubber, rubber type ball... But when I went up there, I, I pitched a couple to him, just to .... see what he could hit... and.. I was pitching like wiffleballs.*" (p. 378)

Asked about Kassidy, Travis said, "... *she was taking a bath. She got a little upset when he tried to wash her hair but.*" Harakles asked, "*Was she splashing around?... So she looked to you completely normal?*" and Travis said, "*Yeah.*" to both questions. (p. 378) Travis said, "*I saw.. little, little bruises on her check, and that was about it,*" (p. 379) and he said that Kassidy usually says, "*Hi,*" when she saw Travis, and that she said "*Hi,*" on that evening as well. Travis affirmed Harakles' characterization that Kassidy "*appeared to be having just a grand old time?*" (p. 379) Travis continued, "*And then I went in... and played with Kyle or whatever, and he* [Chad] *got her out and got her dressed...*" Travis talked with Kyle, "*I said, '.....Do you want to pitch some balls?' and he said, 'Yeah,' and he said he hit, he had hit Kassidy.*" (p. 379) They played ball for 5-10 minutes, according to Travis, and then he went downstairs to change clothes. He came back upstairs to the first floor around 8:30-8:45 p.m. and Chad and Kassidy were in Chad's office and Kyle was on the couch. Travis said that Kassidy was standing, on her own feet, in Chad's office and eating a "*Popsicle type thing.*" (p. 380)

Asked about the conversation with Chad, Travis said, "*...nothing really. ... He said... Jeff had taught her something: her mom was a bitch or whatever, and she was, she was saying it in her little,... the way she talked was pretty cute or whatever. And...he was ... she'd mimic. She'd say eyes or nose if he said it....stuff like that.... so she was... talking or whatever and, then I was pretty much out the door. I gave her a hug and a kiss good night and that was that.*" (p. 381-82) That was the last time Travis saw Kassidy alive. Travis affirmed Harakles' characterization, "*that she was acting, this was the Kassidy you had always known?*" (p. 382) and it was about 8:45 p.m.

The officers then showed Travis several pictures, and he saw the ballhitting bruise, but there were new bruises as well that he said he not seen before. Harakles characterized Travis's reaction, "*Okay. So it's safe to say that her face changed since you saw her.*" "*Absolutely,*" affirmed Travis.(p. 384)

Rockey pointed out "*...how about this? There were a couple of bruises on her right arm which would have been right here below the elbow. On the lower arm,*" and Travis said, "*I didn't see that either.*" (p. 385) They did not ask Travis which way Kassidy was facing, but most people face the faucets and drain when they bathe, and for a person standing in the door of Chad's upstairs bath, the faucets and drain were on the right. Therefore, Travis would have seen the right side of Kassidy's body, at least initially. She likely turned her head toward him, so he could see the ballhitting injury under her left eye, as well. Travis saw Kassidy again on the first floor, she was wearing long sleeved pajamas, so he would not have been able to see any bruise on her right elbow. In 2011, Chad confirmed that Kassidy was facing to Travis's right and he initially saw the right side of her body.

Travis said that when he arrived home around 11:30-12:00 a.m., all the lights in the home were out, except the outside light, and everyone was in bed. Thursday morning, he awoke and there was no one home and he left for his 11-7 shift at the Portsmouth McDonald's, which is about 40 minutes away. He said that his first contact with Chad or Amanda that day was when Chad called him at work between 4-5:00 p.m., and that he was on his way to Kittery. Travis understood Chad to say that he was on the way to a hospital, but there is none in Kittery, and Chad knew he was going to the Kittery Police station. During the call, Chad confirmed with Travis what he had heard the previous evening about the ball hitting Kassidy and that he had seen the resulting injury. Travis said "*you could tell in his voice*" that Chad was nervous. (p. 389-B) Harakles asked several times in several ways, "*...did he at that time ask you to cover for him?*" and each time Travis said, "*Never...No... No*" and "*Yeah,*" he was "*sure about that.*" (p. 389-D)

Travis said that he didn't learn that Kassidy had died until he arrived home after work, and Chad's sister told him. She had come to Chad's home after learning of Kassidy's death from her mother.

Harakles was trying to persuade Travis that there was something wrong with Travis's understanding of the situation, and of Chad,

Well, here you are, at McDonald's, and you got this phone call from this guy that you know pretty well, about a baby whose situation you know quite a bit about. What were you really thinking? What were your suspicions? What were your fears? You couldn't have not been thinking anything.... Did you think that maybe someone had gone too far with this kid? ... while you're at McDonald's you don't ... kinda smell a rat? Kinda feel like some-someone went too far? Maybe not know who but was that your feeling, or are you telling me you didn't....

Travis said several times the same message, "*... I didn't. I didn't. I had no idea..*" (p. 389-E)

Travis said that Chad said nothing during that call about the DCYF call that morning, but that Travis, without knowing the details, had listened to the DCYF phone message before leaving for work and he recalled it as, "*...'This is for Chad Evans. Can you please contact us?' It gave a phone number, and it said who they were.... and they said it was referring to the kids.*" (p. 389-F)

Detective Rockey echoed Harakles' interpretation of Chad's call as a sign of guilt, saying, *Does it seem unusual to you that here's a person whose girlfriend's child has been injured or is so ill that she's taken to a hospital and he's driving to be there and he's calling you at work to make sure that you remember what happened last night?*
Travis replied, "*I didn't think anything of it.*" (p. 389-H) If he had thought more, he might have considered Chad's nervousness very reasononable considering that Chad was on probation and that it was very possible that whatever was ailing Kassidy might have been blamed on him. That's exactly what happened.

What Harakles and Rockey and Travis didn't realize was that when Chad had called Jeff's number earlier, and before Jeff gave the phone to a policeman, Jeff appeared to challenge Chad about the ballhitting incident. Thus, it was on Chad's mind.

Harakles continued, "*Was he also telling you, 'You remember, she gave you a hug and a kiss? You remember she said, Hi?' You remember she was pointing out her nose?' Did he refresh your memory on any of that stuff?*" and Travis said that was correct. Apparently, Harakles found it hard to believe that Travis didn't share his suspicions of Chad and his motives, saying, "*Okay... you're truly sitting here with me now and don't feel like he was trying to pressure you that you need to remember this stuff?*" and Travis remained consistent, "*I didn't feel pressured at all.*" (p. 389-U)

Without saying whether she had children or not, Rockey then asked Travis if he had children, and at that time he did not. Then she told Travis how parents behave and if, "*You find out a kid is injured, your primary function is to get to that kid. That's all you're thinking about..... every parent has their worse nightmare going through their head when they are headed to the hospital... I assure you, you're not calling other people to make sure they remember things that happened the night before?*" (p. 389-J) She was right about a "*worse nightmare*" going through a scared parent's mind, but who is to say what the contents of that nightmare must be. Chad's nightmare at the time was that his parenting of Kyle would be affected, and that nightmare came true. The double irony of Rockey's sermon about parenting, and without any reference to her own experience, if any, is that Chad was a known parent and stepparent, and he wasn't actually Kassidy's parent. By Travis's recollection, part of Chad's call could be considered as seeing reassurance that Kassidy was okay the previous night. As Det. Harakles said in the beginning of Travis's interview, he was the best witness on what happened at Chad's and Amanda's home, aside from them, and they were both considered by the police to be at fault.

Travis said that after his call with Chad, he talked briefly with Jeremy, who had also talked with Chad, and said, "*I hope she's all right.*" (p. 389-K) Travis worked until 7:00 p.m. and then drove home to Rochester. Nicole was there with her husband, Brandon, and told him about Kassidy's death, and then Jeremy called from the Kittery Police station and told Travis that the police would like to talk with him. Brandon, Nicole and Travis went to Kittery together.

Knowing how important Travis's recollections and potential testimony were, Harakles tried to break through what he thought was Travis's reluctance to incriminate Chad. Said Harakles,

I have to ask you, Travis, because... I do think that you're being honest. And that's the truth.... but one thing that I'll never do is I'll never lie to you. I'll tell you to your face what I think of you at all times....and I am concerned that if I'm missing anything here, it's that you're covering up, right? ... I don't know you're doing it, but you might be. You might have saw a little more than your're saying. He might have tried to prep you... so that you were like an alibi for him. And I'm concerned that because of loyalties... your're really confused.... now, you're gonna tell me, look me in the eyes, and tell me that in no way shape or form he tried to prep you at all?

Travis responded, "*Absolutely not.*" (p. 389-O) Coincidentally, Harakles had come tantalyzingly close to understanding Chad Evans's belief in the importance of **eye contact** when he asked Travis to "*look me in the eyes.*"

Jill Rockey joined in the pressure, "*And you saw those pictures of her. You know that child suffered. She suffered.*" (p. 389-P)

Harakles then asked about Jeremy's contacts with Chad after November 9, and they had seen each other a few times,

But you know what I want to know... who's talked about this and what did they say? Is there anything out ther that has raised your eyebrows or thought, "Gee, that's a little screwed up that he said that?" ... when you've been in his presence has been in complete denial like, "I didn't do anything," and "they, they'd better not be after me?" I mean I don't want to put words in your mouth. (p. 389-Q)

Of course, Harakles did want Travis to say what he wanted to him to say and he gave him the words and phrases, despite his saying "*I don't want to put words in your mouth*" for the sixth time during the interview.

Travis said that Chad had "*said he didn't do it...he said he didn't hit that girl, ever.*" (p. 389-Q) Harakles asked if Chad had told Travis "*who he thought might be involved?*" and Travis told the officers, instead what he, Travis, thought, "*I thought Jeff Marshall obviously, because he was the only one with her that day.*" Harakles responded, "*Yeah.*" (p. 389-Q)

Still trying to convince Travis of Chad's guilt, more than trying to learn as much as they could from their interviewee, the officers showed Travis photographs of the bottoms of Kassidy's feet, and called the abrasions, "*pin pricks is what they appear to be. We're not sure what caused them.*" Travis said he had not seen them before, or heard Kassidy complain about them. (p. 389-R)

Travis had said earlier that he understood that Jeff Marshall stepped on Kassidy's toe, but he thought that Kassidy "*seemed to walk all right.*" (p. 389-T)

Finally, Travis told the officers of an anonymous message left on Chad's phone machine after Kassidy's death which said something like, "*How could you live with yourself? How could you live with yourself?*" Travis thought it was left by Amanda's stepfather because

Travis had talked to him recently when Chad asked him to call the Conley home in an effort to talk with Amanda.

At the end of the interview, Harakles asked Travis, "*...before we do wrap up, though, I just want to clarify that at no time during this interview have you felt like you had to be here with us? That you couldn't leave?*" Travis said, "*No,*" but if he had been less polite, he might have pointed out to Det. Harakles that his request that Travis remember what Harakles told him at the beginning of the interview sounded like he was tryng to protect himself, showing the same behavior that Harakles attributed to Chad.

Even though Travis was, after the primary-four, the best witness of Kassidy's last 24 hours, and even though the police believed that Travis was covering up for Chad, they did not ask him if he was willing to take a lie detector test. In 2010, he said he was willing to take a brainscan MRI lie detector test, but sufficient funds are not available for the $4,000 test.

The interview ended shortly after noon, at 12:06 pm.

Travis's quiet nature misled some people, including Chad, to think that he wasn't paying attention as much as he was. Chad wrote in his Nov. 2000 letter to his attorneys

Travis made a point to me right after I got home from jail and was pretty upset about things that made me really think. He said, "Chad, I know you didn't do this man. Most nights you aren't even here until well after I get home and Kassidy was in bed by the time you got here. The only nights you get home early are Tues. and Weds. When you have Kyle. (I didn't realize he was so observant.) I have only ever seen you be nice to that little girl." I guess I consider this a good point because I hadn't really thought of it, but I was never home and rarely had her. On Mondays and Thursdays, I worked out until 9:30 pm. Fridays I never got home before 8 pm. Tues and Weds. I usually got home by 6 pm although in the very beginning of October, I took up candlepin bowling with my friends Bruce and Jeremy. We were going all the time. Sometimes, 2-3 times per week. Saturdays and Sundays that I didn't have Kyle I spent mainly with Bruce figuring out our betting game plan and watching football. On the weekends that I did have Kyle, the four of us (Kyle, Amanda, Kassidy and myself) would take off and do something. I was simply never around.

Later in the afternoon, in her cruiser, Jill Rockey interviewed a co-worker of Amanda at Old Navy, Raymond Aguila, age 23. He worked full time for the U.S. Navy, aboard the U.S.S. Corpus Christi, then docked at the Portsmouth Naval Shipyard, and part-time at Old Navy. According to Rockey's summary, he recalled one conversation with Amanda, "*a few days before Kassidy Bortner died,*" when he and Amanda were folding clothes after the store closed for the day. (p. 390) He remembered one night when Amanda received a call at work, but had to leave, and his other recollections were vague and scattered.

Foster's Daily Democrat published on page 1, the story, "One toll-free call could have saved Kassidy" by Jennifer Saunders, which reported "*allegations she suffered ongoing abuse - abuse people knew was happening.... friends and family members of the child's mother, 18-year old Amanda Bortner, have stated they knew or suspected the child was being abused... however, they said they did not report it.*" Then, returning to the headline's theme, "*According to state officials in Maine and New Hampshire, all it takes is a toll-free phone call to report suspicions of child abuse or neglect.*" In Maine, reported the article, professional people, such as doctors and day care providers who suspect abuse are required to report it to state officials. In New Hampshire, continued the article, "*the mandatory reporting law extends beyond those with professional contact to include anyone who comes in contact and suspects abuse, explained Nancy Rollins,*" who was the director of DCYF. Said Rollins, "*When a call comes in that notifies us of suspicions of sexual and physical abuse, we are required under state statute to contact law enforcement.*" The article did not refer to the Foster's Daily Democrat article three days previous, and noted above, where Rollins's superior, John Wallace, declined to deny that DCYF had actually received such a call. As Tristan Evans had told Chad and the police on the night Kassidy died, she did call DCYF about what she suspected was abuse of Kassidy. Thus, the headline was wrong: one toll-free call was not enough. Also, the article was wrong to state that people "*knew*" Kassidy was being abused. No one knew, although some people thought they knew.

Chad and Amanda knew that Chad had caused bruises when palming Kassidy's face, but the intent of the holding was not to punish. It was to secure Kassidy's attention. It is not abuse to hold a child's face, with the full authorization of the child's parent, in order to get the child's attention. The bruising was the result of easy bruising, and would not have occurred in a child less easily bruised. To Amanda's and Chad's lifelong regret, they didn't seek medical advice about the bruising, because they didn't think it was a serious problem. If they had, they might have uncovered a more serious problem, such as the effect of accumulated head injuries, that might have contributed to her death, if not detected.

Thursday, 23 November 2000

Chad and his parents and brother Jason and sister Nicole and her husband, Brandon, gathered at Chad's home in Rochester for Thanksgiving. Jeremy and Bruce and Jessica Edmands joined them.

Friday, 24 November 2000

New Hampshire State Trooper Shawn Skahan and Sergeant Allen Welch interviewed Barbara Brooks Hamel at her home in Keene. Skahan was from Keene and played football in the Pop Warner League at the same time as Chad. Chad was a good friend of Skahan's brother, Patrick. Trooper Skahan wrote a three page summary of the interview of this "*former girlfriend of Evans, dating him between 1985 and 1991.*" (p. 233) This was when Chad was between the ages of 14 and 20, and all more than nine years before Kassidy's death. She said that she had met Chad for lunch once after that dating period, at which time she was engaged to her current husband, and after Chad had moved to Rochester. Skahan quoted Hamel as describing Chad as "*very jealous,*" "*controlling*" and "*smothering.*" Shakan reported that Hamel said that she and Chad often had heated arguments, but "*she stated that admittedly she knew what buttons to push to get him upset. She added the arguments would usually reach a point where he would push her into a wall or physically assault. She said that Evans never took responsibility for actions and always blamed someone else.*" (p. 233) Hamel recounted several incidents which allegedly showed Chad's anger at work and away from work. Chad disputes these accounts and notes that Barbara is a year older than him, which was a significant part of their difficulties when they were both in high school. Also, at McDonald's he was her supervisor.

As I write this, I recall a former girlfriend telling me after a 20-year gap in communication that I was a "controlling" boyfriend when I, an avowed feminist, was with her. I wasn't convinced, but her memory was her memory.

At the end of the report, Skahan wrote that Hamel had "*spoken to Evans' sister who told her that marriage had changed him. Additionally, the sister told her that he had one child of his own and was attempting to adopt his wife's eldest child.*" (p. 235)

This was the only interview in the case of any of Chad's former girlfriends, including Mary Paquette, the woman he lived with in Rochester before his marriage to Tristan. There were no interviews ever conducted of any of Jeff Marshall's girlfriends.

In a February 18, 2010 letter, Chad wrote about his relationship with Barbara:
Barbara Hamel was probably my first "love." She is incorrect about when we met and how long we were together. We didn't meet until I was in 9th grade. Which was high school. I know this because November 1986 is when I started at McDonald's as a 15 year old. Can you believe that I cannot remember if she was one or two grades ahead of me in school right now? Like every girlfriend previous to Tristan, she was older than I was. We were a bad mix from the start but for some reason kept getting back together. She is correct in that she definitely knew how to push my buttons. I think she enjoyed keeping me on a Yo Yo. I thought I loved her and she kept toying with me, using my insecurities,

saying sweet things one day, horribly mean the next. I didn't know which way was up or down where she was concerned. She remembers the break ups differently than I do. She would break up with me often citing that I wasn't a challenge. She loved confrontation and I was kind of a "yes" man. I always wanted to please her. I lost my virginity to this girl and was convinced starting at 15 years old that I would never find another like her. I would start moving on after we'd split up and she would decide she wanted me back. I dumped a lot of nice girls to go back to her. I think it was really that I hated giving up on things. I always felt that we could be great together not realizing how bad we really were. We had some great times and I always clung to those great times. If you ever talked to ***her*** *best friends of that time, Becky Healey, or Ellen Lounsbury, I am confident that even today, after I have been convicted of this horrible crime, they would paint a very different picture for you, than was presented by Barbara.*

Tuesday, 28 November 2000

Foster's Daily Democrat reported Chad's bail release the previous Wednesday, "Evans' bail terms: No restriction on contact with children." However, as Jennifer Saunders reported, Chad's ability to visit his son Kyle, and stepson, Brent, was now allowed only with restricted supervision by Tristan. Unreported was the requirement that Chad's visits be supervised by a family counselor. The presumption of innocence did not prevent the prosecutors from ensuring that precautions were taken, in case they were right about Chad. Saunders reported that the police would not say "*whether charges will be filed against Kassidy's mother.....* [or] *where Bortner was at the time Evans allegedly inflicted the fatal blow to Kassidy's head.*" The article noted that Amanda "*had left the Seacoast and is residing in Texas*" and that Amanda had spoken, according to friends, at Kassidy's funeral "*service of the difficulties of being a teen mother.*" The companion article in Foster's Daily Democrat that day was "DCYF official: Overwhelming case loads, laws make it hard to fight abuse." Associate DHHS Commissioner still continued to refuse to say whether DCYF had been called about Kassidy, but Kimberly Houghton's article seemed to prepare readers for that conclusion by stating that DCYF had too few resources for too many needs.

Thursday, 30 November 2000

There was a "case briefing" at 3:00 p.m. about the case at the office of the New Hampshire Attorney General. It was attended by officers from the Maine and New Hampshire State Police Dept's and mentioned in a report (p. 1340) by Det. Linscott.

Monday, 4 December 2000

The probable cause hearing was scheduled for this day, but it was postponed at the request of Chad's attorneys who said they needed more time to prepare. The probable cause hearing, in New Hampshire criminal law practice, was required, where a judge would determine whether there was sufficient evidence to support the prosecution's case. If so, and given the seriousness of the alleged crimes, the case would be transferred from the Rochester District Court to the Strafford County Superior Court. Later, the probable cause hearing was scheduled for January 8 2001.

Wednesday, 6 December 2000

NHSP Sgt James White interviewed Will Peirce at the Kittery Police Station, but only a one page summary was prepared. Wrote White,

The purpose of the meeting was to determine the details of a fall Kassidy had taken from Jeff Marshall's truck, which Peirce had observed. Peirce.... believes the fall occurred just a day or two before Kassidy's death.... Kassidy was in her car seat..[and] *was getting out of the car seat under her own power. She kind of rolled forward in a falling motion and Marshall caught her without her striking the ground. Pierce did not believe she struck her head on the truck. Peirce said that Marshall commented, "See, she just falls out of the truck," which Peirce took to mean she had fallen out of the truck before.* (p. 401)

This fall was not the earlier fall described to the police by Amanda, Chad, Jeremy, and Travis, as previously related to them by Jeff. That earlier fall, apparently alluded to by Jeff in his interview with White, was on Saturday, October 28.

Peirce also told White that Jeff had called him on Wednesday evening after Chad had called him, Jeff, about the "baseball" (Tee-ball) incident. Peirce said that Jeff called him again around "*0900 hours*," and told him that "*Kassidy was not walking. She was sitting in front of the television eating cereal.*" It was interesting that Peirce recalled Jeff mentioning Kassidy eating cereal because Jennifer had said that she remembered Kassidy eating cereal as well. Later, however, at the trial, she recanted that recollection. About previous observations of bruises, White wrote, "*Peirce said Marshall had showed him bruises on Kassidy's face about three to four weeks before her death. Peirce described two faded bruises on her cheekbones, below her eyes, and facing grip mark type bruises had darkened again.*" (p. 404) Three to four weeks before Kassidy's death included the period roughly between October 17 and October 24. This period had already been cited by others as a time of noticeable bruises on Kassidy. Unfortunately, it does not appear that he was asked directly about Kassidy's appearance on Wednesday the 8th.

Thursday, 7 December 2000

Sgt. White interviewed Amy Gagne, but the limited purpose of the meeting was stated to be "*to determine when A. Bortner began working at Old Navy.*" (p. 402) Gagne told White that Amanda began work on Monday, November 6. The time slip for Amanda's work at Old Navy also showed work for the four days beginning on that Monday, but it didn't state that this week was Amanda's first.

Tuesday, 12 December 2000

There was a "case briefing" at 3:00 p.m. about the case at the Gray, Maine State Police barracks. It was attended by officers from the Maine and New Hampshire State Police Dept's, the Maine State Police Crime Laboratory, the Maine Medical Examiner's Office and the New Hampshire Attorney General's office, and mentioned in a report (p. 1340) by Det.Linscott.

Thursday, 14 December 2000

A Strafford County, New Hampshire Grand Jury issued multiple indictments and "Information" against Chad Evans for Second Degree Murder of Kassidy Bortner and six counts of second degree assault and two counts of first degree assault against Kassidy Bortner, one count of child endangerment for the period from August 1 through November 9, 2000, and one count of simple assault on evening of November 8-9 against Amanda Bortner. The periods of the six second degree assault charges for "*grabbing and squeezing*" Kassidy's face were: 9/1-9/30, 10/1-10/7, 10/8-10/14, 10/15-10/21, 10/22-10/31, 11/1-11/8. The periods of the two first degree assault charges for causing fractures to Kassidy's arms and legs were from 10/9 through 11/9. As the previous charge against Chad was for manslaughter, the newspapers reported the indictment as an "upgrade" of the charges. Foster's Daily Democrat ran the story as a large banner headline on page one, "**Murder Indictment**" with the sub-heading, "Evans accused of inflicting multiple blows to girl's head and abdomen." Showing the dual-state cooperation and importance assigned to this case, the New Hampshire Attorney General's press release announcing the indictments was joined by the Maine State Police Colonel and the Chiefs of the Kittery and Rochester police departments.

The time-lines of the charges could look like this:

First Degree Assault, arm fracture
|............................|
First Degree Assault, leg fracture
|............................|
Second Degree Assault (6)
|............1............||..2..||..3..||..4..||..5..||..6..|

Child Engangerment

|...|

....

9 Jul**1** Aug**1** Sep**1** Oct**1** Nov**1** **9**

However, to be consistent with the three and six months calendars used here, they are presented below with "C" for Child Endangerment and "A" for Assault and "CA" for the two charges simulteneously.

June 2000

Su	Mo	Tu	We	Th	Fr	Sa
					9	10
11	12	13	14	15	16	17
18	19	20	21	22	23	24
25	26	27	28	29	30	

July 2000

Su	Mo	Tu	We	Th	Fr	Sa
						1
2	3	4	5	6	7	8
9	10	11	12	13	14	15
16	17	18	19	20	21	22
23	24	25	26	27	28	29
30	31					

August 2000

Su	Mo	Tu	We	Th	Fr	Sa
		C	C	C	C	C
C	C	C	C	C	C	C
C	C	C	C	C	C	C
C	C	C	C	C	C	C
C	C	C	C	C		

September 2000

Su	Mo	Tu	We	Th	Fr	Sa
					CA	CA
CA	CA	CA	CA	CA	CA	CA
CA	CA	CA	CA	CA	CA	CA
CA	CA	CA	CA	CA	CA	CA
CA	CA	CA	CA	CA	CA	CA

October 2000

Su	Mo	Tu	We	Th	Fr	Sa
CA	CA	CA	CA	CA	CA	CA
CA	CA	CA	CA	CA	CA	CA
CA	CA	CA	CA	CA	CA	CA
CA	CA	CA	CA	CA	CA	CA
CA	CA	CA				

November 2000

Su	Mo	Tu	We	Th	Fr	Sa
			CA	CA	CA	CA
CA	CA	CA	CA	CA		

The challenge for the defense was to show the police, prosecutors and later, the jury, that in terms of bruising, the last six months of Kassidy's life looked like this:

June 2000

Su	Mo	Tu	We	Th	Fr	Sa
					9	10
11	12	13	14	15	16	NI
NI	NI	NI	NI	NB	23	24
25	26	27	28	29	30	

July 2000

Su	Mo	Tu	We	Th	Fr	Sa
						1
2	3	4	5	6	NI	NI
NI	NI	NI	NB	NB	NB	NB
NB	NB	NB	NB	NB	21	22
23	NI	NI	NI	NI	NI	NB
NB	NB					

August 2000

Su	Mo	Tu	We	Th	Fr	Sa
		1	2	3	4	NI
NI	NI	NI	NI	NB	NI	NI
NI	NI	NI	NB	NI	NI	NI
NB	NB	NB	NB	NB	NB	NB
NB	NB	NI	NI	NI		

September 2000						
Su	Mo	Tu	We	Th	Fr	Sa
					NI	**NB**
3	4	5	**NI**	**NI**	**NI**	**NI**
NI	**NB**	12	13	14	15	16
17	18	**NI**	**NI**	**NI**	**NI**	**NI**
NB	**NB**	**NB**	**NB**	**NI**	**NI**	**NI**

October 2000						
Su	Mo	Tu	We	Th	Fr	Sa
NB	2	3	4	5	6	7
8	9	10	11	12	**B**	**B**
B	**B**	17	18	19	20	**B**
B	23	24	25	26	27	**B**
B	**B**	**B**				

November 2000						
Su	Mo	Tu	We	Th	Fr	Sa
			B	**B**	**B**	**B**
B	6	7	8	9		

Even if the calendar was sufficiently understood, with the solid evidence of good health and no bruising (NB) and no injury (NI) prior to those NB periods, it would still be a challenge for the defense to present explanations for the bruising which was definitely noticeable and specifically identified beginning on October 13.

Friday, 15 December 2000

John Marasco reported that he observed an interview, "*via video telecast,*" of seven-year old Brent Richards [Lincoln] by Nancy Harris in the offices of the Strafford County Attorney. Marasco wrote, "*Richards was extremely hyperactive during the interview, and no new information was gained.*" (p. 1071) There was no other report of that interview and no transcript, in contrast to Nancy Harris's interview with Brent's half-brother, Kyle, a few weeks earlier. She was the Director of the Strafford Country Victim/Witness Program.

Monday, 18 December 2000

Around midnight, Amanda returned to New England from San Antonio, and was met at Boston's Logan Airport by New Hampshire State Police Sergeant James White and Trooper Susan Forey. They went to a motel for the night and the troopers transported Amanda to the Office of the New Hampshire Attorney General in Concord on Tuesday morning.

Tuesday, 19 December 2000

Amanda's first meeting was with Assistant Attorneys General N. William Delker and Christopher Carter at the Office of the New Hampshire Attorney General in Concord. There was no recording made of that meeting.

Amanda was then interviewed by New Hampshire State Police Sergeant James White. Also present was Allison Vachon of the AG's Victim/Witness Advocate's office. The interview was her second longest of five interviews, running from 10:00 a.m. to 11:50 a.m., but it was not recorded. If it had been recorded, the transcript would have run to approximately 75 pages, and would have been very valuable. The summary appeared to have been written two days later, on December 21.

Sgt. White wrote that "*The purpose of the interview was to document, in greater detail, some of the information that A. Bortner had divulged in previous interviews.*" (p. 615) However, even though the best method to capture greater detail in an interview is to record it, he chose to summarize it in his own words. He reported that Amanda said that Kassidy was "*very still*" when Amanda changed her diaper on Thursday morning, November 9, and that she

...carried Kassidy downstairs to the living room couch, where she propped Kassidy up on the couch and turned on the television for her. A. Bortner said Kassidy was not talking or walking...that either she or C. Evans carried Kassidy to the kitchen counter and sat her there... she did not see Kassidy eat anything that morning....A. Bortner told me that on Wednesday, she recalled a mark under Kassidy's right eye, that she sustained after she fell off the couch and struck the coffee table. She also remembered fading (yellowing) bruises around Kassidy's mouth.... On Wednesday evening... she observed redness and swelling around Kassidy's left eye, that she felt could be consistent with being struck by a ball.... A.

Bortner said the swelling wasn't huge. Otherwise she would have applied ice.... A. Bortner did not examine Kassidy for any further bruises, nor did she observe any....
On the Thursday morning trip from Rochester to Dover to Kittery, "*...A Bortner said that Kassidy slept the whole way, which was typical.*" (p. 616)

Regarding the ballhitting incident, "*...she does not know what type of ball"* was used. White wrote that "*C. Evans told A. Bortner that she should take Kassidy to the doctor when the bruises went away, but didn't say specifically why.*" (p. 616)
Amanda told White about the argument she had with Chad on Wednesday night,
...after she told C. Evans how tired she was from working so hard. He told her he worked hard too, and she responded that at least he didn't have to go up and down ladders all day like she did. She told me they were seated on the couch and ... C. Evans then grabbed her by the throat and pinned her down, on her back, on the couch. She pushed him away and then he apologized... A Bortner told C. Evans she was only joking and that he had taken what she said the wrong way. (p. 617)

This was the second time that Amanda had told the police about the argument between her and Chad on Wednesday night. The first time was during Amanda's interview with Angela Blodgett in Gray, Maine on November 12. Chad hadn't mentioned it. Until this December 19 interview, it wasn't an issue. However, what White wrote here became the basis for the First Degree Assault charge against Chad, which was the only charge relating to Amanda, and not Kassidy. By combining the charges at the trial, the prosecution was able to paint a picture of a violent man.

About Kassidy and Chad, "*...at the beginning of the relationship between she and C. Evans, C. Evans ignored Kassidy's jealousy. As the relationship progressed, however, he became more and more frustrated, thinking that she should have been getting used to him....She told me that he was very big on having Kyle and Kassidy look him in the eyes when he was disciplining them. A Bortner told me that C. Evans did not grab Kyle by the face because he would do as he was told and look C. Evans in the eyes. However, Kassidy was a different story. She would not look him in the eyes, so he would get angry and grab her by the face, in an attempt to make her look him in the eyes.*" (p. 617) Thus, Amanda fully understood Chad's use of **eye contact** to ensure effective communication.

Amanda allegedly said, "*that C. Evans would be out of control when he disciplined Kassidy. He would yell and scream at Kassidy, swear at her and call her names, including 'bitch.'* " Regarding Kyle, *"Evans yelled at Kyle also, but did not swear at him or call him names. A. Bortner said she only saw C. Evans spank Kyle once, while he would grab Kassidy by the face and/or arms at least once or twice weekly and even more frequently in the weeks before Kassidy's death.*" To this paragraph, Chad wrote, "*Bullshit*," when he first read it.

Asked if Chad ever disciplined Kassidy in front of Kyle, "*Borter said she is sure he did because she recalled Kyle asking her, 'What's Daddy doing to Kassidy?'*" (p. 617)

White continued, "*She told me that Kassidy was pigeon-toed and did fall a lot, but A. Bortner characterized it as normal baby stuff. She said Kassidy caught herself when she fell and wasn't frequently injured when she fell on her own. A. Bortner told me that Kassidy was fearless and trusting, in that she would jump from the counter into A. Bortner's arms, and once she jumped part way down the stairs into A. Bortner's arms.*" (p. 618)

White summarized Amanda's statement that the "trampoline story" was false, and developed by Chad when Amanda was planning to take Emily Conley to a doctor's appointment, in order to explain the bruises on Kassidy's lower face. Regarding the alleged "*head-butting*" at the washing machine incident, Amanda acknowledged to White that she had told Chad that she "*might*" go on the boat with him, but "*then later decided to spend the day with some friends....While they were in the basement area, C. Evans grabbed A. Bortner and head-butted her. She told him he was 'psycho,' or words to that effect, and he later apologized.*" (p. 618) The alleged head-butting occurred when both Amanda and Chad reached down to pick up the same piece of clothing at the washing machine. This was yet another example of where an accident was construed as an intentional act.

Regarding the argument after the August 25 dinner function at the Exeter Inn, "... *she told me that... he choked her with enough force to cause her to have trouble swallowing for about a week, and the choking caused bruising to her neck. A. Bortner said that C. Evans had drank a lot that night and was very drunk.*" (p. 618) There was no mention of whether White asked Amanda about her alcohol consumption. As Amanda correctly stated to White, the dinner function was to celebrate the re-opening of the Exeter McDonald's. As a company event, with the presence of Chad's managers and company owners, it's very unlikely that he was "*very drunk.*" The assault that White described was not included in the indictments against Chad, and the allegation that Chad's restraint of Amanda was so severe as to cause her difficulty swallowing was never stated again.

After the interview, Sgt White drove Amanda to Springvale, Maine to pick up her car. In a 2008 interview, Amanda talked about the above interviews:

Oh my gosh... which they didn't tape record, it was all handwritten. They didn't want to tape record it - I remember that. I remember going .... saying oh why aren't you tape recording this ... __ so naive, you know, to why they weren't tape recording it, but ya, they actually, um, they tried twisting all my words and they got so frustrated, I remember __ they wanted me to say throw, they wanted me to say, and I couldn't, you know. And then finally, I just agreed with them. (Will Delker) took a hold of his face like this and was getting frustrated ... like arggg. Like I'm driving them nuts. Because I'm not saying what they want me ... to say ... exactly ... you know, they made me feel like __ . So finally, I mean ... I'm pretty sure that's when that happened. They distorted everything differently .... they actually had me use my purse to try to show them how ... um ... Chad would handle Kassidy. And I'm like ... I feel like an idiot, I remember grabbing the purse and just like putting it right here like that ... swear to God .. .like are you sure? .. are you __ Ya! I'm sure, you know, I wasn't sure I'm going to stick up for Chad at all - I wasn't trying to do anything ... I was just trying to say the truth ... but .. apparently that wasn't good enough, you know?

In 2011 Chad remembered that

Amanda left that meeting feeling very frustrated that they [Carter, Delker, White] *wouldn't listen to her. She said at one point, "They kept telling me that I was wrong. It was impossible that Kassidy walked to me on her bed and that she sat on the couch watching TV without falling over. The doctor told them this couldn't have happened because she had a brain injury." I imagine this was both frustrating and confusing to Amanda. Here she is, KNOWING full well what we observed that morning and being told that the experts claim it is not possible. We have this inherent trust in doctors and the police. They cannot be wrong, can they? I imagine Amanda started second guessing herself. I know that I would.* (Letter, July 29, 2011)

Wednesday, 20 December 2000

Foster's Daily Democrat obtained the full text of the indictments and published another front page story by Kimberly Houghton, "Abuse details released - Evans allegedly beat toddler for months before her death."

The article began with an unusual, "*EDITOR'S NOTE: Graphic content in the following story may be unsuitable for some readers.*" Below are excerpts from the article:

ROCHESTER - Chad E. Evans allegedly assaulted 21-month-old Kassidy Bortner several times over a three-month period - beating the child and throwing her into walls - before she died Nov. 9, according to indictments released Tuesday. The court documents state that the Rochester man, indicted on a charge of second-degree murder, also continuously grabbed and squeezed Kassidy's face, and fractured her leg and arm during separate incidents this fall and summer. But it was multiple blows to the girl's head and abdomen that resulted in her death, the indictments state.

Evans is also accused of preventing Kassidy from seeking proper medical treatment for the injuries he allegedly inflicted, said the indictments...

"Evans bruised Kassidy's body and fractured her bones by repeatedly grabbing Kassidy by the face, throat, arms and legs by propelling Kassidy into the walls of the home, causing Kassidy to strike the walls," the court documents state....

Kassidy was repeatedly assaulted from about Aug. 1 until her death, the indictments said....

"Evans recklessly caused the death of Kassidy Bortner... under circumstances manifesting an extreme indifference to the value of human life..." state the indictments.... Evans caused a fracture to Kassidy's arm by grabbing and pulling on her legs. Evans caused bruising to Kassidy by grabbing and squeezing her face," state the assault indictments....

Officials at the Department of Health and Human Services' Division of Children, Youth and Families have said the agency is involved in the investigation of Kassidy's death. However, the agency has not confirmed or denied if it was contacted prior to the girl's death....

The indictments had more dates than the earlier reported charges of an alleged assault by Chad on November 8th. It's unlikely that the grand jury was told by the prosecutors of the report of Kassidy's appointment on September 11, 2000 with Dr. James Timoney. Was it because Dr. Greenwald's November 15 Report of Inquiry and Examination by Medical Examiner" mis-reported the date of that appointment as being in September of 1999, or was it because her office did not forward to the Maine State Police copies of reports from Dr. Timoney which might have been acquired? In any case, the grand jury could not have known. If the grand jury had known of the date of the Dr. Timoney appointment, it would have been more difficult to believe the sensational charges, at least those for the months of August and September. First, as noted earlier, setting the start date of "Child Endangerment" at August 1 would have been unlikely, as would the start of the "Second Degree Assault" charges at September 1. Second, how likely would the alleged abuse by Chad have started the day after a doctor's appointment which he had encouraged Amanda to schedule and attend? Thus, the earliest possible starting point for the alleged abuse would have been September 12.

In its first coverage of the case, the Keene Sentinel ran Kimberly Houghton's Foster's Daily Democrat story with the headline, "Keene native indicted in tot's death - Police allege Evans' assaults on toddler were recurring acts." The Sentinel added to the story that Evans was "*a Keene native and former Keene school board member*." It's not known how many members or former members of school boards are accused of crimes against children, but surely the frequency for such members is lower than that for the average population. Chad had told his interrogators about his Board of Education election during his interview, but the transcript of those police interiews wouldn't become available to the public or the media until after Chad's trial. As Chad and his family were not talking to the media, the information did not appear in the Concord, Portsmouth, or Rochester newspapers. As Foster's Daily Democrat showed when it picked up the information about Chad's "Hero" award from the Union Leader, there was some sharing among newspapers, but the local knowledge of the Keene Sentinel was not shared statewide.

Thursday, 21 December 2000

The next day, the sensational newspaper coverage continued and the allegations of the indictments became transformed into the reported truth. The Portsmouth Herald ran the story as
"*Kassidy's short life of pain*," as if the indictments were fact. Wrote Amy Wallace,
Indictments released by the Strafford County, N.H., grand jury on Tuesday suggest that 21-month-old Kassidy Bortner had been beaten regularly for at least three months prior to her death.
In fact, police say there were several visible signs of abuse including a broken arm and leg.

Chad E. Evans, 29, of 191 Milton Road in Rochester, faces life in prison on a charge of second-degree murder. Kassidy died on Nov. 9 from multiple blows to her head and abdomen, Kittery Detective Steve Hamel confirmed Wednesday....

The court documents say that Evans grabbed Kassidy's throat, face and limbs repeatedly. Hamel confirmed reports that Evans allegedly threw the child against the walls of his home and prevented her from receiving treatment for her wounds, which

Evans inflicted....

Hamel said all evidence points to Evans, who also faces a simple assault charge for allegedly abusing the child's mother."

This article was published 42 days after Kassidy's death, and not a single person interviewed by the police had mentioned a broken bone, let alone an arm AND a leg. The only evidence of fractures came from the Medical Examiner, and the report of the autopsy had not yet been released. Yet, there it was. Perhaps the police meant by "*visible*" that the fractures were visible on an X-ray, but even the York Hospital emergency room doctor did not see signs of fractures on X-rays taken there. To the readers of Foster's Daily Democrat, Chad broke Kassidy's bones and prevented her from getting medical help. Could this be the same person who urged Amanda to take Kassidy to the doctor for the "toed-in" gait. It was ironic that the most inflammatory charge was the breaking of bones when the last doctor seen by Kassidy was an orthopedic surgeon, i.e. a bones specialist.

The Union Leader article by D. Allan Kerr was headlined, "Indictment: Child abused repeatedly," and it again reminded its readers of Chad's previous "hero" award. Kerr listed the possible punishments for the indicted crimes, writing that

Evans, a former McDonald's manager, could face up to life in prison for the second-degree murder charge. He can also receive up 15 years for each of the first-degree assault charges, and up to seven years for each second-degree assault charge.

He can also receive a sentence of up to a year for the misdemeanor charges of simple assault and endangering the welfare of a child.

Amy Wallace wrote the story for the Portsmouth Herald, "Man pleads innocent in killing." The Bortner/Conley family, except for Amanda, continued its support of the indictments against Chad, "*I will not forgive Chad (Evans)," Kassidy's aunt, Lindsey Conley told the Portsmouth Herald. "I think he is guilty — no question. He should be in jail, it's as simple as that.*" Lindsey was a step-sister to Amanda, and hadn't seen Kassidy during her last six months and had never met Chad Evans, and thus had never seen Chad and Kassidy together.

The article stated that Chad's trial had been scheduled to begin on November 5.

Wallace wrote, "*Hamel said the investigation has revealed that Evans allegedly had been abusing Kassidy since Aug. 1 until her death.*" Unfortunately, the reporter surely did not ask Detective Hamel what happened on August 1, or even in that time period. The investigation was woefully inadequate regarding the timing of anything, and no police interview had seen a single event mentioned that occurred in August. No one had told the police that Tuesday, August 1 was the third day of the Evans family, plus Amanda, canoe trip down the Saco River, during which time Kassidy was with her grandmother Jacqueline. Nobody had mentioned the August 10, 15-month old milestone pediatrician appointment for Kassidy with Dr. George Glass. No one mentioned the Wednesday, August 16 trip to Water Country in Portsmouth to which Amanda took Kassidy and her brothers Joshua and Scott who were staying with Amanda and Chad in Rochester.

Tuesday, 2 January 2001

Chad was arraigned at 9:00 a.m. on the grand jury's charges and pleaded not guilty. Kimberly Houghton wrote the story for Foster's Daily Democrat, "Accused baby killer pleads innocent to latest charges - Chad Evans still free on bail after arraignment." Assistant Attorney General N. William Delker represented the prosecution and spoke to the media.

At 11:00 a.m. Sgt. White contacted the Exeter Inn and established that the date of the Colley-McCoy/McDonald's function was Friday, August 25th. He reported, too, that the gathering was attended by 16 people, and that the contact person was Bob McDougall, Chad's boss.

White called Bob McDougall at 1:20 p.m. and confirmed the August 25 function, "*to celebrate the opening of the Exeter McDonald's Restaurant,*" and that Chad and Amanda attended.

Wednesday, 3 January 2001

To this point, the newspapers were relying heavily on the grand jury indictments for the prosecution's theory of the case, but in late December the Keene Sentinel had requested access to more of the documents. In early January, the Keene Sentinel prevailed, and more documents were released to the media, including Sgt. White's affidavits of November 10 and 11.

Relying on the new documents, Foster's Daily Democrat published Kimberly Hougton's and Teresa Robinson's page one story with the banner headlines, "DCYF too late for Kassidy - State tried to contact Evans' house just hours before baby's death." The article said that "*Investigators received information about the call from F. Jefferey Marshall,*" who had told the police in his interview about Chad's call to him on the morning of November 9, "*just after Bortner dropped Kassidy off at Marshall's home, according to the affidavit.*" The author of the referenced affidavit was not identified, but it was one of Sgt. White's two affidavits.

Despite the public release of information about the call to DCYF, that agency continued to decline to comment on whether such a call had been received. However, Associate DHHS Commissioner John Wallace "*did confirm that if a call was made to the agency concerning Kassidy, the case would have been assigned to a protective worker and that an investigation would have begun within 72 hours of the initial call.*"
The article stated,

"*Bortner and her daughter had lived with Evans for only a couple of months. In those two short months, Marshall and his girlfriend, Jennifer Conley, who is also the baby's aunt, saw a rapid decline - 'a marked change' according to court documents - in what they described as a happy, playful baby..... They told investigators that Kassidy became 'fearful and subdued and seemed somewhat reluctant to move about the home,' according to court documents.... She also started to have trouble walking.... Marshall and Conley claimed they often baby-sat for Kassidy because Evans and Bortner were afraid other baby-sitters would report the child's injuries, according to court documents. Marshall told investigators that Kassidy's injuries became so severe that he and Conley became reluctant to bring the baby out in public, according to the affidavit.*
Marshall and Conley told investigators that when Kassidy arrived on Nov. 9, she was 'completely covered with new bruises' and that her condition was worse than before, the affidavit said.

During two searches of Evans' home, authorities seized a number of bats and brushes, such as plastic grill brushes, wire dog brushes and various hair brushes.
Court documents indicate that multiple 'pin prick marks' were found on the bottoms of Kassidy's feet, such as those that could be inflicted by hitting the girl on the bottom of the feet with some sort of brush.

"*Court documents*" and "*court records*" sounded more authoritative than an "*affidavit,*" especially one whose author was unidentified. The picture being painted for readers was horrifying, as the one-sided trial in the media continued.

The Keene Sentinel ran an Associated Press story, which also relied on the newly-available documents, "Ex-Keene man pleads innocent in girl's death." The article said, "*According to court records, Evans had beaten Kassidy repeatedly for three months. The records say Evans threw Kassidy against walls and broke her leg and arm in separate incidents this summer and fall...*"

Thursday, 4 January 2001

The "court records" bubble continued the next day, with the Union Leader's article, "Dead toddler had abrasions, bruises." by D. Allan Kay. He wrote,
While conducting an autopsy on the body of 21-month-old Kassidy Bortner in November, Maine's chief medical examiner noticed "pinpoint" abrasions on the bottom of the toddler's feet.

Dr. Patricia [sic] *Greenwald observed about 10 of the abrasions in the middle of the sole of each foot. According to documents from Rochester District Court, the medical examiner concluded that they were caused by a hairbrush, dull pin or fork used to strike the feet within days of Kassidy's death.*

These and other details seem to support the contention of prosecutors that the little girl was subjected to repeated abuse before she died Nov. 9....

According to court affidavits, Greenwald observed numerous bruises over the back and top of the toddler's head, as well as on the forehead, chin, temple, cheek and lips. She also found hemorrhaging in the muscle tissue of the girl's abdomen which she judged to be consistent with the result of a punch or kick.

The documents written by Sgt. James White of the State Police Major Crime Unit include summaries of White's interview with F. Jeffrey Marshall, the boyfriend of Kassidy's aunt....

As with other news articles, theories were elevated to fact, as with the reported "*cause*" of the abrasions on Kassidy's feet. Sgt. White's affidavit, which was the second of the two similar affidaits on November 10 and 11, said, "*Dr. Greenwald concluded that the abrasions were **likely** caused when a dull instrumentality **such as a** hairbrush, dull pin, or tines of a fork were used to strike Kassidy's feet.*" (emphasis added)
Sgt. White never interviewed Jeff Marshall, as White relied upon the interviews of others for almost all of the information in the affidavits.

Jennifer Saunders' article in Foster's Daily Democrat focused on possible sexual abuse, with the headline, "Sex abuse suspected - Officials say observations won't result in charges at this time." She wrote, after an "*Editors note*" caution about the graphic content in the article,

Recently unsealed affidavits in the murder case of Kassidy Bortner contain suspicions that the 21-month-old girl may have been sexually assaulted, but so far, authorities do not expect to file charges relating to alleged injuries.

The affidavit states that a physician, Dr. Anthony Bock, "made observations of the genital area that he considered to be suspicious, notably it appeared to be an enlarged vaginal vault for the age of the child..

New Hampshire State Trooper Jill Rockey also observed injuires on Kassidy's body, the affidavit states, noting the child's "vagina was irritated and visibly swollen; and there appeared to be irritation to the child's anus."....

In an interview with Foster's Daily Democrat on Tuesday, [Asst. A.G.] *Carter said...."The New Hampshire attorney general's office is not bringing any charge of sexual abuse against Chad Evans or anyone else based on the evidence to date."...*

The affidavit is filled with details about how the little girl's death may have occurred. Bortner...told police after Kassidy's death that she knew of several instances when her boyfriend beat the child....

In several interviews with Foster's Daily Democrat after the child's death, Marshall stated that neither he nor Conley contacted authorities about their suspicions...

Friday, 5 January 2001

The Keene Sentinel's page 3 story, "Child abuse covered up, records say - Ex-Keene man accused in death; mom, sister protected him" reported that it was the Keene Sentinel that had asked the Rochester District Court to unseal the documents. Written by the Associated Press and Sentinel Staff writers, the article confirmed that the transition of the case to New Hampshire was complete, "*While Maine authorities assisted in the investigation, "based on the evidence gleaned thus far... we do not expect to bring charges in the state of Maine regarding the death of Kassidy Bortner or any other offenses against her," said Maine State Police Sgt. Matthew Stewart.*"

The Sentinel reporters interviewed N. William Delker, who "*told the Sentinel this morning that suspicions about sexual assault were raised during examinations immediately following her death. After further investigation, Delker said, no evidence now exists that Kassidy was sexually abused.*"

Said the article, "*Evans admitted to investigators that he 'played with Kassidy in a rough fashion to toughen her up,' court documents said.*"

The words "*rough*" and "*toughen her up*" were from Sgt. James White's November 11 affidavit, and they were not used by Chad, regarding Kassidy, in his interrogation with the police. Below are his references in that interview to playing with Kassidy.

Describing the night of November 8, Chad said,

"You know I fed her, fed KYLE, then we went upstairs, and you know I played with - It's hard because, you know, KYLE is a boy. He's three and she's, you know, 20 months, a girl, you know. So they don't like to do the same things so I tried separating them to do different things with her.... But any ways so you know I played with him for a few minutes and then I go play with her and then you know him and then her... So we just pretty much, we played, did our thing and then my roommate came home...." [1493]

Hear, hear me out. Like one of the things that I was you know getting at before was Amanda said to me before "Jesus she's not Kyle you know, she's not a boy". Because like I'll pick her up like you know and swing her around and go on the bed and wrestle with her and whatever. (p. 1577)

Sgt. White's attribution to Chad of the "*toughen her up*" statement was very likely based on something Amanda said to Det. Angela Blodgett in her interview, "*Yeah, but I've never seen him actually like hurt her...he would just get mad at her. Like he would put her in the corner and... be rough with her and he'd play rough with her saying to, like tough her up, play like a boy, you know?*" (Amanda interview, p. 850) This was Amanda's interpretation of Chad's play, and not what Chad said to his interrogators. There is a big difference, but that quote, "*toughen her up*" as attributed to Chad, was picked up later by the newspapers as a quote from a "court document."

At 4:00 p.m. at the Sanford Police Dept., Detective Linscott interviewed another of Amanda's Sanford friends, Crystal Martin. She was an 18-year old, single mother, and was employed as a chambermaid at a motel in Wells, Maine. Crystal's son, Devin, was the same age as Kassidy, so Kassidy had a playmate when their mothers would visit. Detective Linscott summarized his hour and 45 minute interview with Crystal on two and a half pages:

...Martin said that she babysat Kassidy overnight 3 weeks to a month before her death because Amanda and Chad were going out. Martin stated she gave the kids a bath together and she did not notice any bruises or injuries. Martin said this was the last time she saw Amanda before the death. Martin said that Amanda usually is very prompt, but Martin dropped Kassidy off at Emily Conley's house and Amanda was late in picking Kassidy up. Martin said that Amanda called Emily and told her she couldn't pick Kassidy up until the next day.

Martin said that Amanda told her that Chad threw Kassidy on the bed a little hard. Martin said that Amanda told her that she asked Chad not to do that again and Chad said he wouldn't. Martin said that Amanda called her about three weeks before Kassidy's death and told Martin that Chad told her that he did not want a live-in girlfriend anymore and Amanda asked Martin about getting an apartment together. Martin said that Amanda and Chad patched things up and they never went further on their apartment plans.

Martin stated she has never seen Amanda hit or spank Kassidy. Martin said that Amanda would get frustrated and tell Kassidy to go away. Martin said she has seen Amanda go without food so Kassidy could eat. Martin said she thought the two stories about how Kassidy got her bruises, the trampoline story and the story of Chad dropping her were true at the time, but Emily and Vicki thought Amanda was making them up to cover up abuse.

Martin said that Amanda said that Chad was starting to demonstrate anger and Amanda was concerned. Martin said that Amanda told her that Chad gets angrily [sic] *easily and head-butted her once and they got into a small fistfight. Martin said that on another occasion, Chad and his roommate, Travis, got high and were making fun of Kassidy. Martin said that Amanda took Kassidy upstairs to get away from them.*

...Martin said that Chad was a little rough with Kassidy when he put her in the corner and when he put her on the bed. Martin said that Chad watched Kassidy a lot lately while Amanda worked.

... Martin said she saw Jeff yell at Amanda right after the funeral when Amanda questioned Jeff about giving Kassidy's picture to the press....Martin said she saw Amanda last night in Dover, NH at a dance club called the Inferno. Martin stated that Vicki, who works at VIP, brought Amanda to the dance club. Martin said that Amanda is staying

with Amanda Bullard in Sanford and that Amanda said she is going back to Texas in mid-February. Martin said she talked with Amanda on December 23rd and Amanda said she had been back in Maine 2 weeks. Martin stated she had not seen her until last night at the dance club. Martin said that Amanda said that she had lost her daughter and the mom she loved. Martin said Amanda told her she hasn't seen Chad since the death and that her family has turned against her.

Martin said that Amanda told her about being sexually perpetrated [sic] by her stepfather. Martin said that Kassidy seemed a little slower than other kids did. Martin said that when she last babysat Kassidy, she noticed a burn on Kassidy's foot that looked like a curling iron burn. Martin said she did not notice it during the bath the night before, but only saw it the next day. Martin said the burn could have happened at her house as she sometimes leaves the curling iron on accidentally.

Martin stated she spent the night at Chad's house in August....Martin said she did not see any temper or violent behavior...

When any interviewee makes a mistake about a date, then all the references to time in that interview are suspect. For Crystal, it came when she told Det. Linscott that she saw Amanda on December 23rd and Amanda told her that she had been back in Maine for two weeks. Because it's known that Sergeant White met Amanda at Logan Airport on the evening of December 18 and met with her in Concord on the 19th, what Crystal said was not true. What we don't know is the source of the error. Did Amanda tell Crystal she had been home for two weeks, or did Crystal hear it wrong, or remember it wrong, or did Linscott's summary get it wrong? Whatever the reason, it was a clear mistake, by ten days. The investigation of Kassidy's death would have been dramatically improved if the police had brought a simple tool with them to their interviews: calendars. With a calendar, the police could have referred interviewees to known dates for reference. For Crystal, her birthday in November could have been a reference point. As she referred to "*December 23*" in her interviews, Det. Linscott could have reminded Crystal that Christmas was on a Monday and the 23rd was on the previous Saturday. Another obvious reference date was Thursday, November 9.

The issue of time was became increasingly important during October, and it's likely that Crystal spent the night at Chad and Amanda's on Saturday, October 7, and the babysitting for Kassidy occurred on Sunday evening, October 8, and the babysitting by Emily for Kassidy on Monday the 9th. The absence of bruises on Kassidy would be consistent with the October 1 photo taken of a bruiseless Kassidy at Auburn by Jacqueline Conley. The following week was when the consistent bruising first began to be noticed, and that was when Joshua Bortner Conley noticed bruises in Buckfield on Friday, October 13, and later that weekend by Tracey Foley and Melissa Chick.

If Crystal was right about Amanda being critical of Jeff for his giving a photo of Kassidy to the media, then it's a good example of how the message from Chad's lawyers had infected Amanda, too, which was, "Don't talk with the press, or help them." It would have been helpful to Chad and Amanda if more photos had been given to the press. As the first photo of Kassidy to appear in the newspapers was the 1999 studio photo which appeared in the Saturday, November 18 issue of Foster's Daily Democrat, it's likely that this was the photo that caused Amanda's anger at Jeff. Jennifer Saunders had written that it was given to her "*by a relative*."

Crystal said that Amanda had told her on the night of January 4, that she had not seen Chad since she had been home. That wasn't true, as Amanda and Chad saw each other shortly after her return to New England, and Amanda spent Christmas Day with the Evans family in Keene. The question is whether Amanda lied to Crystal or whether Crystal lied to Det. Linscott, or simply was mistaken, or whether Linscott's summary was incorrect.

Saturday, 6 January 2001

The next day, the Union Leader picked up the same incorrect theme, "Man accused in toddler's death admits he was playing 'rough'." Unlike the other "court documents" stories, this article reported on what the affidavit said about Jeff Marshall.

Though authorities say Evans beat Kassidy sometime between the early evening of Nov. 8 and the morning of Nov. 9, Evans tells a different story in his interviews with police. He appears to blame Conley's live-in boyfriend, F. Jefferey Marshall.
'He stated that he picked Kassidy up at Marshall's house on Nov. 8 and Kassidy was acting funny. Kassidy was quieter than normal. She was leaning forward in the seat in the car and drooling,' Evans told police. Evans then said he called Marshall to ask whether he had beaten Kassidy, the affidavit states.

Evans also told police he was only alone with Kassidy a few times and that "Marshall admitted that Marshall hit Kassidy so hard that his hand stung and Kassidy was black and blue."

Tuesday, 9 January 2001

The Portsmouth Herald's Amy Wallace interviewed the Conley family and Jeff and wrote the story, "Relatives want Amanda Bortner to phone home". The family continued to be split, with Amanda on one side and her entire family, together with the police, on the other. Said the article,

Bob Conley, Amanda's uncle who lives in Buckfield.... "We suspect that her and Chad (Evans) have been in contact again. Knowing his history with women and children, it's not in her best interest to have contact of any kind with him."
Indictments released by the Strafford County, N.H., grand jury suggest that the toddler had been beaten regularly for at least three months prior to her death....
New Hampshire Assistant Attorney General Will Delker said rumors that Evans and Bortner are back together have not been confirmed, but if they are seeing each other, Evans would be violating the conditions of his bail. "The defendant is prohibited from having contact with material witnesses, and (Bortner) is one of the people who the defendant is prohibited from having contact with," Delker said.

Bob Conley said he constantly worries about Bortner. "Mandy does not want to contact her family whenever she is with Chad," Bob Conley said. "We all have a serious suspicion that he has been in contact with her and might even be trying to convince her he's not responsible and she shouldn't testify against him.... The family knows what the results are and who we believe is responsible for Kassidy's death," he said.

Evans told authorities he believes Marshall is responsible for Kassidy's death, but that is absolutely untrue, Marshall said. "We feel that he's obviously a desperate person trying to turn this situation around," Marshall said. "This is about a child and a human life that has been lost."

Bob Conley agrees with Marshall. He said Kassidy responded positively around Marshall, but was submissive around Evans.

Jennifer Conley said she finds it hard to believe that Evans is out on bail. "I don't understand why he's out walking on the streets," she said. "It scares me."
Jennifer's sister, Lindsey Conley, is also surprised by Evans' release. "Kas shouldn't have died, for she was a very innocent child, and I will not forgive Chad (Evans)," Lindsey Conley said in an earlier interview. "I do not understand how someone could take out their anger or frustration or whatever on someone else's child or even their own child. To me, those types of actions are unforgivable, and you cannot mend the wounds, for they are scars that will stay with the victim or the victim's family forever."

Bortner's family is hoping she contacts them to let them know she is doing all right.
As was the case with many other articles about this tragedy, the reporter wrote that a phone call was made to Chad Evans for his response, and it was not returned.

Wednesday, 10 January 2001

Foster's Daily Democrat kept the story in high profile, with top-of-page 1 banner headlines for an article about an interview with Jacqueline Conley, "A grandmother's horror - Kassidy's murder defies logic, Nana says: 'She was so loved.' by Jennifer Saunders. The article said that Amanda and Kassidy lived with the Conleys, "*up until a few months before Kassidy's death.*" Despite her views about Chad, Jacqueline said, " *'As her mother, I can tell you she absolutely loved her daughter,...How could she not?'* " *In the final days of September, Conley said she spent about four days with Kassidy at her Auburn home while Bortner and Evans went to a New York Mets game. Conley said there was not a bruise on Kassidy when the pair brought the child to her home. She also stated that Kassidy was her usual, happy self.....*" This babysitting stint was actually the September 24-27th, Sunday to Wednesday, period that Chad and Amanda went to Martha's Vineyard, and Amanda picked up Kassidy on Wednesday the 27th.

Unfortunately, it does not appear that Jacqueline Conley remembered to tell the reporter that Kassidy was brought back to Auburn by Amanda and Cathy Nuernberg a few days later, on Sunday, October 1, when the Conleys were moving to Buckfield. If she had mentioned that return visit, she might have thought at that time to give Jennifer Saunders a copy of the October 1 photo of Kassidy in a chair at the Conley home holding her bunny rabbit doll.

As the "*final days of September*" were approximately six weeks before Kassidy died, Jennifer Saunders, or her readers or the police and prosecutors, might have wondered about the accuracy of the "*court documents*" which, according to the Foster's Daily Democrat December 20 article (above), had said that Chad had "*fractured her leg and arm during separate incidents this fall and summer.*" They might have wondered about the statement in the December 21 Portsmouth Herald article (above) that said that the grand jury's indictments "*suggest that 21-month-old Kassidy Bortner had been beaten regularly for at least three months prior to her death.*"

Jacqueline filled in more of the chronology by describing Amanda's October 13 visit with Kassidy to Auburn, but she dated it as being "*In October.*" However, she explicitly dated the November 5 shopping day when Amanda "*and Jennifer Conley arrived without Kassidy, telling their mother the child had gone with Evans and his two sons to the zoo. Although Conley was disappointed not to see Kassidy, she said she tried to convince herself it was important for Evans to try to foster bonds between Kassidy and his own two children. At the time, she said, it never occurred to her that the zoo would not be open at that time of year.*" What Jacqueline didn't know was that going to the York Wild Animal Kingdom zoo was, indeed, the plan that day for Chad and the three children. However, Chad also realized that the zoo was closed, and his sons had other plans with their mother that day. This was a very typical family misunderstanding, except for the very untypical circumstance that this was four days before Kassidy died, after which miscommunications and white lies became evidence of murderous intent.

Amanda looked forward to a day with her mother and sister, so Chad took Kassidy to his sister's in Belmont for the day. The police and prosecutors believed that Chad took Kassidy for the day so that Amanda's mother would not see Kassidy's bruises. However, according to Brandon and Nicole Harvey, there was only one fading bruise on Kassidy's right cheek at the time. Also, three days later, on Wednesday morning, November 8, Amanda talked with her mother about babysitting for Kassidy during her upcoming weekend with Chad in Maine.

Thursday, 11 January 2001

At about 10:15 a.m., Sgt. James White interviewed by phone the store clerk at Moonlite Reader in Portsmouth about the double charge that Chad was seeking to correct on the afternoon of November 8, on his way to pick up Kassidy. White's summary report did not state whether he asked any questions about Chad's emotional state at the time. (p. 231) It was the prosecution's contention at trial that Chad's anger and frustration led him to assault Kassidy after he picked her up at Jeff's.

At 10:30 a.m., Sgt. White met with Chad's boss at Colley-McCoy, Bob McDougall. White's summary reported that "*McDougall told me he never saw or heard of C. Evans displaying a temper.*" McDougall said that he had met Amanda only twice, at the company headquarters when Amanda and Chad were returning from their trip to Martha's Vineyard, ("*Cape Cod*") and at the "*grand opening party for the Exeter McDonald's, which was held at the Exeter Inn.*" White already knew the date of the Exeter function from his earlier call with McDougall, but he didn't know the dates of Chad and Amanda's trip to Martha's Vineyard, and he didn't ask. White reported, "*McDougall said that he had only incidental contact with C. Evans and A. Bortner at the Exeter Inn party and he did not make any observations of C. Evans demeanor or sobriety. McDougall was of the opinion that if an assault occurred, it occurred after the party.*" (p. 232)

White did not ask for a copy of Chad's personnel file, where he would have seen the several letters of recognition and bonuses for excellent performance. He would also have had the opportunity to see if there were any comments, perhaps in an annual performance evaluation, about Chad's behavior or management style. He also would have seen references to several dated activities, such as overnight management conferences and training sessions which would have assisted the police in establishing a time-line for the fall.

Monday, 15 January 2001

Amanda traveled again to Texas, after Chad paid for her ticket. Again living in San Antonio, Texas, she worked these two weeks at the International House of Pancakes. On January 28th, she returned to New Hampshire, and stayed with Bruce and Michelle Truell.

Later in 2001, she traveled a third time to Texas, after selling her car to Bruce and Michelle Truell. Amanda had planned to stay in Texas until Chad's trial, but she loved him and missed him, and called Chad soon after arriving in Texas to ask him to help her get back to New Hampshire. Upon her return from Texas from that third trip, Chad and Jeremy met her at Logan Airport.

During these two trips in 2001 to San Antonio, Amanda sought counseling, and her counselor recommended that she write about her life. She finished her "My Life Story" after her return to New England, and Chad gave a copy to his attorneys. The 11-page original begins, "*I don't really know where to start. But I guess I'll start when I was born. It probably doesn't matter but I don't want to forget anything. Just maybe after somebody reads this they might actually understand me.*"

Saturday-Sunday, 20-21 January 2001

Since January 3, the media had access to the unsealed "court documents," i.e. the Sgt. James White affidavits and Sgt. Matthew Stewart's affidavit. However, it wasn't until this date that one of the most explosive statements was published, and it was in an Associated Press article. On the 20th, the Boston Globe's article, "21-month-old girl suffered for months before being killed," quoted the statement, "*It was a **family joke** that only certain people could baby-sit 21-month-old Kassidy Bortner. That's because anyone else probably would have told someone anyone about the girl's bruises and welts.*" (emphasis added) This allegation of a "*family joke*" was attributed by Sgt. White in his November 10, 2000 affidavit to Jeff. White's actual statement was slightly softer, "*Marshall stated that it was **almost a family joke** that no one other than Marshall and his girlfriend Jennifer Connelly could babysit Cassidy, due to concern that anyone else would report the child's injuries.*" (p. 226) (emphasis added) There were only a few changes between the November 10 and November 11 versions of Sgt. White's affidavit, but the November 11 version omitted the reference to a "*family joke.*" Its rephrasing of the allegation of the practice of using only Jeff and Jennifer for babysitting read, "*Marshall stated that based on his discussions with Bortner and Evans, it was understood that no one other than he and Jennifer Connelly could baby-sit Kassidy, due to concern that anyone else would report the child's injuries.*" (p. 319)

That language caught people's attention and the article was published in the Cape Cod Times the following day, as "Family joked about abuse that led to N.H. toddler's death." The article included the October 1, 2000 photo of Kassidy with her bunny rabbit, but the caption said the photo was "*undated.*" Perhaps Jacqueline Conley thought of the photograph after her interview for the January 10, Foster's Daily Democrat article, above, and provided it to the next inquiring reporter, perhaps from the Associated Press.

On the 21st, the Portland Press Herald published the AP story by J.M. Hirsch, as "Family apparently stayed silent as abuse took its toll." Below are excerpts from the story, after the "*family joke*" lead sentence, with details not already published from the White

Affidavits or "court documents." This was the most complete telling of the police version of the case to date.

Someone might have told police she was being beaten, choked and thrown against walls. Anyone else would have said that someone apparently was pricking the bottoms of her feet -- with pins, perhaps, or a hairbrush. Now everyone knows, but it's too late. Kassidy is dead. And no one is laughing at the family "joke."

The Rochester girl's hell began this fall when her 18-year-old mother moved in with her boyfriend, a 29-year-old man already on probation for slapping and choking his ex-wife.

It ended at 1:28 p.m. on Nov. 9. Cause of death was a blow -- perhaps many blows -- to her head and abdomen.

A week later, police arrested the boyfriend. Chad Evans faces a litany of charges, including second-degree murder, alleging he started beating Kassidy in September and didn't stop until she was dead.

"I know you slowly killed my baby," court documents say Kassidy's mother, Amanda Bortner, told Evans the day the girl died. "You wished she had never been born."

Evans, who is free on bail and living in Rochester, maintains his innocence. He did not return calls seeking comment.

"I'm not prepared to litigate this in the press," said Alan Cronheim, one of Evans' lawyers. "We're declining to talk on the record other than to say we are prepared to defend Chad in court."

Bortner, who has moved out of Evans' home, is believed to be staying with friends and could not be reached. The details of this story were gathered from court documents, police affidavits and interviews with neighbors and employers.

Little is known about Evans' life before Bortner and her daughter came into it. His education ended with high school and he since has worked as a manager of several McDonald's restaurants on New Hampshire's Seacoast.

Evans first made news in 1996 when he helped rescue victims of a car crash from their burning vehicle. He was praised as a hero and was given an award by a local newspaper.

In November of that year, he married 20-year-old Tristan Evans, who now works as an X-ray technician in Dover. Eight months later they had a son.

By all accounts, the marriage was tumultuous; they were separated by December 1999. In March 2000, Evans was convicted of assaulting his wife and sentenced to a year in jail. The sentence was suspended on condition of good behavior.

Bortner began dating Evans sometime last summer and moved in with him around September. The trouble for the toddler appears to have started right away.

Bortner's sister, Jennifer Conley, regularly baby-sat Kassidy in her Kittery home. But soon after Bortner moved in with Evans, Conley and her boyfriend, F. Jeffrey Marshall, noticed signs of trouble.

Marshall thought little of Evans, whom he described to police as abusive and a heavy drinker who also used cocaine. He said Kassidy changed from being a normal, energetic child to fearful and subdued during the two months that led up to her death. He and Conley said they noticed extensive bruising to Kassidy's face, apparent choke marks around her neck and that she seemed to have trouble walking.

The girl's injuries were severe enough once that Marshall said he was too embarrassed to take Kassidy out of the house; he was afraid that somebody would accuse him of abuse.

"Marshall stated that it was almost a family joke that no one other than Marshall and his girlfriend, Jennifer Conley, could baby-sit Kassidy, due to concern that anyone else would report the injuries," state police Sgt. James White wrote. It's not clear whether anyone who suspected Kassidy was being mistreated ever told authorities; state law prevents officials from discussing allegations or investigations of abuse.

Bortner told police that when she first noticed Kassidy acting strangely, she asked Evans about bringing her to a doctor. The answer was no.

She said they agreed to lie about her injuries, and routinely said Kassidy hurt herself falling down stairs or off their trampoline.

Around 4 p.m. on Nov. 8, Bortner left Kassidy with Marshall as she headed to work. About an hour later, Evans called Marshall to say he was coming to take the girl home. Marshall said Evans called him around 5:30 p.m., telling him "the retard" was acting strangely, that her head was bobbing around and that she was drooling. Evans later told police he called to ask whether Marshall had beaten the girl.

Marshall said Evans called a second time around 6 p.m. He said one minute Kassidy had been standing next to the car, the next she was face down on the pavement.

Later that evening, Marshall said he called again, telling him that his son and Kassidy had been playing when the girl was hit in the head with a ball. He said Kassidy was unconscious and her eyes had rolled back in her head.

Kassidy woke up crying around 6:30 a.m. the next day. Bortner said the girl's head was bobbing backward and that she seemed tired, ate little or nothing and that her eyes were rolled back in her head. But the mother didn't take her to a doctor.

Instead, shortly after 8 a.m. she dropped off Kassidy at Marshall's home. He and Conley said they immediately noticed new bruises on the girl's face, saying the injuries never had been that severe. Bortner agreed.

Marshall said Evans called shortly after Bortner left, saying he had been called by the state Division for Children, Youth and Families and wanted to know who had contacted them. The court records don't indicate what Marshall said.

During this time, Kassidy was lying on a bed.

When Marshall tried to wake her, she didn't respond. He also noticed that her eyes were rolled back and she was having trouble breathing. He called for help, but it was too late. She was pronounced dead that afternoon.

During the next seven days, the details of Kassidy's painful last weeks were revealed. Now the courts must decide who made them so miserable....

Evans also said the injuries on her face were not caused by him, though he acknowledged once picking her up by her head. He said he did it to keep her from falling off the trampoline. He also said Marshall told him he once hit Kassidy so hard his hand stung and her face was bruised.

Though it's not clear under Maine law whether Marshall and Conley can be charged with not reporting their suspicions of abuse, New Hampshire law leaves open that possibility for Bortner.

Chad's attorney, Alan Cronheim, said he was not going to litigate the story in the press, so the allegations against Chad and Amanda continued to mount and acquire the halo of fact. Above, J.M. Hirsch wrote that Kassidy's "*hell began this fall*," which was not a quote from Sgt. White. This is what happens when allegations are not met with responsive facts. In a sense, Chad was "Swift-boated" to use the analogy from the 2004 presidential campaign where false statements allegations were made about John Kerry's Vietnam service commanding a "Swift Boat" - and he didn't respond soon enough.

Rule 3.6 of the New Hampshire Code of Professional Conduct for lawyers states, generally, that lawyers "*shall not make an extrajudicial statement that the lawyer knows or reasonably should know will be disseminated by means of public communication and will have a substantial likelihood of materially prejudicing an adjudicative proceeding in the matter*." Then, the rule gives specific and narrow examples of what a lawyer can say to the press, such as the upcoming trial schedule, or may publicly request help from the public in gathering information about a case.

Importantly, the New Hampshire rule does not include an exception to its restrictive scope which appears in the American Bar Association's "Model Rules of Professional Conduct." That exception, at Rule 3.6(c) states, "*a lawyer may make a statement that a reasonable lawyer would believe is required to protect a client from the substantial undue prejudicial effect of recent publicity not initiated by the lawyer or the lawyer's client. A statement made pursuant to this paragraph shall be limited to such information as is necessary to mitigate the recent adverse publicity*." Thus, whatever were Alan Cronheim's views of the media, and he firmly distrusted their ability to report facts accurately, there were professional rules in New Hampshire which limited what he could say.

However, there were no rules on what a client could say, and it would have been very helpful if face-to-face interviews with Chad could have been arranged by Chad's attorneys, who could have attended such interviews. Preliminary advice could have been given to Chad about telling the truth and about restricting his answers to what he knew about his own conduct and what he had seen and heard with his own eyes and ears, and to avoid speculating on what might have happened and by whom. Also, his lawyers could have insisted that any interviews be recorded and that a copy be left with them. This strategy is not often used by attorneys, but in a highly publicized case, where the publicity is one-sided, failure to respond can bring disaster. In addition to potentially tainting the future juror pool, bad publicity tends to isolate a defendant from his friends and supporters, and that loss of support can be critical. If "*court documents*" say something, and Chad doesn't respond, what is to be believed?

In such an interview, Chad could have begun with an opening statement to proclaim his love for Kassidy, which newspaper readers might have been astonished to read, and to first present the positive aspects of his life with Amanda and Kassidy. Then, he could debunk the mis-information which had already been published, such as the allegation of his breaking Kassidy's arm and leg, or his alleged beating of Kassidy. A simple one-page timeline could have been started, and reporters could have been confronted with the inconsistencies of their own articles, such as the alleged "*beaten regularly for at least three months*" and the reporting of Kassidy's bruise-free four day stay with the Conleys in late September. Photographs should have been collected and the best given to the reporter. In short, the media could have been viewed as an ally in the search for truth, but instead, it was viewed as an adversary to be avoided.

Among other red flags for Chad's defense in Hirsch's article was the statement that "*Little is known about Evans' life before Bortner and her daughter came into it.*" Well, Chad and his family knew a lot about his life, and so did the Keene Sentinel which had reported on his election to the Board of Education. While the reporters could be faulted for not checking with Chad's hometown newspaper, they were still stymied by the instructions to Chad and, by extension to his family and friends, to say nothing to the media.

As lawyers, prosecutors were subject to the same rule 3.6, but they were also subject to a special rule, 3.8(f), for prosecutors which stated, "*except for statements that are necessary to inform the public of the nature and extent of the prosecutor's action and that serve a legitimate law enforcement purpose, refrain from making extrajudicial comments that have a substantial likelihood of heightening public condemnation of the accused and exercise reasonable care to prevent investigators, law enforcement personnel, employees or other persons assisting or associated with the prosecutor in a criminal case from making an extrajudicial statement that the prosecutor would be prohibited from making under Rule 3.6 or this Rule.*"

One wonders whether A.A.G. Christopher Carter's description of Kassidy to the Union Leader in its November 18 article as "*utterly helpless and defenseless*," had any likelihood of "*heightening public condemnation of the accused.*" This rule is also important because it mandates that prosecutors "*exercise reasonable*" care to prevent other law enforcement officials from making a statement which would violate the rule, if made by a prosecutor. Would it apply to what Kittery Detective Steve Hamel told Amy Wallace of the Portsmouth Herald for her December 21, 2000 article which she summarized, "*Hamel said all evidence points to Evans.*"

January 20 saw the first article devoted entirely to the issue of the requirements in Maine and New Hampshire to report child abuse. Other articles had noted the difference which was that Maine's law applied to professionals, and not babysitters, and New Hampshire's law applied more generally. Nonetheless, movements began in each state to strengthen the requirements to report child abuse, and the reporting that it was a "*family joke that only certain people could baby-sit*" Kassidy heightened the public outcry for better laws. The proposed bills, and resulting laws were informally called, "Kassidy Bortner laws."

The Boston Globe article, by Glenn Adams of the Maine offices of the Associated Press, was headlined, "Abused girl's death prompts legislation in Maine." The next day, the longer version of the article appeared in the Portland Press Herald as "Child's death exposes hole in Maine's reporting law." Adams wrote,

The horrifying death of 21-month-old Kassidy Bortner has brought to light what could be life-and-death differences between Maine and New Hampshire's child abuse reporting laws.

And now some lawmakers, including one representing the Kittery area where the child was last seen alive while in a baby sitter's care, are calling for changes. The Rochester, N.H., child died in November after repeatedly being subjected to physical abuse. Chad Evans, a boyfriend of Kassidy's mother, is charged in the death.

Two of those who noticed a deterioration in the child's condition leading up to the time of her death are Jennifer Conley and her boyfriend, F. Jeffrey Marshall, who baby-sat Kassidy regularly in their Kittery home.

But they apparently never told authorities -- and may well not have been required by law to do so. State Rep. Stephen Estes, D-Kittery, says the case highlights a contrast between the reporting laws in Maine and its neighboring state.

In Maine, specific professionals, including doctors, nurses and other medical practitioners, educators, camp counselors, police, clergy, social workers and others, are required to report signs of abuse to authorities.

Maine's list includes "child care personnel," but it does not appear to apply to baby sitters. "Unless they're clearly professional child care providers, the law is not clear as to whether informal baby sitters are covered," Maine Assistant Attorney General Deanna White said.

New Hampshire's law is all-inclusive; it requires such reports by anyone who comes into contact with children showing signs of abuse.

Estes wants to clarify Maine's law to bring it in line with New Hampshire's. Estes missed the deadline to sponsor a stand-alone bill, but is looking for other legislation that can be amended to include his proposal.

Sunday, 4 February 2001

This day was Kassidy's birthday and the Portsmouth Herald ran the Associated Press story, "Beaten baby would have turned 2 today." Excerpts from the article, which also appeared in the Union Leader, Maine Sunday Telegram, are below:

Maine (AP) — The holidays are hard days for Jacqueline Conley.

The stuffed bunny she bought her granddaughter Kassidy for her first Christmas ended up tucked into the toddler's casket 11 months later. And today marks what should have been another day to celebrate — Kassidy's second birthday.

Nearly three months have passed since 21-month-old Kassidy Bortner of Rochester, N.H., was beaten to death. Her mother's boyfriend, Chad Evans, 29 has been charged with second-degree murder and assault.

According to court documents, the toddler was beaten regularly in the months leading up to her death. Conley remembers being in the delivery room when Kassidy was born. "I will never forget her. There will not be a day in my life I won't think about her," she said from her Buckfield home.

"I can't say good-bye to her," Conley said. "It is so senseless. It is so senseless to have somebody do this. Kass will never grow up. She'll never get to play with Barbies or have another birthday party...."

Bortner's sister, Jennifer Conley, regularly baby-sat Kassidy in her Kittery home. According to court documents, Jennifer Conley's boyfriend told police it was a "family joke" that only certain people could baby-sit Kassidy because anyone else would have reported her injuries.

But F. Jeffrey Marshall said that he doesn't remember making that statement....

Since the original publication of the "*family joke*" allegation in the Boston Globe on January 20, this was the first time a reporter had asked Jeff about it, and he denied making the statement.

Also, the "*family joke*" allegation is not in any of Jeff's transcribed interviews, and, as noted earlier, it appeared only in one of Sgt. White's two November, 2000, affidavits. It may have been that Jeff used the expression in a non-interview setting or that someone else used it. It's unlikely that Sgt. White made it up. Missed in the article and in Jeff Marshall's denial of making the statement was the question whether he ever believed it was true. There were two parts of the statement that were powerful. First, it implied that the bruises and injuries to Kassidy were commonly known among family members, and second, that they were a joke. Certainly, grandmother Jacqueline and all the Conleys, and Chad and Amanda, didn't think that any aspect of babysitting Kassidy was a joke.

The other unsupported statement from the affidavits was White's statement that Chad had admitted playing "*rough*" with Kassidy to "*toughen her up*." The basis for that statement appeared to be a statement by Amanda in her November 9 interview, as noted above. When preparing his affidavits, Sgt. White did not yet have the transcripts, though he did have the audio and video tapes.

Foster's Daily Democrat carried the two-year birthday story on page 1, with Jennifer Saunders' "Sunday, Kassidy would have been 2 - Birthday brings up memories of toddler whose life was cut short by brutal abuse." Again showing the slippery slope from interview to affidavit to "*court documents*" to truth, she wrote,

Although affidavits in the case ***clearly show*** *Bortner was fully aware of the abuse her daughter suffered, she has not been charged with any crime in connection with her baby's death...Pages of court documents* ***illuminate*** *the last weeks of Kassidy's life as* ***a string of beatings and torment that ended only when she succumbed to a blunt force trauma to the head*** *inflicted sometime between Nov. 8 and 9.* (emphasis added)

Noting that Jeff denied making the "*family joke*" statement, the article stated, "*In the months since Kassidy's death, Marshall has said he is haunted by what the child went through and is filled with regret that he ever believed the stories Bortner and Evans made up to explain away the bruises...*" It wasn't revealed if he was asked for any details about these stories. The only untrue story which Amanda and Chad had used was the "trampoline story" to explain the bruises on both sides of Kassidy's lower cheeks which were caused by Chad's palming Kassidy's face in order to obtain **eye contact**. Those bruises appeared about three times since early October. The last such bruise occurred more than a week before Kassidy died, and those bruises had no causal relation to Kassidy's death.

Jennifer Saunders described "*photographs taken during that visit,* [where] *Kassidy smiles back at her grandmother, cuddling her bunny and kicking her bare feet out before her*." The only photograph of Kassidy at the Conleys during that visit, or during the Sunday October 1 visit that was ever released to the media or the prosecution was the photo of Kassidy sitting in a chair with her bunny rabbit. In that photo, which became Exhibit 19 at Chad's trial, her feet are not visible. Even now, it would be helpful to borrow and copy the other photos from the Conleys family.

A companion page one article in Foster's Daily Democrat, "Probation hearing delayed a second time," reported on the parallel legal proceeding whereby the prosecution sought to revoke the suspension of Chad's jail sentence for his 1999 domestic violence against Tristan. One of the two prosecution claims was that the box of live ammunition found in Chad's basement during the search of his home violated the terms of his probation. However, the article, by Kimberly Houghton, reported that the probation requirement was that he not "*receive, possess control or transport any weapon, explosive or firearm or simulated weapon, explosive or firearm.*" Ammunition was not mentioned, although if Chad had remembered that it was in his basement, he would have surrendered it along with the weapons.

The other prosecution claim, according to the article, was that Chad "*signed an agreement stating he would not be arrested for any reason during his probation period.*" Such a probation, by itself, is unfair and violates the presumption of innocence in the judicial process. An arrest does not presume guilt.

In any case, the probation revocation hearing, previously rescheduled for Monday, February 5, was again postponed, and to an undetermined date.

Monday, 5 February 2001

According to her report, trooper Jill Rockey received a call at 8:23 p.m. from a police dispatcher that Strafford County Jail inmate Cory Merrill wanted to talk with her, "*as soon as possible.*" She called him that evening and,

He said he was concerned for Bortner's safety. He had been thinking about Bortner since Sergeant White and I had interviewed him. He said Evans made some comments to him while they were cell mates that made him think Evans may try to harm Bortner.... Merrill said he had spoken to Evans a few times since Sergeant White and I interviewed him. Evans told Merrill he was staying at his parents in Keene and wasn't able to get a job." (p. 1022)

This call was 75 days after Chad had been released on bail from the Strafford County Jail on November 22, 2000. The referenced previous interview with Rockey and Sgt. White probably occurred around the time of that release, but there is no record of it in the Discovery documents. Rockey agreed to meet him the next day.

Tuesday, 6 February 2001

At 1:00 p.m., Trooper Rockey interviewed Merrill at the jail and Rockey reported that he "*said he had time to think since the first time he had been interviewed. He felt there were things Evans had discussed with him that he had to tell us (the police).*" (p. 1022) Merrill recalled accurately that Chad had been released the day before Thanksgiving. The report continued,

...Merrill said Evans told him when the baby wouldn't stop crying, they (Evans and his girlfriend) would spank her. After Evans talked to Merrill about how he disciplined Kassidy, Merrill told me Evans beat Kassidy. He didn't spank her.

...he told Merrill that he walked in on Amanda throwing a baseball at Kassidy.... he and Amanda were coming back from the babysitter's and they dropped the baby on the ground... Merrill said Evans talked about suicide a few times while in the cell with him....Evans told Merrill...Amanda might try to blame him. This upset Evans and Merrill feared for Amanda's safety.

....he picked up the baby in York and said the baby was not responsive when he called her name... he looked over at the baby and she was nodding off. Evans said if he was guilty of anything, it was negligence...

...he started talking about spanking the baby.... Merrill told Evans he might need a job when he got out. Evans said he'd get Merrill a job and a place to stay if he worked hard.

... Evans said he was in love with Amanda and really loved Kassidy. That he and Amanda were planning on getting married.

... Evans said he was walking into the house and saw a baseball go flying across the living room and hit the child (Kassidy)... Merrill assumed Amanda threw it, but Evans didn't say she did. This was the incident Merrill had referenced earlier.

... Evans told Merrill he spanked Kassidy with not only his hand, but with his belt as well.... the baby would wake up crying in the middle of the night. Evans said he'd be totally pissed because he worked seventy to eighty hours and needed the extra sleep, so he'd go in and spank the child....

... he said he came home from work, Merrill thought he said the Rochester store, but he walked in one day and the baby was already crying and Evans said he spanked her....he'd continue to spank Kassidy while she screamed and cried. After a while she'd eventually stop crying and would just shake. Evans would only stop spanking Kassidy when she stopped crying.

...he thought Evans said she [Kassidy] *lost consciousness on the ride home from York that time he picked her up from the babysitter's.*

... he told Merrill his parents put up their house and he was putting up $10,000 cash to get out. If it wasn't his parents' money, he would run."

Like many statements from inmate informants, much of what Merrill said was too good/incriminating to be true. It's very tempting for the police to believe such statements, and there usually is some truth in all of them, because they support the police theories and, if true, would make convictions easier to obtain. Because there was no report of the earlier interview of Merrill by White and Rockey, there was no way to ascertain the consistency of what he said at both interviews.

In several previous articles, Foster's Daily Democrat had shown a belief that bail for Chad was not appropriate. The sub-headline for the January 2 article was, "*Chad Evans* ***still free*** *on bail after arraignment.*" (emphasis added) On February 6, Jennifer Saunders wrote the front page article, "SPECIAL REPORT - Bail: Alleged crime is just one factor in amount set - Evans case prompts examination of criteria\," which began by noting that he was "*free on bail less than a week after his arrest despite the fact that being arrested constituted a violation of his probation for a prior domestic assault conviction...*" Saunders reported there were no restrictions on Chad's contact with children, and she asked A.A.G. Delker why the State has not asked for such restrictions. He responded, "*I really can't comment on that.*"

On March 30, the Foster's Daily Democrat concern about Chad's bail continued, with the story by Jennifer Saunders, "Kassidy's accused killer remains free, despite parole violations"

Wednesday, 7 February 2001

As Merrill had told Rockey that inmate Craig Gautreau and perhaps Adam Tuttle also overheard the above conversation, she interviewed Gautreau. She reported,

Gautreau said Evans wanted to kill himself. He remembered Evans was released the day before Thanksgiving....

Evans told Gautreau it was negligence on his behalf. They should have brought the baby to the hospital....Evans told him he had nothing to do with it. Evans was trying to blame the babysitter.

... But Evans wanted to kill himself. He even asked Gautreau to bang him out. Gautreau explained "bang out" is jail slang for killing someone.

I asked Gautreau if Evans said why he wanted Gautreau to bang him out. Evans again told Gautreau it was negligence on his part. The baby had fallen out of the truck and he didn't take her to the hospital, Evans told Gautreau.....

He asked Gautreau for a Bible and Gautreau gave him one.

Gautreau said at first Evans blamed the babysitter, and then tried to blame ...the mother of the child....

I asked Gautreau if he remembered Evans talking about running after he was bailed if his parents hadn't put up the money. Gautreau said he remembered Evans saying that...

The prison slang term, "*bang out*," actually means to "beat up," and it's unlikely that Chad would have asked Gautreau to assault and beat him up.

In a case where dates were often ignored or confused, it was interesting that both Merrill and Gautreau recalled the correct date of Chad's release on bail, the day before Thanksgiving. There is no question that Chad felt terribly about Kassidy Bortner's death, and felt that he could have prevented it, if only if. Also, Chad habitually took responsibility for mistakes and problems at work, with the philosophy that "*Being a good leader is: accepting responsibility when things go wrong and giving your team the credit for every victory.*" Many people, including the police, and Merrill and Gautreau mistook that regret, sadness and sense of responsibility as indications of guilt.

In a February 18, 2010 letter, Chad wrote about his brief contacts with Merrill and Gautreau:

My recollection of Craig Gautreau and Corey Merrill is similar. We were all housed together in a single cell along with another inmate named Adam Tuttle who incidentally is still here. I was with them for about 5 days after my initial arrest. I didn't know I was with them in almost a protective custody state because they had all molested young children and obviously my stuff was very high profile. I don't remember much of his interview. I think I have it somewhere here. If I remember right, it seemed like the police led him a lot in their interview, and were trying to get him to back Merrill's statements. He is a very rough around the edges guy and out of the two it made sense to put Merrill on the stand. He was more clean cut and well spoken. I confronted Gautreau here once about his false claims and he basically ran from me and right to a cop. While I was in a cell with them they all acted like they were my best friend. Kassidy had just died. I was arrested with no one to talk to. I didn't know any better and talked to them some. I remember specifically talking about picking Kassidy up from the babysitters and how she was acting, etc.

Corey Merrill also was trying to get a deal. He had nothing to say to the police when they first approached him. Then, after several months and having the chance to read the newspaper accounts he seemed to piece together things and ad lib.

...When Merrill was at the prison with me he tried apologizing several times. He said that he didn't want to say anything or testify, but the cops were threatening and pressuring him. I replied, "I don't even care, what hurt me is I helped you when we were housed together for that week and then you lied. Why would you lie?" His only reply was they made him. I just told him that he would have to live with those lies...

There was nothing in the Discovery documents with a transcript or summary of any discussions with Merrill or Gautreau around the time of Chad's release on bail and before these February, 2001 interviews by Jill Rockey. Also, there was nothing to indicate that two investigators also met with the third occupant, Adam Tuttle, of that holding cell around the time of Chad's release.

In April, 2010, Adam Tuttle wrote me a letter from prison, before his August release, and said that Chad was his former employer at McDonald's in Rochester. He said that shortly after Chad was bailed, Adam was called from his cell to an unusual morning visit. It was not with his family but with two state investigators who asked about Chad. Adam wrote that when he told the officers that he believed Chad was innocent, they became "*very upset*," and he was returned to his cell.

If Chad's attorneys had known about the State Police interviews in November with Merrill, Gautreau and Tuttle, they might have been better able to thwart the prosecutors' efforts to have Merrill testify, before the threat of perjury charges forced that charade to stop. The jury heard Merrill's allegations, without any cross-examination on the merits of his allegations.

Thursday, 15 February 2001

Foster's Daily Democrat kept the Kassidy case on page one, with Jennifer Saunders' story, Kassidy tragedy prompts legislation - Proposed law makes child abuse reports mandatory." The article began, "*The beating death of 21-month-old Kassidy Bortner has become the driving force behind legislation to make it mandatory for all Mainers to report suspicious of child abuse and neglect.*" Saunders reported that Kittery State Representative Steve Estes had found an existing bill, to which he sought to add language that would mandate such a requirement.

Estes learned many of the details of Kassidy's life and death after formerly sealed court documents were made public in January.... the affidavits unsealed in Rochester District Court revealed that at least half a dozen individuals ***knew*** *of Kassidy's abuse prior to her death... Estes told Foster's Daily Democrat that he was deeply disturbed that no one who* ***knew*** *of Kassidy's abuse would be facing criminal charges in connection with her death..*" (emphasis added)

Saunders interviewed one "*individual who had witnessed signs of abuse against Kassidy...the individual said he would have called authorities if a mandatory reporting law had been in place.*"

Saturday, 15 February 2001

Continuing the Foster's Daily Democrat page one coverage, Jennifer Saunders interviewed the funeral home driver, Mark Sousa, who transported Kassidy's body from York Hospital to the Maine Medical Examiner's offices, "Girl's death still haunts attendant - Horror of Bortner case prompts action to stop abuse." The article stated that at the hospital Sousa assisted in the taking of photographs of Kassidy's body. In the article, the photo of Kassidy was captioned, "*Child abuse victim,*" and was the undated October 1 photo at her grandmother's home. The article reported how

the sight of Kassidy Borttner's small, bruised body in the hours after her death haunts him to this day....Sousa decided to talk with Foster's Daily Democrat because he hopes the truth about what happened to Kassidy will incense residents in both Maine and New Hampshire enough to call for protection of other children living with abuse."
Sousa said,

I am personally upset at the fact that neither Maine nor New Hampshire has brought charges against the mother of the child....This child went through hell in the last months of her life...

Wednesday, 7 March 2001

The first 819 pages of the "Discovery" documents were sent by the Attorney General's office to Chad's attorneys. In every criminal case, the prosecution is required to provide to the defendant or his attorney copies of all the relevant documents in the case. One goal of that process is to ensure that there are no preventable surprises to either side at the trial. By the time of Chad's trial, the number of Discovery pages would total 3,294. The documents were not in any recognizable order, and the first two pages were the November 16 New Hampshire State Police Arrest Report for Chad, and completed by Sgt. James White. The offense was "manslaughter" and the "*Complainaint/Witness*" was MSP Sgt. Matthew Stewart. Pages three and four were Sgt White's "Continuation of Investigation Report" which outlined his activities on November 9 and 10, 2000, beginning with, "*On Thursday, November 9, 2000, at about 1540 hours* [3:40 p.m.], *I spoke by telephone ... to assist with an investigation into the death of, Kassidy Bortner...*" The third document, on pages 5-6, was Kittery Police Officer Creamer's "Offense Report," the format of which required the listing of a "*Complainant*"and Jeff Marshall's name was written there.

Thursday & Monday, 8 & 12 March 2001

The Maine State Police Crime Lab issued two reports in the Kassidy Bortner case. The March 8 report was for tests performed on items taken from Jeff's house and from Chad's car, but the only results were for the items from Jeff's home. One test concluded that the red stains on the yellow wrapper, #0004, from Wendy's was blood, and the report said that on January 1, "*a cutting from one of these red brown stains was submitted to the Forensic Biology Section of the Crime Laboratory for HemaTrace (a confirmatory test for the presence of human blood and or DNA Analysis.*" Other stains were also found on the napkin, and a cutting from one of those stains was also sent for further testing. A cutting from #0012, the paper towel, was also sent to the Forensic Biology Section for testing, after it was found to be "*soiled.*"

The March 12 report focused primarily on the fingernail clippings from all ten of Kassidy's fingernails, and "*Presumptive chemical tests for the presence of blood were positive on these red brown stains.*" That is, there was blood underneath all ten of Kassidy's fingernails. As with two items from the March 8 test, on January 11, the ten "*fingernail clippings were submitted to the Forensic Biology Section of the Crime Laboratory for HemaTrace and or DNA analysis.*"

These reports were significant enough for Detective Linscott to write on March 28 a separate "Continuation Report" (p. 1183) to acknowledge receipt of the "report." He used the singular form, but it's likely that both reports arrived together and that he addressed them as one. In his own report, he copied Maine Asst. A.G. Fern LaRochelle and New Hampshire State Police Sgt. James White and Assistant Attorney General Christopher Carter.

Thursday, 22 March 2001

The Forensic Biology section issued its report on the four items submitted on January 11, per the reports, above of 8 and 12 March. The DNA tests confirmed that the blood underneath Kassidy's fingernails, and the blood on the yellow Wendy's wrapper belonged to Kassidy. The lab did have a blood sample from Kassidy. The apparent saliva on the paper towel had male DNA, and presumably belonged to Jeff, but no further tests were performed, as the lab did not have a DNA sample from Jeff.

Amy Wallace wrote in the Portsmouth Herald of the progress of Chad's primary criminal case, *"Pretrial conference in toddler case pushed back"* She interviewed Kittery Patrolman Robert Creamer, who was the first officer to respond to the 911 call, and who said,

I think it's appalling that this child had been beaten for at least three months and that other people have not been charged with endangerment to the welfare of a child or failing to report abuse,...It was apparent when I first saw the baby that she had multiple, multiple bruises on her neck, abdomen and face and I immediately suspected ongoing abuse. It was a sickening feeling to know that society, family members and the mother must have been aware that she was being abused for some time.

In a subsequent article about the Estes bill, he said, "*The Kassidy case is a perfect example of continuing abuse,... If this law had been enacted at the time of her death, someone in her family may have felt more obligated to report the abuse.*"

Tuesday, 27 March 2001

Foster's Daily Democrat carried an Associated Press story on page 1, "Kassidy case prompts proposal of Maine death penalty bill" which began, "*The death of a 21-month-old New Hampshire girl last November has prompted a Maine lawmaker to seek to reinstate the death penalty in his state.*" The bill received no other legislative support at a hearing, but the page 1 coverage conveyed the Foster's message to its readers.

Thursday, 29 March 2001

During the Spring, there were four parallel tracks for the Kassidy Bortner/Chad Evans story: the criminal case, the probation revocation case, and the proposed legislation first in Maine, and later in New Hampshire. These four tracks guaranteed that the case would remain highly visible in the media. On this day, Jennifer Saunders wrote the article on page 1 in Foster's Daily Democrat, with the full page banner headline, " 'Kassidy Bill' debated - Maine lawmakers listen to proposal to punish those who fail to report child abuse"

The article stated that Representative Estes told the Judiciary Committee "*about the horrible death of 21-month old Kassidy Bortner... a tragedy that should have and could have been prevented.*" The article said that "*No one called authorities about the abuse,*" apparently forgetting the January 3 Foster's Daily Democrat article which stated that, according to Jeff, DCYF had been called about Kassidy, even if DCYF had not yet publicly acknowledged that call. Wrote Saunders,

During the investigation of Kassidy's death, Bortner and others would tell police that Evans repeatedly threw the toddler into walls and onto the floor. They would tell police that Evans lifted Kassidy up by the head and choked her to keep her from crying. They would say Evans called her the "retard" and said he wished she had never been born. Preliminary autopsy results would reveal, among other injuries, a fractured arm, fractured leg....

Also on page 1 was an example of unusual advocacy for a newspaper, in the form of the article, "How you can help 'Kassidy' law pass," and gave the names and addresses of important legislators to contact. The Foster's Daily Democrat advocacy continued with an editorial on March 31, "Help stop abuse - Tell Maine to pass Kassidy's Bill" which stated, *Kassidy died slowly and horribly from unspeakable brutality. Just as horrible is the fact that while the helpless toddler endured this abuse, many people knew it was happening. Many people knew what was causing the bruises covering her body and why she was withdrawn and having a difficult time walking. Adults in Kassidy's life knew what was going on for six weeks before she died. Yet, no one came to her rescue until she was taken to a hospital in Maine four hours before she stopped breathing. Before that, not a word had been spoken on her behalf so authorities could finally put a stop to the terror.* "

While the facts of Kassidy's death at Jeff Marshall's house were not relevant to the "Kassidy Bill," the editorial's mis-statements were surprising, given its extensive coverage of the case. Kassidy was not taken to a hospital four hours before she stopped breathing, and "*a word had been spoken*" on her behalf to authorities.

Tuesday, 3 April 2001

At 3:00 p.m., Detective Jeff Linscott interviewed Gabe Snyder, age 20, at his place of employment, General Nutrition Center in Sanford. Linscott summarized his 45 minute interview on two pages:

Snyder said that Amanda got frustrated with Kassidy at times, but she would leave the room and pass Kassidy off to Snyder instead of taking out her anger on Kassidy. Snyder stated that he saw Kassidy fall down twice in the time he lived with them and get bruises. Snyder stated he was there both times and no injury was inflicted on Kassidy. All bruising was the result of an accidental fall. Snyder said that Kassidy was a tough kid, and that she did not bruise or cry easily....

Snyder stated he does not know Chad Evans and has never met him before. Snyder said that when he last spoke with Amanda around March 2000, she told him that she was dating Chad Evans and she was bragging about how rich he was. Snyder stated that he does know Jennifer Conley, Amanda's sister, and Jennifer's boyfriend, Jefferey Marshall.... Snyder stated that he "hung out" with Jefferey Marshall and they watched movies together. ...

Snyder said that Amanda and Jennifer argued over anything, like clothes, when they were together and Snyder does not think they got along well or had much to do with each other. Snyder said that Amanda never mentioned herself being abused at all. Snyder stated that Amanda has hit him in anger in the past.... Snyder stated that when Amanda would hit him, he would push her away in self-defense, but he never struck her.

As with Crystal Martin's interview, and others, Gabe Snyder made a substantial date/time error, when he said that Amanda talked with him in March 2000 and bragged about her new boyfriend, Chad Evans. This was because Amanda did not meet Chad until Friday, June 2, 2000.

Again with banner headlines on page 1, Foster's Daily Democrat reported on the "Kassidy Bill" track with, "Kassidy's baby sitter hopes right bill passes - Maine opens debate on law to punish those who fail to report child abuse." Wrote Jennifer Saunders, *When Marshall heard about 'Kassidy's Bill' -- or An Act to Protect Children and Elderly or Incapacitated Adults as it is more formally known - he could not help but think of the blue-eyed little girl who was like a niece to him. "I do want the law to go through, but I want it to be the right one," he said Monday.... In the months since Kassidy's death, Marshall and others close to the child have come under fire for not reporting suspicions of abuse to authorities.*

The article said that Marshall's mother, Janis Marshall, wrote to the Judiciary Committee and asked that provisions be included in the law similar to those in Minnesota where parents and guardians "*are subject to felony charges if a child dies as a result of abuse or neglect.*" Wrote Marshall, "*An example of this is the 'mother' of Kassidy,... knew of the abuse Kassidy endured... and did absolutely nothing to get her out of that situation.*" Ironically, Chad and Amanda were both trying to find a day care placement for Kassidy so she would get out of that situation at Jeff's.

Janis Marshall wrote an observation that would be used by the prosecution at Chad's trial, about Amanda's drive to Jeff's on November 9, "*Upon that ride to Kittery, she passed three hospitals on the way as well as police stations.*"

The article continued,

In the two months that Kassidy lived with her mother and Evans in Rochester, Marshall said, he and [Jennifer] Conley questioned Evans and Bortner several times about marks on Kassidy's face and her withdrawn behavior. Each time, Bortner and Evans had excuses....it was not until after Kassidy's death that all the pieces began falling together." A companion article on page 1 explained the Minnesota law, "Minnesota's tough reporting law spawned from case like Kassidy's," but also contained details about Kassidy, saying, "*Kassidy did not suffer abuse until after her mother moved in with Evans in August, according to all court documents released to date.*"

For the first time, it was reported that "*Bortner was receiving public assistance from the State of Maine at the time of Kassidy's death, although she had been living with Evans in New Hampshire for at least two months*." Even within the same article, it would have been helpful for the reporter to try to reconcile the August "*move-in*" date with "*at least two months*," or to note the inconsistency.

On an inside page, Jennifer Saunders wrote the article, "Failure to report abuse only a misdemeanor in New Hampshire," and reported that the New Hampshire law subjects any resident to misdemeanor penalty if s/he has "*reason to suspect*" abuse, but fails to report it. Saunders wrote that "*no New Hampshire residents who told police after Kassidy's death that they had 'reason to suspect' her abuse are being charged under the law.*"

The next day, Foster's Daily Democrat covered on page 1 the bill's progress, with the article, " 'Kassidy Bill' leaps ahead - Maine law to punish those failing to report child abuse passes first test"

Wednesday, 4 April 2001

Judge Franklin Jones of Rochester District Court, scheduled for July 19, 2001, the trial for the allegation of probation violation due to the possession of ammunition. The trial for probation violation due to the arrest and indictments for Kassidy's death was to be tried by 20 January 2002, i.e. after the Superior Court trial on the substantive charges. The judge accepted Chad's attorneys' arguments that Chad was still innocent of those charges until proven guilty beyond a reasonable doubt.

On this same day, Matthew Coughlin, of the U.S. ATF (Alcohol, Tobacco and Firearms) Office wrote a letter to Kevin (last name unknown) to document a call he received from Jenna Sunderland of the Strafford County Domestic Violence Project about Chad's gun violation and possession of ammunition. Coughlin contacted the Assistant U.S. Attorney Mark Howard, apparently to explore possible Federal charges, but Howard said it would be "Petit Policy," or not worth the trouble.

The April 5 Portsmouth Herald reported the story of the scheduling of the murder trial, "Nov. 5 trial set" by Amy Wallace, which said that a pretrial conference was scheduled for May 7. Foreshadowing an issue that would take a lot of pre-trial time to resolve, A.A.G. Carter said that "*we expect and understand that Evans is complying with the order of the court and conditions of his bail and will not have contact with Amanda or her family*."

Jennifer Saunders wrote the front page Foster's Daily Democrat story, Jail not likely for Evans before trial - One hearing continued; another delayed until after murder case." where she noted that Chad had grown a mustache and a beard. Also, she revealed that "*Several weeks ago, when reached by telephone and asked for his thoughts on the case, Evans said, 'Should I speak with my heart or with my head?' And then declined to comment*." In 2010, Chad wrote his recollection of that exchange,

I remember that call clearly. She called me at my parents' house in Keene. I answered the phone and didn't know at first that she was a reporter when she was looking for Chad. Alan and Mark advised me against ever talking to them. My heart was screaming out, "Tell this lady that you loved Kassidy and didn't kill her." I said the above [head/heart] *and told her, "No thank you," when she asked if I wanted to make a statement....*

It's funny that you found this. Once during my trial or a hearing of some sort, Stephanie Bolduc was talking to Jennifer Saunders. Stephanie told me about their brief conversation at some point. Stephanie was saying to her that I wasn't a monster or anything that the police have made me out to be. Saunders replied, "Yeah, I spoke to him once and he wasn't at all what I expected. He was soft spoken and very polite." (Letters, 20 May 2010)

In 2010, I tried several times to contact Jennifer Saunders, who no longer works for Foster's Daily Democrat. One effort was a call to her home when I talked with her husband, and she was unavailable, and never returned my call.

Thursday, 5 April 2001

Meanwhile, Chad was trying to earn a living, working for Domino's Pizza, and trying to keep in touch with his family, and the supervised visits with Kyle, and court appointments. It was a lot to juggle. On April 5 he received a speeding ticket and on

April 13, he received another ticket and a $72.00 fine for going through a stop sign in Keene.

Friday, 6 April 2001

On this day, Dr. Margaret Greenwald signed the completed 35 page autopsy for Kassidy, but it would be weeks before it was sent to Chad's lawyers, and it was not presented to the media immediately. It was simply another, albeit large, piece to the complex puzzle. Her initial findings were that Kassidy died of "*Multiple blunt force injuries*" and that her death was a "*homicide*." (p. 1103)

There were several errors in the identificaiton section of the report. Kassidy's death was incorrectly stated to have occurred on November 10 (p. 1103), and her residence was stated to be 2 Mousam St., Springvale, but Kassidy, Amanda and the Conleys moved from there to Auburn in the spring of 1999. The autopsy said that the time of death was 1:28 p.m. in the York Hospital Emergency Room, but it was recognized that Kassidy was dead before she arrived at the hospital. As the correct information was easily available, the errors were puzzling and they called into question the accuracy of the entire report.

Addressing one of the most explosive allegations and charges against Chad, Dr. Greenwald found a "*fracture in late reparative to remodeling stage*" on both the left and right forearm "*ulna*" bone. (p. 1122) On the right leg "*tibia*" bone, Dr. Greenwald found a "*Remote injury, remodeling stage with re-injury of acute fracture, inflammatory stage.*" (p. 1121) She also found evidence of a fourth fracture, a "*recent fracture*" in the second metacarpal of her right hand, i.e. the longest bone in her right index finger. She wrote, "*There is prominent subperiosteal callous with fibrovascular proliferation and new bone formation. The callous has not yet enveloped the fracture ends. Reparative stage.*" (p. 1121)

Dr. Greenwald would later provide much information about the autopsy in her deposition on November 28 and in her testimony at Chad's trial on December 13, 2001 and her testimony at Amanda's trial on November 19, 2002.

At 4:00 p.m. in an interview room at the Cumberland County Jail, Detective Linscott interviewed (p. 1176) Robert Sheehan, age 23, who was Kassidy's father. Linscott summarized the 25 minute interview with 22 lines, which are presented below:

Robert Sheehan stated that Kassidy Bortner was probably his child, biologically, but he had no desire to include the child in his life as he already had a child and didn't really know the mother, Amanda (Conley) Bortner. Sheehan knew Amanda Bortner as Amanda Conley and was not even familiar with the Bortner name when initially asked about Amanda. Sheehan stated that Amanda wanted him to take a paternity test to determine who the father was, but he did not take one. Sheehan stated that he slept with Amanda twice, once at his birthday party when he provided her alcohol. Sheehan stated that all sex with Amanda was consensual.

Sheehan stated that he used to go out with Crystal Martin, and Crystal knew Amanda and would sometimes babysit Kassidy. Sheehan stated that Crystal told him that Amanda would sometimes lock Kassidy in a closet when the baby would cry. Sheehan said he saw the baby once at Crystal's apartment when Amanda was visiting and Amanda said, "Did you see your baby?" Sheehan stated that he saw the baby one other time outside a store for just a minute. Sheehan stated he did not see any marks or signs of abuse on the child when he saw it, but that he wasn't looking at the child much.

Sheehan stated he does not know Chad Evans and has never seen him before. Sheehan stated he has heard rumors around town about the death of Kassidy and that Chad Evans caused Kassidy's death. Sheehan commented that he knows a lot of people in Concord State Prison and that people like Chad Evans are not well liked in prison.
Presumably, Linscott did not bother to remind Sheehan that giving alcohol to minors is a crime.

Sheehan's point about the treatment of child abusers and murderers in prison was perhaps significant because years later Chad heard a rumor that some inmates had considered attacking him because of his crimes. Somehow, Chad also heard that those inmates asked Sheehan what he wanted them to do, and he told them that he had heard that Chad was not the murderer, so the anticipated attack was abandoned.

That afternoon's Foster's Daily Democrat returned to the story. Spurred by media representation of the Kassidy Bortner case as the failure of people to report abuse, change was sought for the New Hampshire law, as reported by Jennifer Saunders on the front page, "Kassidy's death spurs reform efforts in N.H. - Grass-roots group calls for revisions to the New Hampshire Child Protection Act" The article began,

A local girl's death has become the catalyst for a grass-roots effort to hold violators of New Hampshire's child abuse reporting law accountable for their inaction... The petition reads, "We the undersigned residents of the state of New Hampshire, wish to express our shock and horror at the brutality and suffering endured by Kassidy Bortner in the weeks prior to her death,...We petition you to seek strict penalties for parents and others who do not report suspicion of child abuse.

As was done earlier to support the citizens effort in Maine, Foster's Daily Democrat published an article, "How to sign 'Kassidy's Petition' "

Not everyone supported a change in the law. On May 7, Ken Goodall of Exeter wrote a letter to the Editor of Foster's Daily Democrat, Kassidy Bill goes "too far". While sharing his abhorrence of child abuse, he wrote,

...Average people are going to have to decide what is and isn't abuse. Will yelling or screaming at your chid be considered abuse? It could be by some people. Is spanking abuse? A lot of people believed it is. What recourse will be available to those that are wrongly accused... Let's not institute a law to report every parent that loses their patience and screams at their kids or slaps a child for mouthing off to them. There's a difference between discipline and abuse.....

Later in May, Foster's Daily Democrat published an update of the campaign, "Momentum builds for 'Kassidy' law" which included the story of a store clerk in Rochester. She told a petition organizer, Howard Hedegard,

"I have never in my life seen a more sad child. She just looked so sad, so withdrawn, curled up in that stroller," recalling the day when a mother came into the Lilac Mall store where she was working, wheeling a small girl in a stroller. The clerk told Hedegard she remembered the child's face was badly bruised and that when she questioned the mother, the parent said the little girl fell and then abruptly left the store. Weeks later, when photographs of Kassidy were published in news accounts of her death, the woman recognized the little girl from the store...

In his May 10, 2011 letter, Chad addressed this alleged encounter with Kassidy,

You talked about a store clerk's claim that Amanda brought Kassidy in a stroller and the clerk saw bruises and a sad child.... This lady is full of B.S. and is confusing Kassidy with another child if she saw her at all. We did have a stroller that we used for Kassidy at times but that was mostly at the beach or during the earlier part of the summer when we went to York's Wild Animal Kingdom. Amanda and I were very adept at carrying Kassidy around but there are times when the stroller is the better choice. Even when carrying Kassidy in our arms, the stroller makes a great caddy to carry things. Our stroller had a nice top that folded over for shade and also a rack to put things underneath. For trips such as York's Kassidy did a lot of walking, we did some carrying, but there was times that she would get tired and sit in the carriage/stroller from exhibit to exhibit. If I'm not mistaken, the stroller that we used was one that Tristan and I had for Kyle.

Anyway, my recollection from the story and clip of the article you sent (clerk saw child weeks before her death.) This lady worked at a store in the Lilac Mall in Rochester. I would say this mall hardly qualifies as a mall. It's tiny. Amanda didn't shop at the 10-15 stores in that particular mall often, but if she had, it wouldn't have been worth the trouble to dig the stroller out of the car and set it up to walk the length of this mall, 200-300 yards. In addition, the anchor store, K-Mart, had carts outside the entrance and if anything, Amanda would have plopped Kassidy into one of them and pushed her around the entire mall as many parents did.

Lastly, I recall reading this article or part of this article back then and paraphrasing its content with Amanda at one point that year and she was livid. She denied taking Kassidy to the mall in a stroller and any clerk EVER asking her what happened to Kassidy's face.

Also on this day, Sgt. White called Amanda in San Antonio, Texas, where she said she was living with Sarah Parker, and no longer with her friend Cathy Nuernberg. Amanda returned his call from a pay phone, and said she was working at the International House of Pancakes and at a second employer, Christy's, and was attending church at the Castle Hills Church. White reported that Amanda told him that "*she had not had any contact with CHAD EVANS either by letter or telephone.... She asked me, 'Why would I do that?'* " (p. 1954) It was an obvious lie, but was aimed at protecting love and not at covering up abuse or a murder. Amanda was increasingly angry at the police for misleading her, and she not longer felt that they cared about what actually happened to Kassidy. The following Monday, White called Cathy Nuernberg and confirmed that she and Amanda had parted ways. (p. 1956)

Wednesday, 12 April 2001

Following up on the issuance of her autopsy findings, Dr. Greenwald completed a "Cause of Death Supplement" for a "Supplemental Certificate of Death." She stated that Kassidy was "*assaulted by another*," but stated that the date and time of the injury were both "*Unknown*." (p. 1097)

Monday, 7 May 2001

A 15 minute pretrial conference was held on this day and Chad's trial was delayed from November 5 until later in the month. According to Jennifer Saunders' article in Foster's Daily Democrat, but off the front page, "Trial for Evans delayed.," Judge Tina Nadeau had a scheduling conflict. A final pretrial conference was scheduled for October 25. Keeping to his policy of minimal comment, Alan Cronheim "*said he is continuing to review the more than 1,400 pages of discovery materials in preparation for the November trial.*"

Wednesday, 9 May 2001

With a story about child abuse, generally, Foster's Daily Democrat marked a milestone with Jennifer Saunders' article, "Six months after Kassidy Bortner's death, her case rings all too familiar" It began,

Six months ago today, a local toddler's death brought home the reality that child abuse does happen here -- fueling an outcry in Kassidy Bortner's name. Residents in both Maine and New Hampshire have written to their legislators and signed petitions expressing their outrage at the abuse 21-month-old Kassidy endured before her death....

On this day, Amanda wrote a handwritten letter to the Strafford Court,

I am looking for a public defender. I have not been charged with anything, but a lot that was said was not true. I was hoping to get my statement thrown out, if that was possible. Seeing I was under duress. Also, maybe look into investigation again. I don't think the detectives did a good investigation at all. If someone could help me, that would be great. (p. 2080)

She included a "State of New Hampshire - Financial Affidavit & Application for Court Appointed Counsel." She wrote that her address was 651 Park Ave., Keene, which was Vanessa Mansson's home, and that,

I just got back from Texas. I have no job and about $200 to live on till I get one. I have no charges against me, but I agreed to things w/the police that weren't true. And I just want to tell the truth at the trial. Thanks. (p. 1952)

Superior Court Clerk Julie Howard responded that because Amanda was a witness in Chad's upcoming trial and

...you may have Fifth Amendment rights (rights against self-incrimination)..., you may be eligible for court-appointed counsel. By copy of this letter, I am asking the Attorney General to inform me whether I need to appoint counsel for you at this time." (p. 2079)

Later, Sgt. James White had Amanda's handwritten letter checked for Chad's fingerprints in his continuing efforts to show that Chad and Amanda were in contact with each other and that Chad was influencing her future testimony at his trial. See the May 23, 2001 New Hampshire Crime Lab Report with negative results.

Friday, 11 May 2001

Sgt. White reported that he received from a New Hampshire National Guard Analyst telephone information about phone calls to and from Chad's Rochester home phone and the phones of his parents and several friends of Chad, Jeremy, and Bruce and Michelle Truell, and one of Chad's employers in 2001, C&S Wholesalers. (p. 2009) He was trying to find evidence of calls with Amanda.

Monday, 21 May 2001

On this day Sgt. White reported that he called the San Antonio Police Department "*to seek assistance in locating Amanda.*" (p. 2011) He also reported that he called the company operating the International House of Pancakes restaurants in San Antonio, and he was told that there were no records of Amanda working in any of its IHOP restaurants. (p. 2017)

Tuesday, 22 May 2001

Sgt. James White reported that he called Cheshire County Attorney Peter Heed, later a New Hampshire Attorney General, about calls made from Jeremy's telephone to the Cheshire County Attorney's office. The City of Keene is in Cheshire County. Heed told White that the call was likely to his employee Vanessa Mansson, who had recently told Heed that she would likely be a character witness for Chad at his trial. White wrote, "*I asked Attorney Heed to keep our conversation confidential and he agreed to do so.*" (p. 1977)

Later in the summer when Heed learned that Amanda had been staying at Vanessa's and that Chad had been there as well, he fired Vanessa.

Also on this day, Sgt. White reported that he received from Asst. Attorney General Chris Carter the cell phone records for Cathy Nuernberg in Texas. (p. 2018) He didn't say how Carter obtained the records.

Wednesday, 23 May 2001

Sgt White reported that he talked with Chad's probation officer, Kevin Callaghan, to whom Chad reported twice a month, on the first and third Thursday. He said that Chad was living with his parents during the week where he worked for Domino's Pizza in Keene, and in his Rochester home on weekends. However, his visits with Kyle were on Wednesdays at Family Strength, in Dover. (p. 2010)

Thursday, 24 May 2001

Sgt. White received a fingerprint analysis report from the Forensics Laboratory of the New Hampshire State Police, which reported that it was not able to find any fingerprints or palmprints belonging to Chad Evans on a "*priority envelope*" or a "*handwritten note*" which White had apparently submitted for analysis. (p. 1979)

Also on May 24, White made several calls to Texas and talked with a person at the holding company for International House of Pancakes and established that Amanda worked for IHOP from January 15-28, 2001. (p. 1982) This contradicted the information noted above.

Monday, 28 May 2001

New Hampshire State Trooper Raymond Tennant reported on this day's surveillance of Chad and Amanda by seven State Police officers, including James White. The three-page report captured the comings and goings of several people in Keene between mid-morning and mid-afternoon.

Tuesday, 5 June 2001

Sgt White reported that he had received from Asst. Atty. General Christopher Carter the telephone records of a Gustavo Guerra in San Antonio, and that the records were procured through a subpoena dated May 17, 2001. However, there was no explanation of the possible connection to Amanda.

Also Sgt. White reported that he had talked with Jacqueline Conley who said that she had not talked with Amanda since before Easter, i.e. April 23.

Wednesday, 6 June 2001

Although A.A.G. Carter was reported by the Portsmouth Herald on April 5 to say that he expected and believed that Chad was complying with the provision of his bail release, the police were working hard to prove that he was seeing Amanda - as, indeed, he was. Instead of asking him, the police resorted to undercover methods. Posing as a friend of Chad, New Hampshire State Police Sgt. Peter Riesenberg conducted undercover surveillance on Chad on this day and visited his place of employment, Dominos Pizza, in Keene. After Chad's work ended for the day, Riesenberg's report said that he then followed cars to Chad's parents' home. In another report, Sgt. Riesenberg said that he had been called that afternoon at 5:45 p.m. by Sgt White to conduct the surveillance and that he, Riesenberg and Trooper Skahan did that work until after midnight and then the next morning. (p. 1986)

At 5:15 p.m. that afternoon Sgt. White called Chad's probation officer, Kevin Callaghan, of the New Hampshire Probation and Parole Dept, and learned about Chad's schedule for the next day so he could "*conduct a surveillance of Evans....*" (p. 1985)

Thursday, 7 June 2001

The next day, New Hampshire State Police Sgt. James White conducted surveillance on Chad Evans and watched him emerge from his lawyers' offices in Portsmouth and then watched him arrive at Family Strength, the social service agency where Chad had his supervised visits with his son, Kyle and stepson, Brent. White's short report of about seven hours of surveillance sounded like a James Bond novel.

On Thursday, June 7, 2001, I conducted a surveillance of Evans in Portsmouth and Dover. In Portsmouth, at the Twomey & Sisti Law Office on Fleet Street, and in Dover at Family Strength on Central Avenue.

I observed Evans arrive alone, on foot, at the law firm at about 1040 hours and leave at about 1140 hours. Evans walked west on Fleet Street toward Congress Street and I was not in a position to observe what vehicle he was using.

Later in the day, while watching Family Strength, I observed Tristan Evans arrive at about 1425 hours in a black compact car. I observed Evans arrive at about 1428 in a gray Volvo station wagon. I did not observe either Tristan or Chad depart from Family Strength.

I checked Evans' Rochester residence but did not observe any further contact with him and concluded the surveillance at 1730 hours. (p. 1988)

Saturday-Sunday, 9-10 June 2001

Sgt. James White talked in August with Alan Noyes, a client of Chad's friend, Michelle Truell. Noyes told White that Amanda was staying with the Truells and that Chad had called her there. Also, Noyes said the Truell's and Chad and Amanda had been together at Bruce and Michelle's camp in Colebrook, New Hampshire, over the weekend of June 9 and 10. White wrote,

Noyes also told me that he believes an 'eight ball' of cocaine was consumed over the weekend and he described Evans as a 'cokehead'." White wrote, "*Truell also told Noyes that she had seen Evans grab Kassidy by the face and that she had seen Evans 'smack' Bortner.*" (p. 1957, 1958)

The police never interviewed Bruce or Michelle even though the police now knew that they had seen Amanda, Chad and Kassidy together.

Monday, 11 June 2001

Sgt. White reported that he received an anonymous call on Monday, June 11, also stating that Chad and Amanda were together for the weekend at the Truell's camp in Colebrook. On this day, he talked with Officer Jones of the Colebrook Police Department who had also received an anonymous call at 2:52 p.m. about "*alleged drug use*" at the Truell's camp. At 4:16 p.m. a second anonymous call was made to the Colebrook Police Dept. to say "*that Chad Evans, the Rochester baby killer, was present at the camp.*" (p. 1989)

Tuesday, 12 June 2001

Sgt. James White interviewed Jacqueline Conley at her home in Buckfield, Maine. She estimated that Amanda moved to live with Chad in August. She told White about the family shopping trip on November 5, 2000, and noted that Jeff Marshall was with her, Jennifer and Amanda. Also, she told White about her call to Chad on October 14, 2000 after learning from Joshua about "*bruises on her* [Kassidy's] *chin area*," and how she was told the "trampoline story," and he heard it from Jennifer, too. (p. 1965) White retrieved Jacqueline's long distance phone bills for November and December 2000, as he was seeking to establish that Chad and Amanda had been in contact. Unfortunately, the November bills began on November 17, because if they had begun on November 1, or if he had received bills for any of the previous months, he would have been able to see perhaps one-half of the near-daily frequency of the calls between her and Amanda. White wrote that "*I also retrieved photographs of Amanda and Kassidy*," so perhaps this was when the police acquired the critically important photo of Kassidy which was taken on October 1, 2000. (p. 1965) There was no further discussion of the photos, or of how many he retrieved. None of these photographs was copied and sent to Chad's attorneys.

Wednesday, 13 June 2001

Relying on "*subpoenaed telephone toll records,*" Sgt White reported that he went to the Holiday Inn in Manchester to see if Chad or Amanda had stayed there between December, 2000 and the present, and there was no such record. (p. 1992)

Thursday, 14 June 2001

Again relying upon phone records, Sgt. White reported that he went to the Presidential Motor Lodge in North Conway and again learned that neither Chad nor Amanda had been guests there since the time period of his inquiry, beginning in December 2000. However, he did learn that Brendan Harvey "*and a guest*" had stayed at the hotel on 12-30-01 through 01-01-01." (p. 1993) Assuming that that he meant December 30, 2000, it's likely that he came across the news that Chad's sister, Nicole, and her husband, Brendan, were at the Lodge to celebrate their first anniversary in North Conway.

This investigation had drifted far away from Kassidy's death in Kittery, Maine on November 9. The police had spent hundreds of hours to prove that Chad was seeing Amanda.

Monday, 18 June 2001

The "Kassidy Bortner bill" was signed in Maine, as "An Act to Protect Children and Incapacitated or Dependent Adults." It required that caretakers report child abuse, and imposed stronger penalties for failing to report such abuse. Amy Wallace wrote the story for the Portsmouth Herald, "King passes laws inspired by N.H. girl's death." The article began,

Gov. Angus King has signed into law tough new child abuse reporting measures that were inspired by the death of a 21-month-old New Hampshire girl....

In New Hampshire, the mandatory child abuse and neglect reporting law states that any resident who has "reason to suspect" abuse from health care and law enforcement professionals to neighbors must report those suspicions to authorities.

Not reporting is a misdemeanor. However, no New Hampshire residents who waited until after Kassidy's death to tell of past abuse are being charged under the law.

But in Maine, where family friends frequently baby-sat the girl and may have suspected she was being abused, the former law requiring that suspicions of abuse be reported applied only to professionals, including teachers, child-care personnel and police.
Amy Wallace wrote a followup story on June 24 about the new Maine law, "Caretakers accountable under new 'Kassidy Bill' ."
KITTERY, Maine — Caretakers of children who do not report suspected abuse may now face felony charges, but police officials and domestic violence experts say a greater awareness of domestic abuse is the real key to prevention.

An Act to Amend the Crime of Endangering the Welfare of a Child became law Monday after Gov. Angus King signed the bill, which was often referred to as the "Kassidy Bortner Bill."

The summary of the new law is as follows:

"This bill creates the crime of aggravated endangering the welfare of a child, which is committed when a parent, foster parent, guardian or person responsible for the care and custody of the child knows that the child has been subject to serious bodily injury by another and fails to protect the child from further injury."...

Kittery Councilor Mark J. Sousa was among those supporting and pushing the bill.

"If common decency doesn't make someone pick up the phone to report suspected abuse, then hopefully being charged with a felony will," Sousa said.

"It's unfortunate that we live in a world where people are more concerned about their privacy than the welfare of a child such as Kassidy. If somebody had come forward after seeing what was going on with this child, I believe she would be alive today."

The bill, sponsored by Rep. Nancy Sullivan, D-Biddeford, was originally drafted to protect elderly or incapacitated adults from neglect and abuse. Rep. Stephen Estes, D-Kittery, proposed an amendment to include the protection of children as well.

After sealed documents were made public in January, Estes said he was shocked to learn the tragic details of Kassidy's beating death. Estes said he proposed the amendment after learning that people either knew or suspected the abuse, but did nothing to stop it.

Tracy Cooley, state coordinator for the Maine Coalition to End Domestic Violence, said it's easy to accuse those who may have known and who are alleged to have known about domestic abuse, but each case should be evaluated carefully and separately."

Amidst this silver lining from Kassidy's death, even if it arose from a distorted understanding of what happened, there was the black fog of the public relations message from Chad's attorneys and from Chad. Chad has said that he rarely read the newspapers as he was advised that they didn't matter in court, which may not have been entirely correct. If he had read them, maybe he would have realized that he didn't look good in what Amy Wallace wrote at the end of this article. It looked like he and his attorneys were hiding. At the very minimum, Chad could have told Amy Wallace that he absolutely did not harm or kill Kassidy. In fact, he loved her. Wallace wrote,

Evans' attorneys refused comment on any pending charges. When the Portsmouth Herald asked Evans at a pretrial conference in May if he killed or beat Kassidy, he declined to answer.

The Portsmouth Herald called Evans at his home on Thursday for comment, but the woman who answered hung up the phone....

The "*woman who answered*" was likely Travis' sister who was living at Chad's home during this period. She understood the lawyers' instructions to Chad which were to avoid the media.

Tuesday, 3 July 2001

Sgt White reported that Chad's probation officer, Kevin Callaghan, called Chad's home in Rochester and a "*female*" answered the phone and said that Chad was not there. Upon request, she declined to identify herself. (p. 2002) It's not known why the woman declined to give her name or what Sgt. Callaghan thought of the refusal. Probably, again, it was Travis Hunt's sister, Tiffany Green, and perhaps she was trying to give the message that the charges against Chad were unfair. In turn, perhaps Sgt. Callaghan thought that she was wrongly shielding a criminal. Open communication throughout this case would have been more helpful on both sides. Sgt. White then went to Chad's home and, together with Detective Paul Callaghan of the Rochester Police Dept. he conducted surveillance from 1:45 p.m. to 4:10 p.m. and recorded the comings and goings at the property. (p. 2003)

That evening, reported Sgt. White, he and nine New Hampshire State Troopers conducted more surveillance "*in an attempt to place Evans with Amanda Bortner, a violation of Evans' bail conditions.*" Chad was followed after his shift at Domino's to his parents' home in Keene and then to his home in Rochester. Then he went to a party, reported White, in Gonic, a section of Rochester. The "*party*" was a wedding reception for Diane Robinson, a fellow employee at McDonald's. At 10 p.m. Chad was pulled over for an "*obstructed license plate,*" and he was also given a field sobriety test as he had been drinking alcohol. This was now permitted, as his one-year probation period had ended, even though he was still being prosecuted for alleged violations during that period. The surveillance ended at 11:00 p.m. and there was no sign of Amanda. One of the nine officers was Trooper James Mayers and he also wrote a report, three pages long. (p. 2005-07)

Saturday, 7 July 2001

Chad attended his last birthday party for his son, Kyle, at Chad's parents' home in Keene. Kyle was four years old.

Wednesday, 11 July 2001

At this second of four pre-trial hearings before Judge Nadeau, Alan Cronheim petitioned the court to sequester the jury during the trial. Jennifer Saunders wrote the Foster's Daily Democrat story, "Evans asks for sequestered jury in murder trial of Kassidy Bortner." The article quoted Cronheim saying, "*There has been some extraordinary publicity,...*" He did not ask for a change in venue, i.e. to move the trial to a location outside the subscriber territory of Foster's Daily Democrat.

Judge Nadeau scheduled future hearings and deadlines with major motions due by September 15, and both sides "*agreed to exchange witness lists during the final pretrial conference on Nov. 15.*" Jury selection was scheduled for the week of November 26. Judge Nadeau decided to appoint an attorney to represent Amanda at her request. Amanda had decided earlier in the summer to fight the charges of child endangerment rather than plead guilty and seek a lighter sentence. Saunders wrote in the article, "SEEKING COUNSEL - Judge to grant counsel to murdered girl's mother", that, "*According to relatives, Bortner has spent the eight months since Kassidy's death staying alternately with friends in southern Maine, southeastern New Hampshire and Texas. Bortner was not present for the proceedings.*"

Thursday, 12 July 2001

Sgt. White reported that he talked with Jacqueline Conley who told him that Amanda "*thinks Jeff (Marshall) 'did it' (killed Kassidy).*" (p. 1975) Jacqueline told White that Amanda had told her that she was calling from Massachusetts where she was living. Jacqueline's phone ID was blocked and Sgt. White's efforts to trace the call failed. Amanda and Jacqueline talked again on the 13th, when Amanda needed information about her Maine driver's license number. (p. 1976)

Friday, 10 August 2001

A hearing was on this date to consider the alleged probation violation due to the finding of ammunition at Chad's home during the November 16 search of his home the previous November. His lawyers argued that Chad's original guilty plea should be vacated because he was not adequately advised that he could not keep his weapons and ammunition. Jennifer Saunders wrote the story for Foster's Daily Democrat, "Evans asks to toss guilty plea in assault Former Rochester man facing murder charges." Judge Franklin Jones later denied the motion to vacate Chad's March 2000 guilty plea. Regarding the revocation hearing on its merits, Chad's attorneys requested more time as they had recently received more "Discovery" documents from the prosecutors. Judge

Jones again postponed the hearing to Friday, September 7.

Saturday, 11 August 2001

In Brattleboro, Amanda was given a motor vehicle warning for going past a Stop Sign without a sufficient stop. Her listed home address was 42 Kimball Avenue in Putney, Vermont.

Tuesday, 14 August 2001

Sgt. White and Sgt. Kelly McClare went to the office of the Cheshire County Attorney, Peter Heed, to interview Vanessa Mansson about her relationship with Chad and Amanda. McClare reported that Vanessa told them that Chad stayed at her apartment in December, 2000. Chad reportedly said to Vanessa, "*I can't believe my life has turned into this mess.*" (p. 2089) Amanda moved in a few days before Christmas, which would have been after her return from her first trip to Texas and the interviews on December 19 in Concord, including with Sgt. White. Vanessa said that Chad would watch her two children for her,

He's watched my kids before, and I had no reason to distrust him. He's like a brother to me... Amanda would come and go. She's a friend, but a bit too irresponsible for me. She forgot to pick up my kids a couple of times. She's not allowed to watch my kids alone. Amanda has a friend from Maine named Mary [Bullard] *who comes down from Maine. I let the two of them take my kids.*" (p. 2089-90)

Vanessa said she hadn't seen Amanda "*for at least a couple of months. She said, 'I'd be devastated if I lost a child. It wasn't there for her. She didn't have the same feelings for a mother who just lost a child.'* " (p. 2090)

Vanessa wouldn't confirm that she had seen Chad and Amanda together since *the beginning of August 2000. They seemed really happy. Chad was devastated by his divorce. I said to him, 'She seems kinda young!' Chad said, 'She's twenty.' I said, 'She's younger than 20!' Ms. Mansson said she saw Chad, Amanda and Kassidy together once.*" (p. 2090)

Vanessa was far better at guessing ages than Chad, who continued, until around this month of August in the summer of 2001, his belief that Amanda was in her 20's, despite all the newspaper articles which said she was 18. He didn't read most of them, and when he asked Amanda about what the newspapers said about her age, she noted that the newspapers often were incorrect about the facts in their stories. Also, a few of his friends told him that they believed Amanda to be younger than he thought, but he ignored them.

Finally, at the Vernon campsite, together with Amanda's high school friend, Mary Bullard, Chad finally learned the truth about Amanda's age. Mary gave her correct age and high school class, and Amanda was forced to acknowledge the truth for her own age. Chad was devastated that he had been lied to, and that he had swept aside all previous indications that Amanda was lying. Importantly, it was yet another indication that Amanda simply viewed lying differently than he did. It's true that he lied about the "trampoline story" to a few others, but that was a lie that he shared with the woman he loved and trusted. Being lied to by Amanda was different.

Vanessa identified one of Chad's high school girlfriends as "*Barbara Brooks, maybe.*" (p. 2090) "*Sgt. White asked Vanessa, 'Have you and Chad ever discussed the case?' She said the following, 'The night he got out of jail, he said, 'No,' when I asked him if he hit the child. I never asked Amanda about it.'* " (p. 2090)

Finally, the officers told Vanessa that they didn't believe her when she claimed not to know that Chad and Amanda had seen each other, and "*After several more minutes of talk and tears, Ms. Mansson said at 1355 hours, 'He's stayed at my house with Amanda several times and I knew it.'* " (p. 2091) At the end of the interview, at 2:20 p.m. Sgt. White served a grand jury subpoena on Vanessa for 9:00 a.m., the next Friday, the 17th. (p. 2092)

Sgt. White reported that he and Sgt. McClare later visited Amanda at the start of her shift at 6:05 p.m. at the Pizza Hut restaurant in Brattleboro where she had been working since July. White wrote that he said, "*Hi Amanda. We haven't talked in a while,*" and

Amanda replied, "***Chad didn't do it. You twisted around everything I said***... *Well, the papers twisted it around. They said he threw her against the wall. He wouldn't do that.*" White wrote that he told Amanda that he couldn't control what the newspapers wrote and that "*we only reported what she told us*." There was insufficient time to explain that he had written the "court documents" and "affidavits" that the newspapers relied upon for their stories, and that there were uncorrected mistakes in the affidavits. According to White, Amanda continued, "*I was confused because of everything going on. Now I know Jeff did it. I dream about things. Chad wouldn't do it. It was Jeff. It was Jeff.*" (p. 1959) White asked Amanda where she was living and she refused to tell him and began crying. She did not yet have an attorney. At her manager's suggestion, the officers and Amanda went to the manager's office and White asked about Amanda's contacts with Chad. When she denied any contact, White told her that she was being untruthful, and served her with a grand jury subpoena for Friday, August 17, at 9:00 a.m. When they left, White and McClare determined that the car Amanda had been driving was registered to Jeremy.

Surprised at work and scared, Amanda was lying, which didn't help her own problems with the police and prosecutors, and it didn't help her support of Chad. (p. 1960)

On the 14th, Sgt. Riesenberg served Chet and Pam Evans at their home in Keene with subpoenas for the same grand jury as for Amanda, and he asked them if they "*would be willing to answer a few questions and both indicated that they would rather not speak to me*." (p. 1961) They were following what they thought were the wishes of Chad's attorney, to say nothing to anyone about Chad or the case. This was a lost opportunity. They could have shown Riesenberg the pool where Kassidy played during her two visits to Keene, and the photographs on their walls of their children, including Chad. They could have shown him Chad's room and pulled out scrapbooks of his achievements, including the election to the School Board. They simply could have told him, and strongly, that the police were making a huge mistake in their prosecution of Chad for the death of Kassidy. They could even have communicated a sentiment that was felt by many which was that it was too bad that the police had not put as much effort into uncovering the truth about Kassidy's last days and health as they had in trying to determine whether Chad and Amanda were seeing each other in 2001.

Also served with subpoenas to appear before the grand jury on the 17th were Bruce Truell's parents, Bruce and Charlene Truell. All the subpoenas were signed by Assistant Attorney General N. William Delker.

Mid-August 2001

Many photographs of Kassidy, and Chad and Amanda were destroyed at the camping site where Amanda was living in a camping trailer on Chad's grandparents' property. Chad described what happened in his February 14, 2010 letter:

As with everything else in this case, (you know, my cosmos lined up quote), we have the worst case scenario regarding pictures of Kassidy. Amanda had almost all photos of Kassidy in a large envelope that we kept in our camper in the woods while living on my grandparents' property in Vernon, Vermont. They were accidently destroyed in a fire. It was a horrible accident. It was really too bad, because we had some awesome shots of Kassidy. She was really a photogenic baby and Amanda was constantly taking pictures of her and Kyle too.

What happened was that a helicopter hovered overhead, and Chad, Amanda and Jason thought it was a police helicopter. As aerial photographs of the property were later provided to Chad's lawyers, it's likely that this helicopter was taking those photographs. Chad, Amanda and Jason panicked, and items were thrown into the fire and Amanda's prized envelope was accidentally included.

In 2011, Chad prepared the list below of the photos that he remembered which are no longer available. Most of them were in the 2001 fire.

1. *I recall several photos that Amanda took of Kassidy and Kyle playing at the house.*
2. *There were some great photos that Amanda took in the boat. I recall one where Kassidy was sitting on the back bench seat by herself as we were stopped in the middle of Baxter Lake.*

3. *I'm positive there was a photo that Amanda took standing in the bow of the boat where I was driving and had Kyle and Kassidy on my lap helping me steer.*
   4. *There was a day that we took Kyle, Kassidy and Brent to Hampton Beach. My mother recently gave you a photo of the boys climbing on the rocks. Amanda took the photo with Kassidy beside her. I took a photo of them together.*
5. *There are several missing photos of Kassidy in the high chair. Amanda was always snapping those photos. I remember we had a few cute ones with food all over her face. In one of them, Amanda ran to get the camera because she was licking the ice cream bowl and had some on her nose.*
6. *There are at least 2 photos of her playing with Kato that I remember.*
7. *Jackie already contacted you about the missing photos of Josh and Kassidy at Water Country that Amanda took.*
8. *There are the missing photos of Kassidy and Malana together in the kiddie pool.*
9. *There are the missing photos of Kassidy and Josh together when he stayed at our house in Rochester. Amanda was always snapping photos. I thought I should buy stock in Kodak that summer. :)*
10. *I'm pretty sure that Amanda had a photo with Kassidy sitting on my lap on the 3 wheeler or the riding tractor.*
11. *I'm fairly certain we had a photo of Kassidy and Ashley, Bruce and Michelle Truell's daughter playing together at the Truell's house, backyard.*
12. *There was at least one photo of Amanda and Kassidy snuggled up in our bed that I took.*
13. *Amanda took photos of Kassidy in her car seat wearing sun glasses.*
14. *There are several more photos missing from the day at York's Wild Animal Kingdom.*
15. *I'm pretty sure that Amanda had a photo of Kassidy and I playing together on the floor from the night Amanda came home from the money mgt. class in Portsmouth. This was the evening I described in a letter to you very early on where Kassidy actually wanted me and pushed Amanda away when she came to play with us. First and only time that happened.*
16. *We had some of Kassidy at the playground in Rochester.*
17. *I remember a really cute one of Kassidy sitting on the couch watching cartoons and had her Teletubby, Tinky Winky, right with her.*
18. *I'm sure Amanda had some of her sleeping. Kassidy was like the most adorable sleeper.*
19. *I know Amanda took some of Kassidy on the trampoline. They both loved jumping together on the trampoline.*
20. *I remember there were several photos of Kassidy framed that Amanda had placed on the fireplace mantle.*
21. *I'm not sure where we were, but Amanda had one of Kassidy sitting on my shoulders. This is how I carried her a lot*
22. *There were some of Kassidy in a dress that Jackie had recently purchased for her.* This dress may have been the red-top dress with a white image of a dog's face, that was cut from Kassidy's body, either on Jeff's porch or later by the EMT's. The lower portion of the dress had horizontal red and white narrow stripes.

Thursday, 16 August 2001

Trooper Jill Rockey served Jeremy Hinton with a grand jury subpoena at 8:32 a.m. and asked him if he was aware of any contacts between Chad and Amanda. According to Rockey's report, Jeremy said, "*No*," and she left. At 11:00, Jeremy called her and said "*he hadn't been completely honest with me and wanted to meet me to talk about it.*" (p. 3128) At 3:00 p.m. Jeremy met with Sgt. White and Rockey at the Greenland Police Dept. Rockey wrote:

Hinton said Amanda stayed at his apartment in Dover for approximately 2 weeks sometime between mid-April and mid-June. ... Hinton said he loaned Evans his car in late April. When Amanda came to stay with him, she was driving the car. While Evans never told him, he knew they must have had contact. He wasn't stupid.

Hinton said he only spoke to Bortner once about the case. He asked her if the stuff in the papers was true. She said, "No." ...Evans told him, "I didn't do this."

...He said both Bortner and Evans have keys to his apartment. One time he came home and they were both there. Hinton thought it was in May, sometime around Memorial Day....Hinton told them when he caught them, "Listen guys, I don't want any part of this. One of you needs to leave." Hinton said he left and came back the next day and they were both gone. (p. 3128)

Friday, 17 August 2001

A Strafford County grand jury began considering the prosecutor's allegations that Chad and Amanda were seeing each other and communicating with each other, despite a condition of Chad's bail that he have no such contact. Friends of Chad and Amanda who were thought to know about, or facilitate, such contacts were subpoenaed to appear before the Grand Jury. There were also allegations of Chad's tampering with a witness, i.e. Amanda.

Sgt. James White met Cathy Nuernberg, who came in response to a subpoena, at the Manchester airport at 10:30 p.m., and began his interview while driving her to the Days Inn motel in Dover, New Hampshire. He continued the interview on Monday, August 20 at the Strafford County Superior Court.

White reported Cathy's recollection of the "headbutting" incident,
Nuernberg told me that one time she accompanied Bortner to Evans' house so Bortner could retrieve something....she, Bortner and some other friends were going out for the evening, dancing....Bortner was in another part of the home with Evans and then came back and told Nuernberg that Evans had just "headbutted" her. Nuernberg said she didn't notice any marks and Bortner didn't seem hurt....sometime around August 2000. Nuernberg told me that Evans and Bortner fought often, yelling and stuff, but Nuernberg never saw anything physical, nor did Bortner describe any physical assaults to her, other than the headbutt. Nuernberg said she wouldn't be surprised to learn that there were physical assaults. She said Bortner knew how to push buttons, and probably fought back. Nuernberg said that Bortner was not generally a "submissive woman." After describing some sexual innuendo, White wrote, "Nuernberg said she went out socially with Evans and Bortner about a half dozen times...Nuernberg told me that generally Bortner controlled the relationships she was involved in, but it was just the opposite with she and Evans. He controlled the relationship.... She told me that Bortner was always on eggshells, afraid that she's be late getting home and make Evans angry. Evans didn't like Bortner to go out "clubbing" so she would lie to him about that.... Nuernberg told me that Bortner couldn't cook, but she tried to for Evans. She was always cleaning the house, and she had to check in frequently...

*I asked about Nuernberg about Evans' relationship with Kassidy. Nuernberg described several observations. She related that she was at Evans' house for a get-together. Kassidy wanted to be held by Bortner. Bortner was in the kitchen, cooking, and couldn't hold Kassidy, who became fussy. Evans grabbed Kassidy by the shoulder, shook her, and told her she was acting like a brat. Nuernberg said it made her uneasy. She also told me that to the best of her recollection, Marshall and Conley were there also....
She said Kyle always seemed to be good, but she didn't know if it was because he was well behaved, or that he was afraid of Evans and complied out of fear.... Evans seemed to be jealous of Kassidy, like he resented her for the time she required of Bortner. Nuernberg said she didn't know if it was just that he didn't like women, or if it was because she wasn't his child. Nuernberg said Kassidy was independent and didn't comply with what Evans expected for behavior, which really frustrated Evans. Nuernberg said that Kassidy was somewhat spoiled. She explained that Bortner was not one to use physical discipline. She would raise her voice and that was about all. Nuerenberg said Bortner may have spanked Kassidy, but not that she recalls. Nuernberg said Bortner didn't like Kassidy to cry because it made her feel like a bad mother.*

Nuernberg related a time she went to Evans' house to meet Bortner, and Kassidy's face was badly bruised and there was what appeared to be a burn on the top of one of her feet. Nuernberg said she believes it was sometime in September 2000, because she remembers it being close to the time she returned to San Antonio, TX. Nuernberg said that she, Bortner and Kassidy left the house, because during that time, Tristan didn't want Bortner there when Kyle was visiting Evans. Nuernberg told me that when they left, she confronted Bortner about the bruises and burn. Nuernberg said there was a bruise above Kassidy's eyebrows. Bortner explained that Evans had Kassidy on his shoulders, was coming down the stairs, and banged her head on the edge of the floor overhang for the stair opening. Nuernberg also described "grab marks" around Kassidy's mouth. Nuernberg said it was clear to her that it was a grab mark becasue she could make out the thumb and finger marks.

Nuernberg said she grilled Bortner for the cause of the grab marks, but Bortner refused to offer an explanation. Nuernberg also described what appeared to be a burn mark on top of one of Kassidy's feet. Bortner explained that a hair curling iron had landed on Kassidy's foot when she was at one of Bortner's friend's in Maine. Nuernberg also said that Bortner would often say that Kassidy had fallen off the trampoline. Nuernberg felt it was possible that maybe Kassidy had fallen off once, but certainly not as many times as Bortner said had happened, particularly because the trampoline was taller than Kassidy and someone would have had to put her up to it....

Nuernberg told me that Bortner had told her that Marshall had spanked Kassidy once and caused redness to her bottom. Bortner also said that Marshall wasn't the best at keeping Kassidy fed. Bortner also said she gave Marshall and Conley food stamps as payment for babysitting. Nuernberg said it was clear that even though Bortner wasn't fond of Marshall, she never blamed him for Kassidy's death.

When Cathy recalled that Kassidy's face was, in White's words, "*badly bruised*," in September 2000, it would have been very helpful if she could have remembered to tell Sgt. White that she had photos of Kassidy. She told the jury at Amanda's trial on November 21, 2002 that "*I took pictures of her in September, and I have them, and she looked fine*." It also would have been helpful if Sgt. White and other investigators had asked Cathy and all the other interviewees if they had photographs of Amanda or Kassidy. In 2011, she declined to provide access to, or copies of, these photos. They would be especially helpful if they were date-stamped.

Saturday, 18 August 2001

With the grand jury considering Chad's and Amanda's living arrangements, it was not a surprise that the media caught at least part of the story. The Keene Sentinel published the article, "Murder suspect, mother in Keene," and reported,

The mother of a murdered seacoast toddler has left the area to take up residence 4 miles from the Keene home of the man charged with the crime.... According to documents in Evans' case file, Bortner has lived at the home of a Vanessa Mansson at 651 Park Ave., Keene, since at least June....During proceedings at Rochester last week, Evans' attorney, Alan Cronheim, said his client currently lives in Keene...

The article said that Amanda had not yet been appointed counsel because she had not yet returned the necessary financial status forms. However, they were sent to the Strafford County Court with her May 9 letter requesting court-appointed counsel.

Sunday, 19 August 2001

Chad was at his parents' home in Keene. He knew that he didn't kill Kassidy and he trusted that the judicial system would reach the correct result of Not Guilty at his upcoming trial. He felt abused by the police who charged an innocent man. It followed that the no-contact condition to his bail was also unfair, and he reasoned that Amanda needed him and he loved her. After the initial secluded rendezvous seemed to help Amanda and didn't result in the revocation of his bail, the second and the third became easier. Finally, by the summer, they were together several days a week and so far, there had been no harm done, as far as Chad and Amanda could see.

He was confident that his, and Amanda's, nightmare would end at his trial, when a jury would see that he did not assault and murder Kassidy, and that the argument with

Amanda on the evening of November 8 would not be seen by the jury as an assault, but as an argument that became mutually physical. His reasoning was similar to what he used when telling the police the "trampoline story," in his police interrogation, which was that he knew it had nothing to do with Kassidy's death, so it didn't do any harm to him or the investigation to continue telling the story that he and Amanda had agreed upon. Similarly, after a trial, everyone would see that it was not a crime for an innocent man to continue to love his girlfriend and help her through their shared tragedy of Kassidy's loss.

However, Chad's closeness to Amanda infuriated the police, who viewed Chad as a very, very bad man and Amanda as a terrible mother, who insulted the memory of her daughter by continuing to associate with the man who allegedly killed her. The dance between the police and Chad became like the plot of a movie drama, with echoes of TV's Grizzly Adams fleeing to the mountains from wrongful accusations of murder. In the movie version, Grizzly returned to prove his innocence. Chad ran out of time, three months short of the trial. The confidence that he would prevail at the trial was shaken.

Monday, 20 August 2001

After a day of grand jury testimony, the prosecutors had enough evidence that Chad was seeing Amanda in violation of his bail conditions. A bail revocation hearing was conducted in response to the prosecutors' petition. Fearing the worst, Chad's parents drove him to the hearing.

Judge James O'Neill III revoked Chad's bail and he was taken to the Strafford County Jail, where he would likely remain until his November trial. It was his last day of freedom. In addition, he forfeited the $10,000 cash which was part of his bail agreement. The Union Leader covered the story on August 23, "Bail revoked in baby death case," and noted, "*Senior Assistant Attorney General William Delker said prosecutors still were investigating the nature of the alleged contact.*" This meant that the grand jury was continuing to hear witnesses as it considered bringing further charges against Chad, such as tampering with a witness, i.e. Amanda.

CHAPTER 6: TRIAL OF CHAD EVANS - PREPARATION 21 AUGUST 2001 TO 3 DECEMBER 2001

"... this is not the normal situation." - Dr. Michael Baden

"When you love somebody so much, what choice do you have?" - Mary Bullard

"I'm too much of a bitch to put up with that." - attributed to Amanda by Tracey Foley

"She was too much of a bitch to put up with that from me" - Chad Evans

With Chad in jail, his ability to assist his lawyers in preparation for his trial was further limited. It's about a half hour from the Fleet Street, Portsmouth office of Alan Cronheim and Mark Sisti to the Strafford County Jail in Dover. Chad had no cell phone and could make few land line phone calls and had no access to computers, and little access to photocopiers.

The cost of Chad's lawyers was significant and mounting. On September 1, he borrowed $38,400 from his parents with an interest rate of 6%, all to be paid within four years, i.e, September 1, 2005. It was an optimistic repayment date.

Thursday, 6 September 2001

Even though Chad's bail had been revoked and he had been jailed on August 21 because of his contacts with Amanda in 2001, Sgt. White interviewed Eric Lepisto of Keene, and "*the purpose of the interview was to determine Lepisto's knowledge of the contact between Bortner and Evans.*" (p. 2992) Lepisto told White that he didn't know Amanda or Chad until he met them through Vanessa Mansson, with whom he was dating, in March 2001. He knew that Amanda and Chad stayed at Vanessa's off and on, and then came to his home to live on a similar basis for a week or two. He described how Amanda and Chad tried to evade detection while staying at his home. He said that later they moved to a camper on Chad's grandparents' land in Vermont.

White wrote,

Lepisto told me he knew they weren't supposed to be together, having been told by both Evans and Mansson... but he knew it wasn't legally wrong. He said Evans seemed like a nice guy so he took Evans at his word when he said he didn't do it (kill Kassidy)...

Lepisto told me that Evans talked about the case a couple of times, but about all he remembered was Evans mentioning pin pricks on Kassidy's feet. Lepisto told me that Evans said he was puzzled about how they got there....

Lepisto told me that about three days before Evans was sent back to jail, Evans and Bortner stayed at his home. Lepisto said he sensed that Evans knew the end was in sight because of [the] *Grand Jury...Evans and Mansson told him to tell the truth...*

Lepisto asked me if this interview was about witness tampering... I explained to Lepisto that I believed Evans had influenced Bortner because of the turnaround in her story. Lepisto said he understood and said he remembers Bortner saying she was under duress when she gave her statement. (p. 2993)

Chad probably "*knew the end was in sight*," that is, the end of his freedom on bail, because of his contacts with Amanda, because of the apparent helicopter surveillance flight earlier in August. The subpoenas sealed his fate, and he urged his friends to tell the truth.

The interview with Eric, even after Chad's arrest and return to jail, showed continued interest by the police in building a case that Chad had seen Amanda during his time on bail and that he was tampering with a witness. Eric was also summoned to the grand jury and testified on September 21. Mary Bullard was the last person interviewed in this effort, on November 20. No charges were ever filed against Chad for witness tampering. Perhaps the police and prosecutors hoped that the use of the grand jury would help them gather evidence for Chad's upcoming trial, but neither side at the trial used the grand jury testimony in any way.

Sgt. White stated in the above summary that he "*believed Evans had influenced Bortner because of the turnaround in her story.*" Until her police interview on November 9, 2000, Amanda did not believe that Chad was hurting Kassidy. Yes, there were real-enough accidents that both Chad and Amanda knew about, and they knew about the palming for **eye contact,** and they knew about Chad's playing with Kassidy as he had played with his son and stepson, but until November 9, she did not believe that Chad was harming Kassidy. From the time of her first interview at 4:20 p.m. on November 9, until approximately the day of Kassidy's burial on Saturday, November 18, the police had partially convinced her that Chad was Kassidy's abuser and killer. After she left for Texas with her friend, Kathy, and even though Kathy, too, believed the police theory, Amanda began to realize that the police theory was incorrect. The actual "*turnaround*" for Amanda was the 10 day period of her apparent acceptance of the police theory, and not her subsequent return to the view that Chad was not responsible. Part of the problem in her understanding of the case was that everyone seemed to accept the police view that Kassidy's death was entirely a homicide, with no allowance for accidents or disease or chronic condition. Thus, by accepting that part of the police theory, she was forced to take the view that Jeff was entirely responsible.

Amanda wanted to be with the man she loved in late 2000 and during 2001 not because she thought that her love for Chad came before her love and loyalty to Kassidy. She wanted to be with him because she loved him and she understood that he was not Kassidy's killer and abuser.

Friday, 7 September 2001

Chad's probation revocation hearing finally occurred on this day, and Jennifer Saunders covered the front page story in Foster's Daily Democrat, "Evans faces probation charge - Murder suspect accused of possessing 1,400 live rounds of ammunition" Accompanying the article was a large color photograph of Chad walking up the courthouse steps wearing an orange Strafford County jumpsuit and handcuffed with a policeman in plainclothes alongside. This was not good publicity for Chad. Saunders wrote,

The ammunition was discovered during the November investigation into the death of 21-month-old Kassidy Bortner. Evans has since been charged with second-degree murder and multiple counts of assault in connection with the child's death.

Cronheim contended Evans did not violate his probation because he had simply forgotten about the ammunition. Cronheim produced a receipt indicating Evans purchased the ammunition from Houston Cartridge Company in 1995 - almost five years before he was placed on probation for assaulting his wife....

Evans rolled his eyes and appeared frustrated when [Asst. County Attorney Hope] *Flynn referred to his past history of domestic violence and described him as a dangerous man. Cronheim countered that if Evans 'was such a dangerous man' his probation officers should have overseen the removal of firearms from his house and should not have allowed Evans to do it himself.*

Not mentioned in court or in the article was how Chad developed his interest in guns, as he described in his May 10, 2011 letter,

I didn't actually go to the gun range with an off duty police officer. Capt. Paul Callahan and I talked about it several times when he was a patrolman and I was the manager of the Rochester McDonald's. He dealt with a theft situation when I started in 1993 and he was a very friendly guy. We seemed to hit it off pretty well. He shared some about his life. I shared some of my life story. I asked what type of sidearm they were now carrying. They had just upgraded to Glock 9MM's I believe and I had just purchased a 10 MM a few years prior. From there, he and I discussed going out to shoot from time to time when I would see him at McDonald's but we never set a firm plan. I did go target shooting at a range in Barrington with my friend, Scott Lane, Larry Lane's brother. Scott had a membership there. I can't recall the name of the range but think it was Major Leanard something. [Major Waldron Sportsmen's Association, Barrington, New Hampshire]

Anyway, to give you a more in-depth understanding to me and guns. As you know, I was introduced to target shooting at a young age by my Uncle Richie, a Vermont Deputy Sheriff. It was one of the bonding things that Uncle Ritchie spent time with me doing. Richie, his stepson, David Gundry, myself and another cousin, would go up behind my cousin's house in Dover, Vermont and target practice in a sand pit. It was a blast. Richie was a great teacher and was all about gun safety. This likely started when I was 9 or 10 years old. My dad hunted some as a boy, but had no firearms and on my grandparents farm there was an old shot gun locked up somewhere, but nothing I had ever seen. As a boy who loved Chuck Norris and Sylvester Stallone action movies, I suspect Uncle Ritchie wanted me to learn that guns were not toys, and are dangerous; but could also be a lot of fun. I'm certain, my mom wished that my interest in guns would wane once Ritchie taught me how to shoot, but it only intensified. I became interested and Ritchie and I would get together as often as he was around to shoot. I didn't get my first gun until I was 16. My parents bought me a Stevens model .22 and I loved it. Around this time, I started working at the Keene McDonald's with Dan Frazier who was an Outdoor Sportsman and gun enthusiast. I have always been interested in investing and around this time, Dan taught me that guns can be a great investment because if they are taken care of, they often appreciate in value. Even as a teenager, I was a diversified investor between tangible and non-tangible goods. For example, I became friendly with a gentleman that owned a comic book store when I found out how much some of the comics appreciated in value over time. (You met Tim at our first Keene committee meeting in Swanzey) Tim would set aside the titles each month that he felt would appreciate and I would purchase them. Boxing and bagging them in my late teens, determined in 25 years I was going to sell them and pay for my unborn children's college tuition.

I digress. So Dan and I started collecting firearms. I purchased some that I felt might appreciate in value and put them away without ever firing. Mostly that was Dan though. I bought a bunch of guns that were a blast to go out and target shoot with and, as long as taken care of, at a minimum would retain their value. Dan and I shot often when we worked together in Keene. Lots of Saturday afternoon's we would cut off early and go shoot for an hour or two at a local gravel bank that at the time allowed shooting or the local fish and game club a few miles from my house. It was relaxing and gave Dan and I a chance to bond, build our friendship, talk work strategies, etc. Dan was like a big brother to me. I also would target shoot at times with my brothers and dad at the farm in Guilford or in the family gravel bank in Vernon, Vt.

My interest in guns continued while living in Rochester, I believe I only made a couple of purchases there in the early years and only one that I can recall after Kyle was born. I shot a few times after Kyle was born, but mostly the guns sat locked up in the oak gun cabinet that my Uncle Alton made. I didn't lose interest in guns but when children come along your priorities change. I imagine if I were home now, I would take Kyle out to the woods to do some responsible target shooting. I think it is a nice way to spend a slow afternoon bonding and talking. It also would allow me to teach him the values that I feel are important and about gun safety.

The last thing I would ever want is for Kyle to be farting around with a friend who just found his dad's gun or something and have no idea how dangerous a weapon it is. Feeling the recoil of the butt against your shoulder, having someone harp about keeping the gun barrel pointing down, and seeing the damage to the target are great teachers.

Thursday, 13 September 2001

Judge Nadeau held the third pre-trial status conference in Ossippee where she was assigned on that day. Jennifer Saunders wrote the story for Foster's Daily Democrat, "Evans' attorney looks forward to trial - No motion filed by defense for change of venue for second-degree murder case" The best news of the day for Chad was that one of his attorneys, Mark Sisti, talked positively to Saunders about Chad's case. She wrote,

The attorney... says he is looking forward to the November trial. "We want this resolved as quickly as possible. We cannot wait to get a fair and impartial jury to try this case before," Mark Sisti said Thursday morning, standing outside Carroll County Superior Court...

"We intend on trying this case in Strafford County. We're intent on getting a jury, and we're intent on getting the facts out in front of the jury." Sisti said.

Friday, 21 September 2001

The "Kassidy Bortner bill," Chapter 345 of the laws of 2001 in Maine, became effective on this date. It required that caretakers report child abuse, and imposed stronger penalties for failing to report. It was signed on 18 June by Governor Angus King. The name of the law is "An Act to Protect Children and Incapacitated or Dependent Adults."

Wednesday, 26 September 2001

The Office of the Attorney General, by Kelly Ayotte, Chief of the Homicide Unit, and N. William Delker, responded to the Chad's Motion to Suppress statements made by Chad after he was arrested on the evening of November 16, 2000. The State responded that it did not intend to use any of those statements, so it was not necessary for Judge Nadeau to further consider the motion. The state's response was reasonable since Chad had said nothing about the case. He said in his short interview at 11:50 p.m. with Maine State Police Detective Jeff Linscott and New Hampshire State Police Sergeant Russell Conte that he wanted to "*answer every question you have, I wanna be as helpful as I can...*" but that he wanted to have his lawyer present. This was the last time that Chad talked with any policeman about the case, and he never talked with a prosecutor or Assistant Attorney General. The defense motion may have been an effort to bring to Judge Nadeau's attention the efforts by the police and Delker to interview Chad, despite Cronheim's telephoned request that he not be interviewed without his presence. However, as the motion was not considered further, it may have had the effect of indicating to Judge Nadeau that Chad had said something incriminating during that very short interview, and he hadn't.

October/November 2001

Each side in the Chad Evans case intensified its preparations for the upcoming trial. With the Chad-bail-chase over, investigators returned again to the main case against Chad Evans.

23 October 2001

The New Hampshire Attorney General offered Amanda Bortner immunity from prosecution in return for her "cooperation" during prosecution of Chad Evans.

Wednesday, 31 October 2001

Approximately on this date, prosecutors met with Crystal Martin to review her prospective testimony. She insisted that when she bathed Kassidy "*2-3 weeks before Kassidy's death*" there were no bruises on Kassidy. This estimate would have covered the period between October 19-26. Perhaps the bruises which had been seen on Friday, October 13 by Joshua Bortner Conley and then over that weekend by others had dissipated by the time of Crystal's bath. Crystal was not called by the prosecution to testify, and Chad's defense team did not interview her.

If the police and prosecutors had requested photographs from Amanda and Chad and their families and friends, they would have located the photograph of Amanda holding Kassidy at Nicole Evans Harvey's home on Friday, October 20, exactly 20 days prior to Kassidy's death and within Crystal's estimate of "*2-3 weeks before Kassidy's death.*" Crystal's recollection of the truth wasn't what the prosecutors wanted the jury to hear, so she wasn't called to testify at Chad's trial. By the rules of the legal game, it wasn't their responsibility to present the defense's case. Because this meeting was with the prosecutors only, there was apparently no obligation to provide the defense a report of this meeting.

At 11:40 a.m. Rochester Detectives Paul Callaghan and Christopher Magnum interviewed Irene Ricci for ten minutes at McDonald's in Rochester, where she worked. This was her first interview with the police about Kassidy's death. Det. Callaghan summarized the interview, in which he spelled Kassidy with a "C":

.... Ms. Ricci told me that Travis Hunt was late that evening and he did not call ahead of time to let her know he was going to be late....

She told me that he arrived between 2100-2130 hours and mentioned he was late because Cassidy had fallen down playing with Chad's son and he waited for her to fall asleep.... Ms. Ricci also stated Travis told her that he felt bad about Cassidy's getting hurt and wanted to make sure she was in bed sleeping before he left. ... he was upset and told her that [he] *felt bad that Cassidy was injured because he liked children.*

At 12:10 p.m. Assistant Attorneys General Delker and Brown and Detective Callaghan interviewed Travis Hunt at the Rochester Police Dept. As the last person outside the primary Four (Amanda, Chad, Jeff and Jennifer) to have seen Kassidy alive, he was a key potential witness. This was his third interview with the police, after the first two nearly a year earlier, on November 9 and 22, 2000. Callaghan summarized the 90 minute interview in his two page report:

...Travis Hunt was extremely nervous throughout the interview. His legs were shaking. He sighed, swallowed, and took deep breaths several times. He kept his arms crossed and against his torso and his voice cracked at times.

Travis Hunt told us that he lived at 191 Milton Road since the Summer of 2000. He now lives there with his sister....

... He told us that [on the evening of November 8] *... he entered the house through the kitchen door and hear noises coming from the second floor... it was just normal noises that people make when they are home....he immediately went upstairs to the second floor bathroom and found Chad Evans giving Cassidy Bortner a bath.... Cassidy was splashing in the bath and was "chipper," ...she was exhibiting more energy than usual and she was fine. He said that Chad Evans pointed out a red circular injury underneath Cassidy Bortner's eye. Chad Evans told him that he was pitching a ball to his three year old son, Kyle and Kyle hit the ball and it struck Cassidy in the face. Travis Hunt believed the ball that struck Cassidy Bortner was a hollow plastic ball.*

...he said Chad was calm and he was sitting on the floor watching Cassidy take her bath....Chad Evans told him in the bathroom that when he was driving Cassidy home tonight, she appeared to have a convulsion in the car as her eyes rolled up into the back of her head while she was in her car seat. Chad Evans also told him that Cassidy fell on her face when she got out of the car at home...Travis Hunt was asked again how Cassidy appeared in the bathtub and he said she was "chipper."... He said that he saw small bruises on each side of her face near her chin and on her leg. He said he did not consider the bruises to be suspicious because Cassidy Bortner fell a lot....

Travis Hunt said that after playing with Kyle he went downstairs... to call Irene to let her know he was coming over....He said that when he was on the first floor he saw Evans carrying Cassidy in the den or near the den while she was eating a "frozen pop." He said she appeared fine and Chad Evans appeared fine. Travis Hunt also told us that he also saw Cassidy Bortner shortly before he left for Irene Ricci's house. He said that he used the second floor bathroom to brush his teeth and Chad Evans was with Cassidy in her bedroom getting her ready for bed and he was reading her a story. Travis Hunt said he left for Irene Ricci's house between 2000-2015 hours....

I asked Travis Hunt if he told Irene Ricci that he was concerned for Cassidy's well-being that night and he said, "No," but he recalled telling her that she got hit by a ball hit by Kyle. I asked Travis if he told Irene that the reason he was late visiting her was because he wanted to make sure Cassidy went to sleep all right. He denied stating that. I asked him if he had any motivation for making that up and he said, "No." ....

I told Travis Hunt that we had concerns with his story. He was asked why he felt it necessary when he got home to go immediately upstairs to the bathroom after hearing noises. He said because he knew Chad was home and he wanted to say, "Hello," to him. Travis Hunt was asked to recall what he saw in the bathroom. He said Cassidy Bortner was in the bath splashing and she was chipper. He said it was unusual for him to see her so active, because she would spend hours at a time watching television. He was asked how Chad Evans appeared and he said Chad was fine. Attorney Delker asked Travis Hunt if he saw any bruises on Cassidy. He stated that he saw the red circular mark underneath her eye. He saw the small bruises on each side of her face near her chin, and he saw a bruise on her leg. Attorney Delker asked him if he saw the bruises on her stomach and he said, "No." Travis Hunt was then asked if he recalled seeing the autopsy photographs of Cassidy Bortner depicting bruises all over her body and he said, "Yes," and added that she did not look like that when he saw her.

Travis Hunt was asked if he ever heard Amanda Bortner and Chad Evans fighting and he said, "No." He did recall one incident that he assumed was a verbal argument because their voices were raised. He was asked if he knew the outcome of that argument and he said, "No."

Travis Hunt was told that there is medical evidence showing the injuries Cassidy Bortner sustained would make it impossible for her to be "chipper" in the tub or be able to eat a popsicle. Travis Hunt explained that he was telling the truth, and that she was playing in the bathtub and she was eating a popsicle when he saw her. Travis Hunt stated that if Cassidy Bortner looked like the autopsy photographs when he saw her in the bathtub, he would have called the police.

Thus, Travis had reported seeing Kassidy in three different settings: in the bathtub, in the den eating a popsicle and in bed with Chad reading her a story and every recollection was of a normal bedtime routine, except for the ball hitting Kassidy's face, which occurred before Travis arrived home.

This was the second time that the police had heard about Kassidy eating a popsicle, but it was the first time they had heard details about the time and place. It was in the den, or Chad's office, sitting on Chad's lap, after her bath and before going upstairs to bed. As noted earlier, the plastic wrapper was discarded in the wastebasket in the den/office, but the contents of that wastebasket were not photographed during the November 10, 2000 search of Chad's home. The first reference to that popsicle was in Chad's interrogation, when he was talking generally about the night of Nov. 8, "*I was all over* [her]*, like just babying the shit out of her. I gave her a popsicle.*" (Interrogation, p. 1591)
From the two prosecutors, only one question had been mentioned, which was the question by Delker about bruises. They, and Det. Callaghan, appeared convinced that Travis was lying.

Travis Hunt was told that there is medical evidence showing the injuries Cassidy Bortner sustained would make it impossible for her to be "chipper" in the bath tub or be able to eat a popsicle.

However, there was no such conclusion in any of the medical reports, including the autopsy. It **was** "*impossible*" for the prosecutors' theory of the case to be consistent with Travis's statements, but the prosecutors chose to stick to their theory and discount Travis's recollections.

One reason the three men felt Travis was lying was his statement that he had called Irene "*to let her know he was coming over"* because Irene had told Detectives Callaghan and Magnum that didn't call. Supporting Irene's memory of the evening is Chad's 2010 recollection that she called Chad's home phone, asking for Travis, after Travis had left. (Letters, January 28, 2010) What's possible is that on October 31, 2001, a year after the night of October 8, Travis recalled such a call to Irene from another night. In 2011, Irene confirmed that she did call Chad's house that evening and talked briefly with Chad. Unfortunately, that fact didn't emerge in the pre-trial interviews, as she would have been an important witness on the issue of Chad's demeanor that evening, even though her call was very short. She could have been asked if Chad sounded stressed or angry, or polite and calm and the answer would have been that he was polite and calm.

No one suggested a polygraph for Travis. In 2010, he said he was willing to take such a test.

Friday, 2 November 2001

The prosecutors sought to ensure Amanda's pro-prosecution testimony at Chad's trial by securing an agreement with her, which gave her immunity from further prosecution in return for such testimony. On this date, a proposed unsigned immunity agreement was faxed to her attorney, Patricia Wiberg, and she signed it. It required, among other obligations that she

must at all times provide information or testimony with the scope of this agreement that is truthful, candid and complete,... making a material false statement or omission will constitute a breach of this agreement. In the event of such a breach, or any other breach of this agreement, the State of New Hampshire will be released from all its obligations hereunder and may initiate prosecution against Amanda Bortner for any crimes relating to the death of Kassidy Bortner or any injuries sustained by Kassidy Bortner before her death. Furthermore, Amanda Bortner will be prosecuted to the full extent of the law for perjury or obstruction of justice or another appropriate offense in the event she is to make a material false statement or omission to investigators, State attorneys, a grand jury or trial jury in the course of fulfilling her obligations hereunder.

After receiving the signed agreement from Amanda's attorney, the prosecutors declined to sign their own agreement because it was becoming clear to them that Amanda was disavowing parts of what she said to the police during her four interviews.

Dramatic proof of the tactics in the Attorney General's office was the subsequent indictment, called "Information" of Amanda. Perhaps the prosecutors thought it was a negotiable item, but Amanda was not intimidated. She knew what she saw and didn't see between Chad and Kassidy, and she would testify truthfully, regardless of what she said to the police the previous year.

Monday, 5 November 2001

The State filed a Motion for Reciprocal Discovery, which meant that it wanted to know what statements by witnesses and all "*books, papers, documents, photographs, tangible objects*" the defense attorneys planned to present at Chad's trial. The defense assented immediately to this motion and asked the same of the prosecution. The goal of this exchange is to preclude, to a reasonable extent, surprises at a trial. Each side know all about the other' case and each side is ready to try to persuade a jury to accept its view of the case. The parties also shared their lists of expected witnesses. The State's, filed on 15 November list had 69 names, nearly all of whom were on Chad's draft list which had 144 names. Only 27 people testified at Chad's trial, and only one of those was a defense witness.

Amanda met with Asst. Attorney General William Delker after signing the immunity agreement of 23 October 2001, and she was advised that the state declined to complete the agreement claiming that Amanda was not cooperating and not being truthful. The prosecutors chose to go ahead, with primary reliance upon Amanda's police interviews rather than slow down the Convict-Chad train and re-investigate at least parts of the case. Crystal Martin's testimony contradicted the police theory. Travis Hunt's testimony was considered impossibly incompatible with the police theory, and Amanda was disavowing a substantial part of what she had earlier agreed to. However, there was no turning back. The schedule had been prepared and the play would continue.

Tuesday, 6 November 2001

As requested by the Office of the Attorney General, the Strafford County Superior Court issued two "Informations" against Amanda, charging that she endangered the welfare of Kassidy Bortner for two specific periods, August 1, 2000 - November 8, 2000, and November 8-9, 2000.

The first "Information" stated,

that between approximately August 1, 2000 and November 8, 2000, at Rochester, NH, [Amanda Bortner] *did commit the crime of Endangering the Welfare of a Child, RSA 639:3 in that, Bortner knowingly endangered the welfare of her daughter Kassidy Bortner, age 21 months, by purposely violating a duty of care or protection which she owed to Kassidy. While Bortner and Kassidy lived with Chad Evans, Evans inflicted bodily injury to Kassidy. Evans bruised Kassidy's body and/or fractured her bones by repeatedly grabbing Kassidy by the face, throat, arms, and legs and by propelling Kassidy into the walls of the home, causing Kassidy to strike the walls. Knowing of Evans' abuse, Bortner violated her duty of care or protection to Kassidy by failing to seek proper medical treatment for Kassidy's injuries and by failing to take steps to protect Kassidy from Evans' abuse."*

The second "information" alleged that Amanda Bortner committed the crime of Endangering the Welfare of a Child,

between approximately November 8, 2000 and November 9, 2000,... in that, Bortner knowingly endangered the welfare of her daughter Kassidy Bortner, age 21 months, by purposely violating a duty of care or protection which she owed to Kassidy. Knowing that Kassidy had sustained severe facial bruising and was ill, Bortner violated her duty of care or protection to Kassidy by failing to seek proper medical treatment for Kassidy's injuries. On November 9, 2000, without taking any steps to seek medical treatment for Kassidy, Bortner dropped Kassidy off at the babysitter's residence. Kassidy died later that day of injuries inflicted before Bortner dropped Kassidy off at the babysitter's residence.

Wednesday, 7 November 2001

At 10:30 a.m. Detective Jeff Linscott and Sgt. James White interviewed Tracey Foley, age 31, at her place of employment in Wells, Maine. This was nearly a year after her first interview on November 13, 2000, which was summarized by Maine State Police Detective Jeff Smith. This interview was transcribed, which was unusual for Sgt White. Out of the 15 interviews he conducted in the case, only three were transcribed. Like this one, the other two were shared with other interviewers: with Det. Blodgett and Amanda on Nov. 16, 2000, and with Det. Linscott and Melissa Chick on Nov. 9, 2001. The rest of Sgt. White's interviews were summarized by Sgt. White.

Tracey described how she unexpectedly ran into Amanda when Tracey was picking up a child at day care at the Sanford YMCA on Friday, October 13, 2000, and Amanda was visiting her friend, Melissa Chick. Sgt. White asked what Amanda said about Chad and Tracey said that Amanda told her, "*How wonderful he was, yeah. Yup, how he had a house and a great job and, he was older and...*" Then Tracey, on her own initiative said, "*I had asked her about the bruises on Kassidy's face.... Kassidy had multiple bruises across the bridge of her nose and her cheek area...And Amanda told me, ... Kassidy fell off a trampoline. That Chad was with Kassidy and he had to catch her so she wouldn't fall and caught her by her face..*" (p. 3152)

The next night Tracey said she saw a bruise on Amanda's face, apparently for the first time, "*....I said something like, 'What the hell happened to you?... and she said, 'Oh, you should have seen me. I fell into a door. You know, klutz that I am'...Later on that night, she said, 'I can't believe that you actually think that I would be with someone that would hit me.*" Tracey offered Amanda a room in her own home if she wanted *"a place to stay, if you need to get away from him."* (p. 3153)

Later Tracey remembered what she thought were Amanda's exact words, "*I'm too much of a bitch to put up with that.*" (p. 3155) Then Tracey explicitly noted that, "*I didn't see the bruise on... Amanda's face that Friday night. I don't know if it was there or not. I didn't see it until Saturday. So I don't know when it happened....a big bruise... a good three, four inches round on the bottom of her jaw. Right side of her jaw.* " (p. 3156) What Linscott and White didn't clarify was that Amanda had not seen Chad since Friday morning, as she and Kassidy spent Friday night at Melissa Chick's home in Sanford. Thus, whatever the cause of the "*big bruise... a good three, four inches round*" on Amanda, it wasn't caused by Chad. If the same bruise was there on Friday afternoon when Tracey saw Amanda, in full daylight, then it wasn't as big as Tracey recalled.

Tracey told the officers of her concerns about Chad and Amanda, but no one in the interview mentioned that there had been a year of bad publicity about Chad, including from supposedly authoritative, "court documents" and "court records." After the weekend of October 14, which the officers never identified specifically, with a calendar, Tracey said that she had no contact with Amanda, as was the plan and expectation, until the following Sunday, which would have been the 22nd, but more likely the 29th. Tracey acknowledged that she didn't have a home phone and was using her neighbor's. Tracey said that when she did reach Amanda, there was this exchange,

I said, "What happened to you? I never heard from you. You were supposed to come over." I was worried. And very sarcastically, she said, "Well, what did you think? I was getting beat?" ... I was a little worried... she's like, "No, I just had a lotta work to do." Some computer survey thing she was doing... And then. I don't know. A week and a half later, Kassidy is dead. (p. 3157)

Tracey described how she learned about Kassidy's death,

I came to work Monday. And I had already spoken with a couple of my co-workers about Amanda. And my suspicions that she was being abused.... my co-worker... handed me the newspaper, that had a picture of Kassidy. "It said. "Toddler's death suspicious...If anything I expected to see Amanda's face on the newspaper...." (p. 3158)

Tracey's recollection was a classic illustration of the tricks of memory, because the first newspaper article about Kassidy which included a photo was the "Who is to Blame?" front page series of stories in Foster's Daily Democrat on the Saturday of her funeral, November 18th. The photo was the studio photo of Kassidy taken in December 1999. However, she did have the date correct, as Tracey then told the officers how she called Melissa Chick at the YMCA, and together they drove to the Kittery Police Dept. Melissa's and Tracey's first interviews were on Monday, November 13, 2000 at Kittery.

Then Tracey described Amanda's surprise arrival at her home on Thursday the 16th,

...Amanda walked in my, kitchen door. Cried and hugged me and said, "and you knew.... and I didn't listen," that sort of thing. And we both cried... she stayed with me that night and she told me bits and pieces of ... the relationship she had with Chad and his abuse of Kassidy... How she looked at Chad like her, her knight in shining armor, her savior... She told me about an incident that Chad threw Kassidy on the bed, in their bedroom. She didn't say why. She told me that Chad was jealous of Kassidy.... I think he was threatened by her [Kassidy] *which seems ridiculous but...* (p. 3158-59)

The idea would have seemed more ridiculous if Tracey had ever met Chad. Tracey said,

Amanda told me that he was jealous. And would want Kassidy to be quiet. And, like push her like up against the wall to get her to be quiet. .... like grab her by the shirt, by the clothes and push her... But again, we were both upset.... we were both crying... we didn't sit down and go in chronological order....But...there was no question in my mind that she was telling me that... Chad did this." (p. 3159)

Sgt. White asked, "*...did she say anything to you about any... of the ... specific bruising to either Kassidy or herself?*" and Tracey responded, "*Not that I can recall. No.*" (p. 3160)

Sgt. White asked general questions about Kassidy and Amanda, "*Did Amanda discipline Kassidy? Did you ever see her discipline Kassidy or? Did you ever see Kassidy misbehave and Amanda have to deal with it?*" and Tracey gave one of the most complete descriptions of the mother/daughter relationship presented in the case,

Amanda was wrapping Chad's birthday presents at my kitchen table. And, Kassidy went over to grab the wrapping paper. Amanda, "Kassidy, No. You don't need that," and took it, and set it down on the floor and off Kassidy went. Works for me. I mean that was great. You know, she's not even two and she listens pretty good. (p. 3162)

Detective Linscott asked if Tracey had ever met Chad, and she said, "*No. She said she would like for me to meet him. I wasn't really that interested... It may have happened. Sooner or later.*"

Tracey described how she last saw Amanda the Friday before Kassidy's funeral when Tracey flew to London for a vacation, and she hadn't had any contact with her since then, saying, "*And now I can understand why, if she's ... with Chad.*" (p. 3164)

Tracey said that Amanda left her car and some belongings and Kassidy's car seat at her house when Amanda went with Cathy Nuernberg's in San Antonio. When Amanda returned, and it would have been on December 19, 2000 when Sgt. White brought Amanda to Sanford to pick up her car, a neighbor of Tracey's let Amanda into her home to retrieve her belongings. Thus, Amanda came close to seeing Tracey, but it remains that Tracey had not seen Amanda in over a year.

Tracey said that when she told Melissa about the newspaper story, her reaction was similar, "*And she, like I was very surprised that it was Kassidy and not Amanda... The last thing I expected was Kassidy's face.*" (p. 3166)

Toward the end of the interview, the officers asked Tracey about what Amanda may have said to her about Kassidy's injuries, and the activity of the night before Kassidy's death, "*cuz,... as you know...Kassidy actually... died in Maine at.... a babysitter.*" Then Tracey recounted what she recalled that Amanda had told her, but she acknowledged that her recollection was of "*bits and pieces... Time sequence I'm not positive about...(Sigh) I need a flow chart (laughs)....*" (p. 3171) Actually, some flow charts or timelines would have helped a lot of people in this case to understand what happened to Kassidy.

At the end, Tracey talked about the night of Thursday, November 16, after she and Amanda had talked for about two hours.

I might have given her a Tylenol PM even, to help her sleep and, she slept in my daughter's room that night.... I felt really motherly, I remember thinking this when I was like tucking her in and we were both crying, and I was tucking her in to bed and I gave her a kiss on the forehead, and she started crying again. Saying, you know, "This is all I ever wanted for Kassidy. I wanted her to have her own room, and she'll never have it." ... It was awful.

After the interview tape recorder was shut off, Tracey recalled, according to a separate report from Sgt. White, "*A. Bortner telling her that Chad's wife, Tristan, had come to her and tried to warn her to stay away from Chad because he was trouble. A. Bortner told Foley that she thought Tristan was only trying to keep Chad for herself, so she disregarded it.*"

In a May 15, 2011 letter, Chad wrote about Tracey's observation of a bruise on Amanda on Saturday, October 14, but not on Friday, October 13,

You also provided some great insight about a bruise on Amanda's jawline from around Oct. 13th. The thing that is interesting is that Tracey didn't see it on Friday the 13th and then noticed it on Sat the 14th of Oct. I didn't see Amanda at all during this period, as she spent the 13th with Melissa Chick. It's too bad that nobody bothered explaining this to Tracey. Anyway, I guess when Tracey asked Amanda about this, Amanda indicated that I didn't do anything to her. ***She was too much of a bitch to put up with that from me****, and the bruise was likely caused when Amanda accidentally walked into a door.*

Friday, 9 November 2001

Sgt. Jim White and MSP Det. Jeff Linscott interviewed Melissa Chick, age 21, at 4:55 p.m. at her home in Springvale. She knew Amanda in school before dropping out in ninth grade, and resumed a friendship around January 2000. Melissa said Amanda had some frustrations with the burdens of raising a child alone,

Like she would just get frustrated with her. I never seen her hit her, never anything like that. But, um, she'd just get frustrated and be like, "Oh, Kassidy, why can't you let me put your sneakers on?"....I remember one time when we were over at Chad's house, she was getting frustrated because... she couldn't put her sneakers on.... she says, "Missy, you don't understand having a child is a lot of work and..." (p. 3183)

Melissa said that Kassidy seemed to become less rambunctious after she met Chad, and seemed to become afraid of men, but Melissa couldn't recall discussing the issue with Amanda.

I was more concerned about the bruises on her face. I just asked her... where's she getting them. And if she is sick, take her to the doctor's. Maybe she's anemic, or leukemia or bone marrow cancer or something...Being young, she was very petite, too, so I was thinking maybe she does fall down a lot, or. But my initiative [initial] *thought... when I had seen the bruises on her face is that I wanted to take a picture of her....and if something had... ever happened..., I wanted to have the picture...I remember the day that she slept*

over...the night she slept over my house that I was looking for my camera just to take a picture of her because I knew there was something going on..." (p. 3184-85)
The officers didn't ask for a date, and it was over a year since that overnight at Melissa's, but it was Friday, October 13, 2000 when Kassidy and Amanda stayed overnight at Melissa's together. Amanda recalls no other overnight when Kassidy stayed at Melissa's, alone. In Detective Jeff Smith's summary of his November 13, 2000 interview of Melissa, he made no mention of any overnight babysitting by Melissa.

It's unfortunate that Melissa was not able to find her camera, because the photograph she intended to take would have been the only photo taken of Kassidy which showed any bruises. If such a photograph had been date-stamped, that would have been better.

Melissa described the bruises,
...were all over her face. Like the bruises that were from before, they just didn't heal very quickly. That's why I thought she was maybe anemic because they just would stay there. She had bruises all over her face, on her nose, across her, one looked like something she got hit with something, and Amanda said that she got hit by...a plastic baseball bat. From the ear to... her chin... some of them were on her body and arms, and on her legs. I never had seen the ones on her like mid area, until I had given her a bath... on her stomach area, on her bottom. They weren't really big, but they were probably... were a half-dollar size.... her knees and stuff like, those were pretty good sizes, like she had fallen down or something." (p. 3185)

It seems unlikely that Melissa would have given Kassidy a bath on a night when Amanda was present and also spending the night. Melissa said that she urged Amanda to take Kassidy to a doctor, "*... there's something wrong with her. And she's like, 'I know... I wish that they'd go away,' she says, ' because I don't want someone thinking that I abuse my child.*' " (p. 3185)

Asked about Amanda's explanations, Melissa answered, "*...she just would always make an excuse...the trampoline, the swings. Stairs...carpeted stairs*." Amanda told Melissa the "trampoline story" "*when I questioned her about... like handprints marks on her face*." (p. 3186) Sgt. White asked about the date of those bruises and Melissa said, "*Three weeks before Halloween. She has spent the night with me. No, it was four weeks before Halloween*." (p. 3186)

Actually, it was Friday, October 13, or 18 days before Halloween. It was the weekend of Chad's birthday, and Melissa said,

Chad's parents were coming over... they were having dinner over there and she didn't want Chad's parents to see Kassidy because she had so many bruises on her face...that's when I started getting a little... suspicious about the whole thing.. I had went over to her house. That's when she started telling me more and more about how he was kind of abusive to her...that night she slept over... she had told me about when he'd headbutted her. He's grabbed her by the chin and headbutted her...held her against the wall... she had the bruise on her chin...three weeks before Halloween...she didn't tell me when... it was kind of an old bruise. It was on her chin, enough to have makeup covering it a little bit...on her chin area, her jaw...jawbone cheek area." (p. 3186-87)

About "*two days afterwards...during the week*" Melissa said she visited Amanda at Chad's, which would have been during the Oct. 16-20, Mon-Fri., week, "*...she told me to lie to Chad and say that I was looking for my ring the day that I had went over to Chad's.*" (p. 3188) The implication seemed to be that somehow Chad would not want Melissa there, and that she needed an excuse.

Melissa continued,
... she told me about a time-out chair that Kassidy had. That...the high chair was her time-out chair.... that whenever she would get too rambunctious.. Chad would reprimand her and Chad had grabbed her by the cheek, the cheeks and would yell at her, and she, Amanda would kinda rebel to Chad and say, "Don't yell at my child. It's my baby." And he would tell Amanda that she, she's young. She needs to learn, she's a very wild child....she's gonna walk over you forever... And he'd make her sit there in the ... high chair and cry. And he'd yell at her until she'd stop crying. (p. 3188)

This recollection, a year after Kassidy died, and after a year of explosive publicity, made Melissa the only person who ever said that the high chair at Chad's home was used as a time-out chair, and the only person who said that Chad would yell at Kassidy for screaming, until she stopped screaming.

Melissa said she met Chad two or three times. "*...he would come and just go. He's met me and then leave. I never really got to see much of him.... he'd be like, 'Oh, I met you once before haven't I?' And then he'd leave....*" (p. 3189)

Melissa said that she had overheard Chad and Amanda arguing and Chad complaining about Kassidy, and that "*he didn't know that I was listening over the speaker phone...*" (p. 3190) The only speaker phone in the house was in Chad's office. Another argument she said she overheard, via the speaker phone, was when Chad was urging Amanda to return to school, after he learned that she dropped out of high school. This argument allegedly continued for half an hour. Whatever was that argument, its logic was somehow warped, because Chad didn't learn until 2011 that Amanda had earned her G.E.D. in 2000, the same year that her former classmates graduated at Sanford High School.

Melissa said that Chad and Jeff would call Kassidy "*retarded*" and comment on how "*she'd fall all the time...she's just a numb child....*" *Then Amanda would say, 'Don't say that about my child.' She'd yell at him for it, but...*" (p. 3191)

Melissa related how she and Amanda and Kassidy were planning to go trick or treating on Halloween, but it didn't happen because Kassidy was sick. According to Melissa, Amanda said that Kassidy "*was falling into her Cheerios. She would pass out into her Cheerios. And that there was something wrong with her, and I was like, 'Well, you need to take her to the doctor's,' She's like, 'Well, I think she's gonna be okay.... she's fine now.*" (p. 3192) This may have been a reference to Kassidy's behavior after she came home from her three day/two night stay with Jeff and Jennifer on October 26-28, when Kassidy was dehydrated and hungry. That was the last conversation Melissa ever had with Amanda before Kassidy's death.

During the same "search for ring" pretext visit, around October 17, Melissa remembered that Chad made the statement that Kassidy was afraid of him, but Melissa said that she didn't ask Amanda about that statement after Chad left to go golfing. Melissa said that Kassidy had become reluctant to play with Chad, like they used to do, and Amanda had said that Chad had said, "*It makes me feel bad that she doesn't like me anymore.*" (p. 3194)

Sgt. White asked what Amanda had said to Melissa about Chad after Kassidy's death and Melissa said that Amanda said, "*he was very rough with her and that she was trying to cover up for that. She says, 'I always wanted them to have a good relationship.'... She just said that he, he grabbed her face. And that's probably where the bruises came from.*" (p. 3195)

Sgt. White said, "*Melissa, ... it sounds like you had pretty frequent contact there... for a pretty good period of time... Did you see bruises every time you saw Kassidy?*" Melissa responded, "*Every time, every time there were bruises. Yeah, she was covered. Her face was covered in them. That's why I thought she was sick.*" (p. 3195) However, the first time that Melissa saw Amanda since the previous spring of 2000 was the Friday, October 13 chance meeting at the Sanford YMCA and the last time she talked with Amanda was by phone on Halloween, October 31, which was an 18-day period.

Melissa recalled, "*I had given her a bath one night...Kassidy slept over her by herself. It was me and Kassidy. She had messed on my couch. She had taken her diaper off, and she was sitting on the couch, and I had to give her a bath. And that's when I noticed all the bruises all over her.... not all over, but she had a few on her abdomen and on her cheek area and her upper thighs.*" (p. 3195) However, Amanda has stated that Melissa never babysat Kassidy for an overnight, and Chad recalls no such occasion either. Melissa was not asked for any further details of that babysitting stint, such as the date, or even relative date, such as before this or after that. There were no details about bringing Kassidy or picking her up, or what Melissa might have known about Chad's and Amanda's activities on the night they needed such babysitting.

Jeff Linscott asked Melissa about bruises on Amanda, and she responded, "*All I know is the bruise she had on her, her jaw. And I remember she had a couple on her thighs, but I didn't really think too much of those.*" (p. 3196) Melissa said that on "*the night that Amanda slept over here,*" which was Friday, October 13, "*... we had gone over to Tracy's house... we had a few drinks over there... she just kinda spilled her beans a little bit to me that night and said that he had grabbed her by the face...That Chad did. That was the only thing she ever admitted to me [as] far as marks on Amanda.*" (p. 3196)

Sgt. White asked about Kassidy's fear of men and how that changed over time since March 2000, and Melissa describe one visit to Olympia Sports with her boyfriend and Kassidy where Kasssidy seemed to be more comfortable with smaller men, and less comfortable with larger men. He asked again about changes in Kassidy's behavior, she again responded about one time period, saying

...when she slept over my house, she didn't do anything. She stayed right on... she was sleeping almost the whole time on my chest. And she didn't do hardly anything and then the next day she was kind of a little bit better. I had brought out some toys and dolls for her. And she'd sit down and play with them. Well, she wouldn't really play with them. She'd just sit there and hold them and, watch TV... and look around the room.... I really didn't spend too much time with Kassidy alone except for that one time. (p. 3197)

Asked about any contact she might have had with Chad since Kassidy's death, Melissa said that after learning about Kassidy's death, (from Tracey, according to Tracey Foley in her interview), Melissa and Tracey came to Kittery to give their statements, which was Monday, November 13. Apparently, at that time, or in the afternoon on Thursday, the 16th when she came to the Kittery P.D. with Amanda for Amanda's fourth interview, "*one of the detectives told me to try to do everything possible to get her* [Amanda] *away from Chad, because she was still with Chad all the time.*" (p. 3198) After Amanda's interview, Melissa and Amanda went to Chad's and Amanda's home in Rochester, before going to the Fox Run Mall to "*pick up Kassidy's funeral clothes so that she could be buried in.*" Melissa said that Chad came home and they talked in the kitchen,

and I was sitting at the kitchen table... and Chad had sat up on the counter... and he was just talking...., saying how sad it was for her [Amanda] *to go through this and she's so young..."I would never hurt that baby. You don't think I'd hurt that baby, do you?" He was talking to me like he knew me forever...we had only... met a few times... he says, "I just wanna let you know, Missy, that of all the friends that she has, you're prob*[ably]*... you're the closest friend that she has and she really needs somebody right now"...he kept saying, "You don't think I'd do something like that," and I said, "I don't know what happened." I said, "I'm not here to blame anybody, but I'm just here for Amanda.*" (p. 3198)

They went to the mall in two separate cars, because afterwards, Melissa and Amanda drove to Buckfield with the clothes for Kassidy's body.

Melissa described Amanda's and Chad's interactions at the mall,

Amanda was kinda like.....we had talked to the detectives that day... And the detective had told her that she needed to get away from him, and she started believing that he had done it. So she was kinda bitter toward him in the...mall. Chad would walk behind us in the mall and Amanda would be like, "I just want him to get away from us...why can't he leave?" ...when were done shopping, he had paid for everything. And she's like, "I can pay for this," ... he's just insisted and he paid for everything.... when we were leaving, ... he started crying and Amanda and him had hugged...And then... he came up to me and hugged me... and he said, "I would never hurt that baby... I would never do anything to harm that baby and, you know that, right Missy?" ... I just was appalled by the whole thing and I didn't have much to say, except for, "I'm here for Amanda"... And I let go and walked off. (p. 3198-99)

Melissa captured well, the effect of the police influence on Amanda, while they were trying to remove Chad's influence on her.

White asked Melissa what Amanda had told her about her relationship with Chad, and she replied,

...she admitted to me... that he was very abusive to her. To Amanda. And that she started thinking that he probably had done it, too [to Kassidy]*...he probably did do this and if he*

did do this, then I shouldn't be with him...she's, "I need to do that for my baby. I can't be with him because if he did this, then I can't be with him".... She just said that he was very abusive and very controlling and that he probably did do it. (p. 3199)

Aside from Melissa's view of Amanda's relationship to Chad, Melissa's didn't appear to be painting a picture of Amanda standing by and watching Chad beat and harm Kassidy, which is the crime for which she was later convicted.

White asked, "*...did Amanda ever have any reservations about... leaving Kassidy either with Chad or with... her sister's boyfriend....?*" Earlier in the interview, Melissa had said that she knew Jennifer very well as she was closer in age to Jennifer than to Amanda, but had never met Jeff and did not know his name. Melissa responded,

She did say she wasn't sure she liked leaving Kassidy with her sister's boyfriend because he would pick on Kassidy and stuff.... she just said she didn't like leaving her there... after she had died she had told me... that they had nails on.... their floor... that were poking up, and that she'd always bring slippers with her...And that she [would] *rather leave Kassidy with Chad at nighttime than bring her over there.*" (p. 3200)

Amanda's stated preference to have Kassidy at home instead of staying with Jeff speaks volumes about her views about Chad and Kassidy. That was why she and Chad specifically decided that Chad should bring Kassidy home from Jeff's on the evening of November 8.

White asked, "*Did Amanda ever... talk about putting Kassidy in a day care?*" and Melissa replied,

Yes, she did.... Amanda would come visit me ...at the YMCA...at that time I knew that Amanda was having problems with Chad... she was kind of getting fed up with it... and that she really loved him and she didn't. She wanted to work it out, and I would try to get her an apartment down below me...she can take her [Kassidy] *to the day cares. I said, "YMCA's offer day care centers..." And she says, "Well... I just got a job at Old Navy," and that she wanted to keep her job and she said, "I wanna make enough money to get my apartment, if possible and... But I'll stay with Chad until then....I don't wanna put Kassidy in a day care. She has too many bruises on her face." So. That's when she had brought her to her sister's. And they babysat her.*

What Melissa didn't appear to know was that Jeff and/or Jennifer had babysat several times for Kassidy at Kittery before the October 13, 2000 sighting by Joshua, and then Melissa and Tracey of bruises on Kassidy. Thus, trying to keep Kassidy where she would not be seen by others was not the only reason for asking Jeff and Jennifer to help with babysitting. Also, Melissa didn't know about the 14 calls that Amanda made on Friday, November 2 and Monday, November 6 to potential day care providers.

Melissa said that she talked with Amanda about three times between Kassidy's funeral and Valentine's Day, February 14, 2001. Melissa knew that Amanda had gone to Texas after the funeral, but didn't remember the name of her friend, Cathy Nuernberg, and didn't know when Amanda had returned from Texas, until this interview. Melissa remembered the Valentine's Day call, which was a phone message, "*Missy, it's Amanda... I just wanna say Happy Valentine's Day.*" (p. 3202) Melissa said she had had no contact with Amanda since then. It appeared that Amanda did not keep in touch with her friends who were siding with the police and against her and Chad.

Monday, 12 November 2001

Assistant Attorneys General Will Delker and Simon Brown wrote a letter to Chad Evans's attorneys to advise that they had met with Amanda Bortner and that they found seven discrepancies between her statements to the police and what she told them about how she would testify at their November 5 meeting. Given the discrepancies, the State had declined to sign the immunity agreement which they had previously drafted. (A copy of that seven-discrepancies letter has not been yet located. It's noted here from the reference to it at page 68 in the transcript of the first day of Amanda Bortner's trial, November 18, 2002.)

In his cruiser, Sgt. White interviewed William Modlin, Jr., age 26, of Rochester who had begun working for McDonald's at the Rochester restaurant in 1997, when Jason Evans was the manager and Chad was the Area Supervisor. In September, 1999, he transferred to the Greenland McDonald's and left in December. The following May, he came back to McDonald's in Hampton and remained there until January 2001. All three restaurants were within Chad's supervision. Modlin returned to work in the Kittery McDonald's from June through August 2001. It was a Colley-McCoy restaurant, but not managed by Chad.

White reported in his four-page, single spaced, summary:

Modlin said he was at Evans' house in Rochester for parties, about five times or so. Modlin said they were McDonald's parties. Modlin said that Evans drank a lot and was easily set off (angered) when he was drunk.

Modlin told me he had observed Evans, Amanda and Kassidy, at the Hampton McDonald's, he believes two days before Kasssidy's death. Modlin was on break, sitting at a table in the dining area. Kassidy was crying and Evans was yelling at her to shut up, which caused her to cry more, which angered Evans more. Modlin said Amanda finally intervened and told Evans to calm down and she would take care of it. ...

He said she [Kassidy] *looked a little yellow and sickly. He saw bruises around one eye and jaw area. Modlin said he asked Evans about the bruises and asked if Kassidy was okay because she didn't look normal. Evans told Modlin that she was okay, and not to worry about it because Kassidy just falls a lot....Modlin said he didn't make a phone call because Evans was a powerful man in McDonald's. Everybody liked him, including Modlin, and Modlin didn't know if he would get fired or if Evans would hurt him physically.... he told me that when Evans is in those drunken rages, you don't mess with him.... he had seen Evans in drunken rages at various parties when he would get mad at someone or something and go off. Modlin said Evans would yell, scream, pick things up, and throw them, or sometimes run after the person and yell at them. Modlin said he never witnessed a physical assault. Modlin said he would back off and leave the party when these things happened.*

Modlin did describe two things he had witnessed between Evans and Tristan Evans' oldest son.... Modlin said at one party, Evans got angry and yelled at the oldest boy for misbehaving... Evans picked up a stick and almost hit the boy. Modlin described a second incident when he was at a party at Evans' house. The older boy was acting up. Evans picked the boy up by his belt buckle and tossed him across the room. Modlin believes they were in the basement. Modlin said Tristan came into the room and said words to the effect of, "What the hell's going on?" Evans said they were just having fun. Modlin said he wasn't sure if Evans was playing around or not.

Modlin said he observed Evans get mad and yell and swear at employees at work when they made mistakes. Evans would say, "Stupid fucking mistakes," according to Modlin.

Modlin said he was told on several occasions not to talk to the police about his observations.... Modlin said on one occasion, Tom Toomey [Toomire] *and Lisa Hanios* [Harnois] *told him not to say anything. Another time, he was called into the office, at Hampton, about one month after Kassidy's death, by Larry Lane and Bob (LNU)* [McDougall] *who is the Vice President of Operations. He was told by them not to talk to the police and to forget it ever happened....Modlin said Bob did most of the talking. Modlin was told, "Be careful what you say and do. If a police officer comes up and asks you, say you don't know anything, because it's none of your business." Modlin said the meeting lasted for ten to fifteen minutes. Modlin also said that sometime during his employment at the Kittery McDonald's, Larry Lane asked him, "Have you said anything to the cops? Please say you didn't."*

Modlin said before he was hired by the Kittery McDonald's, in June of 2001, he met with the Store Manager, Jay Hinton and his brother, Jeremy Hinton. Modlin said one of the conditions of his being hired back was not to say anything to the cops about Evans....

Modlin said Jeremy used to be his boss at the Hampton Beach McDonald's and the Greenland McDonalds' before Melissa (LNU) [Brundage]....

Modlin said Jeremy had called his parents' home a couple of times after he quit the Hampton McDonald's to check up on Modlin. Modlin said no one spoke with him, but he left messages on the answering machine with words to the effect of, "Just checking on you. Hope you're not saying anything about the case to the cops."...

He told me it was noted on a paycheck memo not to discuss the case with anyone, even fellow employees... Modlin said he believed there were two or three memos that referenced the case.

Modlin said when he was first hired by McDonald's, Tristan worked there and he had a crush on her, before he found out she was married to Chad Evans. Modlin said that Tristan told him several times that Evans scared her when he got angry. ..

I asked Modlin how many times he had seen Kassidy. He said he believes it was only the time he saw her at the Hampton McDonald's.... Modlin said he never really liked Amanda... He told me that a month or two before Kassidy died, he overheard a conversation she was having with someone at the Hampton McDonald's.... Amanda was telling someone, "The baby fell on her head the other day. Chad picked her up and shook her. I told him to stop. The baby woke up and I started laughing."

I asked Modlin... about Evans' and Amanda's relationship. Modlin said he saw anger and frustration on Evans' part.... Modlin explained there was yelling, distrust, and anger... Modlin said he never saw anything physical between Evans and Amanda.

I asked Modlin what spurred him to come forward. He told me he had a conversation with Jeff Marshall at BJ's Wholesale Club. Modlin knew Marshall from his doing the lawn care maintenance for McDonald's. Modlin brought up the fact to Marshall that McDonald's management had told employees not to speak with him [Marshall] if he came to McDonald's. Modlin said that they were told that Marshall was the one who actually killed Kassidy, not Evans. He was innocent. Modlin said that Marshall had lost his maintenance contracts with McDonald's because of that.... Modlin said that Marshall encouraged him to contact the police with what he knew... Marshall gave Modlin the phone number for the Kittery Police. Modlin said he called and spoke with a dispatcher. He was told that someone would get back to him, but no one ever did...

Modlin said he was afraid of McDonald's and their employment power... he is physically afraid of Evans and his friends.. "Maybe there's a little revenge for McDonald's for the way they treat people, but I want to do something good for someone who died. She could've had a good life."

Modlin told me he takes medication, Lithium, for bi-polar disorder and also an anti-psychotic medicine, Gendone. (p. 3174-77)

Chad wrote about Modlin in his February 18, 2010 letter.

Regarding William Modlin, it's interesting that the interview took place fully a year after Kassidy died, and that Jeff Marshall encouraged him to contact the police. You can ask Jeremy and Jason about him. It would seem he had all kinds of great information about me. The state would have used him if they could have, but he would have been shredded by my lawyers under cross-examination. Will was at my house one or two times. I had an end-of-summer party and invited everyone. My 40 year old administrative assistant, Melissa Allard, was there. Jeff was also there. My children were not. I don't believe he had ever seen me interact with my boys. Certainly he was never at my house with Tristan and the boys. I know McDougall and Larry Lane would never talk to him about not testifying. They would NEVER put McDonald's in that position. The claim about notes on the paychecks was ridiculous. During that year before my trial, I kept in touch with a lot of former colleagues, and no one ever said anything about corporate messages about me being sent with employee paychecks. The only thing that he said that was truthful was that Kassidy was at the downtown Hampton McDonald's a week or two prior to her death. I remember sitting there feeding her French Fries. The dining room there was the size of your average living room, i.e. tiny. Can you imagine me yelling at her there?? (See also, Chad's May 24, 2011 letter.)

In addition to Chad's response, it can be said that in any customer-oriented corporation, it's unusual for a manager to stay a manager long if s/he hosts parties at his own home and drinks too much and behaves badly. As he could have done when meeting with Chad's supervisor, Bob McDougall, Sgt. White could have sought Chad's personnel records at Colley-McCoy. Was there any indication of bad, belligerent, or bullying behavior? Chad's attorneys should have obtained those records, as well.

When Modlin told Sgt. White that he saw Amanda, Chad and Kassidy at the Hampton McDonald's two days before Kassidy died, that was an opportunity for more questions than he asked. What time of day was it? How long did they stay? Did they eat with anyone else? What did Kassidy eat? How was she dressed?

Modlin's recollection of Kassidy crying and Chad yelling at her at McDonald's doesn't ring true for a manager as image-conscious as Chad. He recalls that when Amanda would visit him at that restaurant and others, they would go to the parking lot at the end of the visit and Chad would not kiss Amanda as he thought it would appear unprofessional, as his employees were surely watching. Also, he didn't want to provoke a jealous response from Kassidy.

There was no indication that Sgt. White made any attempt to corroborate any of what William Modlin told him. White already knew that investigators had talked with Tristan, Jeremy, and Bob McDougall, and Modlin had mention all three of them. Perhaps White had already decided that Modlin's information was not valuable, but it was consistent with the prosecutors' case, and it should have been of interest. The police never asked Bob McDougall, or Colley-McCoy, if there were any memos, which Modlin had referenced, about Chad's case.

Tuesday, 13 November 2001

At 10:04, Sgt White interviewed Stanley Staley, age 26, of Wells, Maine, who "*occasionally works with Jeff Marshall.*" White reported:

Staley told me he had seen Kassidy five to six times over the span of a couple of months, when Marshall was babysitting her. When he first saw her, she wasn't bad at all. She talked a little. She was clean, and she seemed like a normal kid. Staley said he saw bruises on her legs and arms, but he thought they were pretty normal...

Staley told me that about three days before Kassidy's death, he and Marshall went to look at a job, accompanied by Kassidy. Staley said that Kassidy was filthy dirty. Her hair was matted. Her face was dirty, and her clothing looked like it had been worn for several days.... Staley also said he observed bruises on Kassidy's face. He said the bruises were around her neck and chin area and looked as though somebody had grabbed her with their finger and thumb. Staley said Kassidy was very withdrawn, unlike earlier times he had seen her. She didn't talk at all and Staley said it was like she wasn't acknowledging you, and he thought she might be a little slow mentally. (p. 3173)

A major difficulty with this report was the lack of time and date specificity. When WAS the first time that Staley saw Kassidy? Where was that? Who else was there? Where was that job that Jeff and Kassidy and Staley went to "*about three days before Kassidy's death?*" That would have been on Monday or Tuesday, November 6 and 7. None of the primary-Four was asked directly during their interviews about the babysitting arrangements for those days, and Jeff wasn't asked what he did with Kassidy during those two days. Where did Staley see Kasssidy the other four or five times? Why was it that Jeff didn't mention that activity in any of his interviews? Could the time that Staley saw Kassidy in an allegedly unkempt condition have been when Jeff and Jennifer had Kassidy for three days and two overnights on October 26-28?

At 12:10 p.m. Sgt. White interviewed Thomas McNeil, age 52, of York, Maine because he "*was alleged to have witnessed Kassidy fall from Jeff Marshall's truck.*" White wrote, in his one page summary:

McNeil told me he had seen Kassidy a total of four to five times. About four to five weeks before her death, McNeil held Kassidy. He said she seemed to be tentative and slow, and he thought maybe she was slightly retarded....she was slow to react with a smile when one talked to her.... she seemed slow to react in general. McNeil said he did not see any bruises on her at that time.

McNeil said he had never seen Kassidy walk, explaining that the times he saw her, she was either being carried by her mother, or Marshall. McNeil said he never heard Kassidy talk, either.

McNeil said he was present on the day Kassidy died, when the ambulance came to the house and the medics were working on Kassidy.

Regarding the fall from Marshall's truck, McNeil said he doesn't recall that at all.... Marshall said that Kassidy would get up in the night and sleepwalk.

White did not note that the reason McNeil was present at Rogers Road on November 9, was because he had been living in the apartment at 53 Rogers Road, on the northern side of the duplex in which Jeff and Jennifer lived. White wrote nothing about McNeil's employment and why he was at home when the EMT's and police arrived. White did not record any details of what McNeil saw on that tragic November day. As stated earlier in this book, he was interviewed by Foster's Daily Democrat for its November 10, 2000 article, but was not interviewed by the police until this interview by Sgt. White a year later.

Thursday, 15 November 2001

Jody Record of the Union Leader covered the story of Amanda being sent to jail, "Mom of beaten toddler jailed"

DOVER -- The mother of a toddler who was allegedly beaten to death last year was taken away in handcuffs yesterday after appearing in court on misdemeanor charges.

Bail for Amanda Bortner, 19, was set at $5,000 cash or surety by Judge Tina Nadeau in Strafford County Superior Court, where Bortner faced two charges of endangering the welfare of a child....

When asked if she thought the misdemeanor charges lodged against Bortner were an attempt to pressure the young mother into being a witness for the state, Wiberg said it was a possibility that had occurred to her.

"I don't know what the state's motive is in filing the charges so late but that is one I have considered," Wiberg said shortly after Bortner was taken from the Dover courthouse in handcuffs.

She was being held at the Strafford County House of Corrections. As of late yesterday afternoon she had not made bail....

"The terms were theirs. She agreed to everything. They didn't. She didn't change anything," Wiberg said, adding that she could not discuss the terms of the proposed agreement.

Brown had argued for $10,000 bail, contending that there was a risk that Bortner, whose last known address was in Keene, might flee. He also said she had been in contact with Evans, 29, almost constantly since Kassidy's death despite bail conditions for Evans that barred him from having any contact with her.

"The state learned they were having contact," Brown said. "From about Christmas 2000 on, they were living together in Keene. In the summer, they lived in a camper in Vermont on his grandmother's land. They took trips together. They went to Colebrook camping and to New York City to a Red Sox game. It's a chronic pattern of contact."

Brown also expressed concern that, if Bortner was released on personal recognizance, as her attorney suggested, she would flee the state.

Shortly after Kassidy's death, Bortner went to Texas where she stayed for about a month, Brown said. She made another trip to Texas before finally returning to the area. But, according to Brown, in telephone conversations with a victim's advocate at the attorney general's office, Bortner said she was still in Texas.

But telephone records obtained by the state showed the calls were made from Vermont, Brown said.

In addition to the $10,000 bail, Brown asked that Bortner not have contact with 14 people, including Evans, that she be prohibited from leaving the state, maintain a New Hampshire address and report to a probation officer in person at least once a week.

Nadeau granted all of the state's bail conditions except for the $10,000 cash-surety, which she called too high and reduced to $5,000. The judge cited "underlying circumstances" for her unwillingness to agree to personal recognizance.

After the bail was set, Bortner sat in a chair while Evans took her place at the defense table with his attorneys for a pretrial hearing. Evans was indicted about a month after Kassidy died on murder and assault charges.

Friday, 16 November 2001

Foster's Daily Democrat published two front page stories under the banner headline, "State says no deal for mom of slain toddler - Evans trial set to begin on Dec. 5" Dave Pearson wrote one of the two stories under the large headline, "Amanda Bortner will be facing charge of child endangerment"

DOVER - Amanda Bortner, the mother of 21-month-old Kassidy Bortner who was killed last November, spent the night in jail Thursday after the state withdrew an offer of immunity from prosecution. With an escort of Sheriff's deputies, Bortner, 19, of 293 Eindicott Road, Weirs Beach, left the Strafford County Superior Court in handcuffs after her arraignment...

The other story under the two line banner headline was by Dave Pearson and Teresa Robinson,

"Evans trial set to begin on Dec. 5

DOVER - More than a year following the death of 21-month-old Kassidy Bortner, the man accused of killing her is preparing to stand trial... Attorney Mark Sisti... said he wants to take the jury to view two sites involved in the case - a house on Rogers Road in Kittery, Maine, and Evans' one-time home on Milton Road. Senior Assistant Attorney General N. William Delker objected to a viewing at the Kittery home, saying he thought the visit would not add anything to the trial and was unnecessary.

"The request is appropriate," Nadeau said....

Delker's effort to block the jury's visit to the home where Kassidy died is a good example of how the legal game often thwarts the search for the truth. No reasonable person could doubt that seeing Jeff and Jennifer's home was a good idea. During the trial a detective would describe his search of the home. Jeff would describe Kassidy's last day in a bed in a room in that home. Detective Steve Hamel would describe his arrival at the home on November 9. Nonetheless, Delker sought to deprive the jury of that close look at Jeff's and Jennifer's home. For the lawyers, the trial game was not to present the truth to the jury, but for each side to present to the jury only what it felt would help its case, and to seek to prevent the jury from seeing, hearing or learning information favorable to the other side. In European courts, the judge often acts as the seeker of truth, but in the American/English system, the truth is expected to magically appear when the combatants are jousting.

Saturday, 17 November 2001

Approximately on this date, Amanda was released on bail upon posting the $5,000 bail with the assistance of members of her church. Sgt. White later interviewed Bail Commissioner Mike Mone on November 30 about the circumstances surrounding the posting of the bail. According to White, Mone said "*that two younger males arrived at the jail to bail Amanda.... only one of the males was allowed into the jail. The male gave five thousand dollars cash to Amanda.*" One of the men told Mone that Amanda would be living at 43 Mile Hill Road in Belmont, which White identified in his report as the address of Chad's sister, Nicole, and her husband Brandon. Mone did not record the name of either man.

To the police, Amanda's closeness to Chad's family was likely another sign of Chad's manipulation of Amanda. For Amanda, she was going to live with the people she loved and who shared her understanding of Chad and Kassidy and their relationship. Amanda's former friends and family supported the police and prosecutors' theories of the case and she did not feel comfortable with them.

Tuesday, 20 November 2001

Chad's attorneys retained the services of Dr. Michael Baden, a pathologist with a national reputation. On this day he wrote a letter to Mark Sisti stating his view of the case. He wrote,

A complete autopsy by the Maine Chief Medical Examiner, Dr. Margaret Greenwald, showed multiple old and recent bruises of the head, face and body, healing hemorrhages in the retinas in the back of the eyes, healing contusion of the frenulum in the mouth, multiple healing fractures of the extremities and a small subdural hemorrhage around the brain. I agree with Dr. Greenwald's assessment that Kassidy was a battered child and that the battering had occurred over a period of at least many weeks. It is further my opinion that although the fresher bruises to the head and abdomen, and the subdural hemorrhage, could have been inflicted 12 hours before death when Chad Evans was with the baby; they are also equally consistent with having been inflicted 20 hours or even five hours before death when Marshall, and not Evans, was with the child. I agree that the cause of death was multiple blunt force injuries inflicted by an adult.

It is my opinion, to a reasonable degree of medical certainty, based on the autopsy and microscopic findings, that the injuries to Kassidy were inflicted over a considerable period of time and could have been inflicted when the baby was in the exclusive care of either her mother, Mr. Marshall or Mr. Evans. It is further my opinion that, during this time, the injuries Kassidy suffered would have been apparent to any adult who changed her diaper, saw her face or heard her crying from pain caused by the fractures and that she would not have died when she did if any of these injuries had been reported to a physician, social services or to the police when first noticed.

This letter supported the defense attorneys' plan to try to persuade the jury that it was Jeff who inflicted the fatal blows on Kassidy. It's likely that Dr. Baden already knew their strategy, when he wrote that letter. Dr. Baden said nothing about the possibility that incremental accidents, beginning with a fall out of a truck could have been responsible, or partially responsible, for Kassidy's death. The primary reason for that omission was that he was not fully informed of those accidents and their timeline. Also, he did not have any photographs of Kassidy which had been taken during the past two months, and didn't know about the gathering at Chad's sister's home on Sunday, 5 November. Neither he, nor Chad's attorneys, knew about Kassidy's medical appointments on May 9, August 10 or September 11, 2000.

At 10:15 a.m. MSP Detective Rick LeClair and Sgt. White interviewed Mary Bullard at her home in Sanford, with the purpose "*to determine what contact Bullard had with Amanda and Kassidy Bortner and Chad Evans.*"

White wrote:

She had known A. Bortner since about the seventh or eighth grade. She also had contact with Kassidy when she was an infant....she did not know Chad Evans prior to Kassidy's death...Their friendship was rekindled when A. Bortner called Bullard following Kassidy's death.... she felt sorry for A. Bortner because her family was not supporting her...

...she believes it was sometime in July 2001 that she moved to Vermont and lived in a trailer in the woods with A. Bortner.... it was owned by Evans' brother, Jason...on family land, down the road from Evans' grandparents' farm.... She said the logging was being done by Evans' brother, Ronnie Evans... she and A. Bortner even helped by marking hemlocks, in the woods, for cutting.

Bullard said that Evans spent two to three overnights a week with A. Bortner at the trailer... one time Evans' son, Kyle Evans, came out and spent the night...there was also a tent set up for sleeping space.

Bullard said she last saw and spoke with A. Bortner in late July or sometime in August... shortly after A. Bortner was served with a subpoena for court.

Bullard...said that A. Bortner "doesn't know reality, and just wishes it had never happened."...

Bullard said she did know [about the no-contact order] *and stated rhetorically,* ***"When you love somebody so much, what choice do you have?"*** (p. 3212)
Mary Bullard played an important role in helping Chad understand Amanda. He wrote in his February 19, 2010 letter,

It was Mary Bullard, when we were camping all together in Vermont during the summer of 2001, that told me Amanda's real age. It was upsetting because. 1. It was another thing that Amanda deliberately lied to me about. 2. It made me feel like an even bigger "cradle robber." I was already charged at this point and kept thinking this will look great to a jury.

Until that conversation, Chad had chosen to ignore all the newspaper references to Amanda's age of 18, in 2000, and other references to Amanda's age. He preferred to believe Amanda's assurances that she was older: 19 or 20. In a loving relationship, it's unusual to ask a partner for a birth certificate. Chad's inability to acknowledge Amanda's age, despite the strong clues, was similar to the inability of others in this case to acknowledge facts which conflicted with their theory. Perhaps the best example was the October 31 interview of Travis by Det. Callaghan and Asst. Attorneys General Delker and Brown. They told Travis that his observation that Kassidy was appearing normal and even "chipper" in her bath on the evening of November 8, 2000, was "*impossible.*" They chose to disbelieve him, as did, apparently, Chad's jury.

Wednesday, 21 November 2001

At 2:00 p.m., Sgt. White interviewed by telephone, Shannon Gagne, a friend of Amanda. She was first interviewed by phone by MSP Det. Linscott on November 12, 2000. Sgt. White wrote, "*She said she hadn't seen A. Bortner since a couple of days after Kassidy's death,*" (p. 3213) which must have been after Shannon's Nov. 12, 2000 interview and before Amanda left for Texas on November 16.

White reported, "*...she remembers A. Bortner crying a lot and saying, 'I can't believe someone would do this to me.'*" (p. 3213) About Jeff and Jennifer, "*Gagne remembers A. Bortner telling her about J. Marshall and J. Conley, 'They're both so good with Kassidy. I know my sister would never do this to me. I know Jeff would never to do this to me.' Gagne also remembered A. Bortner telling her, prior to Kassidy's death, 'They're both wicked good with Kassidy. Kassidy loves going over there.'* "(p. 3213)

Monday, 26 November 2001

Judge Nadeau held a hearing to consider several of the Motions filed by both sides, or issues about potential testimony.

State Motion to compel Amanda Bortner to testify.

As the prosecution intended to call Amanda Bortner as a witness, and as her attorney, Patricia Wiberg, had indicated that she would decline to testify and assert her Constitutional rights against self-incrimination, Judge Nadeau conducted a "Richards hearing," which was required to determine the legitimate scope of such a Constitutional claim. As Amanda had already been charged by the State of New Hampshire for two counts of child endangerment, her testimony was possibly self-incriminating.

The next day, Judge Nadeau issued an order which required that Amanda testify, because the need for her testimony, as allegedly the only person who witnessed Chad's alleged abuse, outweighed the prejudice against the state's future case against her. However, that anything she said that tended to be self-incriminating could not be used against her in her own upcoming trial.

Jennifer Saunders headlined this story in Foster's Daily Democrat, "Bortner gets immunity; may testify in boyfriend's murder trial" She wrote that Senior Assistant Attorney General N. William Delker said, "*The judge granted immunity and she (Bortner) will be testifying,...Nothing she says during the trial can be used against her,...*" The article said about Amanda that "*Since her daughter's death, Bortner has lived in Texas and New Hampshire, with addresses in Keene, Weirs Beach and, most recently, Mile Hill Road in Belmont....*" As the prosecutors knew, even if Jennifer Saunders did not, that the Mile Hill Road address was the home of Chad's sister, Nicole. As with other indications of the contact between Amanda and Chad and his family, there were several ways to interpret this contact. The prosecutors saw the relationship as an attempt by Chad and his family to influence Amanda's testimony, and Chad and Amanda and his family saw it as helping a virtual member of the family who had lost her child and who was wrongly accused, like Chad, of criminal responsiblity for Kassidy's death. Further, she was being harassed by the very State which could have helped save her child, i.e. by responding in a timely way to Tristan's call to DCYF.

Josh Adams wrote in the Union Leader about the upcoming Amanda testimony, in the article, "Mom gets immunity to testify at trial in daughter's death". He quoted Judge Nadeau as saying in her ruling, "*In this case, the court finds Amanda Bortner's testimony is necessary to the public interest because . . . she was the only person to view the defendant's alleged abuse of Kassidy Bortner.*" Amanda's statements to the police in her interviews were critical to the prosecution's case against Chad, and if Chad was found guilty, then the case against Amanda herself was strengthened as the only witness to Chad's alleged crimes against Kassidy.

State Motion to Consolidate the Charges

Included in the charges against Chad Evans was the charge that on the evening of Wednesday, 8 November, he assaulted Amanda Bortner during an argument. The State argued that it was more efficient for a jury to hear the assault charge during this trial of Chad Evans as the witnesses would be the same as if the assault charge were tried separately. The defense argued that it would be prejudicial to tell the jury about the assault charge as it could imply a motive, or level of anger, for Chad to have assaulted Kassidy earlier in the evening. In 2003, the New Hampshire Supreme Court ruled in State v. Ramos that in such circumstances, the charges must be tried separately so as to avoid such prejudice. However, at the time of Chad's trial, the decision was left to the trial judge's discretion and Judge Nadeau decided to permit the charges to remain joined. Looking back in 2010, defense attorney, Alan Cronheim, believed that this decision nearly sealed the outcome of the trial.

State Motion to present at trial the information that Chad was in contact with Amanda in violation of his bail conditions.

The State argued that it had a right to inform the jury of related bad conduct by a defendant. The defense argued that Amanda's family had abandoned her and that she was essentially homeless. Also, Alan Cronheim acknowledged that he probably should have objected to the "no-contact" provision in the bail conditions, but he didn't do so at the time of granting bail. Further, if the jury learned that a court required that Chad Evans not have contact with Amanda Bortner, while not hearing about such no-contact orders for any of the other adults in the proceedings, it would be unfairly prejudicial to Evans. Judge Nadeau ruled the next day that possible prejudice against Chad, arising from acknowledging to the jury that he violated a court order, was outweighed by the potential importance of the evidence supporting that State's theory that Chad used such contacts to influence Amanda's testimony at trial.

Wrote Jennifer Saunders in her Foster's Daily Democrat article, "Judge says Evans' past to be excluded from trial", Judge Nadeau stated that shortly after Evans' release on bail in December, "*the defendant lived with Bortner and bought her groceries and other personal items... the defendant's contact, especially in light of the court's order, is relevant to prove the defendant's consciousness of guilt and to demonstrate Bortner's bias.*" However, Chad's referenced conduct was ambiguous, and it would just as well be interpreted as that of a man in love with the woman of his life who had lost her child and desperately needed help. During the period of the pending trial, there were no restrictions on the police and the State from contacting any of the potential witnesses and discussing with them their upcoming trial testimony.

State's Motion to preclude introduction of evidence of Jeff Marshall's criminal record.

The State argued that among the several arrest records for Jeff which reported in the Discovery documents, there was only one conviction, which was a guilty plea for the misdemeanor for criminal threatening in 1998. Further, that conviction should have no relevance to the issue of his truthfulness. Implicitly, the State was arguing that his conduct was not at issue.

However, the State did not mention, as it should have, Jeff Marshall's other less-than-innocent findings. In 1994, a York County District Court charge of "harassment" was "continued without a finding" and Marshall paid a fine of $100. In 1995, he pled guilty to violating a "Protection from Abuse" order and paid the Court $220, which payment included compensation to the victim. Also in 1995, a charge of "criminal threatening" was "dismissed without prejudice," but that was after Marshall paid $800 to the victim at the direction of the court.

The State's representation of the 1998 case was a serious understatement. There were two charges in the York District Court: of Violation of a Protection from Abuse order and Criminal Threatening, where he allegedly had stated to a man, *"I'm going to kill you."* These charges were taken to the York County Superior Court, where, in 1999, the Violation of Protective Order was dismissed in view of the guilty plea in the "Criminal Threatening" plea.

On October 12, 2000, about four weeks before Kassidy's death, Jeff appeared in Portsmouth District Court on the charges of "simple assault" and "criminal threatening," which arose from an altercation the previous April. The court continued the assault charge "without a finding," but Marshall was required to compensate the victim for his damaged glasses. The "criminal threatening" charge was "nol-prossed" which meant that Marshall admitted to the truth of the charges, but the state declined to prosecute further. Chad's attorneys were not aware of these charges against Jeff.

Judge Nadeau granted the State's Motion in an order the next day, but specifically advised the defense attorneys to bring the request to her again, if they wished, after hearing Jeff Marshall's direct testimony at the trial. The question at that time would be whether his criminal record would be allowed to impeach anything he said during his testimony. Thus, the jury would be hearing about Chad's alleged assault of Amanda on 8 November, but would not be hearing about Jeff's criminal threatening guilty plea in 1998, nor of the other charges which Judge Nadeau didn't know about, as discussed above. Also it would not hear about Chad's domestic violence against Tristan in 1999.

<u>State Motion to permit it to introduce a statement allegedly made by Amanda Bortner to her friend Tracey Foley on the evening of Chad Evans's arrest on November 16, 2000</u>.

The hearing of this motion required the testimony of Tracey Foley, so consideration was postponed for a day, and later postponed until the judge heard Tracey's prospective testimony, out of the jury's hearing, before deciding whether to permit that testimony to be heard by the jury. The statement, which was attributed to Amanda by Tracey during her November 7, 2001 interview with Det. Linscott and Sgt. White, was *"and you knew.... and I didn't listen,..."*

<u>State Motion regarding Amanda Bortner's statements, and whether they could be treated at trial as statements of a co-conspirator</u>.

The State argued that Chad Evans and Amanda Bortner conspired to hide the bruises and their criminal behavior from others. Brown alleged that the conspiracy began by August 1 and included the joint decision to keep Kassidy away from medical care and from day care. Neither the State nor the defense knew, apparently, of Amanda taking Kassidy to doctors on August 10 and September 11. It they didn't know, it was another casualty to the dual state nature of the investigation, where one hand did not fully advise the other of what it was doing.

The defense argued that whatever statements were made by Chad and Amanda were made independently, and without a conspiracy, and that Amanda had called at least five day care providers, which was a serious understatement of the actual number of 17, during the two days of calls, Friday, November 3, and Wednesday, November 8. (See Chart of Calls.) Neither Chad nor Amanda was charged with a crime of conspiracy, but it made a difference because, according to Brown, "*Now, under the Rules of Evidence, as a co-conspirator, Amanda Bortner's out-of-court statements made during the pendency of the criminal enterprise and in furtherance of the criminal object are admissible, as long as there is independent evidence of a conspiracy.*" (p. 40) Judge Nadeau decided the next day to deny the State's motion as there was little evidence of a conspiracy, but that the State could consider other ways to obtain the testimony, depending upon how the testimony of others proceeded at the trial.

State Motion to exclude evidence regarding Chad Evans's character with other children.

Even though it is intuitively obvious to citizens that one's treatment of one child is relevant, even if not dispositive, to how one treats other children, Brown argued that Chad's treatment of his son and stepson should not be presented to the jury. He argued that under the Rules of Evidence, they were not relevant. Alan Cronheim responded that "*it's not our intent... to introduce single events to show good character. It is, I think, the circumstance in the case that the flavor of Chad's parenting with Kyle is going to come out as a necessary element and a relevant element to Tristan's testimony*." (p. 57) This was an important issue, as there were many witnesses waiting to testify that Chad was a wonderful father. In the real world, away from the Rules of Evidence, wonderful fathers do not abuse other children, and at the very least, such conduct should be considered during a trial of charges of assault against and murder of a child.

That's precisely the question that Judge Nadeau asked Alan Cronheim, "*And how is it relevant to say because I was a good parent before, then I couldn't have committed this crime*?" (p. 58) and Alan Cronheim responded, "*I think it that he's experienced. He understands - - I mean, a possibility would be that he has experience with kids*." (p. 58) Except for Chad's case, I cannot think of a single instance where a wonderful father has been convicted of assaulting and murdering a child in the manner charged in this case. Excluding this information about Chad deprived his jury of a fair opportunity to evaluate the charges against him.

Alan Cronheim did state that Chad's "*parenting is a pertinent character trait. But beyond that, I think it's going to be part of the testimony a whole*." (p. 57) He also noted the irony of how "*as I'm standing here, that anything that's sort of negative about Chad seems relevant. Anything that seems to be helpful to broaden a perspective on who he is, doesn't seem to be relevant, according to the State*."

Judge Nadeau decided in her order, very carefully, as follows:

"*The defendant, however, will be permitted to introduce evidence regarding his experience with caring for children to explain why he could conclude that Kassidy was not well after being in the care of Jeff Marshall. In addition, the defendant may introduce evidence of others' observations of the defendant's parenting of Kassidy.*

Finally, the defendant will not be permitted to introduce general testimony about his parenting style of any other child. Whether or not the defendant abused or did not abuse other children is not relevant to this issue of the defendant's guilt regarding the treatment of Kassidy Bortner." (p. 4-5) This ruling ensured that the jury's understanding of Chad would be limited..

State Motion to exclude information about Kassidy's possible ingestion of Windex at Jeff Marshall's home.

At the hearing, the State withdrew the Motion, and the incident was discussed later at the trial.

Defendant's Motion to Delete "Surplusage" in the language of the indictments

Several of the charges in the indictment said that Kassidy was 20 months old and that Chad committed assault "*with the intention of taking advantage of her age and disability*." The defense argued that it wasn't necessary in the indictments to give Kassidy's age AND to state that she was taken "*advantage of*" was thought by the defense to tend to inflame the jury. Judge Nadeau agreed with the defense.

Other motions were dealt with by agreement or summarily. Regarding a defense motion to exclude certain evidence relating to Chad, the State agreed that it would not introduce evidence of Chad's relationship to Tristan, or of his previous criminal record, which was primarily his guilty plea after assaulting Tristan in 1999, unless the defense opened consideration of the issue through the presentation of its case. This meant, too, that there would be no evidence about Chad's counseling after the 1999 incident and no evidence about his treatment of employees at work. At the time, the defense felt that preventing the jury from learning about the domestic violence against Tristan was a victory, but it prevented the jury from learning about the whole Chad.

The State said it would not introduce affirmatively any evidence about Chad's sex life. In granting a request within the motion not to allow certain information related to Evans' sexual interests to be presented as evidence, Nadeau wrote of a "*high likelihood that the jury will draw unfavorable inferences about the defendant's character once they hear that he is a customer of an adult bookstore.*" The store to which Chad went on the afternoon of Wednesday, November 8, to correct a duplicate charge, was an adult bookstore. It was a curious assumption by the judge that people with active sex lives would be considered child-abuse-prone, or murder-prone.

Judge Nadeau said that the state could potentially present related information during the trial if "*the defendant opens the door to such evidence.*"

There was a question of whether an expert witness could be called by the State who would testify about whether Amanda's behavior fit the profile of "battered-woman syndrome." That expert witness was Scott Hampton, and none of the attorneys was likely aware at that time that Hampton led a court-ordered domestic violence classes which Chad was required to attend in 1999 after his guilty plea to the charge of domestic violence. The defense's position on such testimony was that it would wait until it heard Amanda's testimony, before deciding what position to take on such an offer of testimony by Scott Hampton.

Another issue was the possible calling of an inmate informant, Cory Merrill, to testify against Chad, and whether Merrill would need a new lawyer as his previous defense attorney was Judge Nadeau's husband. That decision was deferred until the State decided with certainty that it would call Merrill as a witness. Although inmate informants are notoriously unreliable, they were not sufficiently unreliable for Judge Nadeau to simply disallow his testimony.

Finally, the hearing dealt with the scheduling matters for deposition of the medical experts. Such scheduling depended, ironically, perhaps, on Mark Sisti's need to care for his children in the evening as his wife was out of state.

This pre-trial hearing ensured that when the jury decided Chad's fate, it would know far less about him than the readers of this book, his website and his letters.

Tuesday, 27 November 2001

Beginning at 9:00 a.m. the process of juror selection began with a pool of 100 jurors. By the end of the day, as Jennifer Saunders Foster's Daily Democrat story stated, "Four jurors picked in Evans murder trial." After hearing the names on the State's list and defense list of potential witnesses, with whom jurors were to have no personal knowledge, 44 jurors were excused and 55 remained for individual interviews. Of the eight potential jurors interviewed, four were selected. Josh Adams wrote in the Union Leader in the article, ""Jury selection begins in case of dead 21-month-old" that Judge Nadeau decided not to order that the jury be sequestered during the trial, but she cautioned the jurors, "*It's very important that you don't allow yourself to see any newspaper reports about this trial.*"

Wednesday, 28 November 2001

The day began with more interviews of jurors by the judge and attorneys and the four selected jurors brought the total to eight. The process would resume the following Monday.

In the afternoon, from the courthouse, Chad's attorneys conducted a deposition, by phone, of Dr. Margaret Greenwald, Medical Examiner for State of Maine

In response to Mark Sisti's question about suffocation as a cause of Kassidy's death, Dr. Greenwald, stated, "*... I don't think it's possible to completely rule out suffocation.*"

She said that the releasing of the fat emboli, which traveled to the lungs and killed Kassidy, could have been caused by blows to the head and the abdomen, and that the blows to the abdomen were likely caused within the last 8-12 hours. The injuries to the head she stated occurred "*somewhere in that 12-24 hour range.*" (p. 15) References to times were usually backwards from the time of Kassidy's death, which was approximately 12:30 p.m., although there was no unaminity regarding that time of death.

Dr. Greenwald identified several bone fractures:

1. The fracture to the left tibia, the leg bone between the knee and the ankle, appeared to have been first fractured 2-3 months previous, and a re-injury "*somewhere two to three day stage.*" (p. 16)
2. The fracture to the second metacarpal of the index finger, i.e. the first bone of the index/middle finger where the finger is connected to the rest of the hand, was estimated to be "*somewhere between one to three weeks."* (p. 16)
3. One fracture on one forearm, the ulna, "*somewhere three to six week time range.*" (p. 17)
4. Second fracture on one forearm, the ulna, "*somewhere three to six week time range.*" (p. 17)

The subdural injuries to the head could have been "*as little as an hour or a few hours, or it could be as long as twenty-four hours.*" (p. 17)

Dr. Greenwald was asked a possible cause of the abrasions on Kassidy's feet that Chad first observed approximately two days before Kassidy died. Dr. Greenwald responded, "*Something like a dog brush, that has, the metal bristles but they would not be very sharp, could cause something of this nature so you would have multiple superficial injuries on the bottom of the foot.*" (p. 18) Importantly, she noted that "*most of them are on the arch of the foot, rather than on the ball or the heel. And if she had stepped on something, more likely it would have been on the prominences of the foot."* Thus, the abrasions, "*do appear to be inflicted.*" (p. 19) Regarding their age, she said, "*they are abrasions. They do appear to be in the healing stage. So they are probably days old.*" (p. 19)

Dr. Greenwald identified hemorrhages to the retinas of both eyes which she believed were "*probably inflicted at or around the same time or using the same mechanism as caused the subdural injury to the brain.*" (p. 19) and "*with evidence of a potential older injury.*" (p. 20) This "same time" was in the 1-24 hour range.

The injury in the abdomen "*involved the mesentery and did extend to the small intestine, but not the large intestine.*" (p. 20) "*So it was hemorrhage or blunt injury affecting the outside of the intestine...approximately twelve hours, it could be anywhere from eight to eighteen hours.*" (p. 22)

Dr. Greenwald described an injury on the inside of Kassidy's lower lip which showed "*acute inflammation and acute hemorrhage, which means that there is blood in there with a reaction to the blood which puts it in the approximately 12-hour time range.*" (p. 26) Earlier she defined terms and "*an acute injury is one that primarily has hemorrhage, with no reaction or minimal reaction*" and "*recent refers to one that should have some reaction, so you've had some time interval that passed: eight to twelve hours or longer than that... An older injury would be one that would actually show fibrosis and in the longer stages of healing where you might be out to a few days or a few weeks.*" (p. 24-5) This was likely the bruise or sore that Chad saw on Wednesday evening, the 8th, and which led him to skip tooth brushing for Kassidy that night, as he didn't want her to exacerbate what appeared to him to be a mouth sore.

Dr. Greenwald agreed that the bruises which were photographed at the time of Kasssidy's death were "*fixed*" (p. 27) or stopped-in-time, and that "*sometimes it takes bruises an hour or so to, to show after someone inflicts them....*" (p. 29)

Mark Sisti asked Dr. Greenwald if 10:00 a.m. might have been closer to the time of death and she responded that if the EMT medics had found no "*pulse or respiration or electrocardiographic activity,*" and they didn't, then "*I can't rule out a ten o'clock time of death....*" (p. 29-30) She noted that death at that earlier time would likely have resulted in the early stages of rigor mortis by the time Kassidy's body arrived at the hospital, and she saw no reports of rigor mortis.

Dr. Greenwald said that she had discussed her autopsy findings with Dr. Michael Baden, the defense pathologist expert and they had only one apparent disagreement which was about the age of the injuries in the backs of the eyes. She called them, "*acute hemorrhages with evidence of prior injury*," and he called them, "*healing hemorrhages in the back of the eyes*." (p. 35)

At 5:00 p.m. Sgt. White and Assistant Attorneys General Will Delker and Simon Brown interviewed Eric Cook at the Strafford County Jail. Cook was the latest of a series of inmates who sought to tell the prosecutors about their acquaintance with Chad Evans. The first series of three such inmates (LaCroix, Merrill, and Gautreau) came after Chad's pre-bail jailing in November, 2000. Cook had written a letter to Delker on November 17, 2001 about his knowledge of Chad after the revocation of Chad's bail in August, 2001. Cook wrote,

I am in a cell right next to Mr. Evans. I know that you may get a lot of people saying they have information, but I really do. He admitted to me that he was at fault. He said he didn't mean to cause her death. I know that he did hit her with something. He wouldn't tell me what. He said the police didn't find it because his friend, Bruce, threw it in the river in Rochester. He also told me that Amanda knew and that he threatened her if she told. I know that he has been talking to Amanda through his parents and that they convinced her to change her story. He also told me that he was so sick when he found out that she died that he threw up at the Police Station.

As with other inmate informant offerings, there was some truth in this one, as Chad did vomit at the Kittery Police Station when told of Kassidy's death.

Sgt. White summarized the meeting with Cook, Delker and Simon in three pages:

I also explained to Cook that ...there was no consideration, either offered or implied, for the information he had. ... Cook said he understood and said, "This is not a great place to be for a rat."

Cook said he had attended school with Evans' ex-wife, Tristan.. Cook said he had also attended school with Joe Lincoln, the father of Tristan's oldest son....

Cook said he remembers Evans crying when he saw Kassidy's picture in the paper and saying, "I let her down." Cook said that Evans also said, "I failed her miserably," and cried often. Cook said he took it to apply to both Amanda and Kassidy when Evans said that.

...At some point between the execution of the first search warrant and the second search warrant, Bruce [Aube] *had gone to Evans' house and retrieved whatever the item was that Evans had used to hit Kassidy in the stomach and head. Bruce then threw the item in the river, downtown where the dam is....*

Evans also told Cook that Bruce is such a straight arrow, he was surprised that Bruce did it for him...

Cook recalled Evans telling him that his son was with him that night. Evans also told Cook that what the newspapers said about him throwing Kassidy into the walls wasn't what killed her. Evans said that was just what the police put together....

Evans told Cook that Amanda makes or breaks the case for him. He told Cook that's why she changed her story around from what it was in the beginning. Cook said Evans' parents helped convince her to do that as well.

Delker, Simon and White apparently thought enough of this story to request another interview with Bruce the following day. There is no record of any of White, Delker or Simon asking each other or Cook, whether it made sense for an accused person to ask another person, not otherwise involved, to help him discard a small object.

Thursday, 29 November 2001

Asst. Attorney General Simon Brown and Sgt White interviewed Bruce in a Rochester Police Dept. Conference Room. As Sgt. White summarized in his report, the purpose of the interview "*was to inquire about the information received from Eric Cook, regarding the throwing of a weapon into the river, by Aube*." Cook was an inmate informant who had met Chad in the Strafford County Jail Wrote White, "*Aube denied any knowledge about throwing any evidence in any river, or anywhere else*."

That was the end of that. As with LaCroix and Gautreau, the prosecutors chose to ignore Cook. They should have ignored Merrill as well, and when they presented him to testify, Judge Nadeau should have blocked his testimony due to its inherent unreliability.

Inmate informants are able to paint their pictures of other defendants by combining information from newspapers with what the fellow inmate, the object of their informing, tells them. For example, in Cook's case, it's very likely that in conversation Chad did refer to his friend Bruce, as a "*straight arrow*," so Cook's characterization was correct. He was also surely correct in his recollection of what Chad said about Kassidy, *"I let her down."* and *"I failed her miserably*." To the willing ears of police and prosecutors, such a statement was surely a sign of guilt, and it confirmed their impressions of Chad from his November 9 interrogation where they mistook his nervousness for guilt. Instead, his remorse was the same as any grieving person who lost a loved-one under circumstances where s/he thought, in hindsight, that more could have been done to prevent the tragedy. Those were not the words one would expect to hear from a child abuser and murderer.

Cook had also heard from Chad, or from the newspapers, that Amanda's understanding of the case, and what happened to Kassidy, was different from when she was interviewed by the police. The police and prosecutors wanted to hear that Amanda had changed from her true recollection to a false recollection under the influence of Chad and his family. They did not want to hear that she had moved from a false recollection under the influence of initial grief and police pressure to a true recollection after reconsidering in hindsight.

The final interview of Bruce was the last interview conducted for the primary case against Chad. During the 13 months of investigation of the death of Kassidy, the police had interviewed 46 people. Of those, 14 had been interviewed twice, and five three times, and one, Amanda, four times. Twenty of the 46 had met Kassidy and 17 of those had seen Kassidy with Chad. As has been mentioned in this chapter and the preceding chapter, there were many who were not interviewed, including the following:

- Amanda Allard. Daughter of Melissa, below, and friend of Chad.
- Melissa Allard. McDonald's employee, working for Chad. Saw him on November 8.
- Chad and Linda Dalessandri. Friends of Chad and Tristan. Day care for Brent and Kyle.
- Lisa DeVoe. Friend of Nicole and Brandon Harvey. Was at November 5, gathering.
- Susan Edgar. Director of Cross Road Kindergarten and School.
- Jessica Edmands. Girlfriend of Bruce and closest friend of Amanda in Rochester. She saw Amanda, Chad and Kassidy many times.
- Chet, Pam and Jason Evans. Father, mother and brother of Amanda.
- Gray Fitzgerald. Private counselor for Chad after court-required counseling concluded.
- George Glass, MD. Kassidy's pediatrician. Saw her on August 10, 2000.
- Gerri and Steve Harvey, Parents of Brandon Harvey. Were at Nov. 5 gathering.
- Diane Hoyt. Maine DHHS/Aspire Case Mgr. for Amanda. Saw her and Kassidy in Oct.
- Frank Marshall. Father of Jeff Marshall.
- Janis Marshall. Mother of Jeff Marshall
- Mary Paquette. Girlfriend of Chad, and lived at Milton Rd., before Chad met Tristan.
- Kevin Picknell. Lived at Chad's parents in summer of 2000. Saw Kassidy and Amanda.
- Jeff Porter. A friend of Jason Evans who was with Amanda and Kassidy at the October 2 court hearing in Portland.
- James Timoney, MD. Orthopedic surgeon. Saw Kassidy on September 11, 2000.
- Bruce and Michele Truell. Friends of Chad and Amanda.
- Tom and Dorothy Urrutia. Friends of Chad and Amanda, who had attended the three financial management classes with Amanda and Nicole. Also, Dorothy

(Dot) was a McDonald's employee in Rochester, who had seen Amanda and Kassidy come to that McDonald's several times.

- o Glen Varney and girlfriend, Deb. Friends of Chad and Amanda. Chad boat at his home.
- o Richard and Ruby Webber. Duplex neighbors of Jeff and Jennifer, until fall of 2000.

Of the above 28 people, 18 had met Kassidy and seen Kassidy with Chad at least once. Thus, there were approximately the same number of people interviewed by the police who had seen Kassidy and Chad together as were not interviewed. Of the total of those approximately 35 people known to me by name to have seen both Chad and Kassidy, only one had stated that s/he had seen Chad abusive to Kassidy, and that was Amanda. Further, Amanda's incriminating statements were only those made to the police during her interviews, which afterwards she had sought to recant or explain.

Friday, 30 November 2001

In its second editorial about the Kassidy/Chad/Amanda case, "EDITORIAL - Chad Evans and the rules of law", Foster's Daily Democrat seemed to want to distance itself from its own one-sided reporting to date.

The case of Chad Evans will soon go before a jury of 12 men and women.... Few of us cherish anything as much as we cherish our children. The death of a child - most especially allegations of the violent death of an infant at the hands of an adult - evokes the kind of anger seldom felt by any of us.

Let's keep something in mind, however. Chad Evans is not guilty of any crime until a jury says he is....

Friday, 30 November and Sunday, 2 December 2001

The deposition of Dr. Michael Baden, the defense's forensic pathologist, was taken by telephone by Asst. Attorney General Delker in two sessions on Friday, November30 and Sunday, December 2. Chad's attorneys participated.

Dr. Baden was the medical examiner for the New York State Police and for Dutchess County, New York. He estimated that he had done exams on over 1,000 children with accidental and intentional traumatic injuries, several hundred of which involved child abuse. (p. 1:8)

Will Delker asked if information gathered from caregivers and parents was used in evaluating whether "battered child syndrome" had occurred. Dr. Baden agreed, saying, *... in addition to the autopsy, there are a lot of other factors that the medical examiner or the examiner would want to know about. The circumstances, the statements made by various caregivers or persons who have knowledge about what was going on in the household.... to evaluate them to see which ones make sense and which ones don't.* (p. 1:11-12)

Other factors to consider included household conditions and conditions at birth and pediatric care. Will Delker asked if there were "*any common sort of explanations that you see from case to case that caregivers give for particular injuries?*" (p. 1:13) Dr. Baden answered,

There is always the story like "I just found the baby dead in the crib."... there is another aspect to it; that the call is usually delayed. That is, typically when a child is battered, the caregiver doesn't call it in right away. And so by the time the ambulance comes or that the baby is brought into the emergency room, there is often the story that, you know, I just fed the baby or just saw the baby a half an hour ago and now the baby is dead, and the signs of death, the texture change, the rigor mortis, the lividity, is inconsistent with the story that's told....and often another part of the pattern is if there are multiple children in the family, often there may be just one child that gets battered, not every child...But... when... a battered child [suffers a fracture], *very commonly the child is not brought for medical attention.* (p. 1:15-16)

Will Delker then addressed Dr. Baden's November 20 letter to Mark Sisti and asked about the extensive records that Dr. Baden had reviewed, and Dr. Baden mentioned his "*understanding was that the baby had been seen last by a pediatrician in July, around July. And I don't believe I have any of those prior records.*" (p. 1:20) Both the prosecutors and the defense lawyers should have reminded themselves to obtain those prior records, as the New Hampshire State Police had intended to do, according to Sgt. White's Investigative Plan. They would have learned about the May 9 and August 10, 2000 pediatrician appointments and the September 11, 2000 orthopedic surgeon appointment. If they had obtained information about Kassidy's conception, and the records of Kassidy's birth, they would have learned that she was born slightly prematurely, or 36.7 weeks after conception. The normal gestation period is 37-42 weeks.

Dr. Baden confirmed that he had reviewed the interviews of Chad, Jeff and Amanda, and Jeff's written statements. He wasn't sure if he had reviewed Jennifer's statement, and he confirmed that he did not talk with Chad. Also, he said that Mark Sisti had told him that "*he felt his client was being unjustly and unfairly accused.*" (p. 1:22.) He said that he had talked with Dr. Greenwald and that he told her that she had done a "*superb job as far as a medical examiner and did a much better investigation report than a great majority of battered child investigations done by other colleagues.*" (p. 1:23) Thus he was implicitly taking the position that Kassidy was a battered child. Later, he agreed explicitly, "*I agree with Dr. Greenwald, this was a battered child. The child was battered over a period of time and finally developed enough injuries that the baby died.*" (p. 2:13)

Dr. Baden estimated that Kassidy died before the EMT's arrived, after seeing "*a very pronounced lividity....*" (p. 1:27) Lividity is skin discoloration that occurs after death, and it increases during those first few hours. He continued, "*... it would have taken many hours for that lividity to develop.,*" before the police photographs were taken. It appears that he saw the photographs by Officer Hackett which were taken at York Hospital around 1:30-2:00, and was not referring to the photos taken of Kassidy on Jeff's porch around 1:00 p.m. Delker said he would like to continue the questioning on this point at a later time, when Dr. Baden had seen photographs taken of Kassidy on the porch. Dr. Baden explained further,

Usually in a child it takes at least two hours before you see a definite lividity. There might be inklings of it in an hour or hour and a half. In two hours one can usually see lividity, and then it gets more and more intense. Two hours is a very faint lividity. And after three, four, five hours, it becomes much more intense. And then after six, seven hours, it becomes fixed. If you press on it, it doesn't go away. In the first few hours, pressure will cause it to go away. (p. 1:28)

Given what he had seen and read, Dr. Baden estimated that Kassidy was "*dead essentially around... for perhaps an hour before the EMT's were called...*" (p. 1:30-31)

Regarding the age of injuries, generally, he said that the microscopic sections that were taken during the autopsy "*could be reflective of some of the injuries being within that three-hour time limit or so, or longer than that, or longer than that.*" (p. 1:33) In other words, some of the injuries could have occurred after Amanda left Kassidy with Jeff and Jen. Then Delker asked about specific injuries, and Dr. Baden said that the injuries to the abdomen could have occurred after Amanda left Jeff's, or before. He said that the *...microscopic slides are helpful but not specific enough in telling when an injury occurred.... The body starts sending live cells, polymorphonuclear cells, polys to the injured site, and then at a later time macrophages, mononuclear cells. Scavengers come in. Various proteins and fibrin comes in, swelling, edema. But this varies from tissue to tissue and from person to person.* (p. 1:36)

Later he said that

Part of our problem with intensity is it depends how many sections are taken, because in the same lesion in the body one can get an area that looks two hours old and another area might be 20 hours old because the whole injury doesn't respond in the same time." (p. 1:37)

Delker then explored the issue of how Kassidy was reacting, or not reacting, to these injuries, and specifically to her subdural, or subdural hemorrhaging. Dr. Baden explained,

Usually there is a subdural that is not a very big subdural. So sometimes there may be no symtoms from a small subdural like this, and sometimes it will irritate the child and make the child more irritable, crying.

And if there were pressure -- as I recall, there was no evidence of pressure on the brain. You see, the subdural isn't what causes the problem. It's the pressing on the brain.

But part of the problem, just so you know where I'm coming from, Mr. Delker, is Kassidy didn't appear to react normally as other children do, or if she did react, nobody noticed it, because remember, when you are talking about the subdural hemorrhage or the fractures of the extremities or the intestinal injuries, some of which clearly were days before or weeks before, most babies yell and scream until a doctor saw the baby.

Whatever happened here, none of those injuries triggered off an examination by a physician. So we can talk about normally what you would expect, but if indeed Kassidy reacted as I would expect from the tibia fracture or from the ulnar fracture, she would have been seen by a doctor, if she had been making such a fuss and the caregiver would have seen the injuries, that a physician would have been called. So that ***this is not the normal situation****."* (p. 1:40-41)

On Sunday, December 2, Dr. Baden resumed his deposition by phone with Delker and Cronheim. Dr. Baden stated that his fee for Chad's case was a retainer of $4,000 and then $4-5,000 per day of testimony, plus expenses. It was lower that his normal fee because of his longstanding relationship with Mark Sisti.

Asked about the internal abdominal injuries, Dr. Baden said that the microscopic slides taken from Kassidy's body showed that the injuries likely occurred the previous afternoon/early evening between 4 p.m. and 8 p.m., thus including the times Kassidy was exclusively with Jeff or Chad. He said it was noteworthy that Chad called Jeff with his observations of Kassidy's aberrant behavior during that time, and that Jeff has acknowledged the call. He said,

I think what's more specific is that apparently Chad makes a call to Marshall around -- after he picks up the baby and says -- allegedly to say what's -- you know, there is something wrong with the baby, what happened. That is very persuasive to me that something happened to the baby before Chad picked her up.... In my experience it's hard to make stories up that fit the pathology....But, as I was advised, instead of eating a full meal, the baby ate half a banana or something which was abnormal, that would speak to the injury already having been there." (p. 2:8-11)

There were also external abdominal injuries which were visible in photographs taken of Kassidy's body on the 9th, but for which there were no microscopic sections taken. As both Amanda and Travis said they saw no evidence of such bruising on the evening of November 8, or on the morning of 9 November,

that would speak to the baby having suffered those injuries after being dropped off at 8 a.m.... that wouldn't account for the injury to the intestines the day before but could account for additional injury after to the abdomen and to the additional hemorrhage in the -- the fresher hemorrhage in the mesentery." (p. 2:12)

In response to Will Delker's followup question, Dr. Baden noted that "*one can get internal injuries without external injuries, especially if someone is wearing clothing.*" (p. 2:12) As for the final cause of death, given the existence of old and new injuries, Dr. Baden said,

That some of the injuries would have occurred -- specifically facial and abdominal injuries would have occurred after the mother dropped the baby off at 8 a.m. and would have been the straw that broke the camel's back; that is, would have been the final cause of death in a child who had had repeated injuries over a period of time previously." (p. 2:14)

Asked about the age of the injuries to the optic nerve and retina of the eyes, Dr. Baden said that they were about the same age as of the subdural hemorrhage, about 3-4 days, or longer. (p. 2:18) As for the subdural itself and its effects on Kassidy's behavior,

It's not a very big subdural... it need not produce much more pain from the injury to the skin because the way subdurals cause symptoms is by pressing on the brain. And it's not clear here that there was much pressure on the brain.....So it can cause lethargy. It can

cause, you know, coma. It can cause the baby going to sleep, you know, being sleepy all the time. It can cause a lot of crying. But it needn't -- it depends how big it is.... But you can also get lethargy from lots of other things including abdominal injuries." (p. 2:21-22) Delker sought to establish the aging of injuries to Kassidy's skin and scalp, based on the microscopic sections taken at autopsy. Of the injuries to her mid-back, Dr. Baden said that because there is "*hemorrhage with no inflammation*" they "*would indicate very fresh. It could be minutes up until two hours, because usually after two hours, you get some kind of inflammation.*" (p. 2:23) However, that understanding was also subject to his earlier observation that if other sections of the same injury had been taken, they might show that the injury was older.

He was asked about the ages of specific injuires or areas:

- right posterior occipital area: older, more than 12 hours, "*twenty-four hours, forty-eight hours... it could even be four or five days old...*" (p. 2:25)
- superior occipital (the top of the head): "*...24 hours or more, also. The* [presence of] *iron would make it 36 hours.*" (p. 2:25)
- left buttock: Eight to twelve. "*...we couldn't rule out 13 and we couldn't rule out 6.*" (p. 2:26)
- right shoulder: "*looks like one of those 24-hour kind of things... or a little bit more than that.*" (p. 2:27-28)
- chin: "*older than 24 hours.... 24 hours, 36 hours, 48 hours.*" (p. 2:30-31) Dr. Baden noted that the closer to the skin surface is an injury, the sooner it would be visible. Thus, an injury to the chin would be more visible than an injury to the buttocks or the intestine.
- salivary glands: "*... a number of days older.*" (p. 2:32)
- frenulum: "*...just a few hours before death.*" (p. 2:33)
- lower lip, above frenulum: "*... could be 10 hours, 12 hours, 14 hours.*" (p. 2:34)
- mucosa (lining) of the left cheek: "*... less than two or three hours since there is no reaction.*" (p. 2:34)
- mid-forehead skin: "*... more than two or three days....*" (p. 2:35)
- right superior subgaleal: "*This has been around for some time, many days, or even weeks.*" (p. 2:37) [Medical terminology, like that of other professions can be obscure. The only reference on the Internet/Google in 2011 to "*superior subgaleal*" was to Kassidy's autopsy at Chad's website.]
- left superior subgaleal: "*...it's not as old as the right one...it could be hours or days old. Not as old as the right, as the one above it.*" (p. 2:37)
- right supraorbital (above right eyebrow): "*There is an area there of old injury that could be weeks and months old. That's the golden brown pigment. There's no reaction around it. Then there is another area with fresh hemorrhage. That could be a day or two old.*" (p. 2:37)

Then the deposition moved to the X-Rays which Dr. Baden received recently and he quickly noted, in the absence of a current question,

... but the x-rays don't show the fractures. They don't show fractures... they also have a report in there from the hospital. The hospital only -- when they took those x-rays, they said there were no fracture[s]. *I agree with that. There are no fractures.*" (p. 2:38)

He said that what Dr. Greenwald saw was

bruising on the bone and not real fractures of the bone.... just thickenings of the outside of the bones....I agree with -- that there is some repair change of some injury in the outside of the bone which could be from twisting the bone, twisting it or a fall or a kick or something. The bone at some point was stepped on or something. There wasn't a fracture in the traditional sense of a break that needed setting..." (p. 2:38-40)

Delker asked about the observation that "*Kassidy had difficulty walking in the days before her death...*" (p. 2:40) and Dr. Baden responded,

The only thing with walking is the tibia -- and that tibia [repair] *is the oldest. The baby would have had that for weeks or months.... if the baby was having difficulty walking, it was not from the bone. It was from the buttocks or arms or whatever or the subdural hemorrhage or other injuries.*" (p. 2:40-41)

Dr. Baden was asked about the reported characteristic of Kassidy's falling, which was that she didn't put her arms and hands out in front of her to block the fall. He said that if she had been blocking falls with her arms and hands and then stopped that response, then the new failure might be a result of injuries to her hands and reluctance to cause them pain. However, he didn't know that Chad's parents had observed that behavior during Kassidy's two visits to Keene.

Delker asked if any of the injuries could have been caused by a baseball, and Dr. Baden said that he had asked Chad's attorneys if that "*roundish area on the face*" had been "*swabbed for DNA because there was a concern that it was a bite mark*" but he had seen no DNA results for a possible bite mark. There was no further discussion during the entire trial of such a DNA test, or of any other DNA test for Kassidy. Regarding the ball, he said, "*a round ball could cause some injury that might be confused with a bite mark. But I can't distinguish the different kinds of blunt force on this child.*" (p. 2:44)

At the end of the deposition, Dr. Baden was asked about the "ultimate cause of death." He responded:

I think the baby died of a... multitude of injuries over a period of time which included the bruises on the body, the subdural hemorrhage, none of which caused death when they occurred, but that the final injuries, the freshest injuries do seem to be the abdominal injuries to the abdomen and mesentery. And I think that those final injuries consistent with something that happened the day before, say Wednesday afternoon or evening time together with whatever additional injuries occurred after the baby came to Marshall, bruises and perhaps additional mesentery, intraabdominal injuries, would have in and of themselves been probably the reason why the baby died when the baby did die. But that's in a constellation of all the other injuries having partially diminished her ability to withstand those injuries." (p. 2:43-44)

Delker asked about Dr. Greenwald's opinion that Kassidy's death was caused by "*a combination of the head trauma and fat emboli.*" (p. 2: 44) Dr. Baden acknowledged that he hadn't seen that conclusion before, and would review it more carefully before trial; but that he was skeptical because fat emboli would have been triggered by bone fractures and he doubted that they occurred. He said,

Yeah, it could be contributing. Usually, fat emboli occur pretty quickly when a bone is fractured. And the only place here where it gets into the fat is the finger bone.... because the fat isn't entered into the marrow on the ulna and tibia.

To the extent that the fat is contributory to the cause of death, it would be very shortly before death. Usually, death occurs within an hour, two, three hours if it's due to fat emboli.... So the fat emboli would speak to a more rapid cause of death and a fresher fracture of the bone. And in this instance, the bone being the hand bone, usually the phalanx, the phalanax doesn't have enough fat to cause a lot of problems. The fat that causes problems usually comes from the tibia or the femur. The femur is the thighbone.

The tibia is fractured, but in looking at the x-rays, one thing that struck me is that ... the fracture doesn't get into the bone marrow cavity, and it's an old fracture. What we are talking about here is fresh fat.... The fat was too little to be of much consequence. However, I will have to look at that more carefully. And I agree with Dr. Greenwald that it might have been a contributory factor. But to the extent that it's a contributory factor, it's a fresh contributory factor, less than a couple of hours old. (p. 2:45-46)

His statement that the "tibia is fractured," seemed to contradict his earlier statement that there were no fractures of Kassidy's bones.

Finally, Delker asked about the possibility of Kassidy being suffocated to death, and Dr. Baden said it was possible, but it was impossible to know, without other support for the theory, such as an eyewitness.

Death for Kassidy in November was never certain. Dr. Baden concluded,

There are many babies that have all kinds of injuries to the body who are not dead; that she had survived all the injuries until the last 24 hours. And it looks to me more like the freshest injuries are the intestinal injuries that would have led to her death. But even then, babies can get intestinal injuries like this and not die. (p. 2:49)

Sunday, 2 December 2001

Two days before the beginning of the trial, Foster's Daily Democrat ran on page 2 a major article, "Child Abuse: DCYF intervention policy aired - Infant death, abuse cases: The facts behind three investigations" The first of the three cases with the "facts" was about Kassidy, and the article essentially presented the police and prosecution's case, with the usual reliance upon "Dr. Greenwald," and "court documents." The bias was clear. The article referred to Amanda's comment about Kassidy's appearance as "derogatory," which wasn't a word from the "court documents." In any other context, if a parent brought a child for babysitting and told the babysitters, one of whom was a sister of the parent that the child looked terrible, that would be a reasonable thing to say. In Amanda's case, there were two differences. First, she said that Kassidy "*looked like shit*," which is a frowned-upon term for women to use, and frowned-upon for parents as a term to describe their children. For others, there is little difference between "terrible" and "like shit." Second, and more importantly, the child died four and half hours later, and hindsight can be terribly correct and judgmental.

The article also said, "*Bortner also stated in affidavits that Evans fractured Kassidy's leg and arm on two separate occasions*." This was a new allegation, and readers would have been shocked and very angry at such monsters who cause fractures to children. However, Amanda never completed an affidavit in the case and during her interviews, she didn't say that. Neither she nor Chad were aware that Kassidy had anything remotely akin to a broken arm or leg. In fact, no one said anything about fractures until after Kassidy's death, and it wasn't until Dr. Greenwald's autopsy that the idea of a fracture arose, and it would be disputed at Chad's trial.

Monday, 3 December 2001

The morning's Portsmouth Herald carried an Associated Press story by J.M. Hirsch, "Trial set to begin for man charged in beating death of baby" which began,

The trial of a former Rochester man accused in the beating death of a 21-month-old girl is expected to focus on the testimony of the child's mother the man's live-in girlfriend before and after the child's death.... Police say she was beaten, choked and thrown against walls repeatedly for at least three months before she died.

Now the time period for alleged abuse was "*for at least three months,*" which meant a starting time of approximately August 9.

Even though the media had interviewed Jacqueline Conley and she had described Kassidy's stay with her in late September, bruise-free. Even though the media now had a photograph of Kassidy from that period, October 1, the articles continued to rely upon the "court documents," i.e. Sgt. White's affidavits, which were written within days of Kassidy's death. The information which reporters had learned, after those affidavits, should have given the media, if not the police, pause. The "three months" allegation was simply not possible. The Maine Chief Medical Examiner had access to Kassidy's medical records, including her September 11 visit to an orthopedic surgeon, and that should have given the police pause. However, it's not yet known when, or if, the Maine police learned about those medical visits, and it seems likely that the New Hampshire State Police and the New Hampshire Attorney General's office never knew about them.

The rest of the 15 jurors were selected on this day.

CHAPTER 7: TRIAL OF CHAD EVANS - THE EVIDENCE FOR THE JURY - 4 DECEMBER TO 17 DECEMBER 2001

"I think we are entitled to present this evidence to give the jury a complete picture of the situation." - Simon Brown

"You can't accuse someone of something if you don't know." - Melissa Chick

"I think that Kassidy Bortner died as a result of multiple injuries over a period of time with the final injuries occurring shortly before she was found dead." - Dr. Michael Baden

U.S. Supreme Court Justice Thomas Clark wrote that "*the solemn purpose of endeavoring to ascertain the truth... is the sine qua non of a fair trial. Over the centuries, Anglo-American courts have devised careful safeguards by rule and otherwise to protect and facilitate the performance of this high function.*" These are high sounding words from the U.S. Supreme Court in 1965, but since then the country has learned what many defendants and defense lawyers have known for a long time, which is that the truth often suffers in a criminal trial. Since 1989, over 272 people have been exonerated by DNA evidence and in every one of those trials resulting in wrongful convictions, the truth was either unavailable or distorted.

The jury at Chad Evans's trial heard several variations of truth, most of it through a prism etched with the word, "guilty." It was what the jurors didn't hear that was most important in the wrongful conviction of Chad Evans.

Although the trial officially began on Tuesday, 4 December 2001, there were many activities beforehand, and described in earlier chapters, which helped determine the outcome.

Chad's trial in the media can be said to have ended at the time his trial in the courtroom began. For the period of the trial, through the verdict on December 21. this chapter will present internet links to the applicable media articles, for further reading, but the trial in the courtroom was now center stage.

MEDIA: 1. "Trial set to begin for man charged in beating death of baby"
2. "Evans trial starts today"

Tuesday, 4 December 2001

All 15 of the jurors selected of the previous several days would hear the evidence together, and after the close of the trial evidence and closing statements, Judge Nadeau would randomly select three to be alternates. The remaining 12 would then decide Chad's guilt or innocence, and the three alternates would then be available in case one or more of the 12 jurors left the jury.

On this first morning of the evidence phase of the trial, the jurors, judge, attorneys, prosecutors and Chad went on a site tour of the homes of Jeff and Chad. Because of the revocation of Chad's bail and his jailing on August 20, every time the jury saw him, he was guarded by uniformed officers, sometimes in handcuffs, instead of seeing him as a defendant walking as a free man into his own trial. Even if, intellectually, a juror can acknowledge the principle of "innocence until proven guilty," the jailing of a defendant prior to trial is an "actions speak louder than words" statement of the strength of the case against Chad Evans. Statistically, defendants who are in jail at the time of their trials are more likely to be found guilty than those who are free on bail.

First, the trial participants went to Jeff's former home at 51 Rogers Road in Kittery, a single floor, one-bedroom apartment. It was vacant, as Jeff and Jennifer had moved to a different home on Rogers Road early in October. The apartment was being renovated by landlord Will Peirce. One juror heard the explanations of the layout and wondered what the unexplained door next to him in the kitchen was for. He opened it and it led to a basement. He turned on the light and walked a short distance down the stairs, and told other jurors about the existence of a basement. He was advised by the judge with other jurors not to discuss what he had seen. Apparently independently, Chad saw a blanket covering the basement door and opened it. With him was Mark Sisti who also looked down into the basement. This was significant because the Maine State Police search of Jeff's apartment missed the existence of the basement entirely, despite that door and the presence of a bulkhead door from the outside. There were only a few internal doors on hinges in the small, one-story, apartment of about 600 square feet.

On the way to Chad's home, the jury and the entourage, including the media, were driven to the Cross Road Kindergarten and School where they were told that Chad's son attended. The apparent point of such a drive-by was the prosecution's view that Chad treated his own son better than he treated Kassidy. The jury was probably not told that Chad's stepson also went to that school, and that Chad paid for all of his tuition for several years, until his imprisonment. During the trial, the jury was never told that around November 1, Chad asked the director of the Cross Road Kindergarten and School, Susan Edgar about admitting Kassidy, but was advised that she could not be accepted until she was toilet trained. The jury finished its site visits at Chad's home, and then returned to the Strafford County Courthouse in Dover.

The trial resumed at the courthouse with an opening statement by Assistant Attorney General Will Delker for the State of New Hampshire. He made many allegations about Chad, Amanda and Jeff during the fall of 2000, which would be presented further by witnesses and documents. Throughout the trial, the jury would be faced with the difficulty of sorting out what happened to Kassidy and when, and the confusion began with Delker's opening. He stated that:

- "*She was learning her ABC's..... but all that changed when the defendant came into her life.*" (p. 1) The jury would never learn that Chad met Kassidy on June 9, 2000, five months before her death, and that he read to her on the night before she died, and on many prior nights.

- "*Now, about the beginning of last summer, the defendant, who was 28 years old at the time, began dating Kassidy's mother.*" (p. 1). The jury would never learn that the first date between Chad and Amanda, which was arranged by Jennifer and Jeff, was in late Spring, on Friday, June 2, 2000.

- "*... towards the end of the summer, Amanda and Kassidy actually moved in with the defendant.*" (p. 2) The jury would never learn that by the **first** full day of summer, June 22, 2000, Amanda and Kassidy were living with Chad almost full-time.

- "...Amanda's *friends and family noticed that Kassidy's behavior changed as well.... Toward the end of her life, Kassidy was quiet and withdrawn.*" (p. 5) The jury did not know that these changes accelerated in late October 2000.

- "And *so, in the late--late October of last year, Amanda asked Jeff Marshall to babysit.*" (p. 5) This date range is correct about the increasingly frequent babysitting by Jeff and Jennifer, but they babysat Kassidy before October as well.

- "*The defendant is also charged with six counts of second-degree assault for knowingly causing bruises on Kassidy by grabbing her time and time again from September until the week before her death.*" (p. 17) The jury heard little about these allegations because Chad attorneys were focusing on the murder charge.

- "*Kassidy was fine when she left Jeff Marshall's house on November 8th...*" (p. 17) However, this was three months after the abuse for which Chad was indicted allegedly began, and it conflicted with the testimony of several upcoming prosecution witnesses.

- "*When this photograph was taken, Kassidy had less than six weeks to live, and those weeks were a living hell, and the defendant was the cause of her misery.*" (p. 18) The jury was told only once the approximate date of the photograph. Importantly, that photograph was taken on 1 October when Amanda brought Kassidy to her mother's while helping her move. It could also have been taken the previous week, when Kassidy was visiting her grandmother, but Jacqueline said that the photo was taken in a nearly empty room with the last chair left available. During both of these visits, no bruises were seen by any member of the family in Auburn, Maine. This was two months after the alleged abuse by Chad began, and before the regular babysitting with Jeff Marshall. No further reference to the date of that photo was made during the trial, and it was the only photo shown to the jury of Kassidy, alive.

Mark Sisti gave the defense's 27 minute opening statement. He said that "*...law enforcement made a choice early in this case, before they knew anything about their little star witness, Jeffrey Marshall, and they picked Chad, because he was convenient, because he was easy.*" (p. 2) Later, Sisti gave the flip side which was that it was "*not convenient for them to pursue Jeffrey Marshall.*" (p. 7) Actually, Jeff was convenient, too, so the reasons for the police early choice were more complicated.

Sisti begged the jurors not to be swayed by the graphic photos of Kassidy's body, but asked them to pay attention to the only photograph at the trial of Kassidy alive which Sisti said was taken six weeks before her death. Thus, he recognized the power of photographs, but before the trial, the available photographs were not gathered.

Sisti urged the jurors to "*be suspect*" of Jeff's upcoming testimony. He told the jurors that of the overnight babysitting by Jeff of October 24-26, but Sisti said incorrectly that it was "*just two days before Halloween...*" (p. 5) It was not a good sign in a case where the timeline was important for the defense to assign incorrect dates to important events.

Sisti was clear about the defense's theory, that Jeff Marshall "*is a killer.*" (p. 3) Further, "*Jeffrey Marshall was an animal.*" (p. 8) That was a strong allegation which would require proof, because Sisti knew that Jeff would be testifying. If you tell a jury that an upcoming witness is an "animal," and fail to prove that allegation, then the overall credibility of the defense case would be damaged, and that's what happened.

Sisti stressed that courtroom was where the evidence would be heard and proved and not in the newspapers. He presented Chad as eager to prove his innocence, "*He wants his trial. He wants this trial more than anything. It's time for the newspaper talk to hit the road. And it's time for witnesses to take the stand.*" (p. 8) The expectation was surely set for the jury that the defense attorneys would present an aggressive and affirmative defense and that Chad would testify.

Sisti told the jurors that Amanda was charged with crimes two weeks before Chad's trial, "*because she didn't give the prosecutors what they wanted to hear.*" (p. 10) On the other hand, Sisti said that Amanda would be immune from prosecution for anything she might say in her upcoming testimony that might incriminate her, and he concluded, "*Folks, we are begging her to tell the truth.*" (p. 10)

The Associated Press article in the Keene Sentinel reported that Mark Sisti said, "*You will find out that only four to five weeks before her death, she started to go to Jeffrey Marshall's... That's not a coincidence.*" With a dramatic Perry Mason-esque flair, Mark Sisti said to the jury,

You're going to see Jeffrey Marshall raise his hand and swear to tell the truth... By the time this is over you're going to deliberate and you're going to ask yourself, "Hey Jeff, is that the hand you used to beat Kassidy Bortner?"

It was good drama, but mocking Jeff Marshall with a clever sleight of hand turned out not to be an effective strategy. The Portsmouth Herald's article, "Murder Blame Game" said about Mark Sisti's presentation,

"The defense will show who really killed Kassidy Bortner," Sisti said, claiming that law enforcement officials were too quick in charging Evans and in fact overlooked the possible guilt of the baby sitter.

Sisti said when Evans picked up Kassidy at Conley and Marshall's Kittery home on Nov. 8, 2000, he noticed she was lethargic, her head was falling forward and she was drooling.

The defense argued before the jury that Marshall was often alone with Kassidy, and Sisti said her bruises only began appearing after she had been in Marshall's care. "Chad (Evans) has waited for over a year to get here," he continued. "It's a very strange feeling for someone falsely accused to wait one year to clear his name."

It's now been 10 years since the death of Kassidy Bortner, and Chad still has a "strange feeling" as he continues to try to clear his name.

Sisti said nothing about the six Second Degree and two First Degree Assault Charges for assaulting Kassidy, and the single Second Degree Assault Charge for assaulting Amanda and the single Child Endangerment charge.

Jacqueline Conley

The first witness was Jacqueline Conley, mother of Amanda and Jennifer and grandmother of Kassidy. She had met Chad only twice, but wasn't asked about the time periods of those two occasions nor of any details about those two occasions. The first was around Tuesday, June 20, and Chad spent the night, with Jacqueline's encouragement, with Amanda and Kassidy in Amanda's bedroom. The second time was around Thursday, July 20. Chad took Amanda, Jeff and Jennifer to eat at Margarita's restaurant in Auburn, and he and Amanda spent the night in a tent in the backyard with Amanda's half-brother, Scott Conley.

Jacqueline testified that she played a large role in Kassidy's first year and a half and that she did not notice that Kassidy bruised easily. "*No, she was normal. ... when children fall, they get a bruise....She didn't bruise easily.*" (p. 11)

Jacqueline said that after living away from home in 1999, and with Jacqueline being the primary caregiver for Kassidy, Amanda moved back to the family home in December. She also said that Jennifer lived in the Auburn home, "*off and on*" (p. 11) However, Jennifer had moved out of the family home the previous spring and was living with Jeff in Kittery.

Jacqueline testified that Amanda's clear move-out date was the end of September, 2000, "*when she told me she was not going to live with us any more, because she didn't want to move to Buckfield.*" (p. 15) However, it was a symbolic date, because Jacqueline said that Amanda didn't stay overnight at Jacqueline's home during the month of September. Jacqueline said of Amanda, "*She came by once or twice to get things, and she'd always run back out to Rochester, or she'd say she was going to a girlfriend's.*" (p. 16) Thus, in practical terms, according to Jacqueline, Amanda had moved out before September.

She said that she last babysat for Kassidy during the week beginning Sunday, September 24. Kassidy stayed with her at her home in Auburn for the entire week, while Chad and Amanda went on a trip. (p. 17) However, Chad recalls that he and Amanda returned from Martha's Vineyard on Wednesday the 27th and that Amanda drove that day to Auburn to pick up Kassidy. Jacqueline recalled that it was the trip to New York City to a baseball game, but it was Amanda's and Chad's trip to Martha's Vineyard. However, Jacqueline was correct in the sense that she did babysit for Kassidy when Chad and Amanda and Jeremy and April and Elaine and Jay Shunk went to New York City to see a baseball game on Sunday/Monday, August 20/21. Kassidy was likely with Jacqueline from Saturday through Tuesday.

She also said that Amanda and her friend, Cathy Nuernberg, came to Auburn on Sunday, October 1, to help Jacqueline and the Conley family move to their new home in Buckfield, Maine. This was the occasion that the trial's only photo of Kassidy, alive, was taken. (p. 18) She said of that last time, "*I saw her October the 1st.*" (p. 17)

If Jacqueline was right that Kassidy was with her from Sunday, September 24, through Sunday, October 1, then that was one entire week of bruise-free observation and care for Kassidy. As the life cycle of bruises is about a week, that meant that there was no substantial or easily observable new injuries or bruising after Sunday, September 17.

Jacqueline recalled a specific call to Chad's home in October. It was Saturday, 14 October, but the jury did not know that was the date. Jacqueline called to ask about bruises which her son, Joshua, had seen on Kassidy the previous day when Amanda came to visit and pick up a check. Bruises on Kassidy were definitely serious business for Jacqueline and were not a "*family joke.*" In fact, there was no references in the entire trial to the "*family joke*" statement in Sgt. James White's two November 2000 affidavits, and in the newspapers. Chad responded to Jacqueline's question about Kassidy's bruises with the "trampoline story," which he recalled in 2010 as the first time he had used the story after he and Amanda settled on that as an explanation for the palming during "eye contact" bruises. Jacqueline also related a conversation with Amanda about that same time, "*a few weeks before Kassidy's death,*" (p. 29) where Amanda said that she planned to move out of Chad's home and get her own apartment. She didn't explain that she talked with Amanda by phone nearly every day.

Jacqueline testified that on the night of November 9, after the police interviews, despite her urging Amanda not to talk with Chad, "*he walked over and they started hugging, and kept telling Mandy he was sorry and he loved her. And she kept telling him she was sorry and that she loved him.*" (p. 30) If this embracing had been observed at any place other than a police station, it would have been viewed as a touching moment for two people who had been struck by tragedy. Kassidy's death was a tragedy that each of them understood that they could have avoided IF, ONLY this and IF, ONLY that.

This was the first time that the jury had heard that Chad had apologized to Amanda, but, as with the other representations of his regret during the entire ten years since Kassidy's death, that regret was not explained. It was likely understood by the jury to be regret that he had harmed and killed Kassidy, but it wasn't. Instead, Chad regretted that he didn't do more to help Kassidy and get medical attention for her and find better day care, and help prevent her death. Also, it was a "sorry," knowing how much Amanda loved Kassidy, and now she was gone forever.

After one of the several discussions among the attorneys and Judge Nadeau about hearsay, Jacqueline related her conversation with Amanda at Kassidy's funeral where she said that now, *"...she was... able to get on with her life, go to college and be like other normal girls; that she was relieved, actually.*" (p. 33) Hindsight, of course is 20/20, and this was one of the many, many times during the Chad Evans case that an ambiguous statement was interpreted to be an indication of guilt. I remember saying when my father was unconscious in the hospital that it was a good time for him to die, as he eventually did. Did that make me responsible for his death?

In January, 2011, Oprah Winfrey disclosed that she had a heretofore unknown half-sister, and in the discussion of the events in her life she said that if the child she had had at the age of 14 had survived, her life would have been entirely different. It was a perfectly normal response to the tragedy of her daughter's death for Oprah Winfrey, but not for a young woman who has been indicted for child endangerment for allegedly watching her boyfriend assault and murder her daughter.

On cross-examination by Alan Cronheim, Jacqueline established an anchor date for 2000 which was August 27, which she said was the date of her operation for a tumor. She testified that she learned about the tumor two weeks beforehand and had the operation on the 27th. (p. 35) However, August 27th was a Sunday, and it's unlikely that, in the absence of an emergency, such surgery would be scheduled for a Sunday. In a case starved for specific dates, it would have been worthwhile for the defense to request from the prosecution or from Jacqueline, directly, a copy of a bill or other document proving that Sunday, August 27 was the correct date. As with other specific dates in the case, it was important for use as a reference date, i.e. for events happening before or after the reference date.

Three years later, for a 2004 sentence review division hearing, Jacqueline wrote, "*The last week in September, she spent a week with me, not long after my operation.... I remember I could not lift her...I just didn't want to pull out my stitches...*" If Jacqueline's doctors had recorded the date that stitches were removed, that would help determine the date Kassidy's last visit with Jacqueline.

Cronhein tried to establish when Jacqueline understood that Amanda could have been said to have moved in with Chad. She acknowledged that Amanda was often away, "*She would say she'd be going to her girlfriend's house for the weekend at first, because she knew I wouldn't approve of her living with any men, number one.*" (p. 35) This was a typical example of a teenager lying to a parent about his or her activities, but it also was an example of a parent trying to convince others of his or her high moral standard. The jury was not told that Jacqueline approved of Chad and Amanda sleeping together during both of Chad's only trips to the Conley's home in July, or one to two months after they met. In many families, it's a much later step in a relationship when an 18-year old daughter is permitted to sleep with a man in her own family's house. The jury did not yet know that Amanda had Kassidy at the age of 17.

Jacqueline agreed that during the time that she last saw Kassidy, October 1st, she saw no bruises and Kassidy had no difficulty walking and no difficulty with her arms. One bruise that Jacqueline might have seen was one that might have been caused a day or two before at the Deerfield, New Hampshire Fair. Chad, Amanda and Kassidy went to this fair with Bruce and Michelle Truell and their daughter. Chad took Kassidy on several rides, including the "Kiddie Roller Coaster." When that ride started, the cart lurched forward, and Kassidy bumped her head on the side of the cart. Chad wrote that "*She cried for a few seconds but seemed fine." (*letter *3/7/10)*

As the trial would show, the relationship between Amanda and her mother after the death of Kassidy was minimal, if not hostile, but up to that tragic day, it was cordial, if not better. However, neither attorney asked Jacqueline about Amanda's call to her on the morning of Wednesday, November 8, at 8:35 a.m. for six minutes. Surely, Kassidy was discussed, but what was said? In 2011, Amanda recalled that she asked her mother during that call to plan to care for Kassidy over the coming weekend of November 11/12 when she and Chad would be in Maine at a Colley-McCoy (McDonald's) business function. If this conversation occurred, it's startling that neither the prosecution or defense ever asked the right question or that neither Jacqueline nor Amanda volunteered the information. Even without knowing about the call from Amanda to her mother, a good question for the police and prosecutors to ask, right on the day she died was, "Who was going to take care of Kassidy during the upcoming weekend?" Amanda told the police about the upcoming weekend, as did Chad and Jennifer. Not only would knowing about that plan have said something to the jury about Jacqueline's care for Kassidy, it would have said something about Amanda's unwillingness to have Kassidy spend another overnight at Jeff's and Jennifer's.

Jacqueline was not asked about her shopping trip with Amanda and Jennifer on Sunday, November 5, and about her understanding of Kassidy's whereabouts on that day. She was not asked how often she talked by phone with Amanda, which was about five times a week.

Steven Hamel

The second witness was Kittery Police Dept. Detective Steve Hamel who, together with Sergeant Ron Avery, was among the officers to come to 51 Rogers Road on 9 November. Asked about his career, Det. Hamel said, "*I started my career with the New Hampshire State Police*." (p. 39) He didn't mention, as he later stated at Amanda's trial that his police career began as a patrolman with the Rochester Police Dept. It was a curious omission, given that Chad was a resident of Rochester and most of his alleged crimes occurred in Rochester. Detective Hamel described to Will Delker the scene of the EMTs and Officer Creamer trying to revive Kassidy and Jeff standing with them. He described Kassidy,

The face was heavily bruised. You could see dots everywhere along the face. You could see some on the head where the hair was thinned out. You could also see some under the chin area here. And the cut, I believe, was on the right, index finger. (p. 46)

Hamel was not asked what he meant by "*dots*," but the "*cut*" on the right index finger was very likely the wart that Amanda and Chad had discussed having removed.

Hamed described about how he brought Jeff to sit in the back seat of his patrol car. He said that Jeff was angry and in disbelief and said,

"This is not me. You need to be talking to Chad. Chad's the one that did this. You guys really need to talk to Chad,".[and that] *the baby was brought to his residence in that condition this morning*. (p. 49)

Mark Sisti cross-examined and Detective Hamel agreed that Jeff had told him in his cruiser that Kassidy "*was wearing red pajamas when dropped off and was eating Cocoa Puffs out of a clear baggie."* (p. 57) Detective Hamel agreed that Jeff had said that he had checked his mail and that at that point, in Mark Sisti's words, "*he found the baby having difficulty breathing and noticed that the baby's eyes were rolled back at or around 12 noon, and then he took the baby from the bed and checked for a pulse.*" (p. 58) Detective Hamel agreed that Jeff told him that he "*found a slight pulse...* [and] *he brought the baby into the kitchen sink in an attempt to wake the baby by splashing cold water on its face, right?*" (p. 59) Then Jeff attempted CPR and then called Jen. Detective Hamel said that he asked Jeff why he didn't call 911, and Jeff responded that "*he thought* [Jennifer] *could give him some advice on the baby, help with the baby.*"

MEDIA: 1. "Murder Blame Game"

2. "Evans defense: Wrong man accused - Lawyers argue evidence points to another suspect"

Wednesday, 5 December 2001

Mark Sisti resumed his cross-examination of Detective Hamel and established that Kassidy was with Jeff the previous day for the hour of 4:30 p.m. to 5:30 p.m. and that, quoting from Det. Hamel's report, and therefore relying upon what he was told by Jeff, "*that the baby seemed normal, and did not have the bruising on her face at that time.*" Detective Hamel stated that Jeff told him that Chad Evans called him when Chad *...was in the area of the Dover toll from his cell phone, I believe, and he indicated that Mr. Evans was inquiring from him if the - - what the baby acted like during the day from the time he had him, only because the baby, in his eyes, was acting weird. Seemed to be out of it.....The second call Mr. Marshall received was Mr. Evans indicating that the baby had fallen on her face out in the parking lot or in the driveway, excuse me, to the residence. The third phone call was between nine and nine-thirty. I believe that phone call, Mr. Evans indicated to Mr. Marshall that the baby had been hit in the face with a baseball while they were playing baseball inside the residence.*" (p. 5-7)

This was the first reference at the trial, to Kassidy's being hit by the Tee-ball on the evening of the 8th, and it was the closest to its real status, by calling it a "*baseball,*" as Det. Hamel did in his original report. Later references at the trial were to a "ball," and most incorrectly as a "*wiffle ball.*"

Then Detective Hamel resumed, from the previous day's testimony, his description of Jeff's phone calls on the 9th. "*He indicated to me on the first phone call, his girlfriend indicated they were extremely busy, that she couldn't talk, if there was a problem with the baby, then Jeff ought to call the baby's mother at Old Navy.*" Jeff tried to call Amanda, but was stuck in a message system and called Jennifer back. "*Again, she was extremely busy. She indicated to him if there's a problem with the baby, then call the ambulance. That's when Mr. Marshall turned and called 911.*" (p. 7) Mark Sisti did not ask Detective Hamel whether Jeff had said anything about his three calls to Chad Evans's cell phone before calling Jennifer, and his three calls to Chad, for one of which he left a message, after calling Jennifer and before calling Amanda.

Detective Hamel agreed that he hadn't asked Jeff whether he had abused or killed Kassidy before Jeff volunteered that the police should talk with Chad.

Will Delker conducted the redirect examination, and reviewed most of Detective Hamel's report and Hamel said that Jeff told him that during the third call the previous evening, about the baseball, that Jeff told Chad that "*he should be talking to the mother, not him.*" (p. 19-20) Also, the next morning Jeff stated that "*the baby was having difficulty walking.... he noticed a bruising on the head and the face. It was obvious that that was, in his opinion, wasn't there last night when the baby left. He indicates that the baby seemed to be out of it.*" (p. 20)

Dr. Anthony Bock

Examined by Will Delker and Simon Brown alternatively, Dr. Bock, the third witness, was the Emergency Room doctor at York Hospital when Kassidy's body was brought to the hospital. Dr. Bock confirmed the EMTs reported arrival at Jeff's at 12:46 p.m. and he said that "*it seemed like she was dead at the time of arrival of the EMTs.*" (p. 29)

He and the jury were shown seven enlarged photographs of Kassidy's body, taken either at the morgue or at the office of the Chief Medical Examiner in Augusta, Maine. Dr. Bock stated that her body looked as it did when he first saw her, with

... bruising, the lesions, the loss of hair on the back of the head...multiple bruising about the face, forehead, the cheeks, the ear which you can see a whole lot in her, which is bruising of really different colors, indicating they're probably different ages...bruising throughout the face, forehead, temple area, cheeks, lips...underneath the chin, the left-cheek area, the left mandible area, more bruising about the left ear, and the forehead. Again, some are bright red, some are dark purple, some are of a lighter tinge, indicating to me that there might have been different ones.... the back of Kassidy's head. The bruising over here and here, and then some alopecia, or just hair that wasn't present compared to the rest of the head....lesions on the feet.... scabs, along her lower abdomen, again there's bruising noted here, and bruising over the lower abdomen on both sides. (p. 33-38)

Dr. Bock believed the cause of Kassidy's death was "*due to blunt trauma or a head injury.*" (p. 39)

Mark Sisti cross-examined Dr. Bock, who then agreed that some of the bruising could have been visible on 8 November. Also, he agreed that a person with a head injury could go back and forth with "*moments of unconsciousness and then coming back into consciousness*...[and could] *include eyes being rolled in back in one's head*"... [and] *just slumping over in a chair or a seat without any particular reason.*" (p. 47-8) Finally, Dr. Bock agreed that if such symptoms appeared after 6:00 p.m., that a head injury could have occurred in the period from 4:30 p.m. to 5:30 p.m. on Wednesday. The goal of the question was to establish that an injury could have occurred at Jeff's prior to Chad's arrival and pickup of Kassidy.

Neither Delker nor Sisti asked Dr. Bock about his examination of the X-rays taken of Kassidy's body at York Hospital. According to Det. Scott Harakles summary of his interview with Dr. Bock on November 9, those X-rays showed no signs of broken bones. The allegations in Chad's and Amanda's trials that Kassidy suffered broken bones were important and inflammatory, and this would have been a good opportunity for Sisti to show the jury that there were no such broken bones. At the very least the jury would have learned that the issue was considered very early in the investigation and that there was a legitimate dispute, and that the alleged bone fractures were not obvious to anyone.

Amanda Bortner

Before Amanda could testify before the jury, the prosecutors, defense attorneys and Amanda's attorney conferred in the judge's office. The judge ruled that the defense could ask Amanda about her allegation that her stepfather abused her sexually. Judge Nadeau said,

I think that the defense has established that it's relevant to demonstrate the bias, if any, of the mother, and to demonstrate why she might not have stayed with her parents. Because the jury could easily presume that she had a place to stay. What I'm going to allow the defense to ask her about is that she - - whether or not she was sexually abused by her step-father, whether she told her mother about it, and whether her mother did anything about it. That's it. (p. 55)

Alan Cronheim advised the judge that he had acquired a copy of Amanda's 11-page "My Life Story" which she wrote in the Spring of 2001. Chad explained the history of the essay in his January 10, 2010 letter, which, incidentally, was his first letter to me,

As I mentioned at our meeting, "My Life's Story by Amanda Bortner," was written by Amanda at the suggestion of some therapist her friend Cathy took her to see while she was in Texas shortly after my arrest in November of 2000. Within two weeks I was home and Amanda called me from Texas one night, indicating she felt so much better having gotten away from the police and all the people pressuring her. She could see clearly now and knew that I hadn't killed Kassidy. She had been discussing it with some therapist. At the suggestion of the therapist, she contacted my lawyers when she got back to NH, who put her in touch with my P.I, a guy named Jon Morgan. At some point she handed Morgan this paper she created while in Texas. Ironically the PI forgot about it or something and never turned it over to my lawyers until the start of my trial.

The prosecutors and the judge were given copies and each was working to determine how it would fit into Chad's trial and Amanda's trial and the immunity from prosecution for what she said at Chad's trial. In that document, Amanda reiterated her belief that Chad did not cause Kassidy's death, and that she made statements to the police about Chad which were not true. She wrote,

I guess the reason I thought that Chad was responsible originally (besides the fact that they basically told me I was dumb and a bad mom because I let Chad kill her), was that I had seen him get mad and lose his temper with her. When I think about it now though I could not think straight. I mean really what were they thinking? My little baby had just died and they wouldn't leave me alone. I could not even see straight. Everything was a blur to me then and is a blur to me now, and I guess one of the reasons that I decided to write this was because I do know that I said some things that were not true about Chad. When I say that I saw him get mad and lose his temper that is true. But when I think about it. He never hit her or anything. He would just yell and try to get her attention. Also they took me saying he put her in the corner, to throwing her into walls. I don't really know how it turned into that, but it did, and I guess it's my job to fix that. And one time probably a month and a half before she died, Kassidy was screaming throwing one of her fits and Chad grabbed her face and said look in my eyes, and said cut it out. Then attempted to put her in the corner. But she would throw herself down and hit her own face into the wall and kick and scream. So he got more angry picked her up and put her in her bedroom on the bed, then she threw herself off the bed and he grabbed her face again. That's when I jumped into the picture and took her from him. As I was pulling her from him. He still had one of her legs so I just let go. So it wouldn't hurt her. Then I yelled I will do the disciplining, go away. He then realized he was starting to lose his temper so he muttered something under his breath, and walked away. I still don't remember what he said. I don't think he said it loud enough for me to hear. She was never all beat up like the papers are trying to say. Actually that whole month before she died and week, I was in and out of the Department of Human Services quite frequent with her. If she was all banged [up] they would be the people to report something. He probably put her in the corner like 4 or 5 times.

I mean I liked Chad a lot, but I love my daughter more than anything in the world as if I would stay and put up with that. So basically I did a lot of agreeing with the cops to get them to leave me alone and that is not really fair to Chad. From time to time I remember bits and pieces of my conversation with the cops. It seemed like every time I said anything about Jeff that [they] didn't want to hear it. This makes me really mad because now that I have had time to really think about things.

.....and the cops were not even smart enough to ask me questions about Jeff, or listen to me. The only thing they brought up constantly was Chad and the fact that they were positive he was responsible. At one point when they had me convinced he did it (deep down inside knowing he didn't) I said stuff I know wasn't true. The cops kept accusing me of downplaying everything when in fact I was making it worse than it was. Also they did a terrible job investigating.

She also wrote about Jeff and his care of Kassidy.

Let's see, he watched her twice when my sister and I landscaped for him. And after that, we'd go shopping. Also, a couple days Jen and I just went shopping. The weird thing was Jeff would say, "Why don't you guys just go. Kassidy's fine here." I thought he was just being nice. Also, Chad and I went out maybe twice and they took her overnight. Jen worked most of the time. Also, I went job hunting a couple of times and he watched her then too. I also started a money management class, and he watched her those nights too. Then one day I got a job interview at Old Navy. I wasn't going to take it, cause they needed me to work a lot of night hours. I didn't have a babysitter at night. The state would only pay for a daycare during the day. Then I told Jen and Jeff about it and he said, "I'll watch her for you." And I said, "It's not as easy as it sounds." He said, "No problem." But the only reason he agreed to baby sit is so he could get my food stamps and sell them for money. He said he knew someone that buys them. And I know for a fact he did it too, cause he told me. Chad doesn't even know I got them. He never would have let me use them. I did use them once with my sister. And I said, "Well maybe just until I find a daycare, and then you could pick her up at 5:30 and me or Chad would pick her up after." I knew then that Kassidy didn't really like him. She would just stand in their house and barely move. Then, I thought nothing of it. But now after all of this it makes sense. She was scared to move around. She barely even said a word. Another thing is everyone we'd ever meet, Kassidy would say their name at least once. She knew Jeff for a pretty long time and never said his name once. Or even attempted to. Also if Jen wasn't there when I would drop Kassidy off I would have to run out the door or she would cry. And it got really bad the last week. I remember now that it was a different sounding cry. It was a real cry. With real tears, I'm sure. I was just so busy with my new job, looking for a daycare, trying to get through Chad's whole divorce, all of a sudden taking care of two babies, and still have a good size house to keep up with. I was so blinded, and totally clueless about everything. I feel so stupid.

Well strange things happened when Kassidy was at Jeff's house. Things that didn't seem strange to me then until now. For example. One time Kassidy came back with a big bruise on the side of her face. He said he was teasing her and said, "Mama's home," so she ran off the bed to get me and fell on her face. I wasn't even there. She must've been so upset. Also, one time he dropped her off and she had 2 small bruises on the side of her face and he had put women's cover up on to hide them. He said that the dog had knocked her over. Why did I believe those stupid stories?

Also, one time he said he told her to go against the wall for some reason and he said he purposely went outside to look in the window to see if she'd moved and she did. She went into the kitchen and started touching things, and he said he ran back in the house, made her jump a mile, and made her go back in the corner. She must have been so scared. I feel horrible.

Now here are two big things I do remember quite clearly. One time Jeff had her over night. I can't remember exactly what we did that night, but the next afternoon Jeff dropped her off. When he walked in Chad was outside and Travis was inside with me. That's when Jeff said,"Her ass might be a little sore, she was being a little shit! So I gave her a spanking." Then Chad came inside and he and Jeff went up North to pick up my 3 wheeler that Chad had bought me. Then I went to change Kassidy's diaper, and that's when I saw it. Her butt was covered in black and blues. Bruises all over her butt. Dark ones. I started freaking out. I immediately started to cry because I never saw anything that bad before. Really, on anyone. Then my sister came over, and I showed her it. She practically started crying, and said, "I am going to kill Jeff." She also said, "He didn't mean to do it that hard, and I'm sure he is going to feel bad."

Later I put her to bed, and my sister and I jumped on the trampoline and had girl talk. That's when she showed me the bruise on her leg....

We also decided we were going to have a talk with the boys and they are not to discipline Kassidy anymore (mainly focused on Jeff). That is for the mother to do, not the babysitter. When they got home from Maine, we were all sitting at the kitchen table, and started talking about things. I was kind of giving Jeff shit. I didn't really come right out and talk about it because Chad was there and Jen didn't want him to know because she knew he would freak and kill Jeff. A day later or so I showed Chad the bruises and he was bullshit. He said something like "No wonder you were so cold and being mean to Jeff when we got back. Jeff made it look like he felt bad and didn't mean to do it that hard. I have to live with the fact that I continuously brought her over after that incident. Am I just an idiot? There is not a day that goes by that I picture her screaming while he smacks her butt.

Oh yeah, and I thought he was kidding when he said he holds a pillow over her head when she cried cause it was so annoying. He must've really did that. And that is why none of the neighbors heard her cry. Or did they? Who knows anymore.

None of this stuff is in any real order. It's just things I have remembered here and there. Okay another time, I do remember it was about 2 weeks maybe less, before she died. I had a money management class to attend, and he said he'd babysit. My car was in the shop then so I couldn't drop her off. So he came and picked her up, and said he'd drop her off after. So after the class I got home called him. He said he was tired and didn't feel like driving and he'd bring her in the morning. It was kind of good for me at the time, cause I was doing surveys on the computer and had a deadline. The next day he said he was gonna drop her off never did. Then finally again he said he'd drop her off in the morning. He never did. Then he said, "Afternoon." Finally he brought her over around 4 or 5:00. She was so sick. She kept saying, "Mama, hungry, hungry!" So I gave her a bowl of cereal and she stuck her face into the bowl and sucked the milk out. She was so dehydrated. Then I gave her water, which she puked up. Because she was drinking so fast. I let her eat a little, gave her Tylenol, and then gave her pedialyte to help with the dehydration. It was like he never fed her. Then I saw the 2 huge bruises on the back of her head. Jeff was still standing there watching the whole thing. He then said she fell out of the truck. He said she was standing on her car seat, and the door was opened, and she fell out and landed right on his driveway and hit her head. I then put ice on her bruises. The only thing I knew about hitting your head, was you should wait awhile to sleep. Now I know that dehydration is a sign of concussion. But, why did Jeff wait around for that long. It was like he was worried I might figure out what he did to her, and when he felt for sure I believed his story. Then he left. Because when he first dropped her off he said he was in a real hurry, cause he had to clean a playplace.

That night when she was starting to fall asleep, I noticed her eyes roll up and then back down. She had never done that before, so I was worried. But I told myself to stop overreact[ing], *and that she was just falling asleep. A lot of babies do that. Boy was I wrong! That night when Chad got home, he was really concerned. He said should we take her to the doctors? And I said, "Well, she's starting to feel better now. If she's still feeling yucky tomorrow I will take her." The next day she was feeling better. One thing that surprised me was she said 6, 7, 8, 9, 10 after Kyle said 1, 2, 3, 4, 5. Maybe I was so impressed by this so I didn't really notice much. I was also very busy with a lot of other things. Like, the deadline on the computer project I was doing. A couple things I did notice was her appetite decreased after that. And she was sleeping very irregularly, and long too. Especially the last couple of days before she died.*

Oh yeah, and her feet had little like scabs, which to me looks like pin pricks. And I asked Chad to put her shoes on one day, and he asked me what happened to her feet. I had never seen that ever before, and she had just came back from Jeff's house that day. I then called Jeff up and asked him why she had that on her feet, and he said, "Oh that would be the top of the nails in the doorway on the floor." So I don't know why it sounded okay, but now that I think about it, that is such a lame excuse.

Also one time Chad was playing with her, swinging her around by her legs and arms. Just playing. And she was laughing. He did that with Kyle a lot and didn't always remember she was a lot younger than him. Then, I think it was the next day, I don't really know, but Jeff said she was standing behind him and he didn't see her, and he stepped on her. Then she was walking with a limp. When she was home that night I squeezed up and down her legs to see if it hurt, and she just giggled. So stupid me, I thought it was just a pulled muscle. She never cried about it either.

.....one time I picked her up [at Jeff's] *and she was butt naked. And at first there was suspicion about that. I also yelled and said, "What about her black and blue butt, and are you sure she fell out of the truck?"*

Well all these things might seem obvious ....Also it happened so fast. I think if I hadn't been so busy working, I wouldn't have been so blinded by everything. Now I have to live with the fact that my baby......, and I didn't protect her. And that cost her life.

Neither the prosecutors nor Chad's lawyers proposed that the court make "My Life Story" an Exhibit, and it wasn't referenced again during the trial. Thus the jury never learned of this important document.

Patricia Wiberg, Amanda's attorney, then related what she had seen in the hallway, when Amanda's mother, Jacqueline Conley, and her step-aunt, Katherine Conley Jackson, loudly told Amanda to tell the truth, " *'You need to tell Kassidy's truth... and if you don't I can disown you.'* " This was said "*with the aunt glaring at Amanda..... The mother was very nasty, and then she just stomped away.*" (p. 57) There was little question that strong feelings were aroused by this case. In this instance, it was mother against daughter, with the mother siding with the police and the daughter siding with the defendant whom she believed to be innocent. Wiberg asked that the court ensure that Amanda's mother and step-aunt not be in the courtroom during Amanda's testimony, and Judge Nadeau agreed.

Returning to the public courtroom, Simon Brown began his direct examination of Amanda who reviewed her basic biographical information including the receipt of her GED high school equivalency degree in January, 2000. She actually received the GED degree from Edward Little High School in May, 2000, which may indicate that she finished her GED classes the previous winter or that she didn't have a good recollection of time and dates.

When asked about meeting Chad, she correctly identified the date as June 2, and she noted, "*I really liked him. I thought he was really nice. Had a good personality. The one thing that really did attract me to him was he was a really good father.*" (p. 67) Amanda said that she told Chad that she was 19 years old, even though she was 18, and that she moved to Chad's in mid-July. (p. 68) Simon Brown confirmed that timing when he asked, later, "*Now, you've been in Chad's house July onward, right?*" and Amanda agreed. (p. 73) She testified that she understood that Chad's divorce was final after Kassidy's death, which shows how little Amanda and Chad actually talked about the case in the one year since, because the divorce was final on October 4th. It was after Kassidy's death that Chad received the formal notification that the divorce was final a month before her death.

Asked about Kassidy's health, Amanda said it was good, and when asked about her walking, she said,

She was always pigeon-toed... Chad was the one that pointed that out to me, or she walked inward, and maybe I should bring her to the doctor's. And his mother said something to me also. So I brought her in July to check her feet, because she did - - she was pigeon-toed, and the doctor said that she was pigeon-toed, but she might grow out of it. (p. 72)

Significantly, the date of that appointment was not in July, but the jury would never learn the truth about Kassidy's medical appointments in 2000. Kassidy's last appointment with her pediatrician was on August 10, 2000, and at that appointment, Amanda discussed with Dr. Glass the "pigeon-toed" problem. It was thought to be sufficiently significant that Amanda and Kassidy were referred to a specialist, Dr. James Timoney, who is an orthopedic surgeon. That appointment was on September 11, and Amanda's recollections at trial of his recommendations were correct.

Simon Brown asked Amanda about her interviews with the police, and specifically about New Hampshire State Trooper Angela Blodgett. Amanda said,

She was okay at first, and then she started getting really harsh saying that -- basically telling me that Chad killed my daughter, and I watched him slowly kill my daughter. She said those same words. And I was like -- just in so much shock at that time, and I was really overwhelmed. (p. 77)

Brown asked Amanda what sorts of things would upset Kassidy after they moved in with Chad, and Amanda stated,

If Chad would kiss me, she would get mad. She was really jealous. If I would pick up Kyle, that was his son, she would get jealous over that.... She would throw a temper tantrum. She would kick and scream and throw her head back and just throw a fit.... In the beginning, it happened a little bit. And then she stopped for a while. And then the last month before she died she started doing it again.... Maybe twice a week. Maybe three times a week. (p. 81)

Amanda stated that Chad's response was that

....he would get frustrated and mad. And at first we started putting her in her room for a time out... He would say things like, "This is stupid." Just stuff like that. And he would grab her face.... He would grab her face like this, and he would say, "Look into my eyes," just to get her attention.

Asked about how hard Chad grabbed Kassidy's face, Amanda said, "*Pretty hard. He left bruises a couple of times.*" (p. 81-2) Later she said, "*five or six times.*" Asked about the timing, she said, "*...he didn't start grabbing her face until towards the end, because he was just getting more and more frustrated. He didn't understand why she was throwing* *the fits, still, because she had stopped for a while.*" (p. 82) What Amanda didn't say, and what Brown didn't ask, perhaps to avoid an objection by defense counsel for asking for hearsay, was what Chad actually said to Kassidy when he held her face to get her attention. In 2010 Chad recalls saying to Kassidy on a few occasions something like, "*Your mother and I love each other, and I love you, too. There is no need to act this way when we show affection. You need a time out to calm down.*"

Asked about other times that Kassidy might get upset, Amanda described a typical toddler,

If she couldn't get her own way. Like one time she did it on the couch. Kyle had the blanket. She wanted the blanket, so she did it then. Sometimes she was eating, and I'd take her tray away after she was done. She threw it then, too. At the grocery store, I spoiled her. I would always give her candy. Almost every time we'd do that. We'd go to the grocery store, and one time I didn't have enough change, so I didn't get her any candy, and she threw a fit, and I remember that was embarrassing. (p. 83)

Simon Brown asked Amanda about her reaction to Chad's palming Kassidy's face and she responded as parents often do when stepparents, or potential stepparents appear to be disciplining his/her child, "*I would get mad, and say, 'Don't do that.' I would just tell him to stop. I would say, 'I'm going to do the disciplining'.... After he got her attention, usually he would stop grabbing her face.*" (p. 84-5) Asked about Kassidy's reaction to the "eye contact" grabbing, Amanda said, "*She would scream, cry.... it didn't look like it hurt. I never thought it hurt her until I saw bruises.... I can remember two times I could see bruises.*" (p. 85)

Amanda was asked to describe in what other ways "*would the defendant discipline Kassidy,*" and she replied, "*...a month before she died, he started -- we started putting her in front of the wall, kind of like a corner, for a time out, because the bedroom wasn't working, I thought, and he thought, also, because she would just cry until I could come in there, and then she'd stop.... I remember a time in front of the closet door in the bedroom.... he would pick her up and roughly put her there. He would put one arm underneath her armpit and one arm -- once he grabbed her arm and sit her in front of the -- plop her down in front of the closet door.*" (p. 85-6) This was in the master bedroom.

Then Brown asked a question based on Amanda's police interviews, "*Did he ever grab her by the neck and toss her into the corner*?" Amanda replied that, "*He might have.*" This was perhaps an example of Amanda torn between what she recalled as the truth, and her definition of the word, "*toss*," and what she said to the police during the interviews where they convinced her that Chad murdered Kassidy. At the trial, she was stuck between that truth and the understanding that she was scheduled for a trial herself, and that she could be prosecuted for the earlier exaggerations or misstatements to the police. Brown then followed her lead, "*I'm going to refer you to one of your statements*." Amanda stated, "*Yes, I know I said that, but, at the time, I was overwhelmed, and I don't know.*" (p. 86-7) Brown read to the court her interview response to Angela Blodgett's question of November 9, "*Toss her into*?" when Amanda said, "*Like bang her head on the closet door so that it would keep her there.*" (p. 90) At the trial, Amanda responded to Brown,

I've seen -- one time, I saw him when he sat her in the corner, roughly put her there. She hit her head on the closet door. The closet door is hollow in the bedroom, and it didn't -- I didn't think it hurt her. And I think that's what I meant when I said that." (p. 90)

Seeking to show that Amanda was minimizing Chad's behavior, he reminded Amanda of her statement to Angela Blodgett that over the last month of Kassidy's life Chad put Kassidy into the corner three times a week, or more. At the trial, Amanda said, "*He never did it that often. I can probablyh remember four or five times.*" (p. 90)

Simon Brown asked Amanda if Kyle ever threw tantrums, and she responded that he did, but Brown did not ask the followup question of how Chad responded to Kyle's tantrums. The answer would have been that Kyle would be sent to his room or to a corner for a time out. Chad didn't need to hold his face to obtain eye contact, because Kyle was already taught by Chad to look at his father, and Chad didn't need to carry Kyle because he went voluntarily. This is one example of how the U.S. system of adversarial trials works. One side tries to present only the facts that support its case, leaving to the other side the challenge of presenting the "rest of the story," as the late radio commentator, Paul Harvey, would say. In a trial, where the judge is pressed to conserve resources and keep trials to a minimum length, and defense lawyers are limited by the resources of their clients, it's often the case that only one side of several stories is left presented. In a case where all but one of the witnesses is a prosecution witness, it's the direct testimony which usually stands for the jury to remember, with only some pieces challenged or supplemented by the defense.

Amanda was asked about an incident involving their bed, and she said that Chad, "*got frustrated with her because she wasn't standing in the corner. She was just throwing a temper, so he threw her on the bed...he just kind of plopped her on the bed....*" and she would land on her back, "*kicking and screaming.*" (p. 92-3) Amanda continued, "*... I came over and I said, 'Don't touch her.' And he grabbed her leg, and then I let go, and then that was it. And then I just yelled at him.... I grabbed Kassidy, and Chad grabbed her leg saying, 'No, she needs to be disciplined. And I said, 'No, I'm going to do the disciplining.' I let go and then he got up and left, went downstairs.*" Afterwards, "*she was fine, because I was there with her. She stopped crying automatically.*" (p. 93-4)

Amanda testified that Chad, "*muttered something under his breath. I wasn't quite sure exactly what it was. Something like, "I wish she wasn't here. He really got frustrated with her.*" (p. 94) Brown asked, "*Did he say that he wished she was never born*?" and Amanda said that he might have. Then she concluded, "*He was frustrated. He knew he lost his temper, so he just got up and went downstairs.*" (p. 95) Simon Brown didn't ask what conversation Amanda and Chad had afterwards.

Brown then moved to another incident involving Kassidy: splashing water on her face. Amanda explained.

I was in the bedroom, and I didn't know what was going on. I heard the faucet running. When I walked in, while I was walking in, he was walking out, and he said he splashed water on her face to get her [to] *stop screaming,.....He said, "I was just splashing her face with water because -- to get herself* [to] *stop screaming, because she was screaming so much".... He was frustrated with her. He was mad.* (p. 95-6)

Amanda was asked how Kassidy reacted to water after the incident, and she said, "*...one time I remember she was scared of the kitchen sink when I went to wash her hands,*" (p. 96) and not any time after that. Brown pursued this question, as he had understood from the statements of others that the "faucet incident" made Kassidy afraid of water, generally. Amanda responded to Brown, "*She loved baths. Always. She was fine. She would hand me the bubble bath, just so I'd give her bubble baths some days.*" (p. 96) In addition to statements from others, Simon Brown reminded Amanda that she, too, told the police that since the faucet incident, Kassidy was afraid of water, and he asked, "*What's the truth*?" (p. 96) Amanda did not waiver and said that Kassidy loved baths. Thus, the perception of fear of water arose from one instance where Amanda brought Kassidy to the sink to wash her hands. The prosecution's theory was that Chad's splashing water in Kassidy's face had made her afraid of water. Amanda repeated, "*She loved baths, always. And she was afraid of the sink when I brought her out to the sink. She always wanted a bath.*" (p. 97). Amanda said she gave Kassidy a bath, "*Almost every day. Every other day.*" (p. 107) Brown never asked if Chad's technique succeeded in calming Kassidy down. It did, and the defense never asked that question during cross-examination, either.

In 2011, Chad wrote about his own experience with Kassidy's possible fear of water.

Incidentally, did I ever tell you about Kassidy flinching by the kitchen sink? I had given Kassidy something sticky to eat and she got it all over her hands and face. So after she was done I brought her to the kitchen sink to wash up. I sat her on the counter and wet the washcloth to wash her up. In the process I guess I must have moved quickly or something and Kassidy pulled back and flinched, quickly closing her eyes and putting her hands up as if she thought I was going to slap her in the face! I wanted to cry right then. I said, "Oh my God baby, I would never hit you." Kassidy didn't make a peep. She just made that flinching. It melted my heart. I pulled her into my chest and gave her a soothing hug and then washed her up. I thought about this a lot right afterwards. I was crushed that she felt that I would slap her then I dismissed it as her natural reflexes until it popped in my head again. I don't believe I ever held her cheeks after that: thinking that I had somehow made Kassidy afraid of me. Kassidy died a short while after this. I remember discussing the flinching with Amanda one night and how odd it made me feel to see her do this. I can't recall if I asked her prior to Kassidy's death what she thought might have caused Kassidy to flinch like that, but I know I discussed it with Amanda while we were staying at Bruce's after Kassidy's death. (Letter, March 22, 2011)

Brown then asked about the names that Chad would use for Kassidy. Amanda stated, "*Some days he would say, 'She's being a little bitch today.' Said that a couple of times*," and "*'She seems like she doesn't know that much. She's kind of slow, retarded.' He said that once, I can remember.*" Amanda said that she responded, "*I would yell at him. I'd get mad and say, "No, she's not.*" (p 97) She said that she was not concerned about Kassidy's development,

Not until after she died. I thought she was just sick, because Kyle had the flue two weeks before she died, and I thought maybe that was why she was really tired all the time. I started working a week before she died all day and all night, so I really didn't get to observe her that much the week before she died. (p. 98)

Amanda said the bruising on Kassidy was "*pretty obvious*," but that she "*still went grocery shopping with her and did regular things. It didn't concern me that much. I think a couple of times it did, though.*" (p. 98) Implicit in this exchange was Amanda's belief that all the bruises she could see were explained by accidents or by Chad's too-forceful palming of Kassidy's face, and that, too, had a reasonable explanation.

Then Brown turned to the "trampoline story," and Amanda described its origin, "*... Emily* [Conley] *and I, she was going to the doctor's, and she* [Kassidy] *had bruises right here from him grabbing her face. And Chad and I made up that excuse.*" (p. 99).
He told me that someone's going to think that someone does something to her because of the bruises on her face...we both thought we should make up an excuse for it, because I didn't feel like explaining that he grabbed her face to Emily.... He said we were there jumping on the trampoline and he grabbed her face to pull her in, because she fell off. (p. 101)

When asked, Amanda said that she couldn't remember whether it was she or Chad who originated the story.

Amanda could have added that the story did have a basis in fact, in that Chad and Kassidy did play on the trampoline together and Chad did catch her to prevent her from falling off on one occasion. Still, he did not grab her by the face at that time. The "trampoline story" was one of those "white lies" that took on a life of its own. In hindsight, it would have been so much easier to simply say to Emily and others, "*Chad palmed Kassidy's face in order to gain* ***eye contact*** *and he regrets that he squeezed it hard enough to cause bruises. We're going to take Kassidy to see her pediatrician to see why she bruises so easily. Her 24-month pediatrician appointment should be coming up soon.*" In fact, following the three month schedule beginning with the May 8 appointment (15 month checkup) and August 10 appointment (18 months checkup), the next appointment, the 24-month checkup, was to have been scheduled in six months, i.e. February 10th, but there is no record of it.

Emily Conley's obstetrician appointment was likely in the week beginning Monday, October 9, because on Sunday, October 8, Amanda's friend, Crystal Martin babysat for Kassidy. Crystal bathed Kassidy and her own son, Devin, and saw no bruises. The following Friday, Amanda took Kassidy to her mother's home in Buckfield where her brother, Joshua saw bruises on Kassidy. Thus, Chad's holding of Kassidy's face likely occurred early that week, and Emily's appointment was a day or two later.

Amanda acknowledged that she told the "trampoline story" to several people, including several upcoming witnesses. Thus, she acknowledged that she made up a story about something she and Chad thought embarrassing at the time. If Kassidy Bortner hadn't died on November 9, 2000, and were now 12 years old, the "trampoline story" might only be remembered as a family fantasy or legend. But she died, and the magnifying glass of the law seemed to transform a fib into the key to a solving a child's death. Paraphrasing Sigmund Freud, sometimes a story is just a story. There was never any evidence that the bruises Chad caused on Kassidy's cheeks when obtaining **eye contact** had anything whatsoever to do with her death.

Missed in the exchange between Simon Brown and Amanda about her telling Emily the "trampoline story" on that day was that Amanda took Kassidy to a doctor's office with Emily, where there was likely a receptionist and others in a waiting room. Amanda was not hiding Kassidy, and this was three weeks before she died.

Then Brown explored other statements that Amanda had made about the bruises and implied that they were all fictional, like the "trampoline story." Amanda acknowledged that, yes, she had told her friend Shannon Gagne that "*while Chad was carrying Kassidy, he hit her head against the wall by accident*," but that "*... I've done that before, too. Just like walking quickly with her, bumped her and not a mark or anything, but just being careless*." (p. 103-04) However, Amanda agreed that at the time she had told Shannon about such an accident, she was using that incident to explain an **eye contact** bruise and not the bruise caused when Chad carried Kassidy on his shoulders and she hit her head on the stairway ceiling.

Amanda agreed that she probably or could have told Emily Conley and Shannon Gagne that bruises on Kassidy's face were "*from another child throwing a toy at her*." (p. 104) Amanda also agreed that she told Tristan Evans that bruises on Kassidy's face were caused by Kassidy falling down the stairs. As Tristan would later testify, that explanation seemed so unlikely to her that she made her anonymous call to DCYF. However, Amanda testified that those bruises, in late October, were caused by Chad's **eye contact** grabbing, but she added that there were "*other things that happened with Jeff, also, she had different other things*." (p. 105)

The difficulty for a listener when one learns, at some point, that what s/he heard was a lie, is that the truth is unknown. It becomes a <u>tabula rasa</u>, a blank canvas on which some fanciful version of events can be painted. That's what happened to Chad when all the people who had heard the "trampoline story" from Chad and Amanda, and other stories from Amanda, realized that they were likely not true. As the police and prosecutors were sure that they knew what the truth was, they painted the canvas for the witnesses, the jury and the media.

The questioning then turned to Amanda's efforts to find day care for Kassidy, and she acknowledged her ambivalence that "*I didn't want people to think that I was doing anything to Kassidy*." (p. 105)

Amanda denied that anyone, including her friend, Melissa Chick, had urged her to see a doctor about the bruises.

Simon Brown asked if Amanda had kept Kassidy away from other people because of the bruising and she recalled the weekend of Chad's birthday, which was on Sunday, October 15, when she took Kassidy to visit her friends in Maine,

because I didn't want her [Chad's mother] *to think I was abusing Kassidy. And also, I didn't want to go down there because Tristan was coming over. It was kind of like a family thing. That's his ex-wife. And I just didn't want to feel uncomfortable*." (p. 108-09)

At the time, Amanda and Chad thought Tristan was still his wife, as the notice about the October 4, 2000 date for his divorce had not yet been sent to him. So, both of them felt that their relationship was somehow more illicit because he was still legally married.

One of the prosecution themes about Chad and Amanda was that Chad was the dominant figure and that he told Amanda what to do and what to say. This was one reason for the bail condition prohibiting contact with Amanda and for the police fervor in 2001 in ferreting out their continued relationship. Brown asked Amanda if she "*had a discussion with Chad about Kassidy being there when his family was over*" and did "*Chad tell you what to do with Kassidy that weekend*?" (p. 109) She said that, "*No*," he didn't tell her what to say, but that, "*Yeah, he was a little concerned about it, but after that he was like, "No, just stay. I'll explain it to her... His mother. But I went anyway, because I hadn't gone out in a long time, either, and I went out that night with Tracey Foley*." (p. 109-10)

After a lunch break, Simon Brown returned to the exact description of Chad's picking up of Kassidy and plopping her onto their bed. Amanda stated, "*I've never seen him just pick her up by the face and throw her onto the bed*." (p. 113) Missing from the questioning were the times when Chad and Kassidy played on the same bed, sometimes with Kyle, in fake wrestling.

The prosecutor asked "*was there ever conduct by the defendant involving Kassidy's throat*?" and Amanda explained, "*Yes. One time he stuck his finger like here* [pointing to her own throat], *and she gagged while she was screaming, crying. And he didn't do it out of anger. She changed her scream and then she stopped crying because she was like, what I am doing. But he didn't hurt her when he did it... I think she was startled, because it changed the tone of her scream, and she kind of thought that was like, I don't know if she thought it was funny or not.*" (p. 113) Whether if was funny or not, Amanda said "*...it made me angry, and I said never to do it again. And he never did.*" However, she conceded that she did tell the police a year earlier that it may have happened "*a couple of times*," but that it did, in fact, only happen once.

Brown returned to the subject of the weekend of October 14-15, Chad's birthday, when Amanda went to Maine, and the question was about a discussion with Chad about whether Amanda was going to visit her mother. Amanda said, "*Yes. She had a bruise on the side of her face, and I don't know if it was from Jeff's house or if it was from Chad grabbing her face, but I didn't want to bring her up there, because I didn't want my mom to think anything was going on, or whatever.*" Amanda testified that Chad said, " *'You can if you want, but she might think something, something like that.'* " and that Chad "*might have*" told her not to take Kassidy to see Jacqueline. She may have already left for Maine when Jacqueline called Chad's home on Saturday, October 14 because Joshua Bortner had told her about bruises on Kassidy's face. When Jacqueline called Rochester, Chad told her the "trampoline story." Thus, Jacqueline already knew about the bruises, but Amanda may not have yet known that she knew, and even if so, she simply may not have wanted to have the discussion with her mother.

Brown then asked about the babysitting of Kassidy, beginning with when and how often. Amanda responded, "*A lot. Couple of times Jennifer and I went shopping. I landscaped twice for him while he watched Kassidy. Every day before she died while I worked. We* [Chad and Amanda] *went to a couple of concerts, and he watched her then overnight, also. And money-management classes I was going to, he watched her overnight one time for that.*" (p. 117) She said that her memory of November 8th was vague, but that "*I was looking for day cares that day. I was on the phone. I worked. I dropped off Kassidy around like 1:30, 2:30 at Jeff's house before I went to work. But I was looking for a dress, because I was supposed to go to dinner with Chad that weekend....*" (p. 118) Previously, it was thought that Amanda left Kassidy at Jeff's around 4:30 p.m. As the difference between a 1:30 or 2:30 dropoff and a 4:30 dropoff, together with Chad's picking up of Kassidy at 5:30 is the difference between one hour at Jeff's on the 8th or 3-4 hours, the question of when Amanda left Kassidy at Jeff's on that day is important. During Amanda's third interview with the police, on November 12, Angela Blodgett asked what time Amanda left Kassidy at Jeff's and Amanda recalled, "*...like three o'clock (3:00) I think. Three (3:00), three-thirty (3:30). Because I remember going to my sister's work and I was going to look for a dress because I was supposed to go to dinner this weekend with Chad.*" Later, Brown asked Amanda what she did after dropping Kassidy off at Jeff's, "*And then you went to work?*" and she responded, "*Yes, Well, no. I went shopping for a dress. Then I went to work.*" (p. 122)

Later, under cross-examination by Alan Cronheim, Amanda stated that she went shopping for a dress "*after leaving Kassidy with Jeff.*" (p. 185) The question still remains unresolved in 2011, which is remarkable, given the importance of every hour of the 48 hours before Kassidy's death. Jennifer has stated that Amanda came to visit her at Perfumania around 3:00, but did not state whether Kassidy was with her or not. At Amanda's trial in 2002, Jennifer said that she did not see Kassidy on Wednesday, November 8th. Also at that trial, Heather Hamilton Lavalley said that she only saw Kassidy once, and that was earlier, in October. Thus, it's likely that Amanda dropped Kassidy off at Jeff's closer to 3:00 p.m. than 4:00, and thus Kassidy was with Jeff for closer to 2 1/2 hours than 1 1/2 hours.

Another question which wasn't asked of Amanda was who was going to babysit Kassidy on the upcoming weekend when Chad and Amanda were in Maine for a Colley-McCoy management social weekend. The question was not asked of Amanda or Chad during their police interviews, either. The answer, according to Amanda in 2011, would have been that she had asked her mother, Jacqueline Conley, to babysit Kassidy for that weekend, and the likely time of that request was Amanda's six minute call with her mother on Wednesday morning, November 8 at 8:35 a.m. If the jury had known that Amanda had made such arrangements, the jurors would likely have looked more skeptically at the prosecution's claims that Amanda was trying to keep Kassidy away from her mother. Also, the answer would have supported Amanda's claim that she believed she understood the reasons for the bruises which she had seen as of that time, and didn't feel they were serious, and she was willing to have her mother make her own evaluation, too.

Returning to Amanda's testimony, she was asked about Kassidy's health on Wednesday, November 8, and Amanda testified, "*She was really tired. She didn't -- she was talking to me. She didn't -- nothing really concerned me that was wrong with her. And I said Kyle had the flu* [a] *little bit, so I thought maybe she had the flu a little bit, too. She was walking and talking. I was just saying* [to Sergeant James White in her December 19, 2000 interview] *she took a little bit longer of a nap. She was a little sleepy that day.*" (p. 120) Asked about Kassidy's face that day, Amanda said, "*... She had a little thing right here from when I saw her fall off the couch onto the living* [room] *table, coffee table.... maybe four days before that. Couple days before that. She started to be a little more klutzier like two weeks before she died... She was getting off the couch... and the coffee table was right there and she hit her eye right here. Right underneath her eye like right here.*[pointing to cheeks]" (p. 120-21) Also, "*I think there was a little bit of fading right here* .[pointing to eye] *from where Chad was grabbing her face....It was going away.*"

The questioning then turned to the evening of November 8th. Amanda said,

I went to Perfumania where my sister works, like a second away from my work. Walked in. The first thing she says to me - - she was on the phone with Jeff -- the first thing she says to me is, 'Jeff doesn't want to babysit any more....And then I was just like, 'I'm on a waiting list for day care, you know, thanks a lot.' Just kind of -- thought that was kind of weird. And then I called Chad and just asked how Kassidy was doing, and he told me about the wiffle ball....He said that they were playing wiffle ball in the bedroom, Kyle, Kassidy and him, and Kassidy was sitting on the bed and he was throwing balls to Kyle and he was batting in the bedroom, and that's normally what they do actually quite a lot. And he said that Kyle hit the ball right into Kassidy's eye right here [pointing to eye]" (p. 122-23)

Simon Brown asked, "*Did he tell you it was a wiffle ball*?" and Amanda replied, "*No, he didn't tell me what kind of ball. But I had a bunch of balls right next to the bed in a wheel barrow. There were all sorts of different kinds of balls that I put in there, so I don't know what kind of ball it was. He never told me actually what kind of ball it was.*" This was important, because it shows that despite the police and prosecutors' concern that Chad was seeking to influence Amanda's testimony in 2001 during his freedom on bail, he never clarified with Amanda what kind of ball it was that hit Kassidy that night. Throughout the trial, the issue of the type of ball was never resolved and different witnesses made references to "*ball*," "*baseball*," and "*wiffle ball*." The important difference was that being hit by a batted wiffle ball will sting, but not likely do damage. However, being hit by a batted Tee-ball, or "*hard rubber ball*" or "*starter baseball*" to use the terms Chad used in his police interview, can cause damage and potentially death, whether by itself, or when accompanied by other injuries.

Trying to set a foundation for challenging the batted-ball-hitting-Kassidy story, Brown asked whether Chad said what kind of bat was used. Amanda didn't say whether Chad specified the type of bat, but she did say, "*It was a wiffle ball bat. That's all the bats that we had at the house.*" (p. 123) She said that Chad, like Jeff a few minutes earlier, said,

"I don't know if I want to babysit any more. It seems like every time I have her something happens where she hurts herself or something happened".... He just sounded concerned. And, to tell you the truth, I was -- I needed to leave to go back to work, so I

was only half listening to him. It was just kind of like a lack of communication there that night.... I was mad. I didn't want another bruise on her, because I wanted to take her to day care.... I said, "I'm sick of her getting hurt." I meant Jeff and Chad, probably... I went back to work.... I worked until 11:00... And I probably got home around midnight. (p. 124-25)

Later in her testimony, Simon Brown returned to this phone call and asked about what Chad said about taking Kassidy to see a doctor, and Amanda responded that he said, "*That, 'you should take her to the doctor's as soon as the bruises clear up.' Something like that.*" (p. 146) What wasn't clear to the jury was which bruises was Chad referring to. Chad believes in 2011 that none of the bruises on Kassidy's face on November 9 were caused by his holding her face to obtain **eye contact**. The previous Sunday, there was only a bruise on one cheek and, according to Brandon Harvey's subsequent pre-sentencing letter to Judge Nadeau, and that bruise was fading. Chad had already resolved to be even more careful about squeezing Kassidy's cheeks too hard, just as he had done after he and Amanda first noticed that he could cause bruising in that way. He forgot that lesson once or twice, but not again during her last week. In 2011, Nicole recalled that that particular bruise was on Kassidy's right cheek and it was about at the middle of her cheek. Thus, it was not a bruise caused by Chad's palming for **eye contact** for two reasons. First, the palming bruises were on the lower cheek, just above the jaw line, and second, when the bruises from palming Kassidy's cheeks appeared in October, they came on both sides of her face, as the pressure was equal from his thumb and from his fingers.

In 2011, Chad wrote about this bruise,

... my belief is the bruise was a very small bruise toward the middle of Kassidy's cheek. Not sure of which side of her face. This was around the time that Kassidy was having some issues with a slight limp on and off when walking and I think that was the explanation we were given [which] *was that Jake* [Jeff's dog] *was running to the door and knocked Kassidy into something. Kassidy as just over 20 pounds and in an excited state, I have seen our dog, Kato, knock her down.* (Letter, July 17, 2011)

Returning to Amanda's testimony, she said that she came home, and talked with Chad about the "*wiffle ball, the whole thing again, what happened. Then I went upstairs and checked on her and it looked exactly* [like] *what he said. She had like a little red mark.*" (p. 125) Amanda then said that her eyesight is not good, and she recalled that she thought she was wearing only one contact lens at the time. The light in Kassidy's bedroom was off, but "*The hallway light was on, though, so I could see a little bit. And I think I gave her a kiss on the cheek and then I went downstairs.... I saw the little red mark, I think around her left eye from the ball hitting her face.*" (p. 126) Also, "*I saw a little bit of fading from him grabbing her face, or from Jeff, I don't know which one. And I saw the little scratch that she had right here* [pointing to right side of face] *from falling on the table from the couch.*" Then she went downstairs, and Brown asked about their interaction.

She testified,

We just -- first we hugged and talked about our day, and then I started talking about ... how I had a long day and I was working 12 hours and that wasn't that easy for me, because I just started working and it had been a while. And I had to go up and down ladders all day... I was just kind of starting something saying he doesn't work as hard as me, just, I don't know, being an eighteen-year old, I guess, and he started arguing and I threw a mug at him that was sitting on the coffee table. We were in the living room on the couch. And then he grabbed me and said, "Cut it out." (p. 127-28)

She said she was just about two feet away from Chad and

...just tossed it at him... He grabbed my throat and said, "Cut it out. What are you doing?"... He had me against the couch... He just had one hand on me. I don't know, he might have had two. I can't remember... for about a second.... Maybe two seconds.... He realized when he lost his temper, and then he would stop.... other people saw me the next day, obviously because that's when she died, and I didn't have a mark on me, or anything.... He said, "You know what gets me going. You know what makes my temper. It's like you're looking for it." (p. 129-31)

When asked, Amanda acknowledged that she didn't tell the police about her throwing the mug at Chad, "*because I was embarrassed. I don't know. I didn't want to get in trouble for it. I believe*[d] *that I would.... Well, I started it.*" (p. 131-32) Amanda testified that she and Chad both apologized to each other for both losing their tempers and they went to bed around 1-1:30.

The next morning, she awoke around 6-6:30 a.m.

I usually would pick Kyle's clothes out and Chad's too... I picked out Kyle's outfit and gave it to Chad so Chad could get him dressed. I got Kassidy ready. I changed her. She had a messy diaper when she woke up. And I got ready. I can't remember if I took a shower or not. (p. 136)

Chad remembers in 2011 that she did take a shower. Amanda said that Kassidy "*would usually walk into Chad and I's bedroom and hop into bed with us,*" (p. 136) but that she didn't do that on the morning of the 9th. Amanda said that Kassidy was crying, and

...she said, 'Mama,'... and I picked her up.... She had a messy diaper, and I brought her into our bedroom, laid her on the bed and changed her.... She was laying down. She was quiet... I was a little concerned, but I rationalized it in my head. I don't know why I did, but just because Kyle had the flu, so I figured she did, too. (p. 137)

She described the rush to get a running breakfast and pack food, Reese's Peanut Butter Puffs for Kassidy, and get out the door as she was running late for work. She described Kassidy as "*really tired. She wasn't talking much. Not like usual.*" (p. 139) When they arrived at Cross Road, and dropped Kyle off, "*I left her in the car. She was sleeping, and I brought Kyle in to the day care.*" (p. 140) Kassidy slept during the drive to Jeff's and

I brought her into the bedroom. My sister was there, and he was there, and I said, "Her eye, or her face looks like shit." I said something of that. And I was only in there for a second, and then I left, because I was running late. And my work was like five minutes from their house. (p. 140)

Amanda cried when she explained that Kassidy "*was wearing a red fleece dress and a sweatshirt, and she was wearing red matching pants...*[and] *a pink jacket,*" (p. 140) and Judge Nadeau offered to order a break, but Amanda said she could continue. This was the first time during the case that Kassidy's dress had been mentioned. It's a distinctive piece of clothing and either she was wearing it when she arrived, or she wasn't. No other witness mentioned the dress, but it was seized, and was an exhibit at the trial. Perhaps because of Amanda's emotional distress, there was no attempt to identify Kassidy's clothes which were admitted as Exhibits at the court. What she described as "*red matching pants*" was Exhibit #2 and called "Red Pajama bottoms." There was no Exhibit of red pajama tops or what Amanda called a "*fleece sweatshirt,*" as it was not recovered during the search of Jeff's apartment. Exhibit #5 was called a "*red fleece dress,*" which was a red-top dress with a white image of a dog's face on the chest. Amanda was not asked if the dress was over the pajamas, or whether Kassidy was wearing it that morning when she was left at Jeff's and Jennifer's.

She said that she carried Kassidy into Jennifer and Jeff's bedroom and they were just getting up. Jeff was in bed watching television and Jennifer was just getting out of bed and ready for work.

Amanda said she was at work and "*My sister calls me at work and she tells me that something happened, or there was an accident and Kassidy's eyes rolled back. And she said, 'but she's fine. She's like, don't worry about it. She's fine. And she told me to go to the Portsmouth Hospital.*" (p. 142-43)

After briefly noting her interviews at the Kittery Police Station, the questioning shifted to the hotel that Amanda, Jeff and Jennifer stayed in that night, and Amanda was asked about her phone call with Chad. She said, "*We had a long conversation. I was on the phone with him all night. It was just like I couldn't believe it happened, and asking him questions. And he was just upset. He was really upset. He was crying. He couldn't believe it happened either. Just in so much shock. I was saying, 'They're telling me that you killed Kassidy.' I was telling him what they were telling me. And I don't know what I believed then. I was just so overwhelmed and* [in] *so much shock. It was crazy.... he said he felt really bad about grabbing her.... Yeah, he might have said that.*" (p. 145-46)

After Simon Brown refreshed Amanda's memory about her fourth interview with Officer Angela Blodgett and Sergeant James White, Amanda remembered, "*Yes. Yeah, I said that I don't know why I want to be with him because of that, because they had convinced me that he did it. Not truly, but....*" (p. 147)

Amanda was at Chad's home when he was arrested, picking up her car. Kassidy's funeral was two days later. Amanda testified, "*I went to Texas right after the baby*['s] *funeral, just to get away, everything. And then I called him from Texas, because I just felt awful, and I knew something wasn't right. And I was just remembering other things about Jeff and just other things. And I called him up and he didn't want to talk with me, and then I started crying. I'm like, 'I really need you.' And finally he started talking with me.*" (p. 148-49)

Amanda acknowledged that she ended up living again with Chad in 2001, even though she knew that was in violation of the conditions of his bail release. She explained, "*Chad was the only one I felt comfortable with, and he was the only one who helped me through everything. I don't really have a family much. I don't really have many people to help me.*" (p. 149) She described the several living arrangements they had during 2001, which ended when several of Chad's friends and relatives were subpoenaed to a grand jury. During that year Amanda said that she called Officer Angela Blodgett and Sergeant James White each "*a couple of times*," and that she told White that she was in San Antonio when she was in New Hampshire.(p. 152)

Alan Cronheim began his cross-examination of Amanda and began with questions about Jeff and established that he began babysitting Kassidy in October, before which time Kassidy had no problems with her health. Amanda said that there were times that Jeff babysat Kassidy at his home while she and Jennifer were doing his company's landscaping work. At other times, when she and Jennifer were shopping, and when Amanda went to the money management classes, and when Amanda was looking for a job. Alan Cronheim didn't specify any dates, but the three Thursday money-management classes were on October 19, October 26, and November 2. It was during for the October 26 class that Jeff kept Kassidy for two nights and three days. The jury did not have the specific dates and did not have a time-line to reference.

Alan Crohneim asked about the unspecified time when Jeff brought Kassidy home from babysitting with bruises on her buttocks. It was Sunday, October 22. Amanda described them, "*They were really bad bruises. They were dark and blue -- black and blue.*" (p. 158) He asked who pointed those injuries out to her, and she responded, "*Myself. I was changing her diaper. My sister was right there and saw it, also. And she was just like, oh my gosh. Shocked.*" (p. 158) "*Her whole butt was black and blue.*" (p. 177) However, Cronheim didn't ask Amanda about Jeff's explanation for those injuries.

On Sunday, October 22, Chad and Jeff drove to Maine in Jeff's truck, as Jeff was helping Chad bring a newly purchased 3-wheeler back to Rochester. Chad wrote in a March 23, 2010 letter,

He told me on the way up to Maine that he had spanked her but I assumed it would have been pretty age appropriate, knowing that she was just a baby. The day after I found out that he had spanked Kassidy's butt, I called him up and said, "Gee, I guess you spanked her butt!" I was expecting him to apologize and act like he felt back as he had when talking to Amanda the previous day. Even though I didn't often address things with him because Kassidy was Amanda's daughter, I did on this occasion because it was so severe. Instead of apologizing and being remorseful for his obvious loss of control he started bragging and laughing, "Yeah, I spanked her so hard my hand stung." I lost it on the phone. I said something to the effect of, "You dumb shit, she is a baby and you hit her so hard through her diaper that it caused bruises. If you ever touch her again, I will beat your ass."

Chad's call to Jeff was on Monday, October 23, because, "*Amanda kept it away from me at Jennifer's request. The next day Amanda showed me the bruising that he caused. I couldn't believe it!*" (Letter, March 23, 2010)

Regarding a second incident addressed by Attorney Cronheim, Amanda confirmed that she had conversations with Jeff after finding marks on Kassidy's feet, but Cronheim did not ask her when this happened.

Chad recalls that he discovered the abrasions on Kassidy's feet approximately on Monday evening, November 6. He wrote in his January 7, 2011 Letter,

You asked in a letter last week and we spoke again yesterday about how I was able to discover the pin pricks on Kassidy's feet by flying her up the stairs like Superman. Sometimes at night this is how I would "fly" the kids up the stairs to bed. Kyle and Kassidy would giggle and I guess it just took some of the stress away from having to go to bed. On the evening that I discovered the pin pricks, Amanda was in the office on the computer working on scoring the survey project for our friend, Bruce. I was in the living room with Kyle and Kassidy playing and watching The Disney-Tarzan Movie (It was Kyle's favorite at the time and he watched it at least once a week). Amanda yelled in from the office that Kassidy needed to go to bed. So I scooped her up and said, "Mama says it's bedtime, baby." At this point, I had Kassidy cradled across my arms as if preparing to haul a bundle of firewood and ran with Kassidy through the dining room into the office so Amanda could kiss her "Good Night." Kassidy was lying with her backside against my arms and as we left the office I tossed her up about 6 inches so that her front side was now against my arms and parallel to the floor. From there, I "flew" her over the dining room table, around the living room, over Kato, and swaying side to side to avoid oncoming "meteors." Once we reached the stairs, I slid my left hand down to Kassidy's feet and my right hand up near her belly/chest area to make the flight up the stairs. (My back was against the wall vs. against the railing side.)

Once I touched Kassidy's feet I could feel these rough bumps all over the soles of her feet. They weren't in any particular pattern they just seemed to be on the surfaces of the foot that would actually hit the ground when stepping. I guess you could say it kind of startled me. I yelled to Amanda. Amanda didn't hear me the first time so I yelled a little louder. Amanda hearing the unsettling tone of my voice on the stairs came running in. As soon as I was able to make eye contact with Amanda as she reached the living room, I asked something to the effect of, "What the hell is wrong with Kassidy's feet?" It was clear from Amanda's dumbfounded look, that she had no idea what I was talking about. From touching, it felt like a bunch of misc. little "pin pricks," for lack of a better description. I turned Kassidy over so she was sitting in my arms and Amanda picked her leg up so that she could see the bottom of Kassidy's feet. Amanda could see them, a bunch of these tiny little holes as if Kassidy had been walking on something, perhaps a hair brush, except they weren't in the pattern of a hair brush. Amanda started tearing up and I had this almost angry feeling surging through me. The only good thing was these pricks didn't seem to affect Kassidy or hurt her in anyway. They weren't very deep. I started firing questions at Amanda. "What has Kassidy been doing today? Was she down in our basement at all? Could she have gotten into something at our house?" etc. Amanda replied, "No" to everything and we searched around looking for anything that could have been dangerous at our house that she could have been stepping on. It looked to me like Kassidy had been walking on "carpet strip" the material used in wall to wall carpeting so I checked all of ours. I couldn't find any bare spots or an area where she could have stepped on it so I knew this wasn't it, (at our house at least). Amanda informed me that she was at Jen and Jeff's earlier in the day and Jeff watched Kassidy for a short time while Amanda and Jen went somewhere. I assumed from this that it had to have happened while Kassidy was with Jeff. I was a little irritated and said not very nicely to Amanda "God damn it, find out what happened over there and tell that idiot that she is a baby and he has to watch her more closely." I shared what it looked like to me with Amanda and she indicated she would be talking to Jeff or Jen tomorrow about it. Kassidy seemed fine so I continued on bringing her upstairs to bed. I never gave it a second thought that this was anything but accidental. It just seemed like carelessness not maliciousness.

The next evening when I got home Amanda informed me that she had spoken to Jen about it and that in Jen and Jeff's apartment, they had some small nail heads sticking up in the linoleum floor or something to that effect and that was "probably" what happened. Jeff

was going to go around and pound them in. This really irritated me. I said something similar to, "If you know that you have things sticking up, you don't let a baby walk around barefoot. Either fix the damn problem or make sure that Kassidy always has shoes or slippers on." I had this bad habit of stating the obvious and sounding a bit "preachy" when something bothered me.

Again, I don't recall at that time considering that this was anything other than accidental. From that point on, we made sure that Kassidy always had her Elmo slippers with her when she went to Jen and Jeff's.

Amanda testified that she talked with Jeff about the abrasions, and "*He said that there's -- in the middle of the bottom of the floor in between the doorway, sometimes -- he said he has old carpet, which he did, and there's like old nails sticking up from the bottom of it. Sometimes they have that at places I've done that.... So I believed him.*" (p. 173-74) She said that she never saw such nails at Jeff's and Jen's, but that thereafter she brought Kassidy to that home with slippers.

Cronheim asked Amanda about a third incident, when Jeff returned Kassidy with bumps on her head, and she said, "*He brought her back and she was really sick. This was about two weeks before she died. He didn't tell me. He waited until I saw the black and blues on her head, and then I was like, 'what is this?'*" (p. 159-60) She asked Jeff what happened and "*He said that she fell out of his truck.... I think he said that she fell out of his car seat. That's not something she would normally do.*" (p. 171

Amanda testified about a fourth incident, arising from the same babysitting stint, *She really was dehydrated also. So I gave her -- she kept saying "hungry," "hungry," "Mama"...She wanted a drink. I gave her water.... She acted like she was starving, like really hungry. I sat her in her highchair and I gave her a bowl of cereal and she like stuck her head in the bowl to suck out the milk... because she was so thirsty. So I was like, "My Gosh." I gave her Pedialyte because that helps for dehydration. And I gave her Tylenol... And then when I picked her up, I saw the bruises... Right on the back of her head. There were two, and they were really big.*" (p.170) The cereal was Cheerios. Amanda said that Kassidy had never acted like that before, and that Jeff was still at Chad's with her and Kassidy during Amanda's efforts to respond to Kassidy's needs. With both of these third and fourth incidents, the time was stated to the jury to be "*about two weeks before she died.*" However, it was actually the three day/two night babysitting from Thursday, October 26 through Saturday, October 28, and the jury would have benefitted from that precise information and also more information about why a night's babysitting turned into a three day period of hunger and thirst.

In further explanation of Kassidy's behavior or condition, Amanda described a fifth incident relating to Jeff, during that same babysitting stint, "*He said that she drank Windex. He said that she may be acting a little funny because she drank Windex. And I said, 'Well, did you call the poison-control center?' And he said, 'Yeah, and they said to give her milk, but we didn't have any milk, so I gave her water.'* " (p. 171-72)

Alan Cronheim asked how Kassidy acted during the rest of the day, and Amanda said, "*She was quiet. That night when she was falling asleep, I just kind of held her all night. Her eyes went back*" Amanda answered "*Yes*," to the question "*Was there a point in time that her eyes started going toward the back of her head*?" and said "*She was with me... on the couch*," and the phenomenon happened for "*like a second*," and Amanda had never seen anything like that before. (p. 172) She continued, "*I was like, 'Oh my gosh.' And I think I asked a few people and I rationalized into my head that babies do that when they're falling asleep, because she was falling asleep when she did it. And I wish I didn't do that, but I did.*," (p. 172-73) meaning that she wished she didn't rationalize the observation, instead of seeking medical help.

Amanda responded, "Yes," when Attorney Cronheim asked about a sixth incident, "*Is there a time when Kassidy comes back from Jeff Marshall's care and she's walking funny*?" Amanda said she asked Jeff about the change for Kassidy, and Jeff said that accidentally "*he tripped over her*" and stepped "*on her foot or leg.*" (p. 175) By Chad's recollection in 2010, this incident occurred around Tuesday, November 7.

Alan Cronheim asked about a seventh incident, after which "*Kassidy came back with some bruises*." He asked, "*Is there a time that Jeff Marshall told you that Kassidy was hurt running -- running off her bed*?" and Amanda responded, "*Yes, his bed*." (p. 175) Amanda said, "*He said he was teasing her, and he said, 'Mama's home,' and I wasn't home. And she just always got excited when I would get there. And she ran off the bed, and he said she was retarded or something, and she had bruises on the side of her face from that. That's what he told me*." (p. 175-76) Amanda testified that she had never before seen Kassidy running off the end of a bed, and agreed, "*Yes*," with Attorney Cronheim's statement/question "*But it's another time that she ended up with bruises after coming home from Jeff Marshall's?*" (p. 176)

In his November, 2000 letter to his attorneys, Chad recalls that this was the first indication of difficulty with Jeff's babysitting. He wrote,

The first sign of trouble came somewhere during the week of Oct. 6-8. Jeff brought Kassidy home one of those nights with three little bruises on her cheek. The odd thing was he had tried to cover them with makeup. He told Amanda, when he brought Kassidy home, that she was standing on the bed and he said to her, "Mamma's here." She repeated, "mamma, mamma" and walked off the edge of the bed. I know it was that weekend because I went to Bruce's (one of my best friends) for football on Sunday and was bitching to Jeremy (my other best friend) about the whole makeup thing.

Alan Cronheim asked about a eighth incident, "*where Kassidy came home from Jeff Marshall's care with makeup on her face*," and Amanda said she recalled the incident. She said that makeup covered up a bruise that did not exist when Jeff's babysitting began, and she asked Jeff about it. "*He said that the dog knocked her over,*" accidentally. (p. 177) Not known to the jury were the dates of these accidents, bruises, incidents or injuries. The above eight are listed in roughly chronological order, with the "~" used to mean "approximately." and "+" means "after." On the left is given the order in which they were discussed in court, and above.

7th	+10/8	Fall from bed when Jeff said, "Mama's here," but then Amanda was not there.
8th	+10/15	Kassidy knocked over by Jeff and Jen's dog, Jake. Makeup applied to cover bruise.
1st	~10/21	Jeff Marshall spanked Kassidy, causing black and blue marks on buttocks.
5th	~10/26	Kassidy drank unknown quantity of Windex at Jeff's.
3rd	~10/27	Kassidy returned with two large bumps on back of head, from fall from Jeff's truck.
4th	~10/28	Kassidy returned home severely dehydrated (same return day as 3rd)
6th	~11/6	Jeff tripped over Kassidy, stepping on her foot, causing limp.
2nd	~11/7	Minute marks found on Kassidy's feet. Also called "abrasions," or "pin pricks"

Alan Cronheim did not ask Amanda about other incidents which involved the quality of Jeff's babysitting for Kassidy.

One incident, called here the ninth, which Jeff related to Chad was that he would put Kassidy in the corner for a time-out and then would look through the window to see if she was complying. Chad wrote in his March 13, 2010 letter,

Jeff described to me once how he put Kassidy into the corner once for a timeout and then went out to get the mail. He watched her from outside the window to see that she hadn't moved from where he put her. After a few minutes Kassidy wandered away and he went and he told me that he yelled at her for moving. I expressed that I thought that was "uncool" and he backed away as he always did, saying, "I only did it once."

A tenth incident was where Jeff allegedly covered Kassidy's face to muffle her crying so the neighbors would not hear her. Chad wrote of this incident in his November, 2000 letter to his lawyers, where Jeff

... described an incident at his house where he was teaching Kassidy a lesson about listening. When watching her the previous week, she started crying and he threw her in on the bed; and she started crying louder. So he then threw a pillow over her head and said,

"Cry into that you little bitch. I have neighbors you know." He let Kassidy get up once she was quiet and she sat still in the chair until it was time to go home after that.
Later in that same letter to his attorneys, Chad estimated that this incident occurred in August,

I remember Jeff telling me when he was watching her early on in the summer that she would sit there and cry. He would take her into the bedroom because he had neighbors and he didn't want them to hear the crying. He told me once, "She tripped and fell and then started screaming. (This must have been August or so) I picked her up and put her on the bed lying face down so that she was screaming into a pillow rather than out loud. I didn't want anyone to hear here and think I was beating her or something. Sometimes though when she is just being a bitch I will throw her onto the bed and put a pillow down onto her face until she shuts up." I remember being pretty unimpressed with this comment and said, "What the hell is wrong with you. She could suffocate you know." He would come back with a big classic Jeff Marshall smile and say, "I didn't really do it hard. I just wanted her to stop. I would just set it there for a second, you know what I mean?" As crazy as it sounds, he is one of those people that can kind of tell you something horrible, and then cover it up in a way with humor or seriousness that would put your mind at ease so it was never questioned again.....

Amanda described both of these incidents in "My Life Story," copies of which Cronheim had recently shown to Judge Nadeau and the prosecutors.

Another, here called the eleventh, was on Tuesday, October 24, when Kassidy was returned home from babysitting by Jeff with three bruises on her jaw that were not present that morning. Jeremy was with Chad that day playing golf and confirmed with him that the bruises seen in the evening were not seen in the morning.

A twelfth was descrbed in Chapter 3, where Jeff "*was changing her diaper, and leaving her standing on the bed while he went to get wipes with her pants around both ankles and she fell face first.*" (Chad, November 2000 letter to his attorneys)
In 2010, Chad could not recall the date of the makeup/dog incident, but remembered that it was after the "Mama's here" incident. In an August 31 letter, he wrote,

In any event, all of this stuff happened after the Oct. 15th time frame. This I'm 99% certain of. Jeff returned Kassidy after an overnight stay I believe and told Amanda he put the makeup on because he had to go to Wal Mart. He would later tell someone, maybe the police? that he put the makeup on because he was trying to cover up bruises I had caused but this was not true. The bruises covered by the makeup occurred while Jeff was babysitting. I recall the Sunday after it happened I was watching football at Bruce's, I believe Jeremy was there and I vented to one or both of them that thought about being disgusted with him having nothing better to do than pick on a baby. Perhaps it was Sunday Oct. 22nd, the day before the golf outing. We know we were all together then. I'm not positive at this time and don't want to guess.

Attorney Cronheim then asked Amanda about Jeff's references to Kassidy and Amanda confirmed that he had called Kassidy a "*retard*" and a "*bitch*" and she agreed with Cronheim's assessments that "*both Chad and Jeff Marshall became frustrated with Kassidy*," and "*that both of them at different points called them names*," and that those names made her angry. (p. 178)

Cronheim brought Amanda back to her earlier conversation where Brown was "*questioning whether there were times that you were essentially hiding Kassidy from others, including your mother*," and Amanda recalled that portion of her direct examination earlier that day. (p. 178) After refreshing her memory by showing her a copy of page 61 of her second interview with the police on November 9, he asked, "*Now, is it the case when Chad said you shouldn't bring Kassidy to your mother's it was because Kassidy had supposedly fallen out of Jeff Marshall's truck?...So it was because of bruises on the back of her head in Jeff Marshall's care that caused Chad's concern?*" and Amanda responded, "*Yes,*" to both questions. (p. 180)

Then Alan Cronheim turned to the issue of Amanda's efforts to find day care for Kassidy. He asked her to identify Defendant's Exhibit A, and she said it was a list of 17 day care centers that she listed on a piece of paper. Then he showed Amanda a list of telephone calls, Exhibit B, made from Chad's home on the morning of November 8th, and established with Amanda that she called seven day care centers on that morning. In addition, as noted earlier, the list shows that she called her mother at 8:35 a.m. for six minutes, but she was not asked about that call. Amanda recalled in 2011 that it was about seeking babysitting care for Kassidy for the upcoming Colley-McCoy weekend meeting on November 11/12. If the jury had known about that plan, it would have significantly weakened the prosecution's charge that Amanda and Chad were consistently hiding Kassidy from people, including Amanda's mother. As is typical with young adults, sometimes Chad and Amanda were comfortable with seeing their parents with Kassidy, and sometimes not.

With leading questions, Cronheim established with Amanda that when she left Kassidy with Jeff, Kassidy appeared to be "*other than being somewhat tired, she was in reasonably good condition*," and "*had some marks and bruises on her face*," and "*she was walking around*," and was "*alert, with her average appetite, which was a pretty healthy appetite*." (p. 184-85)

Cronheim continued to review the chronology with Amanda on the 8th and asked, "*And it's at that time* [7:30 p.m.] *that Chad tells you about the wiffle ball hitting Kassidy's face*." (p. 185) Unfortunately, Cronheim seems to have missed an important aspect of the ball hitting Kassidy's face, which was that it was a Tee-ball, which is almost as heavy and almost as hard as a major league baseball. Such a ball can do damage, whereas a wiffle ball is far less likely to harm a child. Amanda confirmed about Kyle's hitting abilities, saying, "*I've seen the way he hits it, and he hits it a lot*." (p. 186) What the jury needed at this point was for someone to throw a Tee-ball at a sheet of glass in the courtroom and watch it shatter, while throwing a wiffle ball at another sheet of glass would simply bounce off. Without the jury seeing that the ball was more than a wiffle ball, it was useless to argue that the accident playing baseball was even relevant in solving the mystery of Kassidy's death. Also, not knowing the truth about the type of ball, made Chad's statements to the police about the ballhitting accident appear to be lies. As the police knew that Chad lied with the "trampoline story," it was very easy for them to assume that he was lying about other matters, too.

Amanda acknowledged that she first told the police or prosecutors about throwing the mug at Chad at a meeting with Assistant Atty. General Simon Brown, on November 5, 2001. (p. 187)

With an anticipatory apology for the pain it might cause, Alan Cronheim told Amanda that he needed to review with her, and the jury, the events of November 9, 2000. He established with Amanda that after she carried Kassidy downstairs, she put her on the living room couch and turned on the television. However, Kassidy was "*not talking with you the way she usually would?*" and Amanda agreed, "*No*." (p. 190) Amanda could not confirm that Kassidy ate or drank anything before going out the door to the car. Chad recalled in 2010 more details about Amanda's departure that morning, as noted in the first chapter, and his details are consistent with those in Amanda's testimony. As he has noted, because of his conviction, his memory is frozen in time - for the second half of the year 2000.

Alan Cronheim showed Amanda a photograph of Kassidy's body on November 9th and Amanda gasped, "*Oh my God. I can't look at that*." She agreed with Attorney Cronheim's leading questions, "*... she did not look like that when I dropped her off*?" and "*it was only with these ugly photographs on that Thursday that you first saw Kassidy in that condition*?" (p. 193) Amanda stated, "*I've never seen her face look like that, ever*." (p. 193) It's likely that she was responding to the numerous bruises and to the discoloration of skin of human bodies after death.

Alan Cronheim asked Amanda about a list "*of friends with whom you spoke and a number of friends who saw Kassidy during the month of October of 2000*." (p. 184) Then the judge ordered a 10 minute recess so Amanda could recover her composure, and the break became the break for the day.

MEDIA: 1. "I never thought it hurt her"
2. "Murdered baby's mother sees photos, cries out"

3. "Mother of beaten baby points finger at baby sitter"
4. "Bortner blames sitter - Admits murder suspect Evans grabbed toddler by face with enough force to leave bruises"
5. "Dead baby's mom: Evans didn't treat girl too badly"
6. "Kassidy's grandmother barred from courtroom, asked her daughter to tell the truth"

Thursday, 6 December 2001

Amanda resumed her testimony, and Alan Cronheim asked about Jennifer's reaction to seeing the photographs of Kassidy's body. Amanda stated, "*She said, 'I don't understand. They showed me the pictures. She didn't look like that when I saw her.*" (p. 5)

Amanda stated that Jeff and Jennifer wanted Amanda to stay with them for the evening of November 9 at Jeff's, "*to sleep at the same house that my daughter died in, and I couldn't do it.... I just want*[ed] *to go somewhere else, go to a motel.*" (p. 5)

Asked about her family, she said that her mother had remarried and that her stepfather had "*molested me when I was younger,*" (p. 9) and that her mother had not helped her. At first her mother did not believe the allegation of sexual abuse, but Amanda told her mother again when she turned 18, and Amanda believed that her mother then believed her. Amanda told the police about these issues when they were urging her to stay with her parents after Kassidy died.

She said that it was she who initiated the resumption of the relationship with Chad with the call from Texas and that, "*...he always told me to tell the truth.*" (p. 11)

After observing that her testimony thus far had been about "*the hard stuff about the problems with discipline,*" Alan Cronheim asked about the good times. (p. 11) She responded, "*He* [Chad]*.... actually, he taught her a lot. He taught her to count. He said ABC's with her more than I did. He read books to her at night before she went to bed, and I would read books to Kyle. So we kind of had our own little bonding with each kid.*"(p. 11) Chad played with Kassidy, and Amanda felt sometimes too roughly for a young girl. In Alan Cronheim's words, Chad would "*throw her up in the air*?" and "*times that he swung her around*?" and "*swung her by her legs*?" Importantly, Amanda agreed with Cronheim that she did those things with Kassidy, too, saying, "*Yes. She would laugh and stuff. She liked that.*" (p. 12) She agreed with Cronheim's words, "*and she didn't show any concern about being with Chad*?" and "*And she was happy, and smiling, and responding in a playful way*?" (p. 12)

Cronheim continued,

Now, focusing on the time that Chad was with Kassidy, and being physical with her, either through play or through discipline, either through holding or grabbing her arms, or holding or grabbing he legs, [was] *there ever a time that you saw her in pain or physical distress so that you thought she was hurt either in her arm or her leg?* (p. 13)

Amanda answered, "*No,*" and there was never a time she thought that Kassidy had a bone fracture. She said "*Yes,*" to Alan Cronheim's questions, "*Were there times that Chad held her and tried to nurturer her*?" and were "*there times that he tried to be supportive of her and loving of her?*" and that the morning routine "*would be her coming into your bedroom and hopping into bed*?" (p. 14)

Before beginning his redirect examination, Simon Brown asked Judge Nadeau during a bench conference, for attorneys, only, to permit him to introduce evidence of other assaults against Amanda, to counter what he called her "*picture of domestic tranquility in the house as far as him being a good father and having family moments in the house.*" (p. 14) After only four pages, using approximately eight minutes of trial time, of testimony about Chad being a good person, the prosecution seemed to think that its case was threatened. He complained that the recollection of "*Jeff Marshall returning Kassidy to her with makeup on her face to cover a bruise,*" was new, and "*was not told to the police, despite five interviews and repeated contact by the police after the death.*" (p. 15) What Brown misunderstood was that the police were not interested in hearing about Jeff Marshall's care of Kassidy, or in his character or history. The police didn't ask Jeff either, about his criminal history. Beginning with the afternoon of November 9, 2000, the police had one goal, which was the conviction of Chad Evans. The police never asked Amanda to describe Jeff's care of Kassidy, and never asked her about any incidents.

The State was trying to paint a picture of Chad, the intimidating child murderer, and woman batterer, who sought to influence Amanda's testimony at his trial. Brown told Judge Nadeau, that

...the jury has heard that she had made the choice, despite the charges, and despite what she has testified to about the defendant's treatment of Kassidy, she made the choice to be reunited with him for about nine months against a bail order of this court. The jury may conclude only on the evidence here that this is a choice she made because she believes that he has nothing to do with the death of Kassidy. (p. 15-16)

Such a conclusion would have been correct, because it was true. Brown argued, "***I think we are entitled to present this evidence to give the jury a complete picture of the situation.***" (p. 16) That's what the jury never received: "*a complete picture of the situation.*"

Simon Brown wanted to present evidence of the dispute between Amanda and Chad after the McDonald's dinner function at the Exeter Inn which he said he believed to have occurred in September. However, it occurred on Friday, August 25th. He wanted to introduce evidence of Chad's allegedly becoming angry and head butting Amanda when she "*told Chad that she was going to go out with her friend instead of him.*" (p. 16) Brown said, "*There was another -- she told Jeff Marshall about an incident when he* [Chad] *chased her around the house into a bedroom. I was not going to get into that one.*" (p. 17) That latter incident was not mentioned in the transcripts of Jeff's interviews of November 9, 10 and 16, but Chad did, from time to time, playfully chase Amanda into their bedroom. Brown may have been thinking of an incident described vaguely in the conversation on November 11, 2000, among Amanda, Jeff and Jennifer, which was secretly taped by Jeff and Jennifer.

Jeff: "*Yeah, but you said he chased you.*"
Amanda: "*Once, I mean, it was just, but it wasn't like abuse. Do you know what I mean? I don't know... you just had to be there...*"
Jeff: "*Me, Jen and Josh have talked about it, you know. You don't chase your girlfriend around that you love and grab her.*"
Jennifer: "*In anger.*"
Jeff: "*Do you think that's right?*"
Amanda: "*No.*"
Jennifer: "*He choked you... Is that right?*"
Amanda: "*No Jen. I don't want to hear about this. You guys don't understand, anyway. (Inaudible) ... you've never even had a kid and I just want some peace of mind and all I keep hearing is shit.*" (p. 1-2)

Later in that three-way conversation, Jeff brought up the "chase" incident again.

Jeff: "*... when you were upstairs today, you were pretty scared about the fact about how he chased you. Were you not?*"
Amanda: "*Just once he chased me upstairs.*"
Jennifer: "*And you locked the door.*"
Amanda: "*I didn't lock the door. He opened the door. I didn't think the door shut. But all he did was say, 'Sorry,' and run up there.*"
Jennifer: "*For doing what?*"
Amanda: "*Yeah.*"
Jennifer: "*(inaudible)... choking you?*"
Amanda: "*Yeah.*" (p. 6-7)

There was no other information about the alleged choking or the nature of the argument, or if Amanda simply said "Yeah," to get rid of the conversation. The jury never learned about the Jeff's and Jennifer's taping of this conversation, two days after Kassidy's death.

Alan Cronheim countered that such evidence would be prejudicial and not relevant to the charges, and that he did not "*open the door*" to such evidence in his cross-examination as he focused his questions on Chad's treatment of Kassidy, not Amanda. The assumption in this legal wrangling was that there actually was credible evidence that Chad assaulted

Amanda, but there was no such evidence. By arguing to prevent the jury from hearing such evidence, which made sense tactically, the defense contributed to the prosecution's confidence that the evidence was actually worth anything.

Judge Nadeau denied the State's motion to introduce evidence of alleged assaults, saying that Amanda "*testified extremely consistently with her police statements; however, there were some inconsistencies that were pointed out.*" (p. 20) She said that "*the relevance of the proffered testimony is substantially outweighed by the danger of unfair prejudice at this time.*" (p. 21) It might have been better for Chad to allow the state to present these incidents, as they were described earlier in this book. If Chad had been advised to testify, he could have explained them. Imagine if the jury had been able to hear Chad's and Amanda's stories of their playful chasing which often ended in their bedroom. People who love each other passionately are not the people who abuse children.

On redirect examination, Simon Brown then questioned Amanda and reviewed the close contact the police had with her, including Sergeant Jim White's picking her up at Logan Airport in Boston on December 18, 2000 and paying for a motel room and interviewing her on the 19th. Despite the State's open attempts to persuade Amanda of the value of its case against Chad, including the offer of immunity from prosecution, Brown still complained of the "*many months*" (p. 24) that she had spent with Chad, allegedly influencing Amanda during the pre-trial period.

For the the police and prosecutors, Chad's violation of the no-contact order reinforced their view of Chad's criminality. However, as Alan Cronheim had noted earlier to the State and Judge Nadeau, the defense could have objected more strongly to the no-contact order for Chad, as it was inherently unfair and one-sided.

Simon Brown asked Amanda, "*when you were secretly living with the defendant, did you and he discuss this case*?" and she responded, "*No. We discussed him going to jail and how it's not fair. But we didn't get into details about the case.*" (p. 24) If they had, Chad might have corrected her understanding about the Tee-ball, rather than a wiffle ball, for example. Or they might have discussed the actual dates of Kassidy's medical appointments.

Brown challenged Amanda on why she hadn't mentioned before tossing the mug at Chad on November 8th, or Jeff's putting makeup on Kassidy to cover a bruise, and she went beyond the requested Yes/No answer, saying "*No. It's hard to tell* [someone] *something when they think the other person did it and they really don't want to hear anything else.*" She explained further the delay in reporting that one detail of Jeff's treatment of Kassidy, "*... I was so confused. It's not easy to be without her, especially her being murdered. Your mind isn't all there. It took a long time to have a clear conscience... and it's still really hard.*" (p. 26) Brown pushed again his theory that Chad was pressuring her, "*So during that time you were with the defendant, things became clearer to you?*" and she responded, "*Actually, it was becoming more clearer when I started going to church and I became Christian and just... God's helped me have a clear mind through all of this. He really has.*" (p. 26) In 2011, Amanda continues to be strongly Christian.

Simon Brown and Amanda jostled about how much bruising she saw on Kassidy on November 9th, and she denied that she had ever seen Chad cause any injury to Kassidy's leg. "*That didn't happen*?" he asked. "*No,*" she responded. (p. 28)

Amanda was asked, "*What are your feelings for the defendant today*?" and she replied, "*I love him and I miss him.*" (p. 28) Apparently hoping to obtain an admission that Chad, or his family, posted Amanda's bail, Brown asked her the question, and she said that members of her church had posted bail. Amanda used the address of Chad's sister, Nicole, because she didn't have a mailing address and she has been staying with Nicole during the trial. The State had charged both Chad and Amanda with serious crimes, but was now trying to allege illegitimate influencing of Amanda by Chad and his family, because Amanda found love and support with the Evans family during this ordeal.

Amanda didn't recall making a statement to her friend, Shannon Gagne, about Jeff's and Jen's good treatment of Kassidy. Amanda added that in the time after Kassidy's death a lot of people were "*trying to get information from me, and trying to just figure out what happened,*" and she couldn't remember what she said to everybody. (p. 31)

On recross-examination Alan Cronheim established that several friends of Chad and Amanda knew about their seeing each other during his bail release in 2001. She reiterated that Chad told her to tell the truth and that she would never "*lie under oath simply because of your feelings for Chad.*" (p. 32)

Amanda's testimony helped Chad, but there was not enough of the good side of Chad. As with the cross-examination of the other prosecution witnesses, most of it was aimed at deflecting the bad representations of Chad and not presenting the good. Maybe this is one reason why there are so many wrongful convictions throughout the country. There were no photographs of Chad and Kassidy, such as a photograph of her on his shoulders, or her being carried, "Superman-style' and flying through the air. There was no discussion of the trips together to Hampton Beach or to York's Wild Animal Kingdom, or of rides on the 3-wheelers or the good times on the trampoline. There were no descriptions of the many boat rides and the walking trips to Lone Oaks for ice cream.

There was no question similar to Det. Rick LeClair's question of Amanda during her first interview, *"Who besides Jeff, Jen, you and Chad has been with the baby in the last week?... Have you gone out to eat? Have you gone to the store?"(p. 868)* Amanda was not asked about her answer to that question which was to describe the dinner on Saturday, November 4 at a restaurant with Chad, Kassidy, Travis and Bruce. The broader question to ask would have been for every one of the 153 days that Chad knew Kassidy. Who saw Kassidy? Where? When? Such a review would have been lengthy, but it would have required the use of a timeline, to which all other testimony could have been referenced.

Sergeant James White

Sgt. White was the lead investigator for New Hampshire on this case, and his official title was Detective Sergeant, but "Sergeant" is used here. In summarizing his career to Simon Brown, he said he spent seven years with the York Police Dept, which may help explain the easy collaboration in this case between the Maine and New Hampshire State Police organizations. As Jeff grew up in York, the coincidence may help explain the police trust in Jeff.

Describing the duties of a lead investigator, Sergeant White said, "*it's very important in the initial states of an investigation to interview as many people as possible that might be able to prove*[provide] *information about a particular case.*" (p. 38) He was not asked if he ever compiled a list of people who had seen Kassidy during the last two weeks (since the 3-day/2-night babysitting by Jeff and Jennifer) or 40 days (since the October 1 bruise-free photograph) or 154 days (since she met Chad) of her life, and how many of those people he interviewed.

Sergeant White interviewed Amanda on December 19, 2000 after her return from Texas and she told him that she had not had any contact with Chad, and thus didn't tell him that she had called Chad from Texas. He described a phone call he had with Amanda on April 6, 2001 during which Amanda had said she was in Texas, but phone records indicated that she was in New Hampshire. Thus, the jury was reminded that Amanda could lie.

Sergeant White presented photographs taken from a helicopter showing the trailer in the woods at Chad's grandparents' farm in Vermont where Amanda and Chad lived during part of 2001. The helicopter surveillance is what led Chad and Amanda to panic and they started a fire to burn any indication of their living. Very unfortunately, Amanda's cache of photographs of Kassidy, including photos of Amanda, Kassidy and Chad were not saved from the fire. Through the loss of those photos, listed earlier in Chapter 5, Chad and Amanda paid a very high price for their decision to be with and support each other and defy the police. They were hiding their relationship from those, in their minds, who were seeking injustice rather than justice.

Sergeant White also presented several charts of phone calls during November 2000 and identified some of the calls, such as Chad's call to Perfumania on the evening of Nov 8. These large five magnified panels, marked as Exhibits 63-67, contained the calls on the "Chart of Calls."

Defense Attorney Mark Sisti cross-examined, and Sergeant White agreed that the police spent "*over 200 hours*" trying to prove that Amanda and Chad were violating Chad's bail conditions. Then, Sisti asked, sarcastically, "*How many hours did you put in determining whether or not Jefferey Marshall beat Kassidy Bortner black and blue from her buttocks down to her knees*?" (p. 62) It was a clever, Perry Mason-esque question, but not one that was designed to obtain a useful answer. Instead, it was likely perceived by the jury as an attack on the police, and it likely encouraged sympathy for the police and the prosecution. Sergeant White responded that "*We put a tremendous amount of investigation into the early stages of this... investigation.*" (p. 62) It's estimated here that by the time the police decided, in the early evening of November 9, 2000, that Chad murdered Kassidy, the Kittery Police, and Maine and New Hampshire State Police had spent a combined total of about 80 hours on the case. Sergeant White was the first New Hampshire State Police to arrive at the Kittery Police Station, and that was at 5:00 p.m. By 7:30 p.m. the police had told Jeff, Amanda and Jennifer that Chad was their primary suspect. It was around that time that New Hampshire assumed the responsibility for the case because of that early decision than a New Hampshire resident was responsible, and that the fatal injuries to Kassidy occurred in New Hampshire. Eighty hours is not a long time, compared to the 83,640 hours Chad has spent in prison, so far.

Mark Sisti asked if Jeff Marshall was denying the spanking of Kassidy, and Sergeant White said, correctly, that he was not, but there were disagreements about "*whether it caused redness or whether it caused bruising.*" Sisti responded, "*Right. A lot of times we call that minimizing the injury, right?*" (p. 63) Again, the sarcasm surely obscured the valid point which is that the police and prosecutors were accusing Chad and Amanda of minimizing, but that the evidence on police/prosecution side of the case was fairly told without such minimizing. However, the best way to make the point about minimizing was to present testimony with the truth, and lots of it. Regarding the black and blue marks on Kassidy after the spanking, allegedly through a diaper, Sisti would soon have the opportunity to ask prosecution witnesses Jennifer, Travis and Jeremy about them. Chad would have been a good witness about the bruises he saw on Kassidy after Jeff brought Kassidy home from an overnight of babysitting.

Sergeant White said that the spanking by Jeff was "*likely within a couple of weeks of Kassidy's death,*" which is close to correct, as it was on Saturday, October 21, or 21 days before November 9. Later he said it was within a "*two to three week time span...*" (p. 72) However, he said that this spanking by Jeff, over six feet tall and over 200 pounds, didn't raise a "*red flag*" for him because, "*I'm the father of four children, and I believe in spanking, as well.*" (p. 64) Missed in the exchange was the difference between the spanking of a child by a babysitter and the spanking by a parent. Also missed throughout the trial was that Chad, who was more of a parent figure to Kassidy than Jeff, did not believe in spanking, and never hit nor even spanked Kassidy. Chad believed in communication and **eye contact**.

Mark Sisti then asked Sergeant White if the alleged fall of Kassidy from Jeff Marshall's truck was investigated and he responded, "*Yes, that was investigated,*" but said, "*I don't believe it was significant bruising. I think it was described as a bump to the head.*" (p. 74). Sisti asked when Kassidy's fall occurred, relative to the date of her death and Sergeant White responded, "*Again, no one was able to pin down an exact date. We had one witness who thought it was as close to a few days before, and another one, generally -- again, it seemed to be to be that two to three week timeframe, but no exact date.*" (p. 75) In this case, the police simply did not ask for exact dates. The fall from Jeff's truck occurred during the two-night, three-day babysitting stint with Jeff and Jen, from Thursday, October 26 through Saturday the 28th. Sisti made the point that an investigation of a death occurring at a babysitter's house ought to thoroughly include all reported accidents, bruises, incidents or injuries which may have occurred in that babysitter's care. About the reportedly two large bruises on the top of Kassidy's head, resulting from her fall from Jeff's truck, the defense attorney asked, "*Now, would that be an important fact to look into and determine whether or not it was intentional or accidental when you are looking at the homicide of that very child while's she's at Jeff Marshall's house?*" (p. 74)

While Sisti was showing the jury that the police did not carefully investigate the allegations of injury and abuse by Jeff, it was not enough to criticize the police. What could have been done would be to create a time-line chart for the jury to see, and that injury occurred between 14 and 12 days from Kassidy's death. Several people could have helped verify the dates, including Amanda, Chad, Jeremy and Travis, and even Jeff and Jennifer. There is no evidence in the transcripts of the police interviews with any of the people involved in the case that the police carefully tried to identify the exact times of any of the injuries to Kassidy, including the fall from Jeff's truck which caused not one, but two large "goose-egg" sized bumps to the back of her head. The only investigative time-line furnished to the defense in the "Discovery" documents was an undated two-page time-line thought to have been prepared by Sgt. James White of the events on November 8 and 9. (p. 447) It was prepared very early in the investigation, because Kassidy's name is spelled with a "C." Given the Rules of Evidence, introducing such a timeline at Chad's trial would have been a challenge. First, it could have begun as an "Exhibit for Identification" and then witnesses could address or verify the dates on the timeline. Alternatively, the defense could have introduced a blank calendar as an Exhibit and then begun filling in the blanks for the jury.

Next, Mark Sisti asked, "*And did you get information that she was returned home after an overnight stay at the Marshall home and her condition was one of dehydration and starvation*?" (p. 75) Sergeant White was familiar with that incident, and said that "*Amanda described her -- she described dehydration. Said she was very thirsty and actually drank from a cereal bowl, milk from a cereal bowl.*" (p. 75-76) He was asked whether he was sure the incident happened and he said that, "*The only evidence I have is what Amanda said.*" Mark Sisti then established that no investigator asked Jeff or Jennifer about that incident. About the date, Sergeant White said, "*...again, the exact date of when that happened is not clear. That was investigated.*" (p. 79) According to Chad, and the "Chronology" on his website, Kassidy came home dehydrated and with the two bumps on her head, noted earlier, on Saturday, October 28. The dates of this unusual two-night, three-day babysitting could have been established relatively easily by the police, prosecutors or the defense. This was because that babysitting stint began on Thursday, October 26, when Amanda and Nicole Evans went to their second money management class, along with Tom and Dot Urrutia, who were friends and fellow employees of Chad. The Urrutias were never interviewed.

For another source of information, the police had the three-page, handwritten document called "flashbacks" which Amanda wrote shortly after Kassidy's death. These are the notes which the police tried to entice Bruce to surreptitiously retrieve for them. When Chad's lawyers received the document, they gave a copy to the police. It would not have taken much work to establish a timeline of events for Kassidy for the last month of her life. Kassidy was returned to Amanda by Jeff on Saturday, October 28, which was 12 days before Kassidy died.

Sisti returned to the subject of the fall from Jeff's truck, and asked Sergeant White what Jeff said about the incident, and he responded, "*Jeff described -- and, again going from reports -- that Kassidy had been in the truck and had rolled forward out of the car seat and had actually, according to Jeff and to another person who was there, she hadn't even struck the ground, she had been caught, is the way Jeff described it.*" (p. 80) However, that "*another person*" was Jeff's landlord and friend, William Peirce, and the incident he described was not the same fall from Jeff's truck, as it occurred, "*just a day or two before Kassidy's death,*" according to Sergeant White's one page summary report of his own interview of Peirce on December 9, 2000. When that latter incident occurred, "*just a day or two before Kassidy's death*, Peirce recalled that Jeff said, "*See, she just falls out of the truck," which Peirce took to mean she had fallen out of the truck before.* (p. 401) A timeline prepared by the police, the prosecutors or the defense would have helped clarify this discrepancy. In 2010 and 2011, it has taken me hundreds of hours to establish the best possible timeline, because many records have been discardes, such as phone and bank records. It would have been much earier in 2000-2001, and the resulting timeline would have been more complete and accurate.

Sergeant White was then asked about the abrasions, sometimes called "pin pricks," on Kassidy's feet and said that nothing was found in Jeff Marshall's home that likely caused the marks. He was not aware that Jeff entered his home, late on November 9th, without an officer being there. (p. 86) This was after Detective Leighton completed two hour and 30 minute search.

Sergeant White explained that it's the preferred method in New Hampshire to obtain a search warrant, rather than asking a person for consent to a search. Thus, by seeking a search warrant for Chad's home, there was no implication that Chad was reluctant to consent to such a search. Also, he agreed that local calls, such as a call from Jeff's home to Jennifer's or Amanda's place of work would not appear on phone records. Mark Sisti closed his cross-examination with a courteous, but awkward, "*Thank you very much for coming in.*" (p. 90)

There was no mention of Sgt. White's affidavits, a.k.a. "*court documents*" or "*court records*," of November 10 and November 11, 2000, which had contributed so much to Chad's trial, and guilty verdict in the press. They were not reliable enough to be presented as evidence, so the jury saw the original documents and heard the trial testimony of the interviewees and the transcripts of their interviews which formed the bases for Sgt. White's affidavits. Nonetheless, Sisti could have had the Sgt. White affidavits entered as Defense Exhibits for identification, and not for the truth of their contents. With that document, Sisti could have asked Sgt. White about its several innacurate statements, and the sources of that inaccurate information.

Frank Jefferey Marshall

Before Jeff's testimony began, Judge Nadeau invited the arguments of both sides about the State's Motion to exclude questions about Jeff's refusal to take a polygraph test. Seeing that it might take longer than she wanted, the judge said that they would revisit the issue after Jeff's direct examination by Will Delker.

Introducing himself as F. Jefferey Marshall, Jeff described how he first met Kassidy when she lived with her grandmother, Jacqueline Conley, in Sanford, Maine and how he and Jennifer would occasionally babysit for Kassidy in Sanford. After Amanda moved to Chad's home in Rochester, which Jeff placed around the time of Jacqueline's surgery, he said that Amanda and Chad would ask Jeff and Jennifer to babysit for Kassidy, sometimes overnight. From Jacqueline's subsequent testimony, the jury learned that her surgery was August 27th, but without a timeline, the dots could not have been connected by the jury.

In his November 2000 letter to his attorneys, Chad mentioned the frequency of babysitting by Jeff and Jennifer, and that it was Jeff who seemed most interested in helping with babysitting,

The summer went pretty well. A couple of times Jen and Jeff would watch Kassidy for the evening so that Amanda and I could go out. He would say, "If you guys ever need a sitter for a night out or whatever we will take her."

Will Delker asked Jeff if he saw bruises on Kassidy, and he responded "*Yes*," and described,

Bruising along her face, her arms, top of her head, around there. You know, just different bruises all of the time.... Some of them, in my opinion, looked like someone had grabbed her... Sometimes they'd start to fade away. They'd start turning a yellowish color and then they'd look like -- kind of look like they're almost disappearing and then, all of a sudden, the next day she'd have the same bruising in the same place as she did the day before." (p. 103-4)

Jeff said that he saw these bruises, "*Every time we had her*," (p. 104) and that he first noticed the bruising "*right after she started moving in. I kind of questioned it, I believe, the first time.*" (p. 105)

Jeff said that he had talked with Chad "*a handful of times*" about the bruises and "*I heard all kinds of things. I heard that she fell off a trampoline... I heard they were over at a friend's house and she tripped into a coffee table...there was always an explanation for bruising.*" (p. 105)

He didn't remember when he heard the "trampoline story," but said that different bruises then appeared, "*Up around here on her forehead.*" (p. 107) Asked whether Chad had expressed concern about the bruises, Jeff said,

Well, he was concerned that people would see the bruises, certainly people would see the bruises and jump to conclusions that he was hitting her or doing stuff to her. Like if he was going to his parent's house, you know, he'd ask, 'Would you guys watch her, we don't want them thinking that something's going on." If they were going to the store: "Can you watch her?" They basically didn't want to bring her out in public... I believe one time they were going to her mother's house, and they didn't want Jackie to see Kassidy because of the bruising. (p. 107)

In 2011, Chad unequivocably stated that he and Amanda went to his parents' house in Keene twice in the summer of 2000 and they brought Kassidy with them both times. They went to visit Amanda's parents twice during the summer and Kassidy was with them both times. In addition, they never left Kassidy with Jeff and Jennifer for babysitting while they went shopping. To late night parties, yes, but for daytime shopping, no. The babysitting on Wednesday afternoon, November 8, began earlier than Amanda's work, so she could go shopping for two hours for a dress for the upcoming weekend, but that was not an occasion when both Amanda and Chad were going shopping and left Kassidy with Jeff and Jennifer.

Delker asked Jeff to estimate how often Kassidy stayed "*over your house all together*," meaning overnight, and Jeff replied, "*Probably a handful of times. I don't know exactly. To be honest, I can't give you a number. I don't know.*" (p. 108) Asked about any unusual behavior by Kassidy, Jeff responded,

I remember exactly one night we heard some noise in the living room after we had put her to bed. She would sleep on the couch. And we went into the living room, and she was standing there in the dark. And we said you have to get back to bed. You know, we put her back in the bed. And the next morning, we woke up, and she was standing there again.... Just staring at the wall. Standing up straight, staring at the wall... It happened so many [times] -- *practically every time she came over, and it got worse and worse.*" (p. 108-09)

Jeff said that he talked with Chad about this behavior,

... I don't like to admit to it, but I said she's acting a little retarded. She's standing there just lost. And he says, "Well, that's because I put her in the corner when she's bad. And she'll come in our bedroom at night and, you know, if she's trying to come into bed with us, I'll put her in the corner and make her stand up against the wall, and make her stand there." And I told him -- I said you've got to stop that, because she's doing it at our house. She'd get right out of bed and stand up. (p. 110)

The jury never heard from Chad, and Amanda wasn't asked to return to testify, but both would have have firmly said that Kassidy was welcomed into their bed, as often happened. Below is what Chad wrote in 2010,

Do you know how awesome it is to have this cute little blonde snuggle up to you or to wake up with one arm wrapped around "Tinky Winky" and the other wrapped around your neck? Most nights she started out in her bed, but halfway through the night she would wind up with us. Amanda and I usually slept with the door open and Kassidy would sometimes wander in and stand at the bottom of the bed. I would sometimes feel her at our feet early on. She was too small to crawl in, so I would lift her onto the bed. Other times she would have a bad dream or something and start crying. One of us would go to her room and pick her up, and bring her in, usually me. I have always been a very light sleeper.

I would guess that it was once or twice a week on average that she slept part of the night with us. Amanda and I loved it. I think we both thought of it as a guilty pleasure. If you were looking down from the ceiling, Amanda would be on the left closest to the bathroom and I slept on the right, closest to the front of the house. I loved to sleep on the right so that I could wrap my left arm around Amanda's back if she wasn't sleeping in the crook of my right arm with her head on my chest. Man do I miss this. When Kassidy came in she usually would slip right in between us, in the middle of the bed. Occasionally she would sleep on Amanda's or my side wrapped in our arms (more often Amanda's than me). It was great to cuddle with her this way but we would transfer her to the middle of the bed after she fell asleep. Our bed was pretty high, and we were worried about her rolling out of it. Once she was with us, she usually stayed until the morning, similar to the way Jeremy described seeing her in our bed the morning of the golf outing.

Some of the best nights Amanda and I had, and I am confident Amanda would agree, were when both Kyle and Kassidy ended up in our bed. They were so cuddly then. It's hard to describe but to me it was what life was all about. I'd get to make love to this beautiful woman, and several hours later we had these two tired little babies sleeping between us; looking for protection for whatever was chasing them in their dreams. It's too bad we weren't so good at protecting one of them in real life. Thinking back, I really loved watching Amanda and Kassidy sleep together. Amanda had long hair and Kassidy was always somehow wrapped up in it. Some of my best memories of Kassidy are mornings where it was just she and I awake, she'd open her little blue eyes as happy as could be, and breathe her pungent breath in my face. I'd say, "You want to go get some breakfast" and she would have this huge smile on her face and in her eyes and say "yaaa" in a whisper. (Letters, April 6, 2010)

Returning to Jeff's testimony, he was asked to describe Kassidy's behavior after she began living with Chad,

She got to be real slow. Not very active. Just kind of lost. Like if she was going to run around and stuff, she -- she was going to trip or something, she would never put out her arms, you know like a normal person would do as far as to try to catch themselves. She just basically was coming slowly -- not very -- not with it all the time. (p. 110)

Jeff compared that behavior to what he saw of Kassidy before she lived with Chad, "*Day and night. You know, from someone sleeping to a road race,*" (p. 110) but he described the transformation as gradual. He testified that he asked Chad about Chad taking Kassidy to a hospital and Jeff related, "*He said he couldn't bring her there because she had bruises and they would suspect stuff,*" (p. 111) but there was no followup question about when such a conversation might have taken place. That would be left for the defense.

Will Delker asked about any disciplining at Jeff's home and he said that he had spanked Kassidy when she "*had gotten into a bottle of Windex that was on the kitchen table. I took the bottle away from her. I patted her on the butt... just like that.*" (p. 112) Kassidy was wearing a diaper and Jennifer witnessed the episode. Afterwards, said Jeff, there was no bruising, but he did see bruising on her buttocks about a week or two later, presumably from other causes.

Jeff was asked about "*an incident at your house where Kassidy fell out of the truck,*" (p. 113) and Jeff described the incident, witnessed by his neighbor, Will Peirce, where he had released Kassidy from the car seat and she had started to fall out of his truck; but he had caught her, and there was no injury. Jeff was not asked the date of that incident, but Will Peirce would later testify that the date was the same as he stated in his December 6, 2000 interview which placed the incident as "*just a day or two before Kassidy's death.*" (p. 401)

Jeff said that he began babysitting Kassidy more regularly when Amanda began work at Old Navy, which he described as "*pretty close to the time of Kassidy passing away... Within a couple of weeks of time.*" (p. 115) Thursday, November 9, was Amanda's fourth day of work at Old Navy, but she may have spent several hours in training the previous week. He said that

the understanding I had [was that] *they couldn't take her to day care because of her bruises. They didn't want anyone to see her, especially at day care, because, obviously, they're going to see the bruises...They kept telling me that they were going to put her into day care. They just have to wait until the bruises go away. That's what they kept telling me and Jennifer.*" (p. 117)

Jeff recalled that on November 8, 2000, Amanda brought Kassidy around 4:30 p.m. and she stayed until about 5:30 p.m., when Chad picked her up. (At Amanda's trial a year later, he testified that the babysitting for Kassidy on this day was for "*an hour or two,*" and that it began "*later in the afternoon. I would say after 2:00, maybe 3:00, something like that.*" (p. 1-112-13)) That was much closer to Amanda's recollection of approximately 3:00 p.m.

Will Delker asked how her "*situation*" was at that time and Jeff replied, "*...it wasn't very good. She had a problem with her leg. She'd kind of limped... didn't put a lot of pressure on that -- that one leg.*" (p. 121) He said that "*I actually believe Amanda had told me about that incident...*" (p. 121) "*She called up and she was pretty upset about what had happened. She said that Chad had hurt Kassidy's leg. She described it as he was playing rough with her...She was pissed off at Chad. She was quite angry with him at that time.*" (p. 123). A few hours earlier, the jury had heard Amanda say that Chad never hurt Kassidy's leg. Will Delker then asked, "*Was there an incident when something happened and Kassidy got knocked down at your house*?" He said that he thought Kassidy was in the bedroom watching cartoons, but that

...she had gotten up, and did the same thing standing there like she'd become used to, I guess. And the phone rang, and I ran out to the kitchen... and when I came around the corner, I tripped over Kassidy, and I fell on the floor myself." (p. 123-24)

He said this was a week after Kassidy's limping had started, and he noticed no additional injury to her, and that he told Amanda what had happened. "*I told Amanda everything that ever took place.*" (p. 124-25)

Will Delker returned to Wednesday afternoon when Chad picked up Kassidy. After searching for Kassidy's car seat, both men determined that Amanda hadn't left it at Jeff's. Rushed for time, as he had to be at Kyle's day care by 6:00 p.m., Chad seatbelted Kassidy in the back seat as if she were an adult. Kyle would later use the booster seat, for older children. Jeff said that he did nothing to hurt Kassidy that afternoon, "*absolutely not.*" (p. 132)

About 15 minutes after Chad and Kassidy left, Jeff said that Chad called him from around the Dover toll booth, and "*He says, 'Something's wrong with Kassidy. She's acting weird.' I said, 'What's the matter?' And he said, 'I don't know, you know. She's kind of, you know, bobbin' around and stuff....The little bitch is acting weird again.... that's basically the way he referred to her most of the time, anyway.*" (p. 132) Will Delker followed up, asking, "*What do you mean by that*?" and Jeff stated, "*He'd call her a little bitch, little jerk, stuff like that.... little bastard*" (p. 133) In response a general question, Jeff recalled Chad saying, "*She's a little retard. You know, she acts just like her mother. Stuff like that.*" (p. 133) Jeff returned to the call from Chad which he said began, "'*The little retard's... You know, the little bitch is..... Do you know what's wrong with Kassidy?' And I said, 'No.' It was pretty quick. He didn't seem like he was that concerned, you know what I mean. Never came across as being that concerned about it.*" (p. 135) Then the conversation turned to politics and the election.

Delker asked about Chad's next call to Jeff, where Chad said,

"You won't believe this... I took Kassidy out of the car, and I went around to get my son, and I went around to get her out of the car, and she was on her face on the ground..... " He said that he brought her in the house and had to wipe rocks and stuff out of her hair." (p. 136)

Jeff said that Chad told him about Kassidy, "*She was upset, crying, stuff like that,*" (p. 136) and Jeff believed that the call ended with conversation about the elections, again. Then Jeff described the third call, later in the evening where Chad described the batted ball accident. Delker asked a question which didn't get asked enough at the trial, which was, "*What kind of ball was he playing,*" and Jeff replied, "*I believe he said, 'baseball.'* " (p. 137) Jeff continued,

...at one point, he was talking to me pretty frantically that she [Kassidy] *was kind of out of it. Her eyes were in the back of her head, and she was kind of -- he kept yelling out her name, "Kassidy, Kassidy, Kassidy, wake up. Wake up." And I kind of said, "What's wrong? You know, you need to bring her to the hospital." He then said, "Oh, she's come out of it She's fine, now.*" (p. 138)

In response to questions, Jeff said that calls from Chad were unusual, but the circumstances that Chad faced that afternoon were unusual, too. Jennifer came home around 9:00 p.m. and they went to the local Wendy's Restaurant and brought dinner home to eat.

The next morning around 8:00 a.m., Amanda brought Kassidy into Jeff's and Jen's bedroom, with Jeff still in bed. "*I don't know if she handed her to us, or put her right on the bed.*" (p. 143) Then, Jeff testified that Amanda said that Kassidy, *" 'looks like shit, doesn't she? And look what Chad did.' ... I looked, and I mean, it was definitely different than the day before.... It was bruised all over. Just everywhere....*" (p. 142) Delker asked "*Did Kassidy have any of those bruises on her face when she left your house the day before?*" and Jeff said, "*No, she didn't.*" (p. 142-3) Responding to Delker's questions, Jeff described what Kassidy was wearing, "*She was wearing a winter coat and her pajamas.*" The coat "*was pink, with ruffles on it.*" Asked to describe the pajamas, Jeff said, "*They were red,*" and then, in tears, he motioned for tissue paper, but the judge said there was no more available. (p. 143)

Jeff tried to pick Kassidy up off the bed to show Jennifer how her walking was impaired, but Kassidy didn't want to be moved. Jeff described Kassidy's behavior, *"...she was tired. She looked tired. She was kind of out of it. ... She just kind of laid there.*" (p. 144-45) He didn't see her eat any of the cereal she brought with her in the baggie.

It was time for lunch, and the judge repeated the frequent caution to the jury, "*Ladies and Gentlemen, please, again, do not discuss the case, yet, amongst yourselves. Do not decide the case until you've heard all the evidence.*" (p. 146)

Before the jury returned, Judge Nadeau reserved 15 minutes to discuss the State's motion to preclude any questions about Jeff's decision not to take a polygraph test. Mark Sisti argued that the issue was whether Jeff Marshall was cooperative with the police, as he and the prosecutors had represented, and the refusal to take the polygraph would contradict that representation. Will Delker argued that New Hampshire court precedents made polygraph tests inadmissible, as should be the decisions on whether to take or not such a test. Judge Nadeau granted the State's Motion to preclude the defense from raising the issue. Not discussed during the arguments was whether Chad had been offered such an opportunity to prove his truthfulness.

After the lunch break, Will Delker resumed his direct examination of Jeff, and asked if "*you remember a time when you tried to give her a bath or a shower?*" As there was apparently only one time to his recollection, Jeff responded,

> *Yes.... She got sick at the house. She had... kind of puked on her clothes, so I kind of cleaned her up and I went to go put her into the bathtub and she freaked right out as soon as I turned the water on.... instant freak... I know kids don't like water and stuff, some kids, but this was terror.*" (p. 166)

There was no effort to establish a date for this sickness and/or the attempted bath and there was no followup question about how Jeff knew that children don't like water. Maybe he didn't as a child?

During Amanda's testimony the previous day, the jury had heard her say that Kassidy never had a problem with baths, and that she or Chad gave her a bath every night or every other night. Also, the jury had not yet heard specifically about Kassidy's bath on the night of November 8.

Delker returned to the morning of November 9th. Jeff described how his cat, Toby, had taken something off his desk in the living room and ran into the bedroom, and under the bed where Kassidy appeared to be sleeping, but Jeff said that he was "*not specifically checking on Kassidy at that point.*" (p. 169) Right after his visit to the bedroom, Chad called, and Jeff said that Chad began by asking, " ' *How's Kassidy?* ' " (p. 171) Then Jeff related the rest of the conversation which was about the call to Chad from DCYF. Continued Jeff, "*He said, 'If this shit's going to... keep up, Mandy and the little bitch is going to have to get out of my house. I can't put up with this. I got two boys I have to watch out for.*' (p. 172) "*He was very angry about having the, you know, DHS or the Town of Rochester call him.*" Jeff said that Chad speculated that the caller to DCYF was Amanda's friend, Emily Conley, but that Jeff said it probably wasn't and that the call was probably related to his divorce. Ironically, it was related to his divorce, because it was Tristan who made the anonymous call to DCYF.

Then Jeff returned to the television, and checked the mail on his porch, and returned to check on Kassidy.

She was laying there. Her eyes were in the back of her head, and she just looked as if she was in shock. I went over. I looked at her. You know, I didn't know what the... hell was going on. I called people. I called Chad. I called Amanda, I called Jen.... She didn't know what to do. I went back in, tried to see if anything was in her mouth. She was choking -- anything was wrong. I tipped her upside down, started patting her back. Tried CPR. I didn't know how to do CPR. I just kept pumping on her. You know, it seemed, at that point, that, you know, she was kind of gargling or... (p. 174-75)

Delker asked, "*Was she responsive? Was she conscious*?" and Jeff said, "*No*." (p. 175) At Amanda's trial a year later, Jeff testified that "*...it was like she was taking deep breaths..*" (p. 1-128) He said that he didn't think to call 911 because "*I've never been in that kind of situation... It all happened so quick." (p. 175) Meanwhile he, "Just kept trying to see if something was in her mouth.... I didn't know what was wrong. I just tried to pump on her, you know, as far as trying to get her to breathe, trying to get her to come to, check for a pulse*." (p. 175-76) He said that he used a Wendy's napkin to try to check her mouth to see if she was choking on anything, and then "*splashed a little bit of water on her face trying to wake her up, trying to get any response I could. I kept asking the operator, 'Is there anything I can do*?' " (p. 176) The prosecutors were presumably satisfied with splashing water to try to revive a child, even though they viewed splashing water on a child having a temper tantrum, and gasping for breath, as the work of a child abuser and a murderer.

Then Jeff took Kassidy out onto his porch to meet the police and EMTs who arrived quickly. Delker then showed the jury photographs of the bedroom at Jeff's home, including the Wendy's wrapper and pieces of Kassidy's clothing and the mail that Jeff retrieved. The State also showed the jury the actual items of Kassidy's clothing, and Jeff identified them. Delker held up Exhibit 5, which had been labeled by the prosecutors in their "Partial Exhibit List" as "*Red/White Dress*" and Jeff referred to it as Kassidy's "*pajamas*," and Delker referred to the dress as "*top to her pajamas*." (p. 183) The day's transcript referred to Exhibit 5 on the "Index" page (p. 2) as "*pajamas*." Delker said that the pajamas "*appeared to be ripped,*" and Jeff said that they were not ripped when Kassidy was brought to his home by Amanda. I looked at the dress in 2011 and it was cut in the front, from top to bottom, and the length of the left sleeve. The cuts were most likely made by the EMTs with scissors to remove Kassidy's dress-like pajama tops, but there was no explanation for the jury for how and when Kassidy's clothes were taken off or how or when they were cut.

Delker then skipped to ask about the evening at the Kittery Police station, after most of the interviews, and asked what happened when Jeff saw Chad for the first time that day, in the parking lot. Jeff related that he was in the parking area when Chad came out the door,

He came up to me and he said, "I can't believe you did this to me. I can't believe you are doing this to me. You know, basically really angry.... I don't know how you can do this to me. How can you tell them everything..." (p. 185-86)

Delker asked Jeff, "*What was his demeanor*" and the predictable answer came, "*Angry*." The prosecution was painting the picture of an angry, out-of-control man, so it sought favorable interpretation of ambiguous statements in the hope that the picture was convincing. Because of the way the adversarial process works in criminal trials, the jury will have to wait to hear, if at all, that anger is the perfectly normal response of a man who lost a young child he had come to regard as a future stepdaughter and whom he loved deeply and, to make matters far worse, was just accused by the police of killing her. He would have been far angrier if he had any real understanding of what the legal system had in store for him - and he is still paying. The anger picture painted by the prosecutor had another devastating effect which was to discourage him from testifying in his own defense. His lawyers would later be concerned that he would show his anger on the stand, and that such anger would be misinterpreted by the jury. Rather than persuade the jury that his anger was correctly aimed and justly strong, they advised him not to testify at all. But that came later. He remained in his defendant's chair as the prosecution painted their picture of him. With each cross-examination, the defense lawyers would change the hue of this stroke or that stroke, or even the removal of some paint, but the picture would remain the same for the jury unless a different picture was painted.

Returning to Jeff's testimony, he said that Chad and Amanda talked and, "*He was just telling her, you know, 'I didn't do this. I couldn't do this to Kassidy,' and stuff like that.*" (p. 187) Afterwards, "*we went back, not to my house, but to Will's house with Amanda and Jen... and then we decided that we weren't going to stay at the house.*" (p. 187) At his house, Jeff met a Maine State Trooper, who was Detective Herbert Leighton, who just finished searching the home. Jeff said that the trooper said he could re-enter the house if he wanted to, so Jeff went inside and retrieved some clothes and other overnight items.

At the motel, said Jeff, Amanda talked with Chad on the phone, and "*She was upset with him.*" Delker asked Jeff to describe Amanda's emotions. Jeff responded, "*Oh, yeah, she... said, 'You killed my baby. You said you were going to do this.*" (p. 189) The response did not answer the question, but was hearsay and Sisti objected, and the Judge ordered that the statement be "*stricken*" from the record. Of course, however, the jury heard it and it's in the transcript. If the State wanted to introduce evidence of what Amanda said to Chad on that phone call, it could have asked Amanda that question, but it chose not to do so because they knew that Amanda would not support their case. Chad's lawyers chose not to call her back to the stand, either. As with the testimony earlier about Chad's anger, this testimony by Jeff about Amanda's statements would have to wait many minutes, perhaps more than an hour for the defense to counter it with evidence and argument. What needed to be said at the time of Jeff's testimony was that Amanda had been told by the police that Chad had killed Kassidy. The police had convinced her mother, and her sister and potential future brother-in-law, although they were supporting the police's version from 12:47 p.m. onward, that Chad assaulted and killed Kassidy. Thus, one way to interpret Amanda's alleged statements to Chad over the phone is that the police convinced her. She respected the police, who are in the business of solving crimes, and they told her how Kassidy died. She wrote in "My Life Story," about her conversation with Chad, "*I was telling him what they told me how they said, 'You slowly killed my baby,'* "

The next morning, testified Jeff, Chad came to the motel with his sister, Nicole, and Amanda went with them.

Delker returned to the days before Kassidy died, and said to Jeff, "*You described for the jury many times when Kassidy would come to your house with bruises. Why didn't you do anything?*" (p. 192) Jeff responded that, "*... there's no excuse, but it was Jen's sister, number one. Number two, this is a guy that we did business with. He was a friend of mine.... I've got to live with it. It's the worst thing I've ever done.*" (p. 192) He might have added, "and not done." Also, he could have added, "Number three, I was responsible for some of the bruises on Kassidy, Number four, Jennifer and I babysat for Kassidy for approximately 10 days(40 awake hours) and four nights during the month of October and six days (40 awake hours) of November, for a total of 16 days(80 awake hours) and four nights. Perhaps like Chad, I didn't realize the seriousness of Kassidy's condition, and didn't realize that Kassidy was anywhere close to dying."

At the end of this direct examination, Jeff again tried to explain why he didn't do anything to save Kassidy, "*Once again, it's Jen's sister. You think that the parents will do the right thing....*" (p. 193) Whatever the level of Jeff's intent regarding the eight incidents relating to his babysitting about which Alan Cronheim asked Amanda, that parent was trying to do the right thing and find other day care arrangements. Incidentally, Delker asked Jeff about only three of those eight incidents. At this trial, the prosecution was not interested in holding accountable everyone who failed Kassidy Bortner. This trial was only for the one man they picked to shoulder that responsibility. During Amanda's police interviews she was told that after Chad was convicted, they would prosecute Jeff for his role, but that never happened.

After her own trial later in 2001, Amanda appeared on the national "John Walsh Show" and he framed the issue on the flip side of Will Delker's question. Stated John Walsh at the end of the segment about Amanda, Kassidy and Chad,
I'm going tell you what. If I dropped my little boy off, and he had a bruise every time I picked him up, I'd find another babysitter, I'll tell you what.... I don't know if I would buy those excuses, whether it was the carpet tacks or not. I wouldn't take my 21-month old little girl back to the same guy for any reason. I don't care if it was my brother. I wouldn't take her back there.

Amanda was trying to be a responsible parent, and Chad was trying to be a responsible stepfather-to-be.

Following Jeff Marshall's contrite closing, "*I definitely messed up,*" Mark Sisti began his cross-examination aggressively and sarcastically, "*You definitely did mess up, Jeff. You messed up very seriously on November 8th, and you messed up significantly more on November 9th of 2000, do you agree with me?*" Jeff responded firmly, "*Absolutely not,*" and the struggle of the trial was joined. Having decided on its strategy to accuse Jeff of murdering Kassidy, and skipping other theories, such as the role of accidents and chronic illness or disease or a combination of those factors, the defense needed to convince the jury that Jeff should have been placed in the defendant's chair and not Chad. The strategy was to accuse Jeff rather than present and defend Chad's actions and behavior. To this point, Jeff was polite, contrite and seemed to present a coherent story. (p. 193)

Sisti attacked with, "*Oh, by the way, you messed up by telling people different things, too, during the course of this investigation,*" and Jeff countered, "*I don't believe so... I told the truth, and sometimes the truth hurts, but it has to be told.*" (p. 194)

Sisti attacked again with a sarcastic hypothetical that was not aimed at generating any new information about the case, which is the purpose of a trial. He asked, "*If someone came to your house with a dog in that condition on November 9th, 2000, would you just sit there and watch the dog die*?" Jeff responded, "*Like I said, there's no excuse,*" and then he noted that he felt he was protecting Amanda and Chad by not doing anything. (p. 194) He said he "*looked up to Chad,*" thus assuring the jury that he, Jeff, was not here to disparage Chad, but to present truth, and achieve justice. Jeff again agreed that he didn't do enough to help, or even watch Kassidy on November 9th. And again, "*Obviously, we knew what was going on. We did the wrong thing by not saying anything.*" (p. 196)

Sisti asked Jeff another rhetorical question, "*Are you more important than Chad*?" (p. 196) and then asked other hypothetical question about who would cover up for whom. Jeff began to answer questions with "*Sir,*" as in "*Yes, sir,*" and "*No, sir,*" and about a bruise, "*It was fading away, sir.*" (p. 199) Sisti ended another series of hypothetical questions, saying,

Well, we're trying to determine here a few things. I'm going to be fair with you, okay, because I'm sure you've already heard. You see, we're blaming you for the death of that child." (p. 200)

Sitting in his defendant's chair, Chad must have felt some sense of deja vu, as that's almost exactly what Maine State Police Detective Lance McCleish said to him 13 months before. Jeff responded, "*If that's what you must do to try to get somebody off that did it, yes... I think he knows the truth...I have given honest answers, thank you.*" (p. 200)

One key to winning this case was to lead the jury to consider accidents, bruises, incidents, and injuries and their dates. Sisti began doing that by asking, "*Prior to October 1st, 2000, are you telling this jury that Kassidy exhibited bruising about her body*?" (p. 201) Jeff responded not with a "Yes" or "No," or even with his estimation of the dates when he remembered that the bruises began. He responded with his solution to the case, "*Like I said, she started getting bruises when she started moving in with Chad. I can't say an exact date.*" (p. 201)

Sisti then asked, "*If I told you that she moved in with Chad in July of 2000... does that kind of fit up with your memory*? Jeff said, "*I'm not quite sure.*" (p. 201) Sisti then showed Jeff the State's Exhibit 19, which was the October 1, 2000 photo of a bruise-free Kassidy, and he asked, sarcastically, "*And who is that*?" (p. 202) Jeff responded politely that it was Kassidy and he stated that he did recall Kassidy looking as she did in the photo, but he was stuck on the solution that Chad was guilty before the trial was over. However, it wasn't his job to solve the case. It was his job to recollect facts as best he could.

Sisti continued, "*What if I told you that she was with Chad in July and in August and in September, all of those months, and she looked like that*?" (p. 206) What would have been helpful here would have been a timeline, already introduced as a Defendant's exhibit, with Amanda's help and confirmation. Then Sisti could have pointed to a trial Exhibit instead of asking hypothetical questions. Jeff would not budge, "*No, she had bruising when she was living at Chad's house*." (p. 206)

Mark Sisti then invited Jeff to come down from the witness stand, and closer to the photograph of Kassidy and point out the bruises that he thought must be there. At first, he said that "*I don't see any bruising, no*," but then he tried, "*There might be. I'm not.... that's where some of the incidents of bruising happened along ... the side there, which is in this picture*," and he struggled to see bruising. (p. 207)

Having effectively used the only photograph at the trial of Kassidy, alive, Sisti established that Jeff did not know who took the photograph. Sisti then tried more sarcasm, "*Do you know if she's got a grandmother*?" Jeff responded politely, "*Yes, sir*." The jurors could be forgiven if they thought that polite people don't abuse and murder children. The prosecution was painting the picture that it's angry people who abuse and murder children and an angry person who assaults his girlfriend on the same evening of a murderous assault.

Sisti then accused Jeff of knowing dates more than he admitted in court, saying, "*... you know what the problem is? You know, don't you*." (p. 209) Seeking to anchor Jeff Marshall's recollections with concrete dates, Sisti asked Jeff when he introduced Chad and Amanda and Jeff replied, "*I don't know the exact date,*" and wouldn't even confirm that it was summertime, even though Sisti knew that the June 2 date was even before the official beginning of summer. Jeff remembered the restaurant, Applebee's, where he, Jen, Chad and Amanda had dinner on June 2, 2000, but not the date, saying "*I don't think there was snow on the ground. There might have been.*" (p. 209) Without the electronic recordings, it's hard to know if he was also becoming sarcastic, too.

Sisti then sought to establish the approximate dates for Jeff's babysitting, and asked first about when Jeff began to "*regularly care*" for Kassidy, and Jeff responded, "*Probably right up pretty close to the time she passed away*." (p. 210) Then Sisti asked, "*When did you start?*" and Jeff demurred again, "*I don't know an exact date*." Sisti pressed him to tell the jury when his seasonal business shut down for the fall, and Jeff agreed, "*usually the end of September, October, something like that*." (p. 210) In addition to a timeline, a simple poster-sized calendar for the months of October and November would have been helpful. Sisti told Jeff that Amanda said that the babysitting started at the beginning of October, but Jeff would not confirm.

Sisti then asked, "*When Kassidy was first presented to you for child care, she was a perfect baby. She looked like that picture, didn't she*?" Jeff responded, "*No, she didn't*," but Sisti didn't ask the followup question, "How was she different?" (p. 211)

After agreeing that there were photographs of Kassidy in their home, but as a younger baby, Sisti asked if Jeff took any photos of Kassidy in October or the beginning of October, and Jeff said he didn't know. Sisti then sarcastically said and asked, "*You don't know. Well, would you look into that and see if you got any*?" Jeff responded, "*I will*." (p. 212) That question about photographs would have been an excellent question for Chad's defense attorneys to ask of Chad and Amanda, and their parents and friends, and even Jeff and Jen, before the trial. Now, there was only one photo of Kassidy, alive, at the trial, which Sisti used effectively, but more photos could have saved Chad from conviction. If Chad's lawyers had requested all the available photographs of bruise-free Kassidy during her 153 days with Chad, he could have made the same point several times.

Sisti asked Jeff about several people involved in the case, beginning with Will Peirce, "*Just who is this guy? He's a neighbor*?" (p. 212) Referring colloquially to Will Peirce as a "guy" seemed to lower the level of courtroom discourse, as if Sisti was talking down to Jeff, who responded that Peirce was a neighbor who had sometimes worked for Jeff to earn some extra money. Thus, Will was an employee, friend, landlord and neighbor. Jeff stated that he pulled Kassidy's diaper down to show Will Peirce the bruising on her buttocks. However, the date of that bruise-check was not presented to the jury, but maybe it would be later, with Will Peirce's testimony. Pierce did not see such bruising on Kassidy's buttocks.

Sisti then returned Jeff to the afternoon of November 8 "*And your claim to this jury is that she essentially had no bruises on her face, except for some little fading one, right*?" and Jeff responded, "*Yes, sir.*" (p. 217-18) Sisti then asked if "*she appeared fine, normal?*" and Jeff carefully qualified,

When I say normal, I mean normal for Kassidy. You have to understand that her behavior had diminished for a period of time. So when I say, 'normal,' it wasn't normal like a usual toddler. It was a situation where she was still kind of acting tired, and stuff like that so I wouldn't want you to put words in my mouth..." (p. 218)

Sisti seized the opportunity for sarcasm, "*I don't want to put any words in your mouth, and hope you don't put any in your mouth, as well,*" but this didn't present any more information to the jury, and it likely increased its sympathy for Jeff. (p. 218)

Sisti told Jeff that Kittery Detective Steve Hamel had testified before him and had stated in his report that Jeff had told him on November 9, while Jeff was in Hamel's car, that Kassidy seemed "*normal*," and Jeff, once again, tried to clarify what he meant by "*normal*" for Kassidy, but said, "*...as far as bruising goes, no, she didn't have bruises all over her face. It wasn't consistent with a full-out bruise, but it was, you know, disappearing on her*." (p. 221)

Sisti asked Jeff about his statements to Detective Hamel about Kassidy's leg, but the questioning bogged down on the issue of Jeff using Sisti's words or his own. Sisti then asked Jeff to explain to "*this jury what you did when you found this baby unresponsive... Let's get a base line here*." (p. 224) Jeff repeated what he had said earlier and that he tried to perform CPR, which he didn't know how to do. Sisti asked him, "*Do you know that the child on autopsy was found to have a significant abdominal injury*? Jeff said, "*I'm not aware of that, no*." (p. 225) He acknowledged that he was pushing on Kassidy's stomach in his CPR effort. This would have been a good time for Sisti to ask Jeff about his membership in the Police Explorers and to ask what CPR training was given. As with the regular Boy Scouts and Girl Scouts, Police Explorers were taught in the 1990's about mouth-to-mouth resusitation with rhythmic pressure on the chest

Given that Jeff had already acknowledged that he only checked on, or, rather, had seen, Kassidy once the entire morning, before getting the mail around noon, it was not difficult to establish that he was not a good babysitter. So it must have been tempting for Mark Sisti to be sarcastic. He said, "*... you would let the condition of a 21-monthold baby, who's laying lifeless on your bed, give you any kind of interference with the election results, would you*? (p.228-29) and again, two minutes later, "*You wouldn't let her condition get in the way of you watching the elections*?" (p. 229)

Judge Nadeau called for an afternoon 15-minute break and Sisti asked that Jeff be "*sequestered during the course of cross-examination, and not confer with any attorneys or witnesses*." (p. 230) She agreed.

The questioning resumed at 3:28 p.m after a 23-minute break. Jeff said, about the initial placing of Kassidy on the bed, "*I don't know who laid her down. I mean, I think I did.*" (p. 231) Jeff agreed that, given the condition that he said Kassidy was in, it was "*unthinkable*" and "*neglect at its highest level*" not to check on her more often, with the only time he saw Kassidy being when he pursued his cat into the bedroom. (p. 232) Jeff agreed that he didn't ask her how Nickelodeon was, or whether she was even breathing, or if she had a pulse and that what he did was "*I looked over at her*." (p. 233)

Sisti then referred Jeff to State Exhibit 28 which was a photograph of his bed, and it showed the mail which Jeff had retrieved on the 9th, underneath a pair of pants. However, Jeff said that he didn't put the pants over the mail. Perhaps the police did. Jeff said that he had met the previous week with Assistant Attorneys General Brown and Delker and told them at that meeting that the photograph did not accurately represent what the bed looked like on the morning of the 9th. The prosecutors did not recall the correction for that photograph, though they did recall discussion about another photo. The problem, according to Sisti, was that the photo represented an altering of a "crime scene," and he requested all notes from that meeting.

Returning to Jeff, Sisti asked about Jeff's efforts to revive Kassidy. After finding her in distress after he retrieved the mail, Jeff agreed that he did not have medical training, but that he checked Kassidy's pulse. In court, he couldn't remember if he detected heartbeats or not. "*I don't think I did.*" (p. 245) Sisti reminded him that he told Detective Hamel "*that you found a slight pulse in the baby, right,*" but Jeff couldn't remember. (p. 246) Sisti reviewed with Jeff what he had said to Detective Hamel, which Sisti emphasized, "*was right after the event.*" (p. 247) which, by implication, should have made the earlier report more credible. Sisti added, sarcastically, "*This was before you could make anything up, okay?*" and Jeff responded, "*Nobody made anything up. Thank you.*" (p. 248) Then Sisti gave Jeff a copy of Detective Hamel's four page report, for Jeff to read, and the court waited.

Resuming the questioning, Sisti asked about the sequence of Jeff's efforts for the lifeless Kassidy: checking pulse, CPR, splashing water on face, etc. Jeff wasn't sure about the sequence that was in Detective Hamel's report. He said that he did the CPR on the bed, but did not remember that the CPR came after the splashing of water on her face. After those steps, he called and talked with Jennifer, and "*I asked her what I should do.*" (p. 255) Sisti didn't ask Jeff about his three initial, but unanswered, efforts to call Chad's cell phone.

Sisti reminded Jeff that in his testimony under direct examination by Will Delker, he had said that it was his "*belief that responsible people who would have seen Kassidy in that condition, even before you checked for the slight pulse, would have brought her to the hospital.*" (p. 255) Jeff pleaded again, that "*It happened quick.*" (p. 255) Jeff couldn't remember how many times he called Jennifer, but he said, "*I believe I called Chad and Mandy, too, and they're the guardians of Kassidy.*" (p. 258) Again framing a hypothetical question, Mark Sisti asked, "*Well, would it have been a lie that you told your girlfriend that she* [Kassidy] *was alert, awake, and okay*?" and Jeff responded, "*It would have been a lie if I told my girlfriend that*? *Yes.*" (p. 259) Jennifer would testify later, but in her police interview she already said something close to what Sisti was asserting.

Sisti asked how long did Jeff take between his first call and finally calling 911, and Jeff said it was "*real quick,*" and thought it was a matter of seconds, not minutes. The questioning would have been more effective if Mark Sisti had shown Jeff a timeline of the calls he made on November 9th, and the length of time before Jeff called 911. Such a timeline is presented below.

1.	12:25 p.m.	Chad	no discussion	(actually 12:24:49)
2.	12:25 p.m.	Chad	no discussion	
3.	12:25 p.m	Chad	no discussion	
4.	12:26 p.m	Jennifer	discussion	
5.	12:28 p.m.	Chad	no discussion	
6.	12:28 p.m.	Chad	no discussion	
7.	12:28 p.m.	Chad	left phone message	
8.	12:32 p.m.	411	to get phone number for Amanda at Old Navy	
9.	12:34 p.m.	Amanda	no discussion	
10.	12:37 p.m	Jennifer	discussion	
11.	12:38 p.m.	unidentified		
12.	12:39 p.m.	911		

The gap between his first call at 12:25 p.m to Chad's cell phone, and the last of his 12 calls to 911 at 12:39 p.m., was 14 minutes, or approximately 840 seconds. In that amount of time, Jeff could have picked up Kassidy and walked with her to the police station. The 12 calls included six to Chad, two to Jennifer, one to 411-information, one to an unidentified number, and finally the call to 911. Sisti could also have asked why there were so many calls to Chad. Of the first seven calls, six were to Chad. Jeff finally left a message on the sixth call, as recalled by Chad, "*Chad, this is Jeff. Call me as soon as you get this. Bye.*"

Jeff agreed that he wasn't a doctor, and said that several times, and that he didn't know what the problem was with Kassidy. Sisti then reminded Jeff that "*without being asked whether you caused the injuries, without being asked how the baby was in this condition, without being asked anything about it, you blamed Chad Evans?*" (p. 263) Mark Sisti quoted Detective Hamel's report, with Jeff's statement, "*...' This isn't me. I didn't do anything like this. Chad Evans did,*' " and Jeff said he didn't recall saying that, "*I don't think I did.*" (p. 263)

By his questions, Sisti argued with Jeff that Chad had called him more often about Kassidy than Jeff had told the police or than he had just testified on direct. The debatable question was how central to each call was Kassidy. Jeff responded, "*I mean, you can try to turn around all you want, but the truth's the truth.*" (p. 264)

The questioning returned to the time when Chad picked up Kassidy on November 8th.

Q All right. While you and he and Kassidy were there, he wasn't angry, was he?
A While me and Kassidy were there, no. He didn't seem to be
Q Pleasant conversation, right?
A Seemed to be. He told me about where he was and stuff and everything.
Q Yeah. Small talk, right?
A I suppose.
Q Not frustrated, or mad, or angry, or anything like that?
A I guess not, no, not at that point....
Q He wasn't exhibiting any violent tendencies? Nothing? Nothing?
A Didn't seem to be. (p. 267)

Later, Jeff said that Chad was "mad" because Amanda didn't leave the car seat there for him to use for Kassidy, and Sisti asked for clarification, "*He's not mad at the baby, right?*" and Jeff responded, "*I would guess not.*" (p. 268)

This was an excellent point for Sisti, but more could have been said about these moments before, according to the State's theory, Chad hit or beat Kassidy on the way to Kyle's day care. In addition to the "angry man" theory, another part of the prosecutors' case was that Chad and Amanda were keeping Kassidy away from the public and day care professionals. Why, then, would Chad want to pull up to the front door of his own son's school with a beaten or crying Kassidy? It makes little sense that he would stop on the way to Kyle's day care to hit Kassidy. Sisti could have noted that there was no evidence found in Chad's car which indicated any kind of an assault.

That afternoon, Chad had worked with his secretary, Melissa Allard, on a labor report. She could have testified about his demeanor that afternoon. After leaving work, Chad went to the Hampton Shop 'n' Save and purchased an energy bar and spoke briefly with Melissa's daughter, and Chad's friend, Mandy Allard, and she also could have testified about his demeanor that afternoon. Even the clerk at Moonlite Reader, with whom Chad was frustrated because of the slow pace of a refund request, could have testified about Chad's calm demeanor that afternoon. All these witnesses could have supported Jeff's assessment that Chad was not angry on that afternoon.

After Chad left Jeff's at approximately 5:32 p.m., he drove to pick up his son, and he thought he was running late, as parents were asked to pick up their children no later than 6:00 p.m. Mapquest calculates the reasonable time to drive that 18.6 mile trip is 30 minutes, which makes the trip very tight. Stopping or slowing down to assault the daughter of your lover while rushing to pick up the son you love doesn't seem to be a likely scenario.

Twelve minutes into this trip to Dover, according to Sisti, Chad called Jeff, and, according to Jeff, Chad said, "*The little bitch is acting weird.*" (p. 270) In Sisti's words, "*... But he called you and he was concerned about the baby's condition. He described the condition, right?*" and Jeff responded, "*He described the condition, yes.*" (p. 270)

Then, the dialogue shifted to Chad's second call to Jeff, after Chad had arrived home. Jeff confirmed what Chad had told him, including Sisti's statement, "*and he also said, well, he had to bring her inside and there was*[were] *and dirt in her hair and everything, right?"* (p. 271) For the first time, Sisti offered an explanation of how Kassidy may have been injured before Chad picked her up, saying to Jeff, *"If baby Kassidy would have been dropped out of a pickup truck on your gravel and dirt driveway, she would have gotten stones and dirt in her hair, wouldn't she?"* Jeff responded, *"I don't know, because it didn't happen."* (p. 271) Sisti rhetorically and sarcastically asked, "*You got a dirt driveway, you know that*?" and "*Where there's stone, and dirt, and sand and stuff like that*?" Jeff responded, "*Yes, I do*," and "*Yes sir*," respectively. They sparred about the paved driveway at Chad's and how there are stones and dirt on the sides of the driveway.

Judge Nadeau then closed the trial for the day, as there were some matters for the attorneys to work on. She scheduled the next day to begin at 9:00 a.m., and gave the jury the daily mantra not to discuss the case, and also advised the jury to, "... put your notebooks back in the envelopes and hand them in to the bailiff." (p. 273)

Mark Sisti asked Judge Nadeau to issue a no-contact order between Jennifer Bortner and Jeff Marshall. Judge Nadeau agreed to the goal, and asked the State's attorneys to find a solution, as Jeff and Jennifer lived together. Sisti asked the court to give the jury instructions regarding Jeff Marshall's mis-statements about the photograph of his bedroom, State Exhibit 26. Judge Nadeau said she would respond to the request after hearing Jeff's testimony on redirect examination.

MEDIA: 1. "Sitter Remorseful - Defense laying blame on baby sitter for Kassidy's death"
2. "Babysitter denies harming Rochester baby"
3. "Baby sitter: I did not hurt Kassidy"

Friday, 7 December 2001 Jeff Marshall (continued)

Mark Sisti continued his cross-examination of Jeff by showing that Jeff recalled very little of his conversation with Kittery Detective Steve Hamel while Kassidy was being worked on by the EMTs and police. Jeff said, "*I was more concerned about Kassidy being alone in the ambulance, sir.*" (p. 6)

Sisti asked Jeff about Kassidy's overnight with him and Jennifer on Saturday, October 21, 2000, or the night before he and Chad went to Maine to pick up a 3-wheeler that Chad had purchased. First he returned to Jeff's allegations that Chad had called Kassidy a bitch or a retard, and asked Jeff if he had used such words. *"No, I did not,"* he said, but then added, *"I said she acted retarded, sir. That's what I said... I might have swore around her, but I never swore about her, sir."* (p. 10) Sisti asked Jeff about what he said to Amanda and Chad when he returned Kassidy to them on Sunday morning, October 22. He asked Jeff if he said, *"... something to the effect of, 'Her ass might be a little sore. She was being a little shit so I gave her a spanking.' "* Jeff responded, "*Absolutely not. I would never say anything like that*," (p. 11) and he didn't remember walking into Chad's home on that particular day.

Sisti didn't press harder on this issue of the spanking during the overnight babysitting of Saturday/Sunday, October 21/22, despite the physical, black and blue, evidence that it happened, and despite the recollections of four people. Amanda, Chad, Travis and Jeremy had told police that they had seen the bruises and Chad had told the police in his interview that Jeff had told him that, "*he spanked her so hard his hand stung."* (p. 1533) Jeremy had told the police during his interview on November 9 that Jeff had acknowledged the spanking to him that very evening of November 9, with qualification. Jeremy quoted Jeff as saying, *"I just spanked her. I didn't put those bruises on her."* Also, he described his Nov. 9 conversation with Jeff again during his interview on November 14. (p. 293) Thus, after direct examination and cross-examination, the only spanking of Kassidy that Jeff acknowledged was the followup to the Windex-drinking incident. That occurred during the October 26-28 three day/two night babysitting, but the jury did not know that. During these challenges to Jeff, Chad was watching and listening. He would often write notes to Sisti to make a point or remind him about a question to ask. Chad recalls that Sisti didn't pay much attention to these communications, and wrote in his May 27, 2011 letter,

Mark Sisti is a very confident man, loud, with a definite swagger. Mark is the opposite of Alan in almost every way. Mark puts you at ease, comforts you with statements such as, "relax, you are in good hands." And "I'm good at my job and know what I'm doing." And "Relax, I'm in the driver's seat." And "I don't want you to worry or even think about the legal stuff. This is what you hired me for. "It's a bravado that you just feel, "Wow, I'm all set." Then in court, you watch him stumble around. One example is when he cross-examined Jeff and seemingly let him off the hook. And you (me) ask about it and he coolly, indicates that he has everything under control still.

Jeff was asked if made "*excuses like a dog knocked the baby over...?*" and he replied, "*No... Any bruises, from what I recall, came from their house, not our house, sir.... Absolutely.* " (p. 13-14) He was asked, "*Remember bringing the baby home and having had put women's cover-up makeup on the child?*" (p. 14) and he responded, "*No, I do not, sir... No, I do not,*" but moments later he said, "*I know that we probably did put makeup on Kassidy if we went to Wal-Mart. I'm sure Jennifer did, you know, if we went shopping at Wal-Mart or went out.*" (p. 15) Sisti asked if the makeup was covering up bruises, and Jeff responded, "*Yes, sir. That your client inflicted upon Kassidy, yes, that she came to our house with.*" (p. 15) Jeff was asked, "*When,*" and he replied, "*Ever since she started living with them, sir.*" He continued, "*I think there was only one time, sir,*" and he denied that it was to cover up a bruise caused when his dog knocked Kassidy over, an incident which he denied happening. (p. 16)

Jeff said that when they took Kassidy to Wal-Mart, they purchased a doll for her, because, "*well, they brought her over to our house with no toys and no diapers and stuff like that, so, yeah, we had to get stuff for her.*" (p. 16) Sisti did not ask the followup question of what Jeff meant by "*they,*" because Chad never brought Kassidy to Jeff's apartment. Not once. Before picking up Kassidy in the early evening of November 8, he had only been to that apartment once before, the previous week, and never to bring Kassidy for babysitting.

Jeff did acknowledge saying "*Mama's here,*" (p. 20) and that, implicitly, Kassidy did fall when she tripped when trying to run to see her mother. However, he said that he never said, "*Mama's here,*" to tease Kassidy, or when Amanda wasn't, in fact, there.

Jeff reiterated, "*And once again, I never saw her get hurt at our house like that. She would run off with her hands down. That's what you would notice about her as she started to decline. She would run and wouldn't catch herself.*" (p. 17)

Jeff stated, "*...I'm saying she would stand in a corner. If she did fall, it was usually on her bum, you know, because her leg hurt because of what Chad Evans had done... he was playing rough with her...*" (p. 18) Then, the two combatants had an exchange which had been seen before, albeit with different words:

Q When? Give this jury a date.

A I can't give you an exact date, sir. (p. 18)

Sisti asked Jeff, "*Do you ever remember that child being brought home dehydrated and sick?*" (p. 17-18) Jeff said, "*No, sir,*" and he had no recollection of seeing Kassidy, once back at Chad's and Amanda's home, "*putting her face right into a bowl of cereal and drinking all the milk out of it,*" (p. 18) to which Amanda had testified. Jeff responded, "*Absolutely not, sir.*" (p. 18) During this line of questioning, Sisti did not ask about Kassidy's drinking of Windex from a bottle left on the kitchen table, which is likely part of what caused Kassidy's dehydration. Sisti did not ask whether Jeff called a hotline "Poison Control" for help after the Windex ingestion. As the answer was sure to be, "Yes," because Jennifer had said that such a call was made, and lawyers are taught that the best questions to ask in a trial are those to which the answers are already known, Sisti could have asked why if Jeff knew enough to call "Poison Control" only two weeks earlier, it took him 14 minutes and 11 calls before he called 911 on November 9.

Sisti concluded his cross-examination by reviewing how Jeff Marshall's testimony seemed to differ from Amanda's testimony and Detective Hamel's report, but Jeff said that he was confident that they told the truth, and so did he. Sisti's final question was, "*How many times did the baby fall out of your truck?*" and Jeff responded, "*That one time, sir, which I caught her.*" (p. 22)

The challenge now for the defense was to corroborate what Amanda had told the jury about those eight incidents or accidents involving Jeff where his recollection and hers differed widely. Sisti asked Jeff about the first seven of the eight, but did not ask about #8, the abrasions on Kassidy's feet. The eight are again listed below, chronologically:

1	+10/8	Fall from bed when Jeff said, "Mama's here," but then Amanda was not there.
2	+10/15	Kassidy knocked over by Jeff and Jen's dog, Jake. Makeup applied to cover bruise
3	~10/21	Jeff Marshall spanked Kassidy, causing black and blue marks on buttocks.
4	~10/26	Kassidy drank unknown quantity of Windex at Jeff's.
5	~10/27	Kassidy returned with two large bumps on back of head, from the reported fall from Jeff's truck.
6	~10/28	Kassidy returned home severely dehydrated (same return day as #5)
7	~11/6	Jeff tripped over Kassidy, stepping on her foot, causing limp.
8	~11/7	Minute marks found on Kassidy's feet. Also called "abrasions," or "pin pricks"

Another challenge for the defense was to bring to the attention of the jury the other incidents noted below, and not presented during Amanda's testimony, regarding Jeff's babysitting practices with Kassidy.

9	unk.	Put Kassidy into time-out and then watch her through window.
10	Aug.	Cover Kassidy's face with pillow to muffle her crying.
11	10/24	Three bruises on Kassidy's jaw, after return from babysitting on Tuesday, Oct. 24.
12	unk.	Kassidy's fall from the bed at Jeff's when Jeff went to get additional "wipes" and Kassidy had her pants around her ankles.
13	11/7	A fall from Jeff's truck, but without injury, as witnessed by Will Peirce, who testified that Jeff caught Kassidy, and in the presence of Will Peirce. It was not understood at the trial that this incident was different from #5, above.
14	10/24 & unk.	While not an "incident" by itself, Sisti could have asked Jeff about the times during the fall of 2000 that he brought Jennifer, Amanda and Kassidy to a fall cleanup worksite, and then would take Kassidy with him back to his apartment to do some bookkeeping.

Because of the decision to paint Jeff as THE true abuser and murderer of Kassidy, Sisti's cross-examination was viewed by Jeff as a challenge to him and an accusation. The alternative would have been to ask for Jeff's help in exploring what really happened to Kassidy without accusing him. That strategy might have engendered less juror sympathy for Jeff, and would have opened up the other possibilities of causation due to accidents and chronic condition or disease.

Sisti did not ask Jeff about how and when Kassidy's pajamas were removed, even though he would later ask Detective Herbert Leighton about the pajamas, and Leighton would agree that how they were removed could be an important part of the investigation. This was another reason why it would have been helpful to recall Jeff and other witnesses toward the end of the trial as the trial opened up new questions. No witness in the trial was recalled for any reason.

Sisti did not know about, and therefore could not ask, about how Jeff felt after being told by Chad, on about October 26, that his McDonald's contracts would not be renewed, and what percentage of his income was going to be lost. He might have asked whether Jeff was upset or angry and how he showed that anger and to whom. As far as Chad knows, there was no visible reaction or further discussion with Jeff about the decision. There was no anger and no request for reconsideration. It simply was not discussed again during the remaining 16 days before Kassidy died. His feelings about the loss were likely expressed in some way, even before his 2004 lawsuit against Chad.

Jeff was never asked by Sisti about Chad's notifying him around October 24th that his landscaping contracts with McDonald's were not going to be renewed. Sisti may not have known about Chad's decision and communication to Jeff.

Sisti did not confront Jeff with the inconsistency between his testimony on direct examination by Will Delker and what he told Chad on Wednesday evening that, "*You know, you need to bring her to the hospital."* (Transcript, Dec. 6, 2001, p. 138), and what he told the police on the day Kassidy died which was that, "***I should have probably** told him last night" to take Kassidy to the hospital.* (Jeff Interview, November 9, 2000, p. 1308, emphasis added here) The difference is important, because the jury heard that Jeff did say that to Chad and the jury was able to draw the inference that, as the prosecution argued, Chad was especially culpable for not taking Kassidy to the hospital, after Jeff made that explicit recommendation. However, he didn't actually make it, if one believes that what a person says to the police less than a day after a conversation is more reliable than what one says a year later.

Delker began his redirect examination with the circumstances of Detective Hamel's report of his first discussions with Jeff while Kassidy was being treated by EMTs on his porch and being transferred to the ambulance. Jeff said, "*It was just a mess.... I just tried to save Kassidy.... I was upset.*" (p. 22-23) Delker presented the handwritten statement which Jeff made at the Kittery Police Station about two hours after his conversation with Steve Hamel, and Jeff read to the jury where he wrote about Kassidy's condition on the previous day, Wednesday, November 8th. He read, "*She looked fine. Not too many bruises, but she still was acting strange.*" (p. 24) Jeff elaborated on the witness stand, "*...her demeanor had changed, and she was slowly -- she wasn't normal. She kept -- she was slow and got slower and slower.*" (p. 25)

This immediate recollection might be the most accurate of any of Jeff's statements of Kassidy's behavior on the afternoon of November 8. It seems consistent with the behavior that Chad saw later in his car.

Then Will Delker asked Jeff to read from the transcript of his November 9th interview,

She had no real facial bruises, nothing that would, you know, besides her walking problem, and besides these are -- these are starting to clear up, you know, the ones right here. (p. 26)

This was in direct conflict with Amanda's testimony about Kassidy hitting her head on the coffee table on approximately November 5th, and being scratched by her kitty on November 7th. Travis also witnessed the coffee table accident.

In an effort to clear up the alleged discrepancy with the appearance of the photograph of Jeff's bed with a pair of pants on top of mail, Delker showed Jeff two other photographs of the bedroom. Jeff concluded that at the time when he discovered Kassidy in distress, he was,

Frantic. My reaction's not to keep everything where it is. You know. I'm not there to make the bed. First thing is just to try to do what I can to help her." (p. 34)

Jeff was asked again about when he "*first started babysitting regularly*" and he replied, "*When Amanda got her job, sir,"* and that was *"maybe a week, two weeks, something like that,"* before her death. Then, he clarified, "*It was not that long.*" (p. 34) Jeff's vagueness about time and dates was a barrier to his better understanding of what happened to Kassidy, and to the jury's understanding. Amanda seems to have started her job at Old Navy, at 9:00 a.m. on Monday, November 6, exactly four days before Kassidy died. Amanda's job began the first day of the work week. It was the first day after the weekend. It was the day before the election and the Bush/Gore struggle that so fascinated Jeff over the next two days. Jeff's babysitting on those last four days were for 8+ hours on Monday, 12+ hours on Tuesday, 2+ hours on Wednesday and 4+ hours on Thursday, for a total of 26-27+ hours. It was not a week or two weeks.

However, Amanda may have attended one or more training sessions at Old Navy the previous week, during which time Jeff and Jennifer may have babysat for Kassidy. One former co-employee, Kristin Parsons, thought that Amanda started work on Thursday, November 2. Consistent with that recollection, Chad remembers that his "surprise" meetup with Kassidy and Amanda likely occurred the week before Kassidy's death, and Amanda was defninitely working at Old Navy when he took them to the Kittery McDonald's for lunch.

Will Delker continued the uncertainty about dates when he asked Jeff his final series of questions, asking, "*And how was her condition towards the end of her life compared to when she first started staying with Chad*?" (p. 35) Jeff responded, "*They'd be an every-now-and-then occurrence. And then there was more than one bruise. It just progressed. Just like her behavior kept progressing.*" (p. 36) Again, a timeline on a large chart would have been helpful. Kassidy and Amanda were substantially moved to Chad's by early to mid-July, but there was no evidence of bruises or behavior change before October 1, when Jacqueline Conley took that photo of Kassidy, alive, which was State Exhibit 19 at the trial. The onset of bruises and behavior change coincided far more closely with the babysitting at Jeff's than with Kassidy moving in with Chad in July. Of course, coincidence does not always, or even often, determine causation, but if the jury were to comply with Delker's and Jeff's argument that coincidence implied causation, then the State was prosecuting the wrong man.

Mark Sisti, on recross-examination accused Jeff, not of murder, but of not wanting to babysit, "*You didn't want to care for her, did you*?" and Jeff responded, "*I didn't mind taking care of her.... I loved Kassidy, sir.*" (p. 37) Sisti revisited the problem with the photograph showing pants on the bed, with mail underneath, and then closed with a reference to the October 1 photograph where Jeff had thought he saw bruises. His last response was as vague about time as others, "*She did have bruises on her side. I don't know if they were at the time of that picture, but....* (p. 39) When he made that statement he knew, from Sisti's earlier questions, that Jacqueline Conley had taken the photo and that she saw no bruises.

After Jeff stepped down from the witness chair, the lawyers and judge, outside the hearing of the jury, addressed the question of the photo with the pants and mail, and what had been moved before the photograph. The outcome of that argument was an "instruction" to the jury where Judge Nadeau summarized what happened. She said,

If the State's attorney were to testify about the meeting they had with Mr. Marshall last week, the State's attorneys would state that Mr. Marshall did not state that State's exhibit 26 was in inaccurate representation of the room at the time he found Kassidy. The State's attorneys would say, however, that the witness did state that Exhibit 69 was not accurate, because things had been moved." (p. 44)

Patricia Hocter

Assistant Attorney General Simon Brown examined Patricia Hocter, the Assessment Worker for DCYF who responded to the call, then anonymous, from Tristan Evans to DCYF on October 31, 2000. Hocter said that the anonymous report said that "*the child had suspicious marks, bruises on ... the face and neck area.*" and that "*the mother ... reported that the child had fallen down some stairs, and two days later* [the anonymous caller] *asked Chad Evans... and he said that the child had fallen off a trampoline.*" (p. 47) Hocter said that she received the report of the call on November 1 and that she called the Evans home on Monday, November 6, and left a phone message, "*I'm Patricia Hocter. I'm calling from DCYF*," and she said she left her phone number and requested a return call. (p. 47)

Alan Cronheim cross-examined and established that Patricia Hocter didn't receive a return call on November 6, so she called again on Thursday morning, November 9th, arount 9:00-9:15 a.m. She said that Chad called her back, "*The voice mail said 12:30 p.m.*" (p. 54) She said that she heard Chad's voice and he left the message to call him again, Tuesday afternoon, as he would be out of town. One of the five large panel Exhibits (63-67) of the "Chart of Calls" stated that Chad called the DCYF number at 9:32 a.m. and again at 9:35 a.m. It was during that second call that Chad left the message. The jury was left to understand that Chad called DCYF back three and a half hours after the message was left at his home answering machine. While such a delay could have been easily explained, it would have been better if the jury had known that Chad's return call was no more than one-half hour later.

Cronheim was asking Hocter about whether Friday, the day before Veterans' Day was a State of New Hampshire holiday, when Judge Nadeau asked him to speak up as some jurors could not hear him. Alan Cronheim had a different style than Mark Sisti. If Friday was a day off, then asking for a return call on Tuesday was only two-plus work days ahead from Thursday.

There were no questions about why it took so long from the date of Tristan's call on October 31st, to November 9 for DCYF to successfully follow up. State regulations called for prompt reponses to such calls, and the referral form for this call had a handwritten entry for "*48 hours*" in the "*Response Required.*" box. (p. 161) In addition to the use of phones to reach Chad's home, the DCYF office was only three miles away, and a physical visit would have been easy. Coincidentally, the Rochester McDonald's is across the street from the DCYF office. If Kassidy had died without a police theory about the perpetrator, and successful prosecution, DCYF, and individual employees would likely have been held more responsible for her death. Once, however, the purported villain was identified, and the "court documents" began to be quoted about Kassidy's allegedly horrible last three months at the hands of Chad Evans, the pressure on DCYF was minimized.

Joshua Bortner Conley

Before Simon Brown's examination of Joshua, the brother of Amanda, the judge talked with the lawyers about the timing of the day's (a Friday) closing of the courthouse. Alan Cronheim was pleased with the early closing, as he could then go to his son's hockey practice. He appeared to be a good father, just as was Chad, who would soon lose his ability to go to his own son's athletic practices and games.

Joshua, whom Kassidy called, "Osh," was the only witness at the trial who had known Chad but who had not been previously interviewed by the police. On direct examination, Joshua recounted how Kassidy and Amanda lived in the family home off and on until Amanda moved to live with Chad. Joshua often babysat for Kassidy when she was younger and said she had no problems with bruising. He said that Jeff and Jennifer would come to the family home about twice a month and that Jeff and Kassidy got along well, and Jeff would bring her presents.

He said that he had seen Kassidy "*a couple of times*" (p. 69) after Amanda moved to Rochester. One of those times was when Amanda "*brought her there with one of her friends to pick up money to buy Chad a birthday present.*" The friend was not identified in court or in the investigation documents, but she would have been a good source of information. It would have been a good question for the defense to ask Amanda on recall, or simply ask her out of court and summons that person for testimony. Brown established with Joshua that Amanda called first, and that it was a weekday, but he did not establish the date, which was Friday, October 13. Thus, it was a Friday the 13th, a day associated since the 19th Century, with bad luck. There are only between one and three such Fridays a year. If the jury had been told that this sighting of bruises by Joshua was on Friday the 13th of October, it would have assisted them in sorting out the time line in their own minds and notes, even if the lawyers were not going to do it for them. This sighting by Joshua was one of the first, confirmed, now-dated sightings of bruises on Kassidy. The first may have been around October 6, when Chad and Amanda saw bruises on Kassidy after the "Mama's here" incident at Jeff's.

Asked what bruises he saw on Kassidy, Joshua said that he saw "*like brownish bruises, just like kind of close down to her neck, around her chin. Like around the front part and the sides... Both sides.... Dark brownish... They were really noticeable.*" (p. 71) He said that he asked Amanda about the bruises and he was told the substance of what became known as the "trampoline story." He said that at the end of the visit, Kassidy didn't want to leave, which he understood "*because she was crying a lot and stuff before she left.*" (p. 72) When his mother, Jacqueline returned home from a trucking trip with her husband, Paul Conley, the next day, Joshua told her about the bruises. She then called Amanda's and Chad's home, "*within five minutes*" of Joshua's telling her what he saw. (p. 72).

Alan Cronheim cross examined Joshua, beginning with a question about the date of Amanda's visit, and asked, "*...you last saw Kassidy the middle of October, correct, of 2000?*" Joshua replied, firmly, "*No. Not the middle of October, the end of September.*" (p.

73) Even when he agreed that Chad's birthday was October 15, Joshua still insisted that it was the end of September. Then the lawyers discussed with Judge Nadeau how to clarify for the jury that he was wrong. Subsequently, Cronheim asked if he had told the prosecutors in a meeting that very morning of Joshua's testimony that the day was in "*September or October*," and Joshua agreed. While that was a little closer to the correct date, the defense lost the opportunity to clarify that the date was exactly Friday, October 13, the day before Chad's birthday weekend. Establishing that date would have narrowed down the date, finally for the date-starved jury, of at least one set of bruises on Kassidy. This would have enabled the jury to see that the bruises seen by Melissa Chick and Tracey Foley "in October" were exactly the same bruises seen by Joshua on Friday, October 13. Thus, instead of the jury hearing about what might have been two sets or occasions of bruising, they were actually hearing of only one.

Alan Cronheim did establish that Joshua did not notice any other problems with Kassidy and that she was walking around, during her half-hour to an hour visit. Thus, if the jury had known that the date of visit was October 13, the jurors would have understood that only 27 days before Kassidy died, she was fine except for the bruises on her face. The problem was that the jury was left with the impression that the visit could have been as early as September. This they could have thought, if they had remembered Joshua's testimony, and forgotten his mother's previous testimony about the late September visit and the photograph she took. As noted earlier, the jury wasn't told the exact date of that October 1 photograph. Every day into October that Kassidy was healthy is important, and every day bruise-free is important.

Joshua stated that Amanda had called before the trip, and expected that her mother would be there as planned, so there was no intent by Amanda to come to Buckfield when her mother wasn't there. Chad recalled in 2011 hearing one end of a phone conversation between Amanda and her mother when Amanda asked that Jacqueline be sure to leave a check, if she was going to be away when Amanda came to Buckfield. The call that Joshua recalled in his testimony confirmed that Jacqueline had gone on the anticipated trip.

Simon Brown established on redirect that the check Amanda picked up was for $100, and Joshua stated that he and his family had lived in Buckfield for about a month before Amanda's visit. However, that response about dates was also incorrect. His mother had testified that the family moved on October 1, which was the beginning of a month, and a logical time to relocate between rental properties. Thus, Joshua's response, "*about a month*" (p. 79) would have put the Amanda visit at the end of October. He had already acknowledged that Chad's birthday was October 15. The jury would have benefitted immensely from hearing an accurate representation of dates for every one of the events in this case.

Alan Cronheim addressed only one issue on recross-examination, and that was the date of the Amanda visit. He reminded Joshua of his mother's testimony that the previous visit was on October 1, and Joshua agreed. Cronheim stopped there, and settled for a one-month time window. His final question was, "*So the time that you saw Kassidy was sometime in October of 2000*?" and Joshua responded, "*Yes*." (p. 80)

There were four time periods within October for four Second Degree Assault charges. To defeat some or all of them, it would take more than vague determinations of dates. It would take precise dates and a clear understanding of the timeline and what bruises were seen by whom and when.

Jennifer Bortner Conley

Will Delker examined Jennifer and established that she was now an Assistant Manager at Perfumania in Kittery, and had worked there for "*about a year*." (p. 82) As with almost every other witness, the search for truth in this case would have been advanced if testimony about dates had been more precise. The importance of that date would become more clear later in the trial. As Kassidy had died 13 months earlier, Jennifer clearly began working at Perfumania more than a year earlier. Usually, employees of companies have a good idea of their Start Date because that's the date from which some benefits, such as vacation, are calculated. In any case, even if Jennifer did not know the date, the prosecution and the defense should have retrieved her employment records for the case and known the exact date.

Jennifer said that Jeff was her "*boyfriend*" (p. 83), with whom she has continued to live, but that was a change from her police interview in 2000 when she said that she was engaged, and showed her ring to the interviewers. (p. 6) Jennifer stated that she and Jeff introduced Chad to Amanda on a double date in June of 2000, and that date was correct, even if not as precise as June 2nd.

She described how Kassidy and Amanda first lived with Amanda and Jennifer's mother and stepfather, and then Amanda and Kassidy moved to live with a boyfriend, and then they returned, until Amanda, and then Kassidy, moved to live with Chad. Jennifer testified that Kassidy was a normal, healthy baby on whom Jennifer saw no bruising until she moved to live with Chad. The first indication during the trial of the difficult relationship between Jennifer and her sister, Amanda, came when she described the situation in the summer of 2000. "*She lived with my parents, and Mandy would take Kassidy for a little while and then* ***dump*** *her off at my parents' house and leave.*" (p. 90, emphasis added)

Jennifer stated that Kassidy began living full-time at Chad's "*around the time of my mother's hysterectomy.... the end of summer.*" (p. 90) That date, too, was imprecise as it was approximately August 27th. Delker asked Jennifer when she first started noticing bruises on Kassidy and, like Jeff, she answered not with a date, but with the reference point of "*whenever Kassidy started living with Chad full-time,*" which she had just identified as the "*end of summer.*" (p. 91) Asked to describe the bruises, Jennifer said, "*I noticed bruising on her forehead. I noticed bruising on... her cheeks. I noticed bruises, basically, a lot on her face.*" Delker asked, "*Would they be there all the time*?" and Jennifer responded, "*Pretty much, yeah.*" (p. 91)

Delker asked Jennifer to describe what she saw over time, and Jennifer responded,

The first time I saw the bruising, I saw them on the forehead. My sister brought Kassidy into work and mentioned them. And then, you know, they'd start to fade, and then another bruise would appear like around here. [pointing to location on face, unknown in 2011] *And they'd start to fade and then, you know, another bruise would appear, or they'd come back darker.*" (p. 91)

Jennifer was one of several witnesses who had seen bruises on Kassidy's forehead. The others would be Melissa Chick, Tristan, Shannon Gagne and Cathy Nuernberg. Because of the imprecision of dates during the investigation and the trial it's not known if they all saw the same bruise(s) on Kassidy's forehead, and they might have. None of the charges against Chad related to bruises on Kassidy's forehead and no theory was ever advanced to suggest that Chad intentionally inflicted any of them.

This was one point in the trial where knowing Jennifer's exact start date at Perfumania would have been helpful, as it would have established the date, after which she began seeing bruises. In her first police interview, on November 9, 2000, Jen said she had worked at Perfumania, *"About, almost a month. It's more like 3 weeks. I work with Jeff in the summer."* (Interview, p. 913) That would have made her start date at Perfumania around Monday, October 16, or the day after Chad's birthday, and after Joshua's Friday, October 13 observations.

Jennifer was asked the circumstances when she might see Kassidy, and she answered,

We'd be mowing the lawn in Rochester McDonald's and we'd call Amanda and have her come down and meet us for lunch. You know, sometimes me and my sister would go shopping together, and I'd see Kassidy." (p. 92)

However, there were no dates associated with those occasions. The lawnmowing occasion(s) were likely in September or earlier. One such occasion in September was described earlier in Chapter 3, with a description from Chad's Letter of Apr. 18, 2010. He stated there that he was the person, not Jeff or Jennifer, who called Amanda and asked her to come have lunch with him and Jeff and Jennifer. There was certainly no hiding of Kassidy by Amanda or Chad from the public at this time. Also, it was a day where Kassidy and Amanda were at "home" in Rochester and it was during the period of Chad's subsequent charge of Child Endangerment and the September charge of Second Degree Assault against Kassidy.

After stating that she babysat, or "*watched*," Kassidy, Jennifer was asked for the reasons for such babysitting, and she said it was because

...my sister said she couldn't find a babysitter... because the bruises on her face. Mandy didn't want anybody to take the baby away from her, so she couldn't, you know, she didn't want to take Kassidy to -- to a day care, because they were afraid that the State was going to take her from them. I watched Kassidy one time whenever Mandy and Chad went up to Chad's parents' house. And they -- they dropped Kassidy off because they didn't want his parents to see the baby. (p. 92-93)

This allegation about Chad and Amanda not wanting to take Kassidy to Keene to see Chad's parents was just as false when Jennifer said it, just as it was when Jeff said it in his testimony the previous day. Chad's mother, Pam, saw Kassidy during the melded family's two trips to Keene and Pam's two visits to Rochester.

The allegation of Amanda's fear that the state might take Kassidy away from her is belied by Amanda's frequent appointments at the Dept. of Health and Human Services office in Sanford, Maine during the months of September and October.

Asked about overnight babysitting by her or her parents, Jennifer stated, "*To us or to my parents... They just dropped -- my sister would just drop Kassidy off at my parents' house and take off, not even telling them where they were going.*" (p. 93) She said that Kassidy would stay overnight at Jeff and Jen's, "*Probably about two or three times a week. That was after she moved in with Chad full-time.*" (p. 94) If Jennifer was using her mother's operation on August 27 as the starting date, that meant, for the following six weeks, Kassidy would have stayed overnight between 12 and 18 times. Jeff had said it was a "handful" of times, which was far closer to being correct.

Chad recalls, and calendars support, approximately five overnight babysitting stints for Kassidy at Jeff's and Jennifer's between June 9 and November 9, 2000. They were:

1. *On Saturday evening, July 1, Chad and Amanda went boating on Baxter Lake with Chad's friend, Glen Varney, who lived on the lake, and his girlfriend, Deb. As Deb's daughter was elsewhere, Amanda arranged for Kassidy to spend the night with Jeff and Jennifer. This was the first babysitting for Kassidy, since he met her on June 9, that Chad can recall at Jeff's and Jennifer's. It was certainly her first overnight there since June 9.*
2. *On Saturday, August 12, Chad and Amanda went with their friends, Michelle and Bruce Truell, to a party in Newport, New Hampshire, organized by the Freelancers Motorcycle Club. Later, this party was known as the "Harley Party." Kassidy stayed overnight with Jennifer and Jeff Marshall. This was the second overnight for Kassidy at Jeff's and Jennifer's since Amanda met Chad.*
3. *On Friday, August 18, Amanda and Chad and Bruce and Michelle Truell, went to see "Dr. Dirty", John Valby, at the Hampton Beach Casino Ballroom. Kassidy stayed with Jeff and Jennifer for her third overnight with them.*
4. *On Saturday, October 21, Chad and Amanda spent the day and evening with their friends, Bruce and Michelle Truell, in Newport, New Hampshire, and Kassidy had an overnight babysit with Jennifer and Jeff. This was her fourth overnight with Jeff and Jennifer since June 9.*
5. *Thursday and Friday, October 26-27, when Jeff had Kassidy for three days and two nights, during which time she reportedly fell out of Jeff's truck, and, in another incident during this stay, drank some Windex.*

Asked about Amanda's explanations for the bruising, Jennifer said that Amanda "*told me a couple of stories*," and the first was the "trampoline story." Jennifer did not mention that Amanda had told her during the secretly taped conversation in Buckfield on November 11, 2000, that the "trampoline story." was false. Amanda said, "*I told you that wasn't the trampoline. I remember telling you about it.*" (p. 2) Returning to Jennifer's testimony, she said, importantly, "*...that was the first time I saw a bruise on Kassidy...*" (p. 94) As noted earlier, the "trampoline story" was created by Amanda and Chad around the weekend of Chad's birthday on October 15th, which was long after the point which she said a few minutes earlier that the bruises began, i.e. when Kassidy and Amanda moved to

Chad's. Even that date, August 27 (the date of her mother's operation) was later than the actual moving time by about a month and a half.

Will Delker asked for the other explanations, and Jennifer said, "*Kassidy falling, hitting her head on coffee tables. You know, playing, bumping, going down stairs. You know, just random things.*" (p. 94) This was how Amanda had earlier in the week described the origins of Kassidy's bruising to the jury as well. Travis witnessed Kassidy hitting the coffee table, and Jennifer herself had described Kassidy's playful stair descents at her own apartment.

In her second interview, on November 10, 2000, Jennifer said, "*The only thing that I've ever noticed on her butt was, because she used to go down the stairs on her butt. And she did it at my house, too....She slides... instead of walking down the stairs...*" (p. 1159) Jennifer had also described this practice by Kassidy in her first interview which was on November 9, 2000. (p. 917) Thus, Kassidy's butt-down-the-stairs practice was not another "story" from Amanda and Chad to explain bruises on Kassidy's behind.

Will Delker asked about how Chad and Kassidy got along and Jennifer started to describe a time when she saw them interacting at the Rochester McDonald's. Mark Sisti objected as not being relevant to the charges against Chad, and Judge Nadeau said to the State, "*It's a time period question. I need a time period.*" (p. 96) In and out of context, the request for a "*time period*" should have been made far more often. If Chad's jurors had known that they could ask questions during the trial, and most jurors do not, they could have asked that question, too.

Will Delker responded, "*... I think she said that... Kassidy started living with the defendant after her mother's testimony. The hysterectomy was at the end of the summer, so the charges -- September's the first date on the charges.*" (p. 96) However, the imprecision on dates continued. First, just because Jennifer said that Amanda's moving to Rochester with Kassidy occurred around the end of the summer didn't mean that it was the correct date, and second, the time period of the child endangerment charge began on August 1st. In this instance the mutual errors canceled out, but where criminal charges are for actions with specific time periods, it's important that the jury know exactly what happened within those time periods.

The lawyers' bench conference ended and Jennifer continued to describe the occasion at Rochester McDonald's. She testified, "*Chad goes: Look at this. And he started laughing. And he goes: Go away, retard. Go away. And Kassidy...* " (p. 98) Mark Sisti objected because there was nothing about this incident in the Discovery documents. Judge Nadeau then instructed the jury to "*disregard the witness's last answer to the question.. If you wrote it down, scribble it out of your notes.*" (p. 99) Of course, the jury heard what it heard, and would likely remember it. The only way to effectively counteract that testimony would have been to ask, under oath, the other participants at that lunch: Amanda, Chad and Jeff. However, the trial moved on and the legal fiction that the jurors could erase their memories continued. In the real world, outside a courtroom, Amanda, Chad or Jeff could have been asked about their recollections of that day, but in that courtroom, the facts of that gathering were not revisited.

Chad wrote in 2010 about that same lunch at the Rochester McDonalds, which was mentioned in Chapter 3 of this book. He absolutely denies Jennifer's recollection of his actions and statements on that day. Jeff and Jennifer were working at the Rochester McDonald's and Chad, and no one else, invited Amanda and Kassidy to come and have lunch together. Chad, and no one else, took Kassidy to play in the play area. (See his February 22, 2010, Letter)

Will Delker asked Jennifer to describe what Kassidy "*was like before Amanda started dating the defendant,*" and Jennifer said, "*Kassidy was happy. She played dolls with me. We... had fun, basically. And she hung out. It was like, you know, girls' night, you know.*" (p. 99) Delker further asked about "*after*" Chad and Amanda began dating, and Jennifer responded, "*She got quiet. She'd stand and look blankly for numerous minutes. And we'd be like, 'Kassidy, Kassidy.' And then, you know, she'd be like, you know, smiling. But we woke up one time in the...*" *(p. 99)* [missing page 100 of transcript]

Will Delker said the pivotal point was the date "*Amanda started dating the defendant,*" (p. 99) but that was June 2, and Chad didn't meet Kassidy until the following Friday, June 9. Did the jurors understand the problem with the dates? Did they consider that Amanda's mother babysat for Kassidy during the last week of September and took the Exhibit 19 photograph on October 1st? As the jury learned from Joshua's testimony, his mother called Chad on Saturday, October 14, within five minutes of his telling her about bruises on Kassidy. Thus, she showed that she was very alert to such issues as Kassidy's development. Was it likely that she would not have noticed the changes in behavior that Jennifer said she noticed from the time "*Amanda started dating the defendant*"? Of course it is.

Many people observed changes in Kassidy during the fall of 2000, especially during her last 40 days; but the key question was when did those changes begin?

Delker asked Jennifer what Chad said about Kassidy and she stated, "*He said that Kassidy was stupid, and there's something wrong with her. She had a screw or two loose.*" (p. 101) Asked about names that Chad used for Kassidy, Jennifer said, "*He called her a little bitch. He called her a retard. He called her stupid.... He called her, you know, a fucking retard, you know.*" (p. 101) Delker did not ask when and where such statements were allegedly made by Chad, or whether they were made in Kassidy's presence. As there was never a time when Chad and Jennifer were alone, then such comments would have necessarily been made in the presence of others.

Will Delker asked, "*Did Jeff ever use any words like that to describe Kassidy*?" and Jennifer responded, "*Not to describe Kassidy, no.*" (p. 101)

Delker asked Jennifer, "*Did Jeff ever talk about Kassidy's condition or her behavior?*" and Jennifer said that, "... *Chad and Jeff would tease Amanda, calling Kassidy stupid, but they were teasing Amanda about it.*" (p. 102) Delker asked if Jeff ever disciplined Kassidy and Jennifer immediately described one incident, "*He smacked her on the butt... Kassidy was getting into Windex on the kitchen table. We were both sitting in the living room watching TV, and Jeff got up and said, 'No, Kassidy.' He picked her up, just smacked her on the butt.... She was wearing a pair of sweatpants... and a pair of... her diapers.*" and Jennifer stated there was no injury to Kassidy. (p. 102)

Will Delker asked Jennifer if she had ever seen bruises on Kassidy's butt, and said, "*Yes, I have.... They were on the ... top of her butt, and little bit underneath her tailbone... She told me Kassidy got those bruises from sliding her butt down Chad's stairs, because she couldn't walk down the stairs, yet.*" (p. 103) Kassidy's stair navigation technique was discussed above. As with too many other questions from both sides during Chad's trial, there was no effort to give a date, or a range of dates, for these observations.

Delker asked Jennifer what she had noticed about Kassidy's feet, and she said, "*I noticed that there was a blister on her toe once. And I also noticed little -- I don't know what they were, they were little holes or something on the bottom of her feet.*" (p. 103-04) Jennifer and Amanda thought that the "*little holes*" might have been from "*little heads of nails*" on the linoleum in her kitchen, i.e. Jennifer's, and "*Mandy said, yeah, 'maybe that's where they came from.' And that was the end of that conversation.*" (p. 104)

Jennifer stated that she and Jeff began babysitting Kassidy regularly when Amanda started work at Old Navy, "*probably about a week,*" which was close to the correct four days. (p. 105)

Jennifer was asked about how she combined the sharing of the babysitting with her work at Perfumania, and she said, "*I would watch her like half the day before I went to work, and then Jeff would watch her the remainder of the day, or, you know, Mandy would drop her off, and Jeff would watch her in the morning, and I'd watch her when when I got back...*" (p. 105) However, Jennifer acknowledged that she didn't see Kassidy at all on Wednesday the 8th, and she would soon testify that she saw Kassidy for less than an hour on the morning of the 9th. On Monday the 6th, her work schedule (Discovery pages 399-400) was 9-5, and Amanda's schedule (Discovery pages 397-98) on Monday was also 9-5, so Jennifer did not see Kassidy for more than a few minutes, if at all. On Tuesday, Jen's hours were 1:00 p.m. to 9:00 p.m. so she likely saw Kassidy from 8:15 a.m., when Kassidy was likely dropped off, until she went to work, around 12:45 p.m. Thus, the total amount of time Jennifer shared in the babysitting of Kassidy during those four days was Monday (0-.5 hours), Tuesday, (4.5 hours), and Thursday (less than an hour), for a total of about six hours, out of the 26-27+ hours which were calculated above for the total time Kassidy spent at Jeff and Jen's during her last four days of life.

Will Delker asked Jennifer if "*at some point during the day, did Amanda come to your store?*" Jennifer didn't mention the visit by Amanda at 3:00 p.m. during the period when she was looking for a dress, and after she had left Kassidy with Jeff. Jennifer described Amanda's visit to Perfumania at "*7:30, 8:00, maybe closer to 9:00*" (p. 106-07) when Amanda called Chad at home. Jennifer said Amanda was yelling on the phone and "*she was mad.*" (p. 107) Jennifer said that Amanda said after the call, "*I'm sick of my baby always getting hurt when she's with him.*" (p. 107)

Jennifer testified that she was "*lying in bed,*" (p. 109) the next morning when Amanda brought Kassidy to her home, and put Kassidy on the bed and said, about Kassidy's face, "*It looks like fucking shit, doesn't it?*" (p. 110) Jennifer then described what she saw,

...the worst part of her face was the bruise on the side, bruises on the side. The most obvious thing, of course, was around her eye. She had like scratch marks on her cheek. She had bruises on this side, too, on and around her chin." (p. 110)

Will Delker said that he saw that Jennifer was pointing to her forehead and asked if there were bruises there, too, and she said, "*Yes.*" (p. 110) Delker asked what the bruises looked like, without being specific as to which bruises, and she said, "*They looked like finger marks.*" (p. 111) Of course, by this time, a year after Kassidy's death and Chad's arrest, it was somehow easy for people to recall details which they may have missed before. In this case, it was the first time that Jennifer had said to anyone that she thought one or more of the bruises on Kassidy's face looked "*like finger marks.*" As with many prosecution witnesses, Jennifer believed that Chad murdered Kassidy and she knew that Chad had caused some bruiding from paliming Kassidy face, because Amanda had told her. Thus, it was not a surprise when she combined that knowledge into a recollected observation of seeing "*like finger marks*" on Kassidy's face.

Jennifer said that she had last seen Kassidy a couple of days before, which would have been Tuesday morning, and that Kassidy on that day, "*just had the bruises right here, and they were clearing up.*" (p. 111) Without a videotape, it's impossible to know where she was pointing or touching. She said that Kassidy was "*quiet, real quiet. She acted like she was sick, in pain.*" (p. 111) This was the first, and only, time that anyone had indicated in a police interview or testified at Chad's trial that Kassidy might have been in pain on November 9, or any other day between June 9 and November 9. There is a difference between appearing to be sick and appearing to be in pain. Unfortunately, Jennifer was not asked what she meant by "*in pain.*" Did she use that word because she had absorbed the newspapers' and police view that Kassidy was experiencing pain? Or did she actually observe the behavior of Kassidy experiencing pain? We will never know, but if Jennifer did see Kassidy experiencing pain, one would hope that she would have asked Kassidy a normal question, such as *"Can you tell me where it hurts?*" or "*Can you point to where it hurts?*"

Asked about a "*routine that you would do with Kassidy in the morning,*" Jennifer said that she "*would put my lipstick on, my makeup in the bathroom, and I'd sit her on the toilet. And then while I put my lipstick on, she'd stick her lips out like this, and she'd go, 'lips, lips,' and I'd put lip gloss on her...*" (p. 112) However, as noted above, the only morning for that routine during the first three days of Kassidy's last week would have been Tuesday morning, November 7.

Jennifer said that on the morning of the 9th, the fourth day, she asked Kassidy to come into the bathroom with her, and "*She pulled away from me... cried, kind of whimpered a little bit. And I was like, okay. I figured, you know, she was tired, so I covered her back up and went on with my morning.*" (p. 112) Jennifer said that she didn't see Kassidy eat any of her cereal in the baggie, (p. 113), and that Amanda left after about 15 minutes at their house. Jennifer turned the TV on to Nickelodeon and went to work.

Anticipating Mark Sisti's cross-examination of Jennifer, Will Delker asked Jennifer, his prosecution witness, if her just-completed testimony was consistent with what she had told the police on November 9, 2000, and she said it wasn't in at least one respect.

She explained the reason for the discrepancy, "*First, they told me that Kassidy -- Kassidy is dead before I left* [for] *work, and that, you know, that made me feel like I was the blame.... I was under the impression when I first got... interviewed that Kassidy did get hit with a baseball, because that's... what Mandy told me.*" (p. 115) However, Delker did not ask Jennifer what the discrepancies actually were. Jennifer seemed to say that it was okay to lie to the police on November 9 because she thought she was being accused of responsibility for Kassidy's death.

Will Delker then shifted to the scene in the Kittery Police parking lot on the evening of November 9, and Jennifer said that she observed Amanda and Chad hugging, and she heard Chad say to Amanda, "*You know I didn't do it...*" (p. 115) Jennifer said that the police had returned to Jeff and/or her the keys to their home, and they returned to 51 Rogers Road and all went into the house, and her mother was also there. Jeff and Jennifer retrieved clothes for their upcoming stay in a hotel.

At the hotel, Jennifer heard Amanda say to Chad on the phone, "*I know you killed my baby.*" (p. 117) The jurors must have wondered why a mother would say that, and keep talking to such a man and, a few hours later, leave the hotel with him. Finally, Will Delker asked why she didn't report the bruises on Kassidy to anyone, and Jennifer responded that she didn't want "*them to take the baby away from her.*" (p. 117)

Mark Sisti cross-examined Jennifer and asked, "*You described for the jury the bruising on Kassidy's face for the first time when Kassidy was brought in Perfumamia by Amanda*?" and Jennifer replied, "*Yes.*" (p.118) In his second question he repeated the word "*first,*" saying, "*and that's when you first noticed that there was some bruising. Just describe for the jury...*" (p. 118) Jennifer replied, "*bruising on her forehead.*" (p. 118) Sisti repeated "*on her forehead*" and Jennifer said "*Yeah*" and he asked, "*Anywhere else*?" and she replied "*on her forehead.*" (p. 118)

Mark Sisti suggested in a question that her observation would have been three weeks before Kassidy's death, and Jennifer corrected him by saying, "*It was a couple weeks... prior to her death.... I don't remember...It was a couple of weeks prior to her death. I don't remember the exact time.*" (p. 118-19)

Trying to identify the timing of that first sighting of bruising on Kassidy, Sisti tried to establish a baseline and asked, "*You started at Perfumania, just so you remember, about three weeks prior to Kassidy's death, right?*" Jennifer replied, "*Yes,*" and she reaffirmed that she saw the forehead bruises "*a couple of weeks before Kassidy's death.*" (p. 119) Jennifer stated her belief that Amanda and Chad lived together beginning in September. Even though her estimate was 6 weeks after the Amanda's mid-July estimate of the time that she had moved in, including Kassidy, the September 1 date is still six weeks before the time that Jennifer said that she first saw bruises on Kassidy's forehead. Sisti concluded that line of inquiry, "*I just wanted to make sure we had the timeframe defined for the jury,....*" (p. 121) Unfortunately, that defining of the timeframe was not consistently done for all witnesses, and there were no timeline charts to enable the jurors to see the timelines of Kassidy's health and behavior, and the charges against Chad and the other relevant events, such as the taking of photographs, during the period from June 9 to November 9.

Mark Sisti then changed gears to the morning of November 9, and showed Jennifer a photo (State Exhibit 69) of her bed in 2000, with a pair of red pajama bottoms on it, and she identified them as Kassidy's. Then he showed her another photo (State Exhibit 26) showing a pair of Jeff's jeans near the red pajama bottoms, and Jennifer stated twice firmly, "*When I left for work, she was covered up with the pajamas on...Like I said, when I left for work, she had her pajamas -- she had her pajama bottoms on.*" (p. 123-4) During this line of questioning, Sisti was focusing on the pajama bottoms because that was the piece of clothing on the bed in a photograph. The questioning didn't help clarify the question of what Kassidy was wearing for the top portion of her pajamas. Was it a fleece sweatshirt with the fleece/cotton dress over it, or was it only the dress?

Sisti then sought to ask Jennifer about Kassidy's alleged fall from Jeff's truck that caused a bruise and Will Delker objected that Sisti was asking for hearsay evidence. In his argument, Delker said, "*We don't think it's true. We don't think there's a truck incident, okay. We think the bruise got there a different way,*" by which he surely meant that the bumps to the head were caused by Chad Evans.(p. 128) This was an extraordinary statement and the defense should have taken notice and assembled the several witnesses to Kassidy's return and condition on Saturday, October 28, after Jeff brought her home. The prosecution offered no alternate theory as to the origin of those goose-egg sized bumps on Kassidy's head, which were seen by several people.

Judge Nadeau decided that because Sisti didn't confront Jeff with his previous statement he may have told Jennifer about Kassidy falling from his truck, Sisti had to change his questions to Jennifer about the alleged fall-from-truck incident.

Mark Sisti asked Jennifer, "*Did you observe bruises on Kassidy that would have occurred while she was staying at your home*?" and she said, "*No*." Twice. (p. 130) Asked about the forehead bruise, Jennifer responded, "*The only time I ever saw bruising on Kassidy's forehead...* [was]... *when Kassidy fell off the trampoline, supposedly*." (p. 130-31) Sisti pressed Jennifer on what she saw and when, and she said, "*I don't know -- I don't know... I just heard the story of Kassidy falling out of the truck*." (p. 133) Will Delker objected on the grounds of hearsay. Judged Nadeau agreed and asked the jury, "*to disregard the answer to that last question*." (p. 133)

Once again, the jury was asked to engage in a legal fiction, which is to believe that jurors can ignore what they had heard with their own ears. This time, the non-admissible statement was favorable to Chad, whose attorneys were struggling to show the jury that there actually was a fall from Jeff's truck which caused bruising to Kassidy. Unfortunately, they didn't ask Jeff about that issue enough, and what he said to others at the time, when he was on the stand. Amanda, however, did testify that Jeff had said that the bruises to the back of Kassidy's head were caused by a fall from his truck.

Sisti then asked Jennifer about the two calls from Jeff to her at Perfumania on the 9th of November. About the first, she said, "*He said she was acting weird*." (p. 234) She affirmed Sisti's characterization of that call, "*...he says... he was concerned, right about... Kassidy's physical condition...Something's wrong with her...Her eyes are rolling down in the back of her head, right? ...And you're thinking to yourself, well, she must be having a seizure of something*?" Jennifer responded that her "*brother had epilepsy, and that's what I thought. Maybe she was having a seizure*." (p. 135)

Jennifer noted, without being asked, "*... in the ... State of Maine, we really can't bring the baby to the hospital unless the mother's there,*" and then she answered a question about that call, *"Yes, he asked me what he should do, ... and I said, you know, 'Call the hospital.' and he said, 'Okay.' And then we got off the phone. I was really busy at work*." (p. 136-37) Sisti asked if Jeff said, *"...that he checked on her because she was quiet, right,*" and she affirmed, "*Yes, he did*." (p. 137) This assertion implicitly contradicted Jeff's own testimony which was that he checked on Kassidy shortly after noon, because he had taken a break from the television's election coverage to go retrieve the mail. As he was up, it was a good time to check on Kassidy. Also, it was lunch time, and Jeff might have wondered what Kassidy was going to eat.

Then Mark Sisti asked about Jeff's second call, and Jennifer responded, "*He told me that the baby was -- was coming through, and the ambulance was on its way, and not to worry. And I told him that I was going... to call Amanda and tell Mandy that the baby was on the way to the hospital*." (p. 137-38) Sisti reminded Jennifer that she told the police "*that she was alert, sitting up and watching television, right?*" She responded that "*I told the police because I assumed that.... I assumed that the baby was doing better... I assumed, you know, that he was just getting her ready to take her to the hospital*." Referring to the police report of her interview on November 9, 2000, Sisti reminded her that she said, "*... he said she was alert*." On the stand, Jennifer restated, "*I assumed that*." (p. 139) Sisti read more of Jennifer's police interview to her, where she said, "*She was alert, talking, watching TV with -- you know, Jeff hung up, and then he called and said he'd take her to the hospital...*" (p. 140)

After reminding Jennifer that this exchange with the police occurred during the interview which began at 4:15 p.m. on November 9, only four hours after the referenced calls and thus that the statements made during the police interview should be reliable, Jennifer said, "*He -- I assumed the baby was fine, because he was a lot calmer. And he said that the baby was going to the hospital.*" (p. 144)

On redirect, Will Delker asked Jennifer to read a section from her police interview, where she said about the second call, "*And he was all worried and crying and stuff. He was crying. He was wicked upset. And I was like, 'Oh my god,' you know, 'something's wrong with her.' So I went on with my day, you know.*" (p. 145)

In some instances, actions truly do speak louder than words. The true measure of Jennifer's concern, or appreciation of the problem, as communicated to her by Jeff was to go "*on with my day.*" It must be remembered, too, that she saw Kassidy four hours earlier. If Kassidy was as badly bruised and injured as the prosecution claimed, when Amanda left her at Jeff's and Jennifer's, it would seem even more incredible that Jennifer could "*go on with my day*" after receiving two calls from Jeff.

About the bruises she saw, and when she saw them, Delker sought to correct Jen's recent testimony about when she saw the first bruises on Kassidy. In legalese, it's called, impeaching your own witness. Delker asked Jennifer about her second interview, which was on November 10, 2000, "*And do you remember telling the police that, 'I kind of had a suspicion something was going on, because of all the bruises on Kassidy, all the time, ever since she started dating Chad, she started getting bruises*?" and Jennifer replied, "Yes." (p. 150)

Then, as previously agreed at the lawyers/judge bench conference, Judge Nadeau gave the jury her second, "*instruction.*" She said,

Whenever a witness, any witness, is questioned about their prior statement, you cannot use the facts contained in the prior statement as proof of the facts in that statement. What you do is you use the prior statement to judge the witness's in-court testimony, and to decide what of the witness's in-court statement to believe. And that applies to all witnesses." (p. 150)

As it takes legal sophistication or sophistry to understand that distinction, the jurors likely simply concluded that Jennifer wasn't reliable about when she started seeing injuries and that she was either intentionally or unintentionally slanting what she said to the police or to the jury at the trial.

Will Delker apparently preferred the in-court version, so he restated for Jennifer, "*So just so I'm clear, you said the ... first instance you remember seeing bruises was this time in your store, correct?"* and Jennifer replied, *"Yes.*" (p. 151) As the charges against Chad said that his abuse of Kassidy began on August 1, and as that "*first*" that Jennifer saw bruises on Kassidy was after October 15, it's not clear how this testimony helped the prosecution.

Mark Sisti recross-examined and asked Jennifer if she had ever corrected, with the police, her statement the previous year about Kassidy being alert and watching TV. She seemed to say that she didn't realize that such corrections were done, and then said, "*I basically told them, you know, what I thought they wanted to hear...*" (p. 151) Sisti asked whether she was telling the jury the truth or what they wanted to hear and there was an exchange about who wants the truth to be told and Jennifer replied, "*I think Chad knows the truth. I think you know the truth.*" (p. 152)

Certainly, Chad knew the truth about his own actions, but he didn't and still doesn't, know the truth about what others did during those last 40 days of Kassidy's life, from October 1 to November 9. Sisti asked again, "*And the truth is, you talked to the police shortly after your own niece's death, and are you telling the jury you were just giving them words with no meaning*?" Jennifer responded, "*Wait a minute. The police told me that Kassidy was dead before I left work. And I was trying to protect myself.*" (p. 152) She added, "*When I first got interviewed, I believe*[d] *that Kassidy really did get hit with a baseball. I wasn't thinking that she got murdered.*" (p. 153) The implication here was that she no longer believed that Kassidy was hit by a ball the night before her death.

Sisti pressed Jennifer to explain what words she said to the police in 2000 were said in error, and Will Delker objected that Mr. Sisti was going beyond the authorized scope of his own redirect examination, and Judge Nadeau said to the lawyers, tellingly and outside the hearing of the jury, "*.. I think she is going to say anything to protect herself. She said that.*" (p. 154). The court took a lunch break and resumed at 1:34 p.m.

Sisti did not explore further with Jennifer her early statement that she was asked to watch Kassidy while Amanda and Chad went to see his parents. That never happened. Chad and Amanda took Kassidy with them, with pleasure, both times they went to Keene. The defense could have called Chad's parents and siblings to the stand to verify that point. Amanda could have been recalled, too.

William Peirce

Simon Brown examined Will Peirce, Jeff's landlord and friend who lived next door to Jeff and Jennifer. Will told the jury of his background, including six years as a school teacher and "*behaviorial aide in special ed. schools*" in Los Angeles. (p. 160) Since Jeff and Jennifer had moved out of 51 Rogers Road, Will had done some renovations including, and perhaps ironically, the removal of the door to the basement from that apartment. Brown asked generally, "*Was there a time when you saw Kassidy in the company of Jeff Marshall?*" and Will said "*Yes.... October.*" (p. 161) Making no effort to clarify the date more closely, Brown asked for Will's observations, and Will testified, "*I saw two bruises on her cheeks, two bruises on her chin... On her cheeks, they were kind of faded brown...* [and on the chin they were] *two black marks.... The ones on the chin looked fresher.*" (p. 164)

Will said that Jeff asked him whether he, Jeff, should refer Kassidy's bruises to Child Protective Services. Will said that in response to Jeff he picked up Kassidy and "*put her on my left hand, and I lifted up her shirt to look for other marks, and I pulled down her ... diaper to look for other marks,*" and he didn't see any. (p. 166)

Simon Brown then asked about another time, "*after that day*" that Will had seen Kassidy. (p. 166) Will then described an occasion when Jeff pulled into the 51/53 Rogers Road parking area, with Kassidy in the passenger seat. Jeff stopped the truck and went over to the passenger side and,

He unstrapped her out of the seat, and then Kassidy started to get out, and she fell into his hands and --- then -- I was there with Tom McNeil, and we got -- Jeff prompted her to give us a kiss on the cheeks.... And she kissed me on the cheek. And she kissed him, too." (p. 167)

Tom McNeil was working with Will at the time. Will said that Jeff caught Kassidy before she struck anything, and she didn't hit the ground. "*It was inconsequential... No crying or anything.*" (p. 169) Asked about bruises, Will said that it might have been at the time of the truck incident, or non-incident, when "*Jeff pointed out* [that] *the bruise marks were dark again, were a little darker.*" (p. 169) Will's recollection was that he saw, "*the two dark marks, a little darker.*" (p. 169) Presumably, he was referring to the bruises on Kassidy's chin. Will said that the time gap between the two observations was about two weeks, and that the second observation, "*could have been a few days, maybe a week,*" before Kassidy died. (p. 170)

There was no firm determination of the date of the truck incident witnessed by Will and described here in his testimony. In his December 6, 2000 interview, Peirce stated that this incident occurred "*just a day or two before Kassidy's death.*" (p. 401)

The questioning then shifted to the morning of November 9, and Will said he could see, from his window at 6 Johnson Court, when Amanda left Jeff's at 8:20 a.m. and he saw Jennifer get into her truck "*some time before nine...You know, quarter of, maybe...*" (p. 171) That observation had some importance to Will, as he had wanted to borrow that truck, so he went out to the driveway to ask Jennifer about borrowing the truck, and they arranged that he could come to her workplace later to borrow the truck, as she was running late and had five minutes to get to work.

Will testified that shortly after he returned to his home at 6 Johnson Court, Jeff called him and Will said that he remembered three of Jeff's words precisely, " '*She's not walking.*'

" (p. 172) Will continued, "*I asked if she was all right, and he said she was watching TV, and he had given her a bowl of Cocoa Puffs.*" (p. 173) This was likely another example of where memory and assumption are combined into an enhanced memory. Will may have heard "*Cocoa Puffs*" and assumed that Jeff was giving them to Kassidy in a bowl, but Jeff likely said something to the effect that Kassidy had what he thought were Cocoa Puffs in a baggie and was assumed to be eating them. No bowl was found in the kitchen sink which would have been a likely cereal bowl for Kassidy.

Brown asked about the next time he saw Jeff, and Will said that he heard the ambulance come to 51/53 Rogers and he went over to Jeff's and "*I saw... Kassidy, I saw EMTs, at least four of them and Kassidy was laying out on the porch.*" (p. 173)

Mark Sisti then cross-examined Will, and Will agreed that the truck incident occurred "*a day or two before Kassidy's death,*" (p. 176) which was what Sisti said Will had said during his December 6, 2000 interview. Sisti asked what Jeff said at the time, and Will said that Jeff said, " *'See, she just falls out of the truck.*" (p. 181) Will did not have any direct knowledge of any other falls from Jeff's truck, but said that Jeff "*acted as though this is something symptomatic.... that there was something wrong with the child.*" (p. 182) Asked by Sisti if "*Kassidy looked just fine to you?*" Will said, "*Fine. Well, I mean she acted fine.*" (p. 182)

Sisti then asked about the first time Will met Kassidy when Jeff asked him to look at the bruises, and about what Will had written in his police statement on November 9, that Kassidy did not exhibit, in Sisti's words, "*defensive reactions*" to Will's examination of her. (p. 188) After a bench conference about whether Will was an expert, Sisti was allowed by Judge Nadeau to simply ask what he meant by the words in his police statement. Sisti then asked Will to explain what he meant by "*protective-flinching behavior*" and the absence of "*defensive reactions*" in that statement. Will responded, "*Well, if a child's been hit or something,.... they'll be afraid of things. They'll be afraid of people, and... maybe afraid of strangers, afraid of men or something. They might hold their hands up... But she seemed perfectly comfortable.*" (p. 190-91)

In his March 27, 2011 letter, Chad recalled his own, and different, experience with Kassidy's flinching. He wrote,

Incidentally, did I ever tell you about Kassidy flinching by the kitchen sink? I had given Kassidy something sticky to eat and she got it all over her hands and face. So after she was done I brought her to the kitchen sink to wash up. I sat her on the counter and wet the washcloth to wash her up. In the process I guess I must have moved quickly or something and Kassidy pulled back and flinched, quickly closing her eyes and putting her hands up as if she thought I was going to slap her in the face! I wanted to cry right then. I said, "Oh my God baby, I would never hit you." Kassidy didn't make a peep. She just made that flinching. It melted my heart. I pulled her into my chest and gave her a soothing hug and then washed her up. I thought about this a lot right afterwards. I was crushed that she felt that I would slap her. Then I dismissed it as her natural reflexes until it popped in my head again. I don't believe I ever held her cheeks after that: thinking that I had somehow made Kassidy afraid of me. Kassidy died a short while after this. I remember discussing the flinching with Amanda one night and how odd it made me feel to see her do this. I can't recall if I asked her prior to Kassidy's death what she thought might have caused Kassidy to flinch like that, but I know I discussed it with Amanda while we were staying at Bruce's after Kassidy's death.

The trial adjourned early, at 2:25 p.m., as the examinations of the witnesses had not taken as long as the prosecution expected. As it was a Friday, Judge Nadeau spent more time than usual cautioning the jurors not to discuss the case over the upcoming two day break. Then, in anticipation that the jury was soon going to be shown the videotape of the police interrogation of Chad, the lawyers and Judge Nadeau then worked together to redact or excise about six portions that did not conform to the Rules of Evidence, perhaps because they were more prejudicial to Chad than probative. During the discussion, Judge Nadeau took some time to review a U.S. Supreme Court case that Will Delker had used to support his position. By the end of the session, agreement was almost complete, and Judge Nadeau asked the parties to finish the work by agreement.

The problem with this work, in hindsight, was that it appeared that the defense was trying to keep from the jury parts of what Chad had said during his police interview. It may have been more effective for them to have Chad testify and explain everything about the interview that needed explaining. It would have been a stronger position for the defense to say, "Show the whole tape to the jury. Chad Evans is innocent, and he can explain every aspect of this case and his police interview to the jury." The judge, and even the prosecutors may have been impressed by such a strategy. None of the prosecutors had ever talked with Chad Evans, and neither had Judge Nadeau. All they knew about Chad Evans, so far, and aside from the videotape, was what the police and prosecution witnesses and the media had said about him, and that, mostly, wasn't good.

MEDIA: 1. "Relatives take the stand - Kassidy's aunt says bruises began after child lived with Evans"
2. "Agency told toddler was being abused"
3. "Babysitter denies harming toddler in murder trial"
4. "Babysitter, sister, brother testify at Evans trial"
5. "Baby's aunt testifies in murder trial"
6. "Evans trial continues - Today's proceedings begin second week"

Monday, 10 December 2001

Tracey Foley - voir dire examination, without the jury

The prosecutors sought to have Tracey testify about what Amanda said to her when she came to Tracey's home on November 16, 2000, the night of Chad's arrest, and the defense said it was hearsay. The disputed statement was from her November 7, 2001 interview, as noted in an earlier chapter, *"and you knew.... and I didn't listen,"* The question for the judge was whether Amanda's statement to Tracey was an "excited utterance" exception to the hearsay rule.

Will Delker examined Tracey who had known Amanda for about five years, as Amanda used to babysit for Tracey's two children. That babysitting continued after Kassidy was born, which was in February, 1999, but contact ceased after Amanda's parents and the family moved to Auburn. Delker asked Tracey if *"at some point in the fall of last year did you reinitiate or have contact with Amanda, again?"* (p. 9) Tracey explained that she saw Amanda when Amanda was visiting her friend, Melissa Chick, an employee of the Sanford/Springvale YMCA, where Tracey's daughter, Chandler, was in day care. Kassidy was there as well, playing with Chandler. After that rendezvous, all three adults and two children went back to Tracey's house for a couple of hours. Delker asked what Tracey observed about Kassidy, and Tracey testified, "*She had bruising on her face.... Both of her cheeks and across the bridge of her nose.*" (p. 10)

Tracey recalled that the YMCA meeting was on the Friday before Chad's birthday. Amanda left Tracey's that Friday afternoon, or early evening, and returned on Saturday where she and Kassidy spent the night. At Tracey's on Saturday, Kassidy played with Chandler and Amanda wrapped Chad's birthday presents, and Amanda said she was going to Chad's party on Sunday. Tracey said that she asked Amanda about the bruises on Kassidy and Amanda told her the "trampoline story." Tracey said that she offered Amanda the opportunity to come live with her, and that Amanda declined. Amanda and Tracey talked on the phone several times after Amanda left Tracey's home that Sunday, and they made plans to see each other again "*on a couple of occasions*" (p. 12) However, they didn't see each other again before Kassidy's death.

The next time Tracey saw Amanda was on Thursday evening, the evening that Chad was arrested. She said, "*Amanda showed up at my house Thursday evening hysterical. And she walked in my door and she looked at me crying and said, 'And you knew and I didn't listen.' And she hugged me and told me that Chad had been arrested.*" (p. 13) Tracey added, "*She was crying. She was very sporadic in her conversation with me; disheveled; her hair was a mess; she was chain smoking; almost incoherent talking to me...*" (p. 14)

Tracey said that Amanda had told her, "*That Chad was aggressive, that he would get upset with Kassidy and grab her by the shirt and put her in the corner. He would lose his temper....* [because of] *Kassidy crying, wanting her mother's attention.*" (p. 15) Will Delker asked Tracey about what Amanda said that Chad did, and she stated, "*Grab her, put her in the corner. Grab her, throw her in the corner. There was an instance that she told me that he threw her on the bed.*" (p. 16)

Asked what Amanda said about November 8th, Tracey said, "*She told me that Chad had called her at work to tell her that Kassidy had been hit in the eye with a baseball, or a softball, or some sort of ball...*" (p. 16) Amanda slept at Tracey's, in Chandler's room. Tracey said goodnight and recalled, "*She was crying again and said that all she ever wanted was Kassidy to have her own room and have nice things, and that she would never have it.*" (p. 17)

Tracey said she saw Amanda again the following day, Friday for a couple of hours, but not since then.

Alan Cronheim cross-examined Tracey and quickly established the exact date of the Friday, October 13 accidental meeting of Tracey and Amanda at the Sanford/Springvale YMCA. If that date could be presented to the jury during Tracey's upcoming testimony in open court, the jury could connect the dots. Cronheim did not explore with Tracey what Amanda could have meant by *'And you knew and I didn't listen.'* That is, what did Tracey know? It could have been that Amanda credited Tracey with seeing that Kassidy was ill and required medical attention sooner rather than later, or that someone was abusing Kassidy, instead of the assumed meaning that Tracey somehow understood that someone was abusing Kassidy and that someone was Chad. Another alternative is that this was a low point in Amanda's confidence in Chad and in her own judgement.The police had told her during four interviews that Chad killed Kassidy and her family had aligned itself with the police. On the evening of November 16, many policemen and police women dramatically had arrested Chad at his home. Amanda could be forgiven if she did not understand that sometimes innocent people are arrested.

On redirect examination, Will Delker asked about the flow of the conversation Tracey had with Amanda on Thursday evening, October 16th, and Tracey said it was sporadic and uneven.

After hearing Tracey's testimony, and the lawyers' arguments, Judge Nadeau decided to allow the prosecution to ask Tracey about Amanda's statement and to permit that hearsay to be heard by the jury. That left the defense with the option of recalling Amanda as a defense witness to ask her what she meant by that statement and why she said it. Amanda was not recalled.

In fact, none of the witnesses in the trial were recalled. It might have been a useful way to more fully explore the truth. For example, if Jeff Marshall had been recalled after Dr. Greenwald, and her explicit explanation of the locations of bruises and injuries, he could have been asked more explicitly about Kassidy's condition on November 8 and 9.

Even if Amanda had, at the time thought that Chad was responsible and that she had intended to say to Tracey that she credited Tracey with suspecting Chad, recalling Amanda to the witness stand would have given her the opportunity to explain that, at the time, she simply believed what the police had told her. It was not that she believed that Chad was responsible for Kassidy's death because of what she saw, but because at the time she was intimidated by the police and their theory of the case. Tracey's testimony would wait until after Heather Hamilton and Melissa Chick.

Heather Hamilton

Simon Brown examined Heather Hamilton, the store manager at Perfumania, in Kittery, Maine, where Jennifer Bortner Conley worked. Heather said that Jennifer had worked at the store since August 2000. The discrepancy between this statement of Jennifer's start date, and Jennifer's own testimony that she started work at Perfumania around October 16 is significant. Heather said she had met Chad once, when he had come into the store to visit with Jennifer at "*the end of August, I believe.*" (p. 40) At Amanda's trial a year later, Jennifer remembered that Chad had come into Perfumania to purchase perfume for Amanda. Heather also said that after Chad had left, Jennifer told her that he was her sister's boyfriend. Heather did not meet Jennifer's sister, Amanda, until Amanda had come to the store to visit Jennifer, "*a few weeks later*" and that Amanda "*was getting a job at the time at Old Navy...*" (p. 40) As Amanda did not begin work at Old Navy until Monday, November 6, it appears that Heather Hamilton or Jennifer was mistaken about Jennifer's start date. As with other date discrepancies in the trial, the lawyers on both sides should have worked to clear this up. Both sides were busy, but it would not have taken much work to determine Jennifer's actual start date at Perfumania.

Even the judge could have, on her own initiative, asked that the matter be clarified. In our adversarial system, judges do not often bring their own wisdom to bear on gaps in evidence, but she could have, as is the practice in European courts, where judges are more active. In the U.S., some judges encourage questions by jurors, too, and a juror could have asked the same question.

Heather said that she had seen Amanda a total of four times and had met Kassidy once, on the third visit, which Heather said was in October. She said that Amanda carried Kassidy on her hip during the entire visit, of about 15 minutes, and described Kassidy,

She was kind of quiet. I don't remember her ever saying any words. I just remember her [being] *a little bit fussy, kind of pointing at things, and a little bit whiny.* (p. 41)

Heather described the bruises she observed, which were

...brown and tan, and they were oval-shaped, and there were five of them...all over her face. One of them was on a cheek, and that was the darkest one. And a few were on her forehead over here. I believe it was this right side. And I think the lowest one was -- were on her cheek.... what I noticed, a thumb print was on the left cheek, and then the fingers were on the right side.... it looked like a hand print." (p. 41)

Heather asked about the bruises, and Amanda told her the "trampoline story." As the "trampoline story" was first used in mid-October, it's likely that the bruises Heather saw were the same which were seen by Joshua, Melissa and Tracey. Heather described Amanda's manner as "*giggling. She was trying to play it up as if a ... funny thing that happened.*" (p. 43)

Simon Brown then asked about November 9th, and Heather said that after the third phone call, which was the call when Jennifer's mother told her that Kassidy had died, Jennifer left work.

Alan Cronheim cross-examined Heather and tried to clarify the date of the time that Amanda brought Kassidy into her store. She said, "*I don't remember, exactly. I would guess that it was toward the beginning of October, only because I remember it was very shortly after my own birthday, which was* [near the end of September]. *So I remember it being in the beginning of October.*" (p. 46) Asked if it was "*at least more than a week before Kassidy's death,*" Heather said, "*Oh yes, I would say a few weeks.*" If that's 21 days, that would have made the date of the visit Thursday, October 19th, leaving the Friday the 13th sightings of bruises by Joshua and Tracey as the first confirmed sightings of bruises on Kassidy.

Heather stated that she answered the phone for each of Jennifer's first two phone calls on the 9th, and both were from Jeff, but "*on the second occasion that he called, I believe he was calling from a cell phone, because he asked for Jen, and I went to get her, and by the time she got to the phone, he was gone.*" (p. 48) Cronheim told Heather that Jennifer had testified that she received two calls from Jeff, and talked with him on both occasions; and Heather didn't dispute that. If there was a dropped call, that would have meant that Jeff called Jennifer three times. Then Cronheim asked Heather if she had come to work a "*little bit before one when your shift started*?" and Heather said, "*No, I got there right at one.*" (p. 48) Cronheim asked about calls to Jennifer before one o'clock and Heather said she didn't know. What was puzzling was that the phone records indicated that Jeff called Jennifer at 12:26 and 12:37 p.m., and did not show the two calls after 1:00 p.m. that Heather described. In any case, there was no dispute that Jennifer stayed at work after Jeff's two calls and she left work after she received the call from her mother that Kassidy had died.

The prosecution had no questions on redirect.

Melissa Chick

Simon Brown examined Melissa Chick, age 21, who said Amanda had been her best friend since seventh grade, but there were off-and-on times since then. After Amanda became pregnant in 1998, they lost contact. Melissa resumed contact when she learned that she had cancer in January, 2000. At that time, Amanda and Kassidy were living with Amanda's parents and Melissa described Kassidy as "*very spunky. Just a typical one-year-old, you know, just running around, having fun, getting into everything.*" (p. 53) Until the summer of 2000, Melissa saw Amanda about 3-4 times a week.

Brown asked if Melissa saw "*anything change in her* [Kassidy's] *demeanor after Amanda met Chad*?" (p. 55) Melissa responded, "*Yeah, she became very quiet and drawn back...probably about ... three months into the relationship, maybe four...she had bruises on her face... didn't act like a ... normal one-year-old.*" (p. 55)

"*Three months*" into the relationship, would have been September 9 and "*four months*" would have been October 9, and therefore Melissa's observations of changes in Kassidy were a few weeks earlier than those made by others. Again, Kassidy was with Jacqueline and the Conleys for the last week of September, with no observations in that household of a change toward passivity and lethargy. This period was two to three months after Kassidy moved to Rochester, as substantially full-time.

Asked how Kassidy interacted with men, Melissa said, "*She didn't. She would just stare at them. Shock Just stare at them all the time. She didn't move.*" (p. 56) Asked if that differed from her reactions to women, Melissa said, "*she got along better with women -- I didn't see her around many women. When I would see Kassidy, it would be just me and Amanda. So, she.... was normal, but very quiet.*" (p. 56) Melissa wasn't asked to explain how she knew of Kassidy's reactions to men if she only saw Kassidy when the three of them were alone.

Asked about Kassidy's behavior, but without a time period, Melissa said,

She wasn't very active... She didn't do much at all. She just...I'd give her some toys, and she'd just sit there. And if you tried to play with her, she'll play with you a little bit, but she's just very quiet. Very shy." (p. 56)

Melissa said that this behavior, presumably later in 2000, was different from the beginning of 2000.

She said that she saw bruises starting "*probably three or four months into... her relationship with Chad,*" but later said "*I can't really recall.*" (p. 57) However, Melissa's lack of recollection of time was confirmed when she stated that Amanda "*began dating Chad three to four months after January,*" (p. 57) when, in fact, the date of their double date with Jeff and Jennifer was June 2, 2000.

When she did see bruises on Kassidy, they were "*on her face, a little bit on her arms, and her legs.*" (p. 57) Asked about an overnight babysitting with Kassidy, Melissa said that it was around the beginning of September, because it was before she began working at the Sanford/Springvale YMCA, which was on September 8th or 10th. During that babysitting, Melissa gave Kassidy a bath and noticed bruises

on her bottom area and her abdomen area, and her... upper legs... one on her bottom area. That was like the size of maybe a half dollar. It was kind of old. And one on her abdomen area. That was kind of old, too. And on her leg area, it was probably like an inch by two inch.. The one on her bottom area looked kind of new. The other ones looked yellowish, old. (p. 58-59)

She was asked if there were other bruises, and Melissa said,

Yeah, she had them on her face, all over her face.... It looked as if somebody had grabbed her by her face. There was[sic] *...three on one side of her cheek, and one on her jaw area.... She had one on her forehead and her nose, and, also, her ear. ... I sat her in the tub and I just looked at her and I thought there was something wrong. I thought maybe she was sick or that something was going on.... I wanted to take a picture of her so I could be sure that... just to see if somebody else could see her.*

Unfortunately, she didn't find her camera, so she didn't take a photo. It would have been very valuable as the only photograph of Kassidy, alive, with bruises. Melissa testified that she told Amanda that she needed to take Kassidy to see a doctor, "*I said, 'I think there's something wrong with her.' I said, 'I think maybe she's anemic or she's got leukemia or something.'* " (p. 60)

Melissa recounted Amanda's response, "*She said that maybe she does need to go to the doctor's. Maybe there could be something wrong with her, but she didn't want anyone to think that somebody was hurting her because of the bruises on her face.*" (p. 60) After that first babysitting, Melissa said about subsequent visits, "*Every time I'd seen her, she always had bruises on her face.... Old ones and new ones...*" Simon Brown asked if Melissa spoke to Amanda about the additional bruises and *"... she always had excuses for them.... That Chad's children....were rough with her, and... falling down. She was very clumsy..*" (p. 61) Amanda told her the "trampoline story."

In addition to photographs, Melissa's recollection would have been assisted by a timeline chart and very careful explanation of each time that she saw Kassidy and what bruises Melissa saw. Her testimony seemed to indicate that she had seen bruises on Kassidy all the time and that she saw Kassidy frequently, but each claim was exaggerated. Neither Chad nor Amanda remembers Melissa caring for Kassidy before October 13.

Brown asked Melissa if she had been to Rochester and seen Chad and Kassidy interact. Melissa said, yes,

It was probably the middle of September, maybe.... I was in the living room with Kassidy... We were sitting on the couch. She was sitting on a couch diagonal to me... Chad was walking through the living area and he had turned toward me and said that, "Oh, don't mind her, she's just scared of me. She doesn't like me." ... [Kassidy] *was just staring at him the whole time as he was walking through the room.* (p. 62)

Once again, in this case and trial, an observation was made of an ambiguous event and people were left to interpret it as they wished. To some in the courtroom that day, Kassidy was fearfully watching her abuser. To others, she was simply watching Chad and Chad made a flippant remark which related to Kassidy's jealousy, and nothing more.

Melissa related an occasion when she was talking with Amanda, at a time uncertain, but "*when she was living there,*" and "*I heard Chad's voice in the background saying, 'Amanda, come get your child. She's acting stupid and clumsy, again. She's acting like an f'n idiot.' It was something like that.*" (p. 64) There was no effort to ascertain the date, and there was no consideration given to recalling Amanda if she remembered that conversation, or even asking Chad if he were to take the stand. It wasn't clear how this testimony cleared the hearsay rule, but there was no objection, and therefore no instructions to the jury to ignore it.

Brown asked if Melissa had talked with Amanda about getting day care for Kassidy, and she responded affirmatively,

It was probably the middle of September.... she was saying how she'd gotten a new job, and that she needed someone to watch Kassidy. And I was telling her how she could probably put her in the YMCA program, and she said it was too far away. And I told her that she could possibly have a YMCA in that area. And she said that, "I don't want to bring her to day care. Everyone's going [to] *think that someone's beating her, because she has too many bruises on her face." So she said she was going to take her to her sister's house* [and] *see if they would babysit for her.*" (p. 64-65)

Melissa confirmed that this conversation was before Amanda got her new job at Old Navy, but that was in late October, and not "*the middle of September.*" As has been noted before, and given the final results in this case, Amanda's apprehension about what people might think about bruises on Kassidy was entirely reasonable.

Asked when she last saw Kassidy, Melissa said, "*It was probably four weeks before Halloween.... We were in a store. We, all three of us, had gone to Olympia Sports... in Sanford.*" (p. 65) At Amanda's trial in 2002, Melissa recalled that they went to Olympia Sports to return some shoes and that Melissa's sister was with them. However, "*four weeks before Halloween*" was the first week of October, and that was the week of Jacqueline's October 1 photograph of Kassidy. There was no question that Melissa saw

Amanda and Kassidy during the weekend beginning Friday, October 13, when they all met at the Sanford YMCA and Amanda and Kassidy spent the night at Melissa's home.

Asked what she and Amanda did together after Kassidy died, Melissa said that she, "*Went and arranged funeral clothing for her, see what she was going to wear in her casket*," and attended the funeral. (p. 66) After Amanda returned from Texas, where she went with Cathy Nuernberg after the funeral, she didn't contact Melissa.

In his last question, Simon Brown asked, "*Melissa, you saw these, you described the bruising you saw. Why didn't you intervene?*" She responded, "*Because she* [Amanda] *had an excuse for all of them. And you just didn't know.* ***You can't accuse someone of something if you don't know***." (p. 67)

Alan Cronheim cross-examined and began, "*You previously indicated that the first time you saw bruising on her was about -- it was ... about four weeks before Halloween*?" (p. 68) and Melissa agreed. Then he asked, "*And you indicated that you saw her in the bath in mid-October, correct*?" and Melissa said, "*No, it was the beginning of September*." Cronheim then confirmed that it was "*the weekend of October 13 and October 14, when you bumped into... Tracey Foley*." and Melissa agreed. (p. 68) Melissa agreed that she talked with the police on November 13, 2000 and that she indicated to them that she bathed Kassidy on the night that she saw Amanda, Kassidy and Tracey. Then Cronheim reiterated, "*And that the bathing of Kassidy the night you saw the bruising was that night in October*?" and Melissa said, "*No, that was wrong. I didn't know the time. I wasn't in the right frame of mind* [at the time of the interview.]" (p. 69) Cronheim pressed further, "*But it's true that you told the police on November 13th of 2000, that the baby circumstance was mid-October of 2000*?" and Melissa said, "*I don't... remember that.*" (p. 69)

Alan Cronheim then showed Melissa a copy of the summary of her November 13, 2000 interview with the police, and she again said that the date she gave them of mid-October for her bathing Kassidy, "*was wrong*." (p. 70) Cronheim then asked about her November 9, 2001 interview with the police, "*And you indicated to them that it was toward the end, about four weeks before Halloween*?" Melissa replied, "*Yes. That was the real badly bruising on her face*." (p. 71) He then confirmed with Melissa that she was using Halloween [2000] as a reference point and "*there was a time that Amanda was supposed to come up to trick or treat with you*?" (p. 71) Melissa confirmed that Amanda called her to say that she could not come on Halloween because Kassidy was sick. Melissa agreed with Cronheim's characterization that Amanda was very concerned about Kassidy and was "*upset at Kassidy's physical illness*?" and "*said that Kassidy was falling into her Cheerios, correct*?" (p. 74) Cronheim reitereated, "*In fact, she -- used the phrase with you, 'she passed out into her Cheerios... and that she had fallen out of a truck from her babysitter, her sister's boyfriend's truck*?" and Melissa said, "*Yes*." (p. 75) Cronheim continued, "*Did she talk with you about Kassidy's eyes rolling in the back of her head*?" and Melissa responded, "*A little bit*." (p. 75) Thus, it appeared that the referenced conversation was over the weekend of Saturday/Sunday, October 27/28, right after Jeff returned Kassidy after the three day/two night babysitting.

Melissa agreed that her opinion about Kassidy being afraid of men was based on her observation that Kassidy was afraid of her boyfriend, and not of a male sales person at Olympia Sports, so the opinion was refined to mean fear of big men. Finally, Cronheim confirmed that Melissa last saw Kassidy alive during that mid-October visit. Unfortunately, there was no way to line up Chad and the taller and heavier Jeff together so the jury could see the difference.

Simon Brown began his redirect examination by asking "*how sure are you about when you gave that bath to Kassidy about...*" and Melissa said, "*I'm positive that it was the beginning of September, because I was not working*." (p. 76) Brown asked, "*How many times have you seen bruising on her before she made that statement* [about taking Kassidy to be babysat at Jeff and Jennifer's]?" and Melissa answered, "*I'd see bruises on her all the time*." (p. 77)

Melissa was the only witness to firmly give such an early date, "*beginning of September,*" to an observation of multiple bruises on Kassidy. If Chad's defense lawyers had a time-line for June-November, and if they had known of Kassidy's appointment with

Dr. Glass on August 10, and with Dr. Timoney on September 11, they could have reduced the credibility of Melissa's recollection. More powerful would have been the September 2 photograph of Kassidy taken by Jacqueline on the occasion of Scott Conley's birthday. That, too, was not shown to the jury.

According to Chad in a February 19, 2010 letter, Amanda told him that Melissa never babysat Kassidy overnight, except for the Friday, October 13, 2000 overnight when Amanda was there, too, and Melissa did not bathe Kassidy on that night.

There was no attempt to dissect the general allegation of seeing bruises, "*all the time*," which painted a broad picture for the jury. One date certain was that she didn't see Kassidy again after the October 13-15 weekend. This was another occasion during the trial when Exhibit 19, the October 1, 2000 photograph of Kassidy, could have been used. If there were no bruises on Kassidy for the August 10 medical appointment, the September 2 photo, and for her September 11 doctor exam and for the October 1 photo, then what was the meaning of "*all the time*"?

Continuing to focus on the theory that Jeff was responsible for Kassidy's death, Cronheim's short recross-examination was only about Melissa's knowledge of the times of Kassidy's being babysat by Jeff, and she knew nothing. (p. 77)

Tracey Foley

Now before the jury, Tracey was sworn in and examined by Will Delker. Her testimony was the same as before the judge, above. What's presented here will be the variations from that earlier testimony, with some repetition.

Tracey said that she had a stepson who was eleven, as well as her daughter, Chandler. While she didn't make the observation, that made her the adult most similar to Chad in one respect in this case, as she had an older stepchild and her own younger natural child.

Tracey said that Amanda and Kassidy moved away from the Sanford area when Kassidy was eight or nine months old and that contact was resumed when they met at the YMCA. At the "Y," Tracey noticed bruising on Kassidy's face, "across *the bridge of her nose and her cheeks, right here* [pointing to a location on her face]." The bruises were "*yellow, light green. I would say more in a healing end of bruising.*" (p. 82) Tracey asked Amanda about the bruising, and Amanda told her the "trampoline story." Amanda and Tracey made plans to visit the next day, Saturday, and Amanda and Kassidy came with Chad's presents which she had wrapped.

Tracey said that she learned about Kassidy's death on the following Monday, when reading a newspaper at work. She next heard from Amanda when Amanda arrived at her home the following Thursday "*hysterical, crying... She said, 'And you knew, and I didn't listen.*" (p. 85) Amanda then stayed overnight, and for several days at her house. Tracey said that Amanda "*was crying, disheveled, her hair was a mess, like falling out of a ponytail, and she was hysterical.*" (p. 85)

Delker asked what else Amanda told her during their 1-1/2 hour conversation, and Tracey said,

She told me that there had been incidents that Chad had thrown Kassidy on the bed, and that he would get angry and grabbed Kassidy by her shirt and push her into the corner of the room when Kassidy was crying and didn't stop..... (p. 87)

Asked what prompted Chad's responses, Tracey said, "*Kassidy crying, wanting her mother's attention.*" (p. 87) In response to Delker's question, Tracey said that Amanda did not express concern about Jeff's babysitting.

Tracey said that she had to work the next morning, and left for a trip the next night, so she missed Kassidy's funeral. Tracey said that Amanda "*and a friend of hers from Texas*" [Cathy Nuernberg] were buying things for Kassidy's funeral on Friday. (p. 91)

Alan Cronheim cross-examined Tracey and confirmed that the day Amanda came to Tracey's was Thursday, November 16th. However, there was no further clarification of the date that Tracey met Amanda and Melissa at the Sanford/Springvale YMCA. He did not remind the jury that this was the easily memorable Friday the 13th of October, before Chad's birthday on Sunday the 15th. In a date-challenged trial, no one reminded the jury that the bruises that Tracey saw on Friday the 13th were exactly the same bruises that Joshua Bortner saw on the same day.

Interestingly, in contrast to the voir dire examination of Tracey earlier in the day with Judge Nadeau and without the presence of the jury, she made no mention to the jury of bathing Kassidy in September, before she started work, about which she was "positive," earlier that day. The only date references in her testimony before the jury were the mid-October meeting and overnight and Amanda's November 16-18 visit. Thus, from the jury's perspective, the first sighting of bruising to Kassidy was Friday, October 13. Unfortunately, it's doubtful that jurors understood the importance of that date, and other dates in the trial.

Jeremy Hinton

Jeremy was one of Chad's two best friends, but appeared at the trial as a prosecution witness. It was never explained to the jury why witnesses were called as prosecution witnesses or defense witnesses. That might have given jurors some food for thought, as they may have wondered why Chad's friends did not testify at the trial for the defense. They may not have understood that any of the State's witnesses could have been recalled as defense witnesses.

In 2000, Jeremy was the restaurant manager for the Hampton Beach, New Hampshire, McDonald's, which was one of the restaurants for which Chad was responsible. Jeremy said that he first saw Kassidy when Amanda brought her to his restaurant. After that, he saw her about five or six times, and described her,

I never saw her to be what would consider a typical -- any babies or toddlers I've been around have been, you know, a little more energetic, playful. From the very first time I saw her, I never saw that in her. (p. 96-97)

Will Delker then asked about Chad's birthday party, which Jeremy said was on Saturday evening, October 14, at Chad's home, mostly attended by Chad's family, but not including Amanda and Kassidy. The next day, Sunday, Jeremy saw Kassidy and Amanda at the home of Chad's and Jeremy's friend, Bruce, in Rochester. He said,

Amanda drove up. She had some presents and a birthday cake. We were having a little -- I guess a continued birthday party for Chad, watching football the next day. And Kassidy stayed in the car and Amanda gave us the presents... She said she was headed to Maine to drop Kassidy off. (p 97-98)

Jeremy said that Kassidy had bruises on the left side of her face, but he couldn't see more, as it was through a closed car window.

Delker asked when Jeremy saw Kassidy next, and Jeremy recalled it was Tuesday, October 24, 2000, saying,

That morning Chad and I were going to a golf outing in Nashua for our company...I woke up... I saw her in the bed of Chad and Amanda. It was like 4:30 in the morning... I was a bit groggy. I couldn't see her well. And then I saw her again later that evening when we returned home at nine or eight.... she had some bruises on the left side of her neck... They almost looked like fingers.... They looked old. They were black.... Chad called Kassidy over. Kassidy came over to the couch. He pulled down her diaper, and there was bruises from her lower back to just below her knees.... They were bruises on top of bruises... old bruises and there were new bruises... From her lower back to just below her knee, including her butt. (p. 99-101)

Will Delker asked Jeremy about his speaking with Chad on the day Kassidy died, November 9th. Jeremy said

I'm sure I talked with him in the morning just because of work reasons. And then at 3:30, he showed up at my restaurant....He had some soup cookers to drop off.... He talked to Travis Hunt outside, and then I went outside and I talked with him." (p.101)

Travis was Jeremy's Assistant Manager. Jeremy said that Chad looked shaken up and Chad said to him that he had received a page from the Kittery Police Dept., about which "*he had no idea. He said he* [they] *had called him and they said, 'you need to come in person and talk to us.'* " (p. 102)

Jeremy said that about 6:45 p.m., he drove to the Kittery Police station and he saw Bruce, Tristan, Amanda's mother and an uncle.

After Chad's arrest and bail, in early 2001, Jeremy had given both Amanda and Chad keys to his apartment and they stayed there from time to time, and Jeremy knew about the no contact provision in Chad's bail release order.

Will Delker asked about Chad's request that Jeremy register Chad's car under Jeremy's name so it wouldn't be traceable to Chad. Jeremy did register the car, and he believed that Amanda used it. He also recounted a trip to New York City which he took with Chad, Amanda and Jason Evans in the spring of 2001. Delker thus established that Chad and Amanda had seen each other in 2001, in violation of his bail condition. As the Rules of Evidence require that evidence be relevant to the crimes which are charged, it's hard to see how that evidence met that relevance test.

After Will Delker finished his examination of Jeremy, he asked for a bench conference to preemptively prevent Alan Cronheim from introducing any hearsay evidence during his cross-examination. Specifically, he did not want the jury to hear what Chad had told him that Jeff Marshall had told him about bruising on Kassidy's buttocks at the time of the McDonald's golf day on October 24th, as Jeremy dated it. The statement by Jeff was, in Delker's words, "*I spanked Kassidy so hard my hand stung.*" (p. 113) Delker argued that since the defense didn't ask Jeff Marshall that question during his cross-examination, Cronheim could not ask Jeremy about it now, for the purpose of impeaching Jeff's response - as he wasn't asked. Judge Nadeau agreed that it was hearsay and forbade Cronheim from trying to introduce it. If Sisti had asked Jeff about that statement and if Jeff had denied making it, then Chad's attorneys could have asked Jeremy what Chad said to him about Jeff's statement, because it would have been offered to impeach Jeff's credibility and not for the truth of the statement by itself.

Because the prosecution presented, through Jeremy, the incident where Chad showed Jeremy the bruises on Kassidy on the 24th, Cronheim was permitted to ask Jeremy what Chad said about those bruises, i.e. that he didn't do it, even if the jury could not hear what Chad said that Jeff told him.

The loss in this exchange was the truth. The jury should have heard, in some way, what Jeff said to Chad during that truck ride to Auburn to pick up a 3-wheeler on Sunday, October 22. We don't know if Mark Sisti intentionally didn't ask Jeff about what he told Chad on that day, or if he simply forgot to ask. Whatever the reason, they could have considered recalling Jeff to the witness stand in order to ask him that simple question, among others.

Alan Cronheim began his cross-examination of Jeremy by confirming that Jeremy saw bruises on Kassidy twice, when Amanda showed them on October 15, when she brought presents to Chad, and on October 24 when Chad showed bruises on Kassidy's behind to Jeremy. Jeremy recounted one time at Chad's home when he was with Amanda and Chad downstairs and Kassidy was crying upstairs in her room, apparently unable open the door. Jeremy said that Chad went upstairs to get Kassidy and bring her downstairs.

Regarding his seeing bruises on October 24, the time of the golf tournament, Jeremy said that he asked about the bruises on Kassidy, which he had seen on the 15th, and presumably were still there on the 24th, and it was in response that Chad asked Kassidy to come over to him, and Chad showed Jeremy the bruises on Kassidy's behind.

Cronhim didn't ask about bruises on Kassidy's face which he saw on the evening of the 24th, after the golf tournament. Chad's letter of January 11, 2010 describes that day,

Jeremy came into our bedroom that morning, because I didn't wake up. Kassidy was sleeping between Amanda and I. Later that night Jeremy and I returned, and Kassidy came into the living room and had two prominent bruises on her cheek. Jeremy leaned over and asked me what happened to her. I had no idea as I was with him all day but called Kassidy over so I could pull her diaper open. I showed him her butt all black and blue. His eyes went up in disbelief. I told him that Jeff had spanked her and asked his opinion of what I should do. He said something to the effect of, "I'd kill anyone that did that to my kid." I said, that I was thinking same thing but this was Amanda's baby and I didn't want to control her. (Jeremy was friends with Tristan and I and knew I made all decisions in that relationship. At the time I felt like I caused the relationship with Tristan to fail and wasn't going to repeat the same mistakes.) Anyway, Amanda came into room all upset because we were whispering and she thought we were talking about her. Turns out Amanda had spent the day with Jen and Jeff. Jen and Amanda did a landscape clean up job, and Jeff took Kassidy home with him, so he could do some billing or something like that.

Returning to Jeremy's testimony, he confirmed that November 9th was a regular day and his conversations were about work. When Chad told him about the call from the Kittery Police Dept., Jeremy asked Chad why the Kittery Police would be paging him, and they speculated on the reasons, but because of the hearsay rules, Cronheim couldn't ask Jeremy about that conversation. That evening, said Jeremy, he went to the Kittery Police Station on his own initiative as he wondered what had happened to Chad, and it was then that he had learned that Kassidy had died. Jeremy asked the police if they wanted to talk with him, as he had seen bruises on Kassidy.

Cronheim asked about the gathering of people in the Kittery Police Dept. parking lot after the end of several interviews, and asked Jeremy if Chad was upset. Jeremy testified, "*He was -- he was upset that the baby was dead. He said he really loved that girl. He just kept talking about* [how] *he wanted to be with Amanda and support her*." (p. 130)

Asked about Chad's approaching Jeff in the parking lot, Jeremy said, "*He started walking towards Jeff, and I grabbed him and tried to say, 'You know, not a good idea.' And at that point, he got up almost in Jeff's face and said, 'You're going to pay for what you did.'* " (p. 130)

Jeremy said he helped Amanda during 2001 because of friendship, "*I've been blessed with some great family and some good friends, and you know, when I see someone that hasn't had those same fortunes, I try to help them out.*" (p. 131) Jeremy said that Amanda had spoken with him about her problems with her family, and they were not helping her. "*She came to me and she said she had no one. She wasn't allowed to be with Chad, and she had nobody*." (p. 131)

Jeremy said that he helped with the car registration because Chad told him that he had been stopped by the police often, and three times in one day.

Alan Cronheim then asked about Kyle and Jeremy said that he had known him his entire four years of life and that in 2000 while playing with a wiffle ball he could hit a pitched ball "*remarkably well for someone that age*." (p. 133)

Will Delker's redirect contained only one question which was to confirm that it was a wiffle ball, "*one of those plastic, hollow balls*" that Jeremy saw Kyle playing with in 2000. (p. 134) Whatever Delker's intentions, the effect was likely to reinforce the prosecution's message with the jury that if there was a ball that hit Kassidy on November 8, 2000, it was only a wiffle ball. Of course, being able to hit a ball, whether wiffle or not, was the skill that Kyle had, and the important measurement was the diameter of the ball and not its weight. A person could hit a wiffle ball just as easily as a Tee-ball but probably not as easily as a softball and far easier than hitting a ping pong ball. The jury still didn't know that the ball that hit Kassidy was a Tee-ball.

Vanessa Mansson

Will Delker established with Vanessa that she had been a close friend of Chad since childhood and that after his arrest and bail, he stayed at her apartment in Keene for periods of time. Delker asked how it happened that Amanda came to stay at her apartment. Vanessa said that she understood from Chad that Amanda "*was upset and crying and said that she didn't have a place to live... and didn't know what she was going to do. So I offered to Chad to have Amanda stay at my house.*" (p. 138) Vanessa said of Chad, "*He loved her* [Amanda] *very much and missed her.*" (p. 139) She said that Amanda began living at Vanessa's in December 2000, and Chad would stay, from time to time. He helped with phone bills and food, and Amanda helped with babysitting Vanessa's children. Amanda went to Texas twice in 2001, but was with Vanessa most of the rest of the spring of 2001. It was at Vanessa's that Amanda completed her "My Life Story," although the jury did not know about that essay. Delker asked about Chad's and Amanda's relationship, and Vanessa said, "*They were like honeymooners. They were always holding hands and always would sit very close on the couch, and just supporting each other.*" (p. 142) Vanessa said that Amanda moved out in May 2001 because Amanda had forgotten, twice, to pick up Vanessa's children at school.

Delker established that Vanessa knew that Chad did not want the police, or the media, to know that he was seeing Amanda. That was one reason why they stayed at home most of the time when they were together. That is, they didn't go out and do things away from the apartment.

Will Delker then asked about Amanda's interest in finding an attorney, and Vanessa responded, "*She said something to me about that she felt that her initial statements to the police were not correct, that she had just told the police what she thought they wanted to hear so that she could get out ... of there...*" (p. 153-54) Vanessa told Chad that she thought an attorney should be found for Amanda, and Vanessa remembered that the only concern Chad had was "*that when she had an attorney that they wouldn't be able to see each other...* [and] *because he didn't want her to have to go through what she went through the first time,*" i.e. with more police interviews. (p. 158-59)

Alan Cronhein cross-examined and quickly established that Chad's concern was that Amanda wouldn't, in Cronheim's words, "*end up going through another four-hour drill session.*" (p. 159) Vanessa also agreed with Cronheim's question, "*There wasn't any effort that you observed of Chad trying to manipulate the process?*" (p. 159) Cronheim also advised Vanessa that she wasn't the only person to suggest to Amanda that she get an attorney, as Cathy Nuernberg had also made that suggestion. Unknown to the jury, Amanda had also talked with Alan Cronheim about finding an attorney.

Cronheim then reviewed with Vanessa her longterm friendship with Chad, which sparked as romantic as sophomores in high school, but returned to friendship. Vanessa agreed that she worked in the County Attorney's office, and later she agreed that she was fired, because the County Attorney, Peter Heed, later a New Hampshire Attorney General, believed it was inappropriate for her to have permitted Chad to see Amanda in her apartment.

Vanessa agreed that she was with Amanda in Vanessa's apartment when Amanda told Sergeant White that she was calling from Texas. Vanessa also agreed that Chad was there, too. and "*that Chad said that she* [Amanda] *should tell Sergeant White where, in fact, she was.*" (p. 166) Cronheim concluded with Vanessa affirming that she told the truth even though it cost her her job. There was no redirect examination and the jury was dismissed for the day.

The lawyers and Judge Nadeau then discussed the upcoming testimony of Tristan Evans and the extent to which she could relate to the jury what Kyle told her on the evening of November 8. After a voir dire examination and cross-examination of Tristan, Judge Nadeau decided that Kyle's statement to Tristan about the ball hitting Kassidy was an "excited utterance" exception to the hearsay rule and during the next day's testimony, the defense could ask Tristan about that statement. The reasoning behind the "excited utterance" exception is that a person who is excited doesn't have time to calculate lies.

The trial adjourned at 4:03 p.m.

MEDIA: 1. "Ex-wife testifies in Evans' trial"
2. "Evans' ex-wife: I told DCYF of suspected abuse"
3. "They lived like honeymooners - Evans' chjildhood sweetheart recalls his relationship with Bortner after Kassidy's death"

Tuesday 11 December 2001

Cory Merrill

Examined by Will Delker, Cory Merrill said he was a cellmate of Chad Evans at the Strafford County Jail when Chad was first arrested in November, 2000. Merrill said that he had received no benefit from the State for his testimony and that he was currently serving a sentence in the State Prison for sexual assault. Merrill said that Chad was "*mad. He was very depressed. Talked about suicide a lot... very frequently.*" (p. 170)

Delker asked what Chad said about Kassidy, and Merrill responded, "*It was several different occasions that he would talk about that he would spank the baby a lot, not only with his hand, but with a belt*," and that he spanked the baby, "*hard. He said hard....to get her to stop crying.. Basically, he was tired of getting woken up by the baby because he worked 70 to 80 hours a week at McDonald's, I guess and he was tired of kept* [sic] *getting woken up in the middle of the night...*" (p. 171-72) Merrill said that Chad said he was "*pissed off*" at Kassidy, and that when she was spanked by Chad she,

would scream, just really wouldn't stop crying, I know that. Just cry even more and scream, and that's about it?... I believe it was on one occasion he said that he shook the baby... Just basically to get her to stop crying.... He mentioned something about dropping the baby out of their truck, or car or whatever when ... he picked the baby up at the babysitter's. (p. 173)

Delker asked if Chad had told him what he would do when bailed, and Merrill said,

a couple of days before he got bailed out, this was a few days before Thanksgiving of last year, he mentioned that if it wasn't his parents' house that [was] *put up* [for bail security], *then if he had a chance to run, he would.* (p. 174)

Mark Sisti cross-examined Merrill and showed that he was motivated to get into a special class for sex offenders, so he could get his sentence reduced. In response to questions, Merrill named two prison corrections officers who told other inmates that Merrill was going to testify in court against another inmate, thus requiring Merrill to request to be put into PC - Protective Custody. Sisti established that sometime after Chad was released on bail, on November 22, 2000, NH State Trooper Jill Rockey and another person came to talk with Merrill about Chad's case. The police asked, in Sisti's words, "*whether or not you'll help us out here and tell us whether or not Chad said anything to you, anything that will help us solve this case.*" (p. 186)

Merrill said that he told the officers he didn't want to talk with them. However, he subsequently changed his mind because, "*... I was doing a lot of thinking and said that it involves a 20 or 21-month old baby...*" (p. 188)

Merrill was simply doing what several people did in Chad's case, some more consciously than others, which was to tell the police and prosecutors what they wanted to hear. Inmate informants can be especially effective because they come close to providing the Holy Grail of criminal justice: the confession. That is, as yet another exception to the hearsay rule, inmate informants produce statements from defendants that look like confessions, or statements against a person's own interest.

Then Sisti asked about the three charges against Merrill, to which he pled guilty and Merrill said that he did commit two of the three offenses, but he pled guilty to avoid the risk of more prison time. The lawyers and Judge Nadeau then had a long bench conference, along with Merrill's court appointed lawyer, because Merrill had just acknowledged that he had committed perjury by pleading guilty to something he said he didn't do. The bench conference concluded with a plan by the State to provide Merrill with immunity from prosecution for perjury. As it would take some time for the Attorney General to agree and provide such immunity, Merrill's testimony was put on hold, and the next witness was called.

<u>Tristan Evans</u>

Simon Brown examined Tristan, and established that they separated on 13 December 1999 and were divorced on October 4, 2000. Asked about Chad's and Amanda's relationship, Tristan said that "*Amanda had been staying with Chad often, probably four to six weeks prior to Kassidy's death, I'd say, is when I saw her* [Kassidy] *more often in the home with Chad and Amanda.*" (p. 213) Thus, it appeared that Chad's efforts to hide from Tristan the moving-in part of their relationship had partially succeeded. Tristan said that she was at Chad's about every other day, as they shared custody of Kyle and as they communicated often about their parenting.

Asked for her impressions of Kassidy, Tristan said, "*She was very quiet, very withdrawn, inactive.... Once she said, 'Bye,' but other than that, I didn't hear her say anything.*" (p. 214)

Tristan said that over the weekend of October 21-22 she stopped by the house and saw "*bruising on Kassidy's face and down towards her neck... Across her forehead and down by her neck.*"

It was likely on Sunday, the 22nd that Tristan came by, because Kassidy was with Jeff on Saturday, and on Sunday, Chad was with Jeff most of the day in Maine purchasing a 3-wheeler.

Tristan first thought there were dirt marks, but she bent down and said to Kassidy, " *'Hey, baby girl,'* " and saw "*fading brown*" bruising. (p. 215) Tristan asked Amanda what happened, and Amanda said that Kassidy had fallen downstairs. Chad was not home at the time. About two days later, approximately Tuesday, October 24th, Tristan asked Chad, and he told Tristan the "trampoline story." Tristan testified that she told Chad what Amanda said and he stayed with the "trampoline story." Tristan was thus the second person Chad told the "trampoline story." The first was Jacqueline on Saturday, October 14, ten days earlier.

Tristan said that the following weekend, which was the 28-29th, Amanda and Kassidy were again home and Tristan saw a new bruise, "*on her right cheek... a dark purple, about the size of a quarter.*" (p. 217) This was after Jeff had returned Kassidy from the three day/two night extended babysitting. Tristan said she was concerned, but didn't ask Amanda about the new bruise. This bruise became the best known of Kassidy's bruises, because it was observed six days later, on November 5, by Brandon and Nicole Harvey, when Chad brought Kassidy for a daylong visit. Tristan called DCYF about the bruise, and previous bruises, a few days later.

Tristan recounted her call to DCYF, which was on October 31,

That I... saw a couple of instances of bruising. I had given Chad's name and address, phone number. I didn't know Amanda's last name at the time or Kassidy, but I gave their first names. They [DCYF] *had asked ... if I had known who might be doing it. At that time I stated I didn't believe it was Chad, I didn't know if Amanda, possibly the babysitter. But at the time I didn't know who the babysitter was.*" (p. 218-19)

Tristan was sure that she had mentioned a "*babysitter*" as a possible source of the bruising. She continued, "*All I knew is that she had a babysitter. Amanda had recently started working at Old Navy.*" (p. 219) However, Amanda did not start work until one week later, on Monday, November 6th, unless Kristin Parsons was correct that Amanda started at Old Navy on Thursday, November 2. If that was correct, then Tristan's statement could be that she understood that Amanda had recently been hired at Old Navy, but had not yet started work.

Simon Brown asked, "*Would it surprise you if the DCYF intaker had no notes about a babysitter being reported?*" Tristan answered "*Yes*", but probably meant "*No*," and she continued, "*because there were other inconsistencies on her report also.*" (p. 219) However, Brown did not explore those other inconsistencies.

Brown asked if Tristan saw Kassidy again before she died, and Tristan said that she saw Kassidy "*approximately two days*" before she died. Simon Brown asked, "*Did you see anything wrong with Kassidy on that day?*" and Tristan said "*No*." (p. 219) She said that Kassidy "*was sitting on the couch with Amanda crying,*" but Tristan did not know why she was crying. (p. 220)

There were no further questions from Brown about that day. It was probably a Tuesday, when she came to pick up Kyle or bring him to Chad's. Brown did not ask for further clarification of Tristan's "*No.*" He knew what Tristan had said in her November 9 interview about her visit to Chad's on the Tuesday before Kassidy died, but the jury didn't know. In that Interview, Tristan said,

And then I saw her two days ago and she had another bruise on her cheek....I started mentioning to Chad after I saw the bruises... And I said, "she's not acting normal...but is there something mentally wrong with her?" I said, "because she doesn't do things that a one and a half year old do[es]*." .. I said, "She doesn't talk. She doesn't play. She just sits there. You sit her in a chair and she would just sit there for hours. And not move." I'm like, 'you need to start asking some questions here.' Two days ago I said to him, cause... she was just like crying when..."* (p. 1075)

Alan Cronheim cross-examined Tristan and established that she didn't see any change in Kassidy's behavior from the summer through the end of her life. Tristan affirmed Cronheim's summary question that "*she was quiet during the summer, and she was quiet in the October and November timeframe...and not particularly reactive, and not particularly involved?*" (p. 222)

Cronheim then asked Tristan about her concerns about Amanda's parenting practices, including Amanda's "*use of putting Kassidy in her room,*" (p. 225) and not going to retrieve her from her room when she was crying.

After a bench conference with Judge Nadeau and the prosecutors about avoiding hearsay, and staying within the boundaries of the exceptions to the hearsay rule, Alan Cronheim asked Tristan about Chad's phone calls to her on November 8th. He intended to ask about the call with Tristan after the Tee-ball accident, but he made the question so general that Tristan first talked about an earlier call, apparently when Chad was driving Kassidy to Dover to pick up Kyle. Tristan said that Chad said, "*I think you might be right. I think she may be retarded or something. She's in the backseat. She's slumped over. She's dazed and confused. She's blank faced.*" (p. 235)

This was an important call to present to the jury, because the jury had not yet been told that Chad had called anyone else other than Jeff about the drive from Kittery to Kyle's day care. It was the prosecution's theory that Chad's call to Jeff was to somehow set him up, instead of being a genuine call of concern and a plea for help in understanding what was happening. Ironically, that call was similar in intent to Jeff's five calls to Chad the next day.

Tristan then related the second phone call, later in the evening, wherein Chad described the incident when Kassidy fell face first in the driveway, and then he described Kassidy "*had gotten hit with a ball during that time... Kyle had hit a wiffle ball and hit her in the face with it....*" (p. 236) Unfortunately, the confusion about the type of ball that hit Kassidy continued. Tristan said that Kyle was a good hitter and he hit balls "*all the time.*" (p. 237)

Cronheim started to ask Tristan about the conversation with Kyle which occurred during the same call, just discussed, with Chad, and the prosecution objected to hearsay. The question was whether what Kyle said to his mother fit the "excited utterance" exception to the hearsay rule. Judge Nadeau decided to have a "voir dire" hearing with Tristan, with the jury being excused for the day, so the judge could determine if what Kyle said to her was an "excited utterance." After hearing Tristan's description of the conversation with Kyle, Judge Nadeau agreed to allow the defense to ask Tristan about that conversation in front of the jury when the trial resumed the following morning.

Tuesday, 1 December 2001

Tristan Evans (continued)

Alan Cronheim resumed cross examining Tristan and asked what Kyle said to her on the phone on the evening of November 8th. Tristan responded, "*He had told me that they had played ball and that he had hit...Kassidy with the ball and he had told her, 'Sorry,' for hitting her and hurting her...*" (p. 9-10) That was that. There was no question about what type of ball it was, but it was doubtful that Kyle told his mother what type of ball it was, and Kyle was not going to be called to testify.

Cronheim then asked about a call from Chad to Tristan on the afternoon of November 9, and Tristan confirmed that Chad did not remind her of the call the previous evening. This questioning by Cronheim was to pre-empt the prosecution's allegations that Chad had developed a cover story and that he was manipulating others to tell the police what he had told them. At the end of Cronheim's questioning, he revisited Kyle's abilities to hit a pitched ball with a bat, and Tristan reaffirmed her belief that that was exactly what happened on the evening of November 8th.

Simon Brown then conducted redirect examination and confirmed that Tristan had continued contact with Chad because they are the parents of Kyle. Then, Brown explored another prosecution perception of Chad Evans, asking, "*Is the defendant a persuasive person*?" and Tristan appeared to surprise him by answering, "*No*." (p. 17) This was a key part of the prosecution's theory to explain Amanda's disavowal of what she told the police during her four interviews, which was that Chad persuaded her that he was not Kassidy's killer.

Brown again visited the question of Tristan's opinion about the source of the bruises that she reported to DCYF. He asked, "*You testified yesterday that even though you made that call to DCYF on October 31st, you did not suspect the defendant to be causing those injuries*?" and Tristan said, "*Correct*." Brown continued, "*You had no suspicion whatsoever*?" and she said, "*No*." (p. 18-19) Tristan said she didn't believe Amanda's statement that Kassidy's bruises were caused by falling down the stairs. Later she said, "*It's a common answer to say you've fallen down the stairs...*" (p. 21) She testified that she did believe the "trampoline story."

Tristan related how she checked Kyle very carefully for bruises and she said to Chad, "'*If I see one, I'll kill you.' I've never thought he would. He never has*." (p. 24) After several questions,
Tristan said that Chad had told her that the ball that hit Kassidy was a wiffle ball. (p. 25) She simply misunderstood. Perhaps he said to her that they were "**playing** wiffleball."

Tristan said that she had two phone conversations with Chad on November 8th. For the first one, she called Chad, because she was seeking the phone number of a friend. It was in the late afternoon, and from the earlier testimony, it was while Chad was driving, with Kassidy in the back, to pick up Kyle. Simon Brown pointed out to Tristan that there was no telephone record of that first call, and Alan Cronheim interjected that Tristan was not responsible for the accuracy of the State's exhibits. Brown then pointed out that Tristan didn't mention that first call in her police interview either, but she noted that other mistakes were made in that police interview, including getting her birthdate wrong. Also, during that first interview on November 9, she didn't mention the conversation later that evening with Kyle about hitting Kassidy with the ball.

Alan Cronheim then asked Tristan, in recross-examination about the context of her responses to the police questions, which showed her to be more responsive than the prosecutors implied. For example, Brown showed that Tristan mentioned in her police interview only one call with Chad on the evening of November 8, whereas Tristan had testified in court that there were two. Through Cronheim's questions, Tristan explained that the police did not ask her about all her calls. They were only asking her about the one call, which Kyle joined and during which he explained the ball hitting incident.

Cory Merrill

There was another bench conference about the complicated issues surrounding Cory Merrill's testimony, and the potential for him committing perjury if he testifies before the jury. Judge Nadeau decided to conduct another voir dire hearing, without the jury, to determine the nature of his expected testimony so she could decide whether to permit Merrill to testify before the jury.

During that hearing, Mark Sisti asked him several questions and Merrill's counsel, on behalf of Merrill, asserted his Fifth Amendment right not to incriminate himself. Merrill did not respond. Mark Sisti then argued that Merrill's testimony before the jury should be stopped and the jury should be instructed to ignore what Merrill had already said. Judge Nadeau decided that his earlier testimony need not be stricken, and that, pending further reports from corrections officers about other claims by Merrill, he should return to testify. Merrill's testimony was obviously flawed and it's hard to see how the judge and the prosecutors were willing to accept the word of such a man, where the conflict of interest was so large. That is, everyone knew that Merrill wanted favors from the State, even if no one wanted to admit it yet. That would come after Chad's conviction, otherwise not. Inmates are rarely rewarded for snitching unless the government wins its case.

There was a scheduling conflict for Merrill's attorney and Judge Nadeau said, "*The trouble is that we are bumping up against Christmas, and I'm trying to take all steps I can to make sure we don't do that*." (p. 88-89) If the defense called many witnesses, the trial would likely continue into Christmas, but the defense plans were still unknown. This was not the first time Judge Nadeau had shown concern about the length of the trial, and thus brought implicit pressure on the parties to tighten their work. In her July 13 Scheduling Order, she wrote, "*In light of the court's order permitting individual voir dire and in light of the parties' estimate that the trial will take two weeks from opening statements to closing arguments, the court is concerned that the case will not be completed by the time of the Christmas break.*"

The final decision about Merrill would wait.

<u>Shannon Gagne</u>

Simon Brown examined Shannon, who had been a friend of Amanda for about three years, and Shannon had known Kassidy since she was born. She testified that she met Chad once, after Amanda came to her at work at Olympia Sports in Sanford and said that she wanted to bring her to Rochester to introduce her to him. Kassidy was with Amanda on that occasion. Shannon said that her job at Olympia Sports ended in "*the beginning of July, but I'm not positive. It was June/July, somewhere around those areas.*" (p. 94) Shannon saw a bruise on Kassidy's forehead and

I had asked Amanda what had happened, and she said that Chad went to put her to bed one night and Kassidy was fighting because she didn't want to go to bed, and she banged her head off the wall on accident... It wasn't very big; just a little thing. It was starting to discolor, like it had been there for a week or two... It was probably like right above her right eye. Like right around her eyebrow area." (p. 94)

Later that night Shannon went to Rochester to meet Chad.

Shannon said that she saw Amanda a few times afterwards, and asked Amanda about that same bruise another time, "*she did tell me a different story the second time. She had told me that she was playing with a little girl and the little girl had hit her in the face.*" (p. 95) The dates of both of these observations were unknown and unexplored. Perhaps the forehead bruise that she saw was the same as was seen by others, including Jennifer, Melissa, Tristan, and Cathy Nuernberg.

Asked about when she learned about Kassidy's death, Shannon said that a mutual friend, Vikki Normand, had told her on the day Kassidy died. A day later, according to Shannon, Amanda called her, "*...she used to baby-sit for this lady* [Tracey Foley] .... *in Springvale, Maine, ... for a couple of days.*" (p. 96) Shannon visited her at that woman's home for a couple of hours, and related what Amanda said to her about Jeff and Jennifer.

... her first statement was: 'I don't know how anybody could do this.' And then she had stated that Kassidy had loved to go to... Jennifer and Jeff's house.... She loved it over there, Amanda had said to me, "And I knew Kassidy did, because she went to go over there a lot." (p. 97)

Simon Brown returned to Amanda's two explanations for the bruise that Shannon saw in early summer. She said,

Chad Evans went to put Kassidy to bed one night, and Kassidy, being a little girl, didn't want to go to bed at that time. And when Chad was bringing her up the stairs, Kassidy had banged her head off the wall. (p. 98)

Shannon continued,

I talked with her a couple of days after, and I asked how Kassidy was doing. And she went into detail that a little girl had hit her in the face. And I'm assuming she was talking about the same bruise, because I never saw another one on her besides that one that was on her forehead. (p. 98)

Either the bruise was a second bruise with a different cause, or Amanda simply misunderstood its cause. In any case, Shannon saw, at most, two different bruises on Kassidy's forehead during the summer. This was before Kassidy's August 10 and September 11 medical appointments, and before Scott Conley's September 2 birthday party, and the October 1 photo. As Freud might say, sometimes a bruise is just a bruise.

Alan Cronheim cross-examined Shannon, and, once again, the jury saw a friend of Amanda testifying for the prosecution and Chad's attorney challenging what she had said. Cronheim asked about Shannon's November 12, 2000 police interview where Det. Linscott's summary said that she said that she had seen Kassidy three times after Amanda and Chad met. Shannon said that the report was wrong, but she agreed that she was not sure if the two explanations Amanda gave for bruising were about the same bruise.

Simon Brown, on redirect, asked about the timing of Shannon's conversation with Amanda, "*in relation to Kassidy's funeral,*" and Shannon responded, "*It was actually the day after Kassidy got passed. I met her at the lady's house that she had baby-sat for, and she was discussing that she was about to go to Auburn for the funeral.*" (p. 103) While the jurors may have connected the dots, it would have helped if Simon Brown or Alan Cronheim had noted that the "*lady*" was Tracey Foley, who had testified earlier in the trial. As Amanda began that visit on the night of Chad's arrest, November 16, and as Kassidy's funeral was on Saturday, November 18, Shannon's conversation with Amanda was surely on Friday, the 15th. Thus, it was not "*a day later*" after Kassidy died or "*the day after Kassidy got passed.*" It was eight days later. By itself, this date discrepancy doesn't affect the big issues of the trial, but it shows how easily witnesses were confused about dates, and how important it would have been to have a calendar and timeline for the witnesses and the jury.

Shannon was not asked about Amanda's visit with Kassidy to Olympia Sports, which Amanda said was a few days before Kassidy died. Amanda had said that Kassidy was running around and having fun.

Travis Hunt

Examined by Simon Brown, Travis said that he was 27 years old and living in Chad's home in Rochester and that he was working at Burger King as a manager. He said that he met Chad when he was an employee at the Rochester McDonald's in 1992 or 1993. Travis said that he moved to the apartment in Chad's house in mid-September 2000 and that Amanda and Kassidy were living there. He described Kassidy, as

Cute little girl. Little slow I thought, but.... She was very quiet, not like a typical, you know, one-and-a-half-year old... She played like all kids do, but she sat around a lot, also, watching TV." (p. 109-10)

He noticed that "*She wouldn't always necessarily put her hand out to stop her*[self] *from falling.*" Brown asked, "*...would she fall flat on her face, or would she tumble, or...*" and Travis responded, "*Yeah, on her face. Sometimes she fell, you know, to the side, tripped over feet walking, that sort of thing.*" (p. 110) Her arms would be "*To her side.... down.*" (p. 111)

Asked about injuries, Travis said, "*... she always seemed to bruise easily. She had bruises on her arms. I've seen them on her legs before, and on her face right here* [pointing to his lower cheeks]." (p. 111) Regarding timing, Travis said, "*a couple weeks after I moved in. And like probably the night before she died.*" (p. 112)

Chad remembered that Travis moved to his home immediately after the Friday, September 15 seasonal closing of the Hampton Beach McDonald's. If Travis didn't see any bruising until "a couple weeks after" he moved in, that would move his initial sighting of bruises to after September 29, which would have to mean after the October 1 photo of Kassidy by Jacqueline.

Travis said that in a casual conversation, Amanda told him that "*she didn't like the way he* [Chad] *grabbed her* [Kassidy's] *face.*" (p. 114)

On Wednesday, November 8, Travis didn't see Kassidy that morning. He worked on the 11 a.m. to 7 p.m. shift and testified that he arrived home around 7:45-8:00 p.m. He went upstairs and saw Chad giving Kassidy a bath and "*First thing I noticed* [was] *that she had a bruise on her eye. So, you know, I said, "What was up with that?'*" Chad told him that "*Kyle had hit her with a baseball, a wiffle ball.*" (p. 118) Other bruises that he saw included, "*a bruise under her eye. It went like to her nose over here....It was black and blue...she had little bruises here... like a green color...They looked old.*" (p. 119) Kassidy was sitting in the bathtub in a few inches of water, with her knees up, enabling Travis to see bruises on the shin of one of her legs.

Brown asked how Kassidy was behaving in the tub, and Travis said, "*She was smiling. She was splashing in the water.*" Brown was surprised, given Travis's earlier assessment of Kassidy as "*slow,*" so he followed up, and Travis said, "*I don't know, you know, a little kid taking a bath and she's splashing...*" (p. 123-24) Brown pressed about Travis's earlier statements, and Travis said, "*No, I've said she was happy.*" (p. 124) Travis agreed that in his earlier police interview with Det. Callaghan of the Rochester Police Dept., he had described Kassidy as "*active and chipper.*" and he defined "*chipper*" for the jury as being "*happy.*" (p. 124)

Travis testified that after seeing Kassidy, he went into Kyle's room and pitched a few wiffle balls to him which he hit with a "*Yellow wiffle ball bat,*" (p. 126) and agreed with Brown that it was "*one of those long yellow skinny bats.*" (p. 126) Later in the questioning, however, Brown asked if Chad said anything to Travis about "*the bat that was used by Kyle*" and Travis said, "*No,*" and Brown continued, "*So you don't know what bat was involved.*" and Travis again said "*No.*" (p. 137)

Travis said that he had never played baseball in the house with Kyle before, but that he was hitting the balls well, and that Travis didn't catch any of them. Then, after about ten minutes with Chad, Kassidy and Kyle, Travis went downstairs to his basement apartment to change clothes to go out to see his girlfriend, Irene Ricci, in Gonic. After about a half hour dressing, he came to the first floor and saw Chad holding Kassidy, in her pajamas, in his office. Kassidy was eating "*One of those Pop Ice* [frozen juice treats] *in the clear bags.*" (p. 130) Travis said that he could see that she was eating it, and that Chad was talking with Kassidy, "*..he'd say something. She'd say it after, pointing out parts of her face.*" Thus, Chad was teaching her words, and Travis characterized his behavior as "*Normal.*" (p. 131) When Travis left the house around 8:45-9:00 p.m., Chad had already put Kassidy to bed and was back downstairs. Travis said that he left for Irene's and told her that he "*felt bad for Kassidy because she was hurt,*" but he denied that he was upset or that he had purposefully lingered at Chad's just to make sure that Kassidy got to bed okay. (p. 132) Travis said he returned home around 11:30 p.m.-12:00 a.m. and all the lights in the house were out and he didn't see anyone up.

The next morning, November 9th, he arose around 10:00 a.m. and he was alone in the house. He listened to the phone messages, including a message from DCYF "*Just asking Chad to get a hold of them in regards to the children.*" (p. 134) He didn't pass the message on to Chad. Later that day, Chad called the Portsmouth McDonald's and Jeremy answered and passed the phone to Travis and Chad "*told me that Kassidy was in the hospital, and that he was on his way to see her. And he, you know, reminded me that I'd seen her the night before and that she was fine,* [and] *He said, 'Remember Kyle hit her with a ball?' I said 'Yes.'* " (p. 135) Travis said the Chad stopped at the Portsmouth McDonald's after the call and talked with Jeremy, but not with him.

Alan Cronheim began his cross-examination by listing Travis's three interviews with law enforcement: November 9 and 22, 2000, and October 31, 2001, including prosecutors. Cronheim asked Travis, "*So it's true that Kassidy, at one point, fell off the couch and banged herself on the coffee table?*" and Chad wasn't there and Travis agreed. (p. 139) Unfortunately, the question was no more specific about time than "*at one point.*" The jury didn't know that the coffee table injury was one of the three injuries around Kassidy's eyes on November 9th. The other two were the kitty scratch and the Tee-ball. That coffee table accident occurred approximately on Sunday evening, November 5, perhaps on the 6th.

Cronheim confirmed with Travis that he had seen, at least once, Chad take Kassidy upstairs for a time-out, and then "*spoke to her afterwards fooling around.*" (p. 140) Travis agreed that, in Cronheim's words, "*there were times where Amanda would put Kassidy in the room and actually put a sock on the door handle so she couldn't get out?*" (p. 140)

In Chapter 4, the use of a sock in Kassidy's door was introduced, using Chad's October 10, 2010 letter. He supplemented that insight in his January 14, 2011 letter.
You asked for more information about the sock in Kassidy's bedroom door. You enclosed a paragraph from Page 20 of the October "letters." When I purchased the house the bedroom doors all had several problems. For some reason, none of them closed properly. It was as if through expansion and contraction, the doors no longer fit in the frame. The solution was to take the doors off the hinges and shave them a bit, which would enable

them to close. The door in Kassidy's room had two problems. The first was the doorknob needed to be replaced to get it to latch. It had worked for a long time but something happened to it when Tom Mikoski lived in the room. The second problem was that it would swing open when you closed it. It was as if the house had settled a bit so when you closed the door, if it wasn't latched, it would swing open. So the solution was to put a sock in the top of the door and pull it closed which would create enough friction to hold the door against the frame. When using the sock, the door was left open a crack, so that it was quiet for Kassidy during a nap but cracked so that we could easily hear her when she woke. It seemed a perfect solution for when Kassidy was a baby. Surely, I would have fixed it as Kassidy aged and she was able to work the handle herse1f. The other thing that seemed practical is that we controlled the tension of the door. If the door handle was pulled more firmly as you left the room, Kassidy would not be able to open it. Like for example, nap time, when she may not have been as willing to sleep. At night, we would bring the child safety gate up to the top of the stairs, (so she couldn't fall down them if she woke up) and either leave her door open or closed less firmly so Kassidy could either come crawl into bed with us or if one of us heard her, we could go get her.

Alan then asked Travis about "*when Jeff Marshall came back to your Rochester home to leave off Kassidy...*" (p. 141) Simon Brown objected as the question seemed to be going in the direction of hearsay, and a statement by Jeff, that "*her butt might be a little red. She was being a little bitch this weekend...*" (p. 141) Cronheim said that he had the right, by the rules of evidence to ask the question because Mark Sisti had already asked Jeff Marshall on the stand if he had ever called Kassidy a "*little bitch.*" (See transcript, Dec. 7, 2001, p. 10) However, Cronheim said that the "*full statement was that she was acting like a little bitch and I had to spank her ass....*" (p. 142) Judge Nadeau allowed Cronheim to ask about the "*little bitch*" statement, but he could not ask a question that might elicit a response from Travis which might go to the "*spank her ass*" statement, because Mark Sisti had not asked Marshall about that statement when he was a witness. In other words, a question could be asked which could impeach the credibility of something a previous witness said, but not be used otherwise, as it would be hearsay. The rules of evidence are complicated. Although they are designed to protect the integrity of evidence, they sometimes were barriers to the truth.

Cronheim then asked the questions which established that Travis recalled "*three or four weeks*" prior to Kassidy's death that Jeff had brought Kassidy home and called her a "*little bitch.*" The next day, Travis was with Amanda when she was changing Kassidy's diaper and he saw black and blue underneath her diaper, and that the bruise appeared to be a "*day or two old.*" (p. 145) Thus, the jury was able to deduce that an injury had occurred while Jeff was babysitting, but the jury was not told that Jeff had said that he spanked her. Because of similar rules of evidence and criminal procedure, and because Chad did not later testify, the jury did not hear that Jeff had allegedly told Chad, "*Yeah, I spanked her so hard, my hand stung.*" (Letters, March 23, 2010)

Alan Cronheim returned Travis to the evening of November 8, and Travis affirmed Cronheim's description that Kassidy "*was playing as a 21-month-old might play in a bathtub,*" and that she was not afraid of the water. (p. 146-47) Travis agreed that he did not see any bruises on Kassidy's abdomen and that he was inside the bathroom, and not just looking in from the hall.

Cronheim then asked about Kyle, "*You played baseball with him*?" and Simon Brown objected, and Judge Nadeau asked both sets of lawyers for a bench conference. According to the transcript, Judge Nadeau began the discussion, apparently reading Brown's mind or body language, saying, "*I just think that the witness had said, 'wiffle ball'* ", and Cronheim apologized, "*Oh, I'm sorry. I didn't even realize I used the term...*" Judge Nadeau continued, "*They're interchangeable.*" and Cronheim agreed, "*Right.*" (p. 150) However, Judge Nadeau was at least partially wrong. Travis's first reference to the "ball" incident was when he testified that Chad had told him that "*Kyle had hit her with a baseball, a wiffle ball.*" (p. 118) Later, as noted above, Simon Brown emphasized that it was a wiffle ball. Further, Judge Nadeau was significantly wrong when she said that the two words were interchangeable. They are not in real life and certainly not in this case. The term "baseball" is generic and can cover all kinds of activities with a bat and ball, and the ball can be of any type, including hardball, softball, Tee-ball, tennis ball or whatever. On the other hand, a wiffle ball is a very specific, trademarked ball that is white, light and plastic and nearly weightless. The prosecution was seeking advantage by insuring that Travis's belief that it was a wiffle ball that hit Kassidy was imprinted with the jury. Even though Travis was being questioned about his own playing baseball with Kyle, the prosecution wanted the jury to believe that, if there was a baseball incident at all on the evening of November 8th, it was with a wiffle ball. Cronheim's question to Travis about playing "baseball" with Kyle was quite correct as generically stated, and Cronheim need not have apologized, and need not have conceded the point. Other witnesses, to that point had called the ball other names besides "*wiffle ball*." For example, Detective Steve Hamel said that Jeff Marshall had told him that he understood it was a "*baseball*" which hit Kassidy. Jeff had testified that he heard the term, "*baseball*." Amanda had used the term "*wiffle ball*" but she later said that even though there were a number of wiffle balls in the home, she didn't know what kind of ball hit Kassidy.

Returning to Travis, Alan Cronheim asked further about the playing "*ball*" in Kyle's room and asked Travis what Kyle had told him about his hitting the ball that hit Kassidy. Simon Brown objected on the grounds of hearsay. Judge Nadeau said that Travis could not be asked that question because Kyle's response would no longer be an "excited utterance," or "present sense impression" which are two of the exceptions to the hearsay rule. Thus, the jury did not hear what three-year-old Kyle told Travis about the earlier incident with Kassidy. The ball-hitting incident was becoming a keystone to the case. If the jury believed that the hitting of Kassidy with a heavier ball occurred, and was an accident, then it might not find that Chad had intentionally hit Kassidy that night. If the jury didn't believe that there was an accident or believe that there may have been an accident, but that a wiffle ball could not cause serious injury, or even a bruise, then the door was open to conviction. The defense had to convince the jury that the incident was real and with a heavier ball. Without Chad's testimony, it was very difficult.

Alan Cronheim asked about Travis's November 22, 2000 interview with the police where they showed him autopsy photos of Kassidy's body. Travis agreed with Cronheim's assessment,

You indicated that the bruising that they showed you that day... was different from the bruising that you saw on November 8th, 2000, right... And you told them that if you'd seen the bruising that you saw in those photographs, you would have called the police? (p. 161)

<u>Irene Ricci</u>

Simon Brown examined Irene, who said she knew Travis from their working at McDonald's and that their relationship was romantic for a time in 2000. She said that on the evening of November 8th, Travis arrived at her house around 9-9:30 p.m., which was later than usual and that she was annoyed. She said that Travis apologized and explained that "*Kassidy and Kyle were playing together, and she had gotten hurt. So he had stayed to make sure she was okay. He said he stayed, and she was sleeping when he left.*" (p. 168)

Irene said she was sure about the date, because she used to drive by Chad's house every morning to take her child to the babysitter, and on the morning of November 10, she saw the yellow caution tape there, and learned what happened when she arrived at work.

The judge then called for the afternoon break, and during that break there was an altercation between one or more people close to the case. Before the jury returned from that break, Judge Nadeau cautioned everyone to be civil, or she would impose penalties or take other steps.

After the jury returned, Alan Cronheim cross-examined Irene, and confirmed that Travis did not seem "*overly concerned*" about Kassidy when he visited with Irene on November 8th. (p. 174)

<u>Herbert Leighton</u>

Simon Brown examined Maine State Police Detective Herbert Leighton, a crime-scene investigator, who had searched the home of Jeff Marshall on the evening of November 9, 2000. His task was to "*document the residence and look for certain items of evidence.*" (p. 177) Detective Leighton said he arrived around 9:00 p.m. at Jeff's and entered the home through the porch, into the kitchen. He described the apartment, "*To the left of the kitchen was a bathroom. To the right of the kitchen was a living room, and straight ahead was the single bedroom.*" (p. 177)

In describing his work, Detective Leighton said he usually takes photographs of the "*incident scene.*" (p. 179) Then he looked in each room for any protrusions which might have caused the abrasions on Kassidy's feet, and he didn't find any. He described how he took photos of every room and searched for evidence of fluids on every object. For the jury, he described the contents of several State Exhibit photos. Simon Brown asked him explicitly about State Exhibit 69 which showed adult pants over mail on the bed, and Detective Leighton had said that he put those items on that location on the bed. He "*seized*" several items of clothing, and also a bowl of "Spaghetti-O's soup" from the sink. Detective Leighton didn't know, but "Spaghetti-O's" was a typical lunch fare for Kassidy at Jeff's, and she liked them. As she wasn't at Jeff's for lunch on Wednesday the 8th, and didn't eat a prepared meal on the 9th, the bowl in the sink was likely from Tuesday's lunch.

He completed his search at about 11:45 p.m. and then filled out an inventory which listed the items he was taking. He then noticed that a man and a woman were in a vehicle outside, and after identifying the man as Jeff, Det. Leighton told him that the search was over and he returned to him the keys to his apartment and gave him a copy of the inventory of items taken. Also arriving at the scene at the end of his search and at that late hour was Maine State Police Detective Angela Blodgett, who discussed the case with him.

Detective Leighton explained how he looks for trace signs of blood and human fluids and how some items were taken "*to the lab, in their sterile environment,* [where] *they may be able to find some biological fluid on those sheets, and DNA.*" (p. 188) This was the first mention of DNA in the trial, but the prosecution did not ask the Maine State Police Detective the logical followup question, of whether any DNA tests had actually been done. Simon Brown asked Detective Leighton about any items which were taken which might have blood on them. Leighton described "*a wrapper, a yellow, looked like a fast-food wrapper, which was located by the head of the bed by the pillow, and it had a transfer stain on it, red/brown transfer stain, appeared to be blood....*" (p. 190) He did not describe any other items seized with apparent blood stains on them. Specifically, he did not mention that Kassidy's pink jacket appeared to have blood stains.

Mark Sisti thus began his cross-examination with the predictable followup question about "*any other serology stuff you seized, anything for blood?*" Detective Leighton answered, "*No,*" but was asked more specifically, "*Sheets or anything like that?*" and he acknowledged that he "*did seize two sheets so that the crime lab could take a look at it, and look for trace evidence and biological fluids.*" (p. 191) Then Mark Sisti showed Det. Leighton several photographs that he took of seized items including a sheet which had "*red/brown stains.*" (p. 193) In the process, Sisti had the photos marked as Defense Exhibits.

Mark Sisti asked Detective Leighton if he went into the basement and he said that he didn't. He said, "*I could have gone into the basement, but I don't have any recollection.*" (p. 197) It was a curious admission, as there were only approximately five interior doors in the apartment, all within 20 feet of one another, and one of them led to the basement. Detective Leighton said that he would likely have taken one or more photos of the basement, and finally, "*I don't even know that there was a basement.*" (p. 199)

Sisti then asked about the red pajama bottoms in the photo and whether Detective Leighton and posed a hypothetical question, "*Well, if ... there was no reason for those pajama bottoms to have come off that child, then that would have been an important or interesting aspect of your crime scene investigation, right?*" and Detective Leighton agreed.(p. 199-200) He said that he had no information from the investigation at that point that anyone had said anything about taking off Kassidy's clothing. Leighton said he reported no indication of a diaper change at the apartment, and Sisti reminded him that his report said there were no used diapers to be found in the home.

Mark Sisti did not ask about pajama tops, as he seemed to understand that the red/white dress functioned as Kassidy's pajama tops. The solid red pajama tops were never listed as a seized item. Similarly, Detective Leighton's search did not locate the Sippy cup that Amanda brought with Kassidy. He did not mention the diaper bag which was always part of the Kassidy routine at Jeff's. It was used as a general traveling bag, too, and contained snacks that Chad packed that morning.

Sisti did not ask Leighton about his search of Chad's car, during which no evidence of any kind of assault was found.

Detective Leighton said that Jeff Marshall had told him that Kassidy had eaten some of her cereal from her baggie.

MEDIA:
1. "Many saw bruises before tot's death - Evans murder trial continues for seventh day today"
2. "Jury hears more from ex-wife of man charged in baby death"
3. "Judge allows cellmate's testimony to stand"
4. "Testimony will stand - Motion to dismiss account by Evans' former cellmate denied by judge"

Wednesday, 12 December 2001

Cathy Nuernberg

Examined by Simon Brown, Cathy said she knew Amanda from a former workplace, when Cathy was a senior at Sanford High School and Amanda was pregnant. Cathy lived in San Antonio, Texas where she waited on tables and went to college. She said that when Kassidy was a younger baby, she "*was a very good little girl. She was very happy most of the time; playful, but not overly excited. I want to say that.*" (p. 6-7)

Simon Brown asked if Cathy was concerned about Kassidy's development and she said, "*I was always concerned, because just the fact that Amanda was young, and that sort of thing. I wasn't concerned with her immediate health until the very end of the last summer I was here*," which was 2000. (p. 7) Cathy seemed to have a good sense of time, as she correctly stated that Amanda met Chad at "*the beginning of June of 2000.*" (p. 8) and Cathy continued, "*She liked him instantly. I could tell that right off. And it moved very quickly.... I think she moved in within a month of them meeting each other.*" She said that she visited Amanda at Chad's about once a week. She wasn't asked about, and didn't mention, that her first visit to Chad's was Sunday, June 4, when she and Amanda came over from Sanford and they spent the night there.

Alan Cronheim objected to Brown's questions to Cathy about the nature or quality of Amanda's relationship to Chad, stating that it was irrelevant and it was her opinion, rather than evidence. Simon Brown indicated that he wanted to move the questioning to the area of Amanda's alleged submissiveness to Chad. Judge Nadeau permitted the questioning to continue, as she said, and outside the hearing of the jury,

I find that the evidence is relevant because it explains Amanda Bortner's decision to stay with the defendant. It explains Amanda Bortner's decision to hide the abuse of Kassidy. It explains Amanda's minimizing at trial compared to her statements she made pretrial...." (p. 11-12)

Judge Nadeau was reflecting the prosecution's view that Amanda was a battered woman, who was unable to leave. However, as Amanda didn't believe that she or Kassidy was being abused, her decision to stay with Chad could be attributed to softer motivations, such as love and her belief in his character and good parenting skills. Also, there was already evidence that she had considered getting her own apartment, as Chad was having difficulty getting through his divorce with Tristan. Chad still thought until shortly after Kassidy's death, that he was legally married, and he didn't seem entirely ready for an official live-in arrangement with Amanda. This was another issue where it would have been helpful to return Amanda to the stand for further clarification.

In his letter to his attorneys of November 2000, Chad wrote of the situation and his ambivalence,

...but the major mental block I had going through my head was that I was very badly hurt in my relationship with Tristan and I didn't want to fall for anyone again or admit to myself I had. She basically lived with me from July but when she ever talked about moving her dresser in, I had a fit. I would say, "I am not ready for a live-in girlfriend," and she would get pissed and say "What the fuck, I do live here Chad. I haven't been home in months." My feeling on the education front was, I was paying for everything for Amanda and Kassidy and had no problems doing so, but I wasn't about to put another woman through school and have her leave me also. If she moved to Maine and I couldn't have lived without her, I would have brought her back, moved her in, and paid for her education but I wanted to see how things would be first.

Simon Brown continued with his examination of Cathy, who said that in Amanda's relationship with Gabe Snyder, "*Amanda was definitely the dominant of the two. She had control of the relationship.*" (p. 14) "*... when she was with Gabe, she wasn't a household person at all. She was always out. And she was out with him all the time...*" (p. 15) Not said at the trial was the fact that Amanda's control began with her knowledge that Gabe was not the father of Kassidy, though she had led him to believe that he was. Another factor which surely affected Cathy's observation was that she testified that she was "*best friends*" with Gabe in eighth grade and had known him for "*quite some time.*" (p. 14) She didn't know Chad until 2000.

Cathy said that she visited Amanda at Chad's about once a week, and continued, "*When she was dating Chad, she was submissive. She was the exact opposite. She was nervous of being late... or that she had to let him know where she was, things like that.*" (p. 14-15) Asked about changes for Amanda, Cathy said, "*Yes. She started to cook. She became very particular about his house, making sure it was clean. That's pretty much it.*" (p. 15)

Regarding Kassidy and Chad, Cathy said that she often saw Kassidy and Chad at the house together, but she recalled only one

particular instance where... Kassidy was crying and Amanda was going to pick her up, and Chad did not want her to be picked up because he felt as though she was spoiled.... He pretty much told Amanda not to pick her up, and just seemed really kind of harsh about it.... He was angry. (p. 16)

Asked if she saw "*any problems with Kassidy injury-wise,*" Cathy said she visited one day, when Chad was not home and

I could instantly tell when I came in that she [Kassidy] *seemed different that day. I asked Amanda if she was sick or what was wrong, because she was acting very withdrawn.... I instantly noticed bruises on her face... marks on her face that looked like someone had grabbed her. And then she also had a bruise on her forehead... She had two bruises on one side of her face as large as fingerprints, and the other side was -- looked like a thumb print...on the other side of her face... cheeks.* (p. 17)

Cathy said that the bruises on cheeks was "*purple or dark purple*" and the bruise on the forehead was "*larger, but it... didn't seem as recent. It was more faded in color.*" (p. 17-18)

Cathy said that Amanda and she argued about the bruising, "*She told me the* [cause of the] *forehead* [injury] *was that when Chad had had Kassidy on his shoulders he was walking down the stairs and Kassidy had hit her head on the wall coming down the stairs. She wouldn't explain to me what the grab marks were.*" (p. 18) Asked about later explanations given by Amanda, Cathy testified, "*She did give me the story of Kassidy falling off the trampoline.*" (p. 18)

Simon Brown asked Cathy when she saw the bruising and she replied that she left for Texas at the end of September, thus the referenced observation "*was earlier in September.*" (p. 19) If Cathy's recollection about her departure date for Texas was correct, then she must have seen that bruising between the time of Kassidy's September 11 appointment with Dr. Timoney, about which the jury did not know, and Sunday, September 24 which is when Kassidy was with Jacqueline while Chad and Amanda were at Martha's Vineyard. As Cathy said that she visited Amanda about once a week or every other week, and that she made only one observation of the bruises noted above, she must have made her observation at her last visit with Amanda before leaving for Texas. However, according to Amanda in her third police interview (p. 86) and according to Jacqueline in her testimony in court, above, (p. 18) Cathy was with Amanda on Sunday, October 1, when the Bortner/Conley family was moving to Buckfield and when the photo of Kassidy with her bunny rabbit was taken. Thus, Cathy must have left for Texas no earlier than Monday, October 2.

Not only must these injuries have occurred before Sunday, September 24, but they must have cleared up completely by that time, and not been caused after September 17. Thus, they might have been caused between the Sept. 11 doctor appointment and September 17, which is a short window. Travis Hunt moved to Chad's home in mid-September, and he did not report or testify about seeing such bruising at that time.

Cathy then described how she returned to Maine for Kassidy's funeral and then returned to Texas with Amanda afterwards. She said that Amanda returned to New England from Texas around Christmas. It was actually December 18, so she was close.

Alan Cronheim cross-examined Cathy, and reminded her of her testimony before the grand jury in August 2001 about the injury to Kassidy's foot that was thought to have been caused by a curling iron at their friend, Crystal Martin's, house. Cathy agreed that the foot injury and her one day's observations of injuries in September were the only observations.

Cathy agreed that Amanda's learning to cook and keeping Chad's house clean at a time when she wasn't working were "*things that might be part of many typical relationships.*" (p 23) Also, she agreed that she had encouraged Amanda to find a lawyer to represent her.

Simon Brown, on redirect, reconfirmed with Cathy that she first left for Texas at the end of September 2000, and he reconfirmed that Cathy never saw Amanda cook nor clean house when she lived with Gabe Snyder. The State Attorneys General seemed so convinced that they were prosecuting a child murderer and wife/significant-other batterer that they were willing to see significance in any ambiguous behavior that could be interpreted their way. Couldn't Amanda's different responses to her situation with Gabe and Chad been about the difference in her love for each, and her age difference? In my own personal experience, I used to make my bed before I joined the U.S. Army in 1968. After the Army, and its compusory bed making, I didn't make my bed daily. My wife insists that the bed be made daily, so she makes it. What does that mean about my criminal nature? Or about my submissiveness or chauvinism? Not much.

Chad wrote in his Chad January 20, 2010 letter about Amanda and their relationship,

Amanda did a lot for me when we lived in Rochester too. She took great pride in keeping our house clean. She helped a lot with Kyle, picking him up or taking him to school; she loved spending time with him and Kassidy together. I think Amanda felt good about where she was living. Right before she started staying with me, I was thinking of hiring a part-time housekeeper. After my marriage to Tristan fell apart, I realized that there were far more important things to worry about or spend your time on than a clean house and living orderly. Amanda wouldn't hear of it, stating that she would be happy to keep everything up. She did a beautiful job even though I had a white German Shepherd that shed like nothing you've ever seen. Kato was the best dog in the world, but man did he shed hair.

Not caring about the housework was a major sign to me at "how far I had come." I grew up in a house where my mother had everything GI clean....

Amanda's friend Cathy thought that Amanda was submissive to me where she dominated a previous relationship. I'm sure from Cathy's perspective it seemed that way. Cathy hung out with us several times and Amanda alone especially in the beginning. The relationship was new and we both wanted to impress each other as with all new relationships. But anyone that knows Amanda can tell you she is far from submissive. We spent extended periods of time with Amanda's friend Mary Bullard, my brother Jason, Vanessa Mansson, Jeremy Hinton, and Bruce Aube, among others, and they would paint a different picture. Amanda was very assertive. I actually enjoyed this, it was the opposite of what I was used to with Tristan, where it seemed like I decided everything. I made all the decisions all day long at work. It was nice to not have to come home and make them too. Amanda would decide what was for dinner, who we would hang out with on an upcoming day off, (other than when Patriots were playing.) She decided what we would do with free time. Amanda even laid out the shirt and tie that she wanted me to wear the next day.

William Magee

Examined by Simon Brown, New Hampshire State Police Sergeant William Magee was the head of the "crime scene unit" and he conducted the search of Chad's home on November 10, 2000. Sergeant Magee said he was assisted by Sergeant Susan Forey, Trooper Robert Estabrook, and by Trooper Jeff Linscott of the Maine State Police. Prosecutor Brown then introduced several photographs into evidence, along with items seized from Chad's home, including several different types of balls. Magee said he seized every ball in the house that he found. Chad had told the police that the ball that hit Kassidy on the evening of November 8 was a "*starter baseball*" and "*hard rubber ball.*" The State's photograph Exhibit 17 is important because it has such a ball in the photographs marked as #11. Sergeant Magee described it as "*a baseball. It's a hardball. Well, spongy hardball.*" (p. 46) Chad recalls that there were two Tee-balls in the ball collection in the toy wheelbarrow, and that this ball was likely one of them, and may have been the ball that hit Kassidy.

Also seized was every baseball bat (using the term "baseball" generically) and Brown asked Magee if he had found "*a long yellow wiffle ball bat,*" and Magee said "*No, not that I recall.*" (p. 56) The purpose of the question was to impeach the credibility of Travis's testimony about what he heard and saw on the evening of November 8th, and specifically that when he pitched Kyle some wiffle balls that evening, Kyle was hitting them with such a yellow wiffle ball bat. (See above, with reference to page 126 of Travis's testimony.)

Chad wrote about the bat in his April 6, 2010 letter,

I do remember the state trying to make a HUGE deal about Travis testifying that it was a regular wiffle ball bat that Kyle was using. He described it as a skinny yellow bat. I mean, come on, he was testifying a year after the event. The prosecutors went over it in their closing statement, that Travis got the color wrong. As if to say, Travis was lying, or trying to cover for me. Ninety million yellow wiffle ball bat and ball sets are sold each year. Is it really that big of a stretch that Travis would call it a yellow bat? I think the point Travis was alluding to was that it was a PLASTIC bat.

Sergeant Magee said that he listened to the messages on Chad's answering machine, "*the first message being a message from a member of DCYF, Department of Children and Youth Services. And that message indicated that the call was concerning the children, and asked for a return call.*" (p 56) The correct name is "Division of Children, Youth and Families," which is part of the NH Dept. of Health and Human Services, but Magee may have been referring to the Dept.'s former name.

Simon Brown's direct examination concluded with an estimate of the duration of the search, and Sergeant Magee said, "*probably eight to ten hours.*" (p. 56)

Mark Sisti cross-examined Sergeant Magee and established that he searched every room in the house, including the basement. As with other questions, Sisti was trying to persuade the jury that the search of Jeff Marshall's home by the Maine State Police was inadequate. Magee agreed that there were no pieces of evidence that were seized with any indication of suspicious body fluids which might have needed to be sent directly to a crime lab. However, just in case, many items, such as Kassidy's sheets were sent to the lab to see if suspicious fluids could be found. Magee agreed with Sisti that if a stain were detected, "*... you would want it to be thoroughly analyzed to the point where you could determine whether or not that particular stain was human blood... and.. whether or not it had the same DNA characteristics, right*?" (p. 64) This was the second mention of DNA at Chad's trial, and still no reference was made to DNA tests conducted by the Maine State Police Lab of the material underneath Kassidy's fingernails and on the Wendy's wrapper or napkin, and a paper towel.

Mark Sisti asked about a photograph, Defense Exhibit F, of the trash pulled from a bag in Chad's kitchen and Sergeant Magee confirmed that there was a half-eaten banana in the photo. The significance of that banana was not emphasized to the jury at the time, but it corroborated what Chad said to the police during his November 9 interview (p. 14) about Kassidy eating half a banana on the evening of November 8. The jury might have wondered how a man who cared enough about Kassidy to feed her a banana could have beaten her beforehand, or afterwards.

Sisti then asked about the balls which were seized, and Magee agreed that he had been advised that the ball that may have hit Kassidy on the 8th "*was described as a hard, rubber ball*," which description corresponded exactly to what Chad had told the Maine State Police in his interview. (p. 57) Then Mark Sisti asked Magee to describe the ball which was identified as State's Exhibit 17, which he said was a "*Stossaburg T-ball*," (p. 72) and "*it's very flexible, but it's a hard rubber, as well*." (p. 72) This was a ball Chad identified in 2010 which could have been the ball which hit Kassidy. Sisti then showed Magee the ball marked as State's Exhibit 16, which was also identified as a T-ball, and Magee said, "*It's a little firmer, but it's the same basic thing*." (p. 73) Sergeant Magee agreed that he had found those balls on the second floor of Chad's house and that there were balls everywhere on that floor, and agreed with Sisti's characterization that "*It appeared as though they had recently been used...*" (p. 74)

On redirect, Simon Brown specifically opened a new subject, "*Did you see any evidence of mice, or anything like that*?" (p. 77) It was an unusual question, unless Brown already knew the answer. Magee responded, "*Again, I don't recall seeing anything like that. Oh, the mice cubes....*" It appeared that Magee knew of the prosecution's interest in presenting this item to the jury. Brown then asked Magee, "*What is that?*" Magee responded, "*I'm not too certain. I guess it looks like it's to control mice, whether it's a poison or mouse poison.*" (p. 78) Among the other items in the photo of the trash, Brown seemed to want the jury to know that there was poison in the trash. It was apparently discarded along with a half of a banana, perhaps where Kassidy could have retrieved the poison or the banana and eaten either. However, Magee's testimony was incorrect. "Mice Cube" is a brand name for a humane, non-toxic trap for mice, which can then be released outdoors. Coincidentally, it's sold by a New Hampshire company, Pied Piper International in New Castle, and it's manufactured in Manchester. The subject was not addressed again at the trial, so the jury was left with the incorrect impression that Amanda and Chad were careless about the disposal of poisons in a house with young children. It's not known if this point in Magee's testimony was one of those times when Chad passed a short note to Sisti about a problem in a witness's testimony.

Chad wrote in 2011 that

I switched from using traditional "Snap" mousetraps when Tristan moved in with Brent who was then 2 1/2 years old, because I didn't want him to ever accidentally set a off a trap and get hurt. Any harmful chemicals that we had in the cellar were kept in an area that the kids never went into. The cabinet under our sink in the kitchen had child safety latches on it... Back to the traps ... I preferred to use these "Heart" traps because it trapped the mouse alive. About the time I started having children my attitudes about life and other living things changed some. I had nothing personal against these mice. I just didn't want them in my house. When I would catch a mouse I would use it as a lesson for the boys. They could study it in the cube and I would later release it in a small "pull off" wooded area, across from Lone Oaks Ice Cream stand or another location (usually on my way to work the next day). On occasion, if I didn't check on a trap often enough and the mouse apparently suffocated, I would take the mouse body outside and throw it out into the woods, down the steep embankment behind our house where the kids never went. In those instances, I wouldn't even re-use the trap, instead throwing it in our outside garbage can. I wouldn't even throw the trap into our inside garbage because the kids used that trash, who knows what kind of disease the mouse might have been carrying. Both Kyle and Brent have a love and respect for. animals today and I am convinced that this started with our treatment of the mice when they were little. I know I have gotten off the subject of the "poisonous" mousetraps but this kind of things fires me up. It goes back to my question,

"What kind of monster do people think I am." I am human, careless at times, but usually aware where my kids are concerned. It's clear to me that the prosecutors had no clue of who I was. Yeah, some of that may have been our fault for not trying to put on an defense but some of it has to be attributed to the state of prosecutions today. They clearly had no desire to really know who I was either. (Letter, Aug. 2, 2011)

Returning to Magee's testimony, he said that after the initial search on November 10th, his unit had received a report of the abrasions on the bottoms of Kassidy's feet, and his unit went back to Chad's home to search for any objects which could have caused such injuries. Several items were seized, but none were determined to be able to cause the abrasions on Kassidy's feet. Sisti asked Sergeant Magee if Jeff Marshall's home had been searched for any such implements, and Magee said that he didn't know. This was another example of where Sisti could have asked Detective Leighton that same question, but didn't, and Leighton could have been recalled.

At the end of Sergeant Magee's testimony, Mark Sisti made a request to Judge Nadeau saying, *"... I know we haven't been doing this throughout the course of the trial, but could we preserve Sergeant Magee as a witness in the event we have to recall?"* (p. 80) No such request was made for any other witness and no witness was ever recalled in this trial. It would have been a productive way to higthlight and clarify some of the contradictory testimony which had emerged during the trial. For example, Amanda could have been recalled to respond to the testimony of others, including Jennifer, Jeff and Cathy Nuernberg. Sgt. Magee could have been recalled, and a new "Mice Cube" package could have been introduced as an exhibit and he could have been asked again about the product, and been asked to read to the jury the large print on the package: "SAFE, CLEAN, SILENT, RE-USABLE, HUMANE, EASY-TO-USE... AND IT WORKS! WILL NOT HARM CHILDREN OR PETS."

Mary Bullard

Simon Brown examined Mary Bullard, who was a best friend of Amanda in high school, but she had not seen Amanda since Kassidy was only a few months old. Their relationship resumed after Kassidy died, as Amanda needed a friend. Mary described her life with Amanda in the summer of 2001 in a camper in the woods on land owned by Chad's grandparents in Vernon, Vermont. She said that Chad came to the campsite a few days a week. Nothing that Mary was asked had anything to do with the death of Kassidy Bortner. It was all about the State trying to show that Chad was violating his bail condition, and was therefore disrespectful of law, which had already been established the previous August when his bail was revoked.

Alan Cronheim thanked Mary for coming but did not cross-examine her.

Lance McCleish

Maine State Police Detective Lance McCleish was examined by Will Delker, with the purpose of preparing the jury for viewing the redacted videotape of his interview of Chad. McCleish said his role in the investigation was to interview Jennifer Bortner Conley and then Chad. The other interviewer of Chad was Rick LeClair, who had interviewed Amanda before joining McCleish to interview Chad. The jury then watched the videotape, and afterwards the jury was dismissed for the day.

MEDIA:

1. "Evans: I didn't do it - Murder suspect told police during interview he didn't want tot's death 'pinned' on him"
2. Jury hears about Bortner - Evans says in taped statement to police that she would hit Kassidy, call her names"
3. "Jury sees videotape of Evans' interview"
4. "Jury hears taped police interview with Evans"
5. "Jury sees Evans in taped interview with investigators"

Thursday, 13 December 2001

The court opened with procedural issues about the resumption of Cory Merrill's testimony.

In addition to Merrill's allegations that Chad made statements to him when they shared a cell, there was an additional claim that Chad had threatened Merrill when they were inexplicably placed in the same van for the trip back to the jail during the current trial. Delker argued to the judge, "*...I think that threats ... intimidation by the defendant against a witness are exactly the type of evidence probative of the defendant's consciousness of guilt...*" (p. 10) However, even if Chad did have words with Merrill, there is a perfectly reasonable other interpretation which is that Chad was legitimately angry with Merrill for making false statements about him in court. Alan Cronheim argued that there was only one Corrections Officer who made allegations of Chad's threatening actions and she had been working at the prison for only a very short time. Cronheim said that Merrill's lies were the real problem, including his statement that Chad had said that he had used a belt to punish Kassidy. Cronheim noted that no other witness had ever said anything about a belt.

The lawyers and the judge considered the State's motion to have the videotape of Chad's police interview accepted as a "full exhibit," which meant that it could be brought back to the jury room for deliberations. Previously, it had been admitted as an exhibit "for identification." Judge Nadeau ruled that it would be a "full exhibit," to the extent that the jury could have the videotape, but could not bring the copies of the transcript to the deliberations.

The third issue for the pre-testimony bench conference was the State's plan to have Scott Hampton testify about family violence. Simon Brown said that Hampton could be expected to testify about

...the factors which may lead a victim of domestic violence to make inconsistent statements about that violence...[and] *about factors which may lead a victim of domestic violence to remain loyal to the perpetrator despite the abusive acts or not...*[and] *about the factors which may lead a partner who witnessed her partner to abuse another family member to remain with the perpetrator despite the abuse and not take steps to intervene.*" (p. 19)

Alan Cronheim argued that such testimony would be highly speculative and prejudicial and that there were many possible explanations for Amanda's behavior besides the interpretation which Scott Hampton might be expected to present. He said, "*...the State is trying to make... Amanda appear to be a battered woman without a legitimate foundation for it.*" (p. 24) He noted that Scott Hampton led several of the court-ordered domestic violence sessions that Chad attended in 1999 and that Chad has talked with him. Such a previous relationship is not appropriate for a neutral expert. His proposed testimony, said Cronheim, "*was more prejudicial than probative...*" (p. 27) Later, Judge Nadeau declared that Hampton's testimony would not be permitted.

In that continued bench conference, in order to assist Judge Nadeau in scheduling, Mark Sisti told her, "*I'll be pretty candid here. I don't think our case is going to take more than about a day,...*" (p. 32) Later, he said that Dr. Baden might be the defense's only witness.

Before McCleish resumed his testimony, Will Delker observed that Bruce Aube was in the courtroom. As he was on the defense witness list, he had not previously been permitted to attend the trial and hear what other witnesses were saying. Alan Cronheim told the judge and the prosecutors that Bruce would not be testifying for the defense, so his presence in the courtroom was permitted. This was an example of one source of frustration with the trial by Chad's potential witness friends and relatives which was that they had not been allowed to see the trial, and now the reason for that exclusion had vanished, at least for Bruce. It was not yet known that the defense would call only one witness, Dr. Michael Baden.

<u>Lance McCleish (resumed)</u>

Mark Sisti cross-examined Detective McCleish, who stated that his supervisor, Sergeant Matthew Stewart, was monitoring the Chad's interview with a remote video system "*and was aware of the interview as it progressed.*" (p. 47) McCleish acknowledged that he did not tell Chad that the interview was being videotaped, nor that another person was monitoring the interview. Sisti challenged McCleish's quickly-formed belief that Chad had abused Kassidy by showing that he didn't know a lot of the information which pointed to Jeff Marshall. However McCleish did have some information, and said,

The more I spoke to Chad, in comparison to the information that I had been given, it appeared that what he was telling me was minimizing some of the abuse. And, in fact, leaving out some abuse that I'd been briefed about from the Amanda Bortner interviews.... Well, when the discrepancies start to crop up in an interview, it raises suspicions on my part." (p. 72-73)

While acknowledging that he was not an expert, McCleish stated that he understood that Kassidy died of a "*closed-head injury*," which in

...my experience of it, it develops over a period of time.... it doesn't occur within an hour or two. It happens over time..... So when I said that she would ... have had that injury prior to being dropped off at Jeff Marshall's house, that was my experience, that it would have happened over a longer period of time." (p. 86)

Detective McCleish agreed that Chad was cooperative and did not have any problem with a search of his home.

McCleish did acknowedge during Sisti's cross-examination that he told Chad during his interrogation that he, McCleish, had received some of his understanding of Kassidy's death directly from a doctor. In the interrogation, he said to Chad, "*what the **doctors have told me** is ...is some of her symptoms indicate some kind of a, a closed head injury which means something happened in there, in her head.*" (Chad Interrogation, Nov. 9, page 1592) (emphasis added)

At Chad's trial, Sisti challenged McCleish on the reliabilityof what he told Chad about Kassidy's death, "*Well, you didn't speak to the physician, right?*" and McCleish replied, "*No, I did not.*" (p. 52) A few seconds later, there was a similar exchange, "*You didn't talk to a doctor, right?*" and "*No, I did not.*" (p. 53) Thus, McCleish misspoke when he told Chad in his interrogation that "*...doctors have told me...*" This was one of two clear instances of where the police had misrepresented facts in order to obtain answers or cooperation from an interviewee. The other was when Detective Baker told Jeremy Hinton that Jeff had taken a lie detector test. Whether McCleish lied to Chad is a matter of intent. Maybe what he meant to say was, "what the doctors have told **us**," meaning the police, and that would have been more accurate. As was noted earlier in this book, Angela Blodgett once told Amanda, "*I think everybody lies.*"

On redirect examination by Will Delker, Detective McCleish said,

The information that I had been given was that he had -- the abuse was more -- was at a greater extent than what Mr. Evans had indicated to me. I had been briefed that he actually held her, the baby under water, not just splashed water in her face. And now that the baby was afraid of water. because of that; that ...when he was angry, he would grab her by the face; that he had thrown her into a hollow door three-plus times a week; that he called her stupid, a bitch, brat, things of that nature; that he had choked her on one occasion....And the information that Mr. Evans was giving me seemed to be minimized..." (p. 100)

The alternative, which wasn't fully explored at the trial was that the other information receied by the police was "maximized," to coin a new term, or greatly exaggerated. For example, how did McCleish's belief in Jeff's statements of Kassidy's alleged fear of water fare when confronted with the reality of nearly-nightly baths for Kassidy, including a fear-free bath given to Kassidy by Chad on the evening of November 8? This was another example of where allegations about Chad would have been found wanting when matched with the relevant evidence. Similarly, if Kassidy had been thrown "*into a hollow door three-plus times a week*" there surely would have been some tissue or mark or something on that door at Chad's home. None was found, because none existed and no such throwing occurred.

Will Delker did ask McCleish about specific Questions and Answers in the transcript, and on recross-examination, Mark Sisti did the same. One disputed section was where Chad seemed to indicate that he wanted the interview to end, but then seemed to indicate otherwise after some water was brought to him, but these were issues about the fairness of the interview and not about the content.

Sisti did ask about one response by Chad in the interview where he expressed his hesitancy about taking Kassidy to the hospital with bruises, saying, "*I don't want anybody thinking I'm bringing this kid to the hospital*" [and thinking that I abused her] (p. 115) Lance McCleish's interpretation was that, "*He's concerned of his own well-being, instead of the child,*" and Sisti responded, "*He was concerned - you know what? He was concerned the night before that they may falsely accuse him, right?*" (p. 115) and McCleish agreed. This was a key irony in the case which that Chad's partial reluctance to seek medical attention in order to avoid false accusations by medical people, led to what he considered false accusations by the police and prosecutors. His fears were very reasonable and he continues to pay a price for those false accusations.

Margaret Greenwald

Will Delker examined Dr. Greenwald, the Maine Chief Medical Examiner who performed Kassidy's autopsy. She said that she was certified as a forensic pathologist, which she defined as specialists in "*determining the medicolegal causes of death, primarily death that might occur from trauma, or suicide or very sudden and unexpected deaths. And we have a special expertise in looking at wounds and injuries.*" (p. 120) Of the 2000-plus autopsies that she had performed in her career, she estimated that about 100 involved the deaths of children, and about 25-30, the deaths of children due to child abuse.

Of the types of death, Dr. Greenwald said "*There are four major classifications: homicide, suicide, accident and natural, and then there is the occasional death which we, as medical examiners, have to put in the category of undetermined.*" (p. 124) In this case, she determined, "*Kassidy's death was a homicide,*" (p. 126) which was due to "*Multiple blunt-force injuries.*" (p. 127)

Using photographs and diagrams, and in response to questions from Will Delker, Dr. Greenwald identified 100 injuries or bruises which are listed and numbered below:

1, 2. "*...up on the forehead... these are all essentially on the top of the forehead. These are all bruises. They are somewhat variable in color...The middle of the forehead, you can observe an oval-shaped, brown bruise,...* (p. 132)

2. "*...similarly, in between the two eyebrows, it's a little more elongated.*" (p. 132)

3. "*Here, in between these two, there's sort of curvilinear. It's more of a reddish bruise that goes up around from above the left eyebrow up the middle of the forehead....but is sort of comes down almost in a tent-like shape, and there's for of an empty area here. It looks like this may be one uninterrupted bruise, but it may be two, as well.*" (p. 132-33)

4, 5. "*...a couple of lighter bruises above the right eyebrow.* (p. 134)

6. "*Underneath the right eye, there are a number of abrasions.....a bruise should not have a break in the surface. It should be bleeding under the skin. It may be red, it may be blue, it may be purple. If' it's older, it may be a different color. An abrasion is a scrape, an actual break in the skin surface, usually just superficial. And that's what was seen here underneath Kassidy's eye. ...* (p. 135)

7. "*There is an area of bruising underneath that abrasion. It's just slightly discolored underneath that abrasion...there's discoloration under the areas of the abrasion that you see the multiple scratches on the skin.*" (p. 135-36)

8, 9, 10. "*...there were a few small bruises over the left eyelid on Kassidy.*" (p. 136)

11. "*...there's this large area here that extends from the bridge of the nose along the cheek bone here, the zygomatic ridge, all the way over underneath her eye. That's almost two inches long....you could see that there's almost a straight edge on the bottom area right in here.*" (p. 136)

12,13 "*Underneath this elongated bruise here, there's sort of a cluster of little hemorrhages, petechial hemorrhages, which may be another bruise.*" (p. 135)

14. "*...then you lose it.. but you have this second curvilinear injury that kind of comes from the angle of the lips here up underneath this bruise that extends across from the bridge of the nose. This curvilinear injury also has two sort[s] of tiny, little parallel lines that go down from towards the bottom of the chin.*" (p. 136)
15, 16, 17. "*There are a few other small bruises there.*" (p. 136-37)
18, 19. "*On the left forehead, there are two larger bruises up here that you can see,...*(p. 137)
20. "*...there are a couple of smaller ones in that area.."* (p. 138)
21. "*You can see that there is a bruise that goes to the side of the left eye here. ...this area here under the eye is the extension of that bruise that you saw across the left cheek. So this is the same one...*" (p. 138)
22, 23 "*There are also two smaller --just pinpoint little bruises on the cheek there.*" (p. 138)
24. "*And then this area here, this bruise is actual*[ly] *what was documented on the diagram over there on the chin, on the left side of* [the] *chin. This is a larger bruise there.*" (p. 138)
25. "*And then this area, this bruise here on the chin is represented on the diagram, on the chin diagram.*" (p. 138)
26. Moving to the right side of her head...."*Kassidy still has the neck brace on that we put on in the hospital.*" "*...one of the bruises... is a little bit obscured by the neck brace.*" (p. 139)
27, 28, 29. "*But there are a few smaller bruises that are here in front of the ear.*" (p. 139)
30. "*..there's a big purple bruise on the ear, which you can actually see on both sides of the ear.*" (p. 139)
31. "*There is another oval-shaped bruise on the right-hand side.*" (p. 140)
32,33, 34 "*...right under the chin and extending over on the right side, there are some bruises here. I think you can see better in the smaller picture*
35. *that the bruises under the chin are almost entirely surrounded by a very light bruise....*" (p. 142)
36, 37. "*...and then, within that area, there are two darker bruises not quite as obvious on the larger photo.*" (p. 142-43)
38. "*There's this large area right underneath the front of her chin, and you can see -- and between the two rounded bruises there's still some discoloration. So there's a bruise that extends up in both of these bruises.*
39. *And then down underneath... almost underneath the angle of the jaw here.*" (p. 143)
40. "*There is another oval-shaped bruise on the right-hand side.*" (p. 143)
41,42, 43, 44 "*... there were some drying and abrasions on the outside of the lips, both on the upper and lower lip. ..*" (p. 144)
45. "*And then when the lower lip is turned down, there's a large area of bruising, as well as almost a small ulceration on what we call the frenulum, which is the mid-point of the lower lip.*" (p. 144)
46. "*and then there's this large area of bruising on the lower lip.*" (p. 145)
47, 48. "*...allows you to see the bruise on the lips, and, particularly on the upper lip. And this sort of brown crusting is just a scab, a particular type scab that you would see with an abrasion. So there's some abrasion and drying both on the lips.*" (p. 146)
49. "*This is a view of the back of the head, and this... area.. on the lower back we refer as the occipital region....And there's some ... bruising here....*" (p. 146)
50. "*...In sort of the mid-portion of the back of the head, there was an area that looked dry and mottled. We weren't sure whether there was a bruise there or not.*" (p. 146)
51. "*...And then just above that, there was a separate bruise that we could see.*" (p. 146-47)

52. "*You can't actually see, because the* [neck] *collar's there, so you can't really see that injury that's over the right bottom of the head here. But here's the area of redness....*" (p. 147)
53. "*...the other bruise that you can see above that area of redness....*" (p. 147)
54, 55. "*... there were two small bruises on the mid-back.*" (p. 148) "*And then looking at the back... you can see two small bruises on Kassidy's back.*" (p. 149-50)
56. "*...a small bruise over the right-lateral chest..*" (p. 149)
57, 58, 59. "*... There's three small areas of bruising over the right-lateral hip.*" (p. 149)
60, 61. "*.. Going down on the right side, there are two small linear abrasions, basically scratches on the right side of the leg.*" (p. 149)
62, 63, 64. "*...on the same diagram, on the left side, again over the hip area, there are three bruises, tan to red/tan in color.*" (p. 149)
65. "*...there is the little abrasion on the medial aspect of the right knee, ..*" (p. 149)
66. "*...and an abrasion of the medial of the lateral aspect of the left leg.*" (p. 149)
67, 68. "*There are two small bruises on the back of the right arm, and...*" (p. 150)
69, 70"*... two scratches on the back of the right leg.*" (p. 150)
71. *and then there's the injuries on the feet....Extending across both arches of Kassidy's feet, there were multiple, minute, almost pinpoint scratches, really, of the surface. They're abrasions. They do not really appear to penetrate through the skin. And the ones on the left* [foot?] *are slightly bigger than the ones on the right and, appeared almost to be scabbed, to have eschars on the bottom.... the injuries are distributed not only on the heel, but on the balls of the arch.* " (p. 150)
72, 73. "*There were a couple* [of] *small areas of discoloration*" [on the top of Kassidy's feet.] (p. 152)
74. "*...right foot. And there is a little bit of area of bruising, discoloration that you can see between the big toe and the second toe.*" (p. 152-53)
75. " *... left foot.*" *... and you can see some tiny, little brown areas on the top right by the toes. Those are abrasions, just scratches.*" (p. 152)
76, 77. "*There are a couple of small bruises over the right shoulder.*" (p. 154)
78, 79, 80. "*There are multiple red/brown bruises over the abdomen, both sides of the abdomen.*" (p. 154) [counted as three, though number was unspecified]
81, 82. "*And there are a couple of bruises over her right shin, the lower leg...*" (p. 154)
83, 84, 85. "*This is a photograph showing Kassidy's stomach area, her abdomen, ... And you can see the distribution of the bruises, both on the left side and on the right side. Most of the bruises show sort of an oval or rounded appearance, ...*" (p. 155) [counted as three bruises, though the number was unspecified.]
86. "*...even in this area, which is a slightly larger bruise.... this is the larger one I was talking about where there were maybe some rounded, more defined areas inside that larger disk.*" (p. 155)
87. "*...on the right hand, there is a little area of blue discoloration over the knuckle between the middle and distal, the end of the finger.*" (p. 156)
88. "*... And there is a similar area on the index finger.*" (p. 156)
89, 90. "*.. So there's two like areas of bruising over the tips of her fingers.*" (p. 156)
91, 92. injuries on the top of the head, right and left side. (p. 170-71)
93, 94. "*both subdural and subarachnoid hemmorrhage*" to the brain. (p. 181)
95. "*...bleeding around the optic nerves.*" (p. 182)
96. "*...a fracture in the left ulna, which is the typical bone referred to as the funny bone. It's the bone that's on the outside of the lower arm, goes from the little finger to the elbow.*" (p. 197-98)
97. "*...a fracture in the right hand, what was call[ed] the second metacarpal, and that is the bone that connects... the index finger to the hand.*" (p. 198)
98, 99. "*...a fracture noted in the left tibia. The tibia is the largest bone in the lower leg, the bone that is the shin bone. But this fracture was just under the knee.*" (p. 198) "... appear to have two different stages of healing." (p. 200)

100. "*... the right ulna also showed a fracture of a similar age to what was seen on the left.*" (p. 199)

This listing suffers here for the lack of photographs, but they are not provided here in the interest of the privacy of Amanda and of Kassidy's larger family. The diagrams of Dr. Greenwald's markings of bruises on pre-preprinted drawings of generic bodies were shown to the jury as Exhibits 57-62.

The 100 injuries and bruises can be categorized as follows:

41 Face, including forehead, eyes, cheeks, lips, chin.
14 Head, including top, back, sides, including ears.
14 Chest and abdomen, hips.
4 Back, including shoulder
2 Arms
4 Hands
8 Legs, knees
5 Feet
3 Internal, brain. Subdural.
5 Fractures (two in legs, two in arms, and one in hand)

If Brandon's, Nicole's and Chad's recollections are correct, that the only bruise on Kassidy's face on Sunday, November 5 was a fading bruise around the middle of her cheek, then she had no **eye contact** palming bruise on that day. It's even more likely that none of the 41 bruises on Kassidy's face was an **eye contact** palming bruise. Dr. Greenwald's diagrams of the bruises on Kassidy's face do not show any bruises on either side of her face at the jaw line.

During the listing of the bruises, Dr. Greenwald stated that the photographs were taken "*Probably about 12 to 15 hours*" after Kassidy's death. (p. 139) Then she said that it was longer, because the autopsy didn't start until 9:00 a.m. on the morning of November 10. That would mean that the initial autopsy photos were taken approximately 19-20 hours after her death.

Anticipating the question from the defense, Delker asked, "*Would the injuries appear more prominent in the photographs than they might have in life?*" (p. 140) and Dr. Greenwald replied,

Yes, they could.... Well, a living, breathing person has blood that's being pumped through their tissue, and so their face tends to look pink or a reddish coloration. These bruises, most of them have reddish or slightly red/tan appearance. So though you would be able to see them at the time of death, they wouldn't be - - or before death, that they wouldn't be quite as prominent, because after the person dies, that blood begins to drain to the lowest point of the gravity. [sic]. *So if the person is lying down on their neck, most of the blood would drain to the back of their head.*" (p. 140)

Delker asked, "*...did you observe any swelling on the back of her head?*" and Dr. Greenwald said, "*No, I didn't.*" (p. 151) Delker continued, "*And if the defendant had described a goose egg or an egg on the back of Kassidy's head the night before she died, would you have expected to see that during the autopsy?*" (p. 151) Dr. Greenwald responded, "*That description usually, to me, is in reference to a large area of bleeding, a large bruise under the skin, and it should still have... been visible at the time of the autopsy.*" (p. 151) Dr. Greenwald was not informed that the those "*goose eggs*" originated during the period of October 26-28, or 12-14 days before Kassidy died. Thus, they were much smaller on the evening of the 8th, and apparently undetectable on the 9th. Delker was seeking to again show that the alleged "*goose eggs*" never existed, but the jury should have been advised about the normal duration of such bruises and how they likely disappeared by the 9th. The jury could also have been reminded on cross-examination of how many people saw those two bumps on Kassidy's head on October 28: Amanda, Chad, Jennifer and Travis. Maybe what Chad said during his police interrogation about feeling "*a bump the size* [of] *her shoe today.*" wasn't from that earlier incident at all.(Interrogation, p. 1539)

Seeking to further impeach the credibility of Chad's statements to the police in his interview, Delker asked, "*If the defendant described a large bruise or black and blue mark on the top of Kassidy's foot that he observed on the night before Kassidy died, would you have expected to see that during the autopsy?*" (p. 153) Dr. Greenwald responded that she would have expected to have seen such an injury, two days after the observation, and did not.

Delker was apparently referring to Chad's statments during his interrogation where he said,

And she's got a bruise on her foot where. ..Jeff said he stepped back on her but I don't know....She has a - a scar....On the top of her foot. Amanda was over one of her friend's house or something and the - I think she leaned up against the curling iron or something....Burned it. That's what it looks like. Because I don't know, I don't think Amanda would actually no [sic, know] *this - no she wasn't there. Her, this friend was watching her and then I'm like "what the hell happened with her." Oh she must of fell on ...That was a while ago. Probably about a (inaudible). But I don't really know Why. I'm just telling you there might be a scar, I didn't really look for it or nothing. But you could see where it's visibly a big black and blue ...* (Interrogation, p. 1553-54)

As Chad did not testify, he did not have a chance to explain further what he saw on Kassidy's foot that night. Once again, the prosecution had cast doubt on what Chad was heard to say during his interrogation, and there was no rebuttal.

Dr. Greenwald described the wart on the index, or "*pointer*," finger of her right hand, "*This mark here. It says brown and keratosic. That's a wart. It's not an injury*." (p. 156) During the trial, the jury never heard that Chad had urged Amanda to take Kassidy to the doctor to have that wart removed as it was bothering her. The jurors never had to ask each other whether it made sense that the man accused of beating and murdering Kassidy was also recommending to her mother that a wart be removed because it was bothering her. The jurors never had the chance to ask whether people who were attentive enough to observe a wart also were attentive enough to see bruises and other injuries. None of the other witnesses at Chad's trial, including Jacqueline, Jeff and Jennifer, said anything about a wart at the trial, or in their police interiews.

After identifying all the bruises or injuries, Dr. Greenwald was asked if "*any of the injuries you've described... would any of those be a cause of a blood transfer*?" and she responded "*No... Except for the abrasions which were starting to heal, none of the injuries actually cut through the surface, and there wasn't any blood associated with them.*" (p. 157) There was no discussion here of the March 12, 2001 Maine State Police Lab report of blood underneath all ten of Kassidy's fingernails. At the time of the trial, this report was part of the discovery materials provided to the defense by the prosecutors, but it's not clear that Chad's lawyers had noticed that part of the report. Chad certainly hadn't noticed. In addition there was no discussion of the subsequent March 22 DNA test report which indicated that the blood belonged to Kassidy. That report also was provided in discovery, but there was no indication that Chad's lawyers had read it, and it was never referenced in the trial.

Will Delker had asked about blood transfer in preparation for his next questions, about the blood found on the Wendy's yellow wrapper. He asked, "*As part of the dying process, do you commonly see purged fluid from the nose and mouth?*" and Dr. Greenwald responded,

Yes, as a person goes into the final phases of death, the lungs begin to fill up with fluid, and that fluid may be somewhat bloody, because it's coming from the blood vessels. And that fluid may well up and get mixed with some mucous, and ... I won't say commonly - but we do see that there is what we call purge, and it's really just bloody fluid that may come out of the nose or the mouth." (p. 157)

Dr. Greenwald agreed that such purging is, in Delker's words, "*not characteristic of any one particular type of death or injury*" and could occur in non-homicide cases. (p. 158) and she agreed with Delker's that if Jeff "*did check Kassidy's mouth with a napkin and there may have been blood on that napkin, would that be consistent with purged fluid...*" (p. 158)

Without specifically mentioning it, this exchange between Delker and Dr. Greenwald supported the view that Kassidy died at Jeff's and Jennifer's sometime before Jeff began calling for help at 12:24 p.m., and even before he observed her in distress. Dr. Greenwald did not say exactly how close to death such a blood purging stage would be, but she referred to it as one of the "*final phases of death.*"

Will Delker then asked a series of questions about the ages of bruises, and Dr. Greenwald described how you can determine the age of bruises by their color and close examination of tissue excised from the area during autopsy, by looking at such indicators as the presence of white blood cells and whether scarring has begun.

Dr. Greenwald then testified about the ages of 28 of Kassidy's bruises. The ages are given for different bruises or sets or bruises, as of the time of death, which was "*approximately 12:30, when 911 was contacted,*" to use Will Delker's assessment. (p. 168)

Forehead (2): "*three or four days*" and "*around possibly 12 hours*" (p. 165)
Over the right eyebrow (2): "*eight to twelve hours*" and "*two to three, four days.*" (p. 169)
Top of head, left (1): "*eight to twelve hours.*" (p. 171)
Top of head, right (2) "*three to four days.*" (p. 171)
Left cheek (2): about *twelve hours,*" and "*out about a week.*" (p. 172)
Left jaw (1): "*about 12 hours*" (p. 174)
Right jaw (1): "*about eight to twelve hours*" (p. 175)
Middle of the chin (1): "*about eight to twelve hours*" (p. 175)
Lower lip (1): "*about 12 hours.*" (p. 176)
Frenulum, under the tongue (1): "*four or five hours*" (p. 177)
Back of head (1): "*less than four hours.*" (p. 178)
Right back of head (1): "*two to three to eight,*" (p. 178)
Middle back of head (1): "*around 12 hours.*" (p. 178)
Left buttocks (1): "*eight to twelve days.*" (p. 178)
Several bruises, arms legs. Specifically, feet (1): "*probably days old.*" (p. 180)
Brain injury (3): "*...probably hours old, maybe as much as 24 hours.*" (p. 186) [using Will Delker's words] "*anywhere from a few hours to 24 hours old?*" (p. 186)
Abdomen (1): "*around 12 hours*" (p. 194), or "*eight to twelve hours.*" (p. 196)
Fracture to Ulna(2): "*...three to six weeks.*" (p. 199) [both left and right ulna bones]
Fracture to metacarpal finger(1) "*... somewhere between one to three weeks of age.*" (p. 200)
Fracture to tibia(2): "*...we had an older injury, maybe a couple of months old, and then a fresher injury which would have just been, perhaps, days old.*" (p. 201)

When explaining the age of the bruise on Kassidy's left buttock, Dr. Greenwald described how she looked for such a bruise because she believed the case was a "*child abuse case.*" She said that she made "*some incisions in the back of the legs, the back of the buttocks and the person's back, because you may miss bruising that may not be apparent on the surface.*" (p. 179) This was a clear example of how one's theory of a case influenced the direction of an othewise neutral examination. When describing her examination of Kassidy's brain and eyes, Dr. Greenwald said that the eyes are removed "*as a part of the standard autopsy in a child-abuse case.*" (p. 182) Similarly, the X-rays which found the fractures were "*a part, again, of an examination in a child-abuse case.*" (p. 197)

Will Delker asked about the number of blows to Kassidy's head, and Dr. Greenwald responded, "*There were probably at least eight to ten blows if you include both the front and the back of the head.*" (p. 181) and "*at least two*" blows to the abdomen. (p. 181) She said that the head injuries occur when "*either the head hits an object or the object hits the head...*" (p. 182)

Delker asked about the effects on Kassidy's behavior which might have been caused by the "*blunt-force injury*" that Dr. Greenwald said caused the brain injury. She replied, generally about children, "*They become at first just quieter and then almost lethargic. They wouldn't be running around or walking around like normal. They probably wouldn't be speaking in a normal fashion. They may or may not eat.*" (p. 186) She said that such effects occur sooner, depending upon the amount of force that is applied, and the degree of injury to the brain, but "*anywhere from* [sic] *hours to 24 hours.*" (p. 189) [The transcript had no number after the word, "*few*."]

Regarding the progression of symptoms, she said, "*you get more and more swelling, and as the swelling increases, the changes that the child is displaying, the behavior becomes more apparent. They become more lethargic.*" (p. 189)

Delker then asked,

If Kassidy had suffered the type of blunt-force injury that you observed to the brain before 5:30 on Wednesday, when she was picked up from the babysitter's, would you expect to see her later that evening -- and she's described at around that time as being lethargic, and so forth, would you expect her later in the evening to be acting normally, eating a Popsicle, doing her ABC's and playing? (p. 189)

Dr. Greenwald answered, "*No. I mean, if there was a time in between when the injury occurred where she was actually lethargic, I wouldn't expect her to then be perfectly normal after that.*" (p. 190) However, the question was slightly distorted as no one testified that Kassidy was acting "*perfectly*" normally, on the evening of November 8. Travis's testimony came close, when he described Kassidy's behavior in the bathtub, but not "*perfectly normal.*" Dr. Greenwald agreed that Kassidy's lethargy on the morning of Thursday of November 9 was caused by an injury beforehand.

Dr. Greenwald stated that the "*subdural*," i.e. brain injuries, were caused "*somewhere around 24 hours*," before Kassidy's death. "*It did not appear to be older than that.*" (p. 193)

Delker then asked about the injuries to Kassidy's abdomen, which Dr. Greenwald said occurred "*around 12 hours*" before Kassidy's death. (p. 194) He then asked whether Jeff's abdomen-centered CPR technique did not cause the injuries to Kassidy's abdomen. She reasoned that she had seen the video of Jeff's re-enactment of his CPR efforts and he used a flat hand, which was less likely to cause injury. However, that was a video of a re-enactment when Jeff knew that the severity of his pushing on Kassidy's abdomen may have been the cause of some of Kassidy's injuries. The purpose of the videotaped re-eneactment was to determine likelihood of that causation. A flat hand was less likely to cause injuries than a closed hand. In addition, Dr. Greenwald estimated that the injuries to Kassidy's abdomen occurred about "*eight to twelve hours*" before Kassidy's death. (p. 196)

This was Dr. Greenwald's last estimate of the age of an injury. Of the approximately 100 bruises and injuries she identified, she gave aging estimates for 28, five of which were the alleged fractures.

Four hours or less	1
Zero to 8 hours	2
Eight to 12 hours	4
"Around 12 hours"	7
Twelve to 24 hours	3
Twenty-four to 48 hours	0
Two days to a week	6
One week to a month	4
Greater than one month	1

Dr. Greenwald said that the typical "*blunt force*" which causes the external bruising and internal bleeding in the abdomen area is "*often a fist or a foot into the abdomen.*" (p. 196)

Will Delker asked about bone fractures, and Dr. Greenwald said that the radiologist found the four fractures noted above. He asked what could have caused the ulna fractures, and Dr. Greenwald responded, "*... typically in fractures with children, it may either be a compression or a twisting, a torsion kind of motion that might cause the fracture to occur.*" (p. 201) And to the finger, "*... usually grabbing tightly or crushing of that area. Sometimes it's a twisting.*" (p. 201) and to the tibia, "*Again, it would be a twisting or a direct application of force to that.*" (p. 201)

Delker returned to the injuries on Kassidy's face and asked, "*whether the shape of a ball, the convex shape of a ball is consistent or inconsistent with the injuries that you observed on Kassidy,*" and Dr. Greenwald replied that such an impact, "*... should actually not just show the edge of the ball but more of the rounded surface, not just the line, but...*

maybe a whole round area. So it is not completely consistent with those injuries." (p. 210) She said that "*...there were two that I looked at, the one on the forehead here, and then this injury, which is curving up from the lips to the area under the eye.*" (p. 211). It wasn't clear from the transcript which eye she was pointing to, but the Tee-ball injury was definitely under the left eye, so the forehead injury was not a possibility. She said that both of those two possible injuries on the face that might have been caused by a ball, were more likely to have been caused by a concave object, such as "*a cup, or the edge of a spoon, if it's a large enough spoon, or something of that nature which would have a rounded edge.*" (p. 212)

Dr. Greenwald was asked about "*battered-child syndrome*" which she explained as referring "*to a child in which there is repeated trauma inflicted upon them over a period of time.*" (p. 213) Indications of battered-child syndrome are multiple injuries, delay in reporting injuries and "*usually the story is told about how the injury occurs is inconsistent with the severity of the injury.*" (p. 214) Asked about common excuses that parents of children suffering battered-child syndrome give for bruises and injuries, Dr. Greenwald said,

... often we hear that that these parents will say, well, there's a lot of bruises because the child just bruises easily; or if there is fractures, or other injuries, they might say that the child was just very clumsy and fell frequently." (p. 215)

She said that parents who don't take their children to a doctor, "*may actually be trying to either hide the injury or pretend that the injury, as it was inflicted, was not severe, that the child will get over it.*" (p. 216) She said that in a multi-child family, "*there is usually one child that is the scapegoat in that particular family.*" (p. 216) Dr. Greenwald said that in battered-child syndrome cases, the head is usually injured most often, followed by the abdomen. Then Dr. Greenwald concluded that Kassidy's situation was consistent with battered-child syndrome. The defense did not object to Dr. Greenwald's testimony about "battered child syndrome," but there was no qualitification of her as an expert in such matters. During cross-examination, there were no questions, and no requests for documentaion, about her assertion that it was "*usually*" the case that one child is scapegoated. Her expertise was in the analysis of causes of death, as can be determined from examination of bodies.

Asked whether there was an indication of easy bruising, Dr. Greenwald stated, "*There was never any previous description of that from the* ***pediatricians***. *And there was nothing in the sections that I looked at in the bone marrow that would indicate there would be reason for that.*" (p. 218) (emphasis added) This was the only indication at the trial that the prosecution and Dr. Greenwald had any medical records for Kassidy. Such records should have been provided to the defense, but they were not. It is true, however, from records obtained in 2010, that Kassidy's pediatrician did not make any observation of bruises or easy bruising during the appointments of May 9 and August 10. Dr. Greenwald made no mention of records from an orthopdedic surgeon, i.e. the Sept. 11 appointment with Dr. Timoney. All such records from pediatricians and the orthopedic surgeon should have been provided to Chad's attorneys before trial, as part of Discovery. When she mentioned "*pediatricians*," the bells should have begun ringing in Chad's lawyers' heads. They should have asked Dr. Greenwald about those pediatricians. Even if not, they could have remembered later to ask themselves, "Pediatricians? What Pediatricians?" Trial lawyering is difficult, and hindsight can be 20/20.

Dr. Greenwald stated that while "*Any one of the injuries, individually, I could not, perhaps say was not caused accidentally*," (p. 218) In other words, every one of the injuries and bruises could have been caused by an accident. However, she said that Kassidy's accumulation of injuries was not consistent with accidents, because there were so many, and some were in areas not typically associated with accidents.

She stated that the injuries to Kassidy's head could have caused her death by the swelling in her brain, and the abdominal injury by infection or loss of blood,

But in Kassidy's case, there was an additional factor, and that was that she had fat emboli in her small blood vessels in her lungs, and in some of her other organs, as well...usually, we see fat emboli occurring with fractures. But we might also see it occurring with soft-

tissue injuries or with the abdominal injury. And when the fat, which is present underneath the skin and in the abdomen is injured, it can be released into the vessels. And then with the chemical reaction that occurs, they begin to plug the capillaries in the lungs, and that can lead to respiratory distress and death. (p. 219)

Will Delker's final question was "*when Kassidy's fatal injuires were inflicted*?" (p. 219) and Dr. Greenwald replied, "*... the injuries... to the abdomen and to the head, were all consistent with having occurred at some point within the 24 hours prior to her death.*" (p. 219-20)

Delker did not ask Dr. Greenwald to identify the visible bruises to the head and abdomen that could have been caused by the allegedly fatal blows. Thus, out of 100 identified bruises, fractures and injuries, the prosecution did not identify the blows that killed Kassidy and Dr. Greenwald did not identify them on her own.

Instead of treating the Medical Examiner as a partner in the search for truth, Mark Sisti began his cross-examination with sarcasm and asked if Maine and New Hampshire, "*through their investigative agencies, were they kind enough to tell you who Kassidy was in the care and custody of over this 24-hour period?*" (p. 220) and a few seconds later, "*Did you ever hear of Amanda Bortner*?" (p. 221) Despite the sarcasm, Sisti's point was important, which was that Kassidy was with Amanda, Chad, Jeff and Jennifer during her last 24 hours. Dr. Greenwald agreed that all the fatal injuries could have occurred during the times that Jeff cared for her, i.e. the afternoon of November 8, and the morning of the 9th.

Dr. Greenwald agreed that some of the injuries to Kassidy, which did not show any evidence of "*inflammatory reaction,*" could have been caused "*less than four hours*" before Kassidy's death, which was assumed to occur, for the purpose of the question between 12:30-12:45 p.m. (p. 225) Thus, they could have been caused during the time Kassidy was being cared for by Jennifer and Jeff, and then by Jeff, alone. Later, Dr. Greenwald testified about the time of Kassidy's death, "*...she died around 12:30 p.m.*" (p. 231)

Sisti returned to the effects of the dislodging of fat emboli, and Dr. Greenwald said, "*the capillaries that supply oxygen to the lung are closed off by little, tiny globules of fat.*" (p. 231)

Dr. Greenwald agreed that to the extent that Kassidy's death was caused by the fat emboli, "*It may have taken up to a day or so for that to have effect.*" (p. 232) She agreed with Mark Sisti's assessment that it "*Could have taken an hour, two hours, right*?" (p. 232)

Asked about the "*purged blood,*" Dr. Greenwald explained that the lungs didn't have to be openly bloody to release blood into fluids that reached the mouth.

Regarding the age of bruises, Dr. Greenwald agreed that the "*bruise on the lower lip of Kassidy is entirely medically consistent with having occurred within four hours of her death?*" (p. 234) She agreed that the retinal hemorrhaging could have occurred as recently as one hour before Kassidy's death. She agreed that there were a lot of injuries that occurred on November 8 or 9. She agreed that if "*leaning forward in the car and drooling*" and lack of appetite were behaviors seen in Kassidy around 6:00 p.m., they could have been consistent with being injured in the head or abdomen in the 4:30 p.m. range on November 8. (p. 240)

Dr. Greenwald agreed that there were other "*non-reactive*" injuries to Kassidy, i.e. injuries for which there had not yet been a "*reactive inflammation*" prior to her death. Those non-reactive injuries could have occurred within four hours of death. Dr. Greenwald agreed that "*the blunt injury to the back*" was one such injury. (p. 243) In this line of questioning, Mark Sisti had shown that several of Kassidy's bruises could have been caused within four hours of Kassidy's death.

Sisti did not ask about the October 26-28 "goose-egg" bumps and Dr. Greenwald's testimony that she found no evidence of such bumps. The jury was left with the prosecution's view that Chad's statement in his interrogation that he felt the remnant of such bumps was false. Worse, the jury was left with message that the initial observation of such bumps, and Amanda's testimony about them, was also false.

On redirect examination by Will Delker, Dr. Greenwald agreed that what she described as "*non-reactive*" sections of bruises could possibly have been parts of older bruises, by hours, and thus the bruise may not have necessarily been caused within four hours. Similarly, for the bruises where she had predicted a 12 hour aging, the range could have been between 8-18 hours, which would have, in Delker's terms, have brought the earliest time of occurrence to 6:30 p.m. on the 8th.

On recross-examination, Mark Sisti turned to the basic starting point for all the "*aging*" calculations, which was the time of Kassidy's death. As Dr. Greenwald said that "*you would expect to see rigor mortis beginning around two to three hours*" after death, she agreed that Kassidy could have died as early at 10:00 a.m. on November 9, which would have pushed the "18 hour" range calculation back to 4:00 p.m., and within the time that Jeff Marshall cared for her on the 8th. Surprisingly, there was no documentation on the time that rigor mortis began with Kassidy's body.

Dr. Greenwald was then excused and that was the end of the prosecution's case. There had been 27 prosecution witnesses, 13 of whom had reported seeing some bruises on Kassidy.

Judge Nadeau decided to "*instruct*" the jury at this time that

Cory Merrill will not continue as a witness in this case, and, as a result, I am ordering all of his testimony to be stricken from the court record of this trial, and you are not to consider any of his testimony in your deliberations.

She explained that Merrill declined to answer cross-examination questions, and therefore, "*his testimony cannot be considered as reliable and admissible.*" (p. 252-53) However, to jurors who usually know little, if anything, about the unreliability of inmate informants, the damage to Chad had been done. The jurors had heard that Chad had allegedly admitted to Merrill that he had abused Kassidy and used a belt on her. The best way to counter such testimony if a judge starts to allow it in the first place, in addition to having it stricken, would have been to have Chad testify. In 2010, Chad maintained that Merrill's incriminating allegations were simply untrue. Another way would have been to confront the reliability of Merrill's testimony with the testimony of Adam Tuttle and John Lacroix, two of the other inmates close to Chad during his initial jailing. Chad's lawyers did not know about the police interview with Tuttle.

The jury was dismissed at 4:16 p.m , and was advised that Friday would be reserved for legal issues, and that the next day for the jury would be Monday, December 17.

MEDIA:
1. "State rests in Evans trial - Doctor: baby was victim of battered child syndrome"
2. "Jury gets details of battered girl's injuries"
3. "Autopsy Infant had several broken bones"
4. "Testimony of Evans cellmate thrown out; state rests case"
5. "Testimony Discarded - Witness refuses to answer defense questions"

Friday, 14 December 2001

The lawyers and Judge Nadeau met on Friday, without the jury, to discuss Judge Nadeau's instructions to the jury, and to consider the proposed language submitted by each side. The defense submitted two instructions, on "*Testimony of a Police Officer*" and "*Lack of Evidence.*" (p. 3) Then they discussed the State's requests for Jury Instructions, page by page, beginning with "*Burden of Proof.*" (p. 4) On one issue, Will Delker declared, "*I think that is just legalese,*" which might be said about the fine points of the earlier instructions to the jury and the entire jury instruction which would soon come at the end of the case.(p. 8) Later, Judge Nadeau seemed to agree they may be overconfident on the precision of the words, "*We are word nuts, aren't we?*" (p. 54)

My Torts law professor at law school memorably told us that "*juries have the right to ignore the law and do what's right.*" That sounded good, when considering a case where the law was inadequate to provide justice. However, what's called "jury nullification" can work the other way, too, where a jury will find guilt beyond a reasonable doubt where the evidence didn't support it. A case involving the death of a 21-month-old girl, with widespread publicity, certainly was a candidate for such a jury decision.

During these bench conferences, the lawyers can tell the judge what they really think of the case, without regard to the rules of evidence and Criminal Procedure. One disagreement arose when Will Delker said, "*... and there's nothing in the record at this point that shows that Jeff Marshall made up excuses that he knew were false at the time.*"

Alan Cronheim countered,

Jeff Marshall absolutely made up stuff about the truck, pinpricks, and other things. And... there are very real questions from that perspective about Jeff Marshall's misstatements that can also be argued demonstrate a consciousness of guilt. (p. 10)

They continued, line by line of Judge Nadeau's proposed instructions covering such topics as "*circumstantial evidence*" and "*second-degree murder*" (p. 11-12) Much of it was based on "model instructions" which are available to judges.

Regarding Chad's responsibility, Will Delker argued to the judge that

The Defendant's failure alone, to bring Kassidy to the hospital was the cause of her death. If Jeff Marshall had inflicted the injuries, the defendant caused the death by not bringing her to the hospital." (p. 15)

Fortunately, that theory of responsibility was not included in the judge's instruction, but it shows how strongly the prosecutors felt about Chad's culpability, and how much they wanted to win their case. The defense argued that including anything about Chad's alleged failure to take Kassidy to the hospital was outside the scope of the indictment, which focused on blows to the head and abdomen, and that it was unfair to Chad as this late date to, essentially, add a charge to the indictment. They argued that if such a charge were in the indictment, the defense could have cross-examined witnesses to defend against that charge.

There was a break, and afterwards, Judge Nadeau returned with some of her decisions on the content of the jury instructions. She said, "*First of all, I've left in a section on the defendant not testifying, and I can take that out, depending on what you do with your case.*" (p. 21) Even at this late date in the trial, and the legal game, the defense had not firmly told the Judge its plans for the presentation of the defense case, though it did say earlier, informally, that it might take only a day, which essentially means one witness, and Dr. Baden was that witness.

The defense argued that the jury should be advised of the law regarding "*mutual combat*" as a way of describing the argument between Amanda and Chad on the evening of the 8th, but Judge Nadeau rejected that argument. (p. 25) If Chad had testified he could have related to the jury the true nature of his argument with Amanda on that evening and no reasonable juror would have concluded that it was an assault.

MEDIA: 1. "Defense begins its case in Chad Evans Trial"
2. "Kassidy petition to reach N.H. statehouse"
3. "Inmate injured in fight with Evans"
4. "Chad Evans involved in jail fight"
5. "Defense begins its case today"

Monday, 17 December 2001

The trial began with more discussion with Judge Nadeau and arguments to her by the lawyers about the words of her upcoming jury instruction. It may be a common practice for such discussions to begin before the defense has begun presenting its case, but it seems premature.

At the end of the discussion, Alan Cronheim orally made his motion

to dismiss each and every indictment on the ground that the evidence ... taken most favorable to the State, does not demonstrate each and every element of each offense." (p. 13)

Such motions are made routinely in criminal cases, but they are sometimes effective in removing one or more of the charges. He began with the first degree assault charges against Kassidy, i.e. the fracture charges. He said, "*There's ambiguity in the evidence, ambiguity as to the time, ambiguity as to the place, ambiguity as to what it is that caused those fractures.*" (p. 13)

Simon Brown argued that Amanda had testified that Chad had grabbed Kassidy's leg "*while Kassidy was sitting in Amanda's lap,*" and that Jeff "*had testified that he had a telephone conversation with Amanda where she was angry and described the defendant playing rough with Kassidy and hurting her leg.*" (p. 13) Regarding the arm fracture, playing with a child and accidentally causing an injury, if any, is not usually considered a crime, but in the context of the prosecution's view of Chad Evans, his playing rough was considered criminal. Brown said that Amanda's testimony that Chad, in Brown's words, *"jerked Kassidy's arm back when throwing her onto a bed,*" was "*direct evidence*" and enough to convict Chad of causing a fractured arm, and beyond a reasonable doubt. (p. 15) Brown made these arguments, even while knowing, from Dr. Baden's deposition, that he doubted that there were any fractures at all.

Judge Nadeau denied the Motion to dismiss the charge regarding the injury to Kassidy's left leg, saying that there was enough evidence to show guilt beyond a reasonable doubt, but granted the motion to dismiss the charge regarding the alleged fracture to Kassidy's arm. That was a small victory for Chad and for justice.

Before bringing the jury into the courtroom, Alan Cronheim asked that the time frames of the six second-degree assault charges be explained to the jury in Judge Nadeau's instructions, as the alleged assaults were consecutive beginning in September.

Michael Baden

As Dr. Baden was a defense witness, Mark Sisti examined him first. Dr. Baden was the chief forensic pathologist for the New York State Police and Dutchess County, New York, and had a long history of pathologist positions and tasks and training. He'd written over 80 articles and done over 20,000 medicolegal autopsies, and "*...more than 1,000 would have involved injuries to children, either homicidal or accidental.*" (p. 26) He said that the New York State Police had provided assistance to New York City "*as far as DNA studies and to identify victims in that* [9/11/2001] *incident.*" In short, Dr. Baden was one of the best forensic pathologists in the country. This was the third reference at Chad's trial of DNA, but not a word was said about the Maine Crime Laboratory's DNA tests of the blood underneath Kassidy's ten fingernails.

Chad's expectations were raised. He wrote in his May 27, 2011 letter,

I recall when he [Mark Sisti] *had me all pumped up before Dr. Baden testified. "Dr. Baden is the best in the business. He is going to blow these people away. He has proof that you didn't kill Kassidy."*

Dr. Baden spoke highly of Dr. Greenwald whom he knew, and then Sisti asked him, straight off, for the causes of Kassidy's death, and he replied,

I think that Kassidy Bortner died as a result of multiple injuries over a period of time with the final injuries occurring shortly before she was found dead..*.the final injuries that were the immediate cause of death was the fat embolization to the lungs and other organs of the body that Dr. Greenwald identified...Fat emboli are less common, but occur when fat gets into the blood stream and causes a very quick death.....Kassidy Bortner's death was precipitated by those fat emboli.* (p. 30-31)

Further, "*...she died within minutes or an hour or two after the fat emboli go to the lung,*" (p. 33)

He explained that

the most likely cause [of the release of fat emboli] *would be from squeezing .... of fat during the production of injuries to the skin an underlying subcutaneous tissue. Subcutaneous means the tissue right under the skin. And that's largely fat. And so by injuring that fatting tissue, especially in areas like the buttocks, which has a lot of fat, enough fat can be crushed to get into the blood streams, come into the lungs and cause death. So I think that some of the trauma that Kassidy Bortner suffered, especially that in the couple of hours before death, led not only to the various injuries that she has, but, also, to the fat embolization...* (p. 33-34)

Mark Sisti asked if the release of the fatal fat emboli could have been caused by an injury the night before. He responded negatively, because there was sign of a *vital reaction... the coming in of the white blood cells to take away the fat, ... And my opinion is that this happened very shortly before she died,,, And it's massive. There's a lot of it...if there were no other injuries to the child... my opinion would have been that she died of the fat embolism alone. But in the light of all the other injuries that the child has, my opinion would be it's part of the total picture, but it's the part that caused her death...* (p. 35)

He agreed that absent the fat emboli problem, Kassidy could have/might have survived the other injuries.

Asked about the time of the fatal injuries, Dr. Baden stated,
... that the fatal injuries would have occurred less than two hours before she died. If I assume she dies at 12:30, 12:45, then the fatal injuries would have had to occur after 10:45. Because if they occurred earlier than that, there would have been some reaction that can be seen on the microscope of the polymorphonuclear cells coming to the injured area -- to the areas of the lung that have the fat, which isn't there; there is no such reaction." (p. 36-7)

Dr. Baden noted that Kassidy's behavior changes noted on November 8 had nothing to do with the fat embolization cause-of-death. Dr. Baden stated that Kassidy's behavior changes on the late afternoon and evening of November 8th, could have been due to brain and abdomen injuries and they could have been received in the late afternoon of that day, 4:00 - 5:45 p.m., i.e. when Kassidy was at Jeff Marshall's.

Dr. Baden agreed that Sisti's listed behaviors were consistent with those injuries:
- "*...drooping forward in a car and drooling...*" (p. 38) "Yes."
- "*... looked dazed or confused...*" (p. 39) "Yes."
- "*... losing her balance for no apparent reason...*" (p. 39) "Yes."
- "*... was prepared a grilled-cheese sandwich, but refused it and instead had about a half a banana.*" (p. 39) "Yes."
- "*...later on that night she would have had a .. kind of a Pop Ice Popsicle....*" (p. 39) "Yes."
- "*Can't children like Kassidy that are subjected to these types of injuries... appear really bad at some times, and then appear to recover a bit other times?*" (p. 39) "Yes."

Mark Sisti asked Dr. Baden about the time range for the subdural hemorrhage or brain injury and he answered, "*One to two hours to* [no] *more than three days.*" (p. 41) Dr. Baden dated the abdominal injury as older, "*...would have been a few days, at least a few days.*" (p. 41)

In the context of time-of-death, Mark Sisti asked about the contents of Kassidy's stomach. Dr. Baden noted that Kassidy had 42 cubic centimeters of food in her stomach, "*which is about an ounce and a half.*" (p. 43) The English measurement equivalent for the volume is 2.62 cubic inches. There are 14.5 cubic inches in a cup, so volume of Reese's PB Puffs in Kassidy's stomach at the time of her death was about 1/6 of a cup. Dr. Baden stated that Kassidy "*probably ate something within a few hours before death, because the normal emptying time in the stomach is about two to three hours.*" (p. 43) However, because injury to the abdomen or sickness can slow the digestion process, Dr. Baden was unable to determine if the stomach contents were from the previous night of from breakfast time, i.e. the Reese's Puffs. He was able to say that the stomach contents were consistent in color and consistency to the half-a-banana the previous night and what he was advised were "Cocoa Puffs" but which were actually the similarly looking "Reese's Puffs."

Regarding the time of Kassidy's death, Dr. Baden stated that in his opinion, on the basis of the circumstances and looking at photographs of her body at the hospital, "*she was dead before 12 noon.*" (p. 47)

Then Mark Sisti addressed the question of whether there were fractures in Kassidy's bones. First, for the left tibia, Dr. Baden disagreed with Dr. Greenwald and said that there was no fracture, and thus, he agreed with the York Hospital radiologist who reviewed Kassidy's X-Rays. Dr. Baden attributed the hemorrhaging that Dr. Greenwald saw to the

EMTs who, seeking to install an IV into Kassidy, "*... couldn't get a vein because she was dead....as a desparate attempt emergency attempt, they... put in tubes directly into the bone marrow and tried to provide fluids that way.*" (p. 53) He concluded, "*If there is a fracture, it's a very old fracture that's healed without any signs.*" (p. 54) There were no further questions about the bruises or injuries which the EMTs may have caused when trying to save Kassidy.

Turning to the right tibia, Dr. Baden estimated its age as "*... many months. Months. After about four, five, six months in children, fractures can sometimes heal and not leave any evidence of a fracture.*" (p. 54)

Regarding the ages of bruises, Dr. Baden complimented Dr. Greenwald, but said that he would date some of the older injuries, in terms of hours, as being older than Dr. Greenwald's estimate. "*...those areas... that Dr. Greenwald said the eight to twelve, I think could be, you know, six to twenty.*" (p. 57)

Dr. Baden agreed with Dr. Greenwald that Kassidy's death was a homicide. Answering Mark Sisti's last question, Dr. Baden stated, "*The final injuries would have taken place while Kassidy was in Kittery, Maine, being cared for, and would have occurred during the 9:30 to 12 o'clock period of time.*" (p. 64)

Will Delker began his cross-examination by establishing that Dr. Baden received $4,000 for his retainer and $5,000 for his testimony on that day, which was discount from his normal rate, because he had known Mark Sisti for many years. The inquiry seemed to have one purpose, which was to foster mistrust in the minds of the jurors of people who made more money than they did. This inquiry should have been ruled irrelevant by the judge. No one asked Dr. Greenwald how much she earned per year, or for the time she spent on the case. Both Dr. Greenwald and Dr. Baden were qualified as experts, and that should have been enough. Certainly the court would not have permitted the lawyers to ask each other how much they were being paid for their work on the case, or the judge, or perhaps even the police witnesses. The inquiry added absolutely nothing to the evidence in the case, and prejudiced the jurors against Dr. Baden, who was already identified as being from another state.

A similar conclusion can be drawn from Delker's questions about Dr. Baden's work on the O.J. Simpson case and Louise Woodward. They were intended to inflame the jury against him. Delker asked Dr. Baden about a statement from his 1989 book, Confessions of a Medical Examiner, which was about his views in 1961 about the media, "*I liked the reporters and television cameras.*" (p. 70) Dr. Baden explained that he was now older and wiser about the media, but the question had nothing to do with the evidence in the case, and everything to do about causing prejudice by the jury. In addition, Will Delker has had his own share of publicity.

Returning to the evidence in the case, Delker asked Dr. Baden about the discrepancy between his conclusion about the cause of death during his deposition, two weeks earlier, and at the trial. Dr. Baden answered that it was Will Delker himself who brought the fat embolization part of Dr. Greenwald's report to his attention and he hadn't yet examined the fat stain microscopic slides. Dr. Baden explained that he has a busy schedule, but Delker continued to seek to discredit him by pointing out that he used the name in this trial, "Kathy" instead of "Kassidy" and in another trial in Pennsylvania he confused the names of the victim and the defendant. The goal was to poison the jury against Dr. Baden, and his medical conclusions as well. Right after that contemptuous challenge, Delker referred to Dr. Greenwald's autopsy report as "*Dr. Baden's autopsy report.*" (p. 82) Dr. Baden responded, surely with a smile, "*It's contagious, see.*" (p. 82)

Will Delker then reviewed articles and chapters of books relating to fat emboli and tried to show that Dr. Baden's conclusions about Kassidy's death were not consistent with that literature, but Dr. Baden explained, in each case how his conclusions were, in fact, consistent. The cross-examination paused for lunch, and upon return, Will Delker sought again to discredit Dr. Baden by asking him about his being demoted by the Mayor of New York City from the position of Chief Medical Examiner to Deputy Chief. Delker noted that Dr. Baden wrote about the episode in his book, which, again was written in 1989, and Dr. Baden explained that circumstance as well. Then, Delker said, "*Let me get back to your opinion in this case*," (p. 103) which may have seemed to the jury and court observers to be appropriate.

Will Delker then sought to use Dr. Baden's testimony in the Louise Woodward case against him, but in each effort, Dr. Baden explained the difference between the two fact situations. Delker challenged Dr. Baden's view that there were no bone fractures in Kassidy's body and read a portion of Dr. Baden's November 20 letter to Mark Sisti which said, "*It is further my opinion that, during this time, the injuries Kassidy suffered would have been apparent to any adult who changed her diaper, saw her face or heard her crying from pain caused by the fractures.*" (p. 103) Dr. Baden said that he wrote that before he saw the X-rays, with which you can see the whole bone. He said that what Dr. Greenwald found was scar tissue from a bruise to a bone, but not a fracture.

Will Delker noted that Dr. Baden's November 20, 2001 report didn't explicitly say that some of the injuries to Kassidy could have occurred within less than five hours of her death. Then, he revisited Dr. Baden's testimony about the several injuries which likely occurred about two hours before death, and Dr. Baden explained that with small, new bruises, there was less room for variation as might occur by taking different sections of a larger bruise.

On redirect examination Mark Sisti reaffirmed with Dr. Baden that he had done thousands of autopsies in homicide cases and that Will Delker had focused on three or four. Dr. Baden reaffirmed that he usually testifies for the prosecution, with a ratio of 10 or 20 to one, "*And the testimony's the same...whichever side calls me.*" (p. 123) Dr. Baden explained how his analyses in the cases referenced during the questioning by Will Delker were correct. He said that he thought Dr. Greenwald did an excellent job in her autopsy and that the largest disagreement they had was about whether there were fractures, and those fractures were "*irrelevant to the cause of death.*" (p. 131) Of the fat emboli that killed Kassidy, Dr. Baden said it was "*liquefied fat due to the crushing of the fat in the buttock and under the skin. And that's pure fat that goes right in the blood stream....*" (p. 133)

Mark Sisti revisited the time range of several injuries, putting it in the context of Jeff's babysitting between 4:00 and 5:45 p.m. on November 8. Dr. Baden agreed that the "*small intestine injury*" could have occurred during that period, as could a "*portion of*" the subdural hematoma, "*but ... other portions of it were within a few days older.*" (p. 136) Dr. Baden stated that the fat embolism injury could not have occurred that long before Kassidy's death. He reiterated his view that there were no fractures.

Asked by Mark Sisti to explain more about his work and fees, in response to Will Delker's questions, Dr. Baden explained how he taught many courses including courses in the 1970's for the New Hampshire State Police. He said, "*And there's been a great increase and interest in police agencies on forensic science because of all the developments in DNA and other technologies.*" (p. 140) This was the fourth and last reference in the trial to DNA. By that time, on December 17, 2001, approximately 100 people had been exonerated by DNA testing including Kenny Waters, the subject of the 2010 movie with Hilary Swank, "Conviction."

Mark Sisti's concluding question was about the change in his opinion about the cause of Kassidy's death which changed after his November 20 letter to Sisti and his telephone deposition on November 30 and December 2. Doctor Baden said that his change was not in response to any request from Sisti, but in response to the information he hadn't fully considered before, i.e. Dr. Greenwald's microscopic slides. He said that he had, in his career, changed death certificates after getting new information. "*So, you know, it's an evolving process, and the more information I have, the better an opinion I can have.*" (p. 141)

Will Delker then asked on recross-examination about why Dr. Baden wasn't better prepared for his deposition, and he responded that he had 24 hours notice for the phone deposition, and that he was away from home at the time, in Pennsylvania, and that "*There were hundreds of slides and I had not yet reviewed them all in detail. And I still hadn't received the X-rays.*" (p. 143)

Dr. Baden stepped down, and the defense case came to an end. There were no other defense witnesses. Sisti informed Judge Nadeau that Chad would not be testifying. In 2011, many Americans monitored the Casey Anthony case, and when she decided not to testify, Judge Perry asked her a few questions to be sure that she understood what she was doing. If such questioning were the practice in New Hampshire, Judge Nadeau might have asked Chad if he fully understood that this was his last chance to provide the jury with his side of the story.

Chad's brother, Jason, walked with Dr. Baden to his car and he recalled that Dr. Baden said to him about the jury,

I sincerely hope for your brother's sake they were paying attention. Because of some of the child's older injuries I cannot say for sure who did and did not abuse her but there is no doubt in my mind that Chad had nothing to do with her death. The science just doesn't support it.

Chad's lawyers apparently thought that Dr. Baden's testimony and the testimony by the State's witnesses, including their answers to the defense's questions on cross-examination, were enough to give the jurors the required reasonable doubt to obtain a Not Guilty verdict on the murder charge. One big problem for Chad was that his lawyers focused almost entirely on that murder charge, because it carried the largest punishment, but conviction on the other charges also would mean years in prison. The maximum sentence for each of the six Second Degree Assault charges was 30 years, so the total could have been 180 years in prison if the sentences were given consecutively. The two misdemeanor charges, Endangering the Welfare of a Child and Simple Assault against Amanda carred a maximum penalty of one year each. The defense apparently thought that calling other witnesses, especially Chad himself, would present the risk of admitting more harmful facts than good ones. After working on this case for 18 months, I don't understand that risk. Perhaps I am over optimistic about the amount of positive information the judge would have allowed into the trial. As has been said before, hindsight can be 20/20 and it may well have been that in the emotionally charged period of the trial, with its sensational media coverage, it was reasonable to fear an adverse reaction to more testimony.

They apparently thought that the defense evidence was not likely to be sufficiently helpful. They might have thought otherwise, if they had

- asked Chad and Amanda for all the photos of the melded family between June 2 and November 9,
- obtained all of Kassidy's medical records,
- read the statement about blood under Kassidy's fingernails in the Maine State Police lab report of March 12, 2001, and
- read that Lab's DNA report of March 22, 2001.

The "reasonable doubt" defense was risky in an emotional case where the jury had been shown photographs of a dead baby's body and bruises.

In 2011, Chad remembered his conversation with his attorneys about this issue of defending against the Second Degree Assault charges,

As I recall the conversation took place in one of the side rooms at the Strafford County Courthouse while we were on a break in the trial. It was becoming apparent to me (at least I thought it was) that the state's case was weak on the murder charge for obvious reasons. I was concerned though about some of the misc. assault charges. Not the first degree assault charges because in my mind they were ridiculous. I know I had NEVER done anything so rough with Kassidy as to cause a fracture, let alone two. However, I was concerned with the second degree assault charges because I knew that I had held Kassidy's cheeks, in one hand, to obtain eye contact, and on a few occasions bruises later appeared. It didn't seem to me that we were doing much to dispute the assault charges or at least make the state prove the elements that I understood at the time (when they occurred. I wasn't and still am not very educated in the law but one thing that concerned me is I knew that many people described seeing bruises on Kassidy's cheeks but I knew that MULTIPLE PEOPLE HAD SEEN THE SAME BRUISES! For example, I knew that almost every one of Amanda's friends had seen Kassidy with bruises on her cheeks around

Oct. 13th. I was concerned that the jury wasn't going to understand this, hear all of these people describe these bruises, and then think they were all separate incidents which may lead them to find me guilty on each count!

I described this fear to Mark and my thoughts that we need to do a better job defending the individual assault charges. He basically dismissed my concerns as no big deal. I pressed further saying something like, "It's great if we beat this murder charge because I didn't kill Kassidy but I did hold her cheeks and cause some of this bruising. Each of these charges carries many years in prison and if I am found guilty of the various first and second degree assault charges I could be sentenced to 60-150 years in prison! I'm worried!" [At the time I knew what the cumulative number was if the sentences were all imposed consecutively and shared that number with Mark. It used to keep me up at night thinking about it. The sheer number of potential years scared me almost as much as the murder conviction.] Mark then elaborated more on why he wasn't worried about the charges like I was. He said something very close to- "Relax, you aren't going to do 60-150 years. They charged you with all of that to try and make something stick. You didn't kill Kassidy and that is the bottom line. If we beat the murder charge you'll be going home soon after. You grabbed her cheeks. Walk into any Wal Mart and you'll see 20 parents doing the same thing. You've done enough time for that. Until a few years ago, those charges weren't even felonies, they were misdemeanors. Judge Nadeau isn't going to give you much time if grabbing her cheeks is all you are convicted of." These words from my attorney had a calming effect on me. It is my personality to worry but I figured, "Hey, this guy is the professional, as he is fond of telling me, and he would know better than I would." Not to mention, it was nice to hear something that I viewed as positive. (Letter, Aug. 2, 2011)

A defense on the facts of the six Second Degree Assaults charges would have focused on the lack of evidence that Chad grabbed Kassidy's chin during the alleged time periods. There were three sources of evidence on those charges: Amanda's testimony, Chad's police interrogation and the observation of bruises. Amanda testified that Chad caused bruising when grabbing Kassidy's face to obtain eye contact "*five or six times*," but said that those instances occurred "*towards the end*," i.e. close to the time of Kassidy's death. (Testimony, p. 82) Chad stated during his interrogation that he caused a bruise by grabbing Kassidy's face about a week before her death. (p. 1546) The only remaining evidence of such grabbing were the observations of bruises, but most of those observations were either about bruises on other parts of Kassidy's body, such as her forehead, or were not specific enough to determine that the bruises were from Chad's grabbing Kassidy's face to gain eye contact. Further, without timelines, it was difficult for the jury to understand how many of the observations of bruises were actually of the same bruises. For example, during the Friday-Sunday weekend of October 13-15, several people saw the same bruises on Kassidy's face.

In addition to the weak factual evidence for the six Second Degree Assault charges and their timing, the defense could have argued that Chad's grabbing Kassidy's face was a legitimate form of parental discipline. By explicit discussions between Amanda and Chad, each authorized the other to share in the parenting of their respective children. New Hampshire law states that

a parent, guardian or other person responsible for the general care and welfare of a minor is justified in using force against such minor when, and to the extent that he reasonably believes it necessary to prevent or punish such minor's misconduct.

That right, however, "*does not apply to the malicious or reckless use of force that creates a risk of death, serious bodily injury, or substantial pain.*" (Chapter 627:6, New Hampshire Code.) including discipline authorized by parents.

In 1989, the New Hampshire Supreme Court reversed a lower court decision finding child abuse. In the case, Petition of Jane Doe, the mother hit her 21 month-old son, John, "*in the area of the mouth because, during mealtime, John persisted in throwing food. This punishment cut John's lip, causing it to bleed and swell.*" (p. 272) About 17 months later,

Upon being told he had to go to bed, John had a temper tantrum. When Jane instructed him to stop, he swore at her. Jane then slapped John with the back of her hand, hitting him

in the temple area. The slap left a bruise on John's temple, which lasted approximately two and one-half days. Jane was wearing a ring at the time, a factor which may have contributed to the bruise. (p. 273)

In the 1992 case In re: Ethan H, the New Hampshire Supreme Court again reversed a lower court ruling that found child abuse when a mother struck her son's "*bare buttocks approximately six times with an imitation leather belt.*" (p. 682) The discipline was used because the son had thrown food at the dinner table. In both of these cases, the parent hit the child with the intent of inflicting pain with the hitting being the punishment. In Chad's case, he never hit Kassidy to cause her pain and to punish her. He grabbed her face to ensure eye contact which did, nonetheless, cause bruises on 3-4 occasions. In the criminal law, intent makes a difference, as it should, and Chad's grabbing of Kassidy's face would never have been found to be child abuse by the standard set in the above two cases.

In 1993, in State v. Daniel Leaf, the defendant appealed his conviction for Second Degree Assault for hitting his ten year-old stepson ten times on the back, buttocks and thighs with a belt. At the trial, photographs were shown to the jury of the bruises. Leaf had discovered that his stepson had "*hidden, over a three-week period, a quantity of household dishes which he should have washed. The dishes were stored in a toybox.*" (p. 98) Leaf argued that the parental justification statute, above, gave him the authority to deliver such punishment and that such authorized actions should not have warranted a conviction for Second Degree Assault. He lost the argument because he testified that he had intended to strike his son only three times and that was the intended reasonable punishment. However, he said that he hit his stepson an additional seven times because he moved during the administration of the first three hits. The Supreme Court found that

For the defendant's use of force to have been justified, he must have reasonably believed it necessary to prevent or punish his stepson's misconduct.... we conclude that *a rational jury could have found beyond a reasonable doubt that the defendant's use of force was excessie, unreasonable , and not justified under the statute.*" (p. 99)

(For an analysis of these cases see the 2003 law review article by Patricia Weidler of Maine, "Parental Physical Discipline in Maine and New Hampshire: An Analysis of Two States' Approaches to Protecting Children from Parental Violence")

Again, the prosecutors charged in six counts in Chad's case that he held Kassidy's face and caused bruising. It's not known why his lawyers did not raise this parental justification defense, because the law in New Hampshire permitted parents, and their delegates, to administer intentional discipline of far greater intensity than grabbing Kassidy's face to achieve and maintain eye contact. If Daniel Leaf had stuck to his original, and allegedly reasonable, plan to whip his stepson only three times with a belt, the New Hampshire Supreme Court would likely have found that it was justified parental force.

In each of the three cases above, the parents defended the discipline technique of corporal punishment, but Chad has never believed in it, or practiced it. This was yet another indication that his bruising of Kassidy was unintentional and therefor justified by New Hampshire law.

With the conclusion of Dr. Baden's testimony, the jury had heard very, very little about Chad Evans - the man, the father, the friend. The jury had heard very, very little GOOD about him. Amanda did say that Chad was good with Kassidy and helped teach her the "ABC's," but the jury knew nothing about his siblings and parents and nothing about his saving lives from a burning car in 1996. The jurors knew nothing about boat rides with Kassidy and nothing about her "flying" around the house in Chad's arms as "Superman".

The jury would never hear from any of Chad's friends about him, and about their observations with Kassidy. They had seen several of Chad's friends testify for the prosecution, and they may not have noticed that after their testimony, they sat with Chad's family, rather than on the "prosecution side" of the courtroom with the Bortner/Conley family and Jeff Marshall's mother.

Regarding the six Second Degree Assault charges, the jury heard very little evidence that Chad had "*caused bruising to Kassidy by grabbing and squeezing her face,*" which was the language of each of the charges, which were differentiated only by the periods: September, and then four for each of the weeks of October and then one for the nine days of November.

John O'Connor

The final witness for the State was Dr. John O'Connor, a pediatric radiologist in Boston and a professor of Pediatric Radiology at Boston University School of Medicine. Will Delker asked Dr. O'Connor about Kassidy's left tibia bone, and he said that what he saw on the X-rays was "*all consistent with a healing fracture of some weeks to a month, or so, of age*" (p. 160)

On cross-examination by Mark Sisti, Dr. O'Connor said that he did not "*strongly disagree*" with Dr. Greenwald's opinion, in Sisti's words, that "*it could be from two to three months old?*" (p. 162). Dr. O'Connor was then excused after about ten minutes of testimony.

The jury was dismissed at 3:00 p.m., and there was a bench conference where Alan Cronheim presented the defense motions

to dismiss all the charges on the ground that taking the evidence as a whole, a reasonable juror cannot find by proof, beyond a reasonable doubt, all elements of the charges, so that each and every one ought to be dismissed at this point in time. (p.165)

He focused on the First Degree Assault charge regarding the fracture to Kassidy's left tibia bone. He said the dates of the alleged assaults were ambiguous, and thus no reasonable juror could find guilt beyond a reasonable doubt.

Will Delker argued that the evidence supported all the charges. Judge Nadeau denied all the motions to dismiss and gave her reasons. She gave the lawyers copies of her planned instructions to the jury.

The next day would be for the closing arguments, the judge's instructions to the jury and then the beginning jury deliberations.

MEDIA: 1. "Doctor disputes Evans murder trial testimony"
2. "Defense rests in Evans Trial - Sole witness for defense takes stand to make case that baby sitter is real killer"
3. "Defense rests its case in Chad Evans' trial"

CHAPTER 8. TRIAL OF CHAD EVANS - CLOSING ARGUMENTS, CHARGE/INSTRUCTIONS TO JURY, AND VERDICT - 18 to 21 DECEMBER 2001

"...there's not one shred of physical evidence connecting Chad Evans to the death of Kassidy Bortner." - Mark Sisti

"That was Kassidy living with the defendant. A living hell." - Simon Brown

Tuesday, 18 December 2001

On this tenth day of the jury-attended portions of the trial, both sides delivered their closing arguments, and Judge Nadeau gave her Instructions or Charge to the jury, and selected three alternates and deliberations began.

The day began with a final bench discussion about the judge's draft charge to the jury. Judge Nadeau agreed to add "*possibly*" to her instruction about guilt, so the instruction would be stated, "*It is not enough for the State to prove the defendant is possibly or probably guilty, rather the State must prove the defendant's guilt beyond a reasonable doubt.*" (p. 10)

Judge Nadeau noted that the defense had urged her "*to instruct the jury that the State must prove the time alleged in the indictment as an element of the defense,*" for the first and second degree assault charges. (p. 5) She denied the request, saying, "*.... this has not been a time-based offense, ... because time is not an element of the offense, but the defense is certainly free to argue* [in its closing statement] *that the evidence deviates from the time alleged in the indictment.*" (p. 5) Later she said, in response to Alan Cronheim's strong argument that timing was important, that she would "*not give an instruction that the jury must find, beyond a reasonable doubt, that the incident occurred within the time alleged in the indictment.*" (p. 9-10) This was a curious legal distinction, as the timing of the alleged assaults, together with the observations of bruises were critical aspects of the case that both sides rarely focused on with precision. Again, there were no timelines presented to the jury. One serious time problem came not with an assault charge, but with the charge of Endangering the Welfare of a Child, which declared that the abuse began on August 1, 2000. This charge, by its existence, reinforced the prosecution's view that the abuse began every early in the relationship between Amanda and Chad. In its opening statement, the prosecution said that Kassidy was a "*happy, normal, little girl.... learning her ABC's, but all that changed when the defendant came into her life.*" (p. 1, December 4) As noted before, Kassidy was seen by an orthopedic surgeon on September 11, 2000, but the lawyers and judge, and certainly the jury, didn't know that. They did know, however, of Jacqueline Conley's babysitting in August and September for Kassidy and her strong response to hearing from Joshua that he had seen bruising on October 13. Timing was very important to the understanding of this case, and there was a large risk that the jury didn't understand.

The jury was then brought into the courtroom and the closing statements began.

Defense Closing Argument: Mark Sisti

Mark Sisti delivered the closing statement for Chad. He argued that the investigation of the case was "*shoddy*" (p. 4) and that the police jumped to premature conclusions and that they didn't look closely enough at Jeff Marshall. He said, "*Chad didn't kill Kassidy, period,*" (p. 6) and that when Amanda left Kassidy at Jeff's on the afternoon of November 8,

...the baby wasn't exhibiting weird behavior, strange behavior, abnormal behavior. She wasn't exhibiting any problem with her appetite, with her gait, with anything. Nothing. Nothing." (p. 7)

Then, after Chad picked her up, he observed problems and called Jeff.

Sisti said the State argued that Chad injured Kassidy in his car after leaving Jeff's, but "*They searched his car. They came up with absolutely nothing. Not a hair out of place. No fluids. Nothing. Zero. No implement that would have created a blunt injury.*" (p. 9) Sisti argued that the jury should not speculate about "*could have's*" and "*the possibilities*." (p. 10) Referring to the accident with the ball on November 8, Sisti said, "*...that's not a cause of death or anything like that,*" (p. 11) and noted that the prosecutors focused on that incident to damage Chad's credibility. However, by excluding a role for the Tee-ball accident in Kassidy's death, and it did occur during the ranges of injury for Kassidy's head injury, the defense was putting all of its eggs in the Jeff basket.

Affirmatively, Sisti said that on the evening of November 8, "*...one, she was alive; two, Chad was bathing her; three Chad was holding her and feeding her a Popsicle; four, Chad had given her a banana earlier; five, Chad dressed her for bed; six Chad put her to bed. We call that caring for somebody....*" (p. 11-12) Sisti contrasted that caring with the next morning where "*... she was supposed to be cared for by Jeff Marshall... And she wasn't cared for by Jeff Marshall. She was dealt with at the highest level of neglect, and she was beaten at that house.*" (p. 13)

Sisti recalled for the jury that Jeff offered no explanation for the removal of Kassidy's pajama bottoms before the EMT's arrived. He recalled for the jury Jeff's efforts to show bruises on the face of Kassidy in the photo "*that was taken by her grandmother on October 1st, 2000.*" (p. 15) This was an effective use of that photo and that date, but more were needed.

Sisti reminded the jury that when talking to Detective Steve Hamel, Jeff blamed Chad before he was asked any questions.

Mark Sisti argued that when Jeff called Jennifer, the *"baby"* was already dead, but Jeff left Jen with the impression that she was alive. The most visible proof of that understanding was that Jen went back to work after both calls. "*And what the heck was going through Jeff Marshall's head? We don't know.... I suggest that he was still thinking, still trying to figure it out.*" (p. 18) Sisti called Jeff "*a walking reasonable doubt.*" (p. 18) Sisti often addressed the jury as "*folks,*" saying, in this instance, "*You are left with a case, folks, where* ***there's not one shred of physical evidence connecting Chad Evans to the death of Kassidy Bortner****.*" (p. 19) Sisti reminded the jury of the incomplete search of Jeff's apartment,

If you're doing a search of a residence where a 21-month old baby is found dead, and there's blood that is found in the bedroom... would you not check the basement?" (p. 19) Sisti said the police interrogation and quick accusation were unfair and not intent on finding the truth. About Chad, he said,

...we're not saying please crown him, you know, humanitarian of the year, father of the year. This is not what this case is about, okay?" (p. 21)

Unfortunately, the jury never learned that he was a very good father, and stepfather, and eager to become stepfather to a daughter. Because the jury heard very little that was good about Chad, and very little about his parenting, its decisionmaking was almost doomed to err. If there had been defense witnesses, the jury would have learned that he was a lot closer to being that "*father of the year*" than being a murderer. Very few child abusers and murderers set up education funds for their child and stepchild and inquire about such a fund for a potential stepchild - the alleged murder victim.

Sisti referred to Chad's statement in the police interview,

Chad tells them that he's ashamed of what he's done, you know, he's taken the kid by the jaw, all right, and he say that at least on a couple [of] *occasions, all right, that he left some bruises.... And Chad's not proud of a lot of stuff, okay? ... The trampoline thing, all right? That's a goofy excuse, all right? This, the trampoline thing, those are terrible, terrible. Absolutely terrible. But that's light years, folks, away from killing baby.*" (p. 21)

Sisti did not remind the jury had of the reason for Chad's holding Kassidy's jaw which was to obtain **eye contact**, which was done with Amanda's permission. The "trampoline story" was a white lie that Chad and Amanda used harmlessly enough with friends and relatives, as they had no idea that Kassidy was in danger. The white lie became a big problem when Chad told it to the police. That was "*terrible, terrible, terrible,*" but, to Sisti's point, it still didn't make him a child abuser or a murderer. While never using the words, "eye contact," Amanda had described it this way in her testimony, "*...he would say, 'Look into my eyes, just to get her attention.*" (p. 82) Chad did not grab Kassidy's chin in order to cause her pain as punishment. That idea was "*light years*" away from holding her chin to obtain eye contact, but accidentally holding it too strongly. What would the jurors have thought if they knew that Chad DID play on the trampoline with Kassidy and that he DID catch her once when she almost fell off? What would the jurors have thought if they knew it was a white lie from the beginning? Having his own attorney call it "*terrible, absolutely terrible,*" likely did not help the jury see the real reason for that contact.

Mark Sisti correctly summed up the problems with the police work in the case, "*... let's solve the crime. We'll figure out the evidence later.*" (p. 22) He then reviewed for the jury the injuries that Dr. Baden had said were inflicted within four hours of Kassidy's death. He asked, "*How can it be that she has injuries like that?*" (p. 23) The answer, said Sisti, is that "*Jeffrey Marshall beat her... Wake up, folks. It happened. He beat her, he delayed in reporting. He lied when he talked to his girlfriend. He bought time. He blamed Chad Evans.*" (p. 24)

Mark Sisti reminded the jury of Jeff's spanking of Kassidy and of her falling out of Jeff's truck, not a few days before her death, but two weeks before. He directly addressed the issue of blood on the Wendy's napkin,

... there was blood on that napkin, and that was either blood on that napkin because of a fresh injury that would have occurred at Jeffrey Marshall's house, less than four hours before her death, and you take it that way. Or there was blood on that napkin because of purging fluids." (p. 26)

How much stronger that argument would have been if the defense team had seen the reference to blood under all ten of Kassidy's fingernails in the March 12, 2001 Crime Lab report.

After noting that Jeff Marshall's care for Kassidy was within the time ranges for Kassidy's fatal injuries, Sisti said that it wasn't often in his defense experience "*to have two medical examiners support my client.*" (p. 27) More important, "*...there's one huge problem with the prosecutors' case... It's called fat emboli,*" (p. 28) and it was dislodged in Kassidy's body, "*Within two hours*" of her death. (p. 29)

Mark Sisti argued that the prosecutors' attacks on Dr. Baden were self- defeating as Dr. Baden was working for the prosecution in another case in Los Angeles at the same time he was working for O.J. Simpson. Similarly, the client for whom he spoke in Pennsylvania was declared a wrongfully convicted person by a Federal Court, despite the prosecutors' presentation of the trial judge's critical comments about Dr. Baden.
Sisti told the jury that the prosecution "*put more time and effort in looking for Chad Evans and Amanda Bortner in the woods in Vermont than they did in investigating this case,*" (p. 31) and he asked the jury to note that there were no charges before them for witness tampering or obstruction of justice.

Mark Sisti did not mention the Simple Assault charge against Chad for the incident or argument with Amanda on the evening of November 8. He did not mention the problems with the dates of the Second Degree Assault charge.

The defense's conclusion at end of trial could have included the point that the witnesses did not establish how Kassidy was injured. There was only speculation about causes, but a jury should not convict someone beyond a reasonable doubt, no matter how much it's desired to hold a single person responsible, unless there is considerable certainty about the elements of the crime.

The jury knew, but not with enough evidence, that Chad played with Kassidy. He nurtured her, and YES, to ensure that he had her attention, he held her face tightly enough to cause bruises on about three occasions. On the first occasion, he and Amanda were surprised by the appearance of bruises. On the remaining two occasions, where bruising was caused by his holding Kassidy's face, he had forgotten that bruising could happen so easily. During the intervening days with occasional holding of Kassidy's face, no bruises appeared, by his hand. Aside from accidents, Chad caused NO OTHER bruises to Kassidy.

Sisti did not appear toaddress the point made by Judge Nadeau made during the earlier bench discussion that "*the defense is certainly free to argue* [in its closing statement] *that the evidence deviates from the time alleged in the indictment.*" There were no timelines, and very few of the observations of bruising on Kassidy were anchored by a date. Because of that lack of specificity, several observations by different witnesses were of the same bruise, such as the observation of bruising on Kassidy's forehead.

Prosecution closing argument: Simon Brown

Simon Brown began his closing statement with a broad claim, "*Deciding this case will be easy for you because the evidence of the defendant's guilt is so devastating, so overwhelming and so clear.*" (p. 33)

Then, in the only explicit reference in the trial to "eye contact," Brown said, "*And the defendant insisted on discipline and **eye contact** with children in his household.*" (p. 34) Brown amplified, "*He began to grab Kassidy's face with his hand, hold her eyes to his, and make her look him in the eye. He was disciplining her.*" (p. 34) No one had explained to the jury that Chad sought eye contact to ensure understanding of non-disciplinary messages, too. The holding firmly, was not to punish by hurting, but to ensure eye contact so that the words were understood. The phrase, "eye contact," is commonly understood, and the jury might have empathized with Chad.

As an aside, the only other reference to eye contact at the trial was during a bench conference when Alan Cronheim said to Judge Nadeau, "*And I see the look on your eyes as skepticism, but...*" (p. 228, 10 December) In that context at least, they understood the purpose of "eye contact."

Simon Brown relied upon Amanda's police statements and listed Chad's alleged treatment of Kassidy, "*But the defendant's violence towards Kassidy was not confined to grabbing her face. He hurled Kassidy into a wall. He propelled her into a wall. One time he threw her into a closet door, causing her to bang her head. He picked her up by her armpit and her arm and jerked her arm back and he threw her on the bed. When she cried, he took his finger and he jabbed her in the throat, making her gag, and angering Amanda. He pulled roughly on her leg and fractured it.*" (p. 35) All of this came from police statements which Amanda tried to recant, but was walking the fine line between being charged with making false statements to the police and committing perjury in the trial. As the jury heard only Amanda's version of these incidents, it likely accepted it, except for the medical testimony about the alleged fracture. Chad would pay a price for allowing the jury to hear only one version of several incidents.

Simon Brown reminded the jury of Jeff Marshall's testimony that "*when he tried to give her a bath, she freaked out. She was terrified.*" (p. 35) In the American adversarial justice system, there was no requirement that he also remind the jury that Amanda said that she gave Kassidy a bath at least every other night and that Travis had testified that she saw Kassidy and she was "*you know, a little kid taking a bath and she's splashing...*" (p. 123-24) That correction would have to come in Mark Sisti's rebuttal, if at all.

Brown painted his portrait of a monster, "*Instead of learning to coexist with his girlfriend's daughter and doing something about his out-of-control temper, the defendant's violence continued to escalate.*" (p. 36) The jury heard very little about Chad's love for Amanda, and knew nothing of his work with a private counselor about his anger management and knew nothing about Amanda's taking down his list of preventive actions to take to avoid acting out angrily. The jury knew nothing about the day he and Kassidy went to his sister's on Sunday, November 5. Brown summarized the months between June 9 and November 9, "***That was Kassidy living with the defendant. A living hell.***" (p. 36) If the jury had actually heard about what life was really like for Kassidy living with Amanda, Chad and Kyle, the prosecutor's claim would have been dismissed as highly exaggerated as were many of his claims.

Brown described November 8th when he claimed that Chad, "*... beat Kassidy Bortner to a pulp...,*" (p. 36) but gave no further details, and didn't explain Travis's testimony or Amanda's testimony about Kassidy's condition on the 8th and early morning of the 9th. Later, Brown added, "*Only the defendant knows when and where he struck the first blow, but a first blow was struck in that car.*" (p. 36) Brown continued with the State's version of events, "*He called Jeff and he told him that Kassidy was injured but it was due to a flying baseball. But unfortunately for Kassidy, that first blow would not be the last one she* *would absorb that night. There would be more. Horrible photographs show us there would be more.*" (p. 38) Then he reminded the jury that Dr. Greenwald said that a ball did not create the bruises which she saw on Kassidy's head.

Simon Brown noted that Dr. Baden was not asked by the defense about whether a ball could have caused one of the injuries to Kassidy's head. However, Simon Brown didn't ask him either.

Brown addressed the issue of the timing of the bruises to Kassidy and said, "*Bruising was first seen by other witnesses as early as July*," but he didn't say who made that observation. He mentioned observations in September, but he didn't say anything about the pediatrician appointment on August 10, and the orthopedic surgeon appointment on September 11, because he didn't know about them. (Dr. Greenwald did refer to reports from Kassidy's "pediatricans" but those reports and the names of the pediatricians did not get, apparently, to the prosecutors, and not to the defense lawyers either.) He didn't say anything about the two overnight babysitting visits by Kassidy to her grandmother's, Jacqueline Conley, in early and late September. He didn't say anything about the daytime visit with Kassidy on October 1, which was the day of the State's photograph exhibit of Kassidy with her bunny rabbit. As Jacqueline Conley testified about her call to Chad's home on Saturday, October 14, she was very protective of Kassidy, and the jury could have been certain that if she saw any bruises on Kassidy during those visits, she would have discussed them with Amanda right away.

Simon Brown correctly understood that the trampoline story was, in fact, a story, and he sought to exploit that lie by arguing that Kyle's hit to Kassidy's eye was also a story. He said, "*the defendant topped himself with the baseball story... When you're lying, it gets difficult to keep the details straight. And that's what happened here. Because the defendant told some people it was a baseball, and he told some people it was a wiffle ball.*" (p. 46-47) In fact, Chad never told anyone that the "*starter baseball*" or "*hard rubber ball*", the terms he used in his police interview, was a wiffle ball. Some people, including Amanda, thought it was a wiffle ball, but they misunderstood, or simply made an assumption that it was a wiffle ball. Incidentally, Amanda's continued misunderstanding of the type of ball that Kyle hit is a good illustration of how Chad didn't manipulate Amanda's telling of the story. Similarly, Travis Hunt assumed that that the bat that Kyle was using when he was playing with Kyle was a long yellow bat, but it wasn't; as Kyle had not yet graduated to the thin bats. At age three, he was still using the thicker brown bat, which was one of the bats introduced into evidence by the prosecution.

Simon Brown told the jury that Chad lied to the police many times, beginning with the "trampoline story." He said that the "*baseball story*" was a lie. Brown continued, "*He told the police that Kassidy had a giant goose egg on her head from Jeff, that Jeff had caused. Dr. Greenwald told us that she performed an autopsy on November 10 and she saw no goose egg on that child's head.*" (p. 49). With a timeline, Brown might have seen that the injuries to Kassidy's head, and which were seen by Amanda, Chad, Jeremy and Travis, were seen on Saturday, October 28, and likely occurred on Friday the 27th. Another lie by Chad, according to Brown was that Chad had said to the police that "*Kassidy had a black and blue foot from Jeff stepping on her. She had that on Wednesday night*," (p. 49) and then Brown showed the jury photographs of Kassidy's feet which did not show black and blue. However, a few minutes earlier Brown did tell the jury that Jeff was upfront with Amanda about injuries caused as his apartment, and that "*He told her about tripping over Kassidy when he was answering the phone.*" (p. 43) Thus, Chad's recollection to the police was not as far from the mark as Brown implied. At the end of the segment on lies, Brown said, "*And maybe most incredibly, he told the police that Kassidy on her own would sometimes run into the wall herself and propel herself into the wall, causing bruising, and that he and Amanda had chuckled about it. They couldn't believe it.*" (p. 50) The prosecutors never asked Amanda about this incident, or these incidents. Also, it's another illustration of how the showing of the video of Chad's police interview without having him testify, with the opportunity to explain everything he said to the police on November 9, was a severe handicap to Chad's defense.

Brown was critical of Chad for the length of time it took to come to the Kittery Police Station, after being asked by the police to come. Brown said that the page to Chad came "*just after two o'clock.*" (p. 50) It was actually approximately 2:22 p.m. and Chad left his meeting with his boss immediately and needed to stop for gas and then take a "soup cooker" to the Portsmouth McDonald's. He arrived at the Kittery police station at approximately 4:10 p.m., or an hour and 50 minutes after the page. The website, www.mapquest.com, says that the distance from Chad's Hudson, New Hampshire meeting, to Kittery is 57 miles, which is predicted to take an hour and 12 minutes. Brown continued, "*...Kassidy's father figure, the defendant, shows up at the Kittery Police Department that evening later than anyone else, and he arrived with a posse of loyal friends.*" (p. 51) There was no testimony at the trial about exactly when Chad arrived at the Police Dept., but it was around 4:10, and not "*that evening.*" Chad arrived not with a "*posse of friends,*" but in the company of his ex-wife and prosecution witness, Tristan, who had met him at the Portsmouth traffic circle on Route 1, so she could lead Chad to the Kittery Police Dept, as Chad didn't know where it was.

Then Simon Brown discussed Amanda's testimony and her continued love for Chad, and how she lied to her friends and to Sergeant James White. Brown reminded the jury of Melissa Chick's testimony that she saw bruises on Kassidy when she gave her a bath in early September, but that bath was actually on Friday, October 13th, which was the same day that Amanda's brother, Joshua, saw bruises on Kassidy's face.

Brown summarized the prosecution theme that Chad's relationship with Amanda was unequal with Chad being the dominant person, with money and a house, and "*better educated.*" (p. 53) As Amanda had earned her G.E.D. in May of 2000, their education status as high school graduates was exactly the same. Regarding education, the jury didn't know that he had been elected as a member of the Keene Board of Education in 1992, and didn't know that he had encouraged Amanda to continue her education, including the financial management course that Chad encouraged Amanda to attend.

Brown returned to the theme that Chad was a persuasive person, and that he had persuaded Amanda to come back to him. However, it was Amanda who desperately sought to reunite with Chad and who needed him. Brown did not remind the jury that the only person at the trial who was asked about Chad's power of persuasion was Chad's ex-wife, and a prosecution witness, and she said "*No,*" to the Simon Brown's direct question, "*Is the defendant a persuasive person.*" (p. 17, of her testimony) Brown said it was due to Chad's powers of persuasion that his friends helped him during his time of freedom on bail. The jury never heard from his friends who would have explained, if permitted by the Rules of Evidence, that they helped Chad because they believed he was innocent, and because he was a friend.

Returning to Amanda's continued contact with Chad, Simon Brown said that she had other friends, to whom she could have gone, such as Melissa Chick and Tracey Foley and Cathy Nuernberg in Texas. He didn't explain that Amanda believed in Chad's innocence and her friends did not, and the jury could see that all three of them testified for the prosecution. Amanda sought the comfort of Chad and his family and friends because she was either rejected by her family and friends, or she felt uncomfortable with them. Simon Brown said that Chad's contact with Amanda showed that he "*was being deceptive and that he is conscious of his guilt.*" (p. 55) For sure, he and Amanda were hiding their contacts, but that only showed that Chad didn't want to be returned to jail; and showed nothing about his consciousness of guilt or innocence.

Brown correctly noted that Chad minimized his relationship and love for Kassidy during his police interview. He was concerned about her ASPIRE eligibility and about his own divorce, which he thought was still pending.

Simon Brown discussed the defense's arguments "*that they think show a shoddy investigation. And perhaps the most shameless of those is the one involving these pajama bottoms.*" (p. 56) What the defense did was to ask Jeff how and when the pajama bottoms were removed from Kassidy, and he didn't remember. Brown didn't tell the jury of the media coverage early in the case which included the police consideration of sexual abuse charges against Chad, after early reports of abnormalities in Kassidy's genital area. Those allegations were never committed to charges, as the evidence was minimal. Brown was technically correct when he said, "*And we have heard* [in the trial] *absolutely no medical evidence that anything of the like was going on,*" (p. 56) but he knew of the earlier allegations.

Brown referred to Dr. Baden as "*the last defense witness in this case... and paid handsomely to provide you with an expert opinion.*" (p. 57) He certainly was the last defense witness, and also the first, but the attack on his credibility for receiving $9,000 for several days work was not fair. Brown criticized Dr. Baden for changing his opinion, about the fat emboli, after the taking of his deposition and for his view that there was no fracture to Kassidy's leg.

Brown tried to contrast Dr. Baden with Dr. Greenwald whom he said "*is not a hired gun. Her testimony was hardly biased....*" (p. 58) A few minutes earlier, Brown had cited the testimony of Dr. John O'Connor in support of the view that there was a fracture to Kassidy's tibia, but at that time, Brown didn't use the derogatory description, "hired gun," to describe Dr. O'Connor.

Brown noted that the four injuries that the defense said were recent injuries were all to non-fatty portions of the body, and they had failed, therefore, to show where the injury was which could have caused the quick release of fat emboli as claimed by Dr. Baden. It was a good point, but no one asked that question of Dr. Baden, and Dr. Greenwald was not called back to the stand for an explanation. In fact, no witnesses were recalled to the stand, which was remarkable. In other settings, when about 27 people present conflicting information about a subject, there is an opportunity to revisit what others said about a subject. In a courtroom, the witnesses were not permitted to hear what the others said, in order to avoid infecting their testimony. In some American courts, jurors are permitted to ask questions, which are usually routed through the judge so s/he can ensure that they are legally proper. In New Hampshire, it may be allowed, but that isn't the practice, and the jurors in Chad's case didn't ask if they could ask questions.

If witnessed had been recalled, and available for easy recall, Dr. Baden might have been asked about Simon Brown's most recent point which was why he didn't identify where on Kassidy the fat emboli-releasing injuries actually occurred, and if it couldn't be determined, why not? Travis Hunt could have been recalled to explore his recollection that Kyle was using a yellow thin bat on the night of November 8th. Several witnesses could have been recalled to nail down the specific dates of observations of Kassidy and other events, such as Kassidy's appointment with the orthopedic surgeon. Dr. Greenwald could have been recalled to ask for the pediatrician records that she referenced.

Unfortunately, those exchanges did not take place. The jury was to be given a package of conflicting evidence and asked to make a decision in favor of one version of events beyond a reasonable doubt, and reject the others as false.

Returning to Simon Brown and Kassidy's injuries, he said, "*And you have heard no convincing evidence that Jeff Marshall beat this child that morning.*" (p. 60) If the jurors had been able to ask questions, someone might have asked, "What was the 'convincing evidence' that Chad Evans beat Kassidy in the car on the way to Kyle's day care and again after Kassidy's bath?" as Simon Brown had claimed earlier in his closing statement.

Simon Brown said of Kassidy on that morning of the 9th, "*She couldn't walk. He* [Jeff] *put her in bed.*" but there was no testimony that she couldn't walk. There was testimony that Amanda carried her into the apartment, as she might do when rushing, and placed her into the bed. Jeff had testified at page 144, that he had tried to pick up Kassidy to show Jennifer how she was unable to walk, but Jeff hadn't seen Kassidy since the previous afternoon when, he said, she was "*walking weird.*" (p. 144) Will Peirce had testified that Jeff had told him by phone on the morning of the 9th that "*She's not walking,*" (p. 172) but that could have easily meant that she was cranky or tired, and didn't want to get out of bed. There was no evidence that she had been unable to walk and certainly no evidence that Amanda or Chad knew that she was unable to walk.

Below is a summary List of Brown's statements relating to the substantive facts of the case. Each of them is accompanied by one of four evaluations for truthfulness or accuracy to the best of my knowledge, so far: TRUE (>90% true), M-TRUE (Mostly True, 50-90%

true) and M-FALSE (Mostly False, 10-50% true) and FALSE (<10% true). For a few statements, my clarifications are in brackets []. Finding the truth in this case is still an ongoing process.

FALSE 1. *...what the defendant did in this case, to repeatedly manhandle, beat, and eventually kill a beautiful little girl less than two years of age.*

FALSE 2. *But now you know the defendant is capable of such brutality,*

FALSE 3. *... and you know that he murdered Kassidy Bortner.*

M-FALSE 4. *The time that she lived with the defendant. The time that she was transformed from a vibrant, playful, happy little girl into a withdrawn, quiet, shell of a human being.*

TRUE 5. *When Amanda began living with the defendant, she was attached to her mother. She was jealous of her mother's attention.*

M-TRUE 6. *And when the defendant* [or Kyle or others] *showed affection towards her mother, Kassidy cried, she threw tantrums.*

M-FALSE 7. *She reared her head back and stomped her feet and she cried.*

M-FALSE 8. *She also did this at bedtime.*

FALSE 9. *The defendant could not tolerate tantrums.*

M-TRUE 10. *His son Kyle, his three-year-old son, he didn't throw tantrums. Kyle was disciplined.*

M-TRUE 11. *And the defendant insisted on discipline and eye contact with children in his household.*

M-FALSE 12. *But from Kassidy he got neither of those things. He got tears and tantrums.*

M-FALSE 13. *As Kassidy's crying continued, the defendant's anger erupted.*

M-TRUE 14. *He began to grab Kassidy's face with his hand, hold her eyes to his, and make her look him in the eye. He was disciplining her.*

M-FALSE 15. *But he squeezed her cheeks and he hurt her.*

M-FALSE 16. *Ugly bruises* [caused by defendant] *began to appear on Kassidy's face.*

FALSE 17. *But instead of the defendant being horrified that he caused even one mark on that little girl,...*

FALSE 18. *... his temper continued to erupt.*

M-FALSE 19. *And this grabbing of the face, we heard, happened at least twice a week, and the bruises kept reappearing. When old ones began to fade, new ones took their place.*

FALSE 20. *But the defendant's violence towards Kassidy was not confined to grabbing her face.*

FALSE 21. *He hurled Kassidy into a wall. He propelled her into a wall.*

FALSE 22. *One time he threw her into a closet door, causing her to bang her head.*

FALSE 23. [In anger] *He picked her up by her armpit and her arm and jerked her arm back and he threw her on the bed.*

TRUE 24. *When she cried, he took his finger* [once] *and he jabbed her in the throat, making her gag, and angering Amanda.*

FALSE 25. *He pulled roughly on her leg and fractured it.*

FALSE 26. *One time when she was crying, he couldn't take it, and he took her, brought her to a faucet, put water in her face, causing her to scream, and ...*

FALSE 27. *... after that, Kassidy was terrified of water;*

TRUE 28. *As Jeff Marshall told us in this trial, when he tried to give her a bath, she freaked out, she was terrified.*

FALSE 29. *He* [Jeff Marshall] *described to the police how he* [Chad Evans] *roughly picked up Kassidy off the ground by her neck. He described it as pulling her up like a kitten.* [Jeff may have said this, but it was not true.]

TRUE 30. *And he* [Chad Evans] *told the police that he smacked her in the mouth* [flicked her lip] *when she used bad language. He showed the police. He went like that. Which is pretty ironic. Pretty ironic that the defendant would chastise and discipline Kassidy for bad language, considering how he talked about Kassidy.*

FALSE 31. *During one of his violent outbursts he told Amanda exactly how he felt about her daughter. He told Amanda that he wished Kassidy wasn't around. He wished she had never been born.*

TRUE 32. *The 18-year-old girlfriend was fine with the defendant,* [but he thought she was at least 19]

FALSE 33. *...but he couldn't stand her child.*

FALSE 34. *He couldn't stand her crying.*

FALSE 35. *And this grown man actually referred to a 21-month-old on a regular basis as "a little bitch," as "stupid," and as "a retard." That's how he felt about Kassidy.*

FALSE 36. *Instead of learning to coexist with his girlfriend's daughter and doing something about his out-of-control temper, the defendant's violence continued to escalate.*

FALSE 37. *It got to the point where he and Amanda took steps to keep her away from people who would likely report the abuse.*

FALSE 38. *She wasn't taken to daycare* [because of the bruises].

FALSE 39. *... she wasn't taken to the doctor* [because of the bruises].

[The reason Kassidy wasn't taken to the doctor was because neither Amanda not Kassidy understood that the need was sufficiently serious. They thought that her problems were temporary. Each time medical treatment was considered by Amanda or Chad, Kassidy seemed to improve. During the last eleven days of Kassidy's life, there was no eye contact/face palming bruising from Chad.]

M-FALSE 40. *She was kept away from parents.*

M-FALSE 41. *And then, wild* [false] *excuses started to come from Amanda and the defendant. Stories of trampolines and falls and flying toys.*

M-FALSE 42. *And during this time Kassidy's personality changed.*

M-FALSE 43. *It changed to the point that on an overnight stay at Jeff Marshall's house, Jeff found her out of bed, in the living room, standing in the darkness, staring at a wall.*
[The single incident may have occurred, but ttanding up at night does not necessarily mean the Kassidy's personality had changed. She could have been dreaming or sleepwalking. She did not exhibit this behavior at home.]

FALSE 44. *That was Kassidy living with the defendant. A living hell.*

FALSE 45. *Jeff Marshall became the defendant's fall guy on November the 8th of last year because on that day the defendant went too far.*

FALSE 46. *He beat Kassidy Bortner to a pulp,*

FALSE 47. ... *he didn't take her to a doctor,* [intentionally depriving her of care that he knew she needed]

FALSE 48. ... *and because of that beating, she slowly died,* [Kassidy died, but not because of Chad's beating or hitting her.]

TRUE 49.*On November the 9th,* [sic: 8th] *Kassidy was at the defendant's, I'm sorry, Jeff's house. The defendant was in Portsmouth He wanted Jeff to bring Kassidy down to him. He needed to get to Dover for a six o'clock pickup time. Jeff wouldn't go to Portsmouth, so the defendant had to go north to Kittery to pick up Kassidy. And when he got there, he realized he didn't have a car seat for little Kassidy, so he was frustrated.*

TRUE 50. *He put her in the back seat, strapped her into an adult seatbelt, which you can imagine for a 21-month-old, would not be the most comfortable situation. He straps her in, chit-chats with Jeff, and he drives off.*

FALSE 51. *During that trip, during that trip back to New Hampshire, Dover, something happened in that car. Only the defendant knows when and where he struck the first blow, but a first blow was struck in that car. And the result of him striking Kassidy caused her to become groggy and lethargic.*

TRUE 52.*The defendant noted her behavior,* [grogginess and lethargy],

FALSE 53. ... *and he began his campaign to shift the blame,*

FALSE 54. ... *something that he and Amanda had become practiced at by that point.*

TRUE 55. *He called up Jeff*

M-TRUE 56. *... and he said to him, "The little bitch is acting weird. What did you do to her?"* [Chad did not call her a "little bitch" in that conversation.]

TRUE 57. *Jeff said, "Nothing, nothing, she was fine." The topic is changed. He continues to drive. He picks up Kyle from Dover and then they head to Rochester.*

FALSE 58. *When the defendant gets to Rochester, he observes the result of his blow.*

TRUE 59. *He sees that Kassidy is injured* [or ill].

M-TRUE 60. *And he knows at that point that Jeff knows when that child was picked up she had no new bruises on her face.*

FALSE 61. *He has to explain this. And so phone calls to Jeff kept coming,*

FALSE 62. *... and the story got more and more bizarre* [and more false].

TRUE 63. *He called Jeff and he told him that Kassidy was injured but it was due to a flying baseball.*

FALSE 64. *But unfortunately for Kassidy, that first blow would not be the last one she would absorb that night. There would be more.*

FALSE 65. *Horrible photographs show us that there were more* [blows that night].

TRUE 66. *... and we know that the defendant was the only adult caring for Kassidy for about one hour plus before Travis got home, and then from about nine o'clock to midnight when Amanda got home.*

TRUE 67. *And we know that during that night the defendant called or spoke to Amanda on the telephone and he told her, "Amanda, I don't want to look after her any more. Something always happens when I look after her."*

FALSE 68. *And he told her "We should take her to a doctor once the bruises go away." The bruises.*

FALSE 69. *And what was the defendant's mood that night? Was he the multi-tasked Mr. Mom that he described to the police? Hardly.*

TRUE 70. *When Amanda got home from working at Old Navy, they discussed changing a messy diaper on Kassidy. Neither of them ended up changing it.*

TRUE 71. *And then the subject turned to work. Amanda worked a long shift that day, and she made the innocuous little statement of "I work harder than you."*

FALSE 72. *Incredibly, the defendant's reaction to that innocent statement was to fly into a rage, to grab Amanda by the throat, pin her up against the couch, and to have the gall to say to her, "You know what gets me going. You've got to work with my temper. It's as if you're looking for it."*

FALSE 73. *That is the foul, assaultive mood the defendant was in around midnight on November 8th going into the 9th.*

M-FALSE 74. *Coincidentally, that is in the time range that Dr. Greenwald ages the vast majority of the bruises on Kassidy.*

M-TRUE 75. *We know that Kassidy died from blunt impact injuries to the head, face and abdomen. Dr. Baden made that fat emboli opinion yesterday morning, but he agrees that blunt force trauma caused this child's death.*

M-TRUE 76. *When the defendant picked up Kassidy from Jeff's house on Wednesday evening, she had no new bruises. She had fading bruises around her mouth that Jeff described, but no new bruises.*

TRUE 77. *And the defendant, in his multiple phone calls to Jeff, never says to Jeff, "What the heck! She's covered in bruises! What did you do to this girl? She's got bruises all over her face and body." He never says that.*

TRUE 78. *He says that she's been injured by a flying baseball, a baseball that came off the bat of his three-year-old son, a little indoor baseball, where his three-year-old generated enough bat speed and power to send a line drive right into Kassidy's face. That's how he accounts for injuries on Kassidy that night.*

M-TRUE 79. *And the next morning when the defendant tells the police that Kassidy was fine and mowing cereal, the reality is, she was returned to Jeff Marshall's house a mass of bruises.*

TRUE 80. *Jennifer Conley had never seen anything like it before.*

TRUE 81. *Jeff Marshall said it was the worst ever.*

M-TRUE 82. *She left his house on Wednesday with no new bruises.*

M-FALSE 83. *She returned covered with them.* [Kassidy returned to Jeff's and Jennifer's on the 9th with one new bruise, from the ballhitting, and possibly a bruise from her falling in the driveway.]

M-TRUE 84. *And Dr. Greenwald already told us that the injuries were not* [completely] *consistent--no injury on this child is consistent with a ball. But Dr. Greenwald pointed out circular injuries on this little girl's forehead and her cheek, but she told us that if this was a ball, a baseball, the surface of the ball would cause an accompanying contusion. It wouldn't be clear skin next to the curve.*

FALSE 85. *It makes sense. That's not a ball injury.*

M-FALSE 86. *Another problem is there are 8 to 10 blows to the child's head and face, not a single blow from a ball. The blows that happened in this case would have left corresponding bruises, Dr. Greenwald told us that. And she told us that she painstakingly aged these bruises, and as I said, the vast majority are in the 8-hour range to 12-hour range, the time when the defendant had control of Kassidy.*

TRUE 87. *And I note that even Dr. Baden wouldn't touch the baseball. We heard no opinion from the defendant's expert accounting for the baseball story.*

M-FALSE 88. *And Dr. Greenwald told you it didn't happen.*

M-FALSE 89. *This trial from the defense perspective has been as much about Jeff Marshall as it's been about the defendant. And they told you that he's an animal. That's what you were told in opening. He's an animal, and they told Jeff Marshall to his face "We're accusing you of murder; let's get that straight."*

FALSE 90. *But let me point out something very obvious. Making Jeff Marshall the scapegoat is the defendant's only viable defense in this case. This is not an original defense. It's his only hope of deflecting this evidence.*

FALSE 91. *And the evidence--the defense in this case in a nutshell is basically to acknowledge that the defendant hated Kassidy, hurt Kassidy, abused her over many, many weeks,*

FALSE 92. *... but miraculously on November 8th and 9th, Jeff Marshall.comes in and murders her, and the defendant has nothing to do with it. That's what they want you to believe. How unlucky for Kassidy. How unlucky to have two, not one, unbelievably cruel and violent caretakers. But the evidence doesn't bear that out.*

TRUE 93. *In opening, the defense told you that the ugly bruising that so many witnesses saw in this case began to develop 4 to 5 weeks before Kassidy's death when they say Jeff Marshall was looking after her.*

M-FALSE 94. *Well, there are several problems with that claim. We know now after trial that the ugly bruising was appearing long before 4 to 5 weeks before death, long before Jeff Marshall's slow season in landscaping.*

M-FALSE 95. *Bruising was first seen by other witnesses as early as July. Tammy* [Shannon] *Gagne saw a bruise on Kassidy's forehead in early September. Melissa Chick told us about the bath she gave Kassidy where she saw incredible bruising on her buttocks, on her legs, on her abdomen, and all over her face. Early September, long before Jeff Marshall even semi-regularly looked after Kassidy. Kathy Nuernberg told us that before she went back to Texas in September, she saw grab marks or what she thought were grab marks on Kassidy's face.*

M-TRUE 96. *Amanda only began her job at Old Navy the very week that Kassidy died. And it was that week that Jeff looked after her. And it was during that week, up until Wednesday, that he told you her bruising was clearing up.* [On Monday, Tuesday and Wednesday of that week, Kassidy had the bruise on her face from hitting the coffee table and from the scratch from her new kitten, and several others. One distinctive bruise was on her right cheek. Tristan had seen it, almost new, on October 30, and it was seen as a fading bruise by Nicole and Brandon Harvey on Sunday, November 5. That bruise may have been one of the 100 bruises and injuries observed by Dr. Greenwald.]

M-FALSE 97. *But before that week when she started working at Old Navy, the defendant told the police that Amanda was looking at Kassidy during the day for about three weeks, which takes us into October, folks. And he called it complete Kassidy time for Amanda. Yet in that time period when the defendant's coming home in the evenings and Amanda is looking after Kassidy during the day, she's getting these bruises.*

FALSE 98. *Amanda Bortner accounts for that horrible bruising. She told you in vivid detail how the defendant would abuse her, throw her into walls, jerk her arm, throw her onto beds and grab her face.*

M-FALSE 99. *And in retrospect, Jeff's problem may have been that he was too up front with the defendant and Amanda about each and every mishap that happened at his house. He told Amanda everything. He said he did so because she was his* [sic] *mother. He told her about the fall from the truck. He told her about slapping Kassidy on the bottom after she got into Windex. He told her about tripping over Kassidy when he was answering the phone. He told her everything. He didn't tell her wild stories to account for her bruising. He told her everything.* [The "fall from the truck" that Brown identified, was not the same fall that Jeff testified about. He didn't tell Amanda about Kassidy falling to the floor when he said to her, "Mama's here." He didn't tell Amanda about putting Kassidy's face into a pillow to muffle the her crying, so as not to bother his neighbors."]

FALSE 100. *The bruising was getting so bad that the defendant and Amanda sent Kassidy to Jeff to stash her away, basically, to keep her away from people who might report this.*

FALSE 101. *And the plan was always "Once the bruising goes away, we'll put her in daycare."*

M-FALSE 102. *But the bruising didn't go away. Jeff Marshall said that she had bruising on her face almost all the time.*

M-TRUE 103. *And let's not forget, Jeff Marshall had a relationship with Kassidy. He had known her basically since birth. He drove up to Auburn, Maine, and would visit with her. Josh Conley said that Kassidy loved Jeff, Jeff loved Kassidy. Jackie Conley said the same thing. He had no reason to hurt this child. It was his girlfriend's niece. And if he was hurting Kassidy, he wouldn't be approaching his neighbor, basically presenting his neighbor Kassidy, pointing to bruising on her face and asking the neighbor, "Should I report this?" He wouldn't be doing that if he was the one abusing her.*

FALSE 104. *And in none of the excuses that came from the defendant and Amanda while Kassidy was alive, during none of those excuses about trampolines and falls and things like that do they mention "We think it's Jeff. We think Jeff Marshall is doing this." That didn't happen.*

M-FALSE 105. *They made up wild excuses to cover the defendant's conduct, not Jeff's.*

TRUE 106. *On the night that the defendant was arrested, November 16th, when he was arrested one week after Kassidy died, Amanda was there, she was at his house. The police come in, they serve him with the arrest warrant. She gets into her car and drives to Springvale, Maine. She drives unannounced to Tracey Foley's house, the woman she used to babysit for. She shows up in tears. She shows up, Tracey lets her in. Does she say to Tracey, "They've arrested Chad but they got the wrong guy. It was Jeff MarshalL Let me tell you what he's been doing to Kassidy?" No. She said to Tracey Foley, "And you knew, you knew and I didn't listen."*

M-FALSE 107. *And then for the next two hours she proceeded to tell Tracey Foley exactly what the defendant had been doing to Kassidy.*

TRUE 108. *Not that Jeff Marshall isn't* [sic] *without blame here. He is. He is with blame. Kassidy was delivered to him on Thursday, November 9th, covered in bruises, and he didn't do anything about it. He saw bruises before that; he didn't do anything about it. He told us "I looked up to Chad." That certainly doesn't cut it.*

FALSE 109. *Only one person caused those injuries, and that's the defendant.*

FALSE 110. *The defendant in this case told so many lies it is hard to count them.*

TRUE 111. *He told that trampoline story,* [only to Jacqueline, Tristan and the police]

M-TRUE 112. ... *what we now know as the trampoline lie. He told numerous people that he was on the trampoline with Kassidy, they're bouncing around, and somehow she bounces off the trampoline, and like Spider Man, he's able to grip her by the face and bring her back in. That's the story he concocted with Amanda to tell people to account for that facial bruising.*

M-TRUE 113. *The bruising that some people described as looking like dirt that was all over her face. And amazingly, a lot of people bought that lie. He told it to Kassidy's grandmother. He told it to Jeff and Jennifer. He told it to a lot of people, and he told it to the police detectives who were investigating the death of Kassidy, right there, in an earnest manner, having a great conversation with the police, he out and out lied to them. And he said it in as convincing a manner as you could believe.*

FALSE 114. *But as absurd as the trampoline story was, the defendant topped himself with the baseball story.* [Chad and Kyle told the truth about the T-ball hitting Kassidy.]

TRUE 115. *The baseball stories that he told to the police, where he's letting his child hit baseballs in the bedroom, we were all in that bedroom, he says he's sitting on the bed, Kassidy's to his right, and he's throwing baseballs to three-year-old Kyle. And Kyle whacked one, and you can listen to this on the tape, and the defendant says he reached out with his left hand, couldn't get the line drive, and it went right into Kassidy's face.*

FALSE 116. *That was the story that he was concocting to the police.*

FALSE 117. *And it's a story he told to others as well. He told Jeff the story, and he told Travis and Tristan. You know what?* [Chad did tell Jeff, Travis and Tristan and many others about the T-ball hitting Kassidy, but the story is true.]

TRUE 118. *Because the defendant told some people it was a baseball, [He told the police it was a "starter baseball" and "hard rubber ball" He told others it was a "ball."]*

FALSE 119. ... *and he told some people it was a Whiffle ball.* [Chad never told anyone it was a wiffle ball.]

TRUE 120. *Travis got home that night and Travis tells us that he went up and was talking to the defendant, watching Kassidy splash around in the bath. He described her mood that night as chipper at one point. He said on the stand she was absolutely normal. He saw no bruising on her other than what the defendant told us, the bruise under her eye. But Travis tells us that, yeah, gee, "After that I went into the bedroom with Kyle and I did a little batting practice with him, too." Here's Travis, he's home from work, he's in his uniform, and he goes into that bedroom and he starts tossing Whiffle balls to Kyle. And he's whacking them, he's hitting them pretty good, Travis said.* [Normal, but not "absolutely" normal]

M-FALSE 121. *And he was asked what kind of bat was he using? Well, he was using one of those yellow skinny long Whiffle ball bats. We've all seen them. That's what he said. Well, the police secured that house that night. They wouldn't let anyone in or out. Well, they let them out, but they secured it, and the very next day they searched the house and removed every single ball and bat in that house. And there was no long yellow Whiffle ball bat in that house.* [When asked, a year after Kassidy died, the question about the type of bad Kyle used when Travis tossed balls to him, Travis mistakenly assumed and recalled that it was a typical long yellow bat, instead of the red fat bat which was the one used by Kyle.]

TRUE 122. *And we know that Travis left that house at nine o'clock that night. He went to his then girlfriend's house. He said he wasn't back till midnight.*

TRUE 123. *And during that time the defendant was the only adult with Kassidy.*

FALSE 124. *He told so many lies in that statement it's difficult to count them.* [Chad told the "trampoline story" to the police, which was untrue, and he minimized the strength of his relationship with Kassidy. If the latter representation is considered a lie, then the count is two. Everything else he told the police during his three and a half hour interrogation.]

FALSE 125. *His first one was immediately. He walks in and he tells the detectives he doesn't want to sit down, he's been driving for two and a half hours. And we know that he was in Portsmouth around four o'clock talking with his friend Jeremy. He was in the area. Portsmouth is right down the road from Kittery.* [As this representation was mostly true, it was not a lie told "immediately."]

TRUE 126. *He told the trampoline story,*

FALSE 127. *... he told the baseball story.* [He truthfully related the ballhitting event, so the statement that he lied about it is false.]

FALSE 128. *He said that Kassidy was fine in the morning, she was mowing cereal.* [Chad saw Kassidy open her baggie with the cereal and was reaching into it when she was in Amanda's car and he assumed that she had begun eating that cereal. So impressed was he with Kassidy's opening of the baggie, that he commented to Amanda about it, as she was driving away. It was not a lie.]

TRUE 129. *He gave her a kiss goodbye and he described only limited bruising on Kassidy's face.*

FALSE 130. *Well, even Amanda contradicts him on how Kassidy was behaving that morning. She told us that she didn't even get out of bed. Kassidy normally walked into their bedroom every morning. But this morning she was lying in bed crying, and she was lethargic.* [Amanda's and Chad's recollections of how Kassidy was behaving on the morning of November 9 are substantially the same. Therefore, Brown's statement of contradiction is false. One part of Simon Brown's statement is true, which is that Kassidy "*normally walked into their bedroom.*" One wonders if any of the jurors made a note to ask his or her peers why a girl who was allegedly abused by Chad would "normally" walk into his bedroom. Was Brown now describing Kassidy's "*living hell*" or was he describing a different reality that challenged the basis of his case?]

M-TRUE 131. *That's not what the defendant told police. The defendant says that the night before Kassidy was eating a pop-ice, they were playing games, doing ABCs, having a great time.* [Chad was very concerned that evening about Kassidy's wellbeing. In inelegant, but truthful, language in his interrogation, he said, *"I babied the shit out of her last night, more than usual because she was sick "*(p. 1592) Because Chad never said that Kassidy was "*having a great time*," the statement is mostly false.]

M-TRUE 132. *Dr. Greenwald told us that if that child had sustained a serious subdural prior to that, she wouldn't be going in peaks and valleys behavior. It was a steady decline.* [Dr. Greenwald did say that, but Kassidy's behavior was characterized by "peaks and valleys."]

TRUE 133. *He told the police that Kassidy had a giant goose egg on her head from Jeff, that Jeff had caused.*

TRUE 134. *Dr. Greenwald told us that she performed an autopsy on November 10th and she saw no goose egg on that child's head.* [However, the autopsy was 13-15 days after the injury causing the two bumps on the top of Kassidy's head.]

M-TRUE 135. *He said that Kassidy had a black and blue foot from Jeff stepping on her. She had that on Wednesday night.* [Chad said in his interrogation, *"And she's got a bruise on her foot where....Jeff said he stepped back on her, but I don't know."* (p. 1554)]

TRUE 136. *These are the photographs of her feet. They're not black and blue.*

M-TRUE 137. *And then he began to tell a series of excuses about Kassidy, about the bruises, that she fell a lot, that Kyle, here's Kyle again, hit her with toys, causing bruising. He admitted that he himself grabbed Kassidy by the face to get eye contact. But then he said, "But Kyle touched her face right after me. Kyle did, too, so it could have been from him."*

FALSE 138. *He told the police that he never choked Amanda. Even on Amanda's version at trial when she says she threw a mug at him first, she told us he certainly did choke her and pin her up against the couch, and he told the police he never did it.* [Chad never choked Amanda.]

M-TRUE 139. *And maybe most incredibly, he told the police that Kassidy on her own would sometimes run into the wall herself and propel herself into the wall, causing bruising, and that he and Amanda had chuckled about it, they couldn't believe it. These are the things that he's telling the detectives investigating Kassidy's death.* [Once, when running into the corner, Kassidy fell forward and hit her head against the wall.]

TRUE 140. *Let's look at how he behaved on November the 9th, Thursday the 9th. Kassidy has gone to Jeff Marshall's, and he receives a phone call from DCYF, from Patricia Hawker*[Hocter]. *She leaves him a message saying, "It's about the children. Get back--please give me a call back." Well, he does call her back. This is Thursday morning. And he tells her, leaving her a message, "You know, why don't you call me back on Tuesday afternoon between 3 and 4. I'm going out of town."*

FALSE 141. *This is an effort to buy time, ladies and gentlemen, to buy time for the bruises to go away.*

TRUE 142. *So after the DCYF called, he picks up the phone and calls Jeff Marshall. He calls Jeff and says, "How's Kassidy?" And then he says to Jeff--he tells Jeff about the DCYF call.*

M-FALSE 143. *He tells Jeff that he knows it was Emily, Amanda's friend, who called DCYF on him, and he was angry about that. He wasn't calling Jeff and saying, "Thanks a lot, Jeff. You beat her up last night, she's covered in bruises, and now I'm getting calls from DCYF." He's saying "Emily called on me," And he says to Jeff, "If this is about Kassidy, Amanda and Kassidy are out of my house."*

TRUE 144. *Later that day he's paged by the Kittery Police Department. It's in the phone records and they're in evidence. He's paged after two o'clock, just after two, and asked to come down to the police station. Now, the defendant knows that Kassidy was staying in Kittery that day.*

FALSE 145. *Does he get in his car and immediately drive up to the station as he's asked to do? No.* [Chad did leave his meeting with Bob McDougall immediately and head for Portsmouth and Kittery.]

M-TRUE 146. *He starts contacting all of his close friends wondering, "Hey, what do you think this is about? What do you think?" He actually goes to visit Jeremy Hinton at a restaurant and tells him or talks to him about the situation. He calls Travis. He calls Travis and says to him that he needs to go to the Kittery Police Department and he reminds Travis, he reminds him of the baseball story. He reminds him that Kassidy was hit by a baseball, and he reminds Travis that he was playing games with Kassidy and she was fine. Kind of a curious thing to do, don't you think? Kassidy's father figure, the defendant, shows up at the Kittery Police Department that evening later than anyone else, and he arrived with a posse of loyal friends. Are these the actions of a man with a clear conscience who is totally surprised by this page, or is he circling the wagons?* [It is true that Chad had conversations and made phone calls on his way to Kittery, but he arrived at 4:10 p.m. and not "*that evening*," and not with a "*posse of friends*."]

M-FALSE 147. *Amanda Bortner, let's talk about her a minute. Amanda got on the stand and she told you an incredible eyewitness account of the abuse that Kassidy suffered at the defendant's hands. Her testimony supports all of the assault charges that you have before you. She told you some terrible things that happened to Kassidy. But you've got to look at Amanda and ask yourself if she's telling you everything.*

TRUE 148. *She told you on the stand that she loves the defendant, she misses him, she wants to be with him, she's been staying with the defendant's sister.*

M-FALSE 149. *In this case she over and over again lied to other people to cover for the defendant's abuse.* [Amanda told the "trampoline story" to several people to avoid explaining Chad's palming of Kassidy's face to obtain eye contact, and not to cover for abuse.]

M-TRUE 150. *To Sergeant White, the man she described as kind and nice, she lied. She lied to him when he asked her if she was having contact with the defendant.*

And given her loyalties at this point, she has every incentive to trash Jeff Marshall, to make Jeff Marshall look bad because that's going to help the defendant in this case. To use Attorney Sisti's words, be suspect about her claims regarding Jeff.

FALSE 151. *Be suspect when she tells you that she never, ever saw bruising on her daughter's body. She never did. She bathed her all the time. She never saw that.* [Amanda did not say that she never, ever saw bruising on Kassidy. She discussed the bruises with several people.]

M-FALSE 152. *Well, her very close friend Melissa Chick testified in early September she gave Kassidy a bath and she saw her covered in bruises, her stomach, her bottom, everything. And she approached Amanda immediately. She said to Amanda, "There's something wrong. There's something wrong here. You better take her to a doctor. She might have leukemia. She might be anemic." And Melissa told you that Amanda's response was "I don't want people to think she's being abused."* [While Melissa and Amanda may have had that discussion, it was unlikely to have been in earlier September when Melissa was giving Kassidy a bath, because Amanda does not remember Melissa having Kasssidy for an overnight. More importantly, there were several no-bruise observations of Kassidy in September, including Scott Conley's birthday party on September 2, Dr. James Timoney's appointment with Kassidy on September 11, and Jacqueline's babysitting for Kassidy during the last week of September.]

FALSE 153. *Amanda made her choice a long time ago. She told you about the abuse that she witnessed. She lived that. She saw Kassidy being hurt, she knows that Kassidy has died, and she's still standing with the defendant. She didn't protect Kassidy in life and she's chosen to defendant* [sic] *him in death.* [This was a complicated statement, but it's false in the sense that Amanda didn't believe that Chad was abusing Kassidy, and certainly doesn't believe that he hit her or beat her to cause her death. Amanda chose to defend Chad because she believed, and believes to this day, that he is innocent.]

M-FALSE 154. *Now, the defendant dominated this relationship. Kathy Nuernberg told us about that. She had seen Amanda in a prior serious relationship, and she said Amanda did what she wanted before. But with the defendant it was different. She was afraid to be late, she was afraid to go against him. And it's easy to see why. It's easy to see why the defendant was the dominant one in this relationship. He had the good job, he had the money, he was better educated, he had a lot of close friends, he had a house, and he was 10 years older than her. We all know that there's a big difference between the age of 18 and 28.* [Cathy Nuernberg had a distorted opinion of Amanda's relationship with Chad, and Amanda was not afraid of Chad.]

FALSE 155. *And we know that he's a persuasive person.* [Tristan testified that Chad was not a persuasive person. She was the only trial witness to be asked about Chad's alleged persuasiveness. Also, Chad obviously didn't persuade the police of anything.]

FALSE 156. *When you watch that tape again, you can see that the defendant is very comfortable talking to these detectives.* [Chad was nervous during his police interrogation.]

M-FALSE 157. *He's very comfortable talking about topics not having to do with Kassidy. And he's gone far in his job because he's a schmoozer, he knows how to talk. But when you watch that tape, pay special attention when the questions get pointed, when they start asking him questions about the abuse of Kassidy. You'll see him, when he's asked, "Did you ever cause bruises to that child?" "Is that your cell phone or mine?" Then in mid-stream when he's answering the question, he'll change the topic entirely and they'd have to bring him back to it.* [The "schmoozing" was mostly initiated by the police in a classic effort to make Chad feel comfortable. The changing from subject to subject was done by the police as well as Chad, as important questions and answers came to mind.]

TRUE 158. *He admits to causing bruising on Kassidy's face, but then says Kyle did it, too.*

M-TRUE 159. *He tried to be persuasive to the detectives, but it didn't work. And the detectives told you that they had talked to him for a long time that night and they, in monitoring other interviews that had been going on, and Lance McCleish said that the tough questions had to be asked, and they asked them. They were investigating the death of a 21-month-old girl. We know the defendant is persuasive for other reasons.* [Except for the "trampoline story," Chad tried to help the police with factual information about Kassidy. In terms of Simon Brown's word, "persuasive," Chad tried to persuade the police to learn the truth.]

M-FALSE 160. *We know that he persuaded Amanda to stay with him for nine months in violation of the bail order. We know that he persuaded a close friend of his to do incredible things to help him violate the bail order. And he convinced Jeremy Hinton, a restaurant manager, and Vanessa Manson, who worked in the prosecutor's office, he convinced them to help him out. People gave up their apartments and their own beds so that the defendant can have intimate time with the eyewitness of his abuse. These close friends didn't say to the defendant, "Are you crazy? You're on your own." They didn't do that. They wanted to help him. And it even got to the point where the defendant's own family set up this campsite in the woods of Vermont, a campsite where the defendant could have unfettered contact with the state's star witness, in secret, in violation of the Court's order, and out of sight of authorities. And please don't accept the claim that's been made in this case that, well, the defendant was just helping out Amanda because she had nowhere else to go. He did it out of the goodness of his heart. We know that Amanda had other options. She had her friend, Kathy, in Texas who she actually lived with for a while, and she had Melissa and Tracey in Maine. Tracey Foley had an open invitation for her to stay with her. But instead, she abandoned her close friends, dropped contact with her close friends, and aligned herself with the defendant.* [Amanda's 2001 closeness to Chad was about Amanda's love and need for him and her belief in his innocence. It had nothing to do with Chad's alleged persuasiveness.]

FALSE 161. *The point of this contact for nine months against the Court's order is to show that the defendant was being deceptive and that he is conscious of his guilt.*

M-FALSE 162. *On that tape when he was talking to the police, when he's have a free-wheeling conversation, you know, they start talking about Amanda, and he says, "Well, guys, you know, I'm just getting out of a divorce, and I'm going to take things real slow. You know, I can tell this girl really loves me, but I don't want to jump into it too quickly." He says to the police that Amanda keeps bugging him to tell her "I love you." But he said that he told her, "Well, don't you want it to be natural, Amanda, when I finally do say this to you?" This is what he's telling the detectives. But by the end of that interview, he knew that the police suspected him, and within minutes he's out in the parking lot of the police department approaching Amanda and telling her how much he loves her. This is on the same day that he called Jeff Marshall and said that "They're out of my house if this is about Kassidy."* [The different statements by Chad are taken out of context. It is false to believe that they are necessarily contradictory or inconsistent.]

M-TRUE 163. *The defense in this case has poked and prodded the State's case, trying to hit parts of the case that they think show a shoddy investigation. And perhaps the most shameless of those is the one involving these pajama bottoms. They want you to believe that Jeff Marshall was doing something inappropriate with this child on that morning. What other reason would they point to that? The fact is, Kassidy had a diaper on. Jeff Marshall had pants on, and the photograph of those men's jeans show that it was right below an overloaded laundry basket. And we have heard absolutely no medical evidence that anything of the like was going on.* [Why was it more shameless for the defense to ask questions about Jeff's care of Kassidy than it was for the State to charge Chad with murder, assault and child endangerment? Regarding the possibility of sexual abuse of Kassidy, Brown was right that evidence of that possibility was not heard at the trial, but he knew, or should have known, that such possibilities were disclosed by the police to the media early in the investigation.]

M-TRUE 164. *Dr. Baden was the last defense witness in this case. And Dr. Baden was hired by the defense and paid handsomely to provide you with an expert opinion. Judge Nadeau will tell you that you are not required to accept an expert's opinion. If you weigh it against other expert opinions and against the other evidence in the case, you can find that opinion to be unreliable. In this case, Dr. Baden's opinion is unreliable. In this case, Dr. Baden had known about this case for a long time. And on November 20th he issued a report, he issued a report agreeing with Dr. Greenwald, this child had died from blunt impact injuries of the head and abdomen. That report was a page and a half, and nowhere in that report was there one mention of fat emboli. Sixteen days before today Dr. Baden was deposed. It was the second day of a two-day deposition. And Will mentioned to him Dr. Greenwald's findings as to fat emboli. Dr. Baden expressed surprise at that time that fat emboli was a part of this case, even though it was mentioned several times in the autopsy report of Dr. Greenwald. And yesterday morning he traveled up here to New Hampshire and for the first time in this courtroom yesterday morning he presented his opinion that fat emboli, something that he didn't know anything about two weeks before, caused a sudden death on Thursday morning. Major trauma happened on Thursday morning that caused fat to liquify and go into major organs and cause a sudden death. That's his brand new opinion. But strangely, Dr. Baden did not testify about what this major trauma was. What were these blows on Thursday morning that brought about this rare medical phenomenon? He didn't point to these blows that caused that. In his report of November 20th, he said that the bruising that Dr. Greenwald aged was between 5, 12 and 20 hours old. His new opinion about the fat emboli is totally contrary to Dr. Greenwald's expert opinion about fat emboli in which she said it takes many, many hours for that to develop and is contrary to the treatises that were presented to him. Additionally, he was wrong about the leg fracture. He was emphatic that he did not see a leg fracture to the left tibia, and he disagreed with Dr. Greenwald on that. He said that the fracture, if there even was one, didn't go through the bone marrow. Then you heard from*

Dr. O'Connor, who is a pediatric radiologist, and he told you that there most certainly was such a fracture.

M-TRUE 165. *While you wonder how Dr. Baden earned his $9,000 in this case, let me talk to you about Dr. Greenwald. Dr. Greenwald is not a hired gun. Her testimony was hardly biased. She herself has over 20 years of experience as a forensic pathologist. She has practiced all over the country, and unlike Dr. Baden, she did her homework in this case. She was prepared and she painstakingly aged these bruises. As I said before, using a microscope, she aged these bruises, and the vast majority of them are in the 8 to 12-hour range, 8 to 12 hours before death. Now, Attorney Sisti talked about three injuries, three injuries that could be recent. We're talking about two bruises on the back, one to the frenulum--and let's not confuse the frenulum. This giant injury right here is not the frenulum. The frenulum is that little mark there. And one to the back of the head. None of these injuries, ladies and gentlemen, were to fatty areas of the body, fatty areas where this emboli would originate. And Dr. Greenwald told you that when you take these slides, the bruising ages from the outside in, and there's a possibility that you're not getting a section of the bruise that's started the healing process. And also, in this case Jeff Marshall testified that he was fishing around in her mouth when he was trying to help her. There is photograph--there are photographs where the EMTs are putting tubes into little Kassidy's mouth. A picture right here with an EMT and with his hand in her mouth.*

M-FALSE 166. *And you have heard no convincing evidence that Jeff Marshall beat this child that morning. That child was brought to his house covered in bruises. She couldn't walk. He put her in bed. The defense wants you to believe that in that state he began administering more beatings. It's not credible.* [It's not clear how many bruises Kassidy had on her entire body when Amanda brought her to Jeff's and Jennifer's. Her face had several bruises. If Brown was correct that there was no convincing evidence that Jeff beat Kassidy on November 9, and I agree with that assessment, then there was no convincing evidence that Chad beat her on that day or any previous day either.]

M-FALSE 167. *Dr. Greenwald told us that Kassidy was a battered child. She had injuries of varying ages all over her. An aspect of battered child syndrome is that the parent singles out one child and leaves other children alone. That's what happened in this case. [Dr. Greenwald said in her testimony that "there is usually one child that is the scapegoat in that particular family."* (p. 216) [Even if she was right about the characterization of "usually," that doesn't mean that it's always the case. Brown used the fact that Kassidy was one of a three-child melded family to somehow prove that, therefore, this was a case of battered child syndrome.]

FALSE 168. *The abuser creates implausible stories that don't fit the facts. That's what the defendant did in this case.* [Everything that Chad told the police fit the facts except the "trampoline story," and his minimization of his relationship with Amanda. It was the police and prosecution theory of the case which did not fit the facts.]

FALSE 169. *And the most common area for abuse with battered child syndrome, the head and the abdomen. That's where the defendant struck in this case.*

FALSE 170. *Ladies and gentlemen, the defendant roughly pulled on Kassidy's leg, fracturing her leg.*

M-TRUE 171. *He repeatedly grabbed her face, causing bruising,* [The problem here is the characterization of "repeatedly." Chad estimated that he held Kassidy's face to get eye contact approximately 12 times in September/October and that 3-4 of those led to bruises.]

FALSE 172. *...he assaulted Amanda Bortner on November 8th.*

FALSE 173. *He had repeatedly hurt Kassidy.* [Chad can be said to have hurt Kassidy when he held her face too tightly 3-4 times and caused bruises.]

FALSE 174. *and did nothing to help her.*

FALSE 175. *He finally on November 8th into the 9th, he recklessly caused her death by beating her again.*

FALSE 176. *And he showed an extreme indifference to the value of Kassidy's life.*

FALSE 177. ***Kassidy's life with the defendant was a living hell****. And the abuse only stopped when the defendant finally killed her.*

Categorizing the truth of 177 statements and how they show Chad's innocence or guilt is complicated by the fact that many of the true statements did not point in either direction. For example, with #81, about the bruising he saw on November 9, "*Jeff Marshall said it was the worst ever.*" That was likely true, and it was also likely true that it was the worst bruising that Amanda or Chad saw, too. However, Amanda and Chad thought they understood the causes of all the bruising, and on November 8 and 9, there was no bruising caused by Chad. Another example is #122, as it was true "*that Travis left that house at nine o'clock that night. He went to his then girlfriend's house. He said he wasn't back till midnight.*" This TRUE statement also said nothing about Chad's guilt or innocence.

Nonetheless, even amidst imprecision, it's useful to quantify the truth in the above list. Each of the categories can be assigned values: 10 for TRUE, 7 for M-TRUE, 3 for M-FALSE and 0 for FALSE. There were 40 TRUE statements, 27 M-TRUE, 33 M-FALSE, and 33 FALSE statements, with a total value for the 177 statements of 688. If all the statements were true, the score would have been 1770, and if half of them were true, the score would have been 885. In percentage terms, the 688 score was 39%.

There is no set requirement of how much of a prosecutor's closing statement a jury has to believe in order to find a defendant guilty beyond a reasonable doubt. The closing statement tells the jury the prosecution's theory of the case and why the jurors should find a defendant guilty. One would expect, therefore, that for a jury to find guilt, most of that theory must be found to be true, and the closer to 100% the better.

Charge to the Jury: Judge Tina Nadeau

Follow the law. Judge Nadeau then gave her instructions, or charge to the jury, beginning with the admonition that "*It is your duty to follow all of the instructions that I'm about to give you. Regardless of your view of what the law is, that law that I explain to you is the law that you must use in reaching your verdict.*" (p. 14)

Defendant's right not to testify. She told the jury that "*the defendant has an absolute right not to testify. The fact that the defendant did not testify in this case may not be considered by you in any way in reaching your verdict. The state has the burden of proving guilt, beyond a reasonable doubt, and the defendant has no obligation whatsoever, to prove his innocence.*" (p. 15)

Defining the evidence that could be considered. Judge Nadeau explained that the evidence in the case was the testimony of witnesses and exhibits, and that lawyers arguments and statements were not evidence. She reminded the jury that Cory Merrill's testimony was not to be considered in the jury deliberations.

<u>Types of Evidence - Direct and Circumstantial, and rational conclusions</u>. She defined the two types of evidence: direct and circumstantial, which should be valued the same. "*Direct evidence of a person who claims to have personal knowledge of the facts about the crime charged, such as eyewitnesses. Circumstantial evidence ... is the proof of a chain of facts and circumstances which tend to show whether the defendant is guilty or not guilty.*" (p. 18) "*However,*" said Judge Nadeau when drawing a distinction between the two types of evidence, "*to be sufficient to establish guilt, beyond a reasonable doubt, a case based solely on circumstantial evidence must exclude all other rational conclusions consistent with innocence. This means that if, from the circumstantial evidence, it is rational to arrive at two conclusions, one consistent with guilt and one consistent with innocence, then you must choose the rational conclusion consistent with innocence.... And in determining whether all other rational conclusions have been excluded, you should consider each item of circumstantial evidence in the context of all other ...circumstantial and direct evidence...And if the case rests on circumstantial evidence, then the State must exclude all rational conclusions consistent with innocence. Now the rule requiring you to exclude all rational conclusions applies only to circumstantial evidence and not direct evidence.*" (p. 18-19)

The problem with the "rational conclusions" approach for Chad was that his lawyers' had focused on only one rational conclusion which was that Jeff Marshall beat Kassidy in the head and abdomen, together with blows that caused the fat emboli to move to the lung, all of which caused her death. The defense left the jury with only one other "rational conclusion" to choose on the Second Degree Murder charge, and it didn't fully develop the other "rational conclusions" as alternatives for the other charges.

There was no testimony or suggestion for the jury that there may have been accidents which may have occurred at Jeff's house, but which he simply may not have wanted to admit because they would reflect badly on his babysitting, or for other reason.

There was no expert testimony on the effect of a Tee-ball hitting a child's head. There was no expert testimony on what a fall from a truck might do to a child's head and brain. Although Jeff denied that such a fall occurred, Amanda testified that she was told there was a fall from Jeff's truck and Chad and Jeremy were ready to testify that they were told about it, too. In any case, there was enough testimony about such a fall, that the jury could have heard an expert describe the possible consequences of such a fall. There was no expert testimony about the effect of Kassidy's hitting her head on the glass table in Chad's living room, in the presence of Amanda and Travis. The goal of such testimony would have been to show the jury there were other "rational conclusions" which could be determined besides Jeff being a murderer.

There was no expert testimony regarding the apparent decline in Kassidy's health, or the possibility of chronic condition or disease.

It's not known if any of the jurors made a list of the charges, together with labels of the types of evidence with each. If they had, the simple guideline would have been that for any of the charges for which Amanda testified that she saw Chad commit the crime, that testimony would be the direct evidence. There was no other witness who testified to seeing any of the crimes committed. Such a list of the remaining charges, after the removal of the charge of causing the fracture to an arm, with the time periods and types of evidence provided, might have looked like this, and listed in reverse chronological order:

	Charge	Time Period	Type of Evidence	Description
1.	Second Degree Murder	11/8-9	Circumstantial	...inflicted multiple blows to Kassidy's head and abdomen, thereby causing her death.

2.	Simple Assault	11/8-9	Circum, Direct	caused unprivileged physical contact to his girlfriend, Amanda Bortner. While Evans and Bortner argued, Evans placed his hands around Bortner's neck
3.	First Degree Assault	10/9-11/9	Circum., Direc	...caused a fracture to Kassidy' s leg by grabbing and pulling on her legs.
4.	Second Degree Asslt	11/1-11/8	Circum., Direct (?)	...caused bruising to Kassidy by grabbing and squeezing her face.
5.	Second Degree Asslt	10/22-10/31	Circum., Direct (?)	" "
6.	Second Degree Asslt	10/15-10/21	Circum., Direct (?)	" "
7.	Second Degree Asslt	10/7 - 10/14	Circum., Direct (?)	" "
8.	Second Degree Asslt	10/1 - 10/7	Circum.	" "
9.	Second Degree Asslt	9/1 - 9/30	Circum.	" "
10.	Endangering the Welfare of a Child	8/1 - 9/9	Circum., Direct	knowingly endangered the welfare of Kassidy Bortner, age 20 months, the

daughter of Amanda Bortner, by purposely violating a duty of care which he owed to Kassidy. While Evans lived with Kassidy and Amanda and provided care and supervision for Kassidy, Evans inflicted bodily injury to Kassidy. Evans bruised Kassidy's body and fractured her bones by repeatedly grabbing Kassidy by the face, throat, arms, and legs and by propelling Kassidy into the walls of the home, causing Kassidy to strike the walls. Evans also withheld Kassidy from proper medical treatment for those injuries.

First, addressing the direct/circumstantial issue, there was no direct evidence for the Second Degree Murder charge as no witness testified that s/he saw Chad Evans hit Kassidy in the head or abdomen. There was direct evidence, only through Amanda's testimony, of Chad causing "*bruising to Kassidy by grabbing and squeezing her face,*" as stated in the Second Degree Assault indictments)

Consideration of prior statements for witnesses. Judge Nadeau said that the jurors could "consider whether the witness made statements before trial which were not consistent with what the witness said at trial. If the witness made an inconsistent statement before trial, you may use that pretrial statement in deciding whether to believe the witness's in-court testimony. You may not use the pretrial statement as proof that the facts in that statement are true." (p. 24) If the jury remembered such a fine point of law, they should not, for example have considered Amanda's or Jeff's pre-trial statements as truth, but only as far as they may have subtracted from the credibility of their testimony in court. The judge's caution didn't apply to Chad's pretrial interview, because he didn't testify. Thus the jurors were able to consider his interview statements themselves.

Chad's previous explanations for bruises. Judge Nadeau instructed the jury, "*Evidence has been introduced regarding statements the defendant offered to explain certain bruising on Kassidy. If you find the defendant intentionally made statements tending to demonstrate his innocence, or to influence a witness, and that the statements are later discovered to be false, then you may consider whether the statements show a consciousness of guilt, and determine what significance, if any, to give to such evidence.*" (p. 23-24) This was a major problem for Chad, and it was later one of the two grounds for his appeal to the New Hampshire Supreme Court. The appeal argued that this instruction to the jurors should have been applied to statements made by Jeff as well as to Chad.

Chad's problem with the instruction was that he had told the "trampoline story" to two witnesses, Jacqueline (Oct. 14) and Tristan (Oct. 24), and to the police (Nov. 9). This one lie Chad told three times, and the police also heard the truth about bruises on Kassidy's lower cheeks or jaw, as well as the "trampoline story." Is a lie lessened of you tell someone the true story and an untrue, but partially true, story during the same interrogation? Amanda had testified that she and Chad made up the "trampoline story," and the prosecutors derided the story, and no one testified that it was true. Thus, the jury was nearly certain to find that Chad had lied, just as Amanda had admitted that she had lied to her friends. The problem now at the end of trial was that the jurors were told that they could infer a consciousness of guilt if they believed Chad's stories to be false. Not just a consciousness of guilt about the bruises on Kassidy's chin or cheeks, but a consciousness of guilt for everything charged by the prosecution. If Chad had testified about his belief in "eye contact," to which Amanda had already testified, and explained how he felt embarrassed by the bruises he caused, he might have persuaded the jurors to segregate the acknowledged "white lie" about bruises that had no causal relation to Kassidy's death, from the other stories.

Because the "trampoline story" likely was perceived as a lie, the jurors were enabled to draw an inference of Chad's lying about his explanations for the few other bruises for which he was responsible or aware, which were the bruise under Kassidy's left eye from the Tee-ball accident, and any bruises from falling down in the driveway on November 8. The Tee-ball story was the most in jeopardy, because Travis had said that Kyle used a yellow wiffle ball bat when he hit balls to him, and the police found no such bat in the house. The prosecutors said that the ballhitting story was another lie, but Travis's memory about his playing ball with Kyle a year before his interview and the trial was incorrect. In the absence of Chad's testimony, no one was able to explain to the jury that the bat Kyle used was the thicker, brown bat which Sergeant Magee held in his hand before the jury.

Weighing the evidence of experts. Judge Nadeau advised that jurors "*may reject an expert's opinion if you decide the facts are different from the facts that formed the basis of the expert's opinion. And you may also reject an expert's opinion, if, after careful consideration of all of the evidence in the case, expert and otherwise, you disagree with that opinion.*" (p. 24) There were only three witnesses who qualified as expert witnesses: Dr. Margaret Greenwald and Dr. John O'Connor for the prosecution and Dr. Michael Baden for the defense. As the experts had different opinions on the cause of death and on the existence of a fracture to Kassidy's tibia bone, the jury would have to reject Dr. Baden's testimony if the jurors found guilt beyond a reasonable doubt on the Second Degree Murder and First Degree Assault indictments.

The prosecution chose not to ask a grand jury to amend the indictment to include death caused by blows to other parts of the body which would have caused the fat emboli to move to the lungs. Such a change might have caused a new trial to be required, or forced the prosecution to drop the second degree murder charge altogether. Thus, the jury was in a curious position. Dr. Baden said that it was the fat emboli that killed Kassidy, and not the blows to the head or abdomen, thus there was technically no Second Degree Murder at all by blows to the head or abdomen.

On the other hand, for every indictment for which they found Not Guilty, the jurors would not have to specifically accept or reject the testimony of Dr's Greenwald or O'Connor. A Not Guilty verdict need not be "beyond a reasonable doubt," and such a verdict could have meant that the jurors found other "rational conclusions" other than Chad Evans's guilt "beyond a reasonable doubt."

Chad's Statement concerning the crime charged. (different from "previous explanation for bruises, i.e. "trampoline story," discussed above) from Judge Nadeau began this segment,

"*Now, in this case, evidence has been introduced that the defendant has made a statement concerning the crime charged,*" (p. 25) but she stated "*a statemen*t" and "*crime*" in the singular form. It's not clear to me what "*statement*" she is referencing, so it perhaps wasn't clear to the jury, either. As she advised the jurors that they should evaluate whether Chad's "*statement*" was made "*freely and voluntarily*" (p. 25) it must be assumed that Judge Nadeau was referring to a statement in the nature of an admission. Thus, she was not referring to the "*crime*" of Second Degree Murder to his response of "*Ahh, No Way,*" when Detective McCleish told Chad that "*our investigation clearly indicates that you are the cause of these injuries*" which killed Kassidy. Judge Nadeau was not referring to the First Degree Assault charge, alleging Chad's causing a fracture to Kassidy's tibia, because he wasn't asked about fractures or broken bones during his police interrogation.

Judge Nadeau could have been referring to Chad's description of how he held Kassidy to get eye contact, as those were the only bruises that were caused by Chad's intentional acts. The other statement about bruises were about accidents in the presence of others. Chad said, "*The big thing with me is eye contact..,*" (p. 29, Nov 9 Int.) and hold her face "*just like this with two fingers...That left like a mark on her.*" (p. 67, Nov 9 Int.) Those responses do not appear to be a "statement" however.

Instead of a particular statement, it's more likely that Judge Nadeau was referring to all of Chad's responses to his entire interrogation by the Maine State Police on November 9, 2000. She spent several minutes on the issue of whether Chad's "*statement*" was made "*freely and voluntarily,*" because, if not, "*you must not use it as evidence in reaching a verdict.*" (p. 25-26) Even though the defense in the trial argued that Chad felt intimidated by the process, as he was read his Miranda Rights, even though he was not under arrest, and once he was momentarily told to wait, when he asked about leaving; it seemed clear that he talked with the police "*freely and voluntarily.*" The jury had seen the videotape that was soon to be given to them to take to the evidence room.

It was in the context of this consideration of whether Chad gave his "*statement*" "*freely and voluntarily,*" that Judge Nadeau made the only reference to Chad as a full person. She said, "*You may also consider the age, education, experience, character, and intelligence of the defendant.*" (p.26) Because of the defense decision for Chad to not testify and not to have any more defense witnesses, in addition to Dr. Baden, the jurors knew extremely little about Chad. They knew only a fraction of what's now known by the readers of this book. They had heard, for example, from Amanda who said about Chad, "*I thought he was really nice. Had a good personality. The one thing that really did attract me to him was he was a really good father.*" (p. 67, Dec. 5) Judge Nadeau, and the Rules of Evidence and Criminal Procedure, also were responsible for some of the jury's ignorance, as she determined that the jury could not hear evidence about Chad's parenting, saying "*Whether or not the defendant abused or did not abuse other children is not relevant to this issue of the defendant's guilt regarding the treatment of Kassidy Bortner.*" (p. 4-5 of her order of Nov. 28, 2001) This conclusion defies common sense, even though Dr. Greenwald had testified at the subsequent trial that it sometimes happened that one child in a family could be isolated for abuse. The jury should have had the opportunity to learn about Chad's parenting of his son, Kyle, and his stepson. The love and care for his stepson would have been most helpful, as he, like Kassidy, was not Chad's biological child.

What the jury did not know

The jury did not know a lot of information about Chad and the case which would have been useful and would likely have made the difference between Guilty and Not Guilty. Some information was excluded because Judge Nadeau didn't believe it passed a legal test of relevance, where relevance had to outweigh unfair prejudice. That was why the jurors didn't know about Chad's guilty plea in the March 1999 domestic violence against Tristan, and why it was prevented from hearing anything about Jeff Marshall's criminal record and restraining orders.

Other information didn't get to the jury because the police and prosecutors didn't provide it to Chad's attorneys, or didn't investigate in the first place. Finally, Chad's attorneys could have gathered more information about Chad, especially photographs of Kassidy, and him and Kassidy, and they could have presented a defense with witnesses, including Chad. These commissions and omissions are discussed in the next chapter.

Whatever the reason, the jury didn't know or see the following information, in roughly chronological order, which would have supported Not Guilty verdicts on all the charges.

What the jury didn't know

- Chad's 1991 election to the Keene Board of Education.
- Chad's 1997 "hero" award by the Union Leader and Governor Shaheen for his 1996 lifesaving rescue of three men.
- August, 2000, photographs* of Kassidy at Water Country, and at home in Chad's kitchen with Kato* and in her high chair.* (*All the asterisked photographs can be seen at the "Amanda and Kassidy" subsection of Chad's website, and in the Appendix to this book.)
- August 10, 2000, medical appointment with Kassidy's pediatrician, Dr. George Glass.
- September 2, 2000, photograph* of Kassidy at her grandparents' home.
- Photographs taken by Cathy Nuernberg, probably during September, 2000, and mentioned for the first time during her testimony at Amanda's trial. (See transcript, page 35.)
- September 11, 2000, medical appointment for Kassidy with Dr. James Timoney.
- The dates of Amanda's appointments at the Aspire/DHHS offices in Sanford, Maine, including several in October, to which she brought Kassidy, in open view.
- Information about Amanda's Aspire program status, from her counselor(s) there and from Aspire/DHHS records.
- Chad's recommendation to Amanda during fall, 2000, to have a doctor remove the wart on the index finger of Kassidy's right hand, which Chad saw was bothersome to Kassidy.
- Chad's discussion(s) with his financial planner about the establishment of an education fund for Kassidy, as Chad had already established for Kyle and his stepson, Brent.
- October photograph* of Kassidy wearing her "Elmo" slippers in Chad's kitchen.*
- The date of Emily Conley's obstetrician appointment around October 8, to which she was accompanied by Amanda and Kassidy. (It was after this appt. that Chad suggested caution about bringing Kassidy where people could draw false conclusions about Kassidy's bruises.)
- October 20, 2000, photograph* of Amanda holding Kassidy at Nicole Evans Harvey's home.
- Chad's discussion around October 23 with Jeff that his landscaping contracts with Chad's McDonalds' restaurants would not be renewed.
- Collection of photographs of Kassidy, Chad and Amanda which was destroyed in a fire in August 2001. Included were the only photos of Chad and Kassidy together, and there were several. Other photos in other collections were not requested or saved. See Chad's LIST of missing photographs, as of 2011, in Chapter 5.
- Saturday, November 4, 2000, restaurant dinner in Rochester with Chad, Bruce, Travis, Amanda and Kassidy, as Amanda described in her first interview. (p. 868, 871)
- Sunday, November 5, 2000, gathering at Nicole Evans Harvey's home where Chad brought Kassidy for the day, and the observation by school nurse Gerri Harvey of Kassidy, and of Chad and Kassidy together. Also, on that day, Gerri's son, Brandon Harvey, and daughter-in-law, Nicole Evans Harvey, saw and reported only one bruise on Kassidy which was in the middle of her right cheek.
- Chad's early November conversation with Cross Road School Director Susan Edgar about enrolling Kassidy in her school.
- Plans made by Amanda and her mother, Jacqueline, for Kassidy to be babysat by Jacqueline over the weekend of November 11-12, while Chad and Amanda were in Maine for a Colley-McCoy meeting.

- The location or disposition of items at Jeff's and Jennifer's apartment on November 9, 2000: Kassidy's Sippy cup and diaper bag and red pajama tops if they were worn by Kassidy on that day.
- The existence of reddish brown stains on Kassidy's pink jacket, which was a prosecution exhibit.
- Existence of blood underneath Kassidy's ten fingernails. This information was in the Discovery materials, but was not brought to the attention of the jury.
- March 22, 2001 Maine State Police Crime Lab report of the DNA testing, which showed that the blood underneath Kassidy's ten fingernails was hers, and the saliva on the Wendy's wrapper contained male DNA. This information was in the Discovery materials, but was not brought to the attention of the jury.
- Possible medical explanations for Kassidy's behavior changes during October and November, and easy bruising, including disease, chronic condition and/or poisoning from mold, arsenic, lead (paint), insecticides and makeup. Also, there was no medical testimony for the possible effects of injuries from accidents, including the Oct 26-28 injuries to her head causing two large bumps at the top, and from the Nov. 8 hit by a Tee-ball.
- That Cory Merrill's testimony was inaccurate. His testimony was terminated before cross-examination on the merits. The jury didn't know about the other two inmates in the same cell with Merrill and Chad, including Adam Tuttle, whose interview with the police was not communicated to Chad's lawyers.
- Chad's testimony, so the jury could see and hear him, and his explanation for every charge against him and for every incriminating statement at the trial about him, and his explanation of his love for Kassidy, and his parenting style and skill, and, in particular, his explanation of the "trampoline story," and Kyle's hitting of a Tee-ball into Kassidy's face on No. 8.
- Testimony of Chad's many friends and employer so the jury could learn about his relations with managers and employees and his use of **eye contact** at work..

Among the information about which the jury did hear some testimony, it didn't have sufficient information or clarity about the following.

- Number of calls made by Amanda to day care providers, on November 3 and 8, and the content of those calls. One or more of them had Kassidy on a wait list.
- Type of ball that Kyle hit into Kassidy's head on November 8.
- That inmate informants, such as Cory Merrill, are notoriously unreliable and were the causes of a significant proportion of the 272 wrongful convictions which have been reversed by DNA testing.
- The full extent of Jacqueline's babysitting for Kassidy, during which time Kassidy did not have, or can be presumed to not have, any bruises. During the August 1-November 9 indictment period, those dates were:
  -July 29-Aug. 1, while Chad and Amanda were canoeing on the Saco river with his family.
  -August 19-21, while Chad and Amanda were in New York with friends at a baseball game.
  -August 22-26, while Chad and Amanda went to a Creed Concert in Mass. and the Aug. 25 Exeter Inn event, among other activities.
  -Sept 27-October 1st while Chad and Amanda were at Martha's Vineyard.
- The times and dates of Jeff's and Jennifer's babysitting during the month of October, and especially November, and what Jeff and Jennifer did with Kassidy during that babysitting.
- A time line for every day of the 154 days that Kassidy knew Chad.
- The dates of all the referenced observations of Kasssidy, with and without bruises.

The jury could not have known that ten years later Chad would pass a voice stress lie detector test in July 2010. Below are the 18 questions posed to him, to all of which he answered, "NO"

Did you cause the serious injuries that Kassidy died from?
Did you intentionally injure Kassidy between November 8th and 9th, 2000?
Did you ever punch or kick Kassidy?
Did you ever seriously injure Kassidy?
Did you cause the blunt force trauma to Kassidy?
Did you know how the injuries occurred that killed Kassidy?
Did you know who caused Kassidy's death?
Did you inflict any serious injuries on Kassidy?
Did you know for sure who caused the serious injuries to Kassidy?
Did you in fact cause the blunt force trauma to Kassidy?
Did you cause Kassidy's fatal injuries?
Did you ever intentionally hurt Kassidy?
Did you cause the blunt force trauma on Kassidy?
Did you cause the pin prick injuries to Kassidy's feet?
Did you know who caused the serious injuries to Kassidy?
Did you intentionally injure Kassidy after picking her up from [*the babysitter's*] on November 8th, 2000?
Did you ever punch or kick Kassidy?

Beyond a reasonable doubt, and Elements of a crime. Judge Nadeau instructed the jury that "*all defendants in criminal cases are presumed to be innocent until proven guilty, beyond a reasonable doubt. And the burden of proving guilt rests entirely upon the state.*" (p. 27) She continued, the State must convince the jurors, "*beyond a reasonable doubt, that he's guilty of every element of the alleged offense. It's not enough for the State to prove that the defendant is possibly or probably guilty.*" (p. 27) It wasn't just "reasonable doubt" about each charge in its entirety, it was that "*if you have a reasonable doubt as to whether the State has proved one or more of the elements of a crime charged, then you must find the defendant not guilty.*" (p. 28)

The elements of a crime are basically the core aspects of a crime as defined in the indictment. The Second Degree Murder indictment, read as follows:

Chad Evans... of Rochester, in the State of New Hampshire, on or about November 8-9,2000, at Rochester in the County of Strafford aforesaid, with force and arms, did commit the crime of ***Second Degree Murder*** *(RSA 630:1-b) in that, Evans recklessly caused the death of Kassidy Bortner, age 20 months, under circumstances manifesting an extreme indifference to the value of human life. Evans inflicted multiple blows to Kassidy's head and abdomen, thereby causing her death.*

The elements of the crime charged can be broken into the Who, What, When, Where, and Why parts of a composition or newspaper story: The "Why" can be considered to represent intent.

Who: Evans
What1: recklessly caused the death of Kassidy Bortner,
What2: inflicted multiple blows to Kassidy's head and abdomen,
When: on or about November 8-9,2000,
Where: at Rochester
Why: under circumstances manifesting an extreme indifference to the value of human life.

Thus, by Judge Nadeau's instructions, the jury had to find every element was correctly stated in the indictment beyond a reasonable doubt. The prosecutors argued that Chad inflicted the first blow(s) to Kassidy during the car ride from Jeff's home to Dover where Chad picked up Kyle at day care. As that alleged first blow was not inflicted in Rochester, it should not have been considered as part of the indicted offense. The jury was restricted to the elements of the crime as charged.

For the charge of Simple Assault against Amanda on the evening of November 8-9, the "What" was that "*Evans knowingly caused unprivileged physical contact to his girlfriend, Amanda Bortner. While Evans and Bortner argued, Evans placed his hands around Bortner's neck.*" One key word here, and element of the crime, was "*unprivileged*," for if there was consent by Amanda, then there would be no crime. They might have been engaged a mutual, consensual fight, so if the jury could not agree that Chad's hand placing was "unprivileged" beyond a reasonable doubt, then it would have been required by Judge Nadeau's instructions to find Not Guilty on that charge. It was this instruction that was affected by Judge Nadeau's earlier decision on December 14, 2000, not to advise the jury about the law regarding "*mutual combat.*" Such an instruction would have enabled the jury to consider the level of Amanda's participation as an equal combatant in the argument. Such consideration would have been greatly helped if Chad had testified.

For the six Second Degree Assault charges, which all read the same except for time, it was charged that Chad "*caused bodily injury to Kassidy Bortner, age 20 months"* and that *"Evans caused bruising to Kassidy by grabbing and squeezing her face.*" Missing from these six charges was the term in the Simple Assault charge, "*unprivileged.*" If such a qualification was in the charges, the defense might have been prompted to argue that Chad was "privileged" in the legal sense to hold Kassidy's face to obtain **eye contact.** Even without the prompting in the indictment, this argument could still have been made with evidence.

Nearly every time that Chad held Kassidy's face to obtain eye contact, Amanda was present, and she consented to this part of discipline or a positive message (e.g. "Don't go near the dog when he's eating.") which was that Chad was explaining something to Kassidy that he wanted to ensure that she understood. Presumably, the **eye contact** for positive, calm messages was secured with minimal force, as Kassidy would likely have been more calm. Regarding Chad's privilege to discipline Kassidy as her "father figure," to use Simon Brown's term in his closing statement, above, Amanda testified that on one occasion, at Bruce's house, she objected to Chad's holding Kassidy's face when Kassidy was throwing a tantrum, "*I would get mad, say, 'Don't do that.' I would just tell him to stop. I would say, 'I'm going to do the disciplining. Stuff like that.'* " (p. 84-5, Dec. 5) Otherwise, Chad had her permission.

There was no evidence at the trial that Chad held Kassidy's face, severely enough to cause bruises when Amanda wasn't present, as that was not often. Before Amanda was hired by Old Navy on Monday, November 6, she wasn't working and thus was home every time Chad was with Kassidy, but with four exceptions. One was that Chad babysat for Kassidy on the evening of Thursday, October 19, when Amanda attended, with Nicole and the Urutias, the first of the three Thursday night Financial Management classes. Jeff Marshall babysat for Kassidy for the next class on October 27, and Chad babysat for the last, on November 2. The third exception was when Chad was with Kassidy for most of the day on Sunday, November 5, and the fourth that Chad was with Kassidy alone for part of the afternoon and evening of November 8.

The "Why," or Chad's intent, was contained in the indictment as "knowingly," and this is important, and is discussed below with "*Certain Mental State.*"

The remaining element of the crime was time. As Judge Nadeau had previously decided, she did not specifically address how central to each indictment was the issue of time. As Judge Nadeau had told the attorneys at the beginning of the day, she did not give the jurors instructions on how the timing of each charge was to be considered. This was unfortunate, and hurt the defense, as there was extremely little direct evidence of the time that such grabbing and squeezing occurred. Still, the "*elements of the crime*" instruction should have been enough for the jury to see that time was important, as each indictment was short and time was a large part of each. Further highlighting the issue of timing was the only difference among the six Second Degree Assault indictments. One issue of time, but unrelated to the timing of the incidents in the charges, was the duration of Chad's holding of Kassidy's face, and Amanda said, *"...after he got her attention, usually he would stop.*" (p. 85, Dec 5)

There were only two responses to Will Dekler's questions where Amanda described the timing of Chad's grabbing or holding or palming of Kassidy's chin. She said, "*At first we started putting her in her room for a time out.*" (p. 81, Dec 5) Later, at an unspecified time, after getting more frustrated with Kassidy tantrums, Amanda said that, "*He would grab her face like this... He left bruises a couple of times.*" (p. 81-2, Dec. 5) Later she said, "*five or six times.*" Asked about the timing, she said, "*...he didn't start grabbing her face until towards the end, because he was just getting more and more frustrated.*" (p. 82, Dec. 5) Those were the only references to the timing of Chad's grabbing Kassidy's face - after time-outs didn't work and "*towards the end.*" Beyond those statements by Amanda, the evidence of the timing of the grabbing her face was a question of the circumstantial evidence of when others saw bruises on her face that could have been caused by such grabbing.

Because of those two time-related, direct evidence statements by Amanda, the chart-writing juror might have listed "direct" for the types of evidence for the charges after October 7, i.e. the last month of Kassidy's life. That was after Jacqueline took her October 1 photo, which showed no bruises, and before Joshua's circumstantial evidence observation on October 13 of bruises on her cheeks "*around her chin. Like around the front part and the sides.*" (p. 71, Dec. 7)

Only for the Endangering the Welfare of a Child Charge, was there clearly circumstantial and direct evidence provided to the jury during the time period.

The dating of some of the charges was a problem. The only dates, of all those listed above, which were based on any specific event or action were 11/8 and 11/9, so the Second Degree Murder charge was anchored with a date, as was the end of the charged Endangering the Welfare charge, 11/9. The evidence of the existence of a tibia fracture was ambiguous, as were the possible dates, and the prosecutors picked a one-month window, 10/9 to 11/9. All of the other dates, especially those for the Second Degree Assaults, were apparently chosen at random. The trial did little to clear up that timing confusion, and the jury was left to guess about the dates; but finding guilt beyond a reasonable doubt should not be based on guesses.

One significant date in the case was the date of Jacqueline Conley's photo on October 1, but that didn't lead the prosecution to exclude Sunday October 1, and the days before it from the list. That raises the question of the life cycle of a bruise, from cause to disappearance. In fact, that was one question that was never asked during the trial. Jeff Marshall perhaps most accurately described the visibility cycle, "*Sometimes they'd start to fade away. They'd start turning a yellowish color and then they'd look like -- kind of look like they're almost disappearing..*" (p. 103) For the purpose of sorting out the dates, the life cycle of Kassidy's bruising from Chad's face grabbing might begin on Day 1. Then bruising might appear on Day 2, and that bruising might disappear by Days 5-7, averaged here to be "6". Thus, if no bruises were visible on a certain date, no injury could have occurred within the previous 6 days.

That makes the charges of injury during September, despite Cathy Nuernberg's testimony a problem. Because of the October 1 photo, it's likely that no injury occurred between September 25-30. Because of the September 11 appointment with the orthopedic surgeon, no injury likely appeared between September 5-10. The further complication is that Jacqueline Conley testified that she babysat for Kassidy twice in September. The longest period was when Chad and Amanda went to Martha's Vineyard, from Sunday to Wednesday, September 24-27. As Kassidy could not have had any bruises when she arrived at her grandmother's on Sunday, September 24, that pushes the date of possible grabbing and bruise-causing, from any source, back to September 18, which leaves a short window between the September 11 appointment to the 19th.

Previously, in this book, it's been noted that the period of such "Endangering" could not have begun before Kassidy's September 11 appointment with Dr. James Timoney, as he would have noticed some evidence of such abuse. The point there was that the excessively long time period caused the jury to believe the prosecution's theory that the abuse of Kassidy began when she moved with Amanda to Rochester, which was around the end of June or beginning of July. If the lawyers and judge had known about that doctor's appointment, and the pediatrician's appointment on August 10, the prosecution would likely have moved, on its own initiative, to modify the period to something like September 15 to November 9. It would have made no difference in the possible punishment for "Endangering" as one day's abuse is the same as 60 days abuse, but, again, it would have reduced the power of the prosecution's claim that the abuse began upon moving in. It also would have further impeached the credibility of Jeff and Jennifer who insisted that Kassidy's bruising began when she moved to Chad's home in Rochester.

Certain Mental State. Chad didn't know that his holding of Kassidy's chin and face caused bruising until the bruising appeared at some point in October. After that observation, which he and Amanda discussed, he softened his holding of Kassidy's face, but then he forgot the caution and held it too strongly again, and bruises again appeared. That is, there were only three incidents of bruising on Kassidy's face which were caused by Chad. In 2010, he estimated that he held Kassidy's face about 11 times in October, and perhaps once in early November and of those, three or four of them led to the appearance of bruises. The six indictments were only for the occasions of the holding of Kassidy's face that caused bruising, of which Chad estimates there were three or four. The testimony of witnesses at the trial rarely focused on the bruises on Kassidy's lower face. Sometimes, two or more witnesses described the same bruise. For example, Joshua Bortner saw bruises on Friday, October 13, and Melissa Chick reported seeing bruises the same night, as did Tracey Foley and Jeremy. Given that there were few witness statements about such bruises and that there was some overlap, let's assume that 3-4 is the correct number. If so, then at least two of the indictments were without foundation.

As he had forgotten how easily Kassidy bruised from such holding, the legal question is whether Chad "knowingly" understood when he held Kassidy's face that he would cause a bruise. The term "knowingly" is similar to the term "intentionally" and intent is usually a requirement in the law. Certainly, in every incident of holding Kassidy's face, he intended to hold her face, but he never intended to hurt her and never intended to cause any bruises. His intent was to get her attention in order to communicate a message and not to punish by the act of holding

Without referring to the word "knowingly" in the Second Degree Assault charges, Judge Nadeau instructed the jury that "*The definition of each crime requires that the State prove both that a defendant committed certain acts, and that he acted with a certain mental state... The words 'mental state' refer to what a person mentally believes his physical acts will accomplish. For a person to be guilty of a crime, he must have the requisite mental state....*" (p. 28) Amanda testified that she didn't think that Chad hurt Kassidy when he was holding her face, until she saw the bruises. Chad's intent was to gain Kassidy's attention. Sometimes his frustration led him to squeeze Kassidy's face too hard, but he had no intention of harming or hurting Kassidy, and there was zero testimony that he did. As has been stated earlier in this book, Chad insists that he never spanked nor hit Kassidy Bortner, and he passed a lie detector test on that question. So, he was being prosecuted for holding her face to obtain eye contact, and no one had ever seen him hit or spank Kassidy.

Dropping one of the Simple Assault Charges. Judge Nadeau summarized the names and number of the charges and told the jury that the State only had to prove the content of those charges, beyond a reasonable doubt, but did not have to prove all the allegations made in the trial about other matters. Then she advised the jury that only one of the two First Degree Assault charges remained for the jury to consider. She told the jurors, "*you must not guess or speculate about why only one of the charges involving first degree assault remains. It's simply not relevant to your consideration.*" (p. 30) What Judge Nadeau could have told the jurors was that she decided as a matter of law that there was so little merit to the charge that Chad fractured Kassidy's arm that she removed the charge herself. The jury would not know what she told the lawyers, on the morning of the previous day of the trial, after hearing all of the prosecution's case and before hearing ANY of the defense case, i.e. Dr. Baden, "*Considering the evidence in the light most favorable to the State, I cannot find that there is sufficient evidence for a rational juror to conclude, beyond a reasonable doubt, that the defendant fractured Kassidy's arm.*" (p. 17, Dec 17) Again, this was before she heard Dr. Baden say that he didn't believe that Kassidy had any fractured bones at all. It seems fair to say that to the jurors, the charges regarding the fractures to Kassidy's leg and arm were barely distinguishable in terms of the quality of evidence presented by the prosecution. It surely would have made a significant difference to the jurors if they had known that the arm fracture charge was supported by so little evidence that the judge removed it from the jury's consideration, as a matter of law. Instead, they were not told the reason and were told not to guess. The vision of a trial as an engine of truth fades behind the shades of evidentiary and judicial rules and rulings. Thus, the number of charges being submitted to the jury was ten. One startling aspect of determining that there was only a small number of lower jaw bruises, still a serious problem if they were caused by criminal acts, is that the trial indictments have accounted for a very small number of Kassidy's injuries, which were calculated in the previous chapter as about 90. If the murder charge is about two injuries, and the First Degree Assault about one, the broken bone, and the six Second Degree Assault charge are about one injury/one bruise each (i.e. more than 3-4) then the total number of injuries charged to Chad was nine out of 90. Let's call it ten. What happened to the responsibility for the other 80? Several of them were claimed or acknowledged accidents, such as Kassidy falling into the coffee table, or falling in the driveway on the 8th, or Jeff tripping over her foot or the abrasions on her feet.

Below is a list of the bruises which had been mentioned by the listed observers in the days before Kassidy died, in approximate reverse chronological order of observation.

1. Tee-ball
2. Sore on lower lip (Chad reported, in 2010, observing this bruise on the evening of Nov 8th)
3. Hit on coffee table (observed by Amanda, Travis (the actual accident), and bruise by Chad)
4. Cat scratch. (observed by Amanda, Chad, Travis, Jennifer)

Let's assume there were ten such bruises that Amanda, Chad, Jeff and Jennifer had acknowledged seeing, then that leaves 90 which are unaccounted for. Better, let's assume that these four adults had seen and told the police and jury about 20 such accidents, and that the EMTs accounted for ten. What were the causes for the other 70? The jury was being asked to determine responsibility, again for as many as ten. What does that say about the justice system that it will proceed to determine responsibility for 10% of a problem and think that's enough?

<u>Returning to the elements of the crimes charged.</u>

Second Degree Murder. Judge Nadeau said there were three elements of the Second Degree Murder charge, and each must be proved beyond a reasonable doubt:

1. "*...that the defendant caused injury, which was a direct and substantial factor in bringing about Kassidy's death*";
2. "*...that the defendant's actions occurred in New Hampshire*," and
3. "*...that the defendant acted recklessly, under the circumstances showing an extreme indifference to the value of human life*." (p. 30-31)

Then, to prove recklessness, "*the State must prove first, that the defendant was aware of a substantial and unjustifiable risk. This means that there must be proof that the defendant knew that there was a substantial risk that his conduct would cause Kassidy's death; second is the defendant was aware of the risk. There must be proof that the defendant consciously disregarded the risk... Third, you must examine the circumstances known to the defendant. From what he knew of the circumstances, you must decide whether his disregard of the risk was a gross deviation from what a law-abiding person would have done. The key words here are 'gross deviation.' If you find the defendant's actions were unreasonable or thoughtless, that is not enough. To find the defendant acted recklessly,*

you must find that his disregard of the risk was a substantial departure from the actions of a law-abiding person under the same circumstances." (p. 31) Further, "*... for a killing to be second degree murder, the defendant must not simply act recklessly, but, rather, must act recklessly under circumstances showing an extreme indifference to the value of human life.... The State must prove what may be called a depraved-heart murder.*" (p. 32)
Manslaughter. "*Now, if you find the defendant not guilty of second-degree murder, you may go on to consider whether the defendant is guilty of the lesser-included offense of manslaughter,*" which she defined as the same as second degree murder, but that *"to prove manslaughter, the State must prove the defendant caused Kassidy's death recklessly* [but] *...does not require proof of extreme indifference to the value of human life.*" (p. 33)
First Degree Assault. Judge Nadeau defined this crime, of causing the fracture to Kassidy's leg, as having four elements, each of which must be proved beyond a reasonable doubt:

1. "*...that the defendant acted recklessly,...*"
2. "*...that the defendant caused serious bodily injury to Kassidy Bortner by fracturing Kassidy's leg. Serious bodily injury means any harm to the body which causes severe, permanent, protracted loss of or impairment to the health or function of any part of the body;....*"
3. "*... occurred in New Hampshire...*"
4. "*... that Kassidy was under the age of thirteen years old.*" (p. 34)

Second Degree Assault: Judge Nadeau described the chronology of the six charges in September, one a week in October and one in November, and that the crime also has four elements, each of which must be proved beyond a reasonable doubt:

1. "*...that the defendant acted knowingly...that the defendant was aware his conduct would cause bodily injury. The State does not have to prove the defendant specifically intended to commit the crime,... What the State must prove is that the defendant was aware his conduct would cause bodily injury...*"
2. "*...that the defendant caused bodily injury to Kassidy Bortner.*"
3. "*... occurred in New Hampshire; and*"
4. "*... Kassidy was under the age of thirteen years...*" (p. 35)

Judge Nadeau, again, did say that the time period was an element of each charge, which needed to be proved beyond a reasonable doubt.
Endangering the welfare of a child. Similarly, this crime has four elements, each of which must be proved beyond a reasonable doubt.

1. "*... that the defendant acted knowingly, as I've just defined that term;*"
2. "*...that the defendant endangered the welfare of Kassidy;*"
3. "*...that Kassidy was under the age of eighteen...*"
4. "*...that the defendant endangered Kassidy's welfare by purposely violating a duty of care he owed to Kassidy, to provide her care and supervision.*" (p. 35-36)

Simple Assault. Judge Nadeau said that this crime, against Amanda had two parts:

1. "*...that the defendant acted knowingly;*"
2. "*...that the defendant caused unprivileged physical contact to Amanda Bortner.*" (p. 36)

Judge Nadeau did not define "*unprivileged*" for the jurors, but it means "without consent" or "without authority" or "without permission."

Judge Nadeau concluded, "*you should follow the instructions that I've just given you. And you need to decide this case not out of bias or sympathy, but with honesty and understanding.*" (p. 36)

Then Judge Nadeau selected at random the three Alternate jurors. She told the remaining twelve jurors that their first task would be to elect a foreperson. She advised them of the process for relaying questions back to her, but cautioned, "*...we cannot answer questions about the facts. We can only answer most questions about the law.*" (p. 42) The jury was given a copy of Judge Nadeau's just-completed instructions to the jury. The jury was then "excused to deliberate," (p. 43) at 12:59 p.m.

As noted earlier, the jury lacked significant information which was essential to reach a fair verdict. On the issue of bruising, spread across the six charges for Second Degree Assault from Sept. 1-Nov 9, and Child endangerment from Aug 1 through Nov 8, the jury knew only of three instances of the absence of bruising. Only one of those was known with a specific datr, from the October 1, 2000 photograph of Kassidy in Auburn. The jurors knew that Jacqueline Conley had babysat Kassidy during August and September, but they didn't know the time periods. As the charges were specifically dated, it was critically important that the dates and periods of non-bruising be specifically dated, and they weren't.

If the jury had possessed a calendar like the one below during the trial and if the jurors could have used such a calendar in the deliberation room, their decisions might have been different.

June 2000

Su	Mo	Tu	We	Th	Fr	Sa
					9	10
11	12	13	14	15	16	**NI**
NI	**NI**	**NI**	**NI**	**NB**	23	24
25	26	27	28	29	30	

July 2000

Su	Mo	Tu	We	Th	Fr	Sa
						1
2	3	4	5	6	**NI**	**NI**
NI	**NI**	**NI**	**NB**	**NB**	**NB**	**NB**
NB	**NB**	**NB**	**NB**	**NB**	21	22
23	**NI**	**NI**	**NI**	**NI**	**NI**	**NB**
NB	**NB**					

August 2000

Su	Mo	Tu	We	Th	Fr	Sa
		1	2	3	4	**NI**
NI	**NI**	**NI**	**NI**	**NB**	**NI**	**NI**
NI	**NI**	**NI**	**NB**	**NI**	**NI**	**NI**
NB	**NB**	**NB**	**NB**	**NB**	**NB**	**NB**
NB	**NB**	**NI**	**NI**	**NI**		

September 2000

Su	Mo	Tu	We	Th	Fr	Sa
					NI	**NB**
3	4	5	**NI**	**NI**	**NI**	**NI**
NI	**NB**	12	13	14	15	16
17	18	**NI**	**NI**	**NI**	**NI**	**NI**
NB	**NB**	**NB**	**NB**	**NI**	**NI**	**NI**

October 2000

Su	Mo	Tu	We	Th	Fr	Sa
NB	2	3	4	5	6	7
8	9	10	11	12	**B**	**B**
B	**B**	17	18	19	20	**B**
B	23	24	25	26	27	**B**
B	**B**	**B**				

November 2000

Su	Mo	Tu	We	Th	Fr	Sa
			B	**B**	**B**	**B**
B	**B**	**B**	**B**	**B**		

MEDIA:
1. "Closing arguments begin in Evans Trial"
2. "Evans' fate with jury - Defense says Evans no saint, but not guilty in tot's death"
3. "Evans jury still out"
4. "Lawyer: Evans no killer"
5. "Evans jury begins deliberations"

Thursday, 20 December 2001

One juror was dismissed in the morning for inappropriate discussions of the case outside the courtroom, and was replaced by an alternate juror, and Judge Nadeau ordered the jury to begin deliberations anew.

MEDIA:
1. "Tension high in Evans case"
2. "Jury deliberates fate of Chad Evans"
3. "Evans Juror dismissed - Judge says deliberations in murder trial will start over
4. "Evans juror replaced; deliberations start again"
5. "Juror replaced in baby death case"

Friday, 21 December 2001

After 22 hours of deliberations, with some overlap due to the replacement of a juror, over four days, the jury returned at 4 p.m. with a guilty verdict on the primary charge of Second Degree Murder. Of the six Second Degree Assault charges for squeezing

Kassidy's face, Chad was found guilty of the five with time periods of 9/1-9/30, 10/8-10/14, 10/15-10/21, 10/22-10/31 and 11/1-11/8. He was found guilty of Simple Assault against Amanda on the night of 11/8-11/9 and guilty of Endangering the Welfare of a Child.

Chad was found Not Guilty on the remaining First Degree Assault charge for the fracture of Kassidy's leg, and for one of the Second Degree Assault charges (Kassidy) with the time period of 10/1-10/7, which included the period of the October 1 photo.

Chad began that day with the hope that he might have been released from his nightmare with all Not Guilty verdicts. Instead, he was led back to the Strafford County Jail, with the certain expectation that he would spend many years in the New Hampshire State Prison, and with the certain knowledge that he had done nothing to warrant those verdicts.

MEDIA:

1. "Evans convicted of murder"
2. "Evans guilty in child's death"
3. "Evans guilty - Jury says death of toddler was murder; five assault charges stand"
4. "Evans found guilty in toddler's death - He faces up to a life sentence
5. "Evans guilty in toddler's death"

CHAPTER 9: SENTENCING, PRISON AND APPEALS FOR CHAD; PREPARATION FOR AMANDA'S TRIAL - 23 DECEMBER 2001 TO 17 NOVEMBER 2002

"And my heart feels most heavy for the way that I failed Kassidy."
- Chad Evans

Sunday, 23 December 2001

With the jury finished with its work the case of Chad Evans returned to the people and the media. The Portsmouth Herald published an editorial, "Despite conviction, justice not fully served in Evans case", which is excerpted below.

It is heartening that the jury in the case of Chad Evans — tried on charges that he murdered his girlfriend's not quite 2-year-old daughter — was not swayed by attempts to lay blame on the baby-sitter. It now appears the true perpetrator of the crime will get the punishment he so richly deserves.

It is disheartening, however, to learn in the course of the trial that so many people were aware of what was happening to Kassidy Bortner and yet took no action to stop it. Sadly, no punishment will be meted out to Kassidy's mother, grandmother, uncle and others who saw this poor little girl suffer for so long and did nothing to bring the situation to an end....

It was clear from the testimony at Evans' trial that Amanda Bortner, the child's young, unwed mother, relinquished her responsibilities the first time she noticed bruises on her child and chose to put her affection for Evans above the welfare of her daughter. And it was equally clear other members of this dysfunctional family decided early on it was somehow better to feign ignorance than admit knowledge and have to take the steps that could have saved little Kassidy's life.

We would like to have seen every person who knew or felt Kassidy was being abused tried for her death. As far as we are concerned, they were all complicit.

We understand the prosecutors did what they had to do in giving Amanda Bortner immunity. It is doubtful they would have been successful in prosecuting the individual who actually caused the murder had that not been done. But it sends entirely the wrong message to allow those who were obviously complicit in Kassidy's death to simply walk free. Even for those who believe the individuals involved in this crime will ultimately face a higher justice, this is a difficult pill to swallow.

We urge state legislators to take notice of this case and strengthen the penalties for failing to do what is, hopefully, for most of us, appropriate when confronted with any sort of child abuse. Everything possible must be done to persuade, cajole or threaten those more concerned with their personal gratification than the safety of our children to do the right thing....

With Chad's trial over, the newspaper announced that Amanda was guilty, too, as if her upcoming trial was not anticipated or needed. The editorial illustrated the strong public interest in the case on its own merits, and also as a lightning rod for changing the laws regarding the reporting of child abuse. As with many other articles, it ignored the fact that suspicions of abuse were reported to DCYF 10 days before Kassidy's death.

As was the case at Chad's trial, timing and time-lines were critical.

Thursday, 27 December 2001

New Hampshire Public Radio broadcasted Dan Gorenstein's story which asked one of the right questions in the case, "Could DCYF have done more?" The obvious answer was, "Yes," but that doesn't excuse everyone else from their responsibility for their own actions or inaction.

Tuesday, 1 January 2002

Prior to January 1, 2002, New Hampshire had a Sentence Review law, RSA (Revised Statutes Annotated) 651:58, which provided that "[a]*ny person sentenced to a term of one year or more in the state prison,... may file with the clerk of the superior court for the county in which the judgment was rendered an application for review of the sentence by the review division.*" Effective, January 1, the law was modified to give to the State the same right to request a review of a sentence by the Review Division of the State Superior Court system. Thus, the change came after Chad's arrest and conviction, but before his sentencing.

Foster's Daily Democrat published a "2001 in Retrospect" article which contained a single photograph for the lead story for each month, and the photo for November was of Amanda. It was a major story in 2000, 2001, and likely in 2002.

Thursday, 3 January 2002

Foster's Daily Democrat published the short AP story with a headline almost as long, Evans to be sentenced in March for Kassidy Bortner's death - The same week, trial begins for mom on child endangerment charges.

Early-mid January 2002

With Chad held responsible with his criminal conviction, the media re-addressed DCYF's responsibility. Amy Wallace wrote on January 10, 2002 in the Portsmouth Herald of a 66 page report about DCYF's shortcomings, and about Kassidy's case in particular, "Report: DCYF failed toddler." Said the Director of the New Hampshire Children's Alliance, Steve Varnum,

The state must find out why the DCYF didn't follow its own guidelines in dealing promptly with the anonymous phone call which tipped off the organization that Kassidy may be in danger.... We all failed Kassidy Bortner.

In the Keene Sentinel article on the 11th, from the Associated Press, "Evans' case illustrates dilemma," the DCYF Director, Nancy Rollins, was quoted, "*The agency, in its process of doing assessment, did not meet our policy.*"

The January 20 Union Leader story by Josh Adams was headlined, "Too many cases, too few workers hamper child abuse investigations. Caseworkers say they love the job, despite low pay, negative publicity". It noted that Patricia Hocter continued to work for DCYF in the Rochester office, but that her "*handling of the case was 'not within policy'* " according to DCYF manager, Nancy Rollins. Personnel matters are confidential, but there was never any mention in the related articles that any employee of DCYF was disciplined in any way for the acknowledged lapses. The article reported that

The state of Maine, where Kassidy was regularly babysat by family members, now requires mandatory reporting of suspected child abuse as a result of so many people eyeing the suspicious bruises over three months of abuse that culminated in the young girl's death.

The article reported that Kassidy's grave was still unmarked, as it would remain until 2010, when Amanda was able to purchase a headstone.

Tuesday, 15 January 2002

Amanda was scheduled to appear in Strafford Superior Court for a status conference, for preliminary scheduling matters. Jennifer Saunders wrote for the Foster's Daily Democrat, "Amanda Bortner in court today as trial looms," and summarized the case to date, and noted, "*...At one point in her testimony, Bortner stated she still loves Evans and misses him....During the trial, Bortner changed her story from what she told police previously...*"

Saunders then wrote that Chad's jurors heard him, via his videotaped interrogation, *suggest that Bortner was mistreating the child..."Amanda would sometimes hit her. She bruised from that... I think Amanda .. I think that job at home was hard on her... She had two solid weeks or three solid weeks with Kassidy," Evans told police stating that after Bortner began spending more time with Kassidy, she began calling her a "little bitch... a little s--t.*"

Chad was describing normal parental frustration, and not mistreatment and abuse. He never suggested, and never meant to suggest, that Amanda was mistreating Kassidy.

When describing Amanda's little pats to Kassidy's diaper and to her leg as "hit," Chad used the wrong word. If there had been followup questions by the police on that point, he would have clarified his observations of Amanda. Similarly, using inelegant words about one's child during times of frustration is not unusual. In 2011, Chad recalled that Amanda more likely said, occasionally that Kassidy was "*acting bitchy*," which is different from calling her "*a little bitch*."

The article painted a very dark picture, citing the autopsy photographs and stating, *At the time of her death, Kassidy was also suffering from at least three untreated bone fractures in her arms and legs and pin-prick abrasions on the arches of her feet.*
It didn't mention that no one observed these alleged fractures, which is why they were untreated, and that it was Chad who discovered the abrasions on Kassidy's feet. In response to finding those abrasions, Amanda dressed Kassidy with her Elmo slippers when she went to Jeff's and Jennifer's. Given the shared understanding of what might have caused the abrasions, wearing slippers seemed like a reasonable response. Further, the claim of fractures was disputed at Chad's trial, and he was not convicted of causing any such fractures.

Amanda was not present at the status conference, because she made a scheduling mistake and thought the court date was the following day, so she participated in the conference by phone. Her attorney, Patricia Wiberg, was at the conference.

The next day's Foster's Daily Democrat covered the story, "Mom of slain tot says Evans is innocent." by Jennifer Saunders.

The article reported that Amanda called the newspaper that afternoon and told Saunders, "*Chad is innocent, and Jeff Marshall is guilty - but that's all I have to say right now*." After having her initial faith in Chad's innocence shaken during her police interviews in 2000, and pressure from her family and friends, Amanda had returned to her original understanding, and felt strongly that Chad did not kill Kassidy. From that core belief, she used the same logic that the police used, after the assumption that Kassidy's death was a homicide. As there were two likely suspects, she concluded that the other suspect, Jeff, was Kassidy's killer. Neither Amanda nor the police understood the other possibilities of disease or chronic condition or accidents, perhaps combined with abuse.

Also, it was reported that Assistant Attorneys General Delker and Brown, who participated in the status conference, were not going to prosecute Amanda because she was a prosecution witness at Chad's trial.

Thursday, 24 January 2002

Jennifer Saunders reported in Foster's Daily Democrat that Chad's probation violation trial in Rochester District Court would be held on February 20. She wrote in "Evans to stand trial on probation violation" that Chad would be tried on the charge that he did not remain "*arrest free*" as was required as a condition of his 2000 probation from the 1999 domestic violence with Tristan. Saunders reported that he had been acquitted in August, 2001, "*of a second probation violation charge alleging he possessed ammunition at the time of his arrest*."

Saturday, 2 February 2002

For the first time, Foster's Daily Democrat now referred to Chad in a headline as a "*convicted murderer,*" in the otherwise less consequential article, **"Convicted murderer to sell property in Rochester"** Needing to raise money for his crushing legal expenses, Chad sold an .89 acre slice from his property to the owners of the abutting commercial property, Rochester Security Systems.

Monday, 4 February 2002

Kassidy would have been three years old on this day.

Friday, 15 February 2002

Jennifer Saunders reported in her Foster's Daily Democrat article, "Child endangerment trial set in June for Amanda Bortner" that the new trial date was June 10.

The Attorney General had designated Senior Assistant Attorney General Malinda Lawrence to prosecute Amanda. The article noted that "*the state has indicated it will not offer or accept a negotiated plea with Bortner on the charges.*"

Friday, 1 March 2002

According to Jennifer Saunders' article, "Evans' Probation Trial Again Postponed," the Rochester District Court continued Chad's probation violation trial to an unspecified date, presumably after his upcoming sentencing for the December 2001 convictions.

Monday, 11 March 2002

Stephen Carlisle, a Senior Probation/Parole Officer, completed the 33 page Pre-sentencing Report for Chad. It began with a six-page summary of the "Police Version" of the crimes for which Chad was convicted. The next section was "Defendant's Version:" but it was omitted because, "*At the request of the defense attorney, no discussion of the criminal cases occurred with Chad Evans during the PSI interviews....*" (p. 7)

The "Victim Input" was provided by Jacqueline/Jackie, Jennifer, Kathy Jackson, who was Jacqueline's sister-in-law, Jeff and Amanda. Carlisle reported that "*Jackie had to talk her daughter out of getting an abortion.*" (p. 8) Thus, Robert Sheehan and Jacqueline shared the responsibility for Amanda being an single mother at age 17. Jacqueline told Carlisle that during her shopping trip, which Carlisle referenced as "*Christmas shopping*," with Amanda and Jennifer on November 5, "*Amanda purchased a large amount of Christmas decorations for herself.*" (p. 8) Chad recalls that Amanda purchased clothes, including her pink parka and pajamas, for Kassidy with the $300 he gave her, and that Amanda showed Kassidy her new clothes on the evening of November 5. Thus, they were not Christmas presents. Kassidy wore some of those new clothes on the day she died. Carlisle did not mention that clothes for Kassidy were purchased on that day. In 2011 Chad has no recollection of seeing new Christmas decorations on that day, but says that it's possible that they were among Amanda's purchases.
Carlisle reported that Jacqueline "*expressed her thanks and truest appreciation to police authorities in Maine and New Hampshire... for all the kindness and understanding 'everybody' has shown the family. Her appreciation was also extended to the State of New Hampshire for repaying the family for Kassidy's funeral expenses.*" (p. 9) The source of these reimbursement funds is unknown, as no other reference to them has been found. As Amanda and Kassidy were receiving welfare assistance from the State of Maine, the New Hampshire payments were unusual, and were never disclosed to Chad's attorneys. Jacqueline told Carlisle that she hoped to have Kassidy's face engraved on a headstone at the gravesite, implying that she was purchasing the stone. However, Kassidy's grave remained unmarked until 2010 when Amanda was able to purchase the heart-shaped stone.

Jeff and Jennifer interviewed together with Carlisle, and Jeff told Carlisle what he had told the police about Chad's faults, but "*Jefferey pointed out that the defendant was always good to him.*" (p. 10) Jeff said that one of the things he found "*particularly disturbing*" at Chad's trial was that he learned there that Chad and Amanda were planning to go to Disney World after his hoped-for acquittal. (p. 11) Later, Chad told Carlisle that he had planned to go to Florida. This was yet another example of how plans and intentions could be distorted in the retelling. In 2011, Chad wrote that the plan for the Florida trip was for Chad and Kyle so they could reestablish their relationship, and Amanda was not intended to be part of that trip. During his pre-trial year, Chad's contacts with Kyle had been restricted and supervised.

Both Jeff and Jennifer believed that Kassidy was in heaven, and Jeff said that Kassidy's last few months on earth were "*hell.*" (p. 11) Wrote Carlisle, "*It is clear to Jefferey Marshall that Kassidy had a high tolerance for pain. In spite of repeated beatings, she rarely cried and kept enduring her abusive life.*" (p. 12) Such reasoning showed Carlisle's faith in the police and the judicial system and the conclusions of the prosecutors that Kassidy's last months were a "*living hell.*" Jeff had turned common sense on its head. Whereas most people assume that when a toddler doesn't cry s/he is not in pain. However, Jeff believed that since he knew that Kassidy was in pain, the only way to explain her lack of crying was to theorize that she had a high tolerance of pain. The alternative explanation, that she was not in pain, apparently didn't seem reasonable to Jeff.

Kathy Jackson brought a photograph of Kassidy that she said was taken when Jacqueline babysat for Kassidy in September, 2000. Thus, this was not the October 1 photo which was presented at Chad's trial. Carlisle probably didn't know that the photo he was looking at was not presented at Chad's trial, even though it "*certainly depicted the beautiful smile of Kassidy...*" (p. 12) Kathy told Carlisle that when Amanda drove to Buckfield to get a check from Jacqueline, Amanda took one of Jacqueline's checks and forged her mother's signature. Kathy said that one reason her nephew, Scott Conley, was having difficulty in school after Kassidy's death was because two of his classmates were named "Amanda" and "Kassidy." She said that at Kassidy's funeral, Chad's father, Chet, told her, "*If my son did this, he has to pay*." According to Carlisle, Kathy "*stated that Mr. Evans* [Chet] *and the rest of his family know that Chad is 'an animal.'* " (p. 13) This was the same label that Sisti attempted to stick to Jeff at Chad's trial. Jackson said to Carlisle that Kassidy's burial spot was near another little girl who died 20 years earlier. Carlisle wrote, "*As Kathy said, this seemed perfect so that this other youngster could 'show her the ropes' in heaven*." (p. 13) That other girl, 25 feet away, was a Crystal Martin, not related to Amanda's friend of the same name. The deceased Crystal Martin died 19 months after her birth in February, 1980, which was about the same time as the birth of Jennifer Bortner Conley.

Amanda told Carlisle that her family was "dysfunctional" and she blamed Jeff for Kassidy's death. Carlisle wrote that Amanda told him that

Jefferey Marshall once spanked Kassidy so hard that it caused black and blue marks on her buttocks, and he brought the victim home sick after she drank some Windex. Jefferey wasn't going to tell Amanda about the Windex consumption, though, until she inquired into the reason for Kassidy's condition." (p. 14)

Amanda also brought photographs of Kassidy, but Carlisle did not give the dates of those photographs. He wrote that

Amanda refers to Chad Evans as "awesome," a "great father" to his son and step-son, always wanting to help people, and having treated her and Kassidy well. According to Amanda, the defendant used to buy Kassidy happy meals and chocolate donuts from Dunkin Donuts all the time. Throughout their time together, she and Chad were very much in love.... Her position on sentencing is that Chad shouldn't be incarcerated because he has already paid enough of a price "just for grabbing" Kassidy's face. (p. 14)

Then Carlisle gave a "Personal History" of Chad which was extraordinarily detailed and described the youth and young adulthood of a successful and emotionally grounded man. About the conviction, Carlisle wrote, "*...the defendant feels that it he hadn't reacted to Kassidy's screaming and yelling by grabbing her face, ...he might not be sitting in this chair (jail)*." (p. 19) Carlisle didn't mention the concept of **eye contact**.

Tristan attributed the decline of her marriage to Chad to his spending too much time at work and her working hard for her degree in radiology, and both of them not spending enough time with each other. Carlisle wrote that

Her description of the defendant is as sensitive and always willing to help others. This latter attribute meant people took advantage of him in certain instances. For example, he let people live at his house rent-free.... During their marriage, Tristan was the disciplinarian. Chad never utilized strict disciplinary measures and pretty much let Kyle and Brent do as they pleased. Any efforts to address the kids' behavior by Chad consisted of a time-out, only to change his mind five seconds later by explaining to Kyle and Brent what they did wrong.... With respect to corporal punishment, Tristan never saw Chad hit either of the boys not has she ever known her ex-husband to use steroids or abuse alcohol or drugs. She has seen Chad under the influence of alcohol, but denies that he'd become violent (only obnoxious.) (p. 20)

Tristan told Carlisle a softer version of her fight with Chad in March of 1999, saying that she told the Rochester Police a more violent story so they would remove Chad from the home for the night. She didn't anticipate criminal charges. She said that counseling helped Chad to see that his career and making money were not as important as he formerly thought, but she still insisted on divorce.

Tristan said she was happy with Chad's relationship with Amanda and she denied the reports in the discovery materials that she warned Amanda to get out of the relationship because Chad would abuse her. Carlisle reported that Tristan "*still believes in his innocence.*" (p. 20) About Kassidy,

Tristan felt that she appeared quiet and slow. In her visits to defendant's home, she never heard Kassidy utter a word until a couple of days before her death, when the victim said, "bye-bye" to her. Tristan remembers asking Chad if there was something wrong with Kassidy, and the defendant replied really not knowing. (p. 20)

Then Carlisle devoted two pages to Chad's description of his life with Kassidy and Amanda.

Chad described meeting Amanda and then Kassidy and

...they had a wonderful time together, and in early July 2000, mother and daughter moved in with Chad. His first recollection of Amanda and Kassidy living at the 191 Milton Road residence was for a birthday party for Brent and Kyle on 07-08-00. According to the defendant, the four of them (including Kyle) became a family and enjoyed going on outings....However, still recovering from his failed marriage to Tristan...Chad hesitated to get fully involved... On a couple of occasions Chad told Amanda he loved her, only to ask himself, "What did I just say?" (p. 21)

Regarding Kassidy

The defendant recalls showing much patience with her, playing with and teaching the victim new things, and taking care of her when she was sick. Difficult for Chad to understand is the change in her demeanor. After they played for a period of time, Kassidy, an hour later, would start crying and screaming over Chad showing affection to Amanda....In hopes of "getting her attention" and stopping the behavior, Chad would say Kassidy's name. When this wasn't successful, he grabbed her face and made the victim look at him, usually bringing about success of Chad receiving her attention. (p. 21)

However, Carlisle missed the point of Chad's holding of Kassidy's face. "*Getting her attention*," was not a goal in itself, but it was a way to ensure that she would hear him when he tried to explain something to her such as the fact that his love for her mother did not mean that there would be any less love for Kassidy.

At times beginning to cry in our interview, Chad remembers Kassidy as a "tough cookie." This appears to be a reference to her play with Kyle, who was used to playing with his older half-brother, Brent. In playing with Brent, Kyle and Kassidy, Chad would wrestle with them and use varying amounts of force when playfully throwing the kids on the bed, being the least rough with Kassidy. Missing and thinking about Kassidy all the time, he expressed his love for her. Her absence brings about a longing for her "loves [sic, but Chad recalls in 2011 that he said "hugs"] *and kisses," and Kassidy getting on his lap while Chad ate a bowl of ice cream.* [Chad recalls in 2011 that he said that he would feed Kassidy ice cream at these times, and not that he ate ice cream. Either he said it incorrectly to Carlisle during the interview, or Carlisle misunderstood what Chad said.] *Fond remembrances remain of Kyle and Kassidy playing well with each other and sharing. For instance, if Kyle got something, he would say, "What about Kassidy?... Concerning the face grabbing, Chad is ashamed of the discipline measure and can't understand how he could do something like that to a person he loved.* (p. 21)

Carlisle summarized what Chad told him about how he and Amanda made contact after his release on bail,

...Amanda Bortner was living in Texas but calling Chad's residenc. To avoid violating his bail, he would not answer her calls, but did once by mistake. The two started talking, and she discussed her loneliness and missing him. Chad felt very bad for Amanda, especially considering that she was trying to cope with her daughter's death. Amanda told Chad of her intentions to move back to New Hampshire, and they got together over Christmas 2000 at his parents' home. With Amanda believing in his innocence, it appears that Chad threw himself deeply into their relationship over the next seven months. (p. 21)

Carlisle met with five personal friends of Chad: Vanessa Mansson, Jack Loftus, Stephanie Bolduc, Jeremy Hinton and Bruce Aube. Of the five, Jack and Stephanie had not been previously interviewed by the police.

Vanessa told Carlisle about Chad saved her life from suicide and she believed that he saved Amanda's life in 2001 as well. She commented on Chad's high school relationship with Barbara Brooks who was "*moody one minute and crazy the next minute.*" (p. 22.) Carlisle reported that

A number of times Vanessa witnessed Barbara hit Chad in the head, and his only reaction was to grab her arms for protection purposes....This is important because of allegations of abusive and controlling behavior Barbara (Brooks) Hamel has made against the defendant. (p. 22) (See the summary of the Nov. 24, 2000 Barbara Hamel interview.)

Carlisle wrote that Vanessa described another example of physical restraint, *...Vanessa was the victim of a date rape. In hopes of getting the defendant to beat up her attacker, she asked Chad to do something about it; and his response was that such behavior wasn't going to solve anything.* (p. 22)

In summary, Carlisle wrote, that Vanessa said that Chad "*... is definitely not the monster some people think he is right now...Vanessa is certain it is impossible for Chad to have done this to Kassidy.*" (p. 23)

Jack Loftus, the Comptroller for Colley-McCoy said that Chad was "*always an up and coming star" in the company,*" (p. 23) and explained how good Chad was with his employees. Carlisle wrote,

Over the years, Jack observed how well Chad related to the kids in Special Olympics (sponsored by McDonald's). Chad continues to receive the respect of Jack Loftus who quoted the motto the defendant lives by: "You can get anything you want in life if you help enough other people to get what they want." (p. 23)

Stephanie Bolduc met Chad through a business connection and had known and admired him for about eleven years. Carlisle wrote,

...Stephanie recruited Chad to the organization [Jaycees, Junior Chamber of Commerce] *and saw how he interacted with underprivileged children at the annual Christmas party.... even while he was on bail, Chad offered his assistance to the Jaycees to ensure the kids had a good Christmas party... Stephanie knows Chad Evans to be a "born leader."... To celebrate the grand opening of the Rochester McDonald's Play Place in 1995 or 1996, Chad came up with the idea of inviting the children of St. Charles Orphanage in Rochester and giving them all t-shirts... which the defendant paid for himself.* (p. 24)

Jeremy Hinton described for Carlisle how Chad had helped a McDonald's Manager Trainee find a home and how Chad had purchased cars for several employees. Wrote Carlisle,

Some didn't pay him back, but this didn't stop the defendant from doing the same thing again.... Jeremy believes in his friend's innocence...he is still unable to fathom how an individual with so many positive qualities could end up in this situation.... Jeremy did observe Chad and Kassidy together on occasions and felt that his friend treated the victim (Kassidy) well. (p. 24)

Bruce Aube told Carlisle that he had known Chad for about ten years, and they shared a common interest in their extended families. Carlisle asked Bruce about Chad's alleged use of steroids, perhaps because Jennifer Conley had told Carlisle that Amanda had told her of such use. (p. 10) Bruce said that he didn't know of such a problem, but just before Kassidy's death, he had noticed that Chad had increased his weightlifting ability from 275 pounds to 300, and didn't know "*how Chad was able to do that.*" (p. 25) Perhaps Carlisle was thinking that the alleged use of steroids caused a behavior change in Chad, which may have has some connection to Kassidy's death. Whether or not asked about steroids, Tristan told Carlisle that she didn't know of any use of steroids by Chad. (p. 20) Carlisle had asked Chad about his use of steroids, and perhaps because it related to the forbidden topic of Kassidy's death, Chad's attorney spoke for Chad and denied the use of steroids. (p.

22) Later, Carlisle asked Mary Paquette about Chad's alleged use of steroids and she knew nothing. (p. 28)

Chad wrote in his August 8, 2010 letter,

Let me tell you unequivocally, I have NEVER used steroids! I earned my mass the old fashioned way, hard work, proper rest and eating enough protein. I have always been naturally strong. I believe this is due to the fact that I was lifting heavy trash barrels into the back of my dad's rubbish removal trucks. If I wasn't doing that, I was helping my grandfather in the hay fields or hauling slabs in the lumber mill. The extra strength came in handy when playing my favorite sport, football.

While on the subject, I may as well address weight. As you can see from the photos you've posted on the website, I was always a "hefty" kid. (Though I liked to refer to it as being "farm fed" and "big boned" :) By the time I got into 8th and 9th grade most of my baby fat melted off and I was left with a big chest and wide shoulders. I was already an undersized lineman by height standards and without extra weight I couldn't hold up at the point of attack on the football field so I ate and ate to gain. The problem is, I stayed heavy during those last two years of high school even after I stopped playing football. I carried some of this extra weight with me when I moved to Rochester. I always had a thyroid gland problem and add a McDonald's diet to that and it is easy to stay a few pounds heavier than you'd like.

Carlisle reported that, according to Bruce, "*...when Chad was placed on probation, he did a complete turnaround. While everyone else consumed beer watching football, Chad was satisfied to consume fruit drinks, which surprised his friends.*" (p. 25)

Next, Carlisle interviewed Chad's immediate family, including his parents and Jason and Nicole and Nicole's husband, Brandon. He reported that

The family produced two scrapbooks of pictures showing Chad with friends and family, as well as a video of Chad interacting with Kyle, Brent, Jason's three-year-old daughter and others while celebrating birthdays and different occasions. It was clear from these pictures and the idea that warm and loving relationships are present within the family unit and the defendant cares for the youngsters just mentioned. (p. 25)

Carlisle reported that after the verdict, the Evans family received 73 phone messages in support of Chad. Regarding Barbara Brooks Hamel, Chad's family members reported that they had seen Barbara hit Chad many times. Carlisle wrote that Chet, "*wanting to drop the topic and not speak negative about Barbara, considers it 'a dead issue.'* " (p. 26) Carlisle interviewed Barbara later.

Nicole recalled an incident which occurred when she was 12, and Chad was 16 or 17. Wrote Carlisle,

...Chad was driving through Keene with his twelve-year-old sister as a passenger. Nicole still recalls how her brother stopped the car upon seeing a boy beating up his girlfriend. Proceeding to get between the two, Chad pushed the male aside and left with the female. Chad gave her the option of going to the police station, but since she chose not to, he took her home. (p. 26)

Jason told Carlisle that Chad had set up an education fund for his daughter, Malana, and Chad told Jason that when she reached college age, there would be enough money in the fund to cover her education. As the police did not interview Jason, this act by Chad was not known by the police. They did know that Chad had set up similar funds for Kyle and Brent, and if they had known about the fund for Malana, they might have been more receptive to the claim that Chad was planning to help Amanda set up a similar fund for Kassidy. (Nicole interview, November 9, p. 1816)(Chad letter, Feb. 14, 2010) It's common sense that person who abuses a very young children and murders that child is not likely to be a person who is making plans to establish a college education fund for that same child.

Jason described for Carlisle how Chad rescued three men from a burning car in front of his home and the "Hero" award from Governor. Shaheen. Jason said that he accompanied Chad to the ceremony and recalled that Chad was asked why he risked his life, and he responded, "*What else was I to do?*" Carlisle was impressed by the event and also wrote, "*This writer would like to point out that, at no time during any of the PSI interviews at the Strafford County House of Corrections, did Chad Evans even mention this courageous act occurring a half dozen years ago.*" (p. 27)

Carlisle interviewed Merle Wentworth, the father of Tristan, and wrote,

Mr. Wentworth...sees the defendant occasionally and believes in his innocence. If Chad was a child abuser, Mr. Wentworth is of the opinion that he would have abused Brent. To the contrary, Chad treated Kyle and Brent very well. In essence, none of this makes any sense to Tristan's father. (p. 27)

Mr. Wentworth reported that he had observed Chad drinking excessively when he was married to Tristan, but afterwards that drinking had "*decreased significantly.*" (p. 27)

Next, Carlisle interviewed by phone Mary Paquette, with whom Chad lived for 3 1/2 years before beginning his relationship with Tristan. Carlisle wrote,

Mary found Chad "nice," caring, always willing to help people and never exhibiting any violent behavior. In saying that this is nothing she would tolerate, Mary stated that Chad never abused her and always treated her well, while any arguments occurring during their relationship could be traced to "stupid stuff." (p. 27)

Mary told Carlisle that she was not aware of any substance abuse problems, and was not aware of any steroid use by Chad. She said that she and Chad remained friends and she said that the newspaper accounts of Chad's arrest and trial "*blew her mind.*" (p. 28)

Carlisle interviewed Barbara Brooks Hamel, in person. She explained that her earlier police interview had occurred at her initiative after she saw a favorable piece of a television news broadcast about Chad. She recounted their rocky relationship and violent incidents with Chad and Carlisle wrote that "*she never hit Chad.*" (p. 29)

Carlisle closed with an "*Evaluation and Analysis.*"

The circumstances of Kassidy Bortner's death energize many emotions, especially for anyone having viewed the autopsy pictures of this little girl's bruised body...Her excruciating pain and loneliness... can only be described as horrific and terrible. Unfortunately, Kassidy didn't even have her mother to protect her. How sad!...

It is evident that Chad Evans has done various acts of kindness and charity over the years... [but] *these good deeds and attributes are not real important when considering his cruel and barbaric behavior ending the life of Kassidy Bortner.... Chad bringing a picture of Kassidy to one of our PSI interviews and shedding tears while discussing her leaves this writer unimpressed.* (p. 31)

Carlisle concluded that Chad should be punished harshly and recommended 45 years to life for the Second Degree Murder charge. The other recommended punishments were to be either suspended or run concurrently. He recommended 7 1/2-15 years for the first three Second Degree Assault charges for the periods of September 1-30, October 8-15, and October 16-21. For the last two, for the periods of October 22-31 and November 1-9, he recommended a more severe total of 10-30. There was no explanation for distinguishing among the charges. We will never know what Stephen Carlisle might have recommended if Chad had ignored his lawyers' recommendation and talked with him about the alleged crimes for which he was convicted.

We don't know how Kassidy died, but no one testified about seeing her in "excruciating pain" or even in "pain" at all, except for Jennifer who testified that on November 9, Kassidy "*acted like she was sick, in pain.*" (p. 111) Carlisle referenced Chad's "*cruel and barbaric*" behavior. The only reference to "*cruel*" in the trial was in the November 26, 2001 pre-trial hearing where Judge Nadeau said it would be "cruel" to take a deposition of Dr. Baden over a weekend. (p. 81) The term "*barbaric*" was never used in Chad's trial.

Monday, 21 March 2002

Originally scheduled for this day, Chad's sentencing was rescheduled, at the request of the prosecutors to April 16 at 1:00 p.m. While awaiting sentencing, Chad remained at the Strafford County Jail, across the field from the Courthouse.

Monday, 16 April 2002 - Sentencing Hearing.

A sentencing hearing is the closing scene for one judicial phase of the criminal justice system, and is tightly choreographed, as are the trials themselves. It's the opportunity for the victims and their families and friends to publicly confront the now-guilty defendant, now dressed in an orange jumpsuit, and for the State to recommend the appropriate punishment. For an actually guilty defendant, it is the opportunity for him or her and attorney and his family and friends to plead for a light sentence. For a wrongfully convicted innocent defendant, it's an opportunity, once again, to declare one's innocence.

Simon Brown asked for a sentence of a total of "*60 years to life in State prison.*" (p. 3) For the murder charge, he requested 45 years to life and for the other charges an additional 15 years. Paralleling his closing statement at the trial, Brown said that *Kassidy became the focal point of the defendant's aggression and rage....These assaults were systematic. They occurred over weeks and months, culminating in one final and awful beating which caused Kassidy's death....Evidence was presented that he hurled her into a wall, slammed her into a closet, jerked her arm up behind her back before propelling her into a wall. He jabbed his finger into her throat. He picked her off the ground by her neck. He stuck Kassidy's head under a faucet, and he routinely smacked her in the mouth, allegedly to stop her from using foul language.... And on the night of November 8th,... Chad Evans inflicted a final and fatal beating....he made up ridiculous stories about baseballs and wiffle balls...Kassidy's existence in the last months of her life was a living hell...*

The merits of these allegations have been discussed earlier in this book, but new dimensions were added here. In addition to the previous allegation of throwing Kassidy into a wall, the detail not found earlier in interviews or testimony was now added that Chad "*jerked her arm up behind her back.*" Similarly, whereas Chad told the police that he had flicked Kassidy's lip when she said a bad word, Simon Brown now enhanced the story with "*routinely smacked her in the mouth.*" By themselves, these enhancements may not seem like much, but they were similar to the many other enhancements of memory which added up to a wrongful conviction.

At the trial, the prosecution and the judge kept the evidence of Chad's character and parenting away from the jury, but Brown knew that at this hearing, statements about Chad's good character would be made; so he confronted them. First, he noted that the "*incredibly thorough*" pre-sentencing report "*was full of praise for the defendant from those who knew him well and know him well.*" Then he said that those "*positive traits and his good background... make these crimes all the more inexplicable and senseless.*" Unfortunately, Brown was stuck with the jury's verdict and it was too late for him to try to understand the apparent contradiction. He was right, in the sense that the contradiction was "*inexplicable.*" When he prosecuted Chad, he didn't know a lot of the information about Chad that was in that pre-sentencing report, because that wasn't the truth the police primarily were seeking. They were seeking to prove their theory of the case. Brown didn't have the time to go sit down with Chad and get to know him and find out what really happened and to try to explain the "*inexplicable.*" It appeared to be too late. The system ground on.

Brown acknowledged Chad's good traits at work and with friends, and "*we know these crimes were not fueled by alcohol or drug abuse,*" (p. 7) which was not an issue at trial, so it was good to hear. That, of course, made the crimes even more "*inexplicable.*" He continued, "*Given this background, your Honor, there are simply no excuses for what he did. There is no reasonable explanation why a grown man with the defendant's upbringing would abuse and beat to death an innocent little girl.*" Again, Brown was correct. There was no reasonable explanation for Chad being charged and found guilty of these crimes. The most reasonable explanation was that he didn't commit them, but, again, it seemed to be too late to re-examine that possibility. It never should be too late, however. This book is an effort to provide a "*reasonable explanation*" for the "*inexplicable.*"

Brown cited the police interview with Chad's high school girlfriend, Barbara Brooks Hamel as evidence of his "*Jekyll-and-Hyde*" personality, but "Jekyll" and "Hyde" were fictional characters. Rarely do we see such contradictions in real life. Brown thought that Chad was one of those rare examples. After noting Chad's domestic violence conviction, which was a guilty plea, and the court-ordered "*26 weeks of batterer's counseling*" Brown said that Chad "*did absolutely nothing to curb his volatile tendencies*." In fact, that was wrong. It's not known if the pre-sentencing investigator interviewed Chad's privately-obtained counselor, Gray Fitzgerald, because that pre-sentencing report is not yet available. It should have reported that Chad did seek additional counseling services after the end of the court-ordered sessions. Chad's attorneys didn't seek Fitzgerald's records or assistance either.

Finally, Brown argued that Chad's violation of his bail conditions, by his contact with Amanda, showed that he had insufficient respect for the law, and the recommendation for the long prison sentence was justified. He concluded by describing Kassidy's last months as "*a living hell, a reign of terror.*" (p. 11)

Then spoke four relatives and friends of the Bortner family. First was Kathy Jackson, a sister of Amanda's stepfather, the man Amanda accused of molesting her. She made several correct observations, too,

Violence isn't supposed to happen in families like ours. Children aren't supposed to be beaten to death by successful businessmen. Mothers are supposed to protect their children at all costs. ... but there is no rational explanation for what you did. (p. 13)

Jackson, too, chose to believe what she knew was unbelievable. She told the court that she and Jacqueline went to Wal-Mart to purchase clothes for Kassidy's body, and she described those clothes in detail and how they were needed to cover up Kassidy's injuries. However, she didn't tell the court, perhaps because she didn't know, that Kassidy's body was buried in the clothes that Amanda and Chad purchased for her.

Talking about her close-knit family, Jackson noted that her cousin "*Mary and her husband David had wanted to adopt*" Kassidy when Amanda was a pregnant fifteen-year [sic] old. (p. 15) She was 16 at the time of Robert Sheehan's 20th birthday party and Kassidy's conception in May, 1998.

The death of Kassidy and the investigation and trial of Chad caused deep fractures in the Bortner family, but Amanda was especially bitter about the fervor of family members to speak for Kassidy after her death, in comparison to their attention and love while she was alive. Amanda told Chad that her Aunt Kathy saw Kassidy only a few times in her life and not once during the time that Chad and Amanda were together. Amanda sat behind Chad during his sentencing hearing and he remembered her saying quietly about her sister, Jennifer, and her aunt Kathy as they held photos of Kassidy, "*Neither of you cared about Kassidy so much while she was alive*." (Letter, April 19, 2010)

Next to speak was Paul Conley, Kassidy's step-grandfather. He said, "*The lowest form of human depravity in my opinion is the infliction of torture and death of an innocent child.*" (p. 17) He might have been surprised to learn that Chad had similar views. When Chad was asked during his November 9, 2000 interrogation what should be done with such people, he responded, "*string him up by the nuts or whatever*" (Chad interrogation, p. 1564)

Jacqueline Conley followed her husband, introducing herself as "*Jackie Conley*." She told Chad that he should apologize to her family, and also to Jeff Marshall, "*You were friends with him for many years, what I understand, best friends. What kind of friend are you?*" (p. 19) It was a curious request, to apologize to the man who Chad correctly believed to have immediately pointed the police toward him while Kassidy was still lying on his porch, and who told the police that Chad was a drug abuser, a gambler, a sexual deviant, and a violent man. They were never best friends, but saw mutual advantage to being friendly to the other. They never went to a bar together, never went to an athletic event together and never went to a concert together. The only activity they did together was transport Chad's three-wheelers, and that was because Chad needed Jeff's truck.

The fourth family member was Jennifer, who had introduced Chad to Amanda. She asked Chad to look into "*her* [Amanda's] *eyes and tell her why, and tell her you're sorry. Ask her to forgive you.*" (p. 21) Jennifer, like Chad, understood the importance of **eye contact**. She addressed Chad directly, "*Well Chad, no matter what the outcome of today is, remember a couple of things. This is not about you, me, Jeff, Mandy my parents, your parents. It is about one person. Kassidy. Please, Chad, remember her name, Kassidy, not* *'that baby.'* " As is discussed later, regarding the newspaper publication of this statement, Jennifer often referred in her interview to Kassidy as "kid" and "that kid."

Mr. Brown and the four family members had complete faith in the justice system. It was 2002 and the Innocence project had exonerated about 110 wrongfully convicted people, and it was still not widely understood how the judicial system could wrongfully convict innocent people. None of those exonerations had occurred in New Hampshire, and none has yet occurred there through the spring of 2011. They were sure of Chad's guilt.

Brown asked Judge Nadeau to be allowed to give a rebuttal presentation after Mark Sisti and Chad's friends and relatives spoke.

Mark Sisti noted, apart from the emotion that, "*The reality is that Mr. Brown knows that two years ago, Chad would be looked upon* [as] *a fine, productive American citizen,*" and Sisti asked for a sentence that would permit Chad to return to society and resume being productive. (p. 23) Sisti made no specific recommendation for a sentence for any of the charges.

In addition to the upcoming speakers for Chad, Sisti introduced others who "*wanted to make sure that the Court knew they were here.*" (p. 24) Each stood up and introduced themselves: Brandon Harvey, Tristan, ("*ex-wife and best friend*"), Chet Evans, Pam Evans ("*Chad's mother and proud of my son*"), Stephanie Bolduc ("*Chad's friend*"), Nicole Evans Harvey, and Jeremy Hinton ("*...I'm just lucky to know Chad Evans.*") (p. 24-25)

Chad's brother, Jason, spoke first, and described growing up with his older brother, who was his idol. Jason spoke of Kyle's and Brent's "*love and admiration for their father.*" Apparently unaware of the significance of the type of ball which hit Kassidy on the night of November 8, 2000, Jason said,

I remember going to Brent's T-ball game and Kyle telling me, "Next year, I'm going to play T-ball. You know why? Because my Daddy's teaching me how to hit the ball. " (p. 29)

Jason said Chad was

always thinking of other people around him. Even today as he sits in jail, he gives to fellow inmates.... talked to troubled teens. He tutors uneducated inmates. He helps inmates write letters to loved ones because they cannot read or write..." (p. 30)

This was not the picture of Chad Evans that the Attorney General's inmate informants presented to the police and to trial court.

Without a sense of irony, Jason said, "*Anyone that has known Chad for more than three months can tell you some truth about him, and would love to.*" (p. 30) This was approximately the length of time that prosecutors alleged Chad abused Kassidy.

At the end, he made an unusual plea,

I ask you, Judge Nadeau, if the opportunity presents itself, to spend some time with Chad. You will see. Better yet, spend some time with Brent, Kyle and Malana [Jason's three-year old daughter] *Ask them about their Dad or uncle. Go ahead and ask them questions. They're not timid and they control their own minds. I know us family members are considered biased. However, who controls the children?*" (p. 34)

As he heard this, Chad must have wondered about his discussions with his lawyers before trial about whether Kyle, who was with Chad and Kassidy on the evening of November 8, should testify. Chad decided against it as he didn't want to subject Kyle to the courtroom, but that was before he knew that his lawyers would call only one witness, Dr. Baden.

Jason's suggestion that Judge Nadeau "*spend some time with Chad,*" was a novel idea that had considerable merit, for, until this day of his sentencing, Judge Nadeau had never heard from Chad. Neither had the prosecutors. For all that they said about Chad during the trial, neither prosecutor had ever sat down with Chad and talked with him. Some would scoff that this is not how the system works, but as the Innocence Project has shown, the system doesn't work all the time, and ways must be found to prevent wrongful convictions. It was easier for the prosecution to claim that Chad was a terrible person and had done terrible crimes without their ever talking with him, face to face, with **eye contact**.

Next, Vanessa Mansson began by speaking of her recent six years working in the criminal justice system as a corrections officer and as a legal assistant for an attorney and county attorney. Perhaps she was thinking about how she was fired by the County Attorney, Peter Heed, for offering shelter to Chad and Amanda when she said, "*I ponder the question, what is justice*?" She correctly summarized how Chad came to have that forbidden contact with Amanda,

Shortly after Kassidy's death, Amanda reached out to Chad for help and, in true Chad fashion, Chad put his own freedom at risk to help her. Simply, he helped her because he cared. He had no hidden agenda, nor was he being manipulative. Simply, he helped her because he cared. I do not believe that Amanda would have made it through that traumatic time without Chad's support." (p. 36)

Vanessa explained that she helped Chad and Amanda in 2001 because Chad had helped her and many others, unselfishly, in the past, saying, "*To say I owe Chad my life is an understatement*." (p. 36) Finally, she spoke of Chad's relationship with children,

Over the years, Chad has been the only person besides my family that I have trusted to care for my children. He never belittles their opinions or ideas. He has always encouraged them to be the best they can... (p. 37)

Advised by Chad's attorneys not to criticize the trial or the judicial system, Jeremy Hinton began by praising the justice system,

I think the system is tremendous. I think it's fair, and I think it works. In my opinion, I think Chad received a fair trial of his peers and they made a decision....My opinion of the verdict is of no importance. (p. 39)

Jeremy said that for him, Chad "*has been a mentor, a role model, a best friend and really a brother*." (p. 39) Then he quoted one of Chad's mantras to him about people,

Every person has a value, Jeremy. They're not just workers. No matter what you do for a living, you need to put people first. Reach out to them and make their lives better. It's the most important thing that you do every day.

Except for the video of Chad's interrogation, this was the first time Judge Nadeau had heard a quoted statement by Chad about his beliefs. He would soon get his last chance.

Jeremy asked Judge Nadeau to

Look out in the courtroom, your Honor. There's over 30 people there standing behind him. There's more people trying to get in. There's no room for them because the media [took seats and they] *wanted to make Chad out to be a monster*." (p. 42)

Unfortunately, Chad's jury heard very little about the Chad whom his supporters described.

The speakers on both sides were eloquent, but the idea that they could have an impact on the judge was an illusion. She already likely knew the sentences which she was going to impose. Instead, like eulogies, the benefit was not for the subject of the event but for the speakers and others in the audience.

Then Chad addressed the court. As he was advised not to testify at his trial, this was his opportunity to tell Judge Nadeau and the spectators what really happened in the fall of 2000. It was his chance to explain his love for Kassidy, and his extreme sorrow for her death and for his not doing more, in hindsight, to help her. He prepared his comments in writing, and went through three drafts with his attorneys. He was advised not to proclaim his innocence and thereby anger the judge, so he talked about his failure,

...there has not been a minute since the fall of 2000 that I've not felt anything but shame and regret for the things that I've done. I've hurt my devoted family, all my friends, my beautiful sons, and Amanda beyond comprehension. And my heart feels most heavy for the way that I failed Kassidy. Amanda, I am so sorry for the emptiness and the hurt you have to deal with for the rest of your life. You and Kassidy deserved a lot more. I'm really sorry. And-- I'm sorry. That's all " (p. 43-44)

If Chad had felt that he had more time, he might have explained to Judge Nadeau and the people in the courtroom what he wrote in his letter of May 15, 2011, about what was going on in his life and how he felt about Amanda and Kassidy:

Of course, there is the legal argument that Kassidy wasn't my child and who knows if I could have even gotten her treated. However, from an emotional point of view, that

argument carries little weight with others (including myself.) I loved Kassidy and had I known something was seriously wrong, both Amanda and I certainly would have taken her to be seen. Nothing is ever going to change the fact for me that I failed Kassidy because I failed to see what was happening. I will live with this forever. I am not asking for people to excuse my ignorance, but hopefully if we can provide a sense of what I was going through at the time to understand that there was nothing cut and dry about the situation and at the very least, my lack of focus and attention wasn't malicious. It was a product of my life. My being self-absorbed, etc. I'm talking about getting a reader to understand my mental state and all that I was dealing with. I had so much turmoil in my life. I had a career, a pending divorce that some days I wanted to happen and other days I was sad. I had a new relationship with someone I was very interested in but also included a lot of pressure from this person. Things were not moving at the speed she wanted, and after my past marriage failures, I wanted her to be happy. This new relationship included a beautiful baby girl, which presented its own set of challenges. I was on egg shells with my former wife. I was an emotional wreck because I was not accustomed to failing at things and I had failed at marriage. I was dealing with my fears of a custody battle I was trying to stay active and involved in my stepson's life, even though month by month, I was being slowly edged out. I constantly had my perceived failures floating through my head and was trying to take an completely 180 turn away from my past and make different decisions. I.E. I wasn't going to do anything that my new partner could perceive as slightly controlling. It could all be on her terms. etc. etc. Again, this doesn't excuse my inaction, but I am hopeful will explain to people what I had going on. Perhaps, for lack of a better term. They will realize I was "punch drunk."

I really loved Kassidy and Amanda but in hindsight, I was no where healthy enough to be in a committed relationship at that point. Every time I tried to put the brakes on with Amanda, I felt like I was going to lose her, so I would relent. I knew she was the future I wanted, and if I pushed her away she would be gone forever. I already felt abandoned in my marriage vows.

Returning to his actual statement in the courtroom, he really meant that, and it was truthful, but it was ambiguous about the actions or inaction for which he was apologizing. The problem was that the statement was surely understood by most who heard it, and to the newspaper readers who read it, to mean that he accepted responsibility for killing Kassidy. Instead, he meant, simply, that he regretted not doing more to help her. Alan Cronheim then addressed the proper length of sentence for this second degree murder. He praised the pre-sentencing report by Steve Carlisle, but said that Carlisle's recommendation of 45 years to life was too harsh. He spoke of Chad's character and of the "*more than 30 letters from people who have come to know Chad in ways that we as lawyers and you as the Court will never have that opportunity.*" Cronheim correctly observed that usually, when *somebody is charged, the people who claim to be friends disappear because of the notoriety of the charge, because of publicity, because they have more important things to do in their life, so they move on and they move away.*" (p. 46) Despite the large support received by Chad on that day, the powerful forces that Cronheim described continued to work against Chad thereafter, in the absence of a clear, coherent, comprehensive public statement of innocence.

Cronheim spoke of Chad's meetings with Steve Carlisle and how Carlisle, *found unpersuasive his* [Chad's] *comments about Kassidy, and found even perhaps -- and I don't know if he used this word -- 'contrived,' his comments as he's bringing the photograph of Kassidy -- of Kassidy to one of the meetings between the two of them.*" (p. 47)

It was an interesting reference to the power of a photograph, which Chad's lawyers failed to understand at Chad's trial. As Carlisle saw his job as interviewing the man who killed Kassidy, he misunderstood Chad's statements about Kassidy and his bringing the photograph, too. Chad brought to Carlisle photographs of Amanda, Kassidy and Kyle so that Carlisle could see Chad's melded family. He understood that a photo was worth a thousand words. One of the photographs was of Kassidy smiling in Chad's kitchen with Kato licking her face. Chad believes that the photograph was taken in late August or early

September, which was significantly into the period of the alleged abuse. Unfortunately, Chad and his lawyers didn't realize the power of photographs during the year-long investigation and at Chad's trial.

Returning to the question of the proper length of time in prison, Cronhein referred to Carlisle's recommendation of 20 years in prison, just for the second degree assault charges, in addition to the 45 for murder. Cronheim noted the critical reality of any lengthy prison sentence which was that "*in 20 years Chad Evans will be punished by not having time to raise his son, Kyle.*" This is what Chad has missed the most, and so far, he has missed the active parenting of Kyle between his third and fourteenth year, and still counting. (p. 48) Cronheim mentioned another chilling reality of a long prison sentence for Chad which was that he would likely still be in prison when his parents pass away. (p. 49) One part of the motivation for this book and the Campaign for Justice for Chad is to obtain Chad's exoneration while Chet and Pam are alive.

Cronheim did not give a number for his recommended number of years in prison, but he cited another case where a man with a serious police record was given, effectively, 27 years to life for second degree murder, and then concluded, "*we suggest something less than the 45 years to life sentence would be appropriate under these circumstances.*" (p. 49) This must have come as a shock to Chad. His own lawyers were recommending "*something less than 45 years to life*?" Of course they were part of the system, and they felt that they, too, couldn't still protest that their client was innocent, because the jury and court had found them guilty. Cronheim advised Chad that a defendant who doesn't accept a guilty verdict angers judged because it shows disrespect to the jury and to the courts. On the other hand, what does it say when the defendant and his lawyers stop protesting his innocence?

Then the choreographed proceeding departed from the script. Cronheim and Brown conferred with Judge Nadeau because neither the State nor the defense had called Amanda to testify, but she was in the courtroom and had indicated a desire to speak. Neither attorney told the judge why Amanda didn't speak for his side. For the prosecution, it was clear that Amanda, who was soon to be tried for Child Endangerment, and who had recanted her statements to the police, would not be helpful to their request for severe punishment. It was not clear why Chad's lawyers did not have Amanda speak on Chad's behalf during the defense presentation.

Judge Nadeau asked Simon Brown if he had talked with Amanda recently and he said "*No, no.*" and Judge Nadeau asked, "*You can't?*" and Brown said, "*We can't,*" apparently because Amanda's status had changed from prosecution witness to defendant. It was yet another example where the stove-piped system blocks reasonable communication.

As Judge Nadeau stated, Amanda "*has the right to speak*" as the victim's mother, and so she did. (p. 52) Amanda took the stand and said,

I find it really strange that everyone cares so much about Kassidy now, and not one did when she was alive. She was just another kid. My mother has six kids. I was just another kid... I never knew what love was until Kassidy was born. I pray to God she forgives my lack of motherly instincts.

Amanda spoke of

...the horrible, senseless tragedy that we all have to live with forever. No one will get to see the life she could have had. Instead of pointing fingers and casting blame, everyone needs to look internally. No one is innocent. We all failed Kassidy. I am going to be living with regret for the rest of my life.

Referring vaguely to "*those that acknowledge what they've done and those who won't,*" she said, "*God knows the truth, though. Of that I'm sure.*" She, too, was not able to say in court on that day what she felt about Chad's wrongful conviction. Referring obliquely to the depression she felt in the period in 2001 when Chad was forbidden to see her, she said, "*I know I would not be here today without Chad's loving support,*" and concluded, "*As Kassidy's mother, your Honor,... He* [Chad] *has done too much good to lock him up forever. He is a wonderful, caring father and good-hearted man.*" (p. 54)

Simon Brown responded to Cronheim's citing of an apparently light sentence with a case of his own, with a heavier sentence. Brown concluded with one image,

What comes to mind is some of the testimony that you heard in this case where witnesses testified that Kassidy was literally covered -- her face looked like it had dirt all over it -- with bruises, Melissa Chick's testimony about giving her a bath and seeing her covered in bruises...." (p. 55)

This was a reference to a bath that Amanda doesn't believe occurred, but which Melissa claimed to have occurred in September, during a period sandwiched by the still unacknowledged, September 11 visit to a doctor and photographs of a happy, healthy, bruise-free Kassidy on October 1.

Judge Nadeau then recessed the court for twenty minutes saying,

I've already given this case quite a bit of thought, but I want to take some time to incorporate what I heard this afternoon from everybody who spoke on behalf of Kassidy and Mr. Evans and from the lawyers' presentations. So I'm going to take some time and devise sentences that I hope will be appropriate and fair, and I'll be back as soon as I do that." (p. 56)

Resuming the hearing at 3:15 p.m., Judge Nadeau began by saying that she had "*read ever single letter and statement that's been submitted in connection with this case at least once and sometimes more than that...*" (p. 56) There were approximately 52 letters sent to Judge Nadeau on Chad's behalf. Some of those may have been submitted to Chad's attorneys and not been forwarded to Judge Nadeau, but it's presumed that she received most of them. All the letters struggled with the same problem of how to deal with a terrible verdict about a man thought to have such wonderful qualities.

Amanda wrote a six page letter, excerpts of which are below,

Judge Tina Nadeau

I wanted to take a minute and write to you on behalf of Kassidy. I'm not going to speak to you about justice today because how can there ever be justice? It is not as if when a human life is taken you can ever make up for it. Kassidy was my gift from God that I love very much and miss every minute of every day.... I would be lying if I told you I'm not angry and bitter. Every day I ask God why Kassidy? Why me? Why does God let Chad get blamed for this? This is all still not real to me! I wonder if it ever will be. I cry every time I even think about Kassidy. I will never get to see her grow. Her birthday is February fourth. She will be three this year. I will never get to make her a cake, throw her a birthday party, .watch her open Christmas presents, take her to her first day of school, talk to her about boys, brush her hair, go shopping with her, be her best friend, and etc .. The list goes on. If I could get her for one more day I would hold her in my arms and never let her go. She was all I ever had. I've never had a quote "family" so I had a huge attachment to her. She was a little me. She copied everything I did. She is the sweetest little girl in the world.

The state wanted to paint a picture of me being a bad mother. When I sit here and think of the kind of mom I was, I see that I was a mother way before I was ready to be one. I loved her with all my heart and I was really good with her, but I am not so blind that I can't see I had no motherly instinct. I was 17 and 18 at the time but in many ways I had the mentality of a 15 and 16 year old. Something like this has a way of making you grow up fast. But I don't think it was until I really found God that I was able to look at myself in this situation objectively. Now I feel like I'm 20 going on 28. My whole life has changed. I can see clearly in one aspect the police are correct about me being a bad mom, and that is I didn't protect my daughter. I didn't protect her from Chad grabbing her face, and I certainly didn't protect her from Jeff! This is a scar I will live with for the rest of my life. I can't offer you an excuse for what was going through my head at the time. I have nothing but hate for myself when I think about a couple times Kassidy would have little finger bruises on her cheeks. But I hate myself even more when I think about the times I would continuously bring her over ⌊to⌋ *Jeff Marshall's house and almost everyday she would come back with weird bruises, or little pin pricks on the bottom of her feet, or Kassidy screaming every time I'd drop her off or pick her up, coming home with make up on to cover the bruises. I would believe all of his lame excuses. What was wrong with me? The only thing I can tell you is I would never let it happen again. There are no easy answers. I would like to think I was so blind but that doesn't really make me feel any better. I guess what I'm saying, and this isn't out of love {or Chad, this is out of love for my daughter is that we are all to blame. I know I can't write how I feel about the verdict so I won't. I will just say only God and Kassidy truly know the truth. I can only say I believe in Chad one hundred and ten percent. Not because of what he has said to me but rather because of what he hasn't said. He has always told me I to tell the truth. I finally did in the courtroom. When this entire thing started I was sitting there in the police station being told one minute my baby was dead and the next that Chad was responsible. After hours of sitting there I said some horrible things about Chad, many of them untrue, particularly because they had me convinced and partly so I could say whatever and just get out of there. I didn't want to be there, I just couldn't deal with it all. I just figured it would all go away. I pray that no one ever has to go through that pain. As far as punishment for Chad is concerned I would ask you to have mercy. I have a hard time with the things that Chad did, but honestly no one is harder on himself than Chad. He has punished himself everyday and will for the rest of his life. That is the person Chad Evans is. I realize that you don't know Chad and only got one side in the courtroom. I just want to give you an idea about who Chad Evans really is.*

Our relationship started out as most do. Was attracted to the superficial things, looks, security, good times, etc. I soon found Chad had many qualities that were only talked about. He is romantic, sweet, caring, very generous, and the most GIVING person I have ever met.

You have heard about Chad and Kassidys problem but you haven't heard much about their true relationship. Kassidy loved Chad. It makes me cry when I think about how many times in a day Kassidy would ask, "Where's Chad?" He did so many good things with her. Every morning before I had a job she would come into our bedroom and Chad would put her on his back, And piggy back ride her downstairs to her high chair. He fed her breakfast every morning if he was there when she woke up. Many days I would come around the corner and find him sitting there talking away to Kassidy, playing with her while she ate breakfast. Many days he would come home midmorning and bring her some munchkins or for lunch he'd bring her a happy meal. It was like he couldn't come home without bringing her or me something. He would sit with her for hours and color, play spin art, and do the alphabet and numbers with her. He'd always point out objects and she'd say what they were. That's something we both did with her. She loved it! She also loved getting involved with the boys wrestling on the bed. She loved to play with the boys. One of her favorite things to do with the Chad was pony rides and superman. He would sit and read to her at bed time, and was always affectionate. She gave Chad kisses and hugs all the time. He taught Kassidy to say "ohhhhh," when you gave her a hug. He was always talking about saving money for her future. And he's always a softy. He could hardly ever say no to her when she asked for a cookie, or a piece of candy. When I had a survey job on the computer he spent hours with her playing, holding her, watching Disney movies with her, and etc. so that I could work on my surveys. He was always so patient with her then and if she was sick. As far as the bad things, I honestly think it broke his heart that after 2 or 3 months she started throwing temper tantrums if he'd kiss me again. (After Jeff started babysitting) He and I just couldn't understand how she would be all over him playing, etc. for 4 hours one night and then we'd all be sitting together and he'd kiss me and she'd freak out. He has punished himself over and over for grabbing her face but I can honestly say he did not do it with the intention of hurting her but to get her attention, and to have her listen. I can't tell you how many nights he sat there and just cried about how bad he felt and wished he would have never grabbed her face. Over the past year, I've never seen him so much as raise his voice. Not even with me, no matter what I dished out to him. Last summer I was awful after Kassidy died. I was so bitter towards everyone that was around me. And I was the worst to Chad. He ... always waited on me hand and foot since I met him, but after Kassidy died, I couldn't have found anyone more patient and more supportive. He was my comfort and my everything. I didn't want to live anymore and he's the one that kept me alive and gave me hope that I could get through this. Showing me nothing but love and support.

He is the most caring, giving person I've ever met. When we started dating I thought it was cute at first [and then] *it started to become annoying. Every night it seemed someone was dropping by because they needed fifty dollars to buy groceries for their kids, or 100 to make the mortgage payment because they were a little short that week. If it wasn't money people were stopping by because they needed advice or something, or were having relationship problems and just needed someone to talk to. It doesn't matter who these people were some young some old, some employees, some friends, some ex-employees, they all shared one thing in common. They all needed something and he was there for all of them. Sometimes I would sit there in amazement watching him one time he had this young married couple over the house. The husband had just started working in one of Chad's restaurants. They were struggling with their budget and wanted to buy a house. Chad sat there for 3 or 4 hours explaining things to them helping them set up a budget, etc. The next week he's sitting on the couch talking to a 17 year old being a friend to him and basically talking him out of quitting school. Chad didn't leave it at that though. He had the kid stop by or call him every once in a while to see how he was doing. I remember when our friend Jessica and her boyfriend broke up, she was over all the time bawling. She even slept over one night. Then they got back together. After Chad had talked to her boyfriend and her and helped them work out their issues. I could go on with stories like this but I think you get the point. I guess what I'm saying is he did this because he wanted to help people. I never heard him say to anyone, "Hey pay me back Friday," or "I helped you out, now you owe me one." When I look back I guess it irritated me because I was young and I didn't understand it at the time, until I needed someone he was there for me. After Kassidy died and then Chad got arrested I went to Texas. I missed Kassidy so much I wanted to die. As I got away from everyone I realized and remembered more and more things. He was hesitant at first* [to contact him] *because he didn't want to go to jail. But when I told him I was at my breaking point, and wasn't going to make it without him, again he put me first, risking his life. I know how the police made it sound that he was trying to convince me he wasn't responsible but honestly it couldn't be farther from the truth. He made me eat everyday. I seriously could not eat. I lost so much weight. I wouldn't even drink. My brain thought, if Kassidy isn't eating I'm not either. I was a mess. He made me realize that I had to make it. I really think that God gave us that time together. God knew Chad was the only one that could help me. He always put my wants ahead of his own freedom and ultimately he lost it. But even when that happened he was only concerned about me. He put together a little book of sayings to get me through each day. This is Chad Evans always putting others first. He literally saved my life, and I will never forget that.*

Chad has an impact on everyone he meets. He always has a lesson in life to share whether it's a previous mistake he has made or a subject he knows something about. The thing is he doesn't talk down to people or come off like a know it all. He just has this way of making a situation better without having to be the centerpiece.

I mentioned that Chad has saved my life, but 1'm not the only person he has done this for. When we lived together in Rochester I found a plaque awarded to Chad that said, hero ayvarded for bravery. Along with a couple of pictures of him shaking a ladies hand in the closet. "Then I asked him about it he said oh that's nothing really. When I asked his sister about it several months later, she told me it was an award for pulling 3 men out of a burning car saving their lives. The lady in the picture was the Governor at the award presentation.

I'm very close to Chad's family. They are wonderful supportive people. I have learned even more about Chad from being around them the last several months. Like Chad they are very modest people when it comes to good deeds so they don't talk an awful lot. But they don't have to becauseeveryone else does. Murder is one of the worst crimes you could ever be accused of. The day following the verdict there were so many people calling Chad's family's house with stories of what Chad had done for them, how great he is, how can they help, etc. Lots of people stopped by. There was an old high school friend that said he felt like he owed everything he had today to Chad for driving him through school, helping pass 12th *grade English and coming out one night after midnight to pull him off a bridge. He was going to jump off because the pressures of life were too much to handle. This friend, Ken, I think his name was said he would not have his business, wife or child if it wasn't for Chad making him see how good life is.*

After Kassidy died and Chad got arrested he lost his job as an area supervisor for McDonald's. They did believe in him, but since the publicity was bad they said he could come back when this was all over. Everyone assumed he wouldn't get convicted. He had 29 different interviews. Nobody wanted to hire him cause of the papers. He finally got hired at the Keene Domino's. After the verdict, the owner sent a nice card and a beautiful thing of flowers, also a nice phone call. He said that Chad is an amazing person and in the short time he worked there he had a huge impact on the restaurant and the kids that worked there. He is a great listener, and a great friend to anyone. He told Chad's parents if there was anything he could do to help, please let him know. Chad has his 100 percent support.

It was amazing when I was arrested and put in jail, I can't tell you how many of the guards came up to me and said encouraging words and things, like how much they thought of Chad, how he didn't belong in a place like this, how nice he is, how he helps people, and how much he always talks about me, and etc. Some of these things have been said to Chad's parents when they go to visit him. It just blows my mind. His mom told me how hard it was at first when he went to jail. Being charged with what he was, not treated very well by the guards and the inmates. Now four months later and they all have nothing but good things to say about him. This is the truth. I could give you some names if you wanted to check yourself This is Chad Evans. If he was convincing like prosecutors and police say, many people would see through it. He is genuine. That is what makes him special.

Your honor, I could go on and on with stories about Chad and I have only known him for 2 years. But I just wanted to give you an idea of the Chad Evans that I know. I seriously could fill another 50 pages with all of the kind things he has done for me and others. I would be happy to do that if you care to hear it.

I just wanted an opportunity to show you a little bit of the Chad Evans I am in love with. I know the police and prosecutors would like to pass me off as a naive empty headed 20 year old bubble brain that has no idea about life. But I can assure you that is not the case at all. Yes I am young in years, but I have had to deal with more things than most people twice my age do. I've had to do a lot of growing up fast. I hope you will see Chad for the person that he is. Yes he has made some mistakes as we all do, but he is a wonderful and caring person that is not only my life line, but many others as well. We all miss and need him in our lives. I ask you to please consider the real Chad Evans and show up all mercy. I love and miss Kassidy every single day, I assure you if you could have seen them together day in and day out you would know that she would want nothing to do with punishing Chad. I say that on Kassidy's behalf not Chads. We have suffered so much. It is time to start healing. Thank you for taking the time to read this.

The "Ken" that Amanda referenced was on the railing of a bridge over Route 9 in Keene, when Chad talked him out of his suicide plan. Of all the allegations of Chad's "persuasion" in this case, maybe this one is the best to remember. Of the 52 letter writers, most had known Chad before he had met Amanda, but several had seen Chad with his children and Kassidy. One such writer was Kevin Picknell who lived at the Evans's home in Keene in the summer of 2000. He was at the home during the two times that Amanda and Chad came to Keene with Kassidy in August, 2000, although he was not specific about dates. He wrote,

...He was caring and loving to all three children, Kyle, Brent and Cassidy. I got to spend a great deal of time with his children and him. He was always active with children, always playing and in general just spending time with them. It was very obvious that Chad cared for and loved all three children a great deal. ...It was also obvious the loved between Chad and Brent, and Chad and Kassidy. He was always the first one in the pool and out playing with the children. Chad would be the one getting them food and making sure to keep them all happy. He also was always teaching all three children the basics of

life and anything else they had questions [about]... *I believe that, Chad Evans is the greatest individual that I will ever get the pleasure of meeting and knowing.*
Returning to the hearing, Judge Nadeau didn't say anything specific about the letters, but she must have wondered if she was about to sentence the same person who was convicted in her courtroom four months earlier. It's not known what she thought about the letters for Chad, and specifically about the letters from Brandon and Gerri Harvey and Nicole Evans Harvey, all three of whom referred to the November 5, 2000 at the family gathering at Brandon's and Nicole's home. Brandon's reference began with "*On a Sunday a few days before Kassidy died*," and Gerri's was, "*Several days before Kassidy Bortner died...*" Nicole's was the most explicit about the date, referring to "*...the Sunday he spent with us just four days before she died.*" Paralleling Melissa Chick's statement to Sgt. White and Det. Linscott that she looked for a camera to record bruises, Nicole wrote about Sunday, November 5,

I only wish I had my video camera running that day so that the whole world could have seen the Chad Evans that we all know and love, eating pizza with her on his lap, both saying, "mmmm" after each bite. Or singing ABC's, or just cuddling in a way that I could tell that shared a bond.

If Nicole had taken that video, perhaps Chad would never have been charged with Kassidy's murder. During the entire trial, neither Judge Nadeau nor the jury had heard anything about that November 5, 2000 gathering.

Judge Nadeau stated that
My obligation today is to impose a balanced and proportionate sentence, one that takes into consideration the appropriate punishment and provides an opportunity for rehabilitation." (p. 57)

She discussed Chad's life, and said that from the pre-sentencing report and from evidence at the trial, "*I've seen a man who was convicted of domestic violence against his ex-wife and who has committed similar assaults against Amanda Bortner.*" (p. 57) However, Chad's domestic violence, under the influence of alcohol, against Tristan, for which he pled guilty, bore extremely little resemblance to his restraining and pushing-away actions with Amanda, each of which was over in a matter of seconds.
Judge Nadeau continued,

I've seen a man who had admitted to some abuse against Kassidy when he knows there have been witnesses to confirm it and who has minimized other assaults against Kassidy when he believes his ability to persuade is strong." (p. 58)

There was only one person interviewed by the police and only one person who testified at Chad trial who said that she saw Chad harm Kassidy. That person was Amanda, and she recanted most of her police statements at Chad's trial.
Judge Nadeau's reference to Chad's ability to persuade was another police theory that had little support. No police interviewee and no trial witness said that Chad had tried to persuade him or her to say anything different than the truth. A good example of his non-persuasion is the pervasive misunderstanding by several police interviewees and trial witnesses of the type of ball that hit Kassidy on the night of November 8. Even Amanda, allegedly under Chad's influence in 2001, testified that the ball was a wiffle ball. In response to Simon Brown's specific question, Amanda said, "*He never told me actually what kind of ball it was.*" (Amanda testimony, page 123)

At Chad's trial, the only person to be asked directly about Chad's alleged powers of persuasion was Tristan, who was asked by Simon Brown, "*Is the defendant a persuasive person*?" and Tristan answered, "*No.*" (Transcript, p. 17)
Then Judge Nadeau addressed the dilemma which faces all wrongly convicted defendants: the showing of remorse. She said,

I've seen a man who, until today has shown a disturbing lack of remorse for the death of a child he caused, and I've seen a man who has refused to accept any measure of responsibility for causing the death and murdering Kassidy Bortner. Mr. Evans, I hope that someday you will find the courage to tell your family and your friends and Amanda Bortner what you did to Kassidy, and perhaps if you had from the beginning, you wouldn't be facing the sentence that I feel is appropriate and just today. (p. 58)

In fact, he did tell the police on November 8, 2000 that he caused the only bruises created by an intentional act, which were the bruises on Kassidy's lower cheeks. That is, his holding Kassidy's face to get **eye contact** was intentional, but the bruising was unintentional. However, instead of telling the truth about his seeking eye contact, he continued to present the "trampoline story." Hearing Judge Nadeau's summary, Chad must have wondered if his silence before trial, and then his silence at the trial was a good strategy. How different the case might have been if Chad had not only answered the reporters' questions about the case during the investigation, but had sought out interviews. His message would have been clear: remorse for her death for not doing more, but absolutely no intentional actions which caused her death.

Judge Nadeau came closer to the sentencing, and noted that the "*New Hampshire Constitution says that the true design of all punishments* ...[is] *to reform, not to exterminate mankind,*" and she saw "*Mr. Evans' contributions to society... as a sign and an opportunity for rehabilitation.*" (p. 59)

Then she sentenced Chad as follows:

Second Degree Murder,	28 years to life.
Second Degree Assault, Sept. 1- Sept 30:	5-10 years, consecutive, suspended.
Second Degree Assault, Oct. 8- Oct 14:	10-30 years, consecutive, suspended.
Second Degree Assault, Oct. 15- Oct 21:	10-30 years, concurrent
Second Degree Assault, Oct. 22- Oct 31:	10-30 years, concurrent
Second Degree Assault, Nov. 1- Nov. 9:	10-30 years, concurrent
Child Endangerment	12 months, concurrent
Simple Assault, Amanda	12 months, concurrent

Effectively, Chad was sentenced to a term of 28 years to life for all his charges. If he was released after 28 years and ran afoul of the law, the suspension of his 5-10 year, and one of the 10-30 sentences, could be revoked, which would return him to prison for a minimum of 15 years.

After Chad's sentencing, the clerk advised him that he had the right to appeal his sentences to a Sentence Review Board of three other Superior Court justices. Ominously, the clerk said, "*Review of the sentence may result in a decrease* ***or increase*** *in the minimum or maximum term within the limit fixed by law....*" (p. 64) [emphasis added here]

Chad was then led out of the courtroom while the audience was requested to remain seated. The hearing ended at 3:26 p.m., which was 11 minutes after Judge Nadeau returned from her recess. In his Associated Press story, J.M. Hirsch wrote, "*As Evans left the courtroom, his family offered support, shouting, 'We love you, Chad. We all believe in you!*" Hirsh wrote that Simon Brown "*found the display inappropriate,*" saying "*What we found disturbing today was that ...there were echoes of how much everyone loved Chad, but this case has been about a girl less than two years old who was murdered.*"

Jennifer Saunders wrote the Foster's Daily Democrat story, "Evans expresses 'shame and regret' for toddler's death,", and correctly stated, "*He stopped short, however, of admitting guilt for the death of 21-month-old Kassidy Bortner* " Saunders wrote that Chad was wearing an orange jumpsuit, and wrote what Amanda was wearing, but didn't describe the clothes of anyone else. She said that Jeff held Jennifer "*throughout the hearing as she wept at her mother's recollections of Kassidy - and at descriptions of the child's suffering.*"

Of Jennifer's statement to Chad about his use of the term "*that baby,*" Saunders said that Jennifer "*was referring to a taped interview with police, shown during Evans' trial, in which he repeatedly referred to Kassidy without using her name.*" Here, instead of taking the word of someone as the truth, Saunders could have done some quick research, with the transcripts of the police interviews.

In this emotional case, it sometimes happened that a particular phrase or incident would stand out in someone's mind. In Jennifer's case, she remembered Chad's use of the expression, "*that baby,*" during his interrogation. (Interrogation, p. 1605, 1606) He used that expression twice, toward the end, and after the police had told him that he was the man they suspected of killing Kassidy. The 130 page transcript of Chad's interrogation shows that he referred to Kassidy as "*Kassidy*" 22 times, "*baby*" (5), "*kid*" (16), "*her*"

(166) and "*she*" (223). In her police interview on November 9, recorded on 80 pages, Jennifer referred to Kassidy as "*Kassidy*" 27 times, and "*baby*"(9) and "*kid*" (31), including, "*I'm not with the kid that much.*" (p. 957) It was painful for everyone to talk of Kassidy, who was alive only hours before, in the first person, so the use of words not as intimate as her name can be understood. Jennifer's use of such distancing words was more pronounced than Chad's, so her pointed comment was hypocritical.

After Jeff's first call to Jennifer on November 9 to ask for advice and help for Kassidy, she went back to work. After his second call, she called Amanda and returned to her perfume customers. Perfumania was about two miles from her and Jeff's home.

In another story by Jennifer Saunders in Foster's Daily Democrat, "Victim's family, prosecutor rap sentence as too weak", the schism in the Bortner/Conley family showed. Said Jennifer, "*I don't think the sentence was fair. I think he should have been gone a lot longer. He murdered a baby, and this is the first time I've seen any remorse from him,..I saw more emotion coming from him (Evans) than I did from her* [Amanda, her sister]... *I don't know what to think. She was definitely not a mother,...*" To that point, Amanda had been a mother, and Jennifer had not. Said Chad's father to the press, "*We stand behind Chad. We believe in Chad 100 percent,*" He was the only Evans family member to speak to the press.

Thursday, 18 April 2002

Now the State turned to the case against Amanda. The day after Chad's sentencing, Jennifer Saunders interviewed David Ruoff, the Asst. Attorney General who was recently assigned to prosecute Amanda. Normally, misdemeanor charges are not prosecuted by the State Attorney General, but because of its connection to the Chad Evans murder case, the Attorney General retained the prosecution. Saunders wrote in the Foster's Daily Democrat story, "Bortner may skip trial: Considers guilty plea",

In a March letter to Judge Tina L. Nadeau, Assistant Attorney General David W. Ruoff referenced communication from Bortner's court-appointed attorney that indicated "Ms. Bortner is apparently agreeing to proceed with a naked plea to the two pending misdemeanor charges."

Ruoff explained that a "naked plea" is where a defendant pleads guilty without any previous assurances of lenient treatment. Relying upon the planned guilty plea, Ruoff and Amanda's attorney, Patricia Wiberg, were jointly asking Judge Nadeau to authorize a presentencing investigation, as was done for Chad, after he was found guilty. Amanda's trial was still scheduled to begin on Monday, June 10.

Also on April 18, the Foster's Daily Democrat published Saunders' story, "AG may appeal Evans' Sentence." The article stated that Simon Brown and N. William Delker "*have maintained since Evans' sentencing on Tuesday that 28 years to life in prison is not enough.*"

Friday, 19 April 2002

In its second editorial about the Kassidy Bortner case, Foster's Daily Democrat argued for a heavier sentence, "Justice denied: Kassidy was more than a statistic." The paper was offended by Judge Nadeau's comparison of Chad's case to others and asked rhetorically, "*How many times have we seen the laughing face of Kassidy Bortner on the front page of this newspaper?*" The answer is about twenty, but that's a statistic, too. The editorial continued,

"How many times have we thought since hearing of Kassidy's death have we thought that anyone who might commit such a foul act must be spawned in the bowels of hell? ...All Kassidy Bortner got for the love she gave was a horrible and most likely painful death...What goes through the mind of a 30-year old man when he inflicts such punishment on a child...What offense did she commit against Chad Evans to so infuriate him as to beat the life out of her?

The words of Kassidy's aunt, Jennifer Bortner-Conley... spoke volumes more than Judge Nadeau's statistical drivel.... "She (Kassidy) will look down on you and she will ask you, 'Why, Chad, did you do this to me?' "... Kassidy's family cries for her... Can any of us

do less than agree with the state's call for justice? [i.e. the State's request for 60 years, minimum in prison]

Also on this day of the editorial, the State filed its appeal of the sentence. The following Monday, Brad Morin of Foster's Daily Democrat, wrote the story, "AG appeals Evans decision in murder of Rochester toddler."

Wednesday, 24 April 2002

Foster's Daily Democrat published its third editorial about the case, "60 years for Evans." The paper argued,

The sentenced requested by the state is clearly most in keeping with the nature of Evans' crime. It would keep him in prison until he is 90 years old.... Chad Evans committed a horrible crime.... he did so brutally... It is nonsense to suggest that vengeance is not a factor in the way the people expect the perpetrators of some crimes to be punished....

There is no mitigating the brutality of Chad Evans. Seeing him in prison until he is at least 90 years old is a small price to exact for the murder of 21-month-old Kassidy Bortner.

This was harsh language for a case in which there were only guesses about what types of blows killed Kassidy and from what kind of instrument, if any, and when. There was no witness. It used to be in the newspaper business that articles should answer the basic questions: Who, What, Where, When and Why. The same could be said of criminal investigations and the goal of justice, but the investigation, verdict, newspaper coverage and editorials were based on guesses.

Wednesday, 15 May 2002

Chad filed the appeal of the conviction on five grounds, according to April 16 Foster's Daily Democrat story by Jennifer Saunders, "Evans files appeal of murder trial." Three of the grounds were:

1. That Judge Nadeau should not have allowed as evidence, Amanda's statement to Tracey Foley on November 16, "*You knew, and I didn't listen.*"
2. That Judge Nadeau "*improperly focused the jury on defendant's statements and improperly commented on the evidence by instructing the jury in regard to defendant's statements - and not Jefferey Marshall's statements-- that if they found the defendant had made false statements they could consider whether those statements showed consciousness of guilt.*"
3. That Judge Nadeau was wrong to deny the defense motion to dismiss the case before trial due to the "*absence of testimony as to whether Kasssidy Bortner received her injuries in Maine or New Hampshire....*"

In the appeal, Chad's attorneys Cronheim and Sisti announced that they were withdrawing from the case and that Chad's new attorneys would be from the Office of the Appellate defender. Chad no longer had enough money to defend himself, and asked that the $10,400 cost of preparing the transcript of his trial be paid by the State of New Hampshire.

Later, the Supreme Court accepted the case as reported by Jennifer Saunders in the Foster's Daily Democrat story, "Evans appeal to be heard by state's highest court" Although agreeing to hear an appeal is almost routine, it's not required, so the judge's decision was a micro-victory for Chad, in a case where there were few. Saunders reported that

a significant portion of the testimony referenced in the appeal came from Bortner, who has continued to blame Marshall for Kassidy's death since the trial. During the trial Bortner backed away from statements she made to police the night of Kassidy's death... Bortner did testify to seeing Evans squeeze Kassidy's face with enough force to leave bruises and to witnessing Evans "roughly place" Kasssidy in a corner so that she hit her head against a closet door. However, Bortner said she did not believe those incidents hurt Kassidy.

Thursday, 15 May 2002

There was a status conference for Amanda's case, and, again, she did not appear, but her absence was excused, and her attorney represented her. Jennifer Saunders reported in the Foster's Daily Democrat that Amanda "Bortner Eyeing Plea Bargain." Saunders wrote that "*plea negotiations are ongoing. If a plea is not entered on June 10, the trial will need to be postponed until fall because Wiberg needs additional time to prepare.*"

Monday, 10 June 2002

Amanda came to the courthouse with her attorney, and accompanied by members of Chad's family, and not with members of her own family, and decided to plead "not guilty," and go to trial. The trial was then rescheduled for Monday, November 4, and Patricia Wiberg estimated that it would take 10 days, or roughly the same duration as Chad's trial, which was 11 days.

Jennifer Saunders wrote that afternoon's story for Foster's Daily Democrat, "Bortner changes her mind - Decides against plea, will go to trial in Nov."

Perhaps ironically, if she had pled guilty, and if she had not witnessed any abuse by Chad, which is the view of this book, then a guilty plea would have made her guilty of perjury exactly in the same way that Cory Merrill subjected himself to perjury charges. He had told the court that he had pled guilty to crimes he didn't commit, just as Amanda was considering. It's a "legal fiction" that guilty pleas are always for the crimes charged. People familiar with the criminal law system know every day that defendants plead guilty to crimes they did not commit in order to avoid being convicted of more serious crimes or to avoid extended, harsher sentences, whether or not they are guilty of those more serious crimes.

The next day, Jennifer Saunder's wrote again in Foster's Daily Democrat about the plea change, and new trial date, "Amanda Bortner to stand trial on endangerment charges - Lawyer says she's grieving over slain child" The article quoted Amanda's attorney, "*She's innocent and the circumstances surrounding Kassidy's death are not related to Amanda... I think she feels a lot's been said and she feels a trial will be a chance to speak on Kassidy's behalf and also on her own,... She's grieving. This is a very young woman who has lost her child. She's trying to get her life back on track." Patricia Wiberg, Bortner's court-appointed counsel, said Monday afternoon.*

At the time, it appeared that Amanda was planning to testify at her trial. Saunders again noted that Amanda was accompanied by Chad's family, but she also observed that Jeff Marshall's mother, who had attended Chad's trial, was there as well. Wrote Saunders about Mrs. Marshall,

...she is deeply troubled by Bortner's apparent lack of concern for Kassidy....I hope when it hits her and she has that big void in her life she'll realize it's because she failed as a mother by not seeking medical attention and protecting that child."

Ms. Marshall was not asked about her son's care of Kassidy during the week of November 6-9, and in particular the afternoon of Wednesday, November 8 and the morning of November 9.

As Saunders noted, Asst. Attorney General Ruoff *had a different perspective. "I find it difficult to have sympathy for someone who claims as a mitigating factor the fruits of their own crime," Ruoff said, equating Bortner's 'grief' over Kassidy's death to someone who kills both parents and then seeks sympathy "because he is an orphan.... The family asked me to say they're very disappointed. They had hoped for closure today."... Ruoff said the family, in this case, represents "everyone that was involved with Kassidy" in the months leading up to her death.*

Implicitly, the "*family*" of people "*involved with Kassidy*" did not include Kassidy's mother. It would have been more accurate for Ruoff to say that he was asked by Kassidy's grandmother, Jacqueline, or by Jennifer, to say what he said.

As was the case with Delker and Brown, the prosecutors of Chad, Ruoff never sat down and talked with the defendant he was prosecuting. Such a meeting should be a national ethical requirement for prosecutors, or at least an offer of such a meeting. If he had done so, he might not have so easily referred to Kassidy's death as the "*fruits*" of

Amanda's alleged crime. He might have asked a few questions that might have shaken his righteous view of the case.

Tuesday, 25 June 2002

Amanda's continued closeness with the Evans family seemed to bother the press. Jennifer Saunders wrote in Foster's Daily Democrat, "Amanda Bortner moves into home of her child's killer". Wrote Saunders,

The mother of a 21-month-old girl beaten to death in 2000 has moved back into the home of her daughter's convicted murderer.... Bortner is paying $300 per month to live in the brown two-story house on Milton Road according to the affidavit. The affidavit also indicates that Bortner is working part-time at Yoken's restaurant in Portsmouth.

The referenced affidavit was filed with the court as part of Amanda's financial statement in order to qualify for her court-appointed attorney.

Implicitly, Foster's Daily Democrat was asking the rhetorical question, What kind of mother would continue to associate with the killer of her daughter and his family? For the newspaper, there was only one answer - the world's worst mother. In history and in literature, I cannot think of a mother who had made such a choice, but Foster's Daily Democrat and the prosecutors thought they had found one. Readers of this book are asked:

Have there been any instances or cases in real life or literature or movies where:

1. Significant other1 (SO1) abuses Child of Parent.
2. Parent witnesses the abuse and does nothing substantial to stop it, and Parent is not accused abusing Child.
3. Child dies.
4. SO1 is accused of abusing AND murdering Child AND assaulting Parent.
5. Parent remains in love with SO1 and seeks his comfort and the comfort of his family.
6. SO1 is convicted of abusing AND murdering Child AND assaulting Parent.
7. Parent remains in love with SO1 and seeks his comfort and the comfort of his family, and they are engaged to marry, but are thwarted by the reality of years of prison for SO1.

The closest, perhaps, is Hamlet's mother, Gertrude, who married Claudius, the killer of her first husband, and Hamlet's father, but I don't recall if she knew that Claudius had killed her husband.

The other possibility was that Amanda's understanding of the case, pre-police-interviews, was right about Chad's innocence, and that she was remaining loyal to an innocent man. Of course, if he was innocent of abusing and killing Kassidy, then she was innocent, too. Of the several cases in the U.S. where people have been wrongfully convicted of abusing and killing the children of their partner, perhaps some of them come close to this parallel. More generally, many of the people who have loyally stood by their wrongfully convicted siblings, children, parents, lovers or friends were supporting people who were innocent in the first place.

Thursday, 29 August 2002

Amanda was driving on Sunday, August 18, with friends, and one man asked that the car be stopped so he could relieve himself. She pulled over and a police car behind her suspected alcohol was involved, and stopped. The result, according to Jennifer Saunders in Foster's Daily Democrat, was, "Bortner charged with liquor violation." She was 20 years and 8 months old and had had a child at the age of 17, but society wasn't ready to let her drive when there was liquor in the car. This was the same society that seemed to have little problem with someone giving her alcohol and then having sex with her at the age of 16. As with every other article about Chad and Amanda, several hundred words were repeated from previous articles.

The next step was reported by Jennifer Saunders in Foster's Daily Democrat, "AG seeks to revoke bail for Amanda Bortner" Wrote Saunders,

Based on her actions in recent weeks, the mother of a murdered 21-month-old girl may be headed back to jail pending her child endangerment trial in November.

David Ruoff of the New Hampshire attorney general's office, who is prosecuting the case against Amanda Bortner, confirmed Monday afternoon that he will file a motion to have her bail revoked. The motion is based in part on Bortner's arrest Aug. 29 in Epping on a charge of transporting alcohol by a minor. She is 20 years old.

In addition, Ruoff noted, "two times in the past three weeks she has failed to report to the Department of Corrections as required."....

Transporting alcohol by a minor is a violation punishable by a 60-day license suspension and/or fines. Bortner is scheduled to be arraigned Oct. 4 in District Court.

Thursday, 12 September 20

Judge Nadeau held a bail revocation hearing, and the Union Leader announced the result, "Mother of murdered girl remains free on bail" The Associated Press article said that "*Judge Tina Nadeau ruled there wasn't enough evidence to indicate Bortner is a danger to herself or others, or that she is a flight risk....* " Once again, Amanda was accompanied by several members of the Evans family. The judge said she had *extreme concern...You are not taking these cases seriously. These cases involve the death of your daughter. . . . You have refused to accept the culpability of your boyfriend,...*
At prosecutor David Ruoff's request, new conditions were added to Amanda's bail, including a prohibition of possession and consumption of alcohol and a requirement that she inform the Dept. of Corrections of any address or employment changes.

Monday, 1 October 2002

Foster's Daily Democrat informed its readers on Monday, October 1, that "Bortner faces arraignment on alcohol violation" on Thursday in Exeter District Court. At the hearing, Amanda "Bortner pleads innocent to alcohol violation" and the judge ordered that a lawyer be appointed to represent her in this misdemeanor case where the crime was punishable by a fine and temporary loss of driver's license. Writing both articles, Jennifer Saunders, summarized the status of Amanda's case and reminded readers that Amanda was "*the mother of a murdered 21-month old girl.*"

Thursday, 24 October 2002

The Sentence Review Board or Division, composed of three Superior Court judges, denied the Attorney General's petition to increase Chad's sentence. The Board's ORDER, reasoned,

that the defendant was not informed at sentencing in plain and certain terms that the state could seek an enhancement of his sentence. Accordingly, the Sentence Review Division finds that any relief afforded to the state would violate the defendant's due process rights.

The prosecutors first asked the Sentence Review to reconsider (see below, 8 November) and then appealed that decision to the New Hampshire Supreme Court.

Thursday, 7 November 2002

The final pre-trial hearing was held for Amanda's case by Judge Bruce Mohl. Jennifer Saunders reported that "Bortner case set Nov. 18 in Strafford County Superior Court" After the hearing, David Ruoff said that jury selection would begin on the morning of the 18th, and predicted that the trial would last about five days. The prosecutor filed a list of 17 potential witnesses for his case, but Amanda's attorney had not yet filed a witness list.

Friday, 8 November 2002

The Atttorney General filed with the Sentence Review Division a Motion for Reconsideration of its 24 October 2002 Order. The three grounds for the Motion were:

1. "*... the Division acted beyond its statutory authority when it considered and ruled on a matter of constitutional law which was collateral to the question of the appropriateness of the defendant's sentence.*"

2. "*...the Division erred in ruling that due process requires specific notice to the defendant at sentencing of the State's right to petition for sentence review.*"
3. "*... the Division acted beyond its authority when it raised a constitutional issue for the defense* sua sponte [on its own]."

CHAPTER 10: TRIAL AND SENTENCING OF AMANDA BORTNER 18 NOVEMBER 2002 TO 3 MARCH 2003

"I just want the truth to come out, that's all." **-** Jeff Marshall

"The truth will come out." - Amanda Borter

In several ways, Amanda's trial was similar to Chad's. The time periods for the two counts of Endangering the Welfare of a Child covered the same period of charges against Chad: August 1 through November 8, and November 8 and 9. The portrayal here of Amanda's trial will focus on the testimony and arguments that presented new or different information from what was presented at Chad's trial a year earlier.

Of the ten prosecution witnesses, seven had also testified for the prosecution at Chad's trial. The new witnesses would be Amanda Donnell and Angela Blodgett. Amanda's only defense witness would be Travis Hunt, who had also testified at Chad's trial, but for the prosecution.

MEDIA: "Bortner goes on trial today - Charged with endangerment"

Monday, 18 November 2002

There were two indictments or "informations" against Amanda, and they both began *in that, Bortner knowingly endangered the welfare of her daughter Kassidy Bortner, age 21 months, by purposely violating a duty of care or protection which she owed to Kassidy....*

The first information continued,

While Bortner and Kassidy lived with Chad Evans, Evans inflicted bodily injury to Kassidy. Evans bruised Kassidy's body and/or fractured her bones by repeatedly grabbing Kassidy by the face, throat, arms, and legs and by propelling Kassidy into the walls of the home, causing Kassidy to strike the walls. Knowing of Evans' abuse, Bortner violated her duty of care or protection to Kassidy by failing to seek proper medical treatment for Kassidy's injuries and by failing to take steps to protect Kassidy from Evans' abuse.

The second information continued,

Knowing that Kassidy had sustained severe facial bruising and was ill, Bortner violated her duty of care or protection to Kassidy by failing to seek proper medical treatment for Kassidy's injuries. On November 9, 2000, without taking any steps to seek medical treatment for Kassidy, Bortner dropped Kassidy off at the babysitter's residence. Kassidy died later that day of injuries inflicted before Bortner dropped Kassidy off at the babysitter's residence.

Two years and nine days after Kassidy's death, Amanda's trial began with several motions by Amanda's attorney, Patricia Wiberg. One motion was to exclude some of the prosecution's post-mortem photograph Exhibits because they unfairly showed Kassidy in a condition that Amanda did not see when she was alive, due to the discoloration after death. The photos, argued Wibert, were more "*prejudicial than probative*." (p. 1-12) Judge Nadeau excluded a few of the photos, but allowed the others.

Patricia Wiberg asked the court to exclude Dr. Greenwald as a witness as she never knew Kassidy when she was alive, during which time the alleged abuse of Kassidy began. However, Attorney General David Ruoff argued for the State that Dr. Greenwald could testify about injuries and bruises that Amanda should have known about. Judge Nadeau denied the motion.

Then Judge Nadeau met with the prospective jurors and explained the case to them, and told them the names, with their cities and towns, of the prospective witnesses, and asked if any of the jurors knew the witnesses. Then she interviewed individually the prospective jurors, excusing those with various difficulties, and selected the jury. At the end of the process she asked the jurors to return to the courtroom at 1:00 p.m. to begin the trial.

Before the jury returned, Patricia Wiberg presented a Motion to Dismiss the case because the State should be required, she argued, to respect the immunity agreement that it drafted for Amanda and which Amanda signed; and Amanda testified at Chad's trial for the prosecution. Judge Nadeau denied the motion, saying that the State had adequate grounds to withdraw from its planned immunity agreement with Amanda. Primarily, the State's view was that Amanda was no longer willing to testify with the truth, or what the prosecutors thought was the truth.

At 1:17 p.m., the jury was called into the courtroom, and Judge Nadeau read the two charges aloud, and gave the jurors assorted instructions. Curiously, she said, "*... you will not be permitted to take notes or ask questions, for a lot of reasons that we won't go into now.*" (p. 1-74) At Chad's trial, jurors were able to take notes and keep notebooks during the trial and used them during deliberations. However, at the end of the trial, the notebooks were collected by the court and, presumably, destroyed. This was another way that the judicial system protects its verdicts, by eliminating the possibility that such records might contain grounds for challenging verdicts.

Also, she reminded jurors that once they go into the deliberation room, they cannot ask for a transcript of testimony to be provided. Thus, "*... when a witness testifies, it's your one and only opportunity to see them and hear them and listen to what they have to say.*" (1-75)

Opening Statement - David Ruoff

Despite the minimal and conflicting evidence of bone fractures, Asst. Attorney General Ruoff began the State's opening statement with an emotional appeal,

In the weeks before her death, Kassidy had to wake up every morning and live with the pain of two broken arms, a broken leg, and multiple bruises all over her face,..." (1-76)

Given that Chad was charged with two counts of First Degree Assault for those alleged fractures and that Judge Nadeau withdrew the arm fracture charge before the case to the jury, and that the jury found Chad "Not Guilty" on the leg fracture charge, it was unfair to try to hold Amanda criminally responsible for ignoring such alleged fractures.

Ruoff said that "*In late August of 2000, the defendant took Kassidy to move in with Chad Evans because she was already living there full time,...*" (1-81) He said that Amanda's mother could no longer care for Kassidy full-time because of her health. In fact, the reason Kassidy lived with Amanda and Chad is that Amanda was Kassidy's mother. Chad had told her that he thought a mother should spend quality time with her child, and he encouraged Amanda to bring Kassidy to Rochester to live with them.

Ruoff emphasized that Amanda drove by three hospitals on the morning of November 9 when she drove Kassidy to Jeff's and Jennifer's.

Opening Statement - Patricia Wiberg

Attorney Wiberg described Amanda's tough childhood, and sexual abuse at home and then the birth of Kassidy. She said that Amanda would testify that her mother was receiving the child support checks for Kassidy from the State of Maine, and that the State of Maine seized Amanda's income tax refund as the parent's required contribution to that child support payment.

Wiberg said that Amanda moved in with Chad at the end of June, 2000 and, "*Kassidy and Amanda spent all their time there and officially moved down there in the end of July.*" (1-93)

Wiberg said that when Kassidy's walking difficulties were noticed in July of 2000, Amanda brought her to a doctor, but the date of that appointment was not mentioned. Like Chad's attorneys, Wiberg did not know about Kassidy's August 10 and September 11 medical appointments.

Attorney Wiberg said that Amanda "*had a part-time job and* [was] *going to school.....She did have Mr. Marshall take care of Kassidy for a few weeks. And the bruises did start appearing at that time. And Amanda questioned them.*" (p. 1-94) Wiberg joined the group of people who misunderstood the facts about the ball which hit Kassidy, saying, "*on November 8, Mr. Evans' son, who was five* [sic], *hit a wiffle ball in the bedroom -- a plastic yellow bat with a fat ball with the holes in it -- and it bounced and hit Kassidy in the face.*" (1-94) Wiberg said that Amanda gave cereal and Tylenol to Kassidy on the morning of the 9th, "*and that she had told Mr. Marshall what she'd given her.*" (p. 1-95) Wiberg continued,

Amanda did not witness Chad abusing Kassidy. What she witnessed was what she knew as discipline... She did see Chad... grab [Kassidy's face] *like this. And the occasion that she saw that was when Chad was trying to get Kassidy to look at him when he was reprimanding her for misbehaving. She saw it two times and saw a bruise once and said, 'Never again. I'll discipline my daughter.' ...She did not purposely or knowingly endanger Kassidy.*" (p. 1-96/97)

Jeff Marshall

Examined by David Ruoff, Jeff said he owned a landscaping business and that he dropped out of high school two weeks before he was scheduled to graduate. He said that he and Jennifer began living together "*Probably within a week and a half, two weeks,*" after he met Jennifer, which would have been in 1999. (p. 1-101)

He said that Amanda moved in with Chad soon after they met, "*I think that happened pretty quick.*" (p. 104) Jeff said that Kassidy moved to Chad's because Amanda's mother, Jacqueline Conley, "*had an operation, and she couldn't take care of Kassidy anymore. So she asked Amanda, if, you know, 'You have to take care of Kassidy.' And that's basically what happened.*" (p. 1-105)

Describing his and Jennifer's babysitting for Kassidy, Jeff said, "*You know, she'd come to our house where her fingernails would have to be clipped. And she had a wart. I remember I used to tell her mother all the time about getting rid of the wart.*" Amanda's response, said Jeff, was that she would take Kassidy to the doctor when the bruises went away. (p. 1-110) Interestingly, this was the first mention of the wart on Kassidy's index finger of her right hand, in the criminal proceeding, except for the autopsy. As noted in Chapter 3, removal of the wart was recommended by Kassidy's pediatrician, Dr. Glass, at Kassidy's August 10, 2000 appointment, but only the Maine Medical Examiner seems to have had the documentation for that appointment. It wasn't mentioned in the police investigation and Chad's trial. Chad had mentioned it to Amanda as well, and recalled in 2010 that he gave Amanda money for the procedure, which never happened.

Jeff estimated that he babysat Kassidy for "*... maybe an hour or two,*" on Wednesday, November 8, and that "*It was later in the afternoon. I would say after 2:00, maybe 3:00, something like that.*" (p. 1-112-13) Jeff said that Kassidy "*...was having trouble walking*" on that day," and that her activity was, "*Watching cartoons...sit and watch TV, play with her toys, whatever she had. You know, we had toys over there for her that we bought.*" (1-113)

Jeff said that when Chad came to his home to pick up Kassidy, his demeanor was "*In a hurry, having a bad day.*" (p. 1-117)

When Amanda brought Kassidy to Jeff's on the 9th, Jeff said that Kassidy's lips were "*Chapped. They were always chapped. I think she might have had a scrape or something on her lip...*" (p. 1-124) Jeff testified that when he saw Kassidy, he said, " *'If that was a baseball, that baseball ricocheted off the wall back and forth hundreds of times.' It was just - her whole face was black and blue.*" (p. 1-125) David Ruoff asked for how long did Amanda stay at his apartment and he responded, "*She came in, dropped her off and then left.*" (p. 1-126)

Jeff described what happened after he retrieved the mail, "*I looked over, and Kassidy was laying here, and it was like she was taking deep breaths. So then I just -- I started trying CPR, I tried -- and then I called Jen...*" (p. 1-128) At the end of his examination, Ruoff asked, "*Was there ever a time when Kassidy was physically injured in your presence?*" and Jeff replied, "*No. Never.*" (p. 1-132) He didn't seem to remember when he tripped over Kassidy's leg about two days before she died, as he stated in his November 9, 2000, statement to the Kittery Police.

Patricia Wiberg cross-examined Jeff and he described the partial fall from his truck in Will Peirce's presence, but denied that Kassidy fell from a truck where Kassidy hurt her head. Asked about whether he told Amanda about such an injury, he said, "*It might be something that she's making up. I don't know.*" (p. 1-137) When Wiberg was trying to pin down the dates of when he first met Kassidy, and when Amanda moved to Chad's the questioning became confusing, and Jeff responded, "*I don't know why everything has to be so sneaky.*" (p. 1-141) Asked whether he knew the date of Kassidy's birthday, Jeff said that he didn't. Jeff affirmed Wiberg's characterization that "*there was no time after she moved into Chad's house in Rochester that bruises were not on her face, is that correct?*" He responded, "*She always had some form of bruise on her face, yes, ma'am, that I can remember.*" (p.1 -149)

Patricia Wiberg asked Jeff about a problem Kassidy had walking and he responded, "*After she moved into Chad's house,*" and he didn't know the expression, "*pigeon-toed.*" He said that he had asked Amanda about his concerns about Kassidy's walking and she didn't tell him that she had taken Kassidy to see a doctor about it. He related, "*She said that Chad was rough-housing with her, pulling her around and picked her up by the leg.*" (p. 1-149) Jeff denied that his spanking of Kassidy, after the Windex incident left a bruise, "*...no absolutely not.*" (p. 1-152) Jeff was asked if he was aware of "*the program that Amanda was going through for work and school while you were babysitting.*" and he responded, "*Somewhat, ma'am,*" but he didn't know who sponsored it and didn't know what "*the requirements of the program were for her, why she needed you to baby-sit?*" He said, "*No idea.*" (p. 153)

Jeff testified that when Chad called him on the evening of November 8, after Kyle hit the ball at Kassidy, Chad described the ball as a "*baseball.*" (p. 1-157) Patricia Wiberg asked Jeff to read what he wrote in his seven-page statement to the police on November 9, about Kassidy that morning,

She tried to walk around, and Kassidy fell on the floor. Jen was there. We then tried to let her walk again, but she would not move out of the bed. We put the blankets over her and put on cartoons on the TV so she could lay there and watch them. She was very quiet and not very coherent, but was still watching TV." (p. 1-164)

Jeff affirmed Wiberg's statement that Kassidy was wearing pajamas, but when asked what Kassidy was wearing when Amanda brought her to his home, he responded, "*I don't remember, ma'am.*" (p. 161) During this last section of the testimony for the day, Jeff twice vouched for the truth, "*I mean, let's bring out the truth here.*" (p. 1-165) and "*I just want the truth to come out, that's all.*" (p. 1-176)

Referring to Kassidy's leg, Patricia Wiberg asked Jeff to read a portion of his written statement at the police station, which related to the tripping incident a few days before Kassidy died,

She could not walk around that day. She was in bed most of the day. The one thing that was weird was she must have got out at some time because the phone rang and I got up and ran to get the phone. I was in the living room, and Kassidy was in the bedroom, but when I went around the corner, I tripped over her because she was just standing there." (p. 1-177)

The first day of the trial then recessed at 4:23 p.m.

MEDIA: "Murdered toddler's mom on trial for not protecting her"

Tuesday, 19 November 2002

Before the trial resumed with Jeff's cross-examination, Judge Nadeau observed that one juror didn't return, "*as it has to do with some personal matters,*" which is why, as she noted, "*we pick extra jurors, so we can get through the trial.*" (p. 2-7)

Patricia Wiberg asked Jeff again about injuries and he said, again, that Kassidy had bruises "*Just about every time. I can't remember a time I didn't see a bruise on her after she moved in with Chad and Amanda.*" (p. 2-15) showed Jeff the State's Exhibit 1, the photograph of Kassidy in a chair, holding her bunny rabbit, and Jeff said he didn't know who took the photograph or where it was taken, which Wiberg stated was at Jacqueline Conley's house in Buckfield.

As an aside, Wiberg asked, "*Would you take pictures of Kassidy when she came over* [to] *your house?*" and Jeff replied, "*I'm sure we did. I couldn't give you a number.*" (p. 2-

15) Again, neither the police nor prosecutors not Chad's nor Amanda's attorneys asked any of the parties for their photos of Kassidy. Photos of Kassidy with Jeff and Jennifer and at their apartment would have been especially helpful in understanding her health, and presence/absence of bruises at the time of the photo, and her activities at the apartment. Wiberg could have, even at that late date, asked for a subpoena to request all of Jeff's and Jennifer's photos of Kassidy. If the reminder had been sufficient, it was not too late to subpoena all the photographs of Kassidy in anyone's possession.

Returning to Exhibit 1, beyond asking Jeff when he thought the photo was taken, Wiberg did not establish for the jury when the photo was taken, which was October 1, 2000. As was the case at Chad's trial, this photograph of Kassidy was the only photograph of her alive which was shown to the jury. There were no photos of her with Chad or with Amanda or on Chad's boat or on the trampoline or playing with Chad. Jeff's apparent initial unfamiliarity with the photo was curious because when asked if he saw bruises on Kassidy's face, he said,

I believe there is a bruise on the side of her cheek, underneath here, just like I testified in the last trial, right down in here. But that still doesn't show the rest of her body...It doesn't seem like there's any.... (p. 2-17)

David Ruoff then began his redirect examination of Jeff with the observation, "*...I noticed yesterday and today that you keep looking down at something in your hand.. What is it?*" and Jeff said it was "*Just a charm, a guardian angel and a picture of my brother.*" (p. 2-18) In response to another question, Jeff said that he didn't know if his police interviews were videotaped.

Steve Hamel

Asked by David Ruoff about his work experience, Detective Hamel said that "*I started my career in Rochester, New Hampshire, as a patrolman back in 1982... I worked there a little over a year.*" (p. 2-24) This was the second coincidental connection among the investigating officers in the case and the facts of the case. At Chad's trial, Sgt. White had testified that his first years as a policeman were in York, Maine.

During cross-examination by Patricia Wiberg, Det. Hamel said that he accompanied Jeff to the Kittery Police Station after the ambulance left his home, and was with him most of the afternoon on November 9. Hamel said that he went back to Jeff's residence, accompanied by Jeff, and remembered "*talking to Mr. Marshall back at the residence that evening...*" (p. 2-32) He continued, "*I believe his girlfriend, Jennifer, was with him in the kitchen when -- the time I remember being there.*" (p. 2-33) Hamel said that Jennifer was the second person involved in the case to arrive at the police station. Reiterating with what he stated at Chad's trial, Det. Hamel said that Jeff "*pointed the finger at someone else from the entire time I was talking to him.*" (p. 2-36)

Margaret Greenwald

Examined by David Ruoff, Dr. Greenwald stated that Kassidy died of "*multiple blunt force injuries.*" (p. 2-41) Later she added that the fat emboli, perhaps triggered by the injury to the abdomen, could have been a cause. (p. 2-61) She said that "*there were actually four fractures that we identified,...*" (p. 2-56) and that the age of the left tibia, leg fracture was "*two to three months.*" (p. 2-58) She said that "*the second metacarpal* [hand] *fracture is actually a more recent fracture... somewhere between one to three weeks of age,*" (p. 59) and that the two ulna [arm] fractures were about "*three to six weeks, approximately.*" (p. 2-60) She explicitly referred to X-rays.

Dr. Greenwald described the photo, State's Exhibit 13, as "*the left side of the face. You can see the extensive bruising around the eye area...*" (p. 2-63) Ruoff asked, "*Doctor, do you think those injuries could have been caused by a wiffle ball?*" and she responded, "*A wiffle ball is fairly light. It would be unlikely.*" (p. 2-63) There was no further discussion about the type of ball that hit Kassidy on the 8th.

Apparently seeking to determine what Amanda should have known, David Ruoff asked, "*What would the symptoms be,*" and Dr. Greenwald responded, "*There would be a number of potential symptoms. Certainly, they would be painful, so she might be crying or fussy. The injuries to the head would cause her to probably become sleepy or lethargic... And the injuries to the abdomen would also be painful. .... would probably mean that she would not want to eat very much.*" (p. 2-63-64) She said the fractures to the hand and the arms would have been painful.

Returning to the fat emboli as a cause of death, Dr. Greenwald said, "*It can be the result of any injury that damages fat. So some of the bruises the abdominal injury, potentially the reinjury to the tibal fracture, any of those particular injuries could have led to the fat emboli.*" (p. 2-74) and "*We usually see the symptoms from fat emboli around 24 hours.*" (p. 2-75) By "symptoms" she agreed that she meant "*difficulty breathing,*" to use Wiberg's words. (p. 2-75) There was no reference to Dr. Baden's assessment of the cause of the release of the fatal fat emboli by a recent blow to fatty tissue.

As the "*time of death*" at Amanda's trial, Dr. Greenwald used the time, 1:30 p.m. which was the time she was declared dead at York Hospital. (p. 2-96) Dr. Greenwald agreed that she did not do microscopic sections of all the bruises, so that some of them could have been inflicted within the last four hours of Kassidy's life.

Regarding the food in Kassidy's stomach, Dr. Greenwald said that she did not see any food particles at all, but found "*about 40 milliliters,*[of a brownish mass] *which is a little bit more than a tablespoon of materials, so not a lot.*" (p. 2-102) As parents with children who eat Reese's Puffs know, there is not a lot of substance to them.

David Ruoff, on redirect examination, asked whether Dr. Greenwald found any evidence of "*the condition known as being 'pigeon-toed'* " and she said that she "*did not really notice it in the autopsy, but it's not something... unless it's really obvious, it's not something that we would necessarily see.*" (p. 103-04) Here, Ruoff was apparently trying to discredit Amanda's statement at her trial that she had taken Kassidy to see a doctor about it. He didn't ask Dr. Greenwald about whether she had seen any reports from Kassidy's pediatricians, to which she had referenced at Chad's trial. If he had asked, she would have told him that, indeed, she had such records, and from the hospital of Kassidy's birth, as well, and Ruoff and Judge Nadeau would have recognized the significant problem with the cases against Chad and Amanda. That is, the law enforcement authorities in Maine had important documents which contained the truth about Kassidy's medical history, and those documents were not made available to Chad's and Amanda's attorneys, and, apparently, not to the New Hampshire police and prosecutors either.

Jennifer Bortner

Examined by David Ruoff, Jennifer introduced herself as Jennifer Bortner, which was a slight change from Jennifer Bortner Conley, the name she gave at Chad's trial. Paul Conley was her stepfather, and Jacqueline Conley her mother. Ruoff asked about the general chronology of Kassidy's life and Jennifer's and asked, "*When they* [her mother and stepfather and family] *moved to Buckfield, was that about the same time that you moved in with Jeff Marshall?*" and she said, "*Yes.*" (P. 2-111) However, the Conleys moved to Buckfield over the last weekend in September, 2000, and October 1. Jeff had previously testified that he and Jennifer began living together in 1999. Jennifer may have meant the date that her family moved from Sanford to Auburn, but that was in the Spring of 1999. With several successive questions, Jennifer responded to "Buckfield" as if it was "Auburn," and Wiberg did not notice. If Judge Nadeau or the prosecutors noticed, they said nothing, perhaps thinking that it was an unimportant detail. However, if corrected, it would have reduced Jennifer's credibility to the jury.

Asked about her introduction of Amanda to Chad, Jennifer said that what Amanda liked the most about Chad was

she liked the fact that he had money....she's always wanted to have, like nice things, you know, a nice car...I think she kind of wanted to be a mom towards the...[sentence cut off by defense attorney objection.] *He took her to New York for a weekend of partying and stuff like that....*" (p. 2-114).

David Ruoff asked about things that Chad purchased for Amanda,

I know he bought perfume one time from me. I work at a perfume store. He bought her clothes. He gave her money whenever she wanted. I went shopping with her and my

mother a couple of weeks before Kassidy died, and my sister had hundreds of dollars on her." (p. 2-115)

Chad recalled in 2010 that he gave Amanda $300 for the shopping trip with Jennifer and their mother, Jacqueline, but it was Sunday, November 5, which was only four days before Kassidy died. It was not "*a couple of weeks before Kassidy died...*" That was that day that Chad took Kassidy with him to his sister, Nicole's in Belmont, NH and where they were observed together by Nicole's in-laws.

This is yet another example of how deficient both trials were about time. In Amanda's trial, it was not as important as in Chad's, because her two counts of child endangerment only split Kassidy's time with Chad into two sections: up to and including November 8 and after November 8. If a "*couple of weeks*" is actually four days, or about 90 hours, then what about all the other references to time, such as "*about a month ago*," or "*three weeks before she died?*" The jury needed more precise measurements of time.

Jennifer misunderstood Amanda's part-time survey inputting work she was doing for Bruce Aube, saying, "*Well, she was working, like, maybe once in a while for McDonald's, writing up a -- typing up some kind of, I don't know what -- it was a survey or something like that.*" (p. 2-116) Jennifer didn't recall that Amanda ever worked for Jeff, but when prompted, by Ruoff, "*You guys didn't plant flowers together every now and then?*" she did remember, "*We did once for actually, Applebee's. And she actually brought Kassidy to the job site that one time.*" (p. 2-116)

Jennifer recalled that Kassidy moved in with Chad and Amanda when her mother Jacqueline had a hysterectomy, which she said was in September. However, Jacqueline's operation was actually at the end of August. According to Jacqueline at Chad's trial, it was August 27. Then David Ruoff showed Jennifer State Exhibit 1, the photo of Kassidy holding her bunny rabbit, and Jennifer said that she knew when it was taken and that it was "*at my mother's house in Auburn.*" She was asked, "*Do you know if that picture was taken before or after the defendant and Kassidy moved in with Chad Evans?*" and she responded, "*It was taken before. I think it was about the week before.*" (p. 2-117) However, the photo was taken on October 1. Kassidy had been living in Rochester since July, and at least by the time of Jacqueline's operation by Jennifer's recollection. The photo was taken a full month after Jacqueline's operation, and at least **two months after** Kassidy began living full time in Rochester, and not "***the week before***."

This was yet another substantial mistake about time. Even though these dates were not as important as in the charges, it was a fundamental part of the police theory of the case that bruising on Kassidy began when Kassidy moved with Amanda to Chad's home. Not coincidentally, it was also a core part of what both Jeff and Jennifer said about the bruising on Kassidy - that it began when she moved to Rochester.

David Ruoff asked about the changes that Jennifer observed in Kassidy after she moved to Rochester, and then asked, "*How about any physical changes, did you notice any physical changes?*" Jennifer responded, "*I noticed a bruise on her face, that -- the time that my sister brought her to my work once.... a couple of weeks before Kassidy died.*" (p. 2-117-18) Ruoff asked her to reconfirm, "*Was this the first time since she'd moved in with Chad that you'd seen bruises on her face?*" and Jennifer responded, "*Yes.*" (p. 2-118) Two weeks before Kassidy died would have been Thursday, October 26, which was actually the first day of the three day/two night babysitting for Kassidy by Jeff and Jennifer. This contrasted with Jeff's statements that the bruising to Kassidy began when she moved in with Chad which was in July, but no later, by anyone's estimation, than late August. That's a difference of about eight weeks. It also contrasted with Jennifer's own previous statements.

Ruoff asked, "*...did the defendant ever talk with you about wanting to leave Chad Evans?*" and Jennifer said, "*Yes, ... She said that she was going to take Kassidy and move Kassidy to Texas with her friend, Cathy Nuernberg because of the way Chad treated Kassidy, and actually, the way Chad treated Amanda.*" (p. 2-121) This was the first time that it had been alleged by anyone that Amanda had considered moving with Kassidy to Texas. Such a move was never mentioned before by Cathy Nuernberg or by Amanda.

Not only did Jennifer state that it was a plan, she said it was because of Chad, and that was not true.

David Ruoff then focused on Kassidy's last two weeks, and Jennifer said that Amanda *just asked us to watch Kassidy a couple of days until, you know, the bruises would heal up and, you know, Kassidy could go to day care. She was afraid that if Kassidy went to day care with the bruises on her face, that day care would take Kassidy away from her.*" (p. 2-121-22)

Jennifer testified that "*She was limping once at our house, and she actually had a blister on her toe...She had bruises on her all the time, though.*" (p. 2-122)

Specifically, Ruoff asked "*How many times in the last two weeks Kassidy was alive did you or Jeff actually watch Kassidy?*" and she replied, "*About three or four times; it wasn't much.*" (p. 2-122) She said they had Kassidy twice during the last two days of Kassidy's life, but it was actually during each of the last four days of Kassidy's life. It was during such questioning that a calendar, with a pre-existing timeline of some specific events would have been helpful. As noted earlier, "*the last two weeks Kassidy was alive*" included the 3 day/2 night babysitting during the period October 26-28. After that stay, Kassidy was returned to Rochester dehydrated and hungry, and had two large bumps on the top of her head. The next confirmed babysitting by Jeff was on Thursday, November 2, when Amanda was working hard on a home-survey-inputting project before going to her money management class that night with Nicole and the Urrutia's. Jeff transferred Kassidy to Amanda and Nicole that afternoon at the Newington McDonald's and Chad arrived a few minutes later and brought her home for his babysitting.

The full-time babysitting for Jeff began on Monday, November 6 through the 9th. Thus, there were, at minimum, eight babysitting days for Jeff and/or Jennifer during Kassidy's last twoweeks alive, not "*three to four times.*"

Jennifer confirmed that she did not see Kassidy on the 8th, saying, "*I was working the late shift. I didn't get out until 9:00 p.m.*" (p.2-123) She wasn't asked about Amanda's afternoon visit to her, while Amanda was shopping for a dress.

The next morning, said Jennifer, Amanda brought Kassidy to their apartment. Jennifer said that "*Kassidy had a coat on, buttoned up to her neck,*" which was her new pink jacket. Amanda stayed for five to ten minutes and then left "*maybe 10 minutes of 9:00.*" (p. 2-126) However, according to Amanda's time sheet, she clocked in at work at 8:31 a.m. and work was five to ten minutes away. Ruoff asked her "*When did you find out that Kassidy had died?*" and Jennifer responded, "*Around noon.*" (p. 2-126-27) Once again, Jennifer's recollection, apparently not refreshed since her testimony at Chad's trial, was inaccurate about time. She vividly recounted her mother's call when she told Jennifer that Kassidy was dead, but it was around 2:30 p.m. Recounted Jennifer,

She's like, "Kassidy's dead, Jen! Kassidy's dead!" (Witness sobbing) *She goes, "She died at the babysitter's What was the babysitter, Jen? Who was the babysitter?" And I was like, "It's Jeff, Mom." And she told me to go to the police station, so I went to the police station.* (p. 2-127)

Jennifer recounted how she asked for Amanda when she arrived at the police station, and they shared a few crying moments together, with Jennifer asking, "*What happened, Mandy?*'" (p. 2-128) During her testimony the next day, (p. 3-33) Jennifer said that another woman was with them at the time. It was probably Maine State Police detective Angela Blodgett, or Kittery Police secretary, Virginia Grover. After Amanda's and Jennifer's first interviews, Jennifer said that the police put them back in the same room with their mother who had arrived about two hours after their arrival. Jennifer recalled "*And my mom's like, 'It's gonna be all right girls. You know I'm there for you,' and stuff like that.*" (p. 2-130) Jennifer continued, "*Amanda cried and said, 'Chad did it! Chad -- you know, I can't believe he killed my baby!'* " (p. 2-130) The was the first time that it had been alleged that Amanda had made such a statement so early on the day of Kassidy's death. Amanda had not yet been temporarily convinced by the police that Chad had killed Kassidy.

Then they left the police station and they saw Chad in the parking lot. Jennifer warned Amanda not to approach Chad, but they did, and "*After Mandy and Chad were hugging and stuff like that, they -- I was like, 'Let's go,' and I dragged Mandy away from him.*" (p. 2-131)

Jennifer describe that night in the hotel room,

Mandy wanted to call Chad. And I was like, 'Don't call him. Don't talk to him,' you know. And Jeff was like, you know, 'At least, you know, she's gonna do it anyway. She might as well do it while we're here so we can listen to her.' " (p. 2-131)

The next morning, said Jennifer, she woke up and Amanda was gone.

Well, I kind of knew where she went because Chad's sister knocked on our bedroom door and dragged her out of there... maybe 6:00 in the morning. (p. 2-132)

Perhaps there was not enough time to question all the statements of all the witnesses, but the use of the phrase, "*dragged her out of there.*" is significant, because it implies that Jennifer believed that somehow Chad and his family coerced Amanda into joining them. This was also part of the police theory of the case, and why they put so much effort into insisting on a no-contact provision for Chad's bail, and investigating Chad's contacts with Amanda in 2001 and, finally into revoking Chad's bail. No one, except the world's worst mother, would voluntarily associate with the killer of her child, they reasoned, unless there was coercion or extraordinary persuasion. In fact, Amanda talked with Nicole on the phone directly during the calls earlier in the morning and asked Nicole to come get her later. The view that Chad might have been innocent seems to have been erased from their consciousness.

The next night Jeff, Jennifer and Amanda went to Buckfield, and Amanda "*was crying; she was upset. She wanted to talk to Chad, so we all -- we hid the phone from her.*" (p. 2-133) Jennifer said that Amanda was trying to reason through the tragedy and change her mind, back and forth.

She'd just change her story. So we [Jeff and Jennifer] *were like, "Oh, my God!" Me and Jeff were like, "We got to get it on tape," So we got a tape recorder, and we tape-recorded our conversation we had with her...."Cause no one had been arrested for it, and Kassidy died at our house. Mandy was lying---* (p. 2-134)

Ruoff asked Jennifer, "*When was the last time you had a talk with your sister,*" and she responded,

That was the tape conversation that we had, and that was that night. We had gotten in a fight -- the reason me and Jeff thought about the tape recorder, actually was my little brother, Josh, was like, "Someone should record this." (p. 2-134)

This was the first confirmation in the case that Jennifer knew that Jeff secretly tape-recorded a discussion among him, Amanda and Jennifer in Buckfield.

Jennifer said that Amanda accused Jeff of molesting Kassidy, which Jennifer denied, and she hadn't spoken to Amanda since that night, which was Saturday, November 11th, two years previous.

David Ruoff asked Jennifer where Amanda was living, and she said, "*at Chad's house.*" (p. 2-135) He then asked about Jennifer's interviews with the police on November 9 and 10, "*... were you honest with the police in this* [first] *interview?"* and she answered, *"No, I wasn't honest at first. I wanted to protect my sister. I didn't know what was going on. I was in shock.*" (p. 2-136) She continued, "*I didn't tell them about how Kassidy exactly looked the morning she came to my house,"* but *"I was fully truthful the next day, when it finally sunk in that...Kassidy had died.*" (p. 2-136-37) Jennifer said that the only time she ever saw Jeff hit Kassidy was when he spanked her after the Windex incident.

Patricia Wiberg began her cross-examination by establishing that Jennifer and Amanda and their family moved many times, when the children were young, and then more times in New Hampshire and Maine after they moved to New England with their mother's new husband. Asked about her high school, she said, "*I took a -- I got my GED from Sanford High... in '99.*" (p. 2-140) She wasn't asked why she didn't finish with her class of 1999, but she was in the school yearbook for that year. She said that she worked as a "*dietary aide,"* [later defined as *"washing dishes"* (p. 3-56)] at the hospital and that "*my sister and I also delivered papers together, newspapers.*" (p. 2-142) Asked about her high school activities, Jennifer said that she was in a "*Speak Out,*" a public speaking program of the Lions Club. (p. 2-142) Also, she said she was in the Miss Maine pageant during November of her senior year in high school. Wiberg asked if the pageant was while she was "*in high school or right after*?" and Jennifer answered ambiguously that "*it was my senior year of high school.*" (p. 2-144)

She said that she met Jeff in the summer of 1999 when "*I was working at a video store, and I went to Kittery to open the store up, and he came in and we met.*" (p. 2-145) Asked about when she and Jeff decided to live together, she explained that "*... my parents were moving up to Auburn, and I really didn't want to move up to Auburn, so I ended up moving in with Jeff right after we -- a couple of weeks after we met.*" (p. 2-145) This time, she correctly identified Auburn as the city to which her family moved in 1999. She said it was around the time of her participation in the Miss Maine contest of 1999.

The testimony for the second day of Amanda's trial ended at 3:25 p.m.

MEDIA: "Toddler's bruises evident - Little girl's injuries clearly visible as mother drove her to the baby sitters on day she died"

Wednesday, 20 November 2002

On this third day of Amanda's trial, Patricia Wiberg continued her cross-examination of Jennifer, who reaffirmed that Kassidy "*was wearing a jacket when my sister brought her into the bedroom and put her into the bed. ... yeah, she was wearing clothes.*" (p. 3-6) Jennifer explained that on the morning of November 9, Amanda was the person who turned on the TV to the Nickelodeon cartoon channel for Kassidy. Jennifer agreed that "*Whenever I was first interviewed, I would minimize Kassidy's injuries...and I assumed she was eating her Cocoa Puffs. She had a bag with her.*" (p. 3-11) She agreed with Patricia Wiberg's summary, "*And the prior week you said that she had been sick, and you were -- she'd been throwing up, the flu or something.*" (p. 3-11)

Regarding the Windex incident, Jennifer testified, "*She didn't drink the Windex. We didn't see her consume Windex. She spilled it over her face.*" During the trial, the date of this incident was not addressed, but it was during the three-day/two night babysitting of Kassidy from Thursday evening, October 26 through Saturday morning, the 28th. Wiberg then asked Jennifer to read her own statement to the police on November 9, " '*... she got near the Windex, the Windex bottle. She had drank some of it. And we called Poison Control, and they told him what to do and stuff like that. And she was fine...*' " (p. 3-11) Jennifer explained to the court that "*We were under the assumption that she had dranken* [sic] *some. But we didn't see her actually consume it. We were just making* [sic] *precautions.*" (p. 3-11) Then, she agreed that Kassidy's subsequent sickness could have been caused by the Windex consumption.

Patricia Wiberg asked Jennifer about the day after the Windex incident, by which she likely meant Sunday, October 27, which was the day that Chad and Jeff went to Maine in Jeff's truck to pick up a 3-wheeler that Chad had purchased, second-hand.

Q *And the day after that, you were over at Amanda's house, you were gonna go shopping?*"

A *I don't remember.* (p. 3-13)

Q *Do you remember when Amanda changed the diaper and you saw the bruises on Kassidy's bum?*

A *No, ma'am.*

Q *You don't remember saying, "Oh, my God! I can't believe he did that."?*

A *No, ma'am, I don't.*

Q *"He didn't mean to hurt her."*

A *No. I was there when Jeff spanked Kassidy. There's a difference between a beating and a spanking, and he did not leave a bruise. Kassidy had a diaper on.* (p. 3-14)

Unfortunately, Wiberg was uncertain about the timeline for two different events. Sunday, October 22 was the day that Jeff brought Kassidy back from an overnight babysitting with him and Jennifer. That afternoon, Jeff and Chad drove to Maine to pick up Amanda's 3-wheeler.

The Windex incident occurred later that same week, during the three day/two night babysitting from October 26-28. In her questions, Wiberg seemed to be referring to the black and blues on Kassidy's behind on October 22 and Jennifer was responding to the incident five or six days later.

Patricia Wiberg asked about Amanda's statements to Jennifer a few days before Kassidy died about incidents where Kassidy's eyes were "*rolling in her head*," (p. 3-23) and then about the epilepsy afflicting Jennifer's and Amanda's older brother, Chuck. Jennifer said that she and Amanda had been with Chuck when he had had grand mal seizures in the past. Then, Patricia Wiberg revisited Jeff's calls of November 9 to Jennifer at Perfumania, where

he told me he was taking her to the hospital. Her eyes were rolling up in the back of her head. And I thought, "Oh, my God, maybe she's having a seizure... because my brother had epilepsy.... I didn't notice the severity of the bruises. (Witness sobbing) I thought my sister had taken her to the hospital. " (p. 3-24-5)

Later she explained,

I was under the impression that Kassidy had gotten hit in the face with the baseball, and I was under the impression that Kassidy was having a seizure 'cause my brother had epilepsy. I was a mess during the first interview. (p. 3-28)

Regarding the clothes Kassidy was wearing on the 9th, Jennifer reaffirmed, "*she had a coat on... zipped up to her neck...*" and responded "*Yes*," to Wiberg's question, "*And when she was in the bed, under the blankets, she still had her coat on?*" (p. 3-34) and "*I believe so, I don't remember, It was so fast...*" to Wiberg's question, "*And when you took the blankets off to bring her to the bathroom, she still had her coat on?*" (p. 3-34-35) Kassidy's clothes were not at the trial as Exhibits. Probably, Patricia Wiberg never saw Kassidy's pink jacket, because if she had seen it, she would have seen the obvious reddish stains and asked Jennifer about those stains. Perhaps they were blood stains, but they were never tested.

Asked about Kassidy's vocabulary, Jennifer said that Kassidy used the word, " *'kitty' She'd say 'lips' when she wanted me to put lip gloss on her... She'd say 'pease' to say 'please.'* " She "*called* [Jennifer's cat, Toby] *'kitty'.*" (p. 3-39) Jennifer said that Kassidy "*rarely cried.*" (p. 3-40) This observation of rare crying was contrary to the prosecution's allegations that Kassidy was in constant pain when she was living in Rochester with Chad and Amanda.

Jennifer said, "*I didn't change her diaper that often. Maybe once or twice.*" (p. 3-41) Regarding the babysitting logistics, for example, when clothes were dirty, "*Sometimes Mandy didn't bring clothes in the diaper bag. And if she did bring the diaper bag, they'd be dirty clothes from a couple of days before, and I'd have to wash them.*" (p. 3-42)

Patricia Wiberg returned to the afternoon of November 9, and asked Jennifer about when the police separated Amanda and Jennifer, and asked, "*...didn't you also say... 'Don't tell them what Jeff did.'?* " Jennifer responded, "*I don't think so*." (p. 3-43)

Wiberg asked about the morning of November 10, after Chad's sister came to the motel and left with Amanda. Jennifer said that she and Jeff called the police to tell them what happened the previous night about Amanda's calls with Chad; and the police asked them both to return to the police station. Jennifer said that later that day, she and Jeff drove to Buckfield to be with her family. She recalled that her parents came to Kittery, Will Peirce's home, to pick up Amanda and bring her to Buckfield.

Returning to her work history, Jennifer said that she worked at the video store, and then Zales Jewelers, and then Perfumania. She recounted the time that she first heard the "trampoline story," when she was at work.

I was working with Heather, actually, my boss; and Mandy brought Kassidy in, and Kassidy had bruises on her face that looked like a handprint. And she said Kassidy had fallen off the trampoline, and Chad saved the day by catching her by her face." (p. 3-55) The sarcasm of "*saved the day*" was evident.

Wiberg did not attempt to date this use of the "trampoline story" but Jennifer had said during her first Interview, which was on November 9, that she began work at Perfumania "*About, almost a month. It's more like 3 weeks. I work with Jeff in the summer.*" (p. 913) That would have made the start date approximately October 16, so the visit from Amanda, with Kassidy and the "trampoline story" would have been after that. That corresponds to the dates that others first heard the "trampoline story," e.g. Jacqueline, Melissa and Tracey on Saturday, October 14, 2000.

Patricia Wiberg asked Jennifer, "*And isn't it true that your mom had you and Amanda contribute your paychecks to help support the house?*" and Jennifer replied, "*My mother never made us give her our paychecks. I helped out my father a couple of times 'cause my father only made, like 300 dollars a week. And, actually they bought me a car because of it. You know, they were like -- they got me a car when I turned 16.*" (p. 3-56) Then, Wiberg reminded Jennifer of her statement to the police, which Jennifer read aloud, "*...' we had to give my mother every paycheck I had...'* " (p. 61)

David Ruoff then asked on redirect examination about Jennifer's closeness with her mother and family and about the frequency of phone calls. Jennifer said, "*Probably about four, five times a week. I called her all-- talked to her all the time, on my breaks at work and stuff like that.*" (p. 2-65) However, there were no questions about whether they talked with each other about the bruises on Kassidy, especially after Joshua had seen them on Friday, October 13, and Jacqueline had called Chad on Saturday the 14th.

On a different subject, Jennifer said that Amanda told her, before Kassidy died, that the "trampoline" story was false.

Ruoff asked about Amanda's relationship with her parents, and whether Amanda had told Jennifer about alleged molestation by their stepfather. Jennifer responded,
I heard about her accusing my father of molesting her. I heard about it through ... my mother. My mother actually set me aside and said, you know, they were fighting and she's like, "You molested me. You weren't a good mother," to my mother and left the house with her friends, or what not.... That was when she had Kassidy." (p. 3-67)
Jennifer agreed that she did not tell Amanda that their conversation at Buckfield on November 11th was being recorded, by Jeff. Ruoff then asked Jennifer to read from the transcript of that discussion when Amanda said,

"*I'm telling you right now. I've never seen him -- I've seen him bruise her; I've seen him, like get really rough with her. He would, like, throw her in the corner and then throw her on the bed, but not throw her across the room or anything. And I'd yell at him for it, but I never thought it was that serious, that it would internally hurt her..* "
Jennifer said that Amanda, *"loved him and she... liked the fact that he had money and stuff like that.*" (p. 3-71)

On recross-examination, Jennifer said Amanda was distraught and that everyone was in shock, and that during the secretly tape recorded conversation in Buckfield on November 11, Amanda, "*... accused me of molesting Kassidy, of assaulting Kassidy.*" (p. 3-73)

Patricia Wiberg asked Jennifer to read another portion of the transcript of the Saturday, November 11, recording, with Amanda speaking,
"*I never seen him, like hit her head or anything. One time he was walking with her... and .. it was an accident. He hit her in the head, but it didn't, like bruise, or anything, on the door....*" (p. 3-76)

Wiberg asked Jennifer about discipline in the Conley home when she and Amanda were teenagers, "*They'd just take our privileges away, like, our vehicles and stuff like that.*" (p. 3-76) She said that Amanda had a Chevy Corsica and she had a Ford Escort. She said that while there were sometimes threats that punishment would be with a spanking with a boat oar or paddle, "*My father never spanked us.*" (p. 3-77)

The questioning of Jennifer concluded at 11:30 a.m., and the court adjourned for the day.

MEDIA: "Aunt weeps during Bortner testimony"

Thursday, 21 November 21, 2002

The day began with Patricia Wiberg asking Judge Nadeau to ensure that the jurors were not seeing the newspaper and media articles about the case. She said that she had received calls from friends, saying, "*Do you realize what the slant of the press coverage is?*" (p. 3) and she was concerned that the coverage might be intimidating some jurors. Judge Nadeau responded that all a juror needed to do was raise a hand with a concern or say something to the bailiff and s/he could then talk privately with the judge about any concerns.

Heather Hamilton Lavalley

Examined by David Ruoff, Heather was Jennifer's supervisor at Perfumania, a discount perfume retailer in the Kittery Mall. She testified that Jennifer began work at Perfumania in August 2000, and became the assistant manager a few months after that. There was no challenge to this recollection, but, as noted in Chapter 7, it would have been easy to obtain the actual employment records, so the correct date could have been certified.

Heather said she remembered Amanda visiting Jen in the store three or four times, and "*oftentimes for hours,*" (p. 10) and that she brought Kassidy once. On that occasion, Heather saw bruises, which "*... looked like a handprint.*" She was asked to use her hand and demonstrate on her own face what she meant, "*The way they were located, to me it seemed like the lower print was here, and then there were more fingers up towards the top of her-- top right of her forehead.*" (p. 11) She said that Kassidy did not walk into the store that day, as she was held by Amanda.

On cross-examination, Patricia Wiberg asked about Amanda's one visit to Perfumania with Kassidy, and whether Heather remembered "*when Kassidy came in the store in October, she was looking, with Amanda, at all the perfume bottles, the colors?*" and Heather responded, "*Not that I remember.*" Wiberg returned to the question of whether Kassidy was walking during the 15-20 minute visit, "*She* [Kassidy] *walked around the store with Amanda holding her hand, didn't she*?" (p. 18-19) Heather answered, "*No.*"

Cathy Elizabeth Nuernberg

On direct examination, Cathy said that she met Amanda while working at "*Shain's of Maine... a restaurant/ice cream place.*" (p. 22) She said that Amanda lived with her "*for a summer... shortly after she* [Kassidy] *was born... that was the summer Mandy lived with me. And then I moved away. And then... when I came back for a summer, she was like one and a half. And I saw her once a week.*" (p. 23) She said that she came back to Maine for the summer of 2000 to be with her sister. As she stated at Chad's trial, she returned to Texas at "*the end of September of 2000.*" (p. 24) However, Jacqueline Conley testified at Chad's trial that on Monday, October 1, when Amanda brought Kassidy to Auburn for the photograph in the home they were leaving, Cathy Nuernberg was with Amanda on that day. (p. 18, December 4, 2001) Ruoff asked if she had ever been with Kassidy alone, and she responded, "*Yes. We* [presumably Cathy and her sister] *babysat her a few times...*" (p. 24) This was the first time that Cathy had mentioned such babysitting which would have occurred during the summer of 2000, and there was no mention of bruises. Cathy's estimate of the date that Amanda moved in with Chad was "*probably mid-summer, maybe July...*" (p. 25)

Ruoff asked Cathy, "*Did the defendant ever tell you how Chad Evans treated Kassidy?*" and she responded, "*He would ... sometimes ask her for hugs and kisses, and she would go over to him...I'm trying to think... I don't know.*" As that response wasn't helpful to the prosecution, David Ruoff asked to refresh her recollection with page 2112 of a report from New Hampshire State Police Sergeant Jim White of his interview with Cathy on August 17, 2001, which was almost a year after Kassidy's death. As it was not a transcript of her interview, she was not permitted to read it aloud and into the record. Instead, she was to read it, and then respond, realtime, to Ruoff's question.

The relevant paragraph on the report said,

> *I asked NUERNBERG about EVANS relationship with KASSIDY, NUERNBERG described several observations. She related that she was at EVANS' house for a get together. KASSIDY wanted to be held by BORTNER. BORTNER was in the kitchen, cooking and couldn't hold KASSIDY, who became fussy. EVANS grabbed KASSIDY by the shoulder, shook her, and told her she was acting like a brat. NUERNBERG said it made her uneasy. She also told me that to the best of her recollection, MARSHALL and CONLEY were there also.*

Cathy then testified,

One time, there... was going to be a barbecue of some sort held at Chad's house, and her sister was over, and also her sister's boyfriend. And we were cooking, and shewas cooking in the kitchen, or cleaning or something, and Kassidy was whining because she wanted to be held by Mandy, and Chad did not like how -- thought she was being a brat, or something like that, and was just kind of harsh with her. And it just--the--I just didn't like the way it went over.... He just kind of grabbed her real quick and said, "You're being a brat," and didn't let her go to Mandy, and like that. (p. 28)

Cathy said that Kassidy "*was startled and unappreciative...*" (p. 29) but she said that Chad didn't shake her and Cathy didn't notice any resulting bruising. The observed ambiguous behavior would seem typical of "father figure"/daughter-figure relationships, but through the prism of a previous conviction of murder and assault, Chad's behavior could have been misinterpreted by the jurors.

Cathy was then asked about a time she visited Amanda where she saw bruises on Kassidy, "*I believe it was a month before I left for Texas, which was probably about late August, early September,...*" and, in Ruoff's words, "*Well before October?*" (p. 30) She described the bruises, "*...she had grab marks on her face... like somebody grabbed her like this. She had two here, and one -- like a thumb-print here. She also had one on her forehead, and she also had one on her leg... She seemed to be walking fine, but I'm not sure."* (p. 30) Cathy said that Kassidy "*seemed very scared, and she seemed very withdrawn,*" but that Chad was not there at the time, and when he did come home, Cathy did not notice any difference in Kassidy's behavior. (p. 30) After acknowledging that she did not have children of her own, Cathy said that she asked Amanda about the bruising and Amanda explained that "*Kassidy was on Chad's shoulders and... he was walking down the stairs, and she hit her head against the wall, and that he felt bad, and so forth.*" (p. 31) In 2010 Chad recalled this incident in precisely the same way in his March 20, 2010 "Letter." This likely explained the bruise on Kassidy's forehead, which was observed by several people.

Cathy said that Amanda had told her that the bruise on "*Kassidy's leg was from an iron, from when she was at Crystal's* [Martin] *house.*" (p. 31) Later, under cross-examination, Cathy said that this particular bruise "*was on her foot. Sorry.*" (p. 45) David Ruoff did not call Crystal Martin as a witness, nor seek to introduce the summary of her January 5, 2001 interview with Maine State Police Detective Jeffrey Linscott. In that summary Crystal acknowledged that a burn on Kassidy's foot could have been caused by her curling iron, which may have been left ON, accidentally.

Cathy also said that Amanda told her the "trampoline story," and regarding all the bruises, Cathy said, "*At the house when I asked her about it, she didn't seem to make it a big deal.*" (p. 32) Cathy said that she and Amanda talked more about the bruises later and the possible explanations, including "*a lot of different babysitters at that time.*" (p. 33-34) Also, after seeing those bruises, Cathy "*offered for her to move down to Texas with me and bring Kassidy with her. She thought about it, but...* " (p. 34) This testimony corroborated Jennifer's recollection, but neither Cathy nor Jennifer mention this idea in her interview or testimony at Chad's trial.

Cathy said that she last saw Kassidy in September, 2000, and "*I took pictures of her in September, and I have them, and she looked fine.*" David Ruoff asked, "*So the bruises had cleared up*?" and Cathy answered, "*Yeah, as far as I know, it had.*" (p. 35) Neither Ruoff nor Wiberg asked for those photographs, or for them to be subpoenaed.

Cathy testified that Chad sent money to Amanda when she was in Texas at Cathy's via their mutual friend, Vanessa Mansson. She continued,

I actually convinced her to move down with me, and her mother and I think everyone else, including the police, they thought it was a good idea, so that she would be away from him." (p. 39)

Cathy summarized Amanda's situation, saying that all of her childhood friends, and her family believed that Chad abused and murdered Kassidy. That meant, logically, that they thought that Amanda was guilty of the Child Endangerment charges against her. As far as I know, the only close friend of Amanda who thought otherwise was Bruce's girlfriend, Jessica Edmands, but her relationship to Bruce was too close to make her opinion objective. Perhaps her support of Amanda was one reason the police never interviewed her.

In Ruoff's final question he asked about what Amanda said to Cathy about how she felt about Chad, and Cathy responded, "*I think she was really confused, and she talked about him like she still loved him sometimes, but not very often. I don't feel that she was comfortable talking with me about it.*" (p. 40) That would seem reasonable as Cathy had just testified that she and the police had at least similar views about Chad and Amanda. It's hard to stay close to family members and friends who believe that the man you love abused and murdered your daughter.

Patricia Wiberg's cross-examination began with some chronology, and established that Cathy was 17 and Amanda was 16 when they met while working at Shain's and during that time Amanda was pregnant with Kassidy. It must have been the summer of 1998. In the summer of 1999, when Amanda lived with Cathy and Kassidy was with Amanda's mother, they lived in the downstairs apartment in Cathy's mother's house. At the end of that summer, Cathy moved to Texas, and returned for the summer of 2000.

Cathy said that she learned about Kassidy's death from her sister. Subsequently, she said that Amanda called her, while she was at work at a restaurant in Texas, and Cathy went into the restroom, so she could talk with Amanda. Cathy said she flew home, visited with her mother briefly and then spent the night with Amanda at Tracey Foley's home. Although not specified at the trial, that was Friday, November 17, the day before Kassidy's funeral. She and Amanda flew back to Texas after the funeral. While in Texas, Amanda went to a counselor "*One, maybe two times.*" (p. 50) One item that Cathy remembered that Amanda had brought was Kassidy's Teletubby, and that she slept with it at night. (p. 48) Chad remembers this "Tinky Winky" doll as Kassidy's favorite and it was as big as the bunny in the October 1, 2000 photo.

On redirect, David Ruoff asked Cathy more about the fluctuations in her relationship with Amanda, and Cathy responded, "*I never stopped worrying about her. I stopped being able to help her... I felt because she was lying so much that I couldn't help her anymore.*" (p. 51) Patricia Wiberg objected to that last observation and Judge Nadeau sustained the objection and instructed the jury to disregard it, but the jury, of course, heard it, and likely would not forget it. Ruoff asked Cathy if she and Amanda were still friends, and Cathy said, "*No.*" (p. 53) Patricia Wiberg objected, because there was a court order that Amanda not have contact with other witnesses in the trial, including Cathy. Judge Nadeau then advised the jury of that no-contact order.

On recross-examination, Patricia Wiberg sought to ask Cathy if the reason why Kassidy did not move to her apartment with Amanda in the summer of 2000 was because Cathy's mother had just lost a grandchild, who was a niece or nephew to Cathy, and Cathy's mother didn't want to hear a baby crying downstairs. However, amidst the objections from David Ruoff regarding the form of the question, it was never effectively asked.

Melissa Chick (called, but not yet testify)

David Ruoff called for the next witness, Melissa Chick, but before she took the stand, Patricia Wiberg initiated a bench discussion to advise Judge Nadeau that a State witness, Tristan Evans, and a defense witness, Nicole Evans Harvey, had come to her, Patricia, during the break to report that

a number of the State's witnesses that were sitting across from them conferring about their testimony from the Evans trial versus what they're going to say today versus the statements the State gave them to refresh their recollection today with highlighted portions of what they should say, for instance, trying to make their timelines match. (p. 61)

She said that the two were Melissa Chick and Tracey Foley, and Judge Nadeau said that Wiberg could cross-examine any of them to further inquire about this alleged violation of the witness sequestration order and about what was said, but it wasn't grounds for a mistrial. Wiberg asked for a few minutes time to confer further with Tristan to determine what she heard, and David Ruoff said, "*...I don't want this trial to turn into another circus, but we have evidence that there is a sexual ... relationship between Ms. Evans and Ms. Bortner*." (p. 64) It's not clear whether he meant Tristan Evans or Nicole Evans Harvey, but he said, "*It's in the trial -- it's in the discovery. I'm not getting into it, but...*" Aside from Amanda's living at Nicole's home at times during the period before trial, I know of no such evidence in the discovery materials. It was an outrageous and irrelevant accusation, which likely arose as a rumor because Amanda lived at Nicole's home for a while. If the two women were close friends, or even married, and that wasn't yet legal in any state in the U.S., such closeness could have been presented to show loyalty and bias, but it was unnecessary to bring sexuality and alleged sexual preference into the courtroom.

Following the bench conference, Ruoff changed the order of the State's witnesses, and called Tristan Evans to testify.

Tristan Evans

Tristan said she was Chad's ex-wife, and was a CAT scan technician, and affirmed that she knew Amanda and explicitly understood her to continue to have a "*girlfriend*" relationship with Chad. (p. 67) David Ruoff asked about Tristan's conversations with Amanda and about his temper, and she replied, "*I didn't talk about his temper in general...wasn't anything about his temper in particular or in general*." (p. 70) Asked about Chad's "*assaultive behavior*," she said that she had talked with Amanda about "*...one instance, one or two instances that I spoke with her about that...*"

Tristan explained her called to DCYF, after her two observations, about a week apart, of bruises on Kassidy, "*... I wasn't really sure if anything was going on or not. So to make myself more comfortable, I called and made a report*." (p. 74)

On cross-examination Tristan said that she never saw Kyle playing with Kassidy, but "*He talked about playing with Kassidy*." (p. 77) She said that she never saw Kassidy limping or "*moving oddly*." (p. 77)

Without qualifying Tristan as an expert, Wiberg asked if, in her previous work as an X-ray technician, "*Has it ever happened that a patient has come into your office to be x-rayed and it's discovered that they have a broken bone?*" and she replied "*Yes,*" for children and for adults. (p. 77-8) As a significant part of the State's case against Chad and Amanda revolved around the allegation of bone fractures, this was an important issue for the jury to consider. That is, can people have fractures without knowing it? If so, then the strength of the State's charges against Amanda for failing to seek medical attention, and against Chad for the bone fractures is reduced; but that line of questioning ended upon objection by Ruoff. Wiberg should have brought to court an expert witness who could have made the same point.

Such an expert might have been Dr. Michael Lopasata who in 2005 wrote with his wife the article, "Children With Signs of Abuse - When is Not Child Abuse?" The article notes several possible alternate explanations for what appear to be bone fractures, e.g. osteogenesis imperfecta, metabolic bone disease.

Patricia asked Tristan about the phone conversation that she had on the evening of November 8 with Kyle, who was then at Chad's house and "*Excited. You know, happy three-year-old*." (p. 78) Ruoff objected to the anticipated question about Kyle telling his mother about the ball he hit into Kassidy's face on the grounds that Kyle's statements then to Tristan were hearsay. He said, "*But I've got a transcript of an interview with Kyle that I can put in evidence to rebut that*." (p. 79) During the bench conference, he said that Kyle's subsequent interview with Nancy Harris contradicted Tristan's testimony at Chad's trial about the call. Judge Nadeau recalled that she allowed the testimony at Chad's trial, but didn't recall the reason for the exception to the hearsay rule, but did not know there was transcribed, videotaped interview of Kyle available or which contradicted Tristan's testimony. Neither did Patricia Wiberg. As there was no transcript available of Chad's trial, so Judge Nadeau could review her reasons then used for admitting Tristan's testimony about the call. David Ruoff did say that he had the videotape and the transcript there at the courthouse, for review, and Patricia Wiberg dropped this line of questioning.

The interview with Kyle was done by Nancy Harris, Director of the Strafford County Victim/Witness program on November 20, 2000. According to a report by Sergeant James White, he observed the interview, along with Carol Ann Jensen of Nancy's program, Detective Jeff Linscott of the Maine State Police, Patricia Hocter of DCYF, and Kris Keeler of DCYF. During the interview, she told Kyle that it was being "*tape recorded.*" (p. 2) Kyle poignantly said that Kassidy "*lives with God now.*" (p. 6) Joined by Chris Keeler, Nancy Harris asked Kyle about toys and balls, and then asked, "*Did you ever hit Kassidy with one of your balls? By accident or on purpose?*" The transcript records no verbal answer, only Kyle "*(laughing)*" (p. 31) Thus Ruoff's claim that the interview with Kyle contradicted Tristan's expected testimony seems incorrect. It's hard to see how "(laughing)" by a three-year old during a scattered interview can contradict the recollection of a State witness, Tristan. The interview ended a few seconds later with Kyle saying once, "*I'm going to see my mommy,*" and then again after a Nancy Harris question. (p. 32, of 32 page transcript.)

Then Patricia Wiberg asked Tristan about her observations of the two people, whose names she didn't know, she overheard in the hallway discussing their upcoming testimonies, and apparently comparing notes. In her final question, Wiberg asked whether, in her previous discussions with the prosecutors, they had "*talked to you about what they were looking for in this trial...was a statement made to you about who caused Kassidy's death*?" (p. 85) In other words, were they coaching her. Tristan replied, "*Obviously they didn't care who caused Kassidy's death. They just wanted to prove that Amanda failed her.*" (p. 85) On redirect, David Ruoff sought to clarify the conversation he had with Tristan and to rebuff that implication that he was seeking to persuade her to support the prosecution case in her testimony. Tristan agreed that he asked her to tell the truth.

<u>Melissa Rae Chick</u>

At the time of Amanda's trial, Melissa had been working as a veterinary technician for four months, and before that she was an assistant pre-school teacher at the Sanford-Springvale YMCA. Melissa met Amanda around the time of 8th grade. Shortly thereafter, Melissa dropped out of school in the 9th grade and they had an "*off and on relationship.*" (p. 89) She reconnected with Amanda around the time Kassidy was one year old, in February, 2000. Melissa remembered that time because she learned around then that she had cervical cancer. Asked what Amanda said about Chad after first meeting him, Melissa said, "*....she said that he was older, and that he seemed to have a head on his shoulders, and that he had money, and he had a house,...*" (p. 92) She said that after Amanda began seeing Chad, she would see her "*maybe four times a week... She would come to my house, and I would go to Chad's.*" (p. 92) Neither Melissa nor Amanda had said in their interviews, nor in Melissa's testimony at Chad's trial, that she saw Amanda and Kassidy that often.

About the bruises on Kassidy, beyond what was said at Chad's trial, Melissa said, "*I remember bruising on her ear... and that she would touch it always...*" (p. 96) This was the first time that anyone had mentioned in an interview or in Chad's trial a bruise on Kassidy's ear. Melissa remembers telling Amanda that Kassidy might be anemic "*if she is getting all these bruises... She kind of would brush it off and go to something else.*" (p. 97)

Judge Nadeau allowed Melissa to relate what Amanda had told her that Chad had said to Amanda about Kassidy as a "not offered for the truth of the statement" exception to the hearsay rule. Melissa testified,

He would just say mean things about her. He'd just say that "She's acting stupid," and "she's just -- she's falling down. Come get her. I don't want her -- she doesn't like me. Get her away from me," or things like that. And Amanda would protest and say, "Stop saying things like that about my child. (p. 99)

Melissa affirmed that she heard Chad call Kassidy an idiot.

Asked about her observations of Chad and Kassidy interacting, she related a time,

I had gone over [to] *Chad's house to see Amanda and Chad was working. And he had called her prior and asked her to get his things ready for golf. And she* [Kassidy] *was in*

the living room, and he had [come home.] *She was just staring at him..she just seemed very scared...I didn't think it was normal.*" (p. 100-01)

Chad recalls in 2011 that this occasion was the only time that Melissa had ever saw Chad in Kassidy's presence, and he was just passing through, and did not sit down. He insists that he never called Kassidy an idiot.

Melissa said that she and Amanda stopped socializing after the Halloween plans fell through due to Kassidy being sick. They had talked about trick-or-treating together with Kassidy, and perhaps Melissa's younger brother. Before that, she did talk with Amanda about getting her own apartment, and

She said that she...thinks it would be better if ... they weren't living together maybe.. it would be a better relationship if they weren't together, and that if she would get her own apartment, she would be more stable. (p. 103)

Melissa said the last time she saw Kassidy was when they went to Olympia Sports in Sanford, which must have also been before Halloween, and Kassidy "*had bruising on her face... enough* [for a mother] *to be embarrassed about it.*" Asked if there was anything else wrong with Kassidy on that day, Melissa said, "*... I think she was walking a little awkward. She was... running around and playing in there a little bit, and she just seemed to walk a little awkward.*" (p. 104)

On cross-examination, Patricia Wiberg suggested, through a question, that one reason Amanda had considered getting her own apartment was "*because Tristan kept coming by*?" but Melissa did not remember Amanda telling her that. (p. 116)

Expressing some frustration, Melissa said, "*She would just make up excuses about the bruises*." (p. 119)

Regarding the cancellation of their Halloween plans because Kassidy wasn't feeling well, Melissa said, "*I'm not sure if it was before or after her death, but she said something about her falling out of her babysitter's-- her sister's boyfriend's truck.*" (p. 119)

When visiting the Conley home as teenager, Melissa witnessed physical punishment to one of Amanda's brothers, where "*he had a big bag of keys thrown at his eye, and his eye was black and blue.*" (p. 123) Apparently contradicting Cathy Nuernberg's testimony, Melissa said that Amanda walked to work at Shain's and that her parents did not buy her a car, which contradicted Jennifer's testimony that their parents purchased cars for Amanda and Jennifer.

Patricia Wiberg asked, "*What type of mother was Amanda*?" and Melissa said, "*I think she was young and naive*," (p. 125) but that "*yes*," she did care about Kassidy.

<u>Tracey Foley</u>

Tracey said that she was 32 years old and had a six-year-old daughter and was, coincidentally, living in Rochester, New Hampshire at the time of trial, after several years in Springvale. Tracey recalled that she lost touch with Amanda when Kassidy was about six months old, and that the accidental reunion at the Sanford YMCA occurred about "*five weeks before Kassidy died.*" (p. 130) As it was Friday, October 13, it was exactly three weeks and six days before November 9. Tracey asked Amanda about the bruises on Kassidy's head, and Amanda told her the "trampoline story." About Chad, Tracey said that Amanda told her "*That he had a house, and good job and a snowmobile or a four-wheeler or something, he was going to buy her a car...She said he was good to her* [and, regarding his treatment of Kassidy]... *He was a little firm.*" (p. 132-33)

Tracey said she also saw a bruise on a side of Amanda's jaw when she stayed overnight, which was that Saturday, and that was the last time she saw Kassidy alive.

On cross-examination, Tracey said of Amanda's babysitting, "*She was great,*" (p. 136) and after Kassidy was born, Amanda and her boyfriend, Gabe would babysit for Tracey's daughter and stepson. As Wiberg was not representing Chad at this trial, there was no need to clarify that the bruise that Tracey saw on Amanda's jaw on Saturday, October 13, was not seen the previous day by Tracey or Melissa. As Amanda had not seen Chad in the interim, he was not the cause of that bruise.

<u>Amanda Donnell</u>

Amanda was the first witness at Amanda's trial who had not testified the previous year at Chad's trial. She said that she knew Amanda through Amanda's sister, Jennifer, and she knew Chad through her brothers, who lived in Somersworth. In 2011, Chad wrote that he never knew Amanda Donnell's brothers and does not recall knowing anyone named Donell. Her father, who runs Donnell's Auto Repair, "*is good friends with her sister Jennifer and Jennifer's boyfriend.*" (p. 139)

Amanda said that she saw Chad and Amanda Bortner at T.J. Maxx, between Kassidy's death and her funeral, where Amanda Bortner was trying a jacket on, and Chad and Amanda were "*Hugging, kissing, giggling.*" (p. 140) Apparently believing that parents who lose children should act always in a particular way, Ruoff asked, "*Did Amanda, in that time you saw her, ever cry or appear upset or anything like that?*" and Amanda Donnell said, "*No, she did not.*" (p. 140) Ruoff asked another question, to which Wiberg objected, and Ruoff withdrew the question, and Wiberg pressed further, "*What's the relevance on the whole thing*?" The judge said, "*Okay.*" and Ruoff had no further questions. (p. 141)

Angela Blodgett

Maine State Police Angela Blodgett recalled that she interviewed Amanda four times: the first two in the kitchen of the Kittery Police Dept., the third in her office in Gray, Maine, and the fourth in the meeting room at the Kittery Police Dept. She said that of the four interviews, she transcribed one of them herself, though she wasn't sure which one.

David Ruoff asked Detective Blodgett several questions which she often answered by referring to transcript of the interviews and reading aloud from them. After quoting Amanda as saying in the first interview, " *'It looks like it's my fault,'* " (p. 153) Blodgett said, "*She talked about a few incidents at Jeff Marshall's house, but primarily she thought that Chad was responsible.*" (p. 154)

Detective Blodgett said that one reason for the fourth interview was for Amanda to come in "*to sign a release form for the medical examiner's office so that her mother, Jackie, could start making funeral arrangements for Kassidy.*" (p. 168) She testified about her concern about Amanda returning to live with Chad and that she had "*stepped out during the interview and talked with Melissa* [Chick]. *And by the end we had talked about having me arrange for, like, shelter through an abused women's program or something like that.*" (p. 171)

Detective Blodgett testified that she next saw Amanda at Chad's house on the night he was arrested. After the New Hampshire State Police "*took control of the residence*," she felt, as a Maine State Police person, that she could then legally enter the home. (p. 172) She said she found Amanda in the bedroom and that "*She seemed upset and embarrassed about-- we had just had a conversation that afternoon ...about us finding her there. I was a little disappointed in her.*"

If Angela Blodgett and the other police personnel at Chad's that night had taken the time to interview the people who were there with Amanda and Chad, they might have learned about the loving Evans family. If they had talked with Chad's parents, they might have learned about the visit of Chad, Amanda and Kassidy to Keene in August. They might have learned, as they apparently didn't take notice when Chad told them, about his mother's advice, about how Chad's mother encouraged Amanda to take Kassidy to see a doctor about her "pigeon-toed" feet. They might have learned about some of the unusual Kassidy behaviors, such as walking into a wall, and falling without putting hands out in front of her; and these behaviors were appearing in August. Instead, Angela Blodgett knew what her theory of the case was, which was formed on the day Kassidy died; and that was that Chad was a child murderer and a woman abuser. Period. She was going to stick with that theory.

Others there that evening were Chad's sister, Nicole, and his brother-in-law, who had been interviewed already. However, the police didn't ask them specifics about the family social gathering that Chad attended with Kassidy the previous Sunday. They didn't ask about the date of that gathering. They thought they had the facts they needed to support their theory. Instead of talking with the people at the house that night, the police asked them all to leave so the home could be searched.

Another set of parents the police could have interviewed would have been the parents of Jeff Marshall, especially his mother, who lives in a town next to Kittery. She may have seen Kassidy while Jeff and/or Jennifer were babysitting , and she would have other background information.

Back to Detective Blodgett on the stand at Amanda's trial, Patricia Wiberg asked about the initial hours of the investigation. Blodgett said that when she began her interview of Amanda, together with Detective Rick LeClair, Amanda had been sitting, and crying, with a Kittery Police secretary or receptionist.

Detective Blodgett acknowledged that Amanda had told her about her call to Care Link, in her efforts to find day care. Detective Blodgett knew that it was "*a referral service in Maine.*" (p. 183) She said that Detective LeClair knew more about it because his wife provides day care in Maine.

The trial adjourned for the day at 3:30 p.m., and resumed the following morning at 9:36 a.m. the next day.

MEDIA: "Bortner pointed toward Evans as Kassidy's killer, tapes show"

Friday, 22 November 2000

Patricia Wiberg resumed her cross-examination of Detective Blodgett, which consisted primarily of Blodgett reading aloud from several sections of transcripts from her interviews with Amanda. Wiberg asked about Amanda's description of Chad's playing with Kassidy, "*... he'd pick her up and play airplane*?" and, asked to describe "*airplane*," Blodgett said, "*When I play it with nieces and nephews I would hold them kind of under the pelvis and by the chest and go around like this, maybe up and down, and make noises.*" (p. 15) While not explicitly stated, it appeared that Det. Blodgett was not a mother. A few minutes later, Wiberg continued, "*Now, wouldn't that -- another way of playing airplane is swing with their hands, swing them around?...*" (p. 22) Blodgett acknowledged, "*I mean, you could play with a child that way. That's not what I picture as 'airplane.'*" (p. 22-23) Thus, it appeared that because Detective Blodgett's understanding of "*airplane*" was different from Amanda's and Chad's, she was left to assume that Chad's swinging of Kassidy "*by the arms or legs or stuff?*" was more sinister, instead of simply being another form a parent/child play. (p. 22)

In his March 4, 2011 letter, Chad tried to explain this type of play with Kassidy,
I would describe "airplane ride" the way that Angela Blodgett described it. I also would describe it by putting my arms under the child's as they face away from me and swing them around in a circle. Although, I suppose a better description for this is "helicopter" because you, are spinning the child like a rotor on a helicopter. I've used both to describe these actions interchangeably. To me, it was just words to describe picking the children up to spin them around or buzz them around like Superman. Which by the way, I've also used to describe it. This isn't the first time that the state got caught up on a WORD. I wrote in my last letter about another word that they were interpreting differently than I meant. In this instance, it was just meant to describe picking Kassidy up and playing with her in a non-malicious manner.

Blodgett confirmed her understanding that Amanda had said that she had taken Kassidy to the doctor for her "*pigeon-toed walk*" problem "*earlier in the summer.*" (p. 15) Unfortunately, neither Angela Blodgett, nor the Maine nor New Hampshire State Police, nor Patricia Wiberg, sought documentary corroboration of that appointment, which, as seen earlier, was on September 11.

Detective Blodgett recalled about Amanda's third interview, at her office in Gray, "*I think she came with her mom.*" (p. 55)

Blodgett reiterated her concern about Amanda continuing to have a relationship to Chad, "*I felt that Amanda really wasn't making good decisions around her relationship with Chad...I didn't think it* [being with Chad] *was a healthy place to be.*" (p. 81-2)

James White

Examined by David Ruoff, Sergeant James White explained that he was the lead investigator in the Kassidy Bortner case for the New Hampshire State Police. Prior to his 13 years with the State Police, he had worked for seven years with the York, Maine Police Dept., which could have been another reason for the close working relationship between the Maine and New Hampshire police organizations. He first met Amanda when he joined with Detective Blodgett in Amanda's November 16 interview at the Kittery Police Dept.

He described the subsequent interview in Concord, after picking her up the day before at the Boston airport after Amanda's return from Texas on December 18, 2000. He explained that he didn't tape record the interview because he wasn't
planning on covering any new territory, if you will. It was to go into greater detail about things she had already talked about. And there was no reason to tape that. I had plenty of time to take good notes on that interview. (p. 93)
Sergeant White said that fourth interview was helpful. For example, "*we learned, in fact, Amanda had not seen her* [Kassidy] *eat any cereal from that baggie at all that morning.*" (p. 93)

A second or third or fourth interview with Chad Evans would have been helpful, too. On that particular point, he could have told an interviewer that he saw Kassidy open the baggie herself while in the car and begin eating, just before Amanda drove off. In an April 29, 2010 letter, Chad recalled those moments:

As Amanda rolled down her window I said, "I didn't kiss Kassidy yet." I quickly opened the backseat door and kissed Kassidy on the forehead. "I love you, have a good day baby." That is when I noticed she had somehow gotten hold of her Ziplock cereal baggie, had opened it and was eating some of her cereal. I was amazed that she could open it. I believe I said out loud. "You little shit, I didn't know you could open these." I said to Amanda, something like,"Baby, she opened her cereal bag, did you know she could open them?" Amanda sounded a little irritated and replied something like, "She's been able to do that for a while. I am late. I've got to go!"

Returning to White's testimony, he described, without referring to his report of that December 19 interview, what Amanda told him. As she was the defendant, this was not hearsay. He said, relying on Amanda's representations that "*Kassidy didn't eat or drink anything that morning.*" (p. 95) With that testimony, Judge Nadeau ironically ordered a lunch break.

Further relating his December 19, 2000, interview with Amanda, Sgt. White said that Amanda told him that the "trampoline story" was false and that it was developed by Chad for Amanda for Amanda to explain Kassidy's injuries to Amanda's friend, Emily Conley. Amanda and Kassidy were going with Emily to Emily's doctor's appointment. White said, "*He told her that she couldn't take Kassidy because of the bruising. And Amanda told Chad she was going to take Kassidy anyways, so he had better come up with something,*" (p. 101) and that was the "trampoline story." What was missing from that testimony was any effort by Sgt. White to determine the date of Emily's appointment with her obstetrician. I've estimated from other sources that the appointment was around Thursday, October 12th, which was the day before Joshua's, Tracey's and Melissa's observations of Friday the 13th., and therefore a time of known bruising.

Responding to Patricia Wiberg's questions on cross-examination, Sergeant White explained generally how the investigation moved from Maine to New Hampshire, around the time of Amanda's third interview on November 12th. He said,
After receiving witness statements, the evidence that we recovered up to that point, and the medical examiner's findings, along with statements that Chad had made, it was clear that the focus was shifting back to New Hampshire. And that's when the decision was made to relinquish the lead to New Hampshire instead of Maine. (p. 103)

In fact, the decision effectively was made by several officers, apparently by consensus, on the afternoon and early evening of November 9, that Chad was Kassidy's abuser and murderer. He was obviously from New Hampshire. Sgt. White had good reason to want it to appear that the decision was far more deliberative, and far more dependent upon the actual evidence, that was the actual decision. Even his estimate of November 12, only three days after Kassidy's death, was too quick. Below is a list of several aspects of the case, with their date of occurrence, which might have given pause for the decision to transform Kassidy Bortner's death into a New Hampshire homicide.

11/9 Blood stained napkin and sheets and pink jacket were found at Jeff's.

11/9 Nicole, Brandon and Chad told police about the Nov. 5 family gathering w/ Kassidy.

11/10 Search at Chad's home found no signs of abuse.

11/10 Through interviews, Jeff's allegations against Chad of alcohol and drug abuse, gambling losses and sexual deviance, were found to be groundless or greatly exaggerated.

11/10 Criminal records checks for Jeff and Chad performed by this date.

11/14 Jeff declined to take pre-scheduled lie detector test.

11/15 Search of Chad's car found no sign of abuse.

11/16 Second search at Chad's home found no signs of abuse.

Sergeant White said that he believed that Amanda paid for her airplane ticket for the flight back from Texas on December 18th. However, there was no indication that he or any other investigator ever inquired with Amanda how she was paying for her car gasoline and airplane tickets and other living expenses. The answer was that Chad, despite his greatly reduced earnings because of his voluntary resignation from his McDonald's job, was giving Amanda money. It was not enough to explain all her expenses and Chad has always thought that the State paid for Amanda's round trip plane tickets for her first trip to Texas. Her family wasn't helping her.

In her final series of questions, Patricia Wiberg returned to an issue raised in David Ruoff's examination which was why Sgt. White didn't tape his December 19 interview with Amanda, which was conducted, he said, in the presence of Allison Vachon, the Victim/Witness advocate in the NH Attorney General's office. White said that all the words were his own, except that he did put some statements in quotation marks. Through questions, Wiberg pointed out that all of the quoted words were what Amanda had said Chad or Kyle had said, and there was not one quoted word from Amanda herself, except when she quoted her own statement to Jeff and Jennifer when she brought Kassidy to their apartment on November 9th, "*Her face looks like shit, doesn't it?*" (p. 112)

On redirect, David Ruoff reviewed the quotations in Sgt. White's report with Sgt. White. On recross, Patricia Wiberg asked about Amanda's explanation of why Chad didn't grab or hold Kyle's face when seeking eye contact. Sgt. White responded,
The reason she gave was that Kyle would listen when Chad asked him to look him in the eyes when he was being disciplined while Kassidy was a different story. She wouldn't look Chad in the eyes, so he had to grab her ... by the face..." (p. 118)

Further, Sgt. White said that Amanda demonstrated for him how Chad held Kassidy's face, and that ended Sgt. White's testimony.
David Ruoff announced, "*The State rests*." (p. 119)

Patricia Wiberg then made a motion for a "*directed verdict*," which is a determination by a judge that there is no reasonable chance for a verdict of guilty beyond a reasonable doubt, and thus no need to refer the case to the jury. Wiberg stated, "*Taking the evidence in the light most favorable to the State that's been presented, I don't think they have proven..that Amanda knew.. that Kassidy was in need of medical care.*" (p. 120) Secondly, said Wiberg, Amanda believed all the reasons given by others for Kassidy's bruises. David Ruoff objected to the motion, saying, "*we believe we have produced enough evidence during this trial that a reasonable trier of fact* [the jury] *could conclude beyond a reasonable doubt the defendant's guilt.*" (p. 120) Judge Nadeau denied the motion.

The trial adjourned at 2:04 p.m. as Amanda was feeling sick. Wiberg had told Judge Nadeau that her two witnesses would be Amanda's friend, Mary Bullard, for about five minutes, and Travis Hunt for about ten.

MEDIA:1. "Mother blamed boyfriend in hours after Kassidy Bortner's death"
2. "Detective takes turn on stand in Bortner case"
3. "State rests its case in Amanda Bortner child endangerment trial"

4. "Prosecution rests in Bortner trial"
5. "Prosecution rests its case in Bortner child abuse trial"
6. "Jury to hear from slain toddler's mother"

Monday, 25 November 2002

Patricia Wiberg examined the only defense witness, Travis Hunt. There was no explanation of why Mary Bullard was not called to testify, despite Wiberg's representation of the previous Friday.

Travis said that he lived at Chad's home for "*a little over a year*," which would have been from mid-September 2000 through mid-September 2001. (p. 4) He said that on the evening of November 8, he saw Kassidy in the bathtub and the bruises he saw were "*ones on her arm. Right here, like on her chin...On her leg. On her eye.*" (p. 6) He said that she did not seem sick and said " '*Hi*' " to him (p. 8)

Wiberg asked about other bruises he might have seen on Kassidy and he said that he had seen bruising on Kassidy's buttocks, "*It was black and blue and it covered her entire buttocks.*" (p. 8) He said he saw it, "*Just a few months prior,*" (p. 9) but, in fact that was Sunday, October 22, or 18 days before Kassidy died. Travis said that Jeff Marshall had told Travis on the previous day, "*... she was being a little bitch, and he beat her ass.*" (p. 10) Travis said that when Amanda showed him the bruises he responded, "*Well, I--the first I said was, 'Did you do anything?' She said she took care of it,*" (p. 11) and she told Travis that she had talked with her sister and Jeff about it.

Travis recalled the time when he was trying to use the phone, after Amanda had been hired by Old Navy, and Amanda was busy making calls to day care providers. He agreed that he had seen Kassidy have temper tantrums and that she, using Wiberg's characterization, "*threw herself on the floor,*" (p. 14) and he agreed that he had seen "*her run in the house and fall down*?" (p. 14) He said that he wasn't concerned about such falls because she picked herself back up and kept going. He said that Kassidy didn't always go quietly for her naps and she didn't always stay in her room, which implied that she was able to open the door by herself. The only discipline Travis saw was Amanda putting Kassidy in her room or time-outs.

On cross-examination, Travis agreed with David Ruoff's question that Amanda had told him that she thought "*Chad was a little rough with Kassidy at times?*" (p. 15) but he never saw that, and never saw Chad grab Kassidy's face. Travis testified "*I thought she was just waiting to hear back from a day care,*" (p. 16) and that Amanda didn't tell him that the reason Kassidy wasn't in day care was because of the bruises, but he did acknowledge that he agreed with police representations during his 2009 interview that she did tell him the bruising was the reason.

Regarding his observations of Kassidy falling, he agreed with Ruoff's question that he had "*noticed that when she would fall, she wouldn't put her arms out to catch herself?*" (p. 17) He also agreed that he told Irene Ricci on the evening of November 8, though she wasn't named in Ruoff's question, that he was worried about Kassidy.

On redirect examination by Patricia Wiberg, Travis agreed that his reason for concern for Kassidy that evening was because of the "*eye incident*," i.e. the ball hitting Kassidy in the eye. (p. 19) He said that Kassidy's failure to put her arms in front of her was characteristic of most of her falls. He agreed that she picked up her toys and could carry things.

Travis was the last defense witness, and the trial was recessed at 9:32 a.m. Afterwards, there still remained the question of whether Amanda would testify. Patricia Wiberg told Judge Nadeau and Ruoff, "*...she's so back and forth about testifying. Now she said she wants to think about it for five minutes.... I don't think she wants to, though.*" (p. 20-21) Wiberg later advised Judge Nadeau that Amanda would not be testifying, without further explanation. None was required, and judges normally accept such representations by defense counsel. It isn't known precisely why Amanda did not testify. Her lawyer was advising her not to testify. Chad was advising her to testify, as he had already recognized that he had made a mistake by not testifying at his own trial.

Perhaps, in the face of the loud public outcry in the case, and in the face of her own family's support of the police and prosecutors' theories, she was resigned to being sentenced. Perhaps she was reluctant to go through it all again: the direct examination and the cross-examination. She was not able to consult with Chad, her strongest supporter, because the justice system forbade that contact. Chad's family supported Amanda in many ways, but they didn't provide legal advice; they did what families do, which was to support each other, regardless of what they have done or not done.

A welcome reform in American criminal law would be for judges to conduct a detailed voir dire inquiry with defendants, outside the presence of a jury, if they are advised that a defendant is deciding not to testify. Such an inquiry could be similar to what is done to ensure that guilty pleas are willingly given. Regarding decisions not to testify, the defendant could be asked:

1. Do you understand that this may be the last opportunity you have to tell your story?
2. Do you understand that if you are found guilty and you appeal, no appellate court will know your story if you don't testify.
3. Do you understand that jurors **want** to hear what a defendant has to say? This contradicts the "legal fiction" that juries do not hold decisions not to testify against defendants because judges tell jurors that defendants have the legal right not to testify.
4. Do you understand that you can be cross-examined about anything you say?
5 Do you have any questions of me (the judge) about this decision?

In 2011, the judge in Casey Anthony's trial asked her in open court whether her decision to testify was entirely her own decision, but that inquiry was more limited than the inquiry proposed above.

Then there was a hearing or bench conference on the language of Judge Nadeau's upcoming jury instructions. One challenge was to ensure that the language of the "Endangering the Welfare" statute and the indictments and the jury instructions were consistent. There was some discussion of the difference between "*knowingly*" and "*purposely*." At 10:42 a.m. the jury returned for the closing arguments and jury instructions.

Patricia Wiberg - Closing argument.

She began, "*... Amanda Bortner did not purposely or knowingly endanger the welfare of her child. Amanda Bortner loved Kassidy more than anything.*" (p. 36) Wiberg recounted the story to the jury where Kyle and Kassidy were together and Kyle started "1,2,3, 4," for Kassidy and she finished the sequence "up to 10." (p. 37) Even though there was no testimony at this trial of that exchange between Kyle and Kassidy, the prosecutor did not object. Trial lawyers try to minimize their objections to opening and closing statements as they can be viewed as harassment by jurors.

Wiberg said that Amanda thought that Kassidy was okay and that she, Amanda, understood Kassidy's condition, and that it didn't involve abuse or serious illness. Wiberg pointed to several indications that the representations of what happened at Jeff's apartment on November 9 were not reasonable or consistent, but she said that the "*focus of this case really isn't who killed Kassidy.*" (p. 38) She said, "*The whole case is hindsight.... no one realized, least of all Amanda, what was happening to Kassidy... not one person knew she had a broken bone. And she had three at various times.*" (p. 39) Apparently, Patricia Wiberg chose to ignore Dr. Michael Baden's opinion that Kassidy had no broken bones, so the jury was left with the impression that the broken bone diagnosis was undisputed. Still, in terms of the "Endangering the Welfare" charges, the most important aspect was that no one close to Kassidy was aware even of the possibility of broken bones. No one at that trial knew of Kassidy's September 11, 2000 appointment with Dr. James Timoney, an orthopedic surgeon. If he, or any member of Kassidy's family had known there was a possibility of a fracture, Dr. Timoney would have been asked about it, or looked for symptoms. None of the previous pediatric appointments had encountered a fracture, either. The report of the interview on November 9 of Dr. Bock, the York Hospital emergency room doctor, said that he did not see any evidence of fractures, but Dr. Bock was not called as a witness.

Wiberg noted that all of the things that the jury heard that happened to Kassidy occurred "*over a period of a month and a half or so...And in hindsight ... all of that adds up to a terrible picture for Kassidy. But if you take it one at a time, with the explanations that are given by Chad, or by Jeff, or by Jen, to Amanda, how could she know?*" (p. 41)

Wiberg was close to correct about the "*month and a half*" because the consistent appearance of bruises seemed to begin around October 13, which was a month before Kassidy died. If Cathy Nuernberg's observations actually were made during some period of September, those bruises disappeared entirely either before Dr. Timoney's September 11 appointment or before Jacqueline Conley's babysitting of Kassidy from Sunday, September 24 through Wednesday the 27th, or before the bunny rabbit photo of Sunday, October 1. However, Wiberg, like others, had serious misunderstandings about other timing issues. In her closing she said of Kassidy's life at Chad's home, "*she had only been there for a month or so, two months.*" The very real problem with that conclusion was that Wiberg's representation of Amanda's and Kassidy's move-in date nearly coincided with the appearance of regular bruising in mid-October, as noted earlier. Instead, Amanda was living with Chad by early July and Kassidy was living full-time with them soon afterwards. That would mean Kassidy was living with Chad for 17-19 weeks before she died, rather than six to eight. If there was a coincidence in timing for the bruising and something else, it was the coincidence of increased babysitting at Jeff's and Jennifer's, and not moving to Chad's. Of course, coincidence does not mean causation, but in 2000-2002, the coincidence/causation connection was a significant part of the cases against Chad and Amanda.

She urged the jury not to be swayed by the photographs because, they, too "*were taken in hindsight.*" She didn't remind the jury of the point made during Dr. Greenwald's testimony that bruising and injuries look worse in post-mortem photographs than they look before death. Wiberg understood the power of photographs, but, like Chad's attorneys she was looking at photographs defensively, rather than proactively. Wiberg, too, could have asked for, or subpoenaed, many available photographs, including those available now at Chad's website.

Wiberg ended her closing by returning to the original question, "*... did Amanda purposely deprive her* [Kassidy] *of care and protection.*" (p. 49)

David Ruoff - Closing statement

Ruoff opened with, "*The abuse, the grabbing, the throwing that the defendant watched was the price she was willing to pay for living in comfort.*" (p. 50) He characterized the relationship of Chad and Kassidy as "*a violent relationship. It was. Amanda knew it. Her best friends knew it.*" (p. 52)

Ruoff, too, was challenged by the timing issues, as he mentioned bruises and observations by witnesses, allegedly consistently from the time Kassidy moved to Chad's home. However, he didn't mention the timing, and he didn't remind the jury of the photograph of Kassidy, free of bruises, and he didn't remind them of the October 1 date of that photograph. On another issue of timing he represented to the jury that the injuries to Kassidy occurred twelve hours before her death, and emphasized that timing with repetition, "*Twelve hours old, at a minimum. Twelve hours old. Twelve hours old. Twelve hours. Twelve hours. Twelve hours. Twelve hours. Twelve hours.... At about midnight, right around the time, the doctor says, she sustained those bruises.*" (p. 55) Patricia Wiberg objected, because she said that Ruoff was mischaracterizing what Dr. Greenwald had said about the timing of injuries, and Judge Nadeau advised the jurors to use "*your own recollection of the doctor's testimony regarding the ages of the bruises.*" (p. 56)

Ruoff continued. Like so many others involved in the Kassidy Bortner tragedy, he mischaracterized the ball-hitting-eye incident of November 8. Referring to Kassidy's head injuries, he said, "*These weren't caused by a wiffle ball.*" (p. 57) Ironically, he was right. They were not caused by a wiffle ball, as they were caused by a Tee-ball which weighs almost as much as an official hardball baseball. However, his goal was to persuade the jury that the ball-hitting-eye incident was simply another excuse or lie that didn't make sense.

Ruoff referred to Jeff and Jennifer as Amanda's "*sister and brother-in-law*," (p. 57) apparently to make that relationship appear more legitimate to the jury, but Jeff and Jennifer were never married and ended their relationship in the mid-2000's. Jennifer told investigators that they were engaged, and showed her ring during her November 9, 2000, interview, but by the time of Chad's 2001 trial, the relationship was the less formal, "girlfriend/boyfriend." Ruoff didn't know that Chad and Amanda had talked about marriage, too, and about having children together. Jennifer and Jen did not have a child together, and neither has since become a parent.

David Ruoff returned to the issue of fractures, and told the jury

...actually, there were five. One in each arm, one, two; one in her hand, three; and actually two in her leg, one over the older one. Broken in the same spot." (p. 58) Actually, there were zero, but if there were any, they were undetected by parents, doctors and others and even if they had been detected, none were caused maliciously by Chad or Amanda.

Then Ruoff argued that the reason that Kassidy didn't put her hands out in front of her when falling was because she had broken arms. That was an argument that was not supported by any evidence or expert witness.

Nearing the end, Ruoff said,

Well, I've proved that the defendant acted purposely, that she knew it was her duty to care, and she breached that duty of care or protection of her child. Look at her words, her lies, and her inaction. But in this case we have something a little bit extra, that goes a little step further than these three. We have her actually hiding Kassidy, and he mentioned his evidence for that assertion. (p 59) He didn't mention the time that Melissa Chick and Amanda and Kassidy went to Olympia Sports together a few days before Halloween, and Kassidy was running around the store. Melissa testified that Kassidy's bruises were visible enough to be embarrassing, but Amanda brought her to the store, nonetheless, as she didn't think or know that anything was wrong. He didn't mention that Tristan Evans had seen Kassidy several times, and was, in fact, the anonymous person who called DCYF on October 31. He didn't mention Travis Hunt who saw Kassidy on Friday, November 4 when she fell into the coffee table at Chad's, and who saw Kassidy without clothes on November 8th. Finally, Ruoff didn't mention that Chad had taken Kassidy to his sister's home, with several family members present on Sunday, November 5. Perhaps he didn't know about this last event because the defense provided no witnesses to tell the jury, but it was mentioned in three November 9 interviews.

Ruoff reminded the jury that Jeff Marshall denied on the stand harming Kassidy, and Ruoff described him,

...the man that named his own business after his brother, who passed away, who had a picture of him with him up there on the stand, who cried when I showed him the picture. Do you think he was lying to you?" (p 62)

Ruoff concluded by asking the jury to return with a single word sentence, "*like the single-word sentences that she could speak when she died, 'Guilty.'* " (p. 62)

Judge Tina Nadeau - Jury Instructions

As Amanda decided not to testify, and as there was only one defense witness, just as in Chad's case, Judge Nadeau's Instructions to the jury in Amanda's case was very similar to those the previous year in Chad's case, including the law on reasonable doubt, the right not to testify, the role of expert witnesses and what could be considered as evidence.

She said that the crimes of Endangering the Welfare of a Child included four elements:

1. *that the defendant acted knowingly....*
2. *that the defendant endangered the welfare of Kassidy,...*
3. *that Kassidy was under the age of 18 years old, and*
4. *that the defendant endangered Kassidy's welfare by purposely violating a duty of care or protection she owed to Kassidy...* (p. 72-73)

She closed with instructions on the need for unanimity, but with respect for the rights of other jurors' views.

After the instructions, she chose two alternates by drawing paper slips with numbers out of a cup. The jury was dismissed for deliberations at 12:05 p.m.

At 2:09, the jury returned with two Guilty verdicts. Judge Nadeau then, after discussion, said she would schedule a sentencing hearing for about two hours in January. The hearing concluded at 2:11 p.m.

MEDIA:
1. "Bortner defense rests: Mother won't testify"
2. "Bortner silent as child endangerment trial ends"
3. "Borter convicted of child endangerment"
4. "Bortner convicted of child endangerment - sentencing in January for misdemeanors"
5. "Bortner found guilty"

Tuesday, 26 November 2002

The day after the trial's conclusion, Jennifer Saunders wrote for Foster's Daily Democrat,

"Bortner family, prosecution say right decision made". She wrote that,

Chad Evans' brother, Jason Evans, held back tears and gave a statement on behalf of his family. He did not comment on Bortner's guilty conviction, but focused instead on her child. 'We feel deeply for Kassidy... and our thoughts and hearts go out to her,' he said....

The article quoted Amanda as saying, "***The truth will come out,***" and noted that Amanda said she would appeal her conviction.

Allison Vachon, the victim and witness advocate with the Attorney General's office who was assigned to Amanda and the case in 2001, read a statement by members of the Bortner-Conley and Marshall families."... *We first lost Kassidy and then, later, Amanda as well. We really do care for Amanda, but we feel she needs to accept responsibility for her role in Kassidy's death.*" Vachon was in an awkward position, as she was originally assigned to assist Amanda, because if Kassidy truly was a victim of a homicide, then Amanda was the closest surviving family member and the primary surviving victim, unless, of course, she knew about the abuse. However, when Amanda recanted her statements to the police, Vachon shifted her support to the Bortner/Conley family members who supported the police and prosecution's theory of the case.

Jennifer Saunders wrote,

Janis Marshall, who attended the Evans and Bortner trials in support of Kassidy and her son, Jeffe, said she could not endorse the prepared statement by the other family members. "She dragged my son through the mud on unfounded allegations for her own needs. But it's not about Amanda, Chad Evans or what anyone else went through -- including us. It's about Kassidy," she said.

Wednesday, 27 November 2002

The statewide interest in the case continued as Jennifer Saunders wrote, "Child advocacy group applauds Bortner conviction" for Foster's Daily Democrat. Stated Ellen Shemitz, president of the Children's Alliance of New Hampshire,

While we're pleased that Kassidy Bortner's murderer and the mother who refused to protect her will be held accountable for her death, this trial again pointed to the need for New Hampshire's citizens and its state government to be more accountable for the protection of children.

Monday, 2 December 2002

National television began to take an interest in the Kassidy Bortner case, as ABC News broadcast the program, "Is Mom Guilty of Abuse Boyfriend Committed." The program covered two cases, one of which was Amanda's.

The first was about Tabitha Pollock who had served seven years in prison out of a 36 year sentence, for the murder of her three-year old daughter, Jami Sue. The daughter was murdered by Tabitha's boyfriend, Scott English, who was later sentenced to life in prison.

Tabitha was asleep at the time of Jami Sue's murder. According to Tabitha's lawyer, she was convicted not because, *"she knew that her children were being abused, but if she should have known that her children were being abused.*" An appeals court upheld the verdict, and her lawyer resigned. Then Tabitha wrote to the Northwestern University Center for Wrongful Convictions, which is part of the national Innocence Network, together with the New York-based Innocence Project and the New England Innocence Project in Boston.

Said the broadcasts summary, "*They took her case and appealed it to the Illinois Supreme Court. Two months ago, the court overturned her conviction, even though the deadline for an appeal had passed. And, in another rare move, the court ruled the state could not retry her.*" Pollock was released a few days before Christmas, 2002. Then she began to seek to regain custody of her other three children, as the State of Illinois had terminated her parental rights to those children.

Tabitha's attorney, Jane Raley, observed, "*I think society as a general rule, when things go wrong in a family, society always tends to blame the mother.*" The broadcast summary continued,

In Illinois and in many other states, parents can be held legally responsible if they know of threats to their children but do nothing to prevent them. Legal experts say there are hundreds of such cases around the country, but none they know of that involve fathers.

Unlike Amanda's case, there was no indication that Tabitha argued that her former boyfriend was innocent or that she sought to continue her relationship with him after her daughter's death.

The other case of the ABC New program was the Kassidy Bortner case, and Amanda's conviction the previous week. Focusing on the issue of a mother's responsibility to be aware of another's abuse, the broadcast summary stated,

The abuse was only discovered after Bortner took the little girl, Kassidy, to her sister's boyfriend in Maine and asked him to babysit her. That man, Jeffrey Marshall, called 911 after he noticed that the toddler was having trouble breathing. The girl died later that day at a hospital.

Bortner said she would appeal the conviction, but the woman's sister said Bortner needed to accept responsibility for what happened. "I'm just glad Kassidy is finally going to have justice," said Bortner's sister, Jennifer Bortner-Conley.

The broadcast did not state that Jennifer continued to live with Jeff, and that Jeff was the alternate suspect in the case. As neither Chad nor Amanda had testified in their own trials and publicly claimed innocence, the ABC program did not mention the idea that, unlike Tabitha Pollock's case, the abuser and murderer of the mother's children was wrongfully convicted.

There was another difference in the cases, as Scott English had abused Tabitha Pollock's other three children as well, whereas in Chad's case, Dr. Greenwald had testified that it was not unusual for an abuser to abuse only one of several children.

Wednesday, 15 December 2002

Attorney General Philip McLaughlin returned to private practice of law on this day, as Governor-elect Craig Benson considered candidates for his future nomination for the office. Interviewed by the Union Leader, McLaughlin reflected on his term, including the capital punishment and the Kassidy Bortner case, saying,

"....But anger is not a good reason to do the wrong thing."

He said that's the prime emotion every prosecutor feels in a murder case.

Asked if his view of the death penalty has changed in the last five years, he was silent for nearly a full minute before answering.

"I think it has," he said. "What goes unreported in these cases is the incredible visceral anger you go through. Just anger. Anger . . . I've had to discipline myself to not let anger play a role in the decisions of this office, and that's particularly so in regard to the death penalty."

He cited the deaths of children -- 5-year-old Elizabeth Knapp of Hopkinton, raped and murdered in her home; Robbie Mills, 14, of Laconia, killed for a bicycle, and Cassidy

Bortner of Rochester, who died of child abuse -- as deaths that infuriated him and his associates.

"But fury is not a basis for a justice system. Evidence is. Proof is," McLaughlin said.

Tuesday-Thursday, 17-19 December 2002

Amanda and Pam and Jason Evans traveled to New York City by train for a taping session for the John Walsh Show. The session had been scheduled after the show's producer called Chad's family and Amanda. Efforts to include Chad in a remote hookup by phone were not approved by the prison warden.

Pam recalled that during the train ride, she talked with Amanda about her propensity to lie, sometimes when telling the truth would have been easier. It was a problem for Amanda and a big reason for Chad's and her convictions.

Monday, 23 December 2002

Judge Nadeau revoked Amanda's bail and sent her to the Strafford County Jail to await her sentencing hearing, which was coming only 11 days later, on Friday, January 3. Asst. Attorney General Ruoff had requested the revocation after learning that Amanda and Chad had had extensive contact by phone and letters. This contact violated the no contact condition of her bail. An analysis by Sgt. Jim White of recordings of Chad's telephone calls from the New Hampshire State Prison showed 1,587 minutes of calls with Amanda since August, 2002. In addition, there were three hour-long calls since the filing by the state of its revocation motion, including a call on the day of the hearing. Prior to the hearing Jennifer Saunders continued her writing of the story for Foster's Daily Democrat with articles, "State to revoke Bortner bail" and "Phone trail may lead to jail for Bortner".

She reported afterwards in the article, "Bortner gets jail time: Slain tot's mom behind bars after bail violations", that Ruoff had argued to Judge Nadeau, "*There is no doubt that any future contact should be precluded... I would characterize this relationship as dangerous*." The article did not indicate whether Saunders asked Ruoff to be more specific about the alleged danger. Was there any violence during 2001 when Chad and Amanda were seeing each other? Was there any indication in the 1,587 minutes of phone calls of any violence whatsoever? I wasn't there with Amanda and Chad in 2001 and have not listened to any of the 1,587 minutes of recorded conversations, but I have seen many of their hundreds of letters and they show a loving relationship between two people who have suffered a tragic loss and been tragically wronged by their government.

At the revocation hearing, Amanda read a short statement to the judge, apologizing for violating the court's order, but noted that the State had known of her contact with Chad since August. Saunders reported that Amanda said, "*Kassidy was gone, Chad was gone. My family was gone*," and that Chad helped her, "*he gave me a sense of peace*."
Ruoff sought to prevent further contact by Chad's family with Amanda, but Judge Nadeau permitted the family to visit Amanda in jail. The judge said that she would revoke that privilege if she learned that the family was using it to facilitate contact between Amanda and Chad.

Saunders reported that after the hearing,
a friend of the Evans family read a statement in the lobby criticizing the state for seeking to revoke Bortner's bail. She said the family continues to support Evans and that he is innocent. She also alleged the state filed the motion because Bortner is expected to be featured on an upcoming episode of The John Walsh Show.

That "friend" was family friend, Terry Kenny, who went to school with Nicole and Jason in Keene.

Ruoff denied the allegation of retaliation, saying that he only recently learned of the plan for an appearance on the television program.

Saunders reported that Jeff Marshall was at the hearing, and said of Amanda, "*She got what she deserved today*." Marshall's mother was with him, and she agreed.
Judge Nadeau said she would schedule a hearing to consider whether the $5,000 cash bail should be forfeited to the state.

The Portsmouth Herald's story from the Associated Press, "Bortner's calls land her in jail " reported that an Evans family friend *"accused authorities of spending more time trying to catch the couple communicating than investigating Kassidy's death."* This allegation included the investigators' time spent in 2001, which led to the revocation of Chad's bail.

During Amanda's pre-sentencing incarceration in jail, and during her entire upcoming two-year prison term, Amanda received no visits from her immediate family. Chad's family visited her every week, until Amanda was granted work-release privileges and was less isolated in the jail. Chad and Amanda remained in love, and Amanda felt loved in the Evans family.

Thursday, December 26, 2002

Foster's Daily Democrat published its third editorial about the Kassidy Bortner case, "We still weep for Kassidy: There is nothing so brutal as the murder of a child". Here are excerpts:

Amanda Bortner spent Christmas in jail. It is only the beginning of what she deserves....

A man who so abuses a 21-month-old child as to cause her death is little more than a monster. A woman who does not do all she can to protect her child from such abuse is something less than a mother....

Amanda Bortner's illicit telephone conversations with Evans between Aug. 6 and Dec. 12 are inexplicable. Where is there even a hint of reason?...

Chad Evans gave Amanda Bortner "a sense of peace." The man convicted of such terrible crimes as causing her baby's death gave her a "sense of peace."

What form of people are these two? Is it possible justice has gone so awry as to give them any visage of credibility? Juries have said no. What reason is there for anyone to believe otherwise?

Yes, it **was** possible that justice had gone so awry, and the reasons to "*believe otherwise*" were not yet apparent to the courts or to the media, but they are presented in this book and on Chad's website. The "*hint of reason*" comes from love and the goals of truth and justice.

Friday, 3 January 2003

The prosecution's presentation at Amanda's sentencing hearing began with Jeff Marshall who read his statement, presented here in part as he addressed the court and Amanda:

I am tired of your little games and the other family's games. I have had it, and I am not going to take it no more. I am going to be heard. I feel the need to speak out now that the trial has been completed. ... how anyone can still choose the man that killed your daughter over their own flesh and blood is beyond me..... I have been called a lot of things. A big, six-foot-four, 240-pound man with big hands. But I am not a child killer. I despise you and the legal teams that tried to portray me like that. That shows total disrespect for me, and total disrespect for Kassidy. How dare you? And just think, Amanda, you let them disrespect your daughter's name. It doesn't take a rocket scientist to figure out what the two lawyers and you, Amanda, were trying to accuse me of, other than being a murderer....Amanda, if it took them and you having to slander me and my name in order to get the truth, well, it was worth it.... After all, I do not believe you want to see justice for Kassidy. You just want your man. You were not here for her in life, so why should you be here for her in death...And what about the little girl? And God only knows the hell she went through. And you were there and did nothing. ... I am a true believer in karma. What goes around, comes around.....I truly thank God for the truth which Kassidy told us, because I know that you both, you and Chad, tried to set me up. But as I have said, the truth always comes out. I regret and have a lot of guilt that I didn't report things, especially the morning of November 9, 2000. But first and foremost, I regret that I believed all your lies, stories....But unlike you, Amanda, I have taken responsibility for not reporting things....two years is longer than Kassidy's little life. She didn't even get two years....someday, Amanda, you will see Kassidy again. She will look down on you and ask you, "Why did you choose the man who killed me and his money over me?" (pp. 9-13) Jeff's comment about slander, which is oral defamation of character, as compared to libel which is defamation in writing, as an indication of his possible next steps, which included a civil lawsuit for defamation against Chad.

Next was Jeff's mother, Janis Marshall Colby. Attorney Wiberg had objected to her testimony as she was not officially a part of the case and not a member of the victim's family. Wiberg said that Ms. Marshall never had any contact with Kassidy or Amanda.

David Ruoff argued that she was

a very active participant in this case... and was actually part of the investigation. She has been very involved in the prosecution of this case, and has.... been very active in trying to help her son, and coordinating with our office in meetings,... (p. 5)

Curiously, Ms. Marshall was never interviewed by the police. It may be that she never saw Kassidy, or even Amanda, but such non-contact would have been interesting by itself, because she lived only a few miles away. She would have been a good source for background information about Jeff.

Like Jeff, Ms. Marshall addressed Amanda directly as she stated,

.... A mother, a real mother, protects her child from harm....You didn't protect her from harm or endangerment. What you did do, however, was left her in that environment and did absolutely nothing to get her out of there to protect her....On the morning of November 9th, 2000, you drove by three hospitals....What appalls me the most is the fact that you didn't even call that morning to check on her. How sad. Did you kiss her goodbye? Probably not, because you were in a hurry to get to work....I lost a child at the age of 11....I remember the first time I met you, Amanda, at Kassidy's funeral. You made an impression on me I will never forget. I was shocked. There you were, acting like it was a normal day in your life, with your friends watching a video, primping your hair, wondering how you looked, and mainly no true tears....After the funeral, at the cemetery, primping your hair again in the car's side mirror and asking, "Do I look all right? Was I all right? Did I do good?"... You put your sister, Jen, my son, Jeff, and myself through a pure hell... They babysat for you overnight so you could have fun times. They clothed you child. They fed her. They even diapered her, bathed her, cut her nails, and bought her toys. They loved her, and still do....You put my son in a horrible and emotional position on November 9th, and you do owe him an apology for that...I couldn't be at the police station for him. ...you did absolutely nothing, and you alone failed the word, "Mother."...Because you were there, according to the forensics and the timeline, and you know it....We will never really know what happened.... (pp. 13-19)

Ironically, Ms. Marshall referred to "the timeline," but no one had prepared such a timeline.

Next was Jennifer, who also addressed her sister, and stated,

....You knew what was happening to her and never even tried to get her out of that situation... You never loved Kassidy.... What mother would turn her back on her own daughter, even after the man that murdered her was found guilty? ... I would like to know how many times you visited Kassidy since she has died compared to the amount of times you've talked to Chad. It makes me sick that you still talk to that convicted murderer who, quite frankly, has absolutely no respect for the value of human life..... I believe you know exactly what happened to her...You need some help. You need to realize and wake up to the truth. Only then will you start to change your ways, and only then, when you do change, maybe I'll forgive you. I love you and I miss you. But I feel you deserve the maximum punishment for your penalty allowed.... (pp. 19-21)

Kathy Conley Jackson, Amanda's aunt, was last for the prosecution:

Your honor, the last time I spoke in your courtroom, it was to address a stranger whose cold, dark eyes showed no hint of remorse for the horrific crime he'd committed. Today, the defendant is not a stranger. She is my niece, Amanda, and I love her very much... Amanda wasn't always like this... a beautiful young blond mother who allowed her daughter to be brutalized and murdered....I see a beautiful junior bridesmaid walking down the aisle in a red and white dress during her parents' wedding. I see a daredevil flying down the almost bobsled-like track she and her sibling created, along with her dad...And I see Amanda at about five months pregnant, working at a restaurant in Maine...I was convinced that she would beat the odds. She was a goal-oriented achiever with her eyes set on owning a restaurant.... It was clear within months of Kassidy's birth that Mandy really wasn't prepared for the responsibility of parenthood.... So she gave that responsibility to her parents.... Please don't just slap her on the wrist, your honor. Kassidy was slapped enough for both of them....

Then Jackson read from a letter to Amanda from Jacqueline, who who was Jackson's sister-in-law, and Amanda's mother.

Dear Mandy: ... I cannot be there for your sentencing for many reasons, but one of the hardest for me would be seeing my child in prison clothing with handcuffs on....But because you lied and didn't protect our Kassidy, that is why you are in these circumstances today...why did you hide all the bruises from us? ...It made no sense to me, especially when my daughter, who called me practically every day, just disappeared and clung to the man who brutally killed her daughter. ... I remember, after Kassidy died, you stayed in our room, curled up in my bed. You were in a strange trance state. I kept asking you, "What happened?" You repeated, "You don't know, Mom. You just won't understand." Yes, you were right... I don't understand why you still cling to him and his family. He had no regard for Kassidy.... I am haunted by a memory. You called me about a week before Kassidy died. I heard her crying in the background. I asked you, "Is she sick?" You told me she was fine. "Just being a little bitchy." Then you said to me, "I think she misses you, Mom." So I got to talk to Kassidy on the phone. She was crying so hard and fast and kept repeating my name, "Nonna, Nonna." I told her that I loved her, and I missed her, and I'd see her on Sunday. ...I know in my heart, Mandy, that Kassidy wanted to come home to me and her family and to get away from Chad...You talked about leaving Chad on the phone that day. Why didn't you?.... And, Amanda, I want you to know that as long as I live, I will be at every hearing Chad ever has. Every time he tries to get out of his sentence, I will be there, and so will other members of your family, and we will fight to make sure he serves his time....As you are hearing this letter, Josh and I will be at Kassidy's grave, praying to God.... (pp. 21-30)

The "Sunday" that Jacqueline referenced was Sunday, November 5, when she expected that Kassidy would be joining her and Jennifer shopping for the day. Instead, Kassidy went with Chad to his sister's home.

Then, Asst. Attorney General Ruoff argued for the maximum two-year sentence, referring to Amanda's

...absolute refusal from the outset to really accept her position in this, and someone who, as recently as a month ago, was quite adamant about the fact that she is not to blame... at the time Kassidy died, she had two broken arms, a leg that was broken in two places, broken wrist. Bruises over bruises over bruises.... This case has moved just about anybody that has had anything to do with it. Never before has, at least this prosecutor, ever seen the type of public reaction to this type of case...All throughout this case, we have looked for a reason for the defendant's conduct...There's got to be some reason for this. People just don't act like this. Well, this case proves that that point is not true. (pp. 30-37)

The claim of a broken wrist was another example of allegation creep, as there had never been a finding of a broken wrist. Ruoff was actually correct that "*People just don't act like this.*" That is, mothers who have had a child killed by a boyfriend do not continue to voluntarily stay loyal to, and love, that boyfriend. He was wrong to say that this case proves "*that point is not true.*" Here, the exception does not prove the rule. This was not an exception to the rule, or common understanding. He could not even grant Amanda the respect of understanding that she may have believed in Chad's innocence, even if the State's prosecutors thought they knew otherwise, i.e. that Chad was the killer of Kassidy. He was stuck, too, for if he conceded that Amanda believed that Chad didn't kill Kassidy, then she would not be guilty of the two charges of Child Endangerment.

Then, supporters of Amanda took their turn. Terry Kenny spoke first, saying she was

here today for the unconditional love and support of Amanda Bortner, a young lady who has suffered a horrific loss in her life... We as a society are often quick to judge others. I do believe Amanda offered Kassidy what mothering skills she knew. (pp. 37-38)
Mandy Allard said that she had known Amanda for about two years and had lived with her the past six months. She said:

Amanda has suffered many losses over the last two years. Her family, the man she loves with all her heart, and most importantly, her beautiful baby girl, Kassidy.... She had had to overcome many obstacles in her life: Her terrible childhood, her family abandoning her at her time of need...I have seen her cry many times over the terrific losses in her life....She has found Christ, and it has brought her a new peace in her life. ... I pray it is taken into consideration all she is going through and all she will continue to go through. We will always be there for her, by her side, to love and support her. (p. 40-41)
Then Amanda spoke:

Your Honor, I miss Kassidy so much that words cannot describe it. And I realize that I can't change the past. If I could, believe me, I would. I would certainly have made different choices, and Kassidy and I would be outside sledding right now...One of the hardest things for me since the facts surrounding Kassidy's death have been told to me is knowing that she had to be in such terrible pain, and that I, being so young, naive and stupid, whatever you want to call it, wasn't able to realize it and help her. I think about how scared and defenseless she must have felt as she was repeatedly injured by people I trusted to take care of her in my absence?... Believe me, there is really no sentence that can be imposed that will be more punitive than what I am already serving.... (p. 41-43)
Amanda was vague about whom she meant by the phrase, "*people I trusted to take care of her.*" She, like Chad in his pre-sentencing statement, didn't want to anger Judge Nadeau by openly declaring that she was innocent and that Chad was innocent, too. Neither did she want to openly charge Jeff, as she had done on the John Walsh Show.
Patricia Wiberg then asked for leniency for Amanda:

... Your Honor, Amanda has accepted responsibility for Kassidy's death from day one...the fact that she failed Kassidy...a few nights before Kassidy's death, when Kassidy was falling asleep, she saw her eyes do something weird, and then she just thought it was a baby's eyes rolling back...we'd ask that on the first count, ... that Amanda be sentenced for 12 months, House of Corrections, all but three months suspended,.... work release, one year of probation upon release and counseling. On the second charge... all suspended....there are a number of issues she has to deal with... her childhood, the fact that she herself was a victim....since the December after Kassidy died... she has consistently gone back to a local church and become a member of the congregation... She has joined a group called "The Parents of Murdered Children"...the publicity generated by this case has been profound. There has been so much of it all over the State, and I think, sometimes even nationally, but particularly in New England....Her demeanor throughout the trial...has been a subject of much discussion, both in the courtroom here today, during the trial, during the bail hearings, in the media. But these are snips of Amanda's demeanor. No one sees her at home when she is crying, or when she is looking a pictures of Kassidy, or when she is up at the grave site when she is ... home sleeping with ... Teletubby....that was Kassidy's. That's all private. And grief is private. And everyone does it differently. And because she happened to be smiling at one point or another, or flicking her hair back... that doesn't mean that she doesn't care about Kassidy or that she didn't love her..... ask that the court take all of that into consideration as well as the information contained in the letters.... seven of them... (p. 43-49)
Attorney Wiberg showed in her statement that she, too, knew of photographs of Kassidy, but the only photograph of a healthy Kassidy that was shown in Amanda's trial was the same October 1 photo that was Exhibit 19 at Chad's trial.

Ruoff then answered with two points,
...the fact that she has lost her child, I don't think should be considered as a reason for granting leniency.... Secondly, ...I have the WNDS tape... in which she says the police coerced... She specificially names others and denies her accountability. (p. 49)
Judge Nadeau then asked Amanda to stand and then addressed the audience and Amanda,

...I have no doubt about the defendant's love for her daughter or her sincere expression of the grief that she shows for her loss...that jury... found that she behaved in such a way that allowed Chad Evans to kill her daughter... In my view, the defendant is fortunate not to have been charged with accomplice to second-degree murder. Kassidy's death was something the defendant could have, but more importantly was morally obligated to prevent, but she did nothing. Worse, she took affirmative steps to cover up the abuse, and it was that abuse that ultimately led to Kassidy's death. To say that the defendant had a legal duty under the Criminal Code to protect her daughter is nothing compared to the moral obligation that she owed to ensure that Kassidy was nurtured and safe. And although Ms. Bortner was clearly aware of the extent and severity of the injuries that Evans inflicted on a regular basis and over a period of months, she failed to bring Kassidy to the doctor. She prevented family and friends from seeing Kassidy, and she conspired with Chad Evans to lie about Kassidy's bruises.... This is a case where Evans inflicted a pattern of consistent abuse over a period of months, abuse that the defendant regularly witnessed and chose to ignore....the defendant chose loyalty for Evans over saving her daughter.... Ms. Bortner, I hope that someday you will be willing and you will be able to acknowledge for yourself that Chad Evans killed Kassidy, because only then will you be able to heal.... I have read the pre-sentence investigation report...I must depart from the six-month sentence he believes appropriate... I have watched the defendant's behavior over the past two years for myself in this courtroom... the defendant is able to manipulate as well as to endear, to distort facts as well as speak genuinely....I hereby sentence you to two one-year consecutive sentences in the House of Corrections... pre-trial confinement credit of 13 days.... (pp. 49-55)

Judge Nadeau made several statements of fact about Amanda's actions or inaction which the judge believed, but which were false, or partially false. The judge, too, was a victim of the mis-directed police investigation and the prosecutors' and defense attorneys' mistakes and the inherent limits on the justice system to pursue truth. Below are listed, with comments, several of Judge Nadeau's statements about Amanda which brought her to sentence her to the maximum two consecutive years:

- she *behaved in such a way that allowed Chad Evans to kill her daughter*
  Amanda loved Chad and moved to live with him out of that love and also because she felt it was best for Kassidy to have such a man as a father figure, and potential future stepfather. Chad did not kill Kassidy. He never hit nor spanked her.
- [She] *was morally obligated to prevent* [Kassidy's death], *but she did nothing.*

Amanda gave Kassidy Pedialyte when she came home dehydrated on Saturday, October 28. She gave Kassidy Tylenol on the morning of November 9. She enlisted babysitting for Kassidy, not with untrustworthy or unreliable people, but with her sister and her boyfriend. She did not know that Kassidy was seriously ill or at risk.

- [She had a] *moral obligation that she owed to ensure that Kassidy was nurtured and safe.*

Amanda had enrolled in the ASPIRE program to enable her to get more education so could escape the bounds of being an unmarried teenage mother, so she could do more for Kassidy. She had found for Kassidy a loving home, and was teaching her to speak and count and, yes, she believed that more discipline was needed so that Kassidy learned, in the words of the Rolling Stones, "*You can't always get what you want.*" Amanda was looking for day care for Kassidy where she could learn and be more sociable with other children in a safe environment.

- *she took affirmative steps to cover up the abuse, and it was that abuse that ultimately led to Kassidy's death.*

Amanda utilized her sister, Jennifer, and her boyfriend, Jeff, to babysit Kassidy. They offered to help, and the cost was low. Jeff and Jennifer used makeup to hide bruises on one or two occasions. Amanda never used makeup to cover bruises. Amanda had no knowledge of any abuse that put Kassidy at risk of her life.

- [She] *was clearly aware of the extent and severity of the injuries that Evans inflicted on a regular basis and over a period of months.*

Amanda was aware of the minimal bruising caused on a few occasions by Chad's holding Kassidy's face to obtain eye contact, but those were not the injuries that Judge Nadeau had in mind. Amanda was not aware of Chad's harming Kassidy in any other way, and she understood correctly that Chad was seeking to nurture and love Kassidy and certainly not to harm or hurt her. Amanda and Chad thought they understood the causes of every other bruise or injury they knew about, and they both misunderstood the severity of those injuries.

o *she failed to bring Kassidy to the doctor.*

Amanda brought Kassidy to see doctors on August 10 and September 11, and a 24-month checkup was scheduled for February 2001. Not by appointment, but an elementary school nurse saw Kassidy, socially, on Sunday, November 5, and saw no cause for concern.

o *She prevented family and friends from seeing Kassidy,*

Amanda took Kassidy to see friends on October 13-15 (instead of being with Chad's parents and Chad's to-be-ex-wife), and took her to Olympia Sports with Melissa Chick "*before Halloween,*" and to a restaurant with Bruce, Chad and Travis on November 4th, and made plans with her mother to care for Kassidy over the upcoming weekend of November 10-12, 2000. Chad took Kassidy to a gathering of his sister's family and friends on November 5.

o *she conspired with Chad Evans to lie about Kassidy's bruises.*

Amanda and Chad decided on a "white lie" about the eye contact bruises he caused on three occasions. Amanda did not lie to the police about those bruises, and those bruises had absolutely nothing to do with Kassidy's death. Neither Chad nor Amanda lied to anyone about the many other bruises or injuries.

o [She] *regularly witnessed and chose to ignore.... a pattern of consistent abuse over a period of months*

Amanda did not see any actions by Chad which she considered abuse. Regarding the eye contact bruises, Amanda and Chad thought that Kassidy bruised easily, and Chad resolved not to squeeze Kassidy's cheeks so hard. Amanda did speak to Chad about playing too roughly with Kassidy, and she spoke to Jeff about not spanking Kassidy, and about the floor nails in his home. In hindsight, she didn't do enough and wasn't sufficiently aware of what was happening to Kassidy, but she didn't ignore it. Nobody understood what was happening to Kassidy.

o [She] *chose loyalty for Evans over saving her daughter.*

Amanda never felt this was a choice, as she loved both Kassidy and Chad, and Chad loved both Amanda and Kassidy. If Amanda had felt that Chad was abusing Kassidy, she would have left Chad in a second.

o [She] *is able to manipulate as well as to endear,*

Everyone does this.

o [she is able] *to distort facts as well as speak genuinely.*

Everyone does this.

Amanda Bortner would turn 21 years old in jail later that month, January, and finally pass that legal milestone where she could drink alcohol, but that would have to wait for her release in two years. She had been a mother, and lost her daughter, and been told by the State of New Hampshire that her lover had murdered that daughter, and then found her guilty of knowing about the alleged abuse and doing nothing. All this came before the time when she could legally purchase a beer or wine.

The Foster's Daily Democrat story, by Holly Ramer of the Associated Press, summarized the story of the sentencing hearing, "Bortner gets maximum 2-year sentence in baby's death"

Jennifer Saunders wrote a followup story to the trial and sentencing, "Amanda Bortner's family reacts to ordeal" Jennifer Bortner was quoted, "*You don't put up with a man who kills your baby,....She turned her back on her family, we did not turn our backs on her. She turned her back on Kassidy... I think maybe Chad's holding something over her,...*"

Jennifer, and other members of the Bortner family, did not visit Amanda during her time in jail, despite Amanda's efforts to reach out to them.

The article stated that Jeff agreed that Amanda deserved the maximum sentence, and said, *I can't really find sorrow for Mandy under the circumstances,...considering her behavior and everything. I mean, our not saying or seeing certain things, that was bad enough - but she was there. I think it (her sentence) should be longer because I truly believe she knows what happened.*

Kassidy Bortner died on November 9, 2000. Now, on January 3, 2003, the criminal justice system had completed its work by the judgments against Chad and Amanda. Coming ahead were appeals by both Chad and Amanda, although in the minds of most people in New Hampshire, justice had been accomplished. But it hadn't. There was much more to this case than most people knew, including the police and prosecutors.

CHAPTER 11: APPEALS, PRISON, AND NEW HAMPSHIRE "KASSIDY BORTNER LAW" - 2003 TO THE PRESENT

"What kind of a monster do people think I am?" - Chad Evans

"I don't think there is anything worse in life than being accused of things we don't do." - Stephen Brown

Monday, 13 January 2003

The New Hampshire Kassidy Bortner Child Protection Accountability Act was presented at a press conference at 10:30 a.m. Stephen Frothingham's Associated Press article, "Kassidy Bortner Act would reform state agency" was published in Foster's Daily Democrat, and began, "*The death of Kassidy Bortner, a toddler murdered by her mother's boyfriend two years ago, has prodded lawmakers to try to reform the state division that investigates child abuse....*" Kassidy had literally become the poster child for the cause of preventing child abuse in New Hampshire, and the photograph used for the campaign was the December 1999 studio photo which Amanda had arranged. The October 1, 2000 photo of a happy, bruise-free Kassidy during the alleged months of abuse by Chad was not used. Did someone finally realize the conflict between the October 1 photo and Chad's conviction? If so, the answer was simply to use a different photo, rather than to seek justice.

Jacqueline Conley, identified in the article as Jacqueline Bortner, came from Maine to support the bill. She said, "*No case worker ever came to see her swollen face, her broken bones, or the bruises that covered her body... I found out during Chad Evans' murder trial that at least a dozen people thought Kassidy was being abused.*" Jennifer was also at the press conference.

The bill, sponsored by Senator Andre Martel of Manchester, required that DCYF hire more staff in order to meet accreditation standards and that it be required "*to reveal, after the fact, what it knew of child abuse cases that led to death or serious inquiries.*" This provision responded to the long delay of the DCYF admission that it had been contacted about Kassidy 10 days before her death.

Jennifer Saunders' front page Foster's Daily Democrat story, "Kassidy's death spurs reforms - N.H. bill would hold child agency accountable", included her photograph of Jacqueline Conley with four television microphones close by. She reported that the proposed bill began with a preamble:

The 21-month-old child died on Nov. 9, 2000, after being struck in her head eight to ten times and punched or kicked in her abdomen at least twice.... Although the ultimate responsibility for Kassidy's death lies with her convicted murderer, the General Court finds that her death also reveals the inability of the Division for Children, Youth and Families to meet it General Court-mandated responsibility..."

As reported in a previous article, "N.H. eyes Kassidy Law," the proposal was prepared during a one-year process,

by the Child Protection Task Force, a coalition that includes the Children's Alliance of New Hampshire, Child and Family Services, Court-Appointed Special Advocates and Prevent Child Abuse New Hampshire.

The article said that the proposed bill was

the second to be inspired by Kassidy's death. Rep. Robert Ouellette, R-Franklin, sponsored a bill to make child endangerment a felony instead of a misdemeanor when serious injuries or death result...

Support for the new law was quickly established. In a previous Foster's Daily Democrat article, "Amanda Bortner's family reacts to ordeal", Jennifer Saunders reported that Sgt. Stephen Burke of the Rochester Police Dept, "*began seeking legislators to support such a change after he learned the facts of Kassidy's case...*"

The Portsmouth Herald published an editorial about the case and the proposed law, "Bortner bill no substitute for personal involvement" As often happened in the retelling of this story, the details became more exaggerated. The editorial transformed Jacqueline's statement, "*I found out during Chad Evans' murder trial that at least a dozen people thought Kassidy* ***was being abused***" into "*she learned at least a dozen people suspected that her granddaughter* ***was being repeatedly beaten by Evans.***" (emphasis added)

Also on January 13, Douglas Penney of the New Hampshire "Office of Cost Containment" wrote a letter to Chad in prison saying that he must pay for legal expenses and the unpaid balance was $1,350. "Upon your release you must contact this office to discuss your intentions for settling this matter." (underline in original).

Wednesday 22 January 2003

Amanda Bortner appeared on the "John Walsh Show" on national television. The theme of the program was "A mother's responsibility" and the Amanda Bortner/Kassidy case was one of the two featured cases.

Foster's Daily Democrat announced the scheduled program locally on January 21, with Jennifer Saunders' article, "Bortner to appear on television talk show." The article began,

A Rochester woman convicted of failing to protect her young daughter from the abuse that claimed her life is taking her story to the jury of public opinion on a national daytime talk show this week."

Unfortunately, the "*jury of public opinion*" was not courted by Chad or Amanda during the investigation of Kassidy's death and their trials.

On the 22nd, the Portsmouth Herald also covered the story, as Amy Wallace wrote, "Bortner to tell her story on national TV." She wrote,

Amanda Bortner, who was held accountable for the fatal abuse of her 21-month-old daughter, will tell her story today on "The John Walsh Show."

John Walsh, who is well-known for his work as the host of "America's Most Wanted," will explore whether Bortner should be blamed for her daughter Kassidy's death if someone else actually inflicted the abuse. The segment will air at 9 a.m. on WMUR-Channel 9 and WCVB-Channel 5....

Bortner has said she had feelings of guilt, loss and failure, and said she should have taken steps to save her little girl from the ongoing abuse that ultimately caused her death.

However, she later recanted statements she had made to police about Evans in the hours after Kassidy died. Instead, she and Evans accused the baby sitter of inflicting abuse on Kassidy.

A producer from "The John Walsh Show" said the segment was taped in December before Bortner was sentenced.

According to the show's Web site, Walsh will also hear from Pam Evans, Chad Evans' mother. She has been quiet about her son's conviction and has stood by Bortner....

Pam Evans was in the audience when she was interviewed by John Walsh, and Jason Evans was there as well.

On the program, Amanda assertively defended her own and Chad's innocence. See the transcript of the portion of the show devoted to Kassidy Bortner. (Also click to listen to the audiotape (wma format)). The program was taped on December 18, 2002. Here is the last exchange between John Walsh and Amanda.

Walsh *I don't know if I would buy those excuses, whether it was the carpet tacks or not. I wouldn't take my 21-month old little girl back to the same guy for any reason. I don't care if it was my brother. I wouldn't take her back there.*

Amanda *I have to live with that for the rest of my life.*

Jennifer Saunders wrote the January 23 Foster's Daily Democrat article, "Bortner still blames baby sitter - AG calls interview 'totally untrue',"

"*Bortner told Walsh she was wrongfully convicted on two counts of endangering the welfare of a child and her boyfriend, Chad E. Evans, was wrongfully convicted of beating the toddler to death....*

... Assistant Attorney General David Ruoff said Bortner's claims are totally untrue -- and chided the John Walsh Show for not taking the time to research the case....

He said it was unfortunate the show did not focus on the details of the investigation...

including the medical evidence that at the time of her death, the toddler had five fractures of varied ages, one in each arm, two in one leg and one in her hand....

She had bruises over bruises at the time of death. That's all physical evidence of abuse," Ruoff said....

In a strictly legal sense, Amanda was correct, as there was no physical evidence linking Chad to Kassidy's death. Even if Ruoff's claim of fractures was correct, there was no physical evidence linking Chad to those fractures. Some or most of the bruises he mentioned may have been evidence of abuse, but there was no physical evidence connection to Chad. Many of the bruises were correctly attributed to accidents.

The Union Leader covered the broadcast story with the Associated Press article, "Bortner guest on national TV show." and it included Amanda's explanation for her statements to the police, "*I was interrogated for a really long time and just started agreeing with the investigators,... I just wanted to get out of there*."

Foster's Daily Democrat published an editorial the next day, January 24, "EDITORIAL - Amanda Bortner is still guilty of not caring enough - Walsh show was cheap exploitation of Kassidy's death" The paper stated,

Amanda Bortner still doesn't get it. A jury of 12 men and women found her guilty of endangering the welfare of her defenseless 21-month-old child....

Daytime television is designed to sell soap. If they have any social value, it is allowing some of us a better look at the intellectual poverty of some of the participants and producers of the shows....

As for Amanda Bortner and Chad Evans - they received a small measure of what they deserved.

The newspaper's charge against another mass medium was a bit like the pot calling the kettle black. Had not Foster's Daily Democrat exploited the story to sell newspapers?

Thursday, 29 January 2003

The House Criminal Justice and Public Safety Committee held a hearing on the levels of criminal penalties, and two of the jurors at Amanda Bortner's trial spoke. The Union Leader published the Associated Press article by Stephen Frothingham, "Bortner jurors urge stiffer penalties" The same article was published in the Portsmouth Herald, as "Images of toddler haunt two jurors." Below are excerpts from the article...

CONCORD -- The night after a medical examiner showed jurors how 21-month-old Kassidy Bortner died at the hands of her mother's boyfriend, juror Rosemary McDonald broke out in hives and couldn't fall asleep.

A week later, after what she described as "about five minutes" of deliberations, the jury found Kassidy's mother, Amanda, guilty of two counts of child endangerment, for which Bortner was given the maximum sentence: two years in county jail. With good behavior she could serve as little as 16 months.

Yesterday, McDonald and another juror urged lawmakers to stiffen the penalty for child endangerment.

"The vivid pictures of Kassidy, who was used as a human football, flash before me in a never-ending nightmare," McDonald, a former teacher, told the House Criminal Justice and Public Safety Committee.

"How could this crime possibly be a misdemeanor?"

McDonald read testimony from another juror, Leo Callahan of Dover, who wrote that Kassidy's death still makes him weep.

"This woman stood by and allowed her daughter to be murdered," Callahan wrote. "This woman who calls herself a mother deserves to remain behind bars for far more than two years."

Tuesday, 4 February 2003

On this day, Kassidy would have been four years old. Ironically, Amanda Bortner was assaulted by another inmate on this day in the Strafford County Jail. The Dover police chief, William Fenniman, "*said that the assault caused severe bruises to Bortner's face and legs. Fenniman said that he did not believe that Bortner had to be treated by a physician*." ("Fellow Inmate assaults Bortner," Foster's Daily Democrat, by Petra Linnehan.

Thursday, 8 February 2003

On the same day as the article about the assault on Amanda, Foster's Daily Democrat published the most supportive article in the entire case, to date. Supportive, that is, of Chad and Amanda. Written by Ray Carbone, the article, "Slain tot's mom: 'Not my fault' ," was based on an interview with Amanda in the Strafford County Jail. Below are excerpts from the article...

DOVER - Amanda Bortner doesn't look the same.

The woman at the center of one of New Hampshire's most infamous child abuse cases is no longer perfectly made up....

There's a slight mark on Bortner's cheek which she says is the result of a scuffle with another woman at the jail Tuesday - the day that would have been Kassidy's fourth birthday....

After weeks in jail, she maintains that she and Evans have been unfairly treated by the New Hampshire justice system...

...Bortner said "Kassidy is the victim. But I do feel that the system has screwed me over big time. And Chad also. Because they did a horrible investigation... And I feel that Kassidy is a victim in that way as well."...

On Friday, New Hampshire Assistant Attorney General Will Delker disagreed with Bortner's assessment of the police work concerning the baby's death.

"This was one of the most professional investigations I've ever seen," Delker said. "All the points of this case were played out in two separate trials and the juries unaminously agreed twice that (the baby-sitter) wasn't responsible for Kassidy's death."... Bortner says she fills her time now by attending three Bible studies every week, and by studying law books. The law books, she says, will come in handy when's she's released in 16 months on condition of good behavior, and seeks to clear her name, as well as Evans.

Tuesday, 1 April 2003

On behalf of Chad, David Rothstein, the New Hampshire Deputy Chief Appellate Defender filed the appeal brief with the New Hampshire State Court. The brief asked the Court to reverse Chad's conviction because of two errors at the trial:

1. *The Trial Court erred when it gave a "False Exculpatory Evidence" instruction that was applicable to statements made by Chad Evans, but not by Jefferey Marshall*
2. *The State failed to exclude the rational conclusion that Jefferey Marshall killed Kassidy Bortner.*

As noted in Chapter 8, the "false exculpatory evidence" part of Judge Nadeau's instructions to the jury was:

Evidence has been introduced regarding statements the defendant offered to explain certain bruising on Kassidy. If you find the defendant intentionally made statements tending to demonstrate his innocence, or to influence a witness, and that the statements are later discovered to be false, then you may consider whether the statements show a consciousness of guilt, and determine what significance, if any, to give to such evidence.

Chad's appellate attorney, Public Defender David Rothstein, argued that

While it was appropriate for the State to argue an adverse inference from the defendant's false, exculpatory statements, an instruction on the matter unnecessarily and improperly highlighted this evidence. As applied to this case, an instruction that the jury may consider the evidence as it related to Evans, without a similar instruction regarding statements made by Marshall, engendered special prejudice, by implying to the jury that the defense could not use this same type of evidence to attack Marshall's credibility. As a result of the trial court's error, Evans is entitled to a new trial.

The two major statements made by Chad in his police interrogation, that were challenged by the prosecution were the "trampoline story" and the ballhitting incident. If Chad had testified, he would have been able to provide details about the ballhitting incident. Also, he would have acknowledged that the "trampoline story," though based partially on a real event, was a false explanation for the bruises he caused by squeezing Kassidy's face to obtain **eye contact**. He told his lawyers it was false and Amanda told the police it was false. He should not have repeated the story to the police in his interrogation, but he did so because Chad knew that he had never hit nor spanked Kassidy. Chad also knew the face palming bruises he caused had nothing to do with Kassidy's death. Also, Chad assumed that Amanda was telling the same story.

The primary problem with a "false exculpatory statement" jury instruction with respect to the "trampoline story" is that the story, and the bruises that it purported to explain, had absolutely nothing to do with Kassidy's death. She did not die from the bruising at her lower chin. It is true, however, that the "false exculpatory statement" had a lot to do with the six Second Degree Assault charges. By not testifying, Chad allowed the jury to hear his only words about the bruises he caused. Those words were to tell the "trampoline story" and later when he said he did not know what caused other bruises on Kassidy's cheeks, about which he had told the police.

Of the 100 bruises and injuries that Dr. Greenwald pointed out, only two or three could have been attributed to Chad's **eye contact** holding of Kassidy's face. Unfortunately, the jury saw all of the bruises on photographs and Dr. Greenwald told the jury about all of them, but the six charges of Second Degree Assault were only about the bruises caused by Chad's **eye contact** holding of Kassidy's face. Chad estimates that he causes bruising only about three times, of the 12 or more **eye contact** holdings of Kassidy's face.

Rothstein argued first that the instruction to the jury about "false exculpatory evidence" should not have been given at all in this case because such an instruction draws unfair attention by the judge to the allegedly false statements. By giving the "false exculpatory evidence" instruction, Judge Nadeau called the jury's attention to the false explanation for the bruising relating to the six Second Degree Assault charges. Then, relying upon that same instruction, the jury was able to draw inferences about Chad's consciousness of guilt for the murder charge, even though the cheek bruises and the explanatory "trampoline story" had nothing to do with Kassidy's death. It was a dangerous example of judicial leverage.

Rothstein then argued that several of Jeff's statements were possibly false, such as the statement about the nails in his home possibly being the cause of the abrasions on Kassidy's feet. Rothstein then argued that it was "fundamentally unfair" in Chad's case, where Marshall was the alternate suspect, to give the jury the "false exculpatory evidence" instruction with respect to Chad, but not also with respect to Jeff.

The Appellate Brief then addressed the second claim, that "*The State failed to exclude the rational conclusion that Jefferey Marshall killed Kassidy Bortner.*" The argument was summarized in an opinion from a 2001 New Hampshire Supreme Court case, State v. Dugas, where the court stated,

In an appeal challenging the sufficiency of the evidence, the defendant carries the burden of proving that no rational trier of fact, viewing the evidence in the light most favorable to the State, could have found guilt beyond a reasonable doubt... When the evidence presented is circumstantial, it must exclude all rational conclusions except guilt in order to be sufficient to convict.

Rothstein argued that on the basis of the evidence presented at Chad's trial, it was a rational option to conclude that Jeff killed Kassidy. First, she died at his home after being there for four hours, and she was there the day before for about two and one-half hours. Second, Kasssidy's pajama bottoms were removed from Kassidy, and neither Jeff nor Jennifer could explain how or when they were removed. Third, both of the pathologists at the trial said that the blows that killed Kassidy could have come while she was at Jeff's.

These two arguments, jury instruction regarding "false exculpatory evidence" and the rational option that Jeff killed Kassidy, constituted Chad's entire appeal. There was no argument about the jury verdict because no new evidence was presented, unlike what's been presented in this book. If there had been new evidence at the time of the appeal, the proper relief would have been sought with a Motion for New Trial based on new evidence.

Thus, there was no argument that Chad was actually innocent of the charges. It's a curious result of the legal rules that an innocent man can be wrongly convicted, but his appeal need not mention that innocence. In a sense, it's not relevant. Instead, Rothstein was restricted to arguing that there was legal error at the trial, regardless of whether Chad was guilty or not. The judicial rationale for such appeals is that not only must the system find guilty people guilty, it must also find that guilt according to the judicial rules. If there is a legal error and the trial verdict is overturned, then the prosecution can either request a new trial or abandon the case.

The two sides argued the appeal before the Supreme Court judges on November 6, 2003,.Will Delker did the oral argument and he and Simon Brown wrote the brief.

Tuesday, 15 April 2003

The House Committee Children and Family Law Committee held a hearing on the Kassidy Bortner Bill. Warren Hastings wrote the article for the Union Leader, "Lawmakers mull informing public on child abuse cases" The article stated that the committee

considered Senate Bill 86, designed to provide the public limited information on fatal or near fatal child abuse incidents and how they are being handled by the Department of Children Youth and Families,...

Bortner's mother, Jacqueline Bortner of Bryant Pond, Maine, asked the committee to support the bill because it might save other mothers and grandmothers the heartbreak she experienced upon learning of the death of her grandchild....

Friday, 18 April 2003

A few days later, Trooper Jill Rockey was honored by the Rockingham County Attorney for her work on behalf of victim's rights. The event was reported in Lara Bricker's article, "Honored trooper takes one for her advocates team," in the Exeter News-Letter. The article reflected the high visibility of the Kassidy Bortner case,

"I'll never forget that case," Rockey said.

As one of a large team of police investigating the case, Rockey was able to cope with the horrific details uncovered in the investigation by talking with the other investigators.

The hardest part of the case was learning that people around Kassidy suspected she was being beaten and didn't report anything to police.

With Kassidy dead, the investigators saw their job as bringing what happened to the young girl to light.

Friday, 29 August 2003

The 'Bortner Bill' became law in New Hampshire, as Chapter 206 of the laws of 2003. The July 23 Union Leader carried the AP story, Benson signs 'Bortner bill', by Norma Love, about the signing of the new law by Governor Benson. Wrote Love, "*Supporters call the law the "Bortner bill" after Kassidy Bortner, who died of child abuse. ...*"
On April 29, 2008, Norma Love, wrote a followup article, which was published in the Concord Monitor, "Child Advocates Laud State for Abuse Policy" where it was noted that, "*So far, the New Hampshire law inspired by Kassidy's death has not been used. 'There haven't been child deaths that fit within this circumstance,' said Associate Health and Human Services Commissioner Nancy Rollins.*" In doing the research for this book, I invoked the "Kassidy Bortner Law" in order to obtain DHHS records about Kassidy.

6 November 2003

The New Hampshire Supreme Court heard the oral arguments of David Rothstein for Chad and Will Delker for the State of New Hampshrie in Chad's appeal of his conviction. The Union Leader covered the story with an Associated Press article, "Evans appeals guilty verdict in beating death of Kassidy Bortner" The article stated,
Evans' lawyer, David Rothstein, said the conviction should be overturned because the jury was instructed to consider false statements Evans made to police. Rothstein said the jury should have considered similar statements made by Jefferey Marshall, who was caring for

Kassidy at the time of her death....

Prosecutor William Delker said there was never any evidence Marshall lied in any of his statements. However, there were recollections of events and statements that differed from Jeff's.

Friday, 5 December 2003

In the case "Petititon of the State of New Hampshire," the New Hampshire Supreme Court reversed the Sentence Review Board's decision not to consider the Attorney General's petition to review Chad's sentence. Chad's case was combined with the cases of two other defendants, as the Attorney General argued that the Sentence Review Board did not have the authority to decline to hear the State's request for increases in their sentences. The court stated, "*We conclude that the division exceeded its jurisdiction when it ruled that granting the State's petition would violate the defendants' due process rights and, therefore, we vacate the division's order. Thus, the due process issue is not properly before us and we decline to address it on the merits.*" Then, the State's request to increase Chad's sentence went back to the Sentence Review Board, to be heard and decided upon the merits.

Tuesday, 30 December 2003

The New Hampshire Supreme Court issued its decision denying Chad's appeal completely. The court ruled that Jeff's general denials of the defense claim of responsibility did not warrant a "false exculpatory evidence" instruction to the jury. Chief Justice Brock wrote the opinion for the court, which concluded,

Viewing the jury instructions as a whole, we cannot say that the jury was incapable of evaluating the defendant's theory of the case absent a false exculpatory statement instruction that pertained to Marshall.

The court addressed the evidence supporting Chad's guilt and concluded that,

Viewing all of the evidence in the light most favorable to the State, we hold it was sufficient for the jury to exclude all rational conclusions except that the defendant was guilty.

Unfortunately, the jury was offered only one rational alternative to Chad's guilt, which was that Jeff Marshall murdered Kassidy. There was some evidence of accidents to Kassidy, but minimal argument was made that these accidents played a substantial role in Kassidy's death. There was no presentation of a rational alternative of disease or chronic condition or toxin. The New Hampshire Supreme Court reaffirmed this view of circumstantial cases in 2009 in State vs. Joshua Shepard. He had been found guilty of negligent homicide, but when reversing his convictions, the court found that other rational explanations for the three vehicular deaths that he caused had not been excluded.

The court also addressed another issue which Chad raised in his own pro se brief to the court, which was that it was an error for Judge Nadeau to allow into evidence Tracey Foley's recollection of Amanda's statement to her on Thursday, November 16, "*And you knew, and I didn't listen.*" The Supreme Court said that Judge Nadeau's decision was "*a sustainable exercise of discretion.*" The Court said that Chad raised several other issues but that it would not rule on them because they were "*not raised in the appeal, and we did not grant permission to brief them.*"

Because the Court relied entirely upon the trial transcript and upon the appellate briefs it did not address any of the information and arguments in this book about Chad's and Amanda's innocence.

The court began its decision with the statement "*The jury **could have found** the following facts.*" (emphasis added) Those "*facts*" are presented below, and each of them is accompanied by one of the four evaluations for truthfulness or accuracy as used in Chapter 8 to evaluate the prosecution's closing statement: TRUE (>90% true), M-TRUE (Mostly True, 50-90% true) and M-FALSE (Mostly False, 10-50% true) and FALSE (<10% true).

TRUE 1. *Amanda and the defendant began dating in June 2000.*

TRUE 2. *A month later, she and Kassidy moved into the defendant's Rochester home.*

M-FALSE 3. *Shortly thereafter, bruises started appearing on Kassidy.* The first bruises corroborated by more than one person appeared around Friday, October 13. Kassidy was free of bruises on several key days in the early fall, including doctor appts. Aug. 10 and Sept. 11 and visits to her grandmother Jacqueline on September 2 and late September through October 1.

M-FALSE 4. *These bruises were caused by the defendant.* Throughout Kassidy's shared life with Chad, most of her bruises had nothing to do with Chad.

M-FALSE 5. *At first, the defendant bruised Kassidy only occasionally by forcibly grabbing her face out of frustration because Kassidy became jealous when Amanda was affectionate towards him.* Chad held Kassidy's face to ensure **eye contact**, and not to punish or to inflict pain.

M-FALSE 6. *As time went on, his frustration with Kassidy grew.* Kassidy's jealousy of possessiveness for her mother subsided in late summer, but seemed to return in October. This issue was only one of several reasons to seek eye contact with Kassidy, some of them non-disciplinary.

M-FALSE 7. *In the month before she died, the defendant grabbed Kassidy's face hard as often as twice a week.* While Chad may have held Kassidy's face as often as twice a week, it was hard enough to cause bruising only three or four times during October..

M-FALSE 8. *He called her names such as "little bitch" and "f---ing retard."* Chad never called Kassidy a "*f--ing retard.*" Sometimes, he used profane words affectionately as on November 9, when he observed her opening her baggie and eating Reese's Puffs and said *"You little shit, I didn't know you could open these."* Another use of a similar word would have been when he said that "*Kassidy's acting bitchy*," but not to call her names.

M-FALSE 9. *As frequently as three times a week, the defendant disciplined Kassidy by picking her up by the armpits and roughly placing her in front of a wall or in a corner.* Subject to the interpretation of "roughly placing," this happened once or twice during the two month period of September and October, 2000.

FALSE 10. *Once, he grabbed her by the back of the neck and tossed her against a closet door, banging her head against the door.*

M-FALSE 11. *Another time, when Kassidy resisted, he picked her up by the armpits and threw her on the bed. When Amanda intervened, he grabbed Kassidy's leg and then walked away, muttering that he wished Kassidy had never been born.* Amanda testified about an argument where Chad and she were both holding Kassidy and then he released his hold. Chad never said that he wished Kassidy had never been born.

M-FALSE 12. *On another occasion, to stop her from crying and screaming, the defendant pressed his finger on Kassidy's throat, hard enough to make her gag.* Chad and Amanda were both with Kassidy at the time. Chad touched her throat enough to cause her voice to change pitch, and she stopped her temper tantrum, perhaps intrigued by the change. It is true that Amanda used the word "gagged" in her testimony, but she also said immediately thereafter, "*And we* [sic] *didn't do it out of anger. She changed her scream and then she stopped crying because she was like, what I am doing. He didn't hurt her when he did it.*" (Testimony, page 113) However, Amanda was asked, "*Did she gag*?" and Amanda said, "*Yes*." (page 115)

M-FALSE 13. *The defendant and Amanda made up false excuses to explain the obvious bruises on Kassidy's face, including that the defendant grabbed Kassidy's face to prevent her from falling off a trampoline.* The "trampoline story" was the only false excuse that Chad used to explain the bruises on Kassidy's cheeks that he caused. He never made up any false statement to explain any other bruises. He recalls stating the "trampoline story" to Amanda's mother on October 14, and to Tristan around October 30, and to the police on November 9. Amanda told it to others, including her mother, Melissa Chick, and Tracey Foley, but did not state it to the police.

FALSE 14. *They also said that Kassidy was bruised because she was clumsy or because she accidentally bumped her head.* It was true that Amanda, Chad and others believed that Kassidy was sometimes clumsy, perhaps because of her toe-in gait, and that she seemed to fall more often than other toddlers. It was also true that she hit her head, accidentally, at various times, including against the living room coffee table a few days before she died. The statement is labeled "FALSE" here because it's presented by the court as an example of a "*false excuse.*" (#13)

FALSE 15. *Because of the bruises and her fear that Kassidy would be taken from her, Amanda refused to put Kassidy in day care.* Amanda was seeking openings in day care facilities and made 17 calls over two days of such calls, November 3 and 8. The only person at Chad's trial who described apprehension that Kassidy might be taken away from Amanda was Jennifer. Amanda had taken Kassidy to appointments at the DHHS office in Sanford several times during October.

M-FALSE 16. *Instead, she asked her sister and her sister's boyfriend, Marshall, to baby-sit.* There were several reasons for asking Jeff and Jennifer to babysit. They were "family" and trusted, geographically convenient, immediately available, and inexpensive. Also, they volunteered. Amanda's job search was unexpectedly and quickly successful with Old Navy, and she was in a jam without day care. It is also true that she was concerned that people might form the wrong impression from seeing Kassidy's bruises, but that didn't stop her searching for day care.

M-TRUE 17. *On November 8, 2000, the day before Kassidy died, Amanda dropped her off at her sister's and Marshall's home in Kittery, Maine, at around 1:30 or 2:30 p.m.* The time was more likely around 3:00 p.m., as she called Jeff from Chad's home phone at 2:35 p.m.

M-TRUE 18. *When she dropped Kassidy off, Kassidy was fine, although a bit sleepy. She had a couple of scratches and a faded bruise on her face, but nothing more. Her behavior was normal. She spent the afternoon watching cartoons.* Of the 28 bruises and alleged fractures whose ages were estimated by the Maine Medical Examiner at Chad's trial, approximately eleven were estimated to be 24 hours old, or older.

M-TRUE 19. *The defendant picked up Kassidy at around 5:00 p.m. Shortly thereafter, he called from his car to tell Marshall that "...the little bitch is acting weird again." He said that Kassidy was "kind of bobbin' around" in the car.* Chad picked up Kassidy closer to 5:30 p.m. and when he called, his recollection of the statement above was that he told Jeff that Kassidy was having difficulty with her drooling and non-responsiveness, Chad asked, "*What the hell did you do to her?*" During that call, Chad did not refer to Kassidy as "*the little bitch.*" Those were words attributed to Chad by Jeff.

TRUE 20. *An hour or so later, he again called Marshall and said that she fell on her face on the ground when he took her out of the car.*

TRUE 21. *Later that evening, the defendant called Marshall again and told him that while playing ball with his three-year-old son, Kassidy was hit by his son with a ball.*

M-TRUE 22. *During the conversation, the defendant became frantic, telling Marshall that Kassidy's eyes were in the back of her head, and yelling at her to wake up. He told Marshall that Kassidy was out cold.* Chad was very concerned, and did observe the eyes-in-the-back-of-the-head phenomenon, and he did call to her, "*Kassidy, Kassidy,*" as she appeared to be dazed, but not "*out cold.*"

M-FALSE 23. *When Marshall suggested that the defendant take her to the hospital, the defendant said that she had "come out of it" and was fine.* Toward the end of the conversation, Chad was less alarmed, as Kassidy seemed to have recovered. About this time, he had also applied some ice, packed in a cloth, to her face. Jeff did not suggest at that time that Chad take Kassidy to the hospital. In Jeff's police interview on November 9, he said, "*I should have **probably** told him last night* *when she was going in a daze, but 'You need to bring this kid to the hospital,' you know, or something...*" (Interview, p. 1308)(emphasis added here) Chad did discuss the option of a visit to a hospital or a doctor with his wife, Tristan, in a later call. She advised Chad to keep a close eye on Kassidy, and to take her to see a doctor if she didn't seem better.

TRUE 24. *The defendant also called Amanda to tell her about the incident. He told her that he did not want to baby-sit for Kassidy anymore because "...it seems like every time that I have her something happens where she hurts herself."*

M-TRUE 25.*When Amanda came home that night, she and the defendant fought. At one point, the defendant grabbed her throat and pinned her against the couch, telling her to "cut it out . . . you know what gets me going. You know what makes my temper."* When Amanda came home, she and Chad did argue and it became mutually physical. It was very short lived, and they were soon in bed.

M-TRUE 26. *The next morning, Amanda brought Kassidy to Marshall's house. Amanda lay Kassidy on a bed, looked at Kassidy's face, and then said to her sister, "Look what he did. It looks like f----ing s---, doesn't it."* Amanda did say about Kassidy's face that it "*looked like shit.*" To the extent that she said something like "*Look what he did,*" it was a reference to the ball hitting Kassidy's face and to no other action by Chad.

M-FALSE 27. *Kassidy's face was badly bruised; the bruises around her forehead looked like finger marks.* Kassidy's face had several bruises from the kitten scratch, the fall into the coffee table earlier in the week, the fall in the driveway, the ball hitting her on November 8, and a sore on her lower lip. Each of these was thought to be cosmetic, and not a serious problem. There was no testimony at Chad's trial or in police interviews that a bruise on her forehead looked like finger marks. Dr. Greenwald did say, however, of a forehead bruise, "*The middle of the forehead, you can observe an oval-shaped, brown bruise,....*" (Transcript, page 132)

TRUE 28. *Kassidy appeared sick...* On the morning of Thursday, November 9, Kassidy appeared to be very tired, as she was on Sunday, November 5. Amanda and Chad thought she was perhaps suffering from some kind of flu, as was Kyle a week earlier.

FALSE 29. *... and in pain.* Neither Amanda nor Chad nor others who had seen Kassidy over the past days or weeks or months had any idea that Kassidy was in pain, except during recoveries from accidents, such as the collision with the coffee table a few days before her death.

M-TRUE 30. *Marshall and Amanda's sister were concerned about her and put her to bed. When they tried to rouse her, Kassidy whimpered and pulled away from them.* When she was brought to Jeff's and Jennifer's Amanda put her into the bed, still wearing her new pink jacket.

M-TRUE 31. *Amanda's sister went to work and Marshall stayed at home with Kassidy, letting her sleep.* Addressing the implication that Jeff stayed at home in some special response to Kassidy's condition, that was not true. He had previously agreed, during this landscaping off-season, to babysit for Kassidy on this particular week. He didn't "let... her sleep" in the sense that he had other plans for her that had to be shelved. Instead, he thought she was watching cartoons on Nickelodeon, while he was watching the election results on the TV in the living room.

TRUE 32. *At around 9:30 that morning, the defendant called* [Jeff] *and asked how Kassidy was doing.*

M-TRUE 33. *The defendant then told Marshall that he had received a call from the State because "someone had seen Kassidy at his house acting weird."* This was how Jeff characterized the call at Chad's trial, and those are Jeff's words and not Chad's. (Transcript, p. 171)

M-TRUE 34. *The defendant was quite angry, telling Marshall that Amanda and "the little bitch* [are] *going to have to get out of my house."* This was how Jeff characterized the call at Chad's trial, and those are Jeff's words and not Chad's. (Transcript, p. 172)

TRUE 35. *At around 12:30 p.m., Marshall went to the bedroom to check on Kassidy and saw that she was unconscious, her eyes were in the back of her head, and she was making a gargling noise.* This was from Jeff's testimony.

TRUE 36. *While on the phone with 911, he tried to resuscitate her, but could not.*

TRUE 37. *Kassidy was taken by ambulance to a Maine hospital and pronounced dead on arrival.*

TRUE 38. *An autopsy revealed that Kassidy died at approximately 12:30 p.m. from multiple blunt-force injuries that had caused bleeding and swelling in her brain, bleeding in the optic nerve, and internal bleeding in her abdomen.* That is what the Maine Medical Examiner said.

TRUE 39. *The medical examiner estimated that before she died, Kassidy received eight to ten blows to the head and at least two blows to the abdomen from a blunt force, such as a fist or a foot.* That is what the Maine Medical Examiner said.

TRUE 40. *Kassidy's fatal head injuries were inflicted sometime within the twenty-four hours preceding her death.* That is what the Maine Medical Examiner said.

M-TRUE 41. *In addition to her fatal injuries, Kassidy had numerous bruises and multiple fractures in various stages of healing.* That is what the Maine Medical Examiner said. The existence of fractures as disputed.

M-FALSE 42.*Most of the bruises were between eight and twelve hours old.* Dr. Greenwald identified 100 bruises or injuries, including the five alleged fractures. Of those, she estimated the age of 28 of them. Four of the 28 were caused 8-12 hours before Kassidy's death, and seven were caused "*around twelve hours.*" Even if all of the "*around twelve hours*" bruises were less than 12, the total for the 8-12 category would still only be 11, which is less than half of the 28 and only 10% of the 100. Three of the injuries were estimated to have been caused eight or fewer hours before Kassidy's death, and one of those was estimated to have occurred four or fewer hours before death.

M-FALSE 43. *None of the bruises on Kassidy's face was consistent with being hit by a ball.* It is true that Dr. Greenwald stated that the two bruises which she examined, because she thought they looked like ball injuries, were "*not completely consistent with those injuries*." One handicap to Dr. Greenwald's analysis may have been that she may have been thinking that the "*ball*" that prosecutor Delker asked her about was a flexible plastic wiffle ball, instead of the harder T-Ball. Chad's expert witness, Dr. Baden, did not address the question of whether any of the bruising under Kassidy's left eye was consistent with being hit by a Tee-ball. (Testimony, p. 210)

TRUE 44. *On the night of Kassidy's death, the police interviewed Amanda, her sister, Marshall and the defendant. The defendant told the police the trampoline story to explain how he had once bruised Kassidy's face.*

TRUE 45. *He also told them that she would sometimes "throw herself in the corner or throw herself into the wall" or run and "slam right into" a corner.* [See Chad's Annotated Police Interrogation, page 75 for explanation.]

TRUE 46. *He stated that Kassidy was "clumsy" and constantly walked into things like his coffee table.* Others made the same observation.

M-FALSE 47. *That night, Amanda and the defendant spoke by telephone. Crying, Amanda told the defendant, "[Y]ou killed my baby; I know you did this; you wanted her dead."* Jeff and Jennifer alleged that they heard Amanda make those statements, or a similar statement. However, Amanda wrote in her essay, My Life Story, "*Later in the conversation I was telling him what they told me how they said, 'You slowly killed my baby,' and Jeff ran to the cops saying I said that to Chad.*" Amanda was not asked about that alleged statement when she testified at Chad's trial.

Thus, of the 47 "*facts*" that the "*jury could have found,*" I believe that 16 (34%) were TRUE, 10 (21%) MOSTLY TRUE, 17 (36%) MOSTLY FALSE and four (9%) were

FALSE. Of the 16 TRUE, only two, #40 and #44, pointed toward Chad's responsibility for Kassidy's injuries and death. The weighted measure of TRUTH was 60%. Where an upper court presents facts that a jury **could have found** and only 21% of those facts are entirely true, and most of those said nothing about Chad's guilt, then the "guilty beyond a reasonable doubt" verdicts should be questioned. Not necessarily overturned without further investigation, but questioned.

The Keene Sentinel published the story by its reporter, Benjamin Yelle, **"Former Keene man loses appeal."** He wrote,

The N.H. Supreme Court has ruled against a former Keene man convicted in December 2001 of killing his girlfriend's daughter....

"Viewing all of the evidence in the light most favorable to the State, we hold it was sufficient for the jury to exclude all rational conclusions except that the defendant was guilty," Chief Justice David A. Brock wrote in the decision....

Earlier this month, the Court ruled in favor of the State's appeal of a Sentence Review Board decision that had prohibited the State from seeking longer sentences in Evans's case and two others. A law passed in 2001 allows the state to appeal sentences. Senior Assistant N.H. Attorney General N. William Delker told The Associated Press he will seek to lengthen Evans's sentence to 60 years to life."

Monday, 2 February 2004

Two days before what would have been Kassidy's fifth birthday, the New Hampshire Supreme Court denied Amanda's appeal of her conviction.

Judge Duggan began his opinion by stating that the "*jury **could have found** the following facts,*" (emphasis added) and they are separated and numbered below, with TRUE, _M-TRUE, M-FALSE and FALSE notations. There are further comments, where useful and not redundant to similar statements noted above with Chad's appeal.

TRUE 1. *The defendant began dating Chad Evans in the summer of 2000.*

M-TRUE 2. *In September 2000, she and her nineteen-month-old daughter, Kassidy, moved in with Evans and his son, Kyle.* Amanda and Kassidy moved to Rochester in July. Chad recalls that the move was essentially completed shortly after Kyle's early July birthday.

FALSE 3. *Shortly thereafter, bruises began appearing on Kassidy and she had difficulty walking.*

M-FALSE 4. *The defendant later told police that these bruises were caused by Evans.*

FALSE 5. *According to the defendant, Evans banged Kassidy's head into a closet door three times a week,...*

TRUE 6. *...grabbed Kassidy's face hard enough to leave bruises...* This happened three or four times in October.

M-FALSE 7. *...and held her head under running water to stop her from crying.*

FALSE 8. *Evans picked Kassidy up by her face or arm and threw her into a corner hard enough so that she hit her head.*

M-FALSE 9. *He also used his fingers to push down on her trachea until she gagged.*

M-FALSE 10. *During the time that Evans was abusing Kassidy, the defendant concocted numerous stories to explain Kassidy's bruises.*

TRUE 11. *She told her friends and family that Kassidy bruised easily and that she hit her head on a coffee table.*

TRUE 12. *The defendant told another friend that Kassidy hit her head on a wall as Evans carried her down the stairs on his shoulders.*

TRUE 13. *To explain a particularly noticeable bruise on Kassidy's face, the defendant told several people that Evans grabbed Kassidy by the face in order to keep her from falling off a trampoline.* This was the "trampoline story," and it was false.

TRUE 14. *The defendant also explained that a mark on Kassidy's leg was the result of a mishap with a curling iron.*

TRUE 15. *Between September and November 2000, the defendant became concerned that people who observed the bruises on Kassidy would think she was being abused.*

FALSE 16. *For this reason, the defendant did not take Kassidy to a doctor and sent her to a babysitter when Evans' parents visited.*

M-FALSE 17. *The defendant did not bring Kassidy to visit the defendant's mother when Kassidy had bruises on her face and did not put her into formal daycare.* Amanda was not avoiding bringing Kassidy to visit Jacqueline. Amanda and Jacqueline had discussed Jacqueline's anticipated babysitting for Kassidy on the upcoming weekend of November 11-12.

M-TRUE 18. *Instead, the defendant asked her sister, Jennifer Bortner, and her sister's boyfriend, Jeffrey Marshall, to watch Kassidy while she worked.* This arrangement was intended to be only a temporary arrangement, and not "*instead*," and not for avoiding anyone.

M-TRUE 19. *On November 8, 2000, the defendant dropped Kassidy off at her sister's and Marshall's home at around 2:00 p.m.* It was approximately between 3:00 p.m. and 3:30 p.m.

M-TRUE 20. *Marshall watched Kassidy for about two hours and observed her acting normally.*

M-TRUE 21. *At around 5:00 p.m., Evans picked up Kassidy at Marshall's home. Approximately fifteen minutes after he left Marshall's home, however, Evans called Marshall and reported that Kassidy was acting "weird," explaining that Kassidy's eyes were rolling into the back of her head.* It was around 5:30 p.m.

TRUE 22. *Marshall received two more phone calls from Evans that evening.*

TRUE 23. *The second time he called, Evans told Marshall that Kassidy fell "flat on her face" after she got out of his car.*

M-TRUE 24. *In his third call, Evans told Marshall that his son hit Kassidy in the face with a baseball. Again, Evans told Marshall that Kassidy's eyes were rolling into the back of her head but then said that she was "fine.*" Whatever was the word he used, Chad did believe that Kassidy was okay, and not seriously hurt, after being hit by the T-ball. He applied an ice pack to her face.

TRUE 25. *Marshall called Jennifer Bortner at work and described the phone calls he had received from Evans.*

TRUE 26. *Later that evening, the defendant visited Jennifer at her place of work. Jennifer told the defendant about the phone calls Marshall had received from Evans.*

M-TRUE 27. *The defendant called Evans, who told her that Kassidy's tongue was out of her mouth and her eyes were glazed over.* Amanda and Chad did talk by phone, but he did not say to her that Kassidy's tongue was ever out of her mouth. The expression "*glazed over*" is similar to expression frequently seen in this tragedy, "*eyes in the back of her head.*" This quoted recollection came from Amanda's third interview (p. 111) with Det. Blodgett, and was read by Blodgett in her testimony to the jury at Amanda's trial. (p. 164)

M-FALSE 28. *When the defendant suggested bringing Kassidy to the doctor, Evans told her that they should wait until Kassidy's bruises healed.* At some point during October/November Chad and Amanda did discuss bringing Kassidy to see a doctor as she didn't seem well, and it was agreed that the need could wait until her bruises, from whatever sources, subsided. Amanda did state in her testimony at Chad's trial that they had a similar exchange during the phone calls on the evening of November 8, and that Chad said, " *'you should take her to the doctor's as soon as the bruises clear up.' Something like that.*" (p. 146)

M-TRUE 29. *After speaking with Evans, the defendant told her sister that she was "sick of* [her] *f---ing kid constantly getting bruises at his house.*" This was Jennifer's recollection from her testimony at Amanda's trial. (p. 124) At Chad's trial, Amanda testified about her conversation with Chad on Nov. 8, "*I was mad. I didn't want another bruise on her, because I wanted to take her to day care.... I said, 'I'm sick of her getting hurt.' I meant Jeff and Chad, probably... I went back to work.... I worked until 11:00... And I probably got home around midnight.*" (p. 124-25)

M-TRUE 30. *The next morning, the defendant noticed that Kassidy was very still and appeared to be having trouble staying awake.* Kassidy seemed tired and Amanda gave her some Tylenol. This description is almost an exact quote of Sgt. White's testimony at Amanda's trial, (p. 94) but that was his recollection from his interview with Amanda on December 19, 2000, which he summarized and didn't record.

TRUE 31. *The defendant also observed that Kassidy had a mark under her right eye, redness and swelling around her left eye and some faded bruising around her mouth and chin.*

TRUE 32. *Later that morning, the defendant dropped Kassidy off at her sister's and Marshall's home before going to work.*

TRUE 33. *As she brought Kassidy into the bedroom, the defendant commented, "Look at her face. It looks like s---, doesn't it?"*

TRUE 34. *Jennifer and Marshall both testified that Kassidy's face was covered with bruises. The defendant and Jennifer left for work shortly thereafter.*

M-TRUE 35. *Marshall put Kassidy in bed and turned on the television.* Amanda brought Kassidy into Jeff's and Jennifer's bedroom, when she first arrived. Jennifer testified at Chad's trial that she turned on the television to the Nickelodeon channel. (p. 113)

M-TRUE 36. *At around noon, he checked on her and noticed that she was having trouble breathing. Marshall tried to administer CPR and called 911.* This is the sequence described by Jeff. The call to 911 was Jeff's 12th call after her discovered Kassidy in distress.

M-TRUE 37. *A detective who arrived at the scene noted extensive bruising on Kassidy's face, chin and abdomen, as well as a cut on her index finger.* The reference to a cut on Kassidy's index finger was from Det. Hamel's testimony. (p.27) It is almost certain that was this was the wart on that finger, that Kassidy irritated, and that Chad had urged Amanda to have a doctor remove. Det. Blodgett testified (p. 12) that in Amanda's first interview she told Blodgett and Det. LeClair that Kassidy had a wart on her hand, but at the time, she was not specific about the location on her right index finger.

TRUE 38. *Kassidy was pronounced dead upon arrival at York County Hospital in York, Maine.* Kassidy's body arrived at the hospital at 1:17 p.m. However, Kassidy died earlier than that, probably around 12:30 p.m. Dr. Bock testified that Kassidy *was dead at the time of arrival of the EMTs,*" which was at 12:46 p.m. (p. 29) Dr. Baden testified that "*she was dead before 12 noon.*" (p. 47) Dr. Greenwald testified, "*...she died around 12:30 p.m.*" (p. 231)

TRUE 39. *The medical examiner later determined that Kassidy died from multiple blunt force injuries.* She did not, however, identify which injury or injuries on Kassidy's body was the fatal blow or blows.

TRUE 40. *In addition, the medical examiner found that several of Kassidy's bones were fractured and in various stages of the healing process. Specifically, the medical examiner documented fractures to Kassidy's left leg, both arms and her right hand.* While the estimation of fractures was contested at Chad's trial by Dr. Baden, it was not contested by any expert witness at Amanda's trial.

TRUE 41. *Following Kassidy's death, the defendant was interviewed on four separate occasions by Detective Angela Blodgett of the Maine State Police.*

M-FALSE 42. *During the interviews, the defendant told Detective Blodgett that Evans threw Kassidy into a corner, banged her head on the closet door, pinched her face hard enough to leave bruises and called her a "bitch."* Amanda agreed to these characterizations during the interview, but they were not true. She recanted them at Chad's trial.

M-FALSE 43. *The defendant admitted that she did not bring Kassidy to the doctor on the day before her death because she and Evans agreed to wait until Kassidy's bruises went away.* Amanda did not make such an admission. On Wednesday, November 8, Kassidy seemed tired, but relatively okay. Amanda did not realize the seriousness of Kassidy's condition, and her expectation was that Kassidy's bruises were fading, as was the typical cycle.

TRUE 44. *On December 19, 2000, the defendant was interviewed by New Hampshire State Police Sergeant James White. At this interview, the defendant described her observations of Kassidy on the day before her death and the day of her death.* However, in Sgt.White's summary of that interview, there is not a single quote from Amanda about those observations.

M-FALSE 45. *In addition, she described Evans as "out of control" when he was disciplining Kassidy.* This quote was from the testimony of Sgt. White at Amanda's trial, as he was recalling his December 19, 2000 interview of Amanda in Concord. (p.100) It was White's phrase and not Amanda's. Sgt. White used the same phrase in his summary of the referenced interview.

TRUE 46. *The information she provided to Sergeant White was, for the most part, consistent with the information she previously provided to Detective Blodgett.*

The court was not saying that it found the above facts to be true. It said that Amanda's jury "*could have found*" those facts to be true. By my analysis, 21 were TRUE, 12 were MOSTLY TRUE, nine were MOSTLY FALSE and four were FALSE. Of the 21 TRUE statements only two, #6 and #13, seemed to point toward Amanda's guilt for Endangering the Welfare of a Child.

The Portsmouth Herald covered the story with Karen Dandurant's article, "Bortner to remain behind bars" Below are excerpts of the article:

...In Bortner's appeal, defense attorneys argued that the state had violated an immunity agreement offered to Bortner in exchange for her testimony against Evans. The agreement would have protected Bortner from prosecution.

Terms of the agreement, according to the court documents, said that Bortner "was obligated to provide information that was truthful, candid and complete." The agreement further stated that the defendant would be in breach of the agreement if she made a material false statement or omission. The next sentence of the agreement stated that, in the event of "such a breach, or any other breach of (the) agreement," the state would be released from its agreement."

Prosecutors revoked the agreement because of discrepancies in Bortner's testimony during Evans' trial. In several instances, she minimized brutality she had described to police in earlier interviews.

During initial interviews, Bortner told police that she saw Evans bang Kassidy's head into a closet door three times a week, grab her face hard enough to leave bruises and hold her head under running water to stop her from crying. She told police Evans picked Kassidy up by her face or arm and threw her into a corner hard enough so that she hit her head and used his fingers to push down on her trachea until she gagged.

When she was interviewed by prosecutors in November 2001, Bortner altered her description of the time she said Evans held Kassidy under a water faucet, instead describing the incident as one in which Evans simply "splashed water on Kassidy's face."

When Bortner was interviewed by police, she said Kassidy had bruises on her face from Evans grabbing her face and pinching it when he disciplined her. When she was interviewed in 2001, she acknowledged that Evans grabbed Kassidy's face approximately two times a week, but said that only on one occasion did this conduct cause bruising to Kassidy's face....

The immunity agreement became the subject of a New Hampshire Bar Journal article by Kate Morneau, "State v. Bortner: NH Begin to Develop Law on Immunity and Cooperation Agreements in Criminal Cases." The primary question about Amanda's immunity agreement was never resolved: Was she telling the truth when under oath at Chad's trial, or was she reliably telling the truth when being questioned by the police shortly after Kassidy's death. If Chad's voice stress lie detector test in July in 2010 is a valid indicator, Amanda was telling the truth at Chad's trial and therefore the immunity agreement should have been enforceable, and Amanda should not have been prosecuted. She was never asked by the police or prosecutors to take a polygraph, even though she had indicated a willingness to do so.

Wednesday, 4 February 2004

On this day, Kassidy would have been five years old.

8 April/30 June/20 July 2004

On these three days were held depositions in a civil case filed by Jeff Marshall on August 8, 2003, against Chad for defamation. There were two counts. The first was for defamation, alleging that Chad said to others and to the media that Jeff killed Kassidy, and the second claimed damages for intentional infliction of emotional distress. Together with the complaint was a motion to put a lien of Chad's home for the amount of $150,000, because "*The plaintiff believes there is a reasonable likelihood that the plaintiff will recover judgment, including interests and costs, in the amount of $200,000.*"

Jennifer Saunders wrote the article, "Aunt's boyfriend, of Kittery, files lawsuit against Kasssidy's killer," for Foster's Daily Democrat. She stated that Jeff's attorney, Stephen Brown, stated, "***I don't think there is anything worse in life than being accused of things we don't do.****... Alleging a person actually murdered someone and then publicizing that throughout the country, I don't know how you fix that... We'll see what we can do to clear his name."* It was a quote that Chad could adopt as his own, too.

A companion lawsuit was thought to have been considered or filed by Jeff against Colley-McCoy for $500,000 for the loss of his contracts, because of his statements and testimony against Chad in interviews and at Chad's trial. However, records of that lawsuit, if it was ever filed, have not been found.

On April 8, 2004 Chad was deposed at the State Prison, by Jeff's attorney, Steven Brown. In the initial pleadings in the case, Chad represented himself, with the assistance of inmates who were formerly attorneys, and other inmates with a good knowledge of the law.

Chad stated that Amanda and Kassidy moved to his home "*probably the first week of July.*" (p. 13) Attorney Brown said that it was his understanding that Chad continued to work for Colley-McCoy after his arrest in November, 2000, but Chad assured him that he did not work again for Colley-McCoy.(p. 44)

Chad described the events of October 22 when he and Jeff had gone to Maine to get a 3-wheeler and Amanda's showing him, later, the black and blues on Kassidy's buttocks. (p. 53)

Brown asked how many other times Kassidy was returned home from Jeff's with "*bruises or damage, actual physical injury,*" and he answered, "*probably six or seven anyway.*" (p. 55) One observation of three bruises on Kassidy's cheek was shared with Jeremy when they returned from their day of golf on Tuesday, October 25. Chad said, "*I think it was one of the incidents when she had fallen off his bed or the dog knocked her over or something.*" (p. 57)

As Jeff's lawsuit was about statements that Chad allegedly made to others, he responded to questions about such statements by saying that his friends and family had formed their own opinions about what had happened to Kassidy, and that Chad's lawyers had advised him not to discuss the case with anyone. Also, he acknowledged that he probably told others his opinion that Jeff was responsible for Kassidy's death.

Attorney Brown again revealed his understanding of aspects of the case when he asked, in four different ways about Chad's meeting with Bob McDougall and/or Peter Napoli in the summer of 2001. He asked, "*Do you remember having a conversation... where you discussed Jeff having to take the blame because you didn't want to go to jail?*" Chad responded, *"No, Absolutely not.*" He asked again and Chad said, "*No.*" He asked again, "*Did you ever tell Bob McDougall or Peter Napoli that Jeff had to take the blame because of what you did?*" and Chad again responded, "*No.*" Brown asked, "*Did you ever say anything to the effect you were too important to McDonald's to take the blame for murder?*" and Chad again responded, "*No.*" (p. 76-77) Chad denied that Colley-McCoy provided any support to him after his resignation, other than moral support. Later, Brown returned to the same theme, "*You didn't discuss with McDougall that if you blamed Jeff, that you would both get off?*" and Chad responded, "*No.*" (p. 82) Then, and apparently revealing the source of this line of inquiry, Brown asked, "*Do you recall Will Modlin at any time ever coming up to you and saying you couldn't blame Jeff for what you did?*" and Chad answered, "*Never.*" (p. 82-83)

Brown asked Chad about his possible contacts with the "John Walsh Show," and Chad's attorney objected, as he did several times during he deposition.

Brown returned to the earlier theme, "*Did anyone involved with Colley-McCoy or anyone in management ever tell you that they were going to try to pressure Jeff not to testify against you?*" and Chad responded, "*Absolutely not.*" (p. 103) And again, "*Did anyone ever tell you they were going to terminate him or his landscaping services if he testified against you?*" which received the same response, "*Absolutely not.*" (p. 103) People being deposed are not encouraged by their attorneys to offer any information other than strictly what is asked, so Chad said nothing about his conversation with Jeff about the non-renewal of his landscaping contracts. He did say, "*Like I said, I was scaling him down. He knew his contract with me was almost done.*" (p. 104)

On June 30, Chad's Deposition resumed, and also present was a "Commissioner" who had been appointed by a judge to ensure that the deposition was conducted fairly. Brown asked about Chad's conversations with others about the case, and Chad said that he had denied to others the killing of Kassidy. Then Brown asked, "Did you tell them that you harmed her?" and Chad responded, "*I am going to take the Fifth on that,*" which meant that he was going to decline to answer on the ground that it might incriminate him. He had been advised by fellow inmates and by Attorney Fisher that he might be subject to even more criminal prosecution about his **eye contact** palming of Kassidy's face. Also, his Sentence Review Board hearing was coming up in September, and Chad was concerned that anything he said about his actions with Kassidy that seemed to go beyond the charges at his trial would be held against him, so he declined to answer. This was an opportunity to state, under oath in a judicial proceeding what he did and didn't do with Kassidy, but his understanding of the legal system led to his avoidance of that opportunity. As did many others, Chad perceived the legal system as a game to win and not as an opportunity to present truth and then allocate responsibility. He had lost so far, but he was hopeful that his 28 year sentence would not be increased. He also noted in 2010 that he did not want to make life any easier for Jeff, so he was ok with throwing roadblocks where he could.

During his explanation of Chad's taking the Fifth, Fisher noted that everyone in the case "*are all guilty of neglect: Chad, your client, Amanda Bortner, the State of New Hampshire.*" (p. 32) The Commissioner ruled that Chad had to respond to Brown's question, as his invoking of the Fifth Amendment protections didn't apply, as Chad had already been convicted. Chad responded, "*I told them I did some things that I wasn't proud of.*" Brown asked the followup question for more information and Chad again said he would "*take the Fifth.*" (p. 42) The Commissioner again ordered Chad to answer, and he again declined, and added, "*...I am not comfortable right now.... I don't know what to do. I am really getting frustrated.*" (p. 53)

He was asked about his meeting with Peter Napoli in the summer of 2001, which Chad initiated. Chad said Peter noted that horrible things were being said about Chad in the newspapers and Chad said to him, "*something to the effect of, 'Well, just watch everything....Some people in this thing aren't as innocent as they would like to make themselves out to be.' And that was what I said.*" (p. 67)

Brown asked if Chad told Peter Napoli that he didn't kill Kassidy and Chad noted that he didn't believe he did, and added,

"*You know. I don't know if you are going to understand this or not, but a lot of people --- I didn't have to tell anybody. They just -- nobody thought I did this.*" (p. 70)

Brown asked Chad about his conversations with Jeremy, his best friend, and specifically, "*Did you ever specifically tell Jeremy that Jeff was responsible for her death or the assault?*" and Chad responded, "*No. I didn't need to tell Jeremy.*" Then Brown asked the same question as before, "*Did you ever strike or hit Kassidy Bortner?*" and Chad declined to answer, and asserted his Fifth amendment rights, and the Commissioner again ordered him to answer, as it was an inappropriate assertion of those rights. (p. 78)

Brown asked, "*Did you ever shake her*?" and Chad said, "*No*," and "*Did you ever push her against a door?*" or "*throw her against the door*?" and Chad again took "*the Fifth*." (p. 79-80) Again, "*Did you ever hold her face underwater?*" and "*I take the Fifth*." (p. 81) Chad was afraid that if began discussing those allegations that something would be twisted to incriminate him further, even though he knew the allegations were false.

Chad became so committed to the response of "the Fifth" that he gave that answer when Brown asked him, "*Chad, do you deny the allegations contained in the indictments that you were charged with, in other words that you caused her death? Do you deny those allegations in the indictment?*" (p. 82) On all these refusals to answer, the Commissioner ordered him to answer and ensured that Chad understood what he was doing.

A few seconds later, Brown asked a slightly different question, "*Did you ever tell anyone that you were not responsible for her injuries or death,*" and Chad said, "*Yes*," and that was to his family and friends. In his mind, the contradictory responses made sense, but it was a lost opportunity to get the truth about his relationship with Kassidy into a transcript under oath.

Returning to the theme of Colley-McCoy's assistance to Chad, Brown asked if Jack Loftus, the Colley-McCoy Comptroller and friend of Chad's, helped find Attorney Fisher for him. Chad said, "*No, he didn't. My brother did that*." (p. 91) Chad said that it was Jack who "*told me about you guys suing McDonald's for a half a million dollars or something and sending him a thing there...*" (p. 93)

About Will Modlin, from whom many of Brown's questions seemed to come, Chad said, "*He's a nice guy, but his elevator doesn't go all the way to the top....*" (p. 114) Brown continued, "*So if he would say that he confronted you about blaming the murder on Jeff Marshall, that is not true?*" and Chad agreed, "*I am telling you that that's a lie*." (p. 116)

Regarding the "John Walsh Show," Chad confirmed that he called the show after his mother gave him a phone number to call. The show had originally contacted Amanda. Brown asked Chad why he contacted them, and Chad said, "*Well, because there were some things that were wrong about my case...*" and Brown asked, "*What was wrong about your case?*" Attorney Fisher responded for Chad, with an apparent sense of humor or irony, "*He got convicted. He's innocent*." (p. 123) Nonetheless, Chad responded on his own, "*I am going to take the Fifth*." (p. 124)

Chad said that when he talked with the producer of the "John Walsh Show," he told her that he didn't kill Kassidy, and that "*I am assuming that I said*," that Jeff did it. (p. 128) Later, "*I probably said he was responsible. ... I am speculating*." (p. 129-30)

Changing gears, Brown asked, "*Why didn't you take the stand and testify at your trial?*" and Chad responded, simply, "*Good question*." (p. 134) Unfortunately, no further explanation was requested.

Brown asked about Amanda and Kassidy coming to the Hampton McDonald's in October, and Chad responded,

...I think it was early on. We were having something because I remember giving Kassidy a balloon. I think it was there. But that would have been more towards summertime....she came down to the beach a few times to meet me when I was there working. (p. 137-38)

Chad said that he did not discipline Kassidy when she was at the Hampton Beach McDonald's.

Brown returned to the subject of Chad's reducing the number of restaurants for which Jeff was doing landscaping. Brown noted that Jeff did the landscaping for Peter Napoli's home, which Chad didn't know, and he was asked to explain why a landscaper was good enough for the manager's home and not for one of his restaurants. Chad responded, "*Well, he doesn't have customers going to his mansion seeing crabgrass, and weeds, and things like that*." (p. 141)

Brown's last question was whether Will Modlin was "*in management at all?*" and Chad responded, "*No. No. No*." (p. 146)

Jeff's deposition was on July 20 at the law office of Chad's attorney, Robert Fisher, in Dover, New Hampshire. He described the founding of his landscape company and was asked whether he had filed lawsuits as part of that business. Jeff recalled one suit against a trailer company, and observed, "*I'm a Republican, so I don't really like to sue people. It's not my thing.*" (p. 20) Jeff said that he first met "*Mr. Evans*" when he was doing landscape work for Wal Mart in Rochester, and the manager of the McDonald's inside that store liked his work, and suggested that he contact McDonald's or Colley-McCoy. He met Larry Lane, who was then an Area Supervisor for McDonald's and within his area, Chad was the manager of the Rochester restaurant. At the time, Jeff said that his company was "*basically a one-man show... It was me, myself, and I.*" (p. 23)

Jeff said that after Kassidy died, his work with the McDonald's restaurants that Chad used to manage was stopped. Until that time, he said,

Things were definitely -- up until that point in time. There was talk of taking on more jobs, doing more things for McDonald's. And then -- when that whole incident happen[ed] *with Chad, it all changed. (p. 30)*

He didn't mention the conversation that Chad recalls with him around Monday, October 23 about the non-renewal of his landscaping contracts with Chad's restaurants. Maybe he forgot. Maybe he was in denial and didn't believe it, or maybe Chad's recollection was mistaken. Maybe Jeff didn't want to acknowledge the conversation because it might indicate to others that he might have had a reason to be angry at Chad and take that anger out on Kassidy. Such a motivation might be true even if he didn't have such anger about the loss of contracts.

He said that he was told face-to-face at the Dover McDonald's restaurant by Larry Lane that if he testified against Chad at his upcoming trial, his work with McDonald's would cease. (p. 27) He testified at Chad's trial, and Jeff said that Larry Lane called him and left a phone message that his work with McDonald's was terminated. (p. 29) Later, Jeff said that he was also called by Bob McDougall and Peter Napoli, and that he did landscaping for both of their homes. Jeff said that

...store managers... talked to me about the situation....And they told me .... their disagreements with the behavior of McDonald's toward what's going on, but nothing they could do. (p. 31)

Jeff acknowledged that he went to "*three or four*" parties at Chad's over the past several years, one of which was a "cookout" after Amanda and Kassidy had moved to Rochester. (p. 32-33) That would have been a summer gathering.

Jeff said he did some landscaping work for Chad and didn't charge him for it, and Bob Fisher asked if he charged "*Chad or Amanda for the babysitting that you did for them?*" Jeff said, "*No*" and also responded, "*No, sir,*" to the next question, "*And was there ever any discussion of money in relation to the babysitting that you did for them?*" This was contrary to Amanda's statement that she paid Jeff with her food stamps. He continued, "*... Amanda is my girlfriend's sister. I think that should go on the record.*" (p. 34)

Asked about his previous girlfriends, before Jennifer, Jeff said that he was engaged to Nicole Mitchell and Jen Newland was his girlfriend in high school for three years. Fisher asked, "*And have you been convicted of any domestic violence offenses?*" and Jeff responded, "*No, Sir.*" (p. 36) Then Fisher followed up by asking, "*do you recall an incident on May 24, 1996, involving domestic assault?*" Jeff's attorney, Steve Brown, objected, on the grounds that such an offense would not be admissible evidence in a trial, as it was not an allegation involving "*dishonesty, false statements, or felonies which have not been annulled.*" (p. 35)

Fisher asked about fights that Jeff may have been involved in since high school, and Jeff described the most recent,

...when Jen was getting hit on by a guy at her work, and, you know, I stuck up for her....But anything that happened there got thrown out because he was in the wrong. So it didn't matter...She worked at Kay Jewelers at the time...He was a married man that was hitting on her. And bothering her. So I did what any man would do and stuck up for her. (p. 42)

Fisher reminded Jeff of the man's name, Travis Moore, and the location of the encounter was in downtown Portsmouth. Said Jeff,

I believe the situation was he came at me, and we got into it. And I believe he got the worst end of the deal. But it got thrown out...

Fisher asked about domestic violence restraining orders, and Jeff acknowledged "*just cease and desist*" or "*stay away orders*" for Nicole Mitchell and Jen Newland. (p. 44) Jeff denied ever hitting Jennifer Bortner and denied knowing of any bruises on her in the summer and fall of 2000. He said, "*I've never hit a woman, sir....*" (p. 45) Later, Jeff said that Nicole Mitchell had once chased him with a knife and stabbed him. He denied that he had ever threatened to kill her, or that he had ever threatened to kill anyone. (p. 59)

Jeff said that after agreeing to take a polygraph after Kassidy died, he talked with a friend, Ron Donnell, who advised against it. Nonetheless, Jeff said, "*To me, it wasn't a big deal.... I'll take the test.*" (p. 49-50) He didn't recall discussing the issue with Jennifer and did not know if she was asked to take a lie detector test. She wasn't asked.

After the deposition, Attorney Fisher talked with Chad about his taking a polygraph exam, and Chad agreed. However, as will be seen below, Jeff abandoned this lawsuit, and it was before Chad's polygraph had been scheduled by his attorney.

About the investigation at the Kittery Police Station on November 9, Jeff said about Chad's arrival, "*He didn't get there till later at night. I believe it was ten hours after he got told from the cops to go down to the Kittery P.D. he showed up.*" (p. 52) In fact, the first call to Chad from the Kittery P.D. was a page at 2:22 p.m. and he arrived at the station around 4:10 p.m. or in less than two hours. This was perhaps an example of how the force of personal dislike can exaggerate memories. It happened several times in this case.

Jeff said that his father used to hit and be abusive to Jeff's mother and that he "*used to do drugs...*" (p.53) Jeff said that he stood up for his mother, even as a pre-teen, and sometimes was hit by his father during that defense, who called Jeff "*a little bastard,*" and a "*little guinea*" [slang for Italian] (p. 55)

Jeff denied ever telling anyone that "*Kassidy was spoiled and needed discipline.*" Not Chad, not Jennifer and not Amanda. (p. 59)

Fisher asked if Jeff was aware that Amanda received any kind of welfare benefits, and Jeff said that "*Amanda was talking about it. I believe towards the time that Kassidy passed away," but he said that he was not aware that Amanda or Jennifer had ever received food stamps.*" (p. 63) Fisher asked again, and Jeff responded, "*Amanda might have.*" (p. 64)

Jeff said he wasn't aware of Amanda going food shopping with her food stamps and vigorously denied ever selling her stamps, "*Why would I sell Amanda's -- no. Absolutely not.*" (p. 64) Further, he denied ever selling anybody's food stamps.

Fisher asked Jeff about his suspicions that Kassidy might have been abused, and he said,

We had our suspicions because the stories they told us didn't add up...And Jen's sister's a pretty tough cookie. My belief was, if there was something going on, she, first of all wouldn't stay. But now we know differently [because of the convictions of Chad and Amanda]. (p. 72)

Jeff said that he and Jennifer confronted Amanda with their questions about abuse, and he also confronted or asked Chad on a few occasions. During the first such conversation, Jeff said that Chad told him that bruises on Kassidy's face were from what readers now know understand to be the "trampoline story." Jeff didn't date the story, but other reports were that it was first used by Amanda and Chad around October 13.

The second conversation identified by Jeff was when he asked Amanda and/or Chad about a bruise on Kassidy's face,

And they said that it happened when they were over [at] *Chad's friend's... Bruce's house....And I said, "Yeah, right. There's no way. How can she" -- and he said, "If you don't believe me,... you call Bruce...I'll give you the number, you know, blah, blah, blah....*" (p. 74)

A third occasion was when he observed Kassidy "*walking funny. And we confronted Amanda. And she said that Chad was playing rough with Kassidy.*" (p. 75)

The fourth, fifth and six described incidents were the previously described calls from Chad to Jeff on Wednesday November 8, 2000.

In passing, Jeff said that he had a 2003 Corvette at the time of the deposition.

Returning to the issue of defamation, Jeff said that Larry Lane, Jason Shunk and David Heon had told him that Chad had said that Jeff was "*responsible for the death of Kassidy...That I killed Kassidy*." (p. 110-111)

Fisher asked about Jeff's damages from the alleged defamation and the publicity about the Kassidy Bortner case, and Jeff said that he had not discussed the problem with his physician, but that he had lost landscaping jobs because of the controversy and he had to answer a lot of questions from people. He said he lost the Applebee's landscaping contract in that way. Coincidentally, that was the restaurant where Jeff and Jennifer introduced Chad to Amanda. Regarding the McDonald's contracts and the communications from Lane, Shunk and Heon, Jeff said, "*It was told to me that Chad told them to get rid of me, wanted me out of there*." (p. 117)

Jeff denied that he had ever called Kassidy a "*retard*," or "*dumb*," and denied that he had "*ever put a pillow over Kassidy's face when she was crying*." (p. 121) He did, however recall referring to Kassidy as "clumsy." He said that he didn't recall referring to Kassidy as being, in Fisher's words, "*freaky like the characters in the movie, 'Children of the Corn,'*" but he did say that "*She would act strange, yes, sir, because of what they did to her up in Rochester*." (p. 121) He said that he had used the word, "*weird*" rather than "*freaky*." (p. 122)

Jeff was asked about the abrasions on Kassidy's feet and his recollection differed from Chad's and Amanda's,

Amanda brought it up because she was suspicious of Chad over these and she wanted to check if there was any other way besides just Kassidy being in Chad's care that this could have happened before she brought it to Chad's attention... " (p. 123)

Jeff misunderstood the sequence of events after Chad discovered the abrasions on Kassidy's feet, when he was carrying her. Amanda's and Chad's first response was to look around their own house to see if there was anything which could have caused such abrasions. It was not until after that inspection that Amanda called Jeff and Jennifer. It was not because Amanda was "*suspicious of Chad*."

Next, Bob Fisher asked about the alleged fall from Jeff's truck, after which Kassidy developed "*two large eggs on the back of her head?*" Jeff responded,

I don't believe anything happened to her when -- and I don't think she fell out of the truck. She was getting put into the truck I believe is the situation. (p. 123)

Then Fisher asked again about Kassidy getting two large eggs on the back of her head, and Jeff said that he did not recall such an incident. Fisher then asked about what he may have thought was the same incident, but which was an incident a day or two before Kassidy died, "*Do you recall her falling out of the truck and you catching her on the way she fell -- on the way down?*" (p. 124) Jeff said that he couldn't remember, but he did remember that Will Peirce was there. As happened at Chad's trial, the two incidents were confused. Fisher did not explore how Jeff could recall that Will Peirce was present but not more details about the incident.

Next, Fisher asked about the three day/two night babysitting stint, which we know occurred from October 26-28, "...at any time did Amanda ask for you and Jen to return the child and you didn't do it?" and Jeff responded, "*Not that I can recall*." (p. 124) There was no followup question.

Fisher asked "*What was Kassidy going to eat on the day of her death?*" Jeff responded, "*I think Amanda brought cereal, which Kassidy didn't touch.*" It was a good question and one that no one had asked before, especially considering that Jeff checked on Kassidy after noon. Jeff didn't remember any plans for food that day, and didn't remember the planned time of pickup for Amanda, which would have been around 4:00 p.m., after an eight hour day. He said, "*I think she brought a diaper bag or stuff, too..,*" but he said he couldn't recall looking into it to see what other food had been brought with Kassidy. That diaper bag was never found during the search of Jeff's home, or if it was found, it wasn't deemed important enough to be seized as evidence or even to be photographed.

Fisher asked, "*Do you have any knowledge of how often a child the age of Kassidy should be fed from 8:00 or 8:30 a.m. to 5:00 or 6:00 p.m.*"" and Jeff replied, "*No, sir. I guess not.*" Jeff said that he fed Kassidy when she was hungry, "*She knew how to say, 'food, food.' You know, she knew. She knew how to -- if she was thirsty.*"

The deposition was suspended at 1:11 p.m. due to a prior commitment by Jeff's attorney. The completion of the deposition was never scheduled and on December 8, Steve Brown withdrew for unspecified reasons as Jeff's attorney on the case. As no other attorney was retained, the case was dismissed on April 5, 2005.

Except for the legal fees and the large amount of time spent representing himself, pro se, initially, Chad had suffered no harm from the lawsuit, but he missed an opportunity to speak under oath about his relationship to Kassidy and his actions with her. He didn't feel "*proud*" about his past frustrations and anger, but he knew that he hadn't caused her death.

Thursday, 15 April 2004

Amanda was released from jail on this day. During her incarceration, she was never visited by her mother or her sister or other members of her birth family. Chad's parents visited almost every week, as well as some of her friends from church.

Friday, 17 September 2004

The Sentence Review Division held a hearing on the request by the prosecutors to increase Chad's minimum sentence to 60 years. The three Superior Court judges were Particia Coffey, Acting Chair, Robert Morrill and Gary Hicks. The hearing was held at the State Prison. (See selected pages of Transcript.)

David Ruoff argued for the Office of the Attorney General and Christopher Carter of the Appellate Defender Program and Alan Cronheim represented Chad. As Chad was now indigent, Cronheim was assisting him pro bono, as would be the case for all of Chad's future communications with him. He asked Chad for no further payments.

As the initiating party, Ruoff began the argument by noting that

...the State initially requested a 60 year to life sentence... The PSI in this case recommended a 45-year sentence.... Let me talk about the aggravating sentencing factors in this case...It was very severe intimidation and abuse. He threw her into walls. He threw her into a closet. Would jerk her arms around, according to the mother of the victim, maybe about three times a week when she would cry. He held her head under a faucet to keep her from crying. He would pick her up by the head, by the face when she would cry or he would get mad. He would put his hand around her throat and cause her to cough because she couldn't breathe. He would call her an idiot, a retard, bitch." (Transcript, p. 7-8)

As this case progressed, the characterization of Chad seemed to get worse. This was the first time that it had been alleged that Chad had called Kassidy an "*idiot.*" It was not true. He had used the other terms, "*retard*" and "*bitch*" sometimes when talking with Amanda or friends, and usually with a sense of humor, but he never called Kassidy those words to her face. He never put his hands around Kassidy's throat causing her difficulty to breathe. What Ruoff seemed to be referencing was the incident that Amanda described at Chad's trial where he touched his finger to Kassidy's throat at a point where her voice changed in tone. (Trial transcript, p. 113)

Ruoff referred to Kassidy's five fractures, "*and the evidence that those injuries were inflicted within months, a month or two of the death...*" (p. 8) He did not mention, as he did not at Amanda's trial, that the evidence of fractures was minimal and that it was disputed.

Ruoff said that "*...there is no doubt that in the last months of her life, she lived every day in pain. There was also evidence that due to the defendant's ongoing intimidation and abuse of Kassidy that she lived in fear of him. One witness related that when she was over at the apartment one time the defendant walked into a room and she cowered. She looked like a feral cat, afraid of him.*" (p. 9) Assuming for the moment that by "last months," Ruoff meant at least two, that means that, at minimum he told the three judges that since September 9, 2000, Kassidy had been in pain every day, and that there was "*no doubt*" about that. However, there was not one witness at Chad's or Amanda's trial who testified that s/he saw Kasssidy in any pain of any duration longer than the pain caused by a fall into a coffee table. Ruoff apparently did not know about Kassidy's September 11, 2000 appointment with Dr. Timoney, and he said nothing about pain. Ruoff did not remember the October 1, 2000 photo at Amanda's trial of Kassidy holding her bunny.

Regarding observation by a witness that Kassidy watched Chad walk through a room at his home, the terms, "*cowed*" and "*feral cat*" were Ruoff's and not those of the witness. Melissa Chick's testimony was that Kassidy was "*was just staring at him the whole time as he was walking through the room.*" (Trial transcript, p. 62) In short, Ruoff was exaggerating. As with Chad's earlier prosecutors, and at least some of the police in the investigation, he seemed to sincerely believe that Chad was a very evil man, despite the considerable out-of-court evidence to the contrary, including Stephen Carlisle's Presentencing Report. Ruoff had never met Chad before this hearing, and he never talked with him.

Referring to the assault of Tristan, Ruoff said, "*He had already been through batterers' counseling. So he had been through the criminal justice system at least once as a result of his violence and it did not work.*" (p. 10) In fact, despite its faults, the criminal justice system did work for Chad, in the sense that he had resolved not to commit any future violence, and he sought out a counselor, Gray Fitzgerald, to help him better understand the issues, because the "*batterers' counseling*" ordered by the court was insufficient. He had a physical relationship with Amanda with much touching and some jostling, but he never hit her in any way similar to what had happened with Tristan. Ruoff continued with a reference to the wide publicity given to the Kassidy case,

It is no understatement that this case shocked the consciousness of that community in which that little girl was killed. Shocked the conscience. Because as the case unfolded and the facts came to light and the evidence and testimonies testified, it told a story of a worst case scenario for the end of the life of a 22 [sic] *month old little girl....the other function that the court has is to protect the public from people who are very dangerous; those that have a demonstrated history of violence. People who have done something so bad that those factors, the facts of what he did, his conduct, eclipses other factors. Deterrence in this case was not served by a 28 year sentence.* (p. 11)

Alan Cronheim spoke for Chad,

....we have someone who has been involved, and now I'm talking about Chad, in a horrific event, but has some extraordinary strengths and I think the judge was able to see that, whether it be the Union Leader award that he got for saving three people, whether it be his charitable work, whether it be his public service on the School Board, whether it be the community work that he did, that is something that is absent in any other case in which I've been a part of for a serious felony offense. (p. 16)

Cronheim said that the 28-year to life sentence was fair and noted that

....this case has been the subject of a comment by the Attorney General, Attorney General McLaughlin, who was the Attorney General at the time of the case. On October 24, 2002, at the Child Abuse and Neglect Conference, he referenced the sentence in this case. Referenced the fact that the State had requested a greater sentence. Acknowledged that the State did not "win" in terms of getting the sentence it chose, but said that the sentence was a fair sentence, balancing the factors that the sentencing judge must review. (p. 17-18)

Kathy Jackson spoke, "*I'm Amanda's aunt. On behalf of Kassidy, her grandparents, her great grandparents, aunts, uncles...*" she asked for a life sentence "*to ensure that he never again sets foot outside of this facility.*" (p. 19-20) She did not claim to speak for Amanda.

Jennifer Conley was the other family representative to speak,

Hi. I'm Jennifer Conley. I'm Kassidy's aunt. I just want to say that every day that I live I have to think about how I'm not going to spend any time with my niece. And the fact that Kassidy was only alive less than 22 months and he is going to be out in 28 years. (p. 21-22)

Judge Coffey asked for the second time, "*Does your client wish to address the Board?*" (p. 19, 23) and Cronheim responded, "*I think you may have read his remarks in the sentencing transcript itself, and we would rely on that.*" (p. 23)

Until the Campaign for Justice for Chad began in 2010, this was Chad's eighth and last opportunity to speak and present the truth about the case. Those opportunities are listed below:

1. Nov. 9, 2000 interrogation. His minimization of Amanda's role in his life and the use of the "trampoline story" drowned out the truth in the rest of that interrogation.
2. Initial grand jury. It is not known whether Chad was invited to the grand jury, but he had the opportunity to voluntarily appear, and tell the grand jurors what happened during the 154 days he knew Kassidy. It would have been an unusual proactive step, but innocent clients in highly emotional, publicized cases, must affirm their innocence at available opportunities.
3. The night of his arrest, November 16, 2000. The police sought to interview Chad, but he declined on the advice of his attorneys. Subsequently, he and his attorneys could have proactively contacted the police and offered to meet with them to answer questions. Chad could have prepared a statement and brought it to the police. As with volunteering to appear before a grand jury, it would have been an unusual step.
4. His December 2001 trial. He chose not to testify, on the advice of his attorneys.
5. Chad's pre-sentencing interview with Stephen Carlisle, who wrote in his PSI report, "*at the request of the defense attorney, no discussion of the criminal cases occurred with Chad Evans during the PSI interviews....*" (p. 7)
6. The April 16, 2002 sentencing hearing. He spoke, but chose not to proclaim his innocence, on the advice of his attorneys.
7. Amanda's trial in November, 2003.
8. His deposition on April 8 and June 30, 2004, in the civil action by Jeff, where he "took the Fifth" when asked specific questions about Kassidy's death. He chose that course on the advice of counsel.
9. September 17, 2004. Chad chose not to address the three judges, on the advice of his attorneys, with the same reasoning as given at his sentencing hearing. It would not be helpful, they reasoned, to claim innocence when that was not the issue at the hearing, and it would likely anger the judges.

It had now been almost four years since he retained counsel, and he hadn't proclaimed his innocence since his response, without counsel, to Detectives LeClair and McCleish on November 9, "*No Way.*" There were other indirect opportunities to proclaim his innocence such as in the state and Federal appeal efforts to set aside the 15-year increase in his sentence. Innocence just wasn't considered relevant in those proceedings, one of which was still ongoing, at the Federal Court of Appeals in the First Circuit in Boston, as of July 2011.

Returning to the Sentencing Division hearing, Cronheim spoke and compared Chad's case to other cases and then said,

It is a case, contrary to what was stated, where the judge found that there was remorse and I can tell you both from his comments at the sentencing hearing itself and from my time with him that there is no question that there is remorse.... p. 23-24)

Cronheim was trying to walk the same tightwire that Chad walked at his 2002 sentencing hearing, but, once again, the judges had no idea that Chad was feeling remorseful about not doing enough to save Kassidy and that he felt zero remorse for killing her because he didn't.

Cronheim didn't offer Amanda as a witness for Chad, but she was there and Judge Coffey said, "*She can certainly make a statement. She's Kassidy's mother.*" (p. 26)

Amanda was brief,

I just wanted to say on behalf of Kassidy. This has been a huge injustice. I did 16 months at Strafford County and I just got out five months ago. I'm trying to fix things that I said in discovery over an 11 hour interrogation. I haven't had much say in any of this. People don't understand because you really can't understand unless you've been through it. All I have to say is that he's already wrongly convicted, and it might not even matter what I'm saying right now, but he doesn't even deserve 28 to life. One day, justice will be served. I just don't know when. That's all I have to say. (p. 26)

The hearing adjourned.

Amanda wrote a letter to the judges afterwards, which appears below in its entirety, *I'm writing today because I didn't want to leave you with the wrong impression. I wasn't prepared to speak at the hearing September 17, because I didn't know that I could. You see, even though I was Kassidy's mother, the state never wants me to speak on her behalf because I won't paint the picture that they want me to paint. When I talked about fixing my statements at Chad's hearing, what I'm saying is I outright lied when the police questioned me after Kassidy died.*

I was 18 years old when I was told that my baby died while Jeff Marshall was watching her. The last place I wanted to be was sitting in a police station being interrogated by police officers for 11 hours. I said and agreed to many things that just were not true. Much of what I was telling them was what was obvious to me that they wanted to hear so they would leave me alone. I just wanted to leave and hold my baby and they played every trick in the book to guilt me into staying without ever letting me see her again as they had promised.

Did Chad do some awful things? Absolutely. Am I angry with him for that? Absolutely. But the thing that no one wants to look at is that the state's own medical examiner conceeded that Kassidy was "alert", awake, and "watching TV", when medically she was already dead. (EMT's described Kassidy as cool and clammy to the touch with Lividity and Rigor Mortis already setting in upon arrival to Jeff's house). If Jeff didn't kill Kassidy, why would he be calling and lying to Jen, stating that Kassidy was coming around when she was already dead?

The bottom line is Kassidy was my daughter. She was the victim here. Did I fail to protect her? Absolutely. I should have left Chad the first time he squeezed her cheeks. I certainly should have never let her go back to be babysat by Jeff Marshall after he spanked her so hard he put black and blues on her butt because she upset him somehow. I have to live with the knowledge for the rest of my life, that my child died a horrible, senseless death and I was too immature and stupid to see it.

This was far from a "cut and dry" case. As Mr. Cronheim pointed out, the jury deliberated for 5 days before reaching a verdict. This is pretty significant when you consider the emotions involved. I wanted you to know that Chad is not the monster that the state depicted him as. Many of the things Mr. Ruoff attributed to Chad simply are not true and I have to live with the fact that I said and agreed to those things from the beginning and was too scared to go against the police and correct them after.

As Judges I know that you do not see the discovery evidence but let me assure you, there was much more to this case than meets the eye. The state is quick to put my sister Jen on display because she can always muster the crocodile tears, but if you could read her police interviews, you would see for yourself how little she cared for Kassidy. She consistently refers to her as "that kid" or "The Kid" and often in person as a "Whinny pain in the ass." The "drama queen" that refers to herself as my Aunt Kathy, only met Kassidy one time in her life even though she had plenty of opportunity. How dare she speak on behalf of my daughter and equate herself as a victim. I've said it before and I say it again, they are on their high horses now but they didn't give a damn about Kassidy when she was alive. It was a hardship to get any of them to watch her while I worked.

Although I made it clear that I don't agree with the verdict, I think Judge Nadeau's sentencing was fair. She weighed what she believed to be the facts and gave a very thorough explanation of why she chose the sentence that she did. I had the chance to sit before Judge Nadeau twice. Once during Chad's trial and then during mine, (when the state decided to charge me because I refused to tell their version of what happened.) I didn't like the fact that she sentenced me to the maximum of2 years, (I thought losing Kassidy was enough punishment) but I respect how thorough she was in her explanation. She made me realize that loving Kassidy with all my heart wasn't enough and that unintentional or not, I had failed in protecting her.

The important thing to remember is that justice can never really be done. As Judge Nadeau stated, we cannot turn back the hands of time and change all of the horrible things that have happened. Just as sure as I, Kassidy's mother, write this letter today, I would be saying the same thing if it were Jeff Marshall that had been convicted. Being just 22 years old, I cannot fathom all that you will miss in life if you were to spend 28 years locked behind bars. To say that it is not enough time to be punished, think about what you have done wrong, and rehabilitate yourself is absurd. The one lesson my mother did drill into my head growing up was, the world needs more forgiveness not vengeance. That is why I know that my mom had nothing to do with my "aunt" Kathy's statements.

I wrote today because I wanted to be heard and unlike the state, Judge Coffey, you made me feel like my voice matters, so I wanted to take this opportunity to tell you how I really felt.

In 2010 Amanda explained, in a different context, some of her reasoning about what she said in the letter about Chad's squeezing Kassidy's cheeks. She said to me that if Chad had not squeezed Kassidy's cheeks then his wrongful conviction, and hers, would not have happened. She was likely right, because if there had been no bruises from Chad's palming Kassidy's cheeks, there would have been no "trampoline story." Without that story being told to the police by Chad, there would have been less suspicion of his truthfulness. Jacqueline would have been less suspicious as well. Would the absence of any bruises intentionally caused by Chad have been enough to stop the Convict Chad train? We'll never know, but that helps explain Amanda's statement in her letter that she should have "*left Chad the first time he squeezed her cheeks*." It's not known what she meant by Chad's doing "*some awful things*." Unfortunately, the judges didn't write back and ask that question. Judges in the U.S. never respond to such letters on the merits, as their role is to be an umpire between the two sides.

Friday, 4 February 2005

On this day, Kassidy would have been six years old.

Tuesday, 31 March 2005

Jeff Marshall purchased a home in Eliot, Maine and he and Jennifer Bortner Conley moved there.

Tuesday, 26 April 2005

Seven months after the September 17, 2004 hearing, at which Amanda testified on behalf of Chad, the Sentence Review Board issued a decision which added 15 years to Chad's minimum of 28 years. Judge Coffey wrote for the three-judge panel that the increase was warranted "*due to his past history of violence and domestic abuse, the ongoing nature of the assaults on the victim, and for the purpose of general deterrence*."

Later, the New Hampshire Supreme Court summarized what the Sentence Review Board had done, saying that it

"*imposed a sentence of five to ten years in prison on one count of second-degree assault, consecutive to the sentence of twenty-eight years to life for second-degree murder. It imposed an additional ten-to-thirty-year sentence on another count of second-degree assault, consecutive to each of those sentences. It left the remaining sentences unchanged. Thus, the division increased the petitioner's minimum term of imprisonment from twenty-eight to forty-three years.*" (Summary from subsequent, Sept.6, 2006, Supreme Court Opinion, p. 2)

Jason Howe wrote the story for Foster's Daily Democrat, on May 3, 2005, "Kassidy's killer gets a longer sentence" Below are excerpts from the article:

ROCHESTER - State prosecutors say they were stunned four years ago when Chad Evans, convicted in 2000 of murdering 21-month-old Kassidy Bortner, was sentenced to 28 years to life, instead of the requested 60 years to life.

That changed Monday when Senior Assistant Attorney General William Delker received word from the state's Sentence Review Board that Evans' sentence had been extended by at least 15 years....

Amanda Bortner, Kassidy's mother, knew Evans was beating her daughter, but told people Kassidy fell down often and bruised easily, according to testimony.

The beatings were bad enough to prevent Amanda from sending Kassidy to daycare for fear of someone noticing evidence of continued attacks. Nov. 9, 2000, was one such day.

That morning, Amanda dropped off her half-conscious, badly bruised daughter at her sister's apartment in Kittery, Maine.

The baby-sitter contacted 911 within hours of Kassidy's arrival because the child had passed out after a period of struggling for breath...

...Delker said this morning. "Given that the nature of the abuse was so egregious, the sentence the judge handed down seemed disproportionately low."

Evans will now remain in prison until he is at least 73 after losing his 4-year fight against the state's appeal to the Sentence Review Division for more prison time....

"In this case, the new sentences were entirely appropriate considering the extent of the abuse, but I'm sure we haven't seen the end of this case," Delker said.

Delker was correct on that last point. It's not known where the reporter, Jason Howe, found the information that Kassidy died "*after a period of struggling for breath.*" Such a determination was not concluded or even suggested in any of the medical opinions or testimony.

In its fifth editorial about the Kassidy Bortner case, "Justice was Delayed but not Completely Denied," Foster's Daily Democrat contained 707 words with excepts appearing below:

Justice for Kassidy Bortner came late, too late really. The only real justice for Kassidy would be for her to still be alive, smiling and happy, now in her first years of school. But, that's not the way it was for Kassidy. She had to suffer the pain of repeated beatings, beatings which she could neither understand nor protect herself; beatings from which, even 21 months after her birth, she must have wondered why her mother would not protect her.

Finally, a form of justice has been administered more than 4½ years after she succumbed to those repeated beatings from Chad Evans, her mother's boyfriend....

At the same time, Amanda Bortner failed to protect her child. She was the primary enabler. She failed the most fundamental instinct of motherhood. Amanda Bortner allowed events to reach the point at which her child died.

The morning after Chad Evans inflicted that last horrible beating on Kassidy, Amanda Bortner dropped off the half-conscious and badly-bruised child at her sister's apartment in Kittery, Maine. The baby-sitter contacted 911 within hours of Kassidy's arrival, only after the child passed out after struggling for breath....

Animal cubs in the forest get better protection than Amanda Bortner gave to her daughter. No matter the relationship between she and Chad Evans — no matter what she most feared from him — her first duty, even above herself, was to Kassidy.

Amanda Bortner served two years in prison for failing to protect her child in an environment that led up to Kassidy's death. No matter the grief she may feel in the wake of Kassidy's murder, no matter the horrible memories she might have in the future, she deserves little or no pity.

Amanda Bortner could have saved Kassidy's life by taking her out of harm's way. Even on the day Kassidy died, Amanda Bortner might have saved her daughter's life. Why didn't she take her the nearest hospital or doctor's office or call 911 herself?

Chad Evans has come close to getting what he deserves in the murder of Kassidy Bortner and we feel no pity for Amanda Bortner. Kassidy deserved a better mother, a real mother.

One difficulty with this editorial was that there was never any evidence of "*beatings*." Even Amanda's exaggerations, and even as they were misinterpreted by the police and blown out of proportion, did not encompass the concept of beatings, as the term is commonly understood. Another problem is that it repeats the error from the earlier news article that Kassidy "*passed out after struggling for breath.*"

There is a popular saying about being alert to commercial scams, "*If it sounds too good to be true, it probably isn't.*" The flip side of that saying also has merit, "*If it sounds too bad to be true, it probably isn't.*" The Foster's Daily Democrat view of Chad and Amanda was too bad to be true. As Chad wrote in his February 1, 2011 Letter, ***"What kind of a monster do people think I am?"*** The same could be asked about Amanda.

The newspaper had reporters who could have dug into the story far more than they did, even without the assistance of the defendants who were advised to say nothing to the media.

Monday, 19 December 2005

Chad Evans' public attorney, Deputy Chief Public Defender, David Rothstein, filed an appeal with the New Hampshire Supreme Court of the Sentence Review Division 15-year increase in Chad's minimum sentence. The grounds of the appeal were that the application of the Sentencing Review statute was unconstitutional because it became effective after the crimes for which Chad was convicted.

Saturday, 4 February 2006

On this day, Kassidy would have been seven years old.

Friday, 10 February 2006

After five years of struggling to keep his house, and the hope of living in it again, Chad signed a Purchase and Sale Agreement for the price of $185,000. Much of that would go for the remaining mortgage, and the rest to repay his parents for their loans to help him with legal fees and keeping up the mortgage payments since his imprisonment. With his parents in Keene and him in prison, it was extremely difficult to manage the property as a rental home.

Wednesday, 6 September 2006

In the case, Petition of Chad Evans, the New Hampshire Supreme Court upheld the increase to 43 years of Chad's sentence. Judge Dalianis wrote the opinion of the court and said that the statute allowing the State to appeal sentences was a "remedial law" and not essentially punitive in nature, as the State could request lesser sentences as well. Thus, the statute did not violate the prohibition in the U.S. and New Hampshire Constitutions against ex post facto laws, which made legal actions illegal, retroactively. Nearly all of the prosecutor appeals under the statute have been to request additional punishment.

Several newspapers covered the story, including:

Foster's Daily Democrat, "Court rejects Rochester man's bid to reduce sentence in toddler death"

Keene Sentinel, "State Supreme Court upholds Evans' sentence"

Portsmouth Herald, "Killer's sentence is upheld"

Said Will Delker in this article, *"Now this brings some finality to the victim's family."* There can be no "*finality*," when there is injustice to be corrected.

Union Leader, "Court won't reduce murderer's sentence"

Sunday, 4 February 2007

On this day, Kassidy would have been eight years old.

Monday, 26 March 2007

The Supreme Court of the United States denied Chad's appeal of the New Hampshire Supreme Court's ruling upholding the Sentence Review Board's supplemental 15 year sentence.

Thursday, 24 May 2007

In response to a request by Chad and his parents, Dr. Cyril Wecht of Pennsylvania wrote to Chad's father with his OPINION of the case, based on the documents which had been sent to him. Dr. Wecht is a nationally prominent pathologist and is also a lawyer, and he wrote:

Based upon my analysis of all these documents, I should like to set forth my professional opinions as a forensic pathologist. Unless otherwise indicted, each of the following statements is expressed with a reasonable degree of medical and forensic scientific certainty.

1. Kassidy Bortner (KB) died as a result of extensive pulmonary fat embolization. Blunt force trauma of the head and abdomen were unrelated, significant contributing factors. Anoxic encephalopathy and cerebral edema, the terminal pathophysiological events, were produced by the combined effects of the pulmonary fat emboli and the traumatic brain injuries.
2. There were numerous soft tissue injuries of varying ages found at autopsy. It is not possible to determine with any temporal specificity when each of these blunt force injuries was sustained. Inasmuch as KB was in the care of three different adults throughout the period of time in which these injuries would have been incurred, it is difficult to understand why the one or two individuals who may not have been directly responsible for such traumatic events would not have undertaken necessary and appropriate measures to keep the child away from the person(s) who caused or negligently allowed KB to be repeatedly injured.
3. I very much doubt that there were fractures of KB's right and left tibias. If she had sustained true fractures of those significant weight-bearing bones, she would not likely have been able to walk or even stand. I saw no reference in the records to any such complaints by KB, or to any periods of immobilization.
4. There are wide temporal parameters for each of KB's major fatal injuries to have manifested themselves in terms of clinical signs and symptoms prior to her death. Therefore, it is not scientifically possible to determine with absolute certainty exactly when KB sustained the injuries that led to her death. Most probably, the head and abdominal injuries were incurred prior to the morning of her death on November 9, 2000. The fat emboli were of an acute nature, as testified to by Dr. Michael Baden; therefore, they could have been associated with soft tissue injuries that KB sustained sometime after 9:30 AM that day. However, it is quite possible that systemic fat emboli that occurred shortly before her death could have been delayed sequela [after effects] *of injuries sustained several hours or even days before the morning of November 9th*
SUMMARY:

I am puzzled and disturbed by the fact that the prosecutor's office in this case opted to zero in on Chad Evans, while apparently accepting without question the information they obtained from Jeff Marshall. Regrettably, prosecutors have this unlimited power, which I have always considered to be highly immoral, unethical, and intellectually dishonest.

The ruthless, vicious collateral attack by the prosecutor in his cross-examination of Dr. Baden clearly attests to the incontrovertible conclusion that it was not truth and justice that the prosecutor was seeking but rather a conviction of Chad Evans at any cost. Unfortunately, this is not the kind of case in which forensic scientific evidence is able to conclusively prove that someone has been wrongfully convicted, such as has occurred now in more than 200 cases as a result of DNA testing.

When there is a dead child, who has definitely been traumatized, a jury will rarely acquit the defendant. I would be willing to bet any amount that if the prosecutor had selected Jeff Marshall to be the defendant instead of Chad Evans, Marshall would have been found guilty, and your son would be a free man. The prosecutor would simply have "applied" the facts, circumstances, and medical findings in whatever way necessary and appropriate to obtain a conviction, depending on who the defendant was.
So much for the true nature, dignity, and integrity of the criminal justice system in the United States.

As a parent and trained forensic scientist, I can empathize with your family's tragedy and the irrevocable loss of your son's productive years. I wish that it would be possible for me to provide more definitive assistance.

Chad responded with a letter on June 24, 2007 with several additional questions.
1) You stated on page 2 of your report (copy enclosed), that you agreed with Dr. Baden. The fat emboli were of an acute nature therefore, they could have been associated with soft tissue injuries sustained sometime after 9:30 am that day. (She left our house before 7 am.) Then you state in same paragraph that systemic fat emboli could have been delayed sequela of injuries sustained several hours or even days before the morning of November

9th, 2000. These statements seem to contradict each other and are confusing for a layman such as myself. I am hopeful you will elaborate a bit more.
2) Can you think of any reason that the state would neglect to test the fingernail clippings they collected from Kassidy? A report was never provided. I would think it would have been a priority to test them in a case like this...
3) Knowing the information we- have, do you envision a day in the future where science will advance enough to prove...[my innocence]
4) Do you have an opinion on anything else that I should be doing to fight this uphill battle? I have been considering this new brain wave scanning technology that experts claim to be much more accurate than a polygraph but I have no knowledge on the science of it. Do You by any chance? I have no problem hooking up to a machine and telling the truth....

I am under no illusion that I do not bear some responsibility for what happened to Kassidy. I wasn't paying attention like I should have been and failed her miserably. I live with the weight of this everyday. While I'm sure my negligence is deserving of some punishment I do not agree that it should be a 43 year to life sentence for a crime I did not commit. I have two beautiful young sons that I am very involved with and need to find a way to get the truth out so I can go home and raise them. If you can think of anything else, that I should be doing, no matter how small, I would appreciate your input.

Dr. Wecht promptly responded on June 28 with his letter with further clarification, explicitly paragraph by paragraph.
1. There is no contradiction. Fat emboli could have been an acute phenomenon, or a delayed pathophysiological process.
2. Fingernail clippings should have been taken and examined. That is a matter that should have been (and still should be) pursued.
3. Impossible to speculate about such a possibility. In any event, that is not a tangible and meaningful avenue for you to pursue or rely upon at this time.
4. I do not believe that new brain wave scan technology is likely to be utilized in your case. It is not a recognized scientific test like DNA. And you will never get the State to order it.

I wish I would be of more positive assistance to you. I can understand and appreciate the position you are in. True justice was not served in your case. Vicious, incompetent, biased prosecutors are responsible for thousands of innocent people being incarcerated throughout the U.S. That is a problem that our great democratic society fails to fully recognize and accept.

I do strongly recommend that any of your own and your family's efforts in this matter be orchestrated by a knowledgeable, sincere, and courageous attorney. You will never get a review and reconsideration of any aspect of this case unless an attorney pushes for it in a formal and appropriate procedural manner.

At the time of these letters, Chad did not yet know that the Maine State Police crime lab had determined that there was blood underneath all ten of Kassidy's fingernails, or that the blood belonged entirely to Kassidy.

In 2011, Chad reaffirmed his interest in taking an MRI brain scan lie detector test. However, such a test is expensive and can only be taken at a facility in Massachusetts. Travis and Amanda have also indicated their willingness to take such a test, but the $4,000 cost is prohibitive at this time.

Friday, 8 June 2007

Amanda married Craig Chaffee, formerly of Keene. Craig had a daughter, so Amanda became a stepmother of a girl not too far from Kassidy's age. They moved to Mexico, Maine, but the marriage did not last long. Throughout this period, Amanda continued to write to Chad and sometimes talk with him by phone, and help him, where she could, with his appeals. Even though she had been released from jail, Amanda was still suffering from the death of Kassidy and the resulting investigation and court cases. Slowly, she tried to rebuild a relationship with her family, particularly her mother and sister, by agreeing to disagree on the very crucial question of what happened to Kassidy. Until this question is resolved to the satisfaction of those three members of the Bortner/Conley family, the peace among them will be fragile.

Thursday, 25 January 2008

Private investigator Ron Rice interviewed Amanda Bortner at her home in Concord who again denied that Chad had harmed Kassidy in any way. See Interview. During the interview, Amanda told Rice that she still had several photographs of Kassidy, and showed him the photo of her and Kassidy on October 20, 2000 Below are excerpts from the interview, by topic:

RR: *Jeff Marshall stated to the police that you told him Chad held Kassidy's face under a faucet and that was why he observed she was afraid of taking a bath at his house. Is that true or false?*
AB: *False.*

RR: *You never said anything like that?*
AB: *[no]...*

RR: *Did you ever witness Chad throw Kassidy into your bedroom walls?*
AB: *NO!*

RR: *Did you ever observe Chad slam Kassidy's head into bedroom closet door?*
AB: *No.*

RR: *One of your statements mentioned that you witnessed Chad choking Kassidy in the kitchen. Is this true or false?*
AB: *False....*

RR: *Did you ever witness Chad throwing Kassidy into the corners of the house?*
AB: *... No. ... No, he never threw her, he never did that .. so scratch all this throwing stuff out, you know, that's their words not mine....*

RR: *Other than grabbing Kassidy's cheeks in a palming fashion, did you ever observe Chad disciplining Kassidy in a manner that you did not approve of, after you had asked him not to do so?*
AB: *No.*

RR: *Do you believe that Chad cared for Kassidy's well being?*
AB: *Ya.*

RR: *Why?*
AB: *Because he did a lot for her.*

RR: *Did you ever observe Chad hit Kassidy in any fashion?*
AB: *No.*

RR: *He states that regretfully his form of physical punishment was to palm her face to get her to look in his eyes. Is that true?*
AB: *Ya.*

RR: *Why did you tell the police so many things about Chad that you later and now state are not true?*

AB: *Because the police twisted my words and made me feel uncomfortable and I wanted to get the hell out of that room. Basically, in a nutshell that's about it. I was coerced into making a false confession and young and dumb and under a lot of stress. Obviously, I just lost my daughter, so, I don't know how that's credible ... evidence, you know what I mean?*

Monday, 4 February 2008

On this day, Kassidy would have been nine years old.

Tuesday, 12 February 2008

Ron Rice interviewed Shannon Gagne by phone on this day. Much of the interview was about the details of when she observed Kassidy and Amanda eight years earlier and what she saw. There was a discrepancy about when Amanda brought Kassidy to Olympia Sports where she saw Shannon, and the date seemed more likely to be in October, rather than a few days before Kassidy's death as Amanda had recalled. Rice made a few summary comments about the interview.

Shannon stated that Amanda was a good, caring and loving mother and Chad was a good man. Kassidy was always a funny, bubbly, active and outgoing baby..."best kid." While at Olympia Sports, Kassidy was running and having a good time consistent with a baby her age. There were no physical limitations, obvious pain, limping, crying or any other negative signs or indications that Kassidy was suffering from any sort of physical abuse...

Shannon went on to say that she does not believe for one minute that Chad is guilty and that Amanda never did anything wrong and should not have been sent to prison.

Saturday, 6 December 2008

In prison, Chad tries to learn as much as he can about himself and the world. College level classes are not as accessible as they used to be, but there are many other opportunities to learn. On this day, Chad was recognized with a Letter of Recognition, as a "facilitator" in the workshop "Forgiveness One Day," conducted through the Alternatives to Violence Project of Peterborough.

Thursday, 20 March 2008

Continuing to be represented by David Rothstein, Chief New Hampshire Appellate Defender, Chad filed a Motion in U.S. District Court in Concord to set aside the 15-year increase in Chad's sentence on the grounds that it violated the U.S. Constitution's prohibition of ex post facto laws. Such laws make criminal what was previously not criminal. For example, a law passed on June 9, 2011 to make the advocacy for wrongfully convicted people a crime, effective, retroactive to January 1, 2011, would be an ex post facto law. In Chad's case the principle was that the law giving the State of New Hampshire the right to appeal a sentence was effective on January 1, 2002, but was applied to Chad's case which was adjudicated before that date. The Supreme Court of New Hampshire rejected that argument, but Chad had the right to request relief from the Federal Courts as well. We are all citizens of our own states and of the United States and are subject to the judicial systems of each level of government.

Wednesday, 4 February 2009

On this day, Kassidy would have been ten years old.

Saturday, 20 June 2009

For a dedicated father, imprisonment is a double loss: for the father and for his children. Since his August 21, 2001 incarceration, Chad has tried to be the best father he can be, for his son, Kyle, and, to the extent desired by his stepson, Brent, too.
At this time, Chad prepared a unique volume, "KYLE'S MERIT BADGE TO MANHOOD," for his son shortly before Kyle's 12th birthday. The book is a kind of personalized Boy Scout Handbook, with skills and knowledge that Chad hopes that Kyle achieves and absorbs.

Chad wrote to Kyle about the manual:

June 20, 2000

Kyle,

There are so many things I wish I were home to share with you and teach you. Unfortunately, I'm not so I've compiled this checklist of things that I feel are important for you to know. This list is in no way conclusive on what you will need to know in life but it's probably as good a place to start as any. Some of these things are important life skills, others are just fun to know. Together with Brent you are the "men" of the house therefore learning some of these skills will be extremely helpful to your mom. The only thing that I am sure of is that at one point or another you will use all of these skills during your lifetime. (Even if some of them seem crazy to you right now). This is the reason I call this booklet "Kyle's Merit Badges to Manhood." You may already be familiar with some of the items in this booklet. Other tasks will be brand new to you. To earn a "check" you must work with an experienced person on the subject. They will show you the safe and proper way to do a task and then expect you to demonstrate it on your own. At this point they will initial your book for you and that task will be complete. Some of these tasks will be simple and you will earn a check in five minutes. Other tasks may be difficult, frustrating, and take 30 minutes or more to master. This, my son, mirrors life with all its ups and downs and will teach you its own set of valuable skills along the way. (Patience, dedication, follow through, etc.) There is no time limit to finishing this booklet. You can do it as fast or slow as necessary. The important thing is that you learn to do these skills properly. If you set a goal for yourself of getting it done by the end of summer you will need to average completing 4 tasks a day.

You can skip around and do the tasks in any order that you'd like. The only thing that I can tell you is that you will have to earn these checks. There will be no "gimmies". I've enlisted the help of some experts that are eager to help you complete the tasks. Gram, Gramp, Aunt Nicole, Uncle Jason, Uncle Ronny, Uncle Kevin, Great Gram, Tim, Polly & David, etc. It's up to you to navigate through these people and find the best person suited to help you with the task. If you go to the wrong person they will point you in the direction of someone better suited to do the job. For example: You probably aren't going to ask Gram how to check the oil in the car any more than you would ask Gramp to show you how to iron a shirt.

Of course in life we are often rewarded for a job well done. As you work your way through this maze of tasks, I feel that you should be rewarded too. I have set up some nice prizes when you reach certain milestones on your journey to completion.

They are as follows:

» The first 10 tasks you complete and have signed off we will take you to the driving range and let you hit a basket of golf balls.

» When you have completed 20 tasks and have them signed off by your training adult, we will take you out to the batting cages and for ice cream.

» When you have completed 30 tasks we'll take you to Monkey Trunks rope climbing course or Bromley Mountain for the day.

» When you complete 40 tasks, Uncle Jason will rent a canoe with you and spend the day on the Connecticut River.

» 50 tasks completed and Uncle Jason will take you to hike Mount Monadnock.

» 60 tasks completed will earn you a trip to the Christa McAuliffe & Alan Shepard Planetarium! Science Center

» 70 tasks completed will be a day at 6 Flags with a friend.

» 80 tasks completed will be a weekend camping trip at a state park with plenty of fishing or a deep sea fishing trip.

» If you complete every task I have come up with you will get $225.00

cash to do with what you'd like. (In addition to all other prizes, this is the equivalent of earning more than $2.00 for each task you complete.)

Good luck Kyle. I hope you find this challenge as fun to do as I had putting it together. I apologize for not being able to teach you all of these things myself. It would be so much fun. I hope you find comfort in knowing that you are in good hands with people that love you and are excited to help you get started.

Thursday, 4 February 2010

On this day, Kassidy would have been eleven years old.

Thursday, 3 June 2010

Judge Joseph DiClerico, of the U.S. District Court, denied Chad's challenge to the 15-year sentence increase. He concluded,

Although the state's petition for review did result in a longer minimum sentence for Evans, he does not dispute that the sentence was still within the range of punishment that was applicable when he committed the crimes. Therefore, the New Hampshire Supreme Court's decision was not an unreasonable application of federal law.

Because Chad's appeal was only about the 15-year supplemental sentence, and not about his actual innocence, the judge did not address that claim.

Monday, 26 July 2010

Chad took a Voice Stress Analysis (VSA) lie detector test, and the report of that test concluded in November,

After analyzing all of the circumstances and the test results, it was concluded that Mr. Evans was a cooperative, sincere individual who eagerly submitted to VSA testing which revealed No Deception Indicated (NDI) on his part.

In Chapter 8, the 18 questions put to Chad were presented, and they are linked here. Below are the questions that he brought to the test in the hope that he would be asked these as well. However, the test examiner controls the content of the questions, and kept to his 18. Still, Chad's willingness to respond to these questions should indicate something, as does his willingness to subject himself to the test itself. The **bolding** was in his original text with his own sense of importance.

1. Did you truly love Kassidy Bortner?
2. **Did you punch, kick, slap or otherwise hurt Kassidy on the night of Nov. 8th?**
3. **Did you punch, kick, slap or otherwise hurt Kassidy on the morning of Nov. 9th before she left to be babysat by Jeff Marshall?**
4. **Did you want Amanda all to yourself, think of Kassidy as a nuisance, and make it your goal to get rid of her?**
5. **Did you inform Jeff in October of 2000 that his landscaping contracts with McDonald's would not be renewed the following year?**
6. **Did you truly love Kassidy's mother, Amanda Bortner, and have plans of a life together?**
7. **Did you do anything to cause the pinprick type marks on the bottoms of Kassidy's feet?**
8. Were you in fact the person that first found those pinprick marks on the bottoms of Kassidy's feet upon her return from being babysat by Jeff?
9. **Did you do anything that caused Kassidy's death?**
10. **Did you try to persuade Amanda in any way to help you, or lie for you while you were seeing her in violation of your bail condition?**
11. Did you believe that Kassidy had serious injuries and intentionally withhold medical treatment?
12. Did you routinely play wiffle ball with Kyle?
13. **Did Kyle hit a ball, pitched by you, which accidentally struck Kassidy in the face, while playing in his bedroom on the night of November 8th?**

14. Many have questioned the truth of this story and the ability of a 3 1/2 year old child. Is it your belief that Kyle was athletically more gifted than most children his age?
15. Did you call Jeff Marshall on November 8th with suspicions he was hurting Kassidy?
16. Did you abuse Kassidy in the car after picking her up at Jeff Marshall's in the early evening of Nov 8th, 2000?
17. Did Jeff Marshall really tell you all of the things that you allege in your letter to your attorney, Alan Cronheim?
18. **Upon arriving at the Kittery Police station on Nov. 8th, did Jackie Conley truly embrace you in a hug and ask, regarding Jeff, "Oh my God Chad, What did he do to my baby?"**
19. **Did you ever hold Kassidy's face under a water faucet?**
20. Did you ever grab Kassidy by the throat?
21. Have you ever observed Kassidy fall and make no attempt to put her arms or hands out in an attempt to "break" her fall?
22. **Did you ever grab Kassidy in a manner forceful enough to fracture or break a bone?**
23. **Did you ever shake Kassidy?**
24. Were you being truthful during police interrogation, when describing behaviors Kassidy was exhibiting upon picking her up at Jeff's house on evening of Nov. 8th?
25. Did you ever directly call Kassidy a retard?
26. Did you enjoy spending time with Kassidy and having her around?
27. **Have you ever hit Kassidy or Amanda?**
28. **Did you encourage Amanda to seek medical attention for Kassidy when**
    1. she came back from Jeff's after falling out his truck window,
    2. to have her feet checked when she kept falling, and
    3. to have a large wart removed from one of her fingers?
29. Did you speak to your financial adviser shortly before Kassidy's death about setting up an education IRA for her?

There are several types of truth verification tests now available, including voice stress analysis, polygraph, and MRI/brain scan. Each type of test to verify truth has its advocates and detractors, and there is a large number of scholarly and mass media articles which support each position. It is not the position of this book or of the Campaign for Justice for Chad that the test described above proves with certainty that Chad is telling the truth or that he did not commit the crimes for which he was convicted. However, Chad's willingness to take such a test should mean something, just as the police told Amanda and Jeremy in 2000 that Jeff's willingness to take a polygraph test showed that he was being truthful.

Thursday, 29 July 2010

Through his attorney, David Rothstein, Chad appealed the U.S. District Court decision to the U.S. Court of Appeals for the First Circuit in Boston. Assistant Attorney General Elizabeth Woodcock filed the Appellee Brief for the State of New Hampshire. Both attorneys argued the case orally before three judges on April 6, 2011, and a decision by the court is pending.

Friday, 4 February 2011

On this day, Kassidy would have been twelve years old.

CHAPTER 12: CONCLUSION: THE WRONGFUL CONVICTIONS OF CHAD EVANS AND AMANDA BORTNER

"The great enemy of the truth is very often not the lie -- deliberate, contrived and dishonest, but the myth, persistent, persuasive, and unrealistic. Belief in myths allows the comfort of opinion without the discomfort of thought."

- John F. Kennedy

This book has often referred to the quick development of the police/prosecutor theory of the cause of Kassidy's death and apparent abuse. That theory became the "*myth*" in President Kennedy's statement and it was obviously *"persistent"* and *"persuasive,"* as Chad remains in prison. A goal of this book has been to show that the police/prosecution theory, or myth, is *"unrealistic."*

In the New Hampshire Supreme Court direct appeals of Chad's and Amanda's convictions, the court's opinions began the "Facts" section with this introduction: "*The jury could have found the following facts.*" This meant that the jury heard or saw evidence containing the mentioned facts and that the jurors **could have** found them to be true, in the absence of sufficient challenges to their validity. Stated alternatively, on the basis of evidence admitted at the trial, it would have been reasonable for the jury to believe that such a fact was true. For example, if Witness A said that s/he saw bruises, and Witness B didn't mention bruises, or said that s/he didn't see them, the jury could still "*find the following fact,*" because it would have been reasonable to believe Witness A. On the other hand, if Witness A said that the earth was flat, a jury could not "*find the following fact,*" because that is not reasonable.

Here, in this book, I can say that the following facts, which support Chad's innocence, seem to be true with a reasonable level of certainty. Most of these facts or conclusions were not presented or clarified to the juries in Chad's and Amanda's cases.

Chronologically

- Amanda took Kassidy to her pediatrician on September 10, 2000 and to an orthopedic surgeon on September 11.
- Kassidy was generally free of bruising until early October, after the October 1, 2000 photograph, which was seen by the jury as Exhibit 19.
- During October, there were several days of minimal or zero bruising. Crystal Martin saw no bruising during a bath in early October, and Tom McNeil saw no bruising "*four to six weeks*" before she died. The October 20, 2000 photograph showed no bruising.
- Kassidy came home from babysitting at Jeff's and Jennifer's on Sunday, October 22 with black and blue bruises on her buttocks.
- Kassidy was returned home to Amanda on Saturday, October 28, from a three day/two night babysitting at Jeff's and Jennifer's dehydrated and hungry and with two goose egg-sized bumps on the top of her head.
- On November 4, 2000, Kassidy, Chad and Amanda went out to dinner with Travis and Bruce.
- On November 5, 2000 Kassidy was seen by at least six people, other than Chad, and two of those six people noticed a single, fading bruise around the middle of her right cheek. That was the same bruise noticed by Tristan, and reported to DCYF.
- On the evening of November 8, Chad tossed many balls to Kyle for him to hit with his brown Fisher-Price bat. Most of the balls were wiffle balls, but one was a Tee-ball, and Kyle hit it into Kassidy's face below her left eye. Even if Dr. Greenwald did not see a "*completely consistent*" (Trial Transcript, p. 210) matching bruise, the ball did hit Kassidy.
- During Chad's police interrogation on November 9, he did lie about the "trampoline story" and he did minimize his relationship with Amanda, but he told the truth about everything else, including the ball hitting Kassidy, noted above.

Generally

- o No person, other than Amanda, saw Chad hold Kassidy's face in order to obtain eye contact. Chad freely acknowledges that holding and acknowledges that on three or four occasions, out of a much larger number, that holding caused bruises on both sides of Kassidy's face during October.
- o None of the bruises on Kassidy's body at her death, out of the 100 injuries, bruises and fractures identified by Dr. Greenwald, was caused by Chad's palming Kassidy's face for eye contact. Even if there had been residual eye contact palming bruises on Kassidy when she died, they had nothing to do with her death.
- o None of the 100 injuries, bruises and alleged fractures was attributed to an intentional act by Chad by a witness or by other direct evidence.
- o In 2011, Chad recalled and identified approximately ten of the 100 injuries or bruises identified by Dr. Greenwald. On the evening of November 8, and morning of November 9, Chad and Amanda knew about or observed those ten, along with several other smaller bruises. They thought they understood the causes of all of them, or they assumed that they were not serious, and that they were an indication of easy bruising.
- o No person who had seen Kassidy or knew Kassidy had any knowledge that she had any broken bones.
- o There was no indication that Kassidy was in any pain, other than momentary pain following accidents, during her 154 days after meeting Chad.
- o Amanda was the only person who told the police that s/he had seen Chad disciplining Kassidy in any way. At Chad's trial, Amanda recanted much of what she said to the police during her four interviews, and she recanted the rest in her 2002 pre-sentencing letter to Judge Nadeau for Chad, and in her January 2008 interview with a private investigator, and in conversations with me in 2010.
- o Chad did not hit or spank Kassidy.
- o Chad was a good father to his son, Kyle and to his stepson, Brent.
- o Chad loved Kassidy and was a good father-figure for her.

Below are listed the dates or periods of observations of no bruising on Kassidy. The dated photos speak for themselves. Included here are dates of visits with Jacqueline Conley because she showed by her calls to Amanda and Chad's home, and to Jeff's and Jennifer's, on October 14 that she was concerned about any bruises. The same assumption is made for Chad's parents, especially Pam, whose observations of Kassidy in July 2000 were close enough that she saw the problem with toe-in walking, which led to Amanda asking Kassidy's pediatrician about the problem on August 10, and her taking Kassidy to see an orthopedic surgeon on September 11. The codes at the beginning of each entry are NB (No Bruises) 1BF (one bruise on face), 2BF (two bruises on face), ?B (unknown observations of bruises), and MB (multiple bruises)

NB July 12-16	Pam Evans visited Chad, Amanda and Kassidy in Rochester.
NB July 20.	Chad spent evening/night with Amanda and Kassidy in Auburn.
NB J 30-Aug 1	Amanda, Chad, Nicole, Chet, & Jason on Saco River. Kassidy in Auburn.
NB August	PHOTO1 and PHOTO2 of Kassidy in high chair at Chad's and Amanda's.
NB Aug 10	Amanda took Kassidy to Dr. George Glass in Auburn.
NB Aug 16	PHOTO1, PHOTO2 and PHOTO3 of Kassidy at Water Country in Saco.
NB Aug 20-26	Amanda and Chad at concerts and in New York City. Kassidy in Auburn.
NB Aug 27-28	Amanda, Chad and Kassidy at Chad's parents in Keene.
NB late Aug	PHOTO of Kassidy and Kato in Chad's and Amanda's kitchen.
NB Sept 2	Kassidy at Scott's B-day Party in Auburn. PHOTO. (Photo dated by Jacqueline, but Chad believes that photo was later in month at his home.)
NB Sept 11	Amanda took Kassidy to Dr. James Timoney in Lewiston.
NB Sept 24-27	*Chad and Amanda to Martha's Vineyard. Kassidy in Auburn.

NB early Oct. Thomas McNeil held Kassidy in his arms. Saw no bruises. Report.
NB Oct 1 *Amanda, Kassidy and Cathy Nuernberg to Auburn/Buckfield. PHOTO
NB mid Oct Crystal Martin bathed Kassidy. Saw no bruises on Kassidy. Report.
NB late Oct Kassidy in Chad's and Amanda's kitchen with Elmo slippers. PHOTO.
NB Oct. 20 Amanda and Kassidy at Nicole's and Brandon's in Belmont. PHOTO

[All of the photographs listed above can be seen in the Appendix.]

Chad's jury knew only of two (marked with an asteisk*) of the above 19 occasions where no bruising was assumed or seen or photographed. [See the Appendix for 15 photographs of Kassidy between June and November 2000.] First, the jurors knew of the October 1 photograph at Jacqueline's home. Second, they knew from Jacqueline's testimony that Kassidy was with her "*for a week in September, the end of September*," which has been identified here as the week beginning September 24. (Transcript, page 17) Again, the jury did not know about the other 17 days or periods above that Kassidy was observed, or assumed to be, without bruises.

These occasions or observations can be located on the previously created timeline, presented below, with the large zeroes representing the days or periods of no bruising, and the two small zero's representing the four days prior to such observations when there would have been no injury to cause such bruises. On the timeline are represented the occasions of no bruising (NB). Several of the "NB" entries above could not be located on this timeline because their dates lacked sufficient specificity, such as the October photograph of Kassidy in the kitchen with her new Elmo slippers. Even without those events without specific dates, the timeline still has a lot of No Bruise (NB) periods. There is no question in this case that Kassidy had bruises on her body, and most noticeably, on her face in the fall of 2000. What Chad's jury didn't realize was that the bruising was intermittent. As with other symptoms that we now see may have been indications of serious problems for Kassidy, such as the "*eyes in the back of the head.*" observation, the intermittent bruising was viewed as a cosmetic, non-serious problem. At the next pediatrician appointment, expected to be in February, 2001, Amanda would likely have asked Dr. Glass about what she and Chad understood to be easy bruising. If the issue had been presented to Dr. Glass, he would likely have recommended blood tests for inheritable and/or communicable blood diseases. This hypothetical can be added to the many "IFs" and "IF ONLYs" in this case which would have saved Kassidy's life if implemented.

Below are listed the known visits by Amanda and Kassidy to public places, but without clear observations recorded of Kassidy. The codes are "?B" for unknown bruising, "1B", "2B" and "3B" for one, two and three bruises observed, and "MB" for multiple bruises observed. These are listed in response to the prosecution's theory for Chad's and Kassidy's trials that Amanda and Chad were hiding Kassidy from friends, relatives and the public.

?B Oct 2 Amanda appeared in Portland District Ct. with Kassidy who had tantrum.
?B 4 times,Oct Amanda went to appointments at ASPIRE/DHHS office in Sanford, ME.
MB mid Oct Amanda took Kassidy w/ her to Emily Conley's Dr. appt. (Emily observe.)
?B early Nov Amanda took Kassidy to Olympia Sports to return an item.
?B Nov 3 Amanda, Kassidy and Chad to Applebee's or Shorty's and then BJ's.
?B Nov 4 Amanda, Kassidy, Chad, Bruce & Travis had dinner at Spinale's in Milton.
?B Nov 5 Chad took Kassidy through the Dunkin Donuts drive-thru in Alton, NH.

Below are listed the definite and date-specific observations of one or more bruises on Kassidy.

1BFearly Oct Jeff's dog, Jake, knocked Kassidy over. Bruise on face. Makeup used.

2BF Oct 13 — Amanda took Kassidy to Buckfield, and Joshua observed bruises. Also observed by Melissa Chick and Tracey Foley in Springvale in afternoon.
MB Oct 14-15 — Bruises observed by Melissa Chick and Tracey Foley during overnights.
MB Oct 17~ — In her Oct 31 call to DCYF, Tristan reported bruises "two weeks previous"
MB Oct 22-23 — Amanda, Chad, Jeremy & Travis reported bruising on Kassidy's buttocks, after return from Jeff's and Jennifer's.
3BF Oct 24 — Chad, Amanda and Jeremy saw fresh bruises on Kassidy's face.
1BF Oct 30 — Tristan reported to DCYF that she saw a bruise on Kassidy's right cheek.
1BF Nov 5 — Chad took Kassidy to Nicole's and Brandon's in Belmont, NH, and they saw the same, then fading, bruise on Kassidy's right cheek.

Below are listed the five overnight babysitting stints for Kassidy at Jeff's and Jennifer's during the June 9 to November 9 period.

?B July 1 — Kassidy at Jeff's and Jennifer's for first overnight babysitting
?B Aug 12 — Kassidy at Jeff's and Jennifer's for 2nd overnight babysitting
?B Aug 18 — Kassidy at Jeff's and Jennifer's for 3rd overnight babysitting
?B Oct 21 — Kassidy at Jeff's and Jennifer's for 4th overnight babysitting
?B Oct 26-28 — Kassidy at Jeff's and Jennifer's for 5th overnight babysitting (two nights)

The four lists above are combined into the list below:

?B July 1 — Kassidy at Jeff's and Jennifer's for first overnight babysitting, after June 9.
NB July 12-16 — Pam Evans visited Chad, Amanda and Kassidy in Rochester.
NB July 20. — Chad spent evening/night with Amanda and Kassidy in Auburn.
NB J 30-Aug 1 — Amanda and Chad on Saco River. Kassidy in Auburn.
NB August — PHOTO1 and PHOTO2 of Kassidy in high chair at Chad's and Amanda's.
NB Aug 10 — Amanda took Kassidy to Dr. Glass in Auburn.
?B Aug 12 — Kassidy at Jeff's and Jennifer's for 2nd overnight babysitting, after June 9.
NB Aug 16 — PHOTO1, PHOTO2 and PHOTO3 of Kassidy at Water Country in Saco.
?B Aug 18 — Kassidy at Jeff's and Jennifer's for 3rd overnight babysitting, after June 9.
NB Aug 20-26 — Amanda and Chad at concerts and NY. Kassidy in Auburn.
NB Aug 27-28 — Amanda, Chad and Kassidy at Chad's parents in Keene.
NB late Aug — PHOTO of Kassidy and Kato in Chad's and Amanda's kitchen.
NB Sept 2 — Kassidy at Scott's B-day Party in Auburn. PHOTO. (Photo dated by Jacqueline, but Chad believes that photo was later in month at his home.)
NB Sept 11 — Amanda took Kassidy to Dr. James Timoney in Lewiston.
NB Sept 24-27 — Chad and Amanda to Martha's Vineyard. Kassidy in Auburn.
NB early Oct. — Thomas McNeil held Kassidy in his arms. Saw no bruises. Report.
1BF early Oct — Jeff's dog, Jake, knocked Kassidy over. Bruise on face. Makeup used.
?B 4 times, Oct — Amanda went to appointments at ASPIRE/DHHS office in Sanford, ME.
NB Oct 1 — Amanda and Kassidy to Auburn/Buckfield. PHOTO
?B Oct 2 — Amanda appeared in Portland District Ct., with Kassidy who had tantrum.
MB mid Oct — Amanda took Kassidy with her to Emily Conley's doctor appointment.
NB mid Oct — Crystal Martin bathed Kassidy. Saw no bruises on Kassidy. Report.

2BF Oct 13	Amanda took Kassidy to Buckfield, and Joshua observed bruises. Also observed by Melissa Chick and Tracey Foley in Springvale in afternoon.
MB Oct 14-15	Bruises observed by Melissa Chick and Tracey Foley during overnights.
MB Oct 17~	In her Oct 31 call to DCYF, Tristan reported bruises "two weeks previous"
NB late Oct	Amanda in Chad's and Amanda's kitchen with Elmo slippers. PHOTO.
NB Oct. 20	Amanda and Kassidy at Nicole's and Brandon's in Belmont. PHOTO
?B Oct 21	Kassidy at Jeff's and Jennifer's for 4th overnight babysitting, after June 9.
MB Oct 22-23	Amanda, Chad, Jeremy & Travis reported bruising on Kassidy's buttocks.
3BF Oct 24	Chad, Amanda and Jeremy saw fresh bruises on Kassidy's face.
?B Oct 26-28	Kassidy at Jeff's and Jennifer's for 5th overnight babysitting, after June 9.
1BF Oct 30	Tristan reported to DCYF that she saw a bruise on Kassidy's right cheek.
?B early Nov	Amanda took Kassidy to Olympia Sports to return an item.
?B Nov 3	Amanda, Kassidy and Chad to Applebee's or Shorty's and then BJ's.
?B Nov 4	Amanda, Kassidy, Chad, Bruce & Travis had dinner at rest. in Rochester.
?B Nov 5	Chad took Kassidy through the Dunkin Donuts drive-thru in Alton, NH.
1BF Nov 5	Chad took Kassidy to Nicole's and Brandon's in Belmont, NH. Single bruise on Kassidy's right cheek seen by Nicole and Brandon.

If Chad's jury, the prosecutors, and defense attorneys had seen such a timeline, they all could have focused much more specifically on the charges and on the testimony of several witnesses.

The mysterious death of Kassidy Bortner

The subtitle of this book refers to the "*mysterious death of Kassidy Bortner*" and it remains a mystery. As this book has argued that Chad did not kill Kassidy, then how did she die? There are three possibilities, plus a fourth, which would be a combination of the first three:

1. Intentional blows to the head and/or abdomen, or blows which released fat emboli.
2. Accidents which resulted in injuries to the head and/or abdomen, or injuries which released fat emboli.
3. Chronic conditions, or disease, or toxin.
4. Combination of the first three.

As has been described in this book, the jury's understanding of what happened to Kassidy was severely limited by a lack of a timeline for her 154 days with Chad. The efforts since 2010 to construct such a timeline, the "Chronology" in Chad's website, have been impaired by the absence, ten years later, of many documents and photos which would have been very helpful in assembling that timeline.

Nonetheless, while there were some observations of Kassidy's quiet nature during August and September, it seems that Kassidy's behavioral decline can be said to have accelerated after Kassidy's return to Amanda on Saturday, October 28, 2000 from the three day/two night babysitting by Jeff and Jennifer. Kassidy was dehydrated, hungry and she had two large bumps on the top of her head. Over the next twelve days, Kassidy was not her normal self. There is controversy about what her "normal self" was during the period up to October 28, but whatever that standard was, she fell below it after that date. Around that time Kyle had what Chad and Amanda thought was the flu, and they interpreted Kassidy's apparent fatigue as being an indication that she had caught the flu as well.

The possible causes of Kassidy's death are discussed below:

1. Intentional blows to the head and/or abdomen, or blows which released fat emboli.

The police theory of the case was that Kassidy's death was a homicide. That is, someone killed her. Of the four adults with the most contact with Kassidy, the prosecution charged Chad, and the defense countered that Jeff killed her. There was no evidence of any abuse or hitting of Kassidy by Amanda, except an occasional spanking, and none by Jennifer.

Dr. Greenwald identified 100 bruises and injuries, including five alleged bone fractures, but there was no determination of which of those injuries to the head or abdomen was the fatal blow, or one or more of the fatal blows. As the source of the fat emboli was even harder to trace, the blows causing that release were not identified either.

None of the 100 bruises/injuries/fractures identified by Dr. Greenwald was intentionally caused by Chad. He was responsible, accidentally, for the bruise under Kassidy's left eye, even if Dr. Greenwald disputed the claim that it was caused by a ball, but there was no other, of the 100, for which Chad was responsible.

Accepting the police theory that Kassidy's death was a homicide, the defense tried to show that Jeff must have been Kassidy's killer because he was the only other man and he was the person with the most time alone with Kassidy during the two days before her death. The jury was presented with a state-selected defendant and rejected the defense-selected alternative, but that alternative remains to this day as a possibility. As Dr. Cyril Wecht hypothesized in his May 24, 2007 letter to Chad's father, if the prosecution had decided to charge Jeff with Kassidy's murder, it would likely have won a conviction.

Other than Chad, it is still possible that someone delivered blows that caused the release of the fat emboli, and blows to the head and abdomen.

2. Accidents which resulted in injuries to the head and/or abdomen, or injuries which released fat emboli.

There were several known accidents which may have caused brain injury to Kassidy.

- Sudden start on "Kiddie Roller Coaster" with Chad at Deerfield Fair, 9/29 or 9/30
- Falling from Jeff's truck, allegedly, causing 2 large bumps on top of her head, 10/26-28
- Falling from bed to floor while diaper being changed at Jeff's, late October.
- Lurching forward in back seat of Amanda's car at sudden stop, late October.
- Hitting coffee table, 11/5.
- Fall in driveway, 11/8.
- Being hit by Tee-ball, 11/8.

The effects of these accidents may have been tragically underestimated. In 2009, actress Natasha Richardson fell on a ski slope in Canada and hit her head, and no one understood the seriousness of that injury. She died a few days later.

In addition, there may have been other, unknown accidents for Kassidy, unseen by others, such as a fall or collision with a table or a door. Sometimes she was observed not crying after a fall, so that may have happened when not being observed, too.

Symptoms of head injury shown by Kassidy were: disorientation, brain fog, falling a lot, strange behavior, fatigue, crying a lot, eyes rolling in back of head, fever, and easy bruising.

The indications of head injury in the autopsy findings were that there was intracranial pressure, subdural hematoma, and retinal and optic nerve hemorrhages in both eyes. Also, Kassidy showed cerebral edema, which is swelling of the brain with excess fluids, and mild flattening of the sulci and gyri, which are valleys and fissures in the brain. Another symptom was the appearance of petechiae, which are small pinpoint hemorrhages in a tissue. Her eyes were dilated and there were anoxic changes, which showed a restriction of blood flow.

Research in the causes of head-injury-related deaths of children was accelerated by the development of the concept of "Shaken Baby Syndrome (SBS)." Dr. Norman Guthkelch discovered this as a cause of children's deaths when he interviewed parents in countries where shaking children was an accepted part of discipline. According to a

"Rethinking Shaken Baby Syndrome" program on National Public Radio, Dr. Guthhelch has become concerned since his discovery that the diagnosis has become overused to explain the deaths of children when other causes are equally or more likely. In February, 2011, the New York Times Magazine published Emily Bazelon's article, Shaken-Baby Syndrome Faces New Questions in Court which summarized the growing awareness that wrongful convictions had occurred in alleged SBS cases.

One nationally prominent case was of Audrey Edmunds in Wisconsin who was convicted of shaking a baby, Natalie, for whom she was caring. In 2008, a Wisconsin appeals court noted that there was "*fierce disagreement between forensic pathologists, who now question whether the symptoms Natalie displayed indicate intentional head trauma, and pediatricians, who largely adhere to the science as present at Edmunds's trial.*" The court reversed Edmunds's conviction and concluded, "*that the record establishes that there is reasonable probability that a jury ... would have a reasonable doubt as to Edmunds's guilt,...*" In Chad's case, the allegation that he had hit Kassidy in the head or abdomen was derived in a manner similar to the wrongful convictions in SBS cases. That is, the pathologists concluded that there was brain injury and the prosecutors concluded that there must have been hitting, and they looked the likely adults with recent access to the victim. However, there are other possible causes for brain injuries and death, besides SBS and assault.

Since the 1997 "shaken baby" case of Louise Woodward, much more has been learned about the fragility of our brains, and especially children's brains and about how conclusions of homicide have been tragically incorrect. In 2001, Dr. John Plunkett published his important article, "Fatal pediatric head injuries caused by short distance falls," about 18 fall-caused head injuries and he concluded that

A fall from less than 3 meters (10 feet) in an infant or child may cause fatal head injury and may not cause immediate symptoms. The injury may be associated with bilateral retinal hemorrhage, and an associated subdural hematoma may extend into the [brain cavity].

According to an article in 2005, Dr. Plunkett had testified in over 100 SBS cases, usually on the side of the defense which argued for non-SBS causes for the death of a child.

3. Chronic condition or disease or toxin.

a. Chronic condition

Autism. Even before October, there were some observations of Kassidy that were consistent with autism, which has become more frequently diagnosed now than in 2000, and diagnosed earlier in a child's life. The American Autism Association lists 12 indicators of autism in children, and Kassidy seemed to exhibit a few of them: "Poor eye contact," "Doesn't seem to know how to play with toys," and "loses language or social skills." We will never know if Kassidy had any degree of autism, but if so, it might explain her apparent difficulty with eye contact. Jeff and Jennifer testified about seeing Kassidy standing motionless, and staring at a wall during one overnight babysitting stay. Several people had noted that Kassidy would sit placidly among toys, rather than playing with them. It's not known how autism could have been related to her death.

Seizures. Kassidy showed some symptoms of seizures, i.e. bruising, fever, lethargy, falling a lot, crying a lot, difficulty walking, staring and non-responsiveness, pigeon-toed, hands curled up, strange behavior, eyes rolling back, and diarrhea. The seizures might relate to the bumps on the top of her head, allegedly from falling out of Jeff's truck during the October 26-28 babysitting period. There is some family history of epilepsy, which has a tendency to be hereditary. Amanda's brother, Charles, has epilepsy, and began having seizures as a child. When Jennifer received the calls from Jeff on the morning of November 9, one of her fears was that Kassidy might be having a seizure, like her brother. Seizures can occur when people are under increased stress and Kassidy's change from being at home with her mother most of the time to being at Jeff's might have been a source of such stress. Seizures can be associated with flu-like symptoms and with gastrointestinal illness, and Kassidy had both during early November. Kassidy's lethargy and head dropping on the afternoon of November 8 may have been an indication of seizures.

The post-mortem photographs of Kassidy showed some turning inward of her hands and feet, and some distortion of her face, which are indications of seizure. The autopsy found contusions on her tongue and inner cheeks and bloody mucus in her mouth and nose and dilated eyes. One unusual symptom of seizures is that dogs and cats have an ability to sense human seizures and they may respond by running around or whining. On November 9, Jeff's cat, Toby, was running around enough to cause Jeff to follow him into the bedroom, which was Jeff's only visit to that room that morning until the visit after retrieving the mail.

b. Disease

meningococcemia The symptoms of this hard-to-pronounce disease, and cousin to meningitis, are, at least initially, similar to those of influenza. They include fever, nausea, myalgia, headache, arthralgia, chills, diarrhea, stiff neck, and malaise. Later symptoms include septic shock, purpura, hypotension, cyanosis, petechiae, seizures, anxiety, and multiple organ dysfunction syndrome. Acute respiratory distress syndrome and altered mental status may also occur, and may have happened to Kassidy.

Easy bruising (several possible blood disorders)

During the last week of June in 2011 the Public Broadcasting Service (PBS) broadcast a "Frontline" program entitled, "The Child Cases: Guilty until Proven Innocent." The lead story of that program concerned the death of a six-month old girl, Isis Charm Vas, who died at the home of male babysitter, Ernie Lopez, in October, 2000 in Armarillo, Texas. He was convicted in 2003 and sentenced to 60 years for sexual assault and still faces, somehow, the murder charges. As the Lopez case is uncannily similar to Chad's, several excerpts from the PBS website's summary of the program are presented below:

When the ambulance sped her to Northwest Texas Hospital in Amarillo on a Saturday morning in October 2000, doctors and nurses feared that someone had done something awful to her.

A constellation of bruises stretched across her pale skin. CT scans showed blood pooling on her brain and swelling. Blood was found in her vagina. The damage was so severe that her body's vital organs were shutting down. Less than 24 hours later, Isis died. An autopsy bolstered the initial suspicions that she'd been abused. Joni McClain, a forensic pathologist, ruled Isis' death a homicide and said the baby had been sexually violated. McClain would later describe it as a "classic" case of blunt force trauma, the type of damage often done by a beating.

The police investigation that followed was constructed almost entirely from medical evidence. In the end, prosecutors indicted one of the child's babysitters: Ernie Lopez.... Unlike what you see on CSI, many suspicious deaths aren't properly investigated.

But in the years since Lopez was sent to the penitentiary, a growing body of evidence has emerged suggesting that McClain and the hospital staffers were wrong about what happened to Isis — and that her death was not the result of a criminal attack....

Lopez, 40, a soft-spoken man with a slight twang, still can't quite believe he may spend the rest of his life locked up for something he says he didn't do: harming the infant he nicknamed "Little Bird." "Sometimes I wake up and I look at my cell and man, it just hits me: You know, I'm in prison," he said in an interview. "I never thought I would be in prison, never in a hundred years."

At 10:55 a.m. on Oct. 28, 2000, Ernie Lopez grabbed the cordless phone at his house and dialed 9-1-1. "What's going on? What's going on?" asked the operator.

"OK, my ... We're babysitting this little baby girl for Dr. Vas," said Lopez, according to a recording and transcript of the call. A spider, he explained, had bitten Isis a week earlier, "and she's been acting funny ever since."

Lopez and his wife, DeAnn, regularly babysat Isis and her two older siblings, both toddlers. The children's mother, Veronica Vas, was a physician at a nearby hospital, and on that morning she was on her way to Detroit for the weekend.

Lopez, a burly, gregarious man who worked as a mechanic, was looking after the children while DeAnn went shopping for a dress for the annual Lopez family Christmas photo, scheduled to be taken that afternoon. He had been watching the Vas children for 40 minutes when he called for an ambulance.

On the phone, Lopez described his efforts to revive Isis. "I tried to slap her on the bottom and slap her on the face and she won't wake up. She won't do nothing." Blood spilled from her mouth. "She was bit about 14 times. ... She's got all these bruises around her neck and on her face where she was bitten." After the ambulance arrived at his modest one-story home, Lopez rode with Isis to the emergency room. Police detectives, alerted by hospital staffers, quickly showed up at the hospital to question Lopez. He wept as he spoke to the officers. By the time Isis died a day later, police had arrested Lopez.

The body of the baby was transported to Dallas, where McClain performed the autopsy. To the doctor, the evidence pointed to sexual assault and murder. "It is my opinion that Isis Charm Vas, a 6-month-old white female, died as the result of multiple blunt force injuries," McClain wrote in the autopsy report. (McClain declined to comment for this story.)

For police, solving the case was an exercise in elimination. Lopez was the only adult present when Isis collapsed. That made him the sole suspect. Who else could have done it? In October 2001, a grand jury indicted Lopez on charges of capital murder and sexually assaulting a young child....

Forensic pathologists like McClain play a critical role at the intersection of medicine and law enforcement. Employed by medical examiners and coroners' offices, they are called in to figure out how people have died. They scrutinize corpses, searching for clues. If a forensic pathologist says it's a homicide, police will soon be hunting for the killer. Though depicted as glamorous and high-tech on TV shows such as CSI, the field of death investigation is plagued by chronic underfunding, a shortage of specialists, and a lack of national standards, according to a 2009 report by the National Academy of Sciences.... Potter County prosecutors decided to try him [Lopez] *only on the sexual assault charge; the capital murder charge was left pending, allowing prosecutors to try him for that offense at any time. There were no witnesses to the alleged attack, and Lopez had not confessed, so the prosecution's case relied heavily on medical testimony. Over five days, a stream of doctors and nurses who had treated Isis at the hospital told the jury she must have been brutalized.*

Eric Levy, who treated Isis in the hospital's pediatric intensive care unit, said the child's symptoms indicated she had been the victim of a violent attack. Looking at a photo of the baby's lower half, Levy pointed out bruise after bruise.

Michelle Gorday, a veteran nurse who specialized in sexual assault examinations, said it was one of the worst cases she'd witnessed in her 20-year career. "I've never ... ever seen that kind of trauma," she testified.

The defense called no expert witnesses. Lopez chose to take the stand, insisting he had never hurt Isis and testifying about the strange ailments that shadowed the last days of her life. With each day, more health issues cropped up, he said. Blood spots speckled Isis' left eye. Congestion made it hard for her to breathe, prompting the Lopezes to treat the baby with a nebulizer. When Lopez changed her soiled diapers, her fecal matter, he testified, was "black" and "really thick and sticky."...

Veronica Vas, Isis' mother, disputed the Lopezes' account, maintaining that Isis was only mildly ill before she died. "She had about six little bumps on the left side of her forehead, but those were already healing up," Vas testified. The baby's energy level was "quite normal."

Addressing the jury, Assistant District Attorney J. Patrick Murphy summed up the case by saying, "Common sense tells you who had to have done it. ... This child could not fight back. This child could not consent. This child could do nothing but lay there."

The jury found Lopez guilty. It was not until the sentencing phase of the trial that the jury learned Isis had died. McClain, the medical examiner, testified she had ruled Isis' death a homicide. The baby, she said, suffered a "laceration of the vagina area" and injuries to her brain. "In this case," McClain continued, "we know the head has struck something, because we've got bruising in that area." Scrutinizing Isis' eye tissue under a microscope, McClain said, she had discovered more bleeding, which she interpreted as another possible indicator of violent head trauma. Seven other doctors in her office had reviewed the case and concurred with her findings, McClain added....

After learning about Lopez from a relative living in Texas, Kirkwood, [Lopez's current attorney, Heather Kirkwood] *who lives in Seattle, agreed to represent him. For her, Isis' death presented a fascinating jigsaw puzzle to solve. Lopez struck her as "a nice young man" and the "circumstances of the case seemed weird as hell... My gut sense kept telling me this was a sick baby who was neglected," she said.*

Kirkwood started contacting physicians to analyze Isis's medical history. She sent a stack of documents to Richard Soderstrom, an emeritus professor of gynecology at the University of Washington. As an adviser to the Food and Drug Administration, Soderstrom served on a panel that studied the accuracy and safety of the colposcope, a device that can be used to take photos of injuries in sexual assault exams.

Isis Vas had been examined using a colposcope. After Soderstrom reviewed the photos taken of her, he gave a sworn affidavit stating that, in his opinion, the photos did not suggest there had been sexual abuse. Kirkwood also approached Michael Laposata, the chief pathologist for Vanderbilt University Medical Center in Nashville and a leading expert on blood disorders. To gauge how the blood is clotting, physicians typically begin with a pair of basic tests called the PT and PTT. In Isis, the "PT and PTT were markedly abnormal," Laposata said, adding that other tests also suggested a coagulation disorder. Where McClain had seen a "classic" case of blunt force trauma, Laposata saw something entirely different, a "classic picture" of Disseminated Intravascular Coagulation (DIC), a potentially lethal condition that can cause bleeding from sufferers' every orifice.

Based on the baby's "dark, tarry stools," elevated white blood cell count, and abnormal liver function tests, Laposata concluded, "something had to be going on for days" — long before the 40 minutes Lopez was alone with the baby.

An infection could have led to DIC, and, eventually, to a fatal collapse, Laposata said. DIC could also explain Isis' bruises and the bumps on her head that Lopez and others believed were spider bites, he added. "The reality is when your blood is so thin, when you're so unable to make a clot, you can just develop bruises and they can be spontaneous," he said. There is a growing awareness among medical practitioners of "mimics," [which are] *ailments that can cause the kind of bruising and bleeding once assumed to be telltale indicators of child abuse. A 2006 textbook on head injuries in children listed literally dozens of afflictions — including some fairly common illnesses — that can produce hemorrhaging in the brain.*

The Ernie Lopez case was presented here because of the several parallels to Chad's case. Among them, Kassidy and Isis Vas shared several symptoms:

1. They both showed lethargy and loss of energy during the days before their death. Kassidy was assumed by Chad and Amanda to have some type of flu, which may have been contracted from Kyle. Isis was bitten by a spider.
2. They both had extreme, unexplained bruising all over their bodies.
3. They both had feces which were darker and more smelly than usual. Chad first noticed this when he changed Kassidy's diaper on Sunday, November 5, but his changing of the diaper on Wednesday evening was unremarkable. Amanda stated in her November 12 interview that Kassidy "*had a really bad diaper,*" on Thursday the 9th.
4. They both had bleeding in their eyes.
5. They both had unexplained bleeding in their vaginas.

A Texas judge decided in September 2010 that Lopez's trial attorney provided "ineffective assistance of counsel," and ordered a new trial. The prosecutors have appealed and the case is still pending.

The difficulty for Chad in 2011 is that the basic PT and PTT blood tests were not done with Kassidy's blood when she arrived at York Hospital. Dr. Laposata recommends that these tests be performed in all cases of suspected child abuse. In 2005, he wrote with his wife the article, "Children With Signs of Abuse - When is Not Child Abuse?" which noted that blood disorders affect more than 1% of the population. In a 2011 call, he noted that there are about 25 blood disorders that can be mistaken for child abuse, including von

Willebrand's disease and hemophilia A and B, but detection requires blood tests from living, or very recently living, people.

Returning to the other possible non-homicidal causes of, or contributors to, Kassidy's death.

Stroke. Stroke can be caused by blood disorders, trauma, and hypertension. Kassidy's symptoms included: fever, behavioral issues and loss of balance. Her family history of epilepsy may have a connection to stroke and the droop on her face on November 8 may be an indication.

A possible cause of stroke is the application of incorrect CPR to the abdomen. According to the first photos taken at 51 Rogers Road by Robert S. Creamer, Kassidy had no stomach bruising. However, the York Hospital photographs, taken later, showed some bruising. Other autopsy findings indicating stroke were the fresh hemorrhage in the mesentery and small intestines.

Heat stroke. It's not certain what clothing Kassidy was wearing during the morning of November 9, but there was testimony that she was wearing a full set of red pajamas and her new red and white dress-like pajama tops, and her new pink jacket. Depending upon how long she continued to wear all those clothes indoors, and the actual temperature in Jeff's and Jennifer's apartment, she may have suffered heat stroke. Kassidy came with her Sippy cup with her juice, but the cup was not recovered during the police search of Jeff's and Jennifer's. Therefore, it's not known how much she drank on the morning of November 9, if anything, and dehydration may have contributed to her distress.

Syncope (failure of circulation in the heart.) Kassidy's symptom which points toward this problem was her general weakness. Poisoning of some kind is associated with syncope and difficulty of breathing, as reported by Jeff on November 9, may indicate syncope. The autopsy findings of stomach hemorrhage, lung congestion, and heart failure are further indications.

Thrombocytopenia (any disorder in which there is an abnormally low platelet count) Kassidy's symptoms were: bruising, bleeding in the mouth and gums, skin rash, and the petechiae (pinpoint lesions on the soles of her feet.) Other indications, at her death were the

nosebleed, and gastrointestinal bleeding, and blood in her vagina with no sign of trauma.

c. Toxin, Poisoning or allergic reaction

Black Mold. Photographs of Jeff's and Jennifer's bathroom seem to indicate that there may have been mold on the walls. Kassidy's symptoms which were consistent with black mold poisoning were: cold/ flu symptoms, skin rash, hair loss, watery eyes, coughing, fatigue, diarrhea, weakness, fever, brain fog, confusion, and slow reflexes. The best example of the slow reflexes was when Kassidy fell face first in Chad's driveway on November 8, and never put her hands out to stop herself, and didn't cry. The hair loss was noticed by Amanda in late October and Chad asked Nicole about it when they were together on Sunday, November 5. Indications of mold poisoning at Kassidy's autopsy were bleeding in the brain, lung hemorrhaging, internal bleeding, and bleeding in other organs.

Arsenic. Kassidy seemed to show typical symptoms of arsenic poisoning, which is a possibility because the water supply at her grandparents' home in Buckfield was contaminated with arsenic. Kassidy went to that home only twice, and it's not known if she drank any water on either of those two trips. The first occasion was on Sunday, October 1, when Amanda brought Kassidy to Auburn, and then Buckfield, on the last day of the family's moving process. The second occasion was on Friday, October 13, when Amanda brought Kassidy to Buckfield when she came to pickup a check which she used for Chad's birthday presents. When the Conley's became sick months later and learned that the water was contaminated with arsenic, they left that rented home.

Kassidy's symptoms were: confusion, bruising, irritability, fatigue, flu-like symptoms, brittle nails & curling nails, skin rash, hair loss, diarrhea, loss of appetite, drop wrist, and a cough.

The pinpoint marks on the bottom of Kassidy's feet could have been hyperkeratosis, which is a symptom of arsenic poisoning. Another sign was the report by Officer Creamer of a blue line on the gum line in her mouth. The autopsy's finding of congestion of the lungs was consistent with arsenic poisoning, as was cerebral edema.

Lead The possibility of lead poisoning arises from the existence of peeling or chipped paint at Jeff's and Jennifer's apartment. Symptoms of lead poisoning, sometimes similar to those for arsenic, can be: bruising, intense thirst, eye staring, confusion, irritability, dropped hand, and crying a lot. One possible indication of lead poisoning for Kassidy could have opaque bands on bones in an x-ray, which may have been what the Dr. Greenwald understood to be bone fractures. Other indications were her distended abdomen, and the appearance on her lips and mouth of very dry skin and sores. The congestion in her lungs was a possible symptom as were the blue bands on her gums, and the inflamed mucous membrane in her stomach. There was acute inflammation in her small intestines, and symptomatic congestion in her kidneys, lungs, spleen, liver and thymus, pancreas, and lymph nodes. Other indications were her dilated eyes, clenched hands, arched and inverted feet, distended abdomen, and persistence of rigor mortis.

Other poisons: pesticide, makeup and Windex. As Jeff worked in landscaping where he used pesticides, it is possible that his clothing contained residues of pesticides which could have affected Kassidy. For some people, chemicals in makeup can be toxic, and Jennifer applied some makeup to Kassidy in the mornings, and there was one occasion where Jeff and Jennifer used makeup to cover facial bruising on Kassidy.

During the babysitting of October 26-28, Kassidy is believed to have drunk Windex. Later, Jennifer said that Kassidy "*got really, really sick, she kept throwing up.*" (Jennifer interview, p. 925) She came home hungry and dehydrated, and was given Pedialyte by Amanda and Chad. The longterm effects of the Windex are unknown.

4. Combination of the above.

Just as Dr.'s Greenwald and Baden were not able to clearly identify a single homicidal cause of death, it's also likely that there is no single non-homicidal cause. Instead, there may have been a combination of intentional abuse by persons other than Chad, and accidents and chronic conditions, disease or toxins.

In Chad's case, a terrible mistake was made to convict him of murder and several assaults when there were several other likely or possible causes for Kassidy's bruising and her death. If Chad's jurors had known of these other possibilities, they would likely not have found him guilty beyond a reasonable doubt. In Chad's initial direct appeal to the New Hampshire Supreme Court, his lawyer relied upon a 2001 case from that court, State v. Dugas, for the proposition that

When the evidence presented is circumstantial, it must exclude all rational conclusions except guilt in order to be sufficient to convict.

The Court ruled against Chad in December 2003, and responded to the "rational conclusions" argument,

Viewing all of the evidence in the light most favorable to the State, we hold it was sufficient for the jury to exclude all rational conclusions except that the defendant was guilty.

However, Chad's lawyers at his trial presented only one other rational theory of the case, which was that Jeff abused and killed Kassidy. As described in this chapter, there are actually several other rational theories to explain Kassidy's death, and the bruises and injuries.

The Ernie Lopez case is one of many in the U.S. where health problems are incorrectly perceived as the results of criminal actions. The "Frontline" story stated,

An investigation by NPR, ProPublica and PBS Frontline has found that medical examiners and coroners have repeatedly mishandled cases of infant and child deaths, helping to put innocent people behind bars. We analyzed nearly two dozen cases in the United States and Canada in which people have been accused of killing children based on flawed or biased work by forensic pathologists, and then later cleared. Some spent years in prison before courts overturned their convictions. In 2004, San Diego prosecutors moved to dismiss charges against a man who'd been imprisoned for two decades for murdering his girlfriend's son. Others were freed more swiftly but endured hardships nonetheless. An El Paso, Texas, jury acquitted a woman of killing her child in 2010, but after spending 22 months in the county jail, she still had to wage a legal battle to regain custody of her other children.

The questionable prosecutions identified in our joint investigation had common elements:

Often, authorities had little to go on other than autopsy findings. Many of the doctors who conducted post-mortem examinations failed to consult specialists in childhood injuries or ailments, or to thoroughly review medical records that could have affected their conclusions. In several cases, forensic pathologists worked so closely with authorities, they effectively became agents of law enforcement, rather than objective arbiters of scientific evidence. Some experts in the field say worries about mistakes in child death cases are overstated. "The vast majority of forensic pathologists recognize a child abuse case when they see it, and it's not because they want to persecute people," said Mary Case, chief medical examiner for four Missouri counties including St. Louis County. But others say the criminal justice system has yet to confront the full scope of the problem, and that, as a result, more innocent people may be serving time for crimes they didn't commit. "I think it's time to look at these cases again," said Michael Laposata, chief pathologist at Vanderbilt University Medical Center, adding that this could "result in the liberation of a number of falsely accused people."

The death of Kasssidy Bortner may have similarly been one of those unusual cases where the apparent causes of death were not correctly determined and where the convicted alleged perpetrator is innocent. The two pathologists in Chad's case, Dr. Margaret Greenwald and Dr. Michael Baden are both competent and well respected. However, it may have been that the police theory of homicide and the failure to give those two doctors a thorough review of Kassidy's October and November symptoms, and failure to give Dr. Baden the reports of Kassidy's previous doctors' appointments, may have led the pathologists to focus on the possible homicidal causes rather than non-homicidal.

Now, at the end of this book, readers can ask themselves how they might vote, today, if they were on a jury and heard all the evidence, and not just what the jury heard in 2001. Below is a chart to show many levels of belief, certainty and uncertainty about whether Chad murdered Kassidy. The question for reader is: where do you place yourself on this chart?

Percent (%) of certainty of non-involvement.

100-99.9-99-90-------80-------70-------60-------50-------40-------30-------20-------10-1-.1-0

|---**NOT GUILTY**---------------------------------------||*G*|

Below are explanations of the percentages, from left to right:

Chad Evans.....

100% - Did not murder Kassidy. Absolutely not, with total certainty. **NOT GUILTY**
99.9% - Did not murder Kassidy. With much certainty. **NOT GUILTY**
99% - Did not murder Kassidy. With some certainty. **NOT GUILTY**
90% - Very likely did not murder Kassidy. **NOT GUILTY**
80% - Probably did not murder Kassidy. **NOT GUILTY**
70% - Might not have murdered Kassidy. **NOT GUILTY**
60% - Possibly did not murder Kassidy. **NOT GUILTY**
50% - Undecided. Don't have an opinion. **NOT GUILTY**
40% - Possibly did murder Kassidy. **NOT GUILTY**
30% - Might have murdered Kassidy. **NOT GUILTY**
20% - Probably did murder Kassidy. **NOT GUILTY**
10% - Very likely did murder Kassidy. **NOT GUILTY**
1% - Did murder Kassidy. With some certainty. **NOT GUILTY**
.1% - Did murder Kassidy. Beyond a reasonable doubt. ***GUILTY***
0% - Did murder Kassidy. Absolutely, with total certainty. ***GUILTY***

My belief, after 18 months of working on this case is that, with 99.9% certainty, Chad did not kill Kassidy. There is no such verdict as "Not Guilty, beyond a reasonable doubt," but that's what my verdict would be, if available.

Hopefully, readers of this book have moved to the left on the above scale, regardless of where you started. For those who believe that Chad did not murder Kassidy, and even for those who believe that he did, but that he didn't have a fair trial, the answer is that there should be a re-investigation which either will result in a new trial or a complete exoneration.

We should have "zero tolerance" for the conviction of innocent people. Long before that phrase came into use, there has been a favorite among lawyers, from Blackstone's Commentaries in the 1760's, that it is "*better that ten guilty persons escape than that one innocent suffer.*" Benjamin Franklin upped the number according to the essay, "the *n* controversy" to 100, "*that it is better* [one hundred] *guilty Persons should escape than that one innocent Person should suffer.*" Whatever the number is, Americans generally believe that a price should be paid in order to ensure that innocent people are not imprisoned. However, the Innocence Project/DNA revolution has shown that in reality, too many innocent people have been convicted and imprisoned for crimes they did not commit.

Another difficult question is: what happens when doubt about a conviction arises after a trial? Generally, when jurors contact a judge after a trial and advise that they wish to change their previous votes for guilty, to not guilty, they are told that it's too late. The courts developed an expression which they used to minimize the power of such recanting, which is "jurors' remorse." What should happen when jurors read this book and learn a lot about the case that was not presented to them in 2001, and conclude that they either now believe in Chad's innocence or, at least, do not believe in his guilt beyond a reasonable doubt? Shouldn't their voices be heard? A legal purist might say that we cannot stop the system just because doubts arise afterwards.

The question remains, for readers of this book and others who hear the claim that Chad was wrongly convicted: What is to be done? How much doubt must arise before conscientious people insist that Chad be given a retrial or be released by some process, perhaps as was done for Ward Bird?

Below are presented the reasons why Chad should be granted a new trial, and/or his case should be re-investigated. All of the items are based on what has been presented, or referenced in this book. Because the legal standards for granting a new trial are higher than are required for the Attorney General to re-investigate the case, the reasons for a new trial are presented first.

1. Medical records showing Kassidy's two doctor appointments on August 10 and September 11, during the period of Chad's Child Endangerment and Second Degree Assault charges were not provided to the defense.
2. The Maine Medical Examiner's preliminary autopsy report stated that the appointment with Dr. James Timoney was in September,1999, which was false. That appointment was on Sept. 11, 2000, which was 41 days into the period of charges against Chad Evans. Chad's attorneys and defense expert, Dr. Michael Baden, were misled by that incorrect date. Usually the standards of the U.S. Supreme Court case Brady v. Maryland are violated when a prosecutor fails to furnish exculpatory evidence to the defense. Providing misleading information doubles the unfairness at a trial and the argument for retrial is far stronger.
3. Prosecutors knew, or should have known, that when their prosecution witness, Amanda, testified that she last took Kassidy to a doctor for her pigeon-toe exam "in July," that testimony was false. (See above.) That misstatement by Amanda misled the defense and the jury.
4. The misdemeanor Simple Assault case against Chad for his argument with Amanda on the night of Nov. 8, 2000, should not have been joined with the murder and assault cases on Kassidy. In 2003, the New Hampshire Supreme Court ruled in State vs. Ramos that the joining of such charges is more prejudicial than probative. While that Court's ruling was not retroactive to earlier cases, it should be considered in the light of future requests for a new trial.
5. Prosecutors knew, or should have known, that the testimony of prosecution witness, Dr. Greenwald, regarding lack of open wounds was doubtful, given the existence of

blood under Kassidy's ten fingernails, and the report of blood coming from Kassidy's nose, according to Officer Creamer. Although the defense should also have brought these conflicts to the attention of Dr. Greenwald during her testimony, the prosecution should not have remained silent about such apparent conflict in the state's own evidence.

6. Police and prosecutors should have disclosed the presence of a reddish brown stain, possibly blood, on Kassidy's new pink jacket, which she wore on the morning of her death. These stains should have been tested for DNA.
7. After Cory Merrill's testimony was excluded, before cross-examination was conducted on the merits, a mistrial should have been declared, as jury heard incriminating allegations without defense response. Given the notorious unreliability of inmate informants, Merrill should not have been permitted to testify in the first place.
8. Prosecutors should have disclosed an interview at the Strafford County Jail with Adam Tuttle. He was a cellmate of Chad after Chad returned from his arraignment on Friday, November 17, 2000. The prosecutors did provide copies of the interviews of John LaCroix, Eric Cook, Craig Gautreau and Corey Merrill, as all four sought to provide the police information in return for a potential and hoped-for benefit. Adam Tuttle met with two investigators and told them that he believed Chad Evans was innocent, and he told them what Chad had said in his presence and the presence of his fellow cellmates, Gautreau and Merrill. Tuttle knew Chad from before his arrest. No report of that exculpatory interview was provided to the defense. That report, and Tuttle's potential testimony, could have been helpful in the defense arguments to block Merrill's testimony. Later, once Merrill was permitted to testify, the report and Tuttle's testimony would have helped the cross-examination of Merrill.
9. Records of the Portsmouth District Court disposition, one month before Kassidy's death of charges against Jeff of assault and criminal threatening against a third person, were not provided to the defense.
10. The police should have interviewed additional people whom they knew or should have known had seen and/or known Kassidy during the period of the indictment, including:
    Jessica Edmands – close friend of Amanda, and closest friend in Rochester.
    Chet and Pam Evans – parents of Chad, who saw Kassidy several times, most recently
    at their home in Keene over the weekend of August 20-21, 2000.
    Gerri and Steve Harvey - saw Chad and Kassidy on Sunday, November 5, 2000.
    Jeff Porter - was with Amanda and Kassidy at Portland District Court, Oct. 2, 2000.
    Bruce and Michele Truel - friends of Chad and Amanda.
11. The police interviewed Chad's high school girlfriend, Barbara Brooks Hamel, with whom Chad had a troubled, off-and-on, immature relationship. The police did not interview Mary Paquette with whom Chad lived in Rochester for three and one-half years. She was later interviewed for the Pre-Sentence Report, where she said that her relationship with Chad was mutually respectful and non-violent.
12. The jury heard New Hampshire State Police Sergeant William Magee testify that one item found in the kitchen trash basket was a package for "Mice Cube" which he believed to be a mouse poison. This was prejudicial, and may have led the jury to believe that Chad Evans and Amanda Bortner were careless about the presence of poisons around their children. In fact, "Mice Cube" is a New Hampshire-manufactured non-toxic, humane trap for mice, which can then be released outdoors.
13. The prosecutors did not disclose to Chad's attorneys that the State of New Hampshire had reimbursed Jacqueline Conley, a key prosecution witness, for some or all of Kassidy's funeral expenses. As Kassidy and Amanda were receiving public assistance from the State of Maine, the payment to Jacqueline was unusual.
14. Chad's attorneys did not provide sufficient representation to assure a Not Guilty verdict. The legal phrase is "ineffective assistance of counsel." By definition, whenever an innocent person is convicted, the defense is ineffective, but there is not yet a consensus that Chad is innocent. In the past, it was rare that a defendant could

persuade a court that his/her attorneys did such a poor job that s/he should be given a new trial. In colloquial terms, the standard was that if a lawyer was breathing at the trial, the representation was sufficient. In the face of the conventional wisdom that it's better to let guilty people free than convict innocent people, the old standard for evaluating ineffective assistance of counsel showed great confidence in the reliability of the legal system to separate the innocent from the guilty. Now, since the first DNA exoneration in 1989 of Gary Dotson in Illinois, the justice system is becoming more sensitive to claims of wrongful conviction, and the claim of ineffective assistance of counsel.

In February 2011, the New Hampshire Supreme Court reversed Jerome Thompson's conviction for "*aggravated felonious sexual assault*," in part because of "*indisputable and egregious errors of trial counsel, which are apparent from the trial record...*" See Court opinion. The court applied a two prong test:

1. "*first, that counsel's representation was constitutionally deficient*" and,
2. "*second, that counsel's deficient performance actually prejudiced the outcome of the case...*".

The court found in Thompson's case that his lawyer failed repeatedly to object to hearsay evidence as it was presented by two witnesses and that the legally excludable hearsay testimony was the core of the prosecution's case.

Below are listed possible errors or omissions by Chad's attorneys which might be used in a future appeal with the claim of ineffective assistance of counsel. Again, it is noted here that being a defense lawyer is very difficult work, and in most cases resources are limited. Most of the time the innocent clients of defense attorneys are found not guilty and the guilty clients are found guilty. However, sometimes normally adequate representation is not enough.

a. Photographs of bruise-free Kassidy during period of charges were not sought nor presented at trial. Approximately 20 such photographs existed at the time of arraignment, and were in the possession of Amanda, her family, the Evans family, and at least one friend of Amanda's, Cathy Nuernberg. One of those photographs was taken on October 20, which was only 20 days before Kassidy's death.
b. No video recordings were sought. The Bortner/Conley family had at least one video of Kassidy walking, and a clip of that video appeared on the John Walsh show.
c. No medical records for Kassidy were sought or presented at trial.
d. No medical records, including optometrists, were sought for Amanda. Her vision was 20/800, and she has said that she bruises easily
e. No records were sought for Amanda and Kassidy as clients of the Maine Dept. of Human Services, and, in particular, its ASPIRE program. Amanda stated in her "My Life Story" that she brought Kassidy with her during frequent visits/appointments to DHHS during October, 2000, and perhaps once in November.
f. Discovery documents had information about blood underneath Kassidy's fingernails, and about blood coming from Kassidy's nose, but the defense did not present, discuss or argue about the source(s) of that blood at trial. This was particularly evident when Dr. Greenwald was asked about the source of the blood on a napkin and she stated that there were no open wounds from which the blood could have come.
g. The jury was not told that Chad brought Kassidy to a family event four days before she died, on November 5, 2000. There, she was observed, socially, by an elementary school nurse and five others, and only one fading bruise was noted on Kassidy's right cheek. At least four attendees on that day, Gerri and Steve Harvey, Steve's father/Brandon's grandfather and Lisa DeVoe, were not interviewed by the police or by the defense investigator.
h. No timeline was presented to the jury to show important events of Kassidy's life with Chad. Without such a timeline, the defense against the chronologically sequential assault charges was severely hampered. (The only Second Degree

Assault charge which achieved a Not Guilty verdict was for the period between October 1-8, 2000 which included the period of the only photograph of a bruise-free Kassidy in the case. That was Exhibit 19, which was established at the trial to have been taken on October 1, 2000. Such a timeline would have shown the jury the observations of Kassidy with no bruises or with one bruise, and with which the jury could have evaluated the level of bruising throughout the 154 days that Chad knew Kassidy. With such a timeline, the defense could have more effectively questioned witnesses about the times of observations of bruises and of Kassidy in general. There was little effort by the defense to gather all the records, e.g. phone and calendars, of Amanda, Chad and others to establish the outline of Kassidy's life during those 154 days.

i. Only one witness testified for defense, Dr. Michael Baden, a forensic pathologist. Although he is an eminent pathologist, the calling of only one witness appeared to show to the jury that the evidence was overwhelmingly in favor of the prosecution, as it called a total of 27 witnesses. Defense witnesses could have helped establish the timeline mentioned above, and given clear explanations of the times and places of observations of bruises. The defense failed to recall any of the prosecution witnesses as defense witnesses and failed to question some of them about allegations made by other witnesses. For example, Amanda was not recalled to respond to allegations made by Jeff and Jennifer.

j. Chad's financial planner was not called to testify regarding his conversations with Chad about an IRA for Kassidy. Chad's sister discussed such plans in her police interview, November 9, 2000.

k. The director of the Cross Road Kindergarten and School was not called to testify regarding her conversation with Chad, a few days before Kassidy's death, about enrolling Kassidy in her school.

l. The only defense alternative theory was that Jeff committed murder, and Jeff was directly accused of such murder in the courtroom. Instead, the defense should have presented the facts about Jeff and his care of Kassidy to show the jury how the evidence against him was just as strong as it was against Chad, and that evidence was weak. Without directly accusing Jeff of murder, the defense could have presented the jury with the less provocative choice of whether the evidence against Chad was so much stronger than against Jeff as to warrant a finding of guilty beyond reasonable doubt.

m. The defense presented no discussion of "easy bruising" as Kassidy's medical condition. There were no witnesses, discussion or argument that when bruising resulted from Chad's holding of Kassidy's face, it was not abuse, just as it was not abuse when no bruises appeared.

n. Insufficient attention was given to the type of ball (Tee-ball) which hit Kassidy on the evening of November 8, 2000. There was no evidence about the degree of harm that could be caused to a child when hit in the head by such a ball.

o. Defense failed to fully explore the brain injury effects of known accidents, including the alleged fall from Jeff's truck which caused two large bumps on the top of Kassidy's head 14 days before death, and the hit from a Tee-ball the night before her death.

p. There no mention of other possible causes of death, such as disease, chronic condition or toxins.

q. Despite the defense reliance on a single alternative theory for the cause of Kassidy's death, i.e. Jeff's culpability, and despite Jeff's assertive testimony, and despite the showing to the jury of the videotape of Chad's interrogation, Chad was advised not to testify.

r. There were no witnesses, discussion, or argument that Chad's holding Kassidy's face was *in loco parentis*, permitted by Amanda, and was privileged. It was not discipline, *per se*, such as spanking, but was a means to ensure effective communication. Chad never hit or spanked Kassidy. Chad's holding of Kassidy's face to ensure eye contact fit none of those exceptions to the general authorization for parents, and their delegates, in New Hampshire the right to use force when disciplining children. The defense could have argued that face palming was not excessive force, and that it was not the same as using a belt against a child.

s. The defense cross-examination of Jeff omitted several instances of accidents and other conduct which allegedly showed his shortcomings as a babysitter. For example, the jury did not know of the allegation that he covered Kassidy's face with a pillow when she was crying, in order to prevent that crying from bothering the neighbors in the adjoining apartment.

t. The defense cross-examination of Jeff omitted evidence that Chad had told him around October 23, 2000 that his landscaping contracts with Chad's McDonald's restaurants would not be renewed, giving Jeff a possible motive for revenge.

u. The cross-examination of Jeff failed to adequately present the incident where Kassidy drank, or was thought to have drunk, Windex. No pretrial investigation was made to the Maine Poison Control hotline to verify that Jeff had called for assistance, and the time and date of that call. The hotline's record of that call could also have established the content of the advice given to Jeff and Jennifer.

v. The defense failed to question the failure to seize during the search of Jeff's and Jennifer's apartment Kassidy's red pajama tops, Sippy cup, and diaper bag.

w. The defense failed to establish for the jury exactly what Kassidy was wearing on November 9 and how and when those clothes were removed by Jeff or the EMT's.

x. The defense failed to respond proactively to excessive and highly prejudicial pretrial publicity, including newspaper editorial.

y. The defense failed to request a change in venue, given the prejudicial pretrial publicity.

z. The defense failed to present sufficient character evidence to the judge to persuade her that such evidence was relevant in Chad's case. No pretrial psychological testing was conducted for Chad.

aa. The defense failed to present to the jury the facts that Chad recommended to Amanda that she take Kassidy to doctor for toe-in problem and on other occasions, to remove a wart from her right index finger. He was not blocking medical attention for Kassidy.

bb. The defense did not sufficiently argue, and present expert witnesses, that Amanda's testimony was in the nature of "false confession." Too often, police are told what they want to hear, and what interviewees want them to hear, rather than the truth. Amanda's recantation was more truthful.

cc. The defense did not ask about plans made by Amanda and her mother, Jacqueline, for Kassidy to be babysat by Jacqueline over the weekend of November 11-12, 2000, when Chad and Amanda were to be in Maine for a business meeting. The plans for that babysitting were made during the telephone call between Amanda and her mother on Wednesday morning, November 8. That phone call was on the large blownup Chart of Calls, on five Exhibit panels, during November 8 and 9.

dd. The defense failed to obtain and utilize the records of Chad's counseling sessions with Gray Fitzgerald, which ended in the Spring of 2000.

ee. The defense failed to contact the day care providers which Amanda called, and failed to determine which one(s) had listed Kassidy on a waiting list, and which one in Amanda had visited that was too close to a busy road.

ff. The defense did not request DNA testing for the items seized from Jeff's and Jennifer's apartment. Such a request would have led to the discovery that the Maine Crime lab had determined that there was blood under Kassidy's fingernails, and that DNA tests had actually been conducted by the Maine State Police Crime Lab, and that the results had been included in the discovery materials.

gg. Similarly, the defense did not use the DNA test report results which had been provided. That would have been important information for the defense to have during the cross-examination of Dr. Margaret Greenwald, Dr. Baden, Jeff and other witnesses.

hh. There was no attempt by the defense to isolate and separate every one of the 100 bruises, injuries and fractures found by Dr. Greenwald. How many were caused the EMTs in their efforts to save Kassidy's life? How many were caused by accidents at Jeff's and Jennifer's? We know that Chad could identify about ten that he recalled. Probably Amanda knew about others.

Even if Chad's future attorneys are not able to persuade a New Hampshire State or Federal court to order a new trial, the Kassidy Bortner case, and trials of Chad and Amanda must be still be reinvestigated for those above reasons, and for those reasons below:

1. Chad Evans loved Kassidy Bortner. He was planning to marry Amanda and raise Kassidy to adulthood. Thus, there was no motive for harming Kassidy or wanting her to die.
2. Chad had a biological son and a stepson and was, and is, an excellent father. The jury was precluded from hearing evidence of his parenting skills.
3. Chad Evans never hit, nor even spanked Kassidy Bortner. He didn't spank his own son or stepson either. He did not believe in spanking as a method of discipline. He believed in communications and relied upon **eye contact** for effective communication.
4. The police established their theory of the case within about seven hours of Kassidy's death and then gathered evidence to prove their theory, rather than evidence to find causes of death. During those seven hours, they told Chad and others that he was the primary suspect.
5. Chad Evans passed a voice-stress analysis lie detector test in July, 2010. Jeff was scheduled for a lie detector test for November 14, 2000, but he declined. Chad is the only person in the case to have taken a lie detector test.
6. There were only two written statements requested by the police in this case, which were from Jeff and Will Peirce. As he was the alternate suspect, content of Jeff's statements should be analyzed using the technique known as SCAN (Scientific Content ANalysis). SCAN is used by police around the world to evaluate the veracity of statements.
7. Chad was elected to the Keene Board of Education in 1991, a year after graduating from high school. He loved children and helping them learn and grow.
8. In 1997, Chad received a "hero" award by the Union Leader and Governor Shaheen for his 1996 lifesaving rescue of three men.
9. Chad was a successful manager of several McDonald's restaurants and coached many young people into becoming better employees and citizens.

Such a re-investigation should include a thorough medical review of Kassidy's health and death by the New Hampshire Medical Examiner. In some states, there is a provision for an inquest, which is an inquiry into the cause of death of a person, without pre-determined criminal charges. New Hampshire's law providing for such inquests was repealed in 1986. Even without such a law for a formal inquest, the New Hampshire Medical Examiner can re-examine the health and death of Kassidy.

Such an inquiry would look at the case differently. For example, there were three diapers seized at Chad's home and they were sent to the New Hampshire Crime lab for testing for "latent prints/DNA." (Search, p. 3118) A fourth diaper was the one Kassidy was wearing when she died. If the original inquiry had been to establish the status of Kassidy's health and reasons for her death, those diapers would have been analyzed for indications of disease.

This book points out several ways that the police did not fully investigate Jeff. They ignored signs that their belief in the accuracy of his statements was misplaced, such as his decision not to take a polygraph and their failure to corroborate several of his allegations about Chad. These points are made not to accuse Jeff of Kassidy's murder, but to show that the police were rushing to judgment against Chad, whereas there were several reasons to continue to consider Jeff as a suspect. There was no need to rush a decision to pick either man or to proceed entirely on the theory that Kassidy's death was a homicide. As noted here, other potential causes of the bruising and of Kassidy's death should also have been considered.

In conclusion, Chad Evans is innocent of all the charges against him. Not merely "not guilty," but innocent.

1. Murder. Chad did not kill Kassidy with any intentional blows.
2. First Degree Assaults. Chad did not intentionally do anything to Kassidy to cause any fracture of any bone in her body. If he or Amanda had any inkling that Kassidy had a broken bone, they would have taken her to a doctor. The evidence of fractures was uncertain, and disputed. Evidence supporting these charges were so lacking that Judge Nadeau dismissed the charge regarding an arm fracture, and the jury found Chad not guilty regarding a leg fracture.
3. Second Degree Assaults. Chad did not assault Kassidy, but he did cause bruising when holding her face to gain **eye contact**, as he was permitted to do by Amanda. The bruises had no role in Kassidy's death. They may have been the result not of criminally excessive pressure, but of some blood disorder which resulted in what is popularly known as "easy bruising." A key element of criminal responsibility is intent, and Chad's intent when holding Kassidy's face was to gain **eye contact** with Kassidy, and not to punish, harm or hurt her. The jury found Chad not guilty of one of the six charges of Second Degree Assault, for the period of October 1-8, 2000 presumably because of the October 1 photograph at the trial. With a timeline and additional photographs, the jury would found no injury, or that it was the accidental result of permitted contact by Chad.
4. Child Endangerment. Chad did not inflict the harm in this offense and he did not "withhold" medical treatment for injuries he didn't cause.
5. Simple assault. The argument with Amanda on the night of November 8 was an argument with mutual physical actions by Chad and Amanda. It was over in a few minutes and they went to bed together.

Through a unique combination of assumptions and errors by many people, together with a few lies, Chad was charged with crimes he didn't commit, primarily the crime of murdering Kassidy Bortner. The Convict Chad train accelerated and seemed to gather momentum as rumors and misunderstandings became accepted as truth, and ambiguity was always resolved in favor of the theory of abuse and murder by Chad.

What lies? As Angela Blodgett said her first interview with Amanda, *"I think everybody lies,"* (p. 864) and she was right. Chad has acknowledged that the "trampoline story" was a lie. Incredibly, in view of what happened after that story was concocted in October, 2000, it seems today that the truth would have been a more palatable explanation for the small bruises on both sides of Kassidy's chin, i.e. that Chad caused them when obtaining **eye contact** with her. In retrospect, the truth seems as acceptable as the "trampoline story," and there was thus no need to develop the "trampoline story" in the first place. Chad didn't tell the story to everyone because few people asked about the bruises, and the bruises subsided after each of the three or four occurrences. He told the story only to Jacqueline, Tristan and the police. He told the police the "trampoline story," knowing for certain that the bruises that he caused and which were likely no longer even visible on Kassidy's body, had nothing to do with her death. He also told the police about the importance to him of **eye contact**.

Amanda lied to Chad about her age and lied to Sergeant White on April 6, 2001 when he called her in Texas and she denied having any contact with Chad. These lies, too, were unimportant to the solving the mystery of Kassidy's death. I know of no lie told by Chad or Amanda which relate directly to Kassidy's death.

There were likely other lies in this tragic story, but for now they are simply registered here as misstatements, mistakes or inaccurate recollections. Even the statements by Erik Baker and Jill Rockey to Jeremy during his interview (p. 268) on November 14 that Jeff had taken a polygraph test may not have been a lie. Similarly, Lance McCleish told Chad that he had talked to doctors about Kassidy before Chad's interrogation. (p. 1592) To lie, one has to have the intent to be lying. Baker and Rockey may have wanted so much to believe that Jeff was going to pass such a test, that they may have already convinced themselves that he had taken a polygraph. McCleish may have wanted so much to believe his understanding of Kassidy's death that he told Chad that he had talked with doctors.

One challenge in the investigation and prosecution of Kassidy's death was to separate the important misstatements from the unimportant. As the bruises caused by holding Kassidy's chin to obtain **eye contact** had nothing to do with Kassidy's death, the "trampoline story" should have been cast into the "unimportant" bucket. Instead, it was thought to be important.

Why was there such a rush to accuse? Public pressure? There were only a few hours from Kasssidy's death to the verbal accusations of Chad, and only a week to his arrest. Why not wait to be sure? Why not ask Chad's attorney if he and Chad would be willing to meet with the police? Why not ask about a polygraph for Chad? Why not give a polygraph to Amanda and Jennifer? How much would that have cost and how long would those actions have taken?

Part of what happened was self-fulfilling hysteria, like the plague of sex abuse day care hysteria cases in the 1980's and 90's. In nearby Malden, Massachusetts, the Fells Acre Day Center case began in 1984 when a five year old boy told his parents that a day care worker had touched his penis. The tragedy of wrongful convictions of three members of the Amirault family was finally eased with the 2004 release of Gerald Amirault from prison.

In October 1984, in Springfield, Mass., a gay 19-year old day care worker, Bernard Baran, was accused of abusing children and a few months later was convicted and sentenced to life in prison in 1985. He was finally exonerated in 2009.

In both cases, the power of suggestion and fear overcame reason, facts and truth. People were willing to believe the worst about others, including people they previously knew and with whom they were friendly, and into whose care they had placed their children. In each case, the judicial system was unable to correct the flaws in the investigation, and contributed its own errors and omissions.

This is what happened to Chad Evans and Amanda Bortner.

The sequence of events leading to their wrongful convictions is similar to what happened in many of the 270+ Innocence Project exonerations of wrongfully convicted people. The need to find and punish a person to be held responsible for the death of a beautiful blonde toddler girl was more powerful than the need to be deliberate and methodical about determining what caused her death. A similar pattern developed four years previously in the Jon Benet Ramsay case in December, 1996. Why wrongful convictions have happened so often in the U.S. legal system is the subject of many existing and future books, and is beyond the scope of this book.

Chad's wrongful conviction must now be corrected. If Chad is given a retrial, he will testify. If a judge thinks there is enough evidence to give the case to the jury, that jury will see the evidence that Chad's 2000 jury did not see; and Chad will be found not guilty. Alternatively, the Attorney General can make the decision not to retry Chad, because there is almost no chance that a new jury would find him guilty.

With Chad exonerated, Amanda should also be exonerated from the two charges of Child Endangerment for watching Chad abuse Kassidy, which he didn't do.

The State of New Hampshire may never know what happened to Kassidy, as it's now been eleven years since her death. Memories have faded and some evidence has been discarded. This lack of resolution is often the result of a wrongful conviction. Of the 272 Innocence Project exonerations, as of July 4, 2011, the real perpetrator was found in approximately120. In Kassidy's case, we are looking for the real cause of her death.

As has been stated by many participants in this tragic story, Kassidy Bortner cannot be brought back to life. Her death was an enormous tragedy and affected the lives of many. The losses of that tragedy were compounded by the misdirected investigation and the wrongful convictions and imprisonment of Chad and Amanda. What can be brought back to life now are Chad's freedom, his honor and reputation, and his ability to resume being a full-time father and productive, tax-paying citizen.

CHAPTER 13: CAMPAIGN FOR JUSTICE FOR CHAD EVANS AND AMANDA BORTNER

There is nothing so powerful as the truth, and often nothing so strange
- Daniel Webster

The Campaign for Justice for Chad and Amanda can be said to have officially begun with the first meeting of the Chad Evans Wrongly Convicted Committee in Keene on March 24, 2010. The core of the group was Chad's family, along with many of his childhood and adulthood friends.

The Committee agreed upon a statement of its "Mission, Goals, Methods, and Beliefs and Assumptions":

MISSION

To find and present to the people and government of New Hampshire the truth about Chad Evans. That truth will lead reasonable people to see that he was wrongly convicted of murdering Kassidy Bortner. We will find and present the several possible alternate causes of Kassidy Bortner's tragic death.

GOALS. To achieve one or more of the following:

- The judicial exoneration of Chad Evans, and restoration of his reputation.
- The withdrawal by the Attorney General of New Hampshire of the charges against Chad Evans
- The reinvestigation of the death of Kassidy Bortner and, if applicable, the prosecution of the person or persons responsible.

METHODS. To achieve the Mission and Goals above, the Committee will use as many methods of communication and persuasion as possible. Such methods will include:

- Working with attorneys in the state and Federal Courts to overturn the conviction.
- Building a website, www.chadevanswronglyconvicted.org which provides as much of the information about the case as possible, including incriminating information.
- Writing a comprehensive book about the case.
- Writing letters to, and meeting with, elected and appointed government officials.
- Letter writing to the media.
- Encouraging articles in the press, radio and television.
- Continuing the investigation of the case and relentlessly pursuing the truth.
- Circulating a public petition.
- Polling the public.
- Holding public and private meetings for communication and persuasion.
- Developing multi-media means of telling the truth about the case, including music and video.

BELIEFS AND ASSUMPTIONS

- The truth shall set wrongly convicted people free.
- Through honest discussion, with respect for all parties and viewpoints, the truth can emerge.
- Everyone in New Hampshire wants justice.
- Everyone can help in the pursuit of truth and justice in the Chad Evans case
- The men and women in New Hampshire law enforcement are strongly motivated to seek justice.
- No one in New Hampshire wants an innocent person to be imprisoned for a crime s/he did not commit.
- If there is a person, or persons, responsible for intentional or criminally negligent acts which caused the death of Kassidy Bortner, s/he or they should be prosecuted and punished.

Since that first meeting, the Campaign for Justice for Chad and Amanda has grown, as is described below.

Searching for the Truth about the Kassidy Bortner case

The subtitle of this book begins, "The mysterious death in 2000 in Maine of Kassidy Bortner," because it IS a mystery. The way to solve a mystery is to find as much information as possible, and to search for the truth. Too much of Chad's efforts for freedom during the previous ten years saw truth as a secondary goal. The goal of his trial was a "Not Guilty" verdict, and truth was a useful, but not essential secondary goal. When Jeff sued him for defamation, Chad's goal was to defeat that case, rather than use the process as an opportunity to present the truth, and a second bite at the judicial apple. Nineteenth century U.S. Senator Daniel Webster of New Hampshire said, "*There is nothing so powerful as the truth, and often nothing so strange"* and that is a motto of the Union Leader and appears on every page of Chad's website. The search for the truth is an essential part of the Campaign for Justice for Chad, and sometimes the truth was uncomfortable and sometimes strange, but never has it pointed in the direction of guilt in the death of Kassidy.

Below are listed the several ways that the Campaign continues to seek new information about the case.

- Freedom of Information. Much of the new information in this case has been found with Freedom of Information requests, which are called "Right to Know" in New Hampshire.
- Photographs. It is said that a picture is worth a thousand words, and that applies in this case. The Evans family had many useful photographs, but more of Kassidy and Amanda are still unseen and in private collections. As the Campaign for Justice grows, it is hoped that these photographs will be volunteered.
- Records of events, appointments. These are vital to establish and continue to refine the timeline of Kasssidy's life from June 2 through November 9. As it's been 10 years since Kassidy's death, many records have been destroyed, such as the records of Amanda's appointments with her Aspire/DHHS counselors. Chad's tax records were destroyed by his former accountant, according to a routine practice. Other records are maintained for longer periods, such as medical records.
- Lie detector test. The July, 2010 voice stress lie detector test provided new information, even if in an unconventional way. If Chad had been given a polygraph in 2000, the course of the investigation might have changed.
- Medical research. Several Committee volunteers are researching the possible diseases and chronic conditions which Kassidy may have suffered during her life, and especially during her last 40 days, from October 1. It is hoped that one or more pediatricians and other specialists will assist these volunteers.
- Witnesses. Even after ten years, the recollections of some people can be helpful. Some people who saw Kassidy and Amanda together were never interviewed by the police. Even for those who were interviewed, more information can be recalled. Sometimes, it only takes different wording in a question, or a photograph to unleash new information.

The Campaign for Justice for Chad Evans and the Media.

The first ten years of media coverage of Chad's case, except for the Ray Carbone interview of Amanda on February 8, 2003, have been disastrous. Chad was advised in the earlier years not to talk with the media as the results would likely be hostile and inaccurate, and the results became a self-fulfilling prophecy. Amanda had urged Chad in those early years to work with the media, but her voice was discounted.

Today the Campaign for Justice for Chad sees the media as a vital ally in the effort to present the truth about the Kassidy Bortner case.

On June 11, 2010, ten years after Amanda met Chad, the readers of Foster's Daily Democrat first read the news that Chad was claiming that he was innocent. Joey Cresta wrote the article, "Rochester child killer seeks exoneration: Hires private investigator in effort to clear his name."
Cresta wrote,

Evans denies on the website ever striking Kassidy, saying, "I never hit Kassidy. Not for discipline, nor for any reason."

Evans did not testify in his defense and never spoke publicly about the case, which Bonpasse believes was a major mistake. He said the jury never had a chance to hear from a "good man" and "loving father." Evans was also never asked to take a lie-detector test, he said.

After that article there were two interviews, one for Foster's Daily Democrat and one for WMUR-TV with Sean McDonald. For more information about the media coverage to date see Chad's website and its two "Links to Articles" sections: Links to Articles: pre-2002 sentencing and Links to Articles: post-2002 sentencing.

Utilizing the Internet and the "Social Media"

Chad's own website, www.chadevanswronglyconvicted.org, has enabled people around the world to learn about Chad, Amanda and Kassidy. Through the "Online Comments" section, viewers can present their views and ask questions. Many of those answers are in documents which are already posted on the website.

There is an online petition for a re-investigation of Chad's case on the www.change.org website. As of June, 2011, there were 328 signatures.

Chad does not have access to the Internet in prison, so his supporters maintain his personal Facebook page, now with 550 "friends," and a Group Facebook page for the Chad Evans Wrongly Convicted Committee. Another volunteer started a Twitter account in 2011.

A major advantage of the Social Media is that they are nationwide and worldwide. No longer is injustice in one state something that can be isolated to that one state.

This book, EYE CONTACT, and the Campaign

The traditional mass media and the Internet all deliver information to readers and viewers, but each is limited. The most traditional medium to deliver complicated content is a book. A long book is not for everyone, but it's one alternative medium so that people can read the story of the wrongful convictions of Chad and Amanda. Most of the story is contained in these approximately 600 pages and approximately 390,000 words. If there are gaps, please let me know, and they will be considered for inclusion in future editions.

The first Draft Edition was published online on July 18, 2011. The second Draft Edition was published online as a .pdf file on August 10, 2011. It can be downloaded as an e-book on Kindle and Nook. Other means are being pursued to get the story of the wrongful conviction of Chad and Amanda to as many New Hampshire people as possible.

Seeking re-investigation of the Kassidy Bortner case

The primary political effort is to encourage a re-investigation by the New Hampshire Attorney General of the Kassidy Bortner case. In New Hampshire, the Attorney General is nominated by the Governor, and must be confirmed by the Executive Council. With a term of two years, New Hampshire governors are more directly accountable to the people. Vermont is the only other state with a two-year term for governors. As judges are appointed for life, the prosecutors were the only people at the trial directly representing the elected government of New Hampshire.

Attorneys General and prosecutors have considerable discretion in criminal cases, on whether to prosecutor or not prosecute. Less known is that they have the ability to return to any criminal case and request the vacating of a conviction and a retrial or without a retrial. In several of the 270+ exonerations of wrongfully convicted people through the work of the Innocence Project since 1989, the evidence of innocence has been brought to prosecutors and they have then carried the sword of justice toward exoneration. Everyone makes mistakes, and, except for cases where the defendant has been executed, mistakes in the justice system can be corrected. As U.S. Attorney General Eric Holder said to newly sworn Assistant U.S. Attorneys "*Your job is not to win cases. Your job is to do justice. Your job is in every case, every decision that you make, to do the right thing.*" (Boston Globe, April 9, 2009)

A re-investigation of a case can be ordered by an Attorney General just as easily as an initial investigation. It doesn't require the approval of a judge, but it does require political and managerial sensitivity, as the original investigators and prosecutors are often still in office and their professional pride is at stake. However, truth and justice should trump pride.

If such a re-investigation is conducted in the Kassidy Bortner case, and the truth is presented, then it is hoped that Attorney General Michael Delaney will voluntarily seek to have the murder charge against Chad vacated. Alternatively, if the new evidence is not enough to convince him of Chad's innocence, but is enough to convince him that the first trial was unfair due to the absence of critical evidence, he could request a new trial. At a new trial, a jury would be able to see all the currently available evidence, and Chad would certainly testify.

The existence of photographs of Kassidy without bruises, and the availability of witnesses who saw no bruises which could have been caused by Chad's eye contact palming of Kassidy's face and the two doctors appointments in August and September would make the further prosecution of the five remaining Second Degree Assault charges difficult. If a retrial included those charges, the defense that he had Amanda's permission to touch and discipline Kassidy could be used. It wasn't used at Chad's 2000 trial.

Another change from the 2000 trial is that Chad acknowledges that on two or three occasions he and Amanda both realized that his palming of Kassidy's face caused bruising. He also acknowledges that on several other occasions he held Kassidy face to obtain eye contact, but which did not cause bruises. The question is not whether such hold was done, but whether it fit the legal definition of Assault. The same could be said for the single charge of Endangering the Welfare of a Child.

Following the ruling of the New Hampshire Supreme Court in the State v. Ramos case in 2003, the charge of Simple Assault against Amanda would have to be tried in a different proceeding, because combining it with the murder charge would be unfairly prejudicial. In light of all the other circumstances in the case, and the realities of life, it's unlikely that this single charge would be brought by itself.

On October 13, 2011, four members of the Chad Evans Wrongly Convicted Committee met with Senior Assistant Attorney General Jeffery Strelzin to present in-person their reasons for supporting Chad's claim for a re-investigation. They presented to Strelzin a letter with 46 reasons for a re-investigation, which include the issue presented in this book, but in only 15 pages. They also presented a three page outline of the proposed re-investigation, including a new interview with Chad.

Approaching the Leaders of the New Hampshire State Government

Every citizen and every appointed and elected official in New Hampshire has the ability and opportunity to speak and work for justice for Chad and Amanda, and they can contact the Attorney General. The state's motto is "Live Free or Die," which states the case for justice and liberty more strongly than the motto of any other state.

New Hampshire is a small state, famous for its retail politics in the presidential primary every four years. As the late Tip O'Neill said, "*All politics is local,*" and it's true in New Hampshire. Everyone knows somebody in the government who can help or who knows someone else in the government who can help.

A campaign for justice is like any other political campaign, in that it requires person-to-person contact and communication.

Chad and his supporters are writing to their legislators to ask that they get involved and support the request for a re-investigation of the case.

The Chad Evans Wrongly Convicted Committee is always looking for more people to become involved by learning the truth about the case and then trying to exonerate Chad.

The Free Ward Bird Campaign (November, 2010 - February, 2011)

During the first year of Chad's Campaign, another Campaign for Justice for an individual was started in New Hampshire, upon the imprisonment of Ward Bird of Moultonborough for 3-6 years for "criminal threatening." He was convicted in April 2009 of waving his .45

caliber pistol at a woman trespasser on his property in March 2006. When the New Hampshire Supreme Court denied his appeal in November, 2010, he was required to serve his sentence at the State Prison.

There were a few parallels between Ward Bird and Chad. Both men were:

1. represented by Attorney Mark Sisti.
2. advised not to testify at their trials.
3. recognized as "heroes" by the Union Leader for their saving of lives during an emergency. Ward Bird had helped rescue a driver from his submerged automobile in 1989. On November 23, Roger Amsden wrote the story for Union Leader, "21 years ago, now-jailed Ward Bird was a hero"
4. supported by a network of family and friends who believed in them.

The crimes for which the two men were convicted were dramatically different. Bird's supporters felt that it was wrong to convict the family farmer of carrying a gun on his own property. Chad's supporters believe that Chad didn't kill Kassidy Bortner.

Ward Bird's supporters held fundraising events, created a website, and asked their elected representatives for help, and public interest in the campaign went national.

On December 6, Ray Duckler of the Concord Monitor wrote a powerful column, "Judge a man by his character? Bird watchers keep freedom fight alive" He asked, "*Without video or eyewitness accounts, does Ward Bird's apple-pie resume really matter?... A growing number of Bird watchers say yes.*"

For the supporters of Chad Evans, character matters, too.

The "Free Ward Bird" campaign culminated in a petition for a pardon from the New Hampshire Executive Council. On February 2, Bird was released after the Executive Council and the Governor commuted his sentence. It wasn't a pardon, but he was free. It is hoped that Chad's Campaign will eventually be as successful as was the campaign for Ward Bird.

Seeking Justice and Exoneration in the Courts

In addition, as it cannot have all its eggs in one re-investigation basket, the Campaign is seeking legal assistance to obtain a new trial and exoneration in the courts. At some point, enough new evidence will be accumulated to persuade a judge to order such a new trial.

There was no claim of Chad's innocence in his original appeal as that was not an issue for the Supreme Court to decide. There was no claim of Chad's innocence in his efforts to set aside the 15 years added to his sentence by the Sentence Review Board. To put such a claim in an appellate brief would be considered irrelevant by lawyers and, more importantly, judges, but what has the system of justice come to if a wrongly convicted defendant cannot consistently claim his innocence? In this case, as elsewhere, the rules and procedures of the legal system have, so far, trumped truth and justice.

Expansion of the Chad Evans Wrongly Convicted Committee

It is hoped that the Campaign will continue to add chapters and members in New Hampshire and around the country.

The Seacoast Chapter of the Chad Evans Wrongly Convicted Committee held its organizational meeting in Rochester on Wednesday, September 29, 2010. Its members were primarily former McDonald's employees of Chad, and their friends. The chapter is now named the "Rochester Chapter," and it is planning a benefit concert, along with the writing and singing of a song about Chad's case.

Other chapters may be started at the University of New Hampshire Law School, Concord, Manchester, northern New Hampshire, the U.S. and the world, generally.

In September, 2011, the Committee became a member of the New Hampshire Center for Nonprofits. Coincidentally, the Committee joined at the same time as the New Hampshire Bar Association and the New Hampshire Supreme Court Society. All three groups share an interest in justice.

The future of the campaign

As the campaign builds momentum, confidence will grow, and more and more people will feel that it is safe to support the claims of innocence for a man wrongly convicted of a terrible crime - the murder of a child. One of the sources of that momentum is that information which supports Chad's innocence continues to appear. Evidence of abuse and guilt is not appearing.

At some point, the political and legal systems will respond to the will of the people and to what is right and Chad will be exonerated and freed and will return to his son and family.

Appendix: EYE CONTACT

PHOTOGRAPHS OF KASSIDY BORTNER FROM JUNE – NOVEMBER, 2000.

This photo album contains photographs of Kassidy Bortner during the period she lived with her mother, Amanda, and Chad Evans in Rochester, New Hampshire.

The photos are listed below and in this collection in chronological order to the extent possible, as some photos could not be precisely dated. They are printed in Black and White in this appendix, but they appear in color in the "Amanda and Kassidy" subsection of the "Who IS Chad Evans?" section at Chad's website at www.chadevanswronglyconvicted.org.

1-6 June 22. Kassidy at York's Wild Animal Kingdom with Amanda, Kyle and Chad.

7-9 On or before August 16. Kassidy at Water Country in Portsmouth

10-11 August. Two photos of Kassidy in her high chair in Chad's dining room.

12 Mid-late August. Kassidy and Kato in Chad's kitchen.

13 September 2. At the birthday of her uncle, Scott Conley (but perhaps misidentified)

14 October 1. Kassidy at Auburn with bunny rabbit. Photo was at Chad's trial.

15 October. Kassidy in Chad's kitchen with Elmo slippers.

16 October 20. Kassidy and Amanda at Chad's sister's home in Belmont, NH.

None of these photos shows bruises on Kassidy.

Photos 1-6: Kassidy at Yorks Wild Animal Kingdom, Maine (all six photos by Chad)

Photos 1 and 2 is from our day at York's Wild Animal Kingdom. We had a BLAST. It was very hot out and these photos were taken near the end of the day. These were taken at the Prairie dog family exibit. I took this photo from a across the Cement cylinder display. Actually, the prairie dog on the log is alive. It looks close to Kyle but they are actually approx. 10' away. I was using the zoom on the camera. We obviously went at the beginning of the season, because of developing date we know it was 6/22/2000. I took at least an entire roll that day. I wish we had the rest. I had some nice ones toward the beginning with everyone smiling, prior to being hot and tired. We had planned to take them at the end of the season but as you know we missed it. In 2000, the internet wasn't used like it is today to check schedules, opening times, etc.

Photos 3-4   Photo 3 is a closeup of Kassidy from Photo 1, above

Photo 4 Kassidy with animals and people

Photos 5-6
Kassidy, Kyle and Amanda at York's Wild Animal Kingdom

Photos 7-9: of Kassidy at Water Country, Portsmouth, On or before August 16, 2000.

By Chad Evans.
These are awesome photographs of Kassidy. These were taken by Amanda in August of 2000 when she took Kassidy and her brother(s) to Water Country in Portsmouth. I was busy in Hampton so I couldn't make the trip, but I picked up tickets for Amanda to take the kids. Amanda and I did a lot during August. Jackie watched Kassidy a lot. One of the times when Amanda went to pick Kassidy up, she brought her brothers, Scott and Joshua, back to spend a few days with us. Amanda may have gone with one of her friends as well. Obviously from the develop date, it was on or prior to Wednesday, August 16, 2000. The important thing is look how HAPPY Kassidy is!

Photos are close enough to see no bruises. She is wearing a 2-piece bathing suit which shows NO BRUISES on her abdomen.

I wish I had thought of using these photos during the trial. As a matter of fact, I don't recall my attorneys asking for ANY photos. Amanda and the kids had a great day. We grilled out that night, and I believe we walked up to Lone Oaks Ice Cream, less than one-third of a mile from our house, and got ice cream later.

7. Kassidy at end of slides
8. Kassidy on lounge chair
9. Kassidy in locker room

7. Kassidy at end of slides

8. Kassidy on lounge chair

9. Kassidy in locker room

Photos 10-11: Kassidy in High chair, 2 photos (same day?)
Photo 10 by Chad Evans
Here are two different photos of Kassidy Bortner in her high chair in the kitchen in Chad's home. She is wearing the same clothes and shoes as the photo, with Kato, (photo 6) and the hair looks the same, so it may have been taken in late August, 2010.

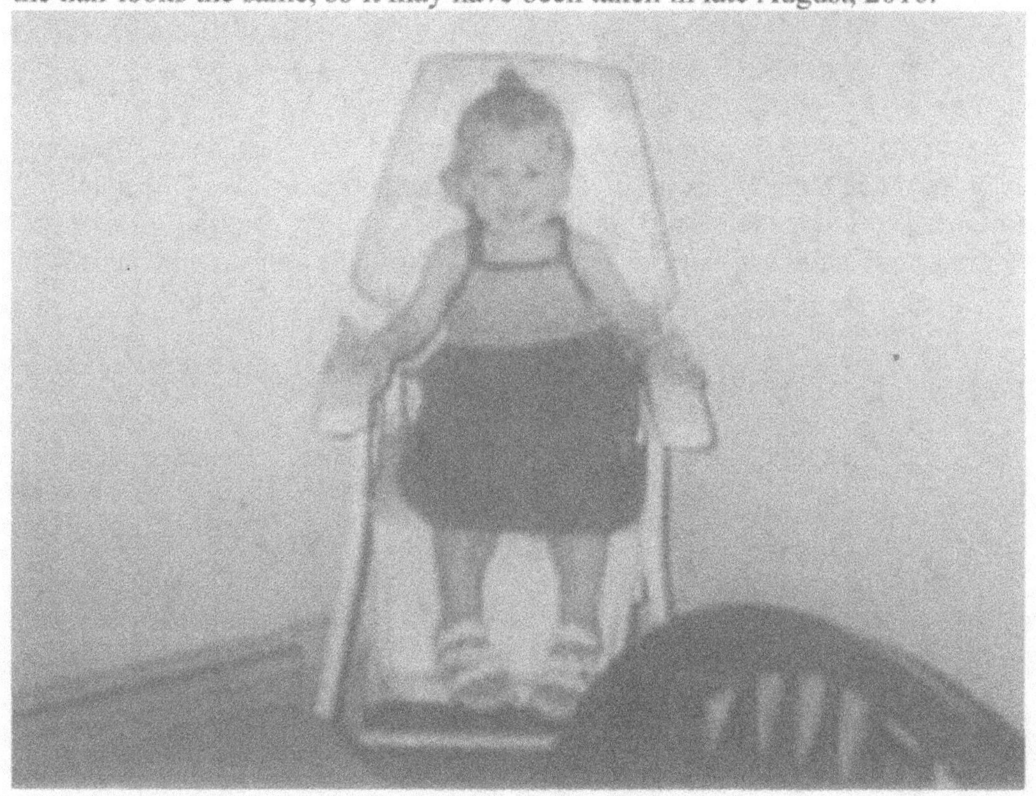

Photo 11 by Chad Evans
This (second) photo was taken by me while Kassidy sat smiling in her high chair in the corner of our diningroom.
Due to Kassidy's face thinning a little, I am going to guess this was taken sometime in August. I think we were just getting ready to have some ice cream and that is why she was smiling so. She was so cute I couldn't resist snapping the photo.

Photo 12. Kassidy with Kato in kitchen in Rochester.

By Chad Evans
I believe by the maturity in Kassidy's face and hair length (compared to York's Wild Animal Kingdom photo taken June 22 +/-), this photo was taken mid to late August. Most importantly, you can see how HAPPY she is in the photo, no bruises and absolutely loved Kato. Amanda took the photo from the dining room entrance facing into the kitchen at our home in Rochester.
… toward the end of the month. Her hair is a bit longer and the white sandals we loved on her couldn't be worn much more after this photo because she outgrew them. The tough thing is that Amanda and I loved that little blue dress and white sandals outfit on Kassidy, and Amanda almost always did her hair the same in that outfit (hair pulled up in one bunch on head).

Photo 13: Kassidy, in Auburn, Maine, September 2, 2000.

Kassidy's grandmother, Jacqueline Conley, believes that she took this photo of Kassidy , at her home in Maine. Kassidy is wearing the same sweater as in the photograph of Amanda holding Kassidy taken on 20 October 2000. According to Jacqueline, this photo was taken on the occasion of the birthday party for Kassidy's uncle, Scott Conley on 2 September 2000.

Chad Evans wrote a note in June 2011 about the photo.
"You know what is weird about this photo? It looks like my livingroom floor with a little view of my entertainment center and those wood TV trays that I stacked in the corner. You can see those TV trays in the corner of my living room in other photos we have looked at.
I know Jackie has indicated she took this photo but…
Also, judging by Kassidy's hair length, this is much closer to the October 1st photo of her holding a rabbit in the chair and the October 20th photo of Kassidy in Amanda's arms. Also, judging by the maturity of Kassidy's face, I really believe Jackie may have confused the photo with others that she may have taken on Sept. 2.

Photo 14: Kassidy in chair with bunny rabbit, Auburn Maine October 1, 2000

This photo of Kassidy was taken by Kassidy's grandmother, Jacqueline Conley on Sunday, October 1, 2000, in the Conley house in Auburn, on the last day of the move to Buckfield. The chair was one of the last in the house. This photo was later used at Chad Evans's trial as Exhbit 19, and it was the only photo shown at the trial of a healthy Kassidy. This was 6 weeks before her death.

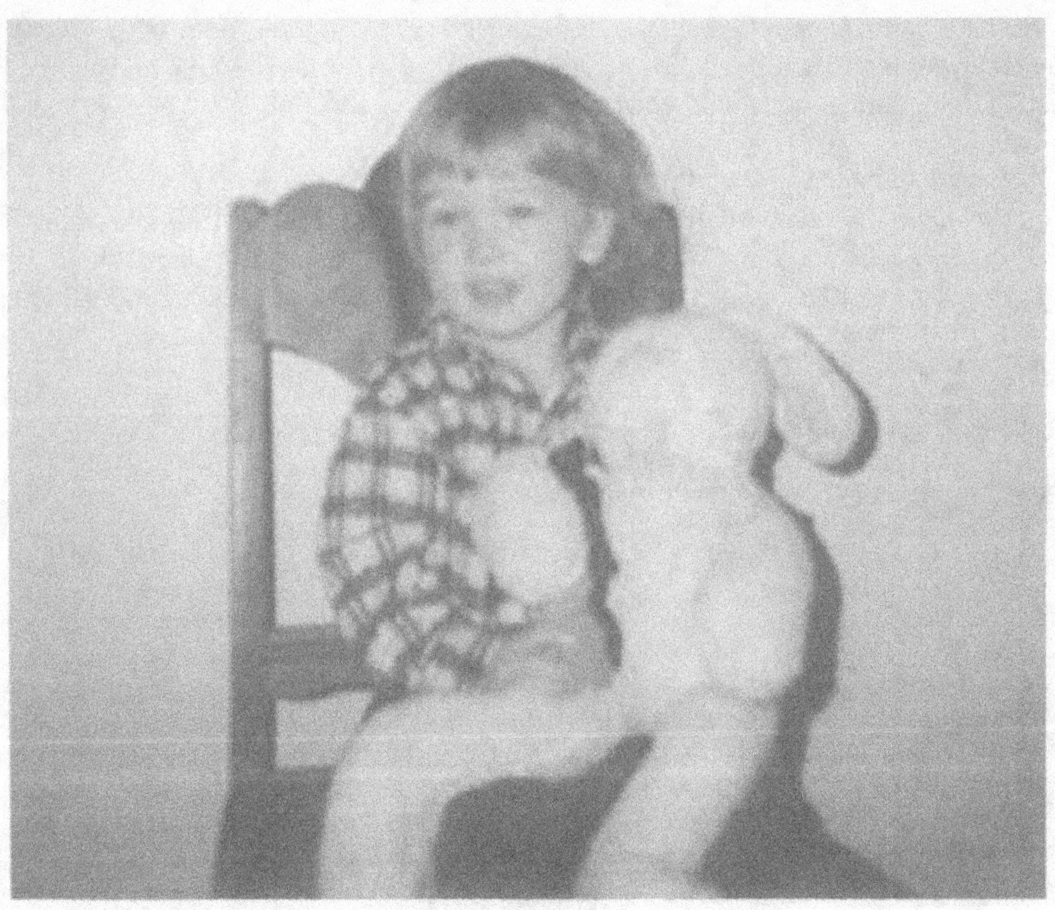

Photo 15: Kassidy in Chad's kitchen, with Elmo slippers, sometime in October, 2000?

by Chad Evans

"OH MY GOD! I had forgotten about this photograph. I will have to find where Amanda mentioned these "Elmo" slippers in her testimony. This picture was taken later in our relationship. Like October. Her interview reference to the slippers may provide a better clue, perhaps which shopping trip she bought that outfit. I believe those are the slippers that Amanda sent to Jeff's so Kassidy wouldn't get any more pin pricks on his floors (if that is what really caused them). Kassidy is bigger in the photograph, her hair is longer.

She is wearing an outfit that Amanda bought shortly before her death. LOOK how HAPPY she was. I'm not sure who took the photo. It was either me or Amanda.

We both were prone to snapping photographs when one of the kids would walk in doing something funny or looking particularly cute. From the angle, I would guess that Amanda snapped this one. I tended to get down more level with the kids to get straight on shots....

God, I wish we had some of the photo's that were taken by Amanda of me holding Kassidy or sitting with her playing or cuddling. The fire in the summer of 2001 was tragic. Sometimes I wonder if accidents like that are signs against me and any efforts I make to right this wrong. It seems like every possible thing that could have gone wrong at the worst possible moment, did in EVERY instance of this case.

… My guess is after October 15, sometime.

Photo 16: Amanda and Kassidy, at Nicole Evans Harvey's home, Belmont, NH, Friday, October 20, 2000.

by Chad Evans
This is an awesome photo, and, I believe, the last existing photo of Kassidy alive. (There were subsequent photos, but they were likely lost in a fire in the Summer of 2001.) I remember the day. We went up to visit Nicole and Brandon. I know, because I was in work clothes. I believe Kyle was with us. I was helping Brandon dig a root or something before the ground froze for the winter. We moved some heavy stuff around and then I took everyone to dinner at "Nothin' Fancy" in Weirs Beach. We decided on Mexican because I wanted the kids to try something a little different. We determined the date of October 20 by the credit card statement for the dinner. This was 20 days before Kassidy died.

I also think this time is likely because I was discussing 3 wheelers with Brandon and I believe I told him I found one in Maine I was going to look at. As we know,, I went to Maine the weekend of the 22nd with Jeff.

Amanda is wearing the brand new Colley-McCoy sweatshirt I had just received in early October to give out as Crew Prizes. These sweatshirts were huge hits with the Crew. Amanda loved the sweatshirt and claimed the one I kept for myself as her own. You can see an earlier photo of Amanda wearing one during our Saco River canoe trip in August. That was my sweatshirt from the previous fall.

You asked about the photo of Amanda holding Kassidy at Belmont on Friday Oct. 20, 2000. I am 99% SURE that it was Nicole that took the photo. I was working with Brandon on the other side of the house trying to dig a trench or something to lay a water pipe before the ground froze. I am pretty sure that Kyle was over with Brandon and me.
(Letter, July 7, 2010)

www.ingramcontent.com/pod-product-compliance
Lightning Source LLC
LaVergne TN
LVHW061234100826
845148LV00008B/958

* 9 7 8 0 9 8 3 7 9 8 5 2 1 *